TABLE B MEASURES OF U.S. INCOME, PRICES, AND FEDERAL DEBT

Year	Net National Product	National Income	Personal Income	Disposable Income	GDP Deflator (1987=100)		CPI (1982-1984=100)		Federal Budget Deficit	Federal Debt
	Billions of Dollars				*Index Number*	*Percent Change*	*Index Number*	*Percent Change*	*Billions of Dollars*	
1929	94.0	85.3	84.2	81.8	12.5	–	17.1	–	0.7	16.9
1933	48.4	40.2	46.0	44.8	9.5	-2.1	13.0	-5.1	-2.6	22.5
1940	91.1	79.9	77.4	75.0	11.0	1.9	14.0	0.7	-2.9	50.7
1945	201.0	181.8	170.0	149.4	13.3	5.6	18.0	2.3	-47.6	260.1
1950	264.6	240.0	227.8	207.7	20.2	1.5	24.1	1.3	-3.1	256.9
1951	306.2	277.7	256.5	228.1	21.3	5.4	26.0	7.9	6.1	255.3
1952	322.5	292.1	273.7	240.2	21.5	0.9	26.5	1.9	-1.5	259.1
1953	340.7	307.0	290.4	255.5	22.0	2.3	26.7	0.8	-6.5	266.0
1954	340.0	307.0	293.0	261.2	22.2	0.9	26.9	0.7	-1.2	270.8
1955	371.5	337.1	314.5	279.9	22.9	3.2	26.8	-0.4	-3.0	274.4
1956	390.1	357.2	337.5	298.8	23.6	3.1	27.2	1.5	3.9	272.7
1957	409.9	373.7	356.5	315.2	24.4	3.4	28.1	3.3	3.4	272.3
1958	414.0	376.0	367.2	326.3	24.9	2.0	28.9	2.8	-2.8	279.7
1959	452.5	410.1	391.2	346.7	25.6	2.8	29.1	0.7	-12.8	287.5
1960	470.2	425.7	409.2	360.5	26.0	1.6	29.6	1.7	0.3	290.5
1961	487.7	440.5	426.5	376.2	26.3	1.2	29.9	1.0	-3.3	292.6
1962	526.5	474.5	453.4	398.7	26.9	2.3	30.2	1.0	-7.1	302.9
1963	556.4	501.5	476.4	418.4	27.2	1.1	30.6	1.3	-4.8	310.3
1964	599.2	539.1	510.7	454.7	27.7	1.8	31.0	1.3	-5.9	316.1
1965	650.7	586.9	552.9	491.0	28.4	2.5	31.5	1.6	-1.4	322.3
1966	712.8	643.7	601.7	530.7	29.4	3.5	32.4	2.9	-3.7	328.5
1967	752.4	679.9	646.5	568.6	30.3	3.1	33.4	3.1	-8.6	340.4
1968	821.5	741.0	709.9	617.8	31.8	5.0	34.8	4.2	-25.2	368.7
1969	884.2	798.6	773.7	663.8	33.4	5.0	36.7	5.5	3.2	365.8
1970	928.3	833.5	831.0	722.0	35.2	5.4	38.8	5.7	-2.8	380.9
1971	1007.3	899.5	893.5	784.9	37.1	5.4	40.5	4.4	-23.0	408.2
1972	1105.7	992.9	980.5	848.5	38.8	4.6	41.8	3.2	-23.4	435.9
1973	1241.9	1119.5	1098.7	958.1	41.3	6.4	44.4	6.2	-14.9	466.3
1974	1334.1	1198.8	1205.7	1046.5	44.9	8.7	49.3	11.0	-6.1	483.9
1975	1433.9	1285.3	1307.3	1150.9	49.2	9.6	53.8	9.1	-53.2	541.9
1976	1602.7	1435.5	1446.3	1264.0	52.3	6.3	56.9	5.8	-73.7	629.0
1977	1789.4	1609.1	1601.3	1391.3	55.9	6.9	60.6	6.5	-53.7	706.4
1978	2019.8	1829.8	1807.9	1567.8	60.3	7.9	65.2	7.6	-59.2	776.6
1979	2248.4	2038.9	2033.1	1753.0	65.5	8.6	72.6	11.3	-40.7	828.9
1980	2430.2	2198.2	2265.4	1952.9	71.7	9.5	82.4	13.5	-73.8	909.1
1981	2701.4	2432.5	2534.7	2174.5	78.9	10.0	90.9	10.3	-79.0	994.8
1982	2780.8	2522.5	2690.9	2319.6	83.8	6.2	96.5	6.2	-128.0	1137.3
1983	3016.0	2720.8	2862.5	2493.7	87.2	4.1	99.6	3.2	-207.8	1371.7
1984	3368.3	3058.3	3154.6	2759.5	91.0	4.4	103.9	4.3	-185.4	1564.7
1985	3599.1	3268.4	3379.8	2943.0	94.4	3.7	107.6	3.6	-212.3	1817.5
1986	3799.2	3437.9	3590.4	3131.5	96.9	2.6	109.6	1.9	-221.2	2120.6
1987	4042.4	3692.3	3802.0	3289.5	100.0	3.2	113.6	3.6	-149.8	2346.1
1988	4374.2	4002.6	4075.9	3548.2	103.9	7.2	118.3	4.1	-155.2	2601.3
1989	4686.4	4249.5	4380.3	3787.0	108.5	4.4	124.0	4.8	-152.5	2868.0
1990	4965.1	4491.0	4673.8	4050.5	113.3	4.4	130.7	5.4	-221.4	3206.6
1991	5114.3	4608.2	4860.3	4236.6	117.6	3.8	136.2	4.2	-269.2	3598.5
1992	5367.3	4829.5	5154.3	4505.8	120.9	2.8	140.3	3.0	-290.4	4002.1
1993	5678.7	5131.4	5375.1	4688.7	123.5	2.2	144.5	3.0	-255.1	4351.4
1994	6011.5	5458.4	5701.7	4959.3	126.1	2.1	148.2	2.6	-203.2	4643.7

SOURCE: *Economic Report of the President, February, 1995.*

PRINCIPLES OF ECONOMICS

FRED M. GOTTHEIL
University of Illinois

SOUTH-WESTERN College Publishing
An International Thomson Publishing Company

Acquisitions Editor: Jack C. Calhoun
Publisher/Team Director: Valerie A. Ashton
Developmental Editor: Dennis Hanseman
Production Editor: Rebecca Roby
Production House: WordCrafters Editorial Services, Inc.
Cover and Internal Design: Craig LaGesse Ramsdell

Photo Researcher: Feldman and Associates
Marketing Manager: Scott Person
Team Assistants: Ronda Faulkner, B.J. Parker, Cory Broadfoot

HB61AA

3 4 5 6 7 VH 1 0 9 8 7 6
Printed in the United States of America

Gottheil, Fred M.
Principles of economics / Fred Gottheil.
p. cm
Includes index.
ISBN 0-538-84020-X
1. Economics. I. Title
HB171.5.G649 1996

330—dc20 95-8566
CIP

International Thomson Publishing

South-Western College Publishing is an ITP Company. The ITP trademark is used under license.

To my wife Diane

To my children, Lisa and Joshua,
who grew up together, not just as
sister and brother, but as best friends

PREFACE

At the end of fall semester a few years ago, I told my class of 1,000 Economics 101 students that I wanted to see how much of the course they would be able to recall four months after the final exam. I asked them to take a post-final exam in early April, covering the same material. A few hundred showed up to take the April exam. The results were instructive, and perhaps not too surprising.

These were very bright students. The scholastic entrance requirements to the University of Illinois are quite high. During the semester, they were able to handle the math and graphs without difficulty. Yet, when it came to the April exam—only four months after the final—there was much confusion explaining, and even more graphing, market equilibrium, national income determination, and other basic ideas.

If I ever thought that the analysis offered in lectures and in the textbook is what students really ingest during the semester, that thought was very quickly dispelled.

Why is the half-life of what we teach so short? Are we trying to teach too much? *Is our basic principles course getting away from being an analysis of basic principles?* Have we forgotten that there is an opportunity cost every time we add material to a course or textbook? Are our textbooks more plumbers' manuals on technique than analyses of a social science subject? What do we want our students to know? Can we talk to our students and be heard?

I wrote this textbook with these questions in mind. It is written for the student, not for the professor. These are two very different readers. To my surprise, I found it difficult to keep the focus on the student who comes to the material without prior knowledge. It was much easier to write to the professor. Most of my rewriting had to do with correcting the focus. Much of the differences in style, content, and depth of analysis between my text and the others on the market reflects this focus. My preference was to sacrifice the number of topics for depth and to present the basics in as nonthreatening a style as possible.

A major problem I confronted in every chapter was what material to exclude while still covering the basic principles with analytic rigor. I chose to challenge the student holding a yellow highlighter. If I could get that student to read without highlighting, perhaps I could light a fire in the student's mind. This book is my answer to that challenge.

MICROECONOMIC ANALYSIS

How do you make fixed and variable costs seem important so that students see the connection between these costs and their own personal experiences? Perhaps by engaging them directly in the world of economic enterprise. In this book, students become the focus of economic activity. I ask them to consider setting up a business, making each of them a decision maker who purchases factors of production, chooses the scale of production, worries about prices, and determines how to calculate profit and loss. In this way, the economic concepts emerge naturally and take on a very real meaning.

The Use of Continuing Scenarios

The microeconomics chapters maintain a continuing storyline. I put the student on an island economy where fish is the staple food and commercial fishing a commonplace economic activity. The student sets up and runs a fishing firm. Fishing is something students can easily visualize and imagine themselves doing. The technology involved is relatively uncomplicated and the product—fish—is familiar and about as close to a homogeneous product as there is. The competition that takes place in the fish market, with price responding to changes in demand and supply, is also very immediate.

The fishing scenario anchors the chapter on supply and demand and several chapters that follow. It is used in analyzing price controls, appears in Chapter 7 on business organization, is the centerpiece in Chapter 8 on costs of production, and appears later in Chapter 9 on maximizing profit. Using this format, the economic concepts build on each other.

In the chapters on price determination, the analysis shifts to the ice-making industry (ice is used by the fishing industry). The student, still in the fishing world of earlier chapters, sees the ice-making firm first as a monopoly. Then, as more firms enter with product differentiation, the monopoly dissolves into monopolistic competition, and finally into perfect competition. In the chapters on factor pricing, the setting changes completely to the coal mining industry in Harlan County, Kentucky. The same coal mining scenario appears in Chapter 15 on wage determination under competitive conditions, in Chapter 16 on monopsony and unions, and finally in Chapter 18 on interest rate determination.

Teaching the *MC* = *MR* Rule

The importance of the profit maximization rule of $MC = MR$ cannot be overstated. In most texts, this paramount idea first appears in the context of price determination in perfect competition. It reappears again in each of the market structure chapters. I was never happy with this traditional approach. Why? It forces students to fight their way through to $P = MR = MC = ATC$, while simultaneously trying to grasp marginal revenue analysis and digest the significance of the $MC = MR$ rule. That may seem like a reasonable enough exercise to professors. However, to beginning students and nonmajors—who were probably warned through the grapevine that economics is difficult and boring—this presentation of the material may be ample confirmation. I think there is a better way to introduce one of the most important ideas we teach in micro theory.

In this book, a complete chapter—Maximizing Profit—is devoted to the idea. This chapter appears before we discuss the intricacies of market structures and price determination. Profit maximization is followed by Chapter 10, Identifying Markets and Market Structures, which examines the outstanding characteristics of each market structure. This allows for an early comparison of market structures. The stage is then set for price determination in each market *which is done in one chapter.* With the $MC = MR$ rule already thoroughly developed and the various markets described, $MC = MR$ is both the organizing principle of the chapter and the universally applied rule. Price analysis focuses on this one central idea.

This approach is not only logical, but even more important, makes it easier for students to understand and retain the principles. Incidentally, I begin price determination in Chapter 11 with monopoly, then move to monopolistic competition, and conclude with perfect competition. Because students are already familiar with the downward-sloping demand curve (from Chapter 3 on supply and demand), I can show its connection to monopoly pricing. Then, I can explain why the demand curve becomes flatter as more firms enter the market. This leads to a discussion of monopolistic competition and finally to perfect elasticity in perfect competition. In this way, I avoid throwing a horizontal demand curve right at them from out of nowhere.

MACROECONOMIC ANALYSIS

Students already have a fair idea of what the macro issues are. Almost every media source comments daily on inflation, the Fed, budget deficits, unemployment, business cycles, and economic growth. Students know that economics affects their lives and they come into the course with strong interest. Our job is to link their lives to the body of economic thought we offer.

Like most texts, this one employs three basic models: aggregate demand and aggregate supply, the Keynesian cross, and variations on the Phillips curve. In each of the theory chapters, the policy issues are never out of reach. In fact, I typically discuss policy before theory. This is an attempt to make students appreciate why we get involved with theory in the first place.

Building the Blocks to Policy Analysis

The same policy issues keep reappearing throughout the macro chapters. I try to avoid pigeonholing ideas into chapter sections and just leaving them there. For example, I introduce the problems of inflation and unemployment early in the first macro chapter to explain why we develop the simple aggregate demand/aggregate supply model. The chapter ends with a section: Can We Avoid Unemployment and Inflation? From the beginning, students know how the basic issues are linked to theory.

The same ideas are recast in the Keynesian model. Fiscal policy is not confined to one chapter, but keeps reappearing, each time presenting yet a new dimension. For example, in the core chapter on fiscal policy the inflationary and recessionary gaps developed in an earlier chapter are reintroduced, but now the question of budget balance is added to the discussion. Fiscal policy shows up again in the chapter on economic growth and business cycles, where it is seen as an instrument to moderate cycles. It reappears in the coverage of the Phillips curve, in the context of the debate on what government can or cannot do.

The money chapters—Money; Money Creation and Banking Policy; The Federal Reserve; and Monetary Policy—approach theory and policy in much the same way, staying close to basic principles. I sacrificed detailed discussion of current debates on target instruments (although they are mentioned). I felt such "up-to-date" discussion didn't really add much to an understanding of how the Fed works or why it does what it does. I want the students' energies directed to understanding the basic principles.

Student Focus Remains in Macro

Perhaps the most distinguishing feature in the macro chapters is the personal involvement of the student. This involvement runs through every macro page. Let me cite just one example that involves the question of how to measure unemployment. The student is presented with some hypothetical data and asked to estimate a rate of unemployment. The student has to think about whether to include the discouraged worker, the underemployed, and the frictionally, structurally, and cyclically unemployed. Each inclusion, of course, produces a different unemployment rate. When we finally get to the official BLS rate, the students knows that it is not some divinely inspired idea but a concept we create ourselves to give us meaningful information. They also know what is left out, and why.

In developing the Keynesian theory of income determination, I recast aggregate expenditures ($C + I$) and aggregate production ($C + S$). The focus of discussion is on what consumers do with their incomes ($C + S$) at various levels of income compared to what producers do (producing $C + I$) at these same income levels. This way of analyzing national income determination splits aggregate expenditures: the consumption spending in aggregate expenditures is the C of the consumers' $C + S$ while the investment spending in aggregate expenditures is the I of the producers' $C + I$. Why do this? Because focusing on the behavior of the consumers and producers personalizes the analysis. It makes it easier for the student to identify the problem of macro disequilibrium. Also, the student can put him- or herself in the shoes of the consumer and the producer and walk through the discussion personally.

Bringing in the Government

The text first presents macro theory in an economy without a government or foreign sector. This simplifies the analysis. The fewer the variables, the easier it is for the student to follow the story. Understanding how national income equilibrium is arrived at is our principal goal. Government comes into the picture later when problems of unemployment and inflation are considered. But that's only the beginning.

My treatment of government is quite different from most texts. Throughout my theory and policy chapters, the focus is on fiscal policy. *G*'s and *T*'s are employed as if that's all there is to government. That makes sense when our aim is to develop the principles of policy, but it obscures a complete picture of government's role in the economy.

I have found precious few texts that make an effort to explain what government really does. In most books, the descriptive analysis of the public sector is put up front, as part of an institutions chapter, with pie charts showing current government data. The sense of how government works in our economy is lost.

Students know that government is a dominant player in our economic life. If we are going to explain how government works, how can we ignore its very raison d'être? Students ought to know and discuss what the different levels of government actually do. They ought to know something about the history of government spending, how specific functions—education, defense, public assistance—grew over time. I think my chapter on government spending is a major plus. The detailed analysis of government spending leads directly to another chapter that discusses how government finances its spending. Here, taxes, government borrowing, and debt are examined. There is a conscious historical bent to these descriptive chapters. They allow the student to see what government does and to appreciate that we can't simply manipulate *G*'s and *T*'s as if they were just numbers in an economics board game.

Discussing the Business Cycle

What else is new? What's old is new. The chapter Economic Growth and Cycles analyzes the business cycle and the history of theories explaining it. I want the student to see how economists struggled, and still do, with the phenomenon of recurring cycles. The innovation cycle, the housing cycle, the war-induced cycle, the population boom cycle, and the multiplier/accelerator cycle are important because they attempt to explain the causes of economic instability. The student reads about these ideas in *U.S. News and World Report* and hears about them on the "CBS Evening News." Business cycle theory belongs in any discussion of economic dynamics. A little history of economic thought is helpful.

Dealing with Lack of Consensus

Many economists avoid macro theory because it is loaded with intellectual landmines. Different schools of thought present competing ideas on fundamentals of macro theory and contentiously challenge one another. To say there is a lack of consensus in macroeconomics is a gross understatement! But that shouldn't be a problem in teaching macroeconomics. Dissension brings engagement, excitement, and intellectual challenge. Economics is not an exact science and we should readily acknowledge that fact to our students. Contentiousness notwithstanding, the issues are real and important. It is our job to stimulate the intellectual nerve of the student. The text tries to present macroeconomics in this light.

THE TEXT'S STYLE

I have emphasized that this text was written for the student, not for the professor. This is a commitment I made to myself when I started the project years ago. If nothing else sets this textbook apart, this does. My idea has been to make economics exciting, to show its importance in our everyday business of life, and to get students to understand the economists' way of thinking. I tried always to keep the analysis within reach of students. Make it real, even personal. Allow them to enjoy the subject matter, not just to think about the coming exam.

We absorb ideas in many ways: through our heads, our hearts, and our innards. An idea that stirs you emotionally has staying power. If you can feel it in your bones, it becomes more than an intellectual exercise. I kept that in mind in every chapter and in every paragraph written. The style is intentionally conversational, but the discussion is always serious. If the story is really understood, it will be remembered. Economists have something to say. That's what my textbook is about.

USE OF PERSONAL NAMES

I believe that economics is about people. As you read through the chapters, you can't help but see many, many names that personalize the discussion. Claudia Preparata buys fish, Diane Pecknold inherits a tobacco farm, Charles Edwards owns a coal mine, Nick Rudd is in the ice-making business. These, along with over 90 more, are real people. They are all friends of my son Joshua who died in 1989, age 19, a victim of lymphoma. The textbook is my way of honoring Josh and honoring as well the beautiful people who were a part of his life.

THE TEXTBOOK'S ACCESSORIES

Study Guide

A Study Guide is the students' principal *reality check*. Do they really know the material? It must be not only student-friendly, but a companion piece that reflects the text's heart and soul. Too often, study guides are written by individuals whose connection to the text author is via e-mail. The study guide becomes generic. Not so here. David Wishart, professor of economics at Wittenberg University, who wrote the Study Guide, is not only a close friend but an outstanding teacher who began his teaching career working with me in the principles course at Illinois. We have worked on this project together for a long, long time. His Study Guide captures the spirit of the text, making it that much easier for students to use.

Instructor's Manual

An Instructor's Manual is the one private connection between the classroom instructor and the author. As the text author, I felt it was important to the instructor, particularly the first-time instructor, that I write the manual myself. The manual is a companion piece to the text. It provides ideas on how to approach each chapter, tips on how to present the chapter's material, and alternative illustrations that can be used to explain points of theory and policy. It also discusses how to turn student questions into teaching opportunities. In each chapter of the manual, the corresponding text chapter outline and its key terms are included for easy reference. The manual also provides detailed answers to the many questions that appear at the end of each chapter in the text.

Test Bank

The Test Bank that accompanies my text includes over 4,000 objective questions, including many that I have written myself. Robert Toutkoushian of the University of Minnesota assembled this test bank, which is available in both printed and computerized formats.

Student Software

In this age of computing, no text package would be complete without tutorial software. The software that accompanies this text will give students a different slant on the material and help draw them into the subject.

Other Supplements

A set of 150 acetate transparencies is available to adopters of the text. These transparencies were chosen to illustrate key ideas in the principles course. They were carefully prepared to ensure that they are legible when projected as overheads.

The same set of images is also available on PowerPoint slides for computer-assisted lecturing. These slides employ transitions that suggest relationships between ideas for maximum presentation impact.

One other ancillary item will be especially helpful to students. The Graphing Primer, prepared by Rob Toutkoushian, takes them step by step through the processes of interpreting, understanding, and creating graphs.

ACKNOWLEDGMENTS

I am grateful to many people for help and encouragement throughout the development of this textbook. Many came to the project in a strictly professional capacity; most ended up as good friends. I owe them more than they believe is their due. At the beginning, George Lobell was enthusiastic about the idea of the textbook and believed that it would make a difference in the profession. He read many chapters, stayed in close touch, and still does. I thank this textbook for introducing me to George. David Wishart was a dear friend before we started the project, and working together on this textbook added another dimension to our friendship. Tricia Nelson and Pat Wakeley were development editors whose skills improved earlier versions of this manuscript immensely. Jack Calhoun, South-Western's economics editor, sold me on the idea of the team concept of publishing. It was Dennis Hanseman, the development editor at South-Western, who saw the project to completion. Responding to Dennis was like taking prelims all over again. But he made it all work. I owe him much, and thank him for his patience and his friendship. Finally, Craig Ramsdell, Rebecca Roby, and

Laura Cleveland played major roles in translating my word-processed drafts and rough sketches into the pleasing book you hold in your hands.

During this book's long gestation period, I have benefited from the comments and suggestions of many reviewers. My heartfelt thanks go to the following economists. This book is much improved because of their efforts.

Michael Bodnar,
Stark Technical College

John Booth,
Stetson University

David Bunting,
Eastern Washington University

Tom Cate,
Northern Kentucky University

Robert Catlett,
Emporia State University

Christopher Colburn,
Old Dominion University

James Cover,
University of Alabama, Tuscaloosa

Jane Crouch,
Pittsburgh State University

Susan Davis,
SUNY College at Buffalo

Abdollah Ferdowsi,
Ferris State University

Carol Hogan,
University of Michigan, Dearborn

Paul Huszer,
Colorado State University

Patrick Kelso,
West Texas State University

Joseph Kotaska,
Monroe Community College

Robert Litro,
Mattatuck Community College

Lawrence Mack,
North Dakota State University

Joseph Maddalena,
St. Thomas Aquinas College

Gabriel Manrique,
Winona State University

G.H. Mattersdorff,
Lewis and Clark College

Henry McCarl,
University of Alabama, Birmingham

James McLain,
University of New Orleans

Norma Morgan,
Curry College

Allan Olsen,
Elgin Community College

Mitchell Redlo,
Monroe Community College

Terry Riddle,
Central Virginia Community College

Richard Schiming,
Mankato State University

Jerry Sidwell,
Eastern Illinois University

Phillip Smith,
DeKalb College

William Stull,
Temple University

Doug Wakeman,
Meredith College

Jim Watson,
Jefferson College

Larry Wolfenbarger,
Georgia College

I also want to thank Peter Schran, my colleague and close friend at Illinois, whose advice always made sense although it sometimes took me a while to appreciate it. To Mark Wohar, professor of economics at the University of Nebraska, Omaha (Mark assisted me in my principles course during the early 1980s), thanks for the help on several chapters. Finally, I'd like to thank my assistant, Sally Campbell, who did considerable work in converting data to tabular and graphical form.

Fred Gottheil
University of Illinois

BRIEF CONTENTS

CONTENTS

Farewell

'His eyes would light up and he'd talk fast and you couldn't help being excited about the band or record he'd discovered, too.'

by P. Gregory Springer

News-Gazette file photo

Part of being young is the feeling of being indestructible. Josh Gottheil, who died last month after a two-year battle against leukemia, probably understood that he wouldn't live forever. But he never stopped working to bring the music he loved to the world around him. Rock and roll would carry on.

The punk movement—simultaneously cynical and realist and suicidal and idealistic—tried in a frenzy to wipe out the commercialism and mass media hallucination which blurred life's realities, even unpleasant ones like death. There were bands named Dead Kennedys, Dead Milkmen, the prototype Dead Boys, and Gottheil's local band, Dead Relatives.

When he was only a sophomore in high school, Gottheil became a drummer for the short-lived band, but he was no angry punk. He heard the message in the music and he set out, ambitious at a tender age, to deliver it to the community.

At 17, he already had promoted dozens of concerts for teens in community centers and church foundations. He was the least pushy music promoter I ever met, enticing me to see at least one political rock and folk concert through his complete, quiet reticence.

It was the music that spoke to and through him.

At one concert he arranged, I watched Billy Bragg and Michelle Shocked get their introductions to the area. And I saw Josh, standing by the door at Mabel's, anxious to see that the message and the feeling came across.

His bands rarely disappointed.

Among the many other national bands he brought to Champaign's clubs were Living Colour, They Might Be Giants, Soul Asylum, Throwing Muses, Jane's Addiction, Dead Milkmen, Husker Du, Let's Active, Timbuk 3, Ministry, and the Pixies.

"The scene wouldn't be what it was today without Josh," said Chris Corpora, an area rock promoter of Trashcan Productions. "He didn't look the part and he risked his own money.

About four years ago he started teen nights when there was a lull in the scene. I don't want to deify him, but he had an incredible will, poise, and the wherewithal to get contracts signed and do things he probably shouldn't have been able to do. When I was 15, I couldn't even read a contract."

Even in the hard-core punk scene, Josh maintained a romantic side, often bringing roses for the girls in his favorite bands, notably Throwing Muses and the Pixies.

"He was always in love with every girl in a band," said Katy Stack, one of many people who considered Josh a best friend.

"He made friends with the Pixies and we flew to California to see them play in San Francisco," Stack said. "They invited him on stage to sing."

For a couple of summers, he worked at the desk at Crystal Lake Pool, announcing the adult swim and checking in bags. After high school, he took some college classes in philosophy and math at Parkland and at the UI, where his father, Fred, is a professor of economics. When he got sick, "it didn't look like he needed to go to college," according to Stack. "He was real busy doing all the music and he always had a lot of money. He was the only 16-year-old that had $2,000 in his checking account."

Another friend, Shara Gingold, actually wrote a book about her crush on Josh.

"He was two years older. The book is called 'I Love You, Josh. Do You Even Know I Exist?'," said Gingold, who lives in Urbana. "I think that it was (the fact that) he was very understanding and caring. We'd meet to play tennis and then we'd just sit and hit the tennis ball against the wall and talk about everything."

Last year, his health started to improve. He gained weight. He was working at Record Swap, surrounding himself in music during the day for the concerts he promoted at night. He had teamed with Chicago promoter Tony Polous, established a limited partnership called Concert One Productions, rented an office in Chicago's Mercantile Building, and developed the financing for big arena shows.

"Josh was destined to be huge," said Polous from the Chicago office. "He was the most effective, easy-going person I ever met. It's not hard to master being pushy and strong. Josh mastered being effective in an unassuming way.

"When he had to go back to the hospital, he never let on how sick he was. Every day I'd call him and he'd ask about what this manager was doing or that agent and he'd make decisions. We never really talked about his health. I never thought he was going to die. I think about him every day."

Despite his illness, Josh moved to Chicago last fall to be immersed in the music business.

"It was a chance, a break, an exciting thing to do. The world was his to conquer," said Fred Gottheil from his UI office. "I remember going up to visit and spend the night. The wind was howling, but he was so proud of the apartment. He was designing tickets on his computer, telling me (about) all the bands he had booked, his new ideas, bubbling with enthusiasm for the possibilities. The move was exhilarating for him. He called home quite frequently, but (Chicago) was where he had to be."

Said former Champaign-Urbana DJ Charlie "The Quaker" Edwards, who shared the Chicago apartment, "He had a real vitality, youth, and infectiousness. His eyes would light up and he'd talk fast and you couldn't help being excited about the band or record he'd discovered, too. Even though there was almost 20 years age difference between us, we'd listen to albums and talk about the bands and share a mutual excitement.

"He was a really good, serious businessman. Much better than I could have been, always dealing with five shows at once. He really loved it, too. He just loved the music."

"Definitely, there are people who are into (punk) because it is a fad," Gottheil said three years ago. "But for the people who really believe in it, it won't die for them."

Josh Gottheil died April 4 at Barnes Hospital in St. Louis, three months short of his 20th birthday. There was a turn-away crowd for his funeral on April 7 at the Sinai Temple in Champaign. Because he did so much to bring a new attitude about music in this area, one of the bands he helped find national prominence, Throwing Muses, has donated its performance at a benefit concert this Sunday at Mabel's, with proceeds going to the Josh Gottheil Memorial Fund for Lymphoma Research.

PHOTO CREDITS

Chapter 1: pp. 2, 7: © Camerique/H. Armstrong Roberts; p. 4, © Chuck Keeler/Tony Stone Images. *Chapter 2:* pp. 26, 29, © Robert Heinzen/SuperStock International, Inc.; p. 28, © Sylvain Coffie/Tony Stone Images. *Chapter 3:* pp. 44, 67, © Hugh Sitton/Tony Stone Images; p. 46, © Jeffry W. Meyers/FPG International, Inc. *Chapter 4:* pp. 74, 80, © SuperStock International, Inc.; p. 76, © MacDonald Photography/Unicorn Stock Photos. *Chapter 5:* pp. 100, 104, © Michael Rutherford/SuperStock Internation al, Inc.; p. 106, © Andy Sacks/Tony Stone Images. *Chapter 6:* pp. 126, 136, SuperStock International, Inc.; p. 131, © Stock Montage. *Chapter 7:* pp. 151, 157, © Charles E. Schmidt/Unicorn Stock Photos; p. 155, © Robert Reiff/FPG International, Inc. *Chapter 8:* pp. 168, 177, © M. Wootton/H. Armstrong Roberts; p. 170, © Ernest Manewal/FPG International, Inc. *Chapter 9:* pp. 198, 215, © Adamsmith/Westlight/H. Armstrong Roberts; p. 200, © Dick Luria/FPG International, Inc. *Chapter 10:* pp. 218, 22 0, © Dave Bartruff/FPG International, Inc.; p. 233, © Mary Kate Denny/PhotoEdit. *Chapter 11:* pp. 242, 263, © Jim Cavanaugh/Third Coast Stock Source; p. 257, © David Young-Wolff/PhotoEdit. *Chapter 12:* pp. 271, 285, Reuters/Bettmann; p. 276, © A. Reininger/Unicorn Stock Photos. *Chapter 13:* pp. 301, 310, © R. Rathe/FPG International, Inc.; p. 309, © Mason Morfit/FPG International, Inc. *Chapter 14:* pp. 327, 331, Reuters/Bettmann; p. 339, © Kathryn Bellifemine/Unicorn Stock Photos. *Chapter 15:* pp. 348, 368, © Terry Qing/FPG International, Inc.; p. 350, © David Hiser/Tony Stone Images. *Chapter 16:* pp. 376, 391, UPI/Bettmann; p. 385, AP/Wide World Photos. *Chapter 17:* pp. 398, 404, © Camerique/H. Armstrong Roberts; p. 402, © L. Powers/H. Armstrong Roberts. *Chapter 18:* pp. 420, 430, © Martin Rogers/Tony Stone Images; p. 422, © Nikolay Zurek/FPG International, Inc. *Chapter 19:* pp. 444, 466, © Cameramann International, Ltd.; p. 446, © Robert W. Ginn/Unicorn Stock Photos. *Chapter 20:* pp. 475, 477, © Andy Sacks/Tony Stone Images; p. 478, © Stephen Johnson/Tony Stone Images. *Chapter 21:* pp. 501, 516, © John Terence Turner/FPG International, Inc.; p. 508, © Royce Bair/Unicorn Stock Photos. *Chapter 22:* pp. 523, 532, © Zigy Kaluzny/Tony Stone Images; p. 525, © Jeff Greenberg/Unicorn Stock Photos. *Chapter 23:* pp. 547, 560, © W. Smith/H. Armstrong Roberts; p. 550, © L. Nelson/H. Armstrong Roberts. *Chapter 24.* pp. 575, 589, © Tom Carroll/FPG International, Inc.; p. 581, © Jeff Greenberg/Unicorn Stock Photos. *Chapter 25:* pp. 603, 613, Reuters/Bettmann; p. 611, © Eric R. Berndt/Unicorn Stock Photos. *Chapter 26:* pp. 625, 633, © Dick Luria/FPG International, Inc.; p. 630, © K. Harriger/H. Armstrong Roberts. *Chapter 27:* pp. 647, 662, © Aneal Vohra/Unicorn Stock Photos; p. 650, © Michael Krasowitz/FPG International, Inc. *Chapter 28:* pp. 667, 682, © Ron Chapple/FPG International, Inc.; p. 672, Reuters/Bettmann. *Chapter 29:* pp. 699, 702, AP/Wide World Photos; p. 70 1, © Jim Pickerell/Tony Stone Images. *Chapter 30:* pp. 727, 731, AP/Wide World Photos; p. 728, © Eric R. Berndt/Unicorn Stock Photos. *Chapter 31:* pp. 753, 764, © Jeff Greenberg/Unicorn Stock Photos; p. 756, © Jean Higgins/Unicorn Stock Photos. *Chapter 32:* p. 778, © Jeff Greenberg/PhotoEdit; p. 783, © Roger Tully/Tony Stone Images. *Chapter 33:* pp. 806, 808, © Michael Simpson/FPG International, Inc.; p. 821, © Jim Pickerell/FPG International, Inc. *Chapter 34:* pp. 833, 845, © Mike Malyszko/FPG International, Inc.; p. 841, © Haroldo & Flavia/FPG International, Inc.. *Chapter 35:* pp. 826, 857 © C. Barr/H. Armstrong Roberts; p. 865, © Jean Higgins/Unicorn Stock Phtotos.

PART I
THE BASICS OF ECONOMIC ANALYSIS

CHAPTER 1
INTRODUCTION

CHAPTER PREVIEW

The way people and societies deal with the problem of scarcity is at the heart of economic analysis. Not only are the goods that we use scarce, but the resources that are used to make the goods are scarce, too. Labor, land, machines, factories, and the human skills associated with directing production are all scarce resources. This introductory chapter will explore the problem of scarcity, the choices scarcity forces on us, and the ways that economists pursue their analysis of scarcity and choice.

After studying this chapter, you should be able to:

- Describe the finite character of the earth's resources.
- Distinguish between renewable and nonrenewable resources.
- Discuss people's insatiable wants.
- Tell how scarcity and choice are related to each other.
- Explain the advantages and limitations of economic models.
- Define and contrast microeconomics and macroeconomics.
- Compare positive and normative economics.

"In the Beginning God Created the Heaven and the Earth" is about as familiar a sentence as any written. The Bible tells us that in the five days that followed the creation of heaven and earth, God separated darkness from light, water from dry land, and brought forth a multiplicity of living plants and creatures to inhabit the newly created land, waters, and skies. And on the sixth day, God created people.

So God created man in his own image, in the image of God created he him; male and female created he them. And God blessed them, and God said unto them, Be fruitful and multiply, and replenish the earth and subdue it; and have dominion over the fish of the sea and over the fowl of the air, and over every living thing that moveth upon the earth.

And God said, I have given you every herb bearing seed, which is upon the face of all the earth, and every tree, in which is the fruit of a tree yielding seed, to you it shall be for meat. And to every beast of the earth, and to every fowl of the air, and to everything that creepeth upon the earth, wherein there is life, I have given every green herb for meat, and, behold, it was so.

NO ONE EVER MADE AN OUNCE OF EARTH

Natural resources

The lands, water, metals, minerals, animals, and other gifts of nature that are available for producing goods and services.

What's the lesson we are supposed to draw from this creation narrative? To an economist, the first chapter of Genesis is both a powerful and humbling account of how our **natural resources** came into being. The message is clear. It doesn't even require particular religious conviction. After all, when you think about it, who ever made an ounce of earth? Who ever created a lump of coal or a nugget of gold? It seems that they have always been here for our use. Nobody ever added to nature's bounty.

Although the scientific interpretation of our resource availability differs dramatically from the biblical one, the message is similar. Natural resources were always here. Physicists express this idea of prior existence and the continuance of matter in the first law of thermodynamics—the conservation principle—which asserts that energy can be neither created nor destroyed.

Economists too, accept as fact that every resource on the face of this earth is a gift of nature. Resources were here before men and women arrived on the scene. Every ounce of iron, tungsten, nickel, petroleum, copper, zinc, asbestos, gypsum, and the many other metals, minerals, and energy sources, including those yet undiscovered, were here long before we learned how to make cement, gasoline, steel, plastics, and aspirin.

The nutrients attached to every grain of soil were already imbedded in the soil before people even began to think about working the land. The herds of goats, the schools of sea bass, the flocks of geese, the reindeer and rabbits, the forests and grasses, and all our other food resources were there for the taking.

Can you describe the finite character of the earth's resources?

And, of course, we took! We learned how to extract natural resources from the earth, how to fish them out of the waters, and how to harvest them from the lands. Most exciting of all, we learned the tricks of transforming resources from their original states into new ones. We transform iron ore into steel, crude petroleum into plastic, trees into furniture, rays of the sun into energy, coal into nylon, sand into glass, limestone into cement, bauxite into aluminum, and water flow into electricity. We are continually discovering newer techniques for transformation. And we have been doing this for a long, long time.

Although we have discovered how to put a man on the moon, we are still nowhere near discovering how to make a carrot. On the other hand, we have taken nature's gift of the carrot—and much more of nature's bounty—and learned how to multiply their quantities. Our harvests today represent one of humankind's greatest success stories!

Are We Running Out of Natural Resources?

We live in a finite world. No matter how seemingly bountiful the quantity of our natural resources may be or how carefully we try to conserve them, if we keep using them, they eventually are going to run out. It just seems reasonable. Or does it?

Renewable and Nonrenewable Natural Resources

What distinguishes renewable from nonrenewable resources?

Many natural resources are renewable. Consider, for example, our supply of forests, sea and land animals, water and grasses. Are not these resources self-renewing? But with rapidly growing human populations, overuse of productive lands can turn them into deserts, and overharvesting of fish and land animals can destroy these living resources. Properly managed conservation, on the other hand, cannot only protect these natural resources but even increase their supply.

Admittedly, our metal and mineral resources are not self-renewing. Gold nuggets don't breed. Because planet earth contains finite space, its mineral resources exist only in finite quantities. You do not have to be a rocket scientist to figure out that mining one ton of copper ore depletes that resource by one ton. In fact, we have been depleting our copper supply ever since King Solomon began mining copper in the Negev desert. However, before we work our way down to the last ton of copper, it is very possible that we will have already abandoned it as a usable resource. In other words, even though copper may not be a renewable resource, we may be well-advised to treat it as one.

Does it mean, then, that we will never run out of any natural resource? No such luck. It just means that our knowledge of a resource's relative scarcity, particularly when we consider its availability in the not-too-distant future, is less than exact.

Thousands of years ago, flint was a primary resource used in the production of tools and weapons. Do you know anyone today concerned about our flint supply? We still produce tools and weapons, but we have moved to other tech-

ADDED PERSPECTIVE

Coal . . . Then (1865), and Now (1993)

In 1865, the celebrated economist, Stanley Jevons, wrote a very sobering book, *The Coal Question*. Jevons set out to prove that England's economic progress and power was on the verge of collapse. The reason? The energy source that powered England's economic growth—coal—was being rapidly depleted. No alternative energy source seemed likely. Jevons estimated that England's commercially available coal supply would run out in 100 years. He warned:

> *. . . I must point out the painful fact that such a rate of [economic] growth will before long render our consumption of coal comparable with the total supply. In the increasing depth and difficulty of coal mining we shall meet that vague but inevitable boundary that will stop our progress. . . . A farm, however far pushed, will under proper cultivation continue to yield for ever a constant crop. But in a mine there is no reproduction, and the produce once pushed to the utmost will soon begin to sink to zero. [pp. 154–155]*

Have we run out of coal? Look at England 128 years later! England's coal problem in 1991, ironically, seems to be too much coal! Read *The Economist* [July 20, 1991]:

> *On July 17th the House of Commons energy committee published a report that underlined the bleak future facing the [coal] industry, despite the fact that its productivity has doubled in the past five years. . . . Britain still has three centuries worth of coal at the present rate of consumption. . . .*

nologies that use very different resources. Is copper's future, then, mirrored in flint's past? If so, we may someday regret having conserved our copper supply. We might end up with mountains of unused, useless copper.

Should we conserve the world's oil supply or instead go full speed ahead, using up as much of it as we need to satisfy our current demands? After all, in a generation or two our energy technologies may have already switched to solar and nuclear power, or to some yet unknown technology. What then do we do with oceans of unused, unwanted oil?

How Do You Satisfy Insatiable Wants?

Suppose we had an infinite supply of natural resources? We would still have an insurmountable economic problem. There simply are not enough hours in a day to allow us to transform those resources into *all* the goods and services we want. That is, the problem ultimately may not be the limited quantity of resources available to us, but rather our limitless or insatiable wants.

Let's go back to the biblical story to illustrate the point. Adam and Eve were happy in the Garden of Eden, not because the garden had so much but because they wanted so little. Their problem was eating the fruit from the Tree of Knowledge: One bite of that apple and they suddenly realized they had no clothes, no air-conditioning, no videocassettes, no quartz watches, no push-button phones, and no Buick. It was a quick trip from the state of ignorant bliss to paradise lost. *Their wants became insatiable.*

We inherited their genes. Our tastes for goods and services are virtually limitless. There is always something else we want. And once these wants are satisfied, our minds are just as capable of conceiving new wants as they are of conceiving ways of satisfying them. In this respect, we differ from lions and tigers who, after a kill, are prepared to rest until hungry again. We instead are perpetually in a state of hunger. Even if we had a never-ending supply of the natural

ADDED PERSPECTIVE

If Not the Depletion of Coal, Then Perhaps Oil

In the 1970s, economists and government people looking at the soaring price of oil panicked. What did they see as cause for rising oil prices? You guessed it! Listen to President Jimmy Carter:

It is obvious to anyone that looks at it [the oil crisis] that we've got a problem that's serious now. It's going to get more serious in the future. We're going to have less oil. Those are the facts. They are unpleasant facts. [May 25, 1979]

Sound familiar? Perhaps President Jimmy Carter should have read Stanley Jevon's 1865 *The Coal Question*. He may have found some reason to be more optimistic about our future and less reason to assert his fears about oil supplies as "unpleasant facts."

resources required to satisfy our limitless wants, it would take more than 24 hours a day to transform them into all the goods and services we want.

Scarcity Forces Us to Make Choices

Why does scarcity force people to make choices in spite of their insatiable wants?

Scarcity

The perpetual state of insufficiency of resources to satisfy people's unlimited wants.

If we can't have everything we want today, what do we do? We are forced to make choices. We must choose to produce some goods and services and not others. Sometimes this kind of choosing can be visibly painful. Have you ever seen contestants on the TV game show "The Price Is Right" blindly choosing among three showcases? What are they thinking of during those few moments of decision? They seem to experience both the joy of anticipating the gifts behind the chosen showcase *and* the pain of frustration, knowing that in choosing one showcase, they have to forfeit the gifts behind two.

Life is like that. **Scarcity** governs us. Because we cannot have everything all at once, we are forever forced to make choices. We can use our resources to satisfy only some of our wants, leaving many others unsatisfied.

WHAT IS ECONOMICS?

Economics

The study of how people work together to transform resources into goods and services to satisfy their most pressing wants, and how they distribute these goods and services among themselves.

What has **economics** to do with Genesis I, Adam and Eve, the first law of thermodynamics, scarcities of resources, and infinite wants? Everything! *Economics is the study of how we work together to transform scarce resources into goods and services to satisfy the most pressing of our infinite wants, and how we distribute these goods and services among ourselves.*

The study of economics focuses on four central issues. Who produces what? How? Who consumes what? And who decides? Taken together these issues form the analysis of how an economy works.

Economics Is Part of Social Science

It is sometimes difficult to separate the study of economics from the study of the other social sciences, such as sociology, anthropology, political science, and psychology. All the social science disciplines, including economics, examine individual and social behavior. While economics concentrates on those aspects of

Our conception about the economic world we live in is inculcated at a very early age. We are taught to respect other people's property and to share, and we are allowed to exercise our well-developed sets of consumer preferences even before we know how to spell *demand* and *supply*.

behavior that affect the way we, as individuals and as a society, produce and consume goods and services, our production and consumption are not done in a social vacuum.

What we consume, what we produce, how we produce, and how we go about exchanging resources and products among ourselves is determined, in part, by the character of our political system, by the customs and traditions of our society, and by the set of social institutions and ethical standards we have established.

Consumer sovereignty
The ability of consumers to exercise complete control over what goods and services the economy produces (or doesn't produce) by choosing what goods and services to buy (or not buy).

Our political and economic rights and freedoms stem from the same root. Our right to vote at the ballot box, for example, is not unrelated to **consumer sovereignty** in the marketplace, that is, our freedom to buy or not buy the goods and services offered. This right to choose what we want dictates what producers will ultimately produce, just as our right to choose our political leaders dictates what kind of government policies we ultimately get.

We grow up in a society whose value system, sometimes described as the Protestant ethic, implants in us a belief in the importance of personal frugality, honest labor, and enterprise. To many of us, any alternative value system is considered deviant or antisocial. In this respect, our ethical standards establish the boundaries of permissible economic behavior. We are also taught from childhood to accept a broad set of social responsibilities, many requiring us to share part of our income, through taxes, with people who are less fortunate than ourselves. These accepted social values and responsibilities contribute to the way we select and meet our economic goals and the role we expect our government to play in the economy.

The contributions that economics as a social science discipline makes to the other social sciences are also fundamental. For example, it is difficult to appreciate what federal, state, and local governments do without understanding the economic circumstances underlying their actions. After all, government budgets are *economic* documents. Taxes and government spending are *economic* tools used by the political system to meet economic as well as political and social objectives. Political debates on issues such as the national debt, budget deficits, and the welfare system require an understanding of economics.

It is difficult, as well, for sociologists to study the role of the family in society without, at the same time, studying how the family behaves as an economic unit. To some extent, even when and whom we marry, the number of children we have, and interpersonal relationships within the family are governed by the dictates of economics.

Using Economic Models

Our real economic world is incredibly complex. Millions of people, making independent economic decisions every day, affect not only their own lives but the lives of everyone around them. In many cases, they influence even the lives of people great distances away. It is one thing to appreciate the fact that we are all mutually interrelating, but quite another to untangle these relationships to draw specific one-to-one, cause-and-effect economic correspondences. It's an imposing intellectual challenge, but economists have been working at it with at least modest success, and in some cases, quite remarkable results.

Where do economists start? *By abstracting from reality*. The purpose of such abstraction is to reduce the complexity of the world we live in to more simplified, manageable dimensions. That is essentially what the economists' models do. The models capture the essence of an economic reality. They try to simplify it without distorting its truth.

In a way, when economists build economic models they are like children playing house. In both cases, it is essentially reduction and imitation. In child's play, many of the household activities are ignored and many of the real problems are overlooked. However, the central figures are there, the accuracy of their behavior is uncanny, and the issues basic to most households are reflected in the children's mimicry of adult conversation.

Economic model

An abstraction of an economic reality. It can be expressed pictorially, graphically, algebraically, or in words.

Most **economic model** builders insist that while their models exclude many economic activities of the real world, overlook the complexities of how people really behave, and ignore many pressing issues that people confront every day, what they portray in their models is nevertheless the quintessence of how the real economy works.

And that's the point of economic analysis. Economists are not really interested in pure intellectual exercise. Their interest is not the economic model *per se* but the real world of economics. Their models are designed to serve only as vehicles to a fuller comprehension of what really goes on.

Ceteris Paribus

Ceteris paribus

The latin phrase meaning "everything else being equal."

One of the most important aids economists use in model building is the assumption of ***ceteris paribus***, which translated means "holding constant" or "controlling for the influence of other factors." *Ceteris paribus* allows economists to develop one-to-one, cause-and-effect relationships in isolation, that is, removed from other potentially influential factors. For example, when the price of filet mignon decreases, economists assert that the quantity of filet mignon demanded increases. But this one-to-one, cause-and-effect relationship between price and quantity demanded holds only if everything else going on in the economy is ignored. If the prices of other foods fell at the same time, then it is questionable whether more filet mignon would be demanded when its price falls. After all, people may be more attracted to the other price-reduced foods than they are to the lower priced filet.

Or suppose people lost their jobs on the very day the filet prices were cut? Chances are fewer filets would be demanded. When you're out of work, filet mignon at any price is probably out of mind.

How then can economists make definitive statements about any economic relationship when so many economic events, all potentially influencing each other, may be occurring at the same time? They do so by assuming *ceteris paribus*. It focuses the analysis. That one-to-one, cause-and-effect relationship between price and quantity demanded, however limited by the exclusion of other considerations, is still highly insightful and turns out to be of critical importance to our understanding of price determination.

Ceteris paribus is not confined to economic analysis alone. When the surgeon general of the United States asserts that smoking causes lung cancer, isn't there a *ceteris paribus* assumption lurking in the background? After all, the smoking–cancer relationship ignores a host of other factors that may explain the cancer. Consider the science of meteorology. When the weather forecast is rain, isn't there a *ceteris paribus* assumption made as well? Weather fronts can and often do change direction.

The Circular Flow Model of Goods and Money

Circular flow model

A model of how the economy's resources, money, goods, and services flow between households and firms through resource and product markets.

Household

An economic unit of one or more persons living under one roof that has a source of income and uses it in whatever way it deems fit.

Firm

An economic unit that produces goods and services in the expectation of selling them to households, other firms, or government.

What are some advantages and limitations of the circular flow model?

Let's look now at an honest-to-goodness economic model. Perhaps the simplest model illustrating how an economy works is the **circular flow model** of money, goods, and services shown in Figure 1.

In this model, people are both consumers and producers. They live in **households,** where they consume the goods and services they buy on the product market, and supply their resources—land, labor, capital, and entrepreneurship—on the resource market to **firms** who use the resources to produce the goods and services that appear on the product market. Entrepreneurs provide the vision and drive associated with the the firm's production of goods and services, anticipating profit in return.

The arrows in the upper-half, orange artery of the model depict the direction of the flow of goods and services from firms, through the product market, to households. Households pay for the goods and services with money earned in the resource market. The arrows in the upper-half, green artery depict the direction of the pay-for-goods-and-services flow of money from households, through the product market, to the firms.

Let's look at households now in their capacity as money-earners. They earn money—wages, interest, rent, and profit—by selling or leasing their resources—labor, capital, land, and entrepreneurship—to firms. The arrows in the bottom-half, yellow artery of the model depict the direction of the resource flow from households, through the resource market, to firms. Firms transform those resources into goods and services that eventually appear on the product market. The money that firms earn by selling their goods and services pays for the resources they buy. The arrows in the bottom-half, green artery depict the direction of the pay-for-resources flow of money from firms, through the resource market, to the households. As you see, for every flow of goods, services, and resources there is a counterflow of money. This circular flow of money, resources, goods, and services continues *ad infinitum*.

How would *you* fit into the circular flow model of Figure 1? Suppose you have a summer job making cotton candy at a neighborhood water slide. The job pays $200 weekly. The bottom-half, yellow artery represents your labor flow to the water slide firm, while the bottom-half, green artery represents the $200 you receive from the firm.

Now let's look at your activity in the upper-half of the circular flow model. Using the $200 you earn at the slide—which is now your household income—

FIGURE 1
The Circular Flow Model
Households supply resources—land, labor, capital, and entrepreneurship—to firms through the resource market in return for money payments—rent, wages, interest, and profit. Firms use the resources to produce goods and services which they supply on the product market. There, households buy those goods and services with the incomes received for the resources they supplied.

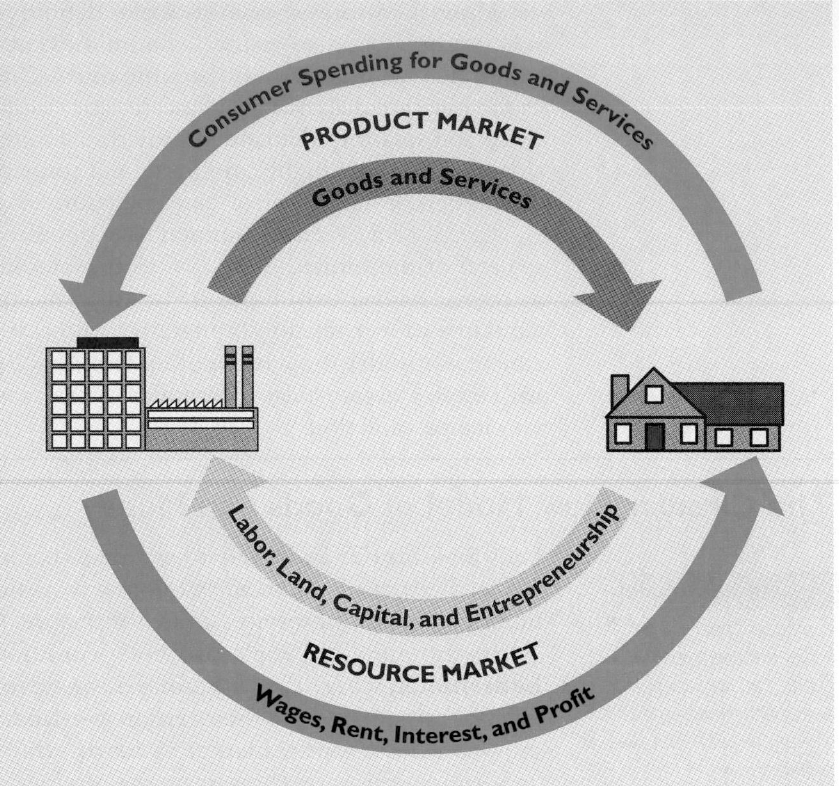

you go to the product market to buy $200 of goods and services that firms have produced for sale on the market. (Among the goods available is cotton candy.) The upper-half, orange artery represents a $200 flow of goods and services to you, while the upper-half, green artery represents the flow of money from you to firms for the goods and services.

Is the circular flow model an accurate reflection of our economic reality? Not really. Where in Figure 1's portrayal of that circular flow are the banks? Where is government? Doesn't government, too, consume goods and services? Where are the unemployed? They consume some of the economy's goods and services, but if they are unemployed, they aren't providing resources. Where, then, do they get the money? How does the model account for retired people? They no longer work, but they continue to consume. Where in the model do we find the economy's exports and imports? Where are savings and investments?

Nowhere! The circular flow model of Figure 1 isn't designed as a *complete* picture of our economic reality. In fact, it ignores a host of major economic institutions and activities.

But far from these omissions representing shortcomings of the model, they illustrate the model's strength. The model is designed to reflect one basic fact about how the economy works: It shows how money, goods, and services flow between households and firms through resource and product markets.

Most of the economic models analyzed in this text are no more complicated than this circular flow model. Some, like Figure 1, are portrayed pictorially, others graphically, and still others take the form of simple algebraic expressions. For example, economists build models of the firm to illustrate how market prices are determined. Other economic models are designed to show how unemployment and inflation arise. Models also serve to illustrate why some nations grow faster than others and why some do not grow at all. Most of these models are expressed graphically. The one thing all of these models have in common is the use of abstraction, that is, the use economists make of simplifying assumptions to distill the essence out of the complicated economic realities they study.

Micro- and Macroeconomics

Microeconomics

A subarea of economics that analyzes individuals as consumers and producers, and specific firms and industries. It focuses especially on the market behavior of firms and households.

Search a newspaper for examples of microeconomic and macroeconomic issues to help get a feeling for the different branches of economics.

Macroeconomics

A subarea of economics that analyzes the behavior of the economy as a whole.

Economists who look at the real world and create simple models to illustrate what they see, do not necessarily look at the same things nor do they ask the same kinds of questions. **Microeconomics,** for example, looks at the behavior of individual households and firms. It asks: Why do firms produce what they do? How do they price their goods and services? How do markets work? What distinguishes competitive from noncompetitive markets? How are resource prices such as wage rates, interest rates, and rents determined? How do firms make profits? What determines people's demands for goods and services?

As these questions suggest, the focus of microeconomic analysis is on the individual. Microeconomists study individuals as consumers and producers. The economy is regarded as a composite of interacting individual economic units. To understand how the economy functions, then, requires an understanding of how each of these individual units behaves and interacts.

Macroeconomics, on the other hand, tries to explain a different set of facts about the economy. It focuses attention on the behavior of the economy as a whole. To macroeconomists, the economy is more than simply a collection of its individual parts. It has character. It has its own vitality and history. It has an identifiable substance. The macroeconomic unit of analysis, then, is the economy.

The macroeconomic questions concern not the behavior and activities of individual households, firms, or markets, but the behavior and activity of the economy itself. They ask, for example, why *national* economies grow? Why do some grow faster than others? What determines a *nation's* savings, its investments, or its consumption? Why does it experience inflation? Why does it generate unacceptable unemployment? Why does it fluctuate from periods of economic prosperity to periods of economic recession?

Positive and Normative Economics

This use of the word "positive" may seem strange to you. Positive means "what is" in this sense—not something good or desirable.

It is one thing for economists to explain why our economy grows at 2.6 percent per year and quite another to advocate that it ought to grow faster. It is one thing to explain why the price of corn is $2.10 per bushel and another to advocate that it ought to be higher. It is one thing to explain what happens to consumer prices when the Federal Reserve System sells government securities and another to advocate that it ought to sell them. It is one thing to explain what happens when firms in certain industries merge and another to advocate that they ought to merge.

You see the differences, don't you? One is a *statement of fact* (the economy grows at 2.6 percent per year) while the other *passes judgment* (it ought to grow faster). Economists are typically very careful about differentiating between analysis of *what is* and *what ought to be.* These are not mutually exclusive, but they are

Positive economics

A subset of economics that analyzes the way the economy actually operates.

Normative economics

A subset of economics founded on value judgments and leading to assertions of what ought to be.

different. Economists refer to *what is* analysis as **positive economics** and *what ought to be* analysis as **normative economics.**

There's nothing inherently wrong with advocacy, although these *oughts* are heavily laden with personal and social values. For example, should we have a minimum wage? What should its level be? Should we subsidize farmers? Should we protect our steel industry? Should we tax the rich more than the poor? Should we provide free school lunches? Should we disallow mergers? Should we regulate bank loans? Should we monitor industrial pollution? Should we control population size?

These are serious economic issues. There is nothing improper about economists applying their own values to economic issues, as long as we know where their value judgments start and their economic analysis ends. It is sometimes difficult to separate the two. Economists, at times, unintentionally disguise advocacy in the language of positive economics. The simple cause-and-effect analysis of positive economics is sometimes taken one step further to advocate policy. For example, analyses of market structures are not always separated from the economists' general view that perfect competition is the most socially desirable market form. Most economists share that view and some will even argue that their analysis of market structures leads inexorably to that view. Their *analysis* of markets may be positive economics, but their *judgment* that competitive markets are more desirable is normative.

Sometimes the elegance of the economists' analysis is so pleasing that proper attention to the theory and policy distinctions associated with the analysis is lacking. For example, economists have reason to be impressed by the elegance of their international trade theory, but they at times combine that theory with free trade advocacy. While their trade theory is positive economics, the free trade advocacy is normative.

WHAT DO ECONOMISTS KNOW?

Does it matter much what policies economists advocate? It matters very much. The White House, for example, has its own Council of Economic Advisers. The Congress and the Federal Reserve System have their own cadres of economists. Corporations, banks, and labor unions all have economists on their payrolls. Economists are everywhere in the media, explaining and advising. Still, what do they know?

We listen attentively each morning to the weather forecast, although few of us fully trust what we hear. We know from experience that if the meteorologist predicts sunny skies, we take an umbrella along for insurance. Meteorologists seem to be forever explaining why yesterday's forecast turned out to be inaccurate. Sometimes we feel that they do not know much more about the weather than we do. But, in fact, they do.

The problem is not their forecast, but our reading of it. We expect too much. The forecast is sunny skies *if* the highs and lows behave properly. Remember *ceteris paribus*? The forecast depends on the fronts moving into our weather region as expected. If they don't, all bets are off. How can meteorologists be held accountable for totally unpredictable changes?

In this respect, economic forecasting is similar to meteorological forecasting. Economic analysis is typically conditioned on the assumption of *ceteris paribus*, that is, that everything else remains unchanged, but it usually doesn't. The econ-

ADDED PERSPECTIVE

Economists, As Wizards of Odds, Are Usually Off

Recession is coming. Recession is coming. Recession is coming. Stephen K. McNees is sick of hearing it. If economists can really see recessions coming, then Boston Harbor's water is as pure as a mountain stream.

The 48-year-old Federal Reserve Board economist has spent a lifetime tracking the performance of his forecasting peers, and one thing he knows for sure—this is no recession, and if it were, few economists would know it.

"The definition of recession is when national economic activity declines for a substantial period of time, and it hasn't," he said. "I predict that historians will not record that the business cycle has peaked."

In fact, if history is a guide, the economists who are saying a recession is here might be eating more crow than scrod come Christmas.

"Econometric" computer models have led to better predictions of economic measures like inflation and gross national product, but major "turning points" have proven extremely hard to call, McNees has found.

Even economists with the most complex computer models, he said, failed to predict the recession which ran from July 1981 through November 1982, and it turned out to be the worst business slump since the Great Depression. Many of them blew it again in 1987 when the economy didn't crash after the stock market did, as they had anticipated. And the recession of 1978 never happened—at least not for two years.

According to McNees, the economics department at the University of Michigan has issued annual economic growth forecasts longer than anyone else, since 1952, with an error average better than other forecasters. But it missed three of four recessions—the 1970, 1974, and 1982 downturns—and correctly forecasted only the 1980 slump.

None of this means economists would do just as well reading tea leaves, McNees allows. Forecasting has improved slightly in the past 20 years, but "the margin of superiority" is surprisingly small between computer users and those who rely on intuition, he said.

In his studies of forecasters who predict GNP, he's found that an "average error" for one-year-ahead predictions is 1.5 percent, which he terms "impressive." What this means is that if an expert predicts the economy will grow at an annual rate of 2 percent, a range of 0.5 percent to 3.5 percent could be expected. "That's not exactly nailing it on the head," he said.

While computers help, McNees feels many forecasters put too much stock in what their machines say. The best seers, he's found, look at the data their computers spit out and then carefully scrutinize it to see if its conclusions gibe with their own. In other words, they give the model's conclusion a specified "weighting" and mix in other factors.

McNees thinks some forecasts would improve if economists put a little more weight on their models and relied a bit less on their judgment. Intuition can be jaundiced, he said, and many economists—especially in Wall Street brokerage houses—have a "vested interest" in optimism.

But even computer models can be flawed by the subjectivity of their human creators. The modelers use equations to link relationships—say, between inflation and interest rates. And the modelers assume that these relationships will recur in the future because they occurred in the past. The trouble is, although these relationships exist, they can change without warning. It's impossible to say why or when.

Sometimes the machine will be wrong simply because even a computer can't tell what's in people's minds. Economists should stress that forecasts are really just "a framework" of possibilities, McNees said. Nowadays, when he hears someone make a precise economic forecast, he shakes his head. "I don't know that they're wrong, but I know that they don't know that they are right," he said.

Source: Bill Hendrick, Cox News Service, September 19,1990.

omists' world is one of uncertainty and they cannot take into account unforeseen future events that come to bear on their analyses. Explaining why previous economic forecasts were inaccurate doesn't build confidence. Instead, people think twice about whether economists really know more about the economy than anybody else. They do.

In the past 50 years, there has been a continuing, dramatic enrichment of our economic knowledge. New and more sophisticated models have been developed to represent our changing world. Also, the growth of economic data, along with the ability to apply modern statistical methods to test models have created a branch of economics called **econometrics.** Econometricians are busy expanding these new and exciting areas of quantitative economic research.

Econometrics

The use of statistics to quantify and test economic models.

In macroeconomics, for example, we now know more about what determines the levels of national income and employment than ever before. Knowing more doesn't necessarily resolve controversy, however. For example, there is no consensus among economists concerning the role government should play in our economy. Much of the debate is founded upon different readings of the same rich data.

In microeconomics, quantitative research on international trade, tax incidence, and market and investment behavior is adding more information to an already rich literature. New theories about uncertainty have given economists new insights into microeconomic questions.

Economists can rightfully claim to have covered an impressive intellectual distance in a very short period of time. Economists really do have something to say, but they realize that they must forever be on guard against claiming too much. As in medical research, the more we know, the more complex are the questions we can ask. Today, the task of the economist is no less difficult than 50 years ago, and the problems encountered no easier. The results of our economic research tell us just a little bit more about ourselves and are well worth the effort.

CHAPTER REVIEW

1. Societies must cope with the fact that resources are finite. Finite resources can be either renewable or nonrenewable.

2. People seem to have insatiable desires for more goods and services. Goods and services are produced from the resources that are available to us.

3. When we couple the facts that resources are finite and human wants are insatiable, it is clear that society must make choices in order to effectively deal with the problem of scarcity.

4. Economics is the social science that describes the way individuals and societies allocate scarce resources for production and distribution in order to satisfy human wants.

5. Economists use models to describe economic behavior. Models are analytical tools based upon simplifying assumptions that allow us to focus on particular economic relationships. One commonly used simplifying assumption is the *ceteris paribus* assumption.

6. Economists look at economic relationships on two levels. Microeconomics explains economic relationships at the level of the individual consumer, firm, or industry. Macroeconomics considers the economic behavior of an entire national economy or a group of national economies.

7. Economic analysis can be either positive or normative, depending on whether the goal is to understand actual economic relationships or to suggest what they ought to be.

8. Positive economic analysis has become more technically sophisticated in the period since World War II. When economists advocate particular economic policies, they practice normative analysis. Normative analysis depends on positive analysis—before economists can consider what ought to be, they must know what is.

KEY TERMS

Natural resources
Scarcity
Economics
Consumer sovereignty
Economic model
Ceteris paribus
Circular flow model
Houschold
Firm
Microeconomics
Macroeconomics
Positive economics
Normative economics
Econometrics

QUESTIONS

1. Does scarcity *always* require us to make choices? Why or why not?

2. Is the idea of insatiable wants unreasonable? Can you imagine a situation in which you have everything you want? What about everything you *need*?

3. What is the difference between renewable and nonrenewable resources?

4. Do you think we should be conserving our oil resources for future generations? After all, there is only so much oil on earth. List the main arguments you can make in favor of conservation. List arguments opposed to conservation.

5. What do you think would happen to our idea of the basic economic problem if we discovered a natural resource that could reproduce and multiply itself any number of times, and could be transformed by labor into any good or service? Before answering, make sure you understand what the basic economic problem is.

6. What is economics? Why is economics considered one of the social sciences? What are some of the other social sciences? What do social scientists study?

7. What does *ceteris paribus* mean? Why is the concept useful to economists? Cite an example.

8. What defines an economic model? In what way is the circular flow model a simplification of reality? Why would economists want to simplify reality?

9. What is the difference between resource markets and product markets? Cite examples.

10. Consider the two statements: "Fifteen percent of our people live below the poverty line," and "Too many people live below the poverty line." Can you

distinguish the positive economic statement from the normative economic statement in these two statements? Compose two additional examples of each.

11. If you looked through the catalog of advanced economic courses and found two that particularly appealed to you: Economics 306, the study of the health care industry, and Economics 359, the study of why economies grow, which would you take to satisfy the college's requirement for a microeconomics course?

12. Suppose your economics professor predicted that the rate of inflation would be 5 percent by the time you took the first economics exam. Instead, the inflation rate was twice the predicted rate. Would you categorically dismiss the professor as a poor predictor and, perhaps worse, an unknowledgeable economist? Why or why not?

Appendix On Reading Graphs

THE ONLY THING WE HAVE TO FEAR IS FEAR ITSELF

It's happened a zillion times: students buy their economics textbooks, flip through the pages, spot the dozens of equations and graphs, and fear, before they start, that it's going to be a losing battle. But it hardly ever is, and certainly not because of the graphs or mathematics. There simply isn't enough information in those graphs or equations to confuse or exasperate.

If you can shake the trauma of the graphic and mathematical form of expression, you will do just fine. As President Franklin D. Roosevelt said during his 1933 inaugural speech, "The only thing we have to fear is fear itself!"

A Graphic Language

Graphs and mathematics are simplified languages. Most of what appears in graphics or mathematics can be described in written form—in fact, most ideas are best expressed that way. In *some* circumstances, however, the written exposition becomes so convoluted that graphs and equations can present the idea more clearly.

Suppose, for example, that the simple arithmetic statement

$$(4)(6) + (8/2) - 12 = 16$$

were written as: 12 subtracted from the product of 4 multiplied by 6 plus the quotient of 8 divided by 2 equals 16. You lose track of the calculations, don't you? The equation form is easier to read. Graphs are like that, too. They are pictorial representations of ideas that could be expressed otherwise, but not with the same degree of clarity.

Know Your Point of Reference

When you read a map, you typically measure out where you want to go from where you are. The where-you-are position is always your point of reference, putting everything else in place.

If you're sitting in St. Louis, Missouri, then Kansas City, Kansas, is 257 miles due west. If you're searching for Louisville, Kentucky, it's 256 miles due east. Kansas City and Louisville are west and east only because you're looking at them from St. Louis. People in Tallahassee, Florida, see Atlanta as due north, but viewed from St. Louis, Atlanta is southeast. In map reading, everything is measured from a point of reference.

Graphs are read the same way. If you can read a map, you can read a graph. Look at Figure A1.

Origin
A graph's point of reference.

The graph's point of reference is called the **origin.** Using our map example, the origin is the graph's St. Louis. Everything on the graph is measured from it. Points can be viewed as lying to the east of the origin, or to the west, or north, or south. More precise readings describe the points as "north by northwest" or "east by southeast." You can see them in your mind's eye.

FIGURE A1
The Four Quadrants

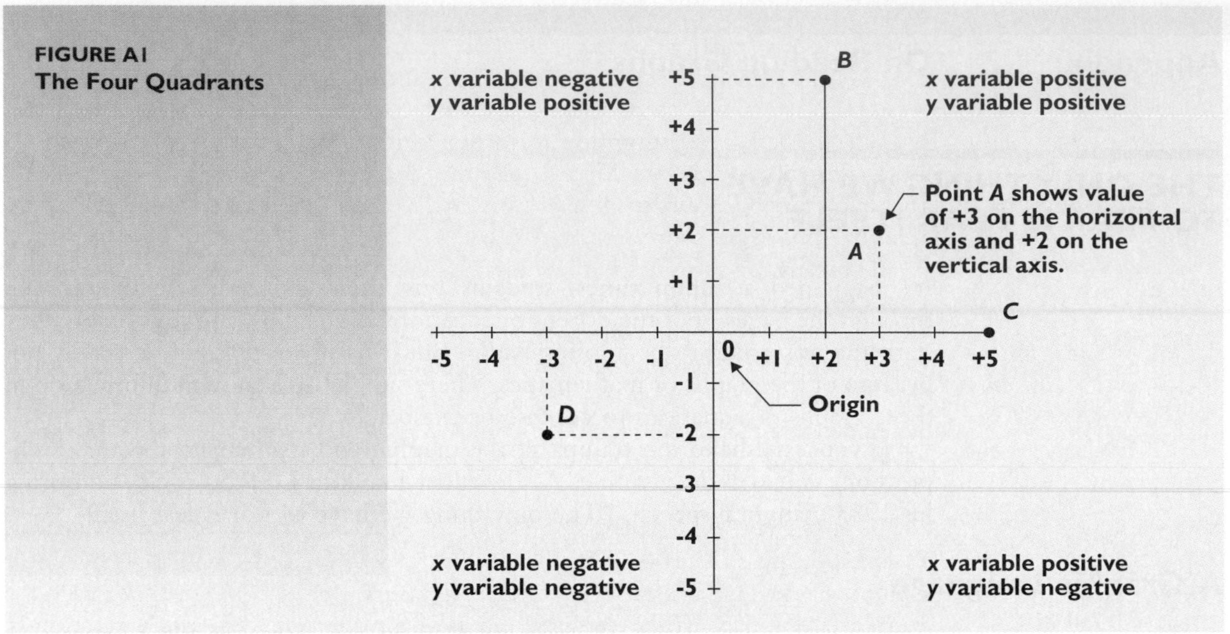

Notice that Figure A1 is divided into four quadrants (or parts). The vertical (Y) axis—running north and south through the origin—and the horizontal (X) axis—running east and west through the origin—are its dividers.

Measuring Distances on Graphs

Have you ever seen a NASA space shot countdown? As you know, its point of reference is blast-off. Typically, NASA starts counting before ignition. If you're watching on TV, you'll see the digital readout register minus 10 seconds, then minus 9, then minus 8, counting down to zero. At zero, ignition occurs and the count continues from zero to +1 seconds, then +2, and so on. The time scale is a continuum, with zero separating the minuses from the pluses.

Graph scaling is also on a continuum. In Figure A1, the vertical scale north of the origin (which is zero) and the horizontal scale east of the origin (which is zero) measure positive values. For example, point *A* located at (+3, +2) reads +3 units away from the origin horizontally and +2 units away from the origin vertically. It marks the intersection of +3 and +2. Point *B*, located at (+2, +5) reads +2 units away from the origin horizontally and +5 units away from the origin vertically. Look at point *C* (+5, 0). It is +5 units away from the origin horizontally and at zero on the vertical scale.

The vertical scale south of the origin and the horizontal scale west of the origin measure negative values. For example, point *D*, located at (–3, –2) reads –3 units away from zero horizontally and –2 units away from the origin vertically. *As you see, every point in every quadrant has its own specific numerical bearings.*

Graphing Relationships

It's generally true that the more you study, the higher your grade. Suppose somebody who is less convinced than you about the relationship between effort and reward insists on evidence. What can you do to make the point? If logic doesn't work, perhaps a test will. For example, you could experiment with Economics 101 and over the course of the semester, compare your exam scores with the number of hours spent studying for them.

The underlying assumption in such a relationship is that exam scores *depend* on the number of hours of study. By varying the hours studied, you vary the scores obtained. Hours studied is described as the **independent variable** in the relationship, exam scores as the **dependent variable.**

Independent variable

A variable whose value influences the value of another variable.

Dependent variable

A variable whose value depends upon the value of another variable.

Typically, economists work with relationships that express dependence. For example, the quantity of fish people are willing to buy depends on the price of fish. The price of fish is the independent variable and the quantity people are willing to buy is the dependent one. The amount of money people spend consuming goods and services depends on their income—again a linkage between a dependent variable and an independent one. Another such dependent relationship is the number of hours people are willing to work and the wage rate offered.

Suppose you find that with zero hours of study, you fail miserably, scoring 20 out of a possible 100. With 2 hours per week of study, you score 50. With 5 hours per week, you raise your grade to 70. With 7 per week, your grade improves to 80. With 10 hours per week, you top the class with the highest score, 85.

If you experimented with Biology 101 exams, the effort-and-reward relationship would still be positive, but the specific payoffs might be different. For example, with zero hours, you still fail, this time scoring only 12 out of a possible 100. With 2 hours per week, you only score 35. With 5 hours, you get considerably better, scoring 55, with 7 hours you score 70, and with 10 hours a week studying biology, you score 75.

That's convincing evidence that increased hours of study produce higher grades, but the written presentation can get confusing, particularly when the number of exams and courses increases. The written form is not always the clearest way to express observations.

Perhaps a clearer presentation of the evidence could be made by converting the information into table form. Look, for example, at the table in Figure A2.

Is it any clearer? The information is the same; it's just displayed differently. It is not only easier to see that the more time spent on study, the higher the score, but comparisons between economics and biology are more readily observed.

Look how the same information is transcribed into graphic form. Panel *a* in Figure A2 records the same information as the table.

As you see, in panel *a*, hours of study are measured along the horizontal axis. Exam scores are measured along the vertical axis. Both variables in our example are positive. Therefore, the corresponding points in the table—such as 5 hours of study and an exam score of 70 in economics—locate in the upper-right quadrant of the graph. Both graphs in Figure A2 show that quadrant.

Connecting Points to Form Curves

The table and graphs in panel *a,* Figure A2 are abbreviated displays of evidence. They record only 10 pieces of data. The experiment could have been expanded to record an exam score for every hour of study, or even every minute instead

FIGURE A2
Test Scores for Economics 101 and Biology 101

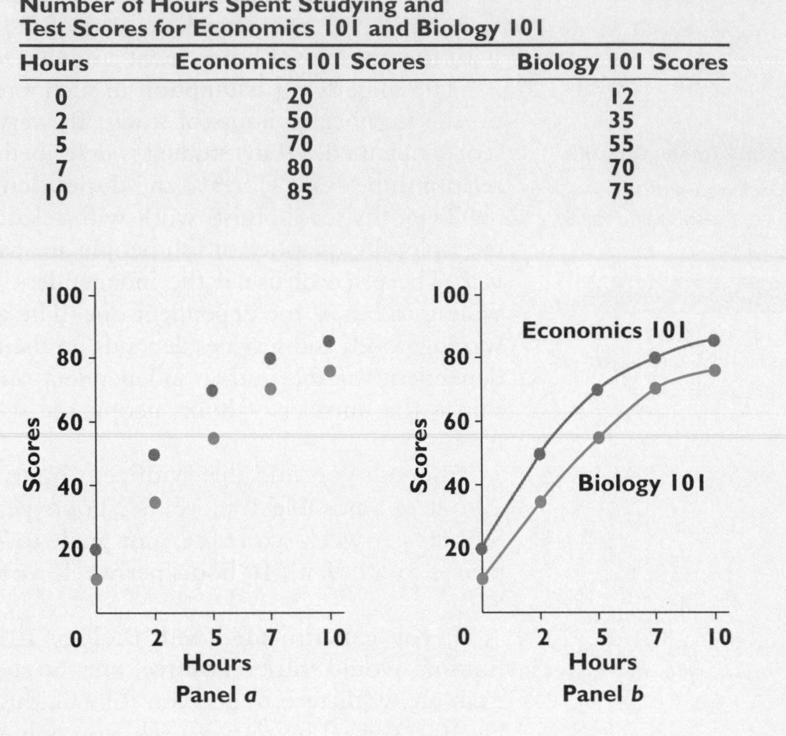

Number of Hours Spent Studying and Test Scores for Economics 101 and Biology 101

Hours	Economics 101 Scores	Biology 101 Scores
0	20	12
2	50	35
5	70	55
7	80	70
10	85	75

of every five hours. That is, if the intervals between the points in panel *a* could be filled in to create a *continuous* series of data points connecting study hours and exam scores (unrealistic, of course, because nobody could take that many exams in one semester), such a completed series would trace a continuous curve on the graph, which is what we see in panel *b*.

But is it necessary to ascertain *every* point to create a curve? Suppose you want to graph the relationship between income and saving. And suppose the table accompanying Figure A3 presents the relevant data.

Note that the data set starts with $40,000 of income. If the graph were to plot *every* income value from $0 at the origin to, say, $43,000 in units of $1,000, 43 units would be marked off on the horizontal axis, but only the last four of the 43 units would bear any data. The graph becomes dominated then by empty, dataless space. And to keep the graph within the bounds of the page, it may even be necessary to make each income unit represent $2,000. By doing so, it becomes even more difficult to read on the vertical axis the increases in saving that are associated with the $1,000 increases in income.

Breaking the axes—as shown in Figure A3—cuts out the empty, dataless space. The break, introduced after the first units on both the vertical and horizontal axes, allows the graphmaker to magnify the data, making it easier for the reader to focus on the relevant part of the graph. The 40th unit of income follows the break on the horizontal axis and the 80th unit of saving—each unit representing $100 of saving—follows the first unit on the vertical axis. The resulting graph maps out a clear picture of the saving curve.

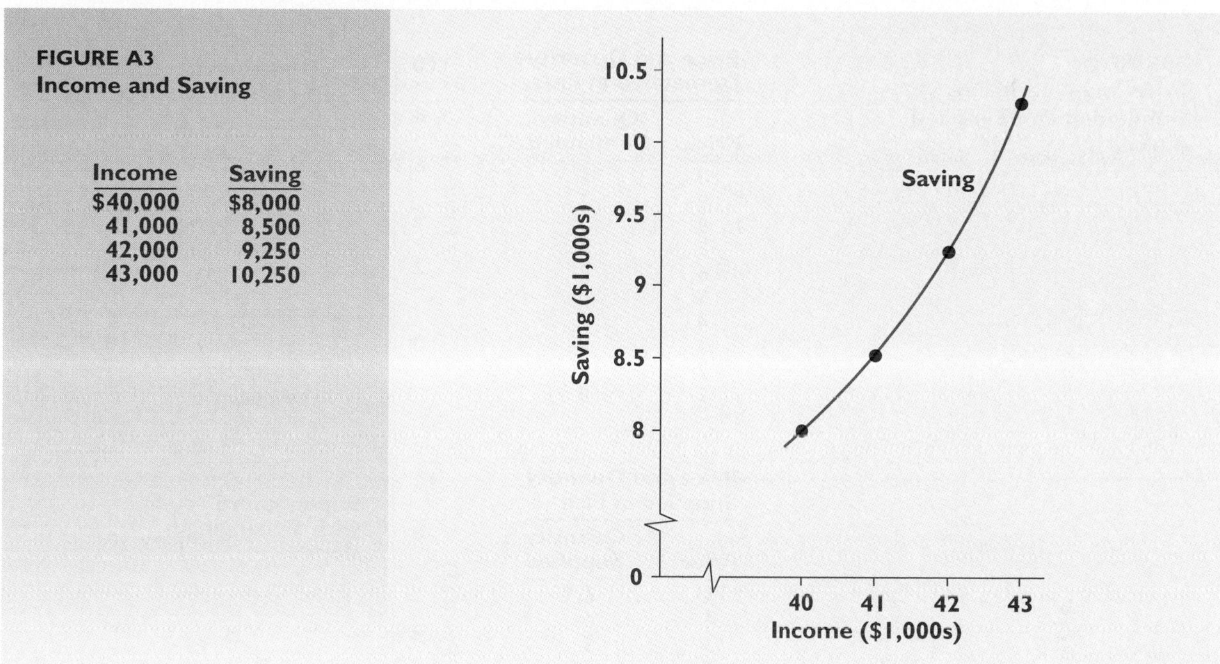

THE SLOPE OF A CURVE

Consider the law of demand: As the price of a good falls, the quantity of the good demanded increases. The table and graph in panel *a,* Figure A4 depict such a relationship between the price of fish and quantity demanded. (The law of demand will be studied more closely in Chapter 3.)

Panel *a,* Figure A4 connects the discrete data given in the accompanying table to form a solid curve which, as you see, is in the form of a straight line.

Slope of a curve

The ratio of the change in the variable measured on the vertical axis to the corresponding change in the variable measured on the horizontal axis, between two points.

The ***slope of a curve*** *measures the ratio of change in the value on the vertical axis to the corresponding change in value on the horizontal axis between two points.*

$$\text{Slope} = \frac{\text{rise}}{\text{run}} = \frac{\text{change in the value on vertical axis}}{\text{change in the value on horizontal axis}}$$

Downward-sloping curves—sloping from northwest to southeast—are considered *negatively sloped;* that is, a positive (negative) change in the independent variable is associated with a negative (positive) change in the dependent variable. Upward-sloping curves—sloping from southwest to northeast—are *positively sloped;* that is, a positive (negative) change in the independent variable is associated with a positive (negative) change in the dependent variable.

Look again at panel *a* in Figure A4. Every $1 change in price generates a one-unit change in quantity demanded. For example, when price falls from $10 to $9 (–$1), the quantity demanded increases from 1 to 2 fish (+1). The slope of the curve, within the $10 to $9 price range, then, is

$$-1/+1 = -1$$

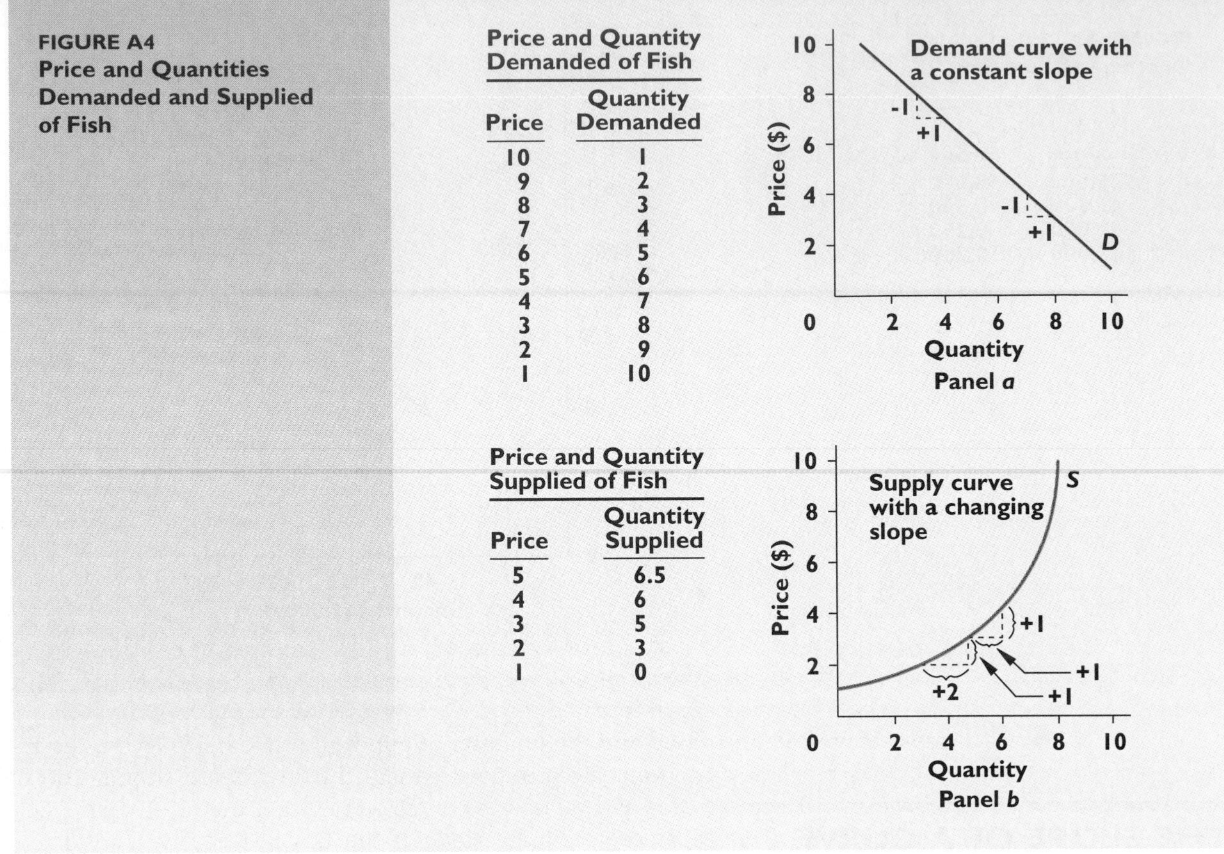

FIGURE A4
Price and Quantities Demanded and Supplied of Fish

Price and Quantity Demanded of Fish

Price	Quantity Demanded
10	1
9	2
8	3
7	4
6	5
5	6
4	7
3	8
2	9
1	10

Price and Quantity Supplied of Fish

Price	Quantity Supplied
5	6.5
4	6
3	5
2	3
1	0

The slope is negative. Note that any other price change within any other price range in this example still generates a negative slope of –1. When price increases from \$3 to \$4 (+\$1), the quantity demanded decreases from 7 fish to 6 (–1). The slope +1/–1 remains –1. *Any curve with a constant slope is a straight line.* That's precisely what we see in panel *a*.

Panel *b* represents a typical supply curve. It depicts the willingness of fishermen to supply varying quantities of fish at varying prices. The curve slopes upward, indicating that higher prices induce greater quantities supplied. Unlike the demand curve in panel *a*, the supply curve here is not a straight line. It is less steep at low price ranges than at higher ones. Let's calculate the slopes within different price ranges. When price increases from \$2 to \$3 (+\$1), the quantity supplied increases from 3 to 5 fish (+2). The slope of the curve, within the \$2 to \$3 price range, then, is

$$+1/+2 = +0.5$$

But when the price rises from \$3 to \$4 (+\$1), the quantity supplied increases only from 5 fish to 6 (+1). The slope of the curve within the \$3 to \$4 price range is

$$+1/+1 = +1$$

There's nothing peculiar or complicated about any curve on any graph or the measurement of its slope. The slope of the curve is only a numerical way of expressing the curve's shape. The numerical value signals the strength of the re-

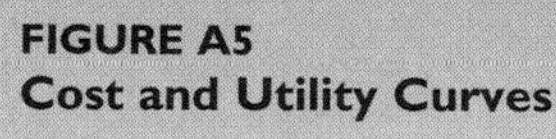

FIGURE A5
Cost and Utility Curves

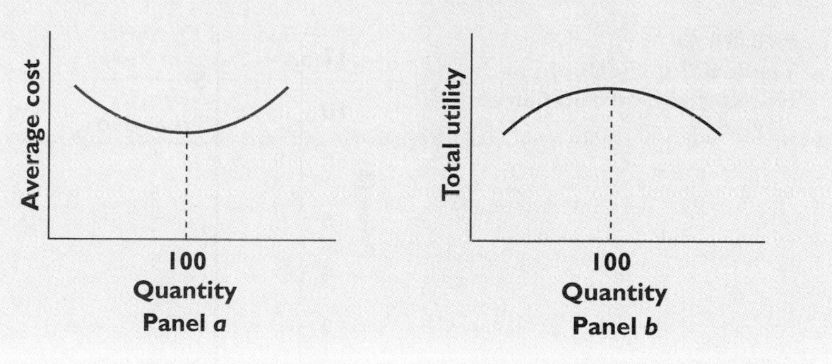

lationship between changes in the variables measured on the vertical and horizontal axes.

U-Shaped and Hill-Shaped Curves

Some curves that are part of the economists' bag of tools contain both positive- and negative-sloping segments. Look, for example, at Figure A5, panels *a* and *b*.

The U-shaped curve in panel *a* shows the relationship between the average cost of producing a good and the quantity of goods produced. Typically, the average cost falls as more units are produced—that's the downward-sloping part of the curve. Beyond some point, however—100 units in panel *a*—average cost begins to increase with production, which is the upward-sloping part of the curve.

From zero to 100 units the slope of the curve, although changing, is always negative. Beyond 100 units, it becomes positive. There's nothing complicated about reading the graph if you consider each point on the curve, one at a time. *Every point on that U-shaped average cost curve represents a specific quantitative relationship between average cost and level of production.* Nothing more!

The hill-shaped curve in panel *b* is much the same. It shows the relationship between the total utility or benefit derived from consuming a good and the quantity of goods consumed. The basic idea is that for some goods—water, for instance—the more consumed, the greater the total enjoyment, but only up to a point. Beyond that point—100 units in panel *b*—the more water, the lower the total enjoyment. Who, for example, enjoys a flood? From zero to 100 units the slope of this curve is positive, but it becomes negative thereafter.

Vertical and Horizontal Curves

Economists also work with relationships that, when graphed, trace out as perfectly vertical or horizontal curves. These are represented in Figure A6, panels *a* and *b*.

Consider the circumstance where fishermen return home after a day's work with 100 fish. Suppose they are willing to supply those fish at whatever price the fish will fetch. After all, a day-old fish isn't something to prize. If the price is $10 per fish, they are willing to sell all 100. If the price is only $9, they are still willing to sell all of them. If the price is $100 per fish, they *still* will supply only 100

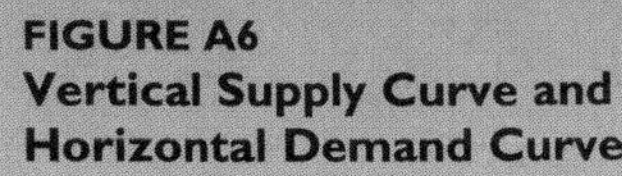

FIGURE A6
Vertical Supply Curve and Horizontal Demand Curve

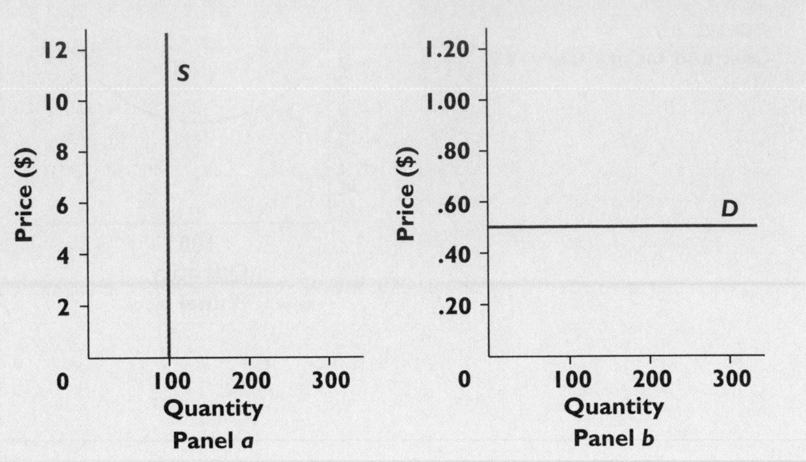

fish, because the day's work is done and there are no more fish available. The supply curve, shown in panel *a*, is a vertical line to denote a supply of 100 fish, whatever the price. Its slope is everywhere infinite. That is, when price changes from \$10 to \$9 (−\$1), quantity doesn't change (0). The slope, then, is −1/0. That's infinity.

What about the perfectly horizontal curve? Suppose you are selling tomatoes in an outdoor market, competing against hundreds of other tomato growers. Suppose also that the price is \$0.50 per pound and you can sell as much as you want at that price. If you were to raise your price by just one penny, or even less, you couldn't sell any tomatoes at all. What a difference a fraction of a penny makes! After all, why would anyone buy your tomatoes when they can buy all they want from your competitors at \$0.50?

How would you graph the demand curve you face? It would be a straight horizontal curve as shown in panel *b*. At \$0.50 you could sell 10, 20, or 200 tomatoes. At just an infinitesimally small increase—approaching zero—in price, you sell zero tomatoes. The slope, then, is 0 divided by any number, which is zero.

FIGURE A7
Measuring the Slope at a Point on a Curve

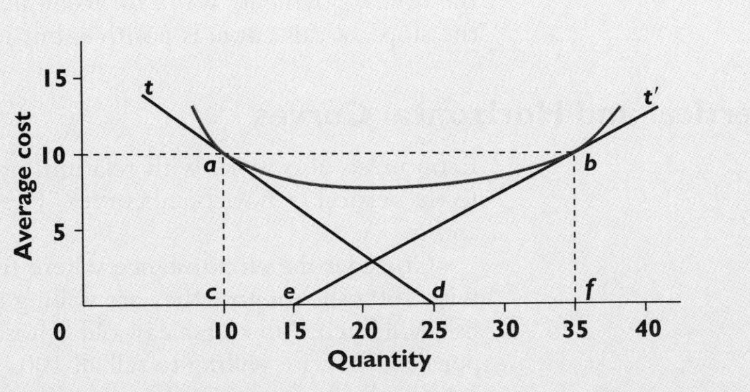

Measuring the Slope of a Point on a Curve

Tangent

A straight line that touches a curve at only one point.

Slope of a tangent

The slope of a curve at its point of tangency.

Look at the U-shaped curve of Figure A7.

To find the slope of any point on the curve, draw a **tangent**—a straight line just touching the curve—at the point where the slope is to be measured. *The* ***slope of the tangent*** *is the same as the slope of the curve at the point of tangency.* What is the slope of the tangent? Look at tangent *td* at point *a* on the curve. Its slope is *ac/cd*, or numerically,

$$-10/+15 = -2/3$$

The minus sign indicates that the point of tangency lies on the downward-sloping part of the curve.

What about the slope at point *b*? Draw the tangent, *et'*. Its slope is *bf/ef*, or numerically,

$$+10/+20 = +1/2$$

Its positive value indicates it is on the upward-sloping part of the U-shaped curve.

KEY TERMS

Origin
Independent variable
Dependent variable
Slope of a curve
Tangent
Slope of a tangent

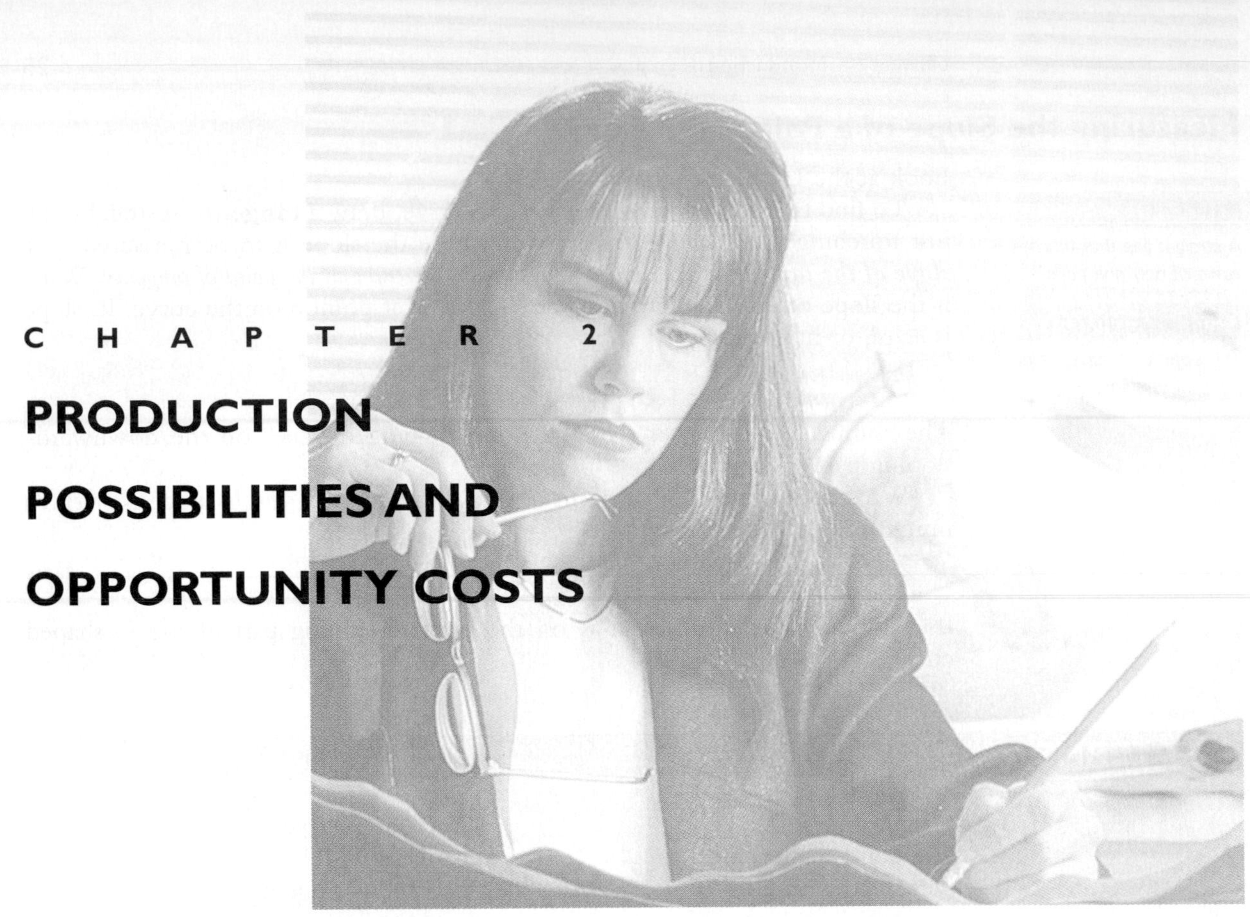

C H A P T E R 2

PRODUCTION POSSIBILITIES AND OPPORTUNITY COSTS

CHAPTER PREVIEW

This chapter considers the variety of ways in which productive resources—labor, capital, land, and entrepreneurship—are combined to make products. It also shows how we model production possibilities. Also, the problem of choice of output, given the scarcity of resources, is posed in this chapter. In order to have more of a particular product, an economy must sacrifice the production of other products. In economists' language, there is an opportunity cost associated with an increase in the output of any product. Furthermore, switching from the production of one product to another may involve increasing opportunity costs. This phenomenon is called the law of increasing costs.

Modern economies experience growth in their productive capacities over time. Economic growth can be the result of increases in the quantity of productive resources or come about through technological innovation. Specialization of labor also results in economic growth over time.

After studying this chapter, you should be able to:

- Name the factors of production.
- Discuss the concept of production possibilities.
- Distinguish between capital goods and consumer goods.

- Define opportunity cost.
- Explain the law of increasing costs.
- Tell how technological change is related to economic growth.
- Explain how specialization of labor contributes to economic growth.

Biologists talk about their field of study without worrying whether people will misunderstand the words they use. A monocotyledon is a monocotyledon—no one ever mistakes it for a screwdriver. Biologists have a language all their own.

Economists, too, have developed their own language, but the vocabulary they chose is rather commonplace. When economists talk about labor, most people feel right at home. People also know what capital, rent, profit, prices, competition, monopoly, money, income, and employment mean.

Unfortunately, what people understand these terms to mean is not always the same meaning that economists use. To understand what economists mean by these terms may sometimes require more effort to unlearn what we already know than to learn what the economists mean.

FACTORS OF PRODUCTION

Factors of production

Any resource used in a production process. Resources are grouped into labor, land, capital, and entrepreneurship.

For example, economists refer to the resources used in the production of goods and services as **factors of production.** The four factors are labor, entrepreneurship, capital, and land.

The two *human* factors are labor and entrepreneurship. The other two, capital and land, are nonhuman factors.

Labor

Labor

The physical and intellectual effort of people engaged in producing goods and services.

Labor is the physical and mental exertion of people engaged in the production of goods and services. Labor willingly sells its skills in the resource market for agreed-upon prices. There is no coercion involved, and the agreements or contracts typically specify price per hour, per week, or per year.

The absence of coercion and the limitations specified in the contract are critical characteristics of the economists' definition of labor. No one sells his or her labor to a firm forever. To economists, slave labor is not regarded as a labor resource at all, since slaves never willingly offer their labor for a price. Bought and sold on slave markets, they are forced to work. Incredible as it may seem, slaves were regarded by slaveowners and the courts as personal property. What about prison labor today? Do inmates willingly offer their services? Who decides the price? If it's not labor, then what is it? You can see that the economists' concept of labor is narrowly defined and can be somewhat more complicated than first imagined. What about peasants in Third World economies who are harnessed to crude, wooden plows? In these economies people and animals are sometimes interchangeable, pulling plows across tough top soils. Certainly a water buffalo isn't labor. What, then, is the peasant who substitutes for the water buffalo?

Not an unfamiliar scene, is it? Microchip technology is everywhere around us. Many of you may end up working in the microchip industry, and all of us will benefit from this modern technology through the goods and services we consume. The microchip is as important to our economic life today as the horse was, years ago, to our great grandparents.

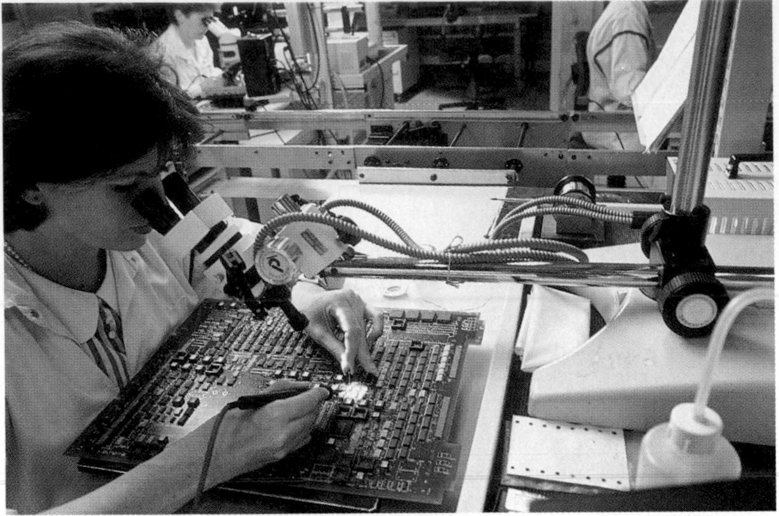

Capital

Capital

Manufactured goods used to make and market other goods and services.

What identifies **capital?** Capital is a *manufactured good used in the production and marketing of goods and services that households consume.* Because capital is not directly consumed by households, it is sometimes referred to as an *intermediate good.* For example, shoemakers' tools and machinery used to produce shoes are not household items. The shoes, of course, are. The stocks of shoe inventory are capital goods. The shoes in inventory become household consumption goods only when they are actually consumed by the household. Obviously, the factory that houses the machinery and inventories is a capital good.

What about robots? Robots that do what labor does are still only pieces of machinery. Store window mannequins are also capital goods because they are used to convert the finished goods inventory into household consumption. In the same way, the thousands of compact discs in record shop inventories are regarded as capital goods because the inventories are as necessary as the disc-making machinery in providing CDs for household consumption. How could you buy a particular CD if the store didn't carry it? It becomes a consumption good only when it is purchased by the consumer.

What about the water buffalo pulling the wooden plow? Even though the buffalo isn't manufactured, economists still define beasts of burden as capital goods. Thoroughbreds running at Churchill Downs are capital goods used to produce horse racing enjoyment.

What about Michael Chang's tennis racket? It is a capital good used to produce a service. The service is our enjoyment at Wimbledon. That same racket in your hand is not capital. After all, it is not in the process of making other goods or services when you play. It is used only for your own pleasure. David Letterman's stylish wardrobe is capital goods. Yours isn't.

Sometimes, capital gets mixed in with labor so we end up with a hybrid factor. For instance, would Linda Marshall, working as a chemical engineer for Dow Chemical, be considered labor? Perhaps the most significant difference between Linda's work and the work of an unskilled laborer is her four years of college education. That education is capital. What then is the engineer, capital or

Studying for that calculus exam? It may not be visual, but this woman is building capital in much the same way that other people build machinery. You're looking at a future mechanical engineer who will forever be endowed with substantial human capital.

labor? Economists refer to special skills, acquired through education or training, as **human capital.**

Human capital

The knowledge and skills acquired by labor, principally through education and training.

As you see, what is obviously labor to other people is less than obviously labor to economists. Is intelligence capital? If so, what's left of labor? Confusing? As you may already sense, differentiations between labor and capital as factors of production, are as much philosophical issues as they are economic.

Land

Land is a natural-state, nonhuman resource that is fixed in quantity. It includes both the real estate and the metals and minerals it contains. For example, an uncut diamond is land. A virgin forest is land. The oceans of oil underneath the North Sea are also land. To the economist, the Gobi desert and the Pacific ocean are land resources.

Land

A natural-state resource such as real estate, grasses and forests, and metals and minerals.

The problem with the economists' definition of land as a factor of production is that we seldom, if ever, see land in its natural state. A tree that is cut and used in production is no longer strictly a land resource. It becomes capital as well. It was cut down by labor and machines. Lumber, then, is a manufactured good. Irrigated land, too, is not strictly land. The irrigation system is capital. Any improved land is a combination of capital and land.

Entrepreneurship

The **entrepreneur** is the only factor of production that does not contract to work for a specific price. Entrepreneurs assume all the risks and uncertainties involved in producing goods and services. Their reward is profit. But they can also incur losses.

Entrepreneur

A person who alone assumes the risks and uncertainties of a business. The entrepreneur conceives the idea of the business, and decides what factors of production to use and how to market the goods and services produced.

No good or service is produced by spontaneous combustion. Resources just don't come together on their own. *Somebody* has to conceive of the essential idea of production, decide what factors to use, market the goods and services produced, and accept the uncertainty of making or losing money in the venture. This somebody is the entrepreneur, a word that comes from the French, to undertake. Although entrepreneurs who own and operate businesses typically do all these things, economists define their entrepreneurial role only in terms of the uncertainties of business they assume.

After all, entrepreneurs can delegate the buying of land, labor, and capital and the overseeing of production to a hired managerial staff. That's precisely

Are the meanings of the terms labor, capital, land, and entrepreneurship that are used by economists different from those you are accustomed to?

what most modern corporations do. Managerial activity is labor. When entrepreneurs manage the production process, they function as laborers. Entrepreneurs can delegate every other function of production to labor, except the function of assuming risk and uncertainty.

We have briefly surveyed the four factors of production. Now let's put them to work.

ROBINSON CRUSOE'S PRODUCTION POSSIBILITIES

Let's begin our analysis of production by imagining Robinson Crusoe alone on an island. We can assume the island has abundant resources and that the stranded Crusoe has access to them. But he also has insatiable wants. After all, why should he be different? What does he do?

A crucial choice for even a one-person economy is what to produce.

He can spend part of the day in leisure and part at work. He could pick mangoes right off the trees or he can fish. He can plant and harvest crops. His principal factors of production are his own labor and the virgin land about him.

Let's suppose he decides to spend his waking hours gathering food for consumption. He climbs trees for mangoes and coconuts and spends the better part of the day trying to pick fish out of the lagoon. He ends each day with six units of consumption. It's enough to keep him going, but, of course, he wants more. How does he get it? *Let's suppose he decides to make a fishing spear.* That requires finding the right materials and fashioning a spear. He sets aside part of the day to find a young tree that will serve as the shank, a stone that can be sharpened to make a spearhead and a length of vine to bind the two together.

This takes time. If he takes the time to produce the spear, he can gather only five units of consumption goods. Why then do it? Because with a fishing spear, he expects to catch more fish in the next round of production. It's a risk, of course. There's no guarantee he will catch more fish. Some expectations are never realized. But let's suppose he catches more. *The spear is Robinson Crusoe's first unit of capital.*

He decides to make a second spear as well to use as an extension tool so that he can reach the bigger, riper fruit at the top of the trees. He discovers that finding the right material for the second spear takes even more time than it did for the first. Why? He had already used the most available tree for the fishing spear's shank, the most available stone for the spearhead, and the most accessible length of vine to tie them together.

While he is producing both the fishing spear and the extension spear, he can manage to gather only three units of consumption goods. Why then do it? Because with both units of capital, he expects to produce considerably more consumption goods in the next round of production.

The Robinson Crusoe economy is simple, yet it contains all the elements of a modern, dynamic economy. It has capital goods production as well as consumption. Land, labor, capital, and entrepreneurship combine to create a set of goods and services.

Production possibilities
The various combinations of goods that can be produced in an economy when it uses its available resources and technology efficiently.

The components of the set are variable. For example, these factors of production can be combined into any of the **production possibilities** shown in Table 1.

The first possibility is for Robinson Crusoe to allocate all his resources to producing consumption goods. If he does that, he ends up with six units of consumption. On the other hand, if he decides to produce a unit of capital, he ends

TABLE 1 Robinson Crusoe's Production Possibilities

Consumption Goods	Capital Goods
6	0
5	1
3	2
0	3

up with only five units of consumption. *As far as he's concerned, then, the unit of capital cost him one unit of consumption.*

Opportunity Cost

Opportunity cost

The quantity of other goods that must be given up to obtain a good.

Is the dollar cost of your college education the same as its opportunity cost?

What economists mean by cost is **opportunity cost,** that is, the quantity of other goods that must be given up to obtain a good. That's a powerful notion of cost. It applies universally. For example, the opportunity cost of watching the LA Lakers play the Boston Celtics the night before an exam is the five points that could have earned an A. The opportunity cost of renovating the high school auditorium is the new biology lab that the school had been thinking about. Opportunity cost applies even where you may least suspect. For example, for a married couple, the opportunity cost of marriage to each partner is the opportunities each gives up that would have been possible had they remained single.

You see the connection, don't you? The thought that goes through Crusoe's mind when contemplating production is the same kind of thinking that you do before studying for an exam. You both think about the opportunities given up. But you make choices. When Crusoe gives up a unit of consumption goods to produce that first unit of capital goods, it's probably because he values that first unit of capital goods more than the consumption good given up. If you spend the evening studying for the exam, it's probably because you value the expected higher grade more than you do the Celtics game.

You may have erred. The game could have been the season's best and the studying didn't make a difference in your exam score. In hindsight, you find that the studying wasn't worth the cost. But what could you have done otherwise? Opportunity costs are typically subjective. How could you possibly know with certainty what opportunity costs are? Even Robinson Crusoe, making simple choices on the island, must rely on calculating *expected* gains and opportunity costs of choices made.

The Law of Increasing Costs

If Robinson Crusoe decides to produce two units of capital, he ends up with only three units of consumption. Measured in terms of its opportunity cost, that second unit of capital costs Crusoe two units of consumption. That is more than he had to give up for the first unit of capital.

What happens if he decides to produce three units of capital? Look again at Table 1. Their production absorbs all the resources available. He ends up with nothing at all to consume! The opportunity cost of that third unit of capital is the remaining three units of consumption.

ADDED PERSPECTIVE

Guns and Butter

Suppose Robinson Crusoe discovers that he is not alone on the island and that his new neighbors are somewhat less than friendly. Suppose they are downright threatening. It would be foolhardy for Crusoe to continue producing only consumption and capital goods. After all, he may wake up one morning to find his uninvited neighbors helping themselves to his consumption and capital goods!

To protect life and property, Robinson Crusoe may have to devote some part of his working day to the production of defensive weapons. Instead of making a fishing spear, he may make several bows and arrows. Or perhaps, remembering what the Chinese had done, build a Great Wall to keep his neighbors out. But Robinson Crusoe knows that every bow, every arrow, and every stone in every defensive wall has an opportunity cost that reflects the quantity of nondefensive goods given up.

Crusoe's guns versus butter choices are the same kinds of choices every society has been forced to make from time immemorial. If an economy is operating on its production possibilities frontier, then guns can be produced only at the expense of butter. More guns means less butter.

What are choices in the Robinson Crusoe tale are also real choices for Americans. Dwight D. Eisenhower, the 34th U.S. President was a five-star general during World War II and also the Supreme Commander of the Allied Forces in Europe. The 1944 invasion of Nazi-occupied Europe under his command and the battles that followed led to Germany's unconditional surrender. But victory is always bittersweet. No one has expressed the costs of war better than President Eisenhower himself:

Every gun that is made, every warship launched, every rocket fired signifies, in the final sense, a theft from those who hunger and are not fed, those who are cold and are not clothed. This world in arms is not spending money alone. It is spending the sweat of its laborers, the genius of its scientists, the hopes of its children. . . . This is not a way of life at all in any true sense. Under the cloud of threatening war, it is humanity hanging from a cross of iron.

Speech before the American Society of Newspaper Editors, April 16, 1953.

Discussion

Can you imagine a situation in which two people, both agreeing on the opportunity costs of war preparedness, would disagree on whether to pursue a policy of preparedness? What other issues do you think they would consider? Do you think nations go to war—or stay out of war—strictly on the basis of economic calculation?

Law of increasing costs

The opportunity cost of producing a good increases as more of the good is produced. The law is based on the fact that not all resources are suited to the production of all goods and that the order of use of a resource in producing a good goes from the most productive resource unit to the least.

Be sure that you can explain why the law of increasing costs causes the production possibilities curve to be bowed out.

Do you notice what's happening? *The opportunity cost of producing each additional unit of capital increases as more of the units are produced.* Economists refer to this fact of economic life as the **law of increasing costs.** It applies no matter what goods are considered. For example, if Robinson Crusoe had started with three units of capital and began adding consumption, the amount of capital goods he would have to give up to produce each additional unit of consumption, too, would increase. Figure 1 illustrates the production possibilities of Table 1 in graphic form.

Look at points *A*, *B*, *C*, and *D* in Figure 1. These are precisely the production possibilities shown in Table 1. Point *A*, for example, represents the choice of devoting all resources to the production of six units of consumption. The curve has a negative slope because any increase in capital goods production comes only at the cost of consumption goods production.

The bowed-out shape to the curve illustrates the law of increasing costs. When Crusoe decides to increase capital goods production from one unit to two, he is forced to use resources less suited to the production of capital goods than the resources employed in producing the first unit. After all, resources are

FIGURE 1
Production Possibilities Frontier
A production possibilities curve depicts the different combinations of goods and services that can be produced in an economy with a given supply of resources and technology. Robinson Crusoe's economy can produce six consumption goods and zero capital goods, shown at point *A*. Alternatively, it can produce five consumption goods and one capital good, point *B*, or any other combination located on the *AD* curve. The law of increasing costs accounts for the balloon-like shape of the production possibilities curve.

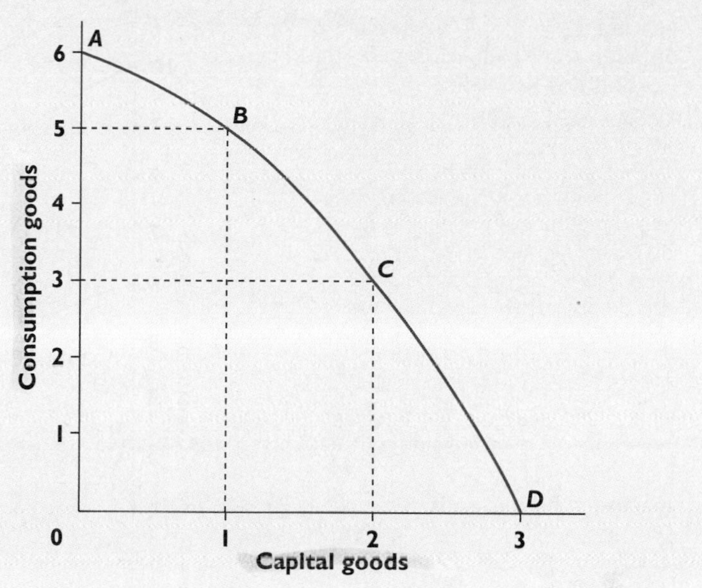

not always of equal quality and he obviously would use the best first. The result is a movement along the curve from point *B* to point *C* which, when plotted in Figure 1, traces out the bowing character of the curve. Suppose Crusoe decides on three units of consumption and two units of capital. He works busily, finishes production, eats the three consumption goods and has available now what he had not had before—two new units of capital.

In the next period of production, he uses the two units of capital along with labor and land. The production possibilities now change. Look at Table 2.

Compare Table 2 to Table 1. Working now with two units of capital, Robinson Crusoe can produce more. For example, 10 units of consumption can now be produced when Crusoe, using the fishing spear and extension tool, devotes all his labor to consumption. Of course, he may again decide to produce more units of capital goods in order to be able to produce even more units of consumption in the following period. This can go on forever *and does in most economies*.

Suppose after deliberating over the production possibilities of Table 2, he selects seven units of consumption and two units of capital. This combination

TABLE 2
Production Possibilities in the Robinson Crusoe Economy, Second Period

Consumption Goods	Capital Goods
10	0
9	1
7	2
4	3
0	4

FIGURE 2
Shifts in the Production Possibilities Frontier
When more resources are available or when more productive technology is used, the quantity of goods and services an economy can produce increases. The increase is depicted by the outward shift to the right of the production possibilities curve.

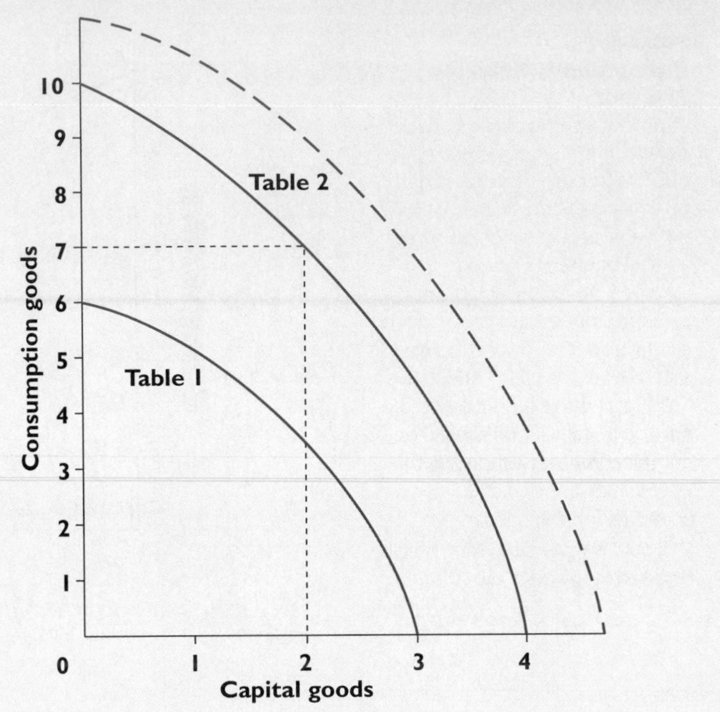

means that he not only adds two more units of capital to his resource base, but he is still able to produce more consumption goods—seven—than he could have produced in the first period, even had he devoted all the resources exclusively to consumption goods production.

Figure 2 illustrates the change in the Crusoe economy over the two periods. The production possibilities curve shifts outward to the right. The shift reflects the changing resource base available to Crusoe. In the second period, capital is added to the land and labor resource base of the first. The dashed curve represents later period production possibilities as long as Crusoe continues the strategy of adding units of capital to his resource base.

Once Rich, It's Easy to Get Richer

This rather simple way of looking at an economy's production possibilities and growth potential is instructive. Imagine two economies, shown in panels *a* and *b* of Figure 3, whose initial production possibilities are described by Table 1. The different selections of consumption and capital these economies make along their identical first-period production possibilities curve trace out their productive growth—or lack of growth—over the course of several production periods.

In the first period, panel *a* people decide to produce three units of consumption and two units of capital, point *C*, while those in panel *b* choose point *A*, six units of consumption and zero capital. Comparing themselves to the people in panel *a*, those in panel *b* may think themselves lucky to have twice the consumption goods. But they won't feel that way in the following period.

The productive powers of the two economies are no longer the same. Panel *a*'s expanded resource base, now containing the two new capital goods, allows

FIGURE 3
Comparative Economic Growth
The same quantity of resources and technology are available in the economies of panel *a* and panel *b*. Panel *a* chooses to produce three consumption goods and two capital goods, while panel *b* uses all its resources to produce six consumption goods. In succeeding years, the additional capital goods created in panel *a* are added to its resource base, shifting its production possibilities curve outward, while the production possibilities curve in panel *b* remains unchanged. The production gap between the two economies widens over time.

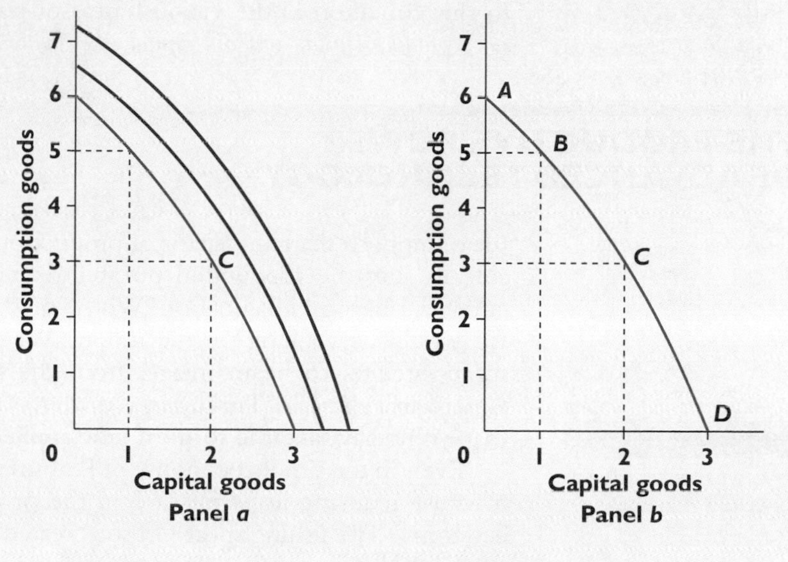

a new and more productive set of production possibilities. Panel *a*'s production possibilities curve shifts outward. Panel *b*, on the other hand, operating on its same resource base, remains locked on its initial production possibilities curve. In fact, the people in panel *a* now actually consume more than those in panel *b* and they can still add to their capital stock.

Time is on their side. After several periods, the outward shifts in panel *a*'s production possibilities curve generate a widening gap between its own curve and that of panel *b*'s. In time, the outward shifts in the panel *a* economy become even easier to obtain. Why? Because a solid consumption base is already in place, the opportunity cost of shifting resources to capital goods becomes less painful. Movements along the economy's production possibilities curve further into the *CD* range—more capital, less consumption—push the curve out even further in succeeding periods.

Once Poor, It's Easy to Stay Poor

Why is it that focusing production on capital goods forces consumers to tighten their belts?

Catching up is hard to do. If the panel *b* people decide to try, it may take some doing. Obviously, they must choose to move away from position *A* on their production possibility curve. The further away from *A* the better. Movements along their curve into the *BC* range—much more capital, much less consumption—may force them to tighten their belts considerably. Where they position themselves along the curve depends upon how well they can tolerate low-level consumption and how quickly they want to catch up.

There are economies with resource bases so underdeveloped that they have little option but to devote their entire meager resources to consumption. It is hard enough just to stay alive! Typically, these economies have high rates of population growth so that it becomes a continuing, dispiriting struggle to feed their own people. The economies simply can't afford to produce the capital needed to shift their production possibilities curves outward. Economists refer to this condition as the vicious circle of poverty: *The economies are so poor they can't produce capital; without capital, they remain poor.* Poverty feeds on itself.

THE PRODUCTIVE POWER OF ADVANCED TECHNOLOGY

Ideas, more so than any factor of production, are the most revolutionizing force able to shift the production possibilities of any economy. Ideas can shift the curve out beyond imagination. Who would have thought just a century ago that we would be walking on the moon? Who would have expected commercial space satellites to beam images from the Superdome in New Orleans to an American airbase in Turkey in a matter of seconds? Economists describe ideas that eventually take the form of new applied technology as **innovations.**

Innovation

An idea that eventually takes the form of new, applied technology.

Even in the simple economy of Robinson Crusoe, innovation can be shown to cause dramatic leaps forward in the production possibilities available to an economy. The fishing spear Crusoe created was an idea fashioned into a unit of capital. Two fishing spears add more to an economy's productive potential than one, shifting the production possibilities curve out to the right, but the technology is still spears.

Suppose Crusoe hits on an altogether new and creative idea: the fishing net. He sketches out this completely new technology for catching fish that requires a different combination of land and labor. Crusoe uses more vine, less wood, no stone, and more labor. The results of this new technology are dramatic. Table 3 compares the production possibilities of using spear and fishing net technologies.

The net technology yields 30 units of consumption goods compared to the 10 units produced with spears when all resources are devoted to the production of consumption goods. Production possibilities based on net technology make it easier to move down along the curve—producing even more capital goods—and, therefore, shifting the curve in succeeding periods out even further to the right.

Innovations creating even more advanced technology are possible. The exciting conclusion we reach, for the simple Robinson Crusoe economy and for our own, is that there are no impassable limits to the growth potential of our economy. Resource limitations may impose a short-run constraint on what we are able to produce in any period of time, but given enough time and enough minds, *new technology reduces the severity of scarcity.* Our grandchildren will no doubt regard our technology as rather primitive, but their grandchildren will consider their technology as hardly more advanced.

How are technological change and economic growth related?

The Indestructible Nature of Ideas

Capital goods can be destroyed, but ideas are far more durable. Wars can bring havoc to any economy's resource base. People's lives are disrupted. Many do not survive the war. Whole factories, complete with machinery, and roads, bridges, railway networks, electric grids, energy facilities, and any other form of the nation's capital stock can be reduced to rubble. But capital goods can also be replaced quickly. Look at Figure 4.

AD represents the economy's prewar production possibilities curve. The destructive effects of war, particularly on its people and capital stock, is shown as

TABLE 3 Production Possibilities Generated by Spear and Net Technologies

Spear Technology		Net Technology	
Consumption	**Capital**	**Consumption**	**Capital**
10	0	30	0
9	1	26	1
7	2	18	2
4	3	10	3
0	4	0	4

an inward shift to the left of the curve to *A′D′*. Recovery, however, can be whole and swift because people, even with minimal capital stock, don't have to reinvent the wheel. Technological knowledge, once acquired, is virtually indestructible. In time, applying known technology, the economy can shift its production possibilities curve back again to *AD* and even beyond to *A″D″*.

The physical devastation of Japan and Europe caused by World War II had some rather paradoxical consequences for these war-torn economies. Because so much of their capital stock in the form of factories and machinery was destroyed, these economies were forced to start over again. But they started over with the most advanced machinery and the most up-to-date factories. The result was an incredible increase in their economies' productivity. Ironically, economies that were spared the devastation of the war had their prewar technology still intact and grew less rapidly than those whose capital stocks were destroyed and replaced with the more modern technology.

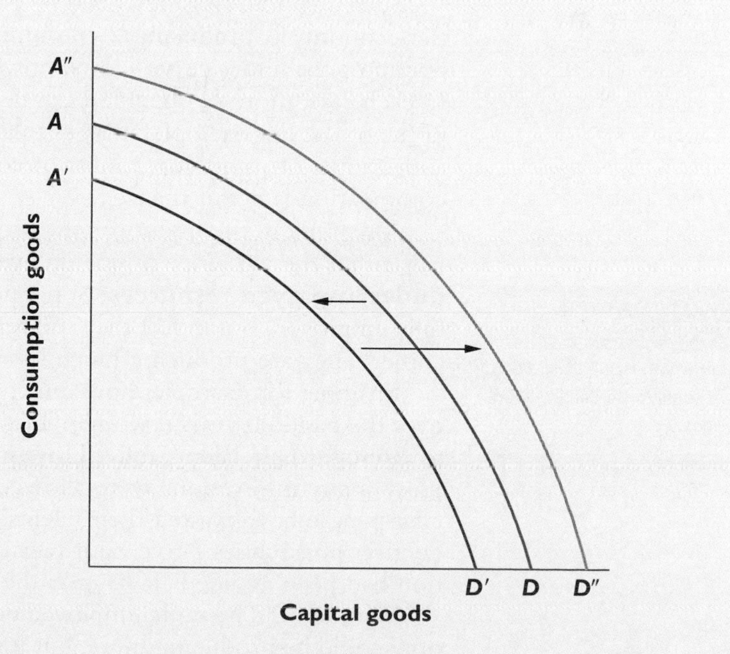

FIGURE 4
Inward and Outward Shifts of the Production Possibilities Curve
With resources destroyed, the economy's production possibilities decrease. The decrease is depicted by the shift to the left of the production possibilities curve from *AD* to *A′D′*. In time, with the rebuilding of resources and the use of more advanced technology, the economy can recoup and even surpass the levels of production previously attained. This is shown in the shift to the right of the production possibilities curve, from *A′D′* to *A″D″*.

FIGURE 5
Possible, Impossible, and Less than Possible
Production combinations, such as *E*, located outside and to the right of the production possibilities curve, are unattainable with the resources and technology currently available. Combinations located within the curve, such as *U*, reflect less than full use of available resources and technology. All combinations that fall on the curve, such as *B* and *C*, represent maximum use, or the full employment of the resources and technology available.

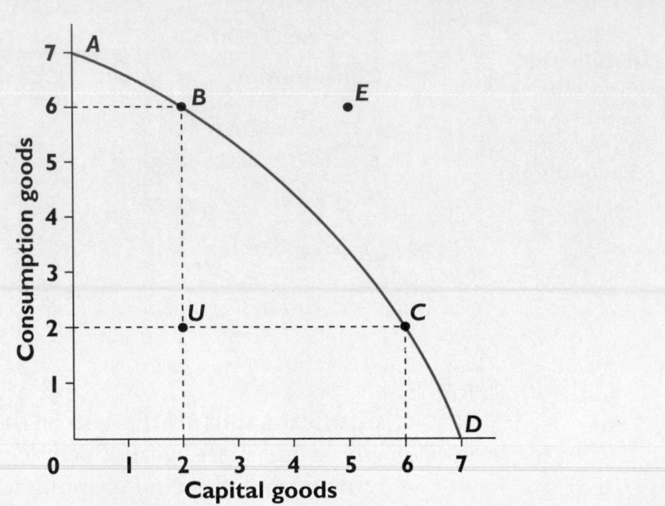

POSSIBILITIES, IMPOSSIBILITIES, AND LESS THAN POSSIBILITIES

What an economy can produce depends upon the availability of resources and the level of technology applied. If the economy's resources are not fully employed, then obviously it cannot be producing as much as possible. For example, if the economy's labor force is not fully employed or if some of its land and capital resources remain idle, the combination of consumption goods and capital goods that it produces will be less than what is possible.

Such a condition is described by point *U* in the economy of Figure 5. At *U*, the economy is producing 2 consumption goods and 2 capital goods. Its production possibilities curve shows, however, that combination *B* or *C* is possible. In each case, more of one good can be produced without having to sacrifice any of the other. For example, it is possible to produce 6 units of consumption goods and 2 units of capital or 2 units of consumption and 6 units of capital. Either combination is better than *U*.

Any point in the interior of the production possibilities curve, such as *U*, signals either the existence of unemployed or underemployed resources. What are **underemployed resources?** Some people working full time *might appear* to be fully employed, but in fact they still represent substantial unused resources. How come? They are producing much less than they are really capable of producing.

Underemployed resources
The less than full utilization of a resource's productive capabilities.

Imagine, for example, how much more our economy could have produced over the past 200 years if women, blacks, and other minorities had been allowed to exercise their talents fully. How many entrepreneurs have we lost forever? How many innovations were allowed to go undiscovered? How many skilled craftspeople have wasted their talents? How much further out would our production possibilities curve be if racial, sexual, religious, and ethnic discrimination had been avoided? It staggers the imagination!

Who loses? The underemployed people and the economy. That is, the economy could be producing more, but it isn't. If these underemployed people were

ADDED PERSPECTIVE

Chickens, Vaccines, and Pushing Out the Production Possibilities Curve

Chicken farmers have a justified dread of Newcastle disease, a kind of fowl pest first identified a half-century ago in Newcastle-upon-Tyne, in northern England. It brings diarrhea, paralysis, and finally death to their poultry. When it strikes an area, they have to kill even the fit chickens to stop the spread of the disease. In the 1971–73 outbreak in southern California, nearly 12 million birds either died or were slaughtered. In developing countries, the disease is endemic; in much of the developed world, it is a constant threat to chicken farms.

Yet vaccines exist against the disease. One was developed by an Australian company, Arthur Webster, as long ago as 1966 after it isolated the harmless V4 strain of the Newcastle virus found in Australian chickens.

The problem is how to use vaccines, especially in developing countries. Conventional vaccines must be stored in refrigerated conditions, which poor villages lack. Administering the vaccines by aerosol spray or by putting them in the water supply is all but impossible at the village level; so is vaccination by eye and nose drops.

In response, scientists from Malaysia's University of Agriculture and Australia's University of Queensland have devised an appropriate low-technology answer. In a joint project funded by the Australian Centre for International Agricultural Research, they have produced a live vaccine that farmers can spray on chicken-feed pellets with a pill-coating machine.

The results of field tests of the new vaccine carried out in Southeast Asia are extremely promising. Pilot studies suggest that simply throwing the coated feed on to the ground is enough to immunize some chickens, which then pass the harmless disease on to their fellow birds. A vaccinated flock of chickens in Java multiplied over a year from 5,300 birds to 12,238—while the birds in an unvaccinated flock exposed to Newcastle disease shrank from 3,867 to 1,400. Since Indonesia has 348 million chickens, everybody stands to benefit: Consumers would get more protein; farmers more income. In Malaysia, which has 49 million chickens and a population willing to pay a premium for tasty village fowls, one economist guesses that the vaccine would increase rural incomes by 25 percent.

Discussion

Draw two production possibilities curves putting units of chickens on the horizontal axis and units of "everything else" on the vertical axis. Use these curves to reflect the story about the use of the vaccine in Java.

Source: "Bird's Eye View of Vaccines," *The Economist*, April 11, 1987.

allowed to exercise their full productive potential, the economy's production would shift from a position inside the production possibilities curve to a position on it.

Economic efficiency

The maximum possible production of goods and services generated by the fullest employment of the economy's resources.

Point *U* in Figure 5 describes an inefficiently producing economy. **Economic efficiency** is defined as the *absence of waste*. Clearly, resources left unused are wasteful. In this sense, the only points of production that represent an efficiently run economy are those *on* the production possibilities curve. No one point on the curve is more efficient than any other, since all of them reflect the full employment and maximal use of the economy's available resources.

Any point lying outside the production possibilities curve in the economy of Figure 5, such as *E*, is an impossible production combination. After all, points on the curve such as *A*, *B*, *C*, or *D* represent production combinations that fully employ the economy's usable resources. How, then, can the economy produce beyond the curve? If the economy is growing, point *E*, impossible now, need not be an impossible dream.

PRODUCTION POSSIBILITIES AND ECONOMIC SPECIALIZATION

Labor specialization

The division of labor into specialized activities that allow individuals to be more productive.

The idea that labor productivity is a function of the degree of **labor specialization** goes as far back as 1776 and Adam Smith. In his *Wealth of Nations,* Adam Smith tells about a visit to a pin factory:

One man draws out the wire, another straightens it, a third cuts it, a fourth points it, a fifth grinds it at the top for receiving the head; to make the head requires two or three distinct operations; to put it on is a peculiar business, to whiten the pins is another; it is even a trade by itself to put them into the paper. . . .

Draw a graph to show how specialization of labor, such as Adam Smith described for the pin factory, affects a production possibilities curve for pins and all other goods.

The reason for such division of labor, he noted, is that these 10 people could make as many as 48,000 pins in a day. If they had each worked separately and independently, they could not have produced more than 200. That's an impressive point and certainly one that would not go unnoticed in the economy of Robinson Crusoe. In Crusoe's economy, shown in Table 1, there is no division of labor. Alone, he is forced to produce everything—to fish, hunt, farm, and repair huts. He may be a talented carpenter, a mediocre farmer, and a terrible fisherman, but he is busy doing it all. The production possibilities shown in Table 1 reflect this circumstance.

Specialization on the Island

But suppose Robinson Crusoe was one of thousands who were stranded on the island. He probably would not have fished a day in his life. The fishing would have been done by people who were good at it. Crusoe would have become the island's carpenter, relieving those who seem only able to hammer their thumbs. Division of labor on that island allows all the castaways to do the specific things each does best.

Labor can be divided and divided again into specialized and even more specialized activities until people are incredibly proficient at doing incredibly minute activities. The result of such specialization and cooperative production can mean enormous production. *The production possibility schedule of an economy with 1,000 people, for example, may be 100,000 times more productive* than a single-person economy.

Of course, with everyone working at specialized jobs, the people will need to create an exchange system that allows them to exchange the goods produced under conditions of specialization. A shirtmaker, for example, producing 1,000 shirts, may keep only one and trade the remaining 999 shirts for goods she needs. After all, working at making shirts all day does not allow her to fish for the evening meal. But her neighbor, fishing all day, would probably want to exchange some of his fish for her shirts. In this way, it is possible for every islander who specializes in production to end up with more of everything.

International Specialization

If specialization among people on the island creates more goods for everyone, then imagine how much more could be produced if there were international specialization and exchange. Suppose contact was made with people on other islands and the practice of exchanging goods with them became commonplace. Now, even more division of labor and specialization would occur. Instead of producing 1,000 shirts for the local island markets, a shirtmaker may produce 10,000 shirts for the larger islands' markets. More people would be engaged in producing shirts. But instead of every shirtworker making a complete shirt, each would specialize in a specific task in the shirt-making process, such as cutting material, sewing pieces, making buttonholes, and folding.

Perhaps four people working at specialized tasks can produce 10,000 shirts in the time it takes one shirtmaker performing all the tasks alone to produce 1,000 shirts. The more islands that joined in international specialization and exchange, the greater are the opportunities for division of labor and specialization. Everyone produces more, exchanges more, and consumes more.

THE UNIVERSALITY OF THE PRODUCTION POSSIBILITIES MODEL

Resource limitations confronting insatiable wants are facts of life that apply to every economic system, large or small, rich or poor, east or west, north or south, and capitalist or socialist.

The universality of the production possibilities model and the law of increasing costs create the same kinds of problems and decision making for all economies. Can the economy fully employ its resources? How much of the resources should be allocated to capital goods formation? Who gets what share of the consumption goods produced?

The same questions are asked about peace and war. Just as the production possibilities curve measures out the possibilities of consumption and capital goods production, it can measure out as well the production possibilities of butter and guns. Israeli economists as well as Egyptian ones knew first-hand the opportunity cost of desert warfare. In no small measure, that knowledge played its part in their 1979 historic peace agreement.

Imagine a couple of Martian economists landing their UFOs undetected on earth, say, one in Beijing, China, and the other in Dayton, Ohio. If their assignments were to detail how Earthlings behave, they would be struck, upon returning to Mars and comparing notes, not by the differences they observed, but instead by the incredible similarities of our experiences and behavior. They would probably be impressed as well by how similar our economic problems and economic choices are to *their own*!

CHAPTER REVIEW

1. Economists refer to the productive resources—labor, capital, land, and entrepreneurship—as the factors of production. Labor is the physical and mental exertion of people who willingly sell their skills on the labor market. Capital is a manufactured good used to produce other goods. Sometimes we speak of a hybrid that economists call human capital. For example, a physician practices medicine only after receiving medical training, which is capital. Land can be unimproved as in a virgin forest or an undeveloped oil reserve, or improved like an irrigated field. Entrepreneurs are people who undertake the risks associated with business enterprises.

2. Factors of production are combined in production processes. A production possibilities curve can be constructed to show the various combinations of goods that can be produced given certain quantities of the factors of production.

3. A production possibilities curve can also be used to illustrate the concept of opportunity cost—the idea that in order to obtain more of one good a certain quantity of another good must be sacrificed.

4. As resources are shifted from the production of one good to another, an economy experiences the law of increasing costs. As more and more resources are shifted, the opportunity cost of producing each additional unit of product increases. The law of increasing costs appears as a bowed-out shape of the production possibilities curve.

5. An economy grows as it accumulates productive resources. Economic growth shows up as an outward shift of the production possibilities curve. An economy that has grown rich has an easier time growing richer because more resources are available for production of capital goods than in a poor economy.

6. Applying new technology to a production process, called innovation, is another way that an economy can grow. Innovation results in greater output from a given stock of resources and helps to overcome scarcity.

7. If the factors of production are not fully employed, then the economy is not producing all that it can. Unemployment or underemployment of the factors of production can be shown by points inside a production possibilities curve. Resources are wasted when they are unemployed. Conversely, if an economy is efficient, then it fully employs its resources and operates on its production possibilities curve.

8. Adam Smith stressed labor specialization as a means toward increased labor productivity in his book, *The Wealth of Nations*. An economy with a bigger labor force can be more productive than an economy with a small labor force because of opportunities for labor specialization.

KEY TERMS

Factors of production
Labor
Capital
Human capital
Land
Entrepreneur
Production possibilities
Opportunity cost
Law of increasing costs
Innovation
Underemployed resources
Economic efficiency
Labor specialization

QUESTIONS

1. What distinguishes entrepreneurship from the other factors of production?

2. Is a four-door 1995 Buick LeSabre taxi capital? Is a four-door 1995 Buick LeSabre parked in your garage capital?

3. Consider your economics lecture. From the point of view of your economics professor, is the lecture capital, labor, or neither? From your own point of view, is it capital, labor, or neither? What is your opportunity cost of that lecture?

4. Explain why the concepts of scarcity and opportunity cost are intricately related.

5. Explain the law of increasing (opportunity) cost. What causes cost to increase?

6. Everybody wants clean air. So why is the air polluted in so many of our cities? (*Hint*: refer to the law of increasing cost in your answer.)

7. Why are most new technologies considered indestructible

8. Suppose you were advising the government of Egypt. What policies would you recommend to achieve economic growth? Why should you expect some resistance to your policy suggestions?

9. Suppose government economists, on the request from the President, construct a production possibilities curve (military and civilian goods) for the United States. Suppose also that two economics professors debate where the United States ought to be on that curve. Which set of economists is engaged in positive economics and which in normative?

10. What factors or events could cause an inward shift of the production possibilities curve?

11. Why does the production possibilities curve bow out from the origin?

12. The Constitution guarantees the right to free speech. Does the "free" in free speech mean that there really is no opportunity cost to free speech? Explain.

13. Fill in an appropriate number (there can be more than one) for the missing number of bushels of oranges in set C and graph the following sets of production possibilities.

Set	Bushels of Grapefruit	Bushels of Oranges
A	200	0
B	150	19
C	100	
D	50	30
E	0	32

14. Graph the following sets of production possibilities and explain why the law of increasing costs is violated.

Set	Bushels of Grapefruit	Bushels of Oranges
A	200	0
B	150	19
C	100	40
D	50	80
E	0	130

CHAPTER 3
DEMAND AND SUPPLY

CHAPTER PREVIEW

Have you ever wondered how the prices that are charged for goods in stores are determined? In this chapter you will explore how buyers on the demand side of markets and sellers on the supply side interact with each other to determine prices for goods.

After studying this chapter, you should be able to:

- Discuss how consumer demand is measured.
- Describe the inverse relationship between price and quantity demanded.
- Discuss how supply is measured.
- Explain in a general way how market prices are determined.
- Describe the concept of equilibrium price.
- Explain how changes in demand, supply, and the equilibrium price are related to each other.

One of the most exciting moments in Shakespearean drama—for economists at any rate—has to be the final scene in Richard III where the king, tired and bloodied at the end of the battle, his horse slain, and standing helplessly alone upon the crest of a hill, sights the enemy about to charge at him. His sword drawn, Richard shouts in desperation: "A horse! A horse! My kingdom for a horse!"

To an economist, that's a dramatic moment, for never has so high a price been placed on a four-legged animal! Not before, and not since. Lassie and Flipper, themselves worth a small fortune, were still well within the reach of any millionaire. The legendary thoroughbred of the 1920s, Man O' War, won every race he ran but one, but even he couldn't command *that* price. Shakespeare was not an economist by profession, yet he understood the market well. In all probability, he picked the right price.

This example raises a more general question about price formation: Why are prices what they are? Why, for example, do oranges sell for 30 cents each? Why not 25 cents? Or 34 cents? Is there something magical about a 30-cent orange? And what about cucumbers? Why are they 49 cents each? Why should they be more expensive than oranges? Why is butter $1.25 per pound? Why is a fresh fish $6?

We can go on identifying thousands of goods that make up our modern economy and ask the same question about each: Why that particular price? From aircraft carriers to salted peanuts, from sweetheart roses to Buick LeSabres, why are the prices what they are?

MEASURING CONSUMER WILLINGNESS

How does price reflect what buyers and sellers are willing to do?

Price formation has to do with people's willingness to buy and sell. There is nothing mysterious about price. It has no life of its own. It has no will. Price simply *reflects* what people are willing to do.

Suppose that people on a small island are busily engaged each day in some productive activity that affords them a livelihood. The variety of their occupations fills up 40 Yellow Pages of their telephone directory. There are auto mechanics, dentists, farmers, plumbers, computer specialists, business consultants, and especially fishermen. After all, it's an island economy, and we should expect the community to take full advantage of its fishing grounds.

Of course, there's no sense in fishing unless some people like to eat fish. Chances are some prefer fish to filet mignon, although there must be others who wouldn't touch fish under any condition. As the Romans used to say: *de gustibus non est disputandum* (there's no disputing taste). But it would be the height of folly if fishermen went out on the water every day only to discover on returning to dock that nobody showed any interest in the fish they caught. Wouldn't you think that even the dullest of them would give up after a while? Fishermen go out every day because they know from long experience that there are always people willing to buy fish.

MEASURING CONSUMER DEMAND

Fishermen also know that when price falls, people's willingness to buy fish increases—it's so obvious and so sensible a response to price that fishermen regard it as natural. They know, for example, that if the price of fish is outrageously

How do you think this fish seller came up with that $2.99 price? You had a lot to do with it. It is quantity demanded as well as quantity supplied (marvelous collection of seafood, isn't it?) that determines price. Anyone care for sushi?

high, say $25 per fish, very few people would be willing to buy. On the other hand, if the price is $10, some people unwilling to buy at $25 now would be willing to buy fish.

Change in quantity demanded

A change in the quantity demanded of a good that is caused solely by a change in the price of that good.

Law of demand

The inverse relationship between price and quantity demanded of a good or service, ceteris paribus.

If the price falls to $5, more people would be willing to buy even more fish. Some who bought a few at $10 would buy more at $5, and those who had not bought before, now get into the market.

When economists refer to ***change in quantity demanded*** *for a particular good, they always mean people's willingness to buy specific quantities at specific prices.* They define the inverse relationship between price and quantity demanded as the **law of demand.** Compare the two statements: "I am willing to buy four fish at a price of $6 per fish" and "I am willing to buy fish." There is considerably more information in the first statement.

Measuring Individual Demand

Let's begin by measuring Claudia Preparata's and Chris Stefan's demand for fish. Claudia is the principal labor relations consultant on the island and Chris is an actress. Table 1 is a **demand schedule** recording their willingness to buy fish at different prices.

Demand schedule

A schedule showing the specific quantity of a good or service that people are willing and able to buy at different prices.

You may not know much about these two women, but you do know that if the price of fish were $10, you wouldn't find Claudia Preparata at a fish market!

Chris Stefan, on the other hand, treats herself to a $10 poached salmon. If the price falls to $9, the quantity of fish demanded by both Claudia and Chris increases. Claudia buys one, and the quantity that Chris demands increases to three. If the price keeps falling, the quantity demanded keeps increasing.

Demand curve

A curve that depicts the relationship between price and quantity demanded.

The **demand curves** in Figure 1 represent Claudia's and Chris's demand for fish at different prices. They contain the same information as that offered in Table 1. It is just a different, more visual way of looking at the information. The demand curves are downward sloping because price and quantity demanded are inversely related. When price falls, the quantity demanded increases.

TABLE 1
Claudia Preparata's and Chris Stefan's Demand for Fish

Claudia's Demand		Chris's Demand	
Price	Quantity Demanded	Price	Quantity Demanded
$10	0	$10	1
9	1	9	3
8	2	8	5
7	3	7	7
6	4	6	9
5	5	5	11
4	6	4	13
3	7	3	15
2	8	2	17
1	9	1	19

Measuring Market Demand

Market demand

The sum of all individual demands in a market.

If we were able to record every person's willingness to buy fish at different prices, we would end up with complete information about the community's demand for fish. We can obtain such information only by observing and recording what quantities people actually buy in the market at different prices. Adding up all the individual demands for fish gives us the community or **market demand.** Table 2 and the corresponding Figure 2 represent the market demand for fish.

FIGURE 1 Individual Demand Curves For Fish

Ceteris paribus, the quantity of fish demanded depends on the price of fish. At a price of $5, the quantity of fish demanded by Claudia is 5—point *a* on demand curve *D*—and the quantity demanded by Chris is 11—point *b* on demand curve *D'*. At a price of $1, the quantity demanded by Claudia increases to 9—point *x*—and the quantity demanded by Chris increases to 19—point *y*.

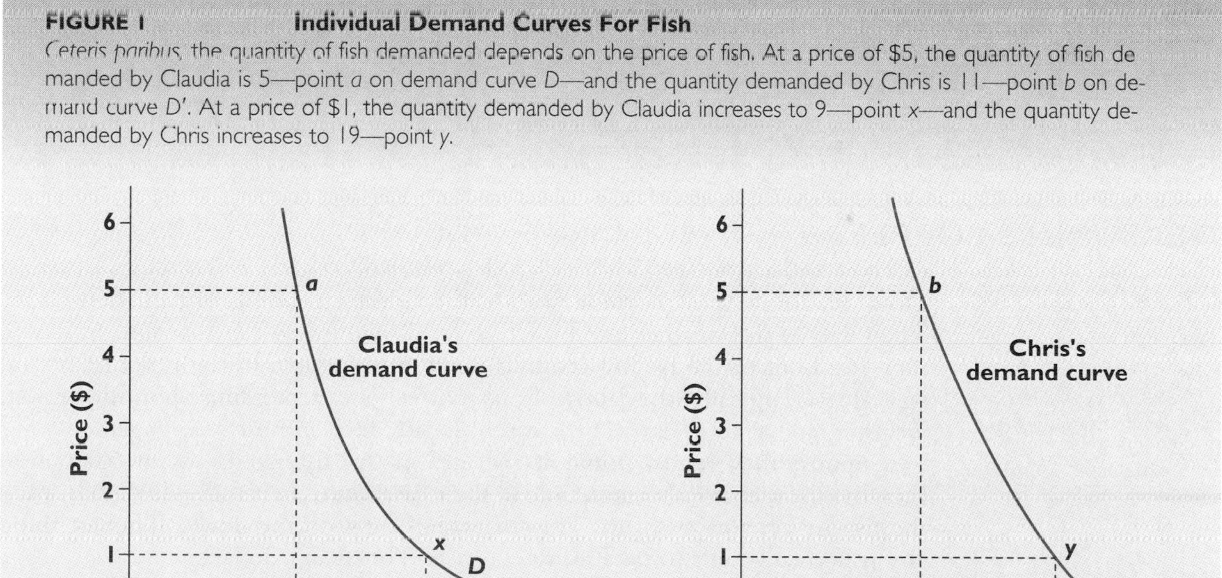

TABLE 2
Market Demand for Fish

Price	Quantity Demanded
$10	3,500
9	4,000
8	4,500
7	5,000
6	5,500
5	6,000
4	6,500
3	7,000
2	7,500
1	8,000

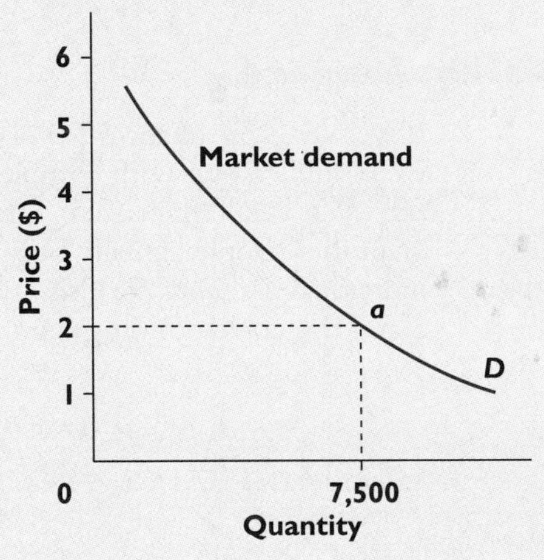

FIGURE 2
The Market Demand Curve
Individual demand curves, including Claudia's and Chris's, are added together to form the community's, or market, demand curve. At a price of $2, the quantity of fish demanded by all demanders is 7,500—point *a*—(which includes 8 demanded by Claudia and 17 demanded by Chris).

MEASURING SUPPLY

On a beautiful April morning we see the fishermen going out in their boats. They live by the weather and by whatever daylight they can manage. At dawn, they head out to the fishing grounds while most people in the community are still asleep. Typically, they move from spot to spot, depending upon the season, weather, and time of day. They search, locate, fish, and move on again.

Suppose they return home at the end of this fishing day with 6,000 fish. Imagine the scene: Fishermen unload their catch into their individual stalls, pack the fish in ice, and wash up. They sell them right on the docks. The last thing any fisherman wants to take home is a fish! They want dollars.

Market Day Supply

Once the fish are in, there's really no decision making concerning what quantity to supply at what price. *Whatever the price,* fishermen are willing to dispose

TABLE 3
Supply Schedule for Fish for the Market Day

Price	Quantity Supplied
$10	6,000
9	6,000
8	6,000
7	6,000
6	6,000
5	6,000
4	6,000
3	6,000
2	6,000
1	6,000

Supply schedule

A schedule showing the specific quantity of a good or service that suppliers are willing and able to provide at different prices.

Market-day supply

A market situation in which the quantity of a good supplied is fixed, regardless of price.

of all 6,000 fish. What else can they do with them? Have you ever handled a day-old fish?

Even if the price were $1 per fish, $P = \$1$, fishermen would be disappointed but still willing to sell all 6,000. Some would probably start thinking about other jobs. On the other hand, if $P = \$10$, the same fishermen would still supply the same 6,000 fish, but this time would be frustrated that they hadn't caught more. But they can't change the quantity supplied once the catch is in. *Regardless of price, the quantity supplied is fixed for the market day.*

Table 3 and Figure 3 represent the **supply schedule** and corresponding supply curve for the **market-day supply.**

FIGURE 3
Market-Day Supply Curve
The market-day supply curve is vertical, reflecting the fact that once the catch is in, fishermen cannot change the quantity they supply. At a price of $9, the quantity supplied is 6,000, point *a* on the supply curve. At a price of $5, the quantity supplied is still 6,000, point *b* on the supply curve.

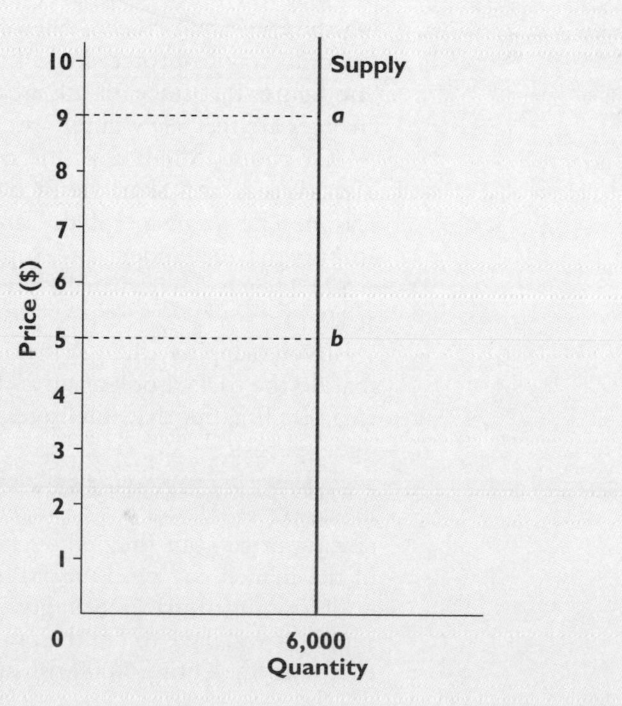

Supply curve

A curve that depicts the relationship between price and quantity supplied.

Just as the demand curve graphs the relationship between price and quantity demanded, the **supply curve** graphs the relationship between price and quantity supplied. The supply curve for the market day shows that whatever the price, the quantity supplied remains unchanged.

DETERMINING PRICE

A fish market is a colorful and bustling sight. Demanders, suppliers, and flies swarm around the fish stalls ready to strike deals. Suppliers busily encourage demanders to buy their fish and demanders take their time looking for the best fish at the best price. But fish are fish, and time is short.

Nobody knows what the other's preferences really are until they become expressed on the market through purchase and sale. But Claudia, Chris, and the many other demanders, as well as the fishermen who are the suppliers, know that 6,000 fish are on the docks for sale.

Suppose the Price Is $8

Let's suppose that the asking price, at least at the outset of the market process, is $8 per fish. This already spells trouble. Look at Table 4 and Figure 4.

Excess supply

The difference, at a particular price, between quantity supplied and quantity demanded; quantity supplied being the greater.

At P = $8, the quantity of fish demanded is 4,500. Of this quantity, Claudia is willing to buy two, Chris five. But the fishermen are already nervous about the weakness they sense in the market. There is insufficient demand to absorb the entire 6,000 fish supplied. People are just not picking up fish as the fishermen had hoped. Look at Table 4. At P = $8, there is an **excess supply** of 1,500 fish that will not be sold. Every fisherman is afraid, in the end, of being left holding the bag. Sheila Reed, one of the many fishermen on the docks, knows that the only way to protect herself from this unpleasant eventuality is to cut price. She figures that since all fish are alike, if she is willing to cut *her own price* to $7, chances are that *she* will sell out.

Of course, Sheila isn't the only fisherman who thinks this way. Fishermen Lisa Muroga and Shari Zernich had already cut their prices to $7 for the same reason. They draw a crowd. Can you imagine what happens when word spreads among the demanders and suppliers that some fishermen are willing to sell at $7? They make it virtually impossible for other suppliers to maintain the price at $8.

Every supplier, then, has no alternative but to reduce the price to $7. Will that do the trick? Look again at Table 4. At P = $7, quantity demanded increases to 5,000 fish, but that still leaves an excess supply of 1,000. The pressure on suppliers persists.

As long as any excess supply exists on the market, there will always be an incentive for suppliers to cut price. The incentive is self-protection. They really don't enjoy cutting prices, but they enjoy even less the prospect of being caught at the end of the market day with unsold fish.

How much price cutting will they have to do? From Table 4 it's clear that suppliers will have to cut the price to $5. At P = $5, quantity demanded increases to absorb the entire 6,000 fish supplied. Excess supply is zero.

TABLE 4
Pressures of Excess Demand and Excess Supply When Market Supply is 6,000

Price	Quantity Demanded	Quantity Supplied	Excess Demand	Excess Supply
$10	3,500	6,000		2,500
9	4,000	6,000		2,000
8	4,500	6,000		1,500
7	5,000	6,000		1,000
6	5,500	6,000		500
5	6,000	6,000	0	0
4	6,500	6,000	500	
3	7,000	6,000	1,000	
2	7,500	6,000	1,500	
1	8,000	6,000	2,000	

Suppose the Price Is $4

Suppose, at the beginning of the market process, price is not $8, but $4. What happens now? Market pressure is on the other side of the market. Claudia Preparata, Chris Stefan, and other demanders are the ones who become somewhat nervous.

For example, at P = $4, Claudia is willing to buy 6 and Chris is willing to buy 13 fish. The quantity demanded by the community is 6,500. Both deman

FIGURE 4
Excess Demand and Excess Supply
At any price other than $5, excess demand or excess supply will force the price to $5. At $1, an excess demand of 500 fish is created, driving up price. At $8, an excess supply of 1,500 fish is created, forcing price downward.

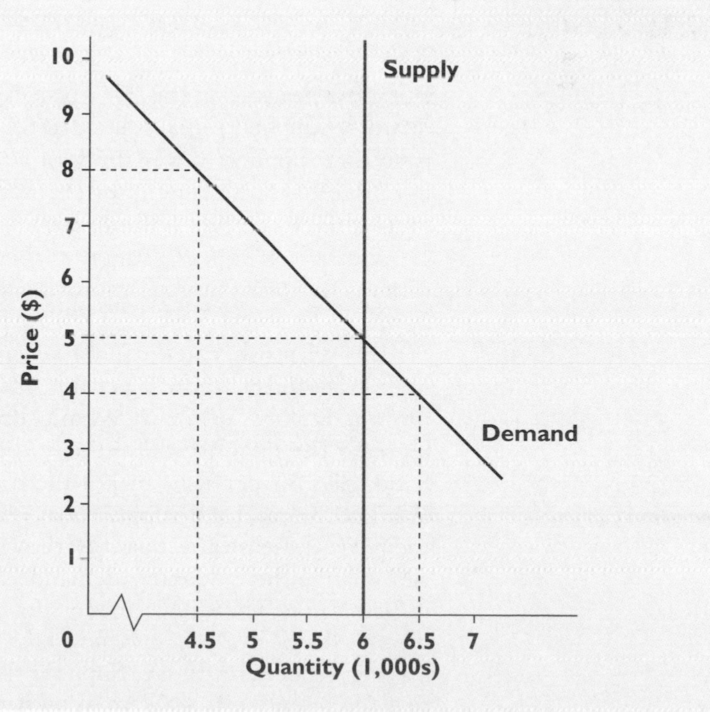

ders and suppliers now sense that there are insufficient fish to satisfy demand at \$4. Fishermen seem less worried about being caught with unsold fish. Now demanders are worried about going home fishless.

Excess demand

The difference, at a particular price, between quantity demanded and quantity supplied; quantity demanded being the greater.

As you see in Table 4, **excess demand** at P = \$4 is 500 fish. What would you do if you were at the docks and really wanted fish? Afraid of getting caught looking at empty stalls, wouldn't you offer a little more? For example, if you announced that you were willing to pay \$5, the chances are that you would draw suppliers' attention. Of course, you're not the only one with fish on your mind; many others are also willing to buy fish at \$5.

The \$4 price, then, becomes untenable. Demanders, competing among themselves for the limited supply of 6,000 fish, will bid the price up. At P = \$5, some buyers drop out. The quantity demanded then falls to 6,000 and the excess demand disappears.

Price Always Tends Toward Equilibrium

In the fish market on this particular day, competition among suppliers to rid themselves of their supply will always force a price greater than \$5 down to \$5. In the same way, competition among demanders will always force a price lower than \$5 up to \$5. Price is stable only at \$5. *Economists refer to that price where quantity demanded equals quantity supplied as the* **equilibrium price.** At P = \$5, the market clears. There is no excess demand or excess supply.

Equilibrium price

The price that equates quantity demanded to quantity supplied. If any disturbance from that price occurs, excess demand or excess supply emerge to drive price back to equilibrium.

Figure 4 illustrates the forces driving price to equilibrium. At any price other than P = \$5, excess demand or supply results, triggering bargaining activity on the part of demanders and suppliers to overcome the market's inability to clear. They force price changes. Price simply reflects their behavior. It gravitates, without exception, toward equilibrium.

MARKET-DAY, SHORT-RUN, AND LONG-RUN SUPPLY

But how realistic is this idea of a fixed supply? In Table 4 and Figure 4, the quantity supplied remains fixed at 6,000, regardless of price. Is it realistic to suppose that suppliers never think of adjusting the quantity they supply to changing prices? Do fishermen, for example, just keep fishing, day after day, bringing their catch to market without regard to the price their fish fetch on the market? Of course not. A fixed supply makes sense only for the market day. Once the catch is in, today's price cannot affect today's quantity supplied. What is done is done.

But what fishermen will do *tomorrow* depends very much on today's price. A high price today, say \$10 per fish, makes fishermen happy and wishing they had more to supply. While they can't supply more today, they can prepare today to increase the quantity they supply tomorrow. A low price today, on the other hand, say, \$3 per fish, makes them less happy and less willing to supply fish. While they can't cut supply today—after all, the catch is in— they can prepare today to decrease the quantity they supply tomorrow. Unlike consumers who can change their quantity demanded instantaneously when prices change, fishermen can't. They have to do something in order to adjust the quantity they supply to price. *Doing something takes time.*

Let's start with today. Suppose fishermen discover when they get to market that today's price is \$10. Are they happy? They're ecstatic! The only regret they

TABLE 5
Market-Day, Short-Run, and Long-Run Supply

Price	Market Day	Short Run	Long Run
$10	6,000	8,500	16,000
9	6,000	8,000	14,000
8	6,000	7,500	12,000
7	6,000	7,000	10,000
6	6,000	6,500	8,000
5	6,000	6,000	6,000
4	6,000	5,500	4,000
3	6,000	5,000	2,000
2	6,000	4,500	0
1	6,000	4,000	0

have is that their quantity supplied is only 6,000 fish. At that price they wish they had more fish to supply. But they can't undo what is done. What is done is their earlier decision to fish today with a certain number of boats, crew, and equipment.

Well, what about tomorrow? With a $10 fish in mind, they would love to supply as many as 16,000 if they could. Look at Table 5, column 4.

But how can they possibly increase the quantity of fish supplied from 6,000 to 16,000 *by tomorrow*? They can't. But perhaps the first thing they can do is add more fishermen to their boats. Where would they find them? Well, suppose you are a potato farmer and not particularly happy about the money you are making in the potato business. To your dismay, the price of potatoes is low. You may be willing to try something else if that something else paid more; that is, if it met your opportunity cost. With fish now fetching $10, it may be just enough to make you switch from potato farming to fishing.

But there are limits to how many people fishermen can add to their boats. If the boats are designed for crews of six, adding one or two more per boat may bring in more fish, but not the 16,000 fish that fishermen are willing to supply. Anyway, hiring more crew takes time and the new crew may have very little experience.

What else can fishermen do to increase the quantity supplied? Another option is to stay out on the water for more hours during the fishing run. But staying out longer means consuming more fuel, more bait, more ice packaging, all of which may be in short supply.

They do the best they can. Suppose their best effort, given the limitation of boat size, increases the quantity supplied from the market day's 6,000 to 8,500 fish. Look at column 3, in Table 5.

Now, 8,500 fish is more than 6,000 but still considerably less than the 16,000 that fishermen want to supply at P = $10. But to reach 16,000 requires more boats (not just more crew or longer hours) and boat making, let's suppose, takes a full year. In other words, for tomorrow at least, they're stuck at 8,500. Until more or bigger boats are available, their only course of action is to produce as much as they can *on the boats they already have*. This time interval during which suppliers are able to change the quantity of some but not all the resources they

Short run

The time interval during which suppliers are able to change the quantity of some but not all the resources they use to produce goods and services.

Long run

The time interval during which suppliers are able to change the quantity of all the resources they use to produce goods and services.

use to produce goods and services is called the **short run.** The 8,500 fish, then, is the quantity supplied in the short run at P = $10.

What about quantity supplied in the **long run?** What distinguishes the long from the short run? In the long run, suppliers have the time to change the quantity of *all* the resources they use to produce goods and services. In the fishing business, the long run is a year—the time it takes to acquire as many boats as fishermen wish. As we see in Table 5, fishermen end up in the long run acquiring enough boats to produce 16,000 fish.

Figure 5 translates Table 5 into graphic form.

The higher the price of fish, the greater the incentive to produce more. As you see for the long run in Table 5, when the price is $9, fishermen are willing and able to supply 14,000, slightly less than the 16,000 they are willing and able to supply at a price of $10. Why do they supply less? Fishermen will tell you that a $9 fish is not as profitable as a $10 fish. As a result, they hire fewer crew. As well, fewer potato farmers would be sufficiently motivated to leave potato farming for a $9 fish. Fewer boats are ordered. Still, $9 is a relatively good price for fish. Compare the 8,000 quantity supplied in the short run to the 14,000 they are willing to and do supply in the long run.

But look what happens at the relatively low $3 price. The market-day supply is fixed at 6,000. If fishermen have time to adjust supply, they will adjust

FIGURE 5 Market-Day, Short-Run, and Long-Run Supply

All three supply curves are upward sloping. The market-day supply curve, *S*, is vertical, depicting the unique circumstance that suppliers do not have time to adjust quantity supplied to price. At *P* = $9, market-day supply is 6,000. The short-run supply curve, *S′*, indicates that suppliers are somewhat flexible in adjusting their quantity supplied to price. At *P* = $9, suppliers are willing and able to supply 8,000. The long-run supply curve, *S″*, reflects the suppliers' ability to adjust completely to price. At *P* = $9, suppliers are willing and able to supply 14,000.

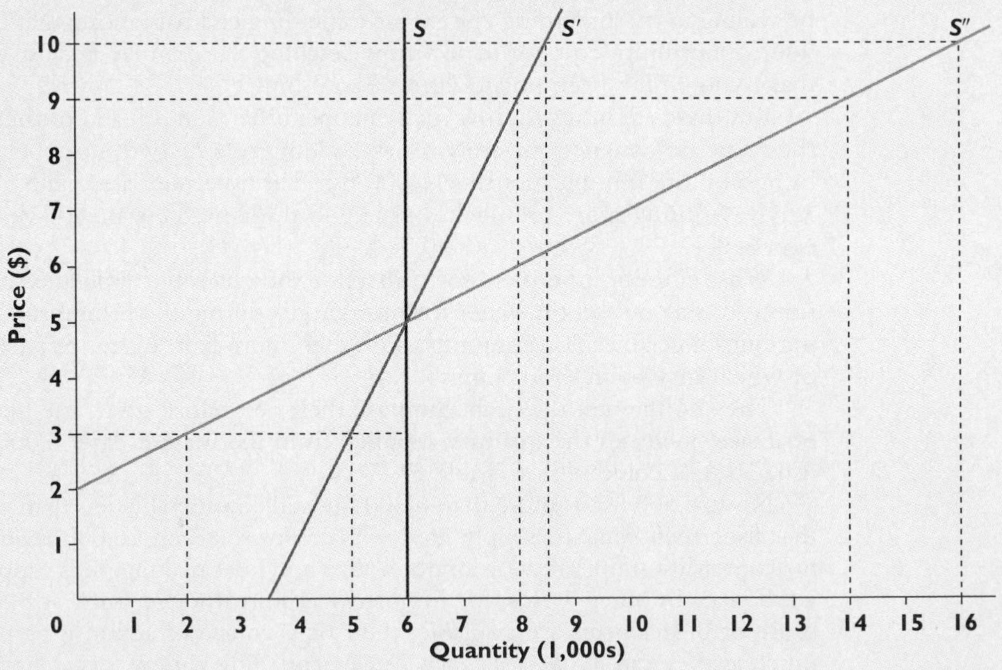

downward. Some who have good options may quit fishing outright (some may end up on a potato farm!). Others may continue to fish, but produce less with smaller crews.

It isn't easy to quit outright even if there are job opportunities for fishermen elsewhere. After all, many fishermen have an emotional investment in their business and little experience at other jobs. (Ask anybody going through job retraining today.) Moreover, they have boats and equipment that represent a substantial financial investment. It may pay them to continue fishing even if the prospects are not very attractive, at least until their boats need substantial overhauling. Then the decision to shut down or stay afloat is forced.

As you see in Table 5, at $P = \$3$, fishermen cut back the quantity they supply in the short run to 5,000 and, given time, in the long run will trim back further to 2,000. At the much lower price of $1, very few fishermen go out on the water, cutting back further in the short run and supplying no fish at all in the long run.

As you see, all three supply curves are upward sloping, but the slope varies with the suppliers' ability to adjust to the different prices. The market-day supply curve is perfectly vertical, with no adjustment to price variations. The short-run supply curve shows moderate flexibility in adjusting quantity supplied to price, while the long-run supply curve has the most gradual slope, reflecting the fishermens' ability to adjust *fully* to price.

CHANGES IN DEMAND

Let's now look at the fish market of Table 6 whose short-run supply (column 2) is drawn from Table 5 and whose initial demand schedule (column 3) is drawn from Table 4. Now suppose that during this short run the demand for fish changes from the schedule shown in column 3 to the one shown in column 4.

Note what happens. At each price, 1,000 more fish are demanded. Prior to the **change in demand,** the quantity demanded at $P = \$10$ was 3,500 fish. It increases now to 4,500. It increases at $P = \$9$ from 4,000 to 5,000, and so on.

Change in demand

A change in quantity demanded of a good that is caused by factors other than a change in the price of that good.

Figure 6 depicts the change in demand shown in Table 6.

Demand curve D, graphing the initial demand schedule (column 3) shifts outward to the right to D', graphing the new demand schedule (column 4). Look at the impact on the equilibrium price of fish of the change in demand from D to D'. The old equilibrium $P = \$5$ is no longer tenable. Now, at that price, an excess demand of 1,000 fish emerges. The pressure of this excess demand forces the equilibrium price up to $P = \$6$, where the 6,500 quantity of fish demanded equals the 6,500 short-run quantity supplied.

What could cause such a change in demand? There are a number of reasons why people change the quantity they demand at the same price. The principal reasons are *changes in income, changes in taste, changes in other prices, changes in expectations about future prices, and changes in population size.* Let's consider each.

Changes in Income

You don't suppose, do you, that when Madonna dines out in one of New York's finest restaurants, she checks the price of poached salmon to see whether

TABLE 6
Fish Market, with Short-Run Supply and Multiple Demand Schedules

Price	Quantity Supplied	Initial Quantity Demanded	New Quantity Demanded
$10	8,500	3,500	4,500
9	8,000	4,000	5,000
8	7,500	4,500	5,500
7	7,000	5,000	6,000
6	6,500	5,500	6,500
5	6,000	6,000	7,000
4	5,500	6,500	7,500
3	5,000	7,000	8,000
2	4,500	7,500	8,500
1	4,000	8,000	9,000

she's willing to make the purchase? Wouldn't you be surprised if she orders the salmon at P = $5 but passes at P = $10?

The more income people have, the more they can afford to buy more of everything. If Claudia Preparata's income were to increase by 25 percent, she might be more willing to buy that first fish at $10. Before, she passed it up. It isn't surprising, then, that when people's incomes increase, the quantity demanded of fish at P = $10 increases from 3,500 to 4,500. It increases as well at every other price level.

Normal good

A good whose demand increases or decreases when people's incomes increase or decrease.

On the other hand, what do you suppose happens to the demand for fish when incomes fall? You would expect that the quantity demanded at P = $10 would fall from 3,500 fish to something less and would fall from 4,000 to something less at P = $9, and so on. To economists, fish is a **normal good;** that is,

FIGURE 6
Change in Demand
Ceteris paribus, an increase in demand from D to D′ raises the equilibrium price from $5 to $6. The quantity bought and sold increases from 6,000 to 6,500. A decrease in demand, say from D to D″, lowers price and reduces the quantity bought and sold.

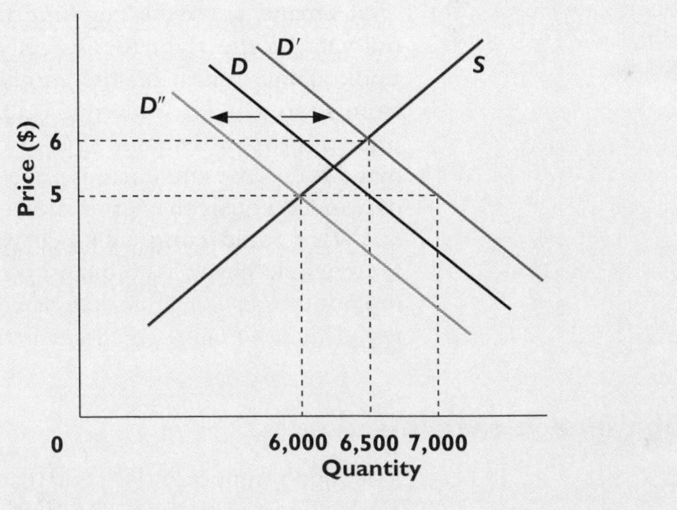

ADDED PERSPECTIVE

De Gustibus Non Est Disputandum

Taste matters. Health and nutrition may be popular with adults, but they're not for children's breakfast cereals. Presweetened cereals with no discernible nutritional value are the key to success in that market. In fact, the latest additions by leading cereal manufacturers, such as Wheaties Honey Gold by General Mills, Frosted Rice Chex Juniors by Ralston-Purina, and Double Dip Crunch by Kellogg, are all presweetened.

Why? Darrin Lynd, retail buyer for Nash Finch of Lincoln, Nebraska, says that launching new nutritional cereals for kids would be a hard sell. "You are going to have to market it to their parents," said Lynd. "They are the ones who are going to pick up on the nutritional value. But it's hard to convince the mom to buy something for the kid, unless the kid sees it and wants it."

Sue Hosey, vice president for consumer affairs for P&C Food Markets, Syracuse, New York, agrees, noting that children have a dramatic influence on parents and shopping choices. Kids have tastes. "Although there have been some indications that the sugar content may have been reduced, there have been no nutritional cereals per se for children," she said.

Rick Friedrichsen, buyer for Holiday Markets, Minneapolis, thinks that manufacturers are hesitant to market more healthful products for fear of jeopardizing their business. The Romans had a saying: *De gustibus non est disputandum.* (Translation: There's no disputing tastes.)

Discussion

Let's introduce normative economics. *Should* children be allowed to dictate tastes? *Should* all cereals be nutritious? Who decides what nutrition is? Answers to these questions are not found in demand and supply analysis. They depend on individual judgment and value systems. Demand and supply analysis helps you understand the economic consequences of making judgments. How would you answer the three questions posed above?

Adapted from *Supermarket News,* November 4, 1991.

a good whose demand increases (decreases) when people's incomes increase (decrease).

Changes in Taste

Tastes seldom change overnight, but they do change. Suppose that the surgeon general reports that the consumption of red meat is detrimental to health. If enough people worry about the quantity of meat they consume and make a conscious effort to cut down, the demand for fish would increase.

Or suppose McDonald's came to the island and introduced its filet of fish. Wouldn't *some* people, tasting McDonald's fish for the first time, switch from meat to fish? Can you picture the McDonald's fish commercials? Advertising tries to shift the demand curve to the right. If a McDonald's commercial pushed fish, people on the island would probably end up buying more fish at each price. At $P = \$10$, for example, quantity demanded might increase from 3,500 to 4,500 fish.

Changes in the Prices of Other Goods

You don't have to be frightened by the surgeon general's report to substitute fish for beef. Prices alone can do it. For example, if the price of hamburger were to jump suddenly from $1.89 to $2.45 per pound, that might be incentive enough

Substitute goods

Goods that can replace each other. When the price of one increases, the demand for the other increases.

Complementary goods

Goods that are generally used together. When the price of one increases, the demand for the other decreases.

for many people to switch from hamburger to fish. After all, fish and hamburger are **substitute goods.** *When the price of one increases, the demand for the other increases.*

Suppose people on the island typically eat fish with fries. And suppose, as well, that the price of potatoes increases from $0.75 to $2.75 a pound. What happens to the demand for fish? It falls. People demand less fish at each price because the "fish 'n fries" combo is more expensive. Fish and fries are **complementary goods.** *When the price of one increases, the demand for the other decreases.*

Can you think of other complementary goods? How about coffee and milk, milk and cookies, peanut butter and jelly, bagels and cream cheese. Coca-Cola once advertised that "Things go better with Coke."® What happens to the demand for Coke when the prices of those "things" increase? It falls.

Changes in Expectations About Future Prices

The demand for fish may change just because people change their expectations about tomorrow's fish price. If you thought that the price of fish would increase tomorrow, you might be willing to buy more fish today; that alone could explain why, at $P = \$10$, the quantity demanded increases from 3,500 to 4,500 (and increases at every price level) in Table 6. Of course, if you had a notion that tomorrow's price would be lower, you might delay consumption by reducing the quantity demanded today. In such case, the demand for fish decreases.

Changes in Population Size

Suppose an immigration wave increases the island's population by 10 percent. How does such an increase affect the demand for fish? With more mouths to feed, the quantity of fish demanded at each price increases. A baby boom on the island would have the same effect.

A Change in Demand or a Change in Quantity Demanded?

Changes in quantity demanded and changes in demand may seem to be two ways of expressing the same idea, but they are not. What's the difference?

Economists define *change in quantity demanded* to mean only the change in quantity demanded that is brought about by a change in price. They define *change in demand* to mean a shift in the entire demand curve.

Look at demand curve D in Figure 7. When price falls from $P = \$10$ to $P = \$7$, the quantity demanded increases from 4,500 to 5,000. Economists describe this increase as "a change in quantity demanded." It traces out a movement *along the demand curve* from point a to point b.

When demand increases for other reasons, such as population growth, the entire demand curve shifts from D to D'. Economists call this shift "a change in demand." At the same price, $P = \$10$, the quantity demanded increases from 4,500 on D to 6,000 on D'. The shift in the demand curve from D to D'— point a to point c at $P = \$10$— occurs because of a determining factor such as a change in people's tastes or income. It is not a result of a change in the price of the good.

It's a matter of precision in terminology. Economists use the specific terms *a change in quantity demanded* and *a change in demand* to help distinguish between two very different ideas.

FIGURE 7
Distinguishing Changes in Demand from Changes in Quantity Demanded
Movement along the demand curve D, from a price of $10 at point *a*, to a price of $7 at point *b*, illustrates a *change in quantity demanded* from 4,500 to 5,000. A shift in the demand curve from D to D′ illustrates a *change in demand*. At a price of $10, the quantity increases from 4,500 on demand curve D to 6,000 on demand curve D′.

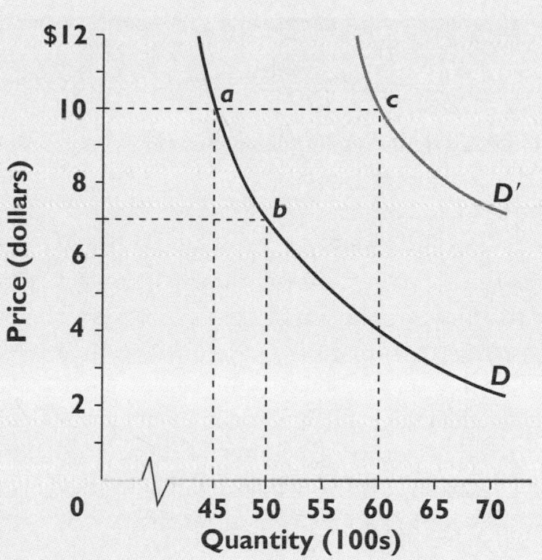

CHANGES IN SUPPLY

Let us now consider what happens to price when changes in short-run supply occur. Let's suppose that the demand schedule is the same as the one in column 4 of Table 6. The change in short-run supply is 1,000 more fish added (at every price) to the supply schedule of Table 6. Table 7 records this market condition.

Change in supply
A change in quantity supplied of a good that is caused by factors other than a change in the price of that good.

Figure 8 depicts the **change in supply** shown in Table 7.

Supply curve S, graphing the initial supply schedule (column 3) shifts outward to the right to S′, graphing the new supply schedule (column 4). Look at its impact on the equilibrium price of fish. The initial equilibrium, $P = \$6$, is no longer tenable. Now, at that price an excess supply of 1,000 fish emerges. The

TABLE 7
Fish Market, with Demand and Multiple Short-Run Supply Schedules

Price	Quantity Demanded	Initial Quantity Supplied	New Quantity Supplied
$10	4,500	8,500	9,500
9	5,000	8,000	9,000
8	5,500	7,500	8,500
7	6,000	7,000	8,000
6	6,500	6,500	7,500
5	7,000	6,000	7,000
4	7,500	5,500	6,500
3	8,000	5,000	6,000
2	8,500	4,500	5,500
1	9,000	4,000	5,000

ADDED PERSPECTIVE

The Weather's Just Too Nice for Some People

Have you ever complained about the weather? Farmers do that a lot! They will tell you that it's either too cold, too hot, or too rainy. Now they have the ultimate weather complaint: Too good! A nice mix of sun and rain is suiting their corn and soybean fields so well that they face the prospect of oversupply. The too-good weather has already depressed prices on the Chicago commodity markets. It may even get worse. Recent crop reports show that farmers have planted more corn and soybeans than economists had estimated. Only livestock farmers are not grumbling. For them, falling crop prices translate into lower feed prices, and that translates into fatter cattle, pigs, chickens, and profits.

Discussion

Draw two graphs, one for the corn market and the other for the livestock market, and show how the good weather in the story affects demand, supply, and price in each.

Source: "The Weather's Too Damn Nice," *The Economist*, July 13, 1991.

pressure of this excess supply drives the equilibrium price down from $P = \$6$ to $P = \$5$, and the quantities bought and sold up from 6,500 to 7,000 fish.

What could cause such a change in supply? There are a number of reasons why fishermen change the quantity they are willing to supply at every price level. The principal reasons are *changes in technology, changes in resource prices, changes in the prices of other goods, and changes in the number of suppliers.* Let's consider each.

Changes in Technology

Suppose Steve Scariano, an electronic tinkerer on the island, invents a sonar device that allows fishermen to detect the presence of fish at considerable depths. What a bonanza! Imagine JoAnn Weber, one of the island's fishermen, using the

FIGURE 8
Change in Supply
Ceteris paribus, an increase in supply, from S to S′, lowers the equilibrium price from $6 to $5 and raises the quantity bought and sold from 6,500 to 7,000. A decrease in supply, say from S to S″, raises price and reduces the quantity bought and sold.

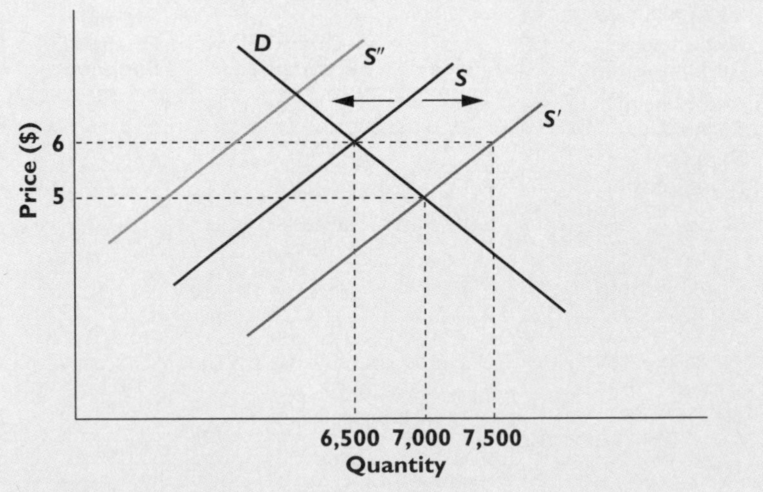

same boat and crew but installing Steve's sonar device on her boat. What do you suppose happens to the quantity of fish she is now capable of bringing home? At every price level the quantity supplied increases.

Why? New technology, such as Steve's sonar device, typically lowers the cost of producing a good. Each fish is now cheaper to produce. That means higher profit for fishermen. That higher profit is an incentive to supply more at every price level.

Changes in Resource Prices

If lower costs raise profit and create incentive to supply more at every price level, then any factor that contributes to lowering costs will increase supply. Consider what happens to the supply curve when resource prices associated with fishing fall. For example, suppose the price (wages) of hiring fishing crews fall. Instead of paying a boat pilot $300 a day, pilots are readily available at $200. Or suppose the prices of bait, fishing gear, fuel, and ice fall. These lower resource prices increase the spread between the market price a fisherman gets for a fish and the costs involved in producing it. That increased spread is greater profit per fish. In other words, lower resource prices increase the quantities of fish supplied at every price level in the fish market.

Imagine what happens to the supply curve if resources associated with fish production become more expensive. The reverse occurs. More expensive resources decrease the quantities supplied at every price level in the fish market. We see this in S'', a new supply curve to the left of S in Figure 8.

Changes in Prices of Other Goods

Many boats, with minor alterations, can serve multiple purposes. For example, a sightseeing boat that transports tourists from island to island can be rigged to fish the same waters. Cargo boats can be scrubbed down and fitted for passengers. Fishing boats can haul cargo.

Suppose faltering island tourism causes the price of sightseeing boat tickets to fall. How long will it take before some of the sightseeing boat operators switch to fishing? And how will that switch affect the supply curve of fish? This change in price of other goods (sightseeing boat tickets) shifts the supply curve of fish out to the right.

Let's digress for a moment. Consider potato farmers. Their fields, too, can serve multiple purposes. If the price of corn skyrockets, many potato farmers may switch from potato farming to corn. How would the switch affect the supply schedule of potatoes? At every price level in the potato market, the quantity of potatoes supplied falls. Graphed, it would show the supply curve of potatoes shifting to the left.

Changes in the Number of Suppliers

Be sure that you are able to think of reasons why supply and demand curves might shift, and in which direction.

Perhaps the first thing that comes to mind when trying to explain what could cause the shift from S to S' is simply more suppliers. Somewhat akin to a change in demand occasioned by a change in taste, a change in supply caused by greater numbers of suppliers might reflect changes in people's occupational "taste." More people choosing to fish means more fish at every price level.

TABLE 8
Market for Fish in the Short Run

Price	Quantity Demanded	Quantity Supplied	Excess Demand	Excess Supply
$10	4,500	8,500		4,000
9	5,000	8,000		3,000
8	5,500	7,500		2,000
7	6,000	7,000		1,000
6	6,500	6,500	0	0
5	7,000	6,000	1,000	
4	7,500	5,500	2,000	
3	8,000	5,000	3,000	
2	8,500	4,500	4,000	
1	9,000	4,000	5,000	

DERIVING EQUILIBRIUM PRICE IN THE SHORT RUN

Is the way equilibrium price is determined really different from the market day to the short run or the long run?

Deriving equilibrium price in the short run involves both demanders and suppliers adjusting their quantity demanded and quantity supplied to price. Table 8 and Figure 9 set up a short-run market condition.

What impact does the fishermen's ability to adjust quantity supplied to price have on equilibrium price? Look at Table 8 and Figure 9.

When price is $9, fishermen are willing to supply 8,000 fish. But demanders at that price are only willing to take 5,000 off the market, creating an excess supply of 3,000 fish.

What happens then? At P = *$9, competition among the suppliers will drive price down.* As price falls, demanders increase the quantity of fish demanded and suppliers, at the same time, reduce the quantity of fish supplied. Excess supply on the market diminishes.

FIGURE 9
Market for Fish in the Short Run
The intersection of the demand and short-run supply curves identifies market equilibrium in the short run. At a price of $6, the 6,500 quantity demanded equals the 6,500 quantity supplied.

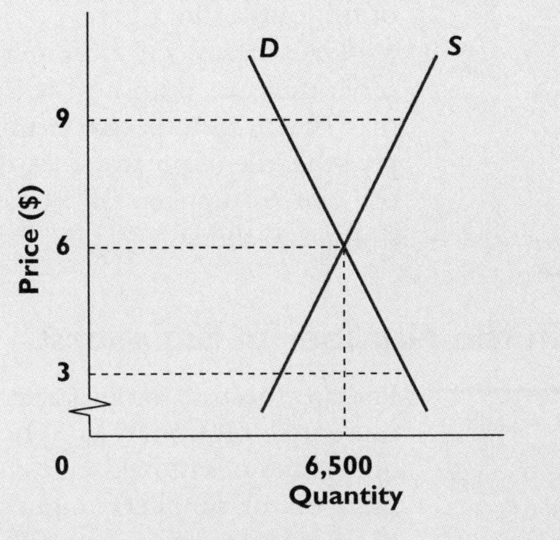

TABLE 9
Market for Fish in the Long Run

Price	Quantity Demanded	Quantity Supplied	Excess Demand	Excess Supply
$10.00	4,500	16,000		11,500
9.00	5,000	14,000		9,000
8.00	5,500	12,000		7,500
7.00	6,000	10,000		4,000
6.00	6,500	8,000		1,500
5.50	6,750	6,750	0	0
5.00	7,000	6,000	1,000	
4.00	7,500	4,000	3,500	
3.00	8,000	2,000	6,000	
2.00	8,500	0	8,500	
1.00	9,000	0	9,000	

When price is $3, an excess demand of 3,000 fish emerges and competition among demanders will force price up. As you see in Table 8 and Figure 9, the market clears at an equilibrium price of $6. There are 6,500 fish bought and sold.

DERIVING EQUILIBRIUM PRICE IN THE LONG RUN

The same market forces of excess demand and excess supply that drove price to equilibrium in the short run drives price to long-run equilibrium as well. Look at Table 9 and Figure 10.

The short-run equilibrium price of $6 becomes untenable in the long run because now fishermen, with more time to adjust their quantity supplied to the

FIGURE 10
The Market for Fish in the Long Run
The intersection of the demand and long-run supply curves identifies market equilibrium in the long run. At a price of $5.50, the 6,750 quantity demanded equals the 6,750 quantity supplied.

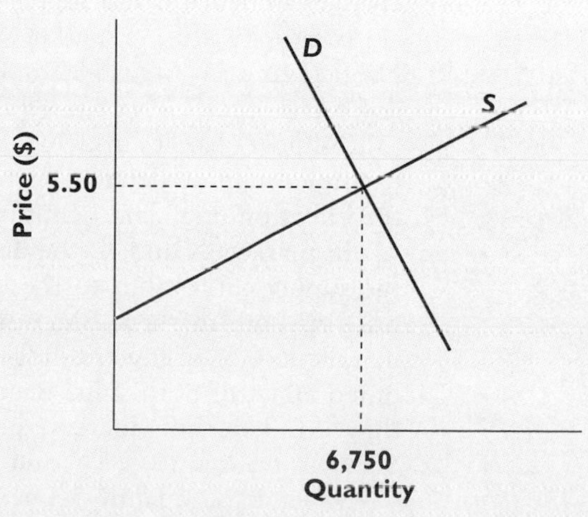

$6 price, are able to supply 8,000 fish. That creates an excess supply of 1,500 fish, which forces the price downward.

As price falls below $6, more quantity is demanded and less is supplied. At P = $5.50, the market clears. The quantity demanded equals the quantity supplied at the long-run equilibrium price of $5.50.

WHEN CHANGES IN DEMAND AND SUPPLY OCCUR AT THE SAME TIME

Figure 11 illustrates how changes in demand and supply generate changes in equilibrium price and quantity.

In markets A and B, increases in both demand and supply shift both the demand and supply curves out to the right, from D to D' and from S to S'.

Be sure that you can draw examples of shifts in supply and demand that occur simultaneously and explain why the equilibrium price rises or falls.

In market A, the more prominent shift is in demand. In market B, the more prominent shift is in supply. Since we know that any outward shift in either the demand curve or the supply curve increases quantity, then the combined effect of both shifting outward at the same time *must* increase quantity. The combined shift increases quantity from 100 to 200 in market A, and from 100 to 300 in market B.

The effect of increases in demand and supply on price is less definitive. An outward shift in the demand curve raises price, but an outward shift in the supply curve lowers price. When both shifts occur at the same time, it is unclear whether price increases or decreases. What ultimately determines the direction of the price change is the comparative intensities of the demand and supply curve shifts.

In market A, the more prominent shift is in demand. When the demand curve shifts from D to D'—holding the supply curve at S—price increases from $6 to $8. But the shift in supply from S to S'—holding the demand curve at D—*decreases* price from $6 to $5. The net effect of changes in *both* supply and demand increases price to $7.

In market B, the intensity of changes in demand and supply are reversed. Note the sizable increase in supply from S to S'. The shift in supply—holding demand at D— decreases price from $6 to $4. The shift in demand—holding supply at S—*raises* price from $6 to $6.50. The net effect of these combined changes in demand and supply lowers price to $5.

In other words, in market situations where both demand and supply increase (as in Figure 11), *quantities increase, but the resulting price changes are indeterminate, depending on the relative strengths of the demand and supply shifts.*

Suppose changes in demand and supply occur in the opposite direction. For example, suppose demand increases while supply decreases. Figure 12 illustrates the effect on price and quantity.

In markets X and Y, the demand curves shift to the right from D to D', but the supply curves shift to the left from S to S'. Consider first what happens to price in both markets. Since we know that either an outward shift in the demand curve or an inward shift in the supply curve increases price, then the combined effect of both shifts occurring at the same time *must* increase price. And they do. The shifts increase price from $6 to $8 in market X and from $6 to $7.50 in market Y.

What about quantity? The effect of an increase in demand and a decrease in supply on quantity is less definitive. An outward shift in the demand curve raises

FIGURE 11 **Increases in Demand and Supply**
In market A, the large increase in demand, from D to D′, and moderate increase in supply, from S to S′ results in higher prices and quantity. When demand shifts from D to D′, supply remains unchanged, quantity increases from 100 to 175, and price increases from $6 to $8. When the shift in supply from S to S′ is added to the market, quantities are pushed further to 200, but price drops to $7.

In market B, the intensity of changes in demand and supply are reversed. The large change in supply from S to S′, with demand remaining unchanged, increases quantity from 100 to 250. Price falls from $6 to $4. When the shift in demand from D to D′ is added to the market, quantity increases further, to 300, and price increases to $5.

Whenever supply and demand both shift outward, we can expect an increase in quantity, but the price effect (up or down) depends on the relative strengths of these demand and supply shifts.

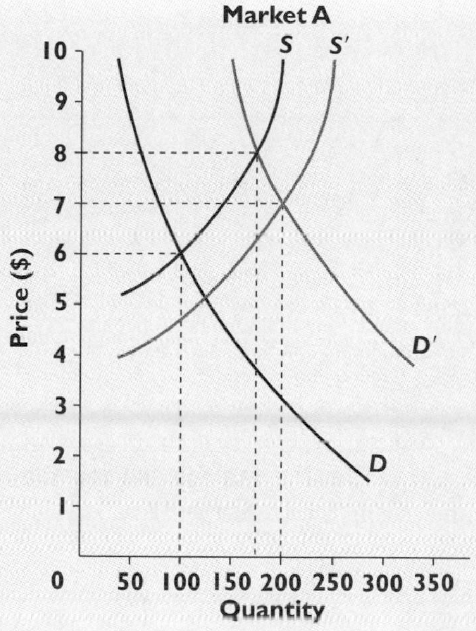

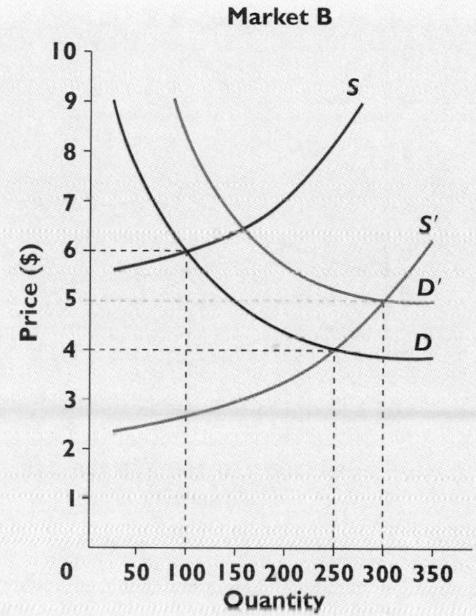

quantity, but an inward shift in the supply curve lowers quantity. When both shifts occur at the same time, it is unclear whether quantity increases or decreases. What ultimately determines the direction of the quantity change is the comparative intensities of the demand and supply curve shifts.

In market X, the more prominent shift is in supply. When the supply curve shifts from *S* to *S′*—holding the demand curve at *D*—quantity decreases from 100 to 50. But the shift in demand from *D* to *D′*—holding the supply curve at *S*—*increases* quantity from 100 to 200. The net effect of changes in *both* supply and demand decreases quantity to 90.

In market Y, the intensity of changes in demand and supply are reversed. Note the sizable increase in demand from *D* to *D′*. The shift in demand—holding supply at *S* increases quantity from 100 to 200. The shift in supply holding demand at *D*—decreases quantity from 100 to 70. The net effect of these combined changes in demand and supply increases quantity to 150.

In other words, when an outward shift in demand is combined with an inward shift in supply (as in Figure 12), *price increases, but the resulting change in quantity is indeterminate, depending upon the relative strengths of these demand and supply shifts.*

FIGURE 12 **Increases in Demand, Decreases in Supply**

When demand increases in market X from *D* to *D′*, quantity increases from 100 to 200 and price increases from $6 to $7. When supply decreases sharply, from *S* to *S′*, quantity falls to 90, well below the initial 100 level. The shift in supply to *S′* also raises the price. In the end, coupling an outward shift of the demand curve with an inward shift of the supply curve, results in a price increase from $6 to $8.

Market Y's supply shift, compared to market X's, is moderate. After the shift in the demand curve to *D′*, the cutback in quantity when supply decreases from *S* to *S′* is to 150, which is still above the initial 100 level. But price rises to $7.50.

With an outward shift in demand and an inward shift in supply, we can expect prices to increase, but the effect on quantity is indeterminate, depending on the relative strengths of the demand and supply shifts.

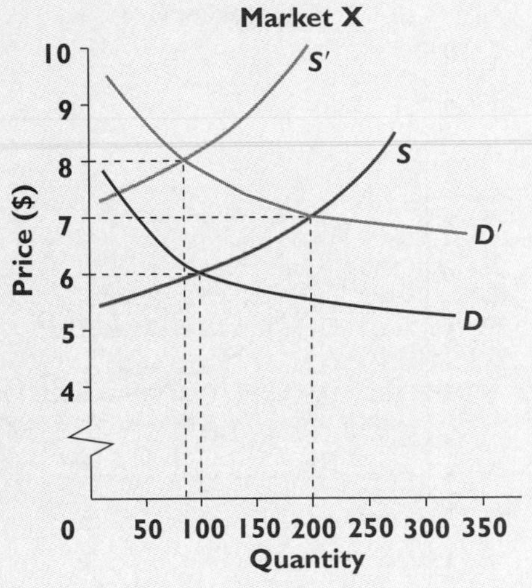

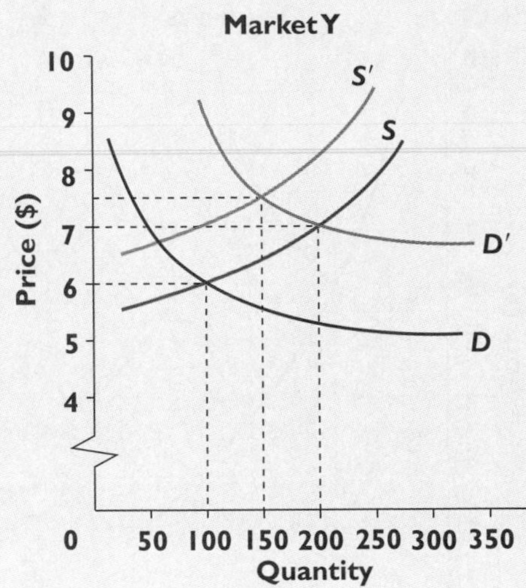

What about the price and quantity effects of other changes in demand and supply, say, a fall in demand and an increase in supply, or a fall in both? Test yourself by graphing these changes using varying intensities of demand and supply shifts.

WHY THE PRICE OF AN ORANGE IS 30 CENTS AT THE SUPERMARKET

The same factors governing the $6 equilibrium price of fish govern as well the 30 cent equilibrium price of oranges. The price of oranges depends upon the supply and demand conditions in the fruit and vegetable market.

If orange imports from Spain, Morocco, and Israel are added to our California and Florida orange supply, the supply curve in the orange market shifts out to the right, forcing the equilibrium price to fall.

Grapefruit and oranges are substitute goods. If the grapefruit harvest in both California and Florida is exceptionally large, resulting in a substantial fall in the price of grapefruit, the demand curve for oranges shifts to the left. The result? The price of oranges falls.

You know what he's thinking. "Gosh, there's an awful lot of perishable goods out here. Where are the demanders? If the goods don't move pretty soon, excess supply will drive the equilibrium price down. Perhaps I ought to lower my price *now,* to beat the rush." What would you do if you were him?

Suppose, on the other hand, that TV commercials sponsored by the orange-growers industry persuade people that orange juice is not only a breakfast drink but an excellent substitute for soft drinks, tea, coffee, or milk at any time of the day. What should the orange growers expect? The demand curve for their oranges shifts to the right, raising both price and quantity.

PRICE SERVES AS A RATIONING MECHANISM

Price serves as our economy's thermostat. In winter, when temperatures in our homes fall below a desired level, the thermostat trips the furnace into action. When temperatures rise beyond a preset level, the thermostat shuts the furnace down.

How does price ration goods and services between buyers?

What is the connection between price and thermostats? Suppose bad weather strikes and the quantity supplied of fish decreases, creating an excess demand. It means people want more fish at the prevailing price than there are fish available. How do you ration fewer fish among all the fish-demanding consumers?

Price solves the problem. How does price ration the fish? *Automatically,* the inward (or leftward) shift in the supply curve raises price, forcing demanders who choose not to or cannot afford to buy at the higher price out of the market. The supply is rationed, then, to those who choose to and can afford to remain in the market at the higher price.

In this sense, price acts as the market's thermostat. By increasing, it shuts down quantity demanded when supply falls, and by decreasing, it increases quantity demanded when supply increases.

Most everyone enjoys strawberries in summer. But very few get to taste them in winter. Would you pay $2 for a strawberry in January? You're not alone. But Madonna loves them!

CHAPTER REVIEW

1. Prices reflect the willingness of people to buy and to sell. People supply goods and services on the presumption that there will be a demand for them. Consumer demand reflects people's willingness to buy.

2. The demand for a good represents people's willingness to purchase specific quantities at specific prices. The law of demand is the inverse relationship between price and the quantity demanded. As the price of a good decreases, the quantity demanded increases and vice versa.

3. Graphs can translate tabular data for quantities demanded at different prices into individual demand curves. Demand curves have negative slopes because price and quantity demanded are inversely related.

4. Market demand curves represent the sum of individual quantities demanded at different prices.

5. Supply involves production activity over a period of time. The market day is a time period so short that the quantity supplied cannot be changed no matter what price is paid to the supplier. Therefore, quantity supplied is constant during the market day, regardless of price.

6. Market price is determined by the intersection of demand and supply. The market price is the price at which quantity demanded equals quantity supplied. Because quantity demanded and quantity supplied are equal at the market price, it is also called an equilibrium price. If the price starts out above the equilibrium, then excess supply will result. If the price starts out below the equilibrium, then excess demand will result. In either case, the price is pushed toward the equilibrium.

7. If supply changes, then the market price has to change also. For example, an increase in supply will cause an excess supply at the existing market price. Thus, the price must fall to a new equilibrium. A decrease in supply will cause an increase in the equilibrium price.

8. Changes in demand also cause changes in the equilibrium price. An increase in demand will result in excess demand at the old price and the price will rise to a new equilibrium. A decrease in demand will lead to excess supply at the old price and the price will fall. The causes of changes in demand include changes in income, changes in tastes, changes in prices of other goods, changes in expectations about future prices, and changes in population size.

9. In a time period longer than the market day, suppliers can respond to changes in the market price. The short run is a time period long enough to allow suppliers to make partial adjustments in production in response to price changes. The long run is a time period long enough to allow suppliers to completely adjust their production to changes in the marketplace. The longer the time period, the more flexible is the response by suppliers to price changes. Thus, as time passes, the supply curve shifts from a vertical line to a flatter, positively sloped line.

10. Determining equilibrium price in the short run and in the long run involves adjustments on the part of both demanders and suppliers. In either case, if the price is above the equilibrium price, then excess supply will exist and price will

fall. As the price falls, quantity demanded increases and quantity supplied decreases. If the price starts out below equilibrium, then excess demand exists and price will rise. As the price rises, quantity demanded decreases and quantity supplied increases.

11. It is possible for both demand and supply to shift at the same time. Simultaneous shifts in demand and supply will lead to changes in price. Whether price increases or decreases depends on the relative strengths of these shifts in supply and demand.

12. Price serves as a rationing mechanism in our economy. As a price increases, the available supply is rationed to those who can still afford to buy it. A decrease in price makes a good available to a wider segment of the market because more people are able to buy it.

KEY TERMS

Change in quantity demanded
Law of demand
Demand schedule
Demand curve
Market demand
Supply schedule
Market-day supply
Supply curve
Excess supply
Excess demand
Equilibrium price
Short run
Long run
Change in demand
Normal good
Substitute goods
Complementary goods
Change in supply

QUESTIONS

1. Draw a demand curve representing King Richard's plea: "A horse, a horse, my kingdom for a horse!"

2. Suppose the communities of Urbana, Champaign, Rantoul, and Danville make up the East Central Illinois market for eggplant. And suppose, at a price of $2, the quantity demanded in Champaign is 2,000, in Urbana 1,000, in Rantoul 400, and in Danville 600. When price falls to $1, the quantity demanded in Champaign becomes 3,000, in Urbana 1,500, in Rantoul 500, and in Danville 700. With these data, graph the East Central Illinois market for egg plant, connecting the points to form a demand curve.

3. Suppose people leave neighboring Indiana and Iowa to settle in East Central Illinois. Show on the graph of question 2 what happens to the demand curve for eggplant in the East Central Illinois market.

4. Would such an influx of people to East Central Illinois change the demand curve for eggplant or the quantity demanded of eggplant?

5. Explain why the market-day supply curve for fish described in the chapter is drawn vertically.

6. Why are the slopes of the short-run supply curve and the long-run supply curve different?

7. "Prices always tend toward equilibrium." Discuss this statement by demonstrating why every other price is unsustainable.

8. Suppose NAFTA (our free trade agreement with Canada and Mexico) allows the neighboring economies to enter our slipper market. Draw a graph showing the probable effects of their entry on price and quantity of slippers demanded and supplied in the United States.

9. When the price of hamburger rises, the demand for fish rises. When the price of hamburger rises, the demand for hamburger buns falls. Why?

10. Hans Gienepp is frustrated every year. In March, the price of tomatoes is $1.75 per pound. That is sufficient incentive for him to plant tomatoes in his yard. But in August, when the crop is ready for picking, prices at the grocer have fallen to 25 cents per pound. "I always run into this bad luck," he laments. Why is his problem not a matter of luck?

11. Because there was a rumor in May that the price of compact disc players was going to increase in August, the demand for compact disc players went up in May. Explain.

12. How would each of the following events affect the international price of oil (in each case *ceteris paribus*): (a) the United States gives economic assistance to oil-rich Ukraine in the form of oil drilling technology, (b) Iraq in a war against Saudi Arabia destroys 50 percent of Saudi oil wells, (c) a U.S. invention uses sea water to fuel automobiles, (d) West European homes are heated solely by solar power, (e) the world's population doubles.

13. Suppose the market for holiday candles was described by the following schedule:

Price	Quantity Demanded	Quantity Supplied
$6	1,000	6,000
5	2,000	5,000
4	3,000	4,000
3	4,000	3,000
2	5,000	2,000
1	6,000	1,000

Draw the demand and supply curves and identify the equilibrium price. What effect would a 1,000 decrease in demand at every price level have on the demand curve, supply curve, and equilibrium price?

14. At what price is quantity demanded equal to 4,000 pairs of shoes? At what price is quantity supplied equal to 5,000 pairs of shoes? What is the equilibrium price for a pair of shoes? At what price is there an excess supply of 2,000 pairs of shoes?

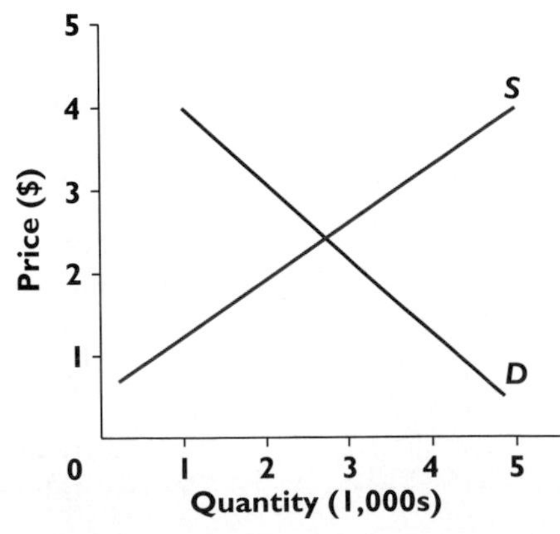

15. Professor Carrie Meyer of George Mason University asks her students the following question: Suppose that a frost affects the coffee harvest in Colombia and destroys much of the crop. What happens to supply and demand for coffee? Equilibrium price and quantity? Suppose also that some consumers take advantage of the coffee crisis to permanently cut down and/or eliminate their consumption of coffee. What will be the result in the coffee market when coffee production returns to normal the following year?

How would you answer her question?

PART 2
INTRODUCTION TO MICROECONOMICS

CHAPTER 4
ELASTICITY

CHAPTER PREVIEW

In Chapter 3 we learned that quantity demanded is inversely related to price. As price increases, quantity demanded decreases. On the other hand, quantity supplied is positively related to price. Given time to respond to price changes, suppliers bring larger quantities to the market at higher prices.

In this chapter, we will study the sensitivity of demand and supply to price changes. For example, if the price of coffee increases by 50 percent, how much will your quantity demanded decrease? If you are a caffeine addict who doesn't like tea or soda, then *your* quantity demanded might be almost unchanged by the price increase. You are quite insensitive to the price change. In other words, your demand for coffee isn't very elastic. Economists have developed methods to compute coefficients for the price elasticity of demand as well as for other elasticity concepts.

After studying this chapter, you should be able to:

- Discuss demand sensitivity to price changes for individuals and for markets.
- List and discuss the determinants of demand sensitivity to price changes.
- Explain the concept of price elasticity of demand.
- Distinguish between the elastic, inelastic, and unit elastic ranges on demand curves.

- Explain the cross elasticity of demand for substitute goods and for complementary goods.
- Distinguish between normal goods and inferior goods using the concept of income elasticity of demand.
- Discuss supply elasticity in the short run and in the long run.
- Explain how tax revenues and the price elasticity of demand for goods that are taxed are related.

Billy Crystal is a very funny man. He makes his living, in fact a very lucrative living, by being funny. When he goes into the routine about his family dynamics, people in the audience respond with genuine laughter. Some of them laugh hysterically, others belly laugh, some chuckle loudly, and a very few manage to just squeeze out a smile.

Comedians understand that. No two people respond the same way to the same humor. Our idea of what is funny is personal. A comedian whose humor is unique could end up facing a very quiet, if not hostile, audience, but seldom more than once!

Have you ever sat through a boring lecture? The response is generally an overpowering urge to sleep, isn't it? Many students succumb, but not everyone at the same time, and there are always some students who actually find the lecture exciting.

What we find funny or boring is not only a matter of personal taste but also a matter of culture. For example, many of us are baffled by British humor, while our own humor is unintelligible to most Russians.

How we respond to humor and to lectures is not unlike our responses to different foods, sporting events, cars, and the myriad of household goods that clutter our different homes. We are individuals, and our responses to acquiring more of these goods, or less of them, reflect our individuality. When we are confronted in the marketplace by changing prices for goods, we typically respond by changing the quantities of the goods we demand. For each of us, however, *how much* we change the quantity we demand when the price of any good changes depends upon our own particular sensitivity to the price change.

For example, when the price of gasoline increases, most people buy fewer gallons of gasoline. But, experience shows, not that much less! On the other hand, if the ticket price of a REM concert were to fall, the quantity demanded of REM tickets would probably increase considerably. These different demand responses to changing prices not only strike us as reasonable but are confirmed by our everyday experience. For some goods, our response is moderate. For other goods, the response can be dramatic. That is, our sensitivity to price changes depends, in large measure, upon the character of the goods.

DEMAND SENSITIVITIES AND INSENSITIVITIES

Consider how you would react to a change in the price of chewing gum. If one morning you woke up to discover that the price of gum had risen 100 percent, from 2 to 4 cents a stick, the probability is very high that if you were a gum-chewer, you would keep right on chewing. Anyone disagree? The 4-cent price tag would hardly deter you. The 100 percent price increase would generate a

"Sale! What a great buy! I surely needed another sweater and had planned on buying one. But at these prices, I'm going to buy two."

zero percent decrease in quantity demanded. That's about as demand-insensitive to a price change as one can get.

Are there goods for which your own demand is particularly sensitive or insensitive to price changes as compared to average consumers? Why do you think your demand differs from the norm for these goods?

Suppose your doctor diagnoses pneumonia and prescribes a unit of penicillin. You rush to the pharmacy only to discover that the druggist just raised the price from \$2 to \$3 per unit. Would you walk away? Or suppose the pharmacy ran a two-for-\$3 special. Would you demand more than the one unit prescribed? It seems reasonable, doesn't it, that your demand for penicillin would be completely insensitive to these price changes.

Gum and penicillin are just two of many goods whose demands are generally insensitive to price changes. The quantity demanded of light bulbs, cigarettes, aspirin, potatoes, shoelaces, nails, sugar, and sparkplugs tends to be relatively insensitive to changes in price. If you think about it, you can probably name hundreds of other goods that fall into this category.

On the other hand, suppose movie prices rose 100 percent, from \$6 to \$12. How would you react? If you were like most people, you would cut down sharply on the number of times you go out to the movies. You would probably switch to videocassettes, or be satisfied with ABC's *Tuesday Night at the Movies*. That is, unlike gum chewing, the quantity demanded of movies tends to be relatively sensitive to price changes.

You can test your demand sensitivities to price changes for a variety of goods by asking yourself how you would respond to a specific percent change in the price of each. Compare your own responses to those of your friends. You will probably find that for a wide range of goods you have much in common.

Expressing Demand Sensitivity Graphically

Figure 1 shows how Misty Coffman reacts to a \$3 to \$2 price cut on three goods: penicillin, sparkplugs, and Coca-Cola.

Look at panel *a*. When the price of penicillin falls from \$3 to \$2, the quantity demanded by Misty remains unchanged. In fact, her quantity demanded is one unit for every price within the price range shown in panel *a*. Why would Misty want two units when only one is prescribed?

FIGURE 1 **Demand Response to Price Change**
Panels *a*, *b*, and *c* depict three different responses to a \$3 to \$2 price cut. In panel *a*, the response is zero for a price cut in penicillin. In fact, at every price in panel *a*, quantity demanded remains unchanged at one unit. In panel *b*, price matters. The \$3 to \$2 cut in sparkplugs generates an increase in quantity demanded from 8 to 10. The demand response to the same price cut in panel *c* is considerably greater. Quantity demanded of Coca-Cola increases from 1 to 3 cartons.

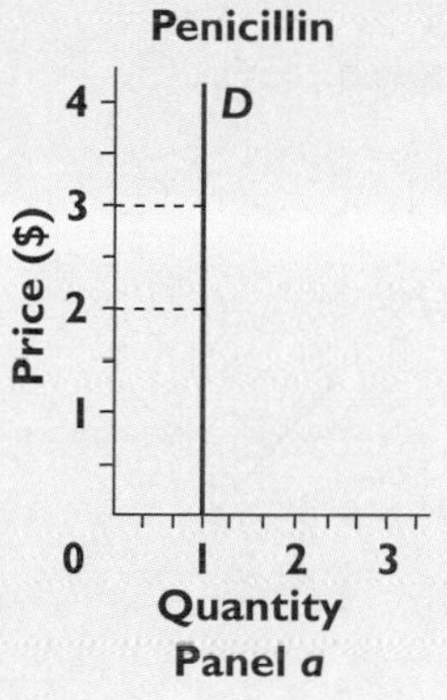

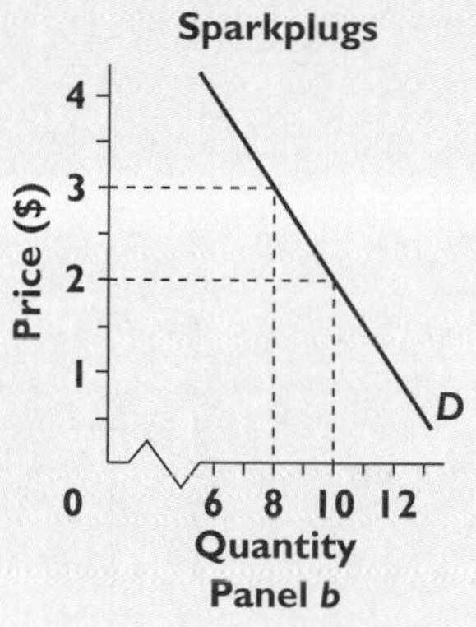

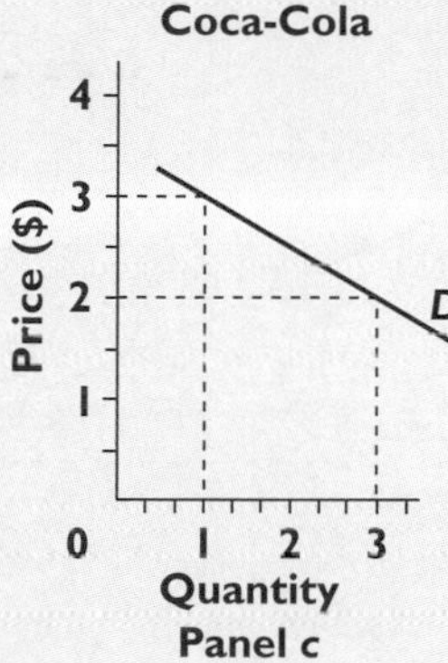

But what about sparkplugs? Look at panel *b*. Misty is not totally insensitive to the \$3 to \$2 price change. The $33\frac{1}{3}$ percent price decrease generates an increase in quantity demanded from eight to 10 sparkplugs, a rise of 25 percent.

Why? Perhaps Misty regards the price cut as temporary and takes immediate advantage of the lower price by buying plugs she otherwise would not buy. Or perhaps, with sparkplugs at \$2, she is inclined to change them more frequently.

Compare her demand for sparkplugs to her demand for Coca-Cola shown in panel *c*. Do you see the difference? When the supermarket cuts the price of a carton of Coke by $33\frac{1}{3}$ percent, from \$3 to \$2, the quantity demanded by Misty increases from one to three cartons, or by 300 percent. As you see, her demand for Coke is quite sensitive to the price change.

How do we explain that sensitivity? Although people's tastes for soft drinks are personal, still most people consider most soft drinks to be very good substitutes for each other. For example, Pepsi-Cola drinkers don't really mind switching to Coke or 7-Up, or most any other brand if the price is right. Some are regarded as very close Pepsi substitutes, others as slightly less so. When Coke, then, cuts its price by $33\frac{1}{3}$ percent, many people *almost* indifferent to brand would make the switch to Coke. How would you respond?

Are Our Demand Sensitivities Alike?

While people are not Xerox copies of each other, there is still a remarkable similarity in the way people respond to price changes across a wide variety of goods. Not everyone responds in the same way, but responses are typically more similar than dissimilar.

For example, Misty's response in Figure 1 to a change in the price of Coke describes most people's response to the price cut. Admittedly, some people are Dr. Pepper fanatics and wouldn't switch even if Coke were given away, but

FIGURE 2 **Market Demand for Coca-Cola and Sparkplugs**
At a price of \$3, the quantity of Coca-Cola demanded, shown in panel *a*, is 50,000 cartons, including Misty's demand for one carton. When price is cut to \$2, Misty and all other buyers increase their willingness to buy Coke. Quantity demanded increases to 150,000 cartons.

The market for sparkplugs is shown in panel *b*. Note the difference in the slopes of the demand curves in panels *a* and *b*. Buyers increase quantity demanded of sparkplugs when price is cut from \$3 to \$2, but by a smaller percentage than in panel *a*.

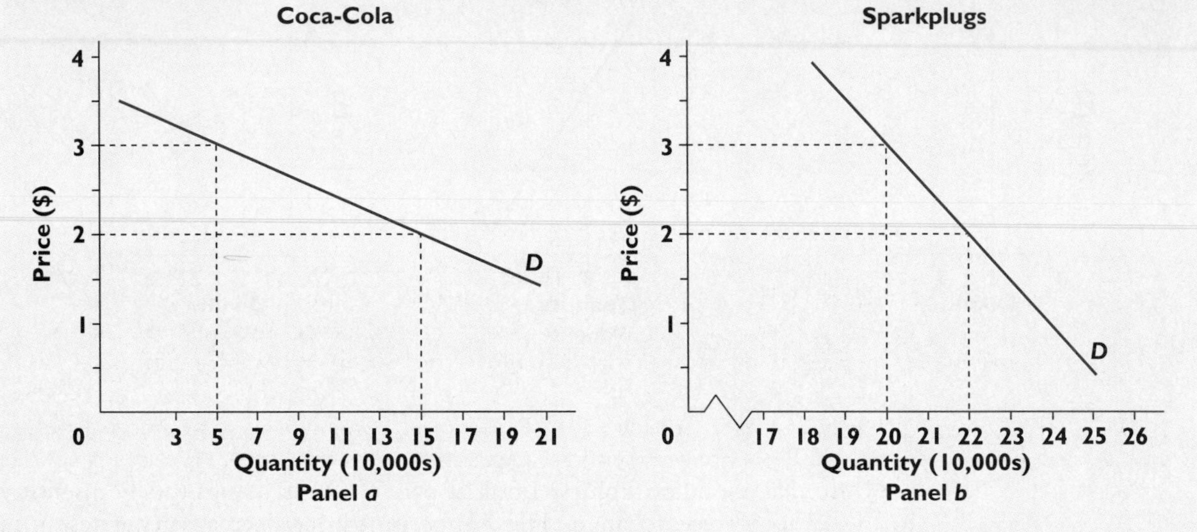

there aren't too many of them around. Adding together people's highly sensitive individual responses to the Coke price cut produces in Figure 2, panel *a*, a highly sensitive market demand curve for Coke.

What about the market demand curve for sparkplugs? It, too, reflects the simple aggregation of individual demand curves for sparkplugs, including Misty's. As we see in Figure 2, panel *b*, the $33\frac{1}{3}$ percent decrease in price creates an increase in the quantity of sparkplugs demanded, but not by much.

How many people do you know who would buy aspirin because the price is right? Few indeed. There is good reason why most people exhibit roughly the same demand sensitivities to price changes.

WHAT FACTORS INFLUENCE DEMAND SENSITIVITY?

How do we explain why demand sensitivities are so commonly held? What influences our reactions to price changes?

Low-Priced Goods

If most people won't even bother to pick up a penny from a sidewalk, why would we expect them to be at all concerned about price changes on nickel and dime items? The fact is, we don't. That's why, in our chewing gum example, a price increase from 2 to 4 cents was anything but earthshaking. Even though it represents a 100 percent increase, the two penny increase goes virtually unnoticed.

Do you suppose a 100 percent price increase on a 25-cent comb would deter many from making the purchase? Would a 10-cent increase on a 10-cent parking meter turn people to public transportation? Because these prices are relatively low, they represent only a tiny fraction of our income. Any price change, therefore, even a 100 percent increase, on these low-priced goods has so little impact on our total spending that the quantities demanded of them tend to be almost independent of their prices.

Income Levels

What may be a little money to some people may be a lot of money to others. We must be careful, then, about making quick assertions concerning demand sensitivities unless we know something about individual income levels. Rich people generally, it is safe to say, are less concerned about price changes than poor people. While a $75 to $200 price change on a graphite tennis racket might deter a university student whose income is $4,000 from making the purchase, the university's chancellor earning $175,000 would make the purchase effortlessly. If you were to draw their demand curves for tennis rackets, how would they look?

What can we conclude? First, poor people are more sensitive to price changes than rich people, and second, as people's incomes increase, their demand sensitivities to these price changes become less intense.

Substitute Goods

Our sensitivity to price changes depends as well upon the alternatives available. After an eventful night, Rolaids, as the TV commercials tell us, spells relief. But so do Tums, Bromo Seltzer, and Pepto-Bismol. Because they are all effective antacids, Rolaids has to be careful about raising its price. Why? Many who prefer Rolaids would switch to another brand if Rolaids raised its price.

If Coca-Cola and Pepsi-Cola are *close* substitutes, and if Rolaids and Tums are *close* as well, what can we say about potatoes grown on two different potato farms in Idaho? An Idaho potato is an Idaho potato, yes? They are *perfect* substitutes. Can you imagine buying the more expensive potato when a cheaper, identical potato is available?

Because Idaho potato farmers produce perfect substitutes, they have no leverage over their prices. Were one of them, say, Steve Coombs, foolish enough to insist on charging a higher price than his competitors—even if the price increase were only a fraction of a penny—the quantity demanded of Steve's higher-priced potatoes would fall to zero. After all, why would anyone buy a single potato from him when a cheaper, perfect substitute is available?

It makes sense, doesn't it, to suppose that our demand sensitivity to price changes depends upon the availability and closeness of substitute goods.

Can you read her mind? "There's the aspirin I wanted. But there are so many choices here, it's getting to be a pain just reading the labels. I guess they're pretty much alike. Perhaps all I should read is the marked-down prices."

Basic Food Goods

How many slices of bread could you eat at a sitting? You know without even trying that it wouldn't take much to reach your limit. Even at bargain prices, the quantity demanded by bread lovers could not really increase significantly.

What about price increases? Bread is a basic food in our diet. Were price to increase, even substantially, the quantity demanded would fall, but not by much. We demand bread for much the same reason that people in Southeast Asia demand rice. It is an important staple in our diet. What about our demand for milk and eggs? They, too, are staples in our diet. Would you expect the demand curve for these basic food goods to look most like the curve in panel *a*, *b*, or *c* of Figure 1?

Basic Nonfood Goods

Food items are not the only goods that represent basic needs in our society. Medicine, obviously, is another. We assumed, in our penicillin example, that the quantity demanded is *totally* insensitive to changes in price. Many other nonfood goods also have demand curves that look like Figure 1, panel *a*. There are considerably more whose demand curves take on the character shown in panel *b*. What about your textbooks? Or your demand for electricity?

Do you suppose business people would be more careful about the number of long-distance calls they make and the time spent on each when the price of these calls increases? Their ability to cut calls is limited by the sheer necessity of business. Telephones are basic items needed to transact business. More calls might be made when prices fall, fewer when they increase, but probably not by much in either case.

Linked Goods

Some goods are coupled. Their particular linked or complementary relationship often determines our demand sensitivities to their price changes. For example, what do you suppose would happen to the quantity of shoelaces demanded if the price of shoelaces increased? Think about it. People can't go about their business with unlaced shoes! It would be silly to stop wearing a $75 pair of shoes because the price of shoelaces jumped from $1.25 to $1.50.

Perhaps a substantial price cut would prompt a few people to change their laces more often. Perhaps a price increase to $2.50 a pair might prompt some to tie a knot or two before buying another pair. But most people do not change their shoelace buying behavior because of price changes.

Automobile dealers tell a story about a prospective buyer of a Rolls-Royce who asked the dealer how many miles per gallon the British import gets. The dealer coldly replied: "Sir, if you ask that question, you don't really want this car." The dealer knew something about linked goods and price insensitivity.

Time to Adjust

In the short run, we are typically less demand sensitive to price changes than in the long run. Given enough time, however, we might modify our tastes and broaden our range of would-be substitutes.

Be sure that you can list and explain the factors that influence demand sensitivity.

How did people initially respond to OPEC's many-fold increase in oil prices? Paralysis! OPEC raised prices from $2 per barrel in 1973 to $12 per barrel in 1974. What could we Americans have done? We were completely locked into our dependence on oil. We found it exceedingly difficult to make any demand adjustment even when oil prices soared to $34 a barrel in 1980.

But we *eventually* switched to smaller cars, lower speed limits, more efficient home insulation, and tolerance of a wider range of living room temperatures. The long-run response surprised OPEC as well as ourselves! We discovered that, given time to adjust, we became rather demand sensitive to oil price changes.

FROM SENSITIVITY TO ELASTICITY

Elasticity

A term economists use to describe sensitivity.

The observation that the quantities we demand of goods are sensitive to price changes, and that these sensitivities are different for different kinds of goods is translated by economists into the concept of **elasticity**. That is to say, elasticity is nothing more than a term economists use to describe sensitivity. If you know how to derive simple percentages, you already know how to measure elasticity. It's a ratio of two percentages. **Price elasticity of demand** (e_d) is the percentage change in quantity demanded generated by a percentage change in price.

Elasticity is another word that has a special meaning for economists. Whenever an economist uses the term elasticity, it means a ratio of percentage changes.

$$e_d = \frac{\text{percentage change in quantity demanded}}{\text{percentage change in price}}$$

Price elasticity of demand

The ratio of the percentage change in quantity demanded to a percentage change in price. Its numerical value expresses the percentage change in quantity demanded generated by a 1 percent change in price.

The percentage change in quantity demanded is simply the change in quantity demanded divided by the original quantity. The percentage change in price is the change in price divided by the original price.

$$e_d = \frac{\text{change in quantity demanded}}{\text{quantity demanded}} \bigg/ \frac{\text{change in price}}{\text{price}}$$

For example, if Wendy's in Campustown cuts its grilled chicken deluxe sandwich from $3 to $2 to attract college students away from McDonald's and discovers that the quantity demanded of its deluxe sandwich increases from 1,000 to 2,000, we know that the price elasticity of demand for that sandwich is:

$$\frac{2{,}000 - 1{,}000}{1{,}000} \bigg/ \frac{\$2 - \$3}{\$3} = -3$$

Simple enough? Perhaps too simple. Economists recognize a problem with such a formulation. Depending upon the direction of the change, different elasticities can be obtained from the same change in price and quantity. For example, a price cut from \$3 to \$2 represents a $33\frac{1}{3}$ percent decrease in price. But if price rises from \$2 to \$3, the percentage change is 50 percent. What number then, should economists use to represent any percent change—direction unspecified—between \$2 and \$3?

Economists resolved the problem by averaging price and quantity over the range of the changes. The equation for price elasticity of demand, then, becomes:

$$e_d = \frac{(Q_2 - Q_1)/[(Q_2 + Q_1)/2]}{(P_2 - P_1)/[(P_2 + P_1)/2]}$$

where Q_1 and Q_2 are the quantities before and after price change, and P_1 and P_2 are the original and new prices. Using this averaging equation, it makes no difference whether the price change measures an increase or a decrease in price, that is, whether the original price was \$2 or \$3. In both cases $P_2 - P_1 = 1$ and $(P_2 + P_1)/2 = 5/2 = 2.5$.

A price increase usually generates a decrease in the quantity demanded. Likewise, a price decrease generates an increase in the quantity demanded. Because the price–quantity relationship is inverse—when one rises, the other falls—demand elasticities are always negative. For example, if a 50 percent decrease in price generates a 75 percent increase in quantity demanded, then the elasticity is $+75/-50 = -1.5$. By convention, economists drop the negative sign, expressing elasticity only by its absolute value, 1.5. From now on, we will follow that convention.

DERIVING PRICE ELASTICITIES OF DEMAND

Let's calculate some more price elasticities of demand. Figure 3 graphs the data in Table 1.

Demand curve *D* in panel *a*, which depicts the demand curve for high school football tickets on Friday nights, is derived from Table 1. Remember those games? At a price of \$4, the quantity demanded is 100. At a price of \$3, quantity demanded increases to 300. At a price of \$1, the 700-person-capacity stadium sells out.

Demand curve *D′* in panel *b* depicts the demand curve for milk. At \$4 per gallon, Josh Gillespie, the proprietor of the grocery just down the street from the high school, sells 100 gallons. At \$3, quantity demanded increases to 140 gallons. On sale at \$1, the quantity demanded increases to 220 gallons.

Let's start with \$4 tickets and milk. Suppose the high school cuts price from \$4 to \$3. Quantity demanded increases from 100 to 300 tickets, from point *a* to point *b* on the demand curve *D* in panel *a*. Price elasticity of demand within this \$4 to \$3 price range, is

$$\frac{(300 - 100)/[(100 + 300)/2]}{(\$3 - \$4)/[(\$3 + \$4)/2]} = \frac{200/200}{1/3.5} = \frac{1}{1/3.5} = 3.5$$

How do we interpret this elasticity of 3.5? It means that within the price range \$4 and \$3, a 1 percent change in price generates a 3.5 percent change in quantity demanded.

TABLE 1
Demand for Football Tickets and Milk

Football Tickets				Milk			
P	**Q**	**Total Revenue**	**Price Elasticity of Demand**	**P**	**Q**	**Total Revenue**	**Price Elasticicty of Demand**
$4	100	$ 400	3.50	$4	100	$400	1.17
3	300	900	1.25	3	140	420	0.62
2	500	1,000	0.50	2	180	360	0.30
1	700	700		1	220	220	

Suppose the high school cuts price again, this time from $3 to $2. Ticket sales jump to 500. What happens to price elasticity of demand in this price range?

$$\frac{(500-300)/[(500+300)/2]}{(\$2-\$3)/[(\$2+\$3)/2]} = 1.25$$

As you see, a 1 percent change in price now generates only a 1.25 percent change in quantity demanded. Note the change in the intensity of the fans' response to price changes. The $1 price change from $4 to $3 generated a 3.5 per-

FIGURE 3 **Price Elasticities of Demand for Football Tickets and Milk**

Elasticity within the $4 to $3 price range is 3.5 for football tickets, shown in panel *a*, and 1.17 for milk, shown in panel *b*. Put differently, a 1 percent change in price within the $4 to $3 range generates a 3.5 percent change in the demand for football tickets but only a 1.17 percent change in the demand for milk. Buyers appear to be less responsive to price changes in the market for milk than in the market for football tickets.

Within different price ranges—$3 to $2, and $2 to $1—elasticities differ. Note that elasticities are lower at the lower end of the price range. Those segments of the demand curve that reflect elasticities greater than 1 are *demand elastic*. Those that reflect elasticities less than one are *demand inelastic*.

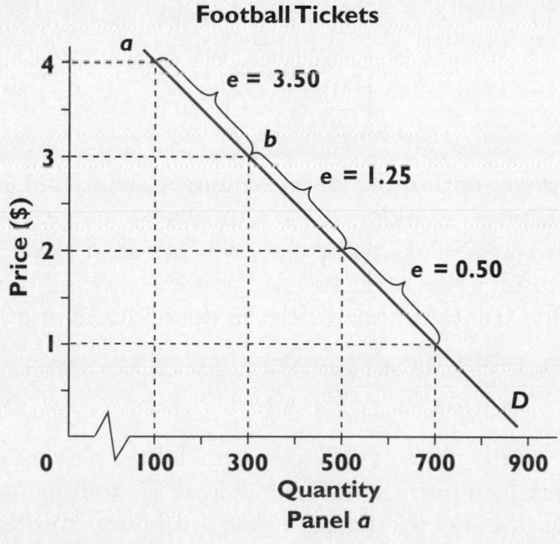

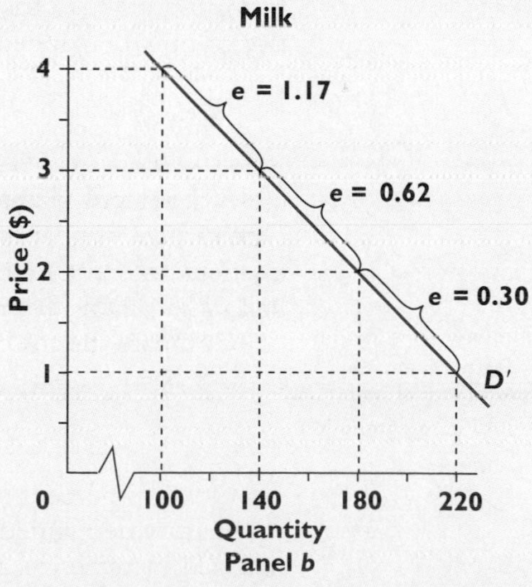

ADDED PERSPECTIVE

Price Elasticity of Demand at the Post Office

Postmaster General Anthony M. Frank looked grim as he stepped before the cameras on November 5. The Postal Service Board of Governors had just killed his proposal to raise the first-class mail rate by one cent to thirty cents, which would have increased annual revenues by $800 million. Frank had won six of the nine votes, but changing the rate required unanimous approval. "I don't want to be overly dramatic about it," said a frustrated Frank, "but you can go to the electric chair on a 5–4 vote."

"I'm the only CEO of a major corporation in America who doesn't have control over his own prices."

Discussion

Setting aside the issue of whether the raise should have been approved, what can we say about the price elasticity of demand within the price range $0.29 to $0.30? Is it elastic, inelastic, or unit elastic? What information in the *Business Week* story gives you the clue?

From *Business Week*, November 25, 1991.

Be sure that you can both compute and interpret values for the price elasticity of demand.

cent change in quantity demand, but the $1 cut from $3 to $2 generated a milder 1.25 percent change in quantity demanded.

Look what happens when price is cut from $2 to $1. The price elasticity of demand falls to 0.50.

$$\frac{(700 - 500)/[(700 + 500)/2]}{(\$1 - \$2)/[(\$1 + \$2)/2]} = 0.50$$

The 1 percent change in price now generates only a 0.50 percent change in quantity demanded. *Note that the price elasticities of demand for football tickets differ in different price ranges and fall—from 3.5 to 1.25 to 0.50—as we calculate them downward along the demand curve.*

In panel *b*, the demand curve for milk reflects what Josh Gillespie knows from long experience: People are relatively insensitive to price changes in milk. For most, milk is a basic food. When Josh cuts the price from $4 to $3, the quantity of milk demanded increases from 100 to 140 gallons.

$$\frac{(140 - 100/[(140 + 100)/2]}{(\$3 - \$4)/[(\$3 + \$4)/2]} = 1.17$$

A 1 percent change in price, within the $4 to $3 range, creates a 1.17 percent change in quantity demanded. Looking at the same price change, the price elasticity of demand for milk is less—1.17 compared to 3.50—than it is for football tickets. Does it make sense?

Compare the milk and football tickets elasticities in the $3 to $2 price range.

$$\frac{(180 - 140)/[(180 + 140)/2]}{(\$2 - \$3)/[(\$2 + \$3)/2]} = 0.62$$

Now a 1 percent change in the price of milk generates a 0.62 percent change in quantity demanded. When Josh puts the milk on sale at $1, the quantity demanded increases to 220 gallons. The elasticity of demand within this $1 to $2 range is 0.30.

TABLE 2 Elasticities, Price, and Revenue Changes

When Elasticity Is	If Price Increases	If Price Decreases
e > 1.0	revenue decreases	revenue increases
e < 1.0	revenue increases	revenue decreases
e = 1.0	revenue doesn't change	revenue doesn't change

$$\frac{(220-180)/[(220+180)/2]}{(\$1-\$2)/[(\$1+\$2)/2]}=0.30$$

A 1 percent change in price now generates only a 0.30 percent change in quantity demanded.

ELASTICITY AND TOTAL REVENUE

Total revenue

The price of a good multiplied by the number of units sold.

Unit elastic

Elasticity is equal to 1.0. In this range, price cuts or increases do not change total revenue.

Price elastic

Quality of the range of a demand curve where elasticities of demand are greater than 1.0.

Price inelastic

Quality of the range of a demand curve where elasticities of demand are less than 1.0.

When a 1 percent decrease in price generates a greater than 1 percent increase in quantity demanded; that is, when the price elasticity of demand is greater than 1.0, ***total revenue*** *increases. When price elasticity of demand is less than 1.0, a 1 percent decrease in price decreases total revenue.*

Look at the relationship between price elasticity of demand and revenues in Table 1. In the case of football tickets, price cuts from $4 to $3 and from $3 to $2 produce elasticities of 3.50 and 1.25, both greater than 1.0. As you see, with both cuts revenues increase—from $400 to $900 with the first cut and from $900 to $1,000 with the second. Were the high school to cut again, from $2 to $1, elasticity would fall to 0.50, which is less than 1.0. The high school's total rev enue would fall from $1,000 to $700.

In the case of Josh Gillespie's milk sales, only the price cut from $4 to $3 has an elasticity greater than 1.0. The cut increases his revenue from $400 to $420. Price cuts from $3 to $2 and from $2 to $1 produce elasticities of 0.62 and 0.30, both less than 1.0. As you see, with both cuts revenues decrease from $420 to $360 and then from $360 to $220.

Economists define a price elasticity of 1.0 as being **unit elastic.** It is helpful to think of unit elasticity as the watershed value. Those parts of a demand curve with elasticities greater than 1.0 are described as **price elastic,** and those parts with elasticities less than 1.0 are said to be **price inelastic.**

Table 2 shows how the relationship between price changes and revenue depends upon the elasticities.

ESTIMATES OF PRICE ELASTICITIES OF DEMAND

Price Elasticities for Agricultural Goods

Table 3 provides several estimates of price elasticities for agricultural goods over a wide range of years.

TABLE 3 Price Elasticities for Agricultural Products

	Marschak	Henry Schultz	Mehren	Fox	Spencer & Siegelman
Sugar	0.38				
Corn	0.32	0.70	0.67		
Cotton		0.70	0.60		
Wheat			0.41		
Potatoes		0.61	0.15		
Milk			0.60	0.30	
Chicken			0.89	0.72	
Beef			0.80	0.79	0.92
Turkey			0.55	0.61	

Source: Jacob Marschak, "Elastizitat der Nachfrage," *Beitrage zur okonomischen Theorie,* no.2 (Tubingen, 1931), in Schultz, Henry, *The Theory and Measurement of Demand* (Chicago: University of Chicago Press, 1938), p.119; Schultz, *ibid.,* pp. 253, 275, 413; Mehren, G. L., "Comparative Costs of Agricultural Price Supports in 1949," *Proceedings, American Economic Review,* XLI, 2 (May 1951), in Schultz, T. W., *The Economic Organization of Agriculture* (New York: McGraw-Hill, 1953), p. 190; Fox, Karl, A., "Factors Affecting Farm Income, Farm Prices, and Farm Consumption," *Agricultural Economic Research,* III, 3 (July 1951), in Schultz, T. W., *op. cit.,* p. 189; and Spencer, Milton, H., and Siegelman, Louis, *Managerial Economics,* (Homewood, Ill.: Irwin, 1959) p. 142.

Price elasticities in every year are less than 1.0. Look at Marschak's 0.32 findings for corn, based on German budgetary data for 1907. It is lower than Mehren's 0.67 estimate in 1949 for U.S. corn, but both are less than 1.0. That is, demand for corn appears to be relatively insensitive to price changes. Look at the demand elasticities for sugar, beef, milk, and potatoes. The 0.38 estimate for sugar is relatively inelastic. All three estimates for beef are less than 1.0, although still higher than the elasticities for potatoes and milk.

Short-Run and Long-Run Elasticities

When consumers have more time, they are better able to find substitute goods. How does the time period affect the price elasticity of demand?

Time makes a difference. Table 4 compares price elasticities of demand for the same goods and services over the short run and long run.

For most people, time is a critical factor in their ability to adjust demand to changing prices. Table 4 shows precisely that. In every case, price elasticities in the long run are higher than short-run price elasticities. Some are decidedly

TABLE 4 Price Elasticities of Demand in the Short Run and Long Run, 1954

	Short Run	Long Run
Jewelry and watches	0.43	0.72
Toiletries	0.76	3.13
Chinaware	1.16	1.31
Stationery	0.47	0.53
Hospital care	0.27	3.85
Gasoline	0.15	0.45
Air travel	0.05	2.36
Television	1.19	1.27

Source: Houthakker, H.S., and Taylor, Lester, D., *Consumer Demand in the United States, 1929–1970 (Cambridge, Mass: Harvard University Press, 1970)*

greater. Compare the short-run to long-run elasticities for air travel, hospital care, and toiletries.

CROSS ELASTICITY

Price elasticity of demand measures the percentage change in quantity demanded of a good generated by a percentage change in the price of that good. **Cross elasticity of demand** measures the percentage change in quantity demanded of one good generated by a percentage change in the price of another good.

Cross Elasticities Among Substitute Goods

Cross elasticity of demand

The ratio of a percentage change in quantity demanded of one good to a percentage change in the price of another good.

When Rolaids raises its price, some people switch from Rolaids to Tums. When Coke raises prices, the quantity demanded for Pepsi increases. When *Time* magazine cuts its price, *Newsweek*'s sales fall. When taxi fares in New York increase, more New Yorkers take the bus. These are all pairs of *substitute goods.*

The more perfect the substitute, the more people replace one good with its substitute when the price of the first changes. Cross elasticity measures this cross relationship. For the Rolaids to Tums crossover, cross elasticity is written as

$$e_c = \frac{\text{percentage change in quantity demanded of Tums}}{\text{percentage change in price of Rolaids}}$$

The cross elasticity of Rolaids prices and Tums quantity is illustrated in Figure 4.

FIGURE 4 **Cross Elasticities Between Substitutes**

An increase in the price of Rolaids from $1.50 to $2.25 in panel *a* shifts the demand curve for Tums, in panel *b*, from D to D′. The quantity demanded of Tums at the price of $1.50 increases from 1,000 to 1,500. As with all substitute goods, an increase (or decrease) in the price of one good generates an increase (or decrease) in quantity demanded of the other.

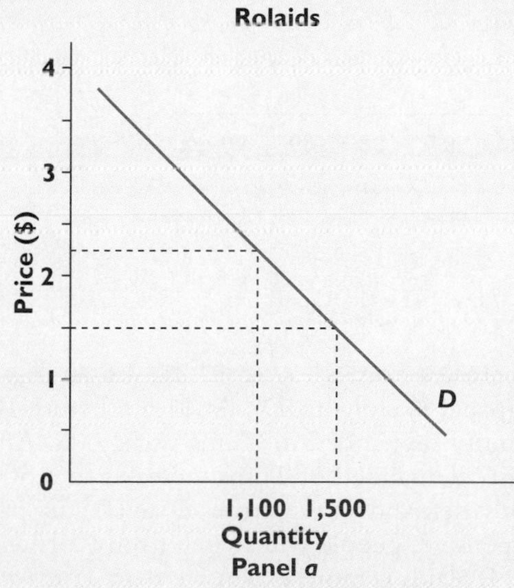

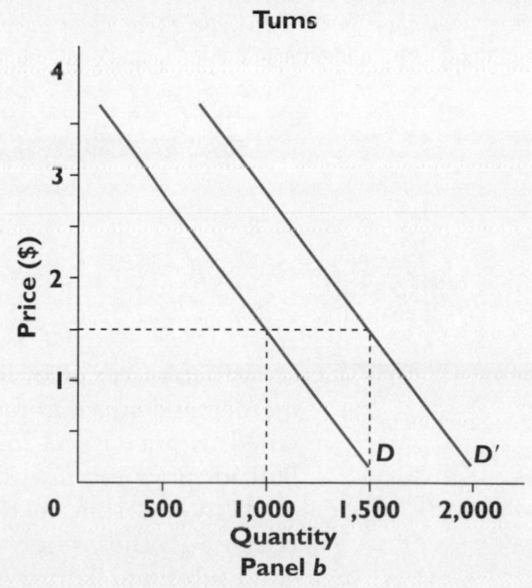

ADDED PERSPECTIVE

Cross Elasticities in the Sound Business

The music we listen to, and the sound equipment on which we listen to it, changed rather dramatically in the 1980s. In increasing numbers, we converted from stereos to tape decks, and then made the switch to compact disc players. Of course, the shift in sound systems impacted our choice of sound format. As the figure shows, we shifted from LPs to tapes, then from tapes to CDs.

Tapes and CDs, at least since the mid 1980s, appear to be good substitutes, while LPs, strong at the beginning of the decade, became less and less attractive as a medium of recorded sound. By 1983, tape sales climbed to 500 million units, matching the sales volume of LPs. CDs were still in their infancy. But look what happened to sales after 1984! LP sales collapsed to under 200 million units by 1990, while CD sales soared to over 700 million units, matching the volume of the slower-growing tape sales.

Discussion

Think in terms of cross elasticities. Would the cross elasticities between LPs and CDs be high in the 1990s? What about cross elasticities between tapes and CDs?

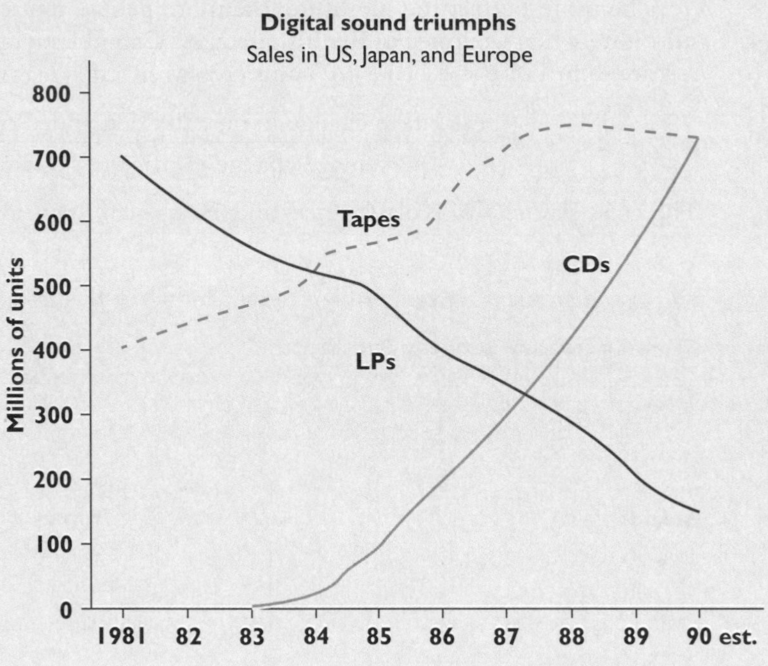

Source: Figure from the "Cacaphony," *The Economist*, June 1, 1991, p. 64. ©1991 The Economist Newspaper Group, Inc. Reprinted with permission..

The cross elasticity is negative for complementary goods and positive for substitute goods. Can you explain why?

When the price of Rolaids increases from $1.50 to $2.25, shown in panel *a*, the demand curve *D* for Tums (panel *b*) shifts to *D′*. At $1.50, before Rolaids raised its price to $2.25, the quantity demanded of Tums was 1,000. After the Rolaids price increase, the quantity demanded of Tums increases to 1,500.

Why the shift in the Rolaids demand curve from *D* to *D′* in panel *b*? Because Rolaids is now more expensive, people will switch from Rolaids to the good substitute Tums. As long as Rolaids is more expensive than Tums at every

TABLE 5
Cross Elasticities of Demand in the Short Run

Change in Price	Change in Quantity	Cross Elasticity
Butter	Margarine	+ 0.81
Margarine	Butter	+ 0.67
Fuel oil	Natural gas	+ 0.44
Natural gas	Electricity	+ 0.20
Pork	Beef	+ 0.14
Beef	Pork	+ 0.28

Source: Wold, Herman, and Jureen, Lars, *Demand Analysis: A Study in Econometrics* (New York: Wiley, 1953).

quantity in Figure 4, then at every price the quantity demanded of Tums will increase.

Table 5 provides some estimates for cross elasticities among a set of agricultural goods.

Note that the cross elasticities for substitute goods are always positive. A decrease (or increase) in the price of one good generates a corresponding decrease (or increase) in the quantity demanded of the other.

Look at the relationship between butter and margarine. When the price of butter falls, many people switch from margarine to butter. When the price of margarine falls, many buy less butter. *But their cross elasticities are not necessarily identical.* When the price of butter increases, we are more likely to switch to margarine than we are likely to switch to butter when the price of margarine increases. As you see, their cross elasticities differ, 0.81 and 0.67.

Cross Elasticities Among Complementary Goods

What about cross elasticities among goods that are linked or complement each other? For example, hotels and air travel. Suppose airlines raise their fares by 15 percent. The quantity of airline tickets would fall, but so too would the quantity of hotel rooms demanded. Why? With fewer people traveling, fewer hotel rooms are needed. Have you noticed hotel advertisements at airports? Hotels and air travel are such obvious complements that travel agents typically book both.

Among *complementary goods* such as air travel and hotels, the cross elasticities—airfares and hotel reservations, and hotel prices and air travel—are still not necessarily the same. Which do you think has the higher cross elasticity? What about VCRs and videocassettes?

Figure 5 illustrates the cross elasticity between plane flights and the decrease in quantity demanded for hotel rooms.

The increase in panel *a*'s airfare from $100 to $150 affects panel *b*'s market for hotel rooms. The demand curve in panel *b* shifts from *D* to *D′* and the quantity demanded of $50 per day hotel rooms decreases from 5,000 to 4,000. Unlike the cross elasticity between substitute goods, the cross elasticity between complements is *negative*; a percentage increase in the price of one generates a percentage decrease in the quantity demanded of the other.

FIGURE 5 **Cross Elasticities Between Complements**

An increase in the price of plane flights from \$100 to \$150 in panel *a* shifts the demand curve for hotel rooms in panel *b* from *D* to *D'*. The quantity demanded of \$50 hotel rooms decreases from 5,000 to 4,000. As with all complementary goods, an increase (or decrease) in the price of one generates a decrease (or increase) in quantity demanded of the other.

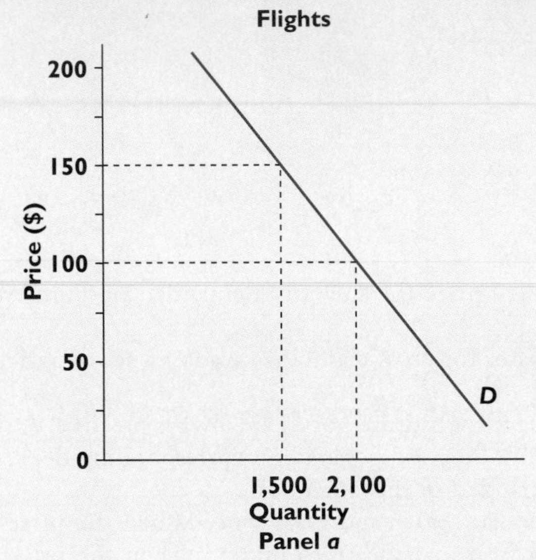

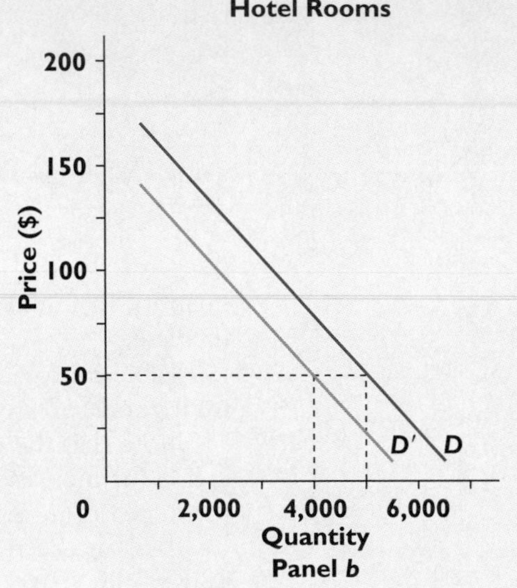

INCOME ELASTICITY

Income elasticity

The ratio of the percentage change in quantity demanded to the percentage change in income.

The concept of elasticity is used not only to measure the relationship between changes in price and changes in quantity demanded, but also the relationship between changes in income and changes in quantity demanded. Economists define **income elasticity** as the percentage change in quantity demanded generated by a percentage change in income.

$$e_y = \frac{\text{percentage change in quantity demanded}}{\text{percentage change in income}}$$

Income elastic

A 1 percent change in income generates a greater than 1 percent change in quantity demanded.

Income inelastic

A 1 percent change in income generates a less than 1 percent change in quantity demanded.

Suppose that after a good season, Andre Dawson, the all-star outfielder for the Boston Red Sox, negotiated a 30 percent increase in salary. Would you not expect that with higher income, the quantities of goods and services demanded by the Dawson family would also increase?

For some goods, the quantities demanded would increase by more than 30 percent. These would be **income elastic.** For goods that are **income inelastic,** the percent increase would be less than 1.0.

Suppose Ms. Dawson decides that with the increased family income, she and their children can afford to see Andre play in more away games than they had the year before. Suppose their demand for airline tickets increases by 50 percent. The Dawson's income elasticity for air tickets, then, is 50/30 = 1.67. Compare this to the Dawson family demand for bread. It is highly unlikely that the family would increase its demand for bread by as much as 30 percent.

FIGURE 6
Air Travel
An increase in a person's income typically results in that person increasing his or her quantity demanded of goods and services. Some increases are greater than others. For example, a 30 percent increase in income shifts the Dawson family's demand curve for air travel to the right, from D_y to D'_y. At a constant $200 airfare, demand increases from 40 to 60 flights.

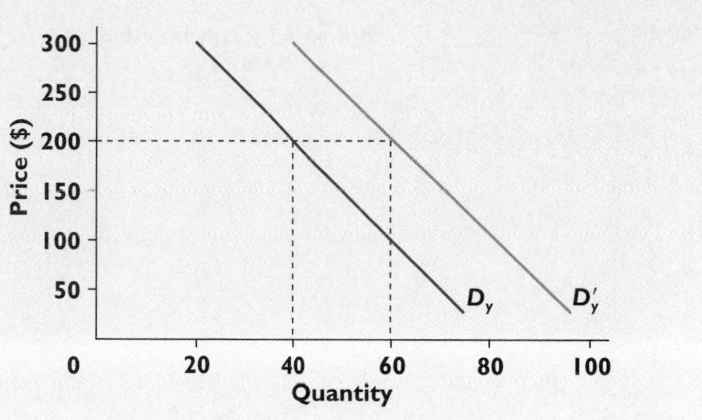

Figure 6 illustrates the Dawson's income elasticity for airline tickets.

The Dawson's demand curve for airline tickets shifts from D_y to D'_y when the family income increases by 30 percent. Note that airfares don't change. The increase in the quantity demanded from 40 to 60 is for the unchanging $200 fares.

Engel's Law

Engel's law
The observation that income elasticities of demand for food are less than one.

Does Engel's law suggest that the demand for food is income elastic or income inelastic? Why?

What do we know about income elasticity? In 1857, Ernst Engel, a Prussian statistician, calculated the income elasticity of demand for food. His 0.70 estimate confirmed the idea that the relationship between income and the demand for food is inelastic. Recognizing his pioneering work, economists today refer to income inelasticities of food as obeying **Engel's law.**

Table 6 provides a set of estimates of income elasticities of demand for agricultural goods. In each case, elasticity is less than 1.0.

In a 1971 Brookings Institution study, Charles Schultze cites income elasticities of demand for food among several countries. His findings are shown in Table 7.

Although Engel's law is confirmed in every case, it appears that income elasticities of demand for food in the more industrialized nations are relatively

TABLE 6
Income Elasticities of Demand for Agricultural Products

	U.S. Dept.of Agriculture	Waite and Trelogan	Wold
Eggs	0.28	0.22	0.86
Milk	0.32	0.41	0.48
Cheese	0.41	0.07	0.37
Butter		0.49	0.69

Source: *Consumer Purchases of Certain Foods, U.S. Non-relief Nonfarm Families, March–November, 1936, Division of Marketing and Marketing Agreements, March, 1940,* U.S. Department of Agriculture, Washington, D.C.; in Schultz, T. W., op. cit., p. 69; Wold, Herman, and Jureen, Lars, op. cit., p. 224; Waite, Warren, and Trelogan, Harry, *Agricultural Market Prices* (New York: Wiley, 1951), p. 41.

TABLE 7 Comparison of Income Elasticities of Demand for Food by Country

Industrially Advanced Nations		Less Industrially Advanced Nations	
United States	0.18	Italy	0.42
Canada	0.15	Ireland	0.23
Germany	0.25	Greece	0.49
France	0.25	Spain	0.56
Britain	0.25	Portugal	0.60

Source: Dewhurst, Frederic and Associates, *America's Needs and Resources* (New York: Twentieth Century Fund, 1947), Table 37, p. 103, in Schultz, T. W., *op. cit.*, p.72.

lower. Compare, for example, Canada's 0.15 to Spain's 0.56. But wouldn't you expect to find demand responses less sensitive to increases in income in the industrial nations?

Income Elasticity of Inferior Goods

Inferior goods

Goods for which demand decreases when people's incomes increase.

Some goods, especially some food items, have peculiar income elasticities. When income increases, the quantities demanded of these goods actually decrease. Economists define such goods as **inferior goods.**

Why inferior? People buy them because the more desirable substitutes are financially beyond their reach. Once richer, these people readily switch from the inferior goods to more attractive substitutes.

Cheap wine isn't just cheap wine, it's downright inferior! When incomes increase, people buy less of it and switch to higher quality wines. Black-and-white television is an inferior good. As income increases, we switch from black-and-white to color. What about drugstore eyeglasses? What about vinyl luggage? Can you think of other examples of inferior goods?

Table 8 provides income elasticity estimates for some inferior agricultural goods.

Income elasticities for inferior goods are negative. A percentage increase in income generates a percentage decrease in quantity demanded. In the case of navy beans, the decrease is 0.52 percent for every 1 percent increase in income. Note that in 1948, before our cholesterol concern, margarine was regarded as an inferior good.

TABLE 8 Income Elasticities of Demand for Inferior Products

Product	Elasticity
Margarine	−0.83
Dried navy beans	−0.52
White potatoes	−0.03

Source: Waite, Warren C., and Trelogan, Harry C., *Introduction to Agricultural Prices* (Minneapolis: Burgess Publishing, 1948), in Schultz, T. W., *op. cit.*, p. 73.

FIGURE 7 **Elasticities of Supply**

Panels *a*, *b*, and *c* depict market-day, short-run, and long-run supply curves in a fish market. The vertical line, which is the market-day supply curve in panel *a*, reflects suppliers' total inability to adjust supply to price.

In the long-run supply curve of panel c, suppliers encounter no obstacles adjusting quantity supplied to price. At a price of $4, suppliers are willing and able to supply 450. At $5, they are willing and able to supply 650.

Not so in the short-run supply curve of panel *b*. Here, at a price of $5, suppliers are willing but not able to supply 650. Suppliers must wait until their productive capacity to produce 650 is available. In the interim—that is, in the short run—suppliers increase production *with existing capacity* to 500.

These differences in ability to adjust supply to price are reflected in the different supply elasticities. Within the range $4 to $5, for the market day, the price elasticity of supply is zero. For the short run, it is 0.47 and for the long run, it is 1.64.

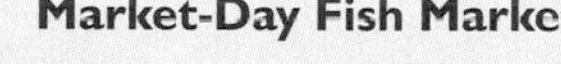

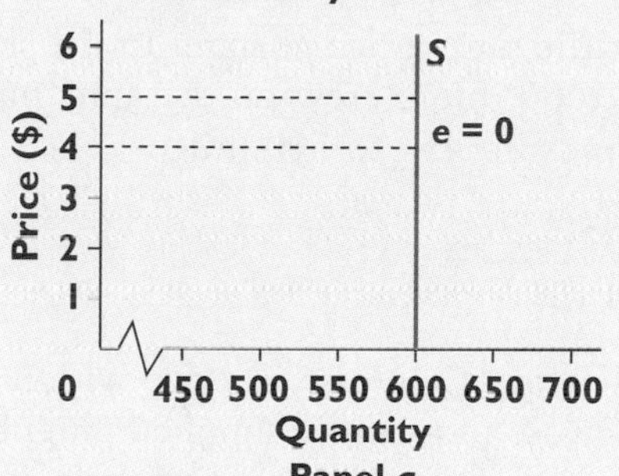

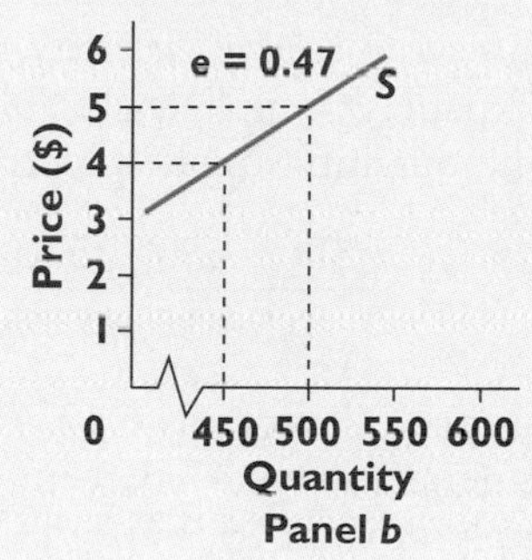

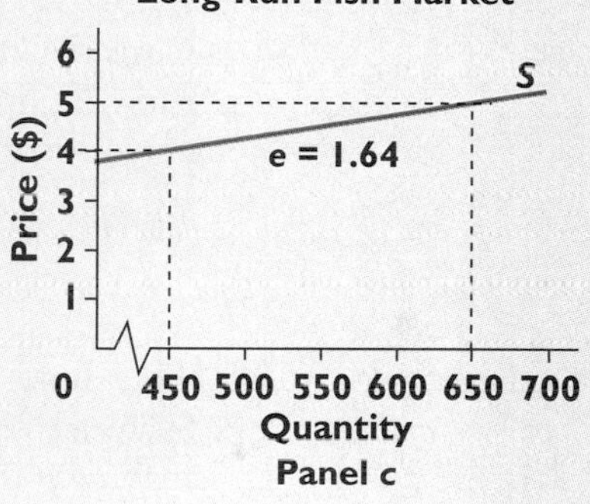

SUPPLY ELASTICITY

Price elasticity of supply

The ratio of the percentage change in quantity supplied to the percentage change in price.

Price elasticity of supply is the percentage change in quantity supplied generated by a percentage change in price. The equation for measuring price elasticity of supply is

$$e_s = \frac{(Q_2 - Q_1)/[(Q_2 + Q_1)/2]}{(P_2 - P_1)/[(P_2 + P_1)/2]}$$

where Q_1 and Q_2 represent quantity before and after the price change, and P_1 and P_2 are the original and new prices. Supply curves are upward sloping, reflecting increases in quantity supplied generated by increases in price. As you see, price elasticities of supply are positive.

What could explain different supply elasticities? Look at the supply curve in Figure 7. These are market-day, short-run, and long-run supply curves for fish.

The sensitivity of supply to changing prices depends upon the time that suppliers have to adjust their supplies to new prices.

Market-Day Supply Elasticity

In Figure 7, panel *a* represents the market-day supply curve for fish. It is vertical at 600 fish. The supply curve tells us that whatever the price, suppliers cannot change the quantity they are able to bring onto the market that day.

When boats return to the docks after a day out on the water, the supply is fixed. Fishermen cannot supply a single fish more than the 600, even if price rises from $4 to $5.

How do we translate this scenario into price elasticity of supply? If price increases from $4 to $5, the quantity supplied increases by zero. Price elasticity of supply on the market day, then, is zero.

$$\frac{(600-600)/[(600+600)/2]}{(\$5-\$4)/[(\$5+\$4)/2]}=0$$

Short-Run Supply Elasticity

Consider the short-run supply elasticity for the same price change. In the short run of Figure 7, panel *b*, suppliers are able to put more crew on the same number of boats. The quantity supplied increases from 450 to 500 units.

$$\frac{(500-450)/[(500+450)/2]}{(\$5-\$4)/[(\$5+\$4)/2]}=0.47$$

The short-run supply elasticity is 0.47. A 1 percent increase in price within the $4 to $5 range, generates a 0.47 percent increase in quantity supplied. Suppliers may *wish* to supply more at $5, but can't because they are limited by their boats' capacities.

Long-Run Supply Elasticity

But suppose fishermen have more time to adjust their supply to price changes. Suppose they can have as many boats as they wish. The capacity of the fishing fleet, then, is no longer a limiting factor. Look at Figure 7, panel *c*. With time to build new boats, suppliers increase their quantity supplied from 450 to 650 fish.

$$\frac{(650-450)/[(650+450)/2]}{(\$5-\$4)/[(\$5+\$4)/2]}=1.64$$

Long-run price elasticity of supply is 1.64. Now, a 1 percent increase in price within the same $4 to $5 price range generates a 1.64 percent increase in quantity supplied. As you see, price elasticity of supply increases when suppliers have more time to adjust price to quantities supplied.

How quickly suppliers adjust supply in response to changing prices depends essentially upon the time it takes to build capacity. And that varies from industry to industry. For example, wouldn't you think Domino's Pizza could produce 20 percent more pizza sooner than Boeing could increase its aircraft production by 20 percent?

Does the time period under consideration affect supply elasticities the same way it affects price elasticities of demand?

If the price of 20-year-old French wine increases by 200 percent, shouldn't the French get busy producing 20-year-old wine? But how do you go about producing it in less than 20 years? On the other hand, you can probably increase the supply of moonshine by 300 percent overnight if price increases by only 20 percent.

ELASTICITIES AND THE BURDEN OF TAXATION

We all understand perfectly well why we have to pay taxes. But understanding is one thing and liking it is quite another. Many people spend a considerable amount of time trying to avoid paying taxes, and many government people spend just as much time devising means of preventing people from avoiding taxes. In truth, few escape.

Avoiding taxes on goods is possible if we can somehow avoid the goods that are taxed. A sure-fire way of escaping a tax on books, for example, is not to buy them. But if people can do without books, it would be silly for the government to tax them. To generate revenues, government typically taxes goods that are essential to households. Years ago, salt was one such good.

Governments seem to understand that in order to raise the most tax revenues, it makes sense to tax goods with price inelastic demands.

Before the advent of modern refrigeration, meat spoilage was commonplace. The primary way people preserved their supply of meat was by salting. Not surprisingly, people's demand for salt was both high and price inelastic. As a result, governments took to taxing salt like the proverbial duck to water. If governments today were looking for a good thing to tax, what would you suggest? How about cigarettes? Cigarettes are relatively demand inelastic, aren't they? It's hard to kick the smoking habit, which is one reason why cigarette taxes work as a steady source of revenue. Look at Figure 8.

Compare the economic consequences of a $2 tax on panel *a*'s cigarettes and panel *b*'s lipstick. For convenience, the supply curves for cigarettes, *S*, and for lipstick, *S*′, are identical. But look at demand. The demand curve for cigarettes, *D*, is relatively inelastic. The demand curve for lipstick, *D*′, is relatively elastic.

Without taxes, the two equilibrium prices are $4. Quantities demanded and supplied in both markets are 100.

Per Unit Tax Shifts the Supply Curve

Suppose the government imposes a $2 per unit tax in each market. How is this done? The government simply instructs the suppliers of cigarettes and lipstick to collect and forward to the government $2 for every pack of cigarettes and every lipstick sold. What happens?

Suppose you were one of the cigarette suppliers in Figure 8, panel *a*. Faced with the $2 cigarette tax, you would charge $6 instead of the $4 equilibrium price. If the equilibrium price had been $8, you would charge $10. That is, your supply curve, S_t, now including the tax, shifts upward by $2. The same shift in the supply curve, from S' to S'_t, is recorded in panel *b*'s lipstick market.

Prior to the $2 tax, the equilibrium price was $4 and quantity sold was 100. The $2 tax raised price to $6, but at $6, an excess supply emerges, forcing price to a new equilibrium at $5.75. That is, the tax shifts the equilibrium price from $4 to $5.75. It also shifts the quantity demanded from 100 to 95. The price cigarette suppliers receive after paying the tax is $5.75 − $2 = $3.75. What about the government? It receives $2 × 95 = $190 in tax revenue.

The effect of the lipstick tax is somewhat different. Look at panel *b*. The demand for lipstick is relatively elastic. The tax shifts the equilibrium price upward from $4 to $4.75. The quantity demanded falls from 100 to 75 because many women would rather go without lipstick than pay the tax. The price lipstick suppliers receive after paying the tax is $4.75 − $2 = $2.75. What about the gov-

FIGURE 8 **What Gets Taxed?**

The markets for cigarettes and lipstick are distinguished by their demand elasticities. A \$2 tax shifts the supply curves, S to S_t in panel *a*, and S' to S'_t in panel *b*. The equilibrium price in panel *a* moves from \$4 to \$5.75, and in panel *b*, from \$4 to \$4.75. The quantity of cigarettes demanded and supplied decreases from 100 to 95, the quantity of lipstick demanded and supplied decreases from 100 to 75.

The relatively low price elasticity of demand in the market for cigarettes results in higher tax revenues than in the market for lipstick, where the \$2 tax results in a relatively large cut in quantity demanded.

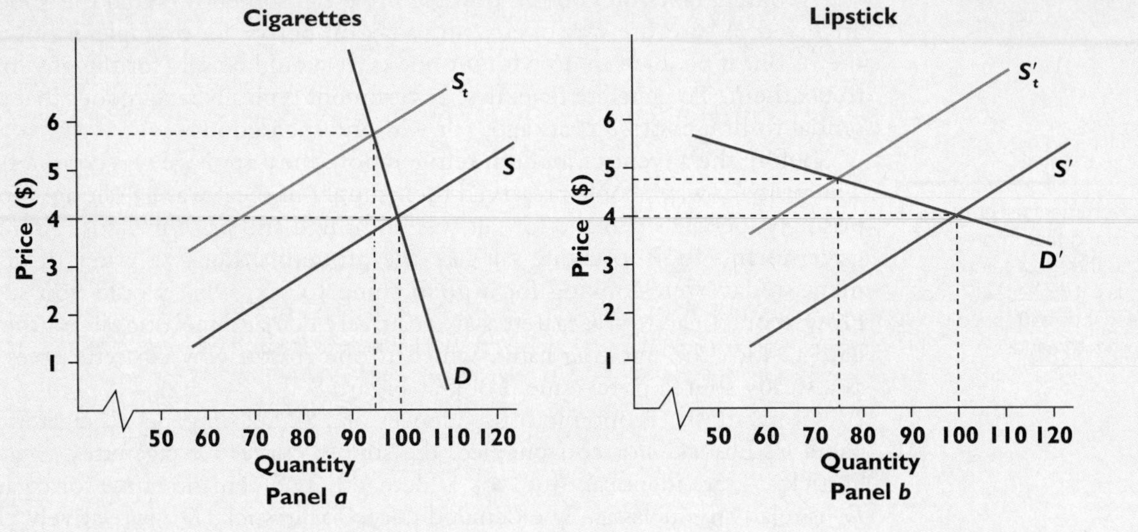

ernment? Because significantly fewer lipsticks are bought, the government receives only \$2 × 75 = \$150.

The Ultimate Per Unit Tax?

To squeeze the maximum tax out of the French population, Jean Baptiste Colbert, the seventeenth century finance minister to King Louis XIV, suggested taxing the air people breathed! He reasoned that because the king was monarch over France's air as well as its land, the tax would be legitimate and absolutely unavoidable. Tyrannical? Perhaps, but he well understood the significance of demand elasticity!

CHAPTER REVIEW

1. When economists consider how sensitive (or insensitive) consumer demand is to price changes, they call this sensitivity the price elasticity of demand. We can consider the price elasticity of demand for an individual buyer or for a market of buyers. Although the price elasticity of demand for a good is likely to vary somewhat from one person to another, people's elasticities are likely to be more similar than dissimilar.

2. Among the factors that influence demand sensitivity or elasticity are (a) the price of the good relative to other goods (i.e., is it expensive or low-priced),

(b) the income level of the buyer, (c) the availability of close substitutes, (d) whether or not the good is a basic item, (e) whether or not consumption of the good is linked to another good, and (f) the amount of time available to adjust to price changes. In general, demand is not very sensitive to price when the price of the good is low or the income of the buyer is high. Demand inelasticity is also characteristic of basic goods and goods that are closely linked to other goods. Finally, the less time the buyer has to adjust to price changes, the more insensitive or inelastic demand is.

3. The price elasticity of demand is computed as the ratio of the percentage change in quantity demanded to the percentage change in price. Because quantity demanded varies inversely with price, computed elasticities always have negative signs. However, economists usually drop the negative sign and refer to elasticities as absolute values.

4. The price elasticity of demand varies along most demand curves. In the elastic range of a demand curve, price cuts lead to an increase in total revenue. In the inelastic range, price cuts lead to a decrease in total revenue.

5. Cross elasticity of demand considers the sensitivity of the demand for one good to changes in the price of another good. If the two goods are substitutes, then the cross elasticity of demand is a positive number. As the price of one good goes up, the quantity demanded of its substitute increases as well. Complementary goods have negative cross elasticities: If the price of one good goes up, the quantity demanded of the complementary good goes down.

6. Income elasticity measures the sensitivity of demand to changes in income. If income increases and the quantity demanded of a good increases too, then the good is a normal good. If income increases and the quantity demanded of a good decreases, then the good is an inferior good. Although Engel's law suggests that agricultural goods are normal goods, they have a low income elasticity of demand.

7. Supply elasticity measures the ratio of the percentage change in quantity supplied to the percentage change in price. Price elasticities of supply are always positive numbers. Supply tends to become more elastic as producers have more time to adjust output to price changes.

8. The price elasticity of demand is useful for the government to know when it formulates tax policy. Goods with price-inelastic demands are the best ones to tax because an increase in their prices is sure to lead to an increase in tax revenues.

KEY TERMS

Elasticity
Price elasticity of demand
Total revenue
Unit elastic
Price elastic
Price inelastic
Cross elasticity of demand
Income elasticity
Income elastic
Income inelastic
Engel's law
Inferior goods
Price elasticity of supply

QUESTIONS

1. The purpose of advertising is to lower the price elasticity of demand for the advertised good. Explain.

2. The 50,000 seat Duke Stadium in Durham, North Carolina, is the home of the Duke University Blue Devils. On Saturday afternoons of football, attendance is typically 40,000. By lowering price, the university could easily sell out Duke Stadium, but it chooses not to do so. Why? *Hint*: Refer to price elasticities of demand and supply.

3. When Exxon moved away from its location at the northeast corner of Wright and Green Streets, Shell, operating on the southwest corner of Wright and Green, promptly raised its prices. Is this a coincidence? Explain.

4. Suppose Wendy's cuts the price of its grilled chicken deluxe sandwich by 25 percent. What do you suppose would happen to the demand for (a) Wendy's hamburger, (b) Wendy's Coca-Cola, (c) McDonald's Big Mac, (d), McDonald's fries, (e) Nike shoes?

5. Suppose you were shown a demand curve for bananas and were asked to calculate price elasticity of demand. Applying the appropriate equation, you came up with 0.80. Your friend was asked to derive price elasticity of demand on the identical demand curve and came up with 0.50. Worried, you asked your professor which of the two answers was correct. The professor checked through both calculations and said both were! How can that be?

6. Suppose Jeff George, quarterback of the Atlanta Falcons, increased his annual income 20 percent by endorsing Selsun Blue shampoo. If his quantity demanded of Selsun Blue didn't change, what can we say about his income elasticity of demand for the product? Suppose he decides to upgrade his housing, moving from his $1 million home to a $1.5 million home. What can we say about his income elasticity of demand for housing?

7. Why are we relatively insensitive to price changes affecting low-priced goods such as bubble gum?

8. Why are price elasticities of demand typically higher for luxury goods such as 35mm cameras than they are for essential goods such as bread?

9. Why is the price elasticity of market-day supply zero?

10. Why is long-run price elasticity of supply greater than short-run price elasticity of supply?

11. The Gillette Razor Company, manufacturer of razors and razor blades, used to sell its uniquely designed razor below cost. Why would it do so?

12. Calculate the price elasticity of supply for a price change from $2 to $3.

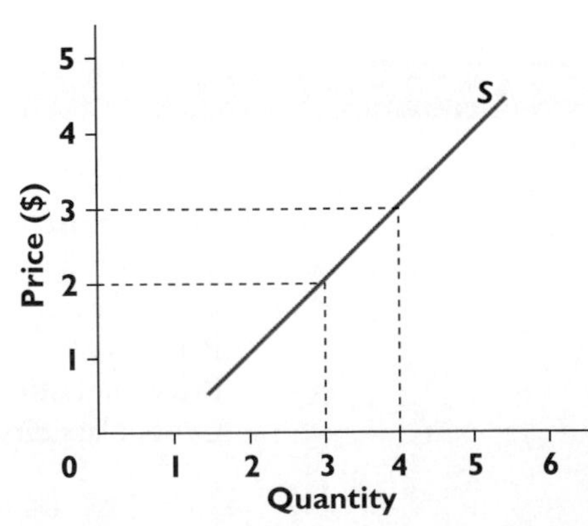

13. Calculate the price elasticities of demand for each one dollar change in price.

Price	Quantity Demanded
$5	20
4	25
3	30
2	35
1	40

14. Suppose, at a party for economics majors, you win a choice among three mystery boxes. You don't know what each contains, but you know that each box has a pair of gifts. You know that one box has a CD and a pair of sunglasses, another has tickets to a Belly concert and a gift certificate to a close-by restaurant for dinner before the concert, and the other has two very similar textbooks on economics. The only clue given is the cross elasticities among the gifts in each box: for the red box, cross elasticity is +1.5, for the blue box, −1.5, and for the white box, 0. If you wanted the dinner and concert pair, which box would you pick?

C H A P T E R 5

MARGINAL UTILITY AND CONSUMER CHOICE

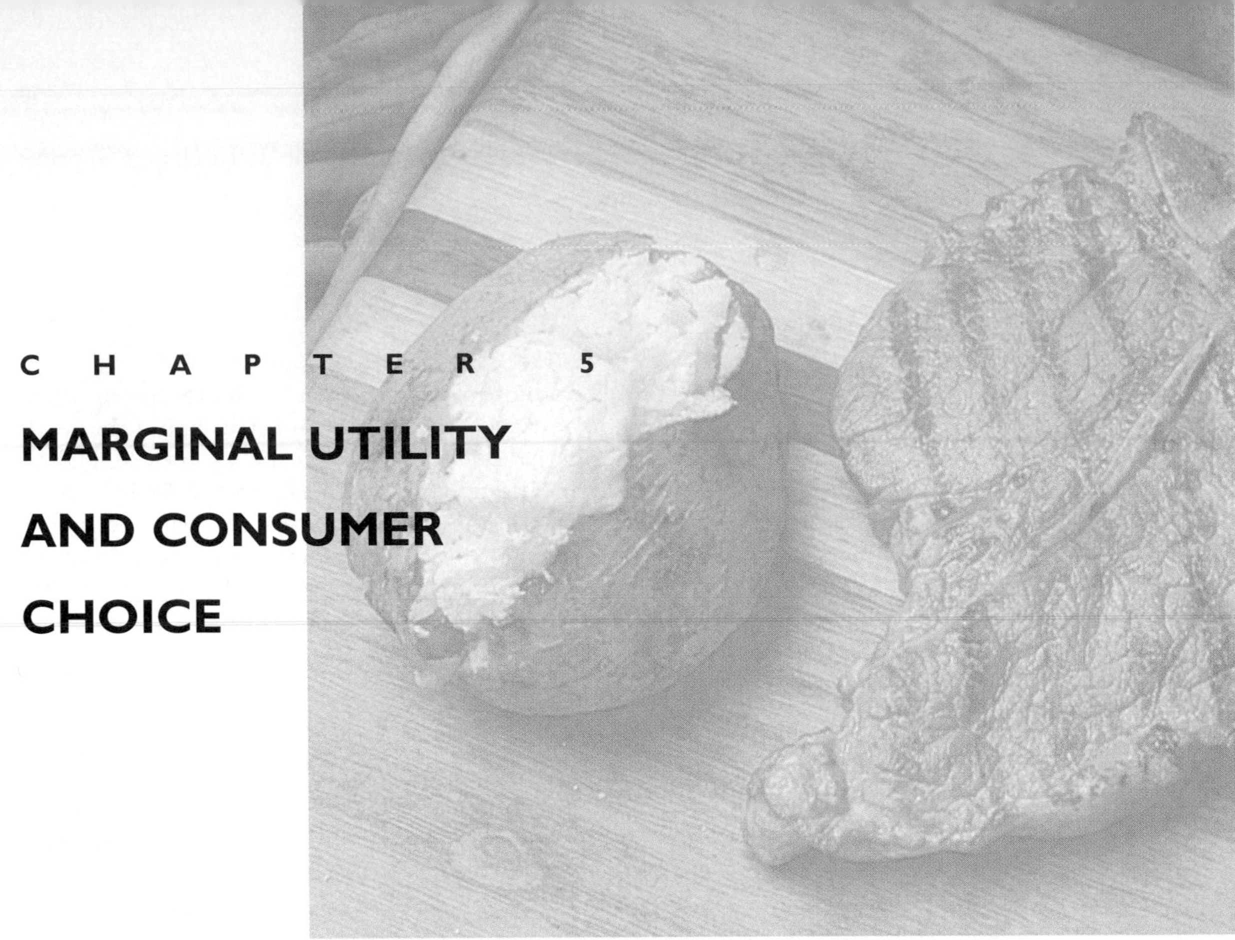

CHAPTER PREVIEW

This chapter continues our examination of demand. So far, we have assumed that as price decreases, quantity demanded increases. This is the familiar law of demand from Chapter 3. Why is it that demand curves display this relationship between price and quantity demanded? The answer lies in the concepts of total utility, marginal utility, and the ratio of marginal utility to price for different goods.

New analytical tools will be developed to analyze consumer choice. These include marginal utility-to-price ratios and consumer surplus. Studying this chapter may change the way you view shopping trips for the rest of your life.

After studying this chapter, you should be able to:

- Explain what is meant by the term *marginal utility*.
- Connect the concepts of total utility and marginal utility.
- Describe the law of diminishing marginal utility.
- Give an explanation for the water and diamond paradox.
- Account for the law of demand using marginal utility-to-price ratios.
- Explain the logic behind the marginal utility-to-price ratio equalization rule.
- Discuss the concept of consumer surplus.

- Explain why interpersonal comparisons of utility are invalid.
- Draw graphs to represent indifference curves and budget constraints.
- Derive demand curves from indifference curves and budget constraints.

Some things are so obvious that you don't think people need to mention them. For example, if you come in out of a sudden summer downpour, your friend might say to you, "Just look at you! You're soaking wet!" As if you didn't know it, standing there dripping all over the floor. Or, if you dart out onto a narrow, one-way street from between two parked cars, and almost run smack into a moving car, an onlooker might say to you, "Gee, that was close!" As if you didn't already know it, your heart pounding like a jackhammer. Economists are sometimes inclined to do the same—point out what *seems* obvious—but they don't apologize for it. For they know that pursuing the obvious can sometimes lead to a more complete and even new understanding of the familiar.

For example, let's take the law of demand. The law states that as price falls, the quantity demanded of a normal good increases. Obvious? Seems so, but economists ask why. *Why do we tend to demand more of a good when its price falls?*

The reason, they discover, is that *the good's marginal-utility-to-price ratio increases above the ratios of other goods.* This higher ratio signals people to rearrange the kinds and quantities of goods they buy with their income—that is, they reduce their consumption of the other goods and increase their consumption of the good with the higher marginal utility ratio. Hence, its quantity demanded increases.

Confusing? Probably so. After all, marginal utility and marginal utility-to-price ratios are new concepts. But don't worry. They, too, will soon make good sense.

WHAT IS MARGINAL UTILITY?

When you were a child visiting family with your parents, you may have been asked by a doting uncle or aunt how much you liked them. They expected an enthusiastic response, and sensing that, you would oblige. Most likely, you would spread your hands apart as far as you could reach, indicating *that* much! They were always happy, weren't they? Imagine how they would have felt if you had paused, thought a while, and then held up your hands just three inches apart!

Util

A fictitious unit of measurement representing how much utility a person obtains from consuming a good.

Utility

The satisfaction or enjoyment a person obtains from consuming a good.

Economists ask the same kinds of questions. But they want to know how much you like tea, coffee, beer, milk, or ginger ale. Or any other set of goods. They don't expect you to indicate your particular likes by spreading your hands apart—although you could do that—but instead they expect you to reckon the **utils,** or the quantity of **utility** you derive from consuming the goods. That's the fictional but very useful measure that economists use to gauge satisfaction. For example, after drinking a mug of beer, your satisfaction or sense of well-being increases by 26 utils. What about a mug of root beer? No more than 3 utils. A weekend on tour with the Breeders? Perhaps 4,000 utils!

ADDED PERSPECTIVE

Beauty and the Beast

An Economist's Abridged Version

Once upon a time there was a merchant who had three daughters. The two older daughters were beautiful, but disagreeable. The youngest was the most beautiful, very loving and kind. Her name was Beauty. One day, just before departing on a business trip to maximize profit, the merchant asked his daughters what gifts they wanted him to bring back. The older daughters asked for highly priced silks, satins, and jewelry. But Beauty, wouldn't you know, just wanted a simple rose.

Entrepreneurs always face uncertainty, and the merchant soon discovered that his trip was a total loss. He could not even afford to buy the promised gifts. On his way home, riding through a giant forest, he got caught in a miserable blizzard. He wandered aimlessly on his horse, looking for shelter, and suddenly came upon a sun-drenched opening in the forest that had at its center a great palace surrounded by beautiful flowers. The palace appeared deserted. The merchant went in, warmed himself by a blazing fire, ate a splendidly prepared meal, and later went upstairs to sleep in an inviting, soft bed.

The next morning he left for home. As he rode among the flowers, he saw the loveliest rose, and remembering Beauty, plucked it from its bed. At that very moment, a terrifying Beast appeared, whose booming voice shook the earth, the horse, and the merchant. "Wretched person," the Beast yelled, "who gave you leave to pick my roses?"

The merchant pleaded forgiveness and explained the circumstances. But the Beast was unmoved. "Last night I granted you all your wishes, and look how you repay me," cried the Beast! "By right I should kill you now. Instead, take the rose home and give it to whichever daughter loves you enough to come back here alone. If no one comes, I will kill you."

Upon returning, the merchant, with much weeping, told the story. Beauty, of course, wanted to go for her father's sake—attaching more utility to his life than the negative utility involved in going to the Beast—but the merchant loved her too much and refused her offer. That night, Beauty stole away on the merchant's horse.

When Beauty first saw the Beast, she was absolutely horrified. Negative utility skyrocketed! But when the Beast spoke to her, she heard a gentleness in his gruff voice that touched her. He told her that everything he had was there for her pleasure. "The only thing I shall ever ask of you," he said, "is to try to love me." She pitied him, but could not love him. For days thereafter, the negative utility vanished and the total utility Beauty gained from her new life grew. And every day the Beast would ask, "Can you love me?" She grew increasingly fond of him, and actually gained considerable utility from his companionship, but could not love him.

One day the Beast saw that Beauty was sad. He knew that the total utility Beauty received was well below the opportunity cost she incurred by not being with her father. He suggested a three-day visit home. He revealed his own set of utilities by saying, "If you stay longer than three days, I shall die of loneliness." She promised to return, and before she left, the Beast gave Beauty a magic ring which she was to keep by her bed. With that ring, she would wake in the morning wherever she wanted to be.

Her visit was joyous, but her sisters, consumed by envy, persuaded Beauty to stay an extra night. That night, in a dream, she heard the Beast sob, "Beauty, you broke your promise and I am dying of loneliness." She awoke, held the ring tightly, and wished to be once more with the Beast.

And just in time! She found him lying in a bed of roses. The Beast whispered, "Beauty, I'm dying." "Oh no," she cried, "you mustn't. I've returned because I love you."

With those words spoken, the Beast changed form and became a young, handsome prince! Beauty was shocked! "Wow," she thought, "I was prepared to spend the rest of my life with the Beast because the utility I gain from being with him is at least equal to the opportunity cost I incur not being with my father." "Gosh," she said, gazing into the eyes of her prince, "just look at my consumer surplus now!"

The More the Better, Up to a Point

Most people would prefer having more of a normal good than less. For example, wouldn't you prefer having two T-bone steaks to one per month? And wouldn't three T-bones be preferable to two? But how much more preferable?

Marginal utility

The increase in total utility a person derives from consuming an additional unit of a good.

Total utility

The total number of utils a person derives from consuming a specific quantity of a good.

Be sure that you are able to explain in words and mathematically what marginal utility means.

Can you quantify satisfaction? For example, how many more utils do you derive from consuming three compared to consuming two? Suppose Table 1 measures the number of utils you derive from consuming T-bones.

Apparently, the more the better! Consuming five T-bones a month gives you 81 utils. That's more than the 80 utils you derive from consuming four. But see what's happening to the number of utils you derive from consuming T-bones as you consume more and more of them. Total utility increases, but by fewer and fewer utils.

That's what the marginal utility of T-bone steaks measures. **Marginal utility** measures the increase in **total utility** a person derives from consuming an additional unit of a good.

$$MU = \frac{\Delta TU}{\Delta Q}$$

where MU is marginal utility, TU is total utility and Q is the quantity of the good. The Greek capital letter Δ, or delta, means "change in."

The Law of Diminishing Marginal Utility

Does the law of diminishing marginal utility apply to all the commodities you consume?

It's clear from Table 1 that the more T-bones you consume during the month, the fewer utils you derive from each additional one. The first excites the taste buds and the enjoyment is heightened by its uniqueness. The second is enjoyable and highly valued, but it lacks the *ummph* of the first. The third is appreciated, but familiar. The fourth becomes commonplace, almost a matter of habit. The fifth is just food, good calories, although a peanut butter sandwich would probably do as well.

Of course, real steak lovers and NFL football players would attach a different set of utils to these T-bones and would probably derive considerable utility even from the twentieth one in a month. But other people would derive few utils after only a second, and vegetarians would derive zero utils from the first.

We are all very different people with very different tastes. But for everyone—yourself, your professor, the defensive tackle for the Indianapolis Colts, and the principal ballerina of the New York City Ballet—the utility derived from consuming additional steaks diminishes as more steaks are consumed.

This is true not only for T-bones, but for T-birds, T-shirts, and T-squares. In fact, it is true for every good. The more that is consumed of any good, the

TABLE 1
Total Utility and Marginal Utility Derived from Consuming T-bone Steaks (Utils)

Number of T-bones	Total Utility	Marginal Utility
0	0	—
1	35	35
2	60	25
3	75	15
4	80	5
5	81	1
6	78	−3

That steak sure looks good to me. I know there are an awful lot of calories in it, but there's also an awful lot of mouth watering enjoyment. Yet, I must confess that every time I'm about to finish such an appetizing dinner, I feel I could do without that next bite. Strange, isn't it?

lower is the good's marginal utility. Economists are so convinced of this that they formulate it into a law: **the law of diminishing marginal utility.**

Law of diminishing marginal utility

The idea that as more of a good is consumed, the utility a person derives from each additional unit diminishes.

Figure 1 maps out the total and marginal utility curves for the T-bones of Table 1.

Note what is measured on the vertical axes. In panel *a,* it is total utility. In panel *b,* it is *changes in* total utility, that is, marginal utility. Total utility reaches its maximum of 81 utils at five steaks. Beyond five, total utility actually falls. Six steaks yield a total of only 78 utils, so the marginal utility of the sixth steak is −3.

Does negative marginal utility seem unreasonable? Think about it. You may pray for snow before a ski weekend, but how much utility would you derive from an additional 10-inch accumulation of snow just when you are trying to get out of your driveway? How much utility would you derive consuming a sixth hard-boiled egg at one sitting? How many utils do you suppose Noah derived from that fortieth day of rain?

Look at the correspondence between the upward-sloping total utility curve and the downward-sloping marginal utility curve in Figure 1. Total utility increases as more steak is consumed, but by smaller and smaller increments. The curve tends to flatten out. These increments are graphed in panel *b.* The curve starts high, at 35 utils, but the marginal utility of the fifth steak is only 1. The curve then cuts the horizontal axis to reach −3 at the sixth steak. Obviously, consuming more than five T-bones is a real mis-steak!

The Water and Diamond Paradox

Some people find it hard to enjoy life because they simply have too much! Sad, isn't it? Can you imagine a rich teenager getting excited about a trip to Europe? You would probably hear the complaint: "What! Again?" The number of utils derived from such a trip may be very few. Why? For the teenager, a trip to Europe is about as routine as eating a slice of white bread. Perhaps that's an exaggeration, but not by much.

How much people value a good depends upon the utils they derive *from the last one consumed.* That explains the paradox between the values we place on water and diamonds.

Would you agree that the total utility we derive from consuming water is infinitely greater than the total utility we could possibly derive from any quan-

FIGURE 1
Total and Marginal Utility
In panel *a*, total utility increases until it reaches a maximum of 81 utils when five steaks are consumed. Additional steaks reduce total utility. In panel *b*, marginal utility falls with each additional steak consumed.

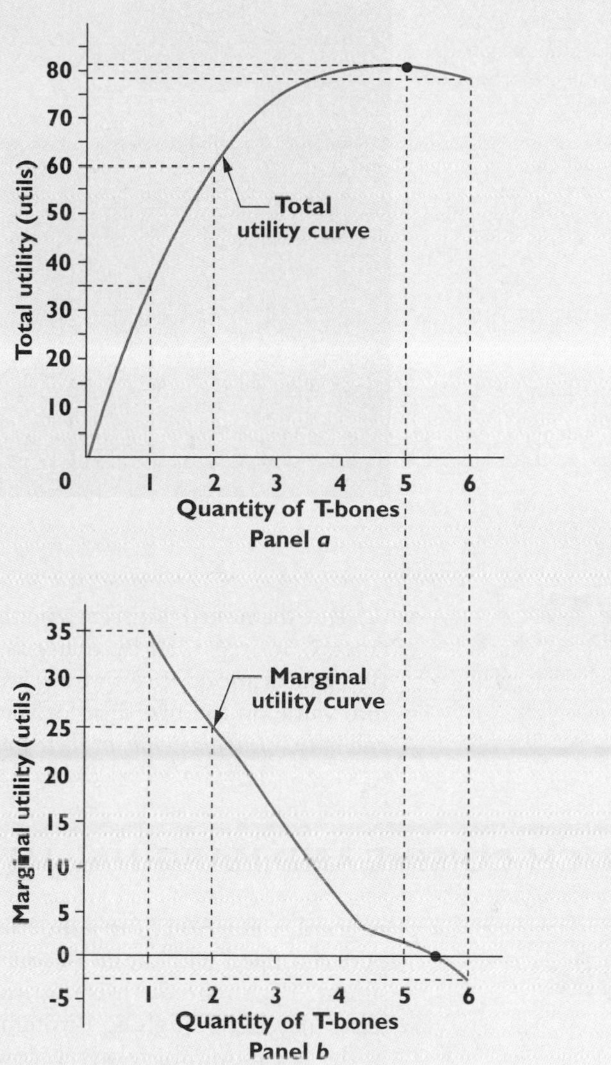

tity of diamonds? And yet, look at the healthy disregard we show for the water we consume and the loving care we show for diamond earrings. Why? Don't our values seem misplaced?

The paradox that we must explain is the high total utility of water and its low marginal utility versus the low total utility of diamonds and their high marginal utility. How does the relative scarcity of water and diamonds help to explain this paradox?

Not really. They simply reflect the quantities available of these two goods. Even though we think nothing of taking leisurely daily showers or baths, or splashing about in our private swimming pools, or watering our lawns, or even washing our automobiles, the marginal utility of the first drop consumed is infintely high. It's just that we're typically far removed from that first drop.

Other people are not quite so fortunate. Desert societies have precious little water available and conserve it diligently. The Israelis, for example, invented *drip irrigation,* a technology that feeds plants one drop of water at a time, with the timing fixed and monitored by a computer system. *The scarcity of water in Israel causes the marginal utility of the last unit consumed to be very high.*

Drip irrigation is a way of conserving scarce water. As a result, the marginal utility of the last drop used is very high.

But diamonds, satisfying neither thirst nor hunger, catering to our frivolous fancies, are regarded by many as being even more precious than water. Why? Because diamonds are more scarce. People who love diamonds still place infinite value on the first drop of water. *But they have water gushing out of their faucets and only a few diamonds in their wall safes.*

FRENCH CUISINE AND MARGINAL UTILITY

A good, solid American dinner consists of a bushel of salad, a 2-pound Idaho potato topped with a pint of sour cream and butter, and a healthy pound of rare sirloin. Each ingredient is nutritious and delicious. But however marvelous the salad may be, ploughing through a bushel of it must make the marginal utility of the last mouthful relatively low. The steak is, perhaps, a tastier cut than anything served in the restaurants of Paris, yet chewing our way through to the last mouthful must make its marginal utility relatively low. What about that giant potato? How many utils do you think you would derive consuming that last bite of Idaho?

The French do it differently. Just a touch of soup. Small enough so that the marginal utility of the last spoonful is still relatively high. Just a touch of salad. Small enough so that the marginal utility of the last mouthful is still high. Just a touch of goose liver appetizer. Just a touch of white asparagus. Just a touch of sauteed mushroom. Just a touch of snow peas. Just a touch of the entree, coq au vin, with a modest serving of potato au gratin on the side. Just a touch of Camembert on baguette. Just a touch of Swiss chocolate. And voila!

The secret of French cuisine, as you see, is in keeping the courses coming but the individual portions minute. The French understand well the law of diminishing marginal utility and play a strategy of never letting any portion's marginal utility get out of hand. We may end up with more total utils at an American table, but the feeling of satisfaction, the sense of well-being, *expressed always by the marginal utility of the goods consumed,* favors French cuisine.

TABLE 2 Marginal Utilities of Clothes and Amusement Goods (Utils)

Quantity	Clothes	Amusement
1	18	23
2	16	21
3	14	17
4	12	15
5	11	14
6	9	13

UNDERSTANDING THE LAW OF DEMAND

Let's take a closer look at that law of demand. When price falls, the quantity demanded of a normal good increases. This seems not only reasonable, but is also confirmed by our experience. *But why?*

Let's suppose you receive a number of birthday gifts from friends and relatives, some in the form of clothes, some in the form of amusement goods, and some cash.

Suppose Table 2 records your utility schedule for clothes and amusement goods.

If you were to pick your birthday gifts from a catalog of clothes and amusement goods in Table 2, your first choice would be an amusement good. It gives you 23 utils. That's 5 more utils than you would get from the first unit of clothing.

With the first amusement good already in your possession, you look to the next best thing, which is still an amusement good. Although the marginal utility of the second amusement good is less than the first—21 utils compared to 23—the marginal utility is still greater than the 18 utils of the first unit of clothes. Next, you would go to that first unit of clothes. The 18 utils is more than the 17 utils the third amusement good generates. You can trace through the rest.

Making Selections from a Given Budget

Suppose, instead of making choices from the catalog, your birthday gifts included $80 in cash—that's your budget—which you decide to spend on clothes and amusement goods. Suppose also, for simplicity's sake, that the price of a unit of clothes and a unit of amusement goods was $10 for either.

How would you spend the $80? You end up buying eight units in the sequence traced out in Table 2. The first $10 is spent on the first amusement good because the marginal utility per dollar of the first amusement good is

$$\frac{MU}{P} = \frac{23}{10} = 2.3$$

This is the most utils per dollar your first $10 could find. The next best buy would be the second amusement good, which gives you 2.1 utils to the dollar. And so on.

ADDED PERSPECTIVE

Are White Rats Rational Consumers?

Have you ever said to yourself, while looking over the dessert menu at an upscale restaurant, "Tonight's the night I splurge! I'm going to treat myself to that $12.50 baked Alaska. I've eaten their $4 apple pie before and it's mighty good, but tonight that baked Alaska, even at that price, is just too good to pass up!"

What you were *really* saying to yourself, of course, was, "Let's see now. The ratio of marginal utility to price of the baked Alaska is higher than the ratio of marginal utility to price of the apple pie. And since I'm a rational consumer, I'll pick baked Alaska."

Well, rats behave—and perhaps even think—the way people do. Consider this experiment. Economists J. H. Kagel and R. C. Battalio put two white rats in separate cages and provided them with "free" food and water. In addition, each cage was rigged with two levers which operated two dipper cups, one cup containing root beer, the other nonalcoholic Collins mix. The rats could get to these drinks by pressing the levers. The "price" of each drink was set by controlling the number of presses required per measured drink. Kagel and Battalio also fixed the total number of presses the two rats were allowed.

What happened? In the initial two-week run, the rats were given 300 presses per day—their "income"—and both drinks were priced at 20 presses. Root beer was clearly their favorite. The first rat ended up consuming 11 units of root beer and 4 units of Collins mix per day. The second rat was really a root beer junkie, averaging less than a unit of Collins mix per day.

Kagel and Battalio then changed the "prices" and "incomes." The "price" of root beer was doubled to 40 presses while the "price" of Collins mix was cut in half, to 10 presses. The rats' "incomes"—the total number of presses they were given—were adjusted to provide each rat the opportunity to make the same choices they made earlier.

Did they make the same choices, or anywhere near the same choices? Not at all. The first rat now chose 8 units of root beer and 17 units of Collins mix per day. The second switched to 9 root beers and 25 Collins mixes per day! They probably still preferred root beer to Collins mix, but what guided their choices were the ratios of marginal utility to price.

Source: Adapted from J. H. Kagel and R. C. Battalio, "Experimental Studies of Consumer Behavior," *Economic Inquiry*, March 1975. Reprinted with permission.

Table 3 transforms Table 2 into the marginal utility price ratios (*MU*/*P*) of the two goods.

It makes sense to keep choosing those goods that yield the highest marginal utility per dollar spent. The first $60 would be spent in the following sequence:

TABLE 3 Marginal Utility-to-Price Ratios of Clothes and Amusement Goods (*MU*/*P*)

	Clothes			Amusement		
Quantity	**Utils**	**Price**	***MU*/*P***	**Utils**	**Price**	***MU*/*P***
1	18	$10	1.8	23	$10	2.3
2	16	10	1.6	21	10	2.1
3	14	10	1.4	17	10	1.7
4	12	10	1.2	15	10	1.5
5	11	10	1.1	14	10	1.4
6	9	10	0.9	13	10	1.3

1st	=	1st amusement good	=	2.3 utils per dollar
2nd	=	2nd amusement good	=	2.1 utils per dollar
3rd	=	1st unit clothes	=	1.8 utils per dollar
4th	=	3rd amusement good	=	1.7 utils per dollar
5th	=	2nd unit clothes	=	1.6 utils per dollar
6th	=	4th amusement good	=	1.5 utils per dollar

With $20 of birthday cash left, you still have two more choices. What will the next purchase be? The marginal utility-to-price ratio of the third unit of clothes is 1.4. But so, too, is the marginal utility-to-price ratio of the fifth amusement good. At this point, you're indifferent. Either one gives you the most utility you can get for a dollar. Suppose you pick the third unit of clothes. The last $10, then, would be spent on the fifth amusement good because its 1.4 utils per dollar is higher than the 1.2 utils per dollar generated by the fourth unit of clothes.

There you have it! Given market prices and the marginal utilities over the range of consumption goods shown in Table 3, the quantity demanded of clothes, at a price of $10, is three units.

IF THE PRICE OF CLOTHES FALLS TO $8

Suppose that the clothing stores begin a 20 percent off sale just as you are about to spend your $80 of birthday money on clothes and amusement goods. You would still check the *MU/Ps* of each of the two goods and choose the highest, then on to the next highest *MU/P* good. Look at Table 4.

Note the differences in the *MU/P* for clothes that the price change made. The first choice now will *still* be the first amusement good. It yields 2.3 utils per dollar, which is still the best buy. But choices change thereafter. The first $60 will be spent in this sequence:

1st	=	1st amusement good	=	2.30 utils per dollar
2nd	=	1st unit clothes	=	2.25 utils per dollar
3rd	=	2nd amusement good	=	2.10 utils per dollar
4th	=	2nd unit clothes	=	2.00 utils per dollar
5th	=	3rd unit clothes	=	1.75 utils per dollar
6th	=	3rd amusement good	=	1.70 utils per dollar

There are still two more choices remaining with the $20 of birthday cash. The marginal utility-to-price ratio of both the fourth unit of clothes and fourth

TABLE 4
Comparing *MU/Ps* after a 20 Percent Off Sale on Clothes

	Clothes			Amusement		
Quantity	Utils	Price	*MU/P*	Utils	Price	*MU/P*
1	18	$8	2.25	23	$10	2.3
2	16	8	2.00	21	10	2.1
3	14	8	1.75	17	10	1.7
4	12	8	1.50	15	10	1.5
5	11	8	1.38	14	10	1.4
6	9	8	1.13	13	10	1.3

TABLE 5 Comparing MU/Ps after a 50 Percent Off Sale on Clothes

	Clothes			Amusement		
Quantity	Utils	Price	*MU/P*	Utils	Price	*MU/P*
1	18	$5	3.6	23	$10	2.3
2	16	5	3.2	21	10	2.1
3	14	5	2.8	17	10	1.7
4	12	5	2.4	15	10	1.5
5	11	5	2.2	14	10	1.4
6	9	5	1.8	13	10	1.3

unit of amusement goods is 1.50. Again, you are indifferent. Either clothes or amusement will do for the seventh choice. If you pick clothes, then the eighth choice would be the fourth amusement good because its 1.50 marginal utility-price-ratio is higher than the 1.38 ratio of the fifth unit of clothes.

With the $80 spent in maximizing utility and with the fall in the price of clothes from $10 to $8, the quantity of clothes demanded increased from three to four units.

Clearly, the price of clothes has fallen and the quantity of clothes demanded has risen.

IF THE PRICE OF CLOTHES FALLS TO $5

If the price of clothes were to fall again, from $8 to $5, the marginal utility-to-price ratios (*MU/P*) for clothes would change again, as shown in Table 5.

Now the utility-maximizing strategy for the $80 of birthday cash buys six units of clothes (assuming *MU/P* for the seventh is 1.0). That is, *when the price of clothes falls from $8 to $5, the quantity demanded increases from four to six units.*

The *MU/P* Equalization Principle

MU/P equalization principle
The idea that a person's utility is maximized when the ratios of marginal utility to price for each of the goods consumed are equal.

The law of demand rests on this **MU/P equalization principle** of consumer behavior. Consumers will always arrange their sequence of choices among goods starting with the highest *MU/P* and running down to exhaust the expenditure budget. In the end, the *MU/P* ratio for each good consumed will be equal.

$$\frac{MU}{P}\text{ (clothes)} = \frac{MU}{P}\text{ (amusement)} = \frac{MU}{P}\text{ (any other good)}$$

In the real world not all goods are divisible into small enough units so that the *MU/P* ratio will be exactly the same for all.

It makes sense because the rational consumer will always shift a dollar from a good whose *MU/P* is lower to one whose *MU/P* is higher. Since consuming one less of a good increases its *MU/P*, and consuming one more of the other good lowers its *MU/P*, the rearranging of goods consumed will drive their *MU/P*s to equalization.

The *MU/P* Equalization Principle and the Law of Demand

While it may be obvious to everybody that when price falls the quantity demanded increases, economists dig deep into the behavior of individual con-

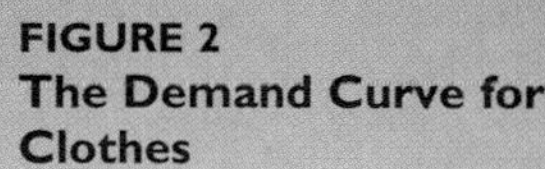

FIGURE 2
The Demand Curve for Clothes

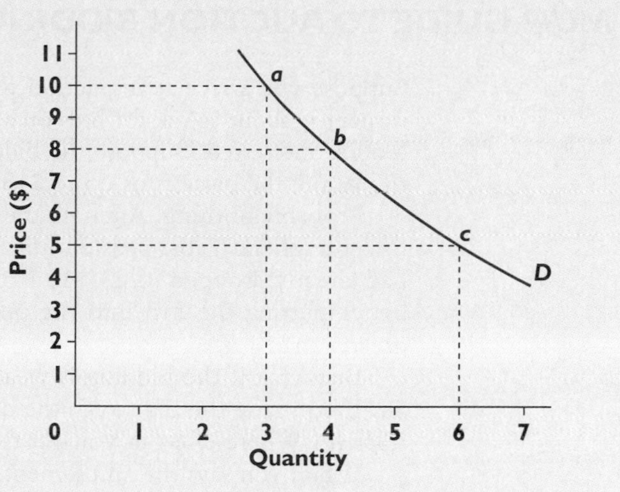

The law of demand derives from the *MU/P* equalization principle—a decrease in price destroys equality of *MU/P* for all goods. Thus, a consumer is induced to buy more of the lower-priced good.

sumers—who are always trying to maximize utility from a given expenditure budget—to explain why the obvious is indeed so.

The demand curve of Figure 2 provides a graphic view of the data offered in Table 3–Table 5.

The three points *a*, *b*, and *c*, on the demand curve correspond to the quantities of clothes demanded at prices of $10, $8, and $5 when the consumer has an $80 expenditure budget and the set of marginal utility-to-price ratios shown in Table 3–Table 5. The three points outline what the demand curve for clothes would look like if other prices for the clothes were considered. This derivation of the demand curve for clothes is simply a more complete explanation of demand determination than that presented in Chapter 3.

Changes in the marginal-utility-to-price ratios (*MU/P*) of any good—caused either by a change in the marginal utility of the good or in its price—changes the quantities demanded. We can summarize here as we did in Chapter 3:

1. *If the price of clothes changes, the quantity demanded of clothes changes.* For example, when the price of clothes falls from $10 to $8 (compare Table 3 and Table 4), the quantity of clothes demanded increases from three to four.
2. *If the price of clothes changes, the quantities demanded of other goods change as well.* For example, when the price of clothes falls from $10 to $8 (look again at Table 3 and Table 4), the quantity demanded of amusement goods falls from five to four.
3. *If consumer taste for clothes changes—reflected in changing marginal utilities for clothes—the quantity demanded of clothes changes.* For example, if the marginal utility of clothes doubles—it's now more fashionable to own a more extensive wardrobe—the marginal-utility-to-price ratio of clothes also doubles, which would prompt consumers to shift some of their dollars out of buying other goods and into buying more clothes.
4. *If consumer income changes, the quantity demanded of clothes changes.* For example, if the birthday cash were $120 instead of $80, more of each good would be demanded.

THE *MU/P* GUIDE TO AUCTION BIDDING

Suppose you arrive at an auction with all your birthday cash just when the auctioneer is about to ask for bids on an amusement good, say a wind-up Elvis doll. You're interested. Suppose the bidding starts at \$3, and before you can get into the game, the price runs up to \$15. What do you do?

Probably nothing. After all, the marginal utility of that first amusement good for you (check Table 5) is 23 utils. Its *MU/P,* then, at that stage in the bidding had already dropped to 23/\$15 = 1.53—too low to get excited. You would do better putting the \$15 into the purchase of some other good whose *MU/P* is greater than 1.53.

But what if the bidding is weak. For example, suppose the bidding stalls at \$4. If you raise the bid to \$5, the doll's *MU/P* is 23/\$5 = 4.6. That's mighty attractive! Where else can you get that many utils for your dollar?

When you saw the amusement good sitting on the auctioneer's table, didn't you mentally fix a maximum price which represented how high you would bid? That's what most people do. Considering that you could get 3.6 utils per dollar by buying the first unit of clothes (check Table 5 again), your top bid for the auctioned amusement good would be \$6.40. A \$6.40 bid would equal the *MU/P* of clothes; that is, 23/\$6.40 = 3.6 utils per dollar. But suppose, to your surprise and delight, the bidding stays at \$4 and when the auctioneer is about to slam the gavel down to signal the sale, you raise the bid to \$5. Nobody tops you. It's yours! You end up paying \$5, although you would have been willing to go as high as \$6.40.

CREATING CONSUMER SURPLUS

Consumer surplus

The difference between the maximum amount a person would be willing to pay for a good or service and the amount the person actually pays.

What happens to consumer surplus as market price falls? As it increases?

Economists call the difference between what you pay for a good and what you would have been willing to pay for it **consumer surplus.** Every consumer walks away from every market with some degree of consumer surplus. For example, suppose Figure 3 represents the market for horseback riding.

The hourly market price for horseback riding is \$6. The demand curve in Figure 3 represents an aggregate of all the individual demand curves of people who make up the market. At \$6 an hour, 720 hours are demanded by them.

Figure 4 represents three individual demand curves that are part of the Figure 3 market. They show how many hours of riding Kim Deal, Tony Poulos, and Randy Seals would demand at varying prices.

In panel *a*, at the \$6 equilibrium price established on the Figure 3 market, Kim ends up demanding four hours of riding. Although she pays \$6 for each hour, *she would have been willing to pay* \$15 for that first hour (point *a*). The consumer surplus she gains, then, from that first hour is \$15 – \$6 = \$9. She would have been willing to pay \$12 for the second hour (point *b*), but pays only \$6. The consumer surplus she receives from the second hour of riding, then, is \$12 – \$6 = \$6. What about the third hour? She pays \$6, but would have been willing to pay \$9 (point *c*). She draws a consumer surplus on this third hour of \$9 – \$6 = \$3. Since she was willing to pay only \$6 for that fourth hour (point *d*), she buys that hour, but it yields no consumer surplus.

The total utility, expressed in dollars, that Kim gains from the four hours of riding is \$15 + \$12 + \$9 + \$6 = \$42. She pays only \$6 × 4 = \$24. She ends up, then, with a total consumer surplus of \$42 – \$24 = \$18.

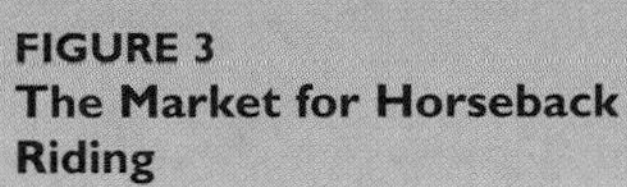

FIGURE 3
The Market for Horseback Riding

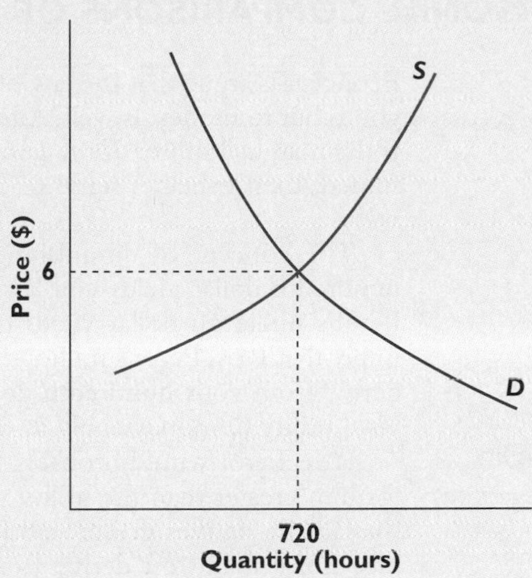

Tony Poulos's interest in riding is, as you see in panel *b*, less intense than Kim's. At a price of $6 an hour, he ends up riding three hours, drawing a total consumer surplus of ($10 + $8 + $6) − ($6 × 3) = $6. Panel *c* shows that Randy takes only two hours of riding and draws a total consumer surplus of ($9 + $6) − ($6 × 2) = $3.

Can you imagine the consumer surplus people gain from consuming water at market prices? Can you imagine how much consumer surplus we derive from everyday consumption of food?

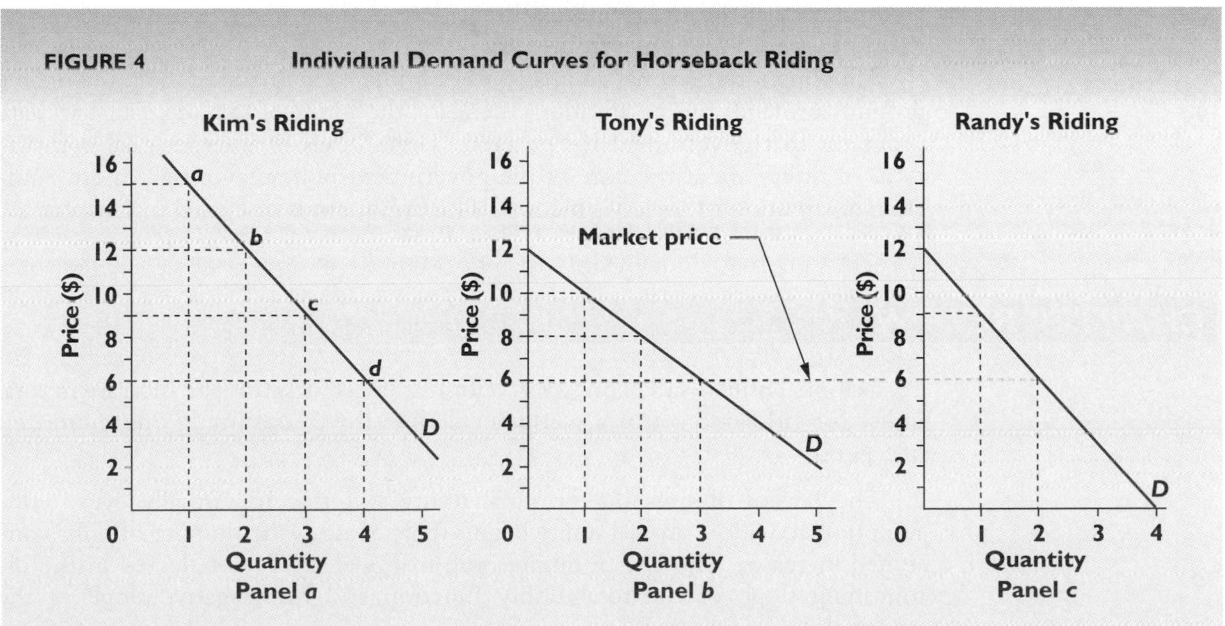

FIGURE 4 **Individual Demand Curves for Horseback Riding**

INTERPERSONAL COMPARISONS OF UTILITY

Economists argue that the law of diminishing marginal utility applies not only to goods but to money as well. After all, money represents the power to buy goods. If the marginal utility of the goods that money buys falls as more goods are consumed, then it makes sense to argue that the marginal utility of money falls as well.

The concept of diminishing marginal utility of money implies that your hundredth dollar yields you less utility than your first. It implies also that Ross Perot's millionth dollar yields him less utility than his hundredth. But does it imply that Ross Perot's millionth dollar yields him less utility than the utility you derive from your hundredth dollar? That is, does the law of diminishing marginal utility of money apply as well to **interpersonal comparisons of utility**?

Interpersonal comparison of utility

A comparison of the marginal utilities that different people derive from a good or a dollar.

Ross Perot would probably insist that his millionth dollar generates a utility for him greater than the utility you derive from your hundredth. He would insist that he derives greater satisfaction from spending his millionth dollar on a race horse than you derive from spending your hundredth dollar on a meal. How can you prove him wrong? How can we compare the satisfaction or utility that different people derive from their money? The answer is, we can't.

Is it necessary to make interpersonal comparisons of utility in order to justify redistributing income from the wealthy to the poor?

Our inability to compare interpersonal utilities of money has sobering implications on tax and social welfare policy. After all, if Ross Perot were right about deriving greater utility from his millionth dollar than you do from your hundredth, then were government to tax that dollar away from him and give it to you, his loss would be greater than your gain. Total utility generated in the economy would fall. If we can't calculate interpersonal utilities of money, how can we justify higher income taxes for the wealthy? How can we justify subsidized housing? Or even aid to dependent children?

However impossible it may be to calculate interpersonal comparisons of utility, many economists nonetheless rely on the *reasonableness* of the idea. Since the marginal utility of money diminishes for each individual, it just seems reasonable to suppose that the utility a Ross Perot derives from his marginal dollar is less than the utility you derive from yours.

Allowing interpersonal comparisons of utility to be made on such reasonable grounds provides the justification, then, for the kinds of tax and social welfare programs that government has enacted. These kinds of interpersonal comparisons of utility are at the core of the government policy favoring a more equitable distribution of society's income. This argument is discussed in Chapter 19.

CHAPTER REVIEW

1. Marginal utility is the concept economists use to describe the increase in total utility (or satisfaction) that a consumer derives from consuming one more unit of a good.

2. The law of diminishing marginal utility says that in virtually every consumption activity, marginal utility begins to decrease as the number of units consumed increases. The law of diminishing marginal utility is reflected in the diminishing slope of the total utility function and the negative slope of the marginal utility function.

3. Water has a high total utility, but the utility of another unit of water in most parts of the world is small. Conversely, diamonds have a low total utility but a high marginal utility. The marginal utility of water is low because it is so abundant in most places. However, diamonds have a high marginal utility due to their scarcity. The French thoroughly comprehend the concept of marginal utility in their eating behavior—they never serve portions that are too large; rather, they serve many courses, each with a high marginal utility.

4. Given a budget and prices for goods purchased, a consumer will arrange purchases so that goods with the highest marginal-utility-to-price ratios are bought first. A decrease in the price of a good alters the order of purchases; more of the lower-priced good is bought because it will have a higher marginal-utility-to-price ratio. At the end of this process, consumers have arranged purchases so that the marginal-utility-to-price ratios are the same for all goods. This is the marginal-utility-to-price ratio equalization rule—the marginal utility per dollar spent is the same for all goods.

5. Because the marginal-utility-to-price ratio changes, consumers will buy more of a good as its price falls. Hence, demand curves are negatively sloped.

6. If a consumer is willing to pay more for a good than its market price, then the consumer receives consumer surplus. For example, consumers are willing to pay much more than the market price for the first, second, and third gallons of water that they consume. Consumer surplus is generated in this market because the price is low relative to what people are willing and able to pay.

7. The fact that the marginal utility of your millionth dollar of income is lower than the marginal utility of your first dollar of income doesn't necessarily mean that the marginal utility of *your* millionth dollar of income is less than the marginal utility of *my* hundredth dollar of income. You may like money much more than I do. Because everyone's tastes differ, economists refrain from making interpersonal comparisons of income. However, some social policies, like the progressive income tax, are based on interpersonal comparisons of utility. The marginal utility of the millionth dollar of income for a millionaire is *likely* to be less than the marginal utility of the hundredth dollar of income to a working mother with three young children. This likelihood is part of the justification for progressive taxation and income redistribution by government.

KEY TERMS

Utils
Utility
Marginal utility
Total utility
Law of diminishing marginal utility
MU/P equalization principle
Consumer surplus
Interpersonal comparisons of utility

QUESTIONS

1. Suppose, at a student/faculty party, you overhear four economics professors make the following comments:

(a) "Did you see the painting George bought? He paid $450 for it! I wouldn't have paid a nickel."

(b) "It's still snowing! That makes 10 inches since last night. I'd gladly offer a student $20 to clear my driveway."
(c) "It's funny, I can recall everything about my first romance, but can't remember the names of those who followed."
(d) "Do I give charity to the poor? Of course!"
Apply utility analysis to each of these comments.

2. Suppose that after drinking four cups of coffee late at night, your close friend, who is studying economics with you, tells you that the total utility of the coffee she consumed is positive, but the marginal utility of the last cup is decidedly negative. Does the comment make sense to you? Explain.

3. An auto mechanic says to you, "I know you like your car and derive great satisfaction driving it. But if I were you, I wouldn't put another penny into it." Explain his reasoning in terms of utility analysis.

4. How can proponents of a more equitable distribution of income use the law of diminishing marginal utility of money to justify their position?

5. What arguments can their opponents use to undermine that position?

6. Stephanie Howard likes mystery novels. Her marginal-utility-to-price ratio for those novels is 60/$10. If the price of the novels falls from $10 to $5, the number of novels Stephanie demands increases. Explain.

7. Mezzanine tickets to hockey games at the St. Louis Arena are $20. When the Montreal Canadiens come to St. Louis, the game usually sells out. Scalpers get as much as $50 a ticket. Most people at the game, including many who paid scalper prices, end up with consumer surplus. Explain.

8. The more people that show up at an auction and the greater their participation in the bidding, the less consumer surplus is realized by the buyers. Explain.

9. Suppose the following table expresses your demand schedule for flowers:

Price	Quantity Demanded
$5	1
4	2
3	3
2	4
1	5

How much consumer surplus would you derive if price were $2? Using marginal utility analysis, explain what is meant by consumer surplus.

Appendix The Indifference Curve Approach to Demand Curves

Although the idea of mooring the law of demand to the law of diminishing marginal utility makes perfectly good sense, the measure of utility developed in this chapter—units of utils—is still somewhat troubling to economists. It just seems so highly unrealistic. After all, who really keeps count of utils? And even if we wanted to, how could we measure out 25 utils of clothes? What kind of yardstick would we use?

Util counting is admittedly indefinite and farfetched. Aware of this credibility problem, economists have devised a rather ingenious, alternative method for tracing demand to its utility roots. How does it work? Instead of counting utils, the new method simply records consumers' preferences between sets of goods offered. The utilities of the goods, then, are not actually measured, they're just rated as greater, less than, or equal to the utilities of other sets of goods.

For example, given a choice between chocolate ice cream and vanilla, you either prefer chocolate to vanilla, vanilla to chocolate, or are indifferent between the two. If you prefer chocolate, then it seems obvious that a pint of chocolate yields greater utility to you than does a pint of vanilla. If you prefer each equally, then it seems equally obvious that their utilities are the same.

IDENTIFYING EQUALLY PREFERRED SETS OF GOODS

If a person is indifferent among various combinations of different goods, then what is true about the total utility of these combinations?

Using the example in this chapter, let's suppose you were offered a choice between combinations of clothes and amusement goods. Among most sets of choices, it doesn't take long to decide which to choose. But there are times when the given choices are so evenly matched, you simply can't make up your mind. That is, you sometimes end up completely *indifferent between the two choices offered*. Look at Table A1.

Table A1 shows combinations of clothes and amusement goods that yield identical utility for you. These equally preferred combinations are determined simply by asking you to compare choices. If you're presented with the two units of amusement goods and 16 units of clothes, *you* decide which other combinations of clothes and amusement goods are equally preferred.

Compare combination *a* to combinations *b*, *c*, and *d*. Declaring complete indifference means that the two units of amusement goods and 16 units of clothes

TABLE A1 Combinations of Amusement Goods and Clothes Yielding Identical Utility (Units of Goods)

Combination	Amusement	Clothes
a	2	16
b	4	8
c	6	6
d	8	5

FIGURE A1
Indifference Curve
The indifference curve, I_1, records combinations of amusement goods and clothes, such as *a*, *b*, *c*, and *d*. When choosing among these combinations, the consumer is absolutely indifferent. Any combination on the curve is preferred to combinations that fall below the curve, while any combination above the curve, such as *t*, is preferred to combinations on the curve. The shape of the curve reflects the declining marginal rate of substitution between the two goods.

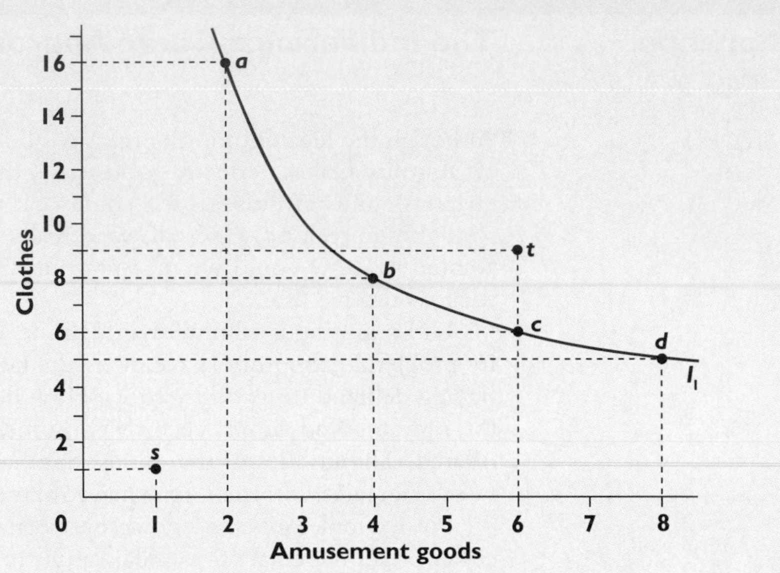

generate the same utility as the 8 and 4, or the 6 and 6, or the 5 and 8 combinations.

Figure A1 graphs these equally preferred combinations into the *indifference curve* I_1.

Points *a*, *b*, *c*, and *d* mark the combinations shown in Table A1. But look at *t*—six units of amusement goods and nine units of clothes—lying off the curve to the right. What about it? It represents a combination of clothes and amusement goods preferred to any combination lying on the curve. Compare, for example, *t* to *c*, the 6 and 6 combination.

Obviously, six units of amusement goods and nine of clothes are preferred to six amusement goods and six clothes. And since *c* is as preferred as any other point on the indifference curve, *t* is preferred to every combination on the curve. Make sense? *Any combination located outside the curve is preferred to any point on it.*

The same logic shows that *any combination located on the curve is preferred to any point inside it.* Compare, for example, *s*—one amusement good and one unit of clothing—to the combination at *c*.

Marginal Rate of Substitution

The marginal rate of substitution is just the slope of an indifference curve.

Why is the indifference curve downward-sloping and convex to the origin? Because it reflects the diminishing marginal utility of goods. As more of a good is consumed, the utility derived from consuming additional units diminishes. Look at Table A2, which just rearranges the information in Figure A1.

Each time you move from *a* to *d* through *b* and *c*, you are willing to give up less and less clothes for each additional amusement good, all the while maintaining the same level of utility. For example, in going from *a* to *b* along indifference curve I_1, two units of amusement goods are substituted for eight units of clothes. That is, because you value the *a* and *b* combinations equally, the two

TABLE A2 Marginal Rate of Substitution between Clothes and Amusement Goods

Rate Going From	Change in Units of Clothes	Change in Units of Amusements	Marginal Rate of Substitution
a to *b*	8 − 16 = −8	4 − 2 = +2	−8/+2 = −4
b to *c*	6 − 8 = −2	6 − 4 = +2	−2/+2 = −1
c to *d*	5 − 6 = −1	8 − 6 = +2	−1/+2 = $-\frac{1}{2}$

units of amusement goods gained are worth the equivalent value of eight units of clothes given up.

But when you move from *b* to *c*, you're now willing to give up only two units of clothes to get the two additional units of amusement goods. The additional two units of amusement goods are now worth to you the equivalent of only two units of clothes. In other words, the amusement goods' utility, expressed in units of clothes, drops from 8 to 2. This is a reflection of the law of diminishing marginal utility. Going from *c* to *d*, the utility of the two additional units drops even further. They're now worth only one unit of clothes.

Economists refer to this decline as the *declining marginal rate of substitution.* This term is a record of the rate at which consumers are willing to substitute one good for another while maintaining the same level of utility.

Constructing Indifference Maps

Look again at combination *t*. Although it is preferred to every combination along the indifference curve I_1 in Figure A1, it is neither preferred to nor not preferred to—that is, indifferent among—the combinations *x*, *y*, and *z* shown in Table A3. They all lie on the same indifference curve.

Compare Table A1 to Table A3. Since *t* is preferred to *c*, every combination in Table 3A is preferred to every combination in Table A1. Figure A2 maps both tables.

In Figure A2, look at point *k*, a 7 and 11 combination. It lies outside indifference curve I_2 and is preferred to any point on it for the same reason *t* is preferred to any point on I_1. The indifference curve I_3 traces out the combinations of clothes and amusement goods that are neither preferred to nor not preferred to—that is, indifferent among—*k*.

TABLE A3 Combinations of Clothes and Amusement Goods Yielding Identical Utility (Units of Goods)

Combination	Amusement	Clothes
x	4	16
y	5	11
t	6	9
z	7	8

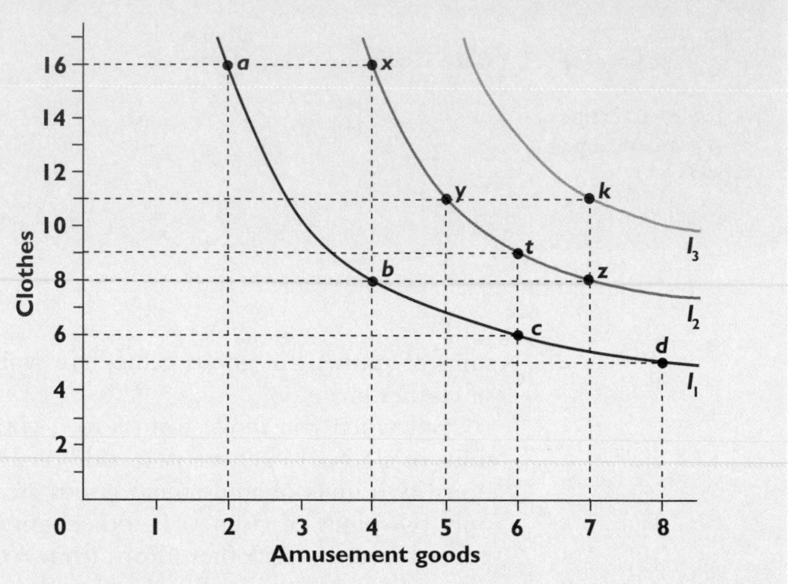

FIGURE A2
An Indifference Map
Any point in Figure A2 falls on an indifference curve. For example, points *x*, *y*, and *z*, combine with point *t* to form the indifference curve I_2. All combinations located on I_2 are preferred to any combination on I_1. Point *k*'s combination falls along the indifference curve, I_3, and is preferred to any point on I_2.

Curves I_1, I_2 and I_3 form a series of ascending indifference curves, with the curve farthermost from the origin representing the combinations of highest utility. Such a set of indifference curves is called an indifference map. Obviously, if you were given the choice, you would prefer a combination of clothes and amusement goods on the curve I_3, since it is farthest from the origin.

THE BUDGET CONSTRAINT

But what choices do you *really* have? Typically, we have to pay for things we consume. Our choices, then, are always limited by our income. Somebody flat broke may have a well-developed set of indifference curves, but still end up without any clothes or amusement goods.

What about yourself? In this chapter, we assumed that your consumption budget was \$80, so you were able to choose \$80 worth of clothes and amusement goods. Let's also suppose—as in Table 5 in the chapter—that clothes are priced at \$5 and amusement goods at \$10. Figure A3 then describes your *ability* to buy combinations of clothes and amusement goods.

The budget line algebraically expresses that income is equal to expenditures.

With a budget of \$80, you have a variety of choices. For example, you can pick *e*—16 units of clothes and zero amusement goods. That adds up to (16 × \$5) + (0 × \$10) = \$80. Alternatively, you can spend the \$80 entirely on eight units of amusement goods. That puts you at point *f*. Of course, these aren't your only options. The \$80 budget allows you to consume *g*, four units of amusement goods and eight units of clothes, or any other combination along the line.

What you can't do is consume eight units of amusement goods and eight units of clothes, point *h* in Figure A3. After all, that costs (8 × \$5) + (8 × \$ 10) = \$120, or \$40 more than your \$80 budget. That is to say, given an income of \$80 and prices of \$5 and \$10 for clothes and amusement goods, the budget line

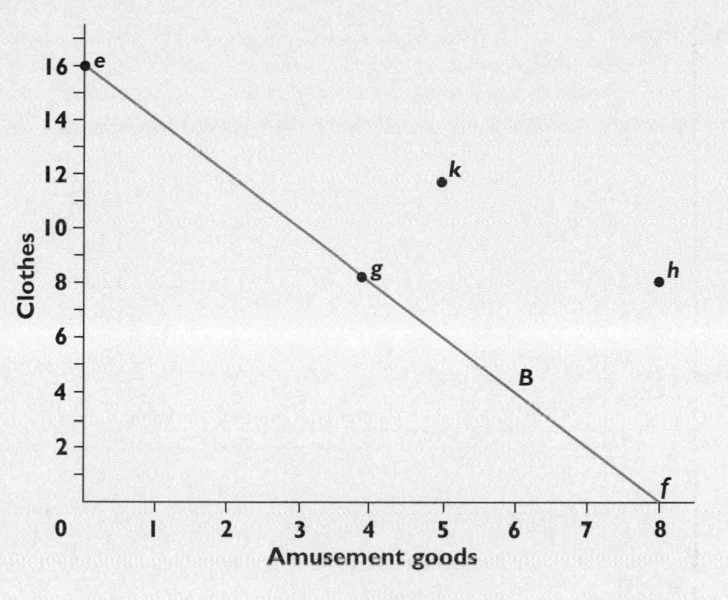

FIGURE A3
The Budget Line
The slope of the budget line *B* depends on the relative prices of clothes and amusement goods. Given these prices, the budget line's polar points, e and *f*, are determined by the size of the budget. At a \$5 price of clothes and \$80 budget, the consumer can buy 16 units of clothes. At a \$10 price of amusement goods, eight units can be bought. Point *g* represents the possible purchase of eight clothes and four amusement goods. What the consumer cannot buy is any combination of clothes and amusement goods that lies above the line. For example, the cost of eight clothes and eight amusement goods—point *h*—exceeds the \$80 budget.

defines the limits of your consumption of clothes and amusement goods. Economists refer to the budget line as a budget constraint.

Price Changes Shift the Budget Constraint

But suppose prices change. For example, suppose all prices increase by 100 percent. You know the consequences, don't you? Your \$80 now just won't buy what it did before. Your new options now shrink from the earlier budget constraint *B* to budget constraint *B*′ in panel *a*, Figure A4.

With amusement goods now \$20 each , your \$80 affords you a maximum of four units. Your position shifts from point *f* on budget line *B* to *f*′ on budget line *B*′ in Figure A4. On the other hand, if you choose to buy only clothes, you end up at *e*′ on budget line *B*′, with eight units of clothes.

But suppose only the price of amusement goods changes. Suppose it alone increases 100 percent to \$20. The price of clothes remains at \$5. What happens to the budget line?

Look at panel *b*, Figure A4, where the budget line shifts from *B* to *B*″. The change in relative prices—the ratio of one price to another—changes its slope. You now have the choice of consuming four units of amusement goods, *f*″, or 16 units of clothes, *e*, or, of course, any other combination along *B*″.

Income Changes, Too, Shift the Budget Constraint

There's just so much you can buy with \$80. If your income goes up enough to increase the consumption budget from \$80 to \$160—prices remaining unchanged—your consumption possibilities increase as well. For example, instead

FIGURE A4 **Effect of Price Changes on the Budget Line**

Panel *a*'s budget line *B*′, reflecting the doubling in prices of clothes and amusement goods, lies closer to the origin than budget line *B* even though the budget remains at $80. Its end points, *e*′ and *f*′ are eight and four units, respectively.

Budget line *B*″ in Panel *b* depicts the same $80 budget, but now only the price of amusement goods doubles, from $10 to $20.

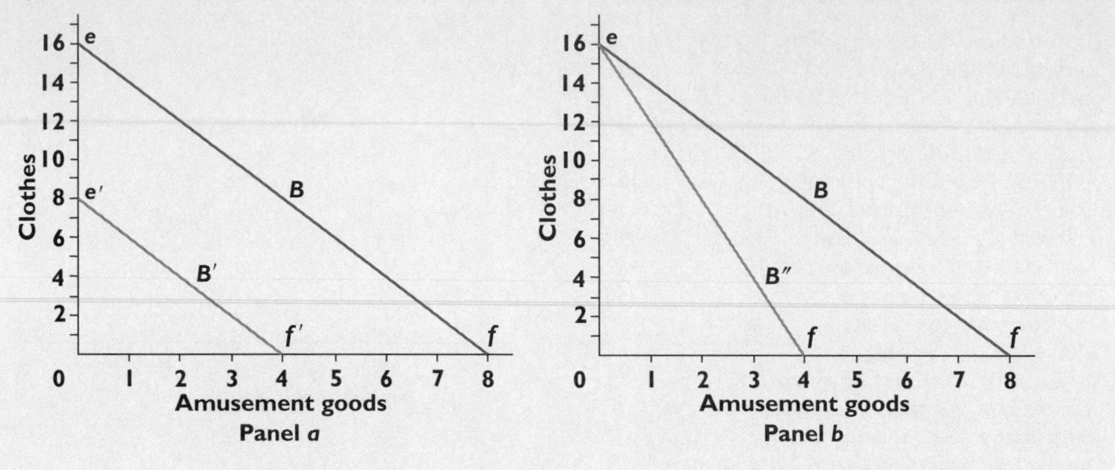

of being able to consume a maximum of eight amusement goods at $10 each, the $160 budget now affords 16. If income increases even more to raise your consumption budget to $240, then 24 amusement goods become possible.

DERIVING THE DEMAND CURVE FOR AMUSEMENT GOODS

The point of tangency of an indifference curve to a budget line represents a price-and-quantity-demanded combination. If the price of one good changes, a new tangent point arises so we have two price-quantity combinations for one of the goods. Hence, we can draw a demand curve for that good.

Everything is in place now to derive the demand curve for amusement goods without having to measure utils. The determinants are your indifference map and budget constraint. Look at Figure A5. Here, the indifference map of Figure A2 and the budget constraint of Figure A4 are brought together to create the demand for amusement goods.

Clothes are priced at $5, amusement goods at $10. With $80 available to spend, you really have no choice but to limit your buying of clothes and amusement goods to those combinations along the budget constraint *B*. What would you end up buying?

Examine the opportunities offered by *p*, *b*, and *f* along the budget constraint. These are all affordable combinations, each summing to $80. But which provides the greatest utility for your budget dollar?

Compare, for example, *p* and *m* (*m* is nonaffordable). Since *p* lies inside I_1 while *m* lies on it, *m* is clearly preferred to *p*. Since *b* also lies on I_1, it, too, is preferred to *p*. As far as best choice, then, *p* is out.

But how do you choose between *m* and *b*? Although you are indifferent between them, one is more expensive than the other. Point *m*, lying off to the right of the budget constraint, costs ($5 × 14) + ($10 × 2) = $90. That's $10 more than the ($5 × 8) + ($10 × 4) = $80 cost of *b* on the constraint. In terms

FIGURE A5
Deriving a Point on the Demand Curve
Facing the budget line, the consumer selects a combination of clothes and amusement goods that is preferred to any other affordable combination. Combination *m*, on the same indifference curve as *b*, is nonaffordable. Combination *p*, on the same budget line as *b*, lies below indifference curve I_1, and is less preferred.

The combination that forms tangency *b* represents the most satisfying combination, given the consumer's budget and the set of prices. Point *b* on I_1 records that four units of amusement goods are demanded at a price of $10. That information locates one point on the consumer's demand curve for amusement goods.

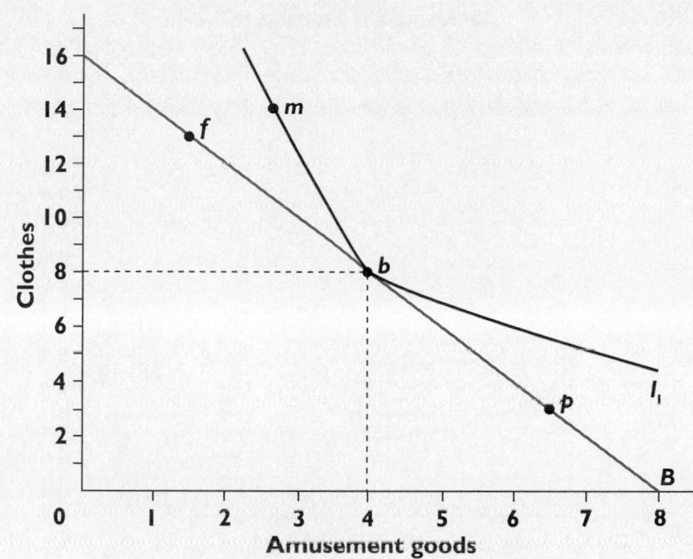

of utility per budget dollar, then, *b* is the best choice. By this same logic, *b* is preferred to *f*.

Think of it this way. Imagine yourself in Figure A5 stepping up to higher indifference curves, one at a time, away from the origin, but still remaining on or within the budget line. How far could you go? You could go only as far as *the indifference curve that is tangent to the budget line.* The point of tangency, then, is your best choice. That's *b*.

Let's transfer this best choice position onto a demand curve. Point *b* tell us that when the price of amusement goods is $10—your income, preferences, and other prices given—the quantity demanded of amusement goods is four units. (*Note:* Point *b* in Figure A5 signals that four units of amusement goods are demanded and eight units of clothes.) This is the first derived price/quantity relationship that makes up the demand curve for amusement goods.

Relating Quantity Demanded to Price

Suppose the price of amusement goods falls from $10 to $5.72. With everything else remaining unchanged, the $80 budget line rotates out from *B* to *B**. Look at Figure A6.

Point *b* in panel *a* is now an interior point to *B**. Given budget line *B**, *b* is no longer your best choice. But what is? The highest utility-yielding indifference curve that still touches the budget constraint *B** is *I**, forming a tangent at *r*. Your highest possible utility-yielding combination now is *r*—six units of amusement goods and nine units of clothes. In other words, when price falls from $10 to $5.72, quantity demanded of amusement goods increases from four to six units.

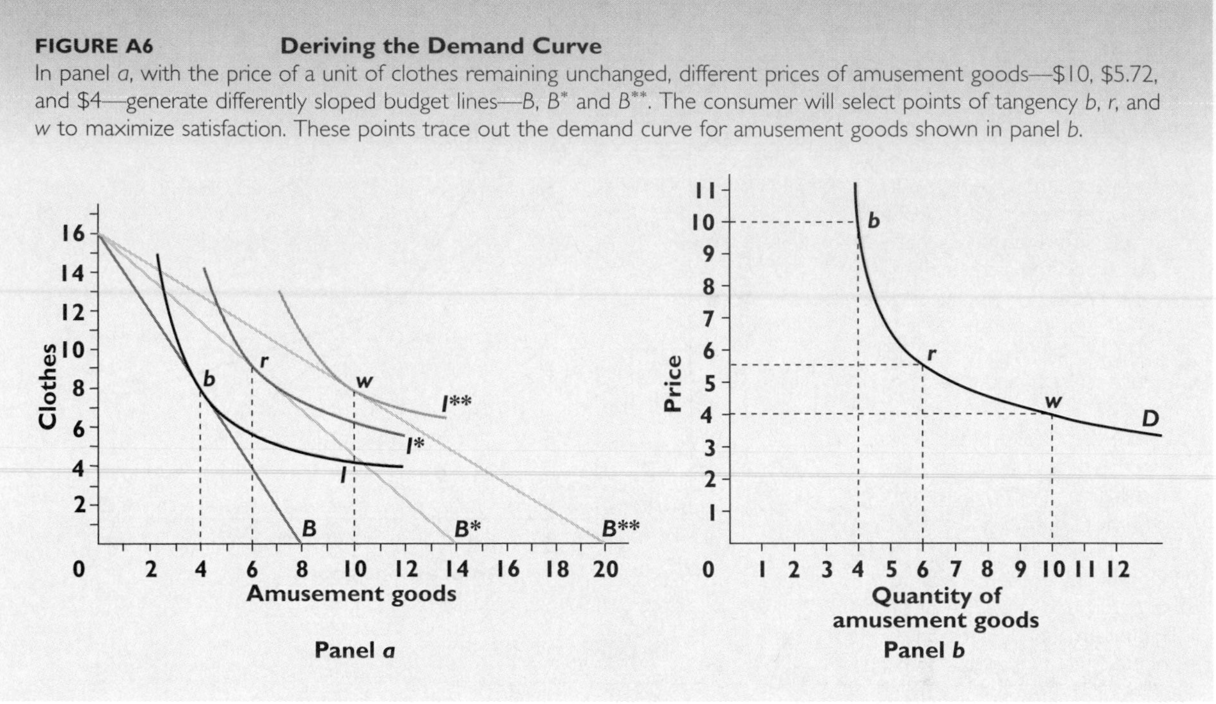

FIGURE A6 Deriving the Demand Curve
In panel *a*, with the price of a unit of clothes remaining unchanged, different prices of amusement goods—\$10, \$5.72, and \$4—generate differently sloped budget lines—*B*, *B** and *B***. The consumer will select points of tangency *b*, *r*, and *w* to maximize satisfaction. These points trace out the demand curve for amusement goods shown in panel *b*.

If price falls to \$4, the budget line rotates to *B*** and the combination chosen is *w*, the new point of tangency between the higher indifference curve *I***, and *B***. The quantity demanded of amusement goods now increases to 10 units.

Panel *b* in Figure A6 transposes these combinations of price and quantity demanded into a demand curve for amusement goods. As you see, with income, preferences, and other prices remaining unchanged, *the quantity demanded increases as price falls*.

Mission accomplished. Demand curves can be generated for any good and for any person by selecting tangency points between indifference curves and budget lines. The need to count utils has been eliminated.

APPENDIX REVIEW

1. The concepts of marginal utility and the counting of utils seem somewhat farfetched. To sidestep the unrealistic character of these concepts, economists have developed another approach to demand derivation based solely on recording consumers' preferences among different sets of goods. Consumers are said to be indifferent among sets of equally preferred goods. Such sets comprise indifference curves.

2. By graphing indifference curves, it is clear that in order to compensate a consumer for the loss of one good, increasing amounts of the second good must be furnished. This is the law of diminishing marginal substitution.

3. An indifference map displays a number of indifference curves. Curves located closer to the origin are associated with less-preferred combinations of goods than are curves located farther away from the origin.

4. A budget constraint represents the choices that are actually available to a consumer. Along a budget constraint, the sum of the prices of goods to be purchased times the quantities of the goods is equal to the income.

5. In a graph of a budget constraint, an increase in income will allow a consumer to purchase more of both types of goods. The budget constraint shifts to the right, given an increase in income.

6. A demand curve can be derived for a good using the indifference curve–budget constraint apparatus. A point on the demand curve is represented by the tangency of the highest indifference curve to the budget constraint. As price is allowed to fall, the intercept of the budget constraint for the good whose price has fallen shifts outward. A consumer can now choose a larger quantity of the good represented by the tangency of another indifference curve to the new budget constraint. Price falls and the quantity demanded increases. The law of demand is supported once again.

QUESTIONS

1. Why are indifference curves called *indifference curves*?

2. What is an indifference map? Why would consumers prefer any combination of two goods on an indifference curve that is farther away from the origin to any other combination of those goods on indifference curves closer to the origin?

3. What is the marginal rate of substitution?

4. Explain why indifference curves are convex to the origin.

5. Explain the significance of the point of tangency between the budget line and an indifference curve.

6. Explain how points of tangency between budget lines and indifference curves create a demand curve.

C H A P T E R 6

PRICE CEILINGS AND PRICE FLOORS

CHAPTER PREVIEW

The types of businesses that are described in this chapter operate in an environment characterized by government intervention. One way that government can influence markets is by setting maximum prices—price ceilings—and minimum prices—price floors. By setting price ceilings and price floors, the government attempts to solve particular problems in certain markets. However, these solutions come with problems of their own.

This chapter highlights two examples in American history where government intervention in markets was particularly dramatic. These were the World War II years, 1941–45, and the agricultural sector of the economy starting with the late 1920s.

After studying this chapter, you should be able to:

- Provide a rationale for government intervention in markets in order to set prices.
- Describe the impact of a price ceiling on a market.
- Discuss the use of price ceilings in markets during World War II.
- Explain how rationing can be used to cope with chronic excess demand.
- Describe the impact of a price floor on a market.

- Discuss how technological success in agricultural markets led to the implementation of price floors.
- Explain what the term *parity pricing* means.
- Distinguish between the old parity system and one based on target prices.
- Give a justification for crop limitation programs.
- Provide evidence to support the claim that the use of price ceilings and price floors is not uncommon but that most prices are market determined.

Have you ever spent a relaxed moment just gazing at the summer midnight sky? If you have (of course you have!), then you've seen that awesome array of hundreds of thousands of brilliant stars suspended in a vast expanse of darkness. If you were particularly lucky, you may even have glimpsed a shooting star cutting across the sky. It's a rare and exciting event. Most nights, the stars just seem to hang there in glittering patterns.

What has all this to do with prices? Each day, hundreds of thousands of prices appear in our markets, each seemingly fixed about an equilibrium point. At any one time, these prices create relative positionings that, like star constellations, appear to be stable. But they really are not. If you were to keep your eyes focused on these prices long enough, chances are you would see some of them shifting out of position.

In fact, the equilibrium prices of most goods continually shift their positions because the demand and supply conditions for those goods are themselves continually shifting. Typically, these price shifts are quite moderate. But there are times when price changes can be sudden and dramatic. Like falling stars, they sometimes seem to shoot right out of the sky.

We cannot control the movement of stars, but our ability and willingness to control prices is quite another matter. In fact, price control—although always an exception to a general rule of allowing markets to determine price—has always played an important role in the functioning of our economic system. This chapter identifies some of the occasions when government has intervened in the market to control prices and examines the economic consequences of such intervention.

THE FISHING ECONOMY, ONCE AGAIN

Consider again our fishing economy in Chapter 3. Recall that every day, weather permitting, fishermen take to their boats, spend the better part of the daylight hours fishing the coastline, and in late afternoon return home to sell their catch.

Some days are good, others less so. Luck and experience have much to do with success. The quantities of fish brought back to market change each day, creating different market-day prices.

This model economy is meant to represent a typical, peaceful community of people going about their honest business, working diligently, earning income, saving some, and spending most on a variety of goods and services, including fish. We probably behave much like these model people.

And like any other group of people living in a productive, peaceful community, they don't really spend too much time thinking about national security

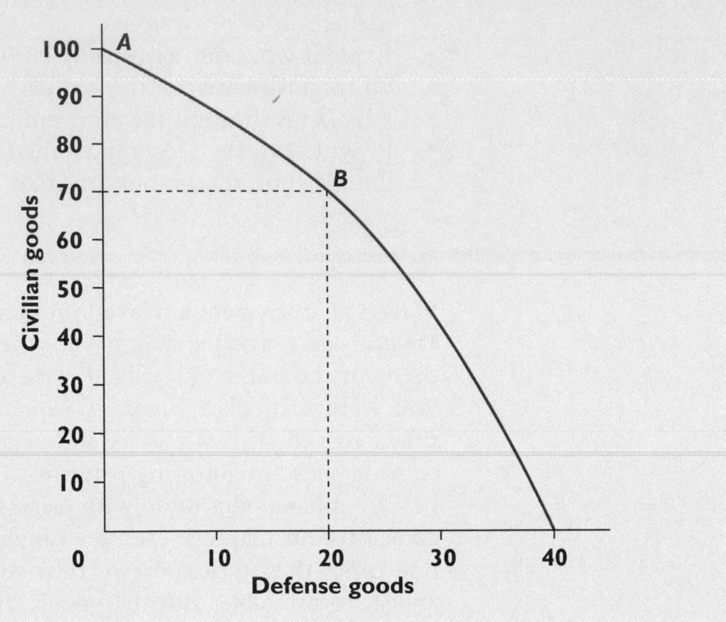

FIGURE 1
Production Possibilities Frontier for Civilian and Defense Goods
The community shifts resources out of civilian production into the production of defense goods. The change is recorded along the PPF from *A* (100 civilian goods and zero defense goods) to *B* (70 civilian goods and 20 defense goods). The opportunity cost of the new 20 defense goods is the 30 civilian goods given up.

issues. After all, why should they? They have been good neighbors and their neighbors have reciprocated. The fishermen have fished in those waters unmolested for generations. No one has ever contested their right to do so.

Now, a National Security Crisis

But let's change that. Suppose their rights to fish the waters are challenged. A neighboring economy decides that those fish-laden waters belong to it. It not only insists on exercising its property rights but threatens our peaceful fishing economy with military force. Out of the blue, there's a national security problem.

How would you expect our fishing economy to respond? Sooner or later it will have to make some hard choices about national security. What can it do? It can mobilize, redirecting some of its resources away from the production of civilian goods to national defense. Such a response to the perceived threat is illustrated in Figure 1.

As shown in Figure 1, the fishing community chooses more defense and fewer civilian goods. The economy shifts from position *A* to position *B* along its production possibilities frontier (PPF). How does it make the shift? One quick way is by drafting people out of civilian occupations, including fishing, into the armed forces.

Mobilizing Fishermen

How would such an armed forces mobilization affect the fishing industry? Fishermen, like everyone else in the economy, would be subject to the draft. One day they're busy fishing, the next day they're on a bus headed for boot camp. Obviously, fewer fishing boats would be out on the water. And, consequently, fewer fish would be supplied.

FIGURE 2 **The Fish Market Before and After the Draft**

In the predraft fish market of panel *a*, demand and supply curves intersect at an equilibrium price of $4 and a quantity demanded and supplied of 10,000. In the postdraft market of panel *b*, the supply curve decreases from *S* to *S'*, raising the equilibrium price from $4 to $10 and lowering the quantity demanded and supplied from 10,000 to 7,000.

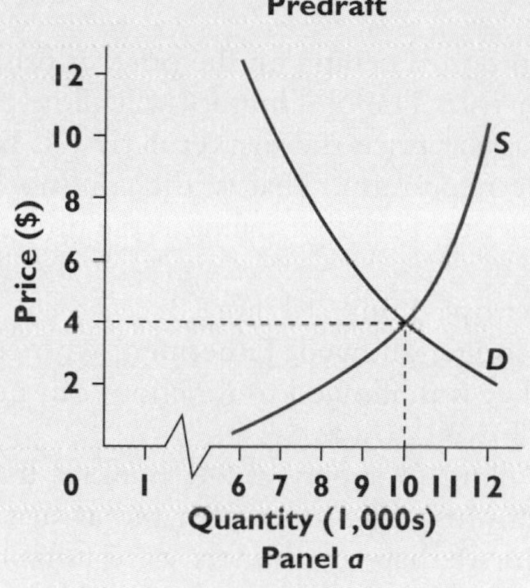

Panel *a*

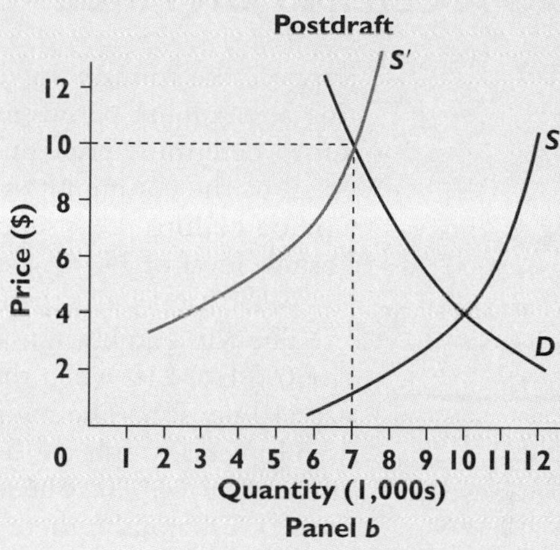

Panel *b*

Panels *a* and *b* in Figure 2 compare the predraft and postdraft conditions in the fish market.

Would the draft affect the economy's demand for fish? Not really. After all, people's tastes for fish don't change just because there's a national security problem. Think about your own demand schedules. Note that the demand curves in panels *a* and *b* are drawn identically.

But what about supply? With fewer boats on the water, the supply curve naturally would shift to the left. That's exactly what we see in panel *b*. We also see that the shift in the supply curve drives the equilibrium price from $4 to $10. And look what happens to the quantity bought and sold. It falls from 10,000 to 7,000 fish. That's a very large impact.

Who Can Afford a $10 Fish?

Obviously, fewer people will be eating fish. A $10 fish, by anyone's count, is an expensive meal. Those with low incomes cannot afford fish at all. They may have had a few fish meals in the predraft days, but at $10 a fish, it becomes unthinkable. The richer people in the economy are still in the market, buying perhaps fewer fish at $10 than they would have in the predraft days. The very rich, on the other hand, if they bought fish before, would buy them still.

In other words, the threat to the economy's security is felt differently by different people. The mobilization of the fishermen into the military means the community has to sacrifice some civilian goods to attend properly to its security needs. But not all citizens sacrifice to the same degree. The poor go fishless. The rich hardly notice the difference.

Is this fair? Should the burden fall disproportionately upon the poor? Suppose some people in the fishing economy find the unequally shared burden both unfair and unacceptable. What can they do about it? The answer is that there is nothing sacred about equilibrium prices. There is no reason in the world why the community has to live with a $10 fish. There are, as we saw in Chapter 3, compelling economic reasons why equilibrium prices are desirable, but there may be compelling *noneconomic* reasons to reject them as well.

SETTING A CEILING ON PRICE

Price ceiling

A maximum price set by government below the market-generated equilibrium price.

Our fishing community made the political decision that the $10 market price for a fish was not sacred. The community simply set a ceiling price of $4 for fish.

Suppose the community decides to impose a ceiling on the price of fish, by setting a maximum permissible price for fish. The community will allow the market to determine price only as long as the price the market derives is below or equal to the community's permissible maximum. That is, the community fixes a **price ceiling.** Let's suppose it decides to set such a ceiling at the predraft equilibrium level of $4.

What happens to the fish market now? Look at Figure 3.

The $10 equilibrium price is no longer allowed. Fishermen, who could sell 7,000 fish at $10 when the free market was allowed to function, can no longer get $10 per fish. The highest price allowed now is $4.

How many fish are fishermen willing to supply at $4? Look at the supply curve. Only 4,000. But see how many fish consumers demand at that price—10,000. Obviously, there's a problem. Perhaps consumers were initially happy to learn that the price was limited to $4, but what's the good of a $4 fish if there aren't many available? As you see, there's an unsatisfied, excess demand of 6,000 fish.

Let's not lose sight of why there are too few fish. The problem was created by drafting fishermen off their boats. Fewer fishermen mean fewer fish. Allowing price to rise to $10 doesn't create more fish. Nor are more fish created by imposing a price ceiling at the old equilibrium price. In fact, the price ceiling merely transforms the problem from living with an intolerable $10 equilibrium price to living with chronic excess demand at $4 per fish.

Living with Chronic Excess Demand

How would you go about rationing the 4,000 fish supplied at the $4 price ceiling when the quantity demanded at that price is 10,000? One practical way is

FIGURE 3
Setting a $4 Price Ceiling in the Fish Market
The postdraft supply curve, *S′* and the demand curve generate a $10 equilibrium price, and 7,000 fish are demanded and supplied. Allowing a price ceiling of $4 to substitute for the $10 equilibrium price, the quantity demanded is 10,000 fish, but the quantity supplied falls to 4,000, creating an excess demand in the market for 6,000 fish.

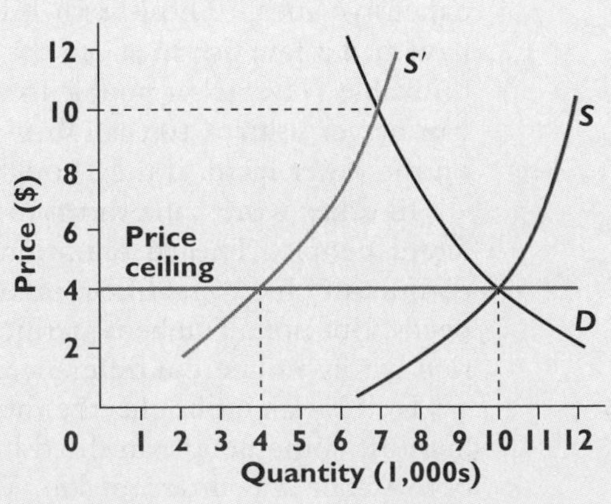

If you were a teenager growing up in the 1940s—during World War II—you would have loved to get your hands on one of these. After all, gasoline was strictly rationed and you would have had no easy access to the family car. Gasoline was rationed by purpose. Cars designated as business vehicles received more gas ration coupons than did family cars.

Ration coupon

A coupon issued by the government entitling the holder to purchase a specific quantity of a good at or below the price ceiling.

The political decision to impose a price ceiling substituted one economic problem for another—the high price for fish was replaced by chronic excess demand.

for the community to print up 4,000 **ration coupons,** each one entitling the coupon holder to buy a $4 fish. The quantity of coupons printed matches the quantity of fish supplied.

But who gets the coupons? What criteria should be used? First come, first served? Imagine consumers' reactions! The 4,000 fish would be gobbled up by the few enterprising early risers. But are they the most deserving? What about distributing the 4,000 coupons by lottery? Chance dictates who gets the coupons. But why leave distribution to chance? Perhaps priority should be given to the elderly. If equity were a criterion, perhaps the distribution should be made among households according to family size. Or to households according to how many persons in the households serve in the military. There is no end to rationing schemes. The only one excluded is the scheme that rations fish to those willing to pay the highest price.

Price Ceilings and Ration Coupons During World War II

The fish story is not too far fetched. The idea of society opting for price ceilings and ration coupons instead of market pricing during periods of national crisis is part of our economic history. In August 1941, President Franklin D. Roosevelt established the Office of Price Administration (OPA), which was given the power to control prices. Why? At that time, when war seemed inevitable, Congress and the administration believed that some form of control over strategic raw materials was essential.

The economy had already mobilized for the war effort. Men, women, and materials were shifted out of civilian pursuits and redirected to military preparedness. Steel, rubber, and petroleum were desperately needed for the production and deployment of aircraft, tanks, and ships. Fats and oils were critical raw materials used in the manufacture of munitions. It was obvious that the new and considerable demands for such raw materials would play havoc with their market prices and, as a result, play havoc with the distribution of these goods among consumers.

What did the government do? On January 5, 1942, within a month after our entry into the war, OPA introduced the rationing system. It was first applied to rubber tires. Shortly after, in May, gasoline was rationed on the East Coast and by the year's end the rationing was extended across the nation. Fuel oil rationing began in the fall of 1942 on the East Coast and became nationwide by the end of 1943.

Other consumer goods also came under OPA price control. The first of the basic foods to come under control were sugar and coffee. Our traditional sugar suppliers—Philippines, Hawaii, and Cuba—were unable to provide adequate quantities because of the increased difficulty of ocean transportation. In May 1942, to avoid the expected soaring of sugar prices, OPA imposed a price ceiling and issued sugar ration coupons to consumers.

By March 1, 1943, prices on foodstuffs such as canned, bottled, frozen, and dried vegetables, fruits, juices, and soups were under OPA control. In fact, by June 1, 1943, price ceilings and rationing affected 95 percent of our nation's food supply. It was a complicated set of price controls. Over 1,000 price ceilings had been placed on grocery items in over 200 cities.

Price ceilings were applied as well to manufactured goods. Back in February 1942, 35 percent of wholesale prices on these items were formally brought under OPA supervision. By mid-October, the system was extended to cover 90 percent of wholesale prices. Because of the almost complete halt in residential housing construction during the war, OPA froze rents in over 450 designated areas. By the war's end, most of our agriculture, manufacturing, and housing markets were under some form of price control.

Did It Work?

Wouldn't you think that implementing such a widespread price control system in such a short period of time under such supply-related pressure would create problems? At best, the task was exceedingly difficult. In some instances, it was next to impossible. As price ceilings were extended throughout the economy, the pressures of excess demand built up dramatically.

How do economists, looking back at the war years, assess OPA's price control policy? As you would expect, reactions range from highly supportive to highly critical. Many economists critical of the effort argue that OPA's price ceiling and rationing cure turned out to be worse than the high equilibrium price disease.

Draw a graph to represent the housing market under rent controls to show the effect of a long-run decrease in the supply of rental housing.

Rent control

Government-set price ceilings on rent.

To make their point, critics cite the distortions created in the housing market. Intentions aside, **rent control,** they argue, was counterproductive. Price ceilings on rent dampened landlords' incentives to properly maintain their existing rental units and discouraged many from investing in new construction. In other words, rent ceilings actually made the housing shortages worse. They decreased the supply of housing in both the short run and the long run.

Critics of rent ceilings would have handled the housing shortage by allowing the market to determine rent and by compensating the low-income renters with rent subsidies. At least such a policy, they insist, avoids the distortions of resource allocation that rent controls generate.

But price ceiling advocates are also persuasive. They argue that market-determined rents coupled with rent subsidies *still* create distortions. After all, the rent subsidies would have had to be financed by some form of taxes, and raising taxes to pay for these subsidies would alter, in some way, what people consume and produce.

Moreover, the kinds of bureaucratic problems involved in deciding who should and who shouldn't receive rent subsidies or whose taxes should be raised might be as distorting as the kinds of problems associated with the administration of rent control.

In retrospect, the decision to create OPA and accept price ceilings and rationing as a policy response to the unavoidable shift from civilian to military production during the war years was, at least, understandable. *If the objective was survival, we survived.* We muddled through the war with chronic excess demand. However uneven our compliance was and however many abuses were created, the population generally accepted the difficulty, the necessity, and the effort involved in putting aside, temporarily, market-determined equilibrium prices for most goods.

THERE'S ALSO REASON FOR PRICE FLOORS

Price floor

A minimum price set by government above the market-generated equilibrium price.

Price ceilings are imposed as alternatives to equilibrium prices "shooting sky-high." But equilibrium prices, for other reasons, can just as well "drop through the floor." And just as unusually high prices are thought to be unacceptable, so too are some unusually low prices. Too low prices are prevented by setting a *minimum* permissible level. That is, the equilibrium market price is allowed only as long as it is above or equal to an established **price floor.**

Imagine again our fishing economy. But this time, rather than a military threat problem, the issue is too much of a good thing. Let's suppose our fishermen are riding a wave of good luck. The weather cooperates, and a new technology is adopted by all the fishermen, producing for each a sizable increase in catch.

The result? The supply curve shifts dramatically outward. Look at Figure 4.

The equilibrium price falls to \$2 and the quantity demanded and supplied increases to 12,000 fish. Fishermen aren't too happy. Look what happens to their revenues. In the old days before the new technology was used, 10,000 fish were

FIGURE 4
Effect of New Technology on the Fish Market
The adoption of new technology shifts the supply curve in the fish market from S to S'. The equilibrium price falls from \$4 to \$2 and the quantity demanded and supplied increases to 12,000.

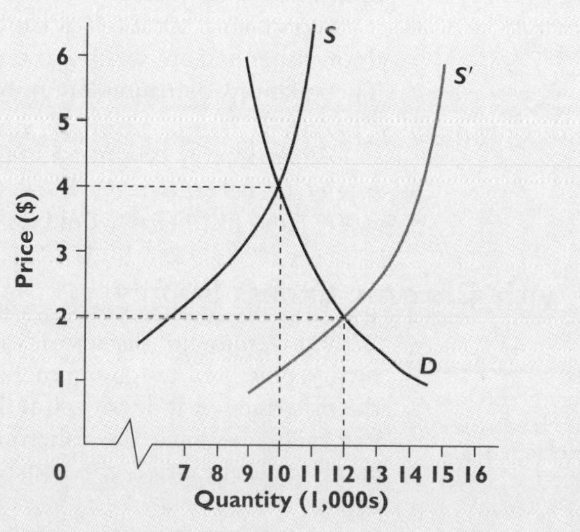

FIGURE 5
Setting a $4 Price Floor in the Fish Market
The posttechnological supply curve, S' and the demand curve intersect at a $2 equilibrium price. Twelve thousand fish are demanded and supplied. Substituting a price floor of $4 for the $2 equilibrium price, the quantity demanded is 10,000 and the quantity supplied is 15,000, creating an excess supply on the market of 5,000 fish.

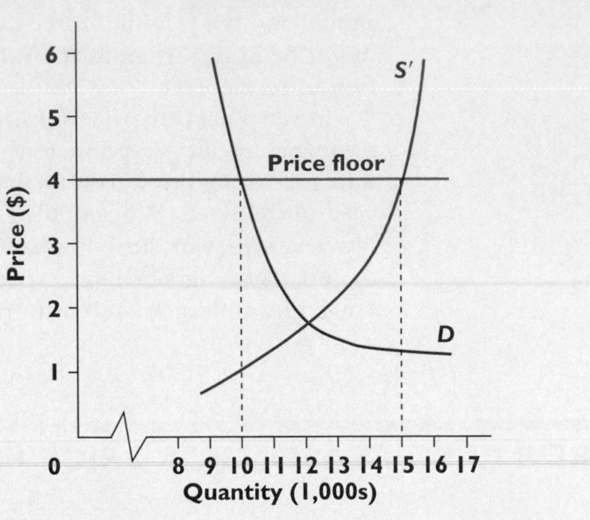

sold at an equilibrium price of $4. The fisherman took home $40,000. Now, with their supply curve shifting from *S* to *S*′, their new revenue is $2 × 12,000 = $24,000. For the fishermen, it's economic disaster. Consumers, on the other hand, are not at all disturbed by the course of events. They pay less and consume more.

Setting a Floor on Price

Fishermen have worked themselves into an uncomfortable position. They can't undo the new technology. There's no retreating to the old way of doing things. They are stuck with the demand and supply conditions of Figure 4. But they can modify its consequences. How?

Again, a political decision is made that there is nothing sacred about the market price for fish—this time, a price that is perceived to be too low.

One way they can overcome the misfortune of being so productive is to abandon equilibrium prices. Just as price ceilings were introduced before as an alternative to the $10 fish, so the community can now introduce some minimum limit to how far prices will be permitted to fall.

Suppose it is set at $4. What happens now? Look at Figure 5. At the $4 price floor, fishermen are willing to supply 15,000 fish. But look at the demand curve. The quantity demanded is only 10,000. Now an *excess supply* of 5,000 fish emerges.

What do you do with 5,000 extra fish? Someone has to absorb this excess supply or fishermen get stuck again. Let's suppose government buys up the 5,000 extra fish. That would do the trick.

Living with Chronic Excess Supply

The problem of too low a price for fish is replaced with the problem of a chronic excess supply of fish.

Why government? Because it's essentially a societal matter. Either the community, represented by government, agrees to support the economic well-being of the fishermen or it doesn't. If it does, government buys the extra fish. That is, the taxpayers lose what the fishermen gain. If the decision is to allow the market alone to dictate price, the taxpayers enjoy lower prices at the expense of fishermen.

Suppose the government decides to protect the fishermen. What could it do with the 5,000 excess fish? One option would be to freeze and store them. Perhaps tomorrow's supply curve will shift to the left, driving future equilibrium prices above the price floor. The government then could release the surplus fish—sell the supply back to the market—to keep future prices from rising much above the $4 target.

A less-complicated option would be to simply dump the excess supply back into the water. Or, it can always be ground up and used as fertilizer. Or, the government can ship it overseas as economic aid. Maybe a new technology can convert the excess fish into an energy source! Actually, there's no want of ideas. You could probably think of a few yourself.

AGRICULTURE'S TECHNOLOGICAL REVOLUTION

We don't have to look too far into our economic history to reproduce the fishing scenario. Agriculture, at least during the last half century, has produced a record of overwhelming productive success. The source of its success is traced out in Figure 6.

FIGURE 6 **Growth of U.S. Agricultural Productivity Throughout U.S. History**
Changes in the dominant energy source technology used on farms, from handpower to horsepower to mechanical power and finally to science power, have generated notable increases in agricultural productivity. The major upward thrust came with the advent of mechanical power during the interwar period (1919–1939), and even more so with the application of new fertilizers, pesticides, and other scientific advances after World War II. These factors more than doubled the growth rate of agricultural productivity from the 1940s to the 1980s.

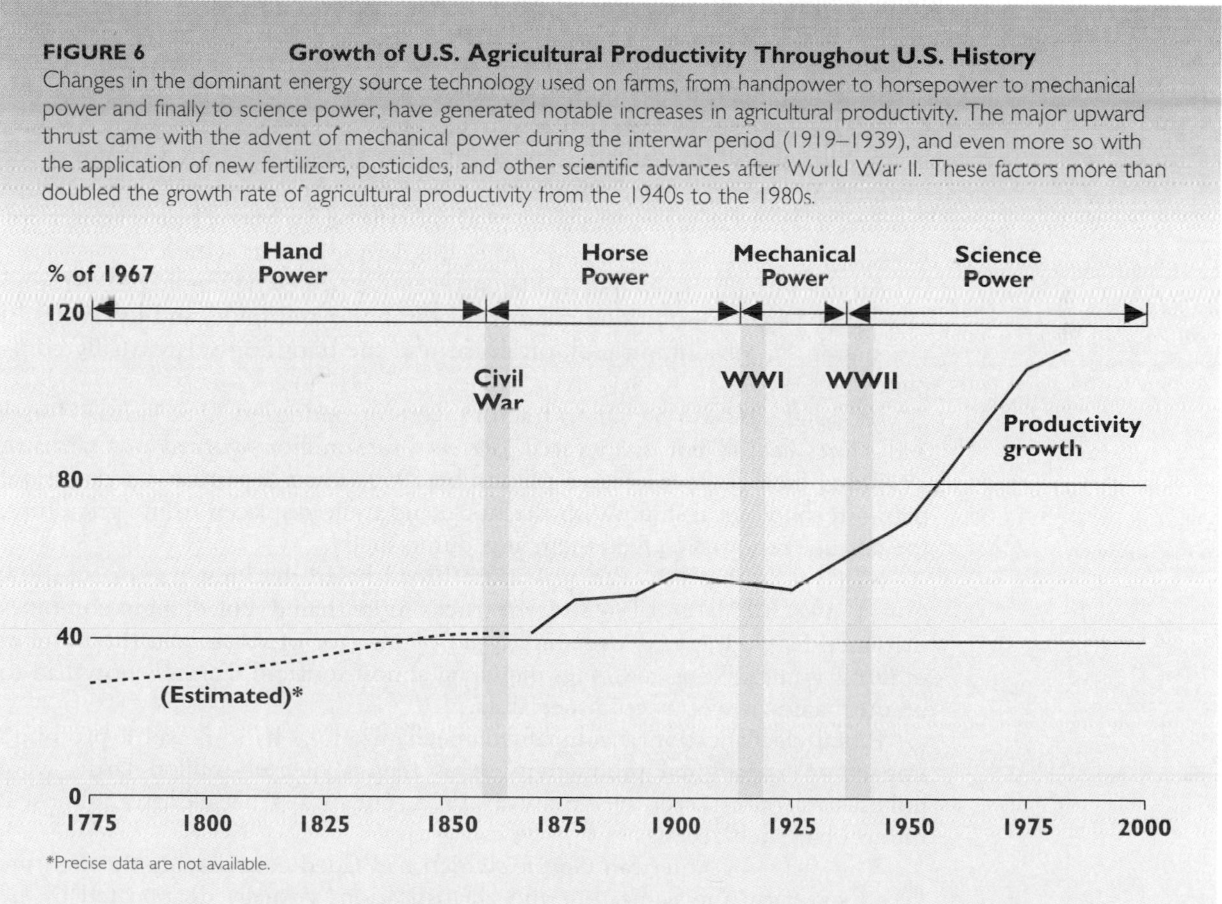

Source: Zelner, James and Lamm, R. M., "Agriculture's Vital Role for Us All," *Food—From Farm To Table, 1982 Yearbook of Agriculture*, Department of Agriculture, Washington, D. C., p. 3.

Environmental hazards aside, crop dusting was not only a thrilling sight to behold—crop duster pilots could just about drop their load on a dime—but it provided a quick and effective delivery system of insecticides, pesticides, and chemical fertilizers that bolstered agricultural productivity.

Note the dramatic take-off after World War I and the distinct shifts in technologies that accompany the years since then. The conversion from human and animal power to mechanical and scientific power separates most of the past century from the earlier 150 years of American agriculture.

But, as with our troubled fishermen and their new technology, the advent of modern agriculture was both good and bad news for the farmer. Productivity soared, but farmers' incomes collapsed. The story is worth telling, partly because it provides us with another example of price controls substituting for free-market equilibrium prices. But it's also a very human story of our ingenuity in creating a system that provides more and more food for an ever increasing population—but creating, at the same time, the demise of that system.

American farmers always have been receptive to new technologies. Around 1920 they began to substitute tractors for the horse and mule, and by 1960, 40 years after the substitution took off in earnest, the transition was virtually complete.

By 1960, close to 5 million tractors were operating on U.S. farms. Horses and mules had all but disappeared. Twenty-five million worked our farms in 1917, but there were less than 5 million by 1960. Their departure signaled more than a technological shift. With the horse and mule displaced from agriculture, the acreage required to feed them also diminished.

Mechanization, however, was more broad-based than just tractor substitution. Between 1910 and 1960, motor trucks more than doubled, grain combines increased fivefold, corn pickers increased by a factor of seven, and the number of farms using milking machines increased almost fourfold. Farmers now had to be mechanics as well as crop specialists.

Rural electrification accompanied mechanization. It, too, had a profound impact on agricultural productivity. Less than a quarter million farms were linked to central-station electricity in 1925, but only a decade later, almost 2 million had such access.

The image of American Gothic, which had faded considerably through the decades of farm mechanization and electrification, virtually disappeared in the petroleum age after World War II.

New chemical insecticides, soil fumigants, weed killers, fertilizers, plant and animal disease inhibitors, defoliants, crop ripeners, and food preservatives—all

ADDED PERSPECTIVE

Substitute Japanese Farmers for American Farmers and Rice for Corn: The Economics is the Same

Five out of six of Japan's 3 million commercial farmers till plots of an average size of 1.2 hectares (three acres). Britain's average farm is 60 times that size, and America's 150 times. But Japan's 2.5 million part-time farmers have started leaving the land in droves. Most of them are aged 60 or so, the usual retirement age in Japan. Within a decade, half of them will be dead from hard work and old age. Brutal though it sounds, this is leaving the 470,000 hard-core professional farmers with more land to lease. Average field sizes are rising dramatically, bringing substantial improvements in productivity.

The government has been quietly nudging along these demographic developments. Since 1986, professional farmers have been given incentives to use combine harvesters and other machinery to transplant five rows of rice plants at a time. Crop rotation—from rice to wheat, barley, and soybeans—has also been encouraged. The aim is to reduce the cost of growing rice by 40 to 60 percent by 1995. The target is not unrealistic.

Suddenly, the unthinkable has happened: Regions that grow inferior rice are finding no one wants their produce—least of all the government agency. Meanwhile, the tasty Koshihikari rice from Niigata and the cheaper Akita-komachi variety from Akita are proving hugely popular. With the beginnings of a free market for rice, price differentials are encouraging growers to become innovative as well as selective. Some have started growing the long-grained Indica variety used in Chinese and Indian cooking. Kirin, a beer company, which entered the rice-growing business in 1988, is expecting Japan's Indica harvest to be 10 times bigger this autumn than last.

Discussion

Japanese rice farmers are facing the same kind of economic future that American corn farmers faced. Graph their story (demand and supply curves).

Source: "Here Comes Farmer Giles-san," *The Economist*, June 8, 1991.

petrochemical based—were mass produced and mass marketed to further increase farm productivity.

Modern chemistry developed nitrogen, phosphorus, and potassium fertilizers. The use of chemical fertilizers, for example, doubled between 1910 and 1940, doubled again between 1940 and 1950, and doubled once more between 1950 and 1970. The quantities applied per acre increased fivefold from 1950 to 1980.

To take full advantage of these farm technologies, farmers increased the size of their farms. They expanded farm acreage by buying out neighbors or by negotiating leases with them. Farms were becoming bigger and they were becoming fewer. The dramatic shift in farm size and number of farms is shown in Figure 7.

The number of farms peaked at 6.8 million in 1935. A decade later, it had fallen to 5.9 million. As Figure 7 shows, the decline continued virtually uninterrupted to fewer than 2.3 million farms by 1990. On the other hand, the size of the surviving farms grew steadily. Average size in 1935 was 155 acres. A decade later, it rose to 195 acres, and by 1990 had reached 456 acres.

THE EFFECT OF TECHNOLOGICAL CHANGE ON AGRICULTURAL SUPPLY

The radical conversion of the farm to mechanization and chemistry made the agricultural sector one of the most productive in the 20th century. As Table 1 shows, productivity per acre accelerated dramatically after World War II.

FIGURE 7 Number and Size of U.S. Farms: 1945–1990
The decline in the number of farms continued virtually uninterrupted from 6.81 million in 1935 to less than 2.3 million by 1990. During this period, the average size of the surviving farms grew from 155 to 456 acres.

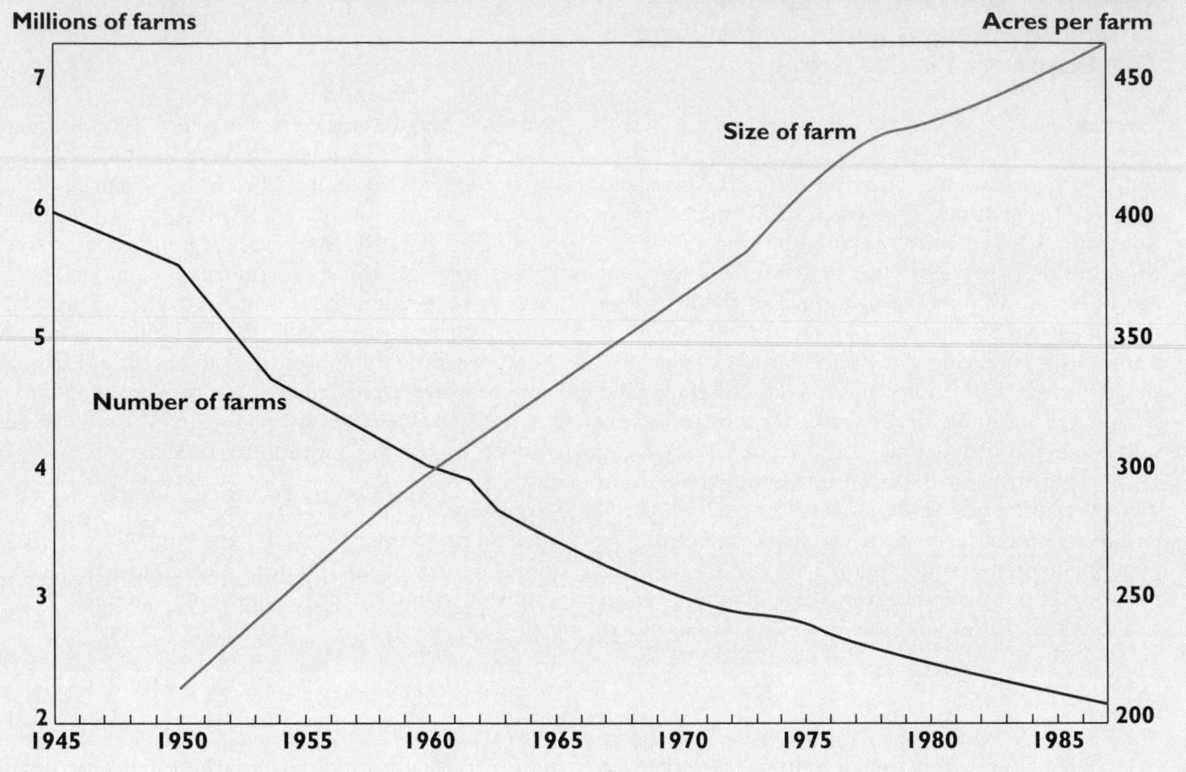

Source: *Public Policy and the Changing Structure of American Agriculture,* Congressional Budget Office, The Congress of the United States, Washington, D. C., September 1978, p. 2; *Statistical Abstract of the United States, 1994,* Department of Commerce, Washington, D. C., p. 667.

By the 1980s, the combination of mechanization and chemical fertilization had more than tripled the yield per acre in corn, tripled the yield per acre in cotton, and almost tripled the yield per acre in wheat. This increase in yield per acre more than compensated for the decline in the number of farms. The total output of agricultural goods increased considerably. Table 2 records the changes in output.

Total farm output, including crops and livestock products, more than dou-

TABLE 1 Yields of Selected Farm Products 1910–14 to 1988

	Corn (bu/acre)	Wheat (bu/acre)	Cotton (lbs/acre)
1988	85	39	600
1964–68	73	27	506
1935–39	26	13	226
1910–14	26	14	201

Source: Schultze, Charles, *The Distribution of Farm Subsidies: Who Gets The Benefits,* The Brookings Institution, Washington, D. C., 1971, p. 5; *Statistical Abstract of the United States, 1990,* Department of Commerce, Washington, D. C., p. 660.

TABLE 2
Indexes of Total Farm Output: 1940–1990 (1977 = 100)

	Total Farm Output	Total Crop Output
1990	119	114
1980	104	101
1970	84	77
1960	76	72
1950	61	59
1940	50	55

Source: *Historical Statistics of the United States: Colonial Times to 1970: Part I*, Bicentennial Edition, Bureau of the Census, U.S. Department of Commerce, Series K, pp. 414–29, 498–99; *Economic Report of the President, 1992*, Washington, D. C., p. 406.

bled between 1940 and 1990. Total crop output of grains, forage, fruits and vegetables, sugar, cotton, tobacco, and oil more than doubled as well.

Figure 8 translates the effects of long-run technological improvement into the familiar shift to the right of the economy's supply curve of farm goods. As you see, the supply curve keeps shifting farther and farther to the right, representing the ability and willingness of farmers to supply much greater quantities at every price.

Unfortunately, the demand for farm goods output simply couldn't keep pace with the farmers' supply. The long-run impact on equilibrium price became abundantly clear and distressing.

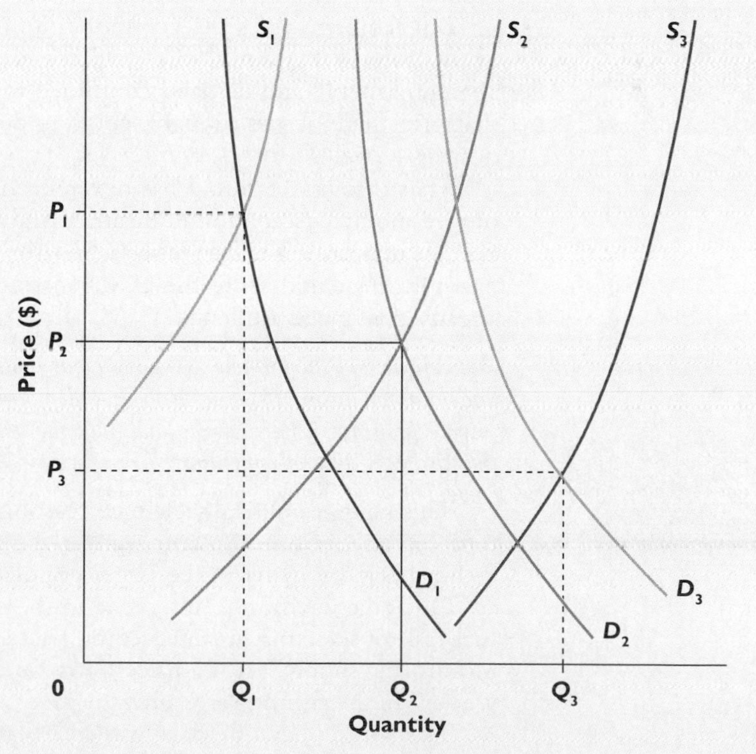

FIGURE 8
Effects of New Technology in Farming
Shifts in the supply of farm goods, from S_1 to S_2 through to S_3, reflecting the new technologies in energy source and modern chemistry, creates price movements from P_1 to P_3. Quantities demanded and supplied increase from Q_1 to Q_3.

But what could farmers do? Go back to horses and mules? Cut out electricity? Discard chemistry? Forget mechanization? Revert to smaller farms? Even if they wanted to, they couldn't. American agriculture seemed to be forever stuck with its incredible productive capacity.

TO INTERVENE OR NOT TO INTERVENE: THAT IS THE QUESTION

To many farmers, this long-term troublesome condition was both unavoidable and unacceptable. Many responded by simply leaving their farms. In the thirty years from 1960 to 1990, farm population declined from over 15 million to 4.5 million. But even this extensive decline did not stop the steady shift to the right of the supply curve. Too many farmers were still producing too many farm goods to generate tolerable incomes for themselves.

The issue was clear enough. Either permit the free market and its harsh consequences to prevail, or rely upon nonmarket strategies to solve the problem of low farm incomes. In 1933, *the choice was made to intervene.*

Many considerations persuaded people in private and public life to support intervention. The combination of high productivity yields and low price and income elasticities of demand for farm goods guaranteed the continuing depression of farm incomes.

Had agriculture not been as significant an industry as it was, affecting so many people directly, the choice might have been different. After all, technological change always involves some unpleasant consequences for some people. If government intervened to redress every economic injury, equilibrium pricing would be an endangered species.

But farming drives the economic life of whole regions of the country, and even more so back in 1933. And the damage could spread. If the forces of changing supply and demand continued to depress prices in the farm economy, that price slide, it was thought, could undermine the vitality of the nonfarm industries as well.

That is to say, farming has never been regarded as just another industry in our economy. Its economic health has always been thought to have very important noneconomic dimensions. Senator Joseph O'Mahoney of Wyoming, for example, in an address to the U.S. Senate on January 5, 1942, put the case to an already convinced audience:

Agriculture and the farmers today represent practically the only bond between this country and totalitarianism. If we wish to save democracy, if we want to save the institutions of private property, if we desire to maintain the basis of free individual life, we must prevent the further decline of agriculture.

This kind of politically charged reasoning prevailed in Congress even among representatives from nonfarm regions. To a large extent, it reflected as well the feelings held by many in the larger population.

Once the decision to intervene in the agricultural market was made, the actual task of selecting an intervening strategy became incidental. Techniques of monitoring supply, setting price floors, and handling the excess supply were, as we saw in the fishing case, after the fact.

The farm policy objective was clearly mandated by Congress in 1933. It was to buttress farm incomes above what the market would have provided. *But to what level?*

PARITY PRICING AS A PRICE FLOOR

There are a number of ways to buttress farm incomes. One quick way is simply to give farmers income subsidies. For example, if the goal is to assure farmers that their annual income will not fall below \$25,000, then for those who sell their farm goods at equilibrium prices and earn less than \$25,000, the government just makes up the difference. If equilibrium prices fall, then income subsidies rise. If we chose to raise the minimum acceptable income level higher than \$25,000, subsidies would be greater.

Another way to buttress farm income is by working on farm prices directly. By substituting price floors for market-determined equilibrium prices, farm incomes can be anything we choose.

The Invention of Parity Pricing

The intent of parity pricing is to maintain farmers' purchasing power relative to nonfarmers' purchasing power.

But how do we go about picking a specific price floor? Why one and not another? What criteria make sense? Many ideas floated about, but the one that stuck in 1933 when Congress passed the Agricultural Adjustment Act was parity pricing. This means simply that farmers "deserve" to get for their bushel of wheat the same value that their fathers and grandfathers got for theirs. It's really quite simple.

Parity pricing asks for a parity, or equality, between the prices farmers have to pay for the goods they buy and the prices they get for the goods they sell. Because farm prices have fallen rather dramatically relative to nonfarm prices, farmers buying nonfarm goods with a bushel of wheat find that as time goes by, they can buy fewer and fewer nonfarm goods with that bushel. The idea of parity pricing, then, was to restore for farmers a parity between farm and nonfarm prices.

The period selected as the benchmark for parity pricing was 1910–14 because farmers believed that this period represented a set of farm and nonfarm prices that traded "equal value for equal value." It seemed to reflect for them an ideal exchange standard. For example, if the market price of corn were \$2 per bushel in 1910–14 and the price of a pair of shoes were also \$2, then farmers could buy a pair of shoes with their bushel of corn. That exchange seemed reasonable. But see what happens in the hypothetical case of Figure 9.

The 1910–14 supply and demand curves for shoes and corn generate for both an equilibrium price of \$2. But look what happens 50 years later. In the shoe market, the demand for shoes shifts from D_1 to D_2, raising the price from \$2 to \$4. On the other hand, in the corn market the shift in the supply curve from S_1 to S_2 lowers the price of corn from \$2 to \$1. Left to the dictates of the market, the farmer in 1964 now finds that he needs to exchange four bushels to buy what his grandfather bought with one. The farmer's lot seemed better in 1910–14.

To restore parity, the government would intervene in the corn market by setting a price floor for corn at \$4. Figure 10 illustrates the economic consequences.

FIGURE 9 **Shoes and Corn: Shifts in Demand and Supply, 1914–64**

In both the 1914 shoe and corn markets, the supply and demand curves—S and D_1 in panel *a* and D and S_1 in panel *b*—generate a $2 equilibrium price for both shoes and corn. Fifty years later, the demand for shoes increases from D_1 to D_2 in panel *a*, raising price from $2 to $4. During the same period, technological change in the farm industry shifts the supply curve of corn from S_1 to S_2 in panel *b*, reducing the price of corn from $2 to $1.

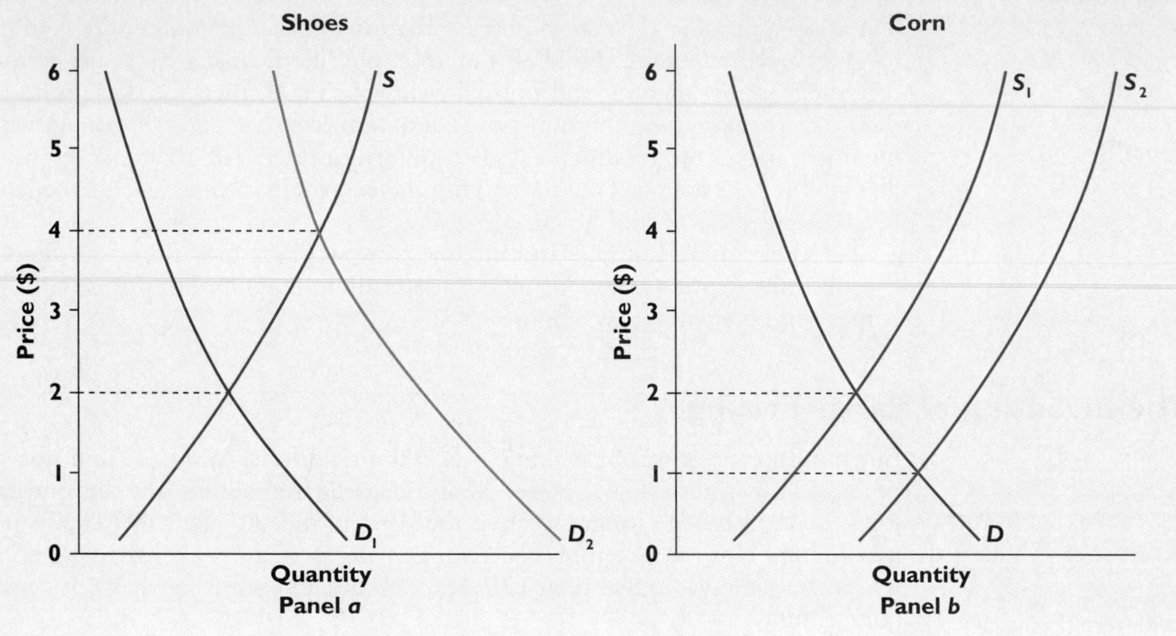

The forces of supply and demand in the corn market generate 110 million bushels demanded and supplied at an equilibrium price of $1. If a $4 price floor is imposed on the market, the quantity supplied by farmers increases from 110 million bushels to 135 million. Consumers, facing the $4 floor price, now take only 85 million off the market. Farmers soon discover that they are left with an excess supply of 50 million bushels. How can they dispose of it? The government buys it up.

Of course, the government may decide not to provide *complete* parity. It could, instead, design a price floor that offers farmers, say, 80 percent of parity. In this case, the price floor is established at $3.20, not $4. At that price, farmers supply 130 million bushels and consumer buy 90 million bushels. The excess supply is thus reduced to only 40 million bushels. Of course, the farmer, then, gets only 80 percent of the pair of shoes his grandfather got with the bushel of corn.

If the government fixed parity at 50 percent, the price floor would fall to $2. But excess supply would again be reduced. As you see, once the market price is abandoned and a price floor established, the price farmers get is subject to political determination—unless of course, the market price is above the price floor.

Deriving Parity Price Ratios

Farmers buy more than just pairs of shoes. The parity price, then, should express the ratio between an index of the prices farmers receive for their goods and the index of prices of goods that farmers buy.

FIGURE 10
Impact of Parity Pricing on Quantities of Corn Demanded and Supplied
The demand and supply curves generate a $1 equilibrium price. The quantity demanded and supplied is 110 million bushels. The government-designed price floor of $4 for corn restores the exchange parity between shoes and corn, but the quantity demanded falls to 85 million bushels while the quantity of corn supplied increases to 135 million. An excess supply of 50 million bushels is created. With 80 percent parity, the price floor drops to $4 × .8 = $3.20. At that price, the quantity supplied is 130 million bushels and the quantity demanded is 90 million bushels. Excess supply becomes 40 million bushels.

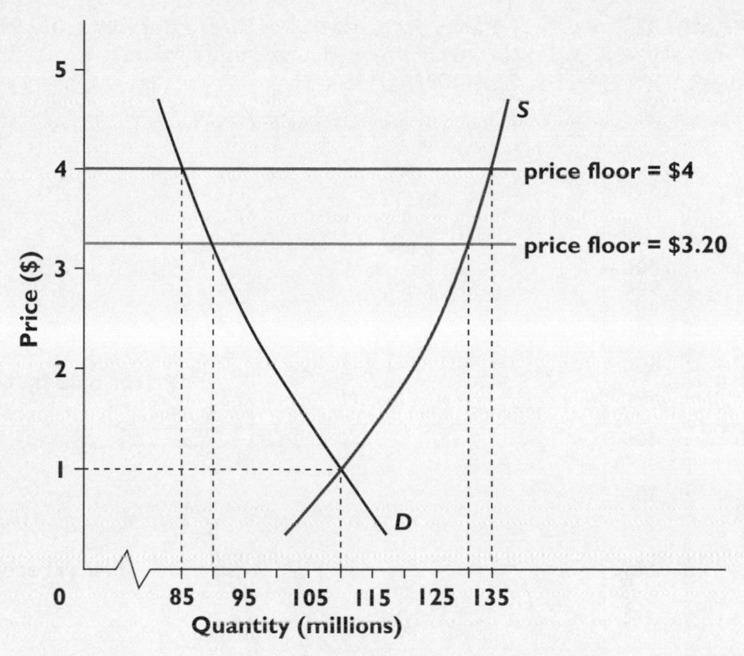

$$\text{Parity price ratio} = \frac{\text{Prices received by farmers}}{\text{Prices paid by farmers}}$$

Parity price ratio
The relationship between prices received by farmers and prices paid by farmers.

Figure 11 traces the persistent downward movement of the **parity price ratio** since 1910.

It isn't hard to spot the "good years." Between 1910 and 1920, the parity price ratio was approximately 100. That is, farm prices were about as firm as nonfarm prices. Note how severely the depression years of the 1930s hit the farmers. The decade of the 1940s—World War II—saw farm prices climb back to 100 percent parity, but it has been an almost steady downward slide since.

Living Under Parity

Why didn't farmers sell all their supply at government-established parity prices? Can you draw a demand-supply diagram to show why?

How does the government intervene? The Agricultural Adjustment Act of 1933 established not only the price floor system, but the Commodity Credit Corporation. The CCC was the agency set up by the government to absorb the excess farm supply created by parity pricing.

How does the CCC work? The CCC provides farmers with loans based on their "expected sales." If the farmers do not sell all their supply at government-established parity prices—and, of course, they typically don't—they pay off their loans to the CCC with the unsold supply. In this way, farmers are subsidized and government ends up with the excess farm supply.

The parity system and commodity support program under the CCC has become quite comprehensive. By 1970, it covered wheat, corn, cotton, rice, tobacco, milk, wool, mohair, barley, oats, grain, sorghum, rye, flaxseed, soybeans, dry edible beans, honey, crude pine gum, and peanuts. Was it effective? Of course! Hundreds of billions of dollars were transferred in this way from gov-

FIGURE 11 **Parity Price Ratios of Prices Received and Paid by Farmers: 1910–90**

Except for war years, 1914–18 and 1940–45, prices paid by farmers for nonfarm goods exceeded the prices they received for farm output. From 1950 to 1980, the parity price ratio declined; by 1980 it was approximately 50 percent of its 1910–14 ratio. From 1980 to 1990, the drop was even more dramatic.

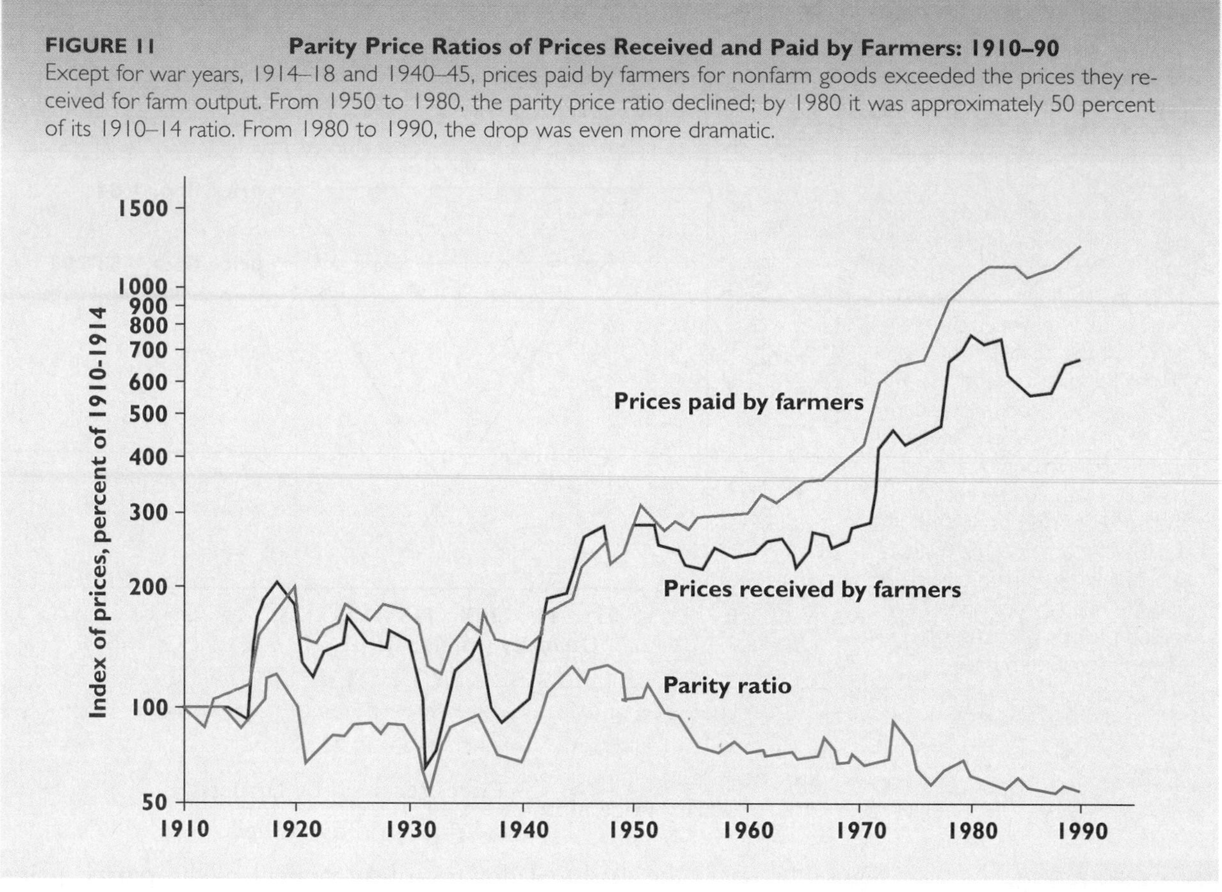

ernment to farmers, while hundreds of thousands of tons of excess farm supplies moved the other way.

Table 3 describes CCC's loan performance. What do you think the CCC did with all its excess supply? Some goods were actually resold on U.S. markets during years of relatively buoyant prices. But there weren't very many of these years. The CCC, operating through federal, state, and private agencies, also do-

TABLE 3 Commodity Credit Corporation's Loans: 1940–88 ($ millions)

	Value of Loans
1988	$13,302
1980	4,228
1970	2,388
1960	1,507
1950	2,203
1940	308

Source: *Historical Statistics of the United States: Colonial Times to 1970, Part 1,* Bicentennial Edition, U.S. Bureau of the Census, Department of Commerce, Series K, 330–43, p. 488, *Statistical Abstract of the United States, 1990,* Department of Commerce, Washington, D. C., p. 652.

nated substantial quantities of farm goods for child nutrition programs and for needy persons. Some of CCC's stockpiled grains were sold at much reduced prices to American livestock farmers who were also experiencing parity price ratio declines. That is to say, the CCC was in the business of virtually giving farm goods away.

And giving it away was precisely what the CCC did through Public Law 480, also referred to as Food for Peace, a piece of legislation enacted by Congress in 1954 that authorized the agency to "sell" its food stocks overseas to Third World countries under terms highly favorable to the buyers. In emergency situations, outright donations were made. The recipient countries paid for our surplus farm goods not with dollars, but with their own currencies. As a result, during the 1950s and 1960s our government stockpiled foreign currencies along with farm goods!

Even though PL 480 was principally designed to help our own farmers, its impact on the Third World countries cannot be ignored. In India, Bangladesh, Pakistan, Egypt, and other countries, our PL 480 farm goods were, at times, the difference between survival and national disaster.

The decade of the 1970s brought a brief respite to the chronic condition of falling parity ratios. The then USSR, a wheat exporter since the early 1960s, became a major wheat buyer in the 1970s. Also, many Third World economies whose incomes had risen during the decade increased their demands for our food exports.

These changes in demand for farm goods occurred at the same time that the world's major food suppliers—Canada, Australia, Argentina, and Russia—were experiencing unusually poor crop yields. The combination of increasing world demand and declining world supply of farm goods translated into relatively high farm prices, reversing the downward drift in the parity price ratio.

Be sure that you are able to compare and contrast the parity pricing scheme in the pre-1973 period with the target price scheme established in 1973.

With the excess supply pressure easing, Congress tackled the problem of overhauling the 40-year-old parity system. In 1973, The Agricultural and Consumer Protection Act, as its name implies, brought our own consumer interests into the picture. What changes did the act make? Instead of consumers having to pay price floor prices, it allowed farm prices to be determined by the market. In a real sense, the act was revolutionary. Consumers once again had access to food at equilibrium prices.

Target price

A minimum price level for specific farm goods that the government sets and guarantees. If the market price falls below this target price, the government pays the farmer the difference between the market and target price for each unit sold.

Farmers, however, were still protected under the act. If market prices were insufficient to provide farmers with incomes regarded by government as acceptable, then cash payments—determined by the difference between the market prices and government-designed **target prices**—were paid to farmers.

The differences between the old 1933 and revised 1973 parity price systems are illustrated in Figure 12.

As you see, under the revised parity system consumers are clearly better off than under the old parity system. Under the 1933 system, consumers paid $4 per bushel. Under the revised system, the price is allowed to fall to $1. And the quantities bought and sold are very different. That's what government had in mind. Under the old system the government ended up with 50 million bushels of excess supply. Under the new system, the market clears.

The 1973 legislation also limited the maximum subsidy that individual farmers could receive to $20,000. That relieved the burden of excess supply on government even more. Before, with no subsidy limitation, rich farmers produced the greater share of farm output and received the larger share of CCC loans. Many poor farmers, on the other hand, with low ouput, received relatively little.

FIGURE 12 **Old and Revised Parity Price Systems**
Under the revised parity price system consumers pay the $1 market price for corn, which is less than the $4 price floor set under the old parity price system. The government pays farmers the difference between the market price and the target price for the 110 million bushels supplied. The $2 target price provides farmers with a predetermined subsidized income, the shaded rectangle in panel *b*. Under the old scheme in panel *a*, the government was obliged to buy up 50 million bushels of excess supply at $4 a bushel. The government's payments are shown by the shaded rectangle.

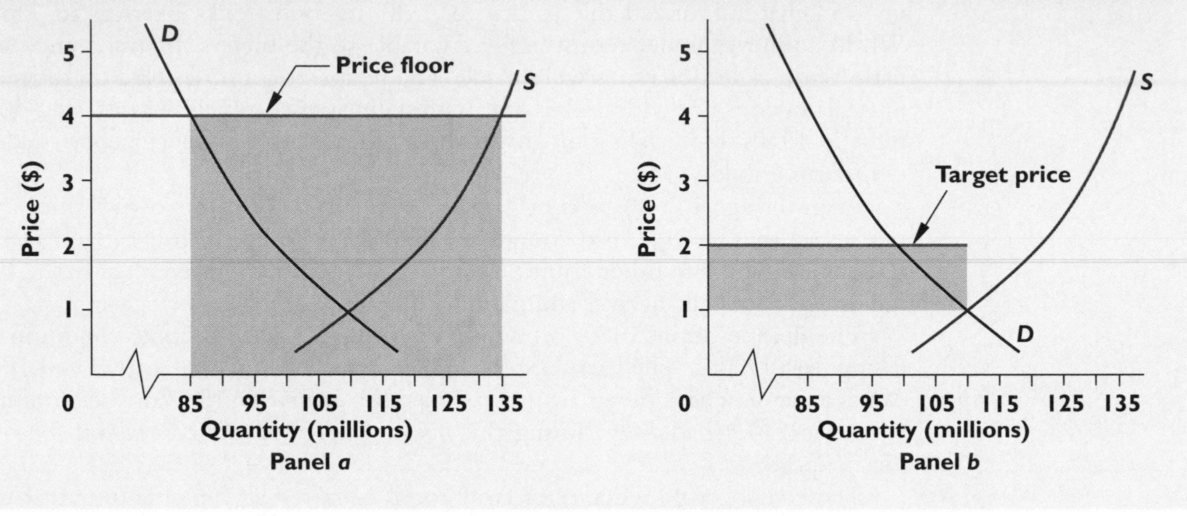

Soil Bank Programs

Another option the government pursued to limit excess agricultural supply was its crop limitation program. The idea was simple. *The government would pay farmers for not producing.*

Rather than have farmers expand output and drive market prices downward even more, as was the incentive under parity pricing, the soil bank or acreage control program would pay farmers to take land out of cultivation. If farmers cut their supply, market prices would increase.

Figure 13 compares the quantities supplied to the market and to the government under a combined system of acreage control and parity pricing.

FIGURE 13
Effect of Acreage Control on Parity Pricing
With an acreage control scheme that shifts the supply curve from S_1 to S_2, the $4 floor price for corn generates an excess supply of 17 million bushels compared to the 25 million bushels generated without acreage control. If the costs to government of acreage control are less than (25) ($4) – (17) ($4) = $32 million, then the combined scheme is less costly to government.

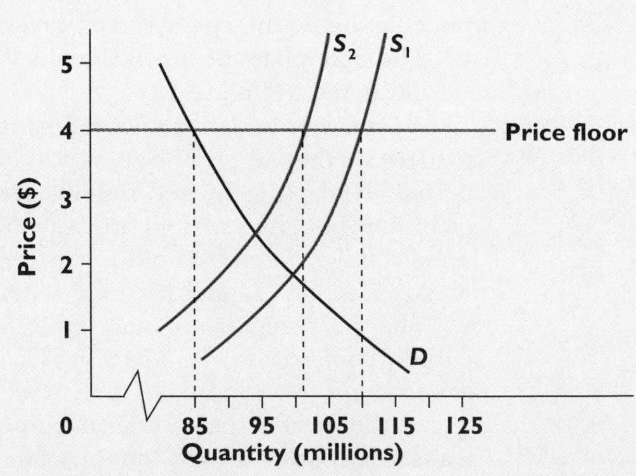

ADDED PERSPECTIVE

How Europeans Cope (Actually, Don't Cope) with Their Excess Supplies of Farm Goods

Perhaps it is no wonder that French politicians fear French farmers. A misconceived food policy—price controls that discouraged peasants from supplying Paris with the ingredients for bread—helped trigger the French Revolution.

There is the fact that French farmers when upset turn to mass demonstrations, as they did yesterday when some 150,000 descended on Paris to object to any European farm policy reform. It was a largely peaceful protest for a change, but in few nations is there greater paranoia among farmers over illusions that they are somehow being cheated.

While all these things are understandable—given the hard past of the French and European peasantry—a questions remains: How long can European governments, especially France, continue to cower in fear of their farmers without doing serious damage to themselves and to their relations with the rest of the world? The European Community (EC), for its own protection and advancement, needs to do several very important things. It needs to open its doors to the rest of Europe, especially the politically and economically shaky European countries newly liberated from communism. It needs to reduce drastically the economic burden caused by subsidies, which boost taxes and government deficits, and disrupt markets.

The EC politicians are unwilling to reform the community's Common Agricultural Policy (CAP) in any meaningful way. By coddling 10 million farmers, the EC is damaging the interests of hundreds of millions of Europeans. And the remarkable thing about all this is that the farmers' claims that a reform will put them out of business are just another one of those rural illusions. The United States already has demonstrated that agricultural policy can be reformed without any economic damage to farmers.

The United States has been through the same nightmare of high market supports and protectionism that now afflicts Europe. In 1981, the U.S. Congress, to protect farmers from the impact of antiinflation measures, jacked up price supports. What that mainly did was price American farmers out of world markets, thus making the plight of U.S. agriculture worse, not better. So in the 1985 farm bill, Congress began a phase-down of supports, substituting direct income supplements to keep farmers whole. Farmers also were paid to set aside land.

This didn't fully solve the problem of overfarming, because the government still was paying people to farm. But it was a successful political solution in that it began reducing government interference in the market without causing undue hardship among farmers. The costs of government agricultural policy, in budgetary terms and to consumers, have been reduced.

The EC, by contrast, has for many years faced the same problem that confronted the U.S. Congress in 1985. To support prices, the EC buys enormous quantities of farm products that, because of the price supports, cannot be sold in world markets. It then dumps them where it can for a fraction of their cost, or stores them, which is also costly.

Whereas the United States responded to the problem, at least in part, the EC has done nothing. EC taxpayers paid $50 billion in direct subsidies to farmers last year and an additional $85 billion in excess food costs brought about by price supports. By contrast, Americans—even though giving direct income supplements to farmers—paid $47 billion in subsidies and their excess food costs were only $28 billion, or less than a third of what their European brethren paid.

More to the point, the U.S. system has helped return United States farmers to the world market to recover some of the enormous market losses during their absence. It has reduced damage to farmers in other countries brought about by the dumping of products bought with U.S. taxpayer money. It has reduced incentives for the United States to protect its markets against foreign imports, since there is less need for protection when prices are no longer supported at artificially high levels.

That EC farmers don't want a U.S.-type dole but prefer to make their living in the market is ludicrous, given the value of the market subsidies EC farmers get. As *The Economist* commented, EC farmers "haven't been near a real market for years."

Discussion

Should mass demonstrations by peasants in Paris dictate European common agricultural policy? If you were a Dutch flower grower, would you insist on equal treatment? Should all governments support all falling prices? How do you pick which ones, if any, to support, and for how long?

Source: Excerpted from *The Wall Street Journal*, September 30, 1991.

When an acreage control agreement is negotiated, the supply curve shifts from S_1 to S_2. The $4 floor price now creates an excess supply of only 17 million bushels compared to the 25 million excess supply generated by the parity price system alone. The government's payments change from $4 × 25 million = $100 million to $4 × 17 million = $68 million, plus the government's negotiated payment for acreage control. As long as that payment is less than the $4 × 8 million = $32 million, the government comes out ahead.

A variation on this acreage control scheme was introduced in 1983 under the Reagan administration. The program, called Payment-in-Kind (PIK), allowed farmers to contract with government to withhold acreage from production—shifting the supply curve to the left. Farmers were paid to do so with crops from the government's excess supply stockpiles. Farmers could then sell these crops on the open market. In this way, farmers get their subsidies and the government gets rid of some of its surpluses.

A LONG TRADITION OF PRICE CEILINGS AND PRICE FLOORS

The use of price ceilings and price floors to undo pure market outcomes is certainly not an invention of the modern world. In fact, ever since markets first came into being, societies have been busy tailoring market prices to conform more closely to their social, political, and religious values.

Consider whether usury laws would actually have made borrowing money less expensive for those who lived under them.

In ancient economies, for example, the market price of borrowing money—the interest rate—was capped by a price ceiling. Usury laws, fixing the maximum price of borrowing money, are at least as old as biblical literature. Such laws are also found in the Islamic Koran and in the descriptions of the ideal society envisaged by Greek and Roman philosophers for much the same reasons. Interest-taking, particularly at market rates, was universally regarded as exploitative, socially disruptive, and morally corrupting.

That view, along with usury laws, survives today. State governments have the constitutional right to enact usury laws and many still do in a variety of consumer lending markets.

Some moneylenders, whose only crime in life is charging what the market allows, just as butchers, bakers and candlestick makers do, are nonetheless still singled out and regarded as unsavory, exploitative loansharks. Their negative image collides with our belief in the virtues of the market system and serves to accent the sometimes contradictory sets of social and economic values we hold.

Although price ceilings and price floors have always played an important role in our economy, they have always represented exceptions to the rule. In most markets, market-determined prices prevail. They do so because we allow them to. Only unusual circumstances prompt their abandonment. A national security crisis or dramatic changes in the fortunes of critical industries in our economy have, at times, allowed noneconomic considerations to dominate over pure market outcomes.

CHAPTER REVIEW

1. Sometimes, market-determined prices move out of line with their historical levels and society will decide to control the price rather than to accept the market outcome. A national security crisis is an example of such a situation.

2. Establishment of a price ceiling below the equilibrium market price results in excess demand. An economy might cope with chronic excess demand through a rationing system.

3. Price ceilings and ration coupons were used extensively in the U.S. economy during World War II to mobilize resources for war production. Resources had to be shifted from civilian production, which resulted in decreased supply in civilian markets and would have caused skyrocketing prices had not price ceilings been imposed.

4. Price floors can be implemented when society decides that a price has fallen too low relative to its historical levels. Setting a price floor above the equilibrium price results in chronic excess supply. Disposing of the excess supply presents a new problem for society.

5. Because agriculture is such a significant industry in the United States, the decision was made in the early 1930s to intervene in farm markets. The Agricultural Adjustment Act of 1933 set parity prices for farmers' products. Parity pricing was intended to restore parity—equality—between farm and nonfarm prices.

6. Between 1933 and 1973, farmers lived with parity pricing, which established price floors for farm products. Excess farm supply was absorbed by the Commodity Credit Corporation. The CCC made loans to farmers which they could repay with unsold crops.

7. In 1973, parity pricing was altered so that it was based on target prices for crops. If the market price is less than the target price, then the farmers are compensated by being paid a subsidy on their products that represents the difference between the two prices. Under target pricing, consumers always face the market price. Crop limitation programs were pursued vigorously in 1983 through the Reagan administration PIK program.

8. Another example of a price ceiling is usury laws that have been imposed worldwide since ancient times.

KEY TERMS

Price ceiling
Ration coupon
Rent control
Price floor
Parity price ratio
Target price

QUESTIONS

1. Some people argue that people are homeless because rents are too high. If the government is willing to impose a price ceiling on rent, the problem of the homeless would disappear. Do you agree? Why, or why not?

2. Why are price ceilings a more practical intervention in times of war than price floors?

3. The reason farmers have not done as well as nonfarm people is because:
   (a) The government has interfered in the agricultural market.
   (b) The government has not interfered sufficiently.

(c) The character of demand and supply in the farm goods market works against the farmer; government interference is not the problem.
Discuss the merit or lack of merit in each argument.

4. Paradoxically, farmers' remarkable success as producers undermines their ability to achieve financial success. Discuss.

5. If the government decides not to interfere in the farm economy, who gains? Who loses?

6. If the government decides to interfere in the microchip industry by imposing a tariff on imported microchips, who gains? Who loses? (*Note*: a tariff is a tax on imported goods.

7. What is parity pricing? How does it work? What is the rationale for using such a mechanism in the agricultural market?

8. How do you view minimum wage laws? Do they represent price floors or price ceilings? Can you make a case for them? A case against them?

9. What are usury laws? Why do you think they have been so universally applied?

10. If a price ceiling were imposed in a fish market whose equilibrium price was substantially above the ceiling, what effect would the price ceiling on fish have on the demand for meat and fowl?

11. Why are ration coupons typically coupled with price ceilings?

12. Given the demand and supply schedule shown in the table below, what would happen to (1) the price students pay for textbooks, (2) the quantity they demand, and (3) the quantity textbook producers supply if (a) the government imposed a $20 price ceiling, or (b) a $10 price floor on textbooks?

Price	Quantity Demanded	Quantity Supplied
$50	250	650
40	350	550
30	450	450
20	550	350
10	650	250

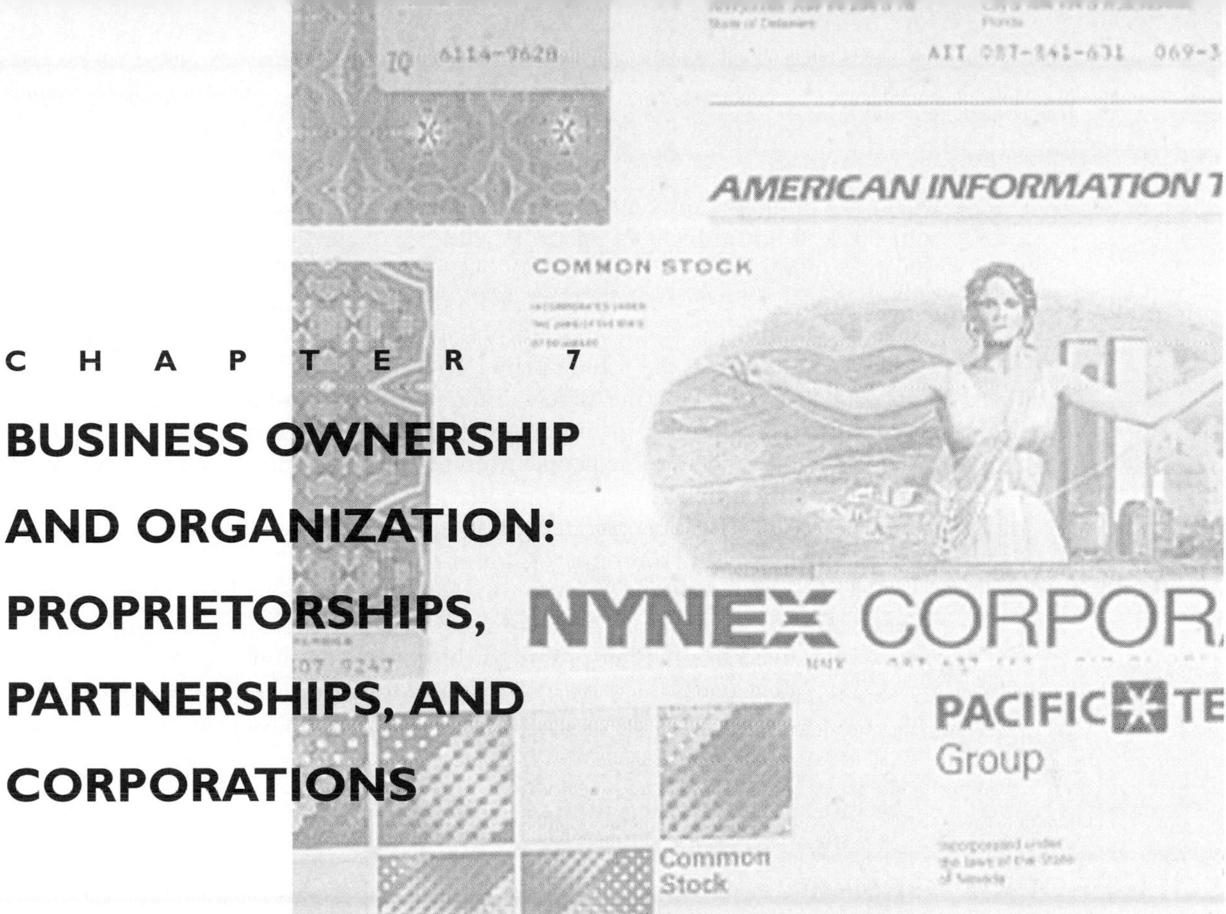

CHAPTER 7

BUSINESS OWNERSHIP AND ORGANIZATION: PROPRIETORSHIPS, PARTNERSHIPS, AND CORPORATIONS

CHAPTER PREVIEW

Chapters 4 and 5 delved into the nature of demand and consumer choice. Chapter 7 moves us back to a consideration of the supply side of the market. Before we begin an analytical treatment of the costs of production in Chapter 8, it is important to have an understanding of how businesses are owned and organized. After all, businesses are the suppliers of goods in our economy. This chapter will introduce you to important characteristics of the three types of businesses that operate in our economy—proprietorships, partnerships, and corporations.

After studying this chapter, you should be able to:

- Describe the way unlimited liability affects a sole proprietorship.
- Discuss the advantages and disadvantages of partnerships versus sole proprietorships.
- Explain why corporations have the security of limited liability.
- Distinguish between stocks and bonds as methods of financing corporations.
- Describe how corporate takeovers occur.
- Outline the characteristics of U.S. business organization.
- Present a profile of stockholders of corporations.
- Compare and contrast international and multinational corporations.

A fishing business can conjure up all kinds of images. For example, picture running a seafood empire—as many Fortune 500 corporations are run—from a plush executive suite at corporate headquarters on the 50th floor of the World Trade Center in New York. That's considerably different, isn't it, from a small fleet of shrimp boats run from a fish-scented, uncarpeted, undersized, cluttered office located just off the fishing pier?

Yet both images are true. These different types of business coexist in the fishing industry, as they do in most other industries. And for good reason. Both offer clear advantages. Some people running businesses prefer the relatively small scale, one-person or two-person operation—in the form of either a *proprietorship* or a *partnership*. These people are willing to forgo the benefits of a *corporate* form of business in favor of a proprietorship or partnership.

Yet, for other people, operating perhaps at a different level of production, the advantages gained from the corporate form of enterprise outweigh the advantages derived from either proprietorship or partnership.

Why? What issues decide which business form to adopt? What are the specific advantages and disadvantages that business people associate with these different forms of business organization?

SOLE PROPRIETORSHIP

Sole proprietorship

A firm owned by one person who alone bears the responsibilities and unlimited liabilities of the firm.

Let's start with **sole proprietorship.** Imagine yourself being the sole proprietor of a fishing enterprise. The business is yours alone. You own the boat, hire the crew, and operate near productive capacity. All decision making belongs to you. You decide whether or not to go out on a fishing run, whether to add crew, or perhaps reduce crew size, whether to purchase new equipment, and whether to add still another boat to your operations.

Of course, much of the day-to-day decision making is routine. But there are times when the decisions you make can substantially change the character of the business. They can even determine whether you stay in business. As sole proprietor, you must assume complete responsibility. That can be downright unnerving. But ask proprietors and they are likely to tell you that the responsibility also gives them a sense of personal pride and control over their working life. It's not suprising, then, that many people who own and run businesses choose to be sole proprietors.

What does it take to set up a proprietorship? Owners typically rely on their own financial means to purchase, rent, or hire physical plant, raw materials, and labor. They hire principally, but not exclusively, family labor. Most produce for local markets.

What do they look like? Proprietorships are typically run as family businesses. If there's a shoe repair shop in your neighborhood, it's probably a proprietorship. So, too, are florist shops, restaurants, travel agencies, taxi services, cattle ranches, and chicken farms. Portrait photographers and scrap metal firms are typically proprietorships. So, too, are many fishing firms. The variety is endless. Just scan the Yellow Pages of your telephone directory.

In many cases, sole proprietorship is the ideal form of business organization. The personal independence it provides the proprietor, its focus on local markets,

Can you list the major advantages and disadvantages of sole proprietorships?

its lack of bureaucratic structure, and its access to familiar and even family labor gives it advantages that, say, corporations do not typically have.

But there are disadvantages, too, and these can become overriding concerns, particularly when proprietors contemplate expanding their production capacities. *In proprietorships, the proprietor and the firm are legally inseparable.* This legal indivisibility of proprietor and firm could result in *personal* losses for the proprietor far beyond the proprietor's own financial commitment to the business.

For example, suppose you set up a fishing business with an initial investment of $100,000. After a few rough years, the firm succeeds only in accumulating debt. By the end of the third year, you discover that your firm owes its creditors $500,000, but has only $75,000 of firm assets to cover the debt. Reluctantly, you decide enough's enough. What happens?

If you liquidate those assets to pay off the debt, you still fall $425,000 short. What do you do? You can't simply walk away from your unpaid obligations. You are personally liable. With the firm's assets depleted, your creditors can make claim to your personal assets. They can, for example, compel you to liquidate personal belongings such as your house, automobile, stocks, bonds, and even home furnishings. In other words, *the proprietorship form of business organization puts in jeopardy the proprietor's entire personal net worth.*

Unlimited liability

Personal responsibility of the owners for all debts incurred by sole proprietorships or partnership. The owners' personal wealth is subject to appropriation to pay off the firm's debt.

You can see, then, why some proprietors would be reluctant to expand their production capacity much beyond its current level, even when the prospects for a successful expansion of business activity seem particularly attractive. The specter of business misjudgments that might trigger **unlimited liability** serves to cramp ambition.

PARTNERSHIP

How, then, can firms run by proprietors expand, without at the same time endangering the species? One option is for sole proprietors to find one or more partners willing to buy into the business. In this way, liability is shared and the firm acquires greater access to capital resources.

Think, again, about your fishing enterprise. Suppose, as sole proprietor, you encounter an excellent expansion opportunity that is simply beyond your own personal means. Suppose you persuade two people, less experienced in the business, to join you in **partnership.** You sell your $40,000 boat and put that sum, coupled with your partners' finances, toward a $400,000 purchase of two larger boats. Your productive capacity increases twentyfold, from 3,000 to 60,000 fish per run. This kind of business expansion would not be possible under a sole proprietorship.

Partnership

A firm owned by two or more persons who each bear the responsibilities and unlimited liabilities of the firm.

But partnership also affects decision making, because business decisions are now made jointly. And although partnerships are founded upon trust, that trust may quickly erode when decisions—made either by yourself or by your partners—are challenged by the other partners.

Can you list the major advantages and disadvantages of partnerships?

There are other problems as well. Although the firm's liability is now shared, partnership makes each partner personally liable for all debts incurred by the business. It is one thing to be held liable for your own mistakes, but partnerships make each partner liable for the other partners' mistakes as well. Some partners, who may have only a minimal share in the business, may end up absorbing considerably more than a minimal share of its losses. Liability is always regarded as

The maximum loss an investor in a corporation can experience is the amount of the investment.

100 percent by each partner. Imagine what would happen if the firm goes bankrupt and your partners claim no personal net worth. The burden of unlimited liability falls solely on you. You can see why people with substantial personal wealth would be reluctant to join partnerships.

CORPORATION

Is there any way of facilitating substantial expansion of the firm and, at the same time, protecting yourself against the possible onslaught of unlimited liability? The corporate form of business organization is designed to do precisely that. How does it work? It's as simple an idea as it is revolutionary.

The Security of Limited Liability

Corporation

A firm whose legal identity is separate from the people who own shares of its stock. The liability of each stockowner is limited only to what he or she has invested in the firm.

The **corporation,** unlike the sole proprietorship and the partnership, is created as a separate legal being, *independent of its owners*. That's the key to limited liability. As a legally created being, it has its own legal rights. It can borrow funds, hire and fire people, produce goods and services, make a profit, and plow that profit back into the business or spend it. Sole proprietorships and partnerships can do these things too, but if a corporation suffers strings of losses instead of making a profit, it alone—not its owners—is liable for its debts.

Of course, if the corporation goes bankrupt, its investors may end up losing their entire investment. But that is all they can lose. Their own personal wealth is not in jeopardy because the owners are not the corporation. And only the corporation is liable. In this way, the separation of the corporation from its owners protects the owners from unlimited liability.

Setting Up the Corporation

Suppose you decide to set up your fishing enterprise as a corporation. The first thing would be to obtain a charter from your state government. The charter is the legal document that recognizes the corporation as an independent person, separate from yourself. Like any other legal person, it is subject to the laws of the state, has the right to organize for business, and can sue and be sued.

OWNERSHIP

Stock

Ownership in a corporation, represented by shares that are claims on the firm's assets and earnings.

Stockholder

A person owning stock in a corporation; that is a share of a corporation.

The corporation is owned by individuals who buy shares of its **stock.** If the corporation decides to issue 1,000 shares at $100 per share, and if you buy all 1,000 shares, then you are the only stockholder. **Stockholders** elect the corporation's board of directors, and the board appoints the corporation's management. By owning 100 percent of the shares, you have complete control over who runs the business. (To maintain unchallengeable control of the business, all you really need is one share more than 50 percent.)

You now make yourself the corporation's chief executive officer (CEO). And the corporation, with its $100,000, buys a boat and equipment and hires a crew. If the firm makes a profit, it can distribute the profit to its stockholders (in this case, just you) in the form of dividends. Or it can use some or all of that profit to buy more equipment, hire more crew, or even buy a second boat. The stockholders decide.

Ready for that interview with Atlantic Records? Its corporate headquarters is on the top four floors in the building set back at the right. The one in front, on the left, is the corporate headquarters for Sony. Good luck!

If stockholders continually decide to allow the corporation to reinvest its profit, then the value of the corporation's stock, reflecting the corporation's growing assets, would become somewhat greater than its original $100,000. Each of the 1,000 shares you own, then, would be worth more than its original $100.

Many small corporations are actually owned and run this way. Many sole proprietors, for example, to protect themselves against unlimited liability, convert from proprietorship to the corporate form of business organization.

STOCK ISSUES

Suppose, as CEO, you encounter an excellent opportunity to expand your fishing operations a hundredfold, but it requires an investment of $900,000. Although the corporation is profitable and enterprising, this is not a sum that can be generated internally out of profit. What can it do?

One solution is to issue another 9,000 shares at, say, $100 per share. Suppose the issue is successfully subscribed. People read the corporation's prospectus and like what they read. The fishing firm's performance record is impressive and the idea for expansion exciting. Many people buy varying quantities of the new issue and within a week, the corporation has at its disposal the necessary $900,000.

The total outstanding stock now rises to 10,000 shares. Your 1,000 shares represent, then, only 10 percent of the total, but when there are many stockholders, 10 percent typically is sufficient to keep control of management. Anyway, there's no reason to suppose that the new stockholders would want to change management. After all, their interest in the corporation is primarily to receive as high a **dividend** as possible. As long as the corporation performs well, why would they even contemplate changing management?

Dividend

That part of a corporation's net income that is paid out to its stockholders.

Corporations have the option of varying the kinds of stock they issue. For example, the $1 million of outstanding stock in your fishing enterprise—entitling each stockholder to a vote that is proportional to his or her share of total

ADDED PERSPECTIVE

What Shareholders Get Depends on Where They Are

Why do some firms pay bigger dividends to their shareholders than others? In November 1991, Japanese and German firms paid shareholders, on average, less than 35 percent of their profits, American firms paid out 53 percent, and British ones a whopping 70 percent. These national differences had widened during the 1980s; in 1975 the rates were closer—47 percent, 41 percent, 48 percent and 51 percent, respectively. In the mid-1970s, America liberalized its financial system; Britain, where dividend controls had applied in the 1970s, did the same in the mid-1980s. So the rising trend is not surprising. The bigger oddity is why German and Japanese payout ratios have fallen so sharply.

Discussion

If you owned corporate stock, where would you prefer to be: Britain, Germany, the United States, or Japan? Why? If you were a corporate manager, what kind of payout policy would you prefer to have? Should the interests of corporate managers differ from those of the stockholders?

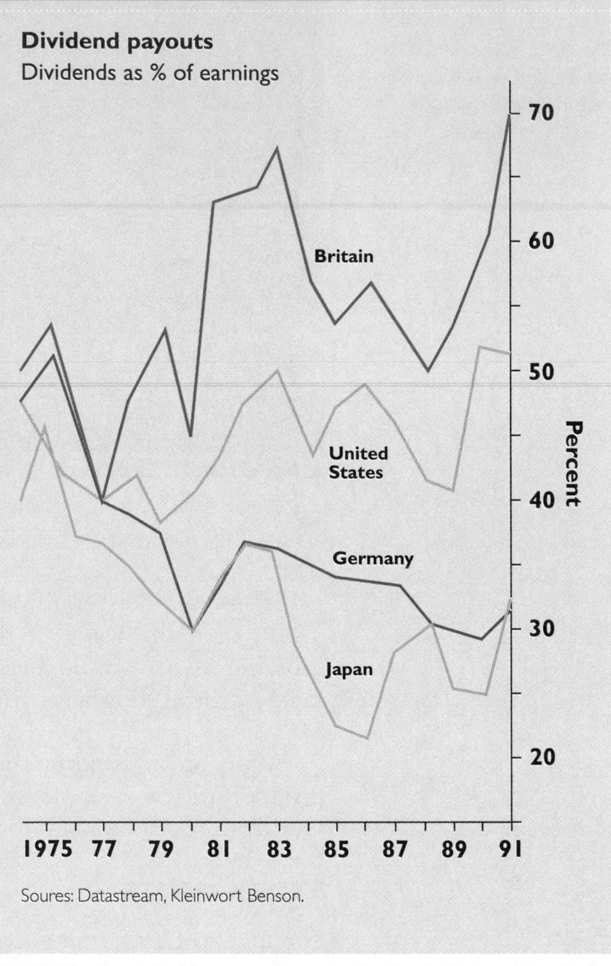

Source: "Economic and Financial Indicators," *The Economist,* November 23, 1991.

outstanding stock—is defined as common stock. Stockholders receive dividends in proportion to the quantity of stock they own, assuming, of course, that the corporation makes a profit and decides to distribute it as dividends.

In addition to common stock, corporations can issue preferred stock. This type of stock differs from common stock in three respects: (1) it does not carry voting privileges, which to most stockholders is only a minor consideration; (2) the dividend yield is fixed; and (3) it has prior claim on dividends; that is, owners of preferred stock receive their dividends before any dividends are distributed to common stock owners. Of course, if the corporation doesn't make enough profit to fully cover the fixed dividends on preferred stock, preferred stockholders end up receiving something less. As you can see, holding preferred stock also involves risk. But compared to common stock, whose dividend returns are not fixed—that is, holders of common stock are more willing to chance greater or lesser gain—the preferred stock option appeals to the more conservative stockholder. It's a matter of preference.

Some people think that owning this stock certificate is equivalent to owning a race track ticket at Belmont Park. After all, we're all betting on the future of "the enterprise." That's not entirely true. The American Information Technologies Corporation, along with *every other corporation* in the race, can win. Your gain does not depend on another's loss.

A third type of stock provides the stockholder further choice. Like preferred, convertible stock carries no voting privileges and yields a fixed dividend. But it differs from preferred stock in two respects: (1) convertible stock has prior claim on dividends over both common and preferred, and (2) it gives stockholders the privilege of converting their stock into common stock. Convertibles, then, offer people yet another way to buy into corporate ownership.

CORPORATE BONDS

Corporate bond

A corporate IOU. The corporation borrows capital for a specified period of time in exchange for this promise to repay the loan along with an agreed-upon rate of interest.

A completely different source of corporate funding is the **corporate bond.** Instead of issuing a new $100 share of corporate stock to a stockholder, the corporation can issue a $100 bond. The person who buys the $100 corporate bond holds the corporation's promise—which is its bond—to pay a specified return on the bond and to repay the principal at a specified time.

The advantage of holding bonds, as opposed to stocks, is that bondholders have first claim on the corporation's profit. Before any stockholder receives one penny in dividends, bondholders must be fully paid. Bonds, then, represent the safest form of participating in corporate business.

Bonds are less risky than stocks from the investor's standpoint, but what about from the standpoint of the issuing corporation?

But this safety comes at a cost. If the corporation's profit increases year after year, stockholders can expect their returns to increase as well. After all, they are the owners. Bondholders do not enjoy this benefit. They are lenders, not owners. It's a question, once more, of people's preferences. Some prefer the security of prior claim on corporate profit and a fixed return, while others are more willing to wager their returns on the performance of the corporation.

The Sky's the Limit in Stock Issues

What about your fishing business? If its performance record is strong enough, there is no reason why you couldn't take advantage of the full range of stock and bond issues to build the corporation into a nationwide enterprise.

It's hard to imagine United Airlines, Exxon, or any of the Fortune 500 companies being run as sole proprietorships. It would be close to impossible to raise the enormous sums of capital required. The value of United Airlines' plant and equipment, for example, is over $8 billion. You couldn't begin to raise that sum as a sole proprietor.

Consider your own case. How could you raise large sums of capital without issuing stocks and bonds? Perhaps a few very wealthy people would come along,

ADDED PERSPECTIVE

Starting a Small Business? What Distinguishes Success from Failure?

Thousands of small firms start up each year but fewer than half survive, and many fewer still become significant employers. British data on the life expectancy of new firms are not encouraging for people contemplating starting up. For the mid-1980s Britain, of every 100 new, small, manufacturing firms, only about 40 survive after ten years, and half the jobs they create end up being produced by the most successful four.

Which firms make it? Is it obvious from the start? Not exactly. Some indicators provide a few clues but mostly it's information after-the-fact.

Small firms are typically director-run, as distinct from management-run, and seem to behave very differently from the larger, more professional corporation. Their early performance record seems to matter. For example, after two years of operations, those that survive will have become three times as large in assets and employment as the average in their original set of starters. They also tend to accept a lower profit margin, and unlike those who don't make it, retain most of the profit. They are also likely to be owned by experienced directors. The family firm or firms run by skilled workers starting up their own enterprises are less likely to last.

Firms with inexperienced managers and directors are disinclined to reinvest profits and are more unlikely to employ many workers, even if they do survive. Success depends not only on experience, but on attitudes and preferences. Many who start up firms prefer to keep them small. That preference, however, makes them much more prone to failure.

Can government help? To some extent. In the first few years of business, these new firms confront barriers that government agencies can help overcome, such as lack of access to overseas markets, to capital, and to skilled labor. The drawback with such government support is that it may undermine the firms' initiative, which is their strength.

Source: "Little Acorns Fail to Sprout," *The Economist,* December 13, 1986.

see the long run potential in your fishing operation, and each invest $10 million. But counting on that possibility must rank among the most unreliable ways of planning a business venture.

One of the beauties of the corporate form of business organization is that it allows people of even modest means to become participants in enterprise ownership. The size of your business organization and its rate of growth isn't intractably tied to the whims of a few people. The corporation is open to hundreds of thousands of people who can afford, say, five shares of a $100 stock. It's your track record that counts. The sky's the limit!

BUT THERE'S A DOWNSIDE TOO!

Why, then, would anyone choose sole proprietorship when they can just as easily incorporate? Even if you decide to remain a small business, why not form a corporation and own all its stock? This way, you avoid unlimited liability.

In many cases, the decisive negative to the corporate form of business organization is that both the owners and the corporation itself pay taxes on the same corporate income. That spells *double taxation.* The corporation, chartered as an independent, legal entity, must pay a tax on corporate profits (also called corporate income tax). But when the corporation's after-tax profit is distributed to its stockholders in the form of dividends, those dividends are taxed as well. This double taxation is enough to discourage many from taking the corporate route.

From the stockholders' point of view, another negative to corporate ownership is that stockholders exercise corporate control only theoretically. In practice, management is in a much stronger position to control the corporation than are the corporation's stockholders. Typically, a stockholder or even a large group of stockholders hold only a minute fraction of the total outstanding stock. It is difficult for them to draw together the necessary 50 percent plus one share to vote out management. It does sometimes happen, but these are rare and notable events.

THE THREAT OF TAKEOVER

Corporate management has its own problem with stockholders. While individual stockholders or groups of stockholders may themselves not have the ability to gather the necessary voting stock to change management, an outsider—typically, another corporation—may decide on a takeover. By aggressively buying up enough of the target corporation's common stock, it can eventually come to own the corporation outright. It's an old rule of the sea. Big fish eat little fish.

Can you list the major advantages and disadvantages of corporations?

How can management defend itself against a hostile takeover attempt? It may resort to an array of anti-takeover or "shark-repellant" activities. One strategy may be to do precisely what the aggressor corporation does: It can buy up its own corporate stock. That is, instead of providing its stockholders with dividends, the threatened management uses the corporation's profits to buy its own stock until the corporation virtually owns itself, making it impossible for a hostile takeover attempt to work.

Management can sometimes avoid a takeover by making the corporation less attractive to the potential acquirer. How? It can purposely accumulate considerable debt by borrowing on the value of the corporation's assets and using the proceeds to pay a one-time cash dividend to its own stockholders. This newly acquired corporate debt may make the targeted corporation less appetizing.

Management could also pursue a "lesser of two evils" strategy, encouraging a friendly corporation, a "white knight," to make a competitive takeover bid. Under friendly new ownership, the threatened management stands a better chance of surviving.

You can see why small, yet successful corporations are attractive targets for corporate takeover. Many of them, with impressive track records, simply cannot withstand a determined, financially well-heeled corporate aggressor.

HOW U.S. BUSINESS IS ORGANIZED

One of the marvelous features of U.S. business is its diversity. Like a fully dressed pizza, where every slice contains every ingredient, you can find on almost every square inch of the U.S. economic landscape almost every form of business organization.

For example, just outside Peoria, Illinois, family farm proprietorships coexist alongside corporate agro-businesses. In Peoria itself, a hamburger place, Steak N Shake, sits in the shadow of one of the world's largest multinational corporations, Caterpillar. Steak N Shake is a corporation, too. It's a 5-minute walk from Caterpillar to Moira's tavern, run by partners Adam Baird and Moira Knight. Next door to Moira's is Brad's Tools. Brad Fish, proprietor and master toolmaker, provides custom-made tools and bolts for Caterpillar. Well over 100 proprietorships, partnerships, and corporations are located within a quarter mile of Moira's. Peoria is a microcosm of the U.S. business world. Look at Table 1.

TABLE 1 Proprietorships, Partnerships, and Corporations, 1970–90 (000s and $ billions)

	1970	1980	1990
Proprietorships			
Number	5,770	11,932	14,783
Receipts ($)	199	411	731
Partnerships			
Number	936	1,380	1,554
Receipts ($)	93	292	566
Corporations			
Number	1,665	2,711	3,628
Receipts ($)	1,751	6,361	10,935
Total Number	8,371	16,023	19,965 *
Total Receipts ($)	2,043	7,064	12,232 *

Source: *Bulletin, Statistics of Income,* Summer 1992, Internal Revenue Service, Washington, D.C., pp. 161–163.

* 1989 data.

As you can see, proprietorships are alive and well in the United States. There were 14.78 million in 1990, representing 74 percent of the total number of operating businesses. Not only are proprietorships far more numerous than other business concerns, they constitute an increasing share of the total. In 1970, for example, proprietorships were 69 percent of the total.

The numbers of firms, however, is a much different matter than the volume of business handled. In 1990, proprietors transacted $731 billion worth of business. That volume represented only 6 percent of the U.S. total. It's like the pennies in a cookie jar, visible from every angle but still adding up to small change.

Clearly, corporations dominate business activity. The 3.63 million corporations in 1990, representing 18 percent of the total number of operating businesses, accounted for fully 89.4 percent—$10.935 of $12.232 billion—of 1990 receipts. This same disparity beween number of businesses and receipts shows up even within the corporate ranks. Look at Table 2.

The 3.06 million corporations with receipts under $1 million made up 82.5 percent of all corporations. But they accounted for only 5.7 percent of total receipts. Big cannons make big noises. Look at the $50 million-or-more class. These 16,000 corporations alone accounted for 67.2 percent of total corporate receipts. Clearly, these corporations are like a few silver dollars in the corporate cookie jar.

PROFILE OF STOCKHOLDERS

Who owns the corporations? How many people actually buy stock? What do they look like? Table 3 gives us some idea about who they are.

Stockholders are certainly not rare animals. The over 47 million stockowners in 1990 made up 26.68 percent of the adult population, 18 years and older. In other words, approximately one out of every four adults held some form of

TABLE 2
Size of Corporation and Corporate Receipts, 1990 (000s and $ billions)

Size	Number	%	Receipts	%
	3,717	100.0	10,914	100.0
Under $1 million	3,068	82.5	625	5.7
$1–4.9 million	484	13.0	1,035	9.5
$5–9.9 million	82	2.0	574	5.3
$10–49.9 million	67	1.8	1,349	12.4
$50 million or more	16	*	7,331	67.2

Source: *Statistical Abstract of the United States, 1994,* Department of Commerce, Washington, D. C., 1994, p. 540.

* = .004

corporate ownership. They have been that visible for a long time. Back in 1970, the 30.85 million stockholders made up 22.8 percent of the population.

But the numbers may be deceiving. Although women's growing participation in the labor force and their increasing financial independence contribute to

TABLE 3
Numbers and Characteristics of Stockholders, 1970–90 (000s)

<table>
<tr><th></th><th>1970</th><th>1980</th><th>1990</th></tr>
<tr><td>Total Numbers</td><td>30,850</td><td>30,200</td><td>47,970</td></tr>
<tr><td>Male</td><td>15,689</td><td>15,666</td><td>30,220</td></tr>
<tr><td>Female</td><td>15,161</td><td>14,534</td><td>17,750</td></tr>
<tr><td>Age</td><td></td><td></td><td></td></tr>
<tr><td>Under 21</td><td>2,221</td><td>2,308</td><td>3,740</td></tr>
<tr><td>21–34 years</td><td>4,500</td><td>6,407</td><td>11,790</td></tr>
<tr><td>35–44 years</td><td>5,801</td><td>5,925</td><td>12,260</td></tr>
<tr><td>45–54 years</td><td>7,556</td><td>5,456</td><td rowspan="2">16,240</td></tr>
<tr><td>55–64 years</td><td>6,084</td><td>5,144</td></tr>
<tr><td>65+ years</td><td>4,330</td><td>4,589</td><td>7,410</td></tr>
<tr><td>Education</td><td></td><td></td><td></td></tr>
<tr><td>1–3 years high school</td><td>3,566</td><td>1,746</td><td>1,910</td></tr>
<tr><td>High school completion</td><td>8,697</td><td>5,737</td><td>9,390</td></tr>
<tr><td>1–3 years college</td><td>5,867</td><td>9,353</td><td>13,280</td></tr>
<tr><td>4+ years college</td><td>9,999</td><td>10,613</td><td>22,450</td></tr>
<tr><td>Income</td><td></td><td></td><td></td></tr>
<tr><td>Under $10,000</td><td>8,168</td><td>1,742</td><td>2,860</td></tr>
<tr><td>$10,000–14,999</td><td>8,346</td><td>3,180</td><td rowspan="2">4,690</td></tr>
<tr><td>$15,000–24,999</td><td>7,670</td><td>6,930</td></tr>
<tr><td>$25,000–49,999</td><td rowspan="2">4,141</td><td>11,623</td><td>20,320</td></tr>
<tr><td>$50,000+</td><td>3,982</td><td>17,910</td></tr>
</table>

Source: *Statistical Abstract of the United States, 1988,* Department of Commerce, Washington, D.C., 1987, p. 487; *Shareownership 1990,* New York Stock Exchange, 1991.

TABLE 4
Stock Portfolio Size, 1990

Portfolio Size	% Stockholders
Under $5,000	34.6
$5,000–24,999	33.7
$25,000–49,999	11.8
$50,000–100,000	9.6
$100,000 +	10.4

Source: *Shareownership 1990,* New York Stock Exchange, 1991, p.19.

the number of those who own stock, many still remain owners only in joint holdings with their husbands.

It's no surprise that income and education count. In 1990, 75.9 percent of stockholders had some college experience and 39.2 percent earned more than $50,000 per year. They weren't all bald-headed, pot-bellied, old fogies either. About 54.0 percent of them were 44 years old or younger. Still, most stockholders cannot even begin to live off their dividends. Look at Table 4.

As you see, about two-thirds of the individuals who owned stock in 1990 held less than $25,000 worth of stock. Only 20 percent held more than $50,000 in stock.

Indirect Stock Ownership

Clearly, direct stock ownership is quite common and, when indirect ownership is also considered, a vast number of people own stocks.

Although people buy into corporate ownership by purchasing stock directly through stockbrokers or through employee stock-purchase plans, there are many more people who come to corporate ownership indirectly. Table 3 describes only those people who themselves own stock. It does not include those who own stock indirectly through pension plans, life insurance policies, and other financial intermediaries.

For example, in 1992 the pension fund for state employees in California, administered by CALpers, owned $68 billion in corporate stock. That is to say, perhaps as many as hundreds of thousands of state employees in California who have never seen a corporate stock certificate, are in fact owners of corporations. If account is made for these people and for the tens of million others who, in the United States, are covered by such pension funds, it is reasonable to argue that corporate stocks are held by a vast majority of our population.

INTERNATIONAL AND MULTINATIONAL CORPORATIONS

Although there's nothing to prevent proprietorships from operating in international markets, and many do, we generally think of corporations when we think of businesses with interests overseas. And we're generally right. Most of our economic relations with other countries—imports and exports—are essentially corporate relations.

TABLE 5 Foreign Revenues as a Percent of Total Revenues and Foreign Assets as a Percent of Total Assets for the 10 Largest U.S. Multinationals, 1985 and 1991

	1985			1991	
	Revenues	Assets		Revenues	Assets
Exxon	69.4	43.0	Exxon	75.9	58.4
Mobil	55.9	41.2	IBM	62.3	54.3
Texaco	50.1	30.1	General Motors	31.8	23.4
Chevron	38.9	31.2	Mobil	68.1	56.6
IBM	40.4	36.1	Ford	39.1	31.6
Phibro Salomon	59.8	9.1	Texaco	49.9	28.6
Ford	29.7	47.4	Chevron	38.2	31.3
General Motors	17.3	21.3	du Pont	44.8	39.8
du Pont	32.0	29.0	Citicorp	52.9	43.2
Citicorp	49.8	53.7	Phillip Morris	27.4	25.6

Source: *Forbes*, July 29, 1985, and July 20, 1992.

Many of these corporate links to overseas markets simply reflect a geographic extension of what these corporations market domestically. For example, the Kellogg plant in Battle Creek, Michigan, produces the same cornflakes for markets in France, Belgium, Australia, and Egypt as it does for its domestic East and West Coast markets. Its sales on the West Coast are regarded as purely domestic trade. But sales in France or Egypt are considered international trade. The cornflakes are all the same, but if Kellogg's exports overshadow its domestic trade, it is viewed as an American-based international corporation.

Be able to distinguish between international and multinational corporations.

But exporting its Battle Creek cornflakes to Egypt is not the only way Kellogg can sell cornflakes there. *It can also build a Kellogg cornflakes plant in Cairo.* Why should Kellogg bother? Because a Kellogg Cairo subsidiary can take advantage of Egypt's lower labor costs, avoid overseas transportation costs, and can circumvent tariffs that Egypt may place on imported foods. That may be enough reason for Kellogg to opt for an Egyptian branch instead of shipping its cornflakes from Battle Creek.

Corporations that rely on overseas production to handle their overseas markets are described as **multinationals.** The difference, then, between an international corporation and a multinational, is the presence of overseas production branches.

Multinational corporation

A corporation whose production facilities are located in two or more countries. Typically, multinational corporate sales are also international.

Imagine your own corporation as a U.S.-based multinational, with a number of fishing subsidiaries overseas. Suppose you own a large fleet and cannery operation in Alexandria, Egypt, that is charged with handling the African markets. You own another fleet and cannery branch, located in Singapore, that handles the Asian markets. Not quite the same business, is it, as a sole proprietorship selling in a local market? Even if you owned a dozen such subsidiaries, you probably still wouldn't rank among the top 100 multinationals based in the United States. Most multinationals are corporations with over $1 billion in foreign revenues.

What is their profile? Table 5 describes some of the financial attributes of the top 10 U.S. multinationals for 1985 and 1991.

Exxon's foreign revenues in 1991, which accounted for 75.9 percent of its total revenues, ranks it top among the U.S. multinationals. Its foreign assets—

representing the asset value of its subsidiaries—are as much as 58.4 percent of its total assets.

As you see, four of the top ten—Exxon, Mobil, Texaco, and Chevron—are oil multinationals. Two others—Ford and General Motors—are automobile corporations. Not included in the top 10, but still prominent, are U.S. multinationals such as Kodak, ranking 15; Coca-Cola, ranking 19; Johnson & Johnson, 25; and Goodyear, 30. Sara Lee ranks 46; McDonald's, 55; and Kellogg, 78.

Living among giants is no guarantee that you'll stay there. For example, TWA ranked 64 and Firestone 87 in 1985, but they both failed to make the top 100 multinational list in 1991. Somebody has to make room for young, dynamic newcomers like Ralston-Purina, ranking 85 in 1991, and Black and Decker, 92. Perhaps, someday, even a fishing multinational.

CHAPTER REVIEW

1. A sole proprietorship is a business that is owned and operated by one person. Proprietorships are often run as family businesses. Proprietorships offer great independence to business owners.

2. One drawback of a sole proprietorship is unlimited liability. Under proprietorship, the owner's entire personal net worth is in jeopardy if the business should fail.

3. If a proprietor takes on a partner in an effort to expand the business, then the firm becomes a partnership. Business decisions are jointly made by both owners and liability is shared. However, the partners can be held liable for each other's mistakes. The risks associated with unlimited liability are the same as with sole proprietorships.

4. Corporations exist as legal entities independent of their owners. An investor in a corporation is subject to losses only as great as the amount of investment. Thus, liability is limited for corporate shareholders.

5. Profits in a corporation can be distributed to the owners (shareholders) as dividends or they can be reinvested in the corporation. Reinvestment results in growth of the corporate assets.

6. Another way to expand a corporation is through new stock issues. Stocks are marketed and sold to new investors who provide funds for corporate expansion. Different kinds of stock can be issued, including common stock, preferred stock, and convertible stock.

7. Sales of bonds represent another way corporations can generate funds for expansion. Purchasers of bonds acquire the corporation's promise to pay a specified return on the bond. Bonds are less risky assets for investors than stocks, since bondholders have first claim to a corporation's profits.

8. Corporations have the advantage of access to funds for expansion through stock and bond sales. However, corporate profits are taxed twice—first as corporate profits and again as personal income for stockholders who receive dividends. Another drawback is that stockholders may have little influence over the way management runs the corporation.

9. Corporate takeovers involve the aggressive buying up of shares of common stock by another corporation so that a majority of shares can be acquired. Management of corporations under threat of takeover may turn to leveraged buy-outs, or seek to be bought by white knights in attempts to avoid the negative consequences of takeover.

10. Seventy-four percent of United States businesses were proprietorships in 1990. However, these firms accounted for only about 6 percent of the total business transacted. Corporations accounted for about 20 percent of the total number of operating businesses in 1990, but they transacted some 90 percent of the business.

11. Over one in four adult Americans owned stocks in 1990. About 70 percent of these stockholders had some college education and about 74 percent earned more than $25,000 per year. If one includes indirect stock ownership through pension funds and life insurance policies, then nearly all adult Americans are stockowners.

12. Most of our economic relationships with other countries are handled by corporations. An international corporation is one that exports a large percentage of its output. A multinational corporation relies on overseas production facilities in its international transactions.

KEY TERMS

Sole proprietorship
Partnership
Unlimited liability
Corporation
Stock
Stockholder/Shareholder
Corporate bond
Dividend
Multinational corporation

QUESTIONS

1. Suppose you were thinking about going into the business of custom-imprinted balloons for birthdays, graduations, weddings, and other special events. Why would you want to own and run the business as a sole proprietor? What disadvantages would you face in choosing that form of business organization?

2. Under what conditions would you think about switching from a sole proprietorship to a partnership? What disadvantages would you now face?

3. Under what conditions would you think about switching from a partnership to a corporation? What disadvantages, compared to the other business forms, face you now?

4. Who are stockholders? Why would anyone choose to become a stockholder?

5. Why would anyone choose to become a bondholder instead of a stockholder in your balloon corporation?

6. Under what circumstances would your balloon corporation be considered an international corporation?

7. Suppose *Fortune* magazine decides to publish a feature story on the evolution of your balloon business. The story's title, "From Sole Proprietorship to Multinational." Why multinational?

8. Suppose the CEO of Exxon, one of the world's largest and richest multinationals, reads the *Fortune* story and, impressed with your business, decides to take it over. How could Exxon do this? How could you prevent it from happening?

PART 3
THE MICROECONOMICS OF PRODUCT MARKETS

C H A P T E R 8

COSTS OF PRODUCTION

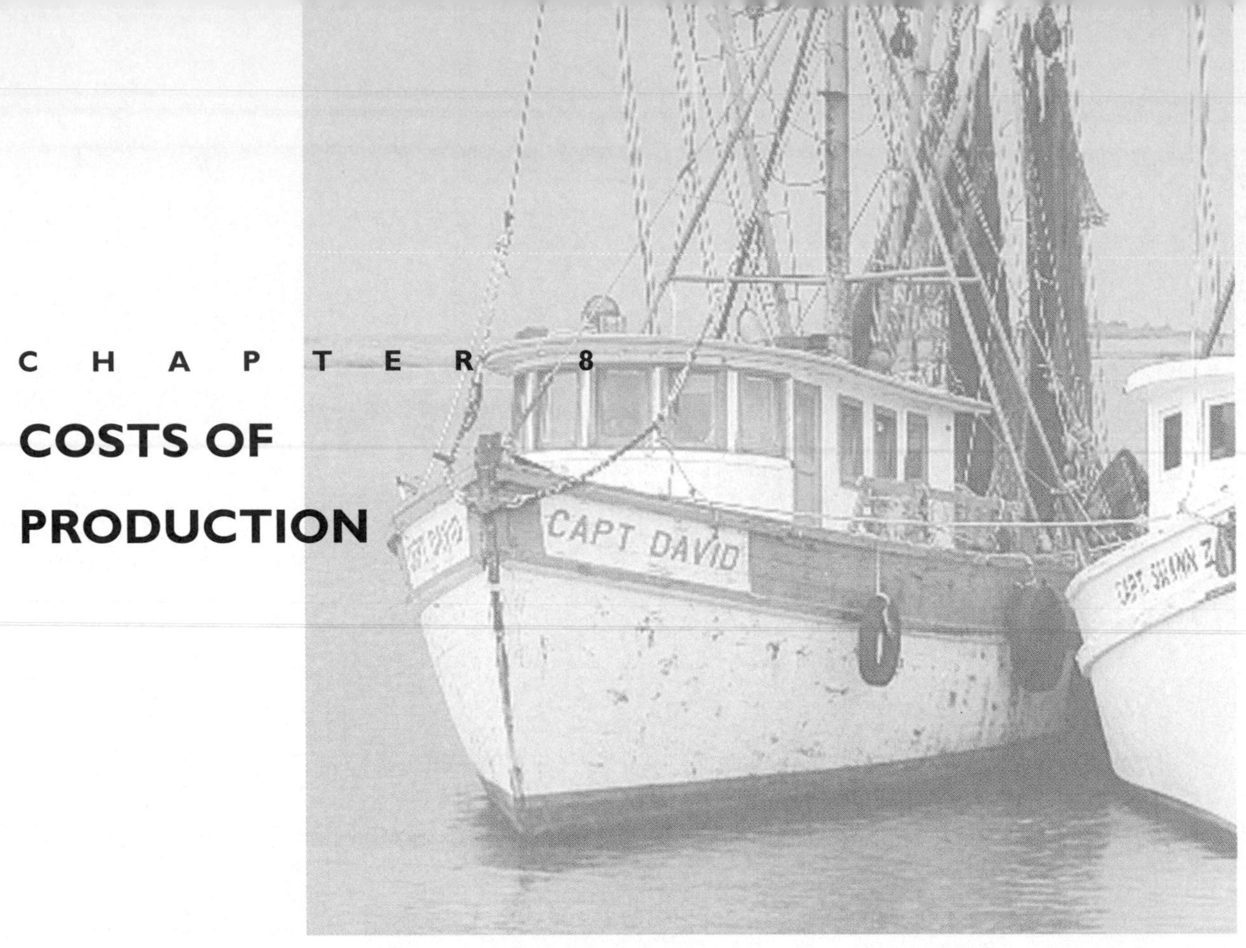

CHAPTER PREVIEW

In Chapter 1 you learned about the circular flow model. This model showed how households supply resources—labor, land, capital, and entrepreneurship—to business firms. Business firms then make payments to households for furnishing these resources to them. The payments that firms make to households represent their costs of production. After all, without labor, land, capital, and entrepreneurship, nothing could be produced.

This chapter details the costs of production for business firms. Costs of production can be categorized as fixed costs and variable costs. The sum of fixed costs and variable costs is total cost. These cost concepts, together with some others you will learn about, are related to each other to form a general picture of the costs of production for businesses.

After studying this chapter, you should be able to:

- Describe the steps involved in becoming an entrepreneur.
- Explain the short run as a commitment to fixed-cost items.
- Link the level of commitment to fixed cost with the level of production a firm will choose.
- Distinguish between fixed costs and variable costs.
- List and explain the determinants of labor costs.

- Draw and explain the shape of a total-cost curve.
- Derive average cost from total cost.
- Derive marginal cost from total cost.
- Draw curves to represent average-cost concepts and marginal cost.
- Understand the difference between economies and diseconomies of scale.
- Distinguish between long-run and short-run costs.
- Discuss short-run and long-run costs for a variety of industries.
- Describe the relationship between costs of production and the socioeconomic environment.

Have you read John Steinbeck's *Cannery Row*? The fishing industry, circa 1920s Monterey, California, comes alive in his wonderful pages. He captures the pulse, smells, and sounds of those canneries and the fishing people who made their living in and around them. But today, his Cannery Row beats with a different pulse. That celebrated row has been converted into a modern shopping mall, catering to the tourist traffic.

Still, the fishing industry along the California coast is alive and well. Modern technology may have changed its character from Steinbeck's day, but there are still honest-to-goodness canneries operating in close proximity to Cannery Row. For example, look beyond the restaurants and gift shops on San Francisco's Fisherman's Wharf, and you'll see commercial fishing boats returning to dock every morning. You'll see tired fishermen unloading their catch, packing their fish in crates of crushed ice, ready for market.

The fishing industry thrives in the Gulf towns of Texas, Louisiana, and Florida, along the New England coast, in the Chesapeake Bay, along the Mississippi River, and in the states of Washington, Oregon, Alaska, and Hawaii. Fishing is a major industry in Canada, Japan, Mexico, Peru, Chile, Iceland, Norway, Italy, France, Spain, Denmark, Finland, Egypt, Greece, China, and Russia. Even Saudia Arabia has a fishing industry. People now eat more fish, and more people everywhere are earning their livelihoods fishing.

Imagine that you were born and raised in the fishing community of Chapter 3. The water, the fishing stories, the canneries, the people working the docks, would be all second nature to you.

GETTING INTO THE FISHING BUSINESS

Now let's suppose you just graduated from the island's college. You could take the first ferry to the mainland and expand your job opportunities at least tenfold. Many people on the island have already done this. But suppose you decide, instead, to make your life's work right there on the island.

Entrepreneurs usually have considerable knowledge of their business before they enter.

What could you do? Fishing is one thing you would probably consider. You have had some summer experience working on the boats and rather enjoyed it. Moreover, it is one thing you really know something about. But how do you convert a familiar and comfortable activity into an occupation?

Any fisherman will tell you that the art of fishing is quite distinct from the art of making money. If you fish commercially, your success indicators are profits and losses, not the beautiful yellowfin tunas that can fight you for the better part of a day. Fishermen—both men and women—like other entrepreneurs,

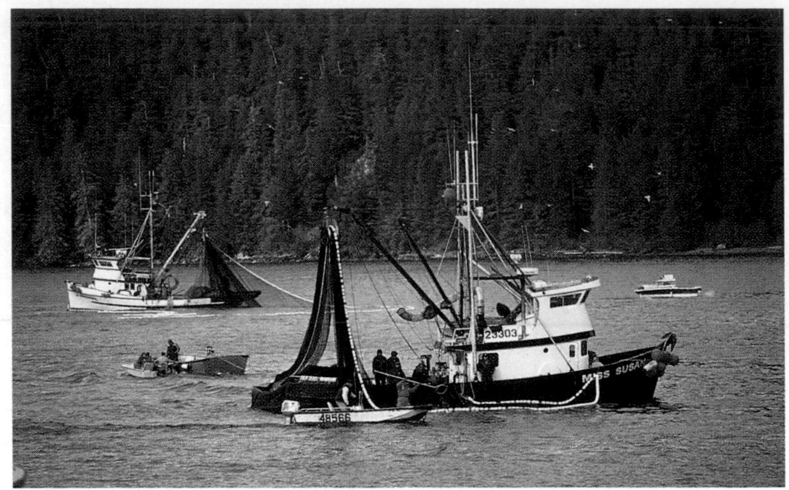

It's a great feeling owning your own boat! But it takes true grit and hard work to keep the enterprise afloat. Some days are quite rewarding. The haul is plentiful and the price of fish is high. On other days—and there are many of them—there seem to be no fish left in the waters.

must confront a world of uncertainty, making decisions about prices, costs, and production. These decisions are critical to survival.

Fishing is a particularly risky business. Not only is the size of the catch a matter of hard-earned experience and downright luck, but the price of fish can be highly volatile. Good fishermen have gone to ruin making inaccurate guesses.

It pays to take a long, hard look at the fishing business before jumping in. It may not be a bad idea to work a year on someone else's boat before committing yourself and your money to setting up on your own. If you keep your eyes and ears open, you can pick up a lot of information about the technical and financial aspects of the business. Of course, time spent working on somebody else's boat is time lost on your own. But, as you already know, most choices involve some opportunity cost.

Let's push the scenario further. Some of your friends have also made up their minds to stay on the island. To no one's surprise, their choices are varied. Some join established crews, intending to remain on permanently. A much smaller number set up their own firms.

Entrepreneurship is not everybody's forte. For many, an honest day's labor for an honest dollar seems right. As working people, they choose to avoid the risk that entrepreneurship entails. Of course, they miss out on the possibilities of profit. Many have no choice. After all, it takes money to start up a business and some talented people who would like to start their own businesses just don't have access to money.

But that's not your situation. After much soul searching and long hours of discussion with people in the industry, you decide to set up your own fishing business. Where do you start?

TOTAL FIXED COSTS

Committing to Fixed Costs

Buying a boat is your first and most expensive single purchase. What kind of boat do you buy? There's more than one kind available. Let's simplify your options. The least expensive, the miniboat, built for a crew of three, costs $40,000.

A more expensive model, the midiboat, built for a crew of five, costs $70,000. The flagship of the industry, the maxiboat, built for a crew of twelve, costs $200,000.

Any fisherman will tell you that once you make a choice, you live with it. *At least, in the short run.* People just don't go about changing boats every day. To a fisherman, it's a commitment no less serious than marriage. In some cases, it's more durable.

Be careful to understand that the short run is not a particular length of calendar or clock time. The length of the short run depends on how rapidly fixed-cost items depreciate.

How durable? Boats, like everything else, depreciate with time. At some point in the future, your boat will need to be replaced. When that time comes, you will have the opportunity, once again, to choose among the different models available. But until then, you're committed.

Fixed cost

Cost to the firm that does not vary with the quantity of goods produced. The cost is incurred even when the firm does not produce.

The firm's short run is defined by the time it takes to depreciate its major fixed-cost items. If its **fixed costs** depreciate in a day, its short run is only a day. If, on the other hand, it takes 20 years for its fixed costs to depreciate fully, then the firm's short run is 20 years. It depends, as you see, on the character of the firm's technology.

How would you decide which boat to buy? Why, for example, would you consider spending $200,000 when a $40,000 boat is available? Obviously, a maxiboat must have features that, for some people, make the additional cost worthwhile. One advantage would be its greater capacity to catch fish.

Now, *if* the weather is cooperative, *if* the fishing grounds are rich, and *if* the price of fish is about as high as it has been in years, you could do well harvesting a lot of fish. But that's a lot of *ifs*! Suppose the price of fish turns out to be lower than anticipated. Or the quantity of fish not as plentiful. You may regret committing yourself to a $200,000 boat. And once you make the $200,000 expenditure, you're fixed to it for as long as 20 years.

Why not go with the $40,000 boat? Because the maximum number of fish you can harvest per fishing run is only 2,000. That's not a lot of fish. Of course, if you go into business expecting to produce within a range of 1,000 to 2,000 fish per run anyway, it's probably the more sensible choice. You simply don't think of a 5,000 or 25,000 fish run with a miniboat.

Calculating Fixed Costs

Suppose boats depreciate in 20 years. Suppose further that five runs are made to the fishing grounds each year. Fishermen calculate fixed cost, that is, cost that does not vary with output. The miniboat's *fixed cost per run,* then, is

$$\left(\tfrac{1}{20}\right)\left(\tfrac{1}{5}\right)(\$40{,}000) = \$400$$

The midiboat's fixed cost per run is

$$\left(\tfrac{1}{20}\right)\left(\tfrac{1}{5}\right)(\$70{,}000) = \$700$$

The maxiboat's is

$$\left(\tfrac{1}{20}\right)\left(\tfrac{1}{5}\right)(\$200{,}000) = \$2{,}000$$

That is, $2,000 of the boat's $200,000 cost depreciates during a run period. *Even if the boat stays in dock during that period, the fixed cost is $2,000.* After all, depreciation of the boat occurs whether the boat is at the fishing grounds or at dock.

Table 1 records these fixed-cost runs for the three boats across the output range of zero to 15,000 fish.

TABLE 1
Fixed Costs per Boat per Fishing Run ($)

Quantity of Fish (000s)	$40,000 Miniboat with 2,000 Fish Capacity	$70,000 Midiboat with 6,000 Fish Capacity	$200,000 Maxiboat with 20,000 Fish Capacity
0	$400	$700	$2,000
1	400	700	2,000
2	400	700	2,000
3		700	2,000
4		700	2,000
5		700	2,000
6		700	2,000
7			2,000
8			2,000
9			2,000
10			2,000
11			2,000
12			2,000
13			2,000
14			2,000
15			2,000

The miniboat has a maximum capacity of 2,000 fish per run. It simply can't handle more fish. (Try loading four cubic feet of topsoil into a wheelbarrow whose capacity is three cubic feet. Can't be done, can it?) That is why the miniboat column in Table 1 is blank after 2,000 fish. Look at the maximum capacity of the midiboat. It is 6,000 fish per run. The maxiboat's capacity is 20,000 fish per run. Fishing anywhere along the output range shown in Table 1—zero to 15,000 fish per run—can be accommodated by the maxiboat alone. The total fixed cost of producing either 1,500 or 15,000 fish on a maxiboat is $2,000. Figure 1 translates Table 1 into graphic form.

The step shape of these three total fixed cost curves reflects the different capacities of the boats. Let's suppose you decide to buy the $200,000 maxiboat that has a 20,000 fish capacity.

TOTAL VARIABLE COST

Variable costs change with the level of output.

A boat is not the only thing you need to run your fishing business. A fishing boat without a fishing crew yields no fish. You also need an arsenal of fishing equipment. Your supply of nets, hooks, lines, and sinkers can quickly diminish in foul weather and at some fishing grounds. You need bait and a stock of crushed ice to keep the fish fresh during a run. Your boat needs fuel to move from fishing ground to fishing ground. These items, and many more, make up the **variable costs** of a fishing business.

FIGURE 1
Total Fixed Cost of Producing Fish on Mini-, Midi-, and Maxiboats
The three straight-line, horizontal curves portray the total fixed costs associated with three boats of different capacities producing quantities of fish ranging from zero to 20,000 per run. The miniboat's total fixed-cost curve is horizontal at $400 through the output range zero to 2,000 fish, its full capacity. The midiboat's total fixed-cost curve is horizontal at $700 per run through the output range zero to 6,000 fish, its full capacity. The maxiboat, with 20,000 fish capacity, can accommodate any level of production in Table 1. The total fixed-cost curve is horizontal at $2,000 per run across the entire output range.

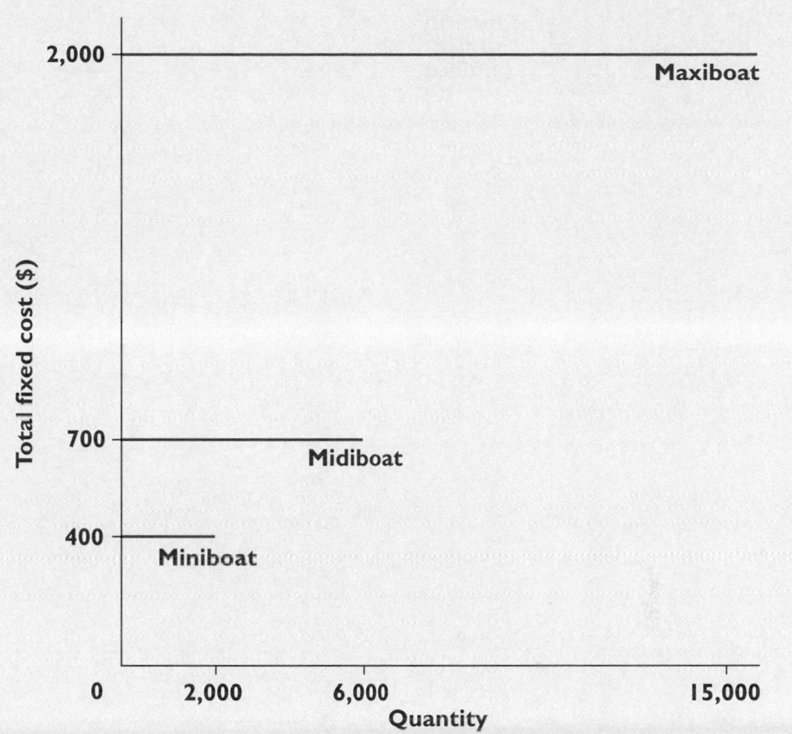

Variable cost

Costs that vary with the quantity of goods produced. Variable costs include such items as wages and raw materials.

Why are these cost items described as variable? Because, unlike the cost of a boat which is fixed regardless of the quantity of fish produced, the costs of labor, equipment, fuel, and ice vary with the quantity of fish produced.

If the maxiboat stays in dock, it still depreciates by $2,000. But at dock, no labor, fuel, equipment, or ice is needed. Variable costs for the fishing firm at an output of zero are zero. Producing 15,000 fish per run, on the other hand, is not costless. Fishermen must venture out to new fishing grounds that are scattered some distance beyond the more accessible ones. It takes time to get there. Time and distance mean higher crew and fuel costs. Moreover, catching 15,000 fish requires large quantities of bait and crushed ice.

Obviously, if you operate within a more modest output range, say 8,000 fish, the more accessible fishing grounds would do. Less labor time, less fuel costs, less bait, less ice are required. In other words, *the costs of labor, fuel, and bait vary with the size of the catch.* This variation in costs is shown in Table 2.

The total variable cost of producing 15,000 fish is $11,500, which represents a $9,405 cost of labor, a $1,345 cost of fuel, and a $750 cost of equipment, including bait. Look carefully at how the particular items of variable cost increase as production levels increase. Look at labor costs over the production range zero to 15,000 fish.

The Cost of Labor

Clearly, if you don't fish, you don't need fishermen. But to get 1,000 fish into the boat requires a crew. The labor cost for a 1,000 fish run is $240. The cost

TABLE 2 Total Variable Costs per Fishing Run

Quantity of fish (1,000s)	Labor	Fuel	Bait	Total
0	$ 0	$ 0	$ 0	$ 0
1	240	50	50	340
2	430	110	100	640
3	575	175	150	900
4	695	245	200	1,140
5	830	320	250	1,400
6	1,050	400	300	1,750
7	1,365	485	350	2,200
8	1,825	575	400	2,800
9	2,380	670	450	3,500
10	3,180	770	500	4,450
11	4,075	875	550	5,500
12	5,115	985	600	6,700
13	6,350	1,100	650	8,100
14	7,780	1,220	700	9,700
15	9,405	1,345	750	11,500

increases with the quantity of fish produced. For example, the labor cost for a 2,000 fish run is $430, and increases to $575 for a 3,000 run.

Do you see what happens to labor costs as greater numbers of fish are added to production? The labor cost per 1,000 fish increases, but by lesser amounts for each additional 1,000 fish until *output reaches 4,000 fish.* Then it begins increasing by increasing amounts. For example, the cost of labor increases by $1,365 – $1,085 = $315 when output increases from 6,000 to 7,000 fish, and it increases even more, by $1,825 – $1,365 = $460, when output increases from 7,000 to 8,000 fish. Why?

Why does the cost of labor increase at a decreasing rate at low levels of output and, at a higher level, begin to increase at an increasing rate? Three factors explain its behavior: changes in labor efficiency, changes in the quality of labor, and changes in the price of labor.

LABOR EFFICIENCY

Labor efficiency

The amount of labor time required to produce a unit of output.

Labor efficiency, the clock time required to catch a fish, depends on the relationship between the size of the crew and the size of the boat. The maxiboat was built for a crew of 12. But the boat can accommodate more. It can also work with fewer.

How many fewer? Well, you couldn't manage it alone. But suppose you had a crew of four. Such a skeleton crew would have to double up on chores. For example, the tasks of navigating, charting, and operating the sonar fish-locating

ADDED PERSPECTIVE

How Driving Costs Can Vary

The difference in costs for drivers of various size cars may surprise you. For instance, an analysis by Rochester, Wisconsin-based Runzheimer shows that as much as $4,000 per year separates the low-cost driver of a compact car from the high-cost driver of a full-size auto who lives in a high-cost driving area.

"It's probably obvious to most that operating cost differences exist between compact, mid-size, and large cars run in different parts of the country, but the degree of cost difference isn't always known," said Runzheimer spokesman Peter Packer.

In its analysis, Runzheimer selected 1992 compact, mid-size, and full-size cars to analyze annual driving costs based on 20,000 miles driven per year. The compact car was a Chevrolet Cavalier with a 110-horsepower four-cylinder engine. The mid-size auto was a Chevy Lumina with a 140-horsepower V-6 engine, and the full-size model was an Oldsmobile 88 with a 170-horsepower V-6 engine.

Car Costs Compared
Runzheimer's Comparison of Annual Car Costs

Car Class	Variable Costs	Fixed Costs	Total Costs
Compact	$1,630	$4,162	$5,792
Mid-size	$1,840	$5,352	$7,192
Full-size	$2,400	$7,620	$10,020

The Cavalier cost $12,200, the Lumina $14,100, and the Olds $20,500. All had automatic transmission, power steering and brakes, air conditioning, tinted glass, speed control, AM/FM stereo, rear-window defogger, and tilt steering wheel. Being a top-line model, the Oldsmobile also had items such as a cassette player and power locks and windows.

"Generally, vehicles with a high purchase price depreciate, in real dollar terms, at a much faster rate," said Larry Snyder, executive vice president of Runzheimer's Transportation Division. "Over three years, the compact depreciates only $2,955, while the full-size car depreciates $4,580." And, he added, all cost components relentlessly add up.

Runzheimer found that the full-size vehicle gets only 19 miles per gallon, but that the compact delivers 24 miles per gallon, and that maintenance costs vary from 3.84 cents per mile at the high end to 1.78 cents at the low end.

Expenses in Runzheimer's analysis included operating or variable costs for fuel, oil, tires, and maintenance, and depend on actual number of miles driven. Fixed costs are for insurance, depreciation, taxes, license and registration fees, and financing, and they are incurred no matter how many miles are driven.

Discussion

Why are items such as insurance, depreciation, taxes, and license and registration fees considered fixed costs? Why are fuel, oil, tires, and maintenance considered variable or operating costs?

Source: "How Driving Costs Can Vary," by Dan J. Slicker. *The Chicago Sun-Times*, July 7, 1992. Reprinted with permission, *Chicago Sun-Times* © 1995.

equipment would most likely be combined into one. And instead of assigning one person to bait nets, three to cast them and monitor their positions, another two to help haul in the catch, and another to pack the fish in ice, these assignments would be handled by two people. However, because few people can master more than one task, the efficiency of each crew member would suffer.

Adding a fifth or sixth crew member creates a more workable environment for everybody. As crew size approaches 12, the greater division of labor allows for a more productive use of each person's talent. Crew and boat become a perfect match.

The boat could take on still more crew. But pushing crew size beyond 12 would, again, adversely affect each person's efficiency. In an overcrowded situation, the mix of labor and equipment becomes less than optimal, damaging labor's performance.

A crew of 16 fishermen would probably bring in more fish than a crew of 12, but the contribution of those four fishermen to output would be somewhat less than any other four on the boat. It's simply more difficult to exercise the full measure of talent under overcrowded conditions.

QUALITY OF LABOR

Not all labor is alike. Ability and experience stamp labor with very different qualities. This fact alone may explain why, as more fish are harvested, the labor cost associated with the fish harvest increases at an increasing rate.

If you were doing the hiring, who would be the first hired? Obviously, the best fisherman available. Someone who can bring more fish into the boat in one hour than anybody else. Who would be second? The second best. And so on. The importance of quality differences in labor depends on the kind of work performed and the availability of the qualified labor. If people exhibit considerable differences in ability and experience, then who you hire and how many you hire very much affects the rate at which labor costs increase.

PRICE OF LABOR

You need more fishermen to catch more fish. But it may be difficult to recruit increasing numbers without raising the wage rate. How much more needs to be offered depends on the availability of labor at varying wage rates. At some level of production, it may require bumping up the wage rate to bid workers away from other boats and even from other occupations.

Moreover, fishermen, like other people, are not eager to work beyond regular working periods. Pushing production to 12,000 or 15,000 fish per run requires staying out longer and working through more than one shift per day. To get fishermen to do that, you may have to offer double the usual wages for the extra hours. Those last few thousand fish, then, come at expensive labor costs.

The Cost of Fuel

Producing 1,000 fish requires a fuel cost of $50. To expand production to 2,000 fish increases this cost to $110. That is, doubling production more than doubles the fuel bill. Every additional 1,000 fish produced requires even larger increases in fuel costs.

Why? At relatively low output levels, the nearby fishing grounds would do. But continually raising the scale of operation involves not only going greater distances from port but also moving more frequently from one fishing ground to another to locate the most productive fishing area.

Look at fuel costs as output increases from 3,000 to 4,000 fish. It increases from $175 to $245 or by $70. Increasing output to 5,000 increases fuel cost by $320 – $245 = $75. The fact that fuel costs keep increasing by greater amounts as output increases reflects the increasing difficulty of finding fish.

The Costs of Bait, Equipment, and Ice

The costs of bait, equipment, and ice vary proportionately with the quantity of fish produced. For example, it requires $50 of bait, ice, and equipment to produce 1,000 fish, $100 to produce 2,000 fish, $150 to produce 3,000, and so on. Fishermen require twice as much ice to handle twice as many fish. The unit cost

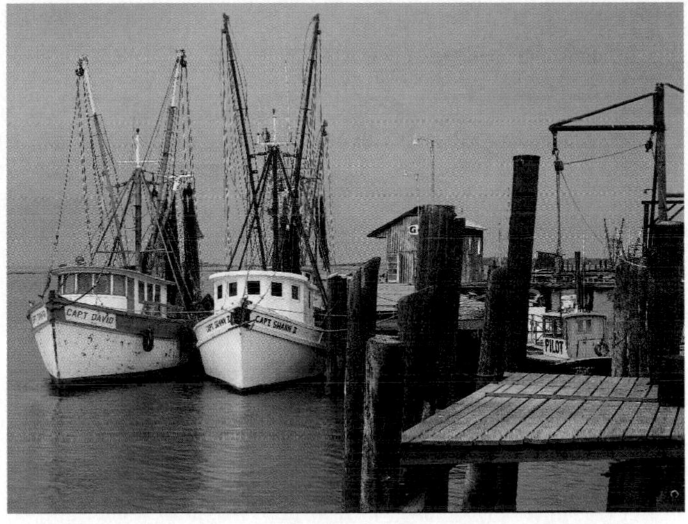

Captains David and Swann know that their variable costs are zero while their boats are tied up at the dock. Good news? Not exactly. Left at the dock, their fixed costs are no less than if they were out on the water fishing.

of these items neither increases nor decreases costs in relation to the scale of production.

Adding Up the Variable Costs

Total variable cost (TVC) sums these specific variable costs in the firm's cost structure. Because labor appears as the most important of the variable cost items, the character of the total variable cost reflects, in large measure, the cost of labor.

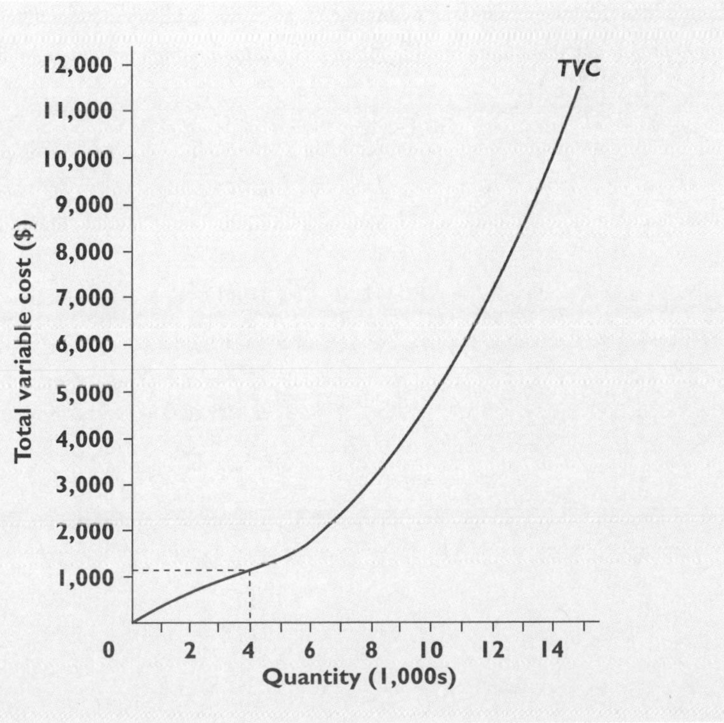

FIGURE 2
Total Variable Cost
The *TVC* curve starts at the origin—zero variable cost at zero output. It increases at a decreasing rate to an output level of 4,000 fish. Above 4,000, it increases at an increasing rate.

Labor efficiency, the quality of labor, and the price of labor cause labor costs to increase at a decreasing rate at low levels of output, but at higher levels of output, labor costs increase at an increasing rate.

This is what you see in Table 2. It isn't that surprising, is it? For many industries, labor is the single most important variable factor of production. Figure 2 maps out the total variable cost curve.

Compare the slopes of the two segments of the total variable cost curve. Between zero output and 4,000 fish, TVC increases but at an ever decreasing rate. Look at how the steps become less steep as output increases to 4,000. But note what happens after 4,000. Total variable cost now increases at an increasing rate. Notice how much steeper the steps have become.

TOTAL COST

Total cost

Cost to the firm that includes both fixed and variable costs.

Total cost (TC) is simply the sum of the total fixed and total variable costs of production.

$$TC = TFC + TVC$$

Why are the total cost and the total variable cost curves parallel?

Table 3 records the total cost of a fish run across the zero to 15,000 production range.

As you see, the *TC* curve is the vertical sum of the *TFC* and *TVC* curves, its shape determined principally by the shape of the *TVC* curve. Compare Figures 2 and 3. Note that the only difference between them is the addition in Figure 3 of the *TFC* curve, the horizontal line at $2,000.

Look at the fishing firm's total cost when $Q = 0$. $TC = \$2,000$. Why? Because even though no fish are being produced, the firm is still obligated to

TABLE 3
Total Cost per Fishing Run (1,000s fish and $)

Quantity of fish (1,000s)	*TFC*	+	*TVC*	=	*TC*
0	$2,000		$ 0		$2,000
1	2,000		340		2,340
2	2,000		640		2,640
3	2,000		900		2,900
4	2,000		1,140		3,140
5	2,000		1,400		3,400
6	2,000		1,750		3,750
7	2,000		2,200		4,200
8	2,000		2,800		4,800
9	2,000		3,550		5,550
10	2,000		4,450		6,450
11	2,000		5,500		7,500
12	2,000		6,700		8,700
13	2,000		8,100		10,100
14	2,000		9,700		11,700
15	2,000		11,500		13,500

FIGURE 3 **Total Cost Curve**

Choosing the maxiboat, the firm's total fixed cost is $2,000 across the entire output range. The *TC* curve is the vertical sum of the *TFC* and *TVC* curves at every quantity of fish produced. Because *TVC* = 0 at zero output, *TC* = *TFC* = $2,000. Beyond zero output, the *TC* curve assumes the shape of the *TVC* curve. This is because at every output level, the only difference between the *TC* curve and the *TVC* curve is the *TFC* curve. At 15,000, *TC* = $13,500. It is the sum of *TFC* = $2,000 and *TVC* = $11,500.

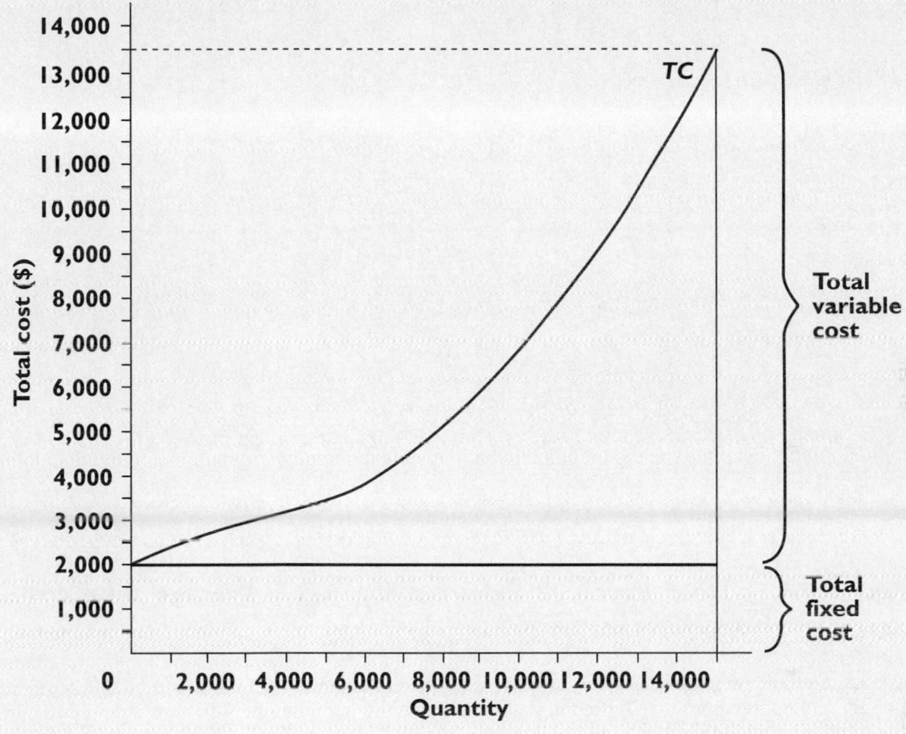

meet its fixed-cost commitment. What about *TVC* at *Q* = 0? It's zero. After all, if no fish are being produced, there are no labor, fuel, ice, or equipment costs to be met.

Note also that at production levels ranging from 0 to 7,000 fish, *TFC* is the dominating factor explaining *TC*. But beyond 7,000, it's clearly *TVC*.

WHAT'S THE AVERAGE COST OF PRODUCING FISH?

We can easily reorganize the data in Table 3 to learn the average cost of producing each fish. It's a piece of information fishermen would want to know. After all, suppose the price of a fish was $0.70. Wouldn't it be useful to know whether the average total cost of producing that fish was greater or less than its price? Obviously, if the fish costs more to produce than it fetches on the market—if *ATC* > $0.70—then it would be silly to fish. No one is in business to lose money. On the other hand, if *ATC* < $0.70, fishermen make money.

TABLE 4 Average Total Cost, Average Variable Cost, and Average Fixed Cost of Producing Fish

Quantity (000s)	*AFC*	*AVC*	*ATC*
0	—	—	—
1	$2.00	$0.34	$2.34
2	1.00	0.32	1.32
3	0.67	0.30	0.97
4	0.50	0.29	0.79
5	0.40	0.28	0.68
6	0.33	0.29	0.63
7	0.29	0.31	0.60
8	0.25	0.35	0.60
9	0.22	0.39	0.62
10	0.20	0.45	0.65
11	0.18	0.50	0.68
12	0.17	0.56	0.73
13	0.15	0.62	0.78
14	0.14	0.69	0.84
15	0.13	0.77	0.90

Average total cost

Total cost divided by the quantity of goods produced. ATC declines, reaches a minimum, then increases as more of a good is produced.

Average fixed cost

Total fixed cost divided by the quantity of goods produced. AFC steadily declines as more of a good is produced.

Average variable cost

Total variable cost divided by the quantity of goods produced. AVC declines, reaches a minimum, then increases as more of a good is produced.

How do you go about deriving *ATC*? **Average total cost** is simply total cost divided by quantity.

$$ATC = \frac{TC}{Q}$$

It can't be simpler, can it? *ATC* is commonly considered the cost of producing a good. What about **average fixed cost**? *AFC* is total fixed cost divided by quantity,

$$AFC = \frac{TFC}{Q}$$

Average variable cost is total variable cost divided by quantity.

$$AVC = \frac{TVC}{Q}$$

Average fixed, average variable, and average total costs are recorded in Table 4.

Note what happens to the averages—*AFC, AVC, ATC*—as output increases from zero to 15,000.

Average Fixed and Average Variable Costs

AFC continuously declines as production increases. Why? The fixed cost is simply spread out over increasing quantities. When Q = 1,000, the $2,000 total fixed cost is divided among 1,000 fish. *AFC* = $2,000/1,000 = $2. When Q = 2,000, *AFC* = $2,000/2,000 = $1. When Q = 15,000, *AFC* = $2,000/15,000 = $0.13.

FIGURE 4 **Average Fixed Cost, Average Variable Cost, and Average Total Cost Curves**
The *AVC* and *ATC* curves are U-shaped. The *AFC* curve is downward-sloping. The difference between the *ATC* and *AVC* curves is *AFC*. As output increases, *AFC* approaches zero, so that the gap between the *ATC* and *AVC* curves narrows.

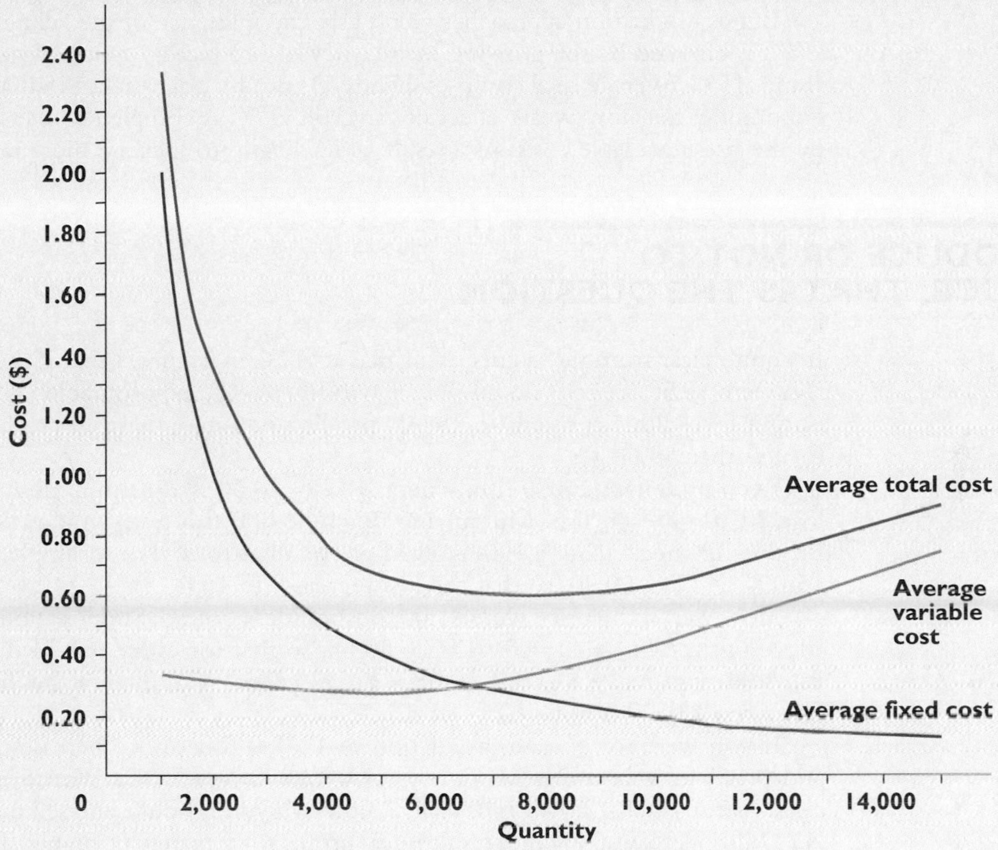

The *AFC* data in Table 4 is mapped into the *AFC* curve in Figure 4. The *AFC* curve is downward-sloping, approaching but never reaching zero.

What about the average variable cost of producing a fish? *AVC* decreases from \$0.34 per fish at Q = 1,000 to a minimum of \$0.28 at Q = 5,000. Beyond Q = 6,000, it rises to \$0.77 at Q = 15,000. Mapped into Figure 4, *AVC* traces out a shallow U-shaped curve.

Average Total Cost

The *ATC* curve combines the *AFC* and *AVC* curves.

$$ATC = AFC + AVC$$

The influence of *AFC* and *AVC* on the character of *ATC* changes markedly depending on the level of production. For example, in the Q = 1,000 to Q = 5,000 range, *AFC* dominates *ATC*. In other words, fixed costs are more important than variable costs at low levels of production. At Q = 1,000, the *AFC* amounts to a whopping \$2.00 share of the \$2.34 average total cost. But at Q = 15,000, only \$0.13 of the \$0.90 average total cost is accounted for by average fixed cost.

In Figure 4, *ATC* is a U-shaped curve. It falls rapidly as output increases from zero. Why? Two factors influence its rate of decline: The rapidly decreasing *AFC* combines with the falling *AVC*, reflecting the firm's increasing efficiency.

But as production approaches 6,000 fish, the influence of the falling *AFC* on *ATC* is checked by the growing inefficiency of production reflected now in the rising *AVC*. Average total cost rises slightly. As production reaches 15,000 fish, the continuing, but now weak, effect of *AFC* on *ATC* is completely overshadowed by the rise in variable costs. As a result, *ATC* begins to increase more rapidly.

TO PRODUCE OR NOT TO PRODUCE, THAT IS THE QUESTION

It's quite clear from just a cursory glance at *ATC* in Figure 4 that if the price of fish were \$0.50, there is no possible way fishing could be profitable. There is no output level along the zero to 15,000 production range that can produce a fish for less than \$0.60.

Even producing 8,000 fish, where *ATC* = \$0.60 is at its minimum, you still lose \$0.10 on each fish. Multiplying this by 8,000 fish gives you an \$800 loss. Producing more than 8,000 is even more disastrous. For example, at Q = 15,000, *ATC* = \$0.90, so that the loss increases to 15,000 × –\$0.40 = \$6,000.

However, if the price were \$1.00, possibilities abound! Suppose you produce 11,000 fish. At Q = 11,000, *ATC* = \$0.68, so that for every one of the 11,000 fish sold, you make \$1.00 – \$0.68 = \$0.32 profit. Multiplying this by 11,000 gives you \$3,520 profit.

If you were to increase production to 12,000 fish, *ATC* increases to \$0.73, and profit now becomes (\$1.00 – \$0.73)(12,000) = \$3,240. Was it worth the extra cost to catch 12,000? Not really. Although you produce and sell more, your *ATC* also increases. The net result is less profit. It's a matter of simple arithmetic.

In either case, you make profit. But what you really want is to make the most profit possible. Look at the cost curves in Figure 4. Can you tell where the most profitable position is on the zero to 15,000 fish production scale when price is \$1.00? Don't bother trying.

MARGINAL COST

Marginal cost

The change in total cost generated by a change in the quantity of a good produced. Typically, MC is used to measure the additional cost incurred by adding one more unit of output to production.

A lot of guesswork or pencil calculations can be avoided by consulting the firm's **marginal cost** (MC). Marginal cost helps you determine precisely where profit can be maximized. Understandably then, marginal cost is one of the most important pieces of information you would want to consult before deciding production levels.

Marginal cost, like average total cost, is just another way of rearranging the total-cost data of Table 3. *Marginal cost measures the change in total cost resulting from a change in the quantity produced.*

$$MC = \frac{\Delta TC}{\Delta Q}$$

TABLE 5 The Marginal Cost of Producing Fish

Quantity	Change in Quantity	Total Cost	Change in Total Cost	Marginal Cost
0		$ 2,000		
1,000	1,000	2,340	$ 340	$0.34
2,000	1,000	2,640	300	0.30
3,000	1,000	2,900	260	0.26
4,000	1,000	3,140	240	0.24
5,000	1,000	3,400	260	0.26
6,000	1,000	3,750	350	0.35
7,000	1,000	4,200	450	0.45
8,000	1,000	4,800	600	0.60
9,000	1,000	5,550	750	0.75
10,000	1,000	6,450	900	0.90
11,000	1,000	7,500	1,050	1.05
12,000	1,000	8,700	1,200	1.20
13,000	1,000	10,100	1,400	1.40
14,000	1,000	11,700	1,600	1.60
15,000	1,000	13,500	1,800	1.80

Be careful to note the difference between marginal cost and average total cost.

Table 5 records the fishing firm's marginal cost over the production range of zero to 15,000 fish.

How do we read marginal cost in Table 5? When output increases from zero to 1,000 fish; that is, when the first 1,000 fish are added to production, total cost increases from $2,000 to $2,340. The marginal cost of each of the first 1,000 fish, then, is the change in total cost divided by the change in quantity, or ($2,340 – $2,000)/(1,000 – 0) = $0.34.

That's not the same as saying that the average cost of each of the first 1,000 fish is $0.34. *ATC* at 1,000 is $2.34. What marginal cost tells us is how much total cost increases when output increases from zero to 1,000. Since sitting in dock costs fishermen $2,000 anyway—$TC$ = $2,000 at $Q = 0$—producing the first 1,000 added only $2,340 – $2,000 = $340 to total cost, or $0.34 for each of the first 1,000 fish. This *add-on* is what marginal cost measures.

Suppose output increases from 1,000 to 2,000. What happens to marginal cost? The total cost of producing 2,000 fish is $2,640, or $300 more than the total cost of producing 1,000 fish. For each of the second 1,000 fish, *MC* = ($2,640 – $2,340)/(2,000 – 1,000) = $0.30.

Look how marginal cost changes across the zero to 15,000 production range. The marginal cost of adding fish decreases to a minimum of $0.24 at 4,000 fish, and increases thereafter, $0.26 to $0.35 to $0.45 and so on. At 15,000 fish, *MC* = $1.80.

Figure 5 maps out the marginal cost of Table 5 and shows the relationship between it and the *ATC* curve of Figure 4.

Note the relationship between the *MC* and *ATC* curves. When $MC < ATC$, *MC* causes *ATC* to fall. Look at any output level within the production

FIGURE 5 **Marginal Cost and Average Total Cost Curves**

Like the *ATC* curve, the *MC* curve is U-shaped. Within the output range zero to 8,000, *MC* is below *ATC*, causing *ATC* to fall. Beyond 8,000, *MC* is above *ATC*, causing *ATC* to increase. At 8,000, *MC* = *ATC*. At that point, *ATC* is at its minimum. The *MC* curve always cuts the *ATC* curve from below at the *ATC* curve's minimum.

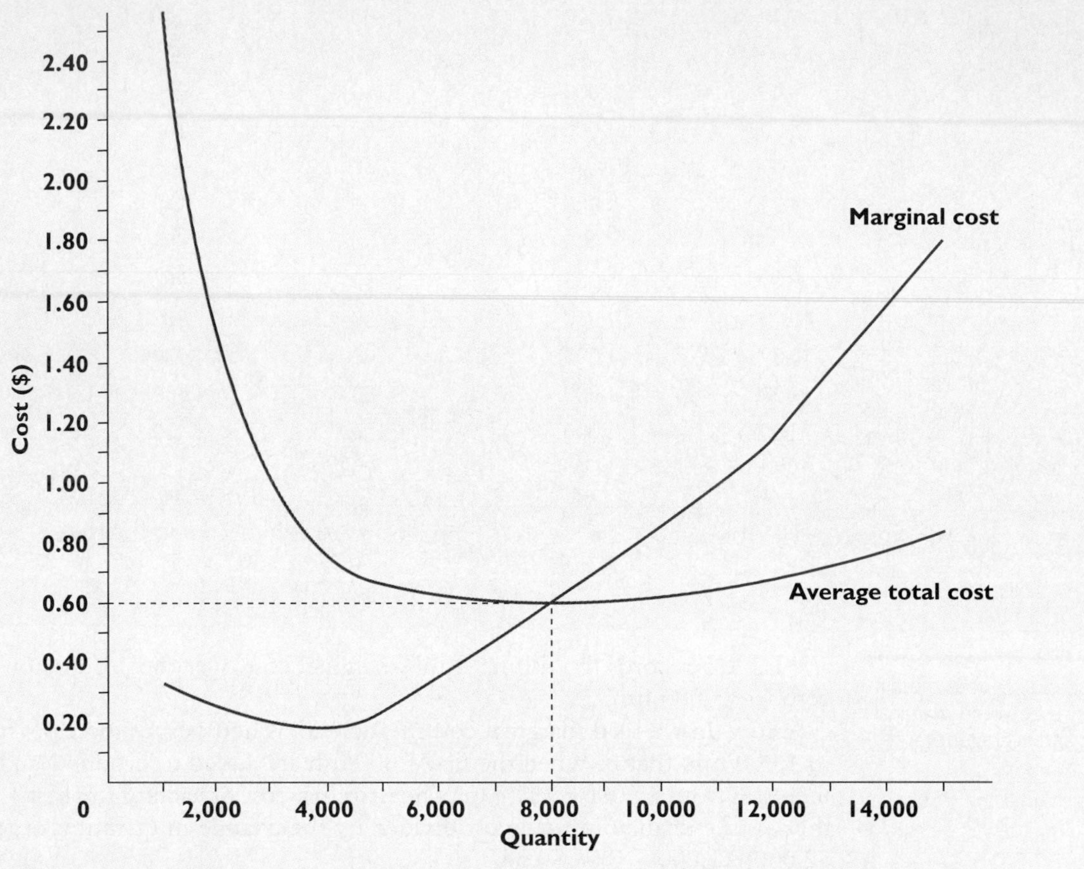

range zero to 8,000. For example, *Q* = 3,000. *MC* is $0.26 and *ATC* is $0.94. And look at the *ATC* curve at that level of production. It's falling. Note also that at production levels greater than 8,000 fish, *MC* > *ATC*, causing *ATC* to rise. Why this causation?

Suppose a class of 100 students takes an economics exam and the average grade is 75. Suppose a new student, the 101st—the marginal student—takes the exam and scores 60. Doesn't the class average fall? Intuitively, we know that when the marginal grade is lower than the average, it pulls the average down.

Look at the *MC* and *ATC* relationship along the upward-sloping segment of the *ATC* curve. At Q = 12,000, MC > *ATC*. When MC > *ATC*—everywhere along the output range beyond 8,000 average total cost is increasing because it is being drawn up by the higher *MC*.

Look at *MC* and *ATC* at Q = 8,000. Here, *MC* = *ATC* = $0.60. Because *MC* is neither greater nor less than *ATC*, it neither lowers nor raises *ATC*. At Q = 8,000, *ATC* is at its minimum point; it is neither rising nor falling.

ADDED PERSPECTIVE

Economies of Scale Wins Out in Mexico's Retailing Industry

The sprawling slum of Netzahualcoyotl, one of Mexico City's "lost cities," does not seem a likely place for a story of retailing success. The barrio's 3 million people earn, on average, $1,200 a year. Disposable income, while not high by U.S. standards, is rising rapidly, and so is consumption. Just in the last four years, Mexicans' personal disposable income has risen over 70 percent.

Jeronimo Arango, the son of a Spanish immigrant who prospered in textiles, is founder and chairman of Mexico's biggest retailer, Cifra, S.A., which had sales of $2.2 billion in 1990. Arango was first exposed to mass merchandising while a university student in America. In 1956, he was inspired by the long lines outside the no-frills E. J. Korvette discount department store in New York, and with his two brothers borrowed $240,000 from their father to open their first Aurrera discount store in 1958. They caused a sensation by offering household goods and clothing at as much as 20 percent below manufacturers' list prices; this infuriated established retailers who were making nice livings on markups of 40 or 45 percent.

"We were called traitors," Arango says. As Mexico City retailers threatened to boycott the Arangos' suppliers, the brothers ventured as far as Guadalajara and Monterrey to find other sources. When a manufacturer threatened to sue Aurrera for selling below list price, the brothers used their sponsorship of the popular TV show *The 64,000 Peso Question* to publicize the threat. The manufacturer backed off.

Discussion

Why do you suppose Arango can discount his merchandise and still profit? Why can't his competitors do the same? If you were in Mexico, what would prevent you from doing what he did?

Source: "Merchant of Mexico," by Joel Millman, *Forbes*, August 5, 1991.

ECONOMIES AND DISECONOMIES OF SCALE

The size of a fixed factor of production—the boat in our example—dictates the relevant range of production.

People in the fishing business, of course, do not all use the same size boat, employ the same crew size, fish the same waters, or combine their fixed and variable cost items in the same way. We can, instead, reasonably suppose that a rich variety of cost structures exist in the industry. Tables 4 and 5, which show *your* *ATC, AVC,* and *MC* across the production range zero to 15,000, represent only one cost structure of many.

Still, the cost variations among the firms would probably not be terribly great. Similar boats with similar equipment and crews probably do have similar cost structures. The cost range within the industry *may,* in fact, be rather narrow.

Figure 6 depicts two fishing firms with different cost structures. Suppose Phil Strang owns a small boat, and his neighbor, Lisa Burnett, owns a larger one.

If you spoke to a member of Lisa Burnett's fishing crew and asked how many fish Lisa's boat produces on a typical fishing run, what would you expect to hear? 2,000? 3,000? 10,000? 14,000? Look at Figure 6 carefully. If all Lisa had on her mind when she headed out on her boat to the fishing grounds was 2,000 fish, she was on the wrong boat! She should have been fishing on a boat similar to Phil Strang's. There's a mighty big difference between the fixed costs of the two boats. Look how the fixed-cost difference affects their *ATC* curves. Look at Strang's *ATC* when producing 2,000. It's $0.70. Compare that $0.70 to Burnett's $1.10 *ATC* when producing the same 2,000 fish on her larger, more expensive boat. It makes no sense for Burnett to use that boat, does it? Not if

FIGURE 6 **Average Total Cost Curves for Two Fishing Firms with Different Fixed Costs**

Strang's *ATC* curve and Burnett's *ATC* curve reflect the different fixed costs associated with the different capacity boats that Strang and Burnett use. For outputs less than 4,000 fish, Strang's operation is more efficient. His *ATC* is less than Burnett's at every output level. But when output exceeds 4,000 fish, Burnett becomes the more efficient. At output levels beyond 4,000 her *ATC* is lower than Strang's.

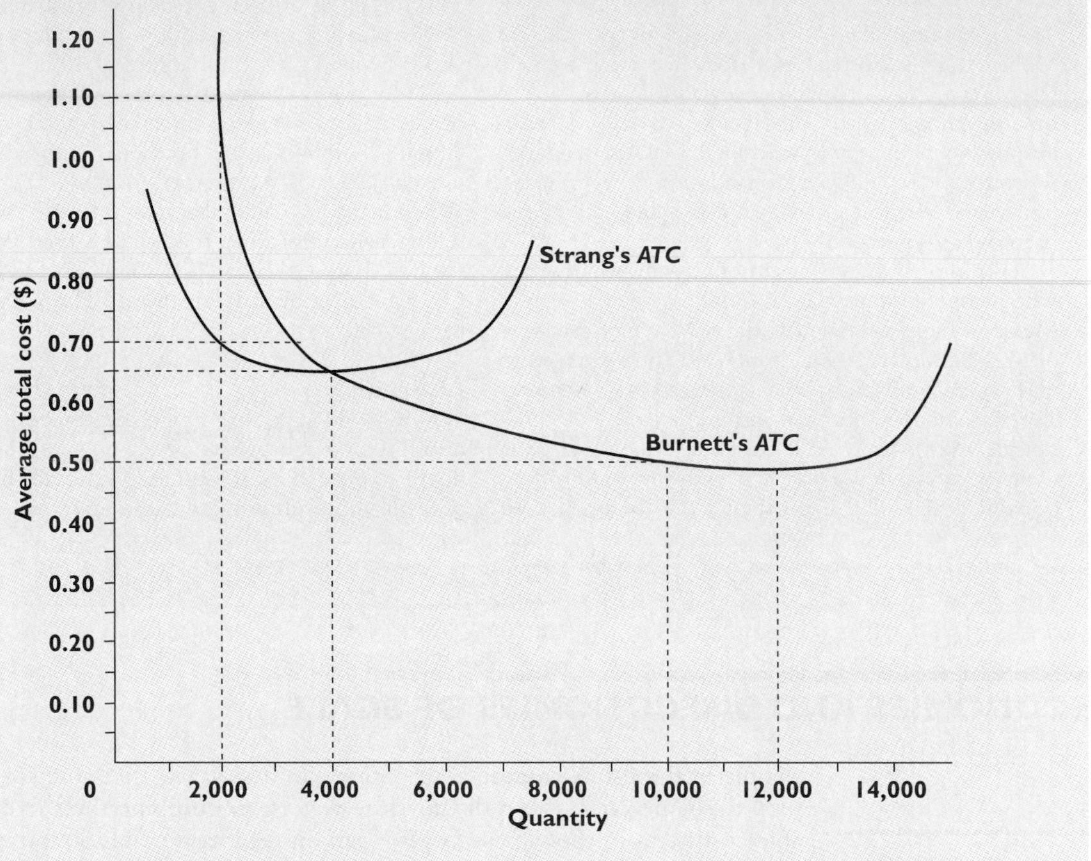

she produces 2,000 or any other output within the zero to 4,000 production range. *But she never intends to produce within that range.* That's why she bought the bigger boat.

As you see in Figure 6, her more expensive boat makes economic sense once production increases beyond 4,000. For example, at an output level of 10,000 fish, Burnett's *ATC* falls to \$0.50 which is \$0.10 lower than Strang's minimum *ATC* (\$0.65).

Strang's production range is limited to 7,000 fish. *But he never intends to produce beyond that range.* In fact, if he produces more than 4,000 fish, he's at a cost disadvantage. Burnett's *ATC* falls below Strang's after 4,000.

Burnett's *ATC* reaches its minimum at $Q = 12{,}000$, well beyond the range that Strang would consider workable. Beyond $Q = 12{,}000$, her *ATC* curve is upward sloping. What set of cost structures is the most appropriate, then, depends on the firm's planned scale of operations.

Let's relax our unrealistic assumption that only three sizes of boats exist. There are, in fact, a variety of types and sizes. Some boats are actually floating

FIGURE 7 **Economies of Scale, Diseconomies of Scale, and Constant Returns to Scale**

Seven *ATC* curves—ATC_1 to ATC_7—represent costs associated with different-size firms. Economies of scale occur within the output range zero to 50,000. Here, increases in firm size from ATC_1 to ATC_4 result in decreases in *ATC* minimums. Constant returns to scale occur within the output range 50,000 to 70,000. Here, firm size increases from ATC_4 to ATC_5. Within that range, the firm's *ATC* minimums are the same. Diseconomies of scale occur beyond 70,000. Here, firm size increases from ATC_5 to ATC_7. As the firm produces more, its *ATC* minimums increase.

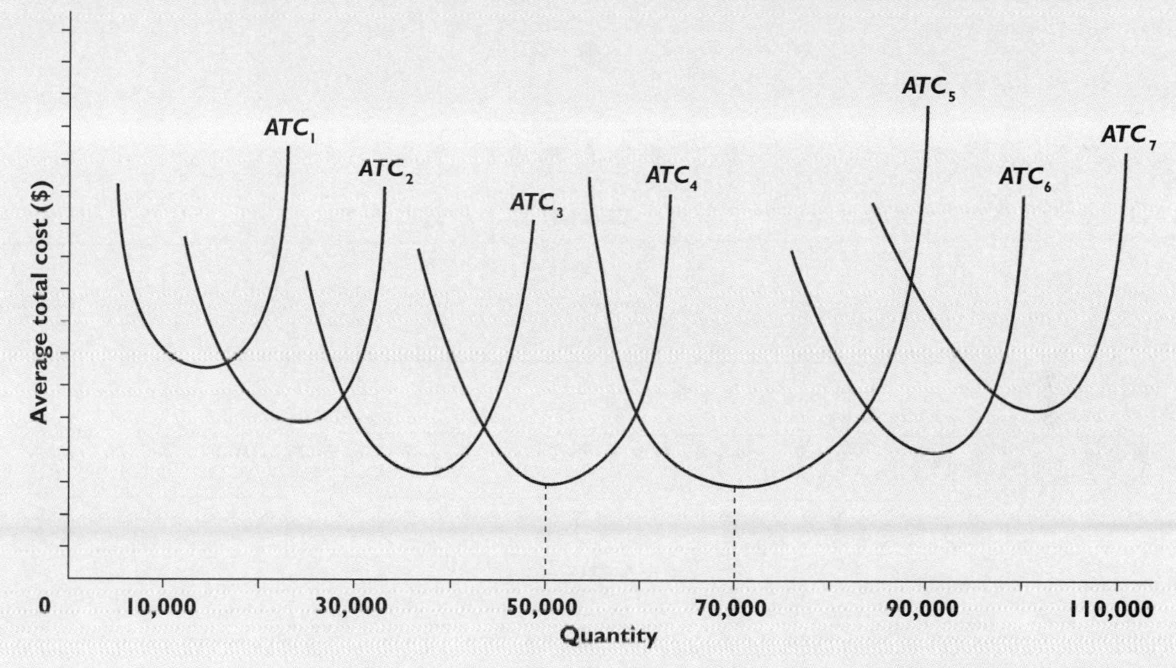

fishing factories, capable of harvesting and dressing hundreds of thousands of fish. For them, production ranges can extend to 1 million fish per run.

What happens to a firm's *ATC* curve when the size of the boats keeps increasing? Do the minimum points on the *ATC* curves keep falling? Not forever. Increases in the scale of operations, that is, larger and larger boats producing more and more fish, can shift a firm's *ATC* curve so that its minimum *ATC* keeps falling, *but only to a certain point.* Beyond that, further increases in the firm's scale of production will eventually cause its *ATC* curve, and the minimum point on the *ATC* curve, to rise again. This effect is illustrated in Figure 7.

Shifting from smaller to larger boats generates a series of *ATC* curves—ATC_1 to ATC_2 to ATC_3—whose minimums, at first, are decreasing. In Figure 7, this phenomenon occurs within the output range zero to 50,000 fish per run. Economists refer to this range as having **economies of scale.** Fishing companies producing at $Q = 50{,}000$, compared to those producing at $Q = 25{,}000$, can take advantage of greater labor specialization, more productive equipment, price discounts through large-quantity purchases, and more cost-efficient methods of marketing.

Economies of scale

Decreases in the firm's average total cost brought about by increased specialization and efficiencies in production realized through increases in the scale of the firm's operations.

By doubling its scale of operations within this output range, a firm's total cost will increase, but not double. That is, by doubling scale, average total cost falls.

But look what happens to the firm's *ATC* minimums within the production range 50,000 to 70,000. The minimums remain unchanged. Economists

FIGURE 8 **Organizational Charts of Working Crew on Boats with 10, 70, and 300 Crew Members**

In chart 1, 10 crew members work under the supervision of one other person. In chart 2, the firm size expands to include two levels of management and a crew of 70. The information flow from crew to top management, or from top management to crew, now gets filtered through a layer of middle managers. In chart 3, the much larger boat supports a crew size of 300. Several new layers of middle management are added to the organizational structure. Once informal procedures become formalized and, at worst, fossilized.

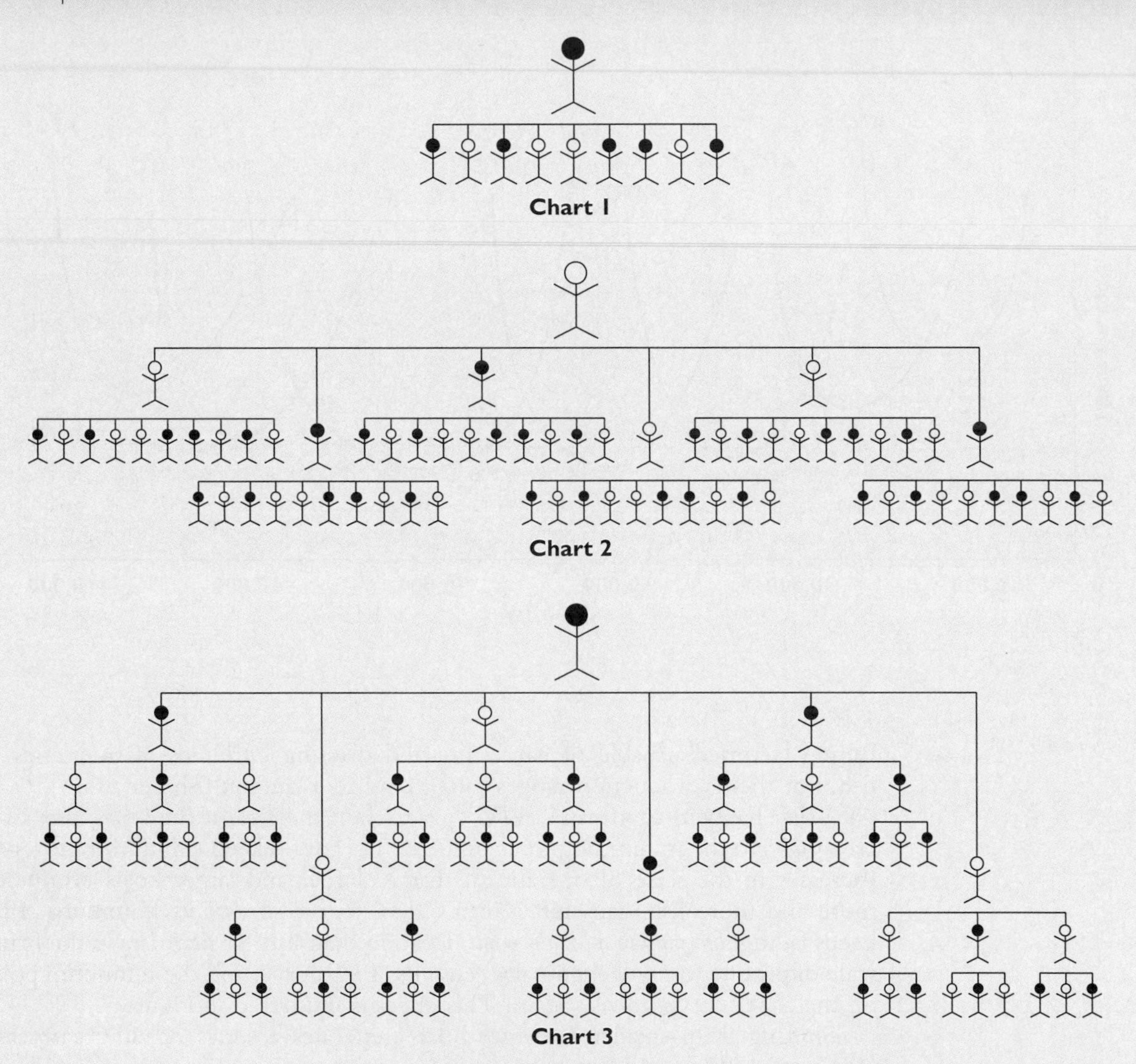

Constant returns to scale

Costs per unit of production are the same for any level of production. Changes in plant size do not affect the firm's average total cost.

refer to this range as having **constant returns to scale.** Increasing the scale of operations within this range just increases the firm's total cost proportionately. The advantages of bigness, seen in the zero to 50,000 output range, have dissipated.

Look at the range of production beyond $Q = 70{,}000$. There, increasing scale from ATC_5 to ATC_6 to ATC_7 generates ATC minimums that actually increase. By doubling the scale of operations in this range, the firm's total cost more than doubles. Economists refer to the range beyond Q = 70,000 as having **diseconomies of scale.** Why? Why has bigness now turned into a disadvantage?

Diseconomies of scale

Increases in the firm's average total cost brought about by the disadvantages associated with bureaucracy and the inefficiencies that eventually emerge with increases in the firm's operations.

Because a firm can get too big for its own good! Problems of management, organization, and information flow emerge. Imagine the kinds of problems management may confront on boats with 10, 70, or 300 crew members. This is illustrated in Figure 8.

In the first chart, 10 crew members work under one person. Bureaucracy is virtually nonexistent. Information about production flows easily and freely from management to crew, from crew to management, and from one crew member to another. Production adjustments are typically made on the spot. Communication is direct and informal.

Chart 2 represents the organizational structure on a larger boat. Here we have two levels of management and a working crew of 70. The new line of management is created to facilitate communication and execute top-level decisions. The information flow from crew to top management or from top management to crew now gets filtered through a layer of middle managers. Information among the 70 crew members, separated by more specific function, becomes somewhat delayed and sometimes misunderstood. A fledgling bureaucracy emerges.

Economies of scale, constant returns to scale, and diseconomies of scale relate to changes in the scale of the firm's operations. If the firm can change its scale of operation, are any factors of production fixed?

In chart 3, a much larger boat supports a crew of 300. Lines of communications between the crew and management become extended as several new layers of management are added. As a result, standard procedures replace on-the-spot decision making. Problems occur, but if unrelated to specific tasks, remain unattended. Information is highly filtered, often misunderstood, and sometimes purposely modified by middle managers who pursue their own agendas. Crew efficiency suffers. In many cases, the gains expected from economics of scale are checked by the bureaucratic inefficiencies inherent in bigness.

LONG-RUN AND SHORT-RUN COSTS

The size of the physical plant is the fixed factor of production in the short run. The physical plant size can be changed in the long run.

How do fishing firms view the variety of ATC structures available to them? Can they pick and choose among them? As we have seen, once the purchase of a boat is made, the firm is committed to the ATC structure associated with that boat. It loses the freedom to move, say, from one ATC curve in Figure 7 to another. It regains that freedom of choice only at full depreciation, when a new boat purchase has to be made. At that time, any boat size—any ATC structure in Figure 7—is viable.

See how Figure 7 is simplified into Figure 9 to illustrate the differences between short-run and long-run costs.

Short run

The time interval during which producers are able to change the quantity of some but not all the resources they use to produce goods and services.

Long run

The time interval during which producers are able to change the quantity of all the resources they use to produce goods and services. In the long run, all costs are variable.

The time interval during which producers are able to change the quantity of some but not all resources they use to produce goods and services is called the **short run.** For the fishing industry, the short run is the time interval in which a fishing firm is unable to change its physical plant, that is, its boat. The firm can still increase or decrease other cost items, such as labor and raw materials, and thereby increase or decrease output. But the range of possible output is limited to the size of the physical plant. Its short-run ATC structure reflects that fixed cost commitment.

In the **long run,** producers are able to change the quantity of all the resources they use to produce goods and services. That is, for the fishing firm in

FIGURE 9 **Short- and Long-Run Cost Curves for a Fishing Firm**

Each of the *ATC* curves represents the firm's short-run cost choices. Once one is selected, the firm is committed to it until the fixed-cost items associated with the chosen *ATC* depreciate. The firm's long-run cost curve is the envelope curve formed by drawing a line enclosing the short-run cost curves. It represents the cost options open to the firm before any specific commitment to boat size is made.

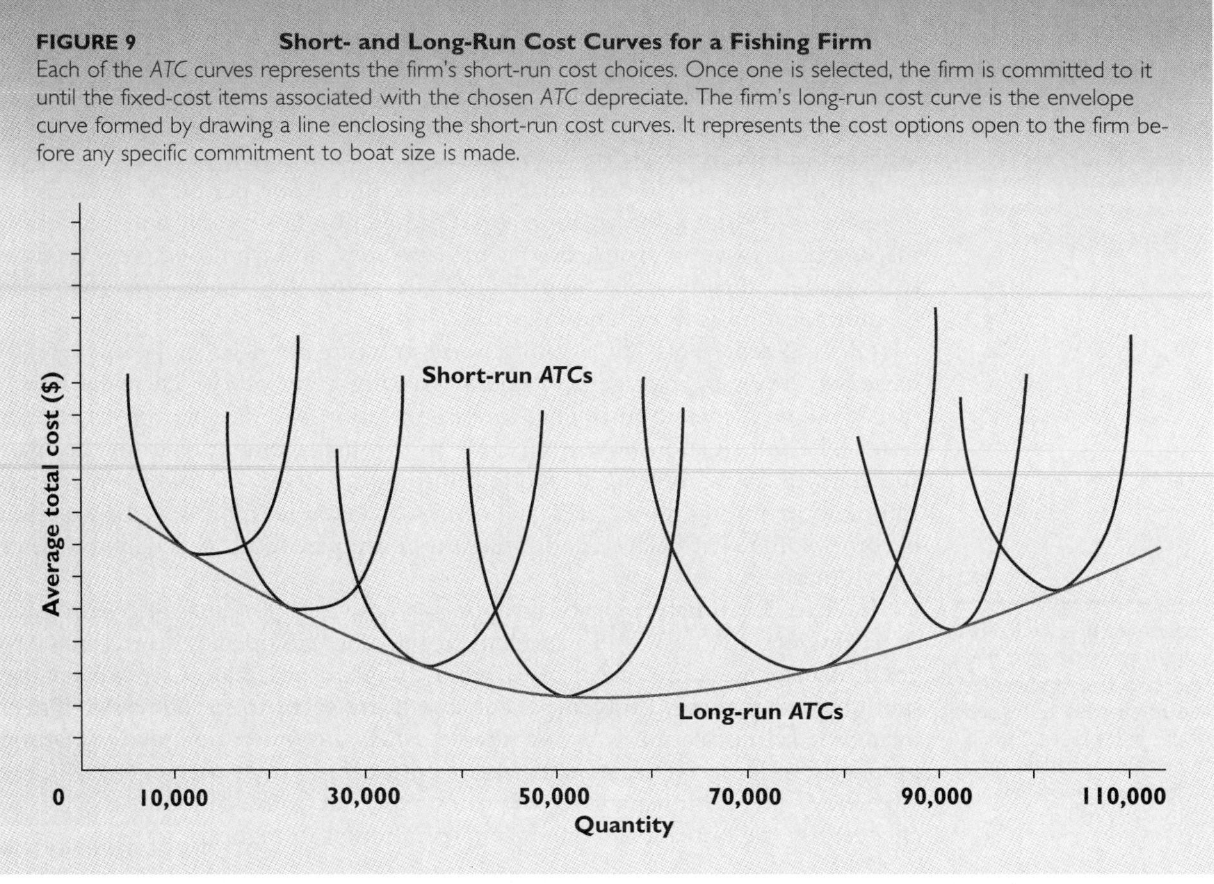

the long run, all cost items, including boats, are variable. When a boat is depreciated fully, the firm can purchase another like it, decide on a bigger one, or even pick a smaller one. *Once the decision is made, the firm is back to the short run.* The firm's long-run *ATC* curve in Figure 9—called the envelope curve—is tangent to the short-run *ATC*s of Figure 7.

WHAT IS TRUE FOR THE FISHING INDUSTRY IS TRUE FOR ALL INDUSTRIES

The *ATC*s and *MCs* for all firms in all industries—fishing, boatmaking, farming, legal services, steel, public relations, plastic tubing—reflect in each the rich variety of short-run and long-run cost combinations. No two Texas farms are exactly alike. Nor should we expect their *ATC* structures to be alike.

J. Patrick Madden of the U.S. Department of Agriculture estimated the average cost curves for different kinds of irrigated cotton farms in the Texas High Plains in 1967. His results are shown in Figure 10.

Each of the six cost curves has the familiar U-shape. They also illustrate economies of scale. Differences in farm size affect the *ATC* of producing Texas cotton. For example, shifting along the curve from a one-man farm to a four-man farm generates progressively lower *ATC* minimums.

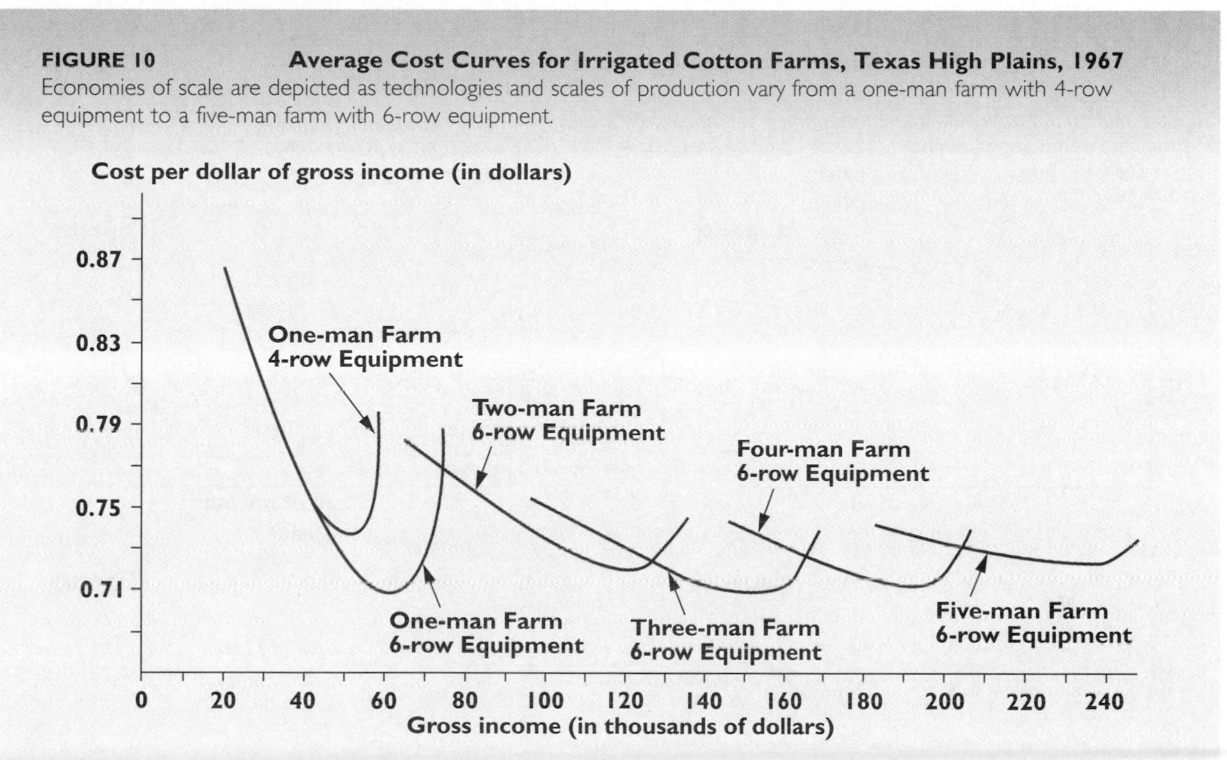

Source: Madden, J. Patrick, *Economies of Size in Farming,* U. S. Department of Agriculture, Washington, D.C., AER No. 107 (February 1967), p. 44.

There's essentially no difference in the general character of cost structures among fishing firms, cotton farms, and automobile firms. In your fishing business, you make decisions concerning the size of the boat, the size of the crew, the types of fishing equipment, the level of production, and so on. On Texas cotton farms, the same kinds of decisions are made.

At General Motors, its board of directors, its research, engineering, finance, and marketing departments do what you do. They too decide on the size of their plants, the number of assembly lines, the size of their labor force, the level of output, and so on. General Motors derives its *ATC* and *MC* in precisely the same manner you do. It, too, confronts economies and diseconomies of scale. If the price of automobiles cannot cover its *ATC,* it closes assembly lines, just as you would put the fishing nets away if the price of fish didn't cover your *ATC.* The only difference between the *ATC* curves of your fishing firm and General Motors is size. General Motors counts in billions, you count in thousands.

WHAT BUSINESS PEOPLE THINK ABOUT THE CHARACTER OF THEIR *ATCs*

Some years ago two economists, Wilford Eiteman and Glenn Guthrie, decided to ask business people what they thought their own cost curves looked like. Were they decreasing, increasing, or constant over their production range?

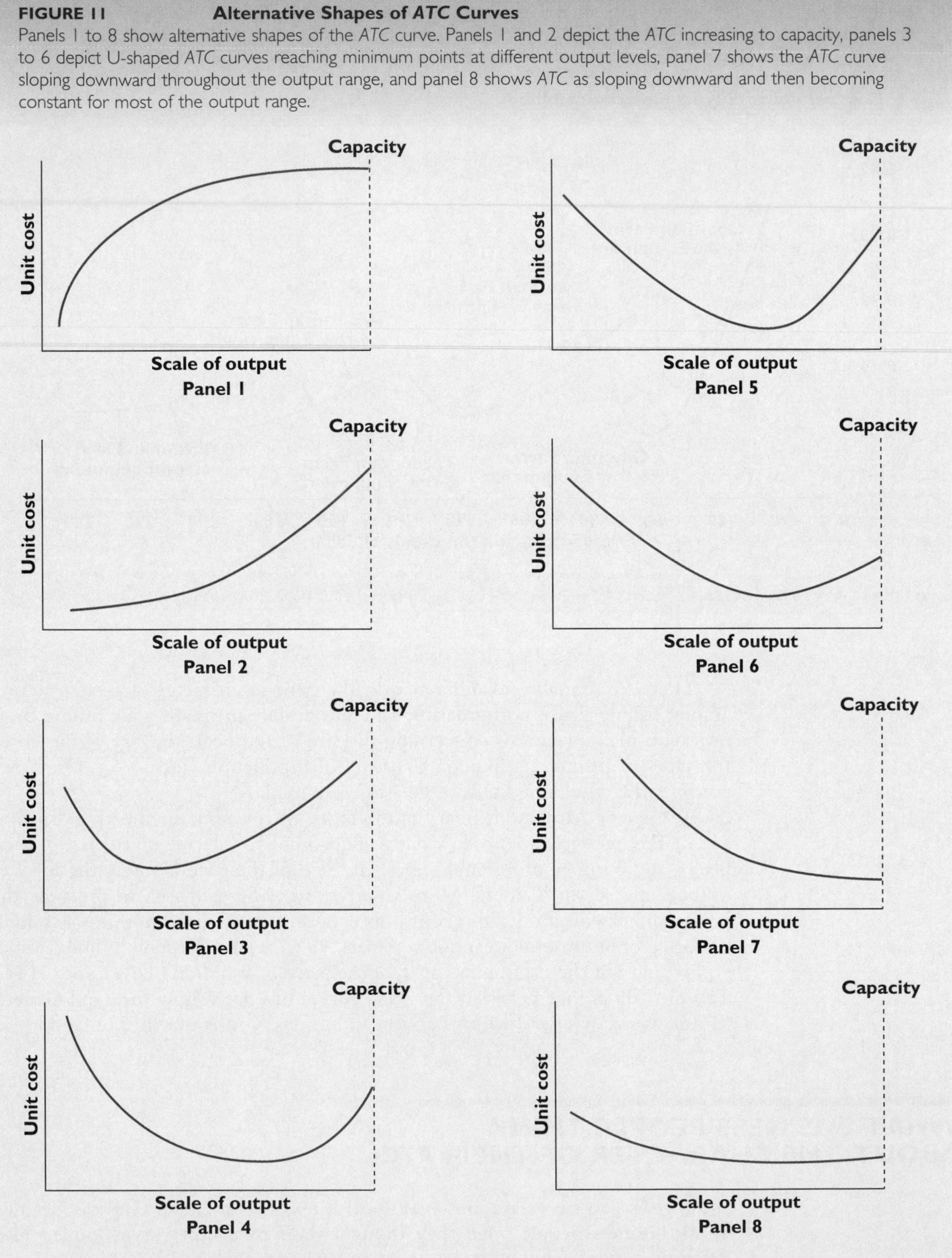

FIGURE 11 Alternative Shapes of *ATC* Curves

Panels 1 to 8 show alternative shapes of the *ATC* curve. Panels 1 and 2 depict the *ATC* increasing to capacity, panels 3 to 6 depict U-shaped *ATC* curves reaching minimum points at different output levels, panel 7 shows the *ATC* curve sloping downward throughout the output range, and panel 8 shows *ATC* as sloping downward and then becoming constant for most of the output range.

Source: Eiteman, Wilford, J., and Guthrie, Glenn, E., "The Shape of the Average Cost Curve," *American Economic Review*, XLII, 5 (December 1952), pp. 832–838.

TABLE 6
The *ATC* Curves Identified by Businesspeople as Representing Their Products' Cost Structure

Panel	Number of Products	Percent of Total Products
1	0	—
2	1	—
3	5	—
4	15	1.3
5	42	3.8
6	381	35.2
7	636	58.7
8	2	—
Total	1,082	100.0

Source: Eiteman, Wilford, J., and Guthrie, Glenn, E., "The Shape of the Average Cost Curve," *American Economic Review*, XLII, 5 (December 1952), pp. 832–838.

Each businessperson was asked to identify, from a set of diagrams offered, the one that best represented his or her situation. The eight diagrams shown in Figure 11 were the choices offered.

Questionnaires were sent to 1,000 manufacturing firms located in 47 states. The companies chosen had more than 500, but fewer than 5,000 employees. Some were multiproduct firms. Together, they produced 1,082 products.

Of the 1,000 firms, 366 responded. The results of the canvass are shown in Table 6.

Of the 1,082 products produced by the firms surveyed, 636 products, or 58.7 percent of the total, were described as having been produced under conditions portrayed by panel 7—that is, continuous downward-sloping until production reaches physical capacity.

For 35.2 percent of the total, panel 6 was identified as representing the character of *ATC*. For these products, *ATC* was essentially downward-sloping, but increased slightly as the firms neared production capacity. Panels 4 and 5, representing only 5.1 percent of the products produced, were also chosen.

One businessperson wrote: "The amazing thing is that any sane economist could consider [panels 3, 4, and 5] curves as representing business behavior." A manufacturer of road-building equipment said: "Even with the low efficiency and premium pay of overtime work, our unit costs would still decline with increased production, since the absorption of fixed expenses would more than offset the added direct expenses incurred."

Were these views rational, or more closely akin to wishful thinking? Several cost structure studies lend support to such a view, although the specific shape of *ATC* curves can vary tremendously from one industry to another.[1]

[1]See, for example, Elzinga, Kenneth, G., "The Beer Industry," in Adams, Walter, ed., *The Structure of American Industry*, 6ed. (New York: MacMillan, 1982), p. 218; Phillips, Charles, F., *Competition in the Synthetic Rubber Industry* (Chapel Hill: The University of North Carolina Press, 1963), p. 185; Kurdle, Robert, T., *Agricultural Tractors: A World Industry Survey*, (Cambridge, MA: Ballinger, 1975), p. 41; and Suits, Daniel, "Agriculture," in Adams, Walter, ed., *The Structure of American Industry*, 6ed. (New York: MacMillan, 1982), p. 14.

BEHIND EVERY COST CURVE IS A SOCIOECONOMIC ENVIRONMENT

Costs are culture-bound. An *ATC* curve for the manufacture of tennis balls in Butte, Montana, may be very different from the *ATC* curve for tennis ball production in Kabul, Afghanistan. It may be economically prohibitive to produce them in Kabul. Why?

Imagine yourself in the foothills of Afghanistan's Hindu Kush with a capital stock of $200 million and a burning desire to produce tennis balls in Afghanistan. How do you begin? Where do you find qualified labor? Where do you find the raw materials? How do you build the plant? If the economic environment isn't cooperative, all the money and ideas in the world won't help.

Let's consider once again your decision at the beginning of this chapter to go into the fishing business. One reason you were able to buy a $200,000 maxiboat is that such boats were being produced. This simple fact presupposes the not-so-simple fact that a boat-building industry exists.

It also means that engineers, welders, steel manufacturers, electricians, accountants, communications people, painters, drydock operators, and a cast of tens of thousands of very productive people are working in thousands of firms. In addition, it assumes that you can arrange payment through a banking system already in place.

How do you come by a fishing crew that can handle sonar and radar, repair engines, and read navigation charts? That assumes the ready availability of qualified people. How do they acquire expertise? Through schools and a system of municipal bonds to finance them. There seems to be a never-ending set of linkages back into every sector of our economy.

The presence of qualified people, institutions, and industries is so familiar to us that it is difficult to realize that without our political, cultural, and social—as well as our economic—system nothing could be produced except perhaps in an economically primitive way. Blueprints and modern technical knowledge may be available, but without a fairly advanced socioeconomic climate, they would be totally unusable. Your maxiboat would remain nothing but a dream.

We take this kind of socioeconomic environment for granted because it is our good fortune to belong to an already highly developed industrialized society. It seems reasonable to us, if we need a skilled crew, to simply telephone the classified department of the newspaper and wait for applicants. In fact, that's what we do.

That is what General Motors does, what Sony does, and what Westinghouse does. But if no telephones, postal service, or newspapers existed, how do you go about organizing a modern labor force? How could you produce automobiles, air conditioners, and fish? Can you imagine how different cost structures would be if *any one* of these factors were absent? And how impossible it would be to produce fish or furniture if they were underdeveloped.

That is to say, the *social and economic environment is as important a factor of production as entrepreneurship, capital, labor, and land.* It is not clear whether people in Afghanistan or Libya can adopt technologies from the United States and Canada as readily as people in Japan and New Zealand can. *Cost structures are very much culture-bound.*

CHAPTER REVIEW

1. Becoming an entrepreneur is an act that requires careful consideration. An entrepreneur usually has considerable knowledge of a business before entering it, as well as the willingness to assume business risks and sufficient access to money to start up a firm.

2. Fixed costs are short-run commitments. Once a fixed-cost item is fully depreciated, the entrepreneur is faced with a long-run situation.

3. Fixed costs are incurred even when production is zero. Fixed costs are spread over the lifetime of the fixed-cost item and the rate at which the item is utilized.

4. Variable-cost items are those that vary with the level of production. For example, in order to catch more fish, more labor must be hired, more bait used, as well as more fuel burned.

5. Labor costs may increase at a decreasing rate and then increase at an increasing rate as production is expanded. Three factors contribute to this labor cost behavior: changes in labor efficiency, changes in the quality of labor, and changes in the price of labor.

6. Average total cost is computed by dividing total cost by the quantity of output. Similarly, average variable cost is total variable cost divided by the quantity of output. Average fixed cost is total fixed cost divided by the quantity of output.

7. Marginal cost is the change in total cost divided by the change in the quantity of output produced. Thus, marginal cost is the addition to total cost when producing one more unit of output. If marginal cost is less than average total cost, then average total cost decreases. When marginal cost is greater than average total cost, average total cost increases. Marginal cost intersects average total cost at its minimum point.

8. Differences in fixed costs, different quantities and qualities of labor and equipment, and different management techniques can lead to differences in costs between firms in the same industry. Yet, the range of these differences is probably not great. Firms in an industry may operate at different levels of production which will create cost differences.

9. Increases in the scale of operations for a firm may result in falling average total costs. If so, then the firm is experiencing economies of scale. Economies of scale occur when an increase in the size of a firm's operations results in a decrease in unit costs. Alternatively, if, say, the firm doubles output and total costs double too, then the firm experiences constant returns to scale. Diseconomies of scale occur when increasing output leads to increases in unit costs. Management problems associated with a big firm are a primary source of diseconomies of scale.

10. The firm's physical plant is fixed in the short run. In the long run, the physical plant can be altered. The long-run average-cost curve is traced out to form an envelope curve of the short-run average-cost curves.

11. A variety of industries exhibit the U-shaped average total cost curves. However, most businesses try to operate on the downward-sloping portion of their U-shaped average total cost curves.

12. The socioeconomic environment influences the nature of costs for all the firms in an economy. The social and economic environment determines whether certain types of production activities are possible or not.

KEY TERMS

Fixed cost
Variable cost
Labor efficiency
Total cost
Average total cost
Average fixed cost
Average variable cost
Marginal cost
Economies of scale
Constant returns to scale
Diseconomies of scale
Short run
Long run

QUESTIONS

1. What is Northwest Airlines' marginal cost of adding an additional passenger to its Boeing 747 flight from Minneapolis to Seattle, assuming seats are available?

2. How long is the long run?

3. Why is labor considered a variable cost?

4. The average fixed cost curve for any firm is downward-sloping, approaching zero. Why?

5. The average total cost curve is U-shaped. Why?

6. At every output level, average total cost is greater than either average fixed cost or average variable cost. Why?

7. Why are there economies of scale, diseconomies of scale, and constant returns to scale? Cite examples.

8. Why does the marginal cost curve cut the average total cost curve from below at the average total cost curve's lowest point?

9. Why would it be much more difficult, perhaps even impossible, to reproduce in the Sahara desert the fixed, variable, and total costs associated with U.S. production of computer equipment?

10. Complete the following table, then plot the *TC* curve on a graph.

Output	***TFC***	***TVC***	***TC***
0	$120	$ 0	
1		60	
2		80	
3		90	
4		105	
5		140	
6		210	

11. Complete the following table, then plot the *ATC* and *MC* curves on the same graph.

Output	TC	ATC	AVC	AFC	MC
1	$1,170			$10.00	
2	1,320				
3	1,450				
4	1,570				
5	1,700				
6	1,840				
7	2,100				
8	2,400				
9	2,750				
10	3,160				

12. Why can't you plot the *ATC* and *MC* curves in question 11 on the same graph as the *TC* curve in question 10?

13. Draw a long-run average total cost curve that shows economies of scale in the lower ranges of outputs, followed by constant returns to scale in the higher ranges, and diseconomies of scale thereafter.

C H A P T E R 9

MAXIMIZING PROFIT

CHAPTER PREVIEW

Entrepreneurs don't want just to make a profit. They want to maximize profits. Once questions of production methods, commitments to fixed costs, employment of labor, and other variable cost inputs have been addressed, an entrepreneur's attention must turn to the revenue side of the business operation. The difference between total revenue and total cost is profit. How should production be arranged to maximize profits? This is the central question to be answered in Chapter 9.

After studying this chapter, you should be able to:

- Discuss the problems entrepreneurs face in correctly anticipating price changes.
- Explain how profit depends on the price of a good once costs are determined.
- Calculate marginal revenue, total revenue, and average revenue given data on price and quantity sold.
- Explain why the "marginal revenue equals marginal cost" rule maximizes profits.
- Show on a graph the area that represents profit for a firm.

- Validate the logic behind the "marginal revenue equals marginal cost" rule for minimizing losses.
- Discuss the implications of a firm's failure to cover its variable costs.
- Present the mark-up theory of profit as an alternative to marginal analysis.
- Describe various empire-building theories of corporate behavior.

There's a story told about a twenty-fifth high school reunion. Those attending were shocked to discover that the most unlikely of their classmates, Jeff Stevens, who had had trouble passing chemistry, literature, history, biology, mathematics, and even gym, turned out to be the only multimillionaire! How had he done it? What was his magic? They gathered around their one outstanding success story to learn his secret. "It's simple," he told them. "Buy at $10, sell at $20, and be satisfied with your 25 percent profit."

The point of this silly story is that you don't necessarily have to be a Nobel Laureate to be successful in the business world. Most entrepreneurs rely on instinct, on their wits, on taking chances, on a great deal of luck, and on extraordinary effort. Perhaps the most important weapon in their profit-making arsenal is *personal drive.*

Profit maximization

The primary goal of a firm. The firm strives to achieve the most profit possible from its production and sale of goods or services.

Vince Lombardi, the legendary coach of the Green Bay Packers, once philosophized about football: "Winning isn't everything. It's the *only* thing." Entrepreneurs understand Lombardi. He wasn't satisfied with just a winning season. It was always a losing season for him if the Packers didn't win the Superbowl. Entrepreneurs are like that. They are never satisfied with just making profit. They want to **maximize profit.**

ENTREPRENEURS AND PROFIT MAKING

Entrepreneurs live in two very different spheres of economic life at the same time. Their survival in each requires them to master very different kinds of knowledge, decision making, and uncertainties. In the sphere of production, entrepreneurs must commit themselves to cost obligations even before production starts. They must make decisions about the kinds of products they will produce and about leasing or buying their physical plant. They need to know what machinery and raw materials to purchase. They must decide on managerial staff before production workers get on the production line. For many firms, the costs of establishing the business are financed by banks, committing the entrepreneur to interest payments on loans as well. All these cost obligations take place before the first unit of goods rolls off the production line.

Entrepreneurs must therefore make production decisions that require some degree of expertise in both the mechanics of production and in accounting. What kinds of technologies are appropriate? What kinds of labor should they hire? How can they arrange these factors of production in the most efficient way? Although costs are committed before production starts, there is no assurance that all the effort and expense will end up generating sufficient revenues to cover costs, let alone provide for profit.

In the other sphere of economic life that entrepreneurs operate in—the world of markets—the problems confronted and the decision making required are very different. The trick here is to *anticipate* what prices will be.

Planning to set up a travel agency in your home town upon graduation? It is inconceivable to think of running such a business today without the use of computers. But, a mountain of computers still cannot substitute for business smarts and cannot assume the uncertainties that businesses confront daily. It's nice to know you're indispensable.

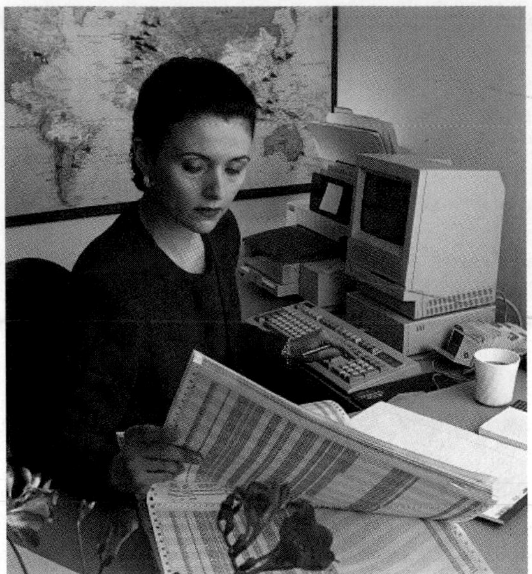

There's obviously no way of knowing. Entrepreneurs rely on their best judgment, sometimes on a sixth sense. Whatever their source of knowledge, it is still basically guesswork. If they guess correctly, if prices turn out to be what they anticipated, or perhaps even higher, they may make a profit. On the other hand, if prices fall short of expectation, they may lose. If they are too far off the mark, they may lose everything. Many novice entrepreneurs do lose everything.

The issues they confront daily concern not only the uncertainties of their own market, but also the uncertainties associated with the state of the economy. After all, even if they know their own markets well, they cannot possibly know how the economy will fare in six months. Will there be prosperity or recession?

What happens to prices if the economy slumps? Typically, national employment, income, and consumption fall. Markets weaken and prices drift downward. But many entrepreneurs have already undertaken cost obligations. Profits, under these conditions, can disappear rather quickly.

On the other hand, if the national economy swings into full employment, demand typically increases and prices bounce upward. The difference now between already committed costs and increasing price widens, creating more attractive profit margins.

PROFIT-MAXIMIZING FISHERMEN

Total profit is just the difference between price and *ATC*, multiplied by output.

Picture fishermen as entrepreneurs. The average total cost of producing a fish depends on the number of fish caught. Table 1 summarizes the average and marginal cost data from Tables 4 and 5 in the previous chapter.

When Costs Are Committed, Profit Depends on Price

Suppose the fishermen return from a fishing run with 11,000 fish. We see in Table 1 that the average cost of producing each of these 11,000 fish is $0.68.

TABLE 1
Average Total Cost and Marginal Cost of Producing Fish per Fishing Run ($ per Fish)

Quantity	Average Cost	Marginal Cost
0	—	—
1,000	$2.34	$0.34
2,000	1.32	0.30
3,000	0.97	0.26
4,000	0.79	0.24
5,000	0.68	0.26
6,000	0.63	0.35
7,000	0.60	0.45
8,000	0.60	0.60
9,000	0.62	0.75
10,000	0.65	0.90
11,000	0.68	1.05
12,000	0.73	1.20
13,000	0.78	1.40
14,000	0.84	1.60
15,000	0.77	1.80

Was it worth the effort? It depends on the price of fish. Suppose the price is $0.75. How much do the fishermen make on a $0.75 fish? The calculation is simple. The profit per fish is $P - ATC$. At a production run of 11,000 fish, profit per fish is $0.75 – $0.68 = $0.07.

What about the fishermen's total profit? Total profit is simply $(P - ATC) \times Q$. With a production run of 11,000, total profit is ($0.75 – $0.68) × 11,000 = $770. What could be simpler than that?

Suppose price increased from $0.75 to $0.80. The fishermen may have been on the water when the price rose, creating a rather pleasant surprise when they return to the docks. Their total profit increases. They still bring in the same 11,000 fish and ATC is still $0.68. But with a price of $0.80, total profit increases from $770 to ($0.80 – $0.68) × 11,000 = $1,320.

Should Fishermen Produce More Fish?

Suppose the $1,320 profit encourages fishermen to increase production. They hire more crew and stay out longer, increasing their catch from 11,000 to 12,000 fish per run. This higher production level means, of course, more $0.80 fish. *But it also means that average total cost changes as well.*

Look at Table 1. The average total cost of producing a fish at a 12,000 production run is $0.73. That is, ATC increases $0.05, from $0.68 to $0.73. The fishermen now get only $0.80 – $0.73 = $0.07 profit per fish. Look what happens to total profit. It decreases from $1,320 to ($0.80 – $0.73) × 12,000 = $840. Did it pay the fishermen to run production up to 12,000?

Obviously not. The increase in total revenue generated by the additional 1,000 fish was not enough to overcome the increase in the total cost of catching those 12,000 fish. Of course, it's not the end of the world. The fishermen are still making $840 profit.

But making profit is not exactly the same as making the most profit possible. Fishermen, like all other entrepreneurs, are in business to *maximize* profit. If their production choices were only 11,000 or 12,000 fish, there's no question where they would choose to produce. But why only two options? Their production capacity, fixed by the size of their boats, allows them to choose *any* output level along the production range zero to 20,000 fish per run. How do fishermen figure out where that profit maximizing output is?

THE *MR* = *MC* RULE

One laborious way of discovering the most profitable level of production is to calculate total profit for each and every output across the zero to 15,000 fish production range and choose the one that yields the most profit. That's 15,000 calculations! A simpler way of arriving at maximum profit is by *looking only at the last unit produced* and calculating whether it adds to or subtracts from total profit.

Thinking on the Margin

Economists define the one unit as the marginal unit. Think of it this way. Imagine yourself playing chess. Your game is always ahead of you, isn't it? The lay of the board is what you face. There's nothing you can do about past moves. It's the one coming up that counts. Whatever decision you make concerns the very next move. That's how entrepreneurs approach choices on production. If a fisherman is already producing 11,000 fish, that is a *fait accompli*. The focus of consideration switches to the next fish, the 11,001st. The 11,001st fish is the marginal fish. Should that fish be produced? It depends on whether the sale of that 11,001st fish adds more to total revenue than its production adds to total cost.

Total, Average, and Marginal Revenue

Let's assume that the market price for fish is $0.90. Table 2 records the fishermen's total, average, and marginal revenue for production ranging from zero to 15,000 fish.

TOTAL REVENUE

Total revenue (*TR*) is simply market price multiplied by the quantity of fish.

$$TR = PQ$$

Total revenue increases by $900 every time fishermen sell an additional 1,000 fish. At zero fish, *TR* = $0.90 × 0 = zero. At 11,000 fish, *TR* = $0.90 × 11,000 = $9,900. At 12,000 fish, *TR* = $0.90 × 12,000 = $10,800. Figure 1 maps the total revenue curve over the range zero to 15,000 fish at *P* = $0.90. As you see, the *TR* curve is a straight line drawn from the origin, its slope determined by price. If the price falls to $0.50, the *TR* curve becomes *TR*′ in Figure 1.

TABLE 2
Total and Marginal Revenue Derived from Selling Fish when P = $0.90

Quantity	Price per Fish	Total Revenue	Marginal Revenue per 1,000 Fish	Marginal Revenue per Fish
1,000	$0.90	$ 900	$900	$0.90
2,000	0.90	1,800	900	0.90
3,000	0.90	2,700	900	0.90
4,000	0.90	3,600	900	0.90
5,000	0.90	4,500	900	0.90
6,000	0.90	5,400	900	0.90
7,000	0.90	6,300	900	0.90
8,000	0.90	7,200	900	0.90
9,000	0.90	8,400	900	0.90
10,000	0.90	9,000	900	0.90
11,000	0.90	9,900	900	0.90
12,000	0.90	10,800	900	0.90
13,000	0.90	11,700	900	0.90
14,000	0.90	12,600	900	0.90
15,000	0.90	13,500	900	0.90

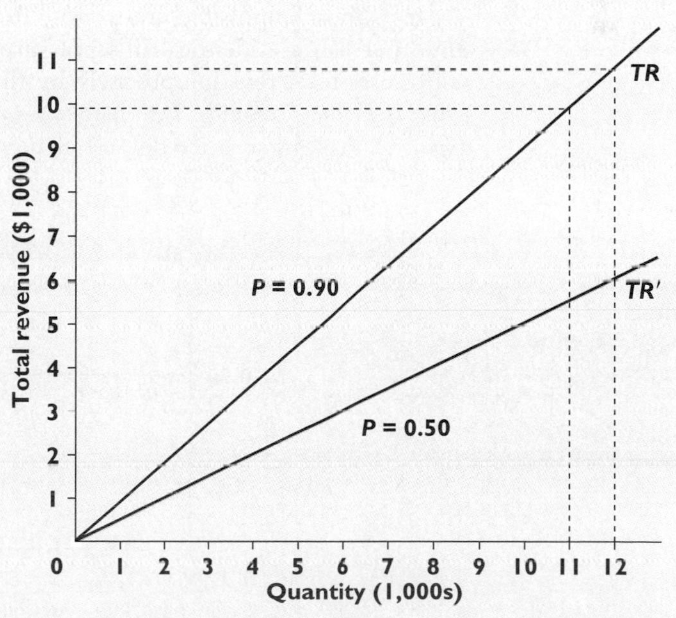

FIGURE 1
Total Revenue Curve
When P = $0.90 and remains unchanged no matter what quantity the firm produces and sells, the total revenue curve, *TR*, takes the form of an upward-sloping straight line from the origin. If price changes to P = $0.50, the total revenue curve is *TR′*.

AVERAGE REVENUE

Average revenue

Total revenue divided by the quantity of goods or services sold.

Average revenue (*AR*) is simply another way of describing price. Every fish sold puts the price it fetches on the market into the fishermen's pockets. That's another \$0.90. With 1,000 fish sold, the fishermen end up with \$900. Just keep adding \$0.90—the price of the fish—every time another fish is sold. If 2,000 are sold, the fishermen end up with \$1,800 total revenue. Average revenue or price is calculated as:

$$AR = \frac{TR}{Q} = \frac{P \times Q}{Q} = P$$

Figure 2 depicts the *AR* curve when price stays steady at \$0.90. As you see, it coincides with the price curve. Because we supposed that price remains unchanged at \$0.90 no matter how many fish are sold, the average revenue curve is a straight-line horizontal curve.

MARGINAL REVENUE

Marginal revenue

The change in total revenue generated by the sale of one additional unit of goods or services.

Just as marginal cost measures the change in total cost generated by a change in quantity produced, **marginal revenue** (*MR*) measures the change in total revenue generated by a change in quantity sold. It is written as:

$$MR = \frac{\Delta TR}{\Delta Q}$$

Look at Table 2, column 4. Every time a unit of 1,000 fish is added, total revenue increases by \$0.90 × 1,000 = \$900. For example, if production increases from 11,000 to 12,000 fish, total revenue increases by \$10,800 – \$9,900 = \$900. If production decreases from 11,000 to 10,000 fish, total revenue decreases by \$9,900 – \$9,000 = \$900. For *each* of these 1,000 additions or subtractions of fish, the *MR per fish* is \$900/1,000 = \$0.90. That's what we see in Table 2, column 5.

The *MR* curve corresponding to column 5 is shown in Figure 3.

It's almost impossible not to note from Table 2 that price and marginal revenue per fish are identical. It's not surprising. After all, adding another fish to sales raises total revenue precisely by the price of the fish. *That is why the MR curve of Figure 3 coincides with the price curve—which is the average revenue curve—of Figure 2.* As long as price doesn't change, then

$$P = MR$$

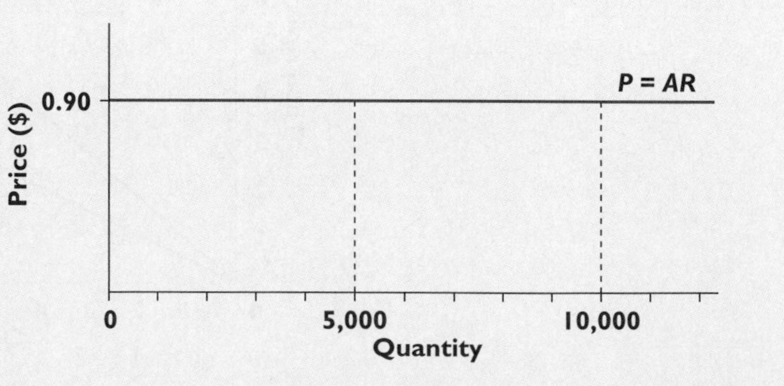

FIGURE 2
Average Revenue Curve
When *P* = \$0.90 and remains unchanged no matter what quantity the firm produces and sells, the average revenue curve takes the form of a horizontal straight line at *P* = \$0.90. The average revenue curve is the price curve.

FIGURE 3
Marginal Revenue Curve
When P = \$0.90 and remains unchanged no matter what quantity the firm produces and sells, the revenue from each additional unit of production is \$0.90. The marginal revenue curve takes the form of a horizontal straight line at P = \$0.90. The marginal revenue curve coincides with the price (and average revenue) curve at $MR = AR = P$.

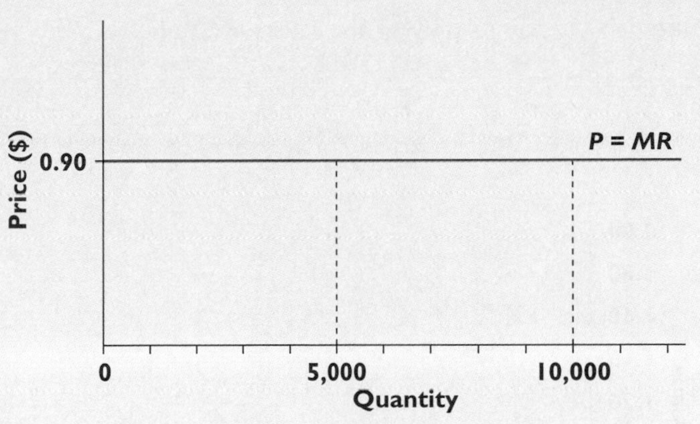

at any production level. As we shall see in the chapter on price determination in perfectly competitive markets, the $P = MR$ identity is characteristic of the perfectly competitive firm's price and marginal revenue curves.

APPLYING THE *MR* = *MC* RULE

Table 3 brings together the five most important pieces of data that a fishing company needs to determine its most profitable level of production. It also tells the fishermen whether or not to stay in business.

TABLE 3
Key Data on Profit Maximization

Quantity	Price	*AVC*	*ATC*	*MC*	*MR*
0	\$0.90	—	—	—	—
1,000	0.90	\$0.34	\$2.34	\$0.34	\$0.90
2,000	0.90	0.32	1.32	0.30	0.90
3,000	0.90	0.30	0.97	0.26	0.90
4,000	0.90	0.29	0.79	0.24	0.90
5,000	0.90	0.28	0.68	0.26	0.90
6,000	0.90	0.29	0.63	0.35	0.90
7,000	0.90	0.31	0.60	0.45	0.90
8,000	0.90	0.35	0.60	0.60	0.90
9,000	0.90	0.39	0.62	0.75	0.90
10,000	0.90	0.45	0.65	0.90	0.90
11,000	0.90	0.50	0.68	1.05	0.90
12,000	0.90	0.56	0.73	1.20	0.90
13,000	0.90	0.62	0.78	1.40	0.90
14,000	0.90	0.69	0.84	1.60	0.90
15,000	0.90	0.77	0.90	1.80	0.90

FIGURE 4 **Applying the *MR* = *MC* Rule**

The firm's marginal cost is *MC*, and its marginal revenue curve is *MR*. At a production level of 6,000 fish, *MC* = \$0.35, *MR* = \$0.90. When *MR* > *MC*, the rule is to produce more. When 7,000 fish are produced, *MC* = \$0.45 and *MR* = \$0.90. *MR* still exceeds *MC*. The firm continues to increase production. At a production level of 10,000 fish, *MC* = *MR* = \$0.90. When *MR* = *MC*, production is at a profit maximizing level.

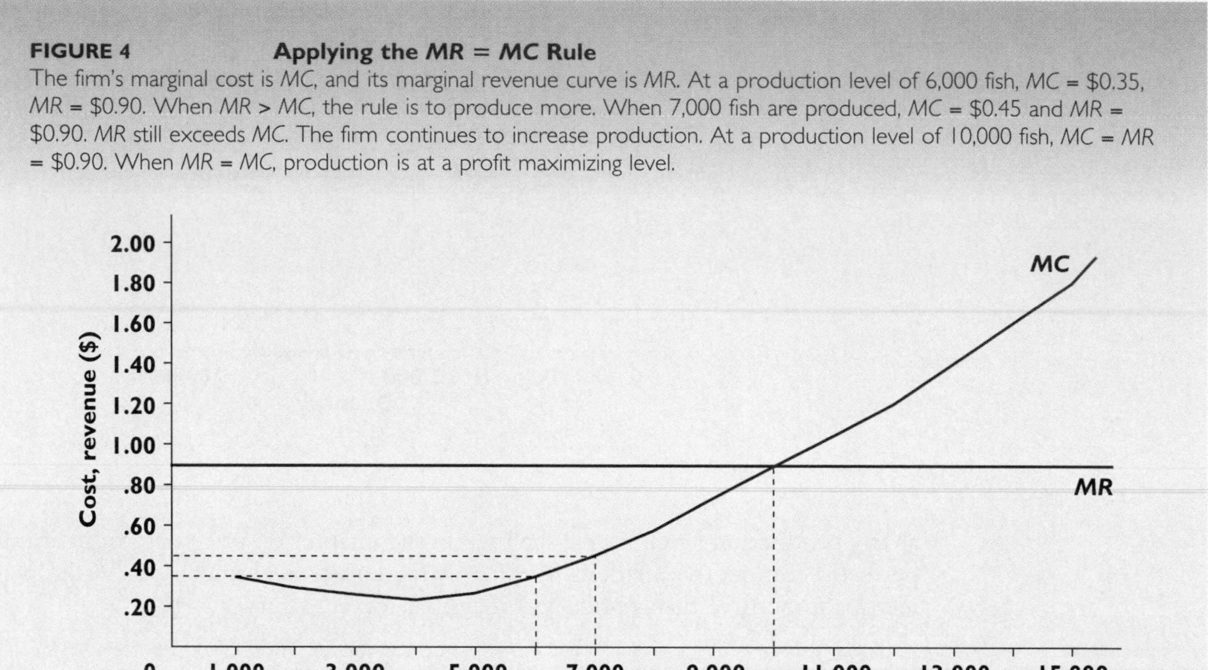

The marginal cost and marginal revenue data alone provide all the information necessary for the fishermen to determine where maximum profit can be made. The price and average cost data determine how much profit—if there's any profit at all—the maximum represents.

The profit maximization guideline is incredibly simple. The rule is to keep adding to production as long as the marginal revenue gained from adding production is greater than the marginal cost incurred from adding it. That is, keep producing more as long as *MR* > *MC*. It stands to reason then that if the marginal revenue gained from any unit produced is less than the marginal cost involved in producing it, you simply don't produce it. Take it out of production and keep subtracting from production as long as *MC* > *MR*.

Be sure that you can explain why profits will be maximized if output is set where *MR* = *MC*.

MC = MR rule

The guideline used by a firm to achieve profit maximization.

Exercising the maxim of adding when *MR* > *MC* and subtracting when *MC* > *MR* leads inexorably to the powerful ***MR* = *MC* rule** of profit maximization. Figure 4 illustrates how the profit maximizing *MR* = *MC* rule is applied.

Suppose the price of fish were \$0.90 and quantity was 6,000 fish. Is the firm maximizing profit at 6,000? Should it produce more or cut back? Look at the marginal cost and marginal revenue of the 6,000th fish. *MC* = \$0.35 and *MR* = \$0.90. The 6,000th fish generates a profit of \$0.90 – \$0.35 = \$0.55. The guideline states: If *MR* > *MC,* keep producing more.

How much more? Look at the 7,000th fish. Compare its *MC* to its *MR*. *MC* = \$0.45 and *MR* = \$0.90. Does it pay to produce that 7,000th fish? Of course. The fishermen *add* \$0.90 – \$0.45 = \$0.45 to profit. That is to say, profit is increasing.

But why stop there? Look at the next 1,000 fish. *MC* increases to \$0.60. Should the fishermen produce that 8,000th fish? Of course. As long as

ADDED PERSPECTIVE

Maximizing Profit on Israel's Kibbutzim

An Israeli kibbutz can claim to be the most collectivized form of political, social, and economic organization in the world. Kibbutzim (plural of kibbutz) are productive communities—engaged in both agricultural and manufacturing activity—in which every kibbutz member contributes to the kibbutz according to his or her ability and receives from the kibbutz according to his or her needs. That is, no link exists between an individual's effort and reward.

How is a kibbutz run? All decision making on the kibbutz, including those associated with managing the kibbutz economy, are rotated among its members. The kibbutz trademark is universal equality.

If you think that people who opt to live and work under such conditions would place less value on acquiring material things than we do, you would be basically right. If you also think that these people would be adverse to profit-maximizing behavior, you would be wrong!

According to Professors David Levhari and Haim Barkai, who are experts on the economics of the kibbutz, the kibbutz behaves as if it were a profit-maximizing firm. Kibbutz members know what marginal cost and marginal revenue are, and they know as well the usefulness of the $MC = MR$ guideline. After all, why wouldn't they keep producing oranges (if that's what they're producing) so long as the marginal revenue is greater than the marginal cost of producing them? If producing until $MR = MC$ makes sense to you, why shouldn't it make sense to members of a kibbutz? What they do with the maximum profit they make is another matter.

When the kibbutz decides what crops to produce, price is an important consideration. If cotton prices increase, it may signal the kibbutz to switch from bananas to cotton. If competition from Spain, Morocco, and other orange-producing economies drives the price of oranges down, it may also drive orange-producing kibbutzim out of producing oranges.

Many kibbutzim shifted their productive focus out of agriculture into manufacturing in the 1960s when the prices of farm goods weakened. Why? Manufacturing, and particularly high-tech manufacturing, pays more than farming. The guideline was $MC = MR$. Kibbutz members see no conflict in maximizing profit and living modestly in an environment of equality.

Discussion

How would you make your case if you were a kibbutz member opposing profit maximization? What kind of an argument could a fellow kibbutz member make to counter your argument? (*Hint*: What the kibbutz does with its profit is another matter.)

$MR > MC$, producing it *adds* to total profit. The \$0.90 – \$0.60 = \$0.30 generated by the 8,000th fish may not add as much to total profit as the 7,000th did, but still, \$0.30 represents \$0.30 more total profit. Even if $MR > MC$ on the next fish yielded only a penny, wouldn't it pay to produce it? It *adds* a penny more to total profit. Why not take the penny?

To take a different example, suppose a friend plays a money game with you, tossing coins in your lap. You get to keep whatever you collect. The only rule is that your friend must keep tossing until you tell her to stop. Suppose she starts by tossing quarters. After a while, she switches to dimes. Soon she's down to nickels and finally pennies. Would you tell her to stop because the last toss was a penny? After all, didn't that last penny still add to your total money?

Suppose the game now costs you a nickel a toss. Wouldn't you keep the game going as long as the coins tossed were quarters or dimes? You could stop when nickels appear, because you break even with each nickel toss. You've maximized your money when the first nickel appears. If your friend tries to continue the game with penny tosses, you would lose four cents on every additional toss.

That's how fishermen play the fishing game. As long as $MR > MC$ on the next unit of production, they produce that unit. In Figure 4, MC increases to \$0.90 when the 10,000th fish is added to production. At the 10,000th fish, $MR = MC$. The fishermen stop.

The profit on the 10,000th fish is \$0.90 – \$0.90 = zero. On the 11,000th fish, $MR < MC$. The *loss* on that 11,000th is \$1.05 – \$0.90 = \$0.15. The fishermen will not produce it. The rule is simple and compelling: Keep on producing until $MR = MC$. At that point, profit is maximized.

HOW MUCH PROFIT IS MAXIMUM PROFIT?

The $MR = MC$ rule gets us to profit maximization, but it doesn't tell us *how much* that maximum profit is. We know that maximum profit is the total of the differences between marginal revenue and marginal cost for each of the 11,000 fish. But that's like knowing when you've reached the top of Mt. Everest. It's a great achievement, but, standing on top, how do you know the height of the mountain?

That's where price, ATC and AVC data come into play. Since we already know that profit is maximized at 10,000 fish and (from Table 3 in the previous chapter) that at 10,000, ATC = \$0.65 and P = \$0.90 then maximum total profit is

$$(\$0.90 - \$0.65) \times 10{,}000 = \$2{,}500$$

It's as simple as that. No other production level yields a profit as large as the \$2,500 generated at 10,000.

Figure 5 provides a graphic illustration of profit maximization.

FIGURE 5 **Measuring Profit Maximization**

The firm calculates the difference between its *ATC* at 10,000 and its price, multiplying this difference by the quantity produced and sold. At 10,000, total profit is (\$0.90 – \$0.65)(10,000) = \$2,500, the shaded rectangle.

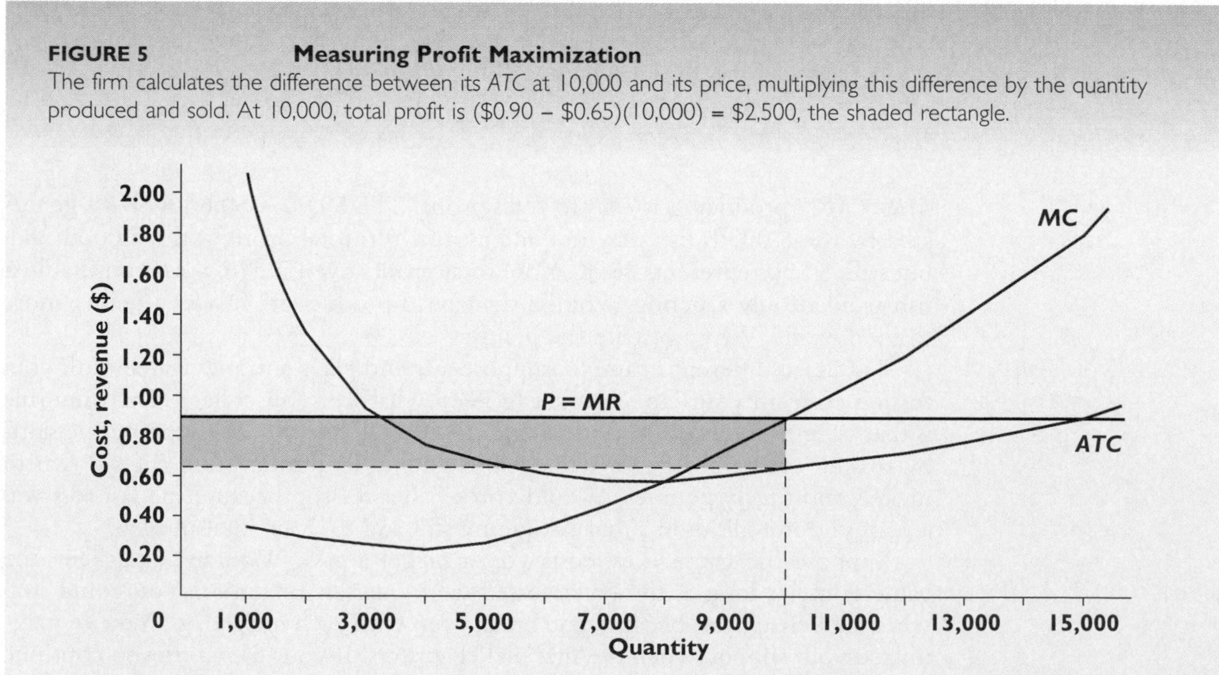

Since we know from the $MR = MC$ rule that maximum profit is obtained at 10,000 fish, then the shaded rectangle showing the difference between price and average total cost at 10,000, ($0.90 – $0.65), multiplied by 10,000 fish generates the $2,500.

MAXIMIZING PROFIT AND MINIMIZING LOSS

Let's now consider some tough problems. In business it's always pleasant searching for maximum profit outputs. It's much less pleasant when the climate of business turns and the problem is deciding whether to stay in business. Entrepreneurs, including fishermen, know that the possibility of incurring losses is always part of business life. And however successful entrepreneurs may be in controlling costs, the one thing most cannot control is price.

Fishermen may *expect* price to remain at $0.90, but that may be wishful thinking. Price responds to market pressures. If these pressures are strong enough, they can drive any price anywhere. Suppose the price of fish drops dramatically to $0.45. What would fishermen do? Look at Figure 6.

Can you explain why the $MR = MC$ rule applies for loss minimization as well as for profit maximization?

Following the $MR = MC$ rule, production should be at 7,000 fish. But there's a problem. At 7,000 fish, $ATC = \$0.60$, and with $P = \$0.45$, total profit is

$$(\$0.45 - \$0.60) \times 7{,}000 = -\$1{,}050$$

Fishermen end up *losing* $1,050! That's not what they had in mind when they went into business. But they never counted on a $0.45 fish. What can they do?

FIGURE 6 **Minimizing Loss**

The $P = MR = \$0.45$ curve is lower than the firm's ATC at every level of output. The firm must incur losses no matter where it produces. The firm's least undesirable level of output—although not desirable—is where losses are minimized. The $MR = MC$ rule still applies. At 7,000 fish, $P = MR = \$0.45$. The loss is ($0.45 – $0.60) × 7,000 = $1,050. No other output level generates as low a loss as 7,000 fish. Producing zero would still involve fixed costs of $2,000.

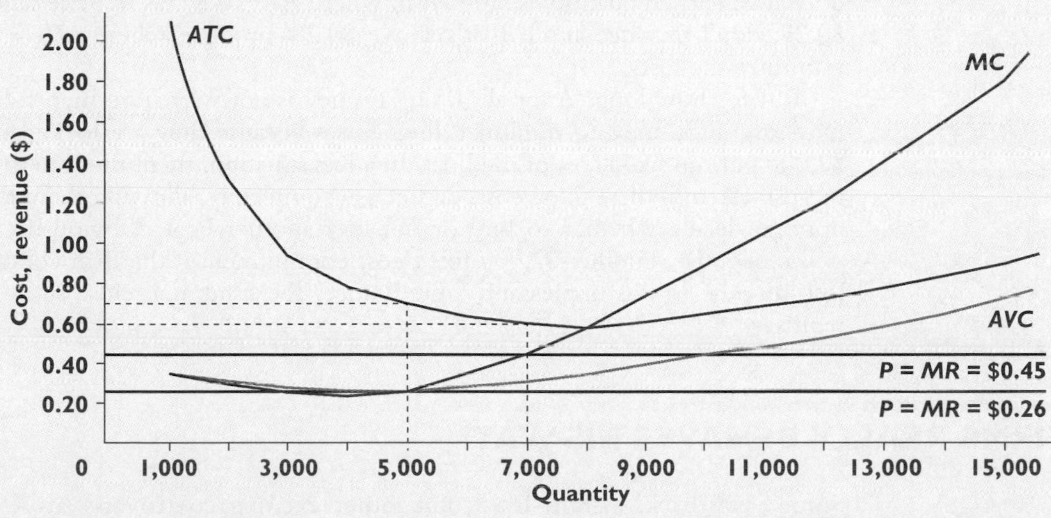

Producing less than 7,000 or producing more than 7,000 *or not producing at all* yields even greater losses. For example, if fishermen were to keep the boats in dock—no fishing at P = \$0.45—they still have costs. *Not producing is not costless.* After all, that \$2,000 fixed cost for the boat has to be paid whether they fish or not. Aren't they better off producing the 7,000 fish and losing \$1,050 than producing zero and losing \$2,000?

Loss minimization

Faced with the certainty of incurring losses, the firm's goal is to incur the lowest loss possible from its production and sale of goods and services.

The MR = MC rule, then, is both a profit maximization and **loss minimization** guide to production. And that, in turn, leads us to another rule: if you can't cover *average variable cost, shut down*!

Since the fixed cost of the boat is already committed, the guiding rule on whether to fish or not, at least in the short run, is determined by whether price covers average variable cost. That is, does the cost of hiring crew, using bait, ice, and fuel per fish add up to more than \$0.45? Is $P > AVC$?

Be careful to note that if price covers average variable cost, then total revenue will cover total variable costs. Can you show why?

Look again at Figure 6. At 7,000 fish, although ATC = \$0.60, AVC = \$0.31. Ignoring the \$2,000 fixed cost, fishermen clear

(\$0.45 − \$0.31) × 7,000 = \$980

This \$980 profit means that producing 7,000 fish is more profitable than not producing at all. After all, producing or not producing, the fishermen are obliged to absorb the \$2,000 cost of the boat.

But suppose price falls to \$0.26. Given the data in Table 5 in the previous chapter, the MR = MC rule guides the fishermen to produce 5,000 fish. At that quantity, AVC = \$0.28. Does it pay to produce? No. Because now $P < AVC$. Producing 5,000 fish creates

(\$0.26 − \$0.28 × 5,000) = − \$100

a loss of \$100. The \$0.26 price does not cover the cost of hiring crew, using bait, ice, and fuel. Why not **shut down** the business and accept the \$2,000 loss on fixed costs rather than incur that \$2,000 cost *plus* the \$100 loss on the variable costs when producing at 5,000? When P = \$0.26, it pays to shut down.

Shut down

The cessation of the firm's activity. The firm's loss minimization occurs at zero output.

Shutting down or not shutting down depends on whether the market price covers average variable costs. Look again at Table 4 in the previous chapter. The critical watershed quantity is 5,000 fish, where AVC = \$0.28. If price falls below \$0.28, don't produce at all. If it's above \$0.28, produce where MR = MC to minimize the loss.

But for how long? After all, losing money is not why fishermen fish. They may stay in business to minimize their losses because they are locked into the \$2,000 per run fixed cost of the boat. In a loss situation, then, the fishermen stay in business until these fixed costs depreciate completely, allowing them the freedom to decide whether to buy or not buy another boat. Obviously, no one will renegotiate another \$2,000 fixed cost commitment if the firm continues to lose money. In this unpleasant circumstance, the fishermen close shop permanently.

DO FIRMS REALLY BEHAVE THIS WAY?

Some years back, a short-lived, but rather exciting controversy arose among economists over this issue of firms' profit-maximizing behavior. Do entrepreneurs *really* think on the margin? Do they really ask themselves whether they should produce the next unit of production? Do they really focus on marginal cost and revenue in making production decisions? In other words, are they actually guided by the $MC = MR$ rule?

The Lester-Machlup Controversy

In the mid-1940s, Princeton's Richard Lester challenged the idea that entrepreneurs look to the margin for production signals. He surveyed entrepreneurs in 58 firms asking them to explain how they chose their production levels. Their response indicated that they did *not* think in terms of marginal units. Lester considered his findings nonsurprising, since he believed insuperable problems are involved in applying marginal analysis to the modern multiproduct firm.

Lester's conclusions, however, did not go unchallenged. Among the defenders of marginal analysis was Professor Fritz Machlup of The Johns Hopkins University. He dismissed Lester's findings on the grounds that the $MR = MC$ theory of profit maximizing doesn't depend on what entrepreneurs *think they do,* but rather on observing what they *actually* do. Entrepreneurs should be seen, not heard!

Milton Friedman's *The Methodology of Positive Economics,* published just a few years later, commented on the Lester-Machlup controversy. To Friedman, the critical issue was whether there was "conformity to experience of the implications of the marginal analysis." And for him, the "experience" was as unmistakable as the "implications" of marginal analysis. In other words, marginal analysis was alive and well.

Most economists share Friedman's view. They accept the idea that no matter how entrepreneurs may describe their own behavior, the $MR = MC$ rule is still the most satisfactory explanation of how they really behave.

The Mark-Up Theory of Profit

But Lester's attack on marginalism was not the only assault on the widely accepted theory of profit-maximizing behavior. Even before the Lester-Machlup controversy, many other economists had challenged the theory.

In the 1930s, R. L. Hall and C. J. Hitch made a systematic study of production and price determination. Their conclusions, too, hit at the heart of marginal analysis. Entrepreneurs, they argued, set prices to cover the full cost of production and a conventional **mark-up profit.** Note that they assume that each firm has the power to set its own prices. And, quite aside from that, they didn't explain how this conventional mark-up was determined.

Mark-up profit
The profit added to cost to determine price.

Michael Kalecki, also in the 1930s, developed a full-cost plus mark-up theory of price and explained why the size of the mark-up is what it is. To him, entrepreneurs are not interested in maximizing profit as the marginalists suggest. Instead, they set a profit mark-up, *m*, to accommodate their investment plans. Since most firms finance their investments by reinvesting their profit, the specific mark-up they choose for profit, then, depends on how much investment they plan to undertake. That is, *the level of planned investment determines the mark-up rate.* (See Figure 7.)

Kalecki's mark-up theory is somewhat more sophisticated because it attempts to explain the size of the mark-up as a function of the firm's planned investment.

In Kalecki's view, the firm's ATC curve over the relevant range of production is constant, $ATC = MC$. The demand curve, *d*, is a given. If the firm plans no investment, it chooses $P = ATC = \$10$ and an output level of 110. If the firm

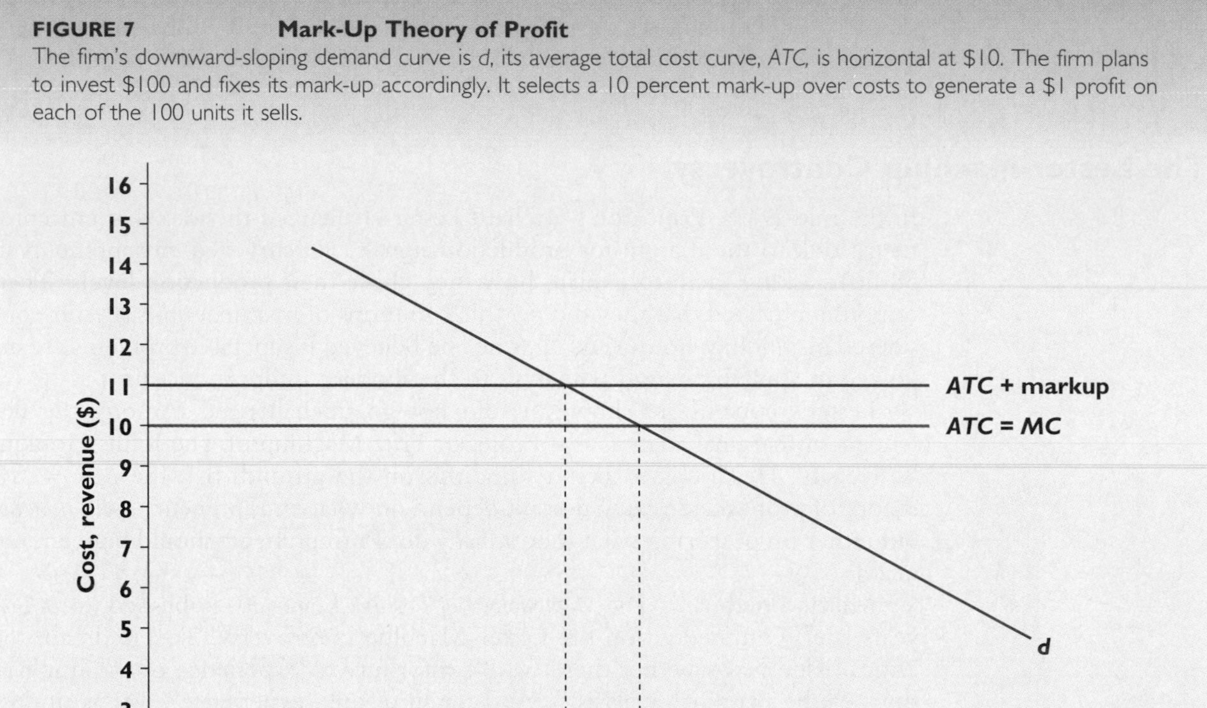

FIGURE 7 **Mark-Up Theory of Profit**
The firm's downward-sloping demand curve is *d*, its average total cost curve, *ATC*, is horizontal at \$10. The firm plans to invest \$100 and fixes its mark-up accordingly. It selects a 10 percent mark-up over costs to generate a \$1 profit on each of the 100 units it sells.

plans \$100 of investment, it chooses a 10 percent mark-up, setting its price at P = \$11 and output at 100.

The mark-up theory attracted few followers until the 1970s, when a number of economists, dissatisfied with the implications of $MR = MC$ behavior, found considerable substance in Kalecki's ideas and incorporated them into a new perspective called Post-Keynesian economics.

Profit Maximizing versus Empire Building

Another perspective on this issue of profit maximization argues that the firm's decision makers are not as one-dimensional as marginalists suggest. According to this view, the idea that a firm goes about squeezing every last bit of profit out of its production run, as the $MR = MC$ rule implies, simply flies in the face of reality.

The advent of the modern corporation changed the character of the firm. The corporation separates owners—stockholders—from decision makers. They are different people with different goals about what the firm ought to be doing.

Stockholders typically want the firm to maximize profit. The firm's managers, on the other hand, have quite a different view of appropriate goals. To

ADDED PERSPECTIVE

Why Profit Maximization?

Of the Origin of Ambition, and of the Distinction of Ranks

For to what purpose is all the toil and bustle of this world? What is the end of avarice and ambition, of the pursuit of wealth, of power, and pre-eminence? Is it to supply the necessities of nature? The wages of the meanest labourer can supply them. We see that they afford him food and clothing, the comfort of a house, and of a family. If we examine his economy with rigour, we should find that he spends a great part of them upon conveniences, which may be regarded as superfluities, and that, upon extraordinary occasions, he can give something even to vanity and distinction. What then is the cause of our aversion to his situation, and why should those who have been educated in the higher ranks of life, regard it as worse than death, to be reduced to live, even without labour, upon the same simple fare with him, to dwell under the same lowly roof, and to be clothed in the same humble attire? Do they imagine that their stomach is better, or their sleep sounder, in a palace than in a cottage? The contrary has been so often observed, and, indeed, is so very obvious, though it had never been observed, that there is nobody ignorant of it. From whence, then, arises that emulation which runs through all the different ranks of men, and what are the advantages which we propose by that great purpose of human life which we call bettering our condition? To be observed, to be attended to, to be taken notice of with sympathy, complacency, and approbation, are all the advantages which we can propose to derive from it. It is the vanity, not the ease, or the pleasure, which interests us. But vanity is always founded upon the belief of our being the object of attention and approbation. The rich man glories in his riches, because he feels that they naturally draw upon him the attention of the world, and that mankind are disposed to go along with him in all those agreeable emotions with which the advantages of his situation so readily inspire him. At the thought of this his heart seems to swell and dilate itself within him, and he is fonder of his wealth, upon this account, than for all the other advantages it procures him.

Discussion

Do you think Smith has a point? Why else would anyone want five Rolls Royces in their garage? What other explanations make sense to you?

Source: Adam Smith, *Theory of Moral Sentiments,* 1759.

them, the firm is more than an economic machine grinding out profit for stockholders. It also has social, political, and historical dimensions that are important to them. The firm is the playing field on which they advance their careers. The firm's status in the industry, not necessarily the profit it produces, is a matter of much consideration.

For example, the owner of a taxi business who, herself, is not involved in running the business, may not care if the taxis are old or new. If more profit can be generated using old taxis, then as far as she's concerned, the old are better. But her salaried managers, who run the business, may think differently about the taxis they use. They may prefer new taxis because this will enhance their own self-image and generate fewer complaints from drivers and passengers. In other words, the managers' interests in the business may not be entirely profit-motivated.

Such a sociological account of a modern corporate economy was first set out in the 1930s by Adolf Berle and Gardiner Means in *The Modern Corporation and Private Property* and later by James Burnham in *The Managerial Revolution.*

More recently, William Baumol's *Business Behavior and Economic Growth* put a new twist on the old argument. To Baumol, the firm that is run by nonowning managers generally chooses to maximize sales, not profit. Success is measured by the size of the production range. But why sales? In Baumol's view, a much sought-after managerial goal is empire building. John K. Galbraith's *New Industrial State* continued the attack on the traditional $MR = MC$ description of firm behavior. He concludes that the managerial bureaucracy controls the corporation and dictates its goals.

How does this come about? In Galbraith's view, the primary goal is the survival of the corporation, and in particular, the survival of its managerial bureaucracy. It aims, then, to reduce the risks and uncertainties that the market tends to generate. The $MR = MC$ rule of firm behavior has been largely overshadowed by these new theories. Corporate stability displaces profit maximization. Industrial planning and cooperative arrangements with government are preferred to the unfettered activity implied in the $MR = MC$ rule.

Lester Thurow of MIT raises the same doubts and criticisms of the $MR = MC$ rule.

American government may be bureaucratic and inefficient, but American industry is just as bureaucratic and inefficient. Who works for a firm that has not added some new layers of management in the last ten years? Who works for a firm that does not generate huge amounts of paper reports—most of which do not get read, much less acted upon? Who works for a firm that has fired secretaries and insisted that managers do their own typing since the introduction of word processors? What firm does not now have a bigger legal staff? What private managers are trying to improve decision making so that they can fire managers?

Where does squeezing the last dollar of profit out of production come into Galbraith's or Thurow's account of business activity? It doesn't. In their view, the preservation of the managerial class, even at the expense of profit, is what managers seek. His and Galbraith's conclusion is inescapable. The modern corporation, owned by a set of stockholders, is run by managers for managers. The $MR = MC$ rule serves fewer and fewer decision makers. To them, the $MR = MC$ rule seems to be obsolete.

WHAT SURVIVES OF MARGINALISM?

What survives of the $MR = MC$ thinking? In a word, *everything*! For most economists, these broadside attacks on the $MR = MC$ profit maximizing theory are parenthetical notes, interesting and perhaps even useful in explaining *some* aspects of corporate behavior. But they offer insufficient evidence to seriously undermine the basic postulate of the marginalist economists: Firms must be guided by the $MR = MC$ rule to maximize profit.

Defenders of the $MR = MC$ profit maximization doctrine argue that our modern economy is still represented by the overwhelming number of firms that look more like our fishing firm than like the corporate giant. For these firms and for most corporations as well, the drive to maximize profit dominates.

Of course, even the strongest advocates of the marginalist view agree that firms are not really as one dimensional as the profit-maximizing rule suggests. But, to them, profit maximizing is only *a first approximation to reality*. They accept the view that other interests, many identified by the critics of the $MR =$

"La Guardia airport? Hey, that's a half-hour there and a half-hour back. I was ready to quit now. But, I'll tell you what. I'll work for an extra hour—without the meter running—if you pay me $50. Otherwise, friend, I go home. What do you say?" . . . "OK, buddy, hop in."

MC rule of behavior, are included in the firm's set of goals. Still, they insist, that as a first approximation, the *MR* = *MC* approach to profit maximizing is not only logical, but empirically verifiable.

CHAPTER REVIEW

1. Entrepreneurs engage in two distinct types of activities. First, they oversee arrangements for production and the production process itself. This involves committing to a variety of cost obligations. Second, entrepreneurs must correctly anticipate prices in order to arrange sales so that profits are earned.

2. The entrepreneur's prior commitment to costs means that the market price will determine whether or not a profit is earned. Profit per unit of output can be calculated as the difference between price and average total cost multiplied by the quantity of output.

3. An entrepreneur's goal is to maximize profits. Profits are maximized by producing where marginal revenue equals marginal cost.

4. Marginal revenue is the addition to total revenue from producing one more unit of output. If the market price is fixed, then marginal revenue is the same as the market price.

5. Average revenue is total revenue divided by the quantity sold. If the market price is fixed, then average revenue is the same as the market price. Thus, when market price is fixed at a particular level, marginal revenue and average revenue are both equal to the market price. A graph of the marginal revenue and average revenue curves shows up as a horizontal line at the level of the market price.

6. Applying the "marginal revenue equals marginal cost" rule involves finding the output level where the two are equal. In a graph, this output level is where the marginal revenue and marginal cost curves intersect.

7. Once profit is maximized at the output level where marginal revenue equals marginal cost, the profit level can be calculated by multiplying the difference between price and average total cost by the quantity. Profit shows up on a graph

as a rectangle with a height equal to the difference between price and average total cost and a width equal to the level of output.

8. The "marginal revenue equals marginal cost" rule applies for minimizing losses as well as for maximizing profits. A firm must cover its variable costs in order to continue producing at a loss in the short run. If price is greater than average variable cost, then variable costs are covered and the firm should produce at a loss in the short run. If price falls to a level below average variable cost, then the firm cannot cover its variable costs and it must shut down.

9. Richard Lester has argued that, based on survey results, entrepreneurs indicate that they do not think in terms of marginal units. However, Fritz Machlup and Milton Friedman argue that what entrepreneurs think they do may not reflect what they actually do. To Machlup and Friedman, the "marginal revenue equals marginal cost" rule is still the best way to explain the behavior of entrepreneurs.

10. Another view of firm pricing is the mark-up over cost theory. Michael Kalecki has developed this theory further by linking the size of the mark-up to a firm's plans for investment.

11. In recent years a number of other economists have developed theories of firm pricing behavior based on the hypothesis that firms are really empire builders rather than profit maximizers. These theories emphasize that firms may have as primary goals the enhancement of their self-image, sales maximization, or long-run survival rather than profit maximization.

12. Despite the variety of hypotheses to explain corporate behavior that have been advanced, most economists agree that the drive to maximize profits is the dominant characteristic of modern businesses.

KEY TERMS

Profit maximization
Average revenue
Marginal revenue
MC = *MR* rule
Loss minimization
Shut down
Mark-up profit

QUESTIONS

1. What talents would you expect to find in successful entrepreneurs? Do you think a college education helps entrepreneurs develop these talents?

2. Consider your own decision making. Do you think in terms of the marginal revenue, or reward, and the marginal cost of doing or not doing things? Cite examples.

3. According to the *MR* = *MC* rule, when *MR* > *MC*, the firm should produce more, and when *MC* > *MR* the firm should produce less. Why?

4. How can the *MC* = *MR* rule be applied by the Boston Celtics of the NBA in deciding whether to sign a college superstar to a first-year $1 million contract?

5. What is meant by loss minimization? What relationship does it have to profit maximization? How does the *MC* = *MR* rule apply in this case?

6. Is it possible for marginal revenue to be zero or negative? Give examples.

7. What rule should the firm use in deciding when to shut down production in the short run? In the long run?

8. What is the mark-up theory of profit? How does it relate, if it does at all, to the *MC* = *MR* rule?

9. Some economists believe the theory of profit maximization expressed in the *MC* = *MR* rule to be an oversimplification of reality. What views do they offer of entrepreneurial behavior? Do these arguments make sense to you?

10. Graph the following table and pick the level of output that maximizes profit. How much profit is maximum profit?

Output	*P* = *MR*	*ATC*	*MC*
100	$5	$10.40	—
200	5	6.20	$2.50
300	5	4.96	2.50
400	5	4.50	3.10
500	5	4.40	4.00
600	5	4.50	5.00
700	5	4.78	6.50
800	5	5.25	8.50

C H A P T E R 1 0

IDENTIFYING MARKETS AND MARKET STRUCTURES

CHAPTER PREVIEW

When should we consider goods to be part of the same market? Clearly, two goods that are the same belong to the same market. But, what about goods that are similar? How similar do they have to be in order to belong to the same market? The first part of this chapter explores answers to this question. The rest of the chapter is devoted to distinguishing different types of market structures. How competitive are different market structures relative to each other? What factors determine the degree of competition in a market structure? We'll try to find answers to these questions.

After studying this chapter, you should be able to:

- Use the cross elasticity of demand to define markets.
- Explain the concept of a perfectly contained market.
- Describe the four types of market structures.
- Discuss the conditions necessary for monopoly to exist.
- Contrast oligopoly and monopolistic competition.
- Account for the existence of advertising in many markets.
- Detail the characteristics of perfectly competitive markets.

To market, to market
To buy a fat pig
Home again, home again
Jiggety-jig

Is the nursery rhyme familiar? Think back! Even as a little child, you were already acquainted with markets. And the nursery rhyme makes it very clear that markets are where you buy fat pigs. What the nursery rhyme does not tell you, however, is the price you pay for fat pigs. It doesn't tell you whether goods are available to substitute for fat pigs, or whether the market's structure is a monopoly or an oligopoly, whether there is perfect or monopolistic competition. Perhaps that is asking too much.

This chapter and the two following go beyond the nursery rhyme. In this chapter we discuss how we go about identifying which goods belong to which markets and how to distinguish among the market structures. The next two chapters analyze how prices are determined in monopoly and oligopoly, and in perfectly competitive and monopolistically competitive markets.

DEFINING THE RELEVANT MARKET

Rose Is a Rose Is a Rose?

When Gertrude Stein wrote her celebrated line, "Rose is a rose is a rose," she was not making a botanical statement nor was she implying that an American Beauty rose and a Peace rose are identical. That idea probably never occurred to her. In all likelihood, she knew the difference, but figured the difference simply wasn't worth noting. Florists, certainly, and perhaps many other people, view roses very differently.

What is true for roses is also true for fish. To some people, and possibly Gertrude Stein, "A fish is a fish is a fish" and "A fish market is a fish market is a fish market." But to fishermen, and many others, differences among fish are worth noting.

After all, fish come in many varieties. Fish are sold in a market, *but what kinds of fish in what markets*? For example, how do you describe the market that sells only cod? Is it a fish market or a cod market? It makes a difference.

Suppose David Holtgrave switches from cod to halibut fishing. When he brings his catch to market, does he become the only fisherman in an exclusive halibut market, or is he still just one of the many fishermen selling fish in a fish market? In other words, are cod and halibut just two different kinds of the same good, or are they two very different goods?

If consumers are completely indifferent about cod and halibut—if they regard these fish as perfect substitutes—then what relevance does a halibut market have? Rather than being the only seller in a halibut market, David Holtgrave quickly discovers that he is actively engaged along with a hundred others in a more inclusive fish market.

Are fishermen in competition only with each other? Not at all. Imagine yourself at a restaurant looking through the menu. Each item competes with every other. You can choose grilled red snapper, broiled cod, fried catfish, or

One thing you know for sure, this isn't a Wednesday before Thanksgiving. Otherwise, this American Airlines terminal at O'Hare would be teeming with travelers. But Thanksgiving traffic along our nation's interstates would be no less congested than this terminal. They are two of many competing ways people travel.

Relevant market

The set of goods whose cross elasticities with others in the set are relatively high and whose cross elasticities with goods outside the set are relatively low.

baked halibut. But you can also choose fried clams, tiger shrimp, or lobster tails. What, then, should fishermen regard as their **relevant market**? Is it strictly the fish market or the broader seafood market?

Yet there's more on the menu. There are cold sandwiches, hearty soups, salads, hamburgers, hot dogs, and pizza. Many who consider seafood as a possible meal can also consider these choices. The fishermen's relevant market may be not only fish or seafood but rather the larger set of goods associated with home-cooked or restaurant meals. In such an inclusive market, David Holtgrave finds himself competing with *thousands* of producers.

Movies and Entertainment

Consider a more commonplace example. Don't you sometimes relax after a long day of classes by going to an evening movie? Suppose four independent theaters are close to campus. Do you think the theater owners regard themselves as competing only with each other for your movie dollar?

Most likely not. They know that home videos offer a viable option. You can also relax at the video arcade, or at the bowling alley in the student union. That is, it may make more sense to describe the good you want as *entertainment*. In the entertainment market, the theater owners are only one group among many competitors.

Automobiles and Transportation

Does the automobile industry make up a relevant market or are automobiles an integral part of the much larger transportation market that includes taxis, buses, railways, and airlines? After all, for most people, the primary purpose of the automobile is transportation.

Do videos compete with stereos, compact discs, television, and books in the home entertainment market? Do chocolate bars, peanuts, licorice, and popcorn compete in the snack food market? Ask interior decorators what they consider competing goods in their market. It's not only wall hangings, but paintings, lithographs, prints, and photographs as well. If Saudi Arabia were the only producer of crude oil, would it still be alone in its market? Probably not. In reality, Saudi Arabia's relevant market is not oil but energy. It competes with countries that produce hydroelectric power, coal, wood, solar, and nuclear energy.

What about the U.S. Postal Service? It's often regarded as a monopoly even though it competes with Federal Express, Emery, United Parcel Service, Airborne Express, Purolator, and with the telephone, telegram, telex, and fax in the communications market. This can hardly be called a monopoly.

COURTS AND MARKETS

Recall that the definition of cross elasticity of demand is the percentage change in quantity demanded of one good divided by the percentage change in price of another good. A positive cross elasticity of demand means that two goods are substitutes and may belong to the same market.

How do you decide what constitutes *the* market? Deciding what goods make up what market is more than just an academic exercise. Unless we understand what makes a market, how can we decide whether or not a market is competitive? And if we decide to encourage competition, how do we know when we have succeeded? These are real issues.

In many cases, courts decide what constitutes the relevant market. In 1953, the government filed suit against Du Pont, charging that it illegally monopolized the cellophane market. It argued that Du Pont produced more than 80 percent of all cellophane and thus undermined the competitive character of the cellophane market.

In defending itself in court, Du Pont did not contest its dominant position in cellophane. Instead, it argued that its relevant market was not cellophane but the much broader market of flexible packaging materials. Because Du Pont controlled less than 20 percent of production in this market, the market's competitive character had not been damaged by Du Pont's cellophane. Impressed by the argument, the court decided in favor of Du Pont. The government appealed the verdict, but the Supreme Court upheld the lower court's decision.

In a similar case a few years earlier, a Circuit Court of Appeals overturned a trial court's verdict on the same issue. The trial court denied the government's charge that Alcoa monopolized the aluminum market, accepting Alcoa's argument that the aluminum market consists of scrap aluminum as well as primary aluminum production. In this broader definition of the aluminum market, Alcoa had only a 33 percent share. In reversing the trial court's decision, the Circuit Court of Appeals redefined the market to exclude scrap aluminum. In this narrower interpretation of the market, Alcoa had a 90 percent market share.

Do the courts possess some inner wisdom that allows them special privilege to decide on matters of market definition? Of course not. The decisions the courts hand down cannot be taken as revealed truth but rather as impartial judgments concerning the issue of what constitutes a relevant market.

Perfectly contained market

A set of goods in which cross elasticities among any two goods in the set are infinite and whose cross elasticities with any other good outside the set are zero.

How do the courts decide on relevant markets? Historically, the court system has borrowed heavily from economic theory. One of the conceptual tools it uses to identify the relevant market is *cross elasticity of demand,* a concept already analyzed in the chapter on elasticity of demand and supply. How are cross elasticities used?

CROSS ELASTICITY DEFINES THE MARKET

In a **perfectly contained market,** all goods in that market are perfect substitutes for each other and no goods outside the market can possibly substitute for them. Put in terms of cross elasticities, *a perfectly contained market is a set of goods whose cross elasticities among any two goods in the set are infinite and whose cross elas-*

FIGURE 1 **Delineating the Market**

Zone A defines the Peace rose market; zones A and B define the rose market; zones A, B and C define the flower market. Zone D lies outside these markets.

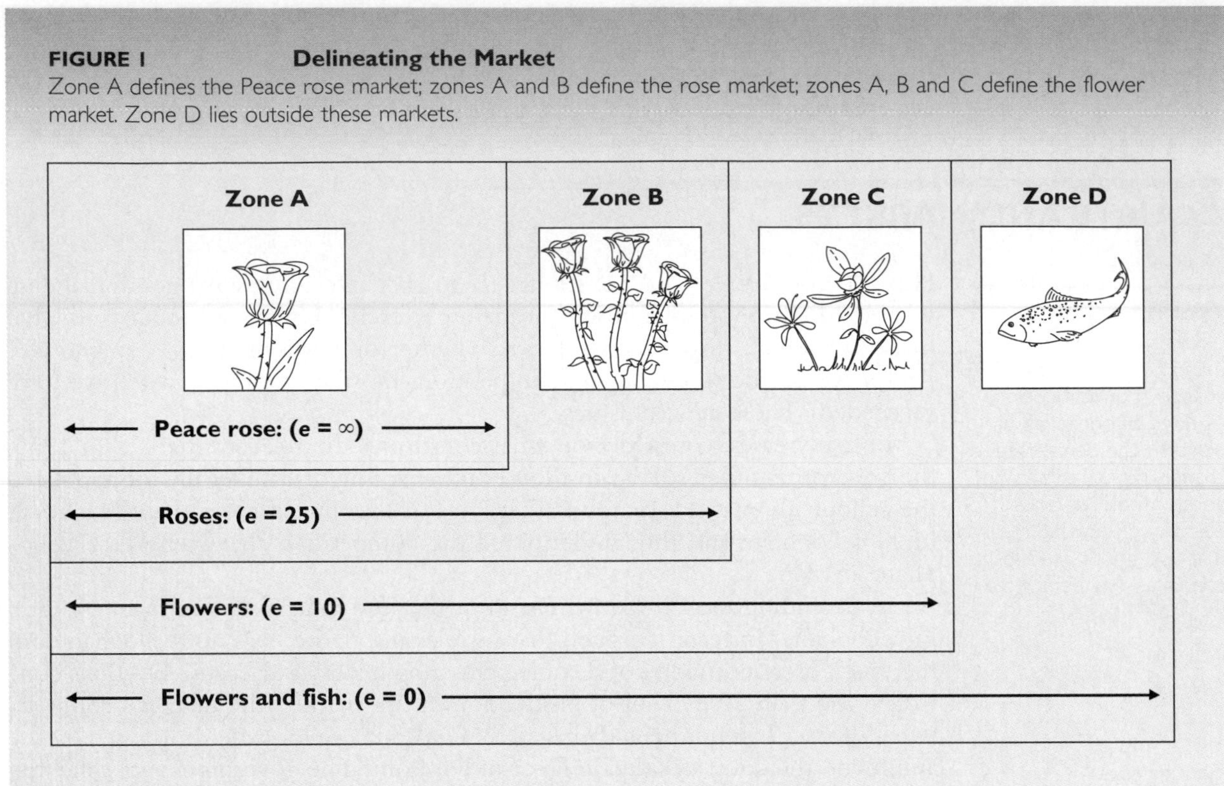

Goods that are perfect substitutes have infinite cross elasticities and goods that are completely unrelated have zero cross elasticities.

ticities with any good outside the set are zero. What examples fit into such a limiting definition?

Perhaps lifesaving drugs come as close as any good does to a zero cross elasticity with any other good. The drug AZT, for example, has for years been the only known drug that is effective in treating AIDS patients. Nothing else in the world works as well. Perhaps the artificial heart also qualifies as having zero cross elasticity with all other goods. Can you think of others?

If this concept of a perfectly contained market—infinite cross elasticities among the goods in the market and zero cross elasticities between them and any other good—is so restrictive, why consider it at all? *Because it provides us with a precise standard against which we can measure real market identities.*

Cross Elasticities in the Flower Market

By considering cross elasticities, we are able to delineate the flower market. Two goods belong to the same market if the cross elasticities between them are relatively high and their cross elasticities with goods outside the market are relatively low.

Let's go back to Gertude Stein's celebrated "Rose is a rose is a rose." Figure 1 shows a spectrum of cross elasticities among a set of goods enabling us to decide—as the court system does—what makes up a relevant market. For example, *if we choose* to define the relevant market as a set of goods whose cross elasticities within the set are infinite and are zero with all goods outside the set, then the market is limited to zone A.

Zone A describes a market whose goods are exclusively Peace roses. Every Peace rose in the market is a perfect substitute for every other, and each is perfectly nonsubstitutable with every other good. Imagine going to a florist on Mother's Day and buying a dozen American Beauty roses only to have them

ADDED PERSPECTIVE

Roses Are Pricey, Violets Will Do

Florists Push Other Buds for Valentines

In October, Pittsburgh Cut Flower, which raised 5 million roses last year, closed its rose-growing division in Richland. The decision left florists without a main supplier of locally grown roses—roses that were known for their freshness, color, and fragrance.

Two weeks ago Frank Bey of Greentree Florist placed an order for Valentine's Day flowers. But instead of the usual 1,400 roses, Bey cut his order by nearly one-third.

The sagging supply of locally grown roses has florists like Bey growing more creative in their offerings for St. Valentine's Day. That's not to say that the old standby—one dozen red roses—won't be available. For $50 to $75—about the same price as last year—you can buy a dozen of the long-stemmed variety. That's up from about $30 or $35, the off-season price.

As an alternative, Bey's staff has designed a Valentine arrangement starting at $35 and called "I love you beary much." The arrangement features a double basket, with one side containing a 12-inch movable stuffed bear, the other a traditional arrangement of red carnations, chrysanthemums, daisies, and baby's breath.

"We're going to try and educate some of the men," Bey said. "We want to let them know there are some nice alternatives to the dozen red roses in a vase."

This year, Chuck Wallace of Wallace Flowers in Mount Washington will suggest that his customers consider a mixed basket, such as one filled with daisies and carnations, and accented with two or three red roses. The cost, depending on the size of the basket, is $25 and up.

For the traditionalist who wants to stick with roses but can't afford this year's prices, Joan Boni of Boni's Flower Shop in McKees Rocks suggests a single bud. "We'd gladly sell one. It doesn't take a dozen to make most women happy," she said.

As an alternative, though, she suggests buying spring flowers. "To have spring flowers inside when there is snow outside can make someone feel just wonderful."

Rick Conley of Oliver Flowers, Downtown and Squirrel Hill, said he, too, had been trying to buy Valentine's Day stock that met any budget. Like Boni, Conley suggested buying a single rose or three roses. Short-stemmed roses, those about 16 inches long, will be sold at his shops for $39.95 a dozen. As an alternative gift, he suggested carnations, irises, tulips, or even Valentine balloons.

George Harris of Harris Brothers Flowers, Downtown, said he was not convinced that the economy would play a role in Valentine's Day. "It's very difficult to dislodge the rose as the flower for Valentine's Day, and I'm of the opinion that love and the recession don't mix," he said.

Nonetheless, for those with hearts bigger than their wallets, Harris suggests giving tulips as a symbol of love. They come in red, pink, or multicolor and right now they're at their peak.

Discussion

These florists may not know it, but their comments on roses, carnations, daisies, and spring flowers touch on the critical concepts that economists use to define the market. Elaborate.

tossed into the trash when you get home because they're not Peace roses! It's as if you had brought home a dozen kangaroos!

If that's how people really feel about Peace roses, then Peace roses make up an exclusive market. If people react the same way about the American Beauty rose, or the Madam del Bard rose or the Koba rose, then each belongs to a unique market. Each variety of rose is a very different good. Does it make sense, then, to refer to a market for roses?

But we don't really think about roses that way, do we? Even for those who can differentiate among roses and prefer the Peace rose to any other, a bouquet of American Beauty roses still is fine. For most people, they are excellent substitutes. Perhaps, then, a more useful definition of a relevant market is this: A set of goods whose cross elasticities among any two goods in the set are *relatively high* but not necessarily infinite, and whose cross elasticities with goods outside the set are *relatively low* but not necessarily zero. This more accommodating definition allows the relevant market in Figure 1 to include goods in zone B as well as zone A. That is to say, a rose market now makes sense.

What about tulips, carnations, and lilies? You don't have to be Dutch to tell the difference between a tulip and a rose. The cross elasticity of demand between roses and tulips is lower than the cross elasticities among the varieties of roses, but probably still relatively high. For many people, flowers are substitutable. Many people partial to roses will switch from a bouquet of roses to a bouquet of tulips if tulip prices fall. In this circumstance, the relevant market expands from zones A and B to include zone C. Zones A, B, and C describe a flower market.

Although people may substitute varieties of flowers, it is highly unlikely that they think of substituting fish for flowers. The cross elasticity of demand between these two goods is zero. Even when the price of fish falls 99 percent, few people stick a fish in a vase. In Figure 1, fish belong in zone D.

How High Is a High Cross Elasticity?

Why is a cross elasticity of 3.0 chosen as high enough for goods to belong in the same market?

But how high is a high cross elasticity? Economists like F. M. Scherer suggest that when any two goods have a cross elasticity greater than or equal to 3.0, they can be regarded as belonging to the same market. In Figure 1, zone B includes a variety of roses whose cross elasticities, although less than infinity, are much higher than 3.0. These varieties qualify as belonging to the same market. But to what market? If the cross elasticities among roses, tulips, and carnations are all greater than 3.0, then according to the 3.0 criterion, the relevant market is the flower market.

Why 3.0? There's nothing magical about a 3.0 cross elasticity; it is simply an arbitrary benchmark along a spectrum of cross elasticities used to divide sets of goods into specific markets.

MARKETS AND MARKET STRUCTURES

Let's look at fish and fishermen again. Suppose the cross elasticities among a variety of fish are relatively high and the cross elasticities among fish and other goods are relatively low, so that fishermen see themselves as operating in a fish market. If you are a fisherman, it probably makes a big difference whether you are the only producer in that market or just one of several hundred. That is because the control an individual fisherman can exercise over the market depends primarily on how many fishermen there are. The number of producers influences how producers respond to decisions consumers make, to decisions other producers in their market make, and to the market prices they face.

Market structure

A set of market characteristics such as number of firms, ease or difficulty of firm entry, and complementarity, or substitutability of goods.

The most direct way to determine how many fishermen make up the market is simply to count them. **Market structure** is defined by the count. With only one fisherman, the market structure is defined as a *monopoly*. On the other hand, if considerable numbers, perhaps thousands of fishermen, are bringing their catch to market, then the market structure is defined as perfectly competitive. With few producers, the market is defined as an *oligopoly*. With more than

FIGURE 2 **The Market Structure Spectrum**

The market structure spectrum consists of a continuum of markets characterized by the numbers of firms in them, the ease or difficulty that firms have in entering them, and the quantity and closeness of substitute goods. At the polar points on the spectrum are monopoly and perfect competition. The monopoly structure consists of only one firm producing goods that have no substitutes. No other firm can enter.

The perfectly competitive market structure consists of a considerable number of firms producing goods that are perfect substitutes for each other. Firms can enter easily into these markets.

The oligopolistic market structure consists of few firms. Entry into an oligopoly is relatively difficult.

The monopolistic competition market structure consists of greater than a few, but fewer than considerable numbers of firms. Firms can enter this market, but typically without the ease allowed in perfectly competitive markets.

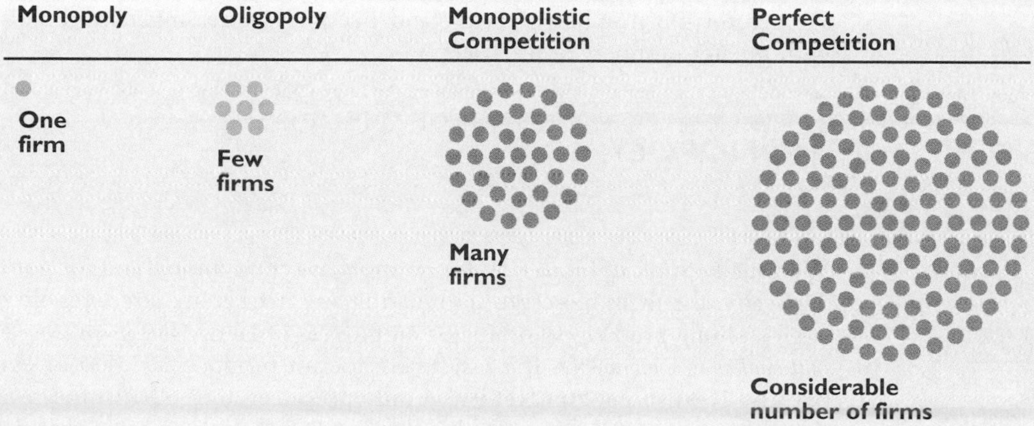

Market structures are defined, in part, by the number of firms in the market. How does the number of firms vary among monopoly, oligopoly, monopolistic competition, and perfect competition?

a few producers, but still less than considerable numbers, the market structure is considered monopolistic competition.

As you see, *the most important characteristic that distinguishes one market structure from another is the number of producers selling in the market.* Figure 2 plots these structures along a spectrum that records numbers of producers in a market—from one to considerable numbers—marking out the ranges on the spectrum that identify specific market structures.

Each market structure is defined by the number of firms, the ease or difficulty with which new firms can enter the market, and the quantity and closeness of substitute goods produced by the firms in the market. Monopoly and perfect competition occupy polar points on the spectrum. A monopoly consists of only one firm, which produces goods that have no substitutes; no other firm can enter the market. The perfectly competitive market structure on the far right in Figure 2 consists of a considerable number of firms producing goods that are perfect substitutes for each other. New firms can easily enter these markets.

Few honest-to-goodness examples of either pure monopoly or perfectly competitive markets exist. *The real world is essentially a world of oligopoly and monopolistic competition,* covering a rich variety of markets, some more monopolistic than competitive, others more competitive than monopolistic.

Oligopoly (*olig* means "few") describes a market with only a few producers. Entry into an oligopoly is relatively difficult. As important a market structure as oligopoly is in our economy—most Fortune 500 firms are oligopolies—economists are less than exact in quantifying "fewness." In fact, fewness is identified not only by the number of producers in the market (typically more than two, but less than 20), but also by the way these few producers arrive at price and output decisions. Economists know that the price an oligopolist sets affects not only the quantity of sales but also the price-making decisions of every other firm in the oligopoly. That is, in oligopoly, the fewness of firms creates **mutual interdependence** among the firms.

Mutual interdependence

Any price change made by one firm in the oligopoly affects the pricing behavior of all other firms in the oligopoly.

To the right of oligopoly in Figure 2 is monopolistic competition. This market structure consists of more than a few but fewer than a considerable number of firms. New firms can enter monopolistically competitive markets more easily than they can enter an oligopoly, but less easily than they can enter a perfectly competitive market. The market structure tends to become more competitive, the greater the number of firms, and becomes increasingly more competitive with greater numbers of producers.

THE WORLD OF MONOPOLY

Size Is Not Important

We usually think of bigness and monopoly as synonymous, and for good reason. Typically, the firms closest to dominating any market are large, highly financed, large-volume producers and major employers of labor. *But it isn't the firm's size that makes it a monopoly.* If a fisherman doesn't produce 100,000 or even 1,000 but just 100 fish per run, yet is the only producer and seller in the fish market, that fisherman is a monopolist. It's the "oneness" in the market that defines the **monopoly.**

Monopoly

A market structure consisting of one firm producing a good that has no close substitutes. Firm entry is impossible.

The Firm Is the Industry

Industry

A collection of firms producing the same good.

An **industry** is a collection of firms producing the same good. If only one firm produces the good, then *the firm is the industry.*

Suppose only one fisherman produces and sells fish in the market. Panel *a* in Figure 3 portrays the market demand curve for fish, and panel *b* portrays the demand curve that the fish monopolist faces. As you see, they are identical.

The monopolist's demand curve is the industry demand curve.

Look at panel *a*. At a price of $1, the quantity demanded by the community is 20,000 fish. When price falls to $0.80, quantity demanded increases to 21,000. Look at panel *b*. *The monopoly rightly regards the community's demand curve for fish as its own.* If the community is willing to buy 20,000 fish at $1, the monopoly correctly identifies that willingness as its own ability to sell 20,000 fish. The monopoly also knows that if it lowers the price to $0.80, it can increase sales to 21,000.

No Entry into the Industry

One reason some monopolies stay monopolies is that would-be competition finds entering the industry impossible. Several additional factors contribute to a monopoly's staying power.

THE NATURAL MONOPOLY

Some markets simply cannot support more than one firm. The fixed cost involved in setting up production for some goods is so high that the firm must

FIGURE 3 **A Monopoly's Demand Curve**

Panel *a* depicts the downward-sloping market demand for fish. At $P = \$1$, the quantity demanded is 20,000 fish. When price falls to $P = \$0.80$, quantity demanded rises to 21,000. Panel *b* shows the monopoly's demand curve. It is identical to market demand since the monopoly is the only firm producing in the market.

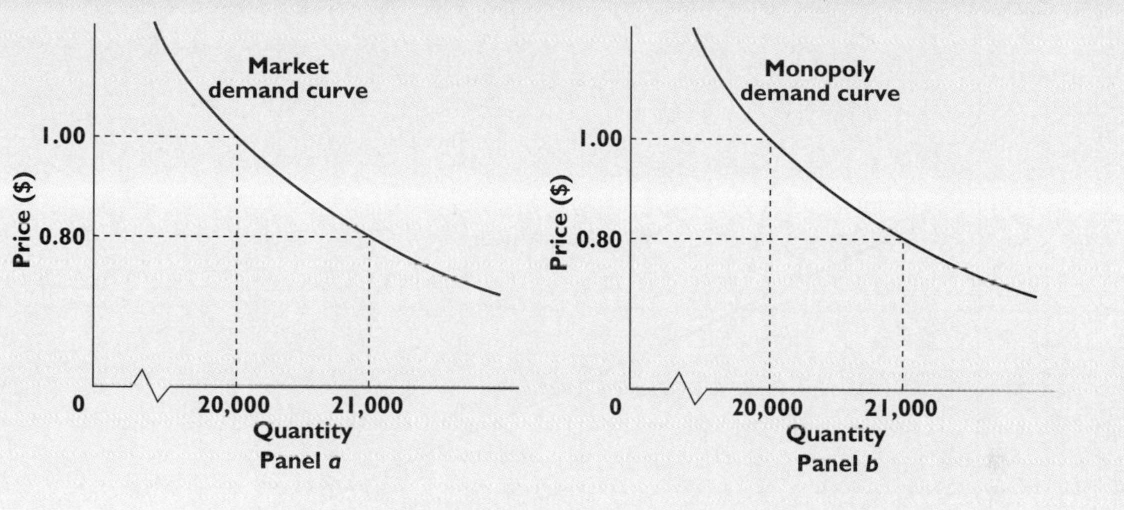

have access to a large market in order to bring its average total cost down to reasonable ranges.

Natural monopolies typically have high fixed costs so that only one firm is able to serve the market at a low average total cost. Why would high fixed costs cause this to be the case? Think about how the average fixed cost behaves as output increases.

Consider, for example, the potential market and the costs involved in bringing another baseball team to Cincinnati. Suppose a new team, the Cincinnati Blues, becomes the next expansion team in the American League. Before the first ball is pitched, it must build a superdome stadium with parking for 20,000 cars. That's an awful lot of building and real estate. The team needs ballplayers, too. A superstar earns $5 million per year whether the ballpark is filled or only 2,000 diehard fans show up at the game. These are examples of fixed costs.

The problem for the Blues is that the Cincinnati Reds at River Front Stadium—a monopolist in Cincinnati until the Blues arrived—have equal access to Cincinnati's baseball market. The bad news is illustrated in Figure 4. The demand curve, *D*, depicts the demand for baseball in Cincinnati. Before the Blues enter the market, the Reds maximize profit by charging $7 and drawing 40,000 to their ballpark. At 40,000, $ATC = \$5$. The Reds' profit is $80,000.

Now suppose the Blues enter the market and can wrestle half of the Reds' fans away to their superdome. Success? Not by a long shot! With 20,000 attendance each for Reds and Blues games, the *ATC* for both climbs to $11. Each now loses $(\$7 - \$11) \times 20{,}000 = \$80{,}000$.

If they price tickets down to $4 and succeed in driving total attendance up to 70,000, they each draw 35,000 fans but have *ATC*s of $5.50. They still incur losses.

Natural monopoly

The result of a combination of market demand and firm's costs such that only one firm is able to produce profitably in a market.

After all, total fixed cost remains the same regardless of market size. The stadiums don't change. The parking lots are still the same size. The ballplayers still earn their attractive salaries. But now, neither the Reds nor the Blues can stay in business at the higher average total cost shown in Figure 4. One team must fold. The survivor becomes a **natural monopoly,** so-called because market

FIGURE 4 **The Natural Monopoly**
As a monopolist, the Reds maximize profit at P = \$7, ATC = \$5, and attendance at 40,000. When the Blues enter the market at P = \$7, each team's ATC = \$11, and attendance is split at 20,000. Both incur losses. If they compete, price falls to \$4, total attendance increases to 70,000, and each ATC = \$5.50. Both incur losses. Only one can survive.

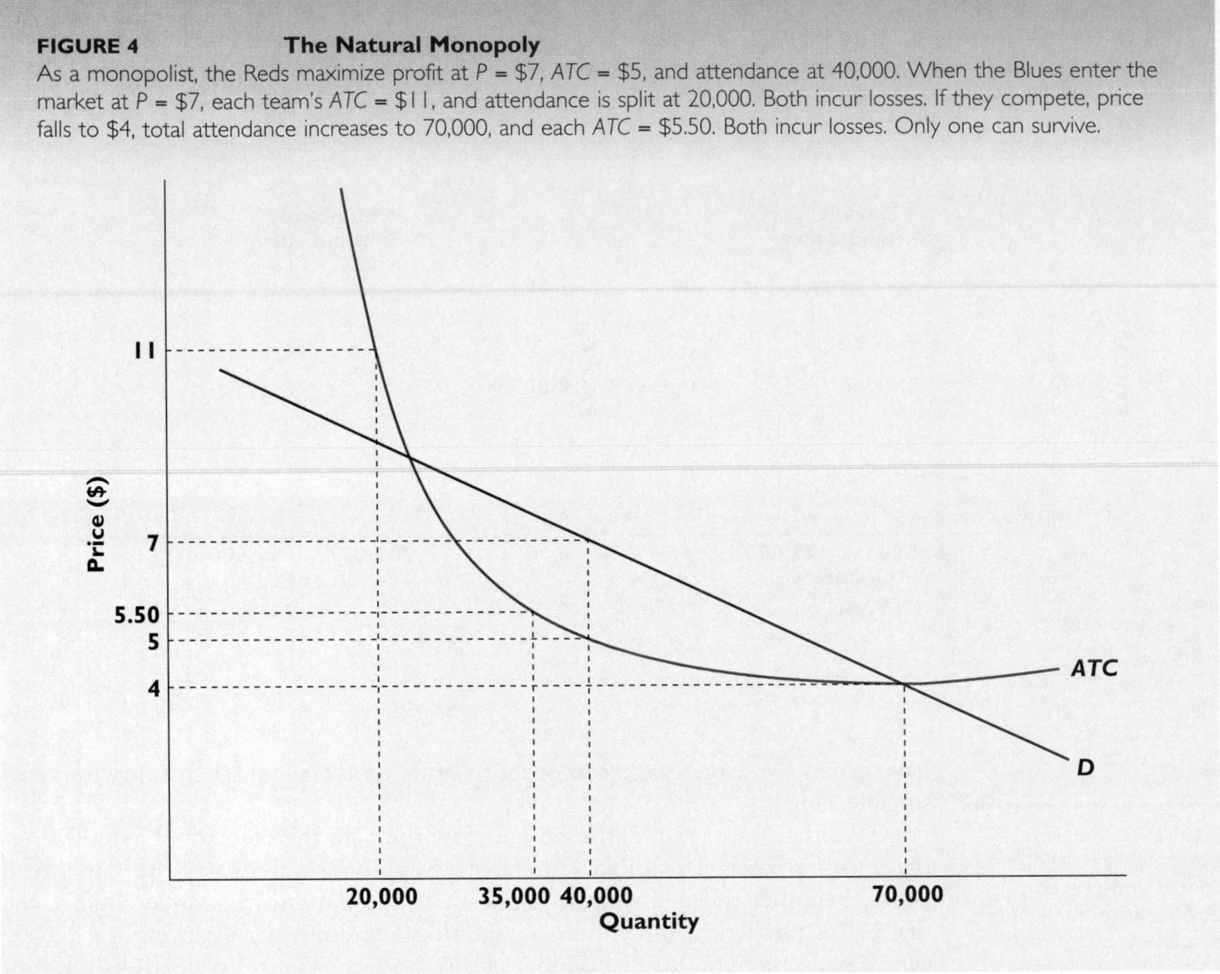

splitting in the industry comes only at the expense of driving up the firms' average total cost to prohibitive levels.

Like baseball teams, city bus companies are natural monopolies. They require heavy fixed-cost expenditures on large garages, staff, and buses. A sizable market for passenger usage is necessary to bring the average total cost per passenger mile within reach of reasonable bus fares. If two bus companies compete in the same community, each with its own garages, staff, and buses, neither can survive by servicing one-half the community's market demand. One must fold. The other survives as a natural monopoly.

That's why we typically find only one water company, only one electric power company, and only one cable televison company in the community market. Public utilities are typically natural monopolies.

EXCLUSIVE ACCESS TO RESOURCES

Some firms, by chance or design, acquire *exclusive* access to a nonreproducible good, such as a mineral resource. For example, if a firm acquires all the diamond mines in the world, it becomes a monopoly. After all, how can any other firm enter the diamond market unless it has access to diamonds? In the same way, any firm acquiring all the oil wells in the world becomes a monopoly.

Just as easily as acquiring exclusive access to resources creates monopolies, new discoveries of these resources by other firms can undo the monopolies. Prior to World War II, the world's entire known supply of helium was located in the Texas Panhandle and New Mexico. Because of helium's strategic role in military preparedness, the U.S. government exercised monopoly control. The result of this monopoly control was dramatically played out in 1937 when Germany, unable to obtain helium, was forced to use highly combustible hydrogen to lift its celebrated zeppelin, the Hindenburg. While attempting to land in Lakehurst, New Jersey, the zeppelin exploded and within seconds was engulfed in flames. Instantly, the world learned about helium and monopoly.

Be sure you can explain why technological change and the discovery of new supply sources threaten the position of a resource monopolist.

Helium is still a strategic military resource. Not only is it an inert lighter-than-air gas, but it has an exceptionally low boiling point. Therefore, aerospace programs use it to chill rocket engines before launch and to pressurize fuels into the rocket engines. But the monopoly has been broken. Since the 1950s, helium has been found in Algeria, South Africa, Canada, and Russia.

Resource monopolies are also destroyed when new technologies create viable alternatives to the resource. Coal made wood an obsolete energy resource. Nuclear and solar energies are now reducing our dependence on coal and oil. Exclusive access to a resource that becomes increasingly substitutable makes the industry increasingly competitive as well.

THE PATENT SYSTEM

Patent

A monopoly right on the use of a specific new technology or on the production of a new good. The monopoly right is awarded to and safeguarded by the government to the firm who introduces the new technology or good.

Monopolies are sometimes government promoted. To encourage firms to develop new technologies and even new goods, the government grants **patents**—monopoly rights—on innovations for 17 years. By law, others are prohibited from producing patented technologies and goods. In this way, the patent holder is assured that imitators will not undermine the profit expected from introducing the new technology or good into the market. Patent holders can, however, license their monopoly rights to others.

Does a patent on a product really guarantee a monopoly on that product?

Polaroid's instant film camera was introduced under the patent system. Xerox's breakthrough in photocopier technology was secured by patent. Most of the miracle drugs, from penicillin to AZT, have been patent-protected. More than 5 million major and minor technological changes have been introduced into our economy by monopolies under the protection of the patent. The familiar and convenient stay-on tabs on beer and soft drink cans were patent protected.

Even patent-bred monopolies, however, are constantly eroded by the creation of newer and technically more advanced close substitutes. Innovations replace innovations. New patents make older ones obsolete. In most cases, the useful monopoly life of a patent seldom reaches its full 17 years.

ACQUISITION, ACQUISITION, AND MORE ACQUISITION

Andrew Carnegie, the first U.S. steel mogul, built his empire by "consuming," or buying out his competition. He devoted his time and energy to organization and financial manipulation. "Pioneering," he philosophized, "don't pay."

Carnegie bought control of his first steel firm in 1873, and by the close of the century owned a fair slice of his competition. When he left the steel business, Carnegie was producing more steel than the combined steel output of

Monopolistic competition

A market structure consisting of many firms producing goods that are close substitutes. Firm entry is possible, but is less open and easy than in perfect competition.

Great Britain. He sold out to his equally aggressive rival J. P. Morgan. By 1901 Morgan had combined 11 large firms, including Carnegie's, to form a new colossus, U.S. Steel.

The strategy that produced the Carnegie and Morgan empires was not unusual during the years of America's greatest industrial growth. Many Fortune 500 giants owe their creation to the simple technique of firm expansion by firm acquisition.

THE WORLD OF MONOPOLISTIC COMPETITION AND OLIGOPOLY

Oligopoly

A market structure consisting of only a few firms producing goods that are close substitutes.

What about monopolistic competition? As the term suggests, **monopolistic competition** is a market structure that has elements of both monopoly and competition. **Oligopoly,** too, has elements of competition and monopoly, but oligopolistic firms have more market power than firms in monopolistic competition.

Monopolistic competitors and oligopolists are monopolist *wannabe's*.

Perhaps the best way to view these hybrid market structures is to consider them as sets of firms struggling unsuccessfully to achieve monopoly positions. *Their lack of success in achieving monopoly status results from their inability to shut out competition.* Other firms actually break into their markets.

No Easy Entry, but Entry Nonetheless

Entry of new firms into monopolistically competitive and oligopoly markets, particularly those markets characterized by firms with substantial fixed costs, isn't easy. Not everybody can compete with USX (formerly U.S. Steel). Imagine how much money it takes to get that first ton of steel rolling off the production line.

Still, as difficult as it is to put together the financial resources required to compete successfully with USX, some firms managed to do it. USX is not the sole provider of steel. The steel industry, which is composed of not one but a *few* firms, might be described as an oligopoly.

High fixed costs may also be a barrier to entry in oligopoly and monopolistic competition.

In reality, however, steel is no longer an oligopoly. The few steel firms in the United States compete not only among themselves but with steel companies in Japan, India, Nigeria, Brazil, Canada, and the European Economic Community. After all, steel produced in Germany or Nigeria can substitute perfectly well for steel produced in Gary, Indiana.

Adding up all the steel-producing companies in the world that have access to the U.S. market means that USX, far from being a firm in oligopoly, operates in a world of sizable competition. But USX's market is even more competitive than the number of firms competing in the steel industry would suggest.

Firms Producing Close Substitutes

Firms that produce close substitutes contribute to the competitiveness of oligopolistic markets even though these markets have only a few firms.

Steel competes with aluminum and fiberglass, both close substitutes for steel, in the automobile market. It also must compete with aluminum and reinforced concrete, both close substitutes for steel, in the construction market. The real extent of competition in an oligopolistic market—in this case the automobile and construction markets—therefore must be measured by the *number of firms in all the industries producing close substitutes*.

This relationship between firms, industries, and markets is illustrated in Figure 5.

The firms that compose an industry in Figure 5 are spaced horizontally. For example, the five steel firms shown in the top row make up the steel industry. The second row shows the five firms producing reinforced concrete; they make up the reinforced concrete industry. The third row shows the firms that make up the aluminum industry.

These 15 firms, representing three industries, make up the construction market, which is spaced vertically in boxes in the last column of Figure 5.

As much as USX would like to be a monopoly in the construction market, it has to compete not only with other steel firms within its industry but also with firms in other industries that produce close substitutes.

We can find close substitutes everywhere. Fire extinguishers, dishwashing detergents, 35mm cameras, sunglasses, stereo receivers, spaghetti, nursing home insurance, garbage bags, blenders, razors, paint, vacuum cleaners, facial tissues, popcorn poppers, microwave ovens, air conditioners, hair dyes, canned tomatoes, clock radios, lawn mowers, clothes dryers, sewing machines, fast foods, VCRs, personal computers, and software are just a few of the familiar goods you own or will own some day.

Product differentiation

The physical or perceived differences among goods in a market that make them close, but not perfect substitutes for each other.

Each good is produced by many firms that offer some degree of **product differentiation.** For example, *Consumer Report* once rated 18 different washing machines sold by 18 different firms in the washing machine industry. No two are exactly alike, although all are considered close substitutes. Of the top four recommended—Sears, Whirlpool, KitchenAid, and Maytag—three were actually produced by Whirlpool. How close can close substitutes be?

Consider the soft drink industry. Can you really tell the difference between Coca-Cola and Pepsi-Cola? Don't be too sure. Blind tests show that many people cannot even distinguish between Coca-Cola and 7-Up once their taste buds

FIGURE 5 **Relationship Between Firms, Industries, and Markets**

Industries consist of firms producing the same good. Markets consist of sets of industries producing close substitute goods. The steel industry's five firms compete with the aluminum industry's five firms and the reinforced concrete industry's five firms in the construction market.

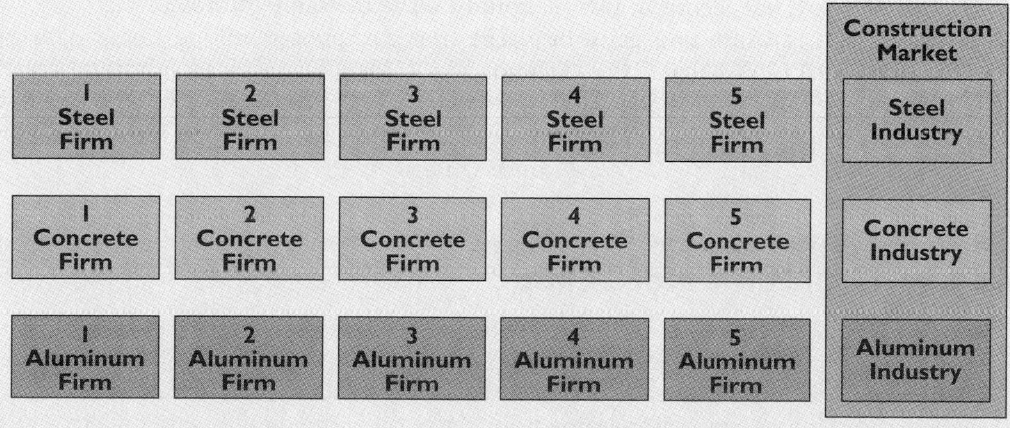

ADDED PERSPECTIVE

It's Hard to Make Profit When You're Competing Against Yourself

When a used-car salesperson tells you that the 1993 Buick you're looking at is as good as new, don't believe a word of it. On the other hand, when a used-CD salesperson tells you that a used Jello Biafra CD is as good as new—and only half to two-thirds the price of a new one—you can believe every word of it! That's what raises the hackles of every record company.

Unlike records and tapes, which wear out after repeated playings and therefore see their value dwindle quickly, there is usually little difference in quality between new and used CDs.

Consumers, of course, are delighted. But record companies, concerned about royalty payments and their own bottom line, see the used-CD encroachment into the music market quite differently. Judging by sales of used CDs and the proliferation of stores specializing in them, they're here to stay.

"It's alarming and a detriment to the music business overall," said Eddie Gilreath, vice president of sales at Geffen Records, which boasts a roster that includes Guns and Roses. "To try and create a want and need for a product and see that product sold two or three times over again undermines our industry. The perception of a product's value is totally destroyed."

Most stores sell previously owned CDs for between $6 and $9. The stores generally give around $5 credit for popular used releases that cost up to $14 new. Cash is given at a rate of 25 percent less than the trade-for-credit amount.

"I don't know how bad it is, but I know it's bad," said Bill Gilbert, senior vice president of sales and distribution at A&M Records. "I don't think there's any way to police it. I mean, they sell used cars, right?"

Discussion

Is there any way CD companies can protect themselves against competition from their own used CDs? What about your textbook? Do you plan to sell it? What should or could book publishers do to protect themselves against competing with their own used textbooks? How should the CD or textbook markets be defined? How does the concept of cross elasticity come into play?

Source: Adapted from "Industry Resents Losing to Used-CD Stores," by Fred Shuster. *Champaign-Urbana News-Gazette,* July 12, 1992. Reprinted by permission of the *Los Angeles Daily News.*

Why don't all people buy Pepsi when it is on sale rather than Coca-Cola?

have been washed by any carbonated drink. But people still have favorites and pay a higher price for their choice. You probably know people who buy Coke even when Pepsi is on sale at the supermarket.

Holiday Inn offers accommodations that, for most people, are close substitutes for accommodations offered at Sheraton, Ramada, Radisson, Best Western, Howard Johnson, Marriott, Hilton, Hyatt, and Hampton Inn. They are not identical, but all seem to serve the same purpose.

And if you get a headache trying to choose among hotels, you can always take MacNeil Lab's Tylenol. But Tylenol is a close substitute for American Home's Anacin, Sterling's Aspirin, Bristol-Myers Bufferin and Excedrin, Rorer's Ascriptin, Burroughs Wellcome's Empirin, and Du Pont's Percogesic.

As More Firms Enter the Market, Firm Demand Curves Become More Elastic

Let's trace the impact of entry on a firm's demand curve in a monopolistically competitive market. Consider the demand for Coca-Cola, the most recognized product in the world. An Atlanta pharmacist, John Pemberton, who made his living concocting homespun "snake oil" remedies, invented Coca-Cola in 1886. In the beginning, Coca-Cola was just another of his medicinal potions. Already

Let's see now . . . this pine-scented deodorant spray claims to provide the best 24-hour protection on the market and that pump-action, musk-scented deodorant claims to provide the best 48-hour protection on the market. Could one of them—or perhaps both—be exaggerating?

in poor health, Pemberton quickly sold two-thirds of his interest in the product for $1,200, and in 1888, just before he died, he sold the remaining third for $500. Ingenious marketing subsequently converted Coca-Cola from a questionable medicine to a popular soft drink.

ADDED PERSPECTIVE

Who Can Be Loyal to a Trash Bag?

Loyalty is a highly valued quality in our society. Friendships and family thrive on it. Loyalty often explains why sports fans endure with love and affection the agony of chronic defeat. Dogs are devotedly loyal to their owners and grateful dog lovers, in turn, are loyal to their pets. But how far does loyalty reach? For example, does loyalty to a particular brand of canned soup make sense? Can you really be loyal to a trash bag? The answers may surprise you.

When generic products were coming on strong a few years ago, J. Walter Thompson, the New York-based ad agency, measured consumers' loyalty to brands in 80 product categories. It found that the leader in market share was not necessarily the brand-loyalty leader. At that time, Bayer aspirin was the market share leader among headache remedies, but Tylenol had the most loyal following.

Thompson measured the degree of loyalty by asking people whether they'd switch for a 50 percent discount. Cigarette smokers most often said no, making them the most brand loyal consumers (see table). Film is the only one of the top five products that consumers don't put in their mouths—so why such loyalty? According to Edith Gilson, Thompson's senior vice president of research, 35-mm film is used by photography buffs, who are not your average snapshooter: "It's for long-lasting, emotionally valued pictures, taken by someone who has invested a lot of money in his camera." Plenty of shoppers will try a different cola for 50 percent off, and most consumers think one plastic garbage bag or facial tissue is much like another.

High-Loyalty Products	Medium-Loyalty Products	Low-Loyalty Products
Cigarettes	Cola drinks	Paper towels
Laxatives	Margarine	Crackers
Cold remedies	Shampoo	Scouring powder
35-mm film	Hand lotion	Plastic trash bags
Toothpaste	Furniture polish	Facial tissues

Discussion

Test yourself. Suppose prices of your favorite brands rose by 25 percent, how loyal would you be to the brands you prefer in the table above?

FIGURE 6 **The Demand Curve for Coca-Cola: Before and After Substitutes Appear on the Market**

Before substitute goods appear on the market, Coca-Cola has a monopoly position, shown in panel *a*. Its demand curve is identical to the market demand curve, *D*. When five new firms enter the market, shown in panel *b*, Coca-Cola's market share falls. Its demand curve, *D'*, shifts to the left. Market demand, *D*, remains unchanged. When five more firms enter the market, shown in panel *c*, Coca-Cola's market share falls even further. Its demand curve, *D''*, shifts further to the left while market demand, *D*, remains unchanged.

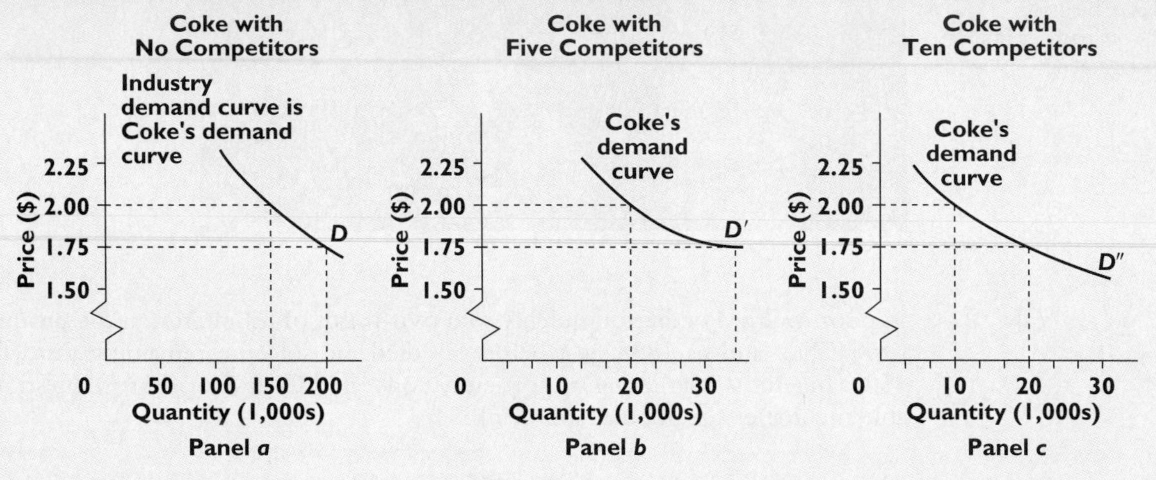

Coke remains an original. As you know, dozens of close substitutes are now on the market, but only Coca-Cola can claim to be the real thing. It is 99.8 percent water and sugar, but it's the remaining 0.2 percent that counts! Coca-Cola's transition from a monopoly to one of many firms in monopolistic competition is traced out in Figure 6.

Because some people buy Pepsi, the demand for Coca-Cola decreases and becomes more elastic when Pepsi is introduced in the market.

Figure 6, panel *a* portrays Coca-Cola's monopoly position before substitutes appear on the market. The industry demand curve is precisely the demand curve that Coca-Cola faces. Coca-Cola is the industry. Suppose Coca-Cola decides to raise its price from $1.75 to $2 per 2-liter bottle. The quantity demanded falls from 200,000 to 150,000 cases per day. The price elasticity of demand within the $1.75 to $2 price range is 2.15. At $2, some thirsty people choose the kitchen faucet over the refrigerator. On the other hand, 150,000 cases are still sold at $2.

Now suppose a dozen soft drink firms enter the market and, after the first year, five actually succeed. What happens to Coca-Cola's market position? Look at panel *b*. Coca-Cola is no longer a monopoly. The industry's demand curve no longer belongs to Coca-Cola alone. With five others competing in the market, Coca-Cola's demand curve falls—that is, shifts to the left—becoming more elastic. The quantity demanded at $1.75 is now only 33,333 cases; the remaining 166,667 cases make up the quantity demanded of its five competitors.

Brand loyalty

The willingness of consumers to continue buying a good at a price higher than the price of its close substitutes.

What happens when Coca-Cola raises its price to $2? Unlike the response shown in panel *a*, consumers react in one of three ways. Some people, even with five good substitutes priced at $1.75, stay with Coca-Cola at $2. It still sells 20,000 cases. That's **brand loyalty**! Price elasticity of demand for Coca-Cola within the price range $1.75 to $2 increases to 3.74. But some customers switch to one of the competing brands that have not raised their prices. When Coca-

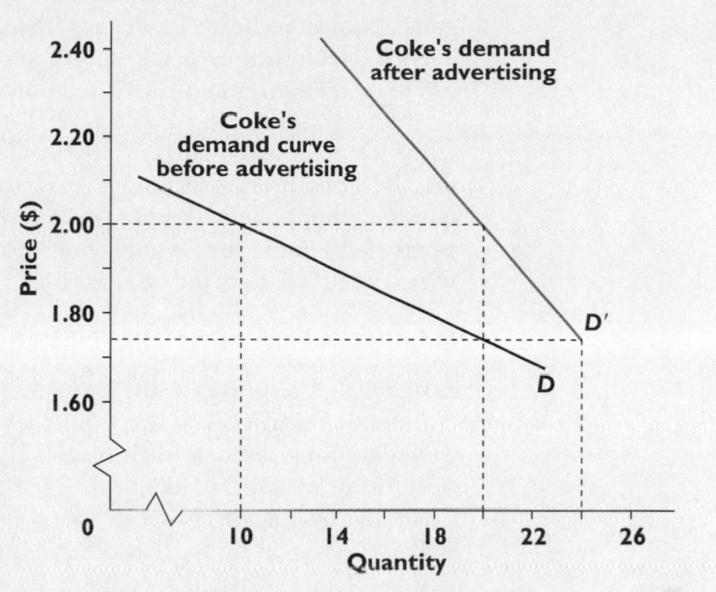

FIGURE 7
The Effect of Advertising on the Firm's Demand Curve
After advertising, Coke's demand curve shifts to the right and becomes more inelastic.

Cola raises its price to $2, other customers don't switch brands, they just switch out of the market completely.

Now suppose the number of firms in the industry increases from six to 11. Coca-Cola's position in the market changes from panel *b* to panel *c*. As you see, its *demand curve shifts further to the left and becomes even more elastic.* Why? Coca-Cola knows that with 10 other soft drinks to choose from, consumers are more likely to find a suitable substitute. At $1.75, quantity demanded of Coca-Cola is now only 20,000 cases, down from 33,333 in panel *b*. At $2, quantity demanded drops to 10,000 cases. Price elasticity of demand within the $1.75 to $2 price range increases to 5.00. As you see, some consumers still remain loyal to Coca-Cola, but these loyalists become fewer and fewer. Coca-Cola cannot help but become aware that consumers who have more choices are more sensitive to price changes.

The Role of Advertising

Be sure you understand the intended impact of advertising on both the shape and the position of demand curves.

Market share

The percent of total market sales produced by a particular firm in a market.

Firms in monopolistic competition, like Coca-Cola, and firms in oligopoly have a strong incentive to advertise. They expect advertising to undo the effects of increasing competition.

Figure 7 compares the before-advertising and the after-advertising position of a monopolistically competitive firm, such as Coca-Cola. The goal of advertising is to increase the firm's **market share** while reducing consumer sensitivity to price changes.

INCREASING MARKET SHARE

Lowering price is one way to persuade consumers already in the market to switch brands, but advertising may engineer that switch without lowering price. It provides consumers with selective information—sometimes misinformation—

that may be the only information available to many in the market. It often suggests associations between the advertised good and such highly valued activities, events, or institutions as sex, sports, and family. It is typically highly repetitious, to create consumer familiarity and confidence.

Not all advertising is slick or sleazy; much is genuinely informative. If Chrysler offers a 7-year or 70,000-mile warranty, that's important information for the consumer. Consumers may have difficulty finding the lowest-priced goods without those double-page newspaper advertisements published by supermarkets. And how would you know what movie is playing where and at what time if theaters didn't advertise?

MAKING DEMAND MORE INELASTIC

Advertising's response to the growing flood of substitutes in a monopolistically competitive market is to deny quite aggressively that any substitutes exist! How can advertising perform such magic? By simply insisting. In almost all cases, the advertising message is identical: *There are no substitutes. Our product is different.* Over and over again, in these efforts at product differentiation, we are told that Coke® is the real thing, that others—notably Pepsi-Cola—are unsatisfying imitations. If its advertised message is successful, a firm can raise its price without much decrease in quantity demanded.

Figure 7 shows that successful advertising can shift a firm's demand curve outward to the right. For example, at $1.75, the quantity demanded of advertised Coca-Cola increases from 20,000 to 24,000 cases, a sizable 20 percent change. Successful advertising lowers the firm's price elasticity of demand. Before advertising, an increase in price from $1.75 to $2 cut quantity demanded from 20,000 cases to 10,000, or by 50 percent. After advertising, the same price increase cuts quantity demanded from 24,000 to 20,000 cases, or only by 16.6 percent. Price elasticity of demand within the $1.75 to $2 price range falls dramatically from a before-advertising level of 5.00 to 1.36 after advertising.

THE WORLD OF PERFECT COMPETITION

Perfect competition

A market structure consisting of a large number of firms producing goods that are perfect substitutes. Firm entry is open and easy.

Perfect competition is monopolistic competition carried to its competitive extreme. In **perfect competition,** increasingly greater numbers of firms invade the market, until so many firms exist and so many substitute goods are produced that neither firms nor goods have any individual identity on the market. In the *perfectly* competitive market, all goods are *perfect* substitutes for each other.

Easy Entry, with Considerable Numbers of Firms Producing Perfect Substitutes

Imagine a market where firms can enter at will. There are virtually no financial or technological barriers to overcome. Of course, not *everybody* enters, but enough firms do so that the goods these firms produce are virtually indistinguishable.

Consider the egg market. Can you really distinguish between the eggs packaged and sold by SunnyFarm, by EggRight, by EggFresh, by MorningStart, or by the hundreds of others that sell directly at outdoor markets or indirectly through groceries and supermarkets?

FIGURE 8 **Market Demand Curve and the Demand Curve Facing a Firm in Perfect Competition**

Panel *a* depicts the market demand curve for roasted peanuts, *D*, in a perfectly competitive market. The market demand curve is downward-sloping. When P = $1.50, quantity demanded is 600,000. Panel *b* shows the demand curve facing a firm in the roasted peanut market. As far as the firm is concerned, it can sell any quantity it chooses—10, 100, or 400 pounds—at P = $1.50. The horizontal shape of the firm's demand curve reflects its ability to sell any quantity it chooses at P = $1.50.

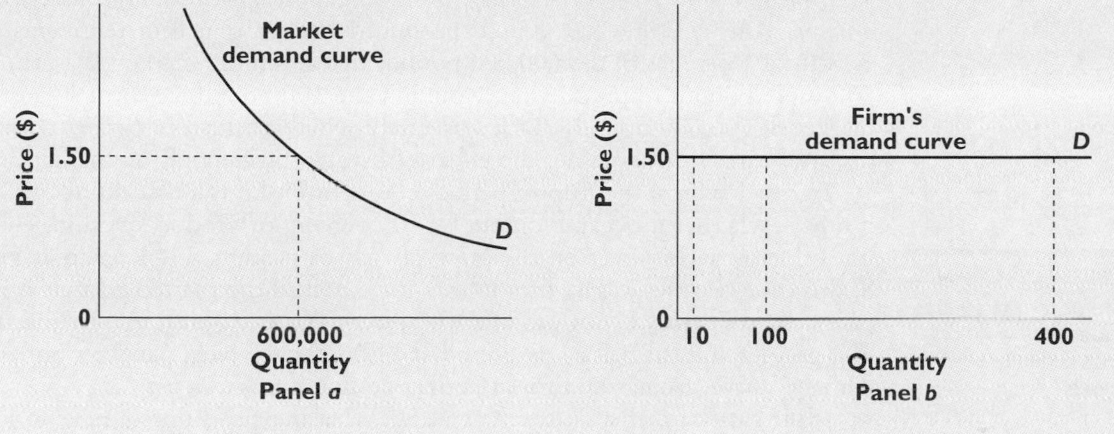

Entry into markets results in a collection of products that are virtually perfect substitutes.

How can anyone distinguish corn grown on Jon Kaufman's 400-acre farm in Newman Grove, Nebraska, from the corn grown on Darla Brown's 1,000-acre farm in Petersburg, some 30 miles away? And hundreds of other farmers are growing corn between them. Identical goods are *perfect* substitutes.

In markets where considerable numbers of firms produce perfect substitutes, firms cannot raise price without inviting disaster. If any firm raises its price by so much as a penny, consumers switch to a competitor because all goods in the market are perfect substitutes. Quantity demanded then falls to zero for the firm with the higher price.

What about the firm's market share in perfectly competitive markets? If market demand remains unchanged as more and more firms enter, each firm's individual share of that demand falls. With considerable numbers of firms entering the market, each firm's share becomes so insignificant relative to total market demand that a firm can double or triple production without worrying about the effect that its increase in production will have on price.

Figure 8 illustrates the perfectly competitive firm's inability to influence market price.

Panel *a* represents the market demand curve for roasted peanuts. At a price of $1.50, quantity demanded is 600,000 pounds. It really makes no difference to people who buy roasted peanuts whether 3, 30, 300, or 3,000 firms produce the peanuts. Why should anyone care? All roasted peanuts are identical. It's strictly price that determines how many pounds of roasted peanuts consumers demand.

Firm's Insignificant Market Share

What about the individual roasted peanut firm? Here, numbers count. Suppose 3,000 such firms each produce 200 pounds. If called on, any of these firms can increase production by 10 percent—to 220 pounds—without exerting noticeable strains on its capacity. It simply hires more labor and purchases more raw peanuts. On the other hand, the firm finds it much more difficult to increase production by 100 percent. It may have to add an entirely new work shift, increase its raw material inventory considerably, and perhaps add a new processing machine. For any one firm to increase its production by 1,000 percent is virtually impossible, at least in the short run.

In other words, the physical quantity that any one of these 3,000 firms can produce, given the size of its productive capacity, is insignificant compared with the market's total demand. After all, the 200 pounds produced by any one firm represents only 1/30th of 1 percent of the 600,000 pounds that reach the market. If a firm adds 100 more pounds to production, wouldn't the 100 pounds be virtually lost in a market of 600,000 pounds? That's precisely why each firm in perfect competition never needs to consider the effect of its own production on market price.

In other words, the firm in perfect competition knows that no matter what it does—whether it expands output by 100 percent or produces nothing—it has no influence whatsoever on the price of roasted peanuts. Look again at Figure 8, this time at panel *b*. The firm knows it can sell all the roasted peanuts it is capable of producing. It can produce 100 pounds or even push production up to 400 pounds and still sell every pound at $1.50. That's what panel *b*'s horizontal demand curve, facing the firm in perfect competition, tells us.

Firms in perfect competition are price-takers—they can sell all they want but the price is determined in the market.

If the firm can sell all it wants at $1.50, what incentive does it have to lower price? None at all. On the other hand, because of the perfect substitutes available from its competitors, it can't raise the price a penny above $1.50. If it did, quantity demanded would fall to zero. For these reasons, the firm views the demand curve it faces as perfectly horizontal.

PUTTING TOGETHER A SCORECARD ON MARKET STRUCTURES

Producers typically know their markets well. They know what kind of competition they face as well as something about the relative ease or difficulty other firms experience in entering their markets. They even have a good idea about the price elasticity of demand for the goods they produce. They know whether it pays to advertise. They can probably locate themselves easily on the scorecard in Figure 9.

Let's review. A monopoly faces no competition, and it has the added security of knowing that no new entry into the market is possible. It views the market as its own. The demand curve it faces is downward-sloping. The incentive to advertise is relatively weak since it need not fight for market share, although it may still choose to advertise in order to shift its market demand curve out further to the right.

A firm in perfect competition operates in a very different world. It is overwhelmed with competitors and faces the prospect of even more competition since entry into its market is open and easy. It produces a good that is identical to those produced by its competition and recognizes its own insignificance as a member of its market. The demand curve it faces is horizontal. Under these conditions, advertising is of no use to the firm.

In the monopolistically competitive and oligopolistic market structures, entry into the market is possible but not always easy. Firms produce goods that

FIGURE 9 **Summary Sketch of Market Structures**

Type of Market	*Number of Firms*	*Type of Product*	*Entry*	*A Firm's Influence over Its Price*	*Does the Firm Worry about the Responses of Its Competition?*
Perfect Competition	Many, many firms	Identical	Easy	None	No
Monopolistic Competition	Many firms	Differentiated	Easy	A little	No
Oligopoly	A few firms	Usually differentiated	Difficult	Considerable	Yes
Monopoly	One	—	Impossible	Complete	No direct competitors

are close but not perfect substitutes, and each firm therefore faces a downward-sloping demand curve for its product. A firm in monopolistic competition can raise its price without having the quantity demanded of its good fall to zero, but the presence of close substitutes raises the price elasticities of demand for its goods. For this reason, firms in monopolistic competition find that it pays to advertise. They advertise to capture a larger piece of the market and to reduce the elasticity of demand.

CHAPTER REVIEW

1. Defining the relevant market depends on identifying the degree of substitutability between goods. Because a positive cross elasticity of demand indicates that two goods are substitutes, this measure is an important conceptual tool for identifying markets.

2. A perfectly contained market consists of goods with infinite cross elasticities among them and zero cross elasticities between them and any other good. A cross elasticity of three is usually considered high enough to put two goods in the same market.

3. Market structures can be scaled along a spectrum, with monopoly at one extreme and perfect competition at the other. Oligopoly, with a few producers, lies closer to monopoly. Between oligopoly and perfect competition is monopolistic competition.

4. Monopoly has only one producer. The firm is the industry. Monopoly is maintained through barriers to entry. These may take several forms, including natural monopoly, exclusive access to resources, and patents.

5. Monopolistic competition and oligopoly are marked by the potential entry of firms, although entry may be difficult in reality. Firms in these markets produce close substitutes. The more substitutable products in these markets become, the more elastic are the demand curves facing individual firms. Entry into these industries reduces each firm's market share.

6. Advertising plays a significant role in monopolistic competition and oligopoly. Firms will advertise in order to increase market share and to make demand more inelastic.

7. Perfect competition consists of many firms producing goods that are perfect substitutes. Entry is easy in perfect competition. The demand curve facing a firm is perfectly elastic. The firm's market share is insignificant, so the decision by the firm to sell more or less has no impact on the market price.

KEY TERMS

Relevant market
Perfectly contained market
Market structure
Mutual interdependence
Monopoly
Industry
Natural monopoly
Patent
Monopolistic competition
Oligopoly
Product differentiation
Brand loyalty
Market share
Perfect competition

QUESTIONS

1. Why would a monopolist choose to advertise? Why wouldn't a firm in perfect competition choose to advertise?

2. What advantages would a firm in monopolistic competition gain from advertising?

3. What is the relationship between cross elasticities of demand and the identification of specific goods to specific markets?

4. What is meant by market structure?

5. What is a natural monopoly? Give specific examples of monopolies you consider natural. Cite examples of monopolies that you think are clearly not natural.

6. Why does the government issue patents and penalize firms who infringe upon the patent rights of other firms?

7. Describe the major factors distinguishing market structures.

8. Explain why an economist and a zoologist, looking at horses, cows, and automobiles, would not choose the same two out of three as having something in common.

9. Why is the size of the firm not a very reliable criterion in identifying monopoly?

10. There is hardly any good that does not have substitutes. Discuss. Can you name goods that don't?

11. What is the relationship between firms, industries, and markets?

12. What distinguishes oligopoly from monopolistic competition?

13. Why is the demand curve for a firm in monopolistic competition downward-sloping?

14. Given the following price and average total cost data, pick the natural monopoly and explain your choice. Convert the data into graphic form.

Firm A			Firm B		
Quantity	**Price**	**Average Total Cost**	**Quantity**	**Price**	**Average Total Cost**
1	$9.00	$6.00	1	$9.00	$6.00
2	8.00	5.00	2	8.00	4.00
3	7.00	4.00	3	7.00	3.35
4	6.00	3.50	4	6.00	3.25
5	4.50	3.00	5	4.50	3.50
6	3.50	2.50	6	3.50	4.50
7	2.00	2.00	7	2.00	5.50
8	1.00	1.75	8	1.00	7.00

15. The following demand schedules are given for the Todd Fletcher Flower Arrangement Company of Logan's Square.

Price	Quantity, With No Competitors	Quantity, With 25 Competitors	Quantity, With 40 Competitors
$10	100,000	4,000	2,500
9	110,000	5,500	3,300
8	120,000	7,200	3,600
7	130,000	7,800	4,550
6	140,000	8,400	4,900
5	150,000	10,500	6,000
4	160,000	11,200	6,400
3	170,000	11,900	7,650
2	180,000	14,400	9,000
1	190,000	17,100	9,500

At a price of $8 per flower arrangement, calculate Fletcher's market share when he has (a) no competition, (b) 25 competitors, and (c) 40 competitors. What is his market share when price is $3?

C H A P T E R 11

PRICE AND OUTPUT IN MONOPOLY, MONOPOLISTIC COMPETITION, AND PERFECT COMPETITION

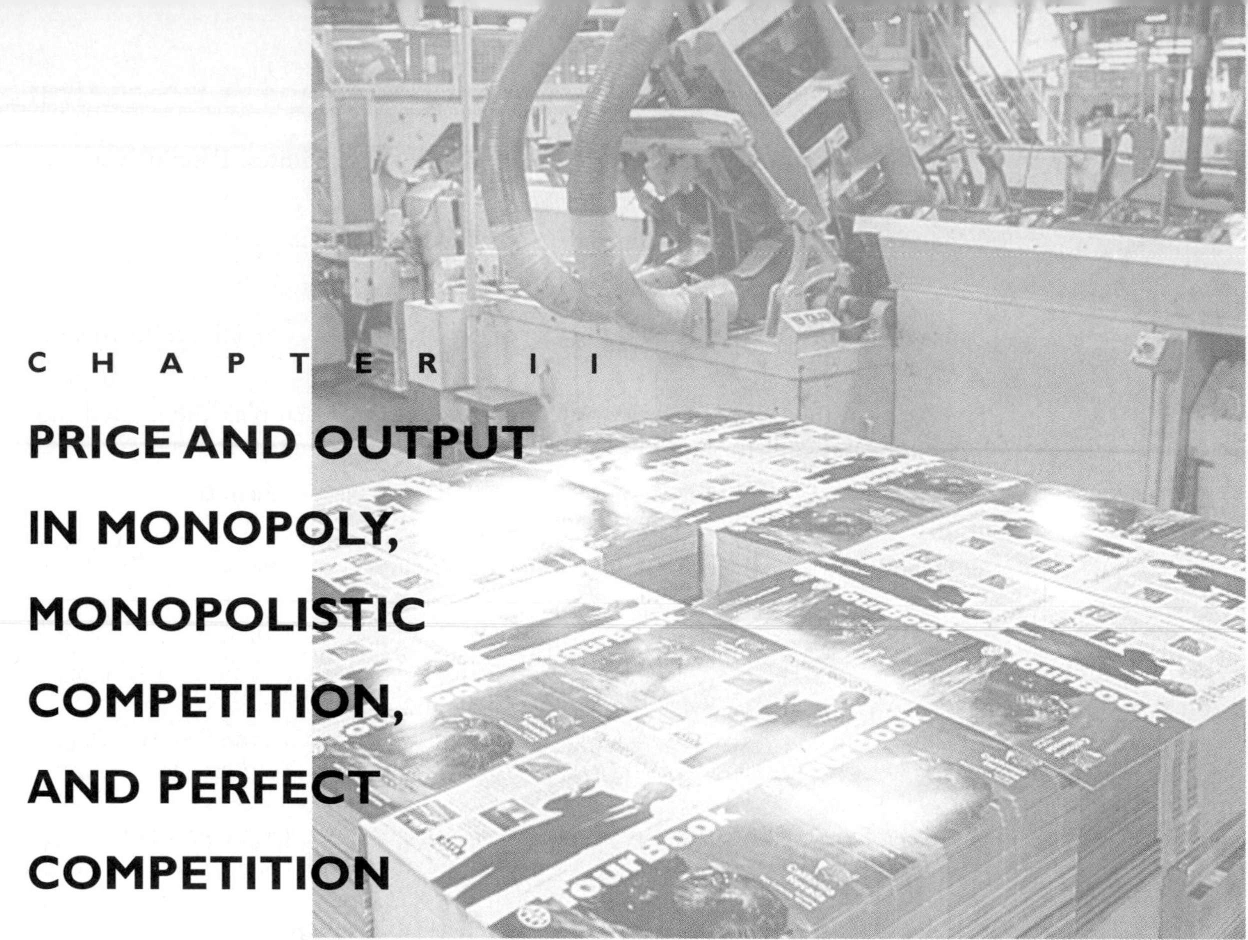

CHAPTER PREVIEW

Now that we understand the characteristics of different market structures, it is time to return to the topic introduced in Chapter 9. That is, how do firms in different market structures compare in their profit-maximizing behavior? More specifically, we want to know how price and output are determined in various market structures. Price and output determination turn out to be fairly straightforward for monopoly, monopolistic competition, and perfect competition. However, price and output determination is another story for oligopoly. We'll save it for the next chapter.

After studying this chapter, you should be able to:

- Derive the monopolist's marginal revenue curve given the demand curve.
- Explain why profit can persist under monopoly conditions.
- Draw a graph to represent a profit-maximizing monopolist earning monopoly profits.
- Discuss the concept of short-run equilibrium in monopolistic competition.
- Show the impact of entry on a monopolistically competitive firm's demand curve.
- Draw a graph to represent long-run equilibrium in monopolistic competition.

- Explain the difference between economic profit and normal profit.
- Contrast marginal revenue for a perfectly competitive firm with marginal revenue for monopoly and monopolistic competition.
- Draw graphs to represent short- and long-run equilibrium in perfect competition.
- Justify the claim that perfect competition leads to maximum efficiency.
- Derive from the marginal cost curve the perfectly competitive firm's and the market's supply curves.
- Compare constant returns to scale and increasing returns to scale.
- Discuss the advantages monopoly might have over perfect competition in advancing technology.

Suppose, after graduation, you land a job as economist on the White House staff. And suppose, on the Friday evening of your first week, just when you are about to leave the executive wing of 1600 Pennsylvania Avenue, the President drops by to chat. In the course of conversation, he tells you that he is concerned about the degree of monopoly in our economy and wonders if there is anything he should do about it. He asks you: "What is it that monopolists *really* want?" What would you say?

Wouldn't you want to emphasize that monopolists, like everybody else in business, simply want to maximize profit? That's it. Nothing more. Yet, were you to take the president's question to the man and woman on the street, or even to members of Congress, or to network news broadcasters, chances are that their overwhelming response would be: "Monopolists want to raise prices." For those unschooled in the principles of economics, raising prices is synonymous with raising profits.

Perhaps that's why George Stigler, 1982 Nobel Laureate in Economics, wrote in the very first sentence of the chapter on monopoly in his *Theory of Price:* "A monopolist is no less desirous of profits than a competitive firm and is in a somewhat better position to achieve them."

Stigler wanted to make the point, early and with clarity, that it is the monopoly's *market position,* not motivation, not morality, not strategy, and not objective, that distinguishes the monopolist from any other entrepreneur. If a monopolist firm discovers that it could increase profit by lowering price, don't you think it would? In fact, many do precisely that. There are even situations where the price chosen by the monopolist is lower than the price that would be obtained if the market were competitive. How do profit-maximizing monopolists go about determining what price to charge and how much to produce?

PRICE AND OUTPUT UNDER MONOPOLY

The rule for profit maximization, $MR = MC$, is the same for a monopolist.

Let's look again at our fishing economy, except this time let's analyze the ice manufacturing industry that caters to the fishermen. Suppose only one firm on the island, the Nick Rudd Ice Company, manufactures ice. Nick Rudd is a monopoly. Fishermen have no alternative but to buy their ice from Rudd.

Suppose Table 1 represents the market demand that the Nick Rudd Ice Company faces. It can charge any price it wishes, but it knows that at higher prices, fewer tons will be demanded.

TABLE 1
Market Demand for Ice

Price	Quantity (tons)
$300	0
275	50
250	100
225	150
200	200
175	250
150	300
125	350
100	400
75	450
50	500
25	550

Although it cannot dictate how much ice people should demand at different prices, it can select price and quantity combinations from Table 1. For example, it can choose $275 per ton and count on people demanding 50 tons or it can lower price to $125 per ton and sell 350 tons.

How does Rudd go about finding the profit-maximizing price and quantity combination? As we saw in Chapter 9, the profit-maximizing rule is simple: Keep producing as long as $MR > MC$. When $MC > MR$, cut back. Profit maximization occurs at $MC = MR$.

The *MC* = *MR* Rule Applied

Let's look at how Nick Rudd Ice Company derives its marginal revenue schedule. The data are shown in Table 2.

Total revenue, *TR*, is price multiplied by quantity,

$$TR = PQ$$

Marginal revenue, *MR*, measures the change in *TR* generated by a change in *Q*

$$MR = \frac{\Delta TR}{\Delta Q}$$

For example, increasing production from 200 to 250 tons, that is, adding 50 tons to production, increases revenue by $43,750 – $40,000 = $3,750. The marginal revenue for each of these 50 additional tons, then, is $3,750/50 = $75.

MR for a monopolist is the addition to total revenue from selling another unit of output. Why is *MR* below market price for a monopolist?

Does it pay Rudd to produce the 250th ton? It depends on the marginal cost of that 250th ton. Rudd consults its cost schedule, shown in Table 3.

Columns 3, 5, and 7 record total cost, average total cost, and marginal cost across the production range zero to 600 tons. Recall that marginal cost is the increase in total cost when an additional unit of ouput is added to production.

TABLE 2 Price and Revenue Schedule for the Nick Rudd Ice Company

Quantity (tons)	Price	Total Revenue	Marginal Revenue
0	$300	$ 0	$ 0
50	275	13,750	275
100	250	25,000	225
150	225	33,750	175
200	200	40,000	125
250	175	43,750	75
300	150	45,000	25
350	125	43,750	–25
400	100	40,000	–75
450	75	33,750	–125
500	50	25,000	–175
550	25	13,750	–225

$$MC = \frac{\Delta TC}{\Delta Q}$$

Economic profit

A firm's total revenue minus its total explicit and implicit costs.

Columns 4 and 8 record the total and marginal revenues derived from Table 2. Column 9 subtracts the total cost of column 3 from the total revenue of column 4; this is the monopoly's **economic profit.**

TABLE 3 Cost and Revenue Schedules for the Nick Rudd Ice Company

Quantity (tons)	P	TC	TR	ATC*	AVC*	MC	MR	Profit
(1)	(2)	(3)	(4)	(5)	(6)	(7)	(8)	(9)
0	300	$ 4,000	$ 0					$ –4,000
50	275	8,500	13,750	$170	$90	$ 90	$ 275	5,250
100	250	11,000	25,000	110	70	50	225	14,000
150	225	12,250	33,750	82	55	25	175	21,500
200	200	13,250	40,000	66	46	20	125	26,750
250	175	14,350	43,750	57	41	22	75	29,400
300	150	15,600	45,000	52	39	25	25	29,400
350	125	17,100	43,750	49	37	30	–25	26,650
400	100	18,950	40,000	47	37	37	–75	21,050
450	75	21,300	33,750	47	38	47	–125	12,450
500	50	24,300	25,000	49	41	60	–175	700
550	25	28,200	13,750	51	44	78	–225	–14,450
600		33,200	0	55	49	100	–275	–33,200

*Figures are rounded to the nearest dollar.

When production is zero, Rudd's total cost is $4,000 because it is still obligated to pay its fixed costs. No revenue is earned at zero production.

Now look what happens when Rudd increases production to 50 tons. Total cost increases from $4,000 to $8,500. Total revenue is $13,750, generating an economic profit for Rudd of $13,750 – $8,500 = $5,250. Is Rudd satisfied? Is 50 tons Rudd's profit-maximizing output? Not by a long shot.

Look at the marginals of columns 7 and 8. At the fiftieth ton, MR = $275 and MC = $90. The profit-maximizing rule counsels Rudd to increase production. As long as $MR > MC$, every additional ton of ice produced adds to the company's profit. As Table 3 records, $MR > MC$ at every output level up to the 300th ton. At the 300th, $MR = MC$ = $25.

Rudd's profit-maximizing output, then, is 300 tons, generating a monopoly profit of $29,400. *Although the monopoly can charge any price it wishes, the price that yields the highest profit is $150.* If Rudd raises price to $200—it can, of course—it would sell only 200 tons and make a profit of $26,750. But why would Rudd choose $26,750 profit instead of $29,400?

Maximum Profit, but Less Than Maximum Efficiency

The profit-maximizing level of output for a monopolist lies to the left of the minimum of the *ATC* curve.

Look at Rudd's average total cost in column 5. At 300 tons, ATC = $52. It is not the most efficient level of output, is it? By expanding output to 450 tons, Rudd could cut its ATC to $47. Shouldn't the monopoly want to produce at its lowest average cost? No! That's not why Nick Rudd is in the ice-making business. If producing at the lowest point on its ATC curve—maximum efficiency—results in the monopoly generating less than maximum profit, why do it? Rudd is interested in maximizing profit, not maximizing efficiency.

Figure 1 translates Table 3 into graphic form.

The ATC and MC curves are U-shaped. The monopoly's demand curve, identical to the market demand curve for ice, is downward-sloping. The downward MR curve cuts the rising MC curve at 300 tons. At that output, price is $150 and the average total cost is $52. The shaded rectangle represents the monopoly's profit.

As long as market demand and Rudd's cost structures remain unchanged, the monopoly will have no inclination to move from producing 300 tons at a price of $150. As far as Rudd is concerned, it is willing to stay at that price and output forever.

PRICE AND OUTPUT IN MONOPOLISTIC COMPETITION

Monopolies, however, don't last forever. And certainly not in this ice-making business. Let's suppose a number of high school graduates decide not to follow their families' fishing tradition but instead go into ice making. It isn't an altogether crazy idea. The ice business looks profitable. And the patent on ice-making technology that has protected Rudd's monopoly position in the market has expired.

With a little imagination, a lot of energy, and a big enough loan from the bank, a number of new ice manufacturers appear on the market. Wayne Coyne,

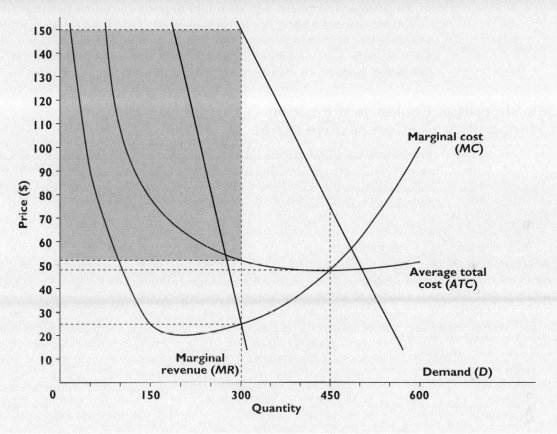

FIGURE 1 **Price and Output Determination in Monopoly**

The monopoly, like all other firms, maximizes profit where $MC = MR$. The MC curve meets the MR curve at an output of 300 tons. At $Q = 300$, the price—read off the demand curve—is \$150 and the average total cost—read off the ATC curve—is \$52. The shaded rectangle represents (\$150 − \$52) × 300 = \$29,400, which is the monopoly's profit.

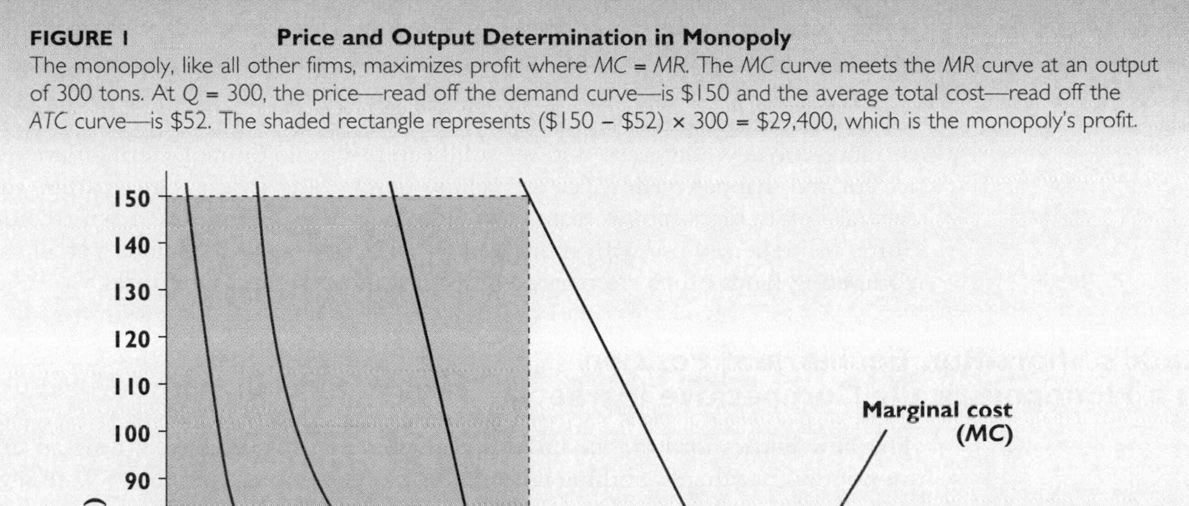

for example, adds a new twist to ice making: color. Fishermen can now buy blue ice, green ice, red ice, and yellow ice, as well as Rudd's clear.

Product Differentiation in Monopolistic Competition

To many people, ice is ice is ice. But to many others, and perhaps to most, product design, color, packaging, and particular taste add to quality. People really do have strong preferences for product differentiations, even though they may agree that the products are functionally equivalent.

Holding such preferences or product loyalties is not necessarily unreasonable. If people are satisfied with the product's performance, they are usually reluctant to experiment with substitutes, even when the price of substitutes is slightly lower. Why tamper with success? That's why newcomers to the industry typically face an uphill struggle for a share of the market.

Product differentiation can be viewed as an attempt to develop brand loyalty.

If new firms are going to break into the market, they must provide something that isn't already offered. *The trick is to differentiate the product sufficiently to claim uniqueness, and yet keep it close enough to existing competition.* In this way, consumers may be coaxed to experiment, knowing that even if they switch, they get pretty much what they got before, and maybe more.

Let's suppose new firms enter the market to manufacture colored ice. A few fishermen, intrigued by the colors, switch from Rudd to its competitors. Their products are new, different, and yet still keep fish fresh. Some fishermen use red ice for red snapper, yellow ice for yellow perch, blue ice for blue marlin, and several colors for rainbow trout. But not everybody is impressed with color. Some fishermen, those with more traditional taste, stay with Rudd. Yet all the competing kinds of ice are regarded by consumers as close substitutes.

Rudd's Short-Run Equilibrium Position in a Monopolistically Competitive Market

The new entries into the ice business must be upsetting to Rudd, now an ex-monopoly. But there's nothing it can do. It has no control over entry. With several competing ice firms now in the market, Rudd's share of market demand dwindles. Look at Figure 2.

FIGURE 2 **Rudd's Demand Curve as New Firms Enter the Market**
When new firms enter the market, the market demand curve remains unchanged at *D* but the competition from the new firms forces Rudd, now an ex-monopoly, to share market demand. Its demand curve shifts from *D* to *D'*, the extent of the shift depending on the strength of competition in the market. Because of the presence of close substitute goods, *D'* is more elastic than *D*.

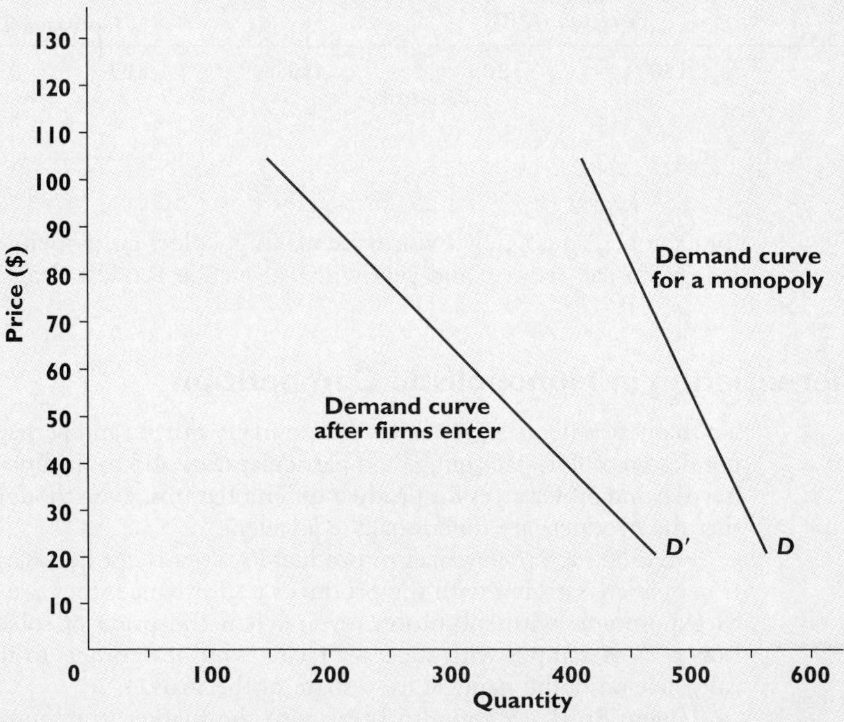

FIGURE 3 **Rudd's Price and Output in a Monopolistically Competitive Market**
As it did in monopoly, the firm in monopolistic competition produces where $MC = MR'$. This occurs at $Q = 200$ tons. Price is \$90 and ATC is \$66, generating an economic profit of \$4,800.

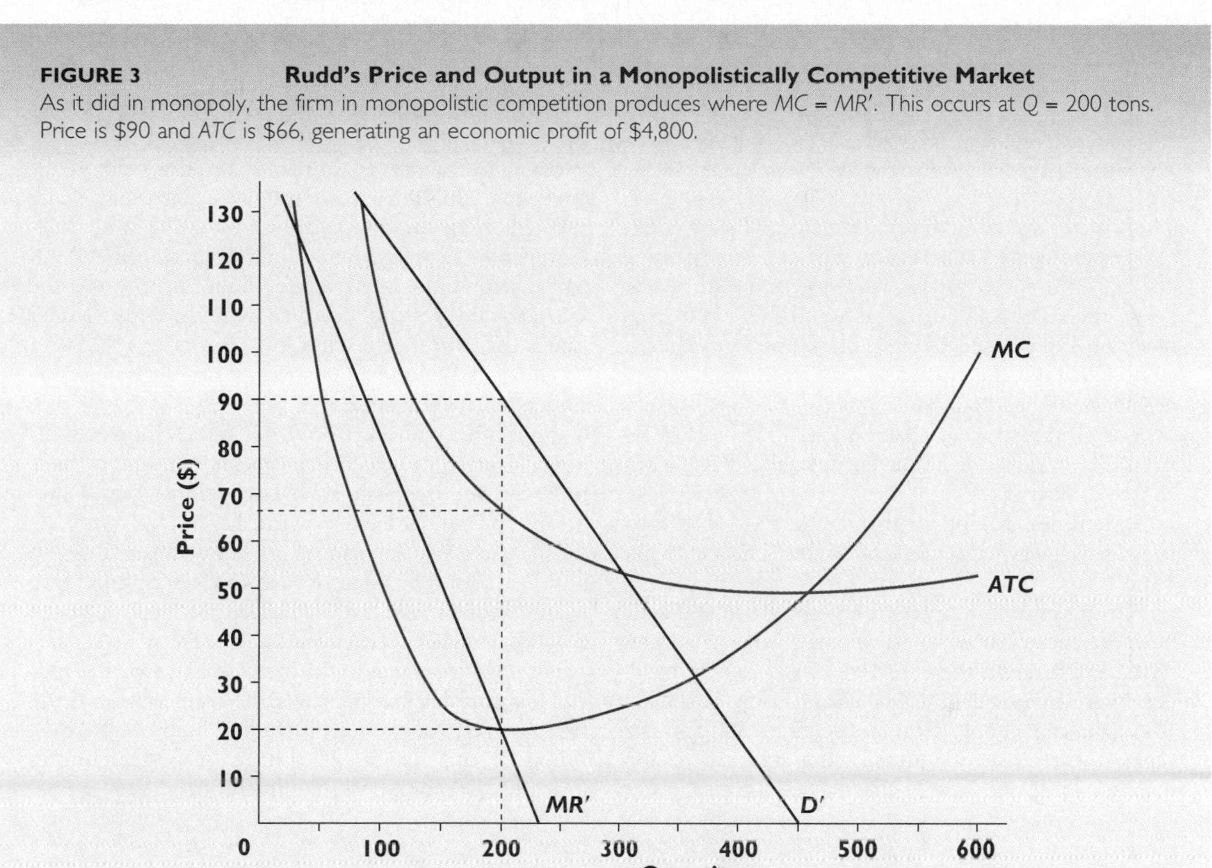

Entry into a monopolistically competitive market shifts demand curves for existing firms down and to the left.

Why do demand curves for an existing firm become more elastic as entry occurs?

Rudd's demand curve shifts to the left, from D to D'—the size of the shift depending upon the number and success of Rudd's competitors—and becomes more elastic. If Rudd raises price above its competitors' price, it must now expect some of its customers to switch to its competitors. Before, as a monopolist, Rudd never had to worry about competition.

What about Rudd's cost curves? They remain unchanged. Picture its ice factory. With or without competition, the same ice-making machines are used. The same quantity of labor is needed to produce a ton of ice. The same insurance policy applies. The same trucks make deliveries. In other words, Rudd's cost curves don't change. The firm may end up producing at *different points on the cost curves,* but the curves themselves remain unchanged.

Under monopolistic competition in Figure 3, Rudd does exactly what it did in the monopoly market of Figure 1. It produces where $MR = MC$.

In Figure 3, $MR' = MC$ at 200 tons. That's where Rudd produces. Its short-run equilibrium price is \$90 and its ATC = \$66. Rudd's economic profit is (\$90 − \$66) × 200 = \$4,800. As you see, losing its monopoly position in the market cuts deeply into Rudd's profit.

What about consumers? They are better off. Compared to the old monopoly market, the price they pay is lower and the quantities they buy are greater.

ADDED PERSPECTIVE

Consumers Face Flood of Products

The in-laws are coming for brunch. You start cooking the omelettes and realize you are out of Swiss cheese. You zoom to the nearest grocery store, run down the aisle to the dairy case, and there you stare, sweating and panting, at eight brands of Swiss cheese, all priced about the same, all made from the same ingredients, all aged 60 days.

You want to yell, "WHAT'S THE DIFFERENCE!!" You want to maybe nuke the entire Swiss cheese industry.

Sometimes, having so many choices is bad. But not always, say experts—not if the choices make sense.

No question consumers are getting deluged with new product choices—new brands, new sizes, new styles. Look down the cereal aisle, where 123 products were unveiled in 1990 alone. Look at the car ads. You can choose from more than 300 models. Open a directory of mutual funds and try to sort through all 2,718. *New Product News* in Chicago says 13,244 consumer products (toilet paper, yogurt, cat food, insect spray, etc.) were introduced last year. *Progressive Grocer* says the average grocery store carries 17,901 items, up from 7,800 in 1970.

The tendency is to say this is terrible. It's frustrating to go to the drugstore and gawk at 41 sizes and varieties of the single brand-name Tylenol. It takes time and effort to figure out what to buy.

But don't look for a backlash. Don't expect relief. Hard as it is to admit, consumers want it this way.

"In most cases, the more choices the better," says Michael Johnson, a University of Michigan marketing professor who studies how consumers decide to buy certain products. A greater variety means shoppers can find exactly what they want. Now you can choose from eight different kinds of Coke: Coca-Cola, Coca-Cola Classic, Caffeine Free Coca-Cola, Caffeine Free Coca-Cola Classic, Diet Coke, Caffeine Free Diet Coke, Cherry Coke, Diet Cherry Coke. Ten years ago, there was just one, regular Coca-Cola.

As Johnson points out, no one has ever been driven insane simply because there were too many choices at the supermarket or mall.

Companies churn out new products or new versions of products for the same reason they do most everything: To make money. Once Tylenol became a hit, its maker, Johnson & Johnson, used the trusted, strong brand name to spin out Tylenol cold medicines and children's pain relievers, expanding sales and grabbing market share. Coke did the same. Companies also create new brands looking for a hit. Miller Brewing Co. invented "light" beer just as the USA started getting health-conscious. Now Miller Lite is the Number 2 seller.

All of it is done under the guise of giving consumers what they want.

So a little whining about too many choices is allowed. Sure, more choices mean consumers have more power over their final selections. But it also means consumers have to work harder.

"It takes a little reading to know what drugs to buy," says John Walden of the Nonprescription Drug Manufacturers Association. There are, he says, about 200,000 brands, varieties, and sizes of over-the-counter drugs available. In the past 15 years, the federal government has approved 400 prescription drugs for sale over the counter, including ibuprofen (Advil, Nuprin) and about 20 kinds of antihistamines (Sudafed, Drixoral). With a little effort, "You get the size you want to buy and it will do what you want it to do," Walden says.

Cars have a built-in anxiety factor: They are typically a consumer's biggest purchase except for a home. A generation ago, a household was typically a "Ford family" or a "Buick family." Brand loyalty ran high. Choices were easy.

Not anymore. Loyalty to an auto make is unusual. If you count all the versions of every make (two-door, four-door, sports coupe, wagon), there are 656 cars to choose from. "Consumers are confused," says J. Ferron of auto consultants J. D. Power and Associates. "There's a tremendous over-choice. You can get a standard luxury car or a luxury standard car." That makes car shopping a burden for many people. Even so, J. D. Power has found that no matter how many models are offered, most buyers consider six models, seriously look at three, then buy one.

The one way to really raise consumers' ire is to offer choices that aren't meaningful—products that have almost no difference in content, packaging, and price. There are, truly, at least eight brands of Swiss cheese in many big supermarkets, all nearly identical. In fact, grocery products are often the worst offenders of over-choice.

"If it's the same old thing, who needs it," says Phil Lempert, publisher of *The Lempert Report* newsletter.

"Gone are the days of unique products. Instead it's all 'me-too's' "—like all the products with "oat bran," "fat-free," or "no cholesterol" labels. The differences become so small that most consumers don't want to take the time to figure out which is the best to buy. So if none are on sale, they grab the brand name their parents used, Lempert says. "That's the safety valve."

Or as Mick Jagger put it: "You can't always get what you want/but if you try sometimes/you just might find/you get what you need."

It even applies to paper towels.

Discussion

In your opinion, are there too many brands—of most everything—on the market? Or is it "the more, the merrier"? Do you think there is such a thing as "too much choice"?

Rudd's Long-Run Equilibrium Position in a Monopolistically Competitive Market

In monopolistic competition, entry occurs until economic profit is eliminated. The demand curve for each firm will then be tangent to the *ATC* curve to the left of its minimum.

But the game isn't over. As long as *any* profit can be made producing ice, other firms, with product differentiations of their own, enter the market. With each new entry, Rudd's demand curve shifts further to the left. How far to the left will it shift? Figure 4 depicts Rudd's price, output, and profit position when its demand curve, because of increasing competition, becomes D'', that is, tangent to its ATC curve.

Rudd produces 150 tons, where $MC = MR''$. At that output, price *and* average total costs are $82. Rudd's economic profit is ($82 – $82) × 150 = 0. Rudd's competitors, too, face the same zero profit situation.

If Rudd makes no economic profit at $Q = 150$, shouldn't it be producing at some other output? No. The $MC = MR$ rule always signals the firm's most profitable output level, even if profit is zero. It simply means that every other output level generates less than zero profit, that is, a loss. *Zero economic profit, then, is Rudd's maximum profit.*

Gone are the days when Rudd was a monopoly making profit. Now, in monopolistic competition because of easy firm entry into the market, it finds itself in long-run equilibrium earning zero profit. Consumers, of course, are happy. They get more ice from the competing firms, and at lower prices.

Making Normal Profit

Normal profit

The entrepreneur's opportunity cost. It is equal to or greater than the income an entrepreneur could receive employing his or her resources elsewhere. Normal profit is included in the firm's costs.

With economic profit at zero, no new firms enter the market. But why would any firm making zero economic profit stay in the ice-making business? Consider the Nick Rudd Ice Company. Although the firm's economic profit disappears in long-run equilibrium, Nick Rudd, as entrepreneur, still draws a **normal profit,** that is, a wage—accounted for in the firm's ATC—which is at least as much as he can earn elsewhere. That is to say, he does as well or better staying in business than he would do elsewhere.

FIGURE 4 **Rudd's Long-Run Equilibrium Price and Output in Monopolistic Competition**
As more firms enter the industry, each firm's demand curve shifts further to the left and becomes more elastic. Rudd produces where *MC* = *MR*″, but output falls to 150 tons. Note the uniqueness of this output level. The demand curve *D*″ is tangent to the *ATC* curve. *P* = *ATC*. The economic profit rectangle shrinks completely away. Because firms no longer make an economic profit, no new firms are attracted into the market.

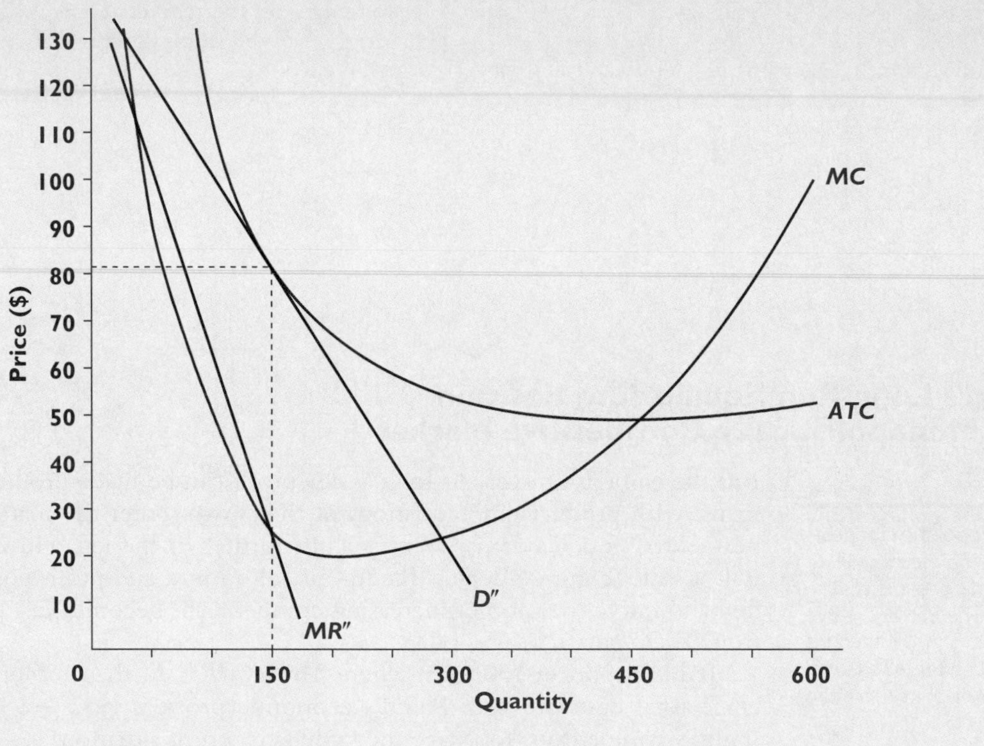

PRICE AND OUTPUT IN PERFECT COMPETITION

There is a limit to the types of *different* products that can be introduced!

Let's change the story slightly. We saw that as more and more firms enter a monopolistically competitive market, the individual firm's market share shrinks. Although the goods these firms produce are very close substitutes, each firm still produces a unique good. Each firm faces its own downward-sloping demand curve. Each can raise price above its competitor's price without losing its entire market to its competitors. But as more firms crowd into a monopolistically competitive market, differences among the goods become less marked. They become more easily substitutable for each other. For example, Coca-Cola and 7-Up differ in taste and color. Still, many consumers regard them as fairly close substitutes. But with Sprite, Slice, Squirt, and Fresca in the market, 7-Up faces an even greater number of even closer substitutes. In every monopolistically competitive situation, as more firms enter, product differentiation narrows and, at the same time, *each firm's demand curve shifts to the left and becomes more elastic.*

ADDED PERSPECTIVE

Explicit and Implicit Costs

For years now, Elaine Rodier had been thinking about going into business. She is not only an excellent cook, but her preparation of appetizers, such as humus, eggplant salad, quiches, stuffed mushrooms, goose liver patés, and cheese canapes are outstanding. Everyone who tried them assured her that she could make a fortune if she went into the business of producing gourmet appetizers.

With that kind of encouragement and with the belief that, in fact, her appetizers were the best in the world, she plunged into the business world. She asked her good friend, Kim Neis, to work with her. She withdrew $20,000 from her savings account, borrowed $30,000 from her neighborhood bank, signed a $5,000 year lease for rather limited space in a shopping mall, had flyers printed announcing her business, hired two neighborhood kids to distribute them, bought the ingredients, utensils, commercial refrigerators, packaging materials, and waited for business.

She didn't have to wait long. People stopped by to place orders almost immediately after she opened her doors. After the first few months of business, she realized that the space she rented was much too small but decided against moving. Instead, she used her own garage as a warehouse for her supplies and her guest room as an office. She also hired Lars Gustafsson as her accountant. He told her to keep account of costs—every monetary payment she made—and record every item of sale.

After one year in business, Lars Gustafsson gave her the good news. She made a tidy profit. He categorized her cost, revenue, and profit in the following way:

Cost of food, in making appetizers	$ 25,000
Cost of labor, Kim Neis, Lars Gustafsson	22,000
Cost of depreciation of equipment	7,500
Cost of borrowing $30,000	3,000
Cost of space, rent	5,000
Cost of advertising	1,000
Cost of insurance	1,500
Cost of utilities	2,000
Total cost	67,000
Total revenue	115,000
Total profit	48,000

Elaine Rodier was very pleased to learn that she made a $48,000 profit. But her friend, Mark Neuman, an economist, examined her accounts and told her that the record of her costs was incomplete. The cost items recorded for Lars Gustafsson, he explained, were explicit costs only, that is, costs in the form of actual monetary payments. She did indeed make payments for wages, rent, interest, and other items shown in the table but these were not her only costs.

For example, her own labor was a cost but, because it did not take the form of a monetary payment she made to herself, it does not appear in the table of costs Lars Gustafsson used. Nor was account taken for the use of her garage, her guest room, or her $20,000 savings. These, he advised her, were all **implicit costs,** that is, the opportunity costs of using resources owned by the entrepreneur. In her case, these costs were not insignificant. He itemized them for her.

Cost of own labor, Elaine Rodier	$23,000
Cost of the use of her $20,000 savings	1,400
Cost of the use of her garage	1,200
Cost of the use of her guest room	3,000
Cost of deliveries, use of her car	2,400
Total implicit cost	31,000

Elaine Rodier gave up a job as a nursery school teacher that paid $23,000. The $23,000 represented the opportunity cost she incurred working for herself. Because she didn't actually pay herself the $23,000—that is, it didn't really take the form of a monetary payment—it did not appear in Lars Gustafsson's table. She also withdrew $20,000 from her savings account at the bank. Since it would have earned her $1,400 (the lending rate was 7 percent), her use of her own savings represented a $1,400 opportunity cost. Garage rental in her community was estimated at $1,200 and her guest room could have been rented for $250 per month. Free delivery service, made in her own car, was valued at $2,400.

To an economist, the costs involved in making $115,000 worth of appetizers include both the $67,000 of explicit costs that take the form of monetary payments and the $31,000 of implicit costs. Her economic profit—the difference between total revenue and the total of explicit and implicit costs of production—was only $16,900, not the accounting profit Lars Gustafsson showed—the difference between total revenue and explicit costs—of $48,000.

Elaine Rodier understood Mark Neuman's distinction between accounting and economic profit but was still glad she went into business. In fact, she told him that if she made no economic profit at all, she would still stay in the gourmet appetizer business because the business covered implicit costs, including the wages she would have earned as a nursery school teacher. Covering those implicit costs to stay in business, Mark Neuman told her, is what economists mean by making normal profit.

Discussion

What are the explicit and implicit costs of your college education?

There's No Product Differentiation in Perfectly Competitive Markets

How far to the left can the demand curve shift? How elastic can it become? Well, let's now suppose there is no product differentiation in the ice-making business. Ice is ice just as a tomato is a tomato, and salt is salt. People can switch from one firm's ice to another's without having to sacrifice preference. That is, the goods produced are identical.

The Firm in Perfect Competition

Let's also suppose that entry into the market is free and open and that ice can be manufactured with relatively low fixed-cost technology. Then the market conditions that the Nick Rudd Ice Company faces as a firm in perfect competition are quite different from those it enjoyed in its salad days as a monopolist.

SMALL-SCALE PRODUCTION

Typically, firms operating in perfectly competitive markets are modest in size. Table 5 describes the cost structure for the perfect competitor Nick Rudd.

The market in perfect competition is split among many firms, each one a small producer relative to the total market output.

The fixed cost associated with this scaled-down version of the Nick Rudd Ice Company monopoly of Table 3 is only 1 percent—$40 versus $4,000—of what it was when the firm was a monopoly. Figure 5 converts the ATC of Table 5 into graphic form.

As you see, minimum *ATC* for the competitive firm is $47 which occurs at production levels of 4.5 tons. If the firm increases production to 6 tons, its *ATC* climbs to $55.

FACING A HORIZONTAL DEMAND CURVE

Price-maker

A firm conscious of the fact that its own activity in the market affects price. The firm has the ability to choose among combinations of price and output.

As one of a considerable number of ice manufacturers, Rudd has no control whatsoever over market price. Before, as a monopoly, Rudd could pick a price and quantity combination that maximized its profit. It was a **price-maker.**

As a perfect competitor, it has no freedom to select price. The competitive firm is a **price-taker.** Suppose panel *a* in Figure 6 portrays the market for ice.

The market demand curve, *D*, is downward-sloping. It is the same demand curve that Rudd once faced as a monopolist. The market's short-run supply

TABLE 5
Rudd's Cost Structure in Perfect Competition

Quantity (tons)	*TC*	*ATC*	*MC*
0	$ 40.0		
0.5	85.0	$170	$ 90
1.0	110.0	110	50
1.5	122.5	82	25
2.0	132.5	66	20
2.5	143.5	57	22
3.0	156.0	52	25
3.5	171.0	49	30
4.0	189.5	47	37
4.5	213.0	47	47
5.0	243.0	48	60
5.5	282.0	51	78
6.0	332.0	55	100

FIGURE 5 **The Competitive Firm's Cost Structure**
This perfectly competitive firm's minimum *ATC* is $47 which occurs at a quantity of 4.5 tons.

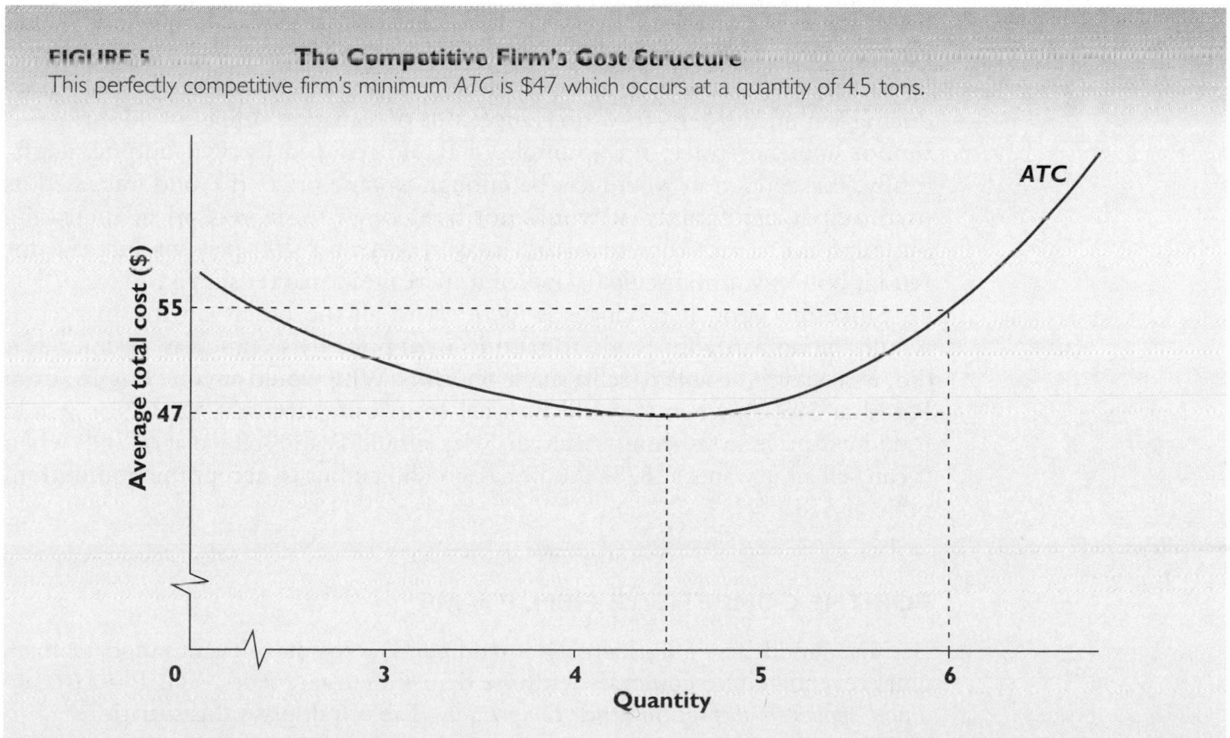

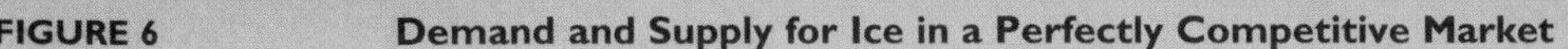

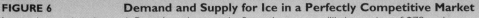

FIGURE 6 **Demand and Supply for Ice in a Perfectly Competitive Market**

In panel *a*, market demand, *D*, and market supply, *S*, produce an equilibrium price of $78 and a quantity demanded and supplied of 440 tons. Once market demand and supply establishes $78 as the price, the competitive firm, a price-taker, takes $78 as its price. The firm, in panel *b*, faces a horizontal demand curve at *P* = $78.

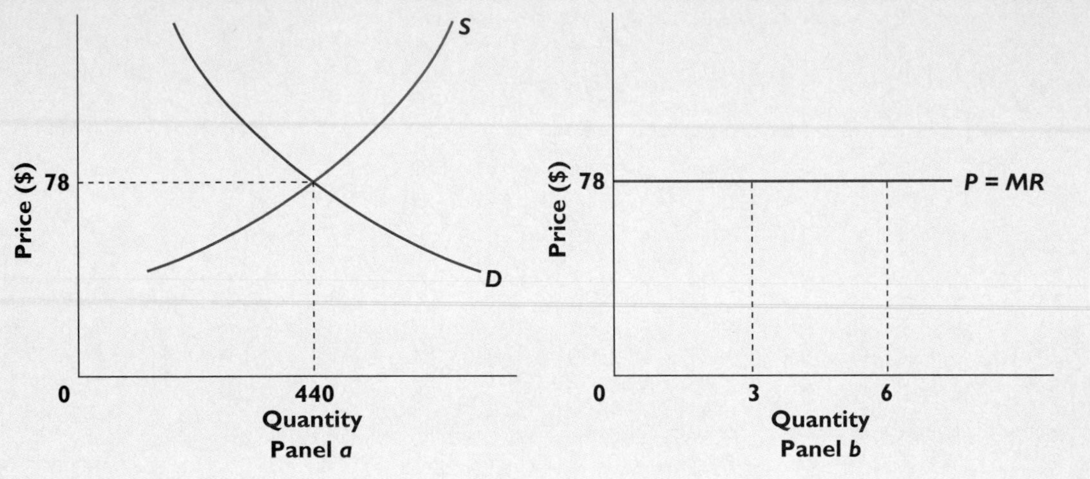

Price-taker

A firm that views market price as a given and considers any activity on its own part as having no influence on that price.

Why is each firm's demand curve horizontal?

curve, *S*, is upward-sloping, reflecting the suppliers' willingness to produce more ice at higher prices. The equilibrium price established in the market shown in Figure 6 is $78. The equilibrium quantity demanded and supplied is 440 tons.

Look at panel *b*, representing the demand curve Rudd itself faces. The demand curve is horizontal across all the quantities—zero to 6 tons—that Rudd can produce. *Rudd sees the same market demand curve that you see in panel a.* However, since Rudd is only a very minor contributor to market supply—producing within the zero-to-6-ton range, out of a market supply of 440 tons—it cannot influence price. For example, if Rudd reduced its own output significantly, that reduction would not be enough to raise price. If Rudd increased its own output significantly, it would not be enough to depress price. Increasing output from, say, 3 tons to 6 tons may represent a 100 percent increase for Rudd, but only a miniscule 0.7 percent increase in market supply.

Since the good it produces is identical to all the others on the market, it would be foolhardy for Rudd to raise its own price by so much as a penny. If it did, it wouldn't be able to sell a single ice chip. Why would anyone buy ice from Rudd at $78.01 when it could buy ice from other firms at $78? Nor would Rudd cut price by a penny. After all, why should Rudd sell ice at $77.99 when it can sell all it wants at $78? Rudd has no choice but to accept the equilibrium price at $78.

FOR THE COMPETITIVE FIRM, *P* = *MR*

Because Rudd faces a horizontal demand curve across its relevant range, its marginal revenue curve coincides with the demand curve it faces. *This P = MR condition applies to all firms in perfect competition.* Table 6 displays this situation.

TABLE 6
Price and Revenue Schedule for Rudd in Perfect Competition

Quantity (tons)	Price	Total Revenue	Marginal Revenue
0	$78	$ 0	$ 0
1	78	78	78
2	78	156	78
3	78	234	78
4	78	312	78
5	78	390	78
6	78	468	78

When Rudd increases production from zero to 6 tons, it increases its total revenue by $78 × 6 = $468. Every ton added to production adds another $78 to total revenue. The added revenue—the marginal revenue—is simply the price the firm gets for selling the additional ton.

SHORT-RUN EQUILIBRIUM PRICE AND OUTPUT FOR THE FIRM IN PERFECT COMPETITION

We have seen that panel *a*, Figure 6 represents the market condition in which the Nick Rudd Ice Company operates. What should it do? As a price-taker, it knows $P = \$78$. But how much ice should it produce?

Table 7 combines the firm's price and revenue schedule from Table 6 with its cost structure from Table 5.

Have you ever gone into a large computer outlet? As you know, choice among computer accessories is highly competitive. Most goods are excellent and almost all are perfect substitutes for each other. It's hard to choose, isn't it? In many cases, price ends up being the deciding factor.

TABLE 7
Demand Schedule and Cost Structure for Rudd in a Perfectly Competitive Market

Quantity (tons)	*TC*	*TR*	*ATC*	*AVC*	*MC*	*MR*
0	$ 40.0	$ 0	—	—	—	—
0.5	85.0	39	170	$90	$ 90	$78
1.0	110.0	78	110	70	50	78
1.5	122.5	117	82	55	25	78
2.0	132.5	156	66	46	20	78
2.5	143.5	195	57	41	22	78
3.0	156.0	234	52	39	25	78
3.5	171.0	273	49	37	30	78
4.0	189.5	312	47	37	37	78
4.5	213.0	351	47	38	47	78
5.0	243.0	390	49	41	60	78
5.5	282.0	429	51	44	78	78
6.0	332.0	468	55	49	100	78

Once again, to maximize profit, the firm sets output where *MR* = *MC*. In this case, *MR* is equal to market price. Why?

There's little question what Rudd should do under the circumstances of Table 7. *MR* = *MC* = $78 at 5.5 tons, and that is the quantity the firm chooses to produce. Its economic profit at 5.5 tons is $429 – $282 = $147, which is more profit than could be generated at any other output level.

Figure 7 translates Table 7 into graphic form. The *P* = *MR* curve facing the competitive firm is horizontal at $78. The *MC* curve cuts the *MR* curve at 5.5 tons. At 5.5 tons, *ATC* = $51. The shaded rectangle, which represents (*P* – *ATC*) × *Q*, measures Rudd's economic profit at 5.5 tons.

Rudd makes $147 economic profit but discovers rather quickly that this profit is short-lived. The profit attracts new firms into the competitive market. Since entry is free and open, these firms add to the market's supply. Look at Figure 8.

Panel *a* of Figure 8 shows what happens to the short-run equilibrium price as more firms join the market. Initially, the market supply curve shifts to the right from S_1 to S_2. The increased competition among the larger number of firms forces price to fall from $78 to $60.

Rudd, under these changing circumstances, is forced to reexamine its production decision. Look at panel *b*. Being a price-taker, it now accepts *P* = $60 and establishes a new level of output at 5 tons, where *P* = *MR* = *MC* = $60. Its profit now is maximized at ($60 – $49) × 5 = $55.

This $55 profit is sufficient to attract even more firms to the market. The supply curve in panel *a* shifts to the right again, from S_2 to S_3 and market price is once more forced downward, this time to *P* = $47.

Back to panel *b*. Rudd has no choice but to accept *P* = $47, and once more reexamines its production decision. It produces now at 4.5 tons, where *P* = *MR* = *MC* = $47. But at 4.5 tons, the firm's *ATC* is also $47. That is, at 4.5 tons, *P* = *ATC*. The firm's profit becomes ($47 – $47) × 4.5 = 0.

FIGURE 7 **The Perfectly Competitive Firm in the Short Run**
To maximize profit, the firm produces where $MR = MC$. The firm's MC curve cuts the $P = MR$ curve at 5.5 tons. ATC = \$51, generating an economic profit—the shaded rectangle — of \$147.

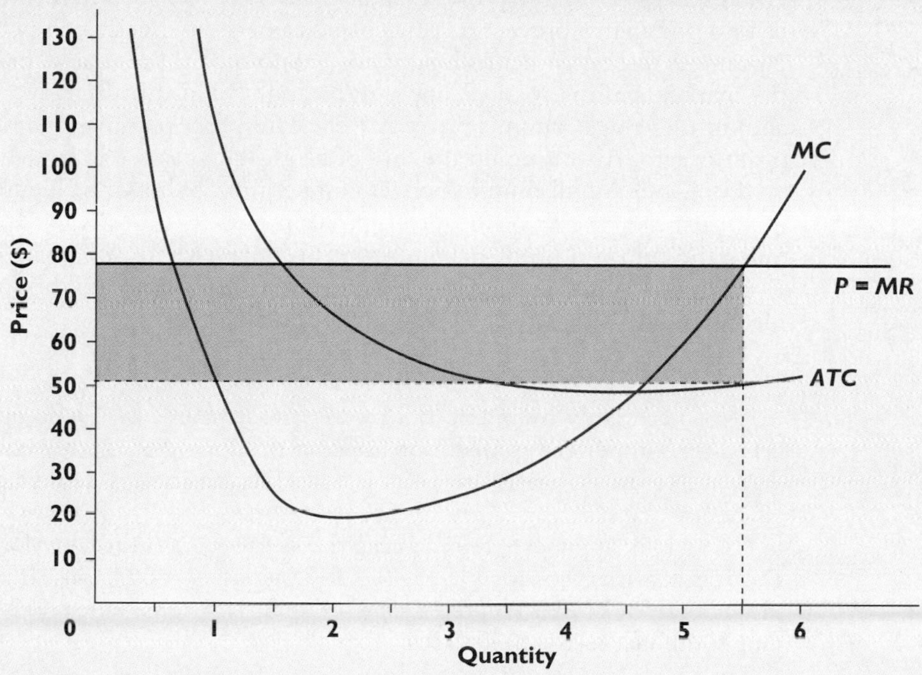

FIGURE 8 **Effects of a Shift in Market Supply**
As more firms enter the market of panel *a*, the supply curve shifts from S_1 to S_2 causing the short-run equilibrium price to fall from \$78 to \$60. The firm in panel *b* produces where $MC = MR$ = \$60, which is at 5 tons. Its economic profit is \$55. Firms continue to enter, shifting the supply curve to S_3. Price falls to \$47. At $MC = MR$ = \$47, Q = 4.5 tons and ATC = \$47. Economic profit disappears and no new firms are attracted to the market.

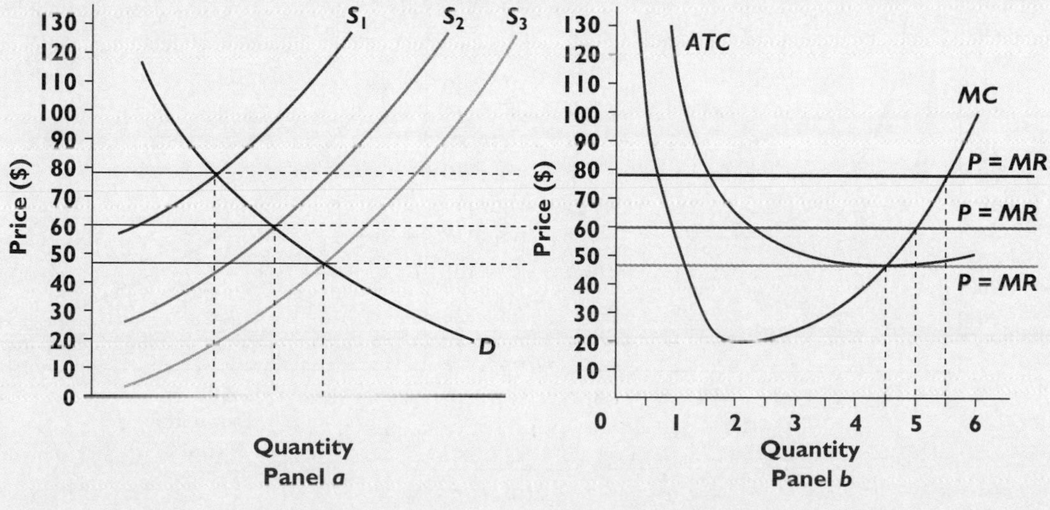

LONG-RUN EQUILIBRIUM PRICE AND OUTPUT FOR THE FIRM IN PERFECT COMPETITION

Entry of new firms has erased economic profit in long-run equilibrium.

Rudd sees its economic profit dwindle from \$147 to \$55, and finally to zero and can do nothing to prevent it. The character of the perfectly competitive market guarantees this outcome. As long as any economic profit is made, firms will enter the market, shifting market supply to the right. This in turn drives down price and, in the end, economic profit as well. This process comes to rest only when profit is zero. At this point, the lure of profit disappears. No new firms appear.

Long-run equilibrium in perfect competition is shown in Figure 9.

Profit is a signal for new firms to enter and in perfect competition they do so easily.

In panel *a*, the firm's no-profit position is $Q = 4.5$ tons, where $P = ATC$. Since the firm is a profit-maximizer, it produces where $MR = MC$. And since $P = MR$ for a firm in perfect competition, its long-run equilibrium position is identified by

$$P = MR = MC = ATC$$

Not necessarily by intent, but by the circumstance of the competitive market, a firm in perfect competition ends up producing at the lowest point on its *ATC* curve. In Figure 9, this point is \$47. This position is defined as maximum efficiency.

Now look at panel *b*, representing the entire market for ice. Market demand, *D*, intersects market supply S_3 at $P = \$47$ and at $Q = 504$ tons. If every firm in the market looks like Rudd—each producing 4.5 tons—then 112 firms would supply the market with 504 tons.

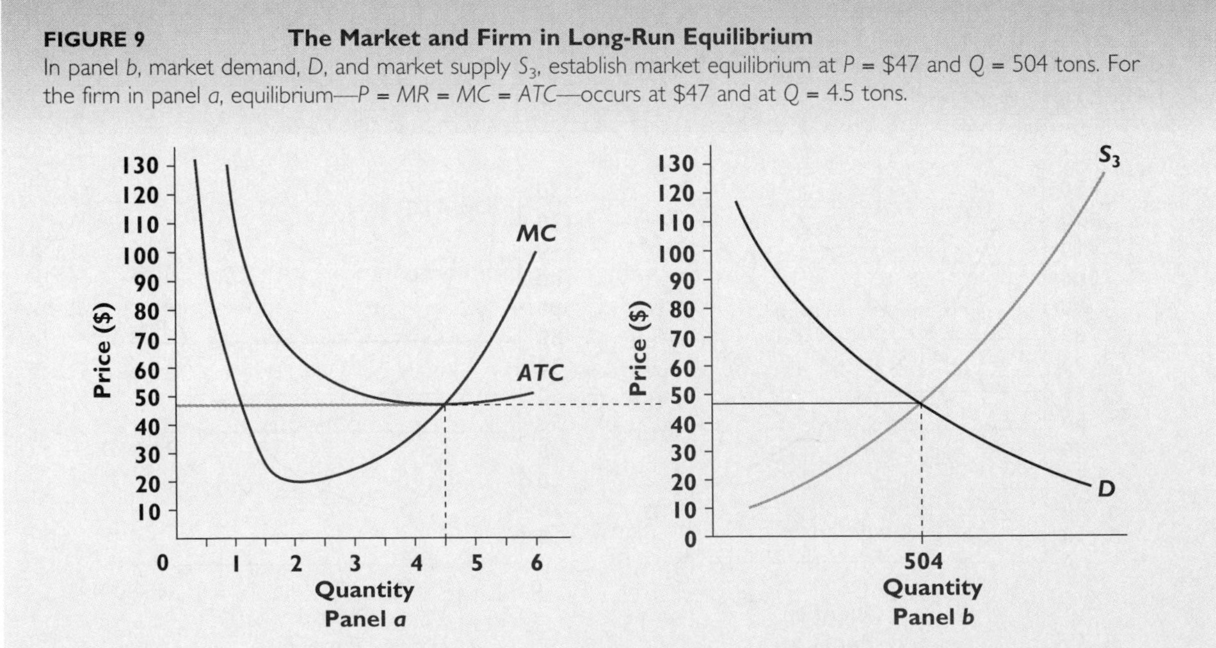

FIGURE 9 **The Market and Firm in Long-Run Equilibrium**

In panel *b*, market demand, *D*, and market supply S_3, establish market equilibrium at $P = \$47$ and $Q = 504$ tons. For the firm in panel *a*, equilibrium—$P = MR = MC = ATC$—occurs at \$47 and at $Q = 4.5$ tons.

Lowest Prices and Greatest Output

Compared to monopoly and monopolistic competition, the perfectly competitive market structure produces the greatest output at the lowest prices. Remember the monopoly outcome. Monopoly price was \$150 and the monopoly produced 300 tons. But when firms gained entry into the market, changing its character from monopoly to monopolistic competition, the market's long-run equilibrium price and output changed as well. Price fell to \$82 and total output increased to 440 tons. Under conditions of perfect competition, the long-run equilibrium price falls to \$47 and market supply reaches 504 tons.

The Firm's Supply Curve

A firm's long-run output level in perfect competition always corresponds to a point on its marginal cost curve above its average total cost curve.

Intuitively, it seems reasonable to suppose that producers would increase the quantities they supply in response to higher prices. It seems reasonable to suppose too that they would be less willing to supply the market when prices fall.

The economic argument underlying the firm's upward-sloping supply curve is related to the $MR = MC$ rule. After all, the quantity firms produce is always determined at the $MC = MR$ output level. In perfect competition, $P = MR$ so that the *firm's long-run supply curve—relating price to quantity supplied—simply traces out the segment of its* MC *curve that lies above its ATC.*

At every price beyond $P = ATC$, the quantity supplied by the firm is determined at its $P = MC$ output level. Look at Figure 10.

When $P = \$100$, $MR = MC$ at $Q = 6$ tons. When $P = \$78$, $MR = MC$ at $Q = 5.5$. When $P = \$60$, $MR = MC$ at $Q = 5$. And when $P = \$47$, $MR = MC$ at $Q = 4.5$. These price and quantity combinations trace out the firm's marginal cost curve. At prices below \$47, the firm will shut down. Why?

Look at the firm's ATC when $P = \$30$. At that price, $MR = MC$ at $Q = 3.5$. At 3.5 tons, the firm's $ATC = \$49$. That is, the firm's most attractive output level when $P = \$30$ is 3.5 tons, but it still generates a $(\$30 - \$49) \times 3.5 = \$66.50$ loss. Why stay in business? That is why the firm's supply curve—what it is *willing to* supply—starts at the $MC = ATC$ point on its marginal cost curve.

The Market's Supply Curve

Can you explain the relationship between an individual firm's marginal cost curves and market supply?

What explains the firm's supply curve, explains as well the market's supply curve. The quantity supplied on the market at a given price is the horizontal sum of the quantities each firm supplies. Each firm's supply coincides with that part of its MC curve lying above its $MC = ATC$. Market supply, then, represents the results of summing all firms' MC curves above their ATCs.

Figure 11 portrays the summing process. Suppose the cost curves of the competitive firms are similar to Rudd's. Panel *a* depicts their individual supply curves and panel *b*, depicting the market, aggregates or sums the supply curves of panel *a*.

When $P = \$100$, the firms of panel *a* are each willing to supply 6 tons so that, together, the 150 firms in the market of panel *b* are willing to supply 900 tons. When $P = \$78$, each firm is willing to supply 5.5 tons, so that market supply in panel *b* for 130 firms is 715 tons. When $P = \$60$, each firm is willing to supply 5 tons, so that the 120 firms in the market are willing to supply 600 tons. When

FIGURE 10 **Anatomy of the Firm's Long-Run Supply Curve**
The firm is a price-taker. Whatever the price, the firm will produce where $MR = MC$. Since $P = MR$, when $P = \$100$ the firm is willing to supply 6 tons. At $P = \$78$, it is willing to supply 5.5 tons. At $P = \$60$, it is willing to supply 5 tons. At $P = \$30$, it is unwilling to supply any because it will incur a loss, $ATC > P$. The firm's supply curve is its MC curve above the $MC = ATC$ point.

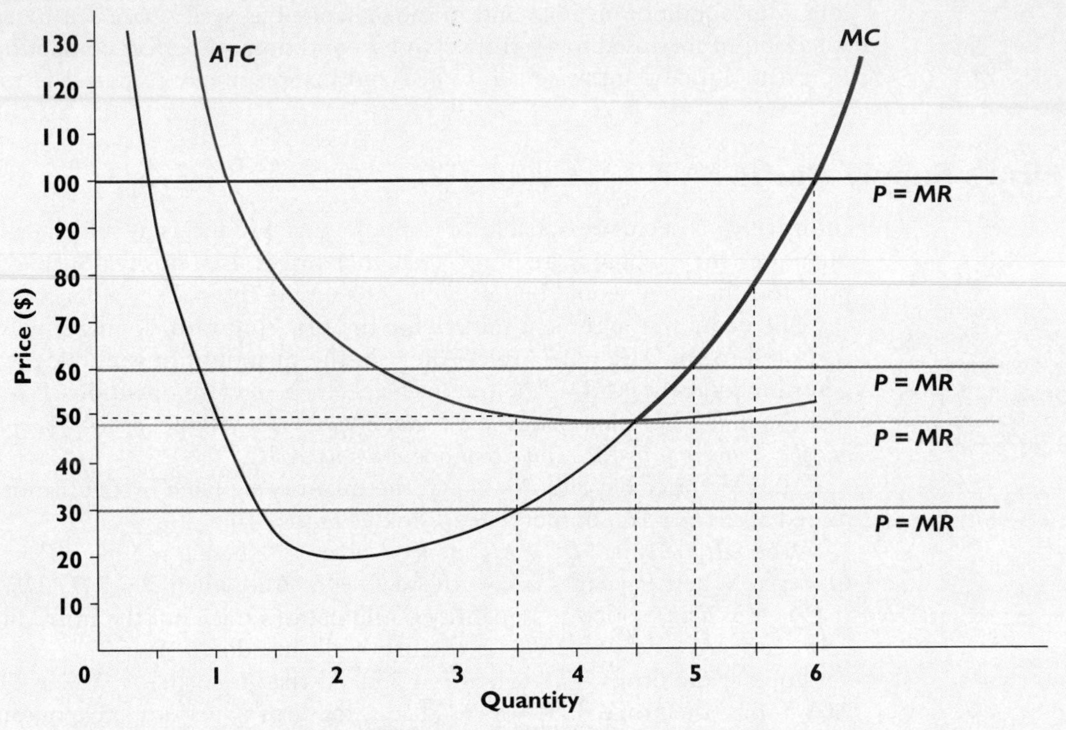

$P = \$47$, each firm is willing to supply 4.5 tons, and the 112 firms in the market are willing to supply 504 tons. At $P = \$30$, market supply is zero, reflecting each firm's decision to shut down at that price.

INNOVATORS AND IMITATORS IN THE PERFECTLY COMPETITIVE MARKET

Suppose one of the firms, struggling along with zero economic profit at $P = \$47$, hits upon a new idea. Adopting a technology that substitutes computers for labor, the firm is able to significantly reduce its costs of producing ice. Figure 12, panel *a* depicts the cost structure of Paola Flygare Ice Works Company, the innovator firm.

Flygare Ice Works faces the same \$47 equilibrium price that its competitors face. It knows that it cannot raise price, nor need it reduce price to sell any

FIGURE 11 **Anatomy of the Market Supply Curve**

The market supply curve is the aggregation of the long-run *MC* curves of the firms in the market. Panel *a* shows the Nick Rudd Ice Works—one among the 150 producing on the panel *b* market. When *P* = \$100, Rudd and the 149 other firms produce a total of 900 tons. When price falls, fewer firms remain in the market and each remaining firm produces less tonnage. The aggregation of their outputs at different prices makes up the supply curve of panel *b*.

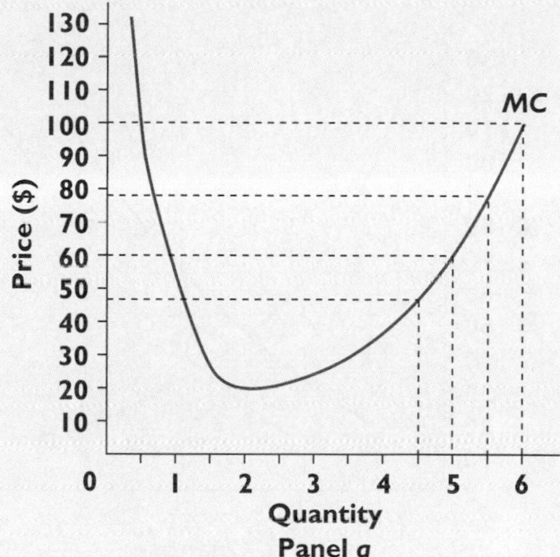

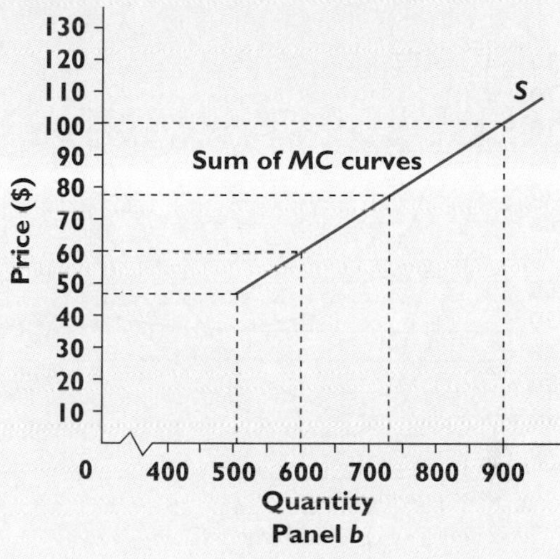

quantity it chooses to sell. It chooses to produce, of course, where its $MC = MR$. This originally occurred at $Q = 4.5$ tons, where $MC_1 = MR = P = ATC_1$. After introducing the new technology, however, Flygare's cost structure changes to MC_2 and ATC_2 and production increases to 5.5 tons, where $MC_2 = MR$. At $Q = 5.5$ tons, $ATC = \$37$. As you see, the Paola Flygare Ice Works Company now makes an economic profit of $(\$47 - \$37) \times 5.5 = \$55$.

Innovation is a means for a firm to generate economic profit. However, the profit is a signal for other firms to imitate the innovation.

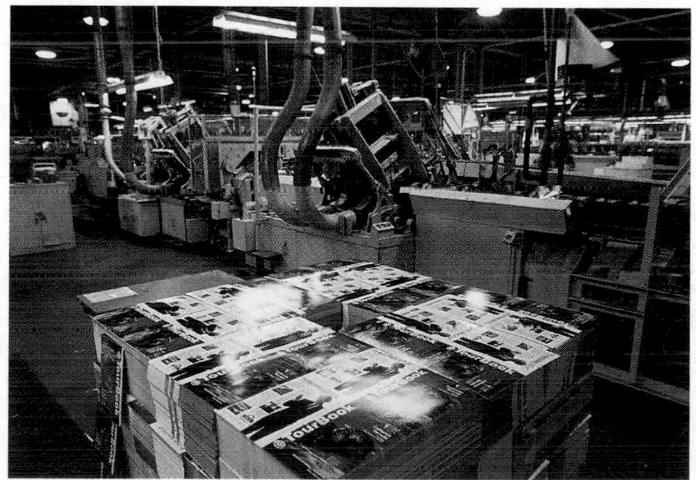

If you're thinking of going into the publishing business, take a look at this outfit. It's hard to compete against a technology that is almost fully automated. The first book coming out of this plant may be very expensive, but if your production range is in the millions, it gets to be increasingly less expensive.

FIGURE 12 The Innovator Firm in Perfect Competition

The innovator firm in panel *a* introduces new technology that lowers its cost structure from ATC_1 to ATC_2 and from MC_1 to MC_2. As a competitive firm, it faces $P = \$47$, produces where $MC_2 = \$47$, and makes an economic profit of $55. Firms in the market adopt the new technology. Other firms, attracted by the prospect of profit, join the market. The market supply curve of panel *b* shifts from S_1 to S_2, driving price down to $37. In panel *a*, the firms' new long-run equilibrium is established at $P = MR = MC_2 = ATC_2 = \$37$.

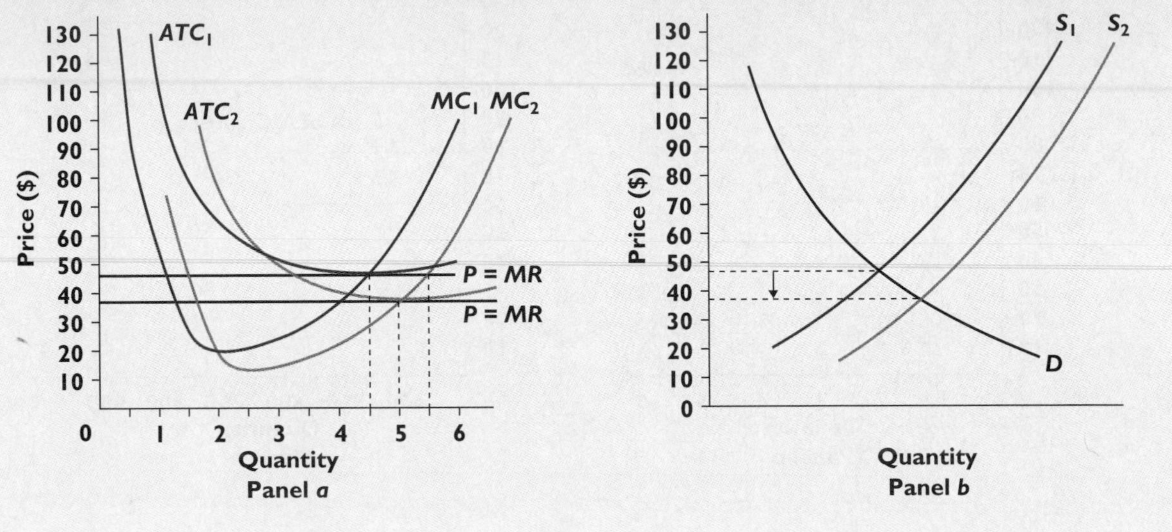

In perfect competition, innovations cannot remain anybody's secret for long. The other firms in the industry become imitators—they mimic the innovator. They, too, adopt the new technology to resemble panel *a*. Still other firms, attracted by the prospects of profit, enter the market. Everybodys's cost structure is now represented by MC_2 and ATC_2.

Now look at panel *b*. These additional firms in the market shift the market supply curve to the right, forcing the market price to fall from $47 to $37. Flygare's economic profit, which emerged through innovation, gets wiped out by imitation. All firms now use Paola Flygare technology. They face a $37 market price and produce at $Q = 5$ tons, where $MC_2 = MR$. There, the new zero-profit equilibrium for firms in perfect competition is established.

DOES COMPETITION ALWAYS GENERATE LOWEST PRICES AND HIGHEST OUTPUT?

Do monopolies always end up charging the highest prices and producing the lowest quantities? Do monopolistically competitive firms always end up producing more than monopoly, but still less than firms in perfect competiton, and charge a price higher than the competitive price? And does perfect competition generate innovative firms that force others to imitate, driving prices even lower and production even higher?

FIGURE 13 **Constant and Increasing Returns to Scale**
Panel *a* illustrates constant returns to scale. It shows cost structures of small and large firms whose minimum *ATC*s are the same. This reflects the assumption that increasing firm size increases total output and total cost proportionately. Panel *b* illustrates a different relationship between output, cost, and firm size. Increasing returns to scale means that increasing firm size increases total output and total cost disproportionately. Average total cost falls as firm size and output increase.

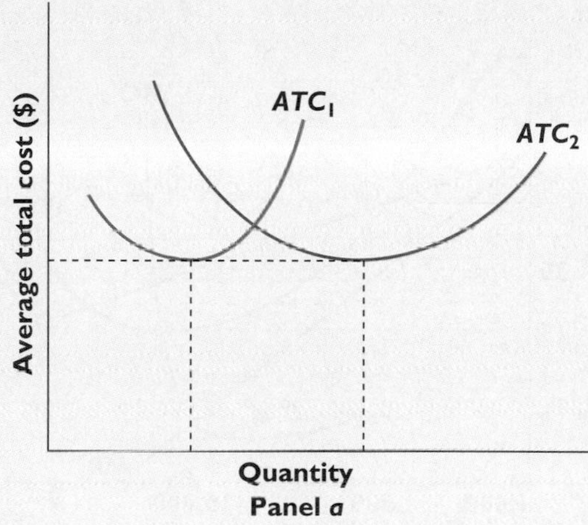

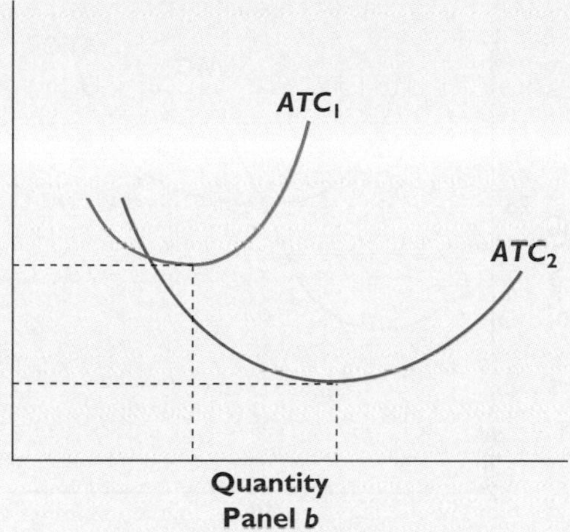

The Schumpeter Hypothesis

Increasing returns to scale
A situation in which a firm's minimum long-run average total cost decreases as the level of production increases.

According to economist Joseph Schumpeter, "It ain't necessarily so!" The idea that monopoly is *ipso facto* bad flies in the face of economic reality. Monopolies don't always end up producing at higher prices. He argues that modern technology creates enormous **increasing returns to scale** that are typically enjoyed by larger firms, many of which are monopolies. Therefore, a more realistic comparison of cost structures is not the constant return to scale depicted in Figure 13, panel *a*, for competitive firms but the increasing returns to scale depicted in panel *b* for monopolies. Although Schumpeter acknowledges that monopolies are defined by their "oneness," not their "bigness," in reality, bigness and oneness are often linked.

Accepting Schumpeter's linkage, the increasing returns to scale *may allow monopolies to maximize profit at market prices lower than those that would obtain under more competitive market conditions*. Look at Figure 14.

If modern technology creates increasing returns to scale, then larger firms may have cost advantages over small firms, leading to lower prices from large monopolistic firms than from small competitive firms.

Panel *a* depicts a competitive book-binding firm in equilibrium, producing 20 bindings at a price of \$25 per binding. If there were 200 competitive firms in the market, the quantity supplied to the market would be 4,000 bindings.

The demand curve facing the monopoly in panel *b* is the market demand. Look at the monopoly's cost structure. It reflects the advantages of large-scale production. At very low levels of output, ATC is exceptionally high. For example, at $Q = 1{,}000$, $ATC = \$600$. But ATC keeps decreasing until it reaches its minimum at $Q = 10{,}000$.

The monopoly, applying the $MR = MC$ rule, produces 10,000 bindings. At that output level, $P = \$20$ and $ATC = \$15$. The monopoly ends up making $(\$20 - \$15) \times 10{,}000 = \$50{,}000$ profit. The increasing returns to scale in the in-

FIGURE 14 **Price and Production in Monopoly and Perfect Competition: Schumpeter's View**

Panel *a* shows a competitive firm in long-run equilibrium. $P = ATC = MR = MC = \$25$. Output is 20 units. With 200 firms in the market, total quantity supplied is 4,000 units. The monopoly in panel *b* supplies 10,000 units; at $Q =$ 10,000, $P = \$20$, and $ATC = \$15$. The firm's monopoly profit is \$50,000. Note that the monopoly price is less than the competitive price—\$20 versus \$25—and the quantity supplied by the monopoly is greater than the quantity supplied by the competitive firms on the market—10,000 versus 4,000 units.

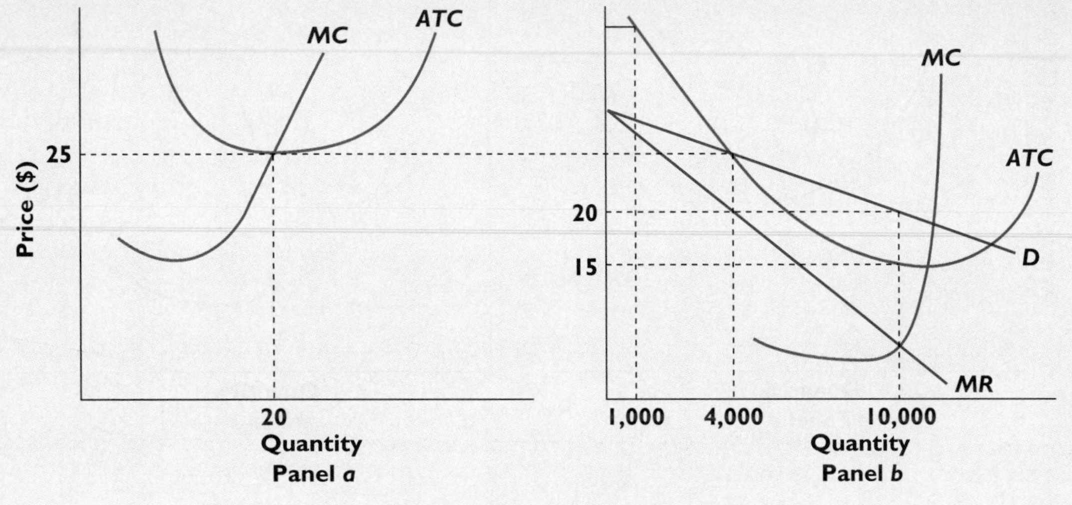

dustry are so pronounced that even with monopoly profit of \$50,000, its $P = \$20$ is lower than the competitive firm's $P = \$25$ and its quantity supplied, $Q =$ 10,000, is greater than the competitive firms' $Q = 4,000$. That's Schumpeter's point.

Monopolies have better access to funds for research and development than do perfectly competitive firms that don't earn economic profit.

To Schumpeter, the increasing returns to scale and the steady flows of technological innovations that occur with monopoly—not with perfect competition—don't happen by accident. *The monopoly, using its profit to experiment with new technologies ultimately creates the new cost structures that promote greater efficiency in production.* The monopoly, like firms in other market structures, is self-serving. It strives to maximize profit. But intent is not the issue. Price and quantity supplied are.

Why can't competitive firms innovate? Because competition undermines profit, which is the source of innovation and experimentation. In long-run equilibrium, competitive firms earn zero profit. Even if a competitive firm had the innovation, why should it go through the innovating effort when it knows that competition will quickly wipe out its rewards? Still another compelling reason why competitive firms shy away from experimenting with cost-saving technology is the possibility of failure. Not every experiment works. If a zero-profit competitive firm in long-run equilibrium tries to innovate and fails, the loss would drive it out of the market. For the competitive firm, then, there's little to gain by innovating and everything to lose.

The monopoly, on the other hand, can afford to make mistakes without having to pay with its life. If a cost-saving technology flops, the monopoly loses a fraction of its profit. That's all. It can try again and again.

Some, But Not All Economists Agree

Many economists share Schumpeter's view. John Kenneth Galbraith, for example, compares the likelihood of innovation among large and small firms:

There is no more pleasant fiction than that technical change is the product of the matchless ingenuity of the small man forced by competition to employ his wits to better his neighbor. Unhappily, it is a fiction. Technical development has long since become the preserve of the scientist and the engineer. . . . Because development is costly, it follows that it can be carried on only by a firm that has the resources associated with considerable size.

Yet Schumpeter's "bigness" hypothesis is rejected as theoretically unsound and empirically invalid by a considerable number of other economists. They are quite reluctant to abandon a conventional wisdom that dates back to Alfred Marshall, the founding father of neoclassical economics.

It was Marshall's view that technical progress was best served in a competitive environment and that entrepreneurial inventiveness and size of enterprise were inversely related.

It has always been recognized that large firms have a great advantage over their smaller rivals in their power of making expensive experiments. . . . But, on the whole, observation seems to show what might have been expected a priori, *that these advantages count for little in the long run in comparison with the superior inventive force of a multitude of small undertakers.*

As you see, Marshall's contention is no less assertive than Galbraith's. The debate on the validity of these conflicting theories continues inconclusively to this day. Volumes of theoretical and empirical research on the subject continue to flow, but they still offer contradictory observations. *Perhaps the only thing we can conclude about innovation and firm size—and in many minds, the long-run price and output comparisons between perfect competition and monopoly—is that we can't conclude.*

CHAPTER REVIEW

1. A monopolist's goal is simply to maximize profits. A profit-maximizing monopolist will set output where marginal cost is equal to marginal revenue. Price is then read from the demand curve.

2. A profit-maximizing monopolist will produce a level of output less than the output of minimum average total cost curve. The monopolist's profit is formed by the rectangle $(P - ATC)Q$.

3. Monopolistic competition consists of several firms selling products that are close but not perfect substitutes. The monopolistic competitor's demand curve is downward-sloping. The firm maximizes profits by setting output where marginal revenue is equal to marginal cost and reading the price from the demand curve, just as in monopoly.

4. A monopolistic competitor may earn economic profit equal to $(P - ATC)Q$ in the short run. However, in the long run, entry by new firms is possible in response to economic profit. As new firms enter, each firm's demand curve be-

comes more elastic and market share declines. Eventually, the demand curve is tangent to the *ATC* curve to the left of the minimum of the *ATC*.

5. Long-run equilibrium in monopolistic competition occurs when no firms earn economic profit. When price is equal to *ATC*, firms earn a normal profit that is equal to or greater than what the entrepreneur could earn elsewhere.

6. Entry into a market results in less product differentiation over time. In perfect competition, firms' products are perfect substitutes for each other.

7. In perfect competition, because each firm is small relative to the market, no firm has any control over price. The firm faces a demand curve that is horizontal at the market price. Thus, price is equal to marginal revenue for a perfectly competitive firm.

8. To maximize profits, the perfectly competitive firm will set output where marginal revenue is equal to marginal cost. In short-run equilibrium, the firm may earn economic profit equal to $(P - ATC)Q$.

9. Economic profit is a signal for new firms to enter a perfectly competitive market. As new firms enter, the market supply shifts to the right and the market price falls. This process continues until only normal profit can be earned by any firm. When all firms earn only normal profit, the industry has reached long-run equilibrium.

10. In long-run equilibrium, perfectly competitive firms produce where $P = MR = MC = ATC$. These firms are producing at the minimum of the average total cost curve. Hence, perfectly competitive firms achieve maximum efficiency, generating the greatest output at the lowest price.

11. In perfect competition, the firm always produces where price equals marginal cost. The price and quantity supplied combinations are all points on the marginal cost curve above the average total cost curve. Market supply is generated by adding the segments of firms' marginal cost curves above their average total cost curves.

12. Innovation is encouraged in perfect competition because the innovating firm can lower average total costs and increase its economic profit. However, other firms will quickly imitate the innovator. New firms enter the market in response to the economic profit, the market supply shifts to the right, and the market price falls.

13. According to Joseph Schumpeter, bigness can be an advantage for an innovating firm. The economies of scale and low average costs of production available to big firms may allow them to charge prices that are actually lower than those charged by small, competitive firms. Monopoly profits permit these firms to experiment with new technologies that ultimately lead to more efficient production.

14. According to Alfred Marshall, the large number of small firms that undertake innovations will lead to the greatest efficiency in production over time. There is disagreement among economists about the exact nature of the relationship between innovation and firm size.

KEY TERMS

Economic profit
Normal profit
Price-maker
Price-taker
Increasing returns to scale

QUESTIONS

1. What does the statement "in monopoly, the firm *is* the industry" mean?

2. If you were an entrepreneur in a perfectly competitive market, would you attempt to innovate? Why or why not?

3. Why do firms produce where $MC = MR$? Why not at the lowest point on their ATC curves?

4. Why is the competitive firm's long-run supply curve identical to its marginal cost curve lying above its ATC?

5. Why is price and marginal revenue identical for the firm in perfect competition?

6. Economists refer to competitive firms as price-takers and to monopolies as price-makers. Why?

7. For competitive firms, profits can exist only in the short run. Why?

8. Why are demand curves for competitive firms horizontal and for firms in monopolistic competition downward-sloping?

9. Can you think of markets in which there is absolutely no product differentiation? If you owned a firm in such a market, what would your demand curve look like? What would the demand curve for the market look like?

10. Why does the firm's demand curve become more elastic in a monopolistically competitive market as more firms enter the market?

11. In perfect competition, imitators dampen the innovating spirit of innovators. Explain.

12. Inevitably, a firm in monopolistic competition ends up producing where its ATC curve is tangent to its demand curve. Explain.

13. Make the argument that consumers are better off when the economy's market structures are more competitive than monopolistic.

14. Why are "economies of scale" central to the argument that monopolies may end up producing more and charging less than competitive firms?

15. Compare John K. Galbraith's and Alfred Marshall's views on innovation and plant size.

16. Perfectly competitive firms in long-run equilibrium produce at the lowest point on their *ATC* curve. They produce at maximum efficiency. Yet, producing at an output that generates maximum efficiency isn't their intent. Why, then, do they end up there?

17. Suppose the cost schedule for a perfectly competitive firm producing brooms is as shown in the following table.

Quantity	Total Cost
0	$ 2
1	4
2	7
3	11
4	16
5	22

If the market price for a broom is $5, how many brooms would the firm produce? Would the firm be making economic profit? How could you tell if the firm is in long-run equilibrium?

18. Suppose the firm is a monopoly and its price schedule is as shown below:

Price	Quantity Demanded
$11.00	1
8.50	2
7.00	3
6.00	4
5.20	5

How many brooms would the firm produce? Would the firm be making an economic profit?

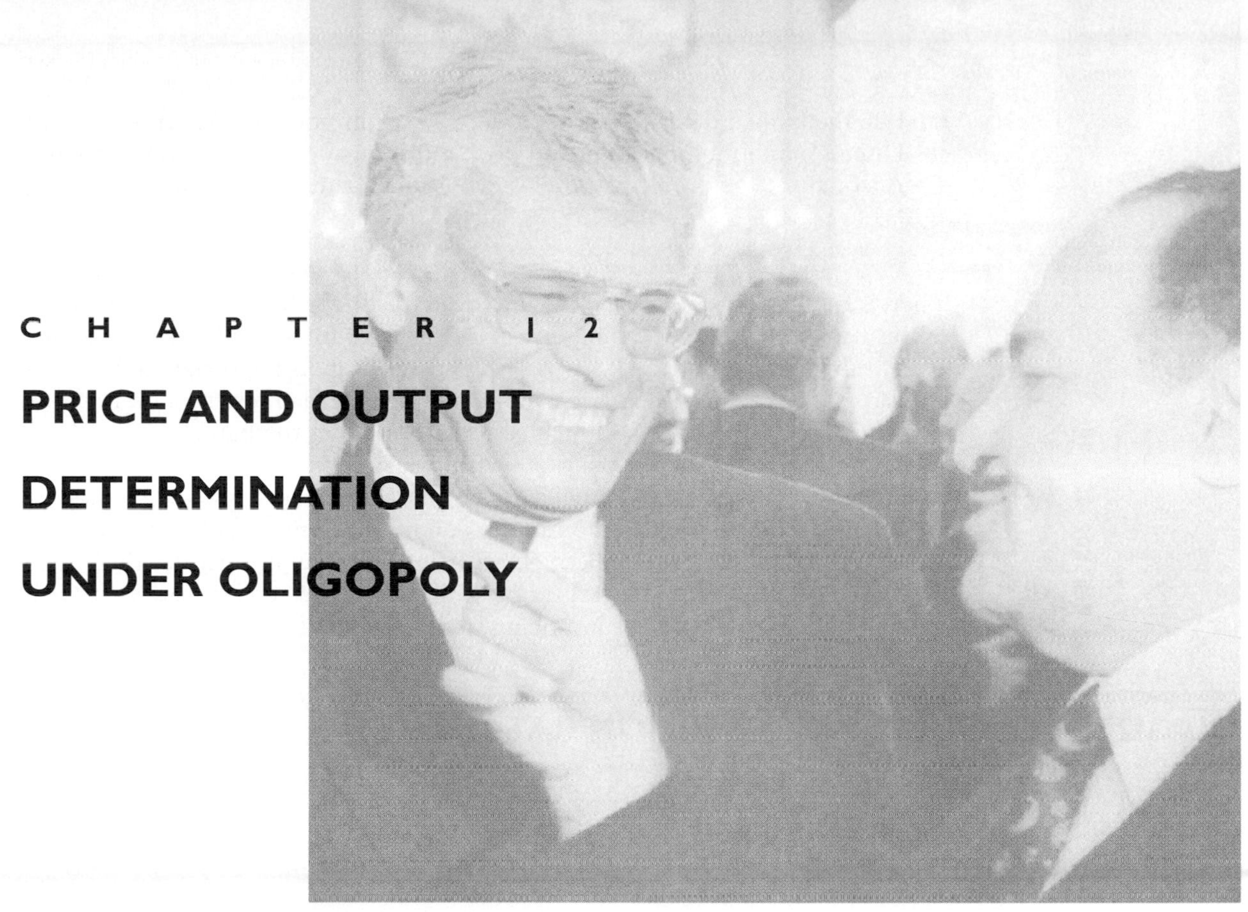

C H A P T E R 1 2

PRICE AND OUTPUT DETERMINATION UNDER OLIGOPOLY

CHAPTER PREVIEW

We left discussion of price and output determination in oligopoly for a chapter all to itself for good reason—it's more complicated than the other market structures. First we'll tackle the problem of describing the degree of oligopoly in a market. Then, several models will be advanced to explain price and output determination under oligopoly.

After studying this chapter, you should be able to:

- Explain how concentration ratios describe oligopoly power in different industries.
- Outline trends in concentration ratios.
- Distinguish between balanced and unbalanced oligopoly.
- Discuss oligopoly power in the United States and other industrialized countries.
- Compare three types of mergers and their impacts on industry concentration.
- Give examples of cartels and collusion.
- Explain the game theory approach to cartel pricing.
- Draw a graph to show the price leadership model.

- Use the kinked demand curve model to explain price stability in oligopoly.
- Discuss brand multiplication and price discrimination as oligopoly strategies.
- Account for the problems cartels have in maintaining high prices.

There's an old story about a slightly intoxicated fellow who was crawling around on his hands and knees searching under a streetlight for a set of keys he had lost at the other end of the block. A passerby chanced upon the scene, and hearing the sad tale, asked why he wasn't looking where he had lost it. The not-too-sober man replied that it was much easier to see under the light.

Let's retell the story just a little differently. Suppose a professor of economics is trying to explain pricing behavior in the U.S. market system. He does so by describing price determination under conditions of monopoly, monopolistic competition, and perfect competition. When asked why he analyzes these market structures when the dominant one is oligopoly, he replies matter-of-factly that it is much easier to explain pricing under the other market structures!

OLIGOPOLY AND CONCENTRATION RATIOS

Is the analogy appropriate? Not entirely. In fact, it's a shameful exaggeration. But like most exaggerations, it serves to emphasize a point. Look, for example, at Table 1. Here, Kaysen and Turner summarize some of their 1954 findings on market structure in the U.S. economy.

There's no sign of perfect competition in Table 1. Nor, it seems, is monopolistic competition a dominant market structure. Instead, manufacturing markets seem to be dominated by large firms whose market behavior more closely approximates monopoly than competition.

Of the 147 industries studied, 58 are defined as Type 1 oligopolies, where the leading eight firms control over 50 percent of industry sales. The leading eight Type 2 oligopolies, which account for 46 of the 147 industries, control over 33 percent of their industry sales. The remaining 43 industries shown in the table are classified as unconcentrated. Of these, the leading eight firms control less than 33 percent of their industry sales.

What can we learn from Table 1? What we probably suspected—the U.S. manufacturing economy is highly oligopolistic. That is to say, in most U.S. man-

TABLE 1 Manufacturing Industries Classed by Concentration and Markets, 1954

Market Structure	Number of Industries	Value of Shipments ($ millions)
Type 1 oligopoly	58	41,819
Type 2 oligopoly	46	68,490
Unconcentrated	43	58,815
Total	147	169,124

Source: Kaysen, C., and Turner, D., *Anti-Trust Policy: An Economic and Legal Analysis* (Cambridge, MA: Harvard University Press, 1959) pp. 26–27.

TABLE 2
Distribution of Manufacturing Industries by Four-Firm Sales Concentration, 1982

Four-Firm Control of Industry Sales (%)	Number of Industries	Percent of Industries
0–19	86	19.2
20–39	163	36.4
40–59	120	26.8
60–79	56	12.5
80–100	23	5.1
Total	448	100.0

Source: F. M. Scherer and David Ross, *Industrial Market Structure and Economic Performance*, Third Edition. Copyright © 1990 by Houghton Mifflin Company. Adapted with permission.

ufacturing industries, control of production and sales is in very few firms. But how few is few?

Concentration ratio

A measure of market power. It is the ratio of total sales of the leading firms in an industry (usually four) to the industry's total sales.

There's no magic number. Measuring oligopoly, as Kaysen and Turner have done, by **concentration ratios** based on eight firms and is quite arbitrary. They could have picked the leading five or six firms, or perhaps the leading nine or ten, to measure the degree to which an industry is dominated by large firms, and still have arrived at the same impressive conclusions on market power.

Market power

A firm's ability to select and control market price and output.

In fact, most studies of oligopoly use the percentage of industry sales held by the leading *four* firms as the identifying concentration ratio. For example, Scherer's 1982 study of **market power,** based on a four-firm concentration ratio, arrives at much the same conclusions as did Kaysen and Turner's. Look at Table 2.

No matter how you look at the U.S. industrial economy of Table 2, oligopoly stares right back at you. In only 86 of the 448 industries do the four largest firms fail to control as much as 20 percent of industry sales. On the other hand, in 199 of the 448 industries, the four largest firms control at least 40 percent of sales.

Is Oligopoly in the U.S. Economy Becoming More Oligopolistic?

Overall, U.S. industry shows no signs of becoming more oligopolistic over time.

If you were a betting person, would you wager any money that the United States is becoming more oligopolistic? Would you, for example, bet that market power is becoming more concentrated in fewer and fewer firms? If your intuition tells you it is, save your money. It isn't.

Don't feel embarrassed. Most people believe that oligopolistic market power increases over time. Karl Marx certainly did. Over a century ago, he was convinced that the industrial giants in Western Europe and the United States would grow at the expense of small firms. This expectation was central to his economic prediction of capitalism's demise. But he was wrong.

There is no convincing evidence to support the contention that the share of industry sales controlled by the largest four firms in the U.S. manufacturing economy is growing. Look at the percentages in Table 3.

You would be hard-pressed to make the case for increasing oligopoly with these numbers. An upward trend appears for the years 1947 to 1963. But it reverses in the succeeding period, 1963–82. The 25.2 percent for 1982 approximates the 24.4 percent for 1947, undermining any attempt to establish long-run trends.

TABLE 3 Percentage of Total Industrial Sales Produced by Industries with Four-Firm Sales Concentration Ratios of 50 Percent or More (1895–1982)

Year	Percent
1895–1904	32.9
1947	24.4
1954	29.9
1958	30.2
1963	33.1
1972	29.0
1982	25.2

Source: F. M. Scherer and David Ross, *Industrial Market Structure and Economic Performance*, Third Edition. Copyright © 1990 by Houghton Mifflin Company. Adapted with permission.

Concentration Ratios and Market Power

Concentration ratios tell us a great deal about market power. In any industry where the leading four firms control 80 percent of industry sales, it's no secret that market power oozes from their corporate windows. But the distribution of that 80 percent among the leading four can vary considerably.

Unbalanced oligopoly

An oligopoly in which the sales of the leading firms are distributed unevenly among them.

Balanced oligopoly

An oligopoly in which the sales of the leading firms are distributed fairly evenly among them.

Why is market power most concentrated in unbalanced oligopoly?

In some cases, the leading firm alone may account for as much as 70 percent. Such an industry concentration is described by economists as **unbalanced oligopoly.** In other cases, the 80 percent of market sales may be dispersed fairly evenly among the four leading producers—say, 20 percent for each—giving such industries the character of **balanced oligopoly.**

Look at Figure 1, which compares two oligopolistic industries with identical concentration ratios.

The leading four firms in each control 80 percent of their industry's sales. But do you see how differently the 80 percent is distributed among the firms?

Look at the unbalanced oligopoly. The largest firm, by itself, controls 50 percent of the industry's sales. Its market share is not only greater than the others combined, but is more than four times as large as the share of the next leading firm. Under these conditions, its market power may be sufficient to force its will upon the other firms in the oligopoly on matters of price and output determination.

The market power within the balanced oligopoly, on the other hand, is quite another matter. Here, the leading firm, with 23 percent of the industry's sales, is hardly more powerful than any of the other three. Under these conditions, price and output are far less likely to bear the imprint of the single largest firm.

There is an air of secrecy when it comes to detailing the character of specific oligopolies. The U.S. Census, which gathers data on concentration ratios in the United States, is reluctant to release the data on concentrations below the four-firm level because it can be easily broken down to reveal confidential data about specific firms in the oligopoly.

Still, some unbalanced cases are well known. Table 4, compiled by Wilcox and Shepard, records examples of oligopolies with substantial one-firm market power.

Do any of these industries surprise you? You could probably name the leading firm in most of the industries listed in Table 4.

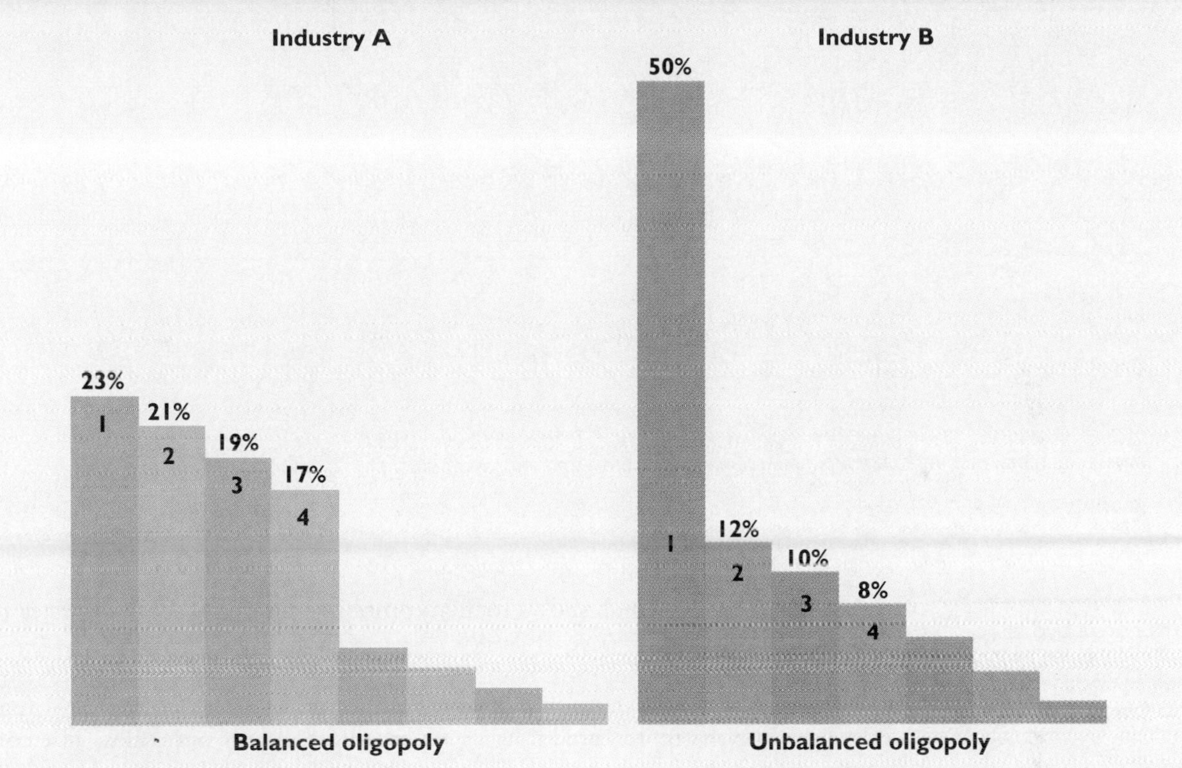

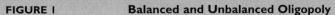

FIGURE 1 **Balanced and Unbalanced Oligopoly**
Industry A is a balanced oligopoly. Sales of its leading four firms—80 percent of the industry's total sales—are distributed fairly evenly among them. For example, the leading firm's sales amount to 23 percent, the second leading firm's sales 21 percent, the third 19 percent, and the fourth 17 percent. Industry B is an unbalanced oligopoly where 80 percent of the industry's sales are concentrated in the leading four firms, but distributed unevenly among them. The leading firm alone accounts for 50 percent of industry sales. The second leading firm accounts for only 12 percent.

Tracking Concentration Ratios Through the U.S. Economy

The 1987 Census of Manufacturers records a series of concentration ratios for a variety of industries. Table 5 is an abridged version. It provides concentration ratio data for 38 specific industries, reporting ratios at the four- and eight-firm levels.

Do any of these concentration ratios surprise you? For example, would you have guessed the ratios for the refrigeration industry? Of the 40 firms that make up the industry, the leading four control 94 percent of total industry sales. The leading eight control 98 percent. For records and tapes, composed of 462 firms, the ratios are 63 and 70. Look at how many of the heavy-goods industries have ratios greater than 70 at the four-firm level.

However useful these concentration ratios are in identifying market power, they can be somewhat misleading. They do not take into account competition from imports or second-hand markets. For example, the concentration ratio of 90 for motor vehicles and car bodies at the four-firm level refers only to motor vehicles produced and sold in the United States. By excluding auto imports, it significantly overstates the actual market power held by the four leading U.S. auto firms.

TABLE 4
U.S. Unbalanced Oligopolies, Percent of Sales

Industry	Approximate Shares of the Largest	
	One Firm	Four Firms
Computers	70	85
Automobiles	45	85
Heavy electrical equipment	50	100
Drugs	50*	90*
Photographic film	70	100
Copying equipment	85	95
Industrial chemicals	45	80
Soaps and detergents	50	95
Aircraft and engines	50	100
Iron and steel	35*	70*
Petroleum refining	35*	70*
Cereals	45	95
Locomotives	75	100

Source: Wilcox, C., and Shepard, W., *Public Policies Toward Business*, 5th ed. (Homewood, Ill.: Irwin, 1975), p. 43.

*indicates an average of regional and product submarkets

Why does including imports and second-hand markets in our analysis dilute the market power of a country's oligopolistic industries?

Look at Table 6 which shows total automobile sales in the United States for 1969–93.

In 1993, 6,674,458 automobiles were produced and sold domestically, but an additional 1,843,680 automobiles were imported and sold on the U.S. market. These imports represented fully 21.6 percent of all U.S. auto sales. The concentration ratio of 90, then, may be overstating the market power of the lead-

This is a big day in the automobile industry. It's early October and the new models are on review. The stakes are high. Design, color, miles per hour, fuel efficiency, safety, and a host of other features can make or break the year. The rivalry is direct. If people prefer Toyota, Buick feels the hurt.

TABLE 5 Concentration Ratios: Percentage of Total Industry Sales Produced by the Leading Four and Eight Firms, 1987

Industry	Number of Firms	Leading 4 Firms	Leading 8 Firms
Food Industries			
Roasted coffee	110	66	78
Malt beverage	101	87	98
Cookies, crackers	316	58	73
Soft drinks	846	30	40
Chocolate	173	69	82
Breakfast cereal	33	87	89
Chewing gum	8	95	100
Household Industries			
Photo equipment	717	77	84
Refrigerators	40	94	98
Furniture	175	43	59
Records, tapes	462	63	70
Sporting goods	1708	13	21
Electronic computers	9148	43	58
Childrens' toys	698	43	55
Heavy-Goods Industries			
Farm machinery	1576	45	52
Textile machinery	475	20	30
Metal cans	161	54	70
Petroleum, coal	92	40	65
Aircraft	137	72	92
Motor homes	141	56	67
Small arms	146	54	73
Tires	114	69	87
Motor vehicles and car bodies	352	90	95

Source: U.S. Bureau of the Census, *1987 Concentration Ratios in Manufacturing,* MC87-S-6 (February, 1992).

TABLE 6 Domestic and Import Sales of Automobiles in the U.S. Market, 1969–93

	Domestic	Import	Total	Import/ Total
1969	8,464,375	1,117,700	9,582,075	11.7
1975	7,050,120	1,577,000	8,627,120	18.3
1982	5,756,660	2,221,517	7,978,177	27.9
1993	6,674,458	1,843,680	8,518,138	21.6

Source: *Automotive News, Market Data Book Issue,* May 31, 1989, p. 33; May 25, 1994, p. 17.

ing firms in the motor vehicles and car bodies industry. And note the trend. In 1969, imports represented no more than 11.7 percent of total sales.

The Largest 100 U.S. Firms

Do you remember the nursery rhyme that ends: "When she is good, she is very, very good, but when she is bad she is horrid"? Table 7 is no nursery rhyme, but it certainly does tell us that when they are big, they are very, very big. Look at the relative sales positions of the 100 leading corporations that top *Fortune* magazine's list of the 500 largest industrial corporations in the United States.

These 100 firms make up approximately 45 percent of the $3,200 billion industrial corporate sales of the Fortune 500. The leading 25 firms—that is, the top 5 percent of the Fortune 500—alone account for 31.6 percent of the sales.

Does the United States Have a Monopoly on Oligopoly?

Oligopoly typifies industrialized economies.

Is the United States unique in the world of oligopoly? Clearly not. The concentration ratios for U.S. industries are not at all out of line with those in other modern industrial economies. Look at Table 8.

Do these ratios look familiar? At the five-firm level, most are above 50 percent. The presence of oligopoly in Japan is unmistakable. What is more, Japanese and U.S. concentration ratios are not unusual. Look at Table 9.

As you see, the control of industry by very few firms is no less a fact of life in Western Europe and Canada than it is in the United States or Japan.

CONCENTRATING THE CONCENTRATION

Fish feed on other fish. Oligopolies, too, have healthy appetites which they sometimes satisfy by feeding on each other. An oligopoly can build market power by reinvesting its profit and painstakingly expanding its production capacity. But for less patient and more aggressive oligopolists, there's another route to enhancing market power. It's through the process of mergers and acquisitions. Overnight, two small firms can become one big one. Or two big ones can become even bigger. Even the biggest can become bigger.

Why do firms merge? Principally, for one of three reasons: (1) to exercise greater market control, (2) to increase their control over the suppliers of their inputs or the buyers of their products, and (3) to expand and diversify their asset holdings. These three reasons explain horizontal mergers, vertical mergers, and conglomerate mergers.

Horizontal Mergers

Horizontal merger

A merger between firms producing the same good in the same industry.

The **horizontal merger** is perhaps the most easily recognized. It's a merger among firms *within the same industry, producing the same product.* When two competing airlines decide to merge, the merger is defined as horizontal. That's precisely what happened on October 1, 1986 with Northwest and Republic. The

TABLE 7
The 100 Largest U.S. Industrial Corporations Ranked by Sales

Rank 1993	1992		Sales, $ millions
1	1	General Motors Detroit	133,621.9
2	3	Ford Motor Dearborn, Mich.	108,521.0
3	2	Exxon Irving, Texas	97,825.0
4	4	Intl. Business Machines Armonk, N.Y.	62,716.0
5	5	General Electric Fairfield, Conn.	60,823.0
6	6	Mobil Fairfax, Va.	56,576.0
7	7	Philip Morris New York	50,621.0
8	11	Chrysler Highland Park, Mich.	43,600.0
9	10	Texaco White Plains, N.Y.	34,359.0
10	9	E.I. Du Pont De Nemours Wilmington, Del.	32,621.0
11	8	Chevron San Francisco	32,123.0
12	13	Procter & Gamble Cincinnati	30,433.0
13	14	Amoco Chicago	25,336.0
14	12	Boeing Seattle	25,285.0
15	15	Pepsico Purchase, N.Y.	25,020.7
16	17	Conagra Omaha	21,519.1
17	18	Shell Oil Houston	20,853.0
18	16	United Technologies Hartford	20,736.0
19	24	Hewlett-Packard Palo Alto	20,317.0
20	19	Eastman Kodak Rochester, N.Y.	20,059.0
21	20	Dow Chemical Midland, Mich.	18,060.0
22	22	Atlantic Richfield Los Angeles	17,189.0
23	32	Motorola Schaumburg, Ill.	16,963.0
24	25	USX Pittsburgh	16,844.0
25	26	RJR Nabisco Holdings New York	15,104.0
26	21	Xerox Stamford, Conn.	14,981.0
27	33	Sara Lee Chicago	14,580.0
28	23	McDonnell Douglas St. Louis	14,487.0
29	27	Digital Equipment Maynard, Mass.	14,371.4
30	29	Johnson & Johnson New Brunswick, N.J.	14,138.0
31	28	Minnesota Mining & Mfg. St. Paul	14,020.0
32	34	Coca-Cola Atlanta	13,957.0
33	31	International Paper Purchase, N.Y.	13,685.0
34	30	Tenneco Houston	13,255.0
35	45	Lockheed Calabasas, Calif.	13,071.0
36	39	Georgia-Pacific Atlanta	12,330.0
37	37	Phillips Petroleum Bartlesville, Okla.	12,309.0
38	36	Alliedsignal Morris Township, N.J.	11,827.0
39	42	IBP Dakota City, Neb.	11,671.4
40	38	Goodyear Tire Akron	11,643.4

TABLE 7
Continued

Rank 1993	1992		Sales, $ millions
41	44	Caterpillar Peoria, Ill.	11,615.0
42	35	Westinghouse Electric Philadelphia	11,564.0
43	41	Anheuser-Busch St. Louis	11,505.3
44	40	Bristol-Myers Squibb New York	11,413.0
45	43	Rockwell International Seal Beach, Calif.	10,840.0
46	47	Merck Whitehouse Station, N.J.	10,498.2
47	46	Coastal Houston	10,136.1
48	50	Archer Daniels Midland Decatur, Ill.	9,811.4
49	48	Ashland Oil Russell, Ky.	9,553.9
50	51	Weyerhaeuser Federal Way, Wash.	9,544.8
51	93	Martin Marietta Bethesda, Md.	9,435.7
52	54	Raytheon Lexington, Mass.	9,201.2
53	53	Citgo Petroleum Tulsa	9,107.4
54	49	Alcoa Pittsburgh	9,055.9
55	61	Baxter International Deerfield, Ill.	8,879.0
56	91	Intel Santa Clara, Calif.	8,782.0
57	63	Textron Providence	8,668.5
58	71	Texas Instruments Dallas	8,523.0
59	66	Abbott Laboratories Abbott Park, Ill.	8,407.8
60	67	American Home Products Madison, N.J.	8,304.9
61	57	American Brands Old Greenwich, Conn.	8,287.5
62	70	Emerson Electric St. Louis	8,173.8
63	68	General Mills Minneapolis	8,134.6
64	56	Occidental Petroleum Los Angeles	8,116.0
65	65	Hanson Industries NA New York	8,111.5
66	55	Unocal Los Angeles	8,077.0
67	76	Apple Computer Cupertino, Calif.	7,977.0
68	64	TRW Cleveland	7,947.9
69	69	Ralston Purina St. Louis	7,902.2
70	60	Monsanto St. Louis	7,902.0
71	62	Unisys Blue Bell, Pa.	7,742.5
72	79	Deere Moline, Ill.	7,693.8
73	73	Whirlpool Benton Harbor, Mich.	7,533.0
74	72	Pfizer New York	7,477.7
75	59	Sun Philadelphia	7,297.0
76	119	Compaq Computer Houston	7,191.0
77	78	Colgate-Palmolive New York	7,141.3
78	80	H.J. Heinz Pittsburgh	7,103.4
79	75	Kimberly-Clark Irving, Texas	6,972.9
80	77	Hoechst Celanese North Somerville, N.J.	6,899.0

TABLE 7
Continued

Rank 1993	1992		Sales, $ millions
81	81	CPC International Englewood Cliffs, N.J.	6,738.0
82	74	Borden Columbus, Ohio	6,700.0
83	85	Campbell Soup Camden, N.J.	6,586.2
84	82	Miles Pittsburgh	6,586.0
85	84	Eli Lilly Indianapolis	6,452.4
86	87	Kellogg Battle Creek, Mich.	6,295.4
87	89	Cooper Industries Houston	6,273.8
88	105	Johnson Controls Milwaukee	6,181.7
89	86	Honeywell Minneapolis	5,963.0
90	99	Levi Strauss Associates San Francisco	5,892.5
91	92	Amerada Hess New York	5,851.6
92	97	Warner-Lambert Morris Plains, N.J.	5,793.7
93	94	PPG Industries Pittsburgh	5,753.9
94	83	W.R. Grace Boca Raton, Fla.	5,736.6
95	98	Quaker Oats Chicago	5,730.6
96	95	Litton Industries Beverly Hills	5,480.2
97	106	Coca-Cola Enterprises Atlanta	5,465.0
98	108	Dana Toledo	5,460.1
99	104	Gillette Boston	5,410.8
100	103	American Cyanamid Wayne, N.J.	5,305.6

Source: *Fortune*, April 18, 1994.

day before, they were two competing airlines. The day after, they were one larger firm. Republic itself had grown out of a horizontal merger—between North Central and Southern—in 1979. In 1980, Republic expanded by acquiring Hughes West. Northwest's growth through horizontal merger was not unusual for the airline industry. TWA acquired Ozark, Piedmont merged with

TABLE 8
Production Concentration Ratios in Japanese Manufacturing Industries by Leading and Five Leading Firms, 1991

Industry	Leading Firm	Five Leading Firms	Industry	Leading Firm	Five Leading Firms
Sugar	12	48	Soy sauce	28	50
Beer	50	100	Crude steel	26	64
Nylon	31	93	Computers	55	93
Polyester	26	80	Tires, tubes	47	98
Gasoline	17	68	Ethylene	13	54
Glass	48	100	Trucks	26	71
Cement	13	56	Automobiles	33	85

Source: *Nippon, A Charted Survey of Japan, 1993/94*, Yano, I., ed., The Tsuneta Yano Memorial Society, p. 163.

TABLE 9 Three-Firm Concentration Ratios for Selected Industries in Canada, Britain, France, and Germany, 1970

Industry	Canada	Britain	France	Germany
Brewing	89	47	63	17
Cigarettes	90	94	100	94
Petroleum refining	25	79	60	47
Cement	20	86	81	54
Steel	80	39	84	56
Refrigerators	75	65	100	72

Source: F. M. Scherer and David Ross, *Industrial Market Structure and Economic Performance*, Third Edition. Copyright © 1990 by Houghton Mifflin Company. Adapted with permission.

U. S. Air, and Continental is an amalgam of Peoples Express, New York Air, and Frontier Airlines.

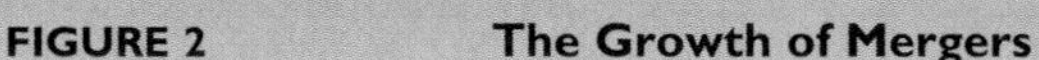

Horizontal mergers are common. Many of the leading firms in leading U.S. industries are products of mergers. The classic example is USX (formerly U. S.

FIGURE 2 The Growth of Mergers
During the 100 year period 1890–1990, growth of horizontal, vertical, and conglomerate mergers was erratic, but progressively reached peaks that pushed mergers to over 1,000 per year for some years before World War II. Merger activity rose rapidly after 1950, reaching peaks of 2,500 per year in the 1970s and 3,000 per year in the 1980s.

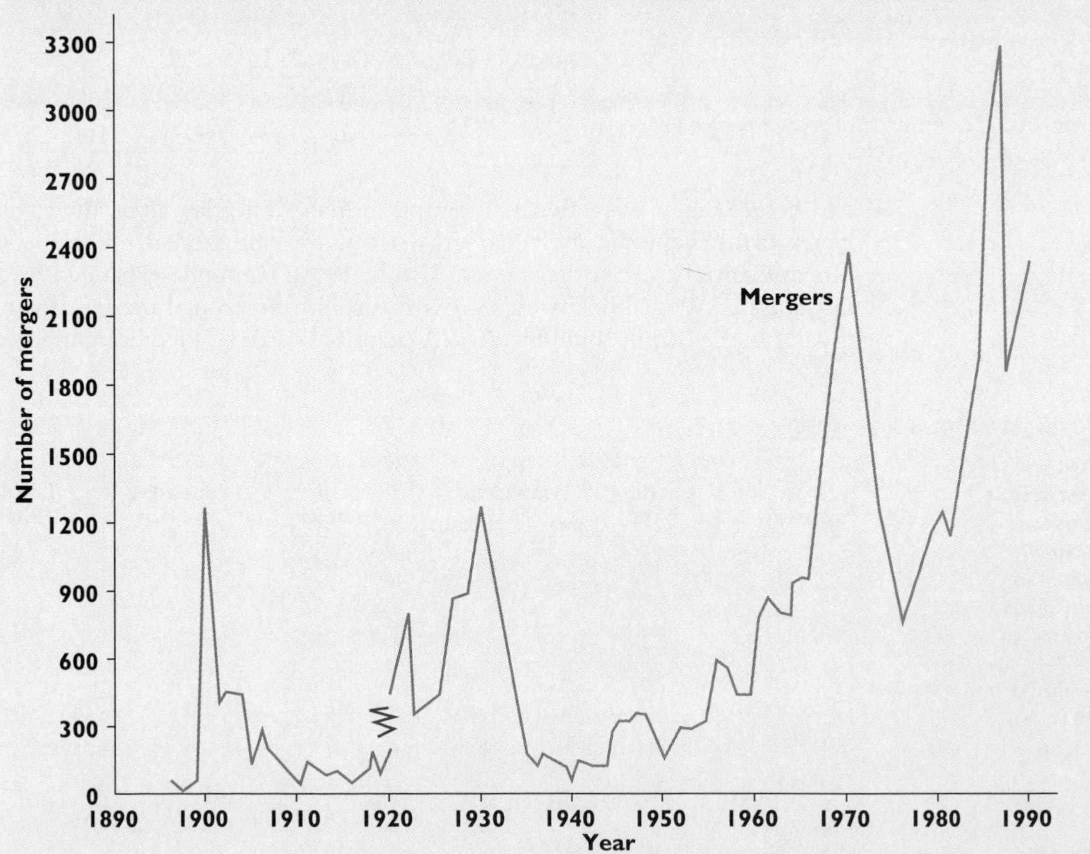

Horizontal mergers directly increase concentration in an industry.

Steel) ranked 24 in the 1993 Fortune 500. As we saw in Chapter 10, J. P. Morgan bought out Andrew Carnegie's enormous steel empire and then proceeded to add eleven more steel and wire combinations—themselves collections of steel and steel-related firms—to form U.S. Steel.

Exxon, ranked third in the 1993 Fortune 500, also owes its primary expansion to horizontal merger activity. As Standard Oil, it was formed in 1870 by the merger of 20 Cleveland petroleum refiners. It then acquired an additional 100 competitors and ultimately controlled 90 percent of the petroleum refining industry.

The American Can Company was organized by an overnight merger of about 120 firms, giving it a 90 percent share of its industry's market. American Tobacco, too, established a 90 percent market share by merging with the industry's five leading tobacco producers. General Electric evolved out of the merger of Edison General Electic and the already-formed-by-merger Thomson-Houston.

During the first major wave of horizontal merger activity—1887 to 1904—horizontal mergers created such firms as U.S. Rubber, United Shoe Machinery, Pittsburgh Plate Glass, Eastman Kodak, U.S. Gypsum, International Harvester, and International Paper.

Vertical Mergers

Vertical merger

A merger between firms that have a supplier-purchaser relationship.

Vertical merger brings together firms that are not engaged in producing the same product. Instead, the vertical merger links firms that are in a supplier-purchaser relationship.

Why would a firm want to merge vertically with another firm?

For example, 24th-ranked USX acquires iron ore firms, coke firms, and mining firms. It owns or leases coal reserves, bulk cargo vessels, and chemical plants. Another example of vertical merging is Anheuser-Busch—ranked 43 in the 1993 Fortune 500—with acquisitions of malt plants, yeast plants, a corn-processing plant, beer can factories, a refrigerator car firm that repairs and maintains refrigerated railroad cars used to ship beer, and a railway that ships freight by rail and truck.

Campbell Soup, ranked 83, is in the canning business. In fact, it ranks among the nation's leading canning firms. If you enjoy its mushroom soup, you may be interested to know that Campbell owns mushroom farms. Firestone, acquired by Bridgestone, not only owns tire manufacturing facilities, but also has rubber plantations in Brazil, the Philippines, Ghana, and Liberia. Uniroyal, its competitor, owns rubber plantations in Indonesia, Malaysia, and Liberia. B. F. Goodrich owns plantations in Liberia and the Philippines, as well as synthetic tire-related chemical plants in Ireland, Holland, New Zealand, Belgium, and Costa Rica.

Conglomerate Mergers

Conglomerate merger

A merger between firms in unrelated industries.

The most common form of merger is the **conglomerate merger.** It brings together firms that are neither in the same industry nor linked to each other in a supplier-purchaser relationship. Why conglomerates? Why would two unrelated firms decide to merge?

One reason for conglomerate mergers is the desire to diversify operations. While horizontal and vertical mergers strengthen the firm's position within the industry, the firm's fate still depends on the health of the industry. That can

Conglomerate mergers don't increase concentration, but they do reduce risks for an oligopolist.

cause sleepless nights. By acquiring unrelated firms, the conglomerate insures itself against catastrophe if the industry itself faces severe problems.

Consider the energy business. What would you have done if you were Shell Oil, earning abnormally high profit in the late 1970s, yet having to deal with the political uncertainties of Iran, Iraq, and Saudi Arabia? Would you reinvest those windfall profits back into the Middle East? Wouldn't you have worried about competition from the nuclear and solar energy industries? Perhaps a safe strategy would be to stay in the energy business, but diversify into hotels, potato chips, movies, publishing, car rentals, frozen foods, and maybe even a football franchise. If you did, you would not be alone. Many Fortune 500 firms are collections of growing conglomerates.

Look at Borden, ranked 82 in the 1993 Fortune 500. If you think only of milk, you don't know the company! Aside from food plants and dairy facilities, it owns chemical plants, soft drink bottling plants, petrochemical firms, and a commercial bakery in Germany.

RJR Nabisco, ranked 25, is a recent merging of R. J. Reynolds, one of the major cigarette producers in the world, with Nabisco and Kraft Foods, two dominating firms in the food industry. R. J. Reynolds had already acquired Del Monte, Hawaiian Punch, Patio (the nation's leading frozen Mexican food), and RJR Archer, a major plastic packaging material supplier for supermarket meats. Gulf & Western Industries owns Paramount Pictures. It owns, as well, the world's largest sugar mill, numerous holiday resorts, docks, shipping facilities, mines, and a railroad system. It owns 250 manufacturing plants and mines in the United States and abroad. It acquired near-controlling shares of Sherwin-Williams, Unisys, Cummins Engine, Jonathan Logan women's apparel, and General Tire. It is about as diversified as the U.S. economy.

Doubleday Book is certainly no Gulf & Western. But it, too, rates as a conglomerate. It owns the New York Mets. Perhaps this connection reflects raw emotion as much as it does business acumen. Nelson Doubleday, with a 51 percent interest in the firm, is descended from Abner Doubleday, the man credited with the invention of baseball.

Cartels: Mergers without Merging

Firms really don't have to buy each other's assets in order to practice merger. They can simply act as if they had. They get together—typically clandestinely—to establish common policy on price and market shares. By agreeing to monitor themselves and abide by joint decisions, they can behave like a monopoly, setting monopoly prices and parceling out the industry's production among themselves. In the United States, such **cartel** arrangements are illegal, but because it is difficult to prove **collusion,** many are operative.

Cartel

A group of firms that collude to limit competition in a market by negotiating and accepting agreed-upon price and market shares .

Collusion

The practice of firms to negotiate price and market-share decisions that limit competition in a market.

"DISGUISED" CARTELS

Just as a rose by any other name is a rose, so too is a cartel by any other name. In many states, agricultural cooperatives producing for regional and even national markets behave like cartels. They control price by voluntary agreement on production limits through quota assignments.

The citrus cooperatives in Florida and California, the dairy cooperatives in Wisconsin, the poultry cooperatives in North Carolina, the corn cooperatives in Iowa, the soybean cooperatives in Illinois, and the peach cooperatives in

Saudi Arabian Oil Minister Hisham Nazer (R) talks to his Libyan counterpart Addullah Salem al-Badri after the opening session of OPEC's summer ministerial conference in Vienna, Austria, on June 15, 1994. Oil prices and oil supplies are the principal issues on their agenda.

Georgia are just a few of the many regional and national cooperatives whose principal function is to control quantities offered on the market in order to regulate price.

GOVERNMENT-SPONSORED CARTELS

Cartels are illegal in the United States, but they still exist in disguised form; in some other countries they have been actively encouraged by government.

Although illegal in the United States, cartels have flourished in other nations, including Western Europe. In some economies, governments have actually assisted cartel formation to replace foreign imports with domestic production and to promote their own national exports. For example, Germany's economic development, beginning in the latter part of the nineteenth century, was essentially built with cartel production. By 1904, 385 cartels, comprising over 12,000 firms, accounted for virtually all of its production of coal, iron, metals, chemicals, textiles, leather, rubber, wood, paper, and glass.

Few people have to be reminded what the Organization of Petroleum Exporting Countries, OPEC, is designed to do. It has been one of the most effective international cartels ever put together. Its membership includes the governments of Algeria, Ecuador, Gabon, Indonesia, Iran, Iraq, Kuwait, Libya, Nigeria, Qatar, Saudi Arabia, the United Arab Emirates, and Venezuela. By setting output quotas and a common price, OPEC raised the price per barrel of crude oil from $2 in 1973 to $34 in 1982. The result was the greatest global redistribution of income—from the rest of the world to OPEC economies—in recorded history.

PRICING AND OUTPUT UNDER OLIGOPOLY

The world of oligopoly is a highly personal one. The decision makers in an oligopolistic industry, so few in number, know each other well. They not only watch over their own business, they spend a great deal of time watching each other. And for good reason. Any action, such as a price cut, taken by any one firm, will affect very directly the market positions of every other firm in the oligopoly.

TABLE 10 Firm Profit, Generated by High and Low Pricing

Ford's Price	GM's Price	GM's Profit	Ford's Profit
High	High	10	10
Low	High	4	14
Low	Low	6	6
High	Low	14	4

For self protection, then, oligopolistic firms learn to react swiftly to market initiatives taken by other firms. For example, they may react to a price cut by cutting price themselves, thus denying the initiator the market advantage that was sought by the cut.

Of course, before any firm would initiate a price cut, it would take into its calculations how the others would probably react to the cut. And just anticipating their reactions may be sufficient to dissuade the firm from initiating the cut in the first place.

Game Theory Pricing

Does the oligopolistic game sound familiar? Firms go through the business day thinking: "If I do this, then they'll do that, then I'll do this, then they'll do that— wait—I'd better not do this!" Or, "If I do this, then they'll do that, then I'll do this, then they'll do that—wait—good, I'll do it!" The mapping out of initiation and response strategies is not unlike the game of chess.

Like chess, there is always a degree of uncertainty in the play. We *really* don't know, do we, what the response will be to any move we make? Thinking a strategy through is actually more like: "If I do this, then they'll *probably* do that. . . ." But what are the probabilities? Each one of us would probably attach different probabilities to the same event. Some players are born risk takers. They play aggressively, forcing the game. But they don't always win.

Decision makers in oligopoly firms recognize the links between the firms' actions and reactions. Price in oligopoly markets may not always tend toward equilibrium as firms react to the actions of other firms.

Decision makers in oligopoly play the same way. Any strategy they adopt must include a careful study of probable reactions. They can cut price in the expectation of capturing a larger slice of the market, and sometimes they succeed. But if they calculated incorrectly, they can trigger a price war among the oligopolists, and everybody may lose.

To illustrate, let's trace out some of the strategy options open to an oligopolistic firm in a two-firm industry where market power is equally shared. We suppose the price options are simple: price either high or low. Suppose the two firms are General Motors and Ford. They price independently, choosing between high and low prices. Table 10 describes the severe profit consequences of this pricing game.

How would Ford price its automobiles? It knows that if it selects a high price and GM does the same, combined profit is 20. With market power equally distributed between the two, Ford's own profit is 10. But another possibility stares Ford in the face. If it chooses a low price while GM chooses a high one, Ford captures the major portion of the market. Its profit becomes 14. People still buy GM models but in fewer numbers, so that GM's profit falls to 4. Their combined profit, in this scenario, is 18.

ADDED PERSPECTIVE

The Prisoners' Dilemma

The assumption, in traditional microeconomics, of many buyers and sellers is all too crucial. When agents are few enough for their decisions to affect others, they are bound to behave "strategically"—i.e., take those effects, and the likely response of other agents to them, into account. In economics, such behavior makes even the simplest transaction difficult to analyze. This is the task of game theory.

In most bargaining circumstances a deal can be struck that will satisfy all sides. But if there is no agreed-upon way to settle on it, everybody may end up unhappy. The classic illustration is one of the simplest games: The Prisoners' Dilemma. Two prisoners are accused of a crime. The prosecutor tells them that if they both confess they will go to jail for 10 years; if neither confesses they will get two years; if only one confesses he (the confessor) will get just one year while his fellow prisoner goes down for 20. If they can come to a binding agreement, the prisoners will both profess their innocence and be sentenced to two years. But suppose they cannot. Each prisoner will then see that—regardless of what the other does—he will be better off if he confesses. Both will confess and get 10 years.

Recently game theory has made strides. Theorists can unravel the structure of extremely complicated games. New research also stresses empirical work, using controlled experiments to see how people behave in real bargaining situations. Fascinating stuff. Unfortunately, it is all too obvious that voluntary agreements among small groups need not be efficient: When the numbers are small, markets are prone to fail.

Discussion

What similarities can you draw between the prisoners' dilemma and the decision making confronting firms engaged in the theory of games? What differences do you see?

But do you think GM would accept a pricing strategy by Ford that undermines its market and profit share? If GM responds by matching Ford's lower price, they each end up with a profit of 6. That's considerably less than the 10 they each generate at high prices.

It seems reasonable to suppose that each would independently select a high price knowing that they understand the unattractive consequences to both firms if either one lowers price. But how well do they sleep? They are both vulnerable operating at the high price.

Their fear is that good sense may not always prevail. Ford may decide to lower its price to capture the higher profit. It may even anticipate GM's response. But its long-run strategy may be to secure quick, short-run gains, calculating that it would provoke a price war that would eventually lead both back to higher prices. In the interim, Ford *may* gain more than it loses. Both understand the strategy, and both fear the other may try it.

Game theory

A theory of strategy ascribed to firms' behavior in oligopoly. The firms' behavior is mutually interdependent.

As you see, this **game theory** explanation of pricing among the few is unlike the price-determining process under conditions of monopoly, monopolistic competition, or perfect competition. In each of those market structures, firms react only to the demand and cost structures they face. They are busy equating marginal cost to marginal revenue. They do not engage in second guessing about how the competition will respond to price decisions they make or about how they, in turn, plan to respond to their competition's reaction. *In monopoly, monopolistic competition, and perfect competition, prices tend toward equilibrium. In the game theory view of oligopoly, prices are subject to fits of change, reflecting firms in the act of* *testing each other's responses.* Although oligopoly prices are typically higher than competitive ones and somewhat stable, price instability is probable. Prices simply don't tend toward equilibrium and stay there.

Godfathers and Price Leadership

Price leadership

A firm whose price decisions are tacitly accepted and followed by other firms in the industry.

The godfather firm sets its price and output by maximizing its own profits, allowing smaller firms to make whatever profits are available in the remaining share of the market at the price it dictates. The godfather's price is an offer the other firms can't refuse!

Game theory is one view of how oligopolists behave. There are others. The godfather or **price leadership** theory explains pricing in unbalanced oligopoly; that is, when one firm in the oligopoly clearly dominates all others. As we saw in Table 4, many oligopolies have a single leading firm where considerable power is vested. These firms sometimes come to play the role of "godfather" in the industry's price-determining process.

There's a long history of price leadership. In the U.S. economy, it included at times General Motors in automobiles, Alcoa in aluminum, Reynolds in cigarettes, General Electric in refrigerators, Kellogg in breakfast cereals, USX in steel, IBM in computers, ATT in telephones, Xerox in copying equipment, International Harvester in agricultural machinery, Standard Oil of New Jersey in petroleum, and many more. Every major industrial economy has its own set of oligopolistic price leaders or godfathers, and in some cases, international "marriages" among them are not uncommon events.

Usually the godfather alone can set the industry's price. The other firms abide by the decision because to challenge it may provoke a price war within the industry that ends up being detrimental to the health of the weaker firms.

In most cases, however, all the firms in the oligopoly go along on the matter of price because they share a sense of common cause. The godfather accepts the responsibility of promoting "peace, prosperity, and tranquility" within the industry. The established price allows the weaker firms in the oligopoly to enjoy a profit that would have been unobtainable under more competitive pricing.

Figure 3 depicts how godfather pricing and firm output levels are determined.

Suppose eight firms make up a chocolate oligopoly dominated by Hershey. The seven smaller chocolate firms acknowledge Hershey as godfather, allowing it alone to determine price. Each accepts the Hershey price as its own.

Suppose also that Hershey's marginal cost curve is MC_h, while MC is the sum of the marginal cost curves of all the other firms in the chocolate industry. The industry demand curve is D. Hershey's demand curve, reflecting a 25 percent market share, is D_h, and its marginal revenue curve is MR_h.

How does godfather pricing work? Hershey maximizes profit by producing 5 tons of chocolate at a price of $5 per pound. The seven other firms, pricing their chocolate at the godfather's $5 per pound, produce where $P = MC = \$5$, or at a combined output of 15 tons, that is, 75 percent of market share. In this way, they avoid conflict with the dominant and more efficient Hershey. The point of accepting price leadership is simple: Prevention of honest-to-goodness price competition.

The Kinked Demand Curve

Aside from the game theory and godfather approaches to price determination in oligopoly, economists offer still another variant on oligopoly pricing that focuses on the unique character of the oligopolist's demand curve. Although downward-

FIGURE 3 **Price and Output under Conditions of Godfather Oligopoly**
D is the industry's demand curve. Hershey's demand curve, D_h, represents a 25 percent market share. Hershey's marginal revenue curve is MR_h. Acting as price leader, Hershey produces where its $MR = MC$; that is, at 5 tons and at a price of $5 per pound. The other seven firms in the oligopoly accept Hershey's price. The *MC* curve is the sum of their marginal cost curves and they produce where $P = MC =$ $5, and at 15 tons. The industry's output is 20 tons.

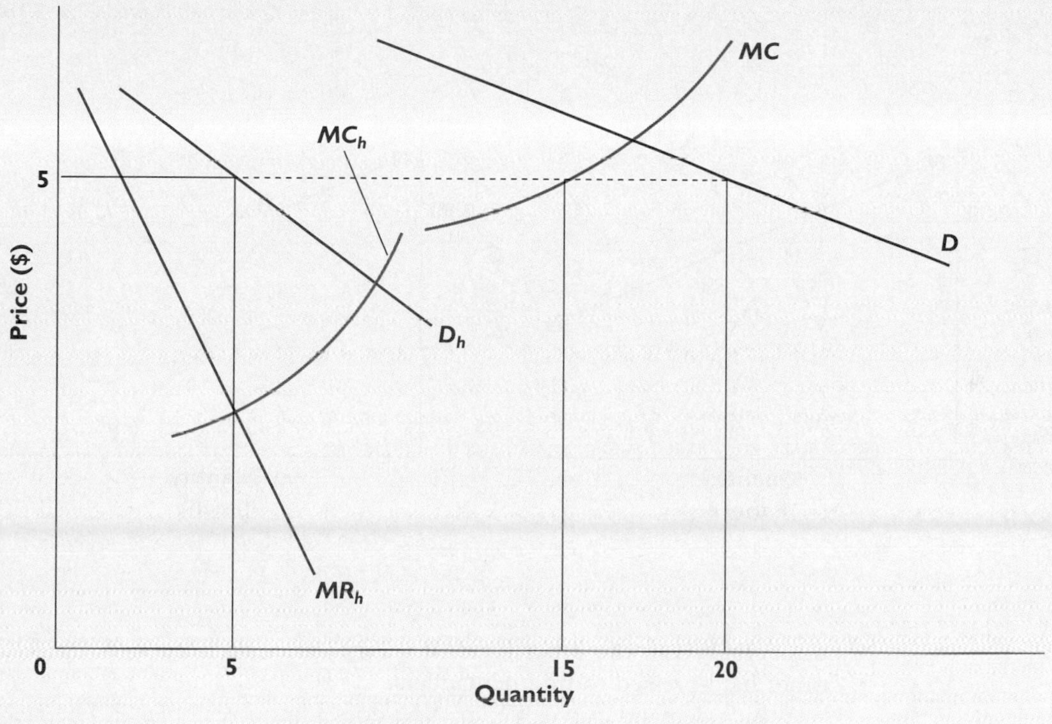

sloping—as all firms' demand curves are in markets other than perfect competition—the demand curve for the firm in oligopoly has a peculiar kink which results from the way firms in oligopoly view each other.

Kinked demand curve

The demand curve facing a firm in oligopoly; the curve is more elastic when the firm raises price than when it lowers price.

The kinked demand curve model embodies two demand curves that the firm must consider. The elastic demand curve presupposes that other firms follow in behavior, while the inelastic demand curve assumes that other firms do not follow each other.

How does the kink emerge, and what significance does it play in oligopolistic pricing? The **kinked demand curve** provides another explanation of why oligopolistic firms do not lower prices to increase market share. Figure 4 illustrates the kinked demand curve's derivation and significance.

Imagine Lipton engaged in price strategy. How does it view its demand curve for instant chicken soup in an industry where Libby and Campbell are its major competitors? Suppose the prevailing price is $0.80 per box. In panel *a*, Lipton's demand curve *YY* (*YY* stands for yes, others follow) depicts what happens to its quantity demanded when it cuts or raises price and its *competitors react by doing precisely what Lipton does*. That is to say, when Lipton cuts, they cut. When Lipton raises price, they raise price.

Lipton's demand curve *NN* (*NN* stands for no, others don't follow) is considerably more elastic. It reflects what happens to quantity demanded for Lipton chicken soup when it cuts or raises price and its *competitors decide not to follow Lipton's lead*. If Lipton cuts price and others don't, quantity demanded increases

FIGURE 4 **Constructing an Oligopolist's Demand Curve**

The two demand curves in panel *a*—*NN* and *YY*—represent two different ways competitors respond to a price cut or price increase initiated by Lipton. If they react by doing precisely what Lipton does—cut price when Lipton cuts, increase price when Lipton increases, Lipton's demand curve is *YY*, relatively inelastic. If competitors react by *not* following Lipton's price initiative, Lipton's demand curve is *NN*, relatively elastic.

Panel *b* combines the two segments of *YY* and *NN* to reflect more realistically how competitors in oligopoly react to Lipton's price changes. When Lipton increases price, its competitors do not follow. Lipton's demand curve above $0.80, then, is *NK*. When Lipton cuts price, its competitors feel compelled to follow. Its demand curve below $0.80, then, is *KY*.

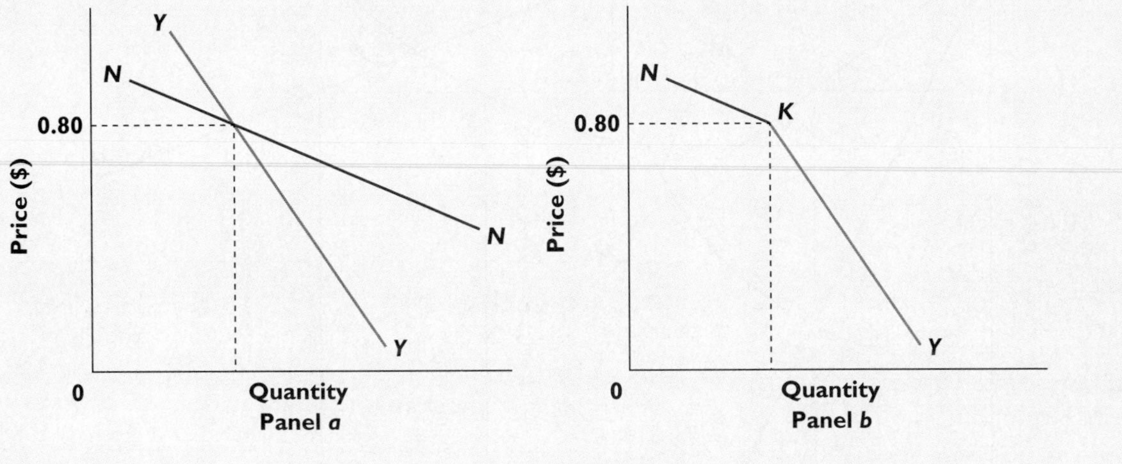

considerably. On the other hand, if it raises price and others don't, Lipton becomes hard-pressed to find demanders.

Which demand curve, *YY* or *NN*, does Lipton really face? The answer is, a bit of both. If price is $0.80 and Lipton decides to raise price to $0.90, the probability is high that its competitors would stay at $0.80. That is, Lipton's demand curve at prices above $0.80 reflects *NN*. On the other hand, if Lipton decides to cut price below $0.80, others would feel compelled to cut as well. In this case, its demand curve below $0.80 reflects *YY*.

Panel *b* puts the two demand curve segments together—*NN* above $0.80 and *YY* below $0.80—to illustrate what Lipton faces when it decides to cut or raise prices. Note that the composite demand curve is kinked at $0.80.

THE MARGINAL REVENUE GAP

What about Lipton's marginal revenue curve? Panel *a* in Figure 5 shows the marginal revenue curve associated with the kinked demand curve.

As you see, the *MR* curve in panel *a* is discontinuous. The *MR* segment above the kink traces the marginal revenue corresponding to the demand curve's *NK* segment in Figure 4, panel *b*. The *M′R′* segment below the kink traces marginal revenue corresponding to the demand curve's *KY* segment. Note that the kink in the demand curve at $0.80 creates a gap, *RM′*, in Lipton's marginal revenue curve. Why are we so interested in understanding the derivation of this *MR* gap? Because it explains why there can be substantial price rigidity in oligopoly despite sizable changes in the firm's costs.

FIGURE 5 **Price Rigidity in Oligopolies with Kinked Demand Curves**

In panel *a*, the oligopoly's kinked demand curve creates a corresponding marginal revenue curve that is discontinuous at the point of the kink. The marginal revenue curve associated with the *MK* segment of the demand curve is *MR*. The marginal revenue associated with the *KY* segment of the demand curve is *M'R'*. Note the *RM'* gap created in the marginal revenue curve.

In panel *b*, the firm's marginal cost curve cuts the marginal revenue curve within the *MR* gap. Applying the *MR* = *MC* profit maximization rule, Lipton will produce 4,000 boxes, priced at $0.80. As long as the firm's marginal cost curve falls within the *MR* gap, price will remain at $0.80. In panel *c*, the firm's marginal cost curve *MC'* cuts the marginal revenue curve along its upper *MR* segment. Output falls to 2,000 boxes and price increases to $0.90.

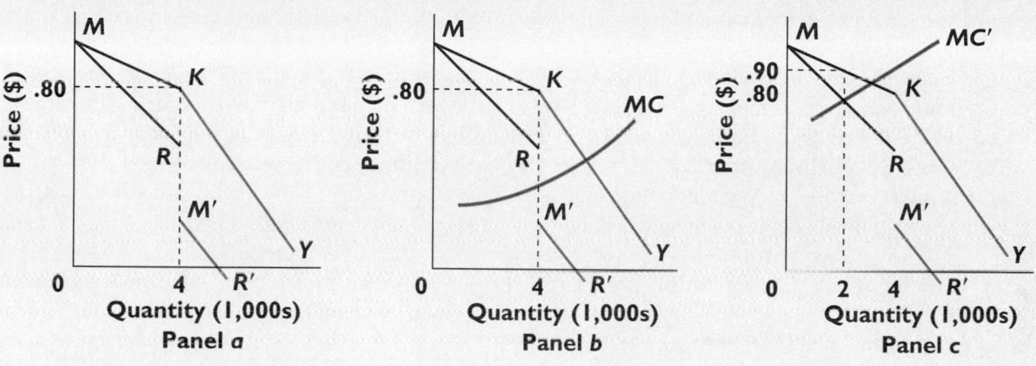

Why don't marginal cost changes cause price to change in the kinked demand curve model?

Why is the *MR* gap bigger as the difference in slopes between the segments of the demand increases?

PRICE RIGIDITY AND PRICE FLUCTUATIONS

Look at panel *b* in Figure 5. Lipton's marginal cost curve can be located anywhere between *R* and *M'* and Lipton will still produce 4,000 boxes and market them at $0.80. Even if its costs—prices of raw chicken, labor, or advertising—were to increase, as long as the resultant upward shift in its *MC* curve still locates *MR* = *MC* within the *RM'* gap, Lipton will maximize profit by producing 4,000 units priced at $0.80.

Even when costs fall, prices may still remain rigid. Suppose a new technology is introduced by Lipton and spreads throughout the oligopoly so that every firm's costs are cut substantially. As long as these lower costs still produce a *MC* curve that locates *MC* = *MR* within the *RM'* gap, price remains at $0.80.

The larger the gap, the greater is the change in costs that Lipton could tolerate without changing price. What determines the size of the gap? As you see in Figure 5, it depends upon the difference in slope between the two segments of the firm's kinked demand curve. This difference reflects both the price elasticity of demand for Lipton's chicken soup and the cross elasticities of demand among all the various brands produced by Lipton and its competitors. The greater the difference in the slopes of the kinked demand, the greater is the gap, and the more resistant is price to changes in cost.

But suppose that rising costs shift Lipton's *MC* curve upward beyond the gap, for example, to *MC'* in panel *c* of Figure 5. Lipton would respond by moving to a new profit-maximizing price and output. Now *MC'* = *MR* at 2,000 boxes. At this output level, Lipton increases price to $0.90.

ADDED PERSPECTIVE

USX Won't Join Rival AK Steel in Raising Prices

USX's U.S. Steel Group reduced the likelihood of a third industrywide price increase for steel this year, saying it won't follow competitor AK Steel Holding Corp.'s planned October price increase.

The nation's largest steelmaker said that instead it would stick by a promise it made to customers last year that it would raise base prices on flat-rolled steel only twice in 1994—once in January and again in July—after raising prices three times last year.

"Even if one player like U.S. Steel is holding on to prices, that would make [an industrywide increase] difficult," said Christopher Plummer, a steel industry consultant with Resource Strategies Inc. in Exton, PA.

And so far no other major steel producer has said it will follow the lead of AK Steel, the seventh-largest steel producer in the United States. But other steelmakers, including Bethlehem Steel and Inland Steel, haven't ruled out a fall price increase, either.

"If no other producers follow, I think it's pretty apparent that the price increase will not stick," said Thomas M. Van Leeuwen, a steel industry analyst with CS First Boston in New York. "But if other producers do follow suit, there's a good chance prices would rise despite U.S. Steel."

AK Steel, based in Middletown, Ohio, announced on June 13 its intention to boost flat-rolled steel prices about 3 percent effective with October 2 shipments. It said then that steep demand and short supply justified the increase.

Indeed, steelmakers are experiencing their strongest demand in two decades. They're running mills at or near capacity to keep up with demand, and they're limiting the amount of steel they ship to certain customers. "Conditions are ripe for a price increase," Mr. Van Leeuwen said.

Mr. Plummer agreed and added that steelmakers need to take advantage of the surging market. "Periods of strong prices are short-lived" in the steel industry, he said. "The name of the game is to maximize your profits during these brief periods."

Discussion

Christopher Plummer may not know it, but he's describing oligopoly behavior in the steel industry in terms of the kinked demand curve. Discuss.

Source: *The Wall Street Journal*, June 20, 1994. Reprinted by permission of *The Wall Street Journal*,

OLIGOPOLY AND BRAND MULTIPLICATION

Have you ever wondered why there are so many breakfast cereals on supermarket shelves? Or why there are hundreds of brands of soaps, toothpaste, soft drinks, laundry detergents, cigarettes, and candy bars? If you read their labels carefully, you will discover that many of these brands are produced by a very few firms. The firms are typically oligopolies in industries with relatively high concentration ratios.

Brand multiplication

Variations on essentially one good that a firm produces in order to increase its market share.

Why would any firm go through the trouble of creating **brand multiplication** of the same product? The answer is market share. Each firm, reluctant to compete in price, tries to increase its profit by capturing a larger share of the market by adding more brands.

Suppose, for example, that Colgate-Palmolive and Procter & Gamble are the only two firms in the toothpaste oligopoly. Suppose, as well, that Colgate's single brand has the same market strength as Procter & Gamble's Crest. Colgate's market share can be expressed as

$$\text{Firm market share} = \text{number of brands} \times \text{brand market share}$$

ADDED PERSPECTIVE

When Patents Expire: Preparing for Market Segmentation

Merck & Company—one of the world's most powerful drug companies—also has one of corporate America's most admired names. But recently it said it would create a new division to produce generic drugs under a different name altogether. Merck's new company, to be called West Point Pharma, based in West Point, PA, will manufacture, at prices rivaling the lowest cost producers, exact copies of Merck drugs after they have lost their patent protection. Generics now account for 40 percent of all prescriptions. West Point Pharma will begin by marketing diflunisal, a low-priced version of Merck's $100 million seller Dolobid, an analgesic. Next: probably, a version of Merck's $565 million veterinary drug Ivermectin, which comes off patent in 1997, to be followed by Mevacor, a hugely successful cholesterol-lowering drug with sales of $1.4 billion. Mevacor loses its patent protection in 1999. "It's possible that we would market a generic formulation of all of our products," said John Doorley, a Merck spokesman.

Discussion

Why would Merck produce *both* a brand name product *and* a generic version of the product? Why would they go into competition with themselves?

Source: "Merck Under Another Name," by Joel Kurtzman, *The New York Times*, September 13, 1992.

Brand multiplication is a means for an oligopolist to increase market share.

With only one brand, Colgate-Palmolive has a 50 percent market share. Now, how would Colgate-Palmolive go about increasing its share of the toothpaste market? Suppose it introduces a second brand, Ultra-Brite, which becomes as successful as Crest and Colgate. It now has two of the three brands on the market. If each brand captures one-third of the market, Colgate-Palmolive's market share rises from 50 percent to 67 percent.

All this was done without Colgate-Palmolive having to cut price a penny. Of course, if Procter & Gamble responds by adding Gleem, its own second brand, then Colgate-Palmolive's market share falls back to 50 percent.

You can see, then, how this market share struggle can get out of hand. The game is to "outbrand" the competitor. An aggressive strategy would be to keep adding new brands, promoting those that succeed, replacing those that don't, and maintaining a greater number of brands on the market than the competition does.

There are limits, however, to a firm's brand multiplication. Each new brand requires physical space, independent management, and advertising expenditures. Unless a new brand can capture a good share of the market, its place in the firm's product line can be detrimental to the oligopolistic firm's profit.

As the number of brands in the industry increases, market share per brand diminishes. Given the relatively high promotional costs associated with each brand's survival, the marginal cost of adding a new brand will eventually catch up to the marginal revenue the new brand generates.

With enough time and testing, oligopolistic firms discover the optimum number of brands to produce. But the brand game is continuous; it requires an ongoing process of weeding out weak brands and strengthening the successful. That's why firms insist that their brands are "new and improved."

WHY OLIGOPOLISTS SOMETIMES PRICE DISCRIMINATE

Picture the scene. Five people in Los Angeles board United Airlines nonstop flight 224 to New York. R. J. Abrams, an executive with MCA records, flies first class. His round-trip fare is $2,022. Tanya Donelly, guitarist for the Rock band "Belly," flies coach. She bought the round-trip ticket just before boarding, paying $1,234. The trip was a last-minute decision. Her agent in New York is putting the finishing touches on a European tour and needs her input. Seated next to her, on the aisle, is Peter Soboroff, a Hollywood stuntman who is going to New York to appear on the *David Letterman Show*. Buying the ticket three days in advance, his round-trip fare was $622. A few rows back is Reesa Rodier. She's a fund raiser for the Leukemia Society of America. Invited to address a New York conference only a week ago, she was able to buy a round-trip ticket, seven days in advance, for $497. Jenny Dibello sits next to Reesa. She is a professor of entomology at UCLA. She planned long in advance to see Susan Dunn in *La Boheme* at the Met. Her round-trip ticket, purchased 14 days in advance, was $318.

Five people buy the *same* product—a round-trip flight between New York and Los Angeles—and yet pay five very different prices. Why would United price the flight so differently? After all, if these same five people went to the same newsstand to buy *The Los Angeles Times,* they would pay the same $0.35. If they went to the same supermarket to buy Hershey almond candy bars, they would pay the same $0.55. Why, then, are their fares so different?

Segmenting the Market

Suppose Table 11 records the demand schedule for the United Airlines flight.

If United Airlines does not segment its market and all costs associated with the flight are fixed—it is a scheduled flight—United would choose to price the flight at $318, earning a total revenue of $119,250.

R. J. Abrams would then enjoy an incredible consumer surplus. He would pay only $318, although he would have been willing to pay $2,022. United knows its market and looks enviously at Abrams' consumer surplus. How can they get Abrams to pay $2,022 even when others pay less? United invents first-class travel. It has several advantages. First-class passengers receive exclusive check-ins. Their seats are wider and more comfortable, their meals are more luxurious, and first-class passengers are physically separated from the common folk.

Why would anyone fly first class? Business and UN people, particularly those on expense accounts, like first class. The wealthy and privileged can afford it. Rock and movie stars enjoy a retreat from recognition. First class guarantees no professor or student in the next seat!

United also knows that some people would be willing to pay much more than $318, although not as much as $2,022. United creates a $1,234 coach fare that can be purchased and cancelled anytime prior to flight without penalty. That's the ticket Tanya Donelly bought. She would have preferred the lower fare, but she only made the decision to fly on the day of the flight. She was willing to pay $1,234. By offering a no-advance-purchase fare at $1,234, United

TABLE 11 Demand Schedule for a United Airlines Round-Trip Flight Between Los Angeles and New York

Price	Seats Demanded	Total Revenue
$2,022	10	$ 20,220
1,500	25	37,500
1,234	40	49,360
1,000	60	60,000
800	110	88,000
622	150	93,300
497	225	111,825
318	375	119,250
200	450	90,000

captured her ($1,234 – $318) consumer surplus. United also set up three different advance-purchase fares—three days, seven days, and 14 days with penalty on cancellation, to capture the consumer surpluses of other passengers.

By segmenting its market in this way, United's total revenue increases substantially. Compare Table 12 to Table 11.

As you see, United's ability to segment its market into a multiple-fare system allows it to capture $210,635 – $119,250 = $91,385 of what would have been its passengers' consumer surplus.

Is it any wonder why there are dozens of rates applied to different categories of people and conditions on international as well as domestic flights? Charter flights to Europe, Israel, Japan, Australia, and other attractive holiday locations compete with each other, and with their own rate schedules. Apex fares, purchased in advance for fixed and unchangeable departure times, and special promotional fares applied to specific periods allow the airlines to discriminate even further.

Price discrimination

The practice of offering a specific good or service at different prices to different segments of the market.

There are so many shades of **price discrimination** on these fares, each airline segmenting the market a bit finer to capture differences between obtainable prices and what people are willing to pay, that airline reservation desks sometimes can't keep up with the complicated airfare schedules.

TABLE 12 Demand by Market Segment for a United Airlines Trip Flight Between Los Angeles and New York

Flight Class	Price	Seats Demanded per Flight Class	Revenue per Flight Class
First class	$2,022	= 10	$ 20,220
Regular coach	1,234	40 – 10 = 30	37,020
3-day advance	622	150 – 40 = 110	68,420
7-day advance	497	225 – 150 = 75	37,275
14-day advance	318	375 – 225 = 150	47,700
Total revenue			$210,635

PRICE DISCRIMINATION ALMOST EVERYWHERE

An oligopolist price discriminates in order to turn consumer surplus into oligopoly profits.

Price discrimination on airfares is just the tip of the iceberg. The profitable strategy of segmenting markets through price discrimination is imaginatively applied to so many consumer and producer markets that it's difficult to think of any markets without some form of price discrimination.

Consider, for example, all the products and services offered to senior citizens at discount prices. That's price discrimination. For each product, two different prices exist side by side. Why should firms introduce senior citizen prices? To capture a thought-to-be untapped segment of the demand curve.

Children sit in the same movie theater to see the same film, but pay only half the adult price. Student rates for magazines are less than regular rates. Doesn't *The Wall Street Journal* offer a student rate? Where do you think you are positioned on its demand curve? Do you see why it would expect its total revenue to increase with a price discrimination policy?

Publishers introduce best sellers in hard cover to capture those willing and able to pay premium prices. When that market is exhausted, the same book appears in soft cover at lower prices. Makes sense, doesn't it? Hotels charge regular, commercial, and convention rates for the same room. Student tickets for theater and sporting events represent another example of market segmentation.

"Gray Area" of Price Discrimination

But is it really price discrimination when box seats at the Chicago Lyric Opera are priced at $150, while you could see the same production of *La Boheme* from the fifth balcony for only $38? Some people who know opera insist that it's not the same *La Boheme* when seen from the fifth balcony. Does location change the product? If it does, then is it really price discrimination? Not necessarily. The question, of course, is not restricted to opera. Is watching a Montreal Canadiens hockey game at the Montreal Forum from a center-ice box seat the same game you watch from an upper-balcony behind-the-goal seat? Probably not. On the other hand, if the Montreal Canadiens offer senior citizens a 10 percent discount on *any* seat, that's clearly price discrimination.

In order for a firm to be truly practicing price discrimination, it must provide *identical* services or products at different prices to different customers.

What about the thousands of quality variations that firms introduce among the products they market? Consider oligopoly's strategy of brand multiplication. For example, how different is General Motors' Buick LeSabre from its Buick Park Avenue? The 1994 LeSabre Custom was priced at $25,430. The 1994 Park Avenue was priced at $31,325. General Motors' 1994 Cadillac Sixty Special V-8 was priced at $42,230. Are they *really* different products?

While the Cadillac may be a superior automobile, General Motors' product line may reflect more price discrimination than product differentiation. It offers higher-priced transportation to those willing to pay the higher price. There is no deception. People who pay for Cadillacs, drive Cadillacs.

What works for General Motors works for General Electric. Consider its line of clothes dryers. It runs from the basic unit to the super deluxe model. Each move up the model range provides a more finely tuned selection of cycles and more dryer conveniences. Each model is designed to segment the demand curve as effectively as it dries clothes. Toaster ovens, personal computers, wristwatches, 35mm cameras, furniture, tennis rackets, lawn mowers, and bicycles are a few among thousands of products that allow for such market segmentation.

FIGURE 6 **Cartel Pricing and Output Allocations**

The cartel behaves as if it were a monopoly. In panel *a*, the industry demand curve, *D*, becomes the demand curve facing the cartel. *MR* is the cartel's marginal revenue curve. The cartel's marginal cost is the sum of the firms' *MC* curves. The cartel maximizes profit for its members by producing 14,000 barrels at a price of $8.

In panel *b*, *MC* and *ATC* represent the marginal cost and average total cost curves of an individual firm belonging to the cartel. The firm's assigned quota is 2,000 barrels. Its profit, then, is (*P* – *ATC*) × *Q* = ($8 – $2) × 2,000 = $12,000. But the firm knows that by raising output to 4,000 barrels, where its *MC* = *MR*, its profit would increase to ($8 – $2.50) × 4,000 = $22,000. Cheating under these circumstances is irresistible.

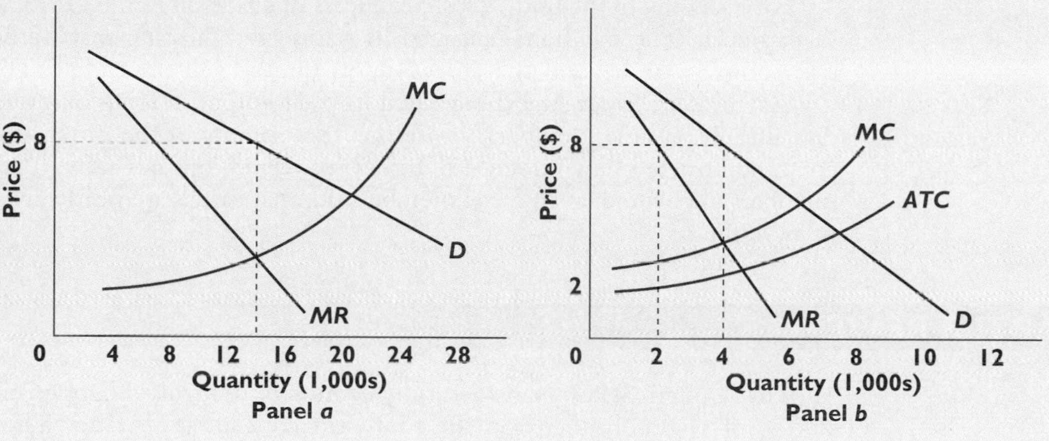

CARTEL PRICING

A firm in a cartel might be able to increase its profits by selling more than its share of cartel output at the cartel price. Or, a cartel member might increase its profits by giving price concessions to a rival's customers.

What about oligopolistic firms bonded together in cartels? How do they determine price? Cartel members put aside their chess-game pricing strategies. There is no need to outguess or outsmart each other. They get together to program common strategy.

Figure 6 depicts how the strategy works for an olive oil cartel.

The cartel takes over the price and output decision making from the firms. It behaves *as if it were* a monopoly. The cartel alone represents the industry. In panel *a*, the cartel's demand curve, *D*, is the industry's demand curve. Its marginal revenue curve is *MR*. The cartel's marginal cost curve, *MC*, is derived by adding together the firms' *MC* curves.

The cartel maximizes industry profit by producing where *MC* = *MR*, at an output of 14,000 barrels and at a price of $8. Each firm is committed to the cartel-derived price of olive oil. They sell at $8, producing only their agreed-upon share of the cartel's output. That output may be allocated among the cartel's firms according to geography—one firm given exclusive rights to the Southwest, another to the Midwest, another to New England—or each firm may be assigned a simple fraction of the industry's output.

Suppose the output quota assigned to the Lynn Eckert Olive Oil Company, a member of the cartel, is 2,000 barrels. Panel *b* depicts Eckert's own demand and cost curves and the price and quantity assigned it by the cartel. If the firm abides by the cartel's rules, its profit is ($8 – $2) × 2,000 = $12,000.

But a serious problem lurks in the shadows of panel *b*. Note that Eckert's own profit-maximizing position—given the cartel price of $8—occurs not at

2,000 barrels but where its own $MC = MR$; that is, at 4,000 barrels. The firm, then, has a strong incentive to cheat on its quota agreement. By producing 4,000 barrels, its profit increases to ($8 – $2.50) × 4,000 = $22,000.

But how does the firm cheat without getting caught? It can produce 4,000 barrels, show 2,000 to the cartel, then launder the other 2,000 barrels through third-party marketing under different brand names or labels. It can also invade restricted markets by giving secret price concessions to the cartel's customers. Of course, what it can do, other firms in the cartel can do as well. And that's why cartels often break down.

For example, in the mid 1980s, producers of crude oil in the OPEC cartel—in particular Iraq and Iran—engaged in semisecret cheating that pushed their own outputs far beyond the agreed-upon quotas. Oil prices fell. To punish OPEC cheaters, Saudi Arabia increased its own output, forcing oil prices down dramatically. OPEC members, aware that the viability of the cartel was threatened, constructed new quotas. Oil prices recovered, but not fully. The OPEC members discovered, as all cartel members do, that cartels are nearly always their own victims.

CHAPTER REVIEW

1. The United States manufacturing economy is highly oligopolistic. Most studies of oligopoly focus on the four-firm concentration ratio. There is no convincing evidence that the degree of concentration in U.S. industry is increasing.

2. High concentration ratios suggest a great deal of market power. However, the market power in a highly concentrated industry may not be distributed evenly, as in an unbalanced oligopoly. Even distribution of market power is observed in balanced oligopoly.

3. Concentration ratios tend to overstate the degree of market power in oligopoly markets because they exclude imports and second-hand markets. U.S. markets are no more concentrated than those found abroad in industrialized countries.

4. Concentration in an industry can increase through horizontal mergers. Vertical mergers link firms that are engaged in supplier-purchaser relationships. Conglomerate mergers link firms in totally unrelated industries. Diversification tends to reduce risk for a conglomerate.

5. Cartel formation involves firms that establish common pricing and market share policies. Cartels are able to behave as monopolists. Although cartels are illegal in the United States, some operate in disguised form. Cartels are observed in other countries and among countries, as with OPEC.

6. Price and output decisions by oligopolists tend to be interdependent. Each firm considers what the other will do if it takes a particular action. Game theory is used to describe this sort of behavior. Game theory predicts some price instability in oligopoly markets as firms attempt to undercut the prices of rivals in order to gain market share.

7. Price leadership models apply to unbalanced oligopoly. A "godfather" firm is a dominant firm in the industry that can dictate price to other smaller firms.

The godfather maximizes its profit by setting output where marginal revenue equals marginal cost. The other firms accept the godfather's price.

8. The oligopolist's demand curve may have a peculiar kink in it arising from the way firms view each other. Above the kink, the oligopolist's demand curve is relatively flat because, if the firm raises its price, rivals will not follow with price increases, so the firm loses significant sales. Below the kink, the demand curve is relatively steep indicating that a price decrease will be matched by rivals and the firm gains little in added sales.

9. The kinked demand curve corresponds to two marginal revenue curves, one flat and one steep, separated by a vertical gap. The firm can maximize profit by setting marginal revenue equal to marginal cost anywhere in the gap. Thus, marginal cost can fluctuate significantly within the gap and the price will not change. The kinked demand curve model suggests price rigidity in oligopoly even if costs change.

10. Brand multiplication is a common oligopolistic strategy to increase market share. Market share is equal to the number of brands times the brand market share.

11. Oligopolists may also price discriminate by segmenting the market in a way that allows the oligopolist to charge consumers what they are willing to pay for the good or service. Price discrimination is readily observable in airfares.

12. Cartel pricing is intended to be cooperative. Each cartel member may be required to restrict output in order to charge the monopoly price. However, individual members may find it in their own profit-maximizing interest to exceed their quotas. When this occurs, the agreed-upon cartel price is difficult to maintain. Secret price concessions also tend to cause cartel agreements to break down.

KEY TERMS

Concentration ratio
Market power
Unbalanced oligopoly
Balanced oligopoly
Horizontal merger
Vertical merger
Conglomerate merger
Cartel
Collusion
Game theory
Price leadership
Kinked demand curve
Brand multiplication
Price discrimination

QUESTIONS

1. Why would firms in oligopoly consider joining a cartel? What do firms give up by doing so? What does the cartel do that oligopolies, acting independently, cannot do?

2. Why is cheating by cartel member firms sometimes irresistible?

3. How does the behavior of an oligopolist differ from the behavior of a monopolist? From a firm in perfect competition? From a firm in monopolistic competition?

4. Why is game theory useful in describing the behavior of firms in oligopoly? According to game theorists, do oligopoly prices tend toward equilibrium? Why, or why not?

5. What are concentration ratios?

6. Is the U.S. economy becoming more oligopolistic? What evidence supports your answer?

7. How have concentration ratios changed in the U.S. economy over the past several decades?

8. Compare concentration ratios in the U.S. economy to those in Japan, Canada, and Western Europe.

9. What is the difference between balanced and unbalanced oligopoly?

10. How does godfathering work? Who decides price? How do other firms in the oligopoly react to the price leader? Why?

11. Explain what is meant by a kinked demand curve. Why is it kinked?

12. Why do prices in oligopolies with kinked demand curves tend to remain rigid even when the firms' costs change?

13. What are the differences among horizontal, vertical, and conglomerate mergers? Give examples of each.

14. Why do firms in oligopoly produce many brands of the same good?

15. What is price discrimination? Why would a firm want to price discriminate? Cite examples.

16. Suppose the demand and supply schedules for watches are as shown in the following table:

Price	Quantity Demanded	Quantity Supplied
$200	1,000	4,000
$150	1,500	3,000
$100	2,000	2,000
$ 50	2,500	1,000

What is the equilibrium price? What is the firm's total revenue? Suppose the firm can price discriminate. Describe what would happen to its total revenue.

17. Graph a kinked demand curve and show its corresponding marginal revenue curve.

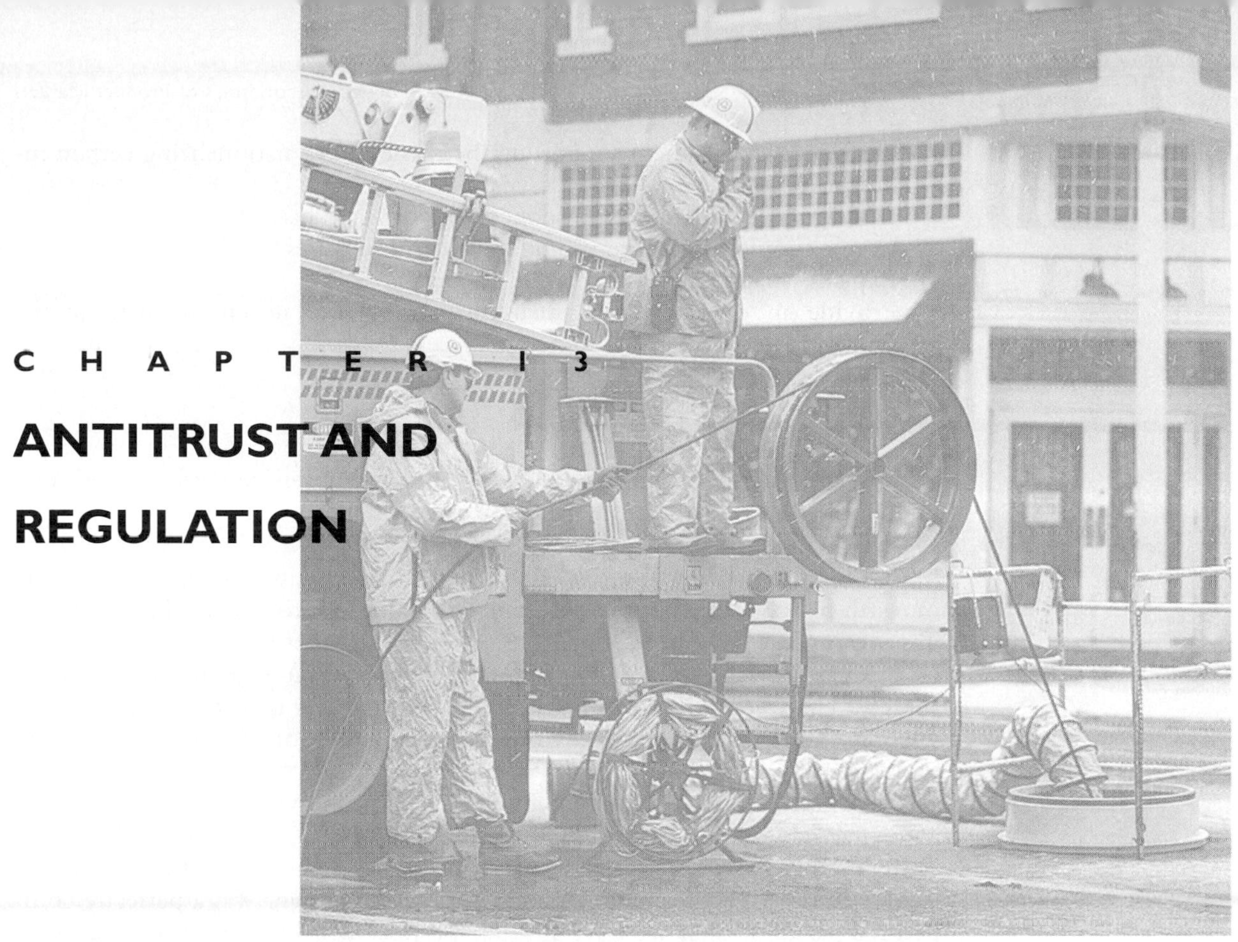

C H A P T E R 1 3

ANTITRUST AND REGULATION

CHAPTER PREVIEW

It is fairly clear after studying the previous two chapters that perfect competition is the exception rather than the rule when it comes to market structures. This scantiness of perfectly competitive markets in the economy makes it virtually impossible for the economy to generate an environment in which firms produce at maximum productive efficiency and at the lowest possible prices. Recall that under monopoly, monopolistic competition, and oligopoly, price is higher and output is lower than under perfect competition. So what should be done, if anything, about monopoly and oligopoly prices? We'll explore this question in the following pages.

After studying this chapter, you should be able to:

- Describe the options available to us for coping with monopoly and oligopoly.
- Draw a graph to depict "fair" price and marginal cost pricing regulation of a natural monopolist.
- Discuss the advantages and drawbacks of each of these types of regulation.
- Explain how deregulation can lead to lower prices for consumers.

- Construct an argument supporting the feasibility of nationalizing certain industries.
- Distinguish contestable from noncontestable markets.
- Give examples of countervailing power in industries.
- Explain what creative destruction means.
- Provide an overview of antitrust legislation and its enforcement in the United States.

Have you ever tried to improve upon an already impressive performance? You know how difficult that can be. Imagine, then, trying to improve upon paradise! Where do you start?

To many economists, the world of perfect competition is the closest thing on earth to economic paradise. It's simply beyond improvement. How can you improve upon $P = MC = MR = ATC$, where all market prices are at their lowest possible levels, all goods are produced at the minimum point on their average cost curves, and the quantities supplied are greater than the quantities that would be forthcoming under any other market condition? No matter how you look at it, *it's magnificent!*

So what's the problem? The only flaw in this otherwise perfect world is the annoying fact that perfect competition does not exist. At least not in our world of high concentration ratios. The real world is essentially one of monopoly, of monopolistic competition, and of oligopoly. If there ever was a perfectly competitive paradise, then we have lost it. We now live in an economic paradise lost.

LEARNING TO COPE WITHOUT PERFECT COMPETITION

How do you regain a lost paradise? Is it even possible? And if it is, do we really want to live in that economic paradise again? There is no consensus among economists on any of these basic questions.

Some believe that perfect competition, if it ever existed, is no longer obtainable. Why not? Because modern technology dictates firm size. The enormous economies of scale that modern technology generates equates bigness with efficiency and at the same time rules out the possibility of easy entry. The idea that our economy today can again be composed of many small firms competing against each other is sheer fantasy. To undo the concentration ratios we observe in modern industry involves the undoing also of the technologies that created them. Of course, that's impossible. To some economists, it's also undesirable.

Because monopoly and oligopoly prices tend to be higher, and their outputs lower, than in perfectly competitive markets, it may make sense in some cases to exercise control over price and output. In other cases, control over oligopoly price and output might not be warranted.

If monopoly and oligopoly are simply inevitable outcomes of modern technology, what then should we do about the monopoly and oligopoly prices they generate?

Even among economists who accept the inevitability of monopoly, very different policies are prescribed concerning what we ought to do. Some insist that government ought to regulate monopoly prices. Others believe government should just take monopolies over, or at least nationalize those particular industries that are absolutely vital to our nation's economic health.

Other economists disagree with the view that monopolies are inherently undesirable. They are convinced that both monopoly and oligopoly present no danger to our economic well-being. They believe we would do better to leave these firms alone. What they advocate as policy is "do nothing," or *laissez-faire*.

Let's survey five competing views on what we ought to do about monopolies and oligopolies. Later, we will examine each in more detail.

Regulating Monopoly

Why regulate? Because monopolies are both inevitable and bad, and regulating what they do is the least disruptive of all effective policy alternatives. That is, if monopoly prices are unacceptable, there's no need to do away with the monopolies. Just do away with their prices. For example, the government can regulate price to conform more closely to the price that would exist if the markets were competitive.

Simple solution? Not exactly. Price regulation may cause other problems and raise a new set of issues. For example, which monopolies should be regulated? Who decides? Government? An independent agency? These issues can create much heated debate even among economists who appreciate the usefulness of government regulation.

Nationalizing the Industry

Other economists accept the inevitability of monopolies and agree they are undesirable but come to different conclusions about how to deal with them. Instead of regulating monopolies, they recommend that the government simply nationalize them, that is, take them over. They believe that compared to regulation, nationalization is less complicated and much less troublesome to administer.

But which monopolies should government take over? All or only some? If only some, then which ones? Who decides what policies these nationalized industries should pursue?

Should government nationalize failing giant monopolies or even oligopolies that despite exercising considerable market power, would still collapse if left alone? That's precisely how Amtrak came into being. Many economists believe that if the government hadn't taken over passenger rail service, the service would have ceased to exist. Creating Amtrak, they argue, was a survival decision.

Laissez-Faire

Laissez-faire

Government policy of nonintervention in market outcomes. Translated, it means "leave it be."

Other economists also see monopolies and oligopolies as inevitable but do not regard them as detrimental to the health of our economy. Unlike the advocates of regulation or nationalization who see a positive role for government, they recommend a **laissez-faire** policy (no government interference) believing that competition and therefore competitive prices exist in markets composed of highly concentrated industries and even monopolies.

To understand their view, think about prizefighters who compete even though there are only two in the ring. The competition is often severe enough to generate knockouts. Admittedly, some fights are fixed, but these are the exception, not the rule. Firms typically behave like prizefighters. Two alone will compete to drive prices to competitive levels.

As well, the *potential threat* of firms entering highly concentrated markets (as distinct from actual entry) is sometimes sufficient to discipline pricing policy. Even monopolies, fearing such *potential* competition, may behave as if there actually were many firms in the market. Economists refer to such markets as **contestable markets.** This potential threat of entry serves to moderate monopoly and oligopoly prices.

Contestable market

A market in which prices in highly concentrated industries are moderated by the potential threat of firms entering the market.

Other economists share the laissez-faire prescription, but see competitive prices as stemming not from contestable markets but from competing economic *power blocs* that cancel out each other's enormous market strengths. Left alone, these competing economic power blocs end up moderating prices to acceptable levels.

Encouraging Concentration

Some economists put a more positive face on the presence of monopoly and oligopoly. These less-competitive markets, they argue, thrive for good reason. They are technically superior. They generate low prices because they are able to capture the economies of scale that bigness offers. Society benefits. Rather than curtail bigness, these economists suggest that the government should do everything possible to promote it.

Splitting Up Monopoly

A very different set of economists reject the idea that bigness is inevitable or technically superior. Instead, they insist that the economies of scale argument regularly used to justify bigness has been overworked and inappropriately applied to most monopoly and oligopoly cases.

Like obesity, they argue, monopolies are neither inevitable nor desirable. If monopolies have no technical superiority, why then do they tend to overshadow competitive markets? *Because monopolies violate the rules of the game.* Monopolies use muscle as well ingenuity to win their way into market control.

If market concentration is neither inevitable nor desirable, what should we do about it? Many economists believe we should shatter monopolies into fragments and establish laws that prevent their restoration. There is no need to regulate monopolies or to run them. Government simply enacts antitrust (meaning antimonopoly) legislation and allows the courts to do the rest. Monopolies who violate antitrust laws now risk becoming criminal offenders.

Hasn't government always been in the business of legislating against undesirable, antisocial behavior? Antitrust advocates believe there is no reason why the marketplace should be exempt. Antitrust legislation should identify anticompetitive market activity as criminal and root it out.

But this is easier said than done. Is the mere presence of monopoly itself sufficient evidence of anticompetitive market activity or must the evidence show intent and *prove* criminal behavior? As you might expect, proponents of antitrust are divided into hardliners and moderates on this issue.

With this cursory outline of the alternative policies behind us, let's look in more detail at the economics of regulation, nationalization, laissez-faire, and antitrust policy.

THE ECONOMICS OF REGULATION

In the state of nature, lions and jackals eat their prey just as monopolies and oligopolies may eat up small competitive firms. We cannot change natural behavior, but there is good reason to believe that we can at least change *what* the predators eat. If you muzzle the lion, you control its diet. This tactic works with monopolies as well. Monopolies will always have a healthy appetite for monopoly profit, but if you take away their price-making function, you take away as well their ability to create monopoly profits.

Regulation

Although ownership of the regulated firm remains in private hands, pricing and production decisions of the firm are monitored by a regulatory agency directly responsible to the government.

That's what government **regulation** of monopoly is about. *It separates monopoly pricing from monopolies.* The price-making function is taken over by government-appointed regulatory commissions. The public utilities commission, for example, decides what rates the electric power company can charge. The price a regulatory commission picks to replace the unregulated monopoly price depends upon its assessment of the company and its market.

Regulating a City Bus Monopoly

Let's begin our analysis of the economics of regulation by supposing that you are the mayor of a fairly large city whose bus company enjoys, as most private bus companies do, a monopoly position. The monopoly is a price maker. It picks its output at $MC = MR$, aiming of course to generate maximum profit. Wouldn't you do the same?

Figure 1 represents the bus company's market. It picks a price of \$1.80 per fare and transports 80,000 passengers per day. Its total revenue is \$1.80 × 80,000 = \$144,000. The average cost per passenger at an 80,000-passenger level is \$1.20. Total cost, then, is \$1.20 × 80,000 = \$96,000. The bus company ends up with a daily profit of \$144,000 – \$96,000 = \$48,000.

A natural monopoly will experience low average total costs of production, which is desirable, but it will charge a higher price than is desirable if left un regulated.

This is a troublesome situation. People without private transportation complain about the high price. A round-trip fare from home to work costs \$3.60, which is prohibitive for many. Since so many retail shops and corner groceries have fallen away to the large franchises and supermarkets at shopping centers, public transportation has become an essential good in the community's life.

There's no reason, of course, to blame the bus monopoly for the \$1.80 fare. It only does what every other firm in the city does. It tries to maximize profit. Competitive firms do the same. Other monopolies do the same. The city's only Triple A baseball team, for example, prices tickets the same way.

But what should you do? If you're like most mayors, you will decide to regulate the public transportation industry, but not the baseball team. Why? Because public transportation directly affects the economic well-being of the entire community, whereas baseball games are a matter of individual leisure-time choice. It's a judgment call, isn't it?

Perhaps the first thing you would want to do is appoint a regulatory commission to decide how to regulate the industry to best serve the community's interests. The focus of the regulation would be on price and output.

If the monopoly fare of \$1.80 is unacceptable, what is appropriate? The regulatory commission knows that if the firm were in perfect competition, it would end up making zero profit. Perhaps that's where to start. It decides to reproduce the competitive $P = ATC$ outcome.

FIGURE 1 **The City Bus Company**

The City Bus Company is a monopoly. The industry demand curve, *D*, is the demand curve the company faces. *MR*, *ATC*, and *MC* are its marginal revenue, average total cost, and marginal cost curves. Left unregulated, the firm prices its fare at \$1.80, providing service to 80,000 passengers.

Deciding that the \$1.80 fare is unacceptable, the community regulates the bus company. It can structure a zero-profit outcome (as in perfect competition), by picking a "fair price" of \$0.90, where $P = ATC$. The number of passenger fares increases to 140,000. The community could instead choose a marginal-cost pricing policy, where $P = MC = \$0.30$. The number of passenger fares increases to 180,000. But at 180,000, $ATC = \$0.70$. The community subsidizes the bus company by \$0.40 per fare to cover losses emerging from its marginal-cost pricing option.

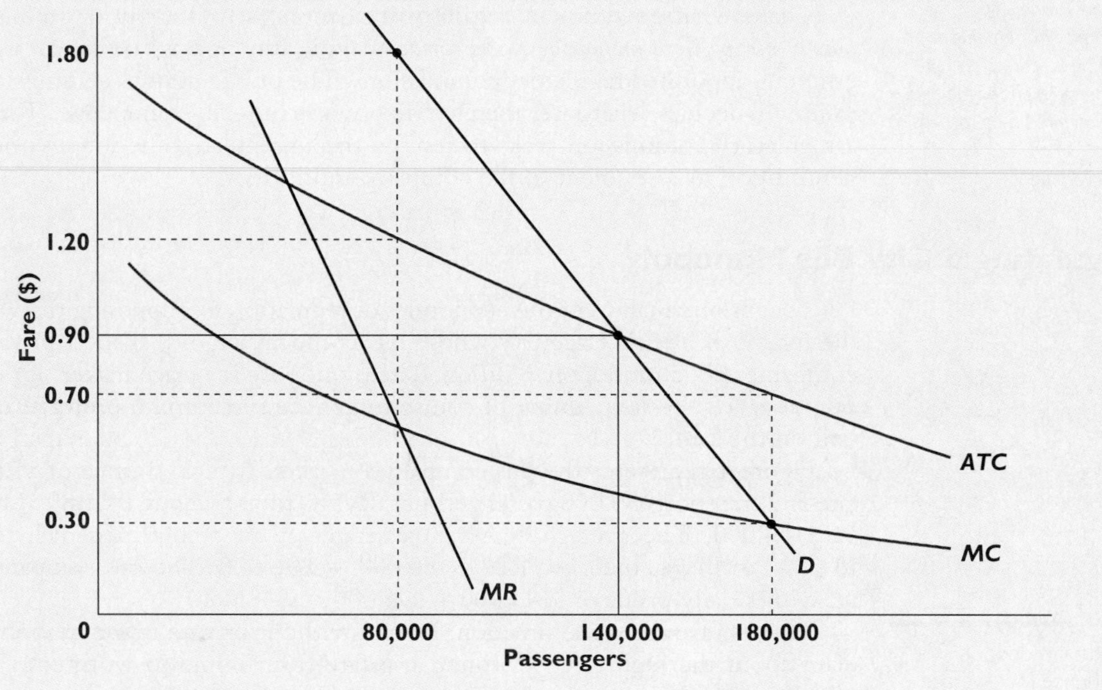

Setting a "Fair" Price: $P = ATC$

Look again at Figure 1. Suppose the regulatory commission sets the bus fare at \$0.90, where $P = ATC$. It considers \$0.90 a "fair" price because the bus company, stripped of its monopoly profits, is entitled to cover its costs. Of course, the company still would enjoy normal profit, as it would under perfect competition.

A price set equal to average total cost is fair to the monopolist because it allows for a normal profit.

What about the passengers? They appear to benefit. After all, the bus fare falls from \$1.80 to \$0.90. As a direct result, the volume of traffic increases from 80,000 to 140,000 passengers.

Is pricing according to the $P = ATC$ rule as uncomplicated as it appears in Figure 1? Not by a long shot. Once price is fixed at average total cost, the question becomes: Who regulates the regulated monopoly's average total cost?

For example, who determines whether new buses are needed? If you were the regulated monopolist and knew that the commission sets price equal to your average total cost, wouldn't you want to buy a string of new buses? The new and most heavily equipped buses might be frightfully expensive, but since the commission sets $P = ATC$ anyway, why not? What's the loss?

Who determines whether bus drivers should receive salary bonuses? Imagine what the average total cost curve of Figure 1 would look like if bus drivers earned the equivalent of NBA basketball salaries. Since the bus company is prohibited from profit making, why should management be concerned about keeping labor costs under control?

The ATC curve, under these conditions, could quickly shift upward, and with it, the $P = ATC$ position. After a while, the "fair" price might begin to look less and less fair.

What has happened here? In an honest effort to control the high monopoly price, the regulatory commission, through price regulation, has simply substituted one form of market inefficiency for another.

But regulatory commissions can read Figure 1 and spot the problem of cost drift just as well as you can. They can, and many do, monitor costs as well. Bus drivers may go on strike just because regulatory commissions are vigilant on cost containment. The firm may want new buses, but it doesn't always get them. The idea of fair price is seldom treated lightly by regulatory commissions.

Applying Marginal Cost Pricing: $P = MC$

Marginal cost pricing

A regulatory agency's policy of pricing a good or service produced by a regulated firm at the firm's marginal cost, P = MC.

Another option the regulatory commission might pursue is **marginal cost pricing,** setting $P = MC$. This occurs in Figure 1 at 180,000 passengers and at a price of \$0.30.

Compare the $P = ATC$ choice of \$0.90 with 140,000 passengers to the $P = MC$ choice at \$0.30 with 180,000 passengers. Why the difference? Why would any commission prefer $P = MC$? Because $P = MC$ indicates society's optimal use of resources.

Look at fair price $P = ATC$. The value that people place on a service is measured by the price they are willing to pay. At 140,000 passengers, the value people place on transportation is higher than the value of the resources used to produce that transportation. The price they are willing to pay for one more trip is \$0.90; the value of the resources needed to produce that trip—measured by marginal cost—is \$0.40. That is, at 140,000 passengers $P > MC$. Wouldn't society be better served if more passengers rode the buses?

$P = MC$ at 180,000. The 180,000th passenger is willing to pay \$0.30, precisely the value society places on the resources used to produce the 180,000th ride. This $P = MC$ condition describes the socially optimum use of resources.

Setting price equal to marginal cost may provide for optimum use of resources, but it requires that the monopolist be subsidized. Do you see why?

But if the regulatory commission agrees to this price, the firm's revenue is only \$0.30 × 180,000 = \$54,000. But now ATC = \$0.70, so that total cost is \$0.70 × 180,000 = \$126,000. You see the problem, don't you? The bus company suffers a loss. If the commission wants the regulated monopoly to produce bus service at $P = MC$, then it must provide the firm with a \$72,000 subsidy.

What about the passengers? Do they really get a \$0.30 bus ride? Not really. The \$0.30 excludes the subsidy. Somebody has to pay it. The \$72,000 subsidy comes from the taxpayers. In other words, the ticketed fare may be \$0.30, but the ATC for the community is \$0.70. Non-bus users now find themselves paying for services they do not use, creating a new kind of inefficiency in the economy.

Who Regulates the Regulators?

Why would a regulatory commission end up protecting the monopolies it is intended to regulate?

Although the intent of regulation is to correct the abuses of monopoly, the outcome can sometimes produce quite the opposite effect. Instead of regulating monopolies, regulatory commissions may end up protecting them.

Who are the regulators? Who gets appointed to commissions? Typically, they include people who can provide useful, specific expertise to the commission's deliberations. It seems reasonable to expect at least some of the commissioners to have a working knowledge of the industry and the finer points of its management problems. This kind of expertise generally comes only after years of experience inside the industry.

These commissioners certainly are not there to undermine the commission's mission, nor do they always represent management's view. But their knowledge and experience command considerable respect on the commission, and their appreciation of management's position—having been there themselves—sometimes creates the impression (if not the fact) that the regulators are the very people whose industry is being regulated.

It is not a question of industry conspiracy, but it can be a delicate matter. For example, should ex-policemen be appointed to a city's civilian police review board? After all, who better appreciates the problems that police confront daily on duty? Who can better advise on procedure? But is that the view that should prevail?

The ICC shielded the railroad industry from the competition the trucking industry presented.

An example of regulators using regulation on behalf of the regulated is the Interstate Commerce Commission's handling of the transportation industry. Congress created the ICC in 1887 to regulate the prices railways were charging along noncompetitive routes. Over the years, the ICC established rate schedules to check the railroad's monopoly power and to protect rural communities against railroad price discrimination.

But by the end of the 1930s, the transportation industry had changed dramatically. The development of extensive highway networks matched the furious output of Detroit's automobile and truck assembly lines. Almost overnight, independent trucking firms mushroomed across the country, providing competitive freight transportation for both long and short hauling.

The railroads' monopoly on transportation was broken. But rather than allow this new trucking competition to force freight rates down, the ICC's response was to contain it. Almost instinctively, the ICC became the protector of the railroads. It expanded its regulatory range to include trucking. The ICC decided how many and which truckers could carry what goods which way on what routes. Truckers were tied to rates that served to protect the railroads. In other words, far from regulating monopoly in the interests of the consumer, the ICC now served to stifle competition.

The ICC's behavior was not unique in the world of regulation. The Federal Communications Commission, established in 1934 to regulate the telephone, telegraph, radio, and later television industries, has also played the dual role of regulator and protector. The Civil Aeronautics Board, established in 1938 to regulate commercial aviation; the Securities and Exchange Commission, established in 1934 to oversee the corporate securities market; the Federal Maritime Board, established in 1950 to regulate intercoastal and international shipping; and the Federal Energy Regulatory Commission, established in 1959 to regulate the energy industry; have all played, at some time, the protector's role.

Pan Am is gone, Eastern Airlines is gone, Braniff Airlines is gone, and several other airlines may well be next on the casualty list as the competitive battle for the air passenger dollar intensifies. On the other hand, Delta and American Airlines still remain strong competitors in the now deregulated industry. Newcomers like Southwest energize the industry's competition.

The Economics of Deregulation

Deregulation

The process of converting a regulated firm into an unregulated firm.

Deregulation of the airline industry actually encouraged greater competition and a lower price for air travel.

"Throwing the engines in reverse" is perhaps the best way to describe the economics of **deregulation.** It reflects a recent and widely held view among economists and government that the regulations imposed over the years for many industries have become obsolete, and in some instances, even counterproductive. As a result, a movement toward deregulation in many parts of the economy took place in the 1980s.

But the dismantling process was never seen as a miracle cure to the problems associated with regulating industry. Nor was there any intention of wiping regulation entirely out of government policy or of allowing a return to monopoly pricing. Industry concentration is still viewed by many economists as a serious economic problem, and the use of regulation to control pricing and output in concentrated industries is still regarded as legitimate and effective.

CLIPPING CAB'S WINGS

The deregulation of commercial aviation is one of President Jimmy Carter's legacies. In 1978 he lured Alfred Kahn out of Cornell University to head the Civilian Aeronautics Board. That appointment was not unlike putting a hungry fox in charge of the chicken house. Kahn immediately went to work dismantling the Board's regulatory powers and ended up doing away with the Board altogether.

Initially, as new airline companies were established and more flights were added to already existing lines, unprofitable routes were dropped and price competition for the growing air traffic was encouraged. Almost instantaneously, the highly rigged airfare schedules disintegrated, resulting in bargain basement prices. At the same time, the innovation of the hub-and-spoke system expanded service by the major airlines and by the newly formed commuter lines.

But not all economists are comfortable with deregulation. Although firm entry and firm expansion did create greater competition and lower airfares during the 1980s and 1990s, it also forced many of the new and some of the well-established airlines into bankruptcy. In the long run, some economists fear, the

A commonplace scene, isn't it? In this case, it's Bell Atlantic, installing fiber optic cable in Roanoke, Virginia.

industry's concentration ratio may recover to its pre-deregulation levels, and airfares may even surpass their pre-deregulation highs.

FOR WHOM THE BELL TOLLS

Perhaps the most dramatic deregulation event of the 1980s was the uncrowning of American Telephone and Telegraph (AT&T), which controlled every aspect of telephone service in the United States. People did not own their own phones. They had to rent them from AT&T and use AT&T's domestic and overseas lines. But the development of satellite technology paved the way for deregulation. It became technologically possible for smaller firms to compete with AT&T on price and service.

In 1978 the Federal Communication Commission ruled that AT&T must provide its competitors who produced telephone equipment with access to its lines. This allowed GTE, MCI, and others to compete with the former monopoly on telephone service. Long-distance rates began to fall almost immediately after these new firms entered the industry.

An earlier ruling by the FCC had disallowed AT&T's monopoly on the sale of telephone hardware and gave AT&T's competitors access to its lines. Consumers now had the choice of buying their phones from a variety of competing firms.

THE ECONOMICS OF NATIONALIZATION

Nationalization

Government ownership of a firm or industry. Price and production decisions are made by an administrative agency of the government.

The economics of **nationalization** is not at all complicated. The government simply buys the shares held by the shareholders of the targeted monopoly. In some economies, nationalizing an industry is an even less complicated procedure. Governments simply confiscate the property.

How do governments buy firms? Typically, they exchange their own bonds for the nationalized firm's shares. Assessing the firm's net worth could be a problem, but as a rule, governments in the business of nationalizing have been rather generous.

The government's main concern is hardly the measure of the firm's net worth. Instead, it is what to do with the firm once it has it.

Price Options Facing Government

Consider the city bus monopoly of Figure 1. Suppose the municipal government, unhappy with the $1.80 fare, decides not to regulate the company, but to buy it out. Once it owns the company, what does the city do?

Who runs the bus company? Most likely the same people who ran it before! Why should the city want to replace an experienced management staff? The reason for the government's takeover was the monopoly's price, not its personnel.

What about management's view of the takeover? Who owns the bus company should make little difference to managers. Their expertise is still applicable. Would the bus drivers feel uneasy? Their paychecks are now signed by the city's financial agent. But if the banks still cash the checks, should they complain? They run the same buses along the same lines to pick up the same passengers. Do you suppose the passengers, paying the same fare, care one way or the other?

Of course, somebody has to decide what the fares ought to be. If it isn't the regulatory commission, then it's some agency of government. The options available to the agency are precisely those that faced the regulatory commission. After all, they both understand Figure 1.

The government is unlikely to run the bus company as a profit-maximizing monopoly, charging a $1.80 fare and making $48,000 monopoly profit. Although it is possible. The mayor could argue that the $1.80 fare is in the "public interest," since the $48,000 profit adds to city revenue, allowing the government to reduce taxes by $48,000. And cutting taxes is always popular. The government agency can also choose either a $P = ATC$ or a $P = MC$ pricing strategy. The issues involved in each are precisely the issues faced by the regulatory commission.

Can the Government Run Industry Efficiently?

Whatever the evidence, many people strongly believe that government-run industry is inherently inefficient. *One reason why government industry often appears to be struggling is that government often takes over a struggling industry!* Amtrak replaced a troubled set of private railroads. Before Amtrak came into being, the railroads that became Amtrak were on the brink of bankruptcy. This situation was not unique. The coal industry in England was in terrible shape when the British government took it over in 1946.

No one, not even the government, believes that nationalizing sick industries is perfect medicine. Why, then, does the government knowingly get itself involved in losing propositions? Because it views the alternatives as worse. Allowing private railroads to go under may get the government off the hook, but it may not serve the economy well.

But not all nationalization is designed to prop up failing private industry. Many economies resort to nationalization for the same reason other economies resort to regulated industry, that is, to control prices. For example, international airlines come in all ownership forms. Some are unregulated private firms, some are government regulated, and others are government owned.

OWNERSHIP AND EFFICIENCY

It is virtually impossible to distinguish ownership on the basis of performance. How would you know that El Al Airlines is owned by the government of Israel? Or that British Airways is privately owned? Have you ever visited Ireland? The

Irish landscape is even greener than the beautiful green depicted in *National Geographic*! You can fly there on Aer Lingus and never know that the government of Ireland owns the controlling interest in the airline.

Do you think the average cost of flying an Aer Lingus passenger from Boston to Dublin is any higher than the average cost of flying that route on a privately owned airline? Do you suppose Aer Lingus uses more fuel? Or its aircrafts depreciate faster? Or its pilots are any less experienced?

Our state university systems are government owned. The University of North Carolina, for example, is administered by the State of North Carolina. The government determines the tuition, fees, and level of student enrollment just as Duke University, a private institution in Durham, North Carolina, decides its tuition, fees, and level of enrollment. Would you suppose professors at the state-owned university are less efficient than professors at Duke? Students at both universities probably use the same text for Economics 101!

Even if you're a football fan, you may not know that NFL's Green Bay Packers is government owned. It is owned by the municipality of Green Bay, Wisconsin. The Packers are, in effect, as government run as the U.S. Post Office is. Do you think the city is less able to hire a credible team? Do you suppose the Packer linebackers are less eager to eat up quarterbacks because the Packers are government owned?

BUT THE GOVERNMENT CAN'T GO BROKE

Why, then, are so many people, including many economists, convinced that government industry naturally breeds inefficiency? The one explanation that makes the view seem so reasonable is the simple fact that governments cannot go bankrupt.

The viability of a private firm depends, ultimately, upon making a profit. The firm can absorb short-run losses and can muddle through with low-level profit in the longer run, but what it cannot do is absorb large losses over long periods of time. One day, it just runs out of money.

Not so with a government-owned firm. It can absorb continuing losses without ever having to face the prospect of closure. Why? Because it can usually rely on tax revenue to subsidize its operation. This possibility—and the certainty of the government's survival—must blunt the cutting edge of its management. By removing the possibility of failure, government managers also lose the incentive to excel. Sound reasonable?

THE ECONOMICS OF LAISSEZ-FAIRE

Other economists see the same industry concentrations very differently from those who advocate regulation or nationalization. They see no reason to follow either. Although they acknowledge the presence and inevitability of bigness, they are not at all disturbed by it. Why not?

The reason is that even with considerable industry concentration, there is still enough competition to generate acceptable price and output levels.

The Theory of Contestable Markets

Many students don't cheat on exams, not because there are so many faculty proctoring the exam but because the few who are proctoring may catch a

A monopolist or an oligopolist can't take full advantage of its market power if there is a threat of entry.

cheater copying someone else's work. That threat alone is enough to keep other students who may think of cheating from doing so.

The theory of *contestable markets* is based on that kind of thinking. The primary consideration that keeps firms in highly concentrated industries from charging a high, noncompetitive price is not the number of firms actually competing in the industry, *but rather the threat of other firms entering the industry to compete.* Many oligopolistic markets are contestable in this way.

For example, the government-owned Canadian National Railways does not stop in every small town served by the privately owned Canadian Pacific Railways, but the government is nonetheless confident that the Canadian Pacific will not take advantage of its monopoly position in those one-railroad communities. What restrains the Canadian Pacific? It's fear that the Canadian National would change its routing to include those communities. After all, the Canadian National has the equipment and labor force to quickly make the shift.

NBC may be the only television network with an affiliate station in Winnemucca, Nevada, but if its advertising rates and profits there were high by industry standards, CBS, ABC, and Fox would probably rush into the market. In other words, the fact that an industry is highly concentrated does not necessarily mean the absence of moderate pricing. As long as markets are contestable, firms still end up with competitive-like pricing.

The theory of contestable markets challenges, then, the necessity of regulating or nationalizing industries that operate in highly concentrated markets. Society, according to this argument, will be better served by a policy of laissez-faire.

Critics of the contestable markets theory find the argument compelling but its applicability terribly limited. The idea that firms can easily switch resources from one line of production to another just doesn't ring true. Examples cited, such as the Canadian railroad competition, are the exception to the rule and even in that market, switching lines involves considerable cost. Firms just don't behave that way. If firms are worried about threats of entry, shouldn't the firms who are threatening entry also worry that by actually entering the market, they will run down profits? What, then, is the significance of the threat? Proponents of regulation and nationalization do not believe that the contestable markets logic applies to the real world.

A market isn't contestable if significant barriers to entry exist.

The Theory of Countervailing Power

If competition doesn't exist among firms *within* a highly concentrated industry, then according to some economists, it may still exist *among* highly concentrated industries. This inter-industry competition may be sufficient to generate acceptable prices anyway.

How does it work? Concentration creates economic power. The economy is a collection of economic power blocs competing with each other. *Power begets* ***countervailing power.*** The economy's markets are polarized into four competing power blocs: industrial, labor, agricultural, and retail. Their prices are determined by their relative strengths.

Countervailing power

The exercise of market power by an economic bloc is ultimately counteracted by the market power of a competing bloc so that no bloc exercises undue market power.

Consider, for example, the relations between the industrial and retail blocs. Suppose the canned food oligopoly, composed of Lipton, Libby, and Campbell, faces a retail market composed of thousands of competitive grocery stores. The oligopoly's market strength *vis à vis* the grocery stores allows it to charge high wholesale prices. It ends up capturing most of the profit in the canned food market.

The existence of opposing power blocs restrains the exercise of oligopoly power.

After all, what choices do the small grocery stores have? If they want to sell canned foods, they can only sell Lipton's, Libby's, or Campbell's. Competition among themselves drives their own retail prices down to the costs fixed by the oligopoly. At best, they end up with normal profit.

But it's precisely that kind of market power imbalance that triggers the creation of a countervailing power. In this case, the power comes not from the small retail grocers, although consumer cooperatives sometimes work, but rather from the transformation of the entire retail grocery industry. Oligopoly replaces competition within retail trade. Kroger, IGA, Jewel, Safeway, Winn Dixie, Grand Union, and other supermarket chains develop to displace the small grocery stores.

While Lipton, Libby, and Campbell can dictate price to a small grocer, they can't dictate to these large chains. Market power checks market power. Wholesale prices are now negotiated between two oligopolies, producing a more equitable distribution of profits between them. *All this happens without government involvement.*

KMart, True Value, and Sears check the market power of oligopolies that produce light durable goods. Corporate agribusinesses replace family farms to restore the power balance between the industrial and agricultural blocs. Labor unions provide the countervailing power in wage rate negotiations with oligopolistic firms in the industrial bloc.

Theory of Creative Destruction

Creative destruction

Effective competition that exists not among firms within highly concentrated industries but between the highly concentrated industries themselves. Such competition assures competitive prices.

Another theory explaining why government intervention in the market is unnecessary—much like the theory of countervailing power—is the theory of **creative destruction.** It argues that although it may be difficult for firms to break into a monopolized industry, it has been much less difficult for them to break the monopolized industry's hold on a market.

For example, while no new steel firms can compete with a steel monopoly, an aluminum monopoly competes with it in the automobile and construction markets. Similarly, in the energy market, oil competes with coal, not new coal firms with an established coal firm.

Technological change might be a very effective regulator of monopoly power over the long run.

Monopolies, then, are destroyed by this creative process. Look at railroads. In the prime of life, their economic power was virtually unopposed. They set discriminatory freight rates that created fortunes for the robber barons. What finally trimmed railroad rates was not more railroads coming into the industry, but rather the new trucking and airline industries.

What brought the coal oligopoly to its knees was not more coal competition but the advent of petroleum. What checked the economic power of the bottling oligopoly was not the influx of more bottling firms, but the aluminum can. Examples abound. They reflect our real competitive life. The role of government? None. Automatically, countervailing powers are created within the economy to assure that even in an economy characterized by highly concentrated markets, acceptable prices still obtain.

THE ECONOMICS OF ENCOURAGING MONOPOLY

Some economists not only reject the view that monopoly is injurious to the economy's well-being, but actually prefer monopoly structures to competition.

FIGURE 2 **Firm Size and Economies of Scale**

ATC_c and ATC_m are the average cost curves of two firms in an industry. The ATC_c curve describes a smaller firm with relatively limited capacity. At low levels of output, the smaller firm's ATC is less than that of the larger firm. For example, at output 100, at ATC_c's minimum, $ATC_c = \$6$, and $ATC_m = \$10$. Note that beyond output of 175, the ATC of the larger firm is less than the ATC of the smaller firm. At 900, the large firm's minimum $ATC_m = \$2$.

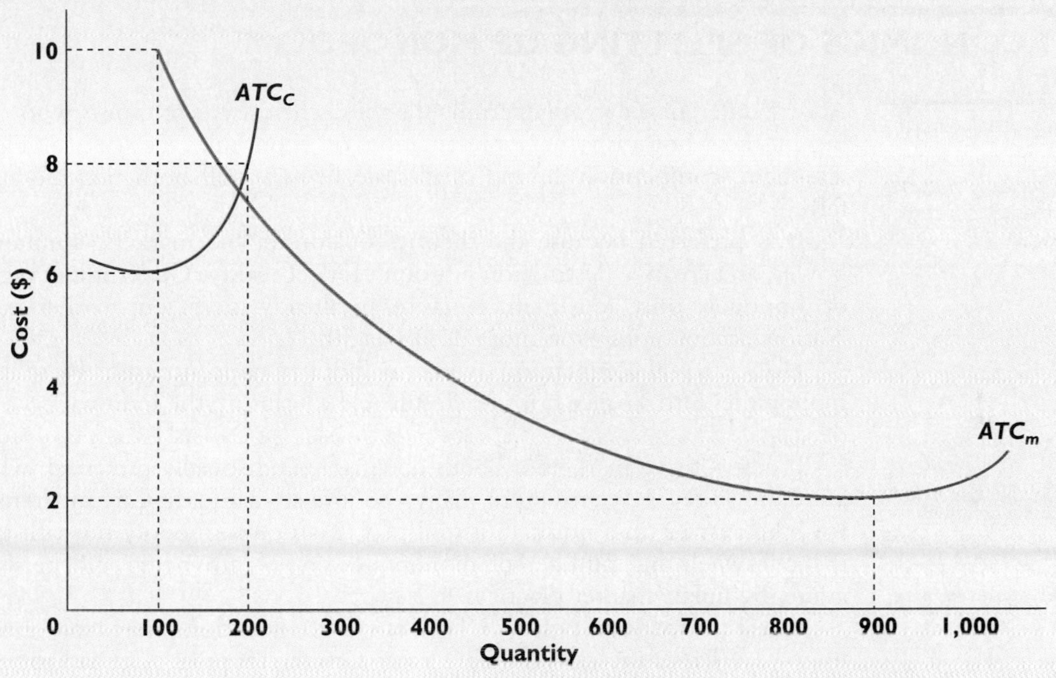

If a monopolist can offer lower average total costs of production than a competitive firm could, then there may be little justification for regulating the monopolist.

Why? Firm size makes a difference. As we saw in Chapter 11, monopoly can take advantage of economies of scale. Figure 2 restates Schumpeter's argument developed in Chapter 11.

Even under the most efficient conditions, the competitive firm in Figure 2 cannot compete with the monopoly. Compare ATC_c and ATC_m. The competitive firm simply cannot produce beyond 100 units without encountering substantial increases in its ATC. Its $ATC = \$6$ at 100 units but increases to $ATC = \$8$ at 200 units. The monopoly's ATC reaches its minimum at 900 units. There, $ATC = \$2$. It's no contest.

If Figure 2 represents our modern economy, you can see why some economists don't believe that the government serves any useful function by controlling prices. If the government is to play any role at all, it should promote bigness.

In fact, that's what government often ends up doing, even while extolling the virtues of competition. Monopolies can turn some of their profits into innovation-producing research. We benefit from newer, higher-quality and lower-priced goods. The proof is in the legislation. The government understands the need to encourage new product development and creates a **patent** system that gives an innovating firm 17 years of legal protection from competition on newly developed technology. The competitive firm usually cannot generate new technology because it lacks the profit cushion for failed experiments.

Patent

Exclusive right granted by government to market a product or process for 17 years.

What role can government play? According to laissez-faire advocates, it can foster an environment favorable to innovating industries. It can encourage basic research and industrial development by providing a wide assortment of tax incentives. In short, it can alter some of the costs associated with dynamic change.

THE ECONOMICS OF SPLITTING UP MONOPOLY

If competition is preferred to market concentration, then it is certainly possible to make market concentration illegal.

A very different view of government's role is held by economists who reject as big-business hogwash the representation of economies of scale in Figure 2. To them, competition among small-scale firms is still both possible and preferred.

It is preferred because the theories of contestable markets, countervailing power, and creative destruction just don't reflect reality. Government regulation of monopoly only adds inefficiency to an already inefficient market structure. Nationalization adds even more dead weight.

How can real competition overcome industry concentration? By splitting up monopolies into smaller firms, each still able to capture the industry's economies of scale.

Antitrust policy

Laws that foster market competition by prohibiting monopolies and oligopolies from exercising excessive market power.

If competitive markets are both obtainable and socially preferred, why then are there so few? According to many economists who advocate **antitrust policy,** the answer, in a nutshell, is foul play. Natural monopoly notwithstanding, the overwhelming number of monopolies come into being and persist, they argue, by unfair market practices.

Is real competition possible? To them, there is nothing inevitable about monopoly. What is the government's role? Crime-stopping. The task of government is to identify unfair market behavior, identify the market violators, curtail their activities, and restore fairness to the marketplace. *This can be done by legislation.*

This view that competition is still doable and preferable is an integral part of our democratic tradition and free enterprise philosophy. Our long and continuing history of antimonopoly legislation attests to our belief in it. Competing views about monopoly's inevitability, even with its economic advantages, have always been outside our mainstream thinking. Let's look at the history of U.S. antitrust legislation.

THE HISTORY OF ANTITRUST LEGISLATION

An 1881 *Atlantic Monthly* article by Henry D. Lloyd, entitled "Story of a Great Monopoly," cited John D. Rockefeller of Standard Oil as the nation's prime trust-maker. Rockefeller epitomized everything that was wrong with our economy. Standard Oil's tyrannical growth to control the nation's petroleum refining industry destroyed any semblance of workable competition and signalled to many what our economic future would look like. Many were frightened.

Lloyd's piece found a ready audience. There was already considerable antimonopoly agitation in the country. By 1888, an election year, both Republicans and Democrats sensed the popularity of this issue and vowed to break the trusts. The Democrats even put antitrust policy into their party platform.

The Sherman Antitrust Act of 1890

In 1890, Senator John Sherman, brother of Civil War general William Sherman, reintroduced a bill he had twice before offered the Senate. The bill was designed to protect market competition from the treachery of monopoly activity. This time, it passed the Senate with only one dissenting vote and cleared the House unanimously. It was signed into law on July 2, 1890 by the Republican President Benjamin Harrison.

The act contains eight sections, but the main thrust is found in Sections 1 and 2. Section 4 invests the Department of Justice with powers to enforce the law.

Section 1. *Every contract, combination in the form of trust or otherwise, or conspiracy, in restraint of trade or commerce among the several states, or with foreign nations, is declared to be illegal.*

Section 2. *Every person who shall monopolize, or attempt to monopolize, or combine or conspire with any other person or persons, to monopolize any part of the trade or commerce among several states, or with foreign nations, shall be deemed guilty of a felony. . .*

Section 4. *The several circuit courts of the United States are hereby invested with jurisdiction to prevent and restrain violations of this Act; and it shall be the duty of the several district attorneys of the Unites States, in their respective districts, under the direction of the Attorney General, to institute proceedings in equity to prevent and restrain such violations.*

The Sherman Act just wasn't specific enough to effectively limit monopoly power in the United States.

It reads tough, but in practice the act seemed to be a paper dragon. At first, the problem was its vagueness. What was meant by "restraint of trade" or by "monopolizing" or by "conspiracy"? And how does the Department of Justice go about proving its case?

In the decade that followed—in spite of Justice's newly created Antitrust Division that successfully prosecuted Standard Oil and American Tobacco—it became increasingly obvious that a better description of what constitutes illegal monopoly practice was needed. This came with the Clayton Act of 1914.

The Clayton Act of 1914

The Clayton Act gave the courts explicit direction. It described four specific anticompetitive activities: (1) price discrimination among purchasers, (2) exclusive contracts where purchasers would agree, as a condition of sale, not to buy from competitors, (3) one firm's acquisition of voting stock in another firm in the same industry, and (4) board members who served on boards of directors of competing firms.

Clayton was on target. Price discrimination was widely practiced. For example, a firm with an already large share of a national market could cut prices in regional markets where it faced competition, leaving its prices untouched in safer, less-competitive markets. This two-price system knocked out competition and made potential competitors think twice about entering.

Exclusive contracts also reduced competition. For example, if a large, nationally known sports equipment firm made sporting goods shops agree not to sell its competitors' equipment, then the large firm's competition disappears. Market muscle creates monopoly, which pumps up more muscle. If such arrangements were standard practice, new firms would hardly stand a chance.

ADDED PERSPECTIVE

Drug Firms Accused of Violating Antitrust Laws

A group of 20 chain and independent drugstores sued seven major pharmaceutical companies, alleging that the drug makers violated antitrust laws by charging different prices to different customers.

The group, which claims to represent 5,000 retail drugstores, alleges that the drug companies illegally discriminated by refusing to give the pharmacies the same deep discounts on drugs that the drug companies offered to mail-order competitors and managed care organizations.

The lawsuit, filed in federal court yesterday, challenges a widespread industry practice of giving managed care customers, such as health maintenance organizations and some big mail-order concerns, steep discounts. Drugstores claim they haven't been able to get the same discounts, putting them at a competitive disadvantage.

The lawsuit "will have a sweeping impact on our industry and benefit millions of American consumers, if we are successful," said Alex Grass, chairman and chief executive officer of Rite Aid Corp. The drugstores said they are seeking redress for an alleged excess "hundreds of millions of dollars a year" they pay because of the discounting. He said the pharmaceutical companies are "making an exorbitant profit on the products we buy."

The drugstore group, led by Rite Aid and Revco D. S. Inc., represents about 10 percent of the country's retail drugstores. The pharmaceutical companies targeted in the legal action are American Home Products Corp., Ciby-Geigy Corp., Monsanto's G. D. Searle & Co., Glaxo Inc., Pfizer Inc., SmithKline Beecham Pharmaceuticals Co., and Schering-Plough Corp.

Managed care organizations have been successful in extracting steep discounts from pharmaceutical companies, in part because they can threaten to substitute one drug for a cheaper, equivalent one on a formulary—the list of drugs the organization recommends (and sometimes requires) its doctors prescribe. In order to get on or stay on a formulary, drug companies often must offer steep discounts to match or better prices of competing, equivalent drugs.

But drugstores usually must carry all the drugs that physicians in their community might prescribe, and they lack the influence over physicians that a managed care organization wields.

According to the drugstores, they pay as much as 1,245 percent more for drugs than managed care concerns. American Home's heart drug Inderal costs HMOs $4.12 for 100 tablets, but community pharmacies pay $48.31, the group claims. Searle's heart drug Calan costs managed care concerns $3.90 for 100 tablets, while drugstores pay $22.91. A Searle spokesman declined to verify the prices.

The lawsuit, which was filed in federal court in Harrisburg, PA, claims the drug companies violated laws against price discrimination and price fixing. Noticeably absent from the list of defendants were some of the biggest drug companies, such as Merck & Co., and Bristol-Myers Squibb Co. Mr. Grass, however, said more defendants may be added later as further evidence is accumulated.

Discussion

What violation(s) of the antitrust laws apply to the drug stores' charge against the drug firms?

Source: *The Wall Street Journal*, October 15, 1993. Reprinted by permission of *The Wall Street Journal*,

Buying voting stock was a more direct strategy of locking up competitive markets. For example, if the same sports equipment firm bought up the voting stock of its competitors, then it could establish monopoly prices for the entire industry.

Another way of killing competition was for people to sit on boards of directors of competing firms associated with the same product. Imagine a board member of the sports equipment firm also sitting as a board member of other sporting goods firms. Convenient? Interlocking directorships of this kind could well affect business decisions. Other firms in the industry—competitors—would have reason to suspect unfair practices.

The Federal Trade Commission Act of 1914

In the same year as the Clayton Act, 1914, Congress created a second means of antitrust enforcement when it passed the Federal Trade Commission (FTC) Act. The FTC was established specifically to monitor markets. It was charged with investigating unfair and deceptive practices, and could, if it believed a situation warranted it, *initiate* complaints. After calling a public hearing on a complaint, it could issue a "cease and desist" order. The cited firm could, of course, appeal the order in court.

The FTC was expected to be a major contributor to the effectiveness of antitrust legislation. Prior to the FTC, the Antitrust Division of the Justice Department handled both the investigation and the prosecution of anticompetitive activity.

Plugging the Loopholes

The Sherman, Clayton, and FTC acts are the core of modern antitrust legislation. Two additional acts extended their coverage.

The Robinson-Patman Act of 1936 amended the Clayton Act on price discrimination. It was designed to help small stores survive the blitz of growing retail chains. Until the act was passed, large firms could offer price discounts to selected buyers, often with the intent to damage their smaller competitors. The smaller firms, naturally, claimed that this practice was unfair. Under Robinson-Patman, *selective* discount deals became illegal.

The Celler-Kefauver Merger Act of 1950 closed a loophole that had been used to circumvent the Clayton Act. Clayton had made it illegal to buy a competitor's voting stock. But it said nothing about buying a competitor's patents, plant, and equipment. The consequences, of course, were the same as if the competition's voting stock had been bought, they produced a disguised merger. The Celler-Kefauver Act put a lid on that activity, but allowed smaller firms the privilege of merging if merging enhanced their ability to survive.

Funding Antitrust Legislation

Why is antitrust legislation only as good as the funding that stands behind it?

It is sometimes easier to pass a dozen laws than to enforce one. This is particularly true when no funds are appropriated by the government for law enforcement.

Imagine, for example, a town council voting unanimously in favor of capital punishment for overnight street parking, *but appropriating zero funds for its enforcement*. How could anyone be arrested, then, if no one is hired to do the arresting? Is the punishment under these zero funding conditions really severe?

How seriously, then, should we take antitrust legislation? Look at Table 1.

The first money budgeted for antitrust enforcement, in 1921, was $147,000. It represented, even then, a rather minor government commitment. Table 1 seems to show that the government's commitment to antitrust enforcement has more than tripled since 1970. But the $165.9 million allocated by Congress in 1994 was still only about what Kellogg spends each year advertising its breakfast cereals.

The costs of investigation and litigation are extremely high. Increasing the government's caseload is futile, whatever the merit of the antitrust cases, if there are no funds to prosecute them fully. And it is foolhardy to go after the big firms when one major legal battle with a giant like IBM, Exxon, or General Motors

TABLE 1 Congressional Appropriations for Antitrust Law Enforcement 1970–1994 ($ millions)

Year	Department of Justice	Federal Trade Commission	Total
1994	71.6	94.3	165.9
1989	45.2	66.6	111.8
1980	47.5	66.0	113.5
1970	10.0	20.7	30.7

Source: *Budget of the United States Government* (Washington, D. C., U.S. Government Printing Office, various years).

could exhaust the better part of the FTC's and Justice's thin budgets. The FTC is simply no match for the army of highly talented and highly paid corporate lawyers that the defendant corporations can field.

But antitrust has gone to court. Its record, over the years, has been rather modest. Nevertheless, it has had its hard-earned victories and has left some mark on the behavior of monopolies.

ANTITRUST GOES TO COURT

Street bullies are typically big. But would you go about calling every big person you meet on the street a bully? That's the issue the courts faced over the years in deciding what constituted violations of antitrust laws.

The Rule of Reason

In its early decisions, the Supreme Court distinguished between acceptable and unacceptable monopolies by examining market behavior. Just being a monopoly was insufficient evidence of guilt.

For example, its 1911 ruling in the Standard Oil case was based on the evidence that Standard Oil's *behavior,* not its size or its share of the market, violated the Sherman Antitrust Act. Because Standard Oil used monopoly power to stifle competition, the Court decided against it. It ordered the breakup of Standard Oil. This criterion became known as the **rule of reason.**

Rule of reason

A judicial standard or criterion by which a firm's size within an industry is insufficient evidence for the court to rule against it in an antitrust suit. Evidence must show that the firm actually used its size to violate antitrust laws.

This same rule of reason was applied against American Tobacco, and in later decisions to find U. S. Steel, Eastman Kodak, and International Harvester innocent of antitrust violations. In the U. S. Steel case, the Court acknowledged U.S. Steel's monopoly position but did not find that the company abused its monopoly power to undermine competition.

The *Per Se* Criterion

In the aftermath of World War II, Supreme Court decisions underwent substantial change. The Court's composition now reflected President Franklin D. Roosevelt's appointees. It became known, by some with anger, by others with admiration, as "Roosevelt's Court." It was precedent-changing in many respects. Among the issues reinterpreted by the new Court was the question of what constituted violations of antitrust laws.

Per se

A judicial standard or criterion by which a firm's size within an industry is considered sufficient evidence for the court to rule against it in an antitrust suit.

In the 1945 decision against Alcoa, Judge Learned Hand wrote that firm size ***per se,*** was the issue. It was his view, shared by the majority of the Court, that the Sherman Act did not mean to differentiate between good and bad monopolies. It outlawed monopolies *per se.* Size was the criterion. Alcoa's 90 percent share of the market was therefore sufficient evidence for the Court to find against the company.

The "rule of reason" holds that monopoly is acceptable if it behaves reasonably. However, the *per se* criterion suggests that simply having a monopoly position is unacceptable no matter how reasonably a monopolist behaves.

The Court was not particularly impressed with the economies of scale argument. Acknowledging that monopolies sometimes result from success in honest competition, not by market manipulation or intimidation, it still ruled that monopoly, whatever its history or intent, was a threat to industrial democracy and therefore in violation of the antitrust laws.

In two landmark 1958 merger decisions, it disallowed Bethlehem Steel from acquiring Youngstown Steel and prevented Pabst Brewing Company and Blatz Brewing Company from merging. In both cases, the Court's message was clear. The competitive character of the industries, already threatened by high concentration, would have been further damaged by the mergers.

In 1962 the Court ruled for the government against the Brown Shoe Company's intended purchase of the G. R. Kinney Company. Here the concern was both horizontal and vertical merging. Both were retail shoe companies, but Brown was also a shoe manufacturer and would have gained access to Kinney's retail outlets.

In the 1965 Von's Grocery case, the Court decided against the merger of two Los Angeles supermarkets, the third and sixth largest chains in the area, because they would have enjoyed a 7.5 percent share of the Los Angeles market. That was a large enough share for the Courts to concur with the government.

Rethinking the Reinterpretation

But the political character of the Supreme Court changed again in the 1970s and so too did the Court's interpretation of what the antitrust acts meant. Once again, it looked at what monopoly does in the marketplace rather than size. The rule of reason criterion again seemed more appropriate than the *per se* criterion.

The transition back to rule of reason could be seen in the government's 1969 case against IBM's control of the computer industry. Initially, the issue was size. The government charged that IBM's market share violated Section 2 of the Sherman Antitrust Act.

The case came to trial in 1975. IBM explained its superior performance record. It argued that its monopoly position was a result of its market success, not an instrument used to achieve it. As the costly case dragged on, it became clear that the old *per se* criterion no longer was sufficient to decide against a company. In 1982 the Reagan Administration simply dropped the suit against IBM.

Conglomerates and the Court

Should conglomerate mergers be permitted under antitrust legislation?

The philosophy of antitrust legislation, from the first days of enactment, was to protect the competitiveness of industry. But a very different kind of antitrust focus has emerged in recent years, a focus on the conglomerate. What distinguishes conglomerates from horizontal and vertical mergers is that conglomerates are not industry-specific. The conglomerate merges firms from totally unrelated industries.

These mergers raise interesting questions concerning the relationship between antitrust and conglomerates. If the antitrust laws were designed strictly to protect the competitiveness of industry, then why should conglomerate mergers be a threat to competitiveness, since the industries affected by the merger are unrelated?

Did Mobil Oil's 1970 purchase of Montgomery Ward in any way affect the competitiveness of either the petroleum industry to which the parent Mobil belongs or the retail industry which it acquired? After all, Montgomery Ward had no intentions of selling petroleum. Nor was Mobil about to go into the department store business.

What sections of the Sherman Act had the Mobil conglomerate violated? Or in what way had Mobil's purchase of Montgomery Ward violated the Clayton or Federal Trade Commission acts? Since the industries involved were left essentially intact, is antitrust really an issue in situations involving conglomerates?

In 1979 the FTC blocked Exxon from purchasing Reliance, an electric motor company. Exxon did not pursue the issue to the courts. But the courts have since indicated that conglomerates are virtually immune under existing law. And Congress seems little inclined to challenge that interpretation.

Yet some members of Congress have drawn attention to this issue. Their concern is that conglomerates may still be a threat, not to the competitiveness of specific industries but to the competitive nature of the entire economy.

The OPEC seige on the U.S. economy in the 1970s made the issue more than academic. The oil companies' financial power and their conglomerate appetite were cited by Senator Edward Kennedy as damaging to our national economy. In 1979 he introduced an amendment to the Clayton Act that would have made it illegal for oil companies to acquire firms holding assets greater than $100 million. The amendment was defeated. Another Kennedy try would have made any merger illegal if it resulted in a combined annual sales volume of $2 billion or more. That, too, failed.

Senator Howard Metzenbaum, fearing as well the corrosive effect of conglomerates on industrial democracy, introduced legislation in 1981 that would have restricted conglomerate mergers to only those cases where the net effect would enhance industry competition. That was defeated.

The mood of Congress and the president on antitrust and conglomerates had unmistakably shifted in the 1980s to reflect a more accommodating view toward large corporations. The economies of scale argument once more became fashionable. It was widely accepted that when conglomerates pooled their financial resources, they could expand output to capture the full measure of economies of scale. Bigness promoted efficiency.

BUT FTC AND JUSTICE ARE STILL IN BUSINESS

Nobody is turning off the lights and locking the doors at the FTC and Justice offices. These agencies are still very much in business, despite limited funding and—according to some antitrust advocates—lackluster leadership. Their concern, as always, is getting the most out of every antitrust dollar. How can they monitor and act upon the flood of mergers that take place each year?

Using the Herfindahl-Hirschman Index

In 1982 the Department of Justice established new guidelines for its merger monitoring. The guidelines are based on the Herfindahl-Hirschman index, which separates contestable from noncontestable mergers. For example, any industry whose index exceeds 1,800 invites antitrust intervention. Mergers that occur in an industry whose index falls in the 1,000 to 1,800 range and result in raising the industry's index by 100 or more may be subject to challenge. Mergers that occur in industries whose values are below 1,000 will be left alone.

Going After the Precedent

Another way FTC and Justice can maximize the use of their budgets and efforts is by the selection of mergers they challenge. A merger may be very highly contestable but remain uncontested by Justice. Why? Because Justice's strategy is not only to contest, but to win. If a highly contestable merger involves an extraordinarily high financial commitment, Justice may decide to bypass that case in favor of challenging a much less powerful adversary where it can set a precedent. That is, the most cost-effective way of challenging the big ones is not by direct legal assault but by setting precedents.

DO WE HAVE A POLICY ON MONOPOLY?

There seem to be nearly as many ideas on what to do about monopoly and oligopoly as there are economists addressing the issue. And all ideas seem to have found a place among the economists' policy prescriptions. Public utilities, for example, are highly regulated industries in the United States and the justification for the regulation has been based primarily on the analysis of price determination under conditions of monopoly and oligopoly.

Not all economists are convinced that regulation has been appropriately applied. Many advocate deregulation in the belief that regulation has been an overworked policy and that in many cases technological change has changed the character of the regulated industry. The United States has shown a clear disinclination toward nationalization of industry. For example, in dealing with the chronic problem of passenger railroad transportation, the Congress passed laws that regulated, deregulated, and finally resorted to Amtrak, a mild form of nationalization. Congress has not yet debated the issue of denationalizing the post office, although the suggestion is often made.

It is difficult to gauge how successful the laissez-faire doctrine has been in formulating policy on monopoly. To some economists, the lack of government aggressiveness against monopoly demonstrates the strength of laissez-faire thinking. Many economists are thoroughly convinced that, left unfettered, monopolies generate prices that are no higher, and perhaps even lower, than prices that would obtain under conditions of perfect competition.

What role has antitrust policy played in our economy? The FTC and Justice have pursued landmark cases which attempted to reduce or at least prevent an increase in an industry's concentration ratio. If the use and effectiveness of antitrust policy on prices in the U. S. economy is controversial among economists, what remains fairly uncontroversial is that no consensus exists among them concerning what we ought to do about monopoly and oligopoly.

ADDED PERSPECTIVE

The Herfindahl-Hirschman Index

In 1982 the Antitrust Division of the U. S. Department of Justice replaced the four-firm concentration ratio with the Herfindahl-Hirschman index (HHI), as its measure of market power. HHI, it believes, more accurately records firms' market power. How does HHI differ from the four-firm ratio? The concentration ratio is the *sum of each of the four leading firms'* market share in the industry, while the HHI is the *sum of the squares* of the market shares of *all the firms* in the industry. The HHI is written as:

$$HHI = (S_1)^2 + (S_2)^2 + (S_3)^2 + \ldots + (S_n)^2$$

where $(S_1)^2$ is the square of the leading firm's percent of market sales (or market share) in an industry composed of n firms. By squaring the percentages, HHI gives greater weight to firms with relatively high market power than the four-firm concentration ratio does. For example, in an industry where the leading firm has 25 percent of the industry's sales and the second-leading firm has 10 percent, the four-firm concentration ratio shows that the leading firm contributes $2\frac{1}{2}$ times the contribution made by the second firm to the concentration ratio. By contrast, the leading firm in the HHI contributes 625/100 or $6\frac{1}{4}$ times the contribution made by the second firm to the industry's HHI.

Table A provides a comparison of HHIs for four hypothetical industries, where one is a monopoly and each of the other three is composed of 10 firms with differing market share distributions.

The most equitable market share distribution is shown in industry A. Each of its 10 firms has a 10 percent market share. Its HHI is 1,000. Market power is at its maximum in industry B. There, the only firm's market share is 100 percent. Its HHI is 10,000. Look at the market share distributions in industries C and D. The leading three firms in each command 79 percent of their industries' market sales. But the leading firm in industry C alone holds 50 percent, while the leading firm in industry D holds 30 percent. Because market share values are squared in the HHI, it is 2,500 for the leader in industry C and only 900 for the leader in industry D. As a result, their HHIs are quite different: 3,204 for industry C, and 2,224 for industry D.

The Antitrust Division uses the HHI as a guideline for action. Any industry whose HHI exceeds 1,800 invites antitrust intervention. Mergers that occur in industries whose values are within the 1,000 to 1,800 range and result in increasing the HHI by 100 or more will be subject to challenge. Mergers that occur in industries whose HHIs are below 1,000 will be left alone.

TABLE A
Herfindahl-Hirschman Indexes for Four Hypothetical Industries

Industry A		Industry B		Industry C		Industry D	
% share	HHI	% share	HHI	% share	HHI	% share	HHI
10	100	100	10,000	50	2,500	30	900
10	100	0	0	25	625	30	900
10	100	0	0	4	16	19	361
10	100	0	0	3	9	3	9
10	100	0	0	3	9	3	9
10	100	0	0	3	9	3	9
10	100	0	0	3	9	3	9
10	100	0	0	3	9	3	9
10	100	0	0	3	9	3	9
10	100	0	0	3	9	3	9
	1,000		10,000		3,204		2,224

CHAPTER REVIEW

1. The advantages that arise from the economies of scale make entry difficult for new firms. As a result, monopoly and oligopoly prices may be higher than competitive ones.

2. One way to cope with monopoly and oligopoly prices is to regulate the industries. Other options include nationalizing industries, allowing them to operate freely, openly encouraging concentration to take full advantage of economies of scale, and breaking up monopolies and oligopolies.

3. Monopoly regulation separates monopoly pricing from monopolies. The monopoly is allowed to persist in order to benefit from economies of scale, but price is regulated to equal average total cost or marginal cost.

4. A fair price equal to average total cost creates a potential problem of cost and price drifting upward. Alternatively, price equal to marginal cost may result in a loss for the monopolist.

5. Regulation has its own problems. Sometimes regulators end up shielding the very industries they are to regulate. Deregulation can sometimes increase competition in such cases.

6. Government simply buys the outstanding shares of a company to be nationalized. Price can then be set equal to either *ATC* or *MC* by a government agency. There is no inherent reason why government-run industry cannot be as efficient as private industry, although government often acquires only those industries on the verge of bankruptcy.

7. A laissez-faire approach to oligopoly may be suitable if markets are contestable. The threat of entry prevents firms in contestable markets from taking full advantage of their market power.

8. The theory of countervailing power suggests that even if there is insufficient competition within an industry, competing power blocs between industries check the exercise of monopoly and oligopoly power.

9. The existence of economies of scale may justify encouraging monopoly and oligopoly power. The patent system can give such encouragement.

10. Competition may arise less from within industries than from technological progress that makes whole industries obsolete. For example, railroads have been rendered obsolete through creative destruction resulting from the growth of the trucking industry and air travel.

11. Antitrust legislation exemplifies the belief that the best way to deal with monopoly and oligopoly power is to break it up. United States antitrust legislation includes the Sherman Act of 1890, the Clayton Act of 1914, the Federal Trade Commission Act of 1914, the Robinson-Patman Act of 1936, and the Celler-Kefauver Merger Act of 1950.

12. Court decisions involving antitrust have changed from the rule of reason in the early twentieth century to the *per se* criterion in the post-World War II period. During the 1970s, the courts shifted back again to the rule of reason. The courts accommodated conglomerate mergers in the 1980s.

13. It is clear from our examination that a variety of policies have been employed over time with respect to monopoly and oligopoly power.

KEY TERMS

Laissez-faire
Contestable market
Regulation
Marginal cost pricing
Deregulation
Nationalization
Countervailing power
Creative destruction
Patent
Rule of reason
Per se
Antitrust policy

QUESTIONS

1. Describe five different views economists hold concerning what to do about monopoly and oligopoly pricing.

2. Discuss the difference between "fair" pricing and marginal cost pricing in regulated industries.

3. Why do some economists favor nationalization rather than regulation of industry? What are the advantages and disadvantages of nationalization?

4. Why would economists argue in favor of allowing monopolies and oligopolies to set their own prices undisturbed by government? What assumptions do they make concerning economies of scale?

5. What is a contestable market?

6. Why do some economists argue in favor of antitrust laws? What assumptions do they make concerning economies of scale?

7. What is the difference between the courts' use of the *per se* criterion and the rule-of-reason criterion in deciding whether firms violate antitrust laws.

8. Outline the principal legislation enacted by Congress since 1890 to monitor and control monopoly in the U. S. economy.

9. Do you think the government and the courts have been too lenient toward big business? Why?

10. "There's no way you'll get your bear if there's no bullet in your gun." How does this saying apply to the Antitrust Division of the Department of Justice?

11. Why deregulate a regulated industry?

12. Who regulates the regulators? Is it a problem?

C H A P T E R 1 4

EXTERNALITIES, MARKET FAILURE, AND PUBLIC CHOICE

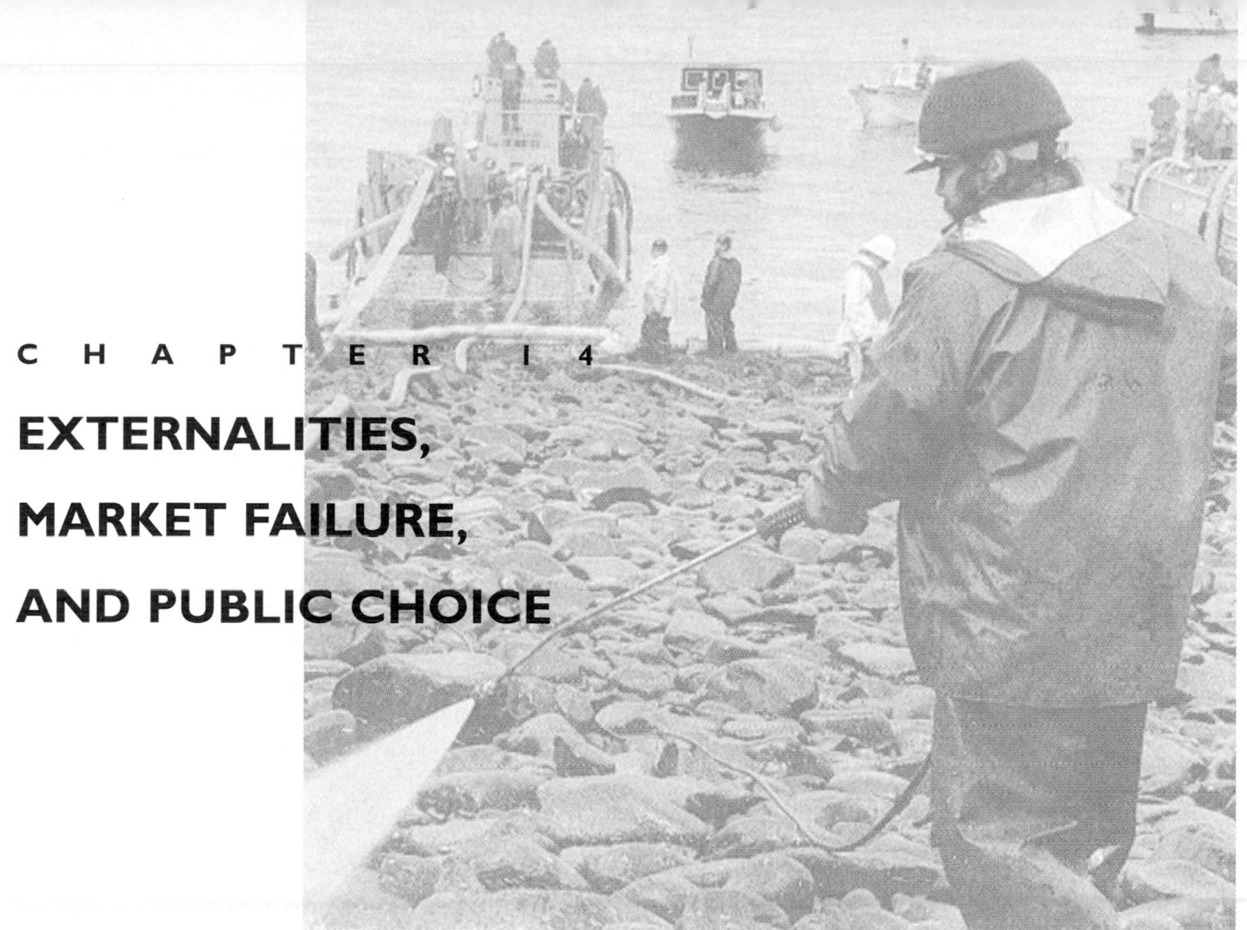

CHAPTER PREVIEW

Thus far, we've described the consumption and production of goods where the costs and benefits of these activities are borne directly by those who do the consuming and the producing. However, there are many activities that spill over to affect third parties. These spillover effects (called externalities by economists) might be costs or benefits for a third party. If they are costs, then the market is encouraging too much of the activity; if they are benefits, the market isn't encouraging enough of the activity. In either case, the market is failing. Fortunately, market failure is often correctable with appropriate government intervention. Unfortunately, government sometimes fails to take appropriate action to deal with market failure. Public choice theory can help us understand the way government will tend to behave. Externalities, market failure, and public choice are exciting and relatively new fields for economic research. This chapter will introduce you to them.

After studying this chapter, you should be able to:

- Explain the difference between external costs and external benefits.
- Discuss why a poor definition of property rights helps create externalities.
- Relate the presence of externalities to the concept of market failure.

- Explain in words and with graphs how market failure can be corrected.
- Contrast the creation of new property forms, pollution taxes, and obligatory controls as approaches to dealing with negative externalities.
- Explain why goods that create positive externalities are often considered to be public goods.
- Distinguish between a pure public good and a near public good.
- Describe the opposing views of public choice.

Imagine what would happen if an Iroquois, hunting for deer on Manhattan Island long before the Europeans arrived, spotted one grazing just about where Times Square would later be. Suppose he took careful aim with his bow and arrow, and missed.

Who would gain from the miss? No question about it, the deer would gain. Who would lose? Obvious again, the hunter. Now imagine that centuries later a New Yorker, spotting a low-flying pigeon in Times Square during rush hour, decides it would make an excellent meal. He aims his high-powered, telescopic rifle and fires. Suppose he, too, misses. Who gains? The pigeon, of course. Who loses? The New Yorker, and perhaps an unsuspecting tourist from Milwaukee who was about to cross Broadway at 42nd Street.

Third parties

People upon whom the unintended externalities are imposed.

The point of the story is that *almost every activity in our modern world involves unsuspecting* ***third parties.*** This point applies to economic activity as well. If people toss their own garbage onto their own front lawns, neighbors would be the losers. Not only would their property values fall, but their views and even their health might suffer.

If people smoke in elevators, others walk away with tobacco-fumed clothing, and sometimes coughing. If paint-making companies eject their gaseous waste products into the air, the surrounding neighborhood smells like a sewer.

If automakers manufactured autos without catalytic converters, carbon monoxide, hydrocarbons, and nitrous oxides would foul our air. If fishermen used boats with gas engines on small inland lakes, many of these lakes would become polluted, denying many vacationers the enjoyment of clean water. If farmers use chemical fertilizers and insecticides on their crops, people in the surrounding areas may develop serious health problems.

Externalities

Unintended costs or benefits that are imposed on unsuspecting people and that result from economic activity initiated by others. Unintended costs are called negative externalities, unintended benefits are called positive externalities.

On the other hand, there is also the possibility of unsuspecting third parties *enjoying* the results of someone else's activities. For example, if a neighbor plants trees, shrubs, and flowers on her property, its beauty and the birds it would attract could add much enjoyment and increased value to a neighbor's property.

Or suppose a greeting card company opened a plant in your neighborhood. It could create a number of well-paying jobs for local people. If you lived directly across the street from Wrigley Field in Chicago, you could see all the Cubs' home games free from your rooftop! And if labor unions are successful in raising wage rates, many nonunionized workers in the same industries may enjoy higher wage rates as well.

ECONOMIC EXTERNALITIES

Economists call these effects on unsuspecting third parties **externalities.** After all, the persons or companies that initiate the activity—the garbage tosser, the paint producer, the farmer fertilizing crops, and the person planting trees—do so to *benefit themselves*. How these actions will affect others is, in most cases, quite beside the point: Which is the economist's point. The activity's effect on others is completely excluded from—that is, it is external to—the decision about whether to undertake the activity.

Identifying External Costs

Private activities sometimes have effects that harm or benefit third parties. The harmful effects are called negative externalities; the beneficial effects are called positive externalities.

As you see, some externalities are negative. The damage and loss of well-being caused by someone tossing garbage onto his *own* property may end up costing a third party $20 just to get someone to clean up the mess. In this simple case, the external cost is easily measured—$20 is what it takes—and perhaps just as easily managed.

But how do you measure the cost of damage caused by a paint company polluting the air? How do you allocate specific costs to specific polluters? Suppose the paint company (1) denies any responsibility, (2) challenges how the cost was measured, or (3) accepts part of the responsibility but claims that other polluters—the airport 30 miles away, the traffic on the highway only two miles away, the smoke from the high school's chimney one block away—are the principal polluters. How would you *prove* that the paint company is responsible? In modern societies, the most important external costs are precisely those that are the most difficult to measure and the most difficult to track to specific offenders.

Identifying External Benefits

What about external benefits? These, too, are not always easily measured or tracked. Perhaps a homeowner can estimate how much benefit is derived from a neighbor's trees, shrubs, and flowers and how much the homeowner would be willing to contribute to that landscaping. But there are other neighbors who derive these positive externalities as well. How much do they gain? And how would anyone go about assessing each other's benefit?

But why should *any* third party contribute to the cost of landscaping, since the benefits the neighbors derive were never considered by the property owner who planted the trees, shrubs, and flowers? And since their sensitivities were not part of the original calculation, it makes sense to suppose that these external benefits would be forthcoming even without their contributions. Economists refer to third-party beneficiaries as **free-riders,** meaning they are in a position to enjoy the ride without paying.

Free-rider

Someone who consumes a good or service without paying for it. Typically, the good or service consumed is in the form of a positive externality.

Imagine a union organizer trying to persuade nonunion textile workers to form a union in their plant. Even if the workers know that it was the International Ladies Garment Workers Union that indirectly won higher wage rates for them, they also know that their personal situation played no role in the union's negotiations with management. Why join? Why not just relax and reap the external benefits of the free ride?

EXTERNALITIES AND PROPERTY RIGHTS

We might ask *why* the property owner planting those beautiful trees, shrubs, and flowers cannot capture any of the external benefits enjoyed by the free-riding

ADDED PERSPECTIVE

Celebrities and Property Rights: A Material View; *T* Stands for "Timber!"

While air rights are well defined in the American legal system, rights to unimpeded views or to picturesque views have not been similarly protected. Typically, these rights are not acquired with the purchase of land, but may be acquired through a covenant or the purchase of an easement.

Popular singer Madonna was involved in a recent lawsuit over an issue less sexy than those typically associated with her, but still controversial. A neighboring Malibu property owner had filed the suit in 1987, before the singer bought the house. He claimed that shrubbery, now belonging to Madonna, blocked his view of the city below and had caused the value of his formerly $3.5 million home to decline by $1 million. Madonna countersued, accusing him of trespassing and of verbal abuse. In December 1990, a California superior court rendered a decision, citing an existing covenant which ensures an unobstructed view to all lots in the neighborhood. Madonna was ordered to trim the hedges and trees surrounding her estate.

Discussion

If you were a member of the California superior court, how would you rule? Does Madonna have a case? Is she entitled to enjoy her property as she sees fit?

ORER Letter, Fall 1991, Office of Real Estate Research, University of Illinois, Urbana.

Property rights

The right to own a good or service and the right to receive the benefits that the use of the good or service provides.

neighbors, or *why* polluters typically don't pay for the pollution costs they generate for others. The reason is because **property rights** in both situations—the rights of the property owner, of the neighbors, of the polluting company, and of those affected by pollution—are poorly defined.

Why the confusion over property rights? If all forms of property—economic resources and final goods—were privately owned by individuals who had clear, recognized, and legal title to the specific properties, there would be no problem. All owners would have exclusive control over their property, the exclusive right to reap the benefits derived from its use, and the right to sue for loss if anyone should damage it.

For example, if an argument resulted in a neighbor chopping down the property owner's newly planted tree, Judge Wapner of *The People's Court* might hear the case, assess the damage, and enforce the penalty.

But who owns the air that the paint factory pollutes? Who has legal title to it? What could Judge Wapner possibly do? Who owns the wild birds that nest in the newly planted trees? Who can claim legal title to them?

Property rights and property claims become complicated on two counts: (1) there are some kinds of resources, such as the sky above and the waters under the earth, that are not easily privatized, and title to them is virtually impossible to claim, and (2) because no one owns these nonownable resources, *no one has an interest in preserving or defending the property.*

For example, you may get upset when you see a driver toss an empty beer can onto the highway, but you would hardly speed up, signal the driver over, and make a citizen arrest. After all, it's only a beer can along a long stretch of road and, anyway, it's not your property. But that is precisely why there are empty beer cans scattered along the highways.

Would you think of checking the exhaust emission system of your neighbor's automobile and making a complaint? Could that one automobile really af-

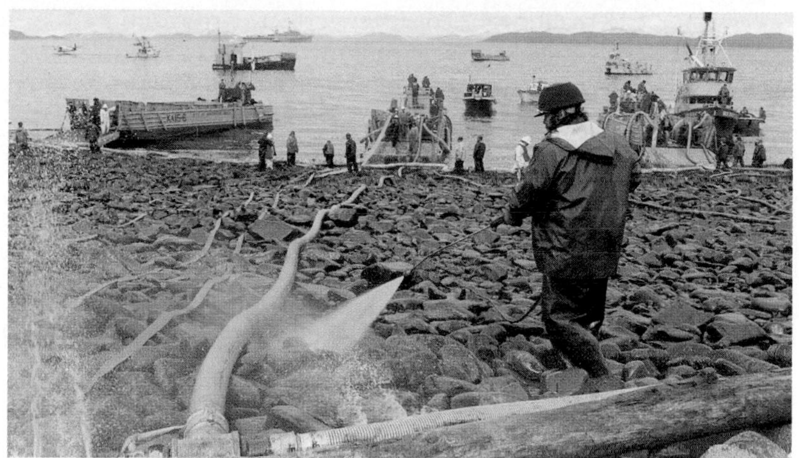

A worker hired by Exxon tests a heated water spray hose to clean oil covered rocks on Smith Island in Prince William Sound in Alaska. The worker, along with 300 others, stayed aboard the U.S.S. Juneau (background) and used its landing craft (left) to clean up the Exxon Valdez oil spill.

fect your well-being? Anyway, is it your air that's being polluted? Do you *own* it? This is a big part of why Denver and Los Angeles are blanketed in smog.

When Exxon's supertanker *Valdez* rammed into a reef off the Alaskan coast in 1988, spilling into the sea the millions of barrels of crude oil it was transporting, it created an economic disaster not only for the Alaskan fishing and tourist industries but for Alaskan wildlife as well. In other words, Exxon's carelessness damaged the economic well-being of thousands of unsuspecting third parties. In the same way, the 1985 accident at Union Carbide's chemical plant in Bhopal, India, and the 1986 meltdown at the nuclear plant in Chernobyl, USSR, resulted in enormous losses of people's livelihoods and lives.

Can you explain why poorly defined property rights result in both negative and positive externalities? Be sure that you can give some examples.

Although the Indian courts ruled that Union Carbide was legally responsible and liable for damages caused to third parties, no suit was brought against the Soviet government, the legal property owner of the Chernobyl nuclear station.

Why not? Because the property issue wasn't the Chernobyl plant. It was the atmosphere! And *who actually has legal title to the atmosphere that the Chernobyl plant contaminated?*

What incentive would lead people, companies, and governments to be careful about creating external costs when they know their actions affect "only" a property form that cannot be claimed? It's frightening, isn't it? How can we begin to address the problem of pollution when our concepts of property make it difficult and sometimes impossible to attach specific costs to specific properties?

Space age technologies that allow us to walk on the moon and send satellites to Mars and Venus also allow us to create even more dangerous threats to our environment than we have yet imagined. An old love song once assured us: "The moon belongs to everyone, the best things in life are free." This may no longer be true. We may now be in a position to pollute the moon just as effectively as we have dirtied our own earthly environment. After all, *who owns the moon?*

WHY SHOULD ECONOMISTS BE INTERESTED IN EXTERNALITIES?

Aside from the fact that economists breathe the same foul air and drink the same contaminated water as everyone else in a polluted environment, their interest in externalities goes one step further. Externalities strike at the heart of the economists' understanding of how the market system works.

Perhaps the issue of property rights and externalities on the moon is still a bit far out, but the presence of positive and negative externalities associated with almost every economic activity undertaken in our economy calls into question the efficacy of our market system. How come?

Defining Market Failure

The allocation of society's resources is inefficient if externalities are ignored.

One of the powerful arguments in favor of allowing markets to determine the economy's resource allocations is the fact that markets allocate society's resources efficiently. Simply put, land, labor, and capital are employed by firms in such a way that we derive the maximum possible utility from their use.

We couldn't do better. For example, if we were to defy the market's resource allocations by just moving one unit of labor—shifting, say, a skilled worker from producing coal-fired electricity to producing F-16 fighter planes—we would have more F-16s, less electricity, *but end up with lower total utility*. If we shifted that worker instead to producing any other good, say automobiles, the result would be the same. We would gain automobiles, lose electricity, and reduce society's total utility.

If we changed the allocation of any other resource, by shifting units of capital or land in directions other than what the market dictates, the results would be the same. Lower total utility. That's a powerful endorsement for letting the market allocate resources, isn't it?

But the argument holds only if we ignore the existence of positive and negative externalities. Otherwise, there is no way markets can guarantee that their allocation of resources will produce the maximum utility for society. But how can you simply ignore the externalities? You see the problem, don't you? That is precisely why economists believe externalities generate market failure.

Too Much Coal-Fired Electricity, Too Low a Price

Let's consider a case of such market failure by looking at the electricity generated by coal-fired plants. Coal used to produce electricity pollutes our atmosphere. One large coal-fired power station, for example, puts out enough dirty ash in a year to cover an acre of land to the height of a six-story building. It also fills our atmosphere with carbon dioxide, suphur dioxide, and nitrogen oxides that come back to earth in the form of acid rain. In addition, coal miners are disabled with black-lung disease.

Now look at Figure 1. The market system establishes the equilibrium price of electricity at $0.07 per kwh (kilowatt hour). Output is 50 million kwhs. The demand curve, *D,* records how much coal-fired electricity people are willing to buy at different prices. What value society places on that 50 millionth kwh of electricity—the marginal utility of electricity—is reflected in the $0.07 they are willing to pay for it.

The supply curve records the quantities of electricity that producers are willing to supply at different prices. The supply curve in Figure 1 sums up the marginal cost curves of all the coal-fired electricity plants. As you see, the marginal cost of the 50 millionth kwh—measuring the value society attaches to the resources used in producing the kwh—that is, the opportunity cost of the resources—is $0.07.

FIGURE 1
Market for Coal-Fired Electricity
The demand curve, *D*, measures the willingness of demanders to buy specific quantities at specific prices. The supply curve, *MC*, reflects the sum of the marginal cost curves of the coal-fired power plants making up the industry. Equilibrium is established at a price of $0.07 per kwh, with output at 50 million kwhs.

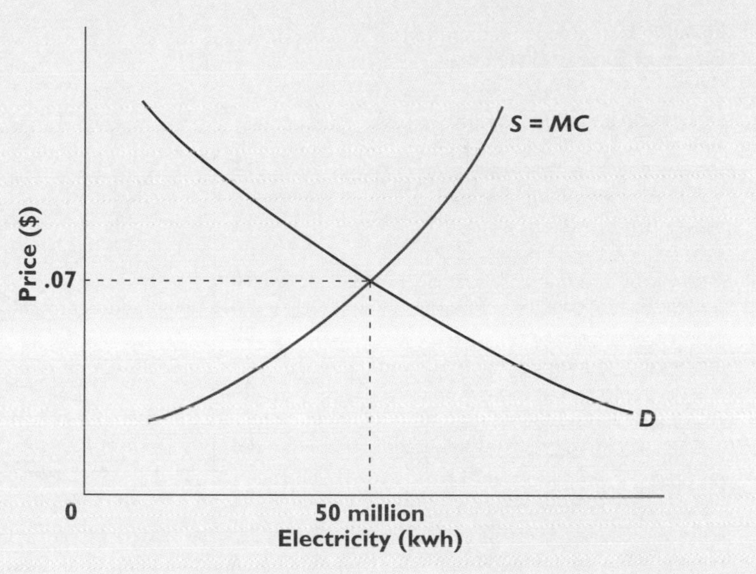

If an activity generates a negative externality and price is set equal to private marginal cost, then too much of the activity will occur. The price is too low.

Figure 1's market for coal-fired electricity satisfies the P = MC efficiency rule of markets. If $P > MC$, society would gain by transferring resources away from the production of other goods to the production of more coal-fired kwhs, because $P > MC$ implies that society values those kwhs more than it values the other goods those resources could produce. On the other hand, if $P < MC$, society would gain by transferring resources out of coal-fired kwhs to other goods. When $P = MC$, no resource transfer can improve the value society derives from its resources.

What About Acid Rain?

But there's a serious problem with this scenario. The $P = MC$ rule does not—it actually cannot—take into account the real costs to society of the acid rain created by the coal-fired plants.

After all, the supply curve in Figure 1 represents only the coal-fired plants' private costs. When a producer sits down to figure out what it costs to produce electricity, only those costs actually incurred in the production are considered—that is, the costs of the labor, land, and capital employed.

Does the producer consider the pollution costs created? Of course not. And probably couldn't even measure them. Do beer companies consider the empty beer cans littering our highways as part of their costs of production? Does the price tag on a new Buick include the cleanup costs of the pollution it will create? Do farmers, in their estimation of farm costs, include the pollution costs caused by the chemicals they use in production?

But these are real costs, aren't they? That is why the cost of producing coal-fired kwhs, calculated by the firms themselves, always understates *society's opportunity costs*—that is, what society must give up for those marginal kwhs.

What does society give up? What resources are used in the production of kwhs? First, of course, those used directly to produce kwhs—the labor, land, and capital that the firms themselves calculate. But a second cost component in pro-

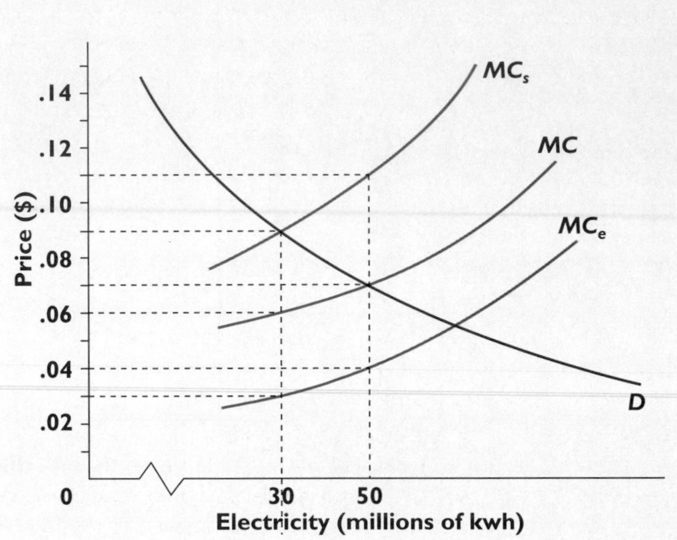

FIGURE 2
Effect of Externalities on Cost
The marginal externality cost curve, MC_e, represents the cost society incurs to clean up the air pollution caused by coal-fired power plants. At zero output, $MC_e = 0$. As the plants generate more kwhs, the marginal cost of the negative externality increases. The marginal social cost curve, MC_s, adds the marginal externality cost curve to the industry's own *MC* curve to reflect the total cost incurred by society in producing kwhs. Under these conditions, the most efficient allocation of society's resources occurs at $P = MC_s = \$0.09$ per kwh. Of the \$0.09 per kwh, \$0.03 is allocated to cleaning up the pollution, and \$0.06 is allocated to the resources used by the power plants to produce the 30 million kwhs.

ducing electricity is the resources society must spend to clean up the polluted environment. For society as a whole, then, the real opportunity cost of producing electricity is the combination of both private (or internal) costs and externality costs.

The difference between the strictly internal or private costs that coal-fired plants incur and the costs that society incurs is shown in Figure 2.

Marginal externality cost, MC_e

The change in an external cost generated by a change in the quantity of a good produced.

Look at the upward-sloping ***marginal externality cost*** curve, MC_e, at the bottom of Figure 2. When output is zero, the marginal externality cost is zero. If no coal-fired kwhs are produced, the plants obviously don't pollute. But once under way, the cleanup costs for the pollution they generate tend to increase at an increasing rate. At high levels of output, these externality costs can become excessive, as pollution builds up to seriously contaminate the atmosphere. As you see, the slope of the MC_e curve increases at higher levels of kwh output.

Marginal social cost, MC_s

The change in the total cost to society generated by a change in the quantity of a good produced. MC_s is equal to the sum of the good's marginal external cost and the marginal cost incurred by the firm producing the good.

Adding these externality costs, MC_e, to the industry's own *MC* curve, which represents the private costs incurred in producing electricity, produces the **marginal social cost** curve, MC_s, of Figure 2. $MC_s = MC + MC_e$.

Suppose pollution costs are ignored. If the market alone dictates price and output, then the equilibrium price is \$0.07 per kwh and output is 50 million kwhs.

But what is the marginal cost of the pollution that society actually incurs producing that 50 millionth kwh? At 50 million kwhs, $MC_e = \$0.04$. Therefore, $MC_s = \$0.04 + \$0.07 = \$0.11$ at 50 million kwhs. The utility society gains from

Market failure

The failure of the market to achieve an optimal allocation of the economy's resources. The failure results from the market's inability to take externalities into account.

the 50 millionth kwh, measured by what consumers are willing to pay—that is, $0.07—is considerably less than the $0.11 cost *society* incurs producing that kwh. Under these circumstances the market is an inefficient allocator of society's resources. The market generates more coal-fired electricity than it should. *To economists, that outcome represents* ***market failure.***

What would be the optimum price and output? Look again at Figure 2. The socially desirable price is $0.09 per kwh and optimum output is 30 million kwhs. Do you see why? At 30 million kwhs, $P = MC_s$.

But There's Still Pollution!

But even at $0.09 and 30 million kwhs, coal-fired plants would still be pumping pollutants into the atmosphere. The cost of repairing the damage inflicted on our environment, that is, the marginal externality cost at the 30 millionth kwh, is $0.03. Only when coal-fired plants shut down is society really pollution-free. But that means no electricity. Not a very attractive alternative, is it?

In other words, because society wants to enjoy the benefits of electricity and because cleaner fuel sources cannot supply the entire demand, it pays society to tolerate some pollution and to clean up the pollution at the same time. *The market fails not because it generates pollution, but because in a world of unavoidable externalities, it cannot signal the proper combination of price and output to give society the most efficient use of resources.*

CORRECTING MARKET FAILURE

If price is set equal to society's marginal cost rather than the private marginal cost, then the external cost will be paid.

Making the case for market failure is easier than correcting it. How do we really know what the marginal externality cost curve looks like for any industry?

Look at Figure 3. Consider again our coal-fired power plants. We know that their marginal externality cost curve begins at the origin, but that's about all we really know. Does marginal cost rise gradually (MC_{e3}), rapidly (MC_{e4}), remain constant (MC_{e2}), or decline (MC_{e1}) as output increases? Do we really have enough information on any set of externalities to make such detailed calculations?

Firms can measure their own private costs to the penny. But measuring externality costs is as much a matter of imagination and conjecture as it is of accurate cost accounting. We simply know too little about environmental impact to confidently trace out MC_e curves for various industries. Yet, we have to try.

After all, what are the alternatives? If we can't be exact about them, we can still be vaguely right. That is to say, if we can't correct the market failure, we can at least try to improve upon it. But how?

Government's Attempt to Correct Market Failure

Typically, we rely upon government. Why? Government may not know exactly what these marginal externality cost curves look like, but it has access to more relevant information than any private firm or individual, and moreover is in the business of collecting that information. Compared to other interested parties, such as the polluting industries and people subject to pollution, government is probably also the most objective.

But what can it do? Government can pursue any or all of three policy options. It can (1) create new property forms to handle externalities, (2) levy a pol-

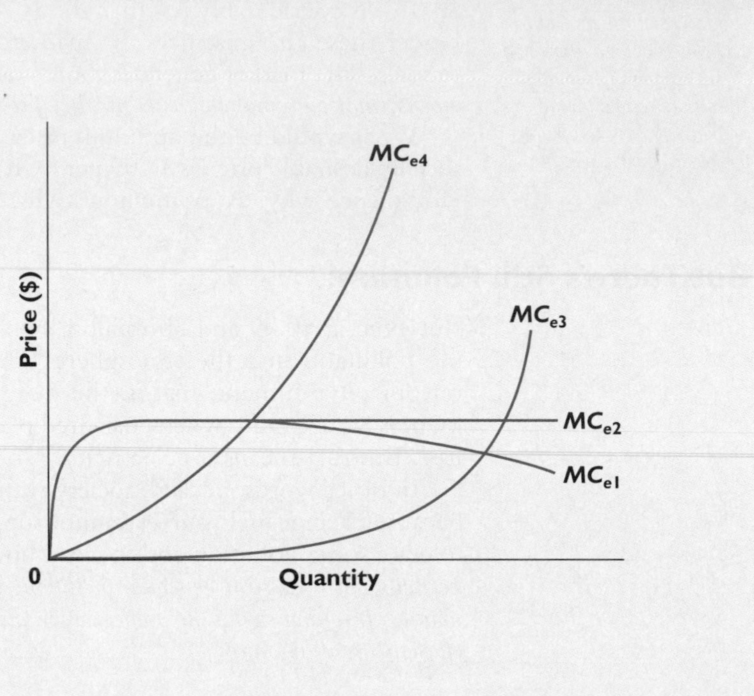

FIGURE 3
The Marginal Externality Cost Curve
The shape of the marginal externality cost curve depends on the rate at which negative externalities are created as more output is produced. At zero output, no pollution is created. The MC_{e1} curve represents a condition where pollution costs increase at a decreasing rate as more electricity is produced. The MC_{e2} curve shows pollution costs increasing at a constant rate as output increases. The MC_{e3} curve represents the situation where pollution costs increase at a gradual rate. At MC_{e4} the curve increases rapidly as more kwhs are produced. The shape of the industry's MC_s, and consequently its efficiently designed price and output, depends to a large extent on the shape of the MC_e curve.

lution compensation tax on the polluting industry, and (3) enforce an environment protecting set of standards on the polluting industry.

Creating New Property Forms

Creating new property forms is a way to define property rights clearly and eliminate negative externalities.

Public beaches are sometimes overcrowded, noisy, littered with trash, and even dangerous to children. The surrounding picnic areas may be torn up by people and by automobiles and improperly parked pick-ups. Just as coal-fired power plants pollute our atmosphere, people can pollute beach areas. Of course, government can patrol beaches and penalize violators of public property. The patrol costs represent the externalities cost.

Another way of reducing abuse of public beaches is to convert them into private property by auctioning them off to private enterprise. If the beaches were privately owned, the owners would have a strong incentive to maintain them. After all, their beach access fees and the number of people willing to pay those fees would depend on how secure, clean, and spacious the beaches are. Having legal title to the beach would assure them that anyone damaging their property would be liable.

In this way, everyone gains. The government's auction brings in revenue, the new property owners earn profit, and the people have access to a more attractive beach.

But can government sell the atmosphere over a coal-fired power plant as easily as it transfers ownership of a beach area? Obviously not. The option of a shift to private ownership, then, has serious limitations.

FIGURE 4
Effects of a Pollution Compensation Tax
If government levies a \$0.04 per unit tax on the industry, the supply curve shifts from the pre-tax *MC* curve to the *MC* + *T* curve. Note that the vertical distance between the two curves is the value of the tax, \$0.04. Price increases from \$0.07 to \$0.10, output decreases from 50 million to 40 million kwhs. Government tax revenue becomes \$0.04 × 40 million = \$1.6 million, depicted by the shaded rectangle. This tax revenue compensates in part for the costs involved in cleaning up the pollution, depicted by the shaded area under the MC_e curve, created by the production of 40 million kwhs.

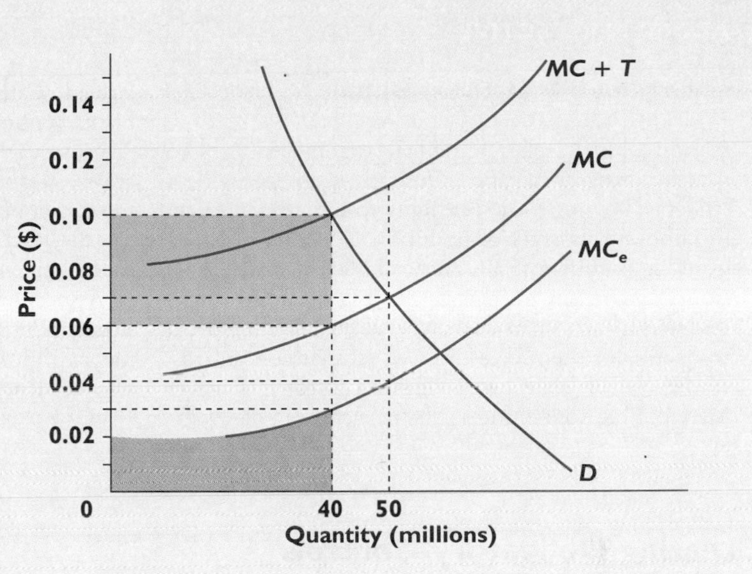

Levying a Pollution Compensation Tax

Pollution taxes add an amount to private marginal costs that approximates the marginal externality cost.

Another option available to government is to tax polluters. The government can impose a tax, then use the tax revenues to clean up the environment. Simple enough? It can do its own environment cleaning or contract the cleaning to private firms. Look at Figure 4.

Suppose government *believes* the MC_e curve looks like MC_e in Figure 4. Suppose also that it has a fair idea about the market demand for electricity and the private costs of producing it. Left unfettered, the market—excluding any thoughts about externalities—establishes a \$0.07 equilibrium price at an output of 50 million kwhs. If government then levies a \$0.04 tax on the coal-fired power companies for each kwh produced, it would shift the industry's supply curve from *MC* to *MC* + *T*, *T* representing the per unit tax.

What would happen to price and output? The coal-fired power plants would respond precisely as would any firm facing a unit tax. The new equilibrium price becomes \$0.10 per kwh and output falls to 40 million kwhs. The government collects \$0.04 of the \$0.10 price. Its tax revenue, then, is \$0.04 × 40 million = \$1.6 million. The coal-fired power plants end up getting \$0.06 per kwh instead of \$0.07, while consumers now pay \$0.10 per kwh instead of \$0.07.

The \$0.04 tax was not a random pick. The revenue it created, depicted by the shaded rectangle in Figure 4, was calculated by government to equal or at least approximate the externality cost of producing the 40 million kwhs, depicted by the shaded area under the MC_e curve.

Moreover, the advantage of such a pollution compensation tax is that it falls squarely on the users of coal-fired electricity. People who heat their homes with solar power don't pay. And people who use very few coal-fired kwhs contribute less to the cleaning-up process than those who consume more.

ADDED PERSPECTIVE

Living in an Imaginary Bubble

Although EPA relies principally upon directives to specific firms in specific industries, it does provide a strategy allowing some flexibility to an individual firm in choosing its level of pollution. For example, in a growing number of cases, instead of setting one emission standard for all plants, the EPA instead assigns one standard to a particular *set of plants,* allowing them to decide for themselves how to satisfy the standard.

This *bubble concept* of pollution control—an imaginary bubble containing all the participating plants involved in the one EPA emission standard—allows plants within the bubble to buy and sell pollution rights to each other. For example, plants that are relatively clean can sell some of their polluting rights to the dirtier plants within the bubble who prefer to pay for the extra rights rather than cut production to meet their share of the emission standard. In this way, EPA succeeds in holding the bubble to a fixed emission standard while allowing internal buying and selling of rights to achieve the bubble's most efficient way of satisfying the standard.

Creating Obligatory Controls

Instead of taxing the polluting industry, the government can impose obligatory controls. For example, it can direct coal-fired power plants to install expensive, giant scrubbers in their smokestacks to control harmful gaseous emissions.

Such obligatory controls are the most common form of government intervention in environmental protection. Think about our municipal ordinances. Aren't leash laws obligatory controls designed to protect the community from the damage that unsupervised dogs can do? What about leaf-burning laws? Aren't they obligatory controls designed to protect the community from polluting its own atmosphere? Or what about sign ordinances? Aren't they obligatory controls designed to protect the beauty of our surroundings?

Why do you think government seems to prefer controls rather than price as a means of reducing negative externalities?

But why controls? Why doesn't government instead just allow people to buy the right to have their dogs roam about freely? Or buy the right to burn leaves? Or buy the right to post any size billboard or grotesque neon fixture? Or buy the right to dispose of garbage in the front yard? Isn't that essentially what the pollution compensation tax would allow industry to do?

If government were to price these rights properly, it could control pollution at any targeted level. For example, if it wanted to eliminate pollution completely, it could price these rights clear out of the market. But it can also set prices at *any* lower level, generating *any* degree of pollution control. In fact, by setting different prices for different industries and regions, government can produce virtually any quality control it wants, assuming it had reliable external cost data.

The Environmental Protection Agency

Government has traditionally controlled externalities by directive rather than by price. That's how the Environmental Protection Agency (EPA) works. Established in 1970 and operating within the executive branch of government, EPA has become *the* environmental regulatory agency of the nation. It administers all of Congress' environmental control acts, among them the Clean Air Act, the Water Pollution Control Act, the Safe Drinking Water Act, and the Toxic Substances Control Act.

Once upon a time, nobody cared how you maintained your automobile. It was your property, and your own business. Not so today. Pollution has become everyone's concern and communities insist you use pollution-reducing devices. Obligatory inspections are designed to see that you do.

Perhaps the most familiar set of obligatory EPA controls are those associated with the automobile industry. They are part of your own automobile. EPA has given you no choice but to buy unleaded gasoline. It directs the automobile industry to install catalytic converters as standard equipment in your automobile. It is illegal for you to remove it even though it's your own property.

The EPA sets the maximum permissible number of hydrocarbon, carbon monoxide, and nitrous oxide pollutants for all automobile emission systems. EPA has made these emission standards tougher through the years and over the objections of the automobile industry.

Through its directives, EPA also controls the quantity and quality of pollutants that firms in other industries discharge into our water, land, and atmosphere. For example, to safeguard our water supply, EPA regulates the pollutants that industry, agriculture, and communities are allowed to discharge into ground and surface water. EPA can direct plants that dump wastes into rivers and lakes to install water purification systems that use the most economically effective technology available.

Although EPA *seems* to be rather busy, many environmentalists argue that it isn't busy enough. Others complain that it's busy doing the wrong thing, focusing far too much on environmental protection but ignoring the opportunity costs that the protection imposes on particular industries and society. For example, if EPA made newer and even more expensive scrubbers mandatory for coal-fired electric production, society might end up with no pollution, but with no electricity either.

EXTERNALITIES AND PUBLIC GOODS

Consider, once again, the homeowner who landscaped her property with trees, shrubs, and flowers. Remember, the entire neighborhood became free-riders, enjoying the landscaping's external benefits.

But suppose, instead, that she had consulted a landscape architect who estimated the cost of that landscaping at $7,000. Suppose she figured that her marginal utility from the landscaping would amount to only $6,000. You already know what would happen. There would be no trees, no shrubs, no flowers, no birds!

Now suppose the next-door neighbor, after watching the landscape architect measure and calculate, asked what was going on. Disappointed after hearing about her calculations of costs and utilities and her decision, he canvassed the neighborhood, and invited each of the other neighbors to contribute $100.

Twenty neighbors estimated that the marginal utility they would derive from the landscaping was $200. They quickly agreed to the $100 contribution. Their combined $2,000 now reduces the homeowner's cost to $5,000, well below the $6,000 marginal utility. The project is now viable!

Everyone—the homeowner, the 20 contributing neighbors, and *even neighbors who didn't contribute at all*—enjoy the trees, shrubs, flowers, and birds. The utility the homeowner derives from the landscaping is worth $6,000. The contributors' utilities are worth $200 × 20 = $4,000. Adding the utilities of the free-riders—say, another $2,000—generates a total utility for society of $12,000, a full $5,000 more than the cost of resources used in the landscaping.

But suppose the contributing neighbors decided differently! Suppose they realized that, although their marginal utility would be $200, each $100 contribution would *by itself* have little effect on the homeowner's decision on whether or not to landscape. They also knew that if the homeowner decided to go ahead with the project, they could not be excluded from the benefits anyway. Pursuing their own self-interest, then, they chose not to contribute. And, of course, there was no landscaping.

Positive Externalities and Public Goods

If an activity generates positive external benefits it will be hard to find volunteers who will pay for the benefits they receive. Why pay if you can ride for free? Production of these public goods must be arranged for by government and funded through taxes.

Public good

A good whose benefits are not diminished even when additional people consume it and whose benefits cannot be withheld from anyone.

Perhaps the community could survive without the landscaping on the homeowner's property. Perhaps they could survive without landscaping anywhere in the community. After all, the same calculation that went into the decision to landscape might make everyone decide not to landscape. The result would be depressingly unattractive, but the community would still exist.

But the issue may be actual survival if people behave the same way with other goods as they do with landscaping. Suppose that the same logic—everyone choosing to be a free-rider—is applied to national defense. There is no way someone can be excluded from its protection. So where is the individual incentive to pay for national defense? Even if the free-riders outnumber the contributors, their protection does not reduce the protection the contributors enjoy. As you see, the benefits society gains from national defense are essentially in the form of externalities. The character of national defense makes it, in the language of economists, a *pure* ***public good.***

For example, suppose a modest defense system is estimated to cost $100 billion. And suppose this $100 billion expenditure generates an estimated utility for society worth $800 billion. That's a good return, isn't it? But it wouldn't matter.

Imagine the president on television asking each of the 50 million households to voluntarily contribute $2,000 to national defense, explaining that each will derive $16,000 of utility. And suppose everyone listening to the appeal accepts the president's estimates. Still, each would decide not to contribute. Why? Because they know that their own $2,000, by itself, is clearly inconsequential. Whether they contribute or not does not influence anyone else's decision to contribute. Moreover, if society does opt for a national defense, the $16,000 of utility they would derive would be forthcoming anyway. The $16,000 is an externality. So why contribute? No one does, and as a result no national defense is provided.

What can society do? It does what all modern societies do. It regards national defense as a pure public good. Its representatives in the government decide how much national defense to produce and tax society accordingly.

Public Goods and Near Public Goods

National defense is about as pure a form of public good as there is. Can you think of any other? What about clean air and clean water? Is it possible to exclude someone from enjoying the benefits of pollution control? Does anyone's consumption of clean air reduce other people's consumption of the air? What about water? Not quite the same as clean air. After all, at some point, continued consumption by anyone could lead to a reduction in someone else's use. Clean water, then, is awfully, awfully close, but not really a *pure* public good.

What about national parks? The benefits, like those of national defense and clean air and water are exclusively external. But national parks are not pure public goods. Up to a point, people can enjoy the parks without reducing the enjoyment others derive. But if too many people visit the parks, congestion will reduce the utility other people derive from the park. Moreover, unlike a pure public good, people can be excluded quite simply if the government charges a high admission fee.

There are many *near-public goods*. For example, everybody can consume nearly as much as they want of a freeway at 2 A.M. without reducing other people's consumption of the road. But not during the 5 P.M. rush hour. Also, people can be excluded from consuming the good if the government changes the road from a freeway to a tollroad.

How can we determine if a good is a pure public good or a near-public good? Think about the role congestion plays.

What about public health? To the extent that government can prevent epidemics, everyone gains and no one is excluded. Even the simple hygiene that the government provides—all those shots that school nurses gave you—created considerable positive externalities in the form of preventive medicine.

What about education? Does everyone's utility increase when children go through the public school system? Education is the single most important contributor to our society's long-run economic growth. Our leadership in technology depends on a continuous investment in basic research. Our ability to use modern technology depends on the education our labor force receives. The flow of goods and services *available to everyone* at relatively low prices, then, is the positive externality that education offers. Our market system cannot exclude anybody, contributors to education or not, from enjoying the increases in societal well-being that education provides.

PUBLIC GOODS AND PUBLIC CHOICE

Most people agree that public goods and most near-public goods properly belong in the government's domain. Why? Because they think that the government, more than any other group of people or institution, can best decide the quantity and quality of public goods that society should consume. Does that view makes sense? Is allowing the government to make the choices about public goods the best way to overcome market failure?

Suppose everyone in the community agrees that national defense is a necessary public good, and agrees as well that everyone should be taxed to pay for its

TABLE 1

	Marginal Benefits of Added Hours to			
Added Hours on	**You**	**Mindy**	**Brad**	**Total**
Sunday	$250	$150	$100	$500
Saturday	200	120	80	400
Wednesday	150	90	60	300
Friday	100	60	40	200
Tuesday	50	30	20	100
Thursday	25	15	10	50
Monday	15	9	6	30

purchase. Does that agreement solve the problem of acquiring national defense? Not entirely. The question then is: How much national defense should the community buy? And is that quantity the socially optimum quantity?

Voting Your Demand for Public Goods

Let's put aside the purchase of national defense for the moment and consider the purchase of another public good, one much closer to home and more directly involved in your daily life: the public library. Suppose the public library in your community is accessible Monday through Friday, 9 A.M. to 5 P.M. And suppose, because you attend school during those hours, you find it rather inconvenient to use the library and you organize a political campaign to extend its hours. How many more hours, if any, will the community buy?

For convenience, let's suppose the community consists of only three people: you, Mindy Manolakes, and Brad Novicoff. Table 1 describes the added or marginal benefit, in dollars, each derives when evenings and weekends are added to the library's hours.

Suppose the cost for each additional extension of library hours is $300. It is shared equally by the members of the community, so that each person pays a $100 tax for each extension. If the issue of the library's extended hours is brought to a vote and if everyone votes to satisfy his or her self-interest, how many units of library-hour extension will the community buy?

Will the community vote for the Sunday extension? Look at the marginal benefit each derives from the Sunday extension. In every case, it is equal to or greater than the $100 tax. For example, Mindy's marginal benefit is $150, or $50 greater than the tax she pays. Brad's marginal benefit is $100, which is equal to the tax he pays. How would you vote? Your $100 tax provides you with $250 of benefit. The community will vote yes for Sunday.

What about Saturday's extension? The vote will be 2 to 1 in favor, Brad alone voting against it. But the vote will be 2 to 1 against Wednesday, you alone voting for it. The community, then, by democratic vote, buys only weekend extensions.

Government Failure

Just as we saw people in the community reacting to market prices and failing to buy the socially optimum quantity of a public good, so we see the same people voting for public goods yet failing to buy the socially optimum quantity. After all, the socially optimum quantity is reached when the community's total marginal benefit equals the total marginal cost—that is, the tax. That occurs in Table 1 with the third extension, Wednesday, where total marginal benefit equals the tax of $300. That is to say, by relying on the political process, less than the socially optimum quantity of library hours is purchased, generating what economists describe as **government failure.**

Government failure

The failure of the government to buy the socially optimal quantity of public goods.

WHEN REPRESENTATIVES VOTE "ON BEHALF OF THE PEOPLE"

Government failure may be worsened when voting on specific issues is delegated to representatives who are elected to political office. Not everyone in the community has the time, the knowledge, or the interest to vote on every public goods issue. As a result, government decision making substitutes for direct voting. But how accurately do the public goods choices made by representatives of government reflect the demands of their constituents for those public goods?

Even with an honest effort, can representatives measure their constituents' specific costs and benefits to reach a yes or no decision on the purchase of a public good? There is another issue. To what extent are representatives, particularly in an off-election year, sufficiently in touch with their constituents to get the information shown in Table 1, however imprecisely it may be expressed? Do they ask for it, or must representatives rely on people making themselves heard? How can representatives assess the costs and benefits to the community of any public good when, say, less than 10 percent of the people make their views known? Should representatives assume that those who didn't participate in the discussion of the issue have no interest in the political outcome?

How well can Mindy, Brad, and you be served when the government makes the decision on the library hours? Is government failure more or less likely when representatives substitute for direct voting?

Let's now turn our attention back to national defense. However difficult it may be for individuals to measure the benefits they derive from extended library hours, it would be even more difficult for them to measure the benefits they derive from public goods more remotely felt, such as national defense. How would Mindy, Brad, or you calculate the individual benefits derived from government's purchase of another F-16 fighter plane? What benefit would you derive from government's $500 billion bail-out of the bankrupt savings-and-loan associations? Unable to make an educated response? Yet, these are the kinds of public goods that representatives buy.

THE POLITICAL POWER OF "SPECIAL INTERESTS"

The prospect of government failure becomes even more apparent when the government's choices of public goods are not intended to reflect the "will of the people."

Public choice

The view that the behavior of government concerning the production and allocation of public goods is dictated mainly by the needs of members of government to keep their jobs.

Economists hold different views about how government functions. Some believe that representatives, accepting the public trust, attempt to produce public goods that enrich the common good. There are always problems, of course, identifying the common good just as there are problems assessing the worthiness of public goods. But the belief held is that at least an honest effort is made to represent the public choice.

Other economists, questioning this view of **public choice,** see these same representatives as people who choose to run for office, whose campaigns are fi-

Public choices can be in the general public's interest or can benefit *special* interests.

nanced by special interests, and who vote for or against legislation depending on how the vote affects the basic support they need to stay in office. That is to say, representatives, like most other people, are guided by self-interest. They are more likely to cater to special interests who depend on government purchases than to the vast majority of the people they were elected to serve.

For example, if a book publishers' association targets its political contributions to receptive representatives, the outcome of a government's vote on library-hour extensions may well be different from the outcome associated with the Table 1 data. What about the government's purchase of defense goods, where billions of dollars are at stake? It is not entirely surprising then that a **special-interest lobbying** industry plays some role in public choice.

Special-interest lobby

A group organized to influence people in government concerning the costs and benefits of particular public goods.

The government's choice of public goods may sometimes reflect only the preferences for public goods expressed by very few people. In this way, government may fail to correct or even improve upon the market's failure to achieve a socially optimum quantity of public goods.

Living with Government Failure

If we can't live without public libraries or public roads or public education or national defense—to name just some of the public goods that are associated with the functioning of a modern economy—then we have to learn to live with some degree of government failure. How responsive representatives are to their constituents, and how willing individuals are to educate themselves on the costs and benefits of buying public goods and to make their choices known, affects the dimensions of government failure.

Economists accept the inevitability of government failure just as they accept the inevitability of market failure associated with public goods. But, as we have seen, they may look to different causes. Some economists see government failure resulting from the impossibility of achieving a socially optimum quantity of public goods even though the government makes every effort to achieve it. Other economists—public choice economists—see the impossibility resulting as well from the nature of the political process itself.

These two differing views about the motivation of government and the effect of that motivation on government's choices of public goods lead invariably to the very striking differences of opinion that economists hold concerning what role government ought to play in our economy.

CHAPTER REVIEW

1. Costs and benefits that affect third parties are called negative and positive externalities. Pollution is an example of a negative externality. Your neighbor's landscaping, which you enjoy as a free-rider, is an example of a positive externality.

2. If property rights were well-defined, externalities would not exist. Polluters would have to pay for the damage they impose on others. People who generate positive externalities would be properly compensated.

3. The presence of externalities suggests market failure. Activities that generate negative externalities impose costs on people for which they are not compensated. For example, polluters don't include pollution costs as part of the marginal

cost of goods whose production creates the pollution. Even though the producer sets price equal to marginal private costs, price is less than marginal social cost, indicating that too much production is occurring.

4. Correcting for negative externalities means forcing producers to face the social costs of their activities. This can be done by creating new property forms, by levying pollution taxes to match the size of the negative externality, or through obligatory controls.

5. Correcting for positive externalities means creating a mechanism to compensate those who create positive externalities. In practice, this is often very difficult, because of the free-rider problem. One solution is to have the government provide these goods.

6. Government may provide pure public goods and near-public goods. One person's consumption of a public good does not exclude others from consuming it, nor does it deplete the good for others to consume. The benefits from pure public goods are exclusively external.

7. The government may provide pure public goods and near public goods in a manner that is consistent with the public interest. Public servants may make enlightened public choices. However, it is easy to envision situations where the government makes choices that are self-serving or that serve only narrow special interest groups. Under these circumstances, one might question government's wisdom in the choice of public goods, that is, public choice.

KEY TERMS

Third parties
Externalities
Free-rider
Property rights
Marginal externality cost
Marginal social cost
Market failure
Public good
Public choice
Government failure
Special-interest lobby

QUESTIONS

1. Everyone knows that cigarette smoking is harmful to your health. But is it also harmful to people who live or work among smokers? Discuss this issue in terms of the third-party economic externalities created and their relationship to the market's ability to allocate resources efficiently.

2. Suppose someone next door plays her stereo so loudly that you complain. However, people living directly across the hall compliment her on her taste in music and ask her to continue playing it. What solution can you suggest?

3. People want more national security, more social welfare, and lower taxes. It just doesn't make sense, or does it?

4. Describe the following in terms of generating positive, negative, or zero externalities: (a) a foot of snowfall in mid-January, (b) living a mile away from an international airport, (c) your neighbor painting a mural on the side of his house

that faces yours, (d) your neighbor's watchdog who is known to have an unpleasant disposition, (e) a super-student in a class in which grades are curved, and (f) high-spirited motorcyclists.

5. Describe why externalities generate market failure.

6. What is a public good? How does it differ from a near-public good?

7. Why do economists believe government failure is inevitable?

8. Can you name your member of Congress or representative to state government? When was the last time you wrote or spoke to either of them? Or they to you? About what issue?

9. What do public-choice economists assume guides the behavior of elected people in government?

10. What is the function of a special interest or lobby?

11. Make the case that government-financed student loans benefit society. Make the case against such loans.

12. The market for oil-based paint is described by the following demand and supply schedules:

Price	**Quantity Demanded**	**Quantity Supplied**
$10	10	75
9	20	70
8	30	65
7	35	60
6	45	55
5	50	50
4	55	45
3	60	35
2	65	20
1	70	10

Graph the market, showing the equilibrium price and quantity demanded and supplied. If the cost of removing the pollution caused by producing paint was $5 per unit of paint, what is the socially optimum price and quantity?

PART 4
THE MICROECONOMICS OF FACTOR MARKETS

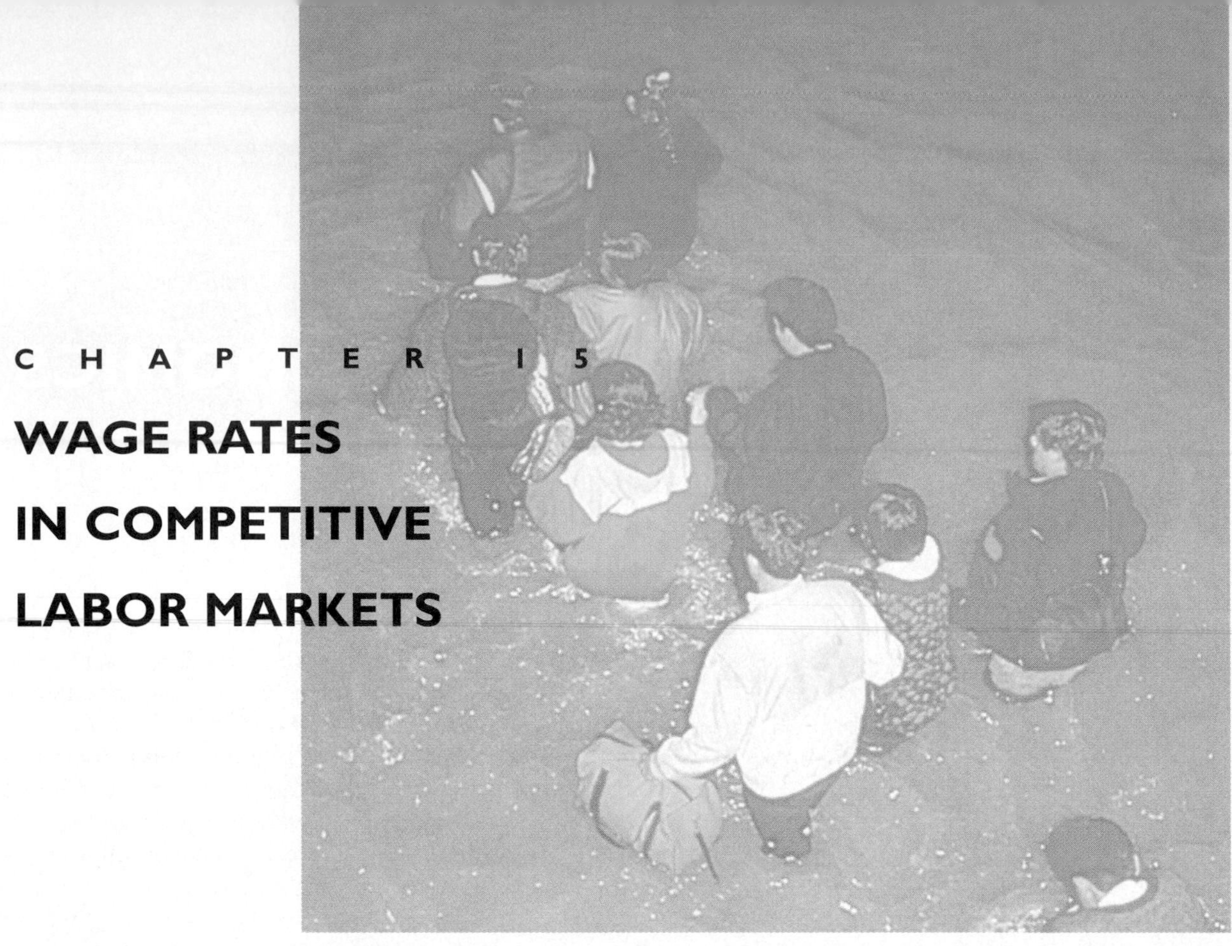

CHAPTER 15

WAGE RATES IN COMPETITIVE LABOR MARKETS

CHAPTER PREVIEW

Remember the circular flow model from Chapter 1? This model showed households purchasing goods and services from business firms in product markets with money earned from supplying resources—labor, land, capital, and entrepreneurship—to firms in resource markets. Beginning with this chapter, our focus shifts from product markets to the resource markets featured in the circular flow model. We'll start by examining how wages and employment are determined in labor markets that are perfectly competitive.

After studying this chapter, you should be able to:

- Explain what the marginal physical product of labor means.
- Give real-world examples of the law of diminishing returns.
- Derive marginal revenue product from marginal physical product.
- Account for the fact that marginal labor cost is equal to the wage rate in a perfectly competitive labor market.
- Draw a graph to show the profit-maximizing level of employment for a firm in a perfectly competitive labor market.
- Give reasons for changes in the demand for labor.
- Describe how the industry demand for labor can be derived from individual firms' demand for labor.

- Explain the shape of and reasons for shifts in the supply curve for labor.
- Discuss the logic behind the backward-bending supply curve for labor.
- Account for wage rate differentials—why they narrow in some cases and persist in others.
- Contrast the impact of a minimum wage law under different assumptions about the elasticity of labor demand.
- Explain why wages set in competitive labor markets can be considered ethical.

The story is told about an old panhandler who regularly worked the corner of Wabash and Adams streets in downtown Chicago. For years, every Friday morning, a generous storekeeper who owned a shop nearby would give him a dollar. One Friday morning, however, the panhandler was refused. Shocked at the rebuff, he asked why. The storekeeper told him that business had been so bad, he couldn't afford to part with the dollar. The panhandler indignantly replied: "Because *your* business is bad, why should I have to suffer?"

Coal miners in West Virginia could ask the same question about their unhappy lot. When oil replaced coal as the primary energy source in the United States, coal prices and output fell dramatically. Mines were forced to shut down. Coal miners, still willing to give the same honest effort down at the mine, nevertheless found their jobs and their wage rate adversely affected.

You don't need to convince Nebraska farm laborers that when the price of corn is down, well-run farms fold, good John Deere equipment goes on the auction block, and their own wage rate is jeopardized. That is no news either to seasonal peach pickers in Georgia or loggers in Oregon.

Why are wage rates what they are? Why do some hard-working, honest folk who have both the capacity and inclination to work earn a decent wage rate while others in the community, no less hard-working, honest, or willing to work take home only a fraction of what their neighbors earn?

Let's pursue these wage rate questions by looking at a simple coal-producing economy and tracing through the factors that seem to explain why coal miners earn what they do. Of course, the factors that determine coal wages are also at work in the steel, automobile, housing, newspaper, and clothing industries. They will help us understand why steelworkers, autoworkers, bricklayers, reporters, and dressmakers earn what they do.

YOU LOAD SIXTEEN TONS AND WHAT DO YOU GET?

Let's set the scene by examining the Charles Edwards Coal Mining Company, located in Harlan County, Kentucky. It is one of 1,000 coal mining firms in the region, and they all face competitive markets both in selling coal and in hiring coal miners.

To begin, suppose that everything required to mine coal—the drilling, blasting, and transport equipment, as well as the coal itself—is on the Edwards site. That is, everything but labor.

Digging energy out of the bowels of the earth. No matter how you look at it, it's hard work. But it beats the old pick and shovel days, hands down!

What would a typical day at the Edwards mine be like? Pretty quiet! It's obvious that without coal miners, no coal can be mined. Machines alone can't mine coal.

Hiring Miners, One at a Time

Charles Edwards will, of course, hire coal miners. It really makes no difference which one the company hires first because we assume that *all miners have equal skills*. Why make that assumption?

With more workers employed, a firm is able to take advantage of specialization of labor so that output expands at an increasing rate.

Because it is probably true. Although no two miners are alike—some are stronger, others brighter, others perhaps more energetic, and others may be more cooperative with fellow workers—still the differences are overshadowed by the similarities of effort and performance.

Let's get the mine operating. Perhaps it is silly to imagine a mining firm functioning with only one miner, but let's do it anyway. The firm can then add a second, a third, a fourth, and so on, while we observe each time what happens to the output of coal as miners are added to the payroll.

Table 1 records output performance.

Look first at column 2. With no miners employed, no coal is produced. When one miner is put to work, coal output increases to 16 tons. When two are employed, output increases to 34 tons. When three miners are employed, output increases to 54 tons. Read down column 2. It records output produced with varying numbers of miners.

Of course, more miners produce more tons. But notice the pattern. At the very beginning, coal output increases by greater and greater tons—0 to 16 to 34 to 54—as more miners are employed. But after the third miner, output begins to increase by fewer and fewer tons—54 to 72 to 88, and so on—as more miners are put to work. Strange? Not at all.

Picture the scene at the mine. With only one miner working, that miner is a very busy person. First comes the task of dynamiting and drilling loose tons of coal. The miner then operates the loading machine that transfers the coal to rail cars. The miner switches function again to ferry the coal out of the mine shaft. Then back to the dynamite. The result is 16 tons.

TABLE 1
Effect of Additional Miners on Output and Revenue

(1) Miners	(2) Output	(3) Marginal Physical Product (*MPP*)	(4) Total Revenue (*P* = $2)	(5) Marginal Revenue Product (*MRP*)
0	0	0	—	—
1	16	16	$ 32	$32
2	34	18	68	36
3	54	20	108	40
4	72	18	144	36
5	88	16	176	32
6	102	14	204	28
7	114	12	228	24
8	124	10	248	20
9	132	8	264	16
10	138	6	276	12
11	142	4	284	8
12	144	2	288	4

With two miners employed, some division of labor occurs. The miners cooperate. One handles the blasting and drilling, the other takes care of loading and transporting. The result is much higher productivity in the mine. By doubling employment from one to two miners, output more than doubles, increasing from 16 to 34 tons.

When Edwards increases employment to three miners, the new division of labor affords even greater productivity. Each miner becomes more specialized, more efficient, and the time lost in switching off and starting up different tasks is reduced. Output increases to 54 tons.

MARGINAL PHYSICAL PRODUCT

Marginal physical product
The change in output that results from adding one more unit of a resource, such as labor, to production. MPP is expressed in physical units, such as tons of coal, bushels of wheat, or number of automobiles.

Another way of reading the information in column 2 is by tracking the **marginal physical product of labor**—that is, the change in output, ΔQ, resulting from a change in the number of miners employed, ΔL. The marginal physical product, *MPP,* is written as:

$$MPP = \frac{\Delta Q}{\Delta L}$$

Column 3 records the *MPP* for the Charles Edwards Company. The same data is shown in graphic form in Figure 1.

The *MPP* of the first miner is 16 tons. Why 16 tons? Because output increases from zero to 16 tons when employment increases from zero to one miner. When the company employs a second miner, output increases from 16 to 34 tons. The *MPP* of the second miner, then, is 34 − 16 = 18 tons. *Because everything else at the mine remains unchanged except for the addition of this second miner, the 18 ton increase in output is attributed to the hiring of this second miner.*

The *MPP* of the third miner is 54 − 34 = 20 tons. The *MPP* of the fourth is 72 − 54 = 18 tons. The *MPP* of the fifth miner is 88 − 72 = 16 tons.

FIGURE 1 **Output and Marginal Physical Product Curves**

In panel *a*, the output curve is upward-sloping, increasing by large amounts until three miners are employed, then increasing by smaller and smaller amounts when more than three miners are employed.

In panel *b*, the marginal physical product (*MPP*) curve maps the increases noted in the output curve. The *MPP* increases for the first three miners—the second miner's *MPP* = 18, the third miner's *MPP* = 20—then falls steadily as more miners are added to production. The *MPP* of the 12th miner is two tons.

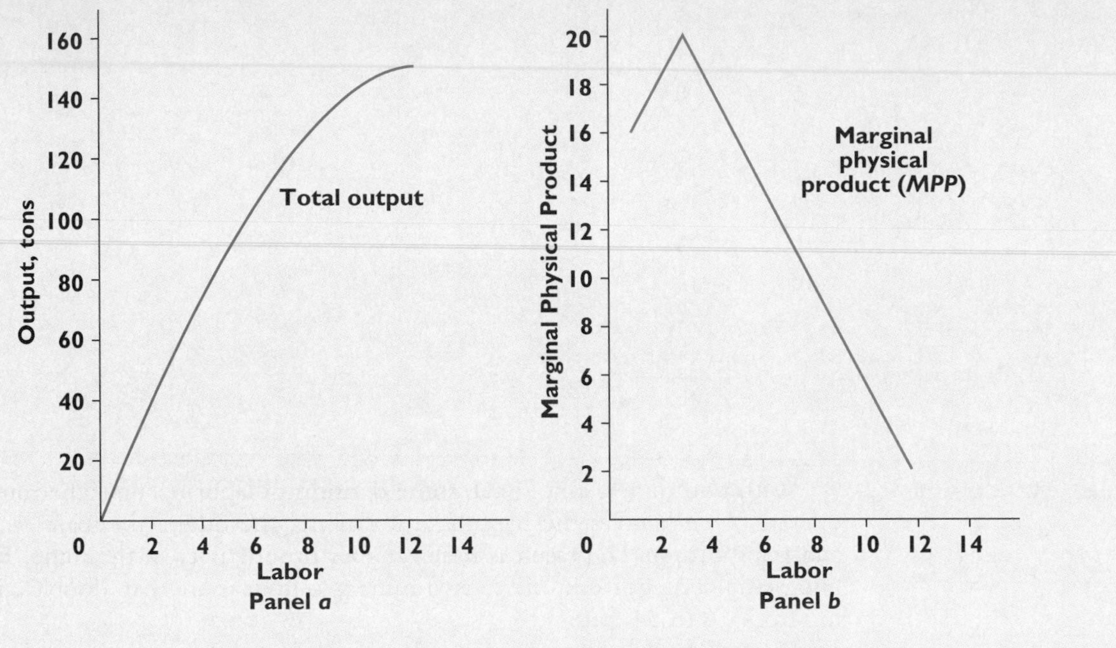

MPP AND THE LAW OF DIMINISHING RETURNS

Output increases with the addition of more workers, but at a decreasing rate if diminishing returns are present.

Note that beyond the third miner, *MPP* declines. As miners are added, one at a time, the additions to output become smaller and smaller. *Total output, of course, continues to increase,* but by diminishing numbers of tons. This is shown by the flattening of the curve in Figure 1, panel *a* and by the negative slope of the *MPP* curve in panel *b*.

Why diminishing returns? Digging deeper into the mine takes more time. Extended mineshafts require more supports, more rail tracks, and more extensive ventilation and communication systems. Adding miners to a given stock of coal-producing machinery must eventually create a less-than-efficient match of labor to capital. Perhaps the most obviously inefficient match of labor to capital in a mine would be two miners working with one pick.

What happens to coal production when more than 12 miners are employed? The *MPP* of the twelfth miner is 2 tons. Could the thirteenth miner's *MPP* fall to zero? Or below zero? Can you imagine so many miners down in the mineshaft getting in each other's way that adding the thirteenth miner *reduces* output? It can happen.

Converting Tons into Revenue

The Charles Edwards Coal Mining Company, although visibly in the business of mining coal, is also in the business of mining money. In the last analysis, it wants dollars, not coal. Suppose that Edwards sells its coal in a perfectly competitive output market. If the price of coal were \$2 per ton, the firm sees the fourth miner adding not just 18 tons to its output, but \$36 to its total revenue. We can convert each miner's *MPP* in Table 1 into **marginal revenue product,** *MRP*, by applying the formula

Marginal revenue product

The change in total revenue that results from adding one more unit of a resource, such as labor, to production. MRP, which is expressed in dollars, is equal to MPP multiplied by the price of the good.

$$MRP = MPP \times P$$

that is, the miner's marginal physical product multiplied by the price of coal. *MRP* can also be written as

$$MRP = \frac{\text{change in } TR}{\text{change in } L}$$

the addition to the firm's total revenue when an additional miner is hired.

Look again at Table 1. This time at column 5. *Since MRP is simply a revenue reflection of MPP,* it, too, starts declining after the third miner. The twelfth miner, for example, adds only \$4 to Edwards' total revenue.

DERIVING THE FIRM'S DEMAND FOR LABOR

Wage rate

The price of labor. Typically, the wage rate is calculated in dollars per hour.

The quantity of labor demanded, like the demand for any good, depends on price. If the price of labor—that is, the **wage rate**—falls, the quantity demanded of labor increases. If the price of labor increases, the quantity demanded of labor falls. In this respect, the law of demand applies to miners just as it applies to microwaves, microchips, and mayonnaise.

Deriving Marginal Labor Cost

Table 2 records Edwards' labor costs when it hires different quantities of miners.

Total labor cost

Quantity of labor employed multiplied by the wage rate.

In a competitive labor market, marginal labor cost is equal to the market wage rate because the firm can hire all the labor it wants at the market wage.

If the wage rate is \$20, the **total labor cost,** *TLC,* of hiring one miner is \$20. *TLC* increases to \$40 when two miners are hired, to \$60 when three are hired, and so on through to \$240 when 12 miners are hired. Because the labor market is perfectly competitive, the Charles Edwards Coal Mining Company is assured that no matter how many miners it hires, it cannot influence the wage rate. For example, if the wage rate for miners is \$20 per hour, Edwards can hire one, two, or 15 miners without worrying that its hiring decision will affect the wage rate. Total labor cost, *TLC,* for Edwards then, is simply the number of miners, *L,* multiplied by the wage rate, *w*.

$$TLC = wL$$

Marginal labor cost

The change in a firm's total cost that results from adding one more worker to production.

What about **marginal labor cost,** *MLC*? The *MLC* allows the firm to read its *TLC* information in a slightly different way. *MLC measures how much the company's total labor cost increases when each additional miner is hired.*

$$MLC = \frac{\text{change in } TLC}{\text{change in } L}$$

Table 2 is depicted in Figure 2, panels *a* and *b*.

When Edwards increases its mining crew from eight to nine miners, *TLC* increases from \$160 to \$180, or by \$20. For the ninth miner, *MLC* = \$20.

TABLE 2
Labor Costs for Coal Miners ($ per hour)

(1) Miners (*L*)	(2) Wage Rate (*w*)	(3) Total Labor Cost (*TLC*)	(4) Marginal Labor Cost (*MLC*)
0	$20	$ —	$—
1	20	20	20
2	20	40	20
3	20	60	20
4	20	80	20
5	20	100	20
6	20	120	20
7	20	140	20
8	20	160	20
9	20	180	20
10	20	200	20
11	20	220	20
12	20	240	20

Look at column 4 in Table 2 and Figure 2, panel *b*. *MLC* = $20 for *every miner*. That is, for every miner Edwards hires at the $20 wage rate, that hire raises Edwards' total labor cost by $20.

Demanding Miners Until *MRP* = *w*

Given the *MRP* data of Table 1 and the wage rate data of Table 2, how many miners will the Charles Edwards Coal Mining Company hire at the $20 wage rate? Let's again consider one miner at a time, starting with the first.

It makes sense for Edwards to hire the first miner. After all, the miner adds $32 to the firm's revenue and only $20 to cost, thereby increasing the firm's revenue by

$$\$32 - \$20 = \$12$$

What about hiring the second? Again, it makes sense. Why? Because the second miner's *MRP* = $36. The second miner adds to revenue

$$\$36 - \$20 = \$16$$

Why stop there? What about the third, fourth, fifth, and so on? In each case, Edwards compares the *MRP* of each additional miner to the wage rate. The hiring rule is simple. If the miner's *MRP* > *w*, hire. If the miners's *MRP* < *w*, don't hire. If this rule is adhered to, Edwards will continue to hire miners until the *MRP* of the last miner hired equals the miner's wage rate,

$$MRP = w$$

At a wage rate of $20, *MRP* = *w* at the eighth miner. The Charles Edwards Coal Mining Company, then, hires eight miners.

FIGURE 2 **Deriving the Marginal Labor Cost Curve**
Marginal labor cost (*MLC*), panel *b*, is the additional cost of hiring an additional worker. In a perfectly competitive labor market where the firm can hire as many workers as it wishes at the prevailing wage rate, the *MLC* curve is horizontal and equal to the wage rate. In the case of Edwards, $w = MLC = \$20$ per hour for any number of workers.

The total labor cost (*TLC*) curve, panel *a*, shows the number of workers multiplied by the wage rate they receive. When one worker is hired at $20 per hour, the total labor cost is $20. When five workers are hired, the *TLC* is $5 \times \$20 = \$100$.

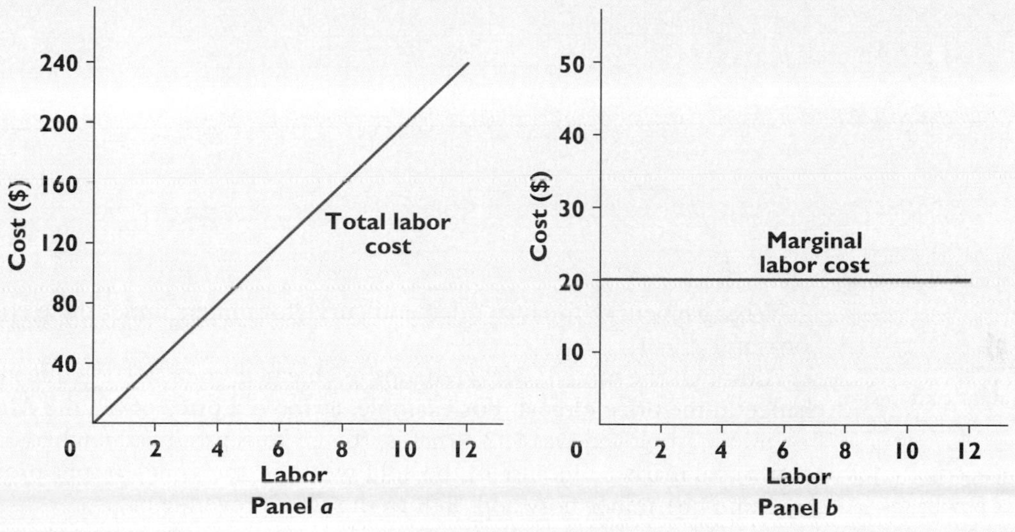

Be sure that you are able to explain why hiring workers until *MRP* = *w* maximizes profits for the firm. Since the *MRP* curve shows what a firm is willing and able to pay for labor, it is the firm's demand curve for labor.

If the wage rate falls to $8, Edwards hires 11 miners since now *MRP* = *w* at the eleventh miner. If the wage rate triples from $8 to $24, will Edwards still hire that eleventh miner? No, because that eleventh miner adds only $8 to Edwards' revenue but costs Edwards $24. Edwards will cut the number of miners it hires to seven.

Table 3 and Figure 3 sum up these *MRP* = *w* hiring decisions to represent Edwards' demand schedule and demand curve for labor.

What we see is that *the demand curve for labor is precisely the laborers' MRP curve.* When *w* = $40, the quantity demanded is three miners because *MRP* = *w* = $40 at the third miner. When the wage rate falls to $4, the quantity demanded increases to 12 because, now, *MRP* = *w* = $4 at the twelfth miner. Each point on the demand curve reflects a *MRP* = *w* position.

What Shifts the Demand for Labor?

A CHANGE IN THE PRICE OF THE GOOD

Imagine a winter with long stretches of below-zero weather. Factory and home furnaces work overtime. The demand curve for coal shifts to the right, creating a new and higher short-run equilibrium price for coal. Let's suppose the price of coal increases to $3 a ton.

Suppose nothing else changes. The miners at Edwards work the same hours with the same equipment producing the same physical quantities. In other words, the miners' *MPP* curve remains unchanged.

TABLE 3
Demand Schedule for Labor

Wage Rate	Miners Demanded
$40	3
36	4
32	5
28	6
24	7
20	8
16	9
12	10
8	11
4	12

The demand for labor increases when the *MRP* of labor increases, due to an increase in either the marginal physical product of labor or the price of the output.

What happens to the firm's demand curve for miners under these conditions? Look at Table 4.

Although the miners' *MPP* remains unchanged, their *MRP* is affected by the change in the price of coal. For example, at the old price of $2, the *MRP* of the first miner employed was $32—that is, the 16 tons produced fetched $2 per ton on the coal market. Because of the cold weather, the same 16 tons produced by that same first miner now adds $48 to the firm's revenue.

As you see, for each of the miners added to employment, the same *MPP* now contributes a higher *MRP*. Figure 4 portrays this *MRP* shift in graphic form.

The *MRP* curve—the firm's demand curve for miners—shifts to the right. At each wage rate, more miners are hired. If the price of coal were to jump to $10, the demand curve would shift even further to the right. *That's why miners like cold weather!*

FIGURE 3
The Demand for Labor
The firm hires workers as long as the worker's *MRP* is greater than or equal to the worker's *MLC*, or wage rate. When the wage rate w = $28, Edwards hires six miners; the sixth miner's *MRP* = $28. When w = $16, Edward hires nine miners; the ninth miner's *MRP* = $16. When w = $4, Edwards hires 12 miners. That is why the demand curve for labor is precisely the firm's *MRP* curve.

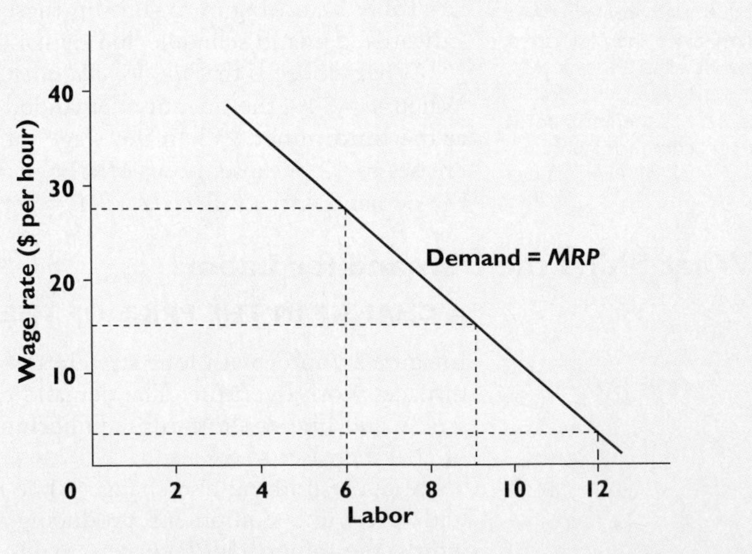

TABLE 4
The Derivation of *MRP* with Price of Coal at $2 and $3

Coal Miners	*MPP*	Old *MRP* = *MPP* × $2	New *MRP* = *MPP* × $3
0	0	$ 0	$ 0
1	16	32	48
2	18	36	54
3	20	40	60
4	18	36	54
5	16	32	48
6	14	28	42
7	12	24	36
8	10	20	30
9	8	16	24
10	6	12	18
11	4	8	12
12	2	4	6

IMPROVEMENTS IN TECHNOLOGY

Imagine what would happen down at the mine if the Charles Edwards Coal Mining Company decided to replace its old coal mining machinery with the most advanced mining technology. Look at Table 5.

FIGURE 4
Shift in the Demand Curve for Labor Caused by an Increase in the Price of the Good
An increase in the price of coal from $2 to $3 causes the demand curve for labor to shift to the right, from *D* to *D'*. At every wage rate, the number of miners demanded by Edwards increases. When the price of coal was $2 and when *w* = $24, Edwards hired seven miners. After the price increases to $3, at *w* = $24, Edwards hires nine miners.

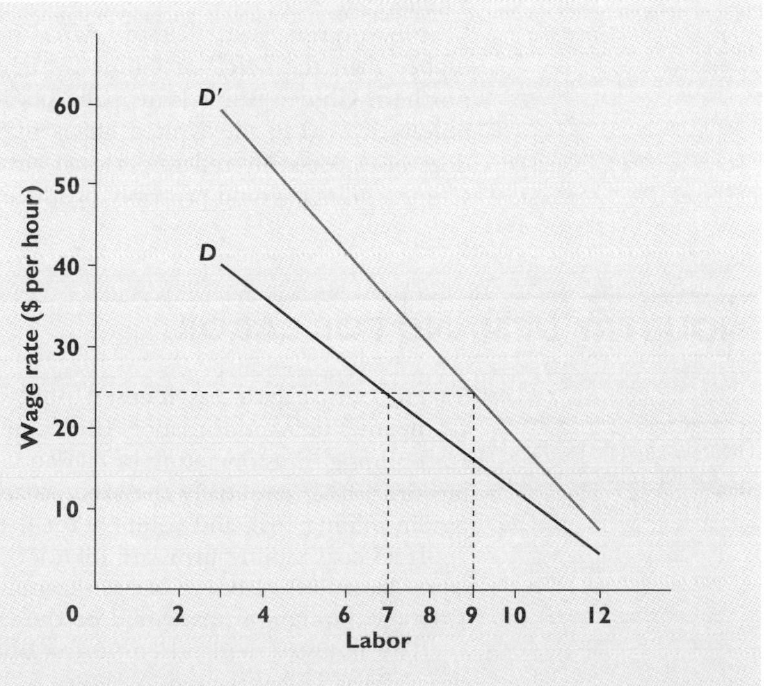

TABLE 5 The Derivation of *MRP* with Old and Newer Technology (price of coal = $2)

Coal Miners	Old Tech *MPP*	New Tech *MPP*	Old Tech *MRP*	New Tech *MRP*
0	0	0	$ 0	$ 0
1	16	32	32	64
2	18	36	36	72
3	20	40	40	80
4	18	36	36	72
5	16	32	32	64
6	14	28	28	56
7	12	24	24	48
8	10	20	20	40
9	8	16	16	32
10	6	12	12	24
11	4	8	8	16
12	2	4	4	8

Compare the *MPP*s. Before the new technology was put in place, the first miner produced 16 tons. After the new technology replaced the old, that same miner produced 32 tons, twice as much.

What about the second miner? Twice as productive, from 18 to 36 tons. What about the third, fourth, and so on? Working with new technology, labor is twice as productive. The *MRP* curve shifts to the right. In other words, *either rising coal prices or employment of more advanced technology will shift the demand curve for miners to the right.*

No surprise, is it, that the *MRP* of West Virginia miners is considerably higher than the *MRP* of Chinese miners working in the Shensi province of northern China? Why? Principally because more and better coal mining technology is used in the United States than in China. The worker's productivity does not necessarily reflect personal effort. Our technology in the hands of the Chinese miner would probably produce equivalent results.

INDUSTRY DEMAND FOR LABOR

The industry demand for labor is the sum of individual firms' demand for labor.

So far, our analysis has focused only on the Charles Edwards Coal Mining Company's demand for labor. But suppose the company is only one of a thousand mining firms operating in Harlan County. And suppose, too, that the mining firms have essentially the same quality coal deposits, use the same technology in mining coal, and compete for the same miners in the same labor market.

If all coal mining firms are identical to Edwards, then each would have the same demand for labor. That is, the miners' *MRP* curve in *any* of the industry's 1,000 coal mining firms would be the same as any other.

The industry demand curve for labor, then, is Edwards', magnified 1,000 times. That's what we see in Figure 5.

ADDED PERSPECTIVE

Wages and Technology

Like so many explanations in the politically charged debate over income inequality, this one raises still another question. Why, after decades of narrowing, did wages shift so decisively in favor of the educated?

Economists have come up with more or less convincing theories, ranging from the decline of unions to the wretched state of public education. But until the publication of a study by John Bound and George Johnson of the University of Michigan in the *American Economic Review,* there had been no comprehensive measure of the relative importance of the leading candidates. And while the Bound-Johnson analysis turns on some daunting econometrics, their conclusions are easily summarized in plain English.

One common sense explanation for the widening wage gap is the decline of industries that for reasons of tradition or unionization or lack of competition, provided all those $12-an-hour jobs that vaulted blue-collar workers into the middle class. This effect is confirmed by number crunching. But the two Michigan economists found that the overall impact on the wage gap was modest: Just one fifth of the change for men and one-eighth for women from 1979 to 1988 seems to have been the consequence of socking it to unskilled labor.

Falling demand for products from industries that paid good blue-collar wages might explain more. It might, but does not. The composition of demand probably did do some damage to Rust Belt icons, notably steel, autos, and rubber. But the effect was offset by growth in demand in a few high-wage industries—health care, for example.

Then there is the question of labor supply. If additions to the labor force had reduced the proportion of workers with college degrees, one might have expected that the changes in relative wages would have favored the educated. Again, a nice try, but no cigar: During the 1980s, the work force became more educated, not less. In fact, econometrics suggests that the trend toward greater education actually slowed the widening of the wage gap by half.

The real culprit, say the two economists, was technological change that made the skills of educated workers more valuable relative to the skills of the uneducated. Just why this happened is unclear. But one way or another, it seems that technology blessed those who already had a leg up in the job market. . . .

While it hardly would have made sense to slow technological change in order to narrow the wage gap, Washington might have responded by making it easier for the economic losers to get the education that leads to better-paying jobs. That would have increased social mobility at a critical moment. And by slowing the rate of growth of the unskilled labor force, it would even have helped those who never made it to college.

In fact, few analysts contend that increased federal interest in public education in recent years has yet improved the quality of the product. And in the one area where money alone would have been most likely to make a tangible difference, the movement has been backward: Higher-education aid was trimmed during a decade when tuition was rising and blue-collar parents were in no position to save for college.

The Michigan economists offer no reason to expect that what technology took from blue-collar workers in the 1980s will be given back in the 1990s. . . .

Discussion

Professors Bound and Johnson could well have described the above analysis in terms of different shifts in the marginal revenue product curves of educated and less educated workers. Explain.

Source: "The Wage Gap: Sins of Omission," by Peter Passell. *The New York Times,* May 27, 1992.

In panel *a*, at w = $20, the quantity of labor demanded by Edwards is eight miners. For the coal mining industry, shown in panel *b*, quantity demanded of labor is 8,000 miners. At w = $4, the quantity of labor demanded by Edwards is 12 miners, the quantity demanded by the coal mining industry is 12,000.

But suppose not all the 1,000 mining firms in the industry are identical. For example, some firms may have access to rich coal deposits while others mine low-quality coal. Or some firms may be using old mining technology while others use the most advanced technology. As a result, the number of tons mined by

FIGURE 5 **Industry Demand for Labor**

In panel *a*, Edwards' *D* = *MRP* curve indicates that it hires 8 workers at a wage of $20 per hour. With 1,000 firms identical to Edwards, the industry demand curve for labor is the horizontal sum of the firms' *MRP* curves. In panel *b*, we see that 8 × 1,000 = 8,000 miners will be hired at a wage of $20 per hour.

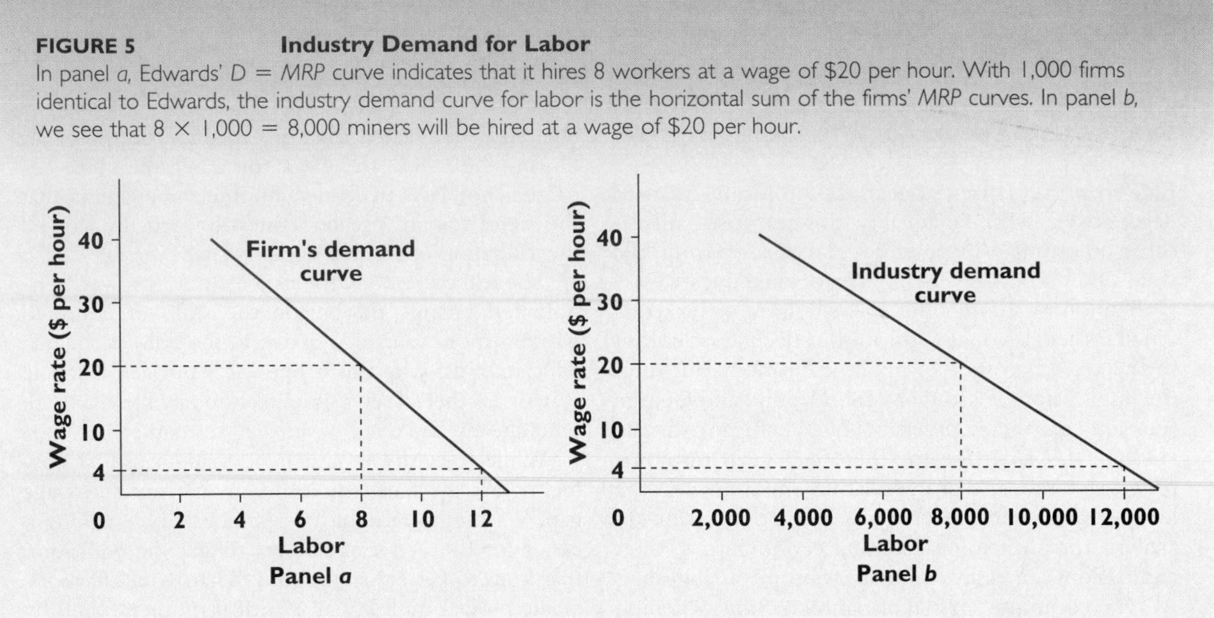

miners—the first, second, third, and so on—in each firm would be different. Each firm's demand curve for labor, then, would be different. For example, while Edwards demands eight miners at w = $20, the Erin Doyle Coal Mining Company, located seven miles down the road, demands 14 (assuming the fourteenth miner's *MRP* at Doyle is $20). Each firm will continue to demand miners as long as the *MRP* of the miner is greater than or equal to the wage rate.

THE SUPPLY OF LABOR

Why does the value placed on leisure cause the labor supply curve to slope up?

Let's now consider how much labor the people of Harlan County are willing to supply to coal mining firms at different wage rates.

Miners have choices. They can choose to work or not to work, and those who choose to work typically face more than one work option. But not all miners have the same work options or share the same preferences for work and leisure. For example, some miners may be workaholics and actually prefer mining to doing anything else with their time. To them, the opportunity cost of mining (the value they place on their next best alternative to mining) is zero. But they are unusual folks. Most people place *some* value on what they can otherwise do with their time. The opportunity cost of working, different for different people, determines how many people in Harlan County would be willing to work at differing wage rates.

Consider, for example, miner Steve Carosello. His next best alternative to mining is the $5.50 per hour he can earn as a school bus driver. A $6 offer at the coal mine, then, exceeds Steve's $5.50 opportunity cost. He is one of the 1,000 people in Table 6 willing to mine at $6. If, on the other hand, the wage rate offered at the mine is $5 per hour, Steve would not be willing to work there be-

TABLE 6
The Supply Schedule Of Coal Miners

Wage Rate ($ per hour)	Quantity of Labor Supplied
$ 0	0
6	1,000
8	2,000
10	3,000
12	4,000
14	5,000
16	6,000
18	7,000
20	8,000
22	9,000
24	10,000

cause the $5.50 he can earn driving the bus is higher. In other words, the $5 wage rate at the mine is below his opportunity cost.

Table 6 records the number of workers willing to work at different wage rates. Nobody goes down into the pits for $5 per hour. At w = $6, 1,000 miners show up. An $8 wage rate meets the opportunity cost of 2,000 miners.

Figure 6 translates Table 6 into graphic form. The supply curve for labor is upward-sloping because the higher the wage rate, the more people's opportunity costs are met.

What Shifts the Supply Curve for Labor?

Note that at a $10 wage rate, 3,000 people are willing to work the mines. That number could increase or decrease depending on changes in the miners' alternative employment opportunities, changes in the population size of the coal mining region, and changes in people's wealth.

CHANGES IN ALTERNATIVE EMPLOYMENT OPPORTUNITIES

If new industries, willing to pay wage rates higher than $10, came to Harlan County, many people who were previously willing to work the mines at $10 would be drawn away from mining to these new employment opportunities. Edwards and other mining firms would soon discover fewer than 3,000 miners available at $10 (and fewer than the numbers shown in Table 6 at each wage rate). The miners' supply curve in the coal industry of Figure 6 would shift to the left, from S to S_1 in Figure 7.

On the other hand, if firms were to leave Harlan County, some people who had been working for those firms would now find the $10 wage rate at the mines their best work opportunity. As a result, more than 3,000 would be willing to work at that wage. With fewer work alternatives for everyone in Harlan County, more miners than those shown in Table 6 would show up for work at each wage rate. The supply curve of Figure 7 would shift to the right.

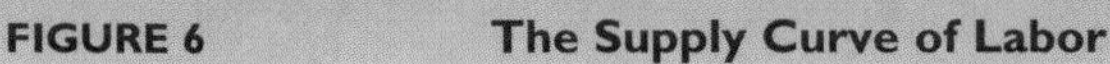

FIGURE 6 The Supply Curve of Labor

The supply curve of labor is upward-sloping. The higher the wage rate, the more willing are workers to supply greater quantities of labor. At w = \$6, 1,000 workers are willing to supply their labor. At w = \$20, 8,000 workers offer their labor. At w = \$24, 10,000 workers are willing to work.

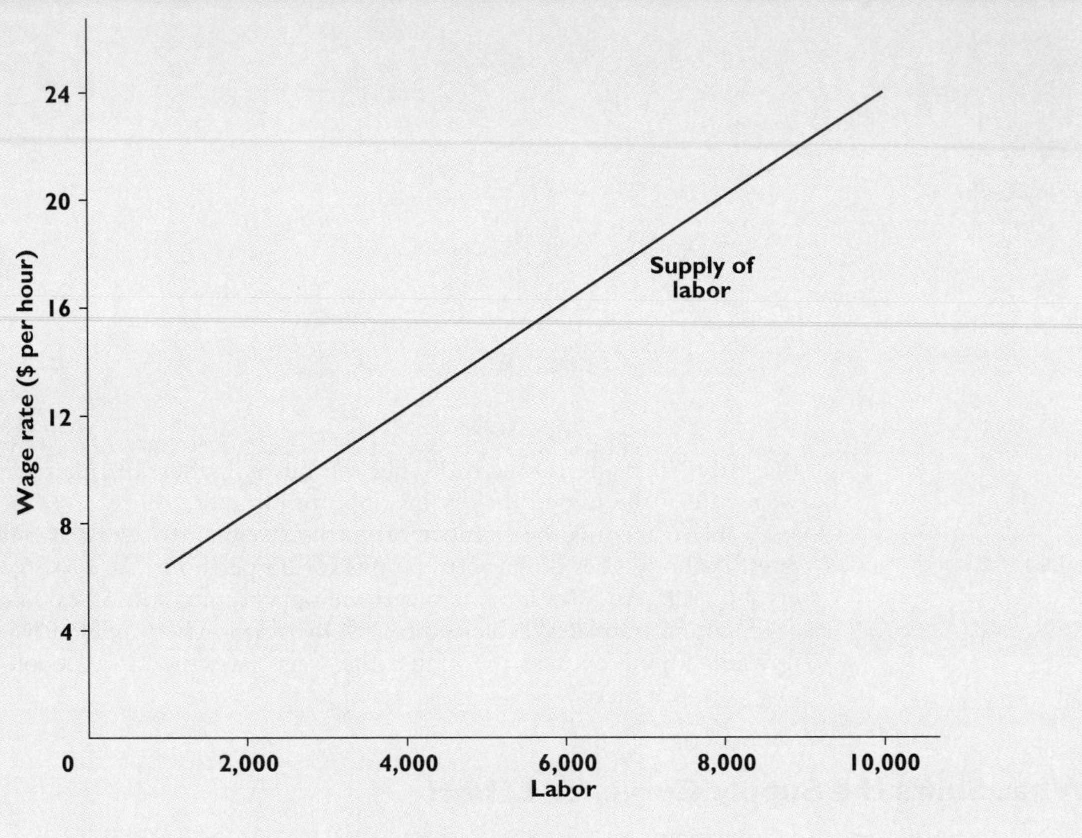

CHANGES IN POPULATION SIZE

Changes in the region's population would also shift the miners' supply curve of labor. For example, if the mining companies continually violate mine safety codes so that a sizable number of miners decide to leave Harlan County, the coal mining firms would soon discover fewer miners than those shown in Table 6 willing to supply their labor at any wage rate. As a result, the supply curve of labor would shift to the left.

On the other hand, what happens to the supply curve of labor in Harlan County if bus-loads of Canadian miners from the depressed mining towns of Nova Scotia migrated in? It shifts to the right, doesn't it?

CHANGES IN WEALTH

Consider as well how changes in people's wealth influence their willingness to supply labor. If you suddenly became a millionaire, how much time would you be willing to spend down in the mine? What wage rate would lure you away from leisure? Let's be more down-to-earth. If an unexpected inheritance tripled

FIGURE 7 **Changes in the Supply Curve of Labor**
Changes in alternative employment opportunities, population size, and wealth affect the number of people willing to work the mines at different wage rates. An increase in alternative employment, a fall in population, and an increase in wealth shifts the supply curve of labor to the left, for example, from S to S_1.

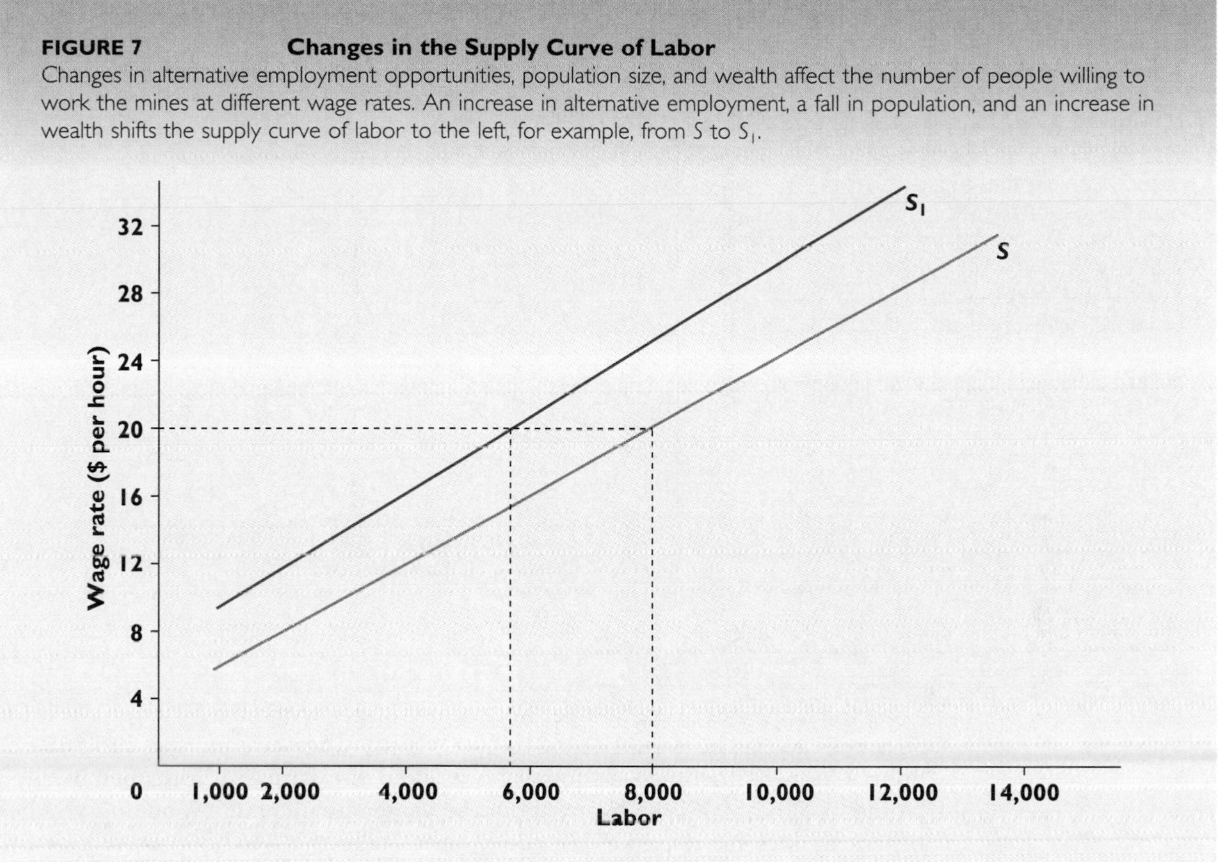

New employment alternatives, changes in population, and changes in wealth cause the labor supply curve to shift.

your wealth, would the mining firm's time-and-a-half wage rate persuade you to give up weekends? Unlikely. Most people are like you. When people have more wealth, they choose more leisure and less work at every wage rate. The result: The supply curve of labor shifts to the left. On the other hand, if fortune fades and wealth falls, the supply curve of labor shifts to the right.

The Backward-Bending Supply Curve

Are all supply curves of labor *endlessly* upward-sloping? Not at all. Suppose you were offered a job paying $10 million, but the job required you to work or to be on call 24 hours a day with no vacations, weekends, or holidays until retirement at age 70. Would you take it?

Not many would. The wage rate is excellent, but the opportunity cost is simply too high. Most people can be enticed by higher wage rates to increase the quantity of labor they supply, but only up to a point. Beyond that, increases in the wage rate may actually result in *less,* not more labor supplied.

For example, Ray Cooper, a miner at Edwards, figures that $100,000 would be more than sufficient to satisfy his needs. Of course, more income is preferred, but not if obtaining more would cut into his leisure time. How would Cooper respond to changes in the wage rate? Look at Figure 8.

FIGURE 8
The Backward-Bending Supply Curve of Labor
Typically, an increase in the rate induces workers to increase the quantity of labor they supply. But once the wage rate reaches a certain level, which may vary for each worker—w = $40 in the case of Ray Cooper's supply curve, S—further increases in the wage rate only encourage workers to cut back on the quantity of labor they are willing to supply.

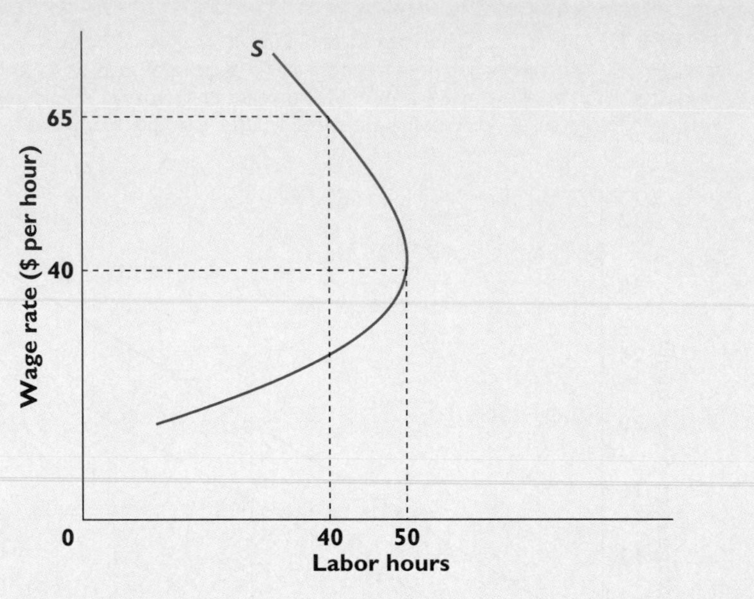

If the wage rate were $40 per hour and Cooper worked a 50-hour week for 50 weeks a year, he would earn $100,000. If the wage rate increased to $65 per hour, Cooper's income—assuming he worked the same 50 hours per week—would be $162,500. Is he happy about the wage rate increase? Wouldn't you be? But how does he respond? He could either take the $162,500 or reduce the hours of work, that is, earn somewhat less but enjoy more leisure. Figure 8 shows what he does. At a wage rate of $65, Cooper cuts back to 40 hours per week and ends up with $130,000. As a result, he gains 500 more hours of leisure. To Cooper, the value of that extra leisure is worth more than $162,500 – $130,000 = $32,500.

The logic behind the backward-bending supply curve for labor rests on the assumption that at a high enough wage people's desires for goods and services other than leisure will be satisfied.

As Figure 8 depicts, at wage rates above $65, Cooper cuts back on the number of hours he supplies even more. That is, Cooper's supply curve of labor at wage rates above $40 is backward-bending.

Conceptually, the backward-bending supply curve makes sense. But we seldom experience it. Typically, workers are willing to supply more labor when wage rates increase.

DERIVING EQUILIBRIUM WAGE RATES

Figure 9 combines the industry demand curve for labor of Figure 5 with the industry supply curve for labor of Figure 6 to create a complete picture of the labor market for miners.

Look at panel *a*. The industry demand for labor, *D*, is the sum of the 1,000 firms' *MRP* curves. The miners' supply curve of labor, S, reflects their willingness to supply varying quantities of labor at varying wage rates. The equilibrium wage rate is $20, and the quantity of labor supplied and employed by the 1,000 coal mining firms is 8,000. At wage rates higher than $20 per hour, an excess

FIGURE 9 The Labor Market
In panel *a*, the supply curve, *S*, shows the number of hours that workers are willing to work at various wage rates. The demand curve, *D*, represents the quantity of labor that firms in the labor market demand at these wage rates. The equilibrium wage rate in the labor market is *w* = $20, the quantity of labor demanded and supplied is 8,000.

In panel *b*, Edwards accepts the *w* = $20 as given. At that wage rate, and with the *MRP* shown as its demand curve for labor, Edwards hires 8 workers, which is where its *MRP* = *w*.

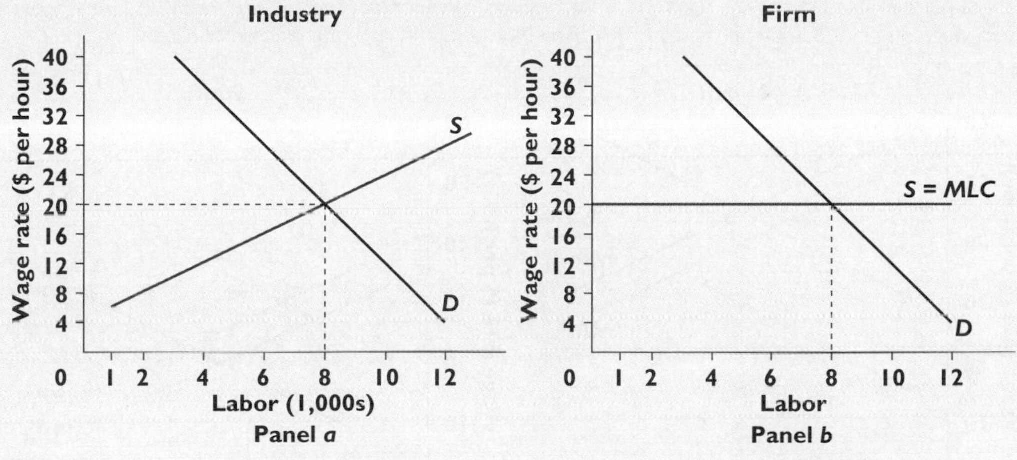

supply of miners emerges, driving the wage rate down. At wage rates below $20, an excess demand for labor emerges, driving the wage rate up.

Picture the scene at the Charles Edwards Coal Mining Company. As far as the firm is concerned, it knows that it is only one of 1,000 firms competing for workers in the miners' labor market. By itself, Edwards has no influence on the miners' wage rate. Hiring one or even five more miners makes no noticeable difference in a labor market of thousands of miners.

That's why Edwards, in panel *b* of Figure 9, faces a horizontal supply curve of labor at w = $20. It can hire one miner at $20 per hour, two miners at $20 per hour each, or as many miners as it wants at $20 per hour. Edwards ends up hiring eight miners because at the eighth miner, $w = MRP$ = $20.

EXPLAINING WAGE RATE DIFFERENTIALS

Understanding how technology and the price of the goods produced by labor affect *MRP,* and understanding as well how the supply curve of labor is affected by the laborer's opportunity cost gives us some insight into why different wage rates exist in different labor markets.

Narrowing Wage Rate Differences

THE CALL OF THE NORTH

If, in the 1960s, you had to guess which of two people's wage rates was the higher, without knowing anything more than that one was working in the South

FIGURE 10 **North-South Wage Rate Differentials**

In panel *a*, the equilibrium wage rate in the North in the pre-immigration period of labor and relocation of factories is \$45. Immigration from the South shifted the labor supply curve from S_{n1} to S_{n2} and the relocation of northern factories to the south shifted the demand curve for labor from MRP_{n1} to MRP_{n2}. As a result, the equilibrium wage rate in the North falls from \$45 to \$35.

In panel *b*, the equilibrium wage rate in the pre-emigration period of labor and before the influx of northern factories to the South was \$20. The emigration of labor to the North shifts the labor supply curve from S_{s1} to S_{s2} and the relocation of northern factories to the south shifts the demand curve for labor from MRP_{s1} to MRP_{s2}. As a result, the equilibrium wage rate in the South increases to \$30. The North-South wage rate differential narrows.

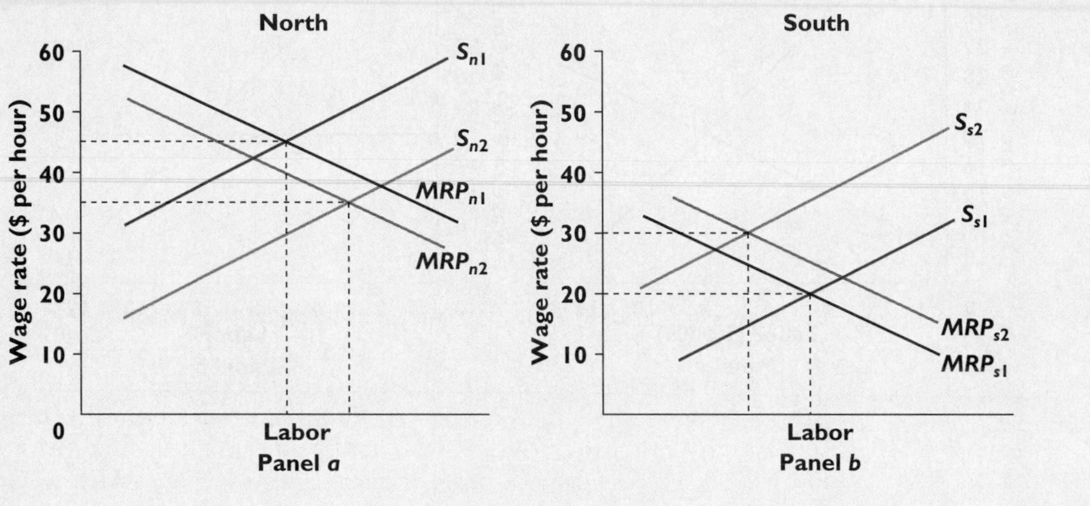

Wage rate differences narrow as workers move to high-wage areas and capital migrates to low-wage areas.

and the other working in the North, you would have been right more times than not to pick the northerner's wage rate.

After all, the manufacturing industries in the North had more capital and advanced technology than those in the South. (Picture their *MPPs*). Moreover, northern industries were typically less competitive than those in the South—oligopoly in the manufacturing North compared to highly competitive agriculture in the South—so that the prices of northern goods were generally higher than those produced in the South. This combination of higher prices and more capital-using technology produced higher *MRPs* for northern workers.

The supply side, too, seems to have worked in the northern workers' favor. They had more attractive job opportunities and, consequently, were much less willing to accept the low wage rates that southern workers accepted coming off low-paying southern farms.

It isn't entirely surprising, then, that southerners would eventually make their way north. Throughout the 1940s, 1950s, and 1960s, millions of people migrated from the small towns of Louisiana, Mississippi, South Carolina, Alabama, and Georgia to the major cities in New York, New Jersey, Ohio, Michigan, and Illinois.

But during these same decades, while people migrated north, industries relocated south to take advantage of the lower southern wage rate. The result is depicted in the shifts in the labor demand and supply curves in both regions, as shown in Figure 10.

In panel *a*, depicting the North's labor market, the supply curve of labor shifted to the right, from S_{n1} to S_{n2}. At the same time, northern industries relo-

TABLE 7
Net Total Migration*: 1970–87 (000s)

By Region		By State	
Northeast	−3,251	New York	−2,144
		Pennsylvania	−752
Midwest	−4,845	Ohio	−1,257
		Illinois	−1,069
		Michigan	−999
South	11,305	Florida	4,526
		Texas	2,626
West	7,190	California	3,740
		Arizona	1,093

*Migration includes net migration from abroad, net interregional, and net interstate.

Source: Bureau of the Census, *Statistical Abstract of the United States, 1989* (Washington, D.C.: U. S. Department of Commerce, 1989), p. 21.

cating in the South shifted the demand curve for labor from MRP_{n1} to MRP_{n2}. Combined, these shifts depressed the North's wage rate from $45 to $35.

Meanwhile, the same labor migration and industry relocations had the opposite effect in the South. There, in panel *b*, the migration of labor shifted its supply curve to the left, from S_{s1} to S_{s2}, while the addition of newly transplanted industries raised the demand curve for labor from MRP_{s1} to MRP_{s2}. Combined, these shifts raised the South's wage rate from $20 to $30. As a result, the wage rate differential between the North and South narrowed. Before it was $45 − $20 = $25. After the migration, the wage differential was $35 − $30 = $5.

As Table 7 shows, the migration shifted in the 1970s; people were leaving the Northeast and Midwest for the Southeast, Southwest, and West Coast.

CROSSING THE RIO GRANDE

As if this Northeast and Midwest migration wasn't enough of a headache for workers in the Southwest and West, they were further upset by the virtually unchecked migration coming across the border from Mexico. How would you feel if you were a worker in Arizona having to compete with newly arrived Northeast, Midwest, *and* Mexican workers?

The less restrictive government policies are with regard to the free movement of labor, the narrower are the wage differentials that will prevail between countries.

It's easy to understand why Mexican workers want to come North. When they compare their situation in Mexico to the employment opportunities north of the border—even for very low-paying U.S. jobs—they have more than enough incentive to cross the Rio Grande.

It's also easy to understand why U.S. industries want to locate south of the Rio Grande. Low wage rates attract industry as much as high wage rates attract workers.

THE MAPLE LEAF FOREVER?

Wage rate differentials also help to explain the migratory traffic on our northern border. Over the years, hundreds of thousands of Canadians have moved south to take advantage of the wage rate differential between Canada and the United States, and at the same time American-owned industry moved north to take advantage of lower Canadian wage rates.

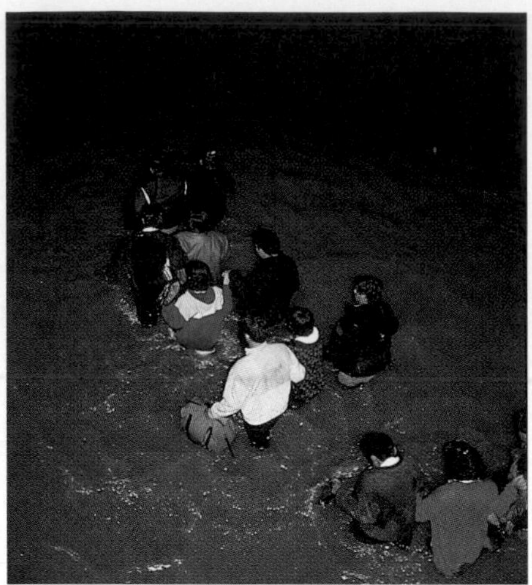

Crossing the Tijuana River in the middle of the night is difficult and dangerous for these and thousands of other Mexican illegals, but the prospect of their getting jobs to feed their families makes their ordeal tolerable.

How do Canadians feel about this? Many in Canada are unhappy about losing so many productive citizens to the United States and see the American "industry invasion" of Canada as undermining Canadian independence. Yet most working Canadians, setting aside national pride, understand the connection between the massive industrial inflow from the United States and the upward shift in their *MRP* and wage rate.

EUROPE'S GASTARBEITERS

Gastarbeiter translates into "guest worker." It has become a common expression in Europe, largely because so many of these people migrated north and east during the 1960s, 1970s, and 1980s to seek higher wages. By 1990, over 5 million *gastarbeiters* were working in northern Europe. Most came from southern Europe and North Africa, the largest numbers from Italy, Turkey, and the former Yugoslavia.

West Germany and France were the principal destinations, and even tiny Switzerland absorbed enough migration to make up fully one-third of its labor force. These *gastarbeiters,* lured away from friends and family by wage rate differentials between their own and the host economies, shifted the labor supply curves in both economies. They were willing to work at jobs others would not touch and at wage rates others would not accept. As wretched as their conditions may have been in the host economy, *gastarbeiters* clearly improved their living standards.

HOW UNIVERSAL IS FIGURE 10?

It really isn't surprising to discover that people everywhere and seemingly *from time immemorial* have responded in much the same way when confronted with regional wage rate disparities. The attraction of higher wage rates elsewhere has always been sufficient to spark even long-distance mobility. The lure of higher wage rates in the United States and Canada enticed millions of European men and women to cross the Atlantic in the 19th century. For the same reason, millions of people in Asia, Africa, and Latin America today leave their villages, friends, and family for the chance to work in the higher-paying overcrowded cities.

THE EFFECT OF IMMIGRATION LAWS

The U.S. constitution guarantees citizens the right to move freely within and between all 50 states. An economics graduate from Purdue University can gather her belongings in West Lafayette and head for the Phoenix labor market, where wage rates are thought to be higher, without having to consider passports, visas, or immigration quotas.

But a graduate of McGill University in Montreal, Canada, with Phoenix on his mind, may get only as far as the international border at Plattsburg, New York. Without a work permit issued by the U.S. Immigration and Naturalization Service, the McGill graduate stays in Canada.

Are the United States immigration laws extraordinarily restrictive? Not really. All governments tend to be selective in admitting immigrants, designing laws to meet domestic concerns.

The supply curve of labor, then, depends not only on the demand and supply conditions in the labor market but also on government's immigration policy. A move to a less-restrictive immigration policy, for example, could shift the supply curve of labor in the receiving economy to the right, creating downward pressure on the wage rate.

PERSISTING WAGE DIFFERENTIALS

If top-seeded tennis players can earn over $250,000 for a few hours' play, why aren't more people playing that brand of tennis? The answer, of course, is that very few people are capable of playing championship tennis.

Although people may be more alike than not, they may still be different in temperament, talent, and intelligence. These differences separate many people into **noncompeting labor markets.** Wimbledon champion Pete Sampras, for example, would be no one's first choice to perform neurosurgery.

Noncompeting labor markets

Markets whose requirement for specific skills necessarily excludes workers who do not have the required skills.

Specific talents, limited to small numbers of people, create unique labor markets that not only allow for relatively high wage rates but also protect the wage rate against erosion. To see this, think about the labor markets for surgeons and butchers.

Suppose that surgeons earn $100 per hour while butchers earn $20. Wouldn't most butchers prefer the $100 wage rate? But can they perform brain surgery? As attractive as the surgeon's wage rate is, the scarcity of people capable of performing surgery keeps the supply curve from shifting to the right.

That is also why NBA basketball players' wage rates are considerably higher than surgeons. Don't you think most surgeons would abandon their operating rooms if they could dunk basketballs like Shaquille O'Neal?

THE ECONOMICS OF MINIMUM WAGE RATES

The problem with persisting wage differentials is not that some people earn millions. It is instead the inability of many people to compete successfully in any occupation that provides an adequate living standard.

Whatever the reasons, individuals become trapped in labor markets where the *MRP* is extraordinarily low and the supply of labor plentiful. The resulting

Can you explain the difference in the impact of a minimum wage law on labor markets with elastic and with inelastic demands for labor?

wage rate is insufficient to provide a decent living. Once in, how do these people break out of the low-wage-rate trap?

Many solutions have been proposed and tried. Perhaps the simplest and most direct way of raising low wage rates is simply to "outlaw" them! That is, the government can legislate minimum wage laws that prohibit employers from hiring people at wage rates below a specific level.

It is not as peculiar a solution as it may appear. After all, almost every economic interest group in our economy has pleaded with government to get into the business of legislating prices. Farmers, for example, have successfully lobbied

FIGURE 11 **The Effects of Minimum Wage Rates**

The minimum wage law generates unemployment among workers willing to supply labor at the minimum wage rate. But the level of this unemployment, and consequently the net effect of minimum wage rates on the incomes of all the workers who would work for minimum wages, depends on the price elasticities of supply and demand for labor. In panel *a*, the net effect of the minimum wage rate legislation is 700 unemployed workers and a decrease in the average worker's income.

But in panel *b*, which assumes different price elasticities of demand and supply, only 100 workers lose their jobs after the minimum wage rate legislation, and the resulting workers' income at the minimum wage rate increases.

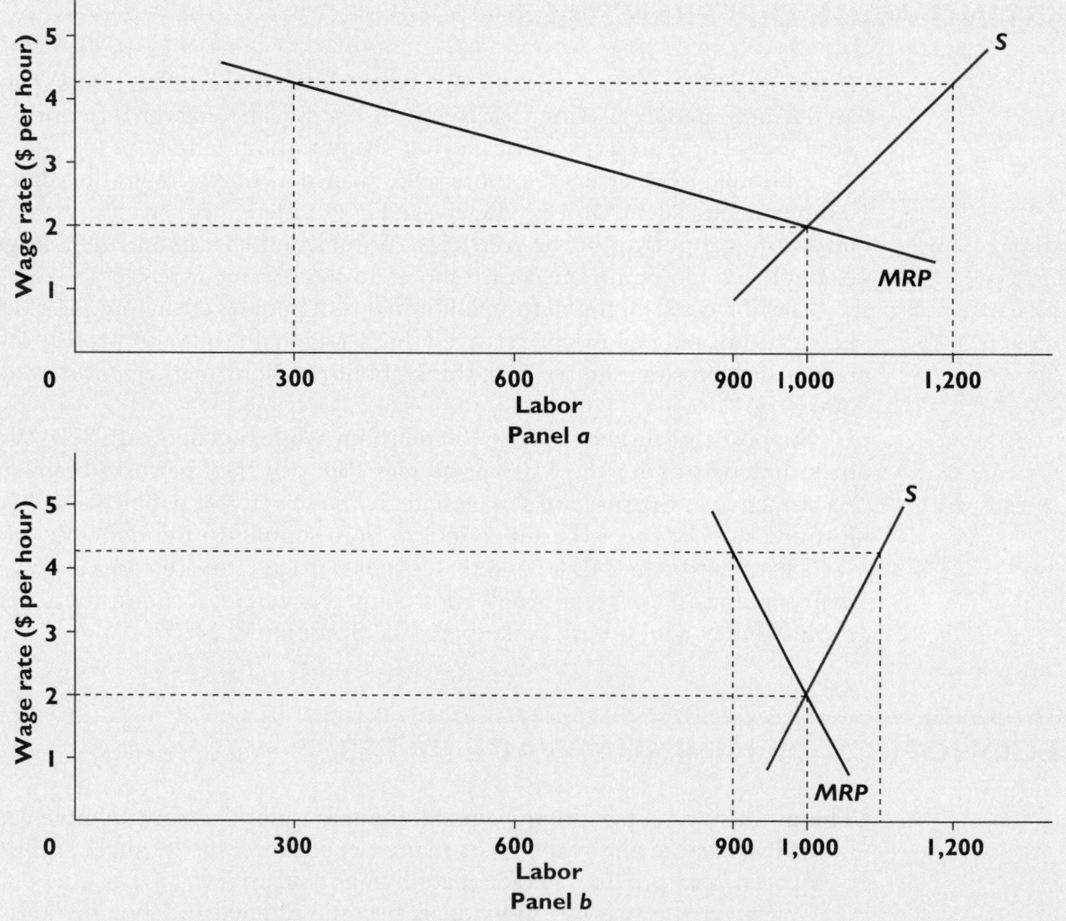

government to set minimum farm prices. Producers of industrial goods have persuaded government to protect their prices by legislating tariffs on imports. The result was to shift income from nonfarmers to farmers in the one case, and from consumers to producers in the other.

But are low-wage-rate earning people really better off with minimum wage laws? Look at Figure 11, which shows the market for low-skilled labor.

In panel *a*, the \$2.00 equilibrium wage rate is inadequate to provide anyone working a 40-hour week with an acceptable living standard. Can you picture yourself trying to make it through the week on \$80?

Suppose government legislated a \$4.25 minimum wage rate. Every working member of Figure 11 now takes home \$170 weekly. It still creates a formidable challenge to make ends meet, but it beats \$80 hands down.

But now a new, perhaps no less severe problem for low-wage-rate earners emerges. *Employers cannot be expected to hire workers whose* MRP *is below the \$4.25 legislated minimum wage rate.* Look at panel *a*. Employers hire only 300 workers at w = \$4.25. They are forced to dismiss 700 of the previously hired 1,000 workers. Why? Because the *MRP*s of the 301st to the 1,000th worker now fall below the minimum wage rate. (Since 1,200 low-wage-rate earning people are now willing to supply their services at \$4.25, the unemployment created by the minimum wage is actually 1,200 – 300 = 900 workers.)

That's not what the government had in mind when it legislated the minimum wage. Not only has the \$4.25 wage rate knocked 700 people out of work, but the total income of low-wage-rate earning people as a group actually falls.

Figure it out. Prior to the minimum wage legislation, total hourly income earned by these people was \$2.00 × 1,000 – \$2,000. After the minimum wage rate was imposed, total hourly income was \$4.25 × 300 = \$1,275.

But suppose panel *b*, not panel *a*, describes the labor market for these low-wage-rate earning people. A very different outcome emerges. The \$4.25 minimum still creates unemployment among those willing to work at minimum wages, but now it's only 100 workers. The total hourly income received by the low-wage-rate earning people of panel *b* is \$4.25 × 900 = \$3,825. (Even if the \$3,825 were distributed among all 1,100 willing to work at the minimum wage rate, the average wage rate would increase to \$3,825/1,100 = \$3.48, considerably better than the previous minimum wage of \$2.00.)

As you see, the impact of minimum-wage-rate legislation on low-wage-rate earning people depends ultimately on the price elasticities of demand and supply of labor. In other words, it depends on whether panel *a* or panel *b* is a more accurate reflection of real world labor demands and supplies. Although economists hold strong views on this critical issue, there is no real consensus.

THE ETHICS OF $w = MRP$

Many working people believe that they should be paid more than they currently earn. This is not surprising. Most people have a well-developed sense of self-worth. But is there any evidence supporting their belief? Should miners, for example, earn more? Should peach pickers in Georgia? Economists typically have shied away from addressing *should* questions. Yet most economists accept market-determined wage rates as ethically defensible, even if wage rates in some labor markets are exceptionally low, because market-determined wage rates are based on individual merit—that is, they reflect workers' *MRP*s.

Consider the labor market for miners in Harlan County, Kentucky. Miners there receive a wage rate equal to their *MRP,* which is the equivalent of what they produce. The ethic underlying this wage rate is expressed as: *From each according to his or her contribution, to each according to his or her contribution.*

A tennis star's $250,000 earnings at Wimbledon is considerably higher than the wage rate earned by a Kentucky miner, yet each individual is paid exactly what that individual contributes. If people with skills not highly demanded in the economy end up earning low wage rates, they are not necessarily underpaid. Underpayment, according to this ethic, occurs only when people receive less than the full measure of their *MRP.*

In a perfectly competitive labor market people get paid a wage equal to their marginal revenue product, which is the value of their marginal physical product.

Why then minimum-wage-rate legislation? The answer may have little to do with the issue of merit. Many economists are driven by compassion to support minimum wage laws. Others accept minimum wage legislation as the lesser of two evils, believing that the intolerable living conditions of low-wage-rate earning people may lead to social unrest and other societal ills that are far less desirable than minimum wage rates.

On the other hand, there are economists, also driven by compassion, who oppose minimum wage laws. To them, such laws serve only to undermine the personal incentives needed to coax people out of low-paying labor markets. Others oppose minimum wage laws because they believe that each individual ought to receive the value of his or her productive contribution.

Yet, both the economists who favor minimum wage rates and those who do not, agree on this: Any wage rate differential between two people producing the same *MRP* signals a gross violation of the $w = MRP$ ethic. This kind of wage rate differential has long hurt women and minorities in many labor markets. Many routinely confront racial, religious, or sexual discrimination that upon examination, shows up as the primary source of their wage rate differentials.

CHAPTER REVIEW

1. A competitive labor market consists of many workers of equal skill offering to work for many employers. Each additional worker adds to total physical product an amount called the marginal physical product. The total physical product increases initially at a increasing rate, then the rate of increase declines, reflecting the law of diminishing returns.

2. Marginal physical product multiplied by the price of the good produced equals marginal revenue product. Marginal revenue product is the addition to total revenue from an additional unit of labor.

3. Just as each worker adds to total revenue, each also adds to total cost. When workers are hired in a competitive market, the firm takes the wage as market-determined. Each unit of labor the firm hires must be paid the market wage. Marginal labor cost for the firm is the market wage. To hire the profit-maximizing number of workers, the firm continues to hire until the marginal revenue product is equal to the marginal labor cost.

4. The marginal revenue product of labor curve is the firm's labor demand curve. The curve shifts due to a change in either the marginal physical product or the price of the good. Therefore, improvements in labor productivity and an

increased price of the good cause the demand for labor to rise, the wage rate to increase, and firms to hire more workers.

5. The industry demand for labor is the sum of individual firms' demand for labor. The market supply of labor curve is the sum of individual workers' labor supply curves. Workers place a value on the leisure they must sacrifice in order to work. Most workers are willing to forego increasing amounts of leisure as the wage rate increases, so the labor supply curve is upward-sloping.

6. Changes in alternative employment opportunities, changes in population size, and changes in wealth shifts the supply of labor curve.

7. The backward-bending supply curve for labor suggests that at some relatively high wage rate, people's needs for goods and services will be satisfied and they will choose to work less when the wage rate increases.

8. The equilibrium wage is set at the intersection of the market demand for labor and the market supply. Each firm can hire as many workers as it desires at the market wage.

9. Wage rates are higher in regions where workers have access to more capital equipment, which makes them more productive. Workers tend to migrate to these high-wage regions. However, capital tends to migrate toward regions where wages are lower. Labor and capital migrations tend to equalize wage rate differentials over time.

10. Government restrictions on the free movement of labor and capital can cause wage differentials to persist. Wage differentials might also persist due to the presence of noncompeting labor markets.

11. Minimum wage laws set a wage floor above the market wage in labor markets. Fewer people will be hired as a result of the minimum wage law.

12. Market wage rates express the underlying ethic that people are paid for the value of what they produce. This ethic suggests that people should be paid equally for equal amounts of production.

KEY TERMS

Marginal physical product
Marginal revenue product
Total labor cost
Marginal labor cost
Noncompeting labor markets
Wage rate

QUESTIONS

1. In explaining how the marginal physical product of labor is derived, economists assume that other factors of production, such as capital and land, are held fixed. Why is this assumption necessary?

2. What is the relationship between the law of diminishing returns and the downward slope of the marginal physical product curve?

3. What is the relationship between the marginal physical product of labor and the marginal revenue product of labor?

4. Suppose the Chris Corpora Coal Mining Company currently employs 17 workers at $14.50 per hour, which is the prevailing wage rate in the perfectly competitive market for miners. Suppose also that the marginal revenue product of the seventeenth worker is $12.50. What should the firm do? Why? What hiring rule should it follow?

5. Farm workers' *MRP* in Canada keeps falling even though they keep producing more output. Explain.

6. Why might a farm worker in Zambia earn less than a farm worker in Canada?

7. Suppose Eastern European economies, following the collapse of Soviet power in Europe, begin to demand more farm goods from Canada. What impact, if any, would you expect this new demand to have on farm wage rates in Canada?

8. Suppose Zambian farmers begin to use more insecticides and chemical fertilizers. What impact would such uses, if successfully adopted, have on Zambian farm wage rates?

9. Recall the analysis of pollution costs in the previous chapter. How would pollution considerations—clean-up costs resulting from increased use of insecticides and chemical fertilizers in Zambia—affect Zambian farm wage rates? *Hint:* Consider price changes resulting from shifts in the supply curve in the farm-goods market.

10. Why is the marginal labor cost identical to the wage rate in perfectly competitive labor markets?

11. What is the relationship between a firm's marginal labor cost and the industry's supply curve of labor?

12. How does the opportunity cost of work influence the character of the supply curve of labor?

13. Suppose yesterday was your lucky day. You won $7 million in the Kentucky State Lottery and the Charles Edwards Coal Mining Company (where you work) raised the wage rate from $12.50 to $17.50 per hour. How would you respond to these pieces of news? What would happen to the quantity of labor you would be willing to supply at the mine? Why? What about your good friend, Adam Schmidt, who works the same shift as you? He didn't win the lottery. What do you suppose would happen to the number of hours he would be willing to work?

14. Two good friends, Mo Jo Nixon and Natalie Merchant, grew up together, went to the same schools, ranked identically in IQ testing, excelled in every subject, and went on to earn Ph.D.'s. Natalie became a professor of finance; Mo Jo became a professor of English. Both teach at the same college. Natalie earns $55,000, while Mo Jo earns $37,000. Is there economic injustice in this story? Perhaps discrimination? How can you explain the income differential?

15. Until very recently almost all the porters at railway stations were black. It seems, then, that black people must have a special talent for that occupation or a preference to work as porters. Discuss.

16. How could one government's immigration policy affect wage rates in other economies?

17. Suppose the price of leather gloves is $12. Graph a demand curve for leather-glove laborers from the following data concerning their total physical product.

Quantity of Labor	Total Physical Product
0	0
1	35
2	65
3	90
4	110
5	125
6	135
7	140

Show what happens to the demand curve for labor when the price of gloves falls to $6. What happens when the price increases to $20?

18. Consider the following perfectly competitive labor market.

Quantity of Labor	Marginal Revenue Product	Total Labor Cost
5	$2.00	$ 5.00
10	1.50	10.00
15	1.25	15.00
20	1.00	20.00
25	0.85	25.00
30	0.75	30.00
35	0.70	35.00

How many laborers would be hired? At what wage rate?

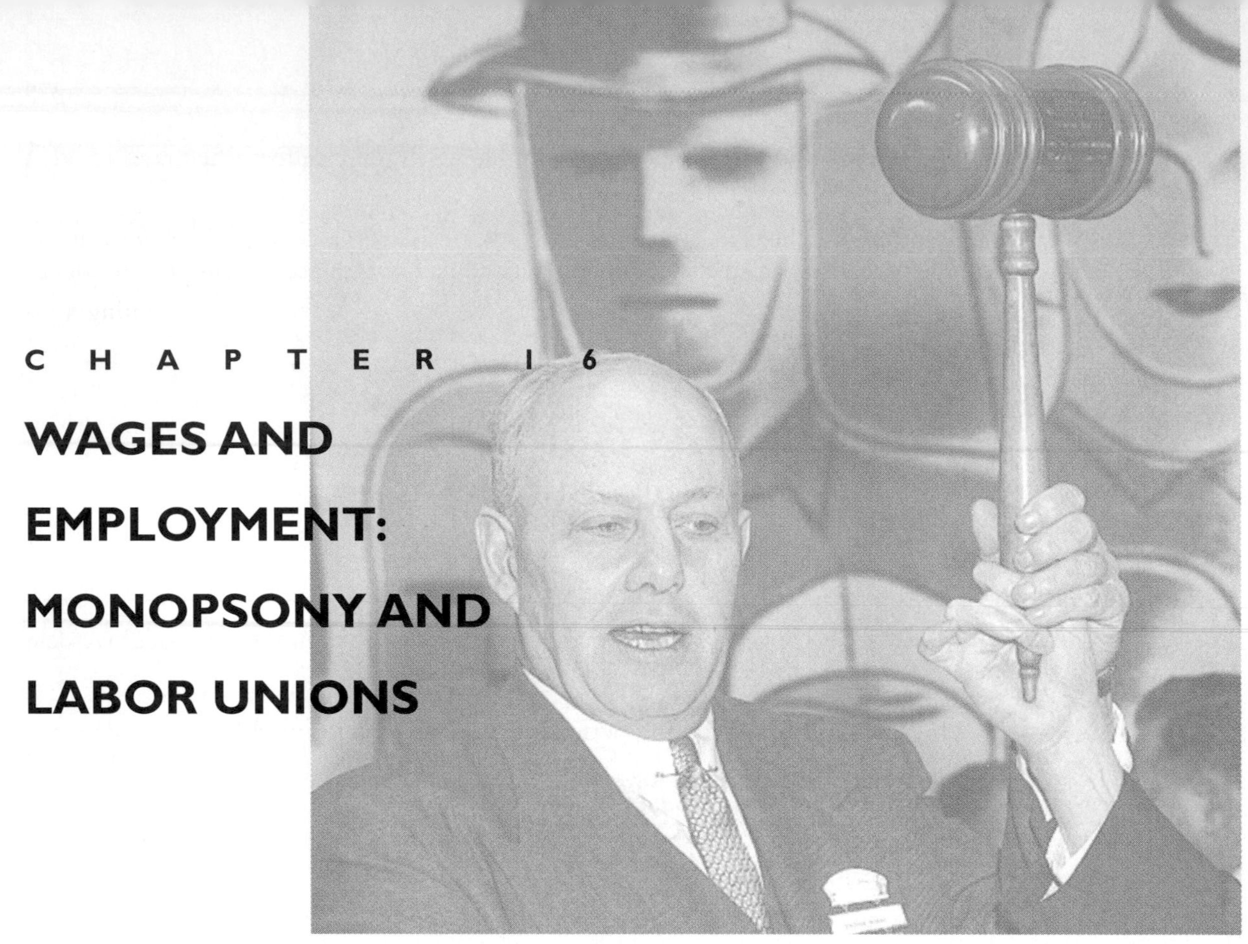

C H A P T E R 16

WAGES AND EMPLOYMENT: MONOPSONY AND LABOR UNIONS

CHAPTER PREVIEW

Not all labor markets are perfectly competitive. A firm that is the sole buyer of labor is called a monopsony. Wage rates and employment determination are different under monopsony compared to perfectly competitive labor markets. Labor unions can play an important role in monopsony labor markets. The interplay between unions and monopsonists can result in intense conflict. Examples of such conflicts are described in this chapter.

After studying this chapter, you should be able to:

- Explain why the monopsonist faces the market supply curve for labor.
- Derive the marginal labor cost curve from the supply curve for labor.
- Account for the fact that the marginal labor cost curve lies above the supply curve for labor.
- Describe how a union can alter the marginal labor cost curve in order to increase wages.
- Discuss the variety of conflicts that arise between unions and monopsonists over wage and employment determination.
- Explain how the elasticity of demand for labor can influence union strategies.
- Outline the historical development of unions in the United States.

Let's continue our analysis of the Charles Edwards Coal Mining Company. But now let's suppose that the firm, in a series of acquisition moves, buys out every other coal mining firm operating in Harlan County. That's a dramatic change. What had been a region with a thousand competitive, thriving coal mining firms becomes through these acquisitions a one-company county.

MONOPSONY: WHEN THERE'S ONLY ONE BUYER OF LABOR

Can you picture the scene? In the beginning, Edwards merely replaces the signs at the mine entrances. The Greg Mechtly Coal Company, for example, is now part of Edwards. No mining operation actually shuts down. Total coal production in the county remains unchanged.

What about the miners? As far as they are concerned, little has changed. They still work at the same mines with the same machinery and are paid the same wage rate. They mine the same tonnage. The only change, at least at the beginning of Edwards' consolidation, is in the name. They are now all part of Edwards.

Monopsony
A labor market with only one buyer

But real change is imminent. Not only do the miners soon realize that their only source of employment in the county is Edwards, *but the firm too realizes that it has become the only firm hiring miners in the county*. Economists define its new labor market position, the only buyer of labor, as **monopsony.**

The Supply Curve of Labor as Seen by the Monopsony

Edwards, as a monopsonist, no longer thinks about hiring only nine or ten miners. It now thinks in terms of thousands. It also knows that because it is the only

TABLE 1
The Supply Schedule of Coal Miners

Wage Rate ($ per hour)	Number of Miners
$ 0	0
6	1,000
8	2,000
10	3,000
12	4,000
14	5,000
16	6,000
18	7,000
20	8,000
22	9,000
24	10,000

FIGURE 1 **Supply Curve of Labor Facing a Monopsonist**

The monopsonist, as the only buyer of labor in the market, faces the market labor supply curve. It has no competitors for that labor. Since the labor market reflects the willingness of workers to supply varying quantities of labor at varying wage rates, the monopsonist is free to choose among the various combinations of wage rates and labor supply. What's available in this case? At w = \$6, the quantity of labor supplied is 1,000 workers. At w = \$8, the quantity of labor supplied is 2,000. At w = \$20, the quantity of labor supplied is 8,000. The supply curve of labor is upward-sloping.

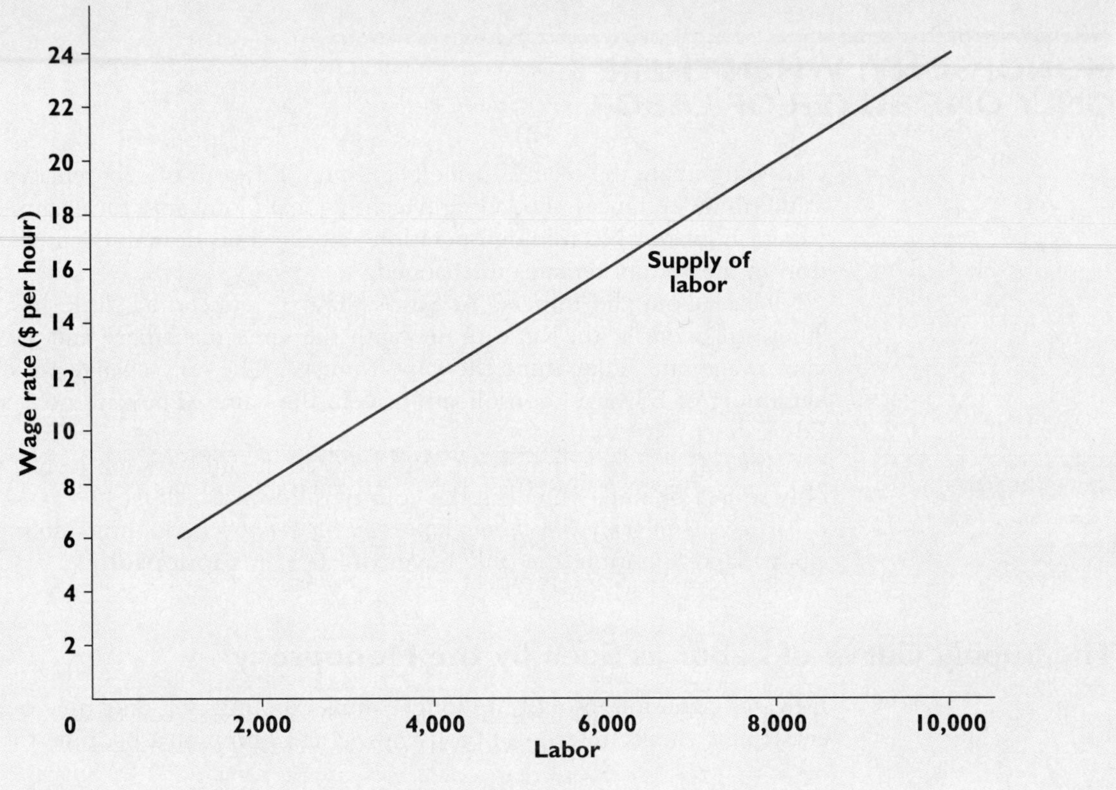

Since the monopsonist is the only buyer of labor in the market, the supply curve of labor facing the monopsonist is the market supply curve of labor. A monopsonist can pick the wage rate it wishes to pay.

firm buying labor in the region, the supply schedule of miners is precisely the market labor supply schedule we saw in the last chapter. That schedule is reproduced here in Table 1 and Figure 1.

When Edwards announces that it is willing to hire at a wage rate of \$10, 3,000 miners show up to work, *as they had before*. Miners' willingness to supply labor does not depend on the number of firms buying labor. Why should it?

If Edwards wants more than 3,000 miners, it will have to raise the wage rate offered. For example, if it needs 4,000 miners, it will have to raise the wage rate to w = \$12. And if w = \$20, 8,000 miners become available.

The labor supply curve of Table 1 changes the way Edwards thinks about hiring. In the old days, when it was just one of a thousand mining firms competing for labor, it took the wage rate given by the market. It had no choice. If it offered less than that market rate, it could hire nobody. Now, Edwards is the market.

TABLE 2
Labor Cost Data

Wage Rate	Number of Miners	TLC	Additional Labor Cost per 1,000 Miners	MLC
$ 0	0	$ —	$ —	$—
6	1,000	6,000	6,000	6
8	2,000	16,000	10,000	10
10	3,000	30,000	14,000	14
12	4,000	48,000	18,000	18
14	5,000	70,000	22,000	22
16	6,000	96,000	26,000	26
18	7,000	126,000	30,000	30
20	8,000	160,000	34,000	34
22	9,000	198,000	38,000	38
24	10,000	240,000	42,000	42
26	11,000	286,000	46,000	46

Edwards can pick the wage rate it wants. But whatever rate it picks, it gets only those miners willing to work at that wage rate. It can't choose w = $6, for example, and hope to get more than 1,000 miners.

What wage rate, then, should it choose? Look at the labor cost options Edwards now faces as a monopsonist. They are shown in Table 2.

Reading Table 2

Because a monopsonist must raise the wage rate in order to hire more workers, even for workers already hired at a lower wage, the *MLC* is above the wage rate.

How does Edwards read Table 2? The wage rate it has to pay to get additional miners and the costs those additional miners add to the firm are not the same. Compare wage rates and marginal labor cost in Table 2.

If w = $6, Edwards can hire 1,000 miners. The firm's total labor cost (*TLC*) then is $6,000, that is, $6 × 1,000. The *MLC* of each of those first 1,000 miners is $6. In this one case, w = *MLC*.

But note what happens thereafter. If Edwards wants to hire more labor, it has to raise the wage rate. Suppose it raises it to w = $8. The quantity of labor supplied increases to 2,000. *TLC* increases to $8 × 2,000 = $16,000, while *MLC* increases to ($16,000 – $6,000)/1,000 = $10.

Do you see what happened? The second group of 1,000 miners hired gets a wage rate of $8, yet each costs the firm $10. Why? Because Edwards is obliged not only to pay those new 1,000 miners $8, but to raise the wage rate of the 1,000 hired earlier at $6 to $8.

When the firm figures the cost of the second 1,000 miners, *both their wages and the cost of bumping up the wage rates of the first 1,000 miners are calculated.* Edwards adds the $2 × 1,000 = $2,000—that represents the bump—to the $8 × 1,000 = $8,000 that is the cost of hiring the new miners. The total is $10,000. Each of those 1,000 new miners, then, costs the firm $10,000/1,000 = $10.

Figure 2 traces the relationship between the wage rates and the *MLC* associated with hiring miners.

FIGURE 2 **Relationship between the *MLC* Curve and the Supply Curve of Labor**

Both the *MLC* curve and the supply curve of labor, *S*, are upward-sloping. The *MLC* curve lies above the supply curve because when the monopsonist increases employment, it must not only offer a higher wage rate to attract more workers but also raise the wage rates of those already working. When the firm increases employment from 3,000 to 4,000, it raises the wage rate from $10 to $12 per hour. Its total labor cost increases from $30,000 to $48,000, or by $18,000 per hour. That is, the 4,000 – 3,000 = 1,000 additional workers cost the firm $18,000, or $18,000/1,000 = $18 per hour per worker. Even though each of these added workers receives only a $12 wage rate, they each add $18 to the firm's labor cost.

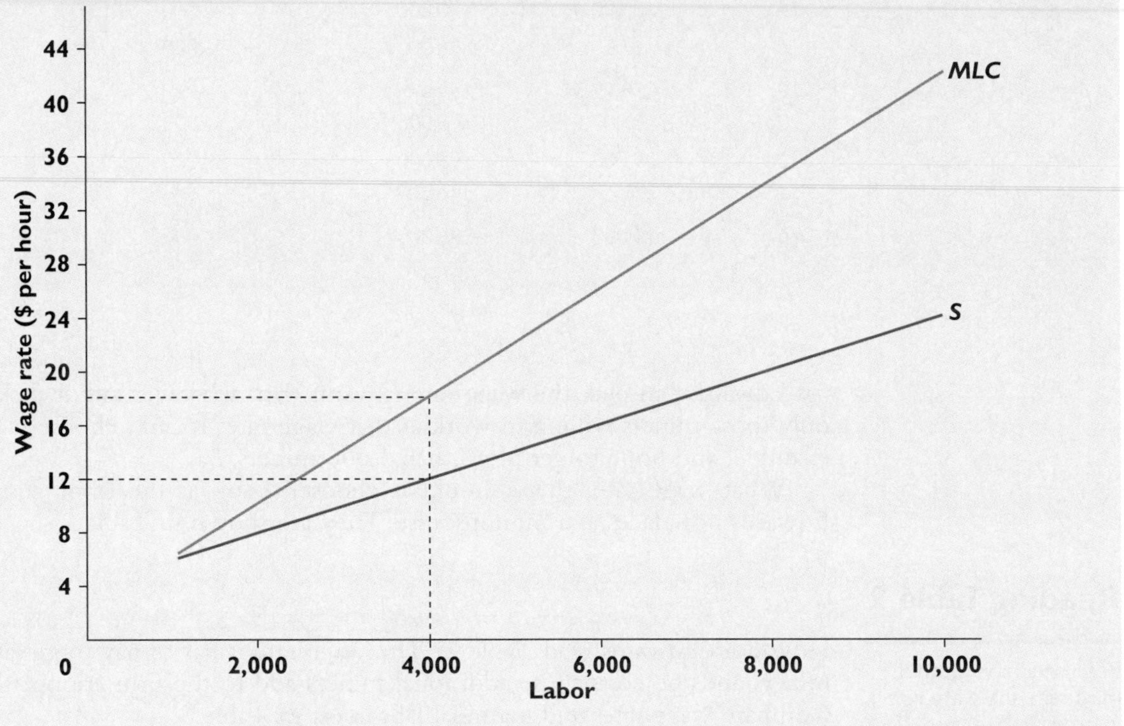

Notice how the supply curve and *MLC* curve diverge as more miners are hired. That's because the need to bump up the wage rates of miners already hired gets to be increasingly expensive as the firm hires more miners.

CHOOSING THE EMPLOYMENT/WAGE RATE COMBINATION UNDER MONOPSONY

The monopsonist hires workers until the *MRP* = *MLC*, then reads the wage rate from the market supply of labor curve. How is this different from a perfectly competitive labor market?

How many miners does Edwards actually hire? Edwards follows the revenue-maximizing rule practiced in the previous chapter. It continues to hire miners as long as *MRP* > *MLC*. It stops hiring when the miner's *MRP* = *MLC*.

Table 3 combines the cost data of Table 2 with the firm's demand for miners. This demand, as we know, reflects the miners' *MRP* which, for simplicity's sake, we assume takes the form shown in column 4, Table 3.

TABLE 3 Determining the Wage Rate and Employment Combination

Labor	Wage Rate	*MLC*	*MRP*
0	$ 0	$—	$—
1,000	6	6	36
2,000	8	10	34
3,000	10	14	32
4,000	12	18	30
5,000	14	22	28
6,000	16	26	26
7,000	18	30	24
8,000	20	34	22
9,000	22	38	20
10,000	24	42	18
11,000	26	46	16

Note that *MRP* = *MLC* at $26 and at 6,000 miners. Edwards hires 6,000 miners, paying them each a wage of $16, which is $10 below their *MRP*.

The Return to Monopsony Power

You can imagine the resentment growing in Harlan County. Remember that during the competitive days of the previous chapter, miners received their *MRP*. But Edwards defends itself, insisting that its behavior hasn't changed. It uses the same employment guidelines it used in the last chapter, employing up to the miner whose *MRP* = *MLC*.

After all, isn't it unreasonable to expect the firm to hire miners who cannot produce sufficient revenue to cover the additional labor cost the hiring imposes on the firm? But that's precisely what happens beyond the 6,000th miner. For example, look at that 7,000th miner. That miner adds $24 to revenue and $30 to the firm's labor cost.

The miners complain that their *MRP* = $26, yet their wage rate is only $16. Aren't they entitled to their *MRP*? In the competitive labor market of the last chapter, *w* = *MRP*. But not any more!

Edwards pays the 6,000 miners a wage rate of $16 because 6,000 miners have indicated—look at the supply curve of labor—that they are willing to work at $16.

The difference between the wage rate that the 6,000th miner is willing to take and the *MRP* of that miner, multiplied by total employment, is the **return to monopsony power.** Edwards' return monopsony power is shown in Figure 3.

Return to monopsony power

The difference between the MRP and the wage rate of the last worker hired, multiplied by the number of workers hired.

The monopsony returns that Edwards is able to capture from its 6,000 miners is (MRP – w) × *L* = ($26 – $16) × 6,000 = $60,000, indicated by the shaded rectangle in Figure 3. The miners argue that the $60,000 would belong to them *if the labor market were competitive.* But it isn't competitive.

FIGURE 3 **The Return to Monopsony Power**

The firm will hire as long as the *MRP* generated by the hired worker is greater than or equal to the worker's *MLC*. The firm stops hiring at 6,000 miners. The *MRP* of the 6,000th worker is $26, but that's not what the firm pays the worker. That 6,000th worker is willing to work for $16, which is what that worker and all the other employed workers receive. The difference between the workers' *MRP* of $26 and their $16 wage rate generates for the firm a return to monopsony power of ($26 – $16) × 6,000 = $60,000, the shaded rectangle.

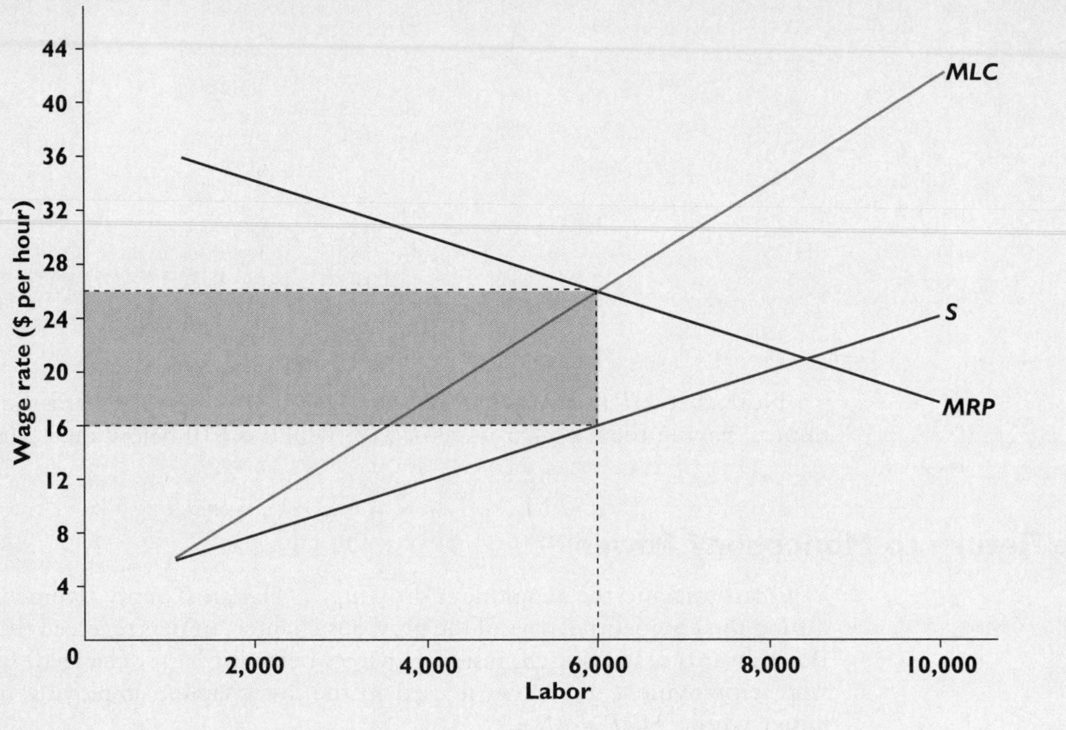

ENTER THE UNITED MINE WORKERS' UNION

Labor union

An association of workers, each of whom transfers the right to negotiate wage rates, work hours, and working conditions to the association. In this way, the union presents itself as a single seller of labor on the labor market.

A union can face the monopsonist with a single wage rate which represents a new supply curve for labor that is horizontal at the wage determined by the union.

What can the miners do? The monopsony condition of Figure 3 is ripe for the United Mine Workers' Union (UMW). Let's suppose the **labor union** sends Michael Kulikowski, an experienced organizer, down to Harlan County, Kentucky, to talk to the mine workers.

His message would be simple. Miners must no longer be willing to offer their labor services at the wage rates shown in Table 1. *They must confront Edwards with a very different supply curve of labor.*

Miners should hold out for $26. Not one miner should agree to work for less. Not even for $25.99. By holding tight at $26, they will get $26. But how do they do that? That's where the union comes in. The miners vote to give the UMW union authority to represent them in negotiations with Edwards. They will work or stay out of work at the union's direction. In effect, the UMW becomes *the* supplier of labor in Harlan County.

Edwards now sees a completely different labor market. What it confronts is the union's offer of labor services shown in Table 4.

TABLE 4
The Supply of Miners Offered by the Union

Union's Supply Schedule		Cost to Edwards of Union-Organized Labor	
Miners	**Wage Rate**	***TLC***	***MLC***
0	–	–	–
1,000	$26	$ 26,000	$26
2,000	26	52,000	26
3,000	26	78,000	26
4,000	26	104,000	26
5,000	26	130,000	26
6,000	26	156,000	26
7,000	26	182,000	26
8,000	26	208,000	26
9,000	26	234,000	26
10,000	26	260,000	26

Employment and Wages in a Unionized Labor Market

Because the union confronts the monopsonist with a single wage, the supply curve for labor and the *MLC* are the same. The monopsonist still hires labor until *MRP* = *MLC*, but the union receives a wage that is now equal to the *MRP*. What happened to the return to monopsony power?

The union is quite willing to allow the monopsonist to choose however many miners it wants to hire. Michael Kulikowski, the union organizer, knows what Edwards will do. The firm will hire the same 6,000 miners, but this time at w = $26 instead of w = $16. The miners will now end up with the $60,000 that had formerly been the return to monopsony power. Why is Michael so sure? Look at Figure 4.

The horizontal supply curve of labor at w = $26 is what the union offers. Edwards can hire one or 10,000 at that wage rate. But not one miner for a penny less! The new, union-designed *MLC* = w is $26. Edwards, resigned to this new labor market, will hire, as it always does, where *MRP* = *MLC*. That, Michael Kulikowski points out, is precisely at the old level of 6,000 miners.

But a problem arises. Look again at Table 2. At w = $26, 11,000 miners are willing to work. That creates an excess supply of 11,000 – 6,000 = 5,000 miners. Edwards, understandably, will hire no more than 6,000 because the 6,0001st miner's *MRP* is less than w = $26. The union, then, must control its labor supply; otherwise the excess supply will undo its collective strength. That's not always easy to accomplish.

The Dynamics of Collective Bargaining

Strike
The withholding of labor by a union when the collective bargaining process fails to produce a contract that is acceptable to the union.

Suppose Edwards decides not to accept the union demand for w = $26. Instead, it offers to increase the wage rate from $16 to $20. The union can ask for w = $26, but asking is not the same as getting.

Edwards simply says it won't hire at w = $26. The union now has two choices. Michael can recommend that miners accept the $20 offer, which is still $4 more per hour than they had earned in the nonunion, unorganized labor market, or he can recommend that miners reject the firm's offer and go out on **strike.**

FIGURE 4 **The Unionized Labor Market**

The union changes the supply curve of labor from the preunion, upward-sloping *S* shown lightly-colored to the unionized, horizontal supply curve of labor, S_u, at \$26. The *S* curve is no longer available to the monopsony. At w = \$26, the monopsony can choose to hire as many workers as it wishes. It hires workers as long as the *MRP* generated by each new worker is greater than or equal to the worker's *MLC*. The firm ends up hiring 6,000 workers, because at 6,000, *MRP* = *MLC*. Now the workers receive \$26, the full value of their *MRP*.

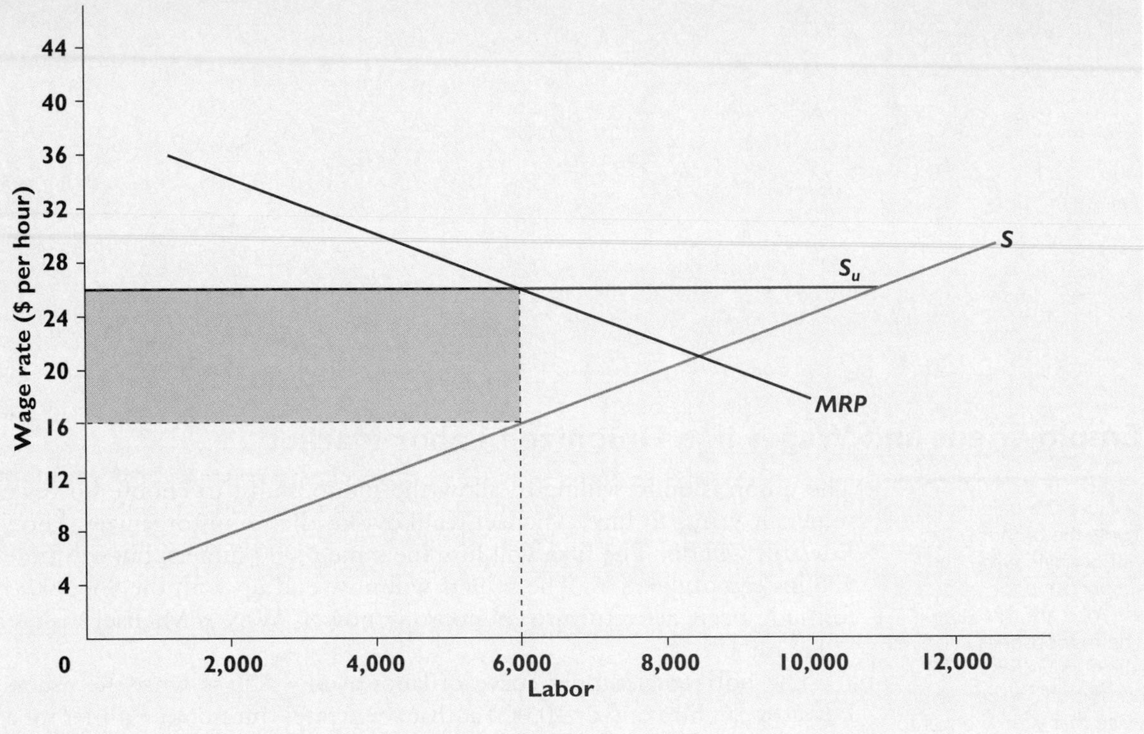

Collective bargaining

Negotiation between a labor union and a firm employing unionized labor to create a contract concerning wage rates, hours worked, and working conditions.

Suppose the miners vote to accept the \$20 offer. Edwards and the miners now share the disputed \$60,000 return to monopsony power. As you can well appreciate, the miners' decision to accept or reject the firm's offer ultimately depends upon their assessment of their own **collective bargaining** power relative to the firm's.

If they sense that they can get more, they reject the firm's offer and go on strike. No coal is mined, Edwards earns no revenue and miners, of course, earn no income.

Miners cannot stay out on strike forever. Nor can mining firms survive without mining. It is only by reassessing each other's ability to tolerate the damaging effects of the strike that the impasse can be broken.

A union doesn't always get the wage it demands from a monopsonist. A union may order a strike if it thinks it can extract a higher wage from the monopsonist.

Does the union have the financial resources to continue the strike? Can the firm stay closed without losing its own customers? Does the firm have enough financial resources to wait out the strike? Playing "chicken" is a nerve-racking business. Strikes are not pleasant for the miners or for the mining firms. But both sides realize that a great deal is at stake.

Unions realize that it takes a long time to make up the revenue lost through a strike. In some cases, they never make it up. But unions also know, as baseball managers do, that you keep arguing with the umpire for the benefit of the *next*

"We buy the drinks!" It's been a hard negotiation session, but the smiles on the faces of these professional baseball negotiators signal success. A strike has been ended.

call. A long, protracted strike is a signal to the firm to reassess the workers' determination. Of course, workers have to make the same reassessments about the firm.

In other words, both firms and unions are involved in a very risky business of signalling, stating intentions, and concealing agendas. They continually reassess all the factors and push for the best wage agreement they can possibly make. The prize is the return to monopsony power.

HIGHER WAGE RATES VERSUS MORE EMPLOYMENT

What happens to the quantity of labor supplied if the union successfully raises wages? What are the implications for the union's control over the supply of labor?

Suppose the union is successful in getting that $26 wage rate and successful in holding the labor force to 6,000. Success, however, may invite the disquieting feeling that perhaps the union miscalculated and should have asked for more.

At the next negotiation round, suppose the union raises its demand to w = $30. But this time, it confronts two circumstances it may not have anticipated.

First, because the supply curve is upward-sloping, at w = $30, more people are willing to work the mines. As a result, the union's ability to control the labor supply weakens. Second, because the *MRP* curve is downward-sloping, at w = $30 (look at Table 3) the firm *cuts* the number of miners employed to 4,000. That is, at w = $30, more people want to work and fewer people are hired.

What does the union do with 2,000 cut from the 6,000 previously working miners? What does it do with the increasing pressure of others wanting to join the labor market?

The union can't just wish them away. But how can it control the labor supply? It can discourage replacements for workers who are retiring. It can create unreasonably long apprenticeship periods. It can impose exceptionally high initiation fees. It can create programs that retrain and relocate miners already in the market. It can simply turn a deaf ear to the unemployed. But whatever the strategy, it is clear to the union, as it is to surgeons in the AMA and basketball players in the NBA, that fewer numbers allow for greater freedom to pursue higher wage rates.

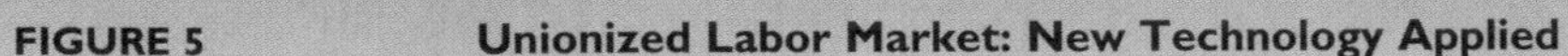

FIGURE 5 **Unionized Labor Market: New Technology Applied**
When new technology shifts the workers' *MRP* to the right, from *MRP* to *MRP'*, the firm and the union may react differently. The firm is prepared to increase employment to 7,000, where *MRP'* = *MLC* = $30. But the union, instead of providing 7,000 miners at a $30 wage rate, may prefer to raise the wage rate from $26 to $32, keeping employment at 6,000 miners.

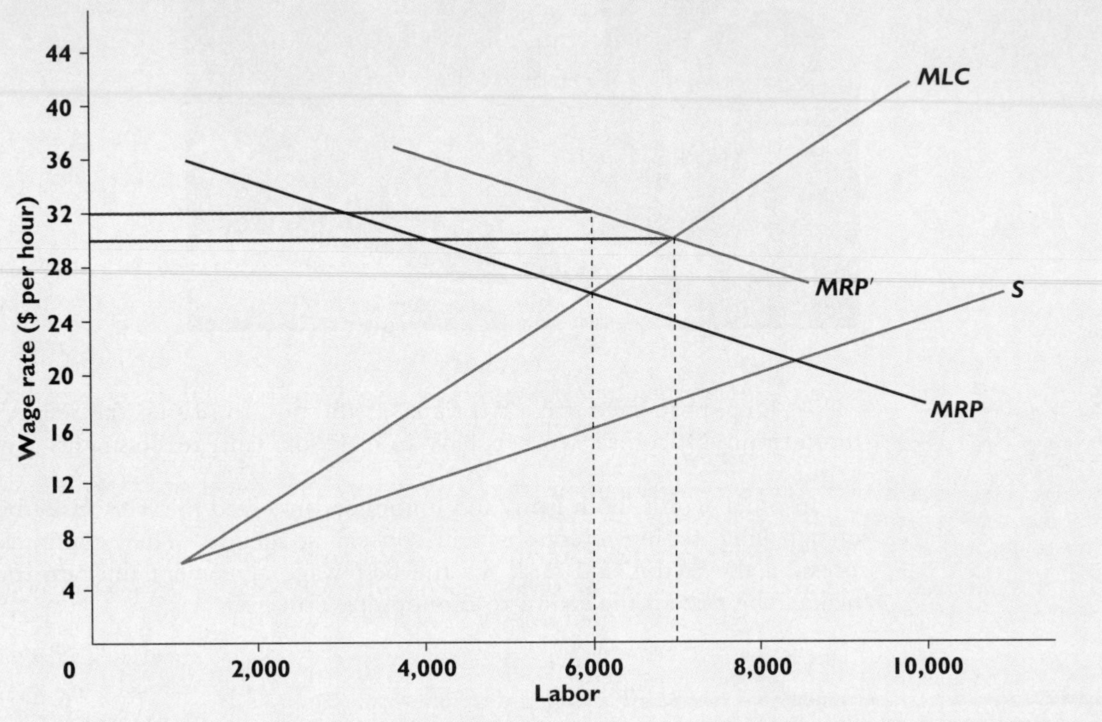

Monopsonist Demands More, Union Reluctant to Supply

An improvement in technology increases the demand for labor. The union is faced with a choice of whether to increase the amount of labor supplied or to restrict the labor supplied in order to raise the wage rate.

Suppose Edwards shifts to a new, more productive form of technology or benefits from a sudden increase in the price of its coal. Either event would shift its miners' *MRP* curve to the right, as illustrated in Figure 5.

Under these new conditions, what would Edwards do? It would want to hire 7,000 miners and would be willing to pay a wage rate of $30. That creates a sizeable increase in the number of miners employed and *in the number of tons of coal produced.*

The union is also delighted with the shift in the *MRP* curve, but it may have other designs. It sees that the *MRP* of its 6,000th miner has increased from $26 to $32. What a great opportunity! If it can hold the quantity of miners it supplies to the firm at 6,000, it can push for a w = $32 contract. Edwards will pay the w = $32 because *MRP'* = *MLC* at $32.

But an aggressive Edwards may challenge such union control over its labor supply. It could appeal directly to nonunion miners and offer them w = $26. Why wouldn't they accept? *You can see, then, that the inherent conflict is not only between the hiring firm and labor, but between nonunion labor and union labor over the issue of employment versus wage rates.*

THE CLOSED SHOP

Perhaps the most effective way of controlling the labor market is for the union to insist that the firm hire only unionized miners. In this way, the union decides whether or not to satisfy the firm's labor demands. Economists call such an arrangement a **closed shop.**

Closed shop

An arrangement in which a firm may hire only union labor.

Although firms relinquish control to the union over their labor supply, the closed shop can sometimes be quite a convenient arrangement for the firm. Relations between the firm and the union aren't always antagonistic. The closed shop can serve as a useful labor filter, providing the firm with a reliable supply of workers.

THE UNION SHOP

But the closed shop, however convenient, still denies the firm the right to choose its own labor. It is one thing to agree on a wage rate contract, but quite another to give up the right to decide on the quantity and quality of labor hired.

The union sees the firm's right to hire anyone, whether union or nonunion, as a potential threat to its ability to raise the wage rate. The firm sees the union's monopoly on the hiring and firing of labor as a barrier to its economic growth.

Union shop

An arrangement in which a firm may hire nonunion labor, but every nonunion worker hired must join the union within a specified period of time.

The **union shop** is a form of compromise. It safeguards the firm's right to employ as many miners as it wants, but it insists that all miners hired must join the union.

How does it work? Suppose Edwards wants to hire more than the union can supply. Under the union shop rules, the firm can recruit anyone from anywhere as long as those recruited join the union. In this way, the union can still decide what wage rate to accept and the firm decides, after negotiating the rate, how many miners to employ.

Elasticity of Labor Demand and the Wage Rate/Employment Trade-Off

A more elastic demand for the product that labor produces translates into a more elastic demand for labor and vice versa. How does an increase in the wage affect employment levels if the demand for labor is elastic? Suppose the demand for labor is inelastic?

The elasticities of the *MRP* curves influence the decisions unions make in negotiating the trade-off between wage rates and employment.

Compare Figure 6, panel *a*, showing a unionized market for coal miners, and panel *b*, showing a unionized market for precision toolmakers. Suppose their labor supply curves were identical but the elasticities of their *MRP* curves were markedly different.

Suppose both the panel *a* market and the panel *b* market initially employ 6,000 workers at w = $26 and in each, the union succeeds in raising the wage rate to w = $30. Look at the consequences. In panel *a*, 2,000 miners are laid off. In the precision toolmakers' market of panel *b*, however, only 500 workers are laid off.

Why the difference? *The MRP curves reflect the demand elasticities of the goods produced.* If the demand for coal is highly elastic, the demand for coal miners tends to be highly elastic as well.

On the other hand, if the demand curve for the firm's product is highly inelastic as it is assumed in panel *b* for precision tools, then the demand for precision toolmakers tends to be inelastic as well.

It is not surprising, then, that price elasticity of demand for goods such as steel, textiles, education, trucking, and coal has much to do with the ability of

FIGURE 6 **Markets For Coal Miners and Precision Toolmakers**

In panel *a*, the high demand elasticity for coal prevents the union from raising the wage rate to \$30. At w = \$30, the firm would lay off 2,000 miners. In panel *b*, the low demand elasticity for precision tools gives the precision toolmakers' union the incentive to demand a \$30 wage rate. At w = \$30, the firm lays off only 500 precision tool workers.

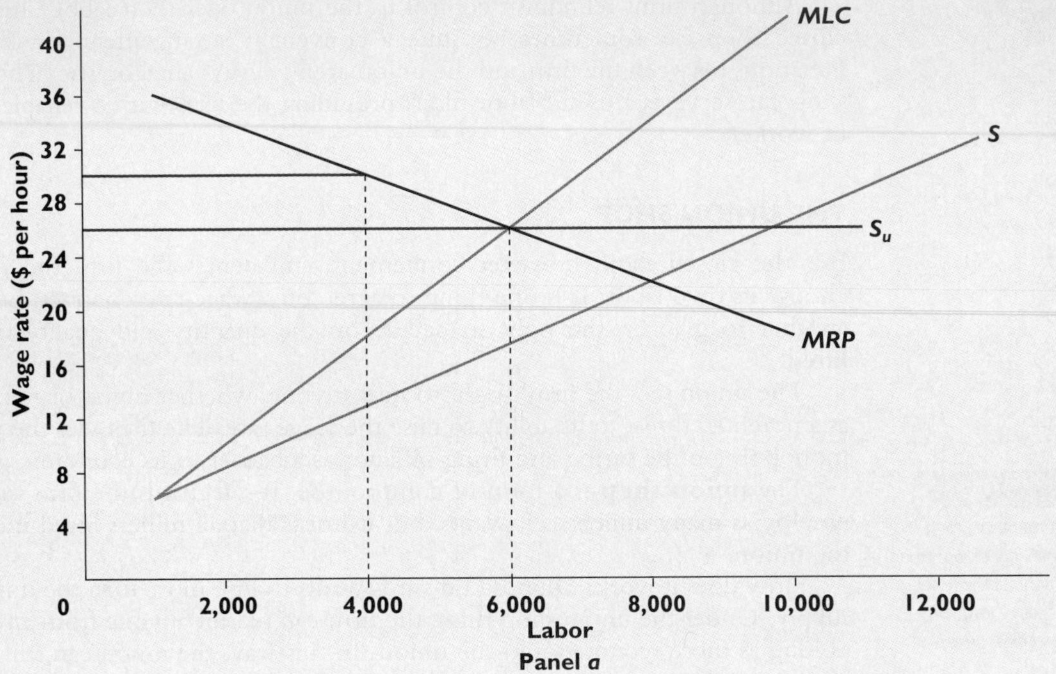

Panel *a*

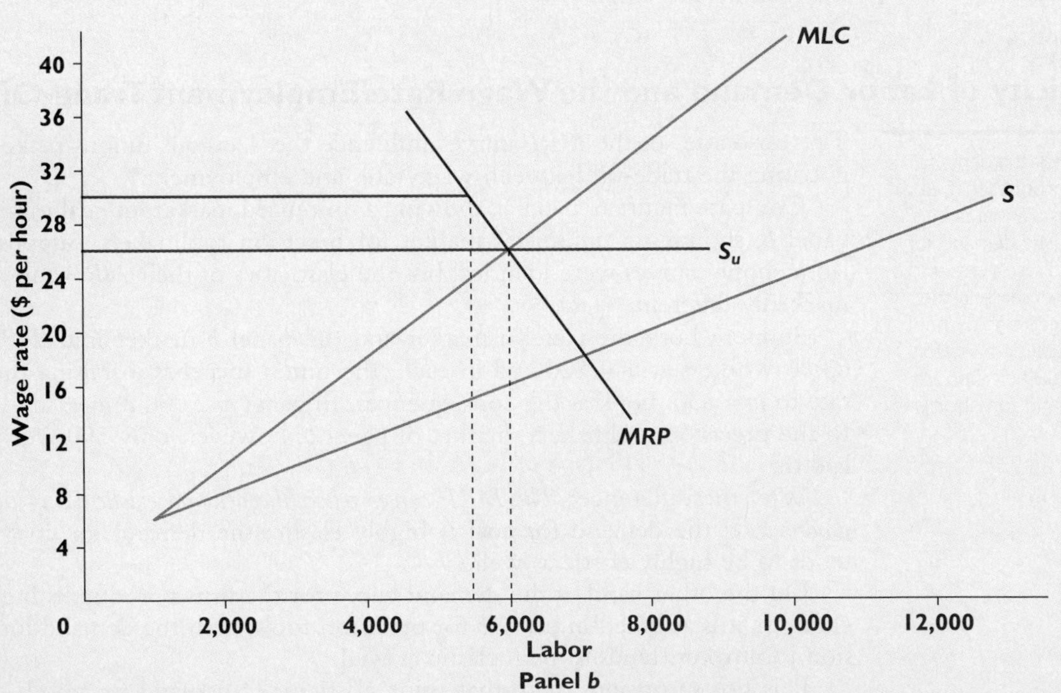

Panel *b*

ADDED PERSPECTIVE

Miners Say Key Issue Is Job Security

The United Mine Workers' $2\frac{1}{2}$-month-old strike against mines in seven states, which has idled 17,000 miners, turned ugly with the shooting death last week of a nonunion worker who crossed a picket line in Lundale, WV.

But no talks are scheduled between the UMW and the Bituminous Coal Operators Association. With utilities' coal inventories above normal, analysts say a settlement could be months away.

Linda Lester, who went into the coal mines at 18, and the other miners on strike in these green mountains and narrow valleys of Appalachia understand how pivotal this strike is.

They've watched the number of union jobs shrink from 120,000 to 70,000 in 10 years as coal production tripled. They know the average miner is 44 and works in a mine with only seven years of production left. They realize more jobs will be lost as Clean Air Act restrictions force companies to close high-sulphur mines.

And they've seen their union's clout wane in the face of nonunion labor: Where once a UMW strike could paralyze the U.S. economy, today union-produced coal accounts for just 30 percent of national output.

No surprise then that the picket line refrain this time is job security—not wages, not health benefits, not safety.

The UMW argues that union labor and concessions over the years have allowed companies to mechanize, to boost production, and to open more mines, so in fairness, union miners should get a guaranteed share of jobs.

"I'm 34 and I've worked for this company since 1979," says Dennis Burress, a mine electrician and Local 2421 president. "All that would be wasted. I'd have to go start over."

The UMW says operators agreed to fill three of five new jobs with union miners, then reneged by spinning off subsidiaries that hired nonunion miners. This "double-breasting" is the core of the dispute. Coal operators say double-breasting isn't illegal and defend hiring nonunion labor.

"Our offer included offering jobs to the UMW at nonunion operations," says BCOA spokesman Thomas Hoffman. "We didn't offer every single job and don't intend to. It limits the worker pool."

Strikers on the picket line here at CONCOL Inc.'s Virginia Pocahontas No. 6 mine, out just two weeks, already worry about money. A union miner may gross $40,000 a year, plus 100 percent medical benefits. The union asks them to work a picket line once a week, so they can look for other work on the side. But there are few jobs to be had outside the mines.

They all know miners who've been laid off for years, some who've taken nonunion jobs. Others head south to the furniture factories, carpet mills, and citrus groves, but more often than not return.

Discussion

To what extent has the shift in energy source from coal to nonfossil fuels such as oil, affected the lives of unionized coal miners? What impact does this energy source switch have on the coal miners' *MRP* curve?

Source: *USA Today*, July 28, 1993.

steelworker, textile worker, teacher, teamster, and coal miner unions to raise the wage rate of their members.

UNIONS IN THE UNITED STATES: A BRIEF HISTORY

It is difficult to identify the beginnings of union activity in the United States because informal arrangements among workers and employers have always existed. Still, the first attempt by workers to organize on some sort of permanent basis seems to have occurred in 1792 when the Philadelphia shoemakers created the Federal Society of Journeymen Cordwainers.

Why did they organize? The shoemakers saw their wage rates and status in the craft threatened by competition from low-paid, unskilled workers that employers were hiring in increasing numbers. In 1799, the union went on strike to counter a wage cut. The employers responded by taking the organized workers to court.

Early unions were considered criminal conspiracies.

On what charges? On conspiring to interfere with employers' rights to operate freely in the labor market. The court obliged, finding the shoemakers guilty of criminal conspiracy. It ruled that union organizing to promote a collective interest was a criminal act. This criminal conspiracy doctrine dictated court decisions until 1842, when the Commonwealth *vs.* Hunt decision ruled that unions were not illegal. It did not, however, bestow legality upon them. For almost a century thereafter, unions fell into a twilight zone, somewhere between legality and illegality.

The Knights of Labor

If solidarity were in the workers' own interest, why not organize all workers into one giant union? That's precisely what the Knights of Labor tried to do. In 1869 it became the first union to organize across all skills, all industries, and all regions.

The Knights of Labor advocated structural changes in the economy to benefit labor in addition to higher wage rates for members.

It was interested not only in pursuing higher wage rates for its members, but also in bringing about structural change in the economy and society. It campaigned vigorously against the use and abuse of child labor and promoted worker-owned cooperatives.

But the Knights had difficulty convincing workers to look beyond their own paycheck. Most workers were more interested in their wage rate than in changing society. Yet, the Knights had its moment of glory. While other unions in the 1880s couldn't deliver, the Knights struck the railroads and won. Nothing succeeds like success. By 1886 it had 700,000 members.

But it was an inglorious slide into oblivion thereafter. It suffered ill-advised and costly strikes, lost money by financing poorly organized cooperatives, and felt the heavy hand of the Pinkerton detective agents hired by employers to infiltrate and disrupt its organizing activity.

But perhaps the major factor in its demise was its inability to convince its own members of the importance of its wider goals. Most weren't interested in social and economic change. They seemed quite prepared to accept the existing economic system, provided the system was generous.

The American Federation of Labor

Although it was difficult for workers to organize during those early antiunion years, many still did. By the end of the 19th century, workers had organized mainly along craft lines, such as unions of welders, painters, or plumbers. Painters and welders working for the same shipbuilding firm, for example, belonged to two separate unions and negotiated two separate contracts.

Samuel Gompers, an official of the Cigar Maker's Union, understood what workers wanted and understood also what it took to get what they wanted. He once remarked that a worker's worst enemy was an employer who didn't make a profit. He knew that a union's ability to win higher wages depended on the firm's ability to pay. And that's all he wanted.

Disenchanted with the Knights of Labor to which his cigar makers' union belonged, Gompers and some other unionists broke from the Knights in 1881 and five years later formed the American Federation of Labor (AFL).

George Meany, president of the AFL, left, joins hands with Walter Reuther, president of the CIO, as the two hold aloft a giant gavel symbolizing the merger of the American Federation of Labor and the Congress of Industrial Organizations. The historic merger ended a 20-year split in the ranks of organized labor.

The AFL stuck to the promotion of strictly economic goals for its members.

Craft union

A union representing workers of a single occupation, regardless of the industry in which the workers are employed.

From its inception, the AFL was designed to promote strictly economic goals, such as higher wage rates, shorter hours, and better working conditions. Its motto was simple and direct: "More More, Now Now!"

Structurally, the AFL was set up as a loose-knit umbrella organization of highly autonomous **craft unions.** The AFL's primary function was to establish general objectives and guidelines and to settle jurisdictional disputes among its craft union members.

For example, when two unions disagreed on which had the right to organize a targeted set of workers, the AFL came in to mediate. With technology constantly changing the character of labor activity, craft identity became highly contested. But AFL mediation didn't always settle jurisdictional disputes.

Because the AFL was craft-related, most of the nation's unskilled workers were left unorganized. Fruit pickers, janitors, farm workers, garbage collectors, and night watch people, for example, hardly involved in craftlike activity, had nowhere to go. Although the focus on crafts meant the AFL lost potential members, it also meant that unskilled, noncraft workers, whose *MRP* was relatively low, would not act as deadweight on the craft unions' efforts to raise wage rates. The AFL showed little sympathy for the growing number of economically powerless workers.

The Congress of Industrial Organizations

The more technology changed, the more craft distinctions blurred. By the 1930s, new manufacturing industries created even more jurisdictional problems as assembly-line production stamped uniformity of skills across craft lines. Many in the AFL saw that its craft orientation was increasingly becoming an impediment to further union growth. But the more successful craft unions felt threatened by industrial growth and stubbornly resisted restructuring.

Industrial union

A union representing all workers in a single industry, regardless of each worker's skill or craft.

What would restructuring mean? The creation of **industrial unions.** That is, unions would be organized along industrial rather than craft lines. For example, all workers in the textile industry would organize as a textile union. Its members would include everyone from fabric cutters, sewing machine operators, finishers, and pattern makers to shipping clerks and janitors at the textile plant. These were people with very different skills, working in different crafts,

FIGURE 7 **Union Membership Since 1900**

Figure 7 depicts the dramatic increase in union membership from the mid-1930s to the early 1980s. The downward slide in membership is even more dramatic in the succeeding short period of the mid-1980s to the 1990s. Note also the percentage of the labor force unionized. The percentage increased rapidly from the 1930s through the 1950s, remained fairly stable at approximately 25 percent until the 1980s, and then dropped dramatically to 11 percent by 1993.

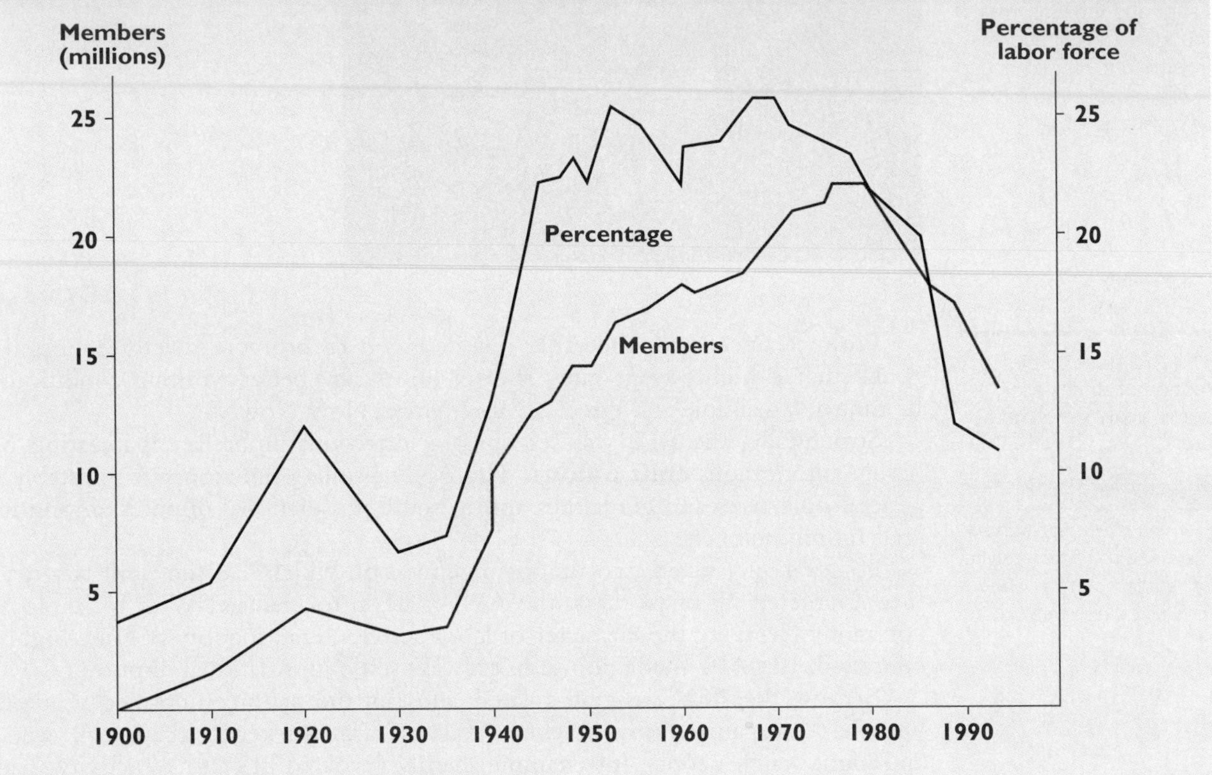

but belonging to a common industry. The AFL's concern was that incorporating all skills in a single organization would weaken the power of the more skilled workers to negotiate a wage contract.

The AFL was a craft union, whereas the CIO was intended to give broad representation to less-skilled industrial workers.

In 1935, a number of industrial unionists, soured by the AFL's refusal to restructure, organized their own association. The Congress of Industrial Organizations (CIO) came into being by first bringing together the mine workers, garment workers, textile workers, and a few others. National industrial unions were founded to reorganize workers. By 1938, the CIO became a competing national labor federation.

AFL-CIO Merger: 1955

The competitive struggle between the AFL and CIO continued throughout and beyond the depression of the 1930s, the World War II years of the 1940s, and into the postwar period of the 1950s. By 1955, both the AFL and the CIO could see beyond their own limited horizons. The future of American unionism depended on union cooperation, not confrontation.

The strengths of these two federations, secured by their own longevity, allowed them to merge in 1955 to form the AFL-CIO. It brought both craft and industrial unions under one roof. The idea was to project one voice for labor and to settle, in a less public arena, the inevitable jurisdictional disputes among specific unions.

Labor, Congress, and Courts

Why did labor unions grow so rapidly during World War I?

Throughout the 19th century and well into the third decade of the 20th century, Congress, the courts, the media, the general population, and even many workers were overwhelmingly antiunion. Figure 7 traces the growth of union membership.

As you see, the growth of union membership was lackluster in its early years but quite robust during the mid-1930s to mid-1940s. It continued strongly, with some backsliding, from the mid-1950s to the mid-1970s, peaked above 21 million in the early 1980s, but declined steadily to 13.3 million in 1993. As a percentage of the civilian labor force, union membership grew until the mid-1950s but after that it declined rather steadily from 26 percent in 1955 to 11 percent in 1993.

The unions' success in attracting membership varied with the economic climate of the times and with the attitude of Congress, the courts, and the media. Between 1900 and 1930, union membership was somewhat erratic, rising and falling with the swings of economic fortune and with political events. It soared to five million during World War I when the high demand for labor overcame businesses' dislike for bargaining with unions. But in the war's aftermath, antiunion business activity combined with an antiunion Congress and the courts to undo whatever gains unions had made earlier. Bitter jurisdictional disputes among the craft unions in the 1920s also compounded the problem, and union membership fell by almost a third.

By 1932, the depression created over 13 million unemployed, accounting for 25 percent of the labor force. Confidence in business was shaken. Considerably more sympathetic to labor's plight, the Roosevelt administration and Congress enacted a series of prolabor laws that shaped a new future for unions. The courts eventually concurred.

NORRIS-LA GUARDIA ACT OF 1932

The first major piece of prolabor legislation was the Norris-La Guardia Act of 1932. It outlawed "yellow-dog" contracts. These were contracts that firms made workers sign as a condition of employment. Typically, the stated condition was that joining a union automatically nullified the worker's employment contract.

THE WAGNER ACT OF 1935

The single most important piece of labor legislation was the National Labor Relations Act of 1935, called the Wagner Act. For the first time, Congress, with the courts concurring, legislated that firms must bargain in good faith with unions. The act was regarded by unions as their Magna Carta. Businesses were forced to accept unions as legitimate institutions in collective bargaining. The act also created the National Labor Relations Board (NLRB) to oversee compliance.

The NLRB guaranteed the unions' right to conduct elections freely among workers and to represent the workers if the majority voted for unionization. The NLRB also conducted investigations of "unfair labor practices." It cited firms for interfering with unions' efforts to organize, for refusing to bargain with recognized unions, and for discriminating against prounion workers in their employ.

Unionism appealed now to the depression-conscious workers. With the creation of the CIO in 1935, total union membership increased to almost nine million by 1940. The high demand for labor during World War II gave unions even more power. By 1950, membership reached 15 million.

THE TAFT-HARTLEY ACT OF 1947

The years following World World II were a period of digestion and ma-turity. Now regarded as an accepted institution in American economic life, unions had to cope with their own success. Congress took a second look at union activity and responded in 1947 with the Labor Management Relations Act, called the Taft-Hartley Act. Although regarded by unions as an antilabor piece of legislation, Congress was responding principally to the unions' abuse of power. The act outlawed the closed shop, replacing it with the union shop.

The act also prohibited unions' "unfair labor practices," and made unions bargain in good faith as well. It prevented unions from pressuring workers during union elections. It prohibited unions from striking in support of other unions' strikes.

LABOR MANAGEMENT REPORTING AND THE LANDRUM-GRIFFIN ACT

In 1959, Congress enacted the Labor Management Reporting and Disclosure Act, the Landrum-Griffin Act, in response to growing concerns about criminal activity by unions. In a real sense, Landrum-Griffin was designed to protect the worker *from the union.* The act specified rules of conduct between the union and its own members. For example, it required full financial disclosure of union revenues and expenditures. It sought to protect the workers from rigged elections. It specified penalties for union leaders guilty of misusing union funds and required full disclosure of the salaries of union officials.

CIVIL RIGHTS ACT OF 1964

Another major piece of legislation affecting union activity directly was the Civil Rights Act of 1964. Again, the legislative purpose was to protect workers from institutionalized union power. The principal issue now was racial and sexual discrimination. Women and minorities, over the years, had been held back by the unions' seniority rules and by union manipulation of the labor markets to protect the status of white men, who dominated unions. The act required unions to adopt affirmative action policies within their own ranks.

CHAPTER REVIEW

1. A monopsonist is the only buyer of labor in a market. Therefore, it faces the market supply curve of labor.

2. A monopsonist can pick whatever wage rate it wants, hiring as many workers as are willing to supply their labor at that wage. In order to hire additional workers, however, the monopsonist must increase the wage rate for all workers, some of whom were hired at lower wage rates.

3. Marginal labor cost for a monopsonist is the addition to total labor cost from hiring another unit of labor. The marginal labor cost is greater than the wage rate because the *MLC* includes the additional amount paid to workers hired at lower wages.

4. To maximize profits, the monopsonist will choose that amount of labor that equates the *MLC* and the *MRP*.

5. The wage rate paid to workers under monopsony is less than the marginal revenue product of labor. Therefore, the monopsonist receives a return to monopsony power equal to $(MRP - w) \times L$.

6. A union presents a monopsonist with a different supply curve of labor. Because the union provides labor at a fixed wage rate, the supply curve of labor and the marginal labor cost curve are the same.

7. A monopsonist and a union face each other in collective bargaining.

8. If a union achieves a wage rate above the wage that equates the *MLC* and the *MRP*, the union attracts more workers into the market. The union loses a degree of control over the labor market.

9. The adoption of new, more productive technology by the monopsonist also presents the union with a choice. The new technology increases the monopsonist's demand for labor. The union perceives this increase in labor demand as an opportunity to limit the amount of labor supplied and increase the wage rate. Under these circumstances, a conflict may arise between the union and the workers who want to work but will not be hired if the the union prevails in its wage demands.

10. A union can secure its control over the labor supply with a closed shop. The union shop represents a compromise over labor's control of the supply of labor.

11. If the demand for labor is highly elastic, an increase in wages secured by the union will cause many workers to be unemployed.

12. Early union activity in the late 18th and early 19th centuries in the United States was halted by court decisions holding that unions constituted criminal conspiracies. The Knights of Labor was the first markedly successful United States labor union, with 700,000 members in 1886.

13. The American Federation of Labor's sole goal is to improve the economic lot of its members. The AFL was organized to represent craft workers.

14. Not until 1935 did unskilled workers gain union representation under the Congress of Industrial Organization. The AFL and the CIO were competing labor unions until 1955, when they merged.

15. The pattern of union membership has been erratic in the 20th century, rising substantially from the mid-1930s to 1955, then falling to 11 percent of the labor force in 1993. The Norris-La Guardia Act of 1932 and the Wagner Act of 1935 served to guarantee the rights of unions and union members. The Taft-Hartley Act of 1947 outlawed closed-shop practices. The Landrum-Griffin Act of 1959 imposed further restrictions on unions to prevent financial and union election abuses. The 1964 Civil Rights Act guaranteed the right to union representation for minorities.

KEY TERMS

Monopsony
Labor union
Strike
Collective bargaining
Return to monopsony power
Closed shop
Union shop
Craft union
Industrial union

QUESTIONS

1. What is a monopsony? How does it differ from monopoly?

2. How is the return to monopsony power derived?

3. Consider two labor markets, each with different price elasticities of supply. Suppose their *MRPs* are identical. Which labor market generates the highest return to monopsony power?

4. Why do some workers choose to join labor unions?

5. How do unions change the supply curve of labor? What effect does the change have on the quantity of labor supplied and the wage rate?

6. Why do unions sometimes strike? Do strikes always benefit all the workers willing to work?

7. Discuss the trade-off unions face between negotiating for higher wage rates and maintaining the level of employment for union members.

8. How does a closed shop differ from a union shop? If you were a union worker already employed, which type of shop would you prefer? If you were a nonunion worker seeking employment, which would you prefer?

9. Discuss the difference between a craft union and an industrial union. If you were a night security guard employed by Ford Motor Company in 1930, would it be likely that you belonged to a union? Why or why not?

10. What do economists regard as the most significant piece of prolabor legislation?

11. Why would unionized workers support legislation that limits the immigration of workers whose skills are in short supply in this country?

12. Do you suppose union workers would be in favor of increases in the minimum wage rate?

13. Nonunionized firms sometimes offer approximately the same wage rates that unionized firms do for the same quality labor. Why do you suppose they do that?

14. What has happened to the number of unionized workers in the United States since the 1970s? What has happened to the percentage of unionized workers in the civilian labor force?

15. Suppose the David Narcizo Drum Manufacturing Company was a monopsonist facing the following supply schedule of labor and the workers' *MRP* schedule.

Workers	Wage Rate	*MRP*
1	$ 7.50	$50.00
2	8.75	35.00
3	10.00	25.00
4	11.25	20.00
5	12.50	17.50
6	13.75	15.00
7	15.00	13.50

How many workers would the monopsony hire? At what wage rate? How much return to monopsony power would the firm receive?

16. Draw a graph illustrating the monopsony labor market of question 15.

CHAPTER 17

WHO EARNS WHAT?

CHAPTER PREVIEW

The two previous chapters laid out the theoretical tools that enable us to understand how wage rates and employment are determined. But, how does the theory translate into real-world situations for workers at their jobs? The following pages provide a closer view of wages and employment, focusing on the factors that determine marginal revenue product curves and labor supply curves in different labor markets. Not surprisingly, the theoretical conclusions worked out in the previous chapters are largely supported by the data discussed in this chapter.

After studying this chapter, you should be able to:

- Describe in some detail the most important factors that determine people's earnings.
- Outline trends in minimum wage rates.
- Explain who earns minimum wages.
- Define unemployment rate.
- Describe patterns of employment and unemployment.

You can't always tell who sits in the box seats, who sits in the grandstands, and who sits in the center-field bleachers when the Cubs play at home in Wrigley Field. But some guesses are better than others. For example, if you had to guess the occupation of someone sitting in a box seat, you would probably be more right than wrong to guess a corporate executive rather than a packing clerk at Marshall Field's.

Corporate executives, of course, are not the only ones in box seats. The person sitting next to her may very well be an accountant or an architect, or perhaps a steelworker from Gary, Indiana. On the other hand, it's not too likely that the executive's box seat neighbor would be a migrant farm worker from downstate Illinois. Not that migrant workers don't like baseball or the Cubs. There are asparagus pickers from Hoopeston, Illinois—die-hard Cubs fans—who make the 120-mile trip north to Chicago just to see a ball game. But they probably end up in the grandstands, or in the sun-drenched center field bleachers along with supermarket cashiers, hospital attendants, and stenographers.

Why this polarizing by occupation? What do the Cubs have against migrant workers? Nothing at all. They don't care who sits where as long as people pay for their seats. But that's the problem. Box seats are more expensive than bleacher seats, and for some people, too expensive. But not for everybody. Some can afford box seats, $125 sunglasses, sports cars, high-resolution televisions, and filet mignon on ordinary Tuesdays. Their salaries are fat.

Let's think back for a moment to the last two chapters. Picture the *MRPs* of corporate executives and migrant farm workers. They work in very different, noncompeting labor markets. Each labor market has its own demand and supply curves that generate unique sets of equilibrium wage rates. As you already know, who in our economy gets what wage rate is not a randomly determined outcome.

In this chapter, we take a close look at who ends up with what incomes, who is employed where, and what counts in determining people's wages and employment. What "people characteristics" lie behind the specific *MRP* curves and supply curves of labor? Many working women, for example, insist that they confront unfriendly and unfair employment competition from men, which translates for them into wages at less than *comparable worth*. What does the evidence show? What about blacks and Hispanics? And does it really pay to get an education? How much are high school diplomas worth? Who has them? Is everyone in the labor market equally vulnerable to unemployment?

WHAT COUNTS IN DETERMINING PEOPLE'S EARNINGS?

Engineers and farm workers earn more today than engineers and farm workers earned 50 years ago. Not surprising, is it? In fact, farm workers today earn more than engineers did 50 years ago.

Productivity Counts

This certainly should make sense to you, particularly after reading the last two chapters. After all, in the last 50 years there's been a long-run upward movement in almost everyone's real output per hour worked. People's *MPP* curves have been shifting outward to the right decade after decade, creating both greater em-

FIGURE 1
Three historical trends are discernible; from 1889 to 1937, when annual productivity growth averaged 1.9 percent; from 1937 to 1973, when average annual productivity grew 3.0 percent; and 1973 to 1989 when it grew 0.9 percent.

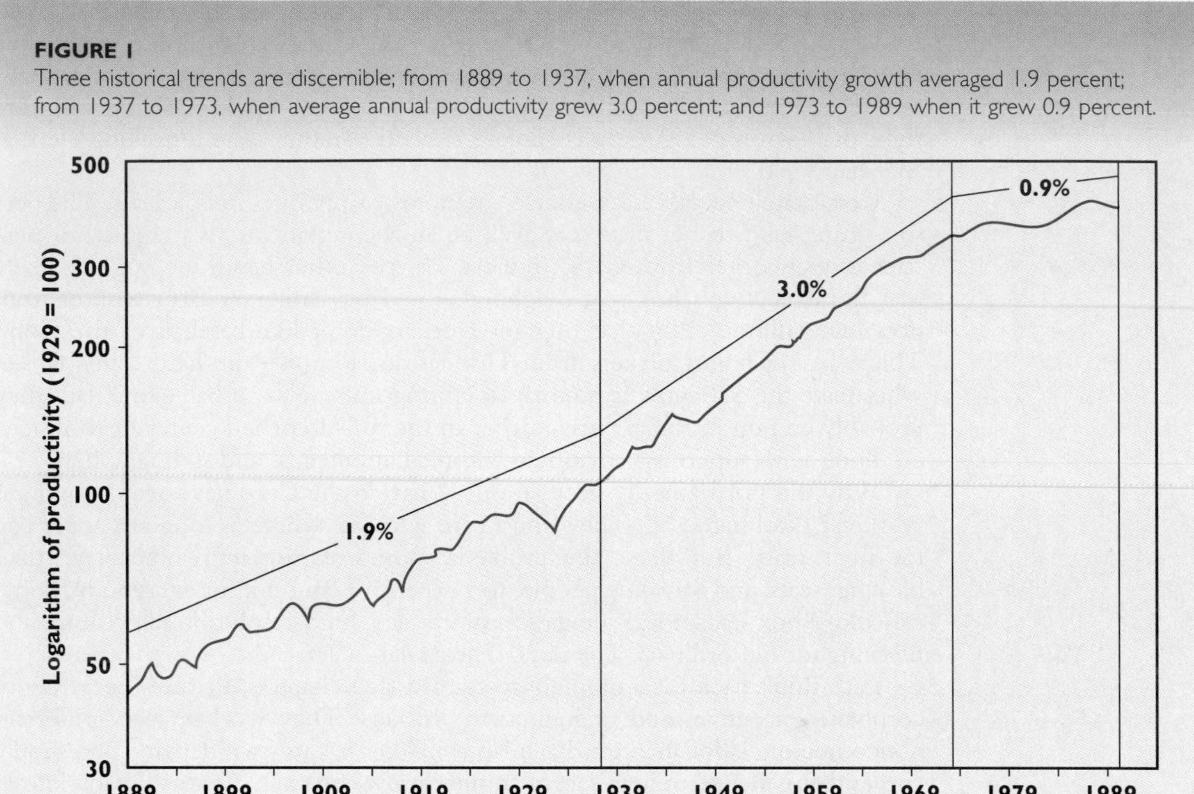

Source: *Economic Report of the President, 1992.* (Washington, D.C.: U.S. Government Printing Office, 1992), p. 91.

Increases in the marginal physical product of labor translate into higher earnings for workers. But increases in the marginal physical product of labor that are coupled with increases in the price of the product yield even higher earnings.

ployment and higher wage rates. Look at the dramatic picture in Figure 1 which shows how productivity has changed through time.

The long-run upward trend is striking. Using 1929 as the base year (= 100), the slope of the curve corresponds to the percentage growth rate of labor productivity. Three segments of the curve are noteworthy: 1889 to 1937, showing an average annual growth of 1.9 percent; 1937 to 1973, showing an average annual growth rate of 3.0 percent; and 1973 to 1989, showing an average annual growth rate of only 0.9 percent. This continuous, although modest, growth means that workers today are over 300 percent as productive as their grandparents were in 1929, and twice as productive as their parents were in 1959. And it shows up in their take-home pay. Look at Figure 2.

The relationship between the growth of compensation and the growth in labor productivity is apparent. Note the break in the compensation growth rate in 1973. It corresponds to the break depicted in Figure 1 for labor productivity. From 1959 to 1973, the average annual real hourly compensation grew at a 2.9 percent rate. After 1973, it grew at only a 0.7 percent rate.

Education Counts

No one could possibly become the chief orthopedic surgeon at the Mayo Clinic without completing medical school. High school dropouts don't typically end up as corporate CEOs either. Look at Table 1.

FIGURE 2
Although most year-to-year changes are modest or even negative, long-run growth of real hourly compensation has been significant, growing 69 percent between 1959 and 1990.

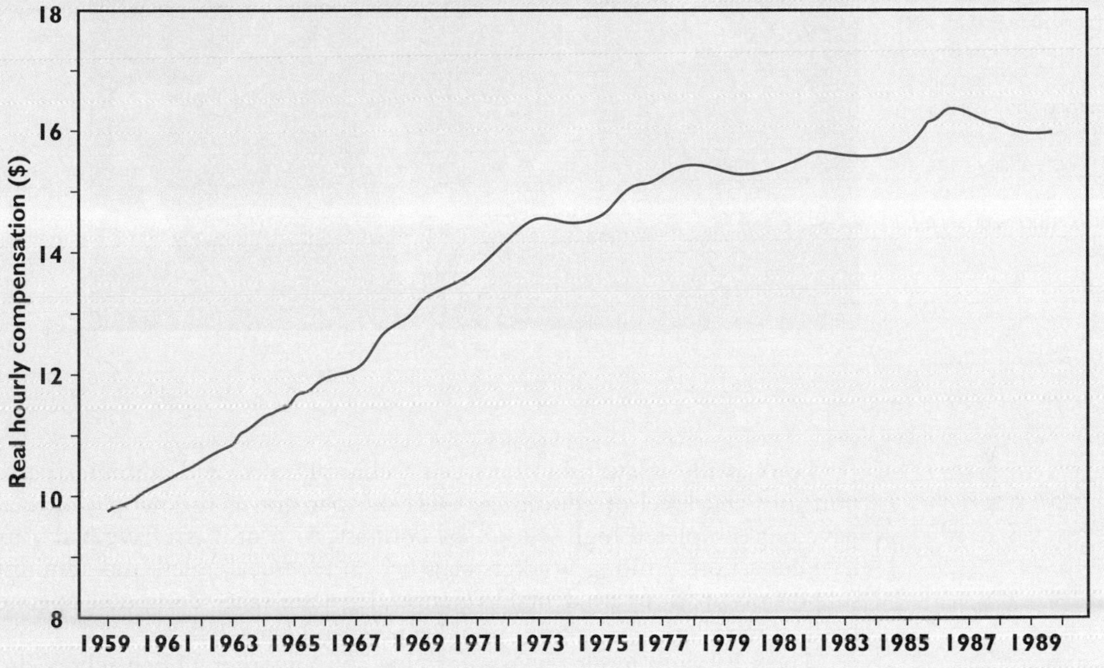

Source: *Economic Report of the President, 1992.* (Washington, D.C.: U.S. Government Printing Office, 1992), p. 96.

The employment opportunities available to people with more education are quite different from those available to people with limited education.

Education counts. It isn't by chance that only 1.9 percent of managerial and professional people have not completed high school, or that 62.2 percent of them have completed four years of college or more. Managers and professionals include such people as engineers, lawyers, computer analysts, accountants, physicians, teachers, and athletes.

TABLE 1 **Occupation of Employed Civilians by Educational Attainment: 1993 (percent)**

	Managerial/ Professional	Technical/Sales/ Administrative Support	Service	Precision Production	Operators/ Laborers/ Fabricators	Farming
Less than 4 years of high school	1.9	4.6	21.6	17.2	25.1	31.8
4 years of high school only	13.9	37.8	44.9	48.9	52.4	40.4
1 to 3 years of college	22.0	35.6	25.5	27.1	18.3	18.4
4 years of college or more	62.2	22.0	8.0	6.8	4.3	9.4

Source: Bureau of the Census, *Statistical Abstract of the United States, 1994*, (Washington, D. C.: Department of Commerce, 1994) p. 412.

These graduates are smiling for a good reason. They studied hard and made it. With college diplomas in their hands, they can venture out into the labor market with full expectations of commanding salaries considerably higher than they would have otherwise been offered. Their ability to move up the corporate ladder is much enhanced as well.

Look at the relationship between technical, sales, and admininstrative support jobs and level of education. Only 4.6 percent of the people in these jobs have not completed high school. By contrast, 57.6 of them have had some college education. Among workers classified in technical, sales, and administrative support occupations are dental hygienists, legal assistants, computer operators, air traffic controllers, sales clerks, bookkeepers, and bank tellers.

The education input reverses for blue collar workers. High school dropouts make up 25.1 percent of operators, laborers, and fabricators. Only 4.3 percent of them completed college. Among workers classified as operators, fabricators, and laborers are people who operate sawing machines, textile machines, printing machines, and who are truckdrivers, construction laborers, and garbage collectors.

Finally, look at educational attainment among precision production workers and service workers. Precision production workers are our butchers, bakers, and candlestick makers. They are also farm equipment mechanics, telephone line installers, brickmasons, oil well drillers, cabinetmakers, and tailors. Occupations classified as service include cooks, housekeepers, firefighters, police, janitors, hospital orderlies, bartenders, barbers, and bellhops.

Does education matter? You better believe it! Table 2 matches people's occupations to people's earnings.

Managers and professionals in 1993 made almost twice the weekly earnings—$675 vs. $365—that people made as operators, fabricators, and laborers. They earned more than double the earnings of people in service and farming.

Experience Counts

Why do you suppose more-experienced workers are more productive?

Experience counts too. Before the advent of the modern factory, production was primarily handicraft, with workers organized within a guild hierarchy of master, journeyman, and apprentice. Craftspeople and artisans customarily started out as apprentices and after acquiring on-the-job training moved up to the rank of journeyman. With more experience, journeymen were eventually

TABLE 2
Median Weekly Earnings by Occupation: 1993

	Earnings	As Percent of Managerial/ Professional
Managerial and professional	$675	100.0
Technical, sales, and administrative support	419	62.1
Service	293	43.4
Precision production	501	74.2
Operators, fabricators, and laborers	365	54.1
Farming	269	39.9

Source: Bureau of Labor Statistics, *Employment and Earnings* (Washington, D. C.: U.S. Department of Labor, January 1994), pp. 243–47.

promoted to master. At each higher level, higher earnings accompanied greater privilege and status.

Although the guild system has given way to the labor market, it still takes time to acquire expertise. Work experience still generates higher earnings. Accountants and attorneys, for example, become more productive as they become more seasoned. Their incomes reflect their experience. Look at Table 3.

Experienced accountants and attorneys earn three times more than accountants and attorneys starting out. Drafters' incomes double as they advance from first to highest levels within their fields.

Gaining experience naturally takes time. Table 4, which highlights the relationship between age and earnings, tells the same story.

It takes a while for working people to reach the peak of their earning power. In 1993, the $543 median weekly earnings of people aged 44 to 54 was just slightly more than the $519 earned by people aged 35 to 44 years, but considerably more than the earnings of people in other age groups.

TABLE 3
Average Annual Salaries for Selected Professional, Administrative, and Technical Occupations, by Level of Experience, 1987–88

	Level					
	1	2	3	4	5	6
Accountants	21,962	26,666	33,028	41,966	53,297	67,950
Attorneys	33,962	42,589	55,407	69,854	89,940	110,489
Chemists	25,314	30,439	37,763	45,760	54,982	65,526
Buyers	22,071	27,863	36,010	43,651		
Drafters	16,691	21,478	26,555	32,701		

Source: Bureau of Labor Statistics, *Handbook of Labor Statistics*, Bulletin 2340 (Washington, D.C., U.S. Department of Labor, August 1989), pp. 427–30.

Note: Some occupations have only four classification levels.

A face in the crowd. Study any carefully. It's our mirror. That face you selected records specific work experiences, education, skills, and characteristics that add up to explain how much that person earns relative to the other faces you see in the crowd.

Minority Status Counts

Regardless of education, age, or experience, or whether you're a manager, technician, or laborer, you would probably fare better in terms of earning power if you also happen to be a white male.

DISPARITIES ACCORDING TO RACE

Race counts. The data in Table 5 are unequivocal. Earnings disparities according to race, in many instances, reflect a combination of discrimination still practiced today as well as the powerful consequences of discrimination practiced generations before.

Racial discrimination, past and present, contributes to the earnings disparities observed among white, black, and Hispanic workers.

Table 5 shows what you probably know or could guess. Black and Hispanic workers are paid lower weekly wages and salaries than white workers are. In 1989 Hispanics averaged only 74.4 percent of white workers' earnings, and blacks fared slightly better, averaging 77.8 percent.

Earnings disparities according to race vary with occupation. For example, Hispanic managers and professionals fared better than black managers and professionals, but less well than white managers and professionals. Hispanic precision production workers earned considerably less than both black and white

TABLE 4 Median Weekly Earnings of Full-Time Wage and Salary Workers by Age: 1993

Age	1993
16 to 24	$283
25 to 34	439
35 to 44	519
45 to 54	543
55 to 64	492
65 and over	394

Source: Bureau of Labor Statistics, *Employment and Earnings* (Washington, D.C.: U.S. Department of Labor, January 1994), p. 250.

TABLE 5 **Weekly Earnings of Workers by Occupation and Race (December 1989)**

	White	Black	Black/White	Hispanic	Hispanic/White
Total	$482.45	$375.38	77.8	$358.78	74.4
Managerial, professional	663.73	540.90	81.5	572.40	86.2
Technical, sales, administrative	427.57	372.22	87.1	373.05	87.2
Service	313.29	275.12	87.8	268.90	85.8
Precision production	494.83	432.25	87.4	399.77	80.8
Operators, fabricators, laborers	381.04	334.39	87.8	304.68	80.0
Farming	279.29	211.83	75.9	241.30	86.4

Source: Bureau of Labor Statistics, U.S. Department of Labor, Washington, D.C., unpublished data.

workers in the same occupation. As Table 5 shows, in all occupation categories, white workers earned the most.

DISPARITIES ACCORDING TO SEX

Chances are, if you're a woman, you're earning less than a man doing the same kind of work. Look at Table 6. The sex gap glares right out at you.

The $395 for women looks pretty light compared to the $514 that men earned. Once off the farm, the sex gap ratios fall below 75 percent. For example, women working in technical, sales, and administrative support jobs make 26.7 percent less than their men co-workers.

The sex gap shows up even more vividly when we compare men's and women's earnings within both low-paying and high-paying jobs. Women are typically overrepresented in the low end of the pay scale and underrepresented in the upper end. We see this in Table 7.

Look at bartending. It's not a particularly lucrative job although some people managed to earn over $500 weekly at it. Who were they? Men accounted

TABLE 6 Women's and Men's Median Weekly Earnings by Occupation Group (1993)

Occupation	Women	Men	Women/Men
Total	$395	$514	76.9
Managerial and professional	580	791	73.3
Technical, sales, and administrative support	376	534	70.4
Service	259	350	74.0
Precision production	344	511	67.3
Operators, fabricators, and laborers	288	399	72.2
Farming, forestry, fishing	242	274	88.3

Source: Bureau of Labor Statistics, *Employment and Earnings* (Washington, D.C.: U.S. Department of Labor, January 1994), pp. 243–47.

TABLE 7
Median Weekly Earnings of Men and Women and Percent Earning Under $200 and Over $500 in Selected Low-Paying and High-Paying Occupations

	Median Earnings	Percent Under $200		Percent Over $500	
		Men	Women	Men	Women
Lowest-Paying					
Waiters	$158	36.1	77.5	6.0	*
Cashiers	176	52.7	66.3	5.4	0.5
Nursing aides	182	43.2	65.1	2.5	0.1
Sales clerks	188	34.5	71.0	8.8	1.2
Bartenders	196	37.9	65.9	4.6	*
Personal service	202	33.2	56.1	7.6	3.1
Highest-Paying					
Lawyers	$626	2.3	3.0	74.8	48.5
Engineers	586	0.4	1.3	71.3	45.0
Computer analysts	539	*	4.6	66.9	35.4
School administrators	517	0.6	20.7	65.2	28.7
Professors	499	2.6	6.4	56.1	32.7
Bank managers	471	0.7	7.6	63.6	18.2

Source: Mellor, E. F., "Investigating the Differences in Weekly Earnings of Women and Men," *Monthly Labor Review*, June 1984, p. 24.

Note: Mellor uses 1982 data. No updated data are available.

* = Less than one-tenth of one percent.

for the 4.6 percent who had the highest earnings. Less than one-tenth of one percent were women! On the other hand, 65.9 percent of women tending bar earned less than $200 weekly compared to 37.9 percent for men.

Look at elementary and secondary school administrators. Six-tenths of one percent of the men and 20.7 percent of the women earned under $200 weekly. At the other end, the ratio reverses. 65.2 percent of the men and only 28.7 percent of the women earned over $500. Does it tell you something?

The disparity between men's and women's earnings holds even when their incomes are compared by age groups. Look at Table 8.

Although the gender gap in wages is pronounced, it seems to have narrowed somewhat in recent years for younger women.

As you see, in every age category, the story's the same. Men earn more than women. Look at 1993. The wage disparity widens with age. Among workers in the 16 to 24 group—that is, among people starting employment or among workers with little experience—women made 94.8 percent of their male co-workers. And as they advance in the workplace with age and experience, women lose out even more. Among workers in the 25 to 34 range, women made only 82.9 percent of the male wage, and that percentage falls to 67.6 for women in the age range of 55 to 64.

The overall earnings disparity nonetheless narrowed from 62.5 percent to 76.8 percent between 1979 and 1993, narrowing even more significantly for younger women. Among older people, the narrowing was considerably less.

ADDED PERSPECTIVE

The Lowdown on Women's Low Pay

When economists talk about "low pay," here's what they mean: Low pay, says the U.S. Bureau of the Census, is $13,091 or less a year—about 8 percent below the U.S. poverty level of $14,228 for a family of four.

In a study of earnings, Jack McNeil, a census analyst, found that almost 20 percent of full-time workers earned low pay in 1992, an increase from 12 percent in 1979. About 23 percent of women and 14 percent of men are low earners.

"Women are more likely to have low earnings than men," the report states. "And low earners tend to have less education than other workers."

Does that mean women earn less money than men because they have less education? "No, the two are not linked," said Heidi Hartmann, economist and director of the Institute for Women's Policy Research in Washington. "Women are disproportionately more likely to make low salaries."

For example, says Hartmann, "Of people with a high school diploma but no college at all, about 17 percent of the men and 30 percent of the women are low earners."

Hartmann says the reason women do so poorly when it comes to paychecks is not education, but that "women face discrimination in wages and in the kinds of jobs open to them."

Those jobs, Hartmann says, are often as clerks, sales personnel, cashiers, and telemarketing representatives. The report shows, however, that "the likelihood of having low earnings has risen faster among men than women," which reflects an economic dynamic of the 1980s.

"During that decade," said the economist, "women did relatively well in wages compared to men, not in outearning them but by not losing as much."

In other words, men's wages fell during the 1980s, while women's were slowly edging upward—though still remaining behind men's. The transition of the U. S. economy to low-paying service jobs from high-paying manufacturing jobs held by men is another reason the wages of men and women moved closer.

"In the 1980s, women didn't have much to lose in salary rates, made some real gains and moved into a broader range of jobs," said Hartmann.

Another gap that's closing between the genders is the percentage of full-time workers. Today, 48 percent of women work full time, compared with 70 percent of men. But in 1972 only 35 percent of women were full-time workers, compared with 75 percent of men.

"More women are working full time, getting more education and reducing the amount of time spent in child rearing," said Hartmann.

Though the report doesn't mention part-time workers, they are a concern of Hartmann's. "Women are more likely to combine a number of part-time jobs to equal one full-time job," she observed. "And, they are much less likely to have benefits."

In 1993, 14.6 million women worked part time compared with 8.3 million men.

Source: "The Lowdown on Women's Low Pay," by Carol Kleiman. *Chicago Tribune*, June 16, 1994.

TABLE 8 Ratio of Median Weekly Earnings of Workers by Age and Sex, 1979 and 1993 (percent)

Age	1979 Women/Men	1993 Women/Men
16 and over	62.5	76.8
16 to 24	78.6	94.8
25 to 34	67.5	82.9
35 to 44	58.2	73.1
45 to 54	57.0	67.2
55 to 64	60.3	67.6
65 and over	78.3	74.0

Source: Bureau of Labor Statistics, *Handbook of Labor Statistics*, Bulletin 2340, August 1989, p. 162, and *Employment and Earnings*, January 1994 (Washington, D.C.: U.S. Department of Labor), p. 250.

ADDED PERSPECTIVE

Must the Union's Success Create Its Own Demise?

Some 31 percent of American workers belonged to a trade union in 1970. By the late 1980s the figure was barely half that, at 17 percent. Union membership is now no higher as a share of the labor force than in the 1920s. The fall in the private sector has been sharper still, offset partly by some growth in public-sector unions.

Though it is generally true that unions are flexing their muscles rather less than they used to, only a few countries have seen significant deunionization. Union membership has fallen in Britain, Japan, Holland, and Italy, though nowhere near as sharply as in America. In most countries membership remained firm in the 1980s, or even rose, as in Sweden and Denmark.

Outside America the average percentage of workers belonging to a trade union rose from 48 percent in 1970 to 55 percent in 1979, and has since remained broadly unchanged. If anything, the increasing importance of trade and expanding production by multinational firms should have caused greater convergence in industrial relations trends. It hasn't: So much, brothers, for all the talk of a world labor movement.

Why has America taken a different path than most? Economists David Blanchflower and Richard Freeman suggest one possible explanation. They argue that American trade unions have been too successful in winning wage increases for their members. Employers have therefore had a greater incentive to oppose unions.

American unions have indeed lifted their wages relative to nonunion pay by more than in other countries. The gap between average union and nonunion pay in America rose from 15 percent in the 1960s to 22 percent by the late 1970s—three times as big as the average union differential in other countries where such data are available. For example, in Britain workers in trade unions earn, on average, 10 percent more than nonunion workers; in West Germany and Australia the gap is 8 percent; in Canada, 15 percent; in Switzerland, 4 percent; in Japan there is no differential for male workers.

The greater "success" of American trade unions might encourage more workers to join them. But this is outweighed by the fact that a wage premium of 22 percent puts unionized firms at a serious disadvantage when competing against imports or nonunionized domestic firms. Employers therefore have greater reason to declare war on unions and to keep them out of the workplace.

The union-pay premium increased in the 1970s at the very time when productivity growth slumped. This inevitably led to job losses and hastened deunionization. Other American studies have found that industries with the biggest wage differentials had the most rapid declines in union membership.

To what extent can the gap between union and nonunion pay account for the movements in union membership in different countries? Unfortunately, data on wage premiums are not available in most countries. Instead, the authors examine trends in union penetration in countries with different types of wage-bargaining systems.

Their assumption is that in countries with centralized wage-setting systems, unions are likely to have a smaller differential impact on wages than under decentralized collective bargaining, so employers will have less incentive to resist trade unions. This is because national unions are more likely to take account of job prospects; they also often set wages for the whole economy, not just for their members.

This seems to fit the facts. In the 1970s and 1980s union membership fared better in countries with centralized industrial relations systems—e.g., Sweden and West Germany—than in countries with decentralized ones, such as Britain and Italy.

Looking ahead, the authors conclude that unless American trade unions change their tactics and develop a new brand of unionism which deals not just with wages but with other interests of workers as well, they are doomed to extinction. This is precisely what the United Auto Workers is doing in its attempt to get America's big-three car makers to agree to job guarantees during the current industrywide contract negotiations. If other unions do not begin to look beyond their pay packets, predict the authors, union penetration in America will drop into single figures, leaving "ghetto unionism" in just a few aging industries and the public sector.

Discussion

Unless American unions change their tactics—that is, push for higher wages—they may be doomed to extinction. Why?

Source: "Workers of the World Disunite," *The Economist,* August 18, 1990.

TABLE 9 **Median Weekly Earnings of Full-Time Wage and Salary Workers by Occupation, 1993**

	Total	Members of Unions	Represented by Unions	Nonunion
Managerial and professional specialty	$675	$696	$688	$670
Technical sales, and administrative support	419	509	501	408
Service occupations	293	478	467	265
Precision production, craft, and repair	501	642	637	453
Operators, fabricators, and laborers	365	501	497	321
Farming, forestry, and fishing	269	436	413	264

Source: Bureau of Labor Statistics, *Employment and Earnings* (Washington, D.C.: U.S. Department of Labor, January 1994), p. 251.

Note: The category "Represented by Unions" includes union members as well as workers who report no union affiliation but whose jobs are covered by a union contract.

Unionization Counts

Does it pay to join a union? If you were counted in Table 9, you wouldn't hesitate answering. Look at the payoff when unions negotiate wage rate and salary contracts.

The amounts by which union wages and benefits exceed those for nonunion workers are readily apparent from the data.

Unions have been instrumental in raising wages and salaries beyond levels obtained by nonunion workers. For example, in technical, sales, and administrative support jobs, union-negotiated wages and salaries were 25 percent greater than nonunion wages and salaries. In service occupations, workers covered by union contracts made 80 percent more than nonunion workers, and among operators, fabricators, and laborers, the premium was approximately 55 percent. Only among managers and professionals did union affiliation fail to achieve substantially higher earnings.

FRINGE BENEFITS

Lefty Grove pitched for the New York Yankees back in the 1920s when New York was a powerhouse in the American League. After a bad season, Grove and the Yankees' owner got together to discuss salary. The Yankees' owner looked hard at Grove then scribbled a number on a piece of paper. He passed it across the desk to Grove. Grove glanced at the proposed salary and is reputed to have said: "Let's make a deal. You keep the salary, I'll take the cut in salary."

Fringe benefits

Nonwage compensation that workers receive from employers.

Like Grove, people today are willing to sacrifice salary for something else. That something else today is the **fringe benefits** that accompany salary. These benefits include a wide variety of items such as contributions to social security, retirement and savings plans, life insurance, medical benefits plans, on-the-job rest periods, vacations, sick leave, employee meals, education and day care. When you add up the monetary value, the dollar value of fringe benefits can be substantial. Some are so substantial that they inhibit low cash-paying job holders from moving to higher cash-paying jobs.

Table 10 shows the percentage of payroll that fringe benefits represent.

TABLE 10 Employee Benefits as a Percent of Payroll, by Industry: 1990

Manufacturing	
Rubber, leather, plastics	48.6
Fabricated metals	43.1
Pulp, paper, lumber, furniture	42.5
Food, beverage, tobacco	41.9
Primary metals	41.5
Machinery (excluding electrical)	41.3
Electrical machinery and supplies	40.6
Transportation equipment	40.3
Stone, clay, glass products	39.3
Instruments & misc. mfg. industries	35.0
Printing and publishing	34.8
Chemical, allied products	34.5
Petroleum industry	34.4
Textile products and apparel	29.9
Nonmanufacturing	
Public utilities	41.9
Insurance companies	37.7
Misc. non-mfg. industries	36.8
Hospitals	35.3
Wholesale and retail trade	34.9
Banks, finance, and trust companies	29.4
Department stores	28.2

Source: Bureau of National Affairs, *Bulletin to Management Datagraph,* U.S. Chamber of Commerce, January 16, 1992, p. 12.

The value of fringe benefits in some industries nears 50 percent of the worker's earnings. Even at the low end of the table data, the value of benefits is still as high as 30 percent of earnings. In 1990 the total annual benefit per worker in manufacturing amounted to $14,286. For workers in nonmanufacturing, the benefit was $11,414.

TABLE 11 Fringe Benefits, by Type of Benefit (percent of payroll)

	Manufacturing	Nonmanufacturing
Medical	11.6	8.9
Time not worked	10.8	10.3
Legally required	9.8	8.8
Retirement and savings	5.6	5.4
Rest periods	2.1	2.5
Insurance	0.5	0.5
Other	0.6	1.0

Source: Bureau of National Affairs, *Bulletin to Management Datagraph,* U.S. Chamber of Commerce, January 16, 1992, p. 12.

TABLE 12 Federal Minimum Hourly Wage Rates 1967–91

Year	Rate
1967	$1.40
1969	1.60
1975	2.10
1977	2.30
1979	2.90
1981	3.35
1990	3.80
1991	4.25

Source: Bureau of the Census, *Statistical Abstract of the United States, 1991* (Washington, D.C.: U.S. Department of Commerce, 1991), p. 418.

The principal form these benefits took is shown in Table 11.

As you see, the value of medical benefits accounts for approximately 10 percent of earnings. Time not worked, such as paid vacations, holidays, sick leave, and parental leave accounts for another 10 percent. Legally required benefits, such as social security and unemployment insurance, are close behind at 9 percent.

Are these benefits important? According to Diane Capstaff, executive vice president at John Hancock Mutual Life Insurance Company in Boston: "We recruit heavily on the benefits we offer. People aren't motivated by money alone."[1] Capstaff estimates that the company's benefits, such as flexible scheduling, dependent-care services, a fitness center, and take-home food from the company's cafeteria had helped trim the company's annual employee turnover—losing and replacing workers—from 14 to 6 percent.

Emphasis on fringe benefits increased in the 1990s. Michael Davis, head of the executive compensation practice at consultants Towers Perrin sums it up: "The '90s is all about life style, as opposed to the '80s, which was about cash."[2]

HOW IMPORTANT ARE MINIMUM WAGE RATES?

For many people, earnings depend more on what government legislates than on what they are able to derive from labor markets. Approximately 87 percent of all workers are covered by minimum wage rate guarantees. In industries such as mining, construction, manufacturing, and utilities, coverage is virtually 100 percent. On the other hand, less than 40 percent of farm workers are covered by the minimum wage. What do those who rely on minimum wage rates actually receive?

Table 12 traces the increase in minimum wage rates from 1967 to 1991. How minimum is the minimum wage? Figure 3 traces the ratio of minimum wages to the average wage.

As you see, the decade of the 1980s has been terrible for those on minimum wages. The ratio fell steadily from a high of 37 percent of the average wage to under 25 percent. It recovered only slightly in 1990.

[1] *Wall Street Journal,* April 22, 1992.
[2] *Ibid.*

FIGURE 3
Although the federal minimum hourly wage increased from $2.10 in 1975 to $4.25 in 1991, this increase was substantially less than the increase in the average hourly wage. As a result, the *relative* earnings position of workers making the minimum wage or less deteriorated, falling from 37 percent of the average wage in 1980 to under 25 percent in 1990.

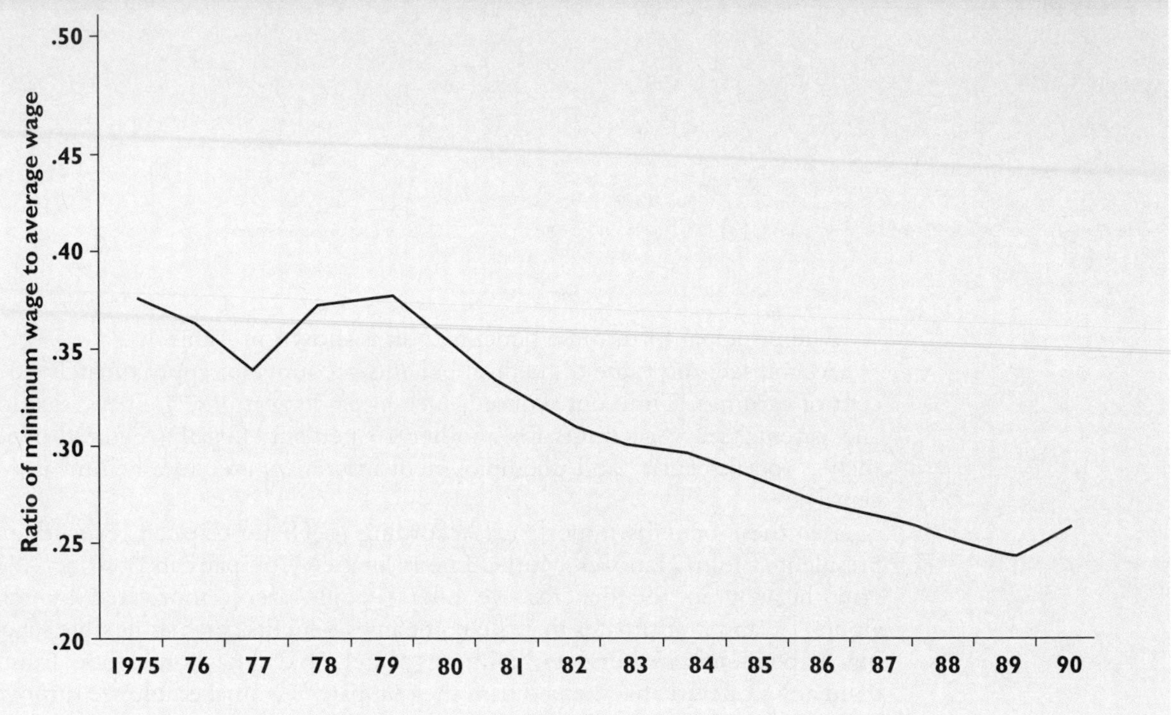

Source: Organization for Economic Cooperation and Development, *OECD Economic Surveys: Canada.* (Paris, France: OECD, 1991), p. 89.

Primarily, young people earn minimum wages. Young women are disproportionately employed at the minimum wage level.

How many workers are at the minimum? How many earn less? Table 13 provides a profile of workers in 1993 at or below the then $4.25 minimum wage.

Of the 63.3 million workers who were paid by the hour in 1993, 6.6 percent were at or below the $4.25 minimum. Broken down by sex, 5.0 percent of men were in this group compared to 8.2 percent of women. The most visible subgroup of minimum wage earners was the young; 18.4 percent of women aged 16 to 24 were earning the minimum or less.

EMPLOYMENT AND UNEMPLOYMENT

Labor force

Everyone over age 16 and willing to work.

Economists define the **labor force** to include everyone over age 16 and willing to work. In 1993 there were 129.53 million such people. But not all of them were working. Over eight million were unemployed but actively seeking work. Not all the employed were working in civilian occupations. About 1.5 million people were serving in the armed forces. Table 14 provides a historical record of the labor force and employment in the United States.

The labor force doubled from 63.37 to 129.53 million during the 43-year period of Table 14, representing a rather modest 1.7 percent annual rate of

TABLE 13 **Workers Paid Hourly Rates with Earnings at or Below the Minimum Wage, 1993 (1,000s and %)**

	Total Paid Hourly Rate	Percent of All Workers Paid $4.25 Hour or Less		
		Total	At $4.25	Below $4.25
Total				
16 years and over	63,316	6.6	4.0	2.6
16 to 24 years	14,331	15.6	10.0	5.6
25 years and over	48,984	4.0	2.2	1.8
Men				
16 years and over	31,699	5.0	3.3	1.7
16 to 24 years	7,385	13.1	9.2	3.9
25 years and over	24,314	2.5	1.5	1.1
Women				
16 years and over	31,617	8.2	4.7	3.5
16 to 24 years	6,946	18.4	10.9	7.5
25 years and over	24,671	5.4	3.0	2.4
White	52,971	6.5	3.8	2.7
Black	8,078	7.1	4.9	2.2
Hispanic	6,047	9.0	7.1	1.9

Source: Bureau of the Census *Statistical Abstract of the United States, 1993* (Washington, D.C.: U.S. Department of Commerce, 1993), p. 432.

Surprisingly, some 70 percent of the labor force is involved in nonmanufacturing jobs.

growth. Perhaps the most notable change occurred in farm employment. In 1950 farm workers made up 12 percent of civilian employment. By 1993, not only had their absolute numbers fallen, but measured against the doubling of civilian employment, they now made up only 2.4 percent of the total. Does the

TABLE 14 U.S. Labor Force and Employment: 1950–93 (millions)

Date	Total Labor Force	Armed Forces	Civilian Employment		
			Farm	Nonfarm	Total
1950	63.37	1.17	7.16	51.75	58.92
1955	67.09	2.00	6.45	55.72	62.17
1960	71.49	1.86	5.45	60.31	65.78
1965	76.40	1.95	4.36	66.72	71.09
1970	84.89	2.11	3.46	75.22	87.67
1975	95.45	1.67	3.40	82.43	85.85
1980	108.54	1.60	3.36	95.94	99.30
1985	117.17	1.71	3.12	103.97	107.15
1993	129.53	1.49	3.07	116.23	119.31

Source: Bureau of the Census, *Statistical Abstract of the United States, 1987* (Washington, D.C.: Department of Commerce, 1989), p. 374; Bureau of Labor Statistics, *Employment and Earnings* (Washington, D.C.: U.S. Department of Labor, January 1994), p. 13.

low number of farm workers compared to the total civilian labor force surprise you?

Perhaps you are surprised as well at the unchanging size of our armed forces. It has hovered around two million since 1950; as a percentage it shrank from 1.9 percent of the civilian labor force in 1950 to 1.2 percent in 1993.

Who Is Employed Where?

The goods and services produced in our economy are produced by men *and women*. In 1989 women made up 45.2 percent of U.S. civilian employment. Black men and women accounted for 10.2 percent, and Hispanic workers accounted for 7.3 percent. Look at the employment profile shown in Table 15.

Managers and professionals represent 25.9 percent of all civilian employment. Another 30.8 percent are in technical, sales, and administrative support jobs. That is, more than 50 percent of all workers are in white collar occupations. The blue collar occupations of precision production and operators, fabricators, and laborers make up another 27.4 percent of employment. Service jobs are 13.3 percent.

EMPLOYMENT BY SEX

For many years, toy manufacturers marketed nurse's kits for girls and doctor's kits for boys. It was as much societal indoctrination as occupational norm. After all, registered nurses were almost exclusively women. Nurses are still predominantly women, although increasing numbers of men have chosen to enter the nursing profession. Most physicians are men, although women have made substantial gains in medicine. In 1975, 9.9 percent of physicians were women; by 1990 the percentage had increased to 17.0. Many other occupations, as we see in Table 15, remain gender-polarized.

Men are employed disproportionately in blue collar jobs. Women are typically found in large numbers in service-oriented support-system jobs.

For example, in precision production there are over ten times as many men as women, and almost three times as many among operators, fabricators, and laborers, even though women account for 45.2 percent of total employment. Where do you find women workers in large numbers? In support occupations associated with technical, sales, and administrative work. Their numbers there are twice those of men.

EMPLOYMENT BY MINORITY STATUS

Minority men are vastly outnumbered by whites in managerial and professional occupations.

For a long time, minority people searching for employment confronted subtle and sometimes not so subtle "need not apply" signs on locked doors. Although the civil rights movement of the 1960s and the subsequent legislation on affirmative action did much to pry open previously restricted occupations, distribution of minority people among the occupations is still very unlike the occupational distribution of whites.

White employed men outnumber black employed men by 9.4 to 1. Yet, in managerial and professional jobs, white men outnumber black men by 18.6 to 1. In fact, managers and professionals are the single most important occupation for white men, and technical, sales, and administrative support jobs are the most important source of employment for white women. The most numerous jobs for black and Hispanic men are as operators, fabricators, and laborers.

TABLE 15 **Distribution of Employment by Occupation, Gender, and Race (1989)**

	Total			White		Black		Hispanic	
Total	**Total**	**Men**	**Women**	**Men**	**Women**	**Men**	**Women**	**Men**	**Women**
	100.0	54.8	45.2	48.0	38.6	5.1	5.1	4.4	2.9
Managerial, professional	25.9	14.2	11.7	13.0	10.4	0.7	0.9	0.5	0.4
Technical, sales, administrative	30.8	10.8	20.0	9.6	17.4	0.9	0.2	0.6	1.1
Services	13.3	5.3	8.0	4.1	6.3	0.9	1.4	0.7	0.7
Precision production	11.8	10.8	1.0	9.7	0.8	0.8	0.1	0.9	0.1
Operators, fabricators, laborers	15.4	11.4	4.0	9.4	3.2	1.7	0.7	1.3	0.5
Farming	2.9	2.4	0.5	2.2	0.5	0.2	—	0.4	—

Source: Bureau of Labor Statistics, U.S. Department of Labor, Washington, D.C., 1989, Unpublished data.

WHERE THE FUTURE JOBS ARE

If you keep score on the fastest growing and fastest declining occupations, check off for fastest growing such jobs as computer programmers, computer systems analysts, medical assistants, electrical and electronic engineers, electrical and electronic technicians, computer operators, radiologic technicians, legal assistants, physical therapists, dental assistants, mechanical engineers, and restaurant cooks.

The fastest declining occupations include stenographers, industrial truck and tractor operators, sewing machine operators, textile machine operators, farm workers, and electrical and electronic assemblers.

If these trends continue, then workers whose background, education, and skills make it difficult for them to shift out of traditional blue collar jobs into the higher paying white collar occupations will be in for a hard time, to say the least.

Unemployment

Half of those unemployed in 1993 lost their jobs. The remaining half were split between those who left their jobs, reentrants to the job market, and new entrants to the job market.

Who are the unemployed? An unemployed person is someone over 16 years who doesn't have a job but is actively seeking one. Not everyone counted as unemployed has actually lost a job. Some quit voluntarily to seek better ones. Others, who were in the labor force but left voluntarily, now try to rejoin the labor market. Still others have never been employed but are actively and unsuccessfully seeking work. These are four very different kinds of out-of-work people contributing to our unemployment totals. Look at Table 16.

Over half the 1993 unemployed had lost their jobs. These people represent the involuntarily unemployed. But 10.8 percent left of their own accord. Typically, they leave to find better jobs. While out looking, they are counted among those not having a job, but who are actively seeking one.

Reentrants are workers who voluntarily left the labor force but now seek reentry. They include women whose children have reached school age and retired people who have decided to work again. While these people were invol-

TABLE 16 Unemployed People, by Reason: 1970 and 1993 (000s and %)

	1970	1993
Total	4,093	8,733
Job losers	44.3	54.6
Job leavers	13.4	10.8
Reentrants	30.0	24.6
New entrants	12.3	10.0
	100.0	100.0

Source: Bureau of the Census, *Statistical Abstract of the United States, 1994* (Washington, D.C.: U.S. Department of Commerce, 1994), p. 417.

untarily unemployed when the count of unemployment was taken, their economic condition and employment prospects differ from job losers.

New entrants, too, represent a different unemployment condition. It takes time and effort to find a first job and these 10.0 percent of the unemployed are the ones finding it difficult.

UNEMPLOYMENT AMONG WOMEN, MINORITIES, AND THE YOUNG

It is no surprise to find women, blacks, and Hispanics, as well as young people disproportionately represented among the unemployed. Still, the size of the disparities may surprise you. Look at Table 17.

The unemployment rates for black men and women in 1993 were twice the unemployment rates for white men and women. Young black men and women have an especially rough time trying to get a job. As many as one-third of young blacks in the labor force have been unemployed. The unemployment rates for young whites are also double-digit, but they are not nearly as severe as those for blacks.

High rates of black unemployment cannot be explained by differences in educational attainment alone.

UNEMPLOYMENT BY OCCUPATION AND EDUCATIONAL STATUS

One factor contributing to the unemployment disparities among races is the kinds of occupations in which whites and minority people are employed. Another is their educational attainment. Look at Table 18.

TABLE 17 Unemployment Rates by Sex, Age, Race, and Hispanic Origin, 1993

		White	Black	Hispanic
Total	16 years and over	6.0	12.9	10.6
	16 to 19 years	16.2	38.9	26.2
Men	16 years and over	6.2	13.8	10.4
	16 to 19 years	17.6	40.1	26.1
Women	16 years and over	5.7	12.0	10.9
	16 to 19 years	14.6	37.5	26.4

Source: Bureau of Labor Statistics, *Employment and Earnings* (Washington, D.C.: U. S. Department of Labor, January 1994), p. 232.

TABLE 18 Unemployment Rates by Occupation and Educational Attainment, 1993

Occupation	
Managerial and professional	3.0
Technical, sales, and administrative	5.3
Service	7.6
Precision production	7.9
Operators, fabricators, and laborers	9.9
Farming	8.2
Educational Attainment	
1-3 years high school	11.0
4 years high school	5.9
1-3 years college	4.8
4 years college or more	2.8

Bureau of the Census, *Statistical Abstract of the United States, 1994* (Washington, D.C.: Department of Commerce, 1994), p. 417–18.

Unemployment rate

The ratio of unemployment to the labor force.

The disproportionate number of minority workers in precision production jobs, and as operators, fabricators, and laborers makes them considerably more vulnerable to unemployment. The **rate of unemployment** for these workers is 9.9 percent. Relatively few minority workers are managers and professionals, who face only a 3.0 percent unemployment rate.

Education counts as well. Unemployment rates among workers who have not gone to college are considerably higher than the rates afflicting workers with some years of college. As you already know, it pays to get an education!

CHAPTER REVIEW

1. Rising productivity has been the primary factor behind the long-run increase in all wages in the U.S. economy. Labor productivity has increased sevenfold between 1890 and 1989. However, some wages do not rise in tandem with productivity increases because the price of the product the labor produces does not rise.

2. Education influences wage levels over time. College graduates have a different, higher-paying set of employment opportunities to choose from compared to high school graduates and dropouts.

3. Experience also influences wage levels. Work experience contributes to labor productivity. Men hit their peak earning period between ages 44 and 54, while women earn most between the ages of 35 and 44.

4. Disparities in earnings also exist between racial groups. Blacks and Hispanics typically earn 25 to 30 percent less than do white workers in similar jobs.

5. A gender gap exists in wage levels. Women earn less than men, the percentage depending on age and occupation. The gender gap in wages appears to be narrowing over time.

6. There is significant difference of opinion among economists as to the effect of unionization on wage rates. More recent data suggest that union workers earn substantially more than their nonunion counterparts.

7. Of all workers who are paid hourly wage rates, 6.6 percent were paid at or below the minimum wage in 1993.

8. The labor force consists of anyone over the age of 16 who is willing to work. The labor force grew at a 1.7 percent annual rate between 1950 and 1993. During the same period farm employment declined from 12 percent of the labor force to 2.4 percent of the labor force. Nearly 70 percent of the labor force is engaged in providing services such as managerial, professional, technical, housekeeping, janitorial, and others.

9. Women account for some 45 percent of total employment. However, they are concentrated in support-system occupations that are technical or associated with sales and administration. In these occuptions they outnumber men two to one.

10. Minority workers are disproportionately concentrated in jobs as operators, fabricators, and laborers.

11. Future jobs will tend to be concentrated in areas involving computers, medical training, electronics, and professional assistants. Blue collar jobs will continue to decline.

12. Workers may be unemployed because they have lost their jobs, because they have left their jobs voluntarily, or because they have just entered the labor force to look for a job. Women, blacks, Hispanics, and young people are disproportionately unemployed. Minority workers who are employed primarily in blue collar jobs are particularly vulnerable to unemployment. But, even if black workers have the same education as white workers and are employed in professional occupations, they are still more likely than white workers to be unemployed.

KEY TERMS

Fringe benefits
Labor force
Unemployment rate

QUESTIONS

1. Suppose you had to defend the argument that no sex or racial discrimination exists in our labor markets. How could you use the data in this chapter?

2. Suppose you had to defend the argument that both sex and racial discrimination exist in our labor markets. How could you use the data in this chapter?

3. Does it pay to get an education? What evidence can you cite?

4. Can you offer two examples (from personal experience) that demonstrate that experience is worth paying for?

5. In spite of the fact that we are producing more goods in our economy, workers are shifting out of jobs that make goods into jobs that provide services. Can you suggest a reason for this occupational shift?

6. What are the major professional/occupational categories analyzed in this chapter? What "people characteristics" apply to each of these categories?

7. What percent of U.S. hourly workers are at or below the minimum wage? What are the economic characteristics of these workers?

8. Distinguish between job losers, job leavers, reentrants, and new entrants among the unemployed.

9. Which occupations are most vulnerable to unemployment? Which are least vulnerable? What age groups are most represented among the unemployed?

CHAPTER 18

INTEREST, RENT, AND PROFIT

CHAPTER PREVIEW

Our examination of resource markets in the previous three chapters has focused entirely on labor. How are other resources like capital, land, and entrepreneurship priced? How much of each of these resources will a profit-maximizing firm hire? This chapter addresses these questions. You will find that many of the same concepts applied to the study of wage and employment determination can be adapted to an examination of interest rate, rent, and profit determination.

After studying this chapter, you should be able to:

- Explain the terms marginal physical product of capital and marginal revenue product of capital.
- Describe the difference between loanable funds and equipment capital.
- Verify that a firm maximizes profit from capital by employing capital until its $MRP = MFC$.
- Graph the demand for loanable funds and the supply of loanable funds to explain interest rate determination.
- Discuss the ethics of interest-payment incomes.
- Use an equation to explain the relationship between interest rates and present values of property.
- Give an economic definition for rent.

- Develop an example to show that the rent per acre of land is strictly demand-determined if the supply of land is fixed.
- Derive differential rents on land of different quality.
- Give examples of wage-related rents.
- Describe how entrepreneurs calculate their profit-related income.

Have you ever seen money work? Think about it. Have you ever seen a dollar bill go to work the way people do? For example, can you imagine a dollar bill getting up in the morning and going to work at the Charles Edwards Coal Mining Company? Can you imagine a dollar bill producing tons of coal? Can you visualize a marginal physical product curve for dollar bills? This may sound absurd, but don't be too sure.

THE PRODUCTIVITY OF CAPITAL

Economists believe that money, in the form of capital, is productive in precisely the same way that people are. In the chapter on wage rates and employment under perfect competition, we saw that as more miners were hired by the Charles Edwards Coal Mining Company, total tonnage increased. Remember how we derived labor's productivity. We assumed that everything required to mine coal—the drilling, blasting, and transport equipment, as well as the coal itself—was already on the Edwards site. Everything but labor.

We then added workers. We saw that without a single miner, no coal could be produced. All the mining equipment in the world couldn't produce a solitary nugget without someone actually working the equipment. And when miners were added, one by one, total output increased. The more miners, the higher the tonnage.

What makes sense for labor makes sense as well for capital. We calculate the productivity of capital the same way. But this time, we assume that Edwards starts with a fixed supply of miners and coal resources. The company has everything required to produce coal except capital.

When capital is added to a production process, output increases. The addition to total physical product from the addition of a unit of capital is the marginal physical product of capital.

Can you picture the scene at the mine? How can miners be expected to mine coal without so much as a pick and shovel? What can they possibly do? They cannot scratch their way into the pits with bare hands. The combination of an ample quantity of miners, an ample quantity of coal resources, and no capital equipment produces no coal. We see this in Table 1.

Does Table 1 look familiar? It should. It shows what happens to output when a resource, in this case, capital, is added to production. You may want to compare Table 1 here to Table 1 in the earlier chapter on wage rates and employment. Do you see the similarity?

Marginal revenue product of capital

The change in total revenue that results from adding one more dollar of loanable funds to production.

Loanable funds

Money that a firm employs to purchase the physical plant, equipment, and raw materials used in production.

Look at capital's total physical product, *TPP*. Working with one unit of capital—$1,000 worth of capital equipment—miners are able to produce a total physical product of 250 tons. If the price per ton of coal is $2, then the **marginal revenue product of capital** is $2 × 250 = $500.

This is a very impressive revenue generated by the first $1,000 employed. Calculating the *MRP per dollar,* each of the first thousand dollars earns $500/$1,000 = $0.50 or 50 percent.

If Edwards decides to use $2,000, then *TPP* = 475 tons. The *MPP* of the second unit of $1,000 **loanable funds** is 475 – 250 = 225 tons. The *MRP per dollar* for each of the second thousand dollars is $0.45 or 45 percent.

Marginal physical product of capital? One person operating that steam shovel can move more tons of earth in one day than 1,000 able-bodied people working with hand picks and shovels can move in an entire month.

From Loanable Funds to Equipment Capital

The addition of equipment capital to a production process can be measured in monetary units, that is, as loanable funds.

But how does Edwards add a second unit of $1,000 loanable funds to the already employed first $1,000? It isn't quite the same as adding a second miner to one miner already employed. The first miner is the same miner with or without the second employed. But in the case of loanable funds, the doubling of loanable funds used in production *may require changing the physical character of the first $1,000 worth of loanable funds employed.*

For example, if the first unit of $1,000 were used to purchase 20 picks and shovels, and an additional $1,000 were later added to buy another 20 picks and shovels, there is no problem. But suppose the most productive use of $2,000 is not 40 picks and shovels, but one pneumatic drill. Here's the problem. *How can Edwards purchase the $2,000 drill when it already has the first $1,000 worth of capital in the form of 20 picks and shovels?*

TABLE 1
The Effect of Loanable Funds on Output and Revenue (price of coal = $2 per ton)

Loanable Funds	Total Physical Product (tons)	Marginal Physical Product (tons)	Marginal Revenue Product	*MRP*/Dollar (%)
$ 0	0	—	—	—
1,000	250	250	$500	50
2,000	475	225	450	45
3,000	675	200	400	40
4,000	850	175	350	35
5,000	1,000	150	300	30
6,000	1,125	125	250	25
7,000	1,225	100	200	20
8,000	1,300	75	150	15
9,000	1,350	50	100	10
10,000	1,375	25	50	05

Edwards has no such problem when it considers hiring more workers. It can hire, lay off, and rehire miners without affecting their individual physical characteristics. A mining crew of 10 miners can be reduced to a mining crew of nine miners without changing any individual miner. But Edwards cannot add to or withdraw loanable funds from production without changing the total stock of equipment that the loanable funds buy. Once any quantity of loanable funds is employed in production, it takes the definite physical form of **capital equipment** and is unalterable in the short run. It is impossible to add $1,000 of loanable funds to $1,000 worth of capital equipment already fixed in the form of picks and shovels and end up with a $2,000 pneumatic drill.

Equipment capital

The machinery that a firm uses in production.

In reading Table 1, then, we assume that the calculations Edwards makes in adding or subtracting units of capital are made while capital is still in its money form.

EDWARDS' DEMAND FOR LOANABLE FUNDS

Interest rate

The price of loanable funds, expressed as an annual percentage return on a dollar of loanable funds.

How much loanable funds will Edwards demand? The quantity demanded depends on the amount of money, that is, the **rate of interest,** firms are obliged to pay to obtain them. After all, nobody lends money for free. The higher the interest rate, the less loanable funds will the firm demand.

Let's suppose the interest rate, r, is 15 percent. That is, Edwards can get as much loanable funds as it desires at $r = .15$.

The marginal factor cost of a dollar of loanable funds is the interest that must be paid in order to borrow it.

Look again at Table 1. Would you advise Edwards to borrow? How much? Consider the first $1,000. For each of the first thousand dollars, *MRP* = $0.50. Since it costs Edwards only $0.15 per dollar to borrow that money, that's a net gain of $0.50 – $0.15 = $0.35 per dollar used in production.

What about the second $1,000? Each of these dollars adds $0.45 – $0.15 = $0.30 to Edwards' revenue. Each of the third $1,000 adds $0.40 – $0.15 = $0.25 to revenue. Although the *MRP* of capital falls as the quantity of capital employed increases, it is not until the 8,000th dollar that *MRP* = $0.15.

The *MRP* = *MFC* Rule

Marginal factor cost

The change in a firm's total cost that results from adding one more unit of a factor (labor, capital, or land) to production.

The *MRP* = *MFC* maximization rule—that is, marginal revenue product equals **marginal factor cost**—applies to capital just as the *MRP* = *MLC* rule applies to labor. Edwards will continue adding loanable funds to production as long as its *MRP* is greater than or equal to the marginal cost of employing loanable funds, *MFC*. Edwards' demand curve for loanable funds, then, is its *MRP* curve. This is shown in Figure 1.

If $r = .15$, Edwards demands $8,000 of loanable funds. If $r = .20$, Edwards demands $7,000. And so on.

LOANABLE FUNDS IN THE ECONOMY: DEMAND AND SUPPLY

The Charles Edwards Coal Mining Company is only one of many thousands of firms operating in the economy. As you can imagine, each of these firms has its own Table 1, with its own *MRP* curve. The economy's demand for loanable

FIGURE 1 **Edwards' Demand for Loanable Funds**
The downward-sloping demand curve for loanable funds is identical to the firm's *MRP* of capital curve. If the rate of interest, *r*, which is the price the firm has to pay for loanable funds, is 15 percent, the quantity of loanable funds demanded by the firm is $8,000. Every one of the first $7,999 produces for the firm a revenue greater than $0.15. The $8,000th produces exactly $0.15. That is why the firm will borrow as much as $8,000 of loanable funds at $r = .15$. If $r = .20$, the quantity of loanable funds demanded by the firm falls to $7,000, because every dollar it buys over the $7,000th, produces a *MRP* that is less than $0.20.

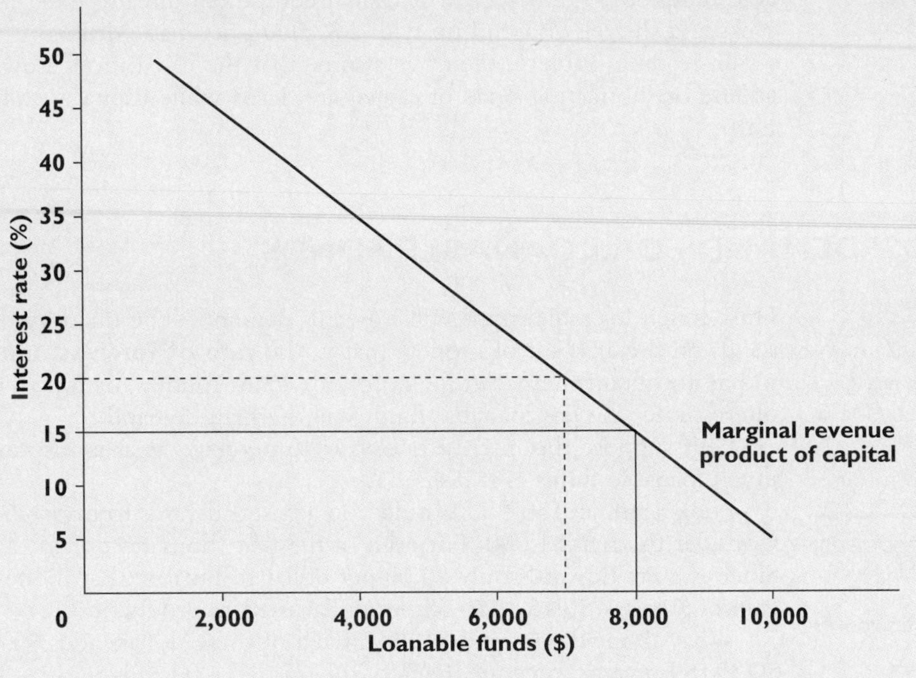

The economy's demand for loanable funds is the sum of all individual firms' demands for loanable funds.

funds, then, at $r = .15$, is the sum of each firm's demand for loanable funds at $r = .15$. This is shown in Figure 2. At $r = .15$, $12 million is demanded.

Where do the loanable funds come from? People supply the loanable funds. They are willing to supply the capital *for a price*. The price, offered by the firms using the capital, is the rate of interest. The higher the rate of interest, the greater is the quantity of loanable funds supplied.

People can do two things with their income. They can spend it or save it. There is, of course, good reason to do some of both. People spend at least some of their income on household necessities. But they also spend part of their income on items whose consumption could be postponed without inflicting permanent damage to body and soul.

Loanable funds market
The market in which the demand for and supply of loanable funds determines the rate of interest.

Why would anyone be willing to postpone consumption? One good reason is that the money saved and supplied to the **loanable funds market** earns a rate of interest. Most people would get excited about the prospect of earning 15 percent on their savings.

Of course, not everybody gets equally excited about interest. You would expect people with different incomes to behave differently. And they do. Low-income people, for example, generally spend most of their waking hours figuring out how to make ends meet. Their ability to save is limited. In some cases,

FIGURE 2
The Economy's Demand for Loanable Funds
The downward-sloping demand curve for loanable funds in the economy reflects the sum, at every rate of interest, of quantity of loanable funds demanded by each firm. At $r = .15$, the economy's demand for loanable funds is $12 million, of which $8,000 is demanded by the Charles Edwards Coal Mining Company.

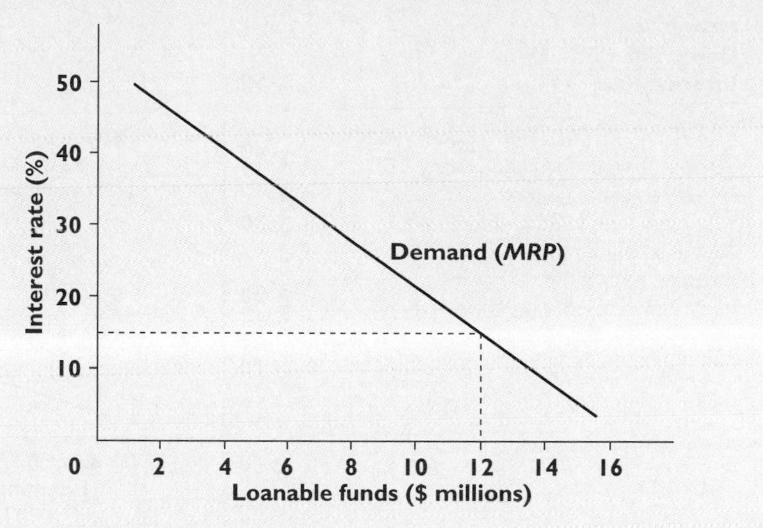

If people don't spend their incomes, they save them. Saving is the act that supplies loanable funds to the economy. At a higher interest rate, people are inclined to save more, supplying a larger quantity of loanable funds to the market.

it is flat zero. The prospect of earning interest by offering their savings to the loanable funds market is, therefore, probably the furthest thing from their minds.

But not for other people. Earning interest is a sufficient inducement for people who have the ability to supply savings to the loanable funds market. Look at Figure 3.

The supply curve of loanable funds is upward-sloping. At low rates of interest, the quantity of loanable funds offered to the market is relatively low. But as the rate increases, the quantity supplied increases as well.

FIGURE 3
The Supply of Loanable Funds
The upward-sloping supply curve of loanable funds in the economy reflects the willingness of people to supply quantities of loanable funds at varying rates of interest. At $r = .15$, the quantity supplied is $12 million. At higher rates of interest, such as $r = .20$, the quantity supplied is larger.

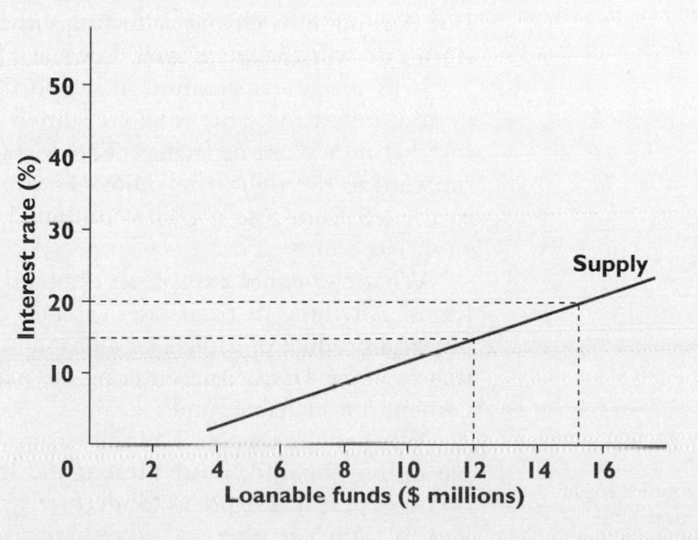

FIGURE 4
Determination of the Interest Rate
The equilibrium rate of interest is determined by the supply of and demand for loanable funds. At $r = .20$, an excess supply of \$15.5 million – \$10.5 million = \$5 million of loanable funds emerges, forcing the rate of interest down to equilibrium.

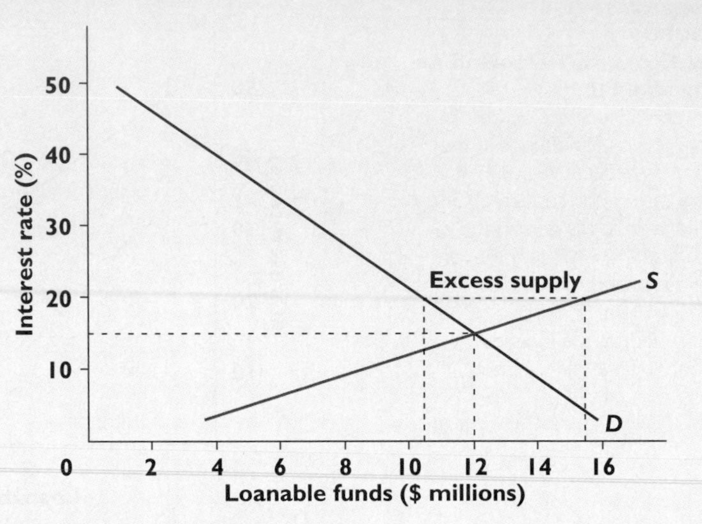

THE EQUILIBRIUM RATE OF INTEREST

What determines the equilibrium rate of interest? Supply and demand. Figure 4 brings together Figure 2, showing the economy's demand for loanable funds, and Figure 3, which shows the economy's supply of loanable funds.

As you see, the equilibrium rate of interest is 15 percent. If the rate were higher, say, $r = .20$, an excess supply would emerge on the market. Competition among suppliers of loanable funds would drive the rate down. If the rate were lower, say, $r = .10$, the excess demand for loanable funds among borrowers would drive the rate up.

The rate of interest remains unchanged as long as the demand and supply conditions in the loanable funds market of Figure 4 are themselves unchanging. But if conditions change, affecting either demand or supply, then the equilibrium rate will change as well. Look at Figure 5.

Let's imagine a situation in which the housing industry is entering a boom period, but at the same time consumers are spending more on housing by taking the money out of savings. The demand curve for loanable funds would shift outward to the right from D to D', while the supply curve would shift inward to the left from S to S'. The combined effect of these shifts drives the equilibrium rate to $r = .25$.

What else could explain an outward shift in the demand curve for loanable funds? Anything that increases capital's *MRP,* such as a change in the marginal physical product of capital, or a change in the price of the product produced by that capital, or new firms entering the market, each adding to the market its own demand for loanable funds.

Be sure that you can explain why the equilibrium rate of interest might change over time.

What about supply? The shift from S to S' usually reflects a change in people's preferences for more present and less deferred consumption. For example, if you expect future prices to increase, you may withdraw your savings from the loanable funds market and take that vacation to Hawaii now.

FIGURE 5
Changes in the Rate of Interest
When the demand curve for loanable funds increases from D to D' at the same time that the supply curve of loanable funds decreases from S to S', the equilibrium rate of interest increases from $r = .15$ to $r = .25$.

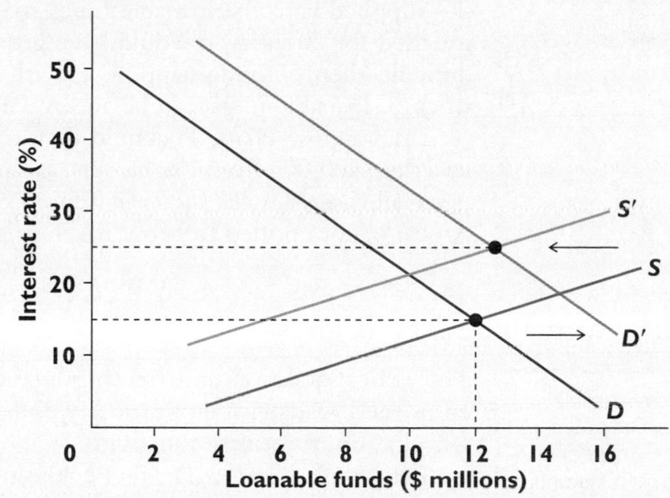

THE ETHICS OF INCOME FROM INTEREST

Is income from interest payments earned or unearned income?

At $r = .15$, suppliers of loanable funds receive as interest payments $0.15 for every dollar supplied. Suppose Diane Pecknold supplies $400,000 to the loanable funds market. At $r = .15$, she receives interest of $60,000 per year.

Let's suppose also that she lives in the coal mining region of Harlan County. But unlike her coal mining neighbors, she does not get up at 6 o'clock every morning to make her way to the coal pits. Instead, she rises at 10, takes her morning coffee in the sun room, and spends the rest of the late morning hours leisurely scanning the financial section of the local newspaper. She frequently lunches with the local banker and typically spends her afternoons fishing in a private lake for smallmouth bass. In other words, life for money supplier Diane Pecknold is not entirely unpleasant.

She is also the topic of conversation among her coal mining neighbors. Down at the pits, they refer to her as "unproductive." Some see her as a parasite, "living off the sweat of the working class." But is Diane Pecknold really unproductive? Is she really a parasite?

While Diane sleeps comfortably during the early morning hours of the work week, *her capital is busy working for her*. It earns its *MRP*, just as miners earn theirs. If Pecknold is not entitled to the fruits of her property, who is? After all, the $400,000 loanable funds advanced by Diane Pecknold is her property, just as the miners' muscle power is theirs.

Somebody Did the Saving

How did Diane Pecknold come by $400,000? Suppose she accumulated the $400,000 of loanable funds over a long period of time. It could represent years of saving. While others were busy spending their income on consumption items, Diane Pecknold saved.

As a result, she managed to put aside $10,000 from her first-year's salary, and she supplied it to the loanable funds market at $r = .15$. If she kept it there untouched for 20 years, it would have grown from $10,000 to $166,664. It is not difficult, then, to understand how, with a determined effort to save, a $400,000 stock of loanable funds can be accumulated.

But suppose Diane Pecknold didn't save at all. Suppose, instead, she inherited the $400,000 from her parents. Is she no less entitled to the interest it bears? After all, *somebody did the saving*. How did her parents come by the $400,000? Are they not entitled to bequeath their savings to their children?

Property and Property Rights

Income from loanable funds is justified in the sense that owners of loanable funds hold a property right to the loanable funds.

The ethical question underscoring Diane Pecknold's claim to interest payments raises the broader issue of property and property rights. What is property? And who has claim to its productivity?

Let's look beyond Diane Pecknold's claim to interest. Is a student who scored a perfect exam not entitled to an A simply because she hadn't studied for the exam? Is it fair to other students that, because she has an exceptional mind, she can exert minimal effort and yet top the class? Her superior performance reflects her high IQ. But what did she do to warrant having one? If she inherited her intelligence from her parents, is she, then, really entitled to the rewards it creates?

Or what about the musical genius of violinist Gil Shaham? Is that not a marketable property? Should he not be entitled to the rewards it affords him? What about Shaquille O'Neal? He's one of the highest-paid basketball players in the NBA. Is it fair that he is rewarded for a natural ability he did little to acquire?

Everyone, it appears, possesses some particular set of physical or mental properties that works for her or him. The A student, blessed with a high IQ, earns a high grade without having to exert much effort. Gil Shaham's genius works the classical concert circuit. Shaquille O'Neal's innate ability works in the NBA.

Should Diane Pecknold's loanable funds be treated differently? It is a property, like intelligence or physical ability acquired through inheritance. It works the loanable funds market. Is not every property holder with legitimate rights to the property entitled to receive the *MRP* the property generates?

Marxist View of Interest-Derived Income

Marxists don't recognize the validity of property rights; hence, they object to income being earned from loanable funds.

Not all economists are willing to justify interest-derived claims to income on the basis of capital's productivity or as a reward for saving. Marxists, for example, are quick to dismiss these arguments as simplistic, self-serving apologies.

While Marxists have no trouble understanding that supply and demand for loanable funds determine the interest rate, they do question how the supply of loanable funds got into the hands of the suppliers in the first place. Their own explanation is radically different. To them, the answer is theft. All private property, Karl Marx asserted, originates in theft.

In this interpretation of history there are no ethical foundations to property claims whatsoever. Diane Pecknold's claim to her $400,000 loanable funds property and to the $60,000 interest it generates annually has about as much validity to a Marxist as an eagle's claim to a bunny rabbit. It's strictly predatory.

PRESENT VALUE

Let's stay, for a moment, with Diane Pecknold's good fortune. Suppose she receives a letter from a law firm in Raleigh, North Carolina, telling her that she has inherited a 40-acre tobacco farm from a distant uncle. The farm, she discovers, generates an annual net income of $28,000. Although nobody, including Diane Pecknold, looks a gift horse in the mouth, she is still curious to know just how much the farm is worth. How would she go about calculating the value of the property?

Her first thought is on the mark. She knows that her $400,000 in loanable funds earns her $60,000 annually in interest. She figures, therefore, that if the farm earns annually a little less than one-half of $60,000, it should be worth a little less than one-half the value of her $400,000 loanable funds.

Once the idea is understood, the calculations become rather simple. She figures her annual interest as follows:

$$R = rPV$$

where, R represents the annual return on the property, PV represents the property's **present value,** and r represents the rate of interest.

Present value

The value today of the stream of expected future annual income a property generates. The method of computing present value is to divide the annual income generated, R, by the rate of interest r. That is, PV = R/r.

In the case of her newly acquired farm, Diane Pecknold knows $r = .15$ and the annual return on the property is $28,000. Rewriting our simple equation, the present value of the property—that is, the farm—is simply

$$PV = R/r$$

or, $28,000/.15 = $186,666.67. As she originally thought, the value of the farm is just a little under $200,000.

Effect of Changing Interest Rates on Property Values

Suppose the rate of interest dropped to 10 percent. What would happen to the value of Pecknold's farm? The arithmetic is simple enough.

$$\$28{,}000/.10 = \$280{,}000$$

At $r = .10$, the value of the farm shoots up to $280,000. The farm's value, then, increases as interest rates fall. Does this inverse relationship between interest rates and property value make sense?

Suppose you wanted to create a bank account that provides steady annual interest of $28,000. If the interest rate were 15 percent, how much would you need to put into the account? The answer is $186,666.67. But if the interest rate were 10 percent, wouldn't more money be needed in the account to generate the same $28,000 annual return? How much would be needed now to generate $28,000 annually? $280,000.

Why does a decrease in the interest rate increase the present value of a property?

Since the farm generates $28,000 year after year, shouldn't its value, at $r = .15$, be equivalent to the value of a $186,666.67 bank account, and at $r = .10$, be equivalent to the value of a $280,000 account?

Property Values and Price Floors

Suppose Diane Pecknold develops a strong interest in this North Carolina tobacco farm. She learns that the farm produces 10,000 pounds of Bright Leaf to-

FIGURE 6
Price and Output in the Tobacco Market
The market demand and supply curves intersect at $P = \$2$ and $Q = 800{,}000$. The market-determined value of the tobacco crop is $\$2 \times 800{,}000 = \$1{,}600{,}000$. The government-imposed price floor is fixed at \$2.80. At that price, tobacco farmers supply 1,000,000 pounds. The value of tobacco farms increases with a price floor.

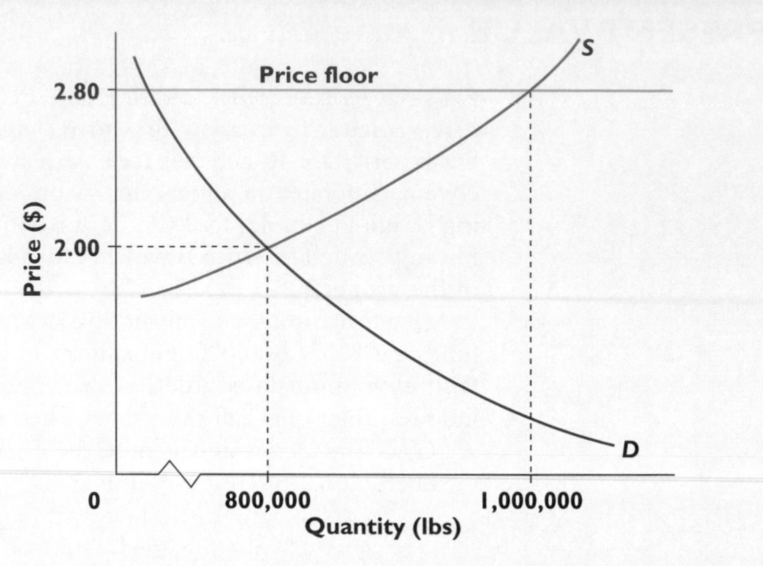

Be sure that you are able to explain why a price floor would artificially inflate the present value of property that produces a commodity whose price is propped up by the floor.

bacco each season which is sold at \$2.80 per pound. But she soon discovers that the price of tobacco has a long and troubled history. The \$2.80 it fetches on the market is a politically determined floor price, set by government to protect tobacco producers. The equilibrium price that would prevail in a free market—if the government didn't interfere—would be \$2. Figure 6 depicts the price circumstance she and other tobacco farmers face.

Diane Pecknold knows that as long as the government keeps supporting the price of tobacco at \$2.80, the value of her annual tobacco crop will stay at $\$2.80 \times 10{,}000 = \$28{,}000$. The value of the farm property, at $r = .15$, then, remains at \$186,666.67.

But suppose the government abandons its price support of tobacco, allowing price to adjust downward to its \$2 market value. The value of her crop falls from \$28,000 to $\$2 \times 10{,}000 = \$20{,}000$.

"Just feel that quality, it's about as fine as you'll ever get," shouts the selling agent (off to the left) for Diane Pecknold's tobacco, in this tobacco auction in Durham, North Carolina. He's waving a handful of uncured tobacco leaves at buying agents representing the major cigarette companies.

What happens to the value of the farm? The present value of a property generating \$20,000 annually is \$20,000/.15 = \$133,333.33. In other words, *Diane Pecknold's tobacco farm is valued at \$186,666.67 only because tobacco prices have been artificially inflated by the government to \$2.80, well above the \$2 price that the market would generate.*

You can see, then, why tens of thousands of farmers today might be uncomfortable. Many bought farms at inflated values. If price supports are withdrawn, property values could come crashing down, destroying much of the loanable funds farmers have tied up in their farms.

Almost Anything Is Marketable Property

A North Carolina tobacco farm fits well into our image of what a property is. It is tangible. A brick house is about as tangible a property as any you could describe. But property, in the world of economics, need not be physical.

Imagine having a bubbling brook surface on your property with water all year round tasting as delightful as Perrier. If you can sell access to the brook for \$10 per year and 1,000 people buy into the deal, the present value of the brook would be \$10,000/.15 = \$66,666.67.

Or imagine owning a popcorn company that nets \$500,000 annually. And suppose Bonnie Blair, U.S. Olympic speedskater who won five gold medals in the 1993 Winter Games, allows you to use her name and face on your popcorn box. Your new designer popcorn now nets an income of \$1.5 million annually. The capitalized value of Bonnie Blair's *name,* then, becomes (\$1,500,000 − \$500,000)/.15 = \$6,666,666.67. That is to say, a name can also be valuable property.

You can see, can't you, why winning at Wimbledon is so financially important to the players? Their names become valuable properties that enhance the market value of the rackets they promote and, as a result, the market value of the firms producing the rackets.

INCOME FROM RENT

If you were playing a word-association game and someone said "rent," what would you say? Most people would say "apartment" or "house." But economists wouldn't. To economists, rent describes a payment for the use of a resource in production. The resource generating the rent can be labor or capital or land. That is, rent is paid to laborers for the use of their labor in precisely the same way that rent is paid to landowners for the use of their land.

Rent

The difference between what a productive resource receives as payment for its use in production and the cost of bringing that resource into production.

Economists define **rent** as *the difference between what the resource receives as payment for its use in production and the payment that was necessary to bring the supply of the resource into being.* Let's see how this works.

The Derivation of Land Rent

Consider rent derived from the use of land. Even without improvements, land is a productive resource. It is the wellspring of our raw materials, our foodstuffs, and our fuels. Perhaps the most remarkable feature about land is its supply price, or cost. We don't have to use any labor or capital to bring land in its natural state

FIGURE 7 **The Derivation of Land Rent**

The supply of land is fixed at 120,000 acres. In panel *a*, reflecting sparse population, the downward-sloping demand curve for land, *D*, falls to zero at 40,000 acres, well below the island's land capacity. The equilibrium price of the land is zero. In panel *b*, the increasing population shifts the demand curve for land to *D'*. The new equilibrium price, determined by the intersection of the demand and supply curves, is $50 per acre. Since the supply price, or cost, needed to bring acreage into being is zero, the difference between what the land receives in payment and the supply price—the rent—is $50 per acre. In panel *c*, with continuing growth in population, the demand curve shifts to *D''*. Now, the equilibrium price, or rent, rises to $60 per acre.

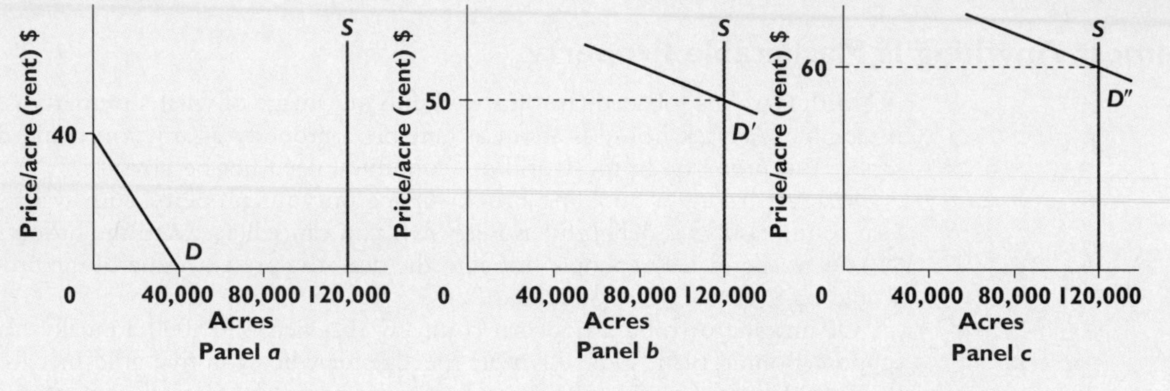

into existence. It is simply there, part of our natural heritage. Economists, therefore, consider the supply price of land in its virgin state to be zero.

Imagine, then, a small island economy where virgin land is divided into small lots of privately owned acres and used exclusively to produce the island's food. Imagine abundance, so that people on the island could well be singing the Rodgers and Hammerstein song from *South Pacific:*

We have sunlight on the sand
We have moonlight on the sea
We have mangos and bananas
We can pick right off the tree

Panel *a*, Figure 7 describes such a situation.

The supply of productive land on the island, *S*, is fixed at 120,000 acres. We assume that the cost of bringing the 120,000 acres under cultivation is zero. The demand curve for land—the *MRP* curve—is downward-sloping. Suppose the island's population is so sparse that the *MRP* curve of land, *D,* falls to zero at the 40,000th cultivated acre. As you see, there is an excess supply of cultivable land even at a land price of zero. How could any landowner get a penny of **land rent** under these conditions?

Land rent

A payment to landowners for the use of land.

But let's suppose that in time population growth in the economy presses upon land supply to draw all 120,000 acres into cultivation. Suppose the increasing demand for food shifts the *MRP* of land—the price of food increases—from *D* in panel *a* to *D'* in panel *b,* Figure 7.

Land rent is entirely demand-determined when the supply of land is fixed.

Landowners now face a very different circumstance. Before, with 120,000 − 40,000 = 80,000 acres left uncultivated, land rent was zero. Now, in panel *b,* the new demand and supply conditions generate a rental price per acre of $50. Why? Although people now pay $50 for the use of an acre, the supply price of land—

FIGURE 8 **Deriving Differential Rent**

The supply curve of land shows step increases to 120,000 acres. The supply price, or cost, required to ready these acres for cultivation varies with the quality of the land. The supply price is zero for the highest quality 40,000 acres, \$50 per acre for the second-grade 40,000 acres, and \$60 per acre for the lowest quality 40,000 acres. In panel *a*, the demand curve, *D*, decreases to zero at 40,000 acres. No rent emerges. In panel *b*, population growth shifts the demand curve to *D'*. The new equilibrium price for land is \$50 and the quantity of land cultivated increases to 80,000 acres. These changes create \$50 – \$0 = \$50 rent per acre on the highest quality 40,000 acres and \$50 – \$50 = zero rent on the second-grade 40,000 acres. In panel *c*, the growing population shifts the demand curve to *D"*. The equilibrium price increases to \$60 per acre and all 120,000 acres are brought under cultivation. Rent on the highest quality land becomes \$60 – \$0 = \$60 per acre. A rent of \$60 – \$50 = \$10 per acre emerges on the second-grade land. Only the lowest quality 40,000 acres yield no rent.

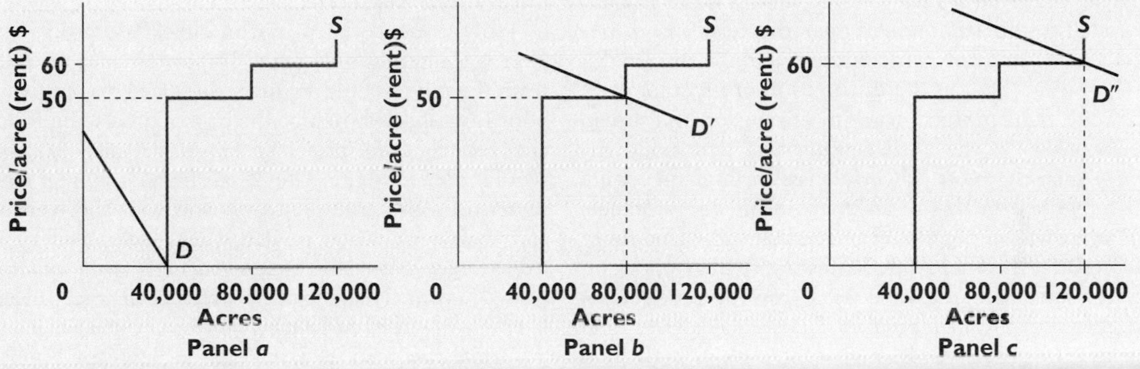

the cost of bringing the land into being—still remains zero. The rent that landowners receive—the difference between the payment the resource receives and its supply price—is the \$50.

Suppose population continues to increase. The increasing demand for food drives up the price of food shifting the *MRP* curve of land further to the right, to *D"* in panel *c*, Figure 7. The new demand and supply conditions generate a new rent per acre of \$60. Landowners who before received a rent of \$50 per acre, now receive \$60 per acre. As you see, *rent per acre is strictly demand determined.*

Differential Rent

When land of lower quality is brought into production, the rent on land of superior quality increases. What does this have to do with differences in costs of production between different types of land?

Now let's add a new wrinkle to the economy of Figure 7. Let's suppose that the 120,000 acres come in three different grades. The first 40,000 acres are the highest quality, the second 40,000 acres are lower-quality, and the third 40,000 acres are lowest-quality, quite inferior to the others. The cost of bringing the first 40,000 acres into cultivation is zero, as we supposed in Figure 7. The second 40,000 acres requires \$50 of fertilizer per acre to ready it for cultivation, while the third 40,000 requires \$60 of fertilizer per acre. Look at Figure 8.

If the island's population is sparse so that the *MRP* curve of land, *D*, falls to zero at 40,000 acres (see panel *a*, Figure 8), only the highest quality acres will be cultivated. The supply price for these 40,000 acres is zero. Landowners owning these highest quality acres are no better off than the other landowners. That is, they receive no rent.

ADDED PERSPECTIVE

The Corn Laws Controversy in 19th Century England

The rent analysis of Figure 8 has historical roots. During the 1790s, the price of corn (which we call grain) in England more than doubled, and it continued to increase during the early decades of the 19th century. This extraordinary upward thrust in corn prices triggered a bitter controversy among English capitalists and landowners over the relationship between the price of corn and rent, and the impact this relationship had on the distribution of income.

The conventional wisdom among pre-Ricardian economists of the 19th century was that landowners—then the most powerful class in England—were the sole benefactors of an unavoidable circumstance: The growth of population made cultivable land more scarce and this increasing land scarcity drove up rent. Since rent was regarded as a cost of production, higher rent meant higher food costs and higher food prices. In other words, high rent *explains* high food prices.

David Ricardo, one of the most brilliant economists of the period (and perhaps since) joined in the discussion on rent and food prices but reversed the order of causation. In his celebrated book, *On the Principles of Political Economy and Taxation* (1817), he developed the theory of differential rent. Ricardo argued that land has nothing to do with the cost of producing food. Labor and capital are the only real costs.

How then does land and rent come into the picture? Since population growth forces farmers to bring more land under cultivation, and since the new lands are typically less fertile than lands already in cultivation (requiring more labor time to produce the same quantity food), and since price is determined by the costs of producing on the least-favorable land, the farmers working the more favorable lands reap the differential between their own costs of producing food and the increasing price of food. That differential is rent. In other words, price is rent-determining, not rent price-determining. That is to say, high food prices *explain* high rent.

How, then, to keep rent in check? Ricardo's answer was international trade. Importing cheaper corn from Europe would reduce the need to cultivate poor English land, reduce the cost of producing food, and reduce corn prices in England; this, in turn, would reduce rent. The English landowning class understood the argument only too well and to protect their rent voted in Parliament—which it controlled—for corn laws that fixed high tariffs on imported corn. Keeping imported corn out meant keeping English rents in.

While the corn laws were good news for English landowners, they were bad news for English capitalists. After all, restricting corn imports kept corn prices high at home. The money wages that capitalists paid to workers, then, had to be raised to keep pace with the rising corn prices. Higher money wages meant lower profit. The trade-off was clear and politically loaded: High rents for landowners or high profits for capitalists.

The struggle between the landowning and capitalist classes over the corn laws raged on until mid-century. In the end, the growing economic and political power of the English capitalist class prevailed, and in 1846 the corn laws were repealed.

But suppose, as we did before, that the island's population increases. The increased demand for food shifts the *MRP* curve from D to D', shown in panel *b*. More acres are put under cultivation. As you see, the *MRP* curve now cuts the supply curve at 80,000 acres, setting price at $50 per acre.

What about rent? For the first 40,000 acres, the difference between the $50 price per acre—what each acre receives as payment—and the zero cost in bringing each acre into use, is $50 per acre. What was formerly no-rent acreage now generates for those landowners a **differential land rent** of $50 per acre.

Differential land rent

Rent arising from differences in the productivity of land.

What about the second 40,000 acres under cultivation? They yield no rent for these landowners because the $50 price that each of the acres receives in payment just covers the cost of bringing the acre into cultivation.

FIGURE 9 **Deriving Location Rent**

Price per acre is measured on the vertical axis, quantities of land *and* their distance from the marketplace, starting from the origin, are measured on the horizontal axis. The demand curve for land use, *D*, is downward-sloping. The transport cost curve, *t*, is upward-sloping, reflecting the increasing cost associated with transporting food from more distant land to market. The demand curve intersects the transport cost curve, creating an equilibrium rental price of $60 per acre. All acreage within 70 miles of the marketplace, or 50,000 acres, is cultivated. Each acre—except the 50,000th—has an *MRP* that is greater than the cost of transporting food to market. Rent on acreage arising from advantages of location is the difference between the $60 price of land and the transport cost associated with each acre. For the 49,999 rent-yielding acres, location rent is marked out by the shaded area between price and the transport cost curve. The 50,000th acre yields no location rent.

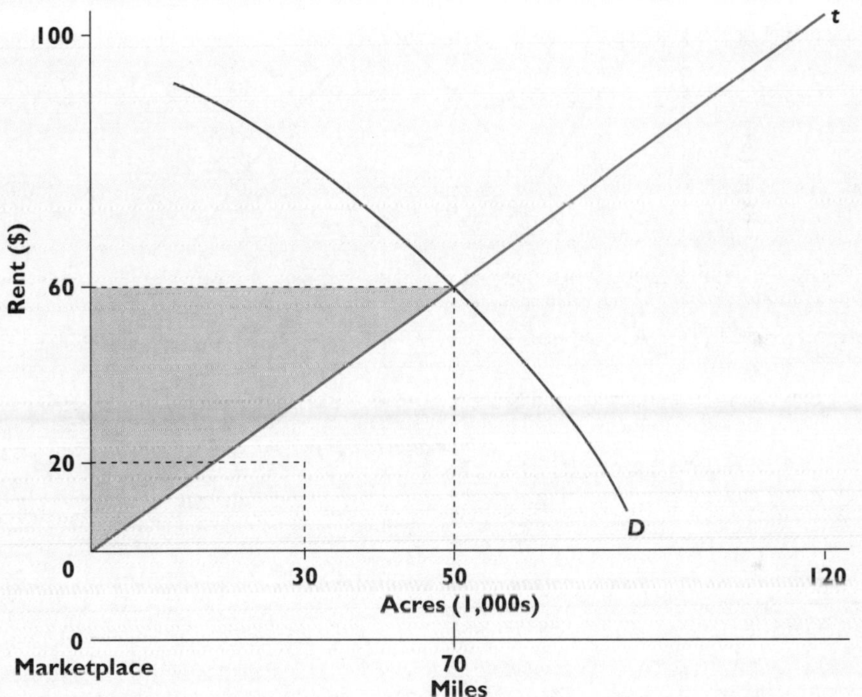

Suppose population continues to grow, shifting the *MRP* curve to *D*″, as shown in panel *c*. Now the *MRP* curve cuts the supply curve at 120,000 acres, setting a new price at $60.

What about rent? Landowners have something to cheer about. Rent on the first 40,000 acres increases from $50 to $60 per acre, while rent on the second 40,000 acres put under cultivation increases from zero to $60 – $50 = $10 per acre. The last 40,000 acres cultivated still yield no rent.

Location Rent

Another source of rent arises from differences in distances between cultivated lands and markets. *Because there's a cost involved in transporting food to market and some acres are located closer to the market than others,* location advantage creates yet another source of rent. Look at Figure 9.

FIGURE 10 **A New Set of Rent-Yielding Acres**

Price per acre is measured on the vertical axis. Quantities of land *and* their distance from the new marketplace, now located 50 miles west of the old marketplace of Figure 9, are measured on the horizontal axis. The demand curve for land, *D*, radiates out from the marketplace in both directions, east and west. The upward-sloping transport curve, *t*, radiates out from the marketplace in both directions as well, reflecting the cost of transporting food from the acreage to the market. The transport cost 10 miles east of the market is the same as the transport cost 10 miles west of the market. The demand curve cuts the transport cost curve 40 miles from the marketplace, bringing into cultivation 60,000 acres—30,000 on each side of the marketplace—and setting price at $15. Location rent emerges on the 29,999 acres on either side of the market. The 30,000th acre away from the market in each direction yields no rent.

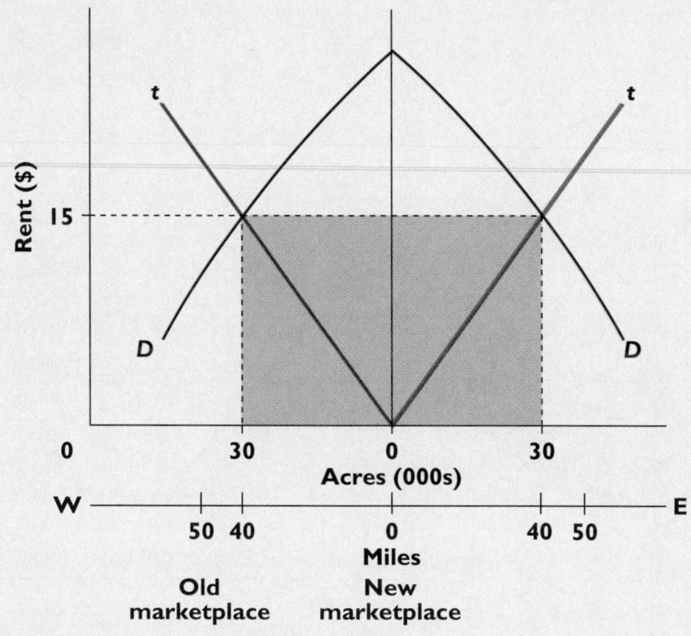

Suppose the marketplace is located at the origin so that each acre along the horizontal axis of Figure 9—from the first to the 120,000th acre—is a greater distance in measured miles from the marketplace. The transport cost curve, *t*, represents the cost of moving an acre's food to market. For example, $t = 0$ for the acre closest to market, while $t = \$100$ for the 120,000th acre farthest away.

In the economy of Figure 9, only those acres within a 70-mile reach of the market will be cultivated. Why? Because the *MRP* curve cuts the transport cost curve at the 50,000th acre—70 miles from market—setting the rental price of land at $60.

Land closer to market earns location rent because of lower transportation costs.

Location rent

Rent arising from differences in land distances from the marketplace.

How can we explain this rent? On the first acre, rent emerges solely because of the acre's location. With price at $60, the difference between the $60 and the zero transport cost in bringing the acre's food to market, is $60. That is pure **location rent.**

Location rent is generated as well on the 20,000th acre, 30 miles from the market. There, $t = \$20$. The location rent yielded to the owner of the 20,000th acre is $\$60 - \$20 = \$40$. The 50,000th acre, located 70 miles from the market, where $t = \$60$, yields its landowner $\$60 - \$60 =$ zero location rent.

As you see in Figure 9 the total sum of location rent generated in the economy is the sum of the differences between price and the *t* curve for every acre within 70 miles of the market. Landowners close to market are fortunate. Those beyond 70 miles might just as well own an acre on the moon.

RELOCATING THE MARKETPLACE CHANGES LANDOWNERS' FORTUNES

Which landowner gets what location rent depends, as we see, on where the marketplace is located. For example, if the marketplace of Figure 9 were replaced by a marketplace 50 miles away from the origin along the horizontal axis, as we see in Figure 10, a very different set of landowners end up with rent. Look at Figure 10.

Look at the acres now closest to market. The first two acres brought under cultivation would be the two acres on either side of the marketplace. Twice as many acres can be cultivated at each measured mile from the marketplace. The transport cost curve, *t,* is zero at the market and extends outward *in both directions*. Because two acres are located at each measured mile from the market, the transport cost for the same number of acres cultivated in Figure 10 is half what it would be in Figure 9.

The *MRP* curve of land (labeled *D* in the figure) radiates outward in both directions along the horizontal curve, starting 50 miles from the origin. As you see, the *MRP* curve cuts the transport cost curve at a distance of 40 miles from the market, bringing into cultivation 60,000 acres—30,000 acres in either direction from the market, at a transport cost on the 30,000th acre of $15.

But look what has happened to the landowner who was closest to the old market in Figure 9. That acre is now 50 miles away from market and left uncultivated. The tables have turned. Now this landowner may just as well have owned an acre on the moon.

SHOPPING MALLS REARRANGE RENTS

It isn't difficult to understand, then, how a new shopping mall, built on the outskirts of town, will create absolute havoc among landowners of downtown property. If Sears, J. C. Penney, and other department stores decide to relocate to shopping malls, rents accruing to downtown properties are virtually destroyed.

What once had been high-rent downtown property, overnight becomes potential urban blight. What once had been a source of substantial location rent, overnight becomes virtually worthless. On the other hand, there are people who by chance own property close to the new shopping mall, and overnight they become high-location rent receivers. In the fast-changing modern world of marketplaces, location rents come and go.

Wage-Related Rents

Rent emerges as a component of wage-related income as well. Consider baseball players' incomes. How many times have you seen a superstar interviewed on television after signing a $2 million contract tell the interviewer that although the money is alright, he really loves the game and, gosh, would have played for nothing?

FIGURE 11
The Rent Component in Coal Miners' Wages
The supply curve of labor, S, reflects the miners' willingness to supply labor at varying wage rates. The equilibrium wage rate is $13 and the quantity of labor demanded and supplied is 125. At a wage rate of $4, the quantity of labor supplied is 10. For these 10 coal miners, the wage they receive is $13 – $4 = $9 more than their supply price—that is, the price they would have been willing to work for. This $9 difference defines the rent component of their wage. Of the $13 × 125 = $1,625 wage income earned by the 125 coal miners, the shaded area represents their combined rent.

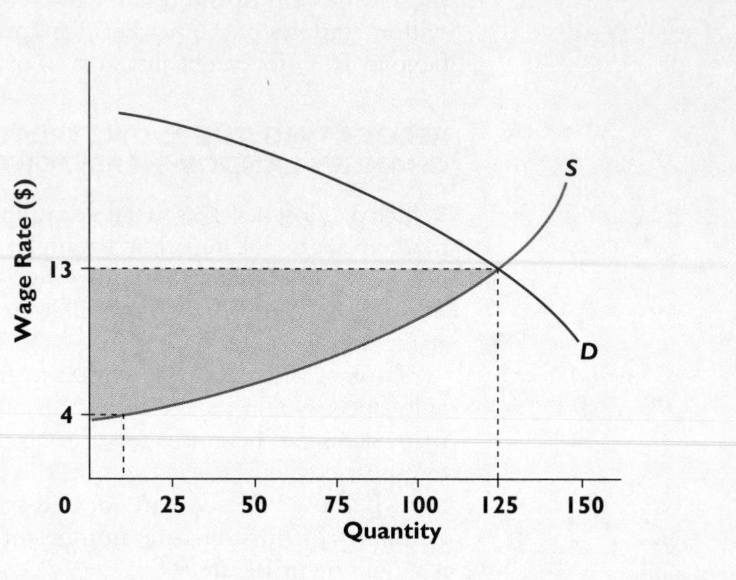

Wage-related rent

The difference between what a resource receives and what it takes to bring the supply of that resource to market.

Is he believable? Of course not! But if he really would play for nothing, his $2 million income would be entirely **wage-related rent.** After all, rent is the difference between what a resource receives and what it takes to bring the supply of that resource to the market. His professed willingness to play for nothing sets his supply price at zero. The difference, then, between his income and his supply price is the full $2 million.

He probably would have signed the contract for something less than $2 million. How much less? Suppose his next-best job opportunity would be selling insurance, which would provide him with an income of $30,000. In this circumstance, he would play baseball for anything above $30,000. The rent component of his $2 million baseball contract then is $1,970,000.

Can you imagine how much of San Francisco 49er quarterback Steve Young's income is rent? But what about opera singers, fashion designers, lawyers, university deans, and corporate presidents? For many, a good part of their incomes are well above their supply price. In fact, almost everyone's income has some element of rent built into it.

For example, consider the incomes earned by the coal miners in Figure 11.

The equilibrium wage rate is $13. But as you see in the supply curve of labor, only the 125th miner has a $13 supply price. Every one of the 124 other miners employed would have worked for less. For example, even at a $4 wage rate, 10 miners would work, although they certainly prefer the $13 wage rate they receive to the $4 they would be willing to accept. The $13 − $4 = $9 difference is the rent component in their $13 wage rate.

What about the other coal miners? The total rent generated in the labor market of Figure 11 is the sum of the differences between the $13 equilibrium wage rate and the specific supply prices of each miner. Of the $13 × 125 = $1,625 wage income earned by the miners, the shaded area in Figure 11 represents their combined rents.

ADDED PERSPECTIVE

Big-Time Dreaming

The fresh sheet of ice gleamed as the Moncton Hawks, in white and blue, began their pregame skate. The rival Fredericton Canadiens, in red, white, and blue, circled at the other end of the Moncton Coliseum rink. The previous night Fredericton had topped Moncton in a memorable overtime duel, taking a 1-0 lead in their best-of-seven American Hockey League (AHL) division semifinal series. "This is great hockey," declared Michael LeBlanc, 31, a teacher from Bathurst, NB, as he sipped coffee and watched the teams warm up for their second encounter. "A lot of these guys could step right into the NHL now." That, in fact, is the burning desire of most players who lace on skates in the American Hockey League.

Although just one step below the NHL, the American Hockey League marks the crossroads on the professional hockey map and provides a pointed contrast to the big-money machinations in the NHL bargaining. The rosters of all 15 AHL teams are filled with blue-chip prospects on the way up, former NHLers on the way down—and dozens of others who will never skate a shift in the top league. The average salary is in the $35,000 range, a far cry from the $379,000 average in the NHL. Players spend up to 12 hours on the team bus traveling to such small cities as Sydney, NS, St. John's, Nfld, and Hershey, PA, where they often stay in second-rate motels. "It's far from glamorous," said Robert Joyce, a 25-year-old Moncton Hawks forward. All the same, they hold fast to their high-flying dreams—even if some will never realize them. "It's a game of inches," declared Robert Cowie, 24, a first-year defenseman with the Hawks. "One guy puts the puck in the net and he is called up. Another guy hits the post and he stays where he is."

Monctonians, like residents of other AHL towns, say that the team helps to bring the community together. "Go to a Hawks game and you see all your old friends," said Ralph Powell, a 56-year-old retired federal government employee living in Moncton. The players are heroes in Moncton, a city of 56,000 where locals recognize them on the street. But all the time the players' eyes remain firmly fixed on the NHL. "Once you get a taste of it, it burns inside of you," said Anthony Joseph, a 23-year-old Hawks forward who played two NHL games for the Jets in 1988. Even such experienced veterans as Moncton player-coach Mark Kumpel, 31, who has played 288 NHL games for Quebec, Detroit, and Winnipeg, say that they have not given up on returning to their former glory. "Playing hockey in the AHL is a great life," Kumpel says. "But the NHL is better."

The players say that circumstances, as much as skill, dictate which minor-leaguers get the call. Earlier this season six members of the Fredericton squad were called up to the Montreal Canadiens to fill in for injured players. On the other hand, chances of moving up are slim for a minor-league player with an organization that has an abundance of talent playing his particular position. Joyce, who has played with both the Boston Bruins and the Washington Capitals in the NHL, declared: "It is all about numbers and being in the right place at the right time."

But few Moncton players were thinking about their long-term futures after last week's heady victory over Fredericton. Each game brings a new opportunity to impress the Winnipeg Jets management. As he stood outside the Moncton dressing room, Rudy Poeschek, who played four games with Winnipeg this season, seemed optimistic about his prospects. "This year, it was a numbers game with the Jets. There was no room for me," he said, his face still swollen from his first-period fight. "I know I can play at that level if someone gives me the chance." With that, he stepped inside the dressing room to join his happy teammates in their shared dreams of NHL glory.

Discussion

What connection can you make between this story and the derivation of wage-related rent described in the text?

Source: *Maclean's*, April 20, 1992. Used with permission.

Think about the work you have done, the wage rate you received, and the minimum rate you would have accepted. Like quarterback Steve Young and the coal miners of Figure 11, wouldn't some part of your wage-related income be pure rent?

INCOME FROM PROFITS

Laborers, loanable funds suppliers, and landowners receive wages, interest, and rent because they provide the resources used in production. What do entrepreneurs provide that explains their source of income?

Profit

Income earned by entrepreneurs.

Profit is the reward for undertaking the uncertainties of enterprise. Many people have great ideas about products and production and some of them actually transform their ideas into successful realities, but if the willingness to take a chance at enterprise is lacking, great ideas remain just great ideas.

We Are a Nation of Thomas Edisons

Everybody knows the story of Thomas Edison. He not only invented the electric light but converted the invention into a massive fortune by creating the General Electric Company. He is *the* classic example of the entrepreneur. But let's play lightly with history and make up another version of the popular Thomas Edison story. Let's imagine he invented the electric light, and stopped right there.

Suppose Edison felt uneasy about committing himself to the financial obligation involved in setting up the General Electric Company. Suppose he was quite willing and able to contribute all his creative and organizational energies to mass-producing the electric light, but he was unwilling to bear the financial uncertainties of enterprise. If that were the Thomas Edison story, we might still be reading by candlelight.

Or, consider still another version of the tale. Thomas Edison's electric light could not long remain a secret. Some energetic entrepreneur heard about Edison's invention, bought the rights to his patent, and even put him on salary as production manager. We still end up with General Electric and the electric light. Thomas Edison, in this version, ends up a millionaire. But no matter how much salary he receives, he never earns one penny of profit. Profit is the reward for entrepreneurship.

While large industrial conglomerates cast giant shadows over the thousands of small firms that make up our economy, these small firms are still very much alive and flourishing. Their successes are forever invitations for others to try. And others always do.

Chef Ra's Pizza House, Julia Johnstone's Shoe Repair, Frances Reedy's Computer Service, Jenny McMahon's Beauty Shop, P. Gregory Springer's Record Swap, Eric Schor's Dry Cleaners, Paul Chastain's Electrical Appliances, Garret Jakobsson's Bookstore, Karen Turk's Plumbing, Jon Ginoli's Construction, and Geoff Merritt's Video are products of entrepreneurship. These firms and thousands of others flood the Yellow Pages of every city's telephone directory.

Each of these firms, at one time, was just a good idea in the mind of a would-be entrepreneur. Making it work took physical and psychological stamina, business acumen, a twist of good luck, and a willingness to accept the inevitable fortunes or misfortunes of enterprise.

Geoff Merritt, for example, founded Geoff Merritt Video with \$200,000, four years' experience as a Blockbuster manager, and some new ideas. In less than three years, his firm showed a net return of \$125,000. But Merritt knew that this \$125,000 was not all a return on entrepreneurship.

After all, he could have stayed at Blockbuster and earned a salary of $50,000. Although he never considered the time spent at his own firm as salaried labor, the labor time he put into the company does nonetheless represent a $50,000 opportunity cost.

Profit-related income is over and above the entrepreneur's opportunity costs of labor and money capital.

But the $50,000 isn't the only opportunity cost incurred. The $200,000 invested in setting up the video store could have been invested instead in the loanable funds market at 15 percent. That would have yielded $30,000. In other words, Geoff Merritt could have earned $80,000 annually in salary and interest if he had chosen not to become an entrepreneur.

What, then, is Merritt's profit? It is his income adjusted for the implicit costs of his labor and money capital. In other words, $125,00 – $80,000 = $45,000 of income is real profit, representing the return on entrepreneurial ability.

The Invisible Entrepreneurs at General Motors

What about the profit earned by large corporations like General Motors? Is any part of their corporate profit a return on entrepreneurial ability? Where would you find entrepreneurs at General Motors? Who, for example, are its visionaries? Who designs the automobiles, gets the auto plants in motion, unravels the knots, acquires financial obligations and risks everything on the uncertainties of consumer choice?

There are people at General Motors who do the same things Merritt does. Although decision making there is not combined in one person, the necessary talent to make decisions on what to produce and how to produce it is there. Decision-making talent is found in the planning and research departments, in engineering and design, and even in the departments of finance and marketing.

But the people working in these departments are not risking their money. It is the stockholders who venture their money. Stockholders own the company and hire corporate managers to run the business. The managers' incomes are strictly salary. In theory, GM's stockholders have the decision-making powers to hire or fire anyone, to produce what they want, and to decide how they want it produced. That is, the ultimate power of entrepreneurial decison making rests with them. GM's corporate profit is their income. Because they alone assume all the uncertainties of the business. Even though stockholders may be silent and perhaps even invisible, they are nonetheless General Motors' entrepreneurs.

CHAPTER REVIEW

1. The productivity of capital can be measured in much the same way that we measured the productivity of labor. Adding dollar increments of capital to a production process increases total physical product. Thus, it is possible to calculate the marginal physical product per dollar of capital employed.

2. The marginal revenue product of capital per dollar is the marginal physical product of capital per dollar multiplied by the price of the product the capital produces.

3. The firm's demand for loanable funds (which it converts to equipment capital) follows the curve of the marginal revenue product per dollar of capital employed.

4. A firm will maximize profits by choosing that amount of capital where its marginal revenue product is equal to the marginal factor cost.

5. The demand for loanable funds in the economy is equal to the sum of individual firms' *MRP* curves. The economy's supply of loanable funds curve comes from people who are willing to supply loanable funds in return for an interest payment. The market rate of interest is determined by the intersection of these two curves.

6. Some individuals earn part or all of their income from interest payments on loanable funds that they supply to loanable funds markets. Loanable funds can accumulate over time through savings that are invested to earn interest.

7. The present value of a property is equal to the annual return on the property divided by the interest rate. Therefore, as interest rates decrease, the present values of properties increase, if the annual return is held constant.

8. Rent is the difference between what a resource is paid for its use in production and the payment necessary to bring that resource into the market. Rents increase as the *MRP* curve of land shifts out. Land rents are strictly demand-determined.

9. Differential rents stem from differences in quality between parcels of land. As the *MRP* of land increases, land of inferior quality with higher production costs is brought into production. When this happens, land of better quality begins to earn rent.

10. Rents can also arise from differences in location. Land that is close to a market earns a location rent equal to its marginal revenue product because transportation costs are zero.

11. Rent may be a component in a person's wage if the wage paid is above the wage necessary to induce the person to supply skills in the labor market.

12. An entrepreneur earns a profit-related income that is calculated by taking the difference between what the entrepreneur earns in net revenue and the entrepreneur's opportunity cost.

KEY TERMS

Marginal revenue product of capital
Loanable funds
Equipment capital
Rate of interest
Loanable funds market
Present value
Rent
Land rent
Differential land rent
Location rent
Wage-related rent
Profit

QUESTIONS

1. Economists use precisely the same tools to analyze rates of interest as they do to analyze wage rates. Discuss.

2. How does a firm decide what quantity of loanable funds it should demand from the loanable funds market when the interest rate is 10 percent?

3. Why would anyone be willing to supply loanable funds on the loanable funds market?

4. Distinguish between loanable funds and capital equipment.

5. What factors change the rate of interest?

6. What arguments can you make to justify people living off interest-derived income?

7. What arguments can you make against people living off interest-derived income?

8. You don't have to work to be productive. Explain.

9. Suppose you were interested in buying the New York Yankees. If the Yankees generated an annual income of $30 million and if the rate of interest were 10 percent, what would be the present value of the New York Yankees? If the rate of interest fell to 5 percent, would you have to pay more, less, or the same for the team? Explain.

10. Government's support of farm prices has affected the value of farm property. Why?

11. A little strip of land by Fenway Park in Boston, which is the home of the Boston Red Sox, is a choice location for a sandwich shop. There, a hot dog sells for $3. Two blocks away, the same hot dog sells for $1. The rent paid by the Fenway Park sandwich-shop owner is much higher than the rent paid by the owner of the shop two blocks away. Is the $3 hot dog price high because rent is high at the Fenway Park location, or is rent there high because hot dogs sell for $3?

12. If the coal mining firms were able to get together and cut miners' wage rates in half, many coal miners would quit the mines. On the other hand, if major league owners were able to get together and cut baseball salaries in half, very few of the ballplayers would quit baseball. Why?

13. When Sears decides to move from its downtown location to a shopping mall on the outskirts of town, some people suffer loss of rent while others end up getting more rent. Why?

14. The market for loanable funds is described in the following demand and supply schedules.

Interest Rate (%)	Quantity Demanded	Quantity Supplied
14	$1,000	$5,000
12	2,000	4,000
10	3,000	3,000
8	4,000	2,000
6	5,000	1,000

Suppliers of loanable funds would prefer 14 percent to any other interest rate in the table. But 14 percent is not what they will receive. Why not? Explain fully.

15. Graph the loanable funds market of question 14. Suppose the government imposes an interest-rate ceiling of 12 percent. What consequences would that ceiling have on the loanable funds market?

C H A P T E R 1 9

INCOME DISTRIBUTION AND POVERTY

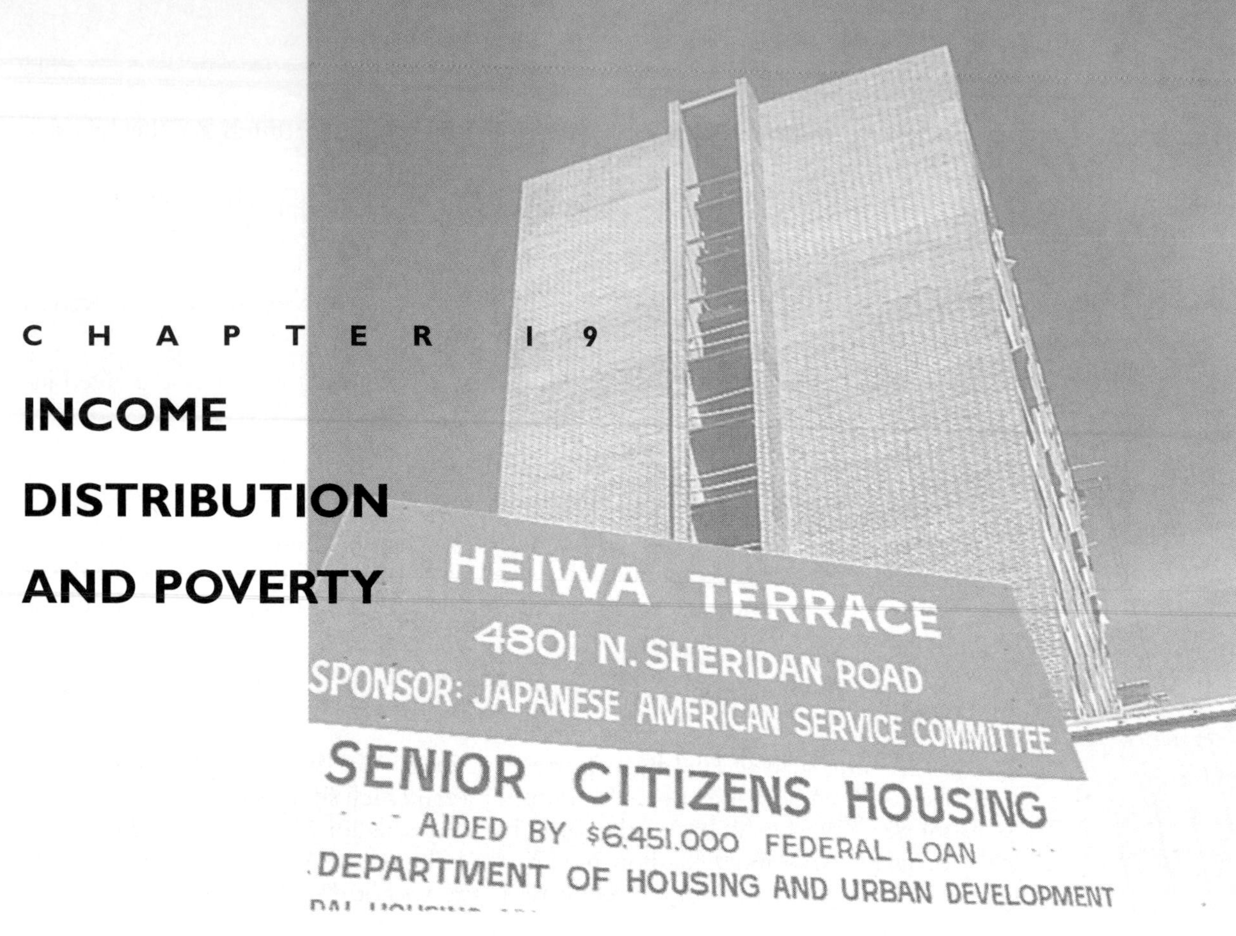

CHAPTER PREVIEW

We conclude our examination of resource markets with a consideration of income distribution and poverty. We touched on these issues in the previous two chapters. However, it is possible to achieve a more complete understanding of income distribution now that we understand how suppliers of all factors of production—savers, landowners, and entrepreneurs, as well as workers—are paid.

At the bottom of the income distribution are those who live in poverty. These unfortunate individuals seem unable to operate effectively in resource markets. Why is this the case? What can be done about poverty? We'll address these crucial questions, which bear heavily on social policies.

After studying this chapter, you should be able to:

- Discuss why some people are rich and some people are poor.
- Measure an economy's income distribution using a Lorenz curve and a Gini coefficient.
- Compare income inequality between countries using Lorenz curves and Gini coefficients.
- Discuss differences in income distribution between industrially advanced economies and less developed economies.

- Describe inequality over time in the distribution of wealth in the United States.
- Present arguments for equality and for inequality in income distribution.
- Define poverty and describe methods for coping with poverty.

Why are some people rich and others poor? Why are there so many more poor? Can anything be done about the distribution of income among people? *Should* anything be done about it? Would it really matter what we do?

These kinds of questions have occupied the minds of many people ever since we began thinking about economic life. In fact, more thought seems to have been devoted to the subject of income distribution than to the subject of how incomes are derived in the first place.

THE RICH AND THE POOR

Questions about the rich and the poor are, of course, not the monopoly of economists. They arise from the political, ethical, and even religious foundations of our society. The Bible, for example, tells us very little about how people come to acquire income, but it is very explicit about what we should do with it once we get it. The one thing we cannot do—and expect redemption—is ignore the poor:

When you reap the harvest in your field, and overlook a sheaf in the field, do not turn your back to get it. . . . when you beat down the fruit of the olive trees, do not go over them again; that shall go over to the stranger, the fatherless, and the widow.

These caring directives are matched by concerns over differences between rich and poor. The biblical text tells us that not only is it unacceptable to ignore the needs of the poor, but it is also unacceptable to condone the wasteful extravagance of the rich.

The Greek philosophers wrestled with the same issues. Plato and Aristotle, no less concerned about the distribution of income among rich and poor, tied their arguments not to sin and salvation but to political instability. Plato, writing in the aftermath of the Peloponnesian wars, saw a functional relationship between income inequality and political discontent.

He argued for policy that would limit the extremes among rich and poor. In his *Laws,* he suggested that the income of the richest citizen should be no greater than five times the income of the poorest. Plato's concerns were shared by Aristotle. He, too, considered poverty the parent of revolution and crime. Unlike Plato, however, he relied on individual benevolence, believing it more important to equalize desires than property.

The questions concerning income distribution haven't really changed that much in 2,500 years. We still ask why some people are rich and others poor, and why there still seem to be so many more poor than rich. Many still ask whether anything can be done about the situation. And there are many who, no less compassionate than others, are uncertain whether anything should be done—assuming that anything could be done.

"Herein lies the tragedy of the age; not that men are poor—all men know something of poverty; not that men are wicked—who is good? Not that men are ignorant—what is truth? Nay, but that men know so little of men."
W. E. B. Du Bois, *The Souls of Black Folk.*

But there is one difference. Although we still wrestle with the same questions concerning income distribution, we are also wrestling with questions concerning income determination. Moreover, the one seems to have direct bearing on the other. A person's income seems to be connected to that person's productive contribution in the market. The rich are rich, then, because they are relatively productive. The poor are poor because they are not.

NOT TOO MANY COAL MINERS ARE MILLIONAIRES

You can generally make a fair guess about a person's economic status merely by knowing the principal source of the person's income. Coal miners are typically 100 percent wage earners. It is unlikely, no matter how successful the United Mine Workers Union may be in raising wages, that a coal miner would be found among the top 500 richest persons in the country.

Other people earn income by other means. For example, for some individuals, the only source of income is the interest they receive. Landowners' income is derived from rent. Some individuals do nothing but cash the dividend checks they receive as corporate stockholders.

These different forms of income—wages, interest, rent, and profit—are not mutually exclusive. An individual's income may be some combination of these four forms of income. Most coal miners' incomes are wage-derived, yet some may invest some loanable funds and generate modest sums of interest. Some may be shareholders in corporations that yield dividends. Some may even own real estate that provides rental income. But no matter how many of these income forms contribute to their total income, most coal miners would still think of themselves as wage earners and not see themselves as particularly rich.

Who are the very rich? They too probably have multiple sources of income, but it is highly unlikely that wages would count as their primary source. What makes them rich, and separates them from coal miners, are their interest, rent, and profit.

When there is a shift in either the supply curves or *MRP* curves of labor, capital, or land, the equilibrium wage rates, interest rates, and rents also change. As a result, people's incomes increase or decrease. A fall in the interest rate or an increase in the wage rate makes some people richer and others less so. Income disparities among people widen or narrow. But such price changes seldom make poor people rich, or rich people poor. You are more likely to identify the rich and poor by their primary form of income than by the ebbs and flows in their income. Rich people become poor—and the poor, rich—most often by changing their occupation or their source of income.

People who derive their income from a variety of sources tend to be richer than those whose incomes are in the form of wages.

MEASURING INCOME DISTRIBUTION

Every society has its own rich and poor. In some the rich are considerably richer than the poor. In others the income disparities between rich and poor are less extreme. Would you suppose that income is more equal in Russia than in Sweden? How about Sweden compared to the United States? How would you measure the differences in income distribution? Has income inequality among rich and poor in the United States changed much since 1950? How would you go about measuring the change?

There are two principal techniques used by economists to measure an economy's income distribution. These are the Lorenz curve, developed by the American statistician Max Lorenz, and the Gini coefficient, developed by the Italian statistician Corrado Gini.

The Lorenz Curve

Lorenz curve
A curve depicting an economy's income distribution. It records the percentage of total income that a specific part of the population—typically represented by quintiles, ranging from the poorest to richest—receives.

The **Lorenz curve** provides a quick visual expression of income distribution. It shows what percentage of an economy's total income each part of the population receives. Typically, the population is divided into deciles—10 groups, each with 10 percent of the population—or into quintiles—5 groups, each with 20 percent of the population—arranged in sequence from poorest to richest.

THE LORENZ CURVE: A HYPOTHETICAL CASE

Perhaps the best way to illustrate Lorenz's technique is to imagine three economies with identical population sizes and total incomes, but with very different patterns of income distribution.

Suppose Washtenau, Springfield, and Holmes each have 1,000 people and $200,000 total income. The per capita income in each economy is $200, but that does not mean that everyone receives $200. Some receive much more, others much less. Table 1 records how the $200,000 is distributed among the 1,000 population in each economy.

The first quintile contains the economy's poorest 200 (of its 1,000 people), the second quintile contains its next 200 poorest, and so on, to the fifth quintile containing its richest 200 people.

Washtenau's distribution portrays *perfect income equality*. Look at the percentage of total income received by each quintile of population. Each 20 percent of the population, each quintile, receives precisely 20 percent of the economy's

TABLE 1
Percent of the Economy's Total Income Held by Each Population Quintile

Quintile	Washtenau	Springfield	Holmes
Poorest	20	0	4
Second	20	0	7
Third	20	0	15
Fourth	20	0	30
Richest	20	100	44
Total $	$200,000	$200,000	$200,000

total income. No one quintile receives more than any other. As you can imagine, there's no distribution equivalent to Washtenau's in the real world, although some economies are closer to perfect income equality than others.

Income distribution in Springfield represents *perfect income inequality*. Look at the percentage of total income received by each quintile of population. Suppose 999 people receive nothing, one person receives the entire $200,000. That is, four quintiles of the population receive zero percent of total income, and they are joined by everyone but one of the remaining quintile who also receive zero percent of total income. One person—the richest in the economy—ends up with 100 percent of total income. Needless to say, there's no distribution equivalent to Springfield's in our real world, although some economies are much closer to perfect income inequality than others.

What about Holmes? Its poorest quintile receives just four percent of the economy's $200,000 income. The next poorest quintile fares slightly better. They receive seven percent. The richest quintile receives 44 percent of the economy's total income.

If you lived in Holmes, you would probably have little difficulty distinguishing the rich from the poor. They live in different neighborhoods, drive different automobiles, go to different schools, eat different foods, take different vacations, work at different occupations, and have different expectations of their children. That is to say, the rich don't just have more money. They have different life-styles and go through life with much higher levels of self-confidence and self-esteem. These are consciously and subconsciously transmitted to their children who, in turn, are more able than others to eventually place themselves in the higher quintiles of the economy's income distribution.

Figure 1 translates Table 1 into a Lorenz curve.

How do we graph Washtenau's income distribution? Its Lorenz curve lies along the diagonal of Figure 1. *Any* 20 percent of the population, which is measured on the horizontal axis, receives 20 percent of total income, which is measured on the vertical axis. *Any* 40 percent of the population receives 40 percent of total income and so on, cumulatively, to 100 percent of the population receiving 100 percent of total income. *On the diagonal the Lorenz curve represents perfect income equality.*

Be sure that you can explain why a Lorenz curve closer to the diagonal represents a more equal distribution of income.

What about the Lorenz curve for Springfield? It lies along the horizontal axis, from the origin to the 100 percent of population, then runs perfectly vertical at that point up to the 100 percent of total income. That is, the *Lorenz curve for Springfield is formed by the two sides of a right angle.* Everyone, except the one

FIGURE 1 **Lorenz Curves for Communities of Washtenau, Springfield, and Holmes**

The percentage of population is measured along the horizontal axis, and the percentage of total income the population receives is measured along the vertical axis. Because everyone in Washtenau receives the same income, the Lorenz curve for Washtenau lies along the diagonal. In the Springfield economy, everyone but the richest person receives no income. The Lorenz curve for Springfield falls along the horizontal axis, up to the 100 percent point of population, then rises vertically to 100 percent of income. The Lorenz curve for Holmes shows that the poorest 20 percent of its population receive 4 percent of its income, the poorest 40 percent receive 4 + 7 = 11 percent, and so on, cumulatively, until 100 percent of the population receives 100 percent of the income.

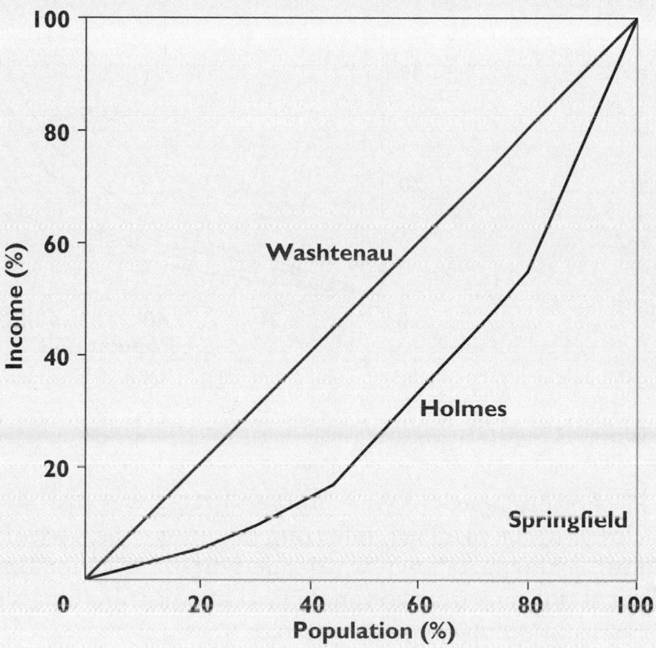

rich person, receives a total of zero percent of the economy's income, tracing out the horizontal segment of the Lorenz curve. That one rich person, receiving all the income, traces out the vertical segment of the curve.

Look at Holmes' Lorenz curve. It lies in the area below the diagonal—its distribution is not as equal as Washtenau's—and above the two sides of the right angle—it's also not as unequal as Springfield's. As indicated in Table 1, the poorest quintile receives only four percent of the economy's income. Eighty percent of the population—all but the richest quintile—receives 56 percent of total income. The richest quintile alone receives 44 percent.

LORENZ CURVES FOR SWEDEN, BRAZIL, FRANCE, AND THE UNITED STATES

Most of the world's distributions are similar to the Lorenz curve for Holmes, positioned somewhere in the area between perfect equality and perfect inequality. But some are closer to the diagonal than others. Look at Figure 2. Do the Lorenz curves surprise you?

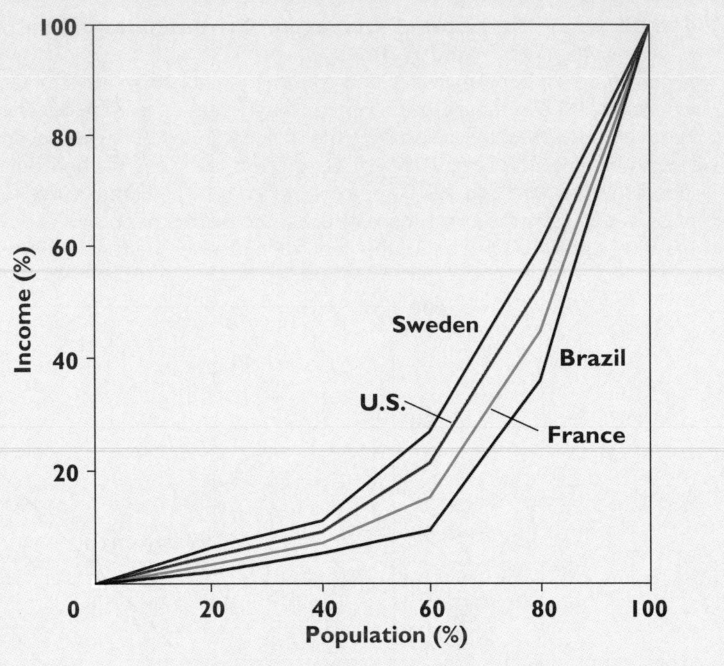

FIGURE 2
Lorenz Curves for Sweden, France, Brazil, and the United States
The poorest quintile in Sweden receives 7 percent of Sweden's income; its richest quintile receives 40 percent. The poorest quintile in Brazil receives 2 percent; its richest quintile 66 percent of Brazil's income. These two sets of data trace out the Lorenz curves for Sweden and Brazil. The U.S. curve lies below the Swedish and the French curve lies slightly below the U.S. curve, but above the Brazilian curve.

For example, are you surprised to discover that Sweden's Lorenz curve lies closest to the diagonal, reflecting the most equal income distribution among the four economies shown here? The Lorenz curve for Brazil reflects the most unequal income distribution. The U.S. distribution, slightly more equal than France's, occupies middle ground.

Many of the Lorenz curves drawn for economies are, at best, only rough estimates of the underlying reality. Income data, particularly for less-developed economies like Brazil are typically incomplete and, in some cases, nonexistent. Even for economies such as Sweden, France, and the United States, Lorenz curve comparisons can be somewhat hazardous.

Some economies have more government-provided goods, such as national security, transportation systems, national parks, health care, education, housing, and food, than others. The distribution of these services among individuals is sometimes impossible to trace. For example, do the rich and poor place the same value on the national security provided them? How much of the national parks or education do the poor receive compared to the rich? Should we simply divide total government spending by total population and *assume* that each person receives the same value? In some economies, these government-provided services make up a larger percent of total income than in others. How, then, can we compare different Lorenz curves with confidence? We can't.

Gini Coefficients of Inequality

Another way to measure an economy's income distribution is by calculating its **Gini coefficient.** The coefficient transforms the Lorenz curve into a numerical value. How is that done? Look at the Lorenz curve of Figure 3.

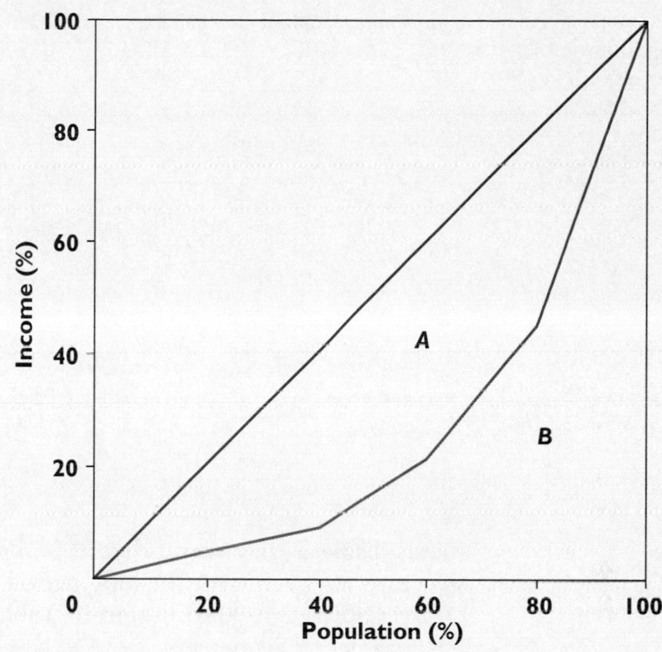

FIGURE 3
The Gini Coefficient
The Gini coefficient is the ratio of the two areas produced by the Lorenz curve, $G = A/(A + B)$. Area A lies between the diagonal and the Lorenz curve. Area B lies below the Lorenz curve. In the case of perfect equality, the Lorenz curve lies on the diagonal, so that area A collapses to zero. The Gini coefficient, then, is zero. In the case of perfect inequality, the Lorenz curve lies on the horizontal and vertical axes so that area B collapses to zero. The Gini coefficient, then, is one. In all real-world economies, the Gini coefficient is greater than zero but less than one.

Gini coefficient

A numerical measure of the degree of income inequality in an economy. It ranges from zero, depicting perfect equality, to one, depicting perfect inequality.

Gini coefficients range from zero to one. The closer to one the coefficient is, the more unequal the income distribution.

The Gini coefficient is simply a ratio of the two areas produced by the Lorenz curve. The first is area A, lying between the diagonal and the economy's Lorenz curve. The second is area B lying below the curve. The Gini coefficient, G, is calculated as

$$G = A/(A + B)$$

If an economy's income distribution is perfect equality, as we saw in the hypothetical example of Washtenau, the Lorenz curve lies on the diagonal, so that A, the area between the curve and the diagonal, compresses to zero. If area $A =$ 0, then $G = A/(A + B)$ is also zero. In other words, *the Gini coefficient expressing perfect equality is zero.*

If an economy's income distribution is perfect inequality, as we saw in the hypothetical example of Springfield, the Lorenz curve would lie along the two sides of the right angle in Figure 3, so that B, the area below the curve, compresses to zero. If area $B = 0$, then $G = A/(A + B) - 1$. That is, *the Gini coefficient expressing perfect inequality is one.*

Although the Gini coefficient is a convenient way to discuss and compare income equality across various economies, remember that it is no more accurate than the data on which it is based.

HOW UNEQUAL IS OUR INCOME DISTRIBUTION?

What about income distribution in the United States? How does it compare to that in other countries? Is it constantly changing, or does it remain relatively

TABLE 2
Percent Share of Aggregate Income, by Quintile (1950–1992)

Year	Q1	Q2	Q3	Q4	Q5	Top 5%
1950	4.5	12.0	17.4	23.4	42.7	17.3
1955	4.8	12.3	17.8	23.7	41.3	16.4
1960	4.8	12.2	17.8	24.0	41.3	15.9
1965	5.2	12.2	17.8	23.9	40.9	15.5
1970	5.4	12.2	17.6	23.8	40.9	15.6
1975	5.4	11.8	17.6	24.1	41.1	15.5
1980	5.1	11.6	17.5	24.3	41.6	15.3
1992	4.4	10.5	16.5	24.0	44.6	17.6

Source: Bureau of the Census, *Current Population Reports, Series P-60,* Table 17, 1984; *and Statistical Abstract of the United States, 1994* (Washington, D.C.; U.S. Department of Commerce, 1994), p. 470.

fixed? Table 2 may surprise you. It shows how rigid our income distribution structure has been over the long period from 1950–1992.

As you see, the distribution in Table 2 is calculated in quintiles. The poorest quintile, or 20 percent, of U.S. families received 4.5 percent of national income in 1950. Forty-two years later it received 4.4 percent. Not much of a change, is it? At the upper end of the distribution, the richest 20 percent received 42.7 percent in 1950, 1.9 percent less than it received 42 years later. Even for the richest five percent of the population, income share fluctuated no more than 2.3 percentage points, from a low of 15.3 percent in 1980 to a high of 17.6 percent in 1992.

Figure 4 graphs the Gini coefficients from 1947 to 1990. Despite year-to-year changes, the 1947 to 1968 period showed a downward trend in the U.S. Gini coefficient. After that, the Gini coefficient rose steadily, reaching a peak of 0.40 in 1990.

Is Income More Unequal in the United States Than in Other Economies?

Gini coefficients are very similar for industrialized countries. Be sure that you can account for the greater inequality of income distribution in less-developed countries compared to industrialized countries.

How does our income distribution compare to that of other economies? For example, how does it compare to the economies of Western Europe, Canada, and Japan? Would you expect disparities between rich and poor in the United States to be greater? Look at Table 3. Note how strikingly close the quintile shares of income are among these industrially advanced economies and how they approximate the quintile shares in the United States. Look at their Gini coefficients.

The range of Gini coefficients, from .260 in the Netherlands to .342 in France, seems particularly narrow when compared to the Gini coefficients for the less-developed economies in Table 4.

Through the eyes of the Brazilian poor, the rich in Brazil must be incredibly rich. Look at the percentage of income Brazil's richest and poorest quintiles receive. The rich receive over 30 times the income of the poor. Brazil's Gini coefficient is .565. Similar inequalities characterize the Ivory Coast, Kenya, and Peru.

FIGURE 4 **The U.S. Gini Coefficient: 1947–90**

Annual fluctuations notwithstanding, the U.S. Gini coefficient declined gradually over the period 1947–68, then climbed fairly steadily thereafter, exceeding in the 1980s the earlier coefficient values of the 1940s.

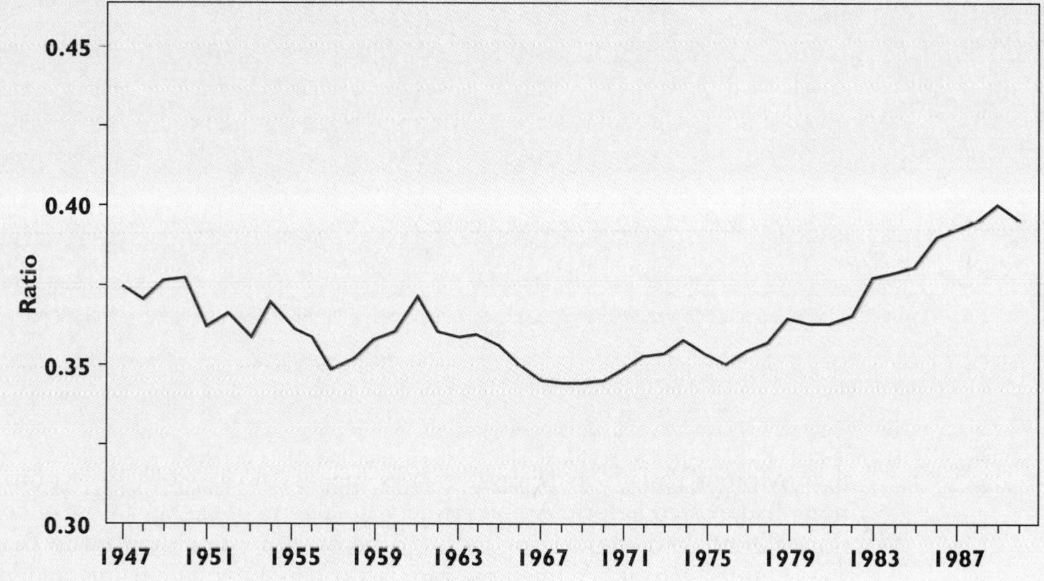

Source: *Economic Report of the President*, 1992. Washington, D.C., p. 123.

Many economists attribute the greater inequalities among many less-developed economies to the character of their economic production. Most are predominantly agricultural. Their relatively strong dependence on agriculture restricts the range of employment opportunities and increases dependence on world commodity markets.

The prospect for breaking out depends on the creation of nonagricultural employment. Firestone in Liberia opens up new and relatively attractive jobs. A

TABLE 3 International Household Income Inequality (by quintile)

Country	Year	Q1	Q2	Q3	Q4	Q5	Gini
France	1975	5.5	11.5	17.1	23.7	42.2	.342
Germany	1978	7.9	12.5	17.0	23.1	39.5	.295
Netherlands	1981	8.3	14.1	18.2	23.2	36.2	.260
Canada	1981	5.3	11.8	18.0	24.9	40.0	.330
Norway	1982	6.0	12.9	18.3	24.6	38.2	.304
Sweden	1981	7.4	13.1	16.8	21.0	41.7	.306
U.K.	1979	7.0	11.5	17.0	24.8	49.7	.315
Japan	1979	8.7	13.2	17.5	23.1	37.5	.270

Source: Sawyer, M., "Income Distribution in OECD Countries," *Occasional Studies, OECD Economic Outlook*, July 1986, pp. 14–16.

TABLE 4 Income Distribution in Less Developed Economies (by quintile)

Country	Year	Q1	Q2	Q3	Q4	Q5	Gini
Philippines	1985	5.2	8.9	13.2	20.2	52.5	.424
Venezuela	1970	3.0	7.3	12.9	22.8	54.0	.470
Malaysia	1973	3.5	7.7	12.4	20.3	56.1	.471
Turkey	1973	3.4	8.0	12.5	19.5	56.5	.470
Kenya	1976	2.6	6.3	11.5	19.2	60.4	.514
Mexico	1977	2.9	7.0	12.0	20.4	57.7	.492
Peru	1972	1.9	5.1	11.0	21.0	61.0	.536
Ivory Coast	1986	2.4	6.2	10.9	19.1	61.4	.524
Brazil	1972	2.0	5.0	9.4	17.0	66.6	.565

Source: Mahler, V., "Income Distribution Within Nations," *Comparative Political Studies*, 22, 1, April 1989, p.18. *World Development Report*,* 1987 (Washington D.C.: World Bank, 1987), pp. 252–3.

*The footnote to the table in *Report* reads: "These estimates should be treated with caution."

new Motorola plant in Malawi creates manufacturing jobs in regions where none had existed before. An oil refinery in Algeria opens up a host of construction, clerical, and engineering jobs. A Volkswagen assembly plant in Brazil creates a mini-Detroit. A modern shirt factory in Egypt demands and pays for skilled labor.

The more diverse the manufacturing activity, the greater the numbers and varieties of skilled, semiskilled, administrative, managerial, and professional jobs created. The industrialization process in less-developed economies draws the agricultural poor from the countryside to the cities, broadening the base of its middle class. The greater income inequalities there reflect the stage of their development process.

Distribution of Net Wealth

Wealth

The accumulated assets owned by individuals.

Net wealth among population deciles tends to be far more unevenly distributed than income. A person's **wealth** reflects not only this year's income but the accumulated assets of a lifetime. People also inherit assets—other people's wealth—so that individual wealth sometimes reflects asset accumulation over several lifetimes. No surprise then, is it, to discover that the difference between people's wealth is even greater than the difference between their incomes?

Life-cycle wealth

Wealth in the form of nonmonetary assets, such as a house, automobiles, and personal clothing.

Almost everybody, including most of the poor, owns some **life-cycle wealth.** Most people own their refrigerators, automobiles, and personal clothing. Many own their own homes. Many have bank accounts. But fewer people own substantial holdings of bonds, corporate stock, commercial real estate, and rental property.

These kinds of wealth holdings tend to be much more unequally held. For example, in 1979 among people who owned common stock or mutual funds, the top 1 percent held over half the total. Most of us have some savings, but did you know that the richest 5 percent of the population in the United States holds 50 percent of the personal savings?

TABLE 5
Distribution of Net Wealth of U.S. Families (1774 and 1973)

Decile	1774	1973
Poorest	–2.0	—
Second	—	—
Third	1.0	—
Fourth	2.0	0.1
Fifth	3.0	0.9
Sixth	5.0	2.6
Seventh	7.0	4.5
Eighth	11.0	7.3
Ninth	18.0	13.8
Richest	55.0	69.8
Gini coefficient	.730	.810

Source: Jones, A. H., *Wealth of a Nation To Be—The American Colonies on the Eve of Revolution,* (New York: Columbia University Press, 1980); Greenwood, D., "An Estimation of U.S. Family Wealth and Its Distribution from Macro Data, 1973," *The Review of Income and Wealth,* Series 29, 1, March 1983, pp. 23–44.

How unequal is unequal wealth? Table 5 measures the distribution of wealth holdings in the United States.

Net wealth is far more unevenly distributed than income.

Even back in colonial days—two years before our political independence—wealth holdings of the colonists were highly unequal. Look at the Gini coefficient for 1774 wealth. It was .730. Did wealth distribution change much in two centuries of accumulation? The Gini coefficient for 1973 was .810, and the wealthiest decile held 69.8 percent of the nation's net wealth. The wealthy seemed to get wealthier; the least-wealthy 50 percent of the population held only 1 percent of net wealth!

IS THERE AN OPTIMAL INCOME DISTRIBUTION?

What an economy's wealth or income distribution *should* be is not really an economic issue. It concerns personal and societal ethics and values. There are, however, economic arguments that people, including economists, make to explain why one kind of distribution might be preferable to another.

The Case for Equality

THE RANDOMNESS OF PERSONAL MISFORTUNE IS A MISFORTUNE

One of the most powerful arguments offered in support of income equality is the belief that good fortune is distributed randomly. Those who have it become rich, those who don't become poor. Income inequality, then, has no more justification than a lottery result.

Some people, no more deserving than others, *chance* into jobs that allow for quick advancement and excellent income. Many, *by chance,* make the right moves horizontally and vertically through the maze of labor markets, layering one success upon another. Others, no less bright and capable, seem to be at the wrong place at the wrong time.

Some people, at least for a while, seem to have that magic business touch. They time their investments just right. They know when to expand production and, while others are expanding, when to cut back. They raise prices at just the right time and lower them at other times to stay ahead of the competition.

To many all this appears to be the result of business acumen. But to others, it is just a matter of luck. Good fortune, ignoring talent and effort, smiles upon some and frowns upon others. Who gains and who loses, then, is randomly determined.

Cases for equality in income distribution can be built around notions of randomness of personal misfortune, conceptions of a just society, the unequal assignment of property rights, and utility maximization.

Even more unsettling than the randomness of good fortune is the random distribution of disaster. A stroke or heart attack can undo years of career building and drive a secure household into instant bankruptcy. Chronic diseases bleed household incomes. There is simply no way to protect a household from accidental misfortune. Can anyone at any time really feel secure? What protection is there against involuntary unemployment? How do you protect yourself against a new technology that makes your particular skill obsolete? Is there *any* level of savings that can guarantee financial security?

These are rather depressing thoughts, aren't they? Shakespeare's Hamlet, facing choice and contemplating his alternatives, forsook chance for the certainty of an anguished future.

For who would bear the whips and scorns of time
Th' oppressor's wrong, the proud man's contumely,
The pangs of dispriz'd love, the law's delay
The insolence of office, and the spurns
That patient merit of th' unworthy takes,
When he himself might his quietus make
With bare bodkin?

Hamlet knew, as so many do, the reason why.

The undiscover'd country, from whose bourn
No traveller returns, puzzles the will,
And makes us rather bear those ills we have
Than fly to others that we know not of.

Many of us, comparing the whims of fortune with the present value of our expected future income, would rather trade fortune for the certainty of moderate income. In this sense, income equality becomes the preferred distribution.

RAWLS' THEORY OF JUSTICE

Harvard philosopher John Rawls comes to the same conclusion. The tyranny of random events and the fear of losing badly in the game of random selection is the reason, he suggests, why people who look objectively at distribution alternatives would choose income equality.

But how can anyone be expected to look objectively at such alternatives? The rich will always prefer inequality and the poor, with little to lose, will always choose income equality.

To overcome this self-interested bias, Rawls imagines a society "in the making." It is in the process of adopting a set of production and distribution rules that will be binding on all members. Since nobody yet knows what the agreed-upon rules will be or what position he or she will occupy in the society, the likelihood of ending up a septic tank cleaner is as great as ending up a film critic.

What pattern of distribution will this society choose? The fear of being in the lowest-paying job will outweigh any other consideration. To prevent such a disaster, people will opt for income equality. If forced, they would accept moderate levels of inequality, as long as the worst-case outcome is still tolerable.

THERE'S NOTHING RANDOM ABOUT INEQUALITY

Many socialists, Marxists in particular, make the case for equality not because inequality is founded in randomness but because inequality has been rigged from the start. To them, everyone is capable of acquiring the skills to do almost anything. Given proper training, anyone can master carpentry, walk on the moon, design hydroelectric dams, run General Motors, or teach classics. People are created equal.

What, then, causes income inequality? Why do some people live off their stocks, bonds, and rents while others live by the sweat of their brow? The socialist answer is property. Unequal distribution of property creates unequal distribution of income. How do people come to have property? The socialist answer is theft. Their idea is eloquently expressed by poet Carl Sandburg:

Get off the estate
Why
Because it's mine
Who gave it to you
My father
How did he get it
He fought for it
OK, I'll fight you for it.

To undo these rigged income inequalities, then, requires the undoing of private property. Marxists are prepared to undo both. Other socialists, while acknowledging the connection between property and unequal income, are not prepared to go that far.

How do you achieve income equality while still adhering to a private-property economy? The socialist prescription is to knock down the barriers to equal opportunity. In this way, the excesses of income inequality are reduced.

But undoing these barriers or the entire property system is merely the *means* to achieve an end. The end is what really counts. And that is income equality. Ultimately, the socialist argument reduces to a simple proposition: People should share equally in the bounty of the earth.

EQUALITY AND MAXIMUM UTILITY

Economist A. P. Lerner makes a case for equality based on the presumption that equality produces the greatest welfare for the greatest number of people. In making the case, he shows that for any two people, equal income distribution maximizes their combined utility of money. Look at Figure 5.

Let's assume that Gen Clark's downward-sloping marginal utility curve of money, *a*, reflecting the marginal utility of the goods and services that money

FIGURE 5 **Equality and Maximum Utility**
Gen Clark's marginal utility curve for money is drawn from left to right. Ben Cohen's marginal utility curve for money is drawn from right to left. The marginal utility of their tenth dollar is 50 utils. At any distribution of the $20 total income other than equality—$10 each—the marginal utilities of their dollars would be unequal. A shift of $1, from the one whose marginal utility for money is lower to the other whose marginal utility for money is higher, would raise their combined total utility. At equality, then, combined total utility is maximized.

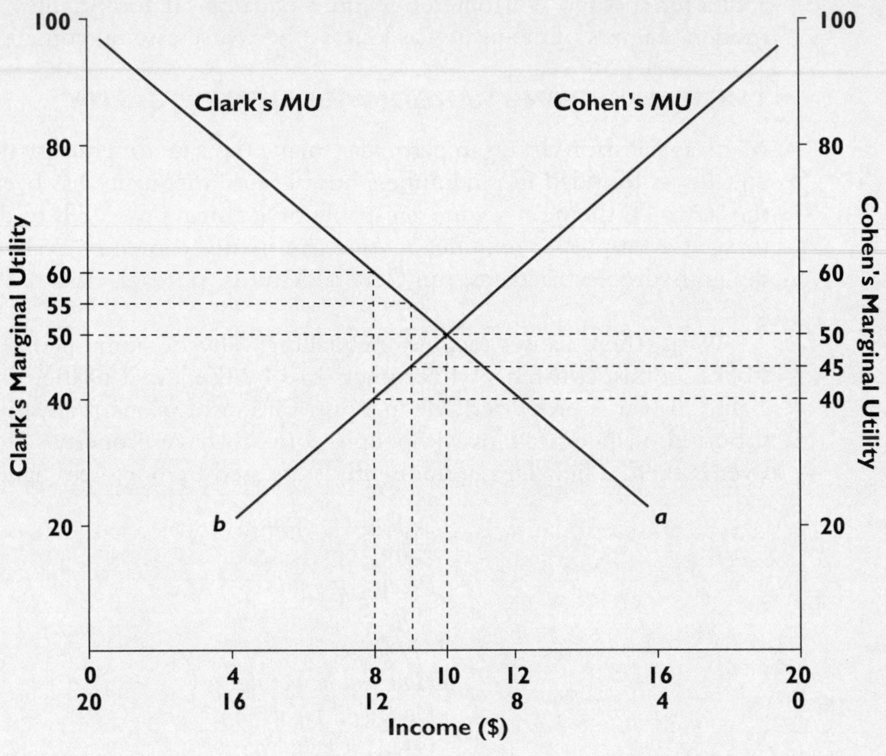

can buy, is drawn from left to right. Ben Cohen's marginal utility curve, *b*, is drawn from right to left. Suppose their combined income is $20. Let's start with income inequality, assuming that Cohen has $12 and Clark only $8. Although Cohen is no doubt pleased with this unequal distribution, the combined utility they derive from their incomes is less than maximum.

Why? Because Gen Clark has fewer dollars, the marginal utility of her last dollar, the eighth, is 60 utils, considerably higher than the 40 utils of Ben Cohen's twelfth dollar. If we take Lerner's advice and give Clark $1 of Cohen's income, the utility she gains from this extra $1—the marginal utility of her ninth—is 55 utils. But Cohen's income is now $1 less. The utility he loses by giving up the $1 is 40 utils. *And that's Lerner's point.* By transferring $1 from Ben Cohen to Gen Clark, their combined utility increases by 55 – 40 = 15 utils.

Income inequality, although reduced, still persists. Gen Clark's income at $9 is still $2 less than Ben Cohen's at $11. There is still room to expand total utility. How? The marginal utility of Clark's ninth dollar is 55 utils, 10 utils greater than the 45 utils of Cohen's eleventh dollar. If yet another $1 were transferred from Cohen to Clark, Clark's utility gain is 50 utils—the marginal utility of her ninth dollar—while Cohen loses the 45 utils of his eleventh dollar. This second transfer of $1, then, added another 50 – 45 = 5 utils to their combined utility.

But that does it. *Total utility is maximized when each has $10 income.* Look at their marginal utility at $10 income. It is 50 utils. If another $1 were transferred to Gen Clark, Ben Cohen would lose 50 utils while Gen Clark gained 45 utils. This last transfer would reduce their combined utility by 5 utils.

Lerner's choice of equality as the preferred distribution, based on this maximum utility rule, applies as well to economies whose populations are greater than two people. But his proof of maximum utility rests on the assumption that everyone's utility functions are alike. For example, he would have to assume that Gen Clark's and Ben Cohen's marginal utility curves were identical to get his results. But why assume that?

Why would Lerner make such an assumption when he knows, as you do, that no two people derive identical satisfaction when it comes to spending money? If you were in his shoes, what assumption would you make? *Realizing it's impossible to know for certain whose utility curve is really higher,* would you guess Cohen's curve to be higher than Clark's? Why? What if his were really lower? That would be the worst possible guess. Assuming Clark's is higher creates the same problem. Why not, then, just assume that they are equal? Wouldn't it be safer? In this way, we minimize the damage of making a mistake. That's precisely why Lerner assumed that they were identical.

HOW THE CHINESE ARRIVED AT LERNER'S CONCLUSIONS

An old Chinese rule on property distribution preceded Lerner's conclusions. How do you bequeath property so that everyone involved acknowledges equality? So that everyone feels he or she has a fair share? Suppose the task is to divide an estate between two children. Neither can be trusted to make a fair division.

Assuming identical utility functions, maximum total utility is achieved by allowing one child to do the dividing and the other to choose first from among the two sections. The divider will be forced to create two equal shares. After all, it would be foolish to divide them unevenly knowing that the other has first choice. The chooser can't complain. After all, if the properties are unevenly divided, having first choice guarantees a higher-valued share.

The Case for Inequality

EQUALITY VERSUS EFFICIENCY

Many economists, acknowledging some merit in the equality arguments, still opt for tolerable levels of inequality as the preferred distribution. They do so by drawing upon the connection between productive contribution and economic reward. People should receive their *MRP*. And since the *MRP*s generated in competitive markets are everywhere different, income inequality is totally justified. The distribution ethic is simple: Contribution merits reward.

But there is more to their case for inequality than its ethic. Many argue that without the reward linkage, productive people would lack the incentive to contribute as much as they do. After all, most productive contributions are not effortless. Denying people the full measure of their contribution, then, will ensure less than the full measure of their energies. In other words, the imposition of income equality breeds a less-than-efficient use of the economy's resources. The economy's output would be less than its productive potential.

FIGURE 6 **Effect of Inequality on National Income**

The vertical axis measures levels of national income and the horizontal axis measures the degree of inequality, expressed in terms of the Gini coefficient. At the origin, $G = 0$, reflecting perfect income equality. The hill-shaped national income curve maps the trade-off between economic efficiency and income equality. At $G = .45$, income is $900 billion. If government policy of redistributing income forces G to .35, production disincentives and inefficiencies emerge that reduce national income to $700 billion. The hill-shaped income curve of the poorest 60 percent maps the income received by the poor at varying levels of inequality. At $G = .45$, the poor receive $300 billion of the $900 billion national income. At $G = .35$, the poor receive $350 billion of the $700 billion national income.

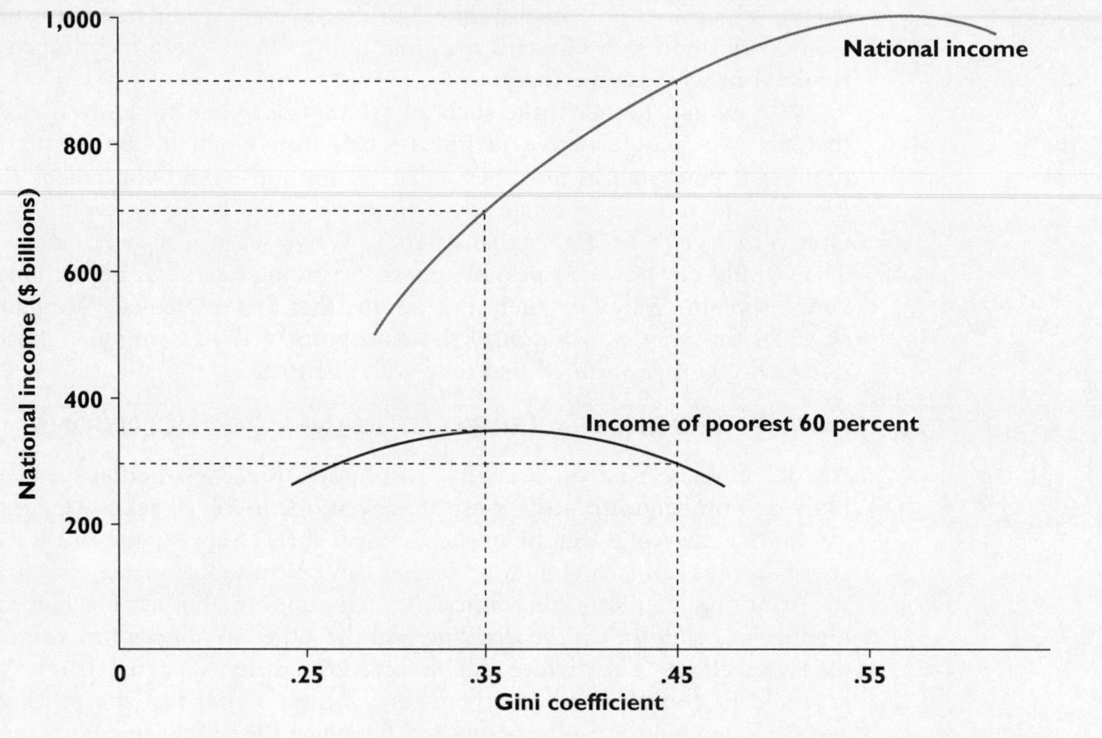

The inefficiency costs of equality become even greater if the equality is achieved by rigging factor prices, as with minimum wage rates or interest rate ceilings. The economy would lose its guide to opportunity costs. How, then, could an entrepreneur make efficient use of resources? Look at Figure 6.

Suppose the economy's national income is $900 billion, and its income inequality, measured by the Gini coefficient, is .45. Let's now suppose that society decides to generate greater income equality. It transfers income from rich to poor, to push the Gini coefficient to .35. However, with G = .35 imposed on the economy, note what happens to the level of national income. It falls to $700 billion. The income transfers discourage maximum production, and inefficiencies take their toll. The national income curve maps the relationship between levels of inequality and levels of national income.

If income were distributed equally, then productivity might suffer.

What may be bad for the economy, however, may still be good for people occupying the lower quintiles of income distribution. Their incomes may increase even though national income decreases as a result of greater equality. Look at the income curve for the poorest 60 percent. It records their income at

FIGURE 7 **Inequality and Economic Growth**
The vertical axis measures levels of national income and the income received by the poor. The horizontal axis measures time. At the origin national income is $900 billion. The curves trace two different income paths for the poorest 60 percent. The high growth curve reflects $G = .45$. The less-rapid income growth curve reflects $G = .35$. In 15 years, the absolute level of income received by the poor with $G = .45$ catches up to the income they would have received with $G = .35$. Beyond 15 years, the poor's income with $G = .45$ is actually higher.

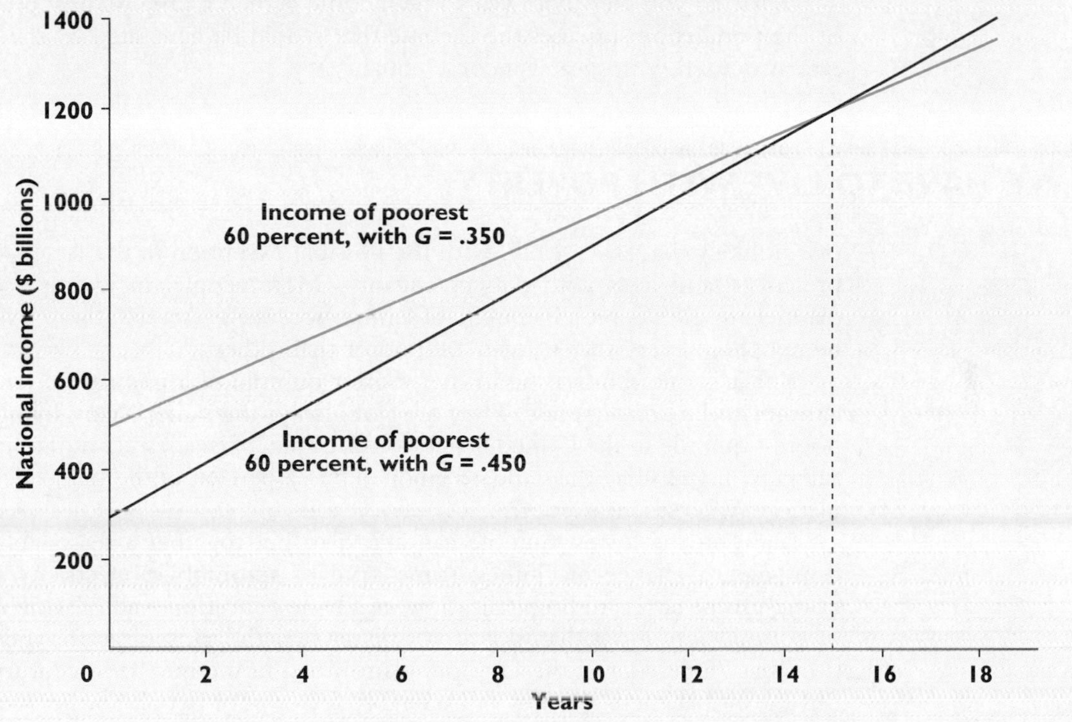

different levels of inequality. As you see, when $G = .35$, these people receive—because of greater income equality—$350 billion of the $700 billion, which is more than the $300 billion they received when national income is $900 billion.

But there is a limit to the gains the poor can receive by such methods of income transfer. If a Gini coefficient of .30 were imposed, the decline in national income would become so pronounced that everyone would be worse off, including the poor. Even though the poor's share of national income would increase, the absolute amount of income they received would fall.

EQUALITY VERSUS ECONOMIC GROWTH

Economic growth depends on investment in the economy, which depends on saving that is undertaken primarily by the rich.

Because the rich can afford to save a higher percentage of their income than can the poor, they tend to do the economy's investing. In this way, the economy's growth rate and investment are linked to income inequality. The richer the rich, the greater the investment and the higher the rate of growth.

Paradoxically, the poor are supposed to benefit from income inequality as well. How? Even though with $G = .45$ their share of national income is relatively small, the investments made by the rich increase the rate of growth of national income, so that eventually the absolute size of the poor's small share becomes larger than before. The rising tide of national prosperity raises all ships, both large and small. This concept is shown in Figure 7.

Again, let's suppose the economy's national income is \$900 billion. The curves trace two different income paths for the poorest 60 percent of the population. The high-growth path reflects high income inequality, $G = .45$. The lower-growth path reflects a state of less income inequality, $G = .35$.

What do you see? In 15 years, the income earned by the poorest 60 percent of the population surpasses the income that would be generated by the growth rate associated with greater income equality.

DO WE HAVE TO LIVE WITH POVERTY?

It is unlikely that any society, with the possible exception of the Israeli kibbutz, prefers to and lives with perfect equality. Most people, including economic planners in the People's Republic of China, accept the fact that there will *always* be people in every society who are poorer than others.

But it is one thing to be in the poorest quintile of a population, and quite another to be *actually* poor. They are not always the same. Many living in the poorest quintile in the United States, for example, have a standard of living considerably higher than the standard enjoyed by 75 percent of the Bangladesh population. Who, then, is poor?

Many in the lowest quintile can afford to put together a reasonably nutritious diet, a change of clothes, some kind of automobile, electricity in their homes, some access to hospitalization, and basic education—all of which add up to considerably more than the food, shelter, health, transportation, and education that 75 percent of the U.S. population had in the mid-19th century. Does this mean that there are now considerably fewer poor people in the country?

Defining Poverty

What does poverty mean? Perhaps the best way to answer this question is by first asking what it is we want to know. But that's the problem. We aren't entirely clear what kind of information we seek.

AS A PERCENT OF MEDIAN INCOME

Median income

The midpoint of a society's income distribution, above and below which an equal number of individuals (or families) belong.

Poverty threshold

The level of income below which families are considered to be poor.

To many people, and many economists, poverty is a relative concept. People are only poor relative to others. One way, then, of defining poverty is to arbitrarily select some percentage of the population's **median income** as the **poverty threshold.** Those with incomes below that threshold level are considered to be living in poverty. For example, if the threshold level selected were 50 percent of median income and if median income were \$10,000, then those earning less than \$5,000 would be below the poverty line. If the government selects a threshold level of 40 percent, fewer people would be classified as living in poverty. If, over time, median income increases more rapidly than the incomes of the poor, the poverty ranks swell. How many live in poverty, then, depends not on a person's particular income, but upon the relationship between that income and the income of others.

MEETING BASIC NEEDS

Another way of identifying poverty is by describing some *minimal acceptable physical standard of living* that people ought to have. Those whose incomes are insufficient to afford that standard are considered poor. As you can imagine, such a definition of poverty can produce as many poverty threshold levels as there are opinions on what constitutes minimal standards of living. In fact, various government agencies have identified as many as 124 different poverty levels.

Be sure that you can explain the two approaches to defining poverty—percentage of median income and basic needs.

Since 1920, the Bureau of Labor Statistics has constructed annual subsistence standard-of-living budgets for U.S. families. Such a budget, you would think, would not change if subsistence were regarded simply in terms of basic needs. After all, a quart of milk contributes as much nutritional value to a poor family in 1990 as it did to a poor family in 1920. But our perceptions of basic needs change. A heated house may have been a luxury in 1920, but it is perceived as a basic need today. High school education may have been a luxury in 1920, but it is obligatory today. Because retail stores were typically interspersed among houses and apartment buildings, people years ago could shop by foot. Today, with residential neighborhoods separated from shopping centers and downtown malls, the automobile has become a basic need. In other words, our concepts of basic needs are always changing.

The most commonly used poverty threshold that reflects basic needs was developed by the Social Security Administration in 1964 and revised in 1981 by the Federal Interagency Committees. It is based on the Department of Agriculture's 1961 Economy Food Plan. Let's see what kind of picture it paints.

Who and How Many Are in Poverty?

The percentage of people who fall below the poverty threshold, as calculated by the Social Security Administration, is shown in Table 6.

Are we making headway? Look at the decade of the 1960s. Between 1960 and 1970, the percentage of people in poverty fell from 22.2 percent to 12.6 percent. The decline among blacks in poverty was even more dramatic. But that substantial progress came to an abrupt halt and since then the percentage of people in poverty has remained almost unchanged.

Who are the poor? Look at the family characteristics shown in Table 7.

TABLE 6
Percentage of Persons below Poverty Level, by Race 1960–1992

	1960	1970	1980	1992
All persons	22.2	12.6	13.0	13.1
White	17.8	9.9	10.2	10.3
Black	55.1*	33.3	32.5	31.0
Hispanic	NA	NA	25.7	26.7

Source: Bureau of the Census, *Statistical Abstract of the United States, 1994* (Washington, D.C.: Department of Commerce, 1994), p. 480.

NA = not available.

* refers to data for 1959.

TABLE 7 Selected Characteristics of Families below the Poverty Level (1992)

	Percent
Families below poverty level	11.7
Age of householder	
15-24 years old	38.2
Size of family	
6 persons	22.6
7 or more	34.7
Education of householder	
less than 8 years	24.1
Single mothers	46.0

Source: Bureau of the Census, *Statistical Abstract of the United States*, 1994, (Washington, D.C.: Department of Commerce, 1993), pp. 478–79.

Not surprising, is it? As you see, poor families make up a little more than 10 percent of the U.S. population, yet 46 percent of all single mothers fall below the poverty line. Young families, large ones, and those headed by someone with only grade school education are also at high risk of living in poverty.

FIGHTING THE WAR ON POVERTY

Do we care? Michael Harrington's *The Other America: Poverty in the United States,* published in 1962, addressed the issue of America's neglected poor. Its message was unmistakable. Life in the United States was not nearly as comfortable as the comfortable would like us to believe. His message was not original. Many had written on poverty before. What was unique about Harrington's book was its reception. The timing was right.

Lyndon Johnson's War on Poverty

In 1964, President Lyndon B. Johnson put the issue of our nation's poor on the national agenda. He called for a "war on poverty." Reaction was mixed. Some people regarded it as unnecessary and even self-defeating. Eliminating poverty, they argued, depended more on the benefits the poor derive from being part of a strong and growing market economy than on government-sponsored income transfers.

Cash assistance

Government assistance in the form of cash.

In-kind assistance

Government assistance in the form of direct goods and services, such as Medicaid or food stamps.

Others applauded the president's recognition of the problem, but viewed his commitment as entirely too weak. More funding was needed for more programs for a longer period of time. It appeared more a measured skirmish than an all-out war.

Whatever the intent of the Johnson war on poverty, it marked the beginning of a broad-based set of programs funded by federal, state, and local governments to address specific poverty issues. The benefits were in the form of **cash assistance** and **in-kind assistance.**

Making an Honest Effort?

How much funding? Since 1964 the number of people eligible for assistance, as well as the funding of the poverty program, has expanded significantly. The principal form of assistance has been in-kind—goods and services *other* than monetary—programs such as health care, food stamps, education, housing, and energy.

MEDICAID

The highest-priced item in the poverty program is *Medicaid,* which provides medical services to the poor. Medicaid pays for inpatient hospital care, physician's services, skilled nursing facilities, medication, and dental care. In 1990, Medicaid expenditures totaled $72.1 billion, which included $41.1 billion of federal matching grants to states. The states contributed the remaining $31.0 billion.

FOOD STAMPS

The *food stamp* program is government's primary way of helping the poor maintain nutritious diets. People eligible for this form of in-kind assistance receive monthly allotments of stamps, based on income and household size, to help them buy food. In 1990, poor people received $15 billion in food stamps.

RELATED FOOD ASSISTANCE

Two government programs distribute food directly to the needy. One is a special supplemental food program for women, infants, and children (WIC) living in poverty, and the other is the so-called commodity supplemental food program (CSFP). WIC focuses on health problems associated with inadequate diets during the critical early stages of child development, including the prenatal months. CSFP administers the transfer of government surplus foods, such as cheese and butter, to food banks, schools, and charitable institutions. 1990 funding for these programs was $2.2 billion.

HOUSING ASSISTANCE

In 1990, $15.9 billion of in-kind assistance was budgeted for housing for the poor in the form of public housing—housing owned and operated by the government's Department of Housing and Urban Development (HUD)—and for rent subsidies, which allow the poor to compete for private housing at market prices.

HOME ENERGY ASSISTANCE

The government also provides grants specifically earmarked to help pay the fuel bills of poor families. The program, administered by the states, can make direct cash payments to eligible families or payments to energy suppliers. In 1990, the government budget for home energy assistance was $1.4 billion.

HEAD START

Since its beginning in 1965, *Head Start* has served more than 11 million economically disadvantaged preschool children. It provides an array of educational and social services designed to compensate for the absence of an intellectually

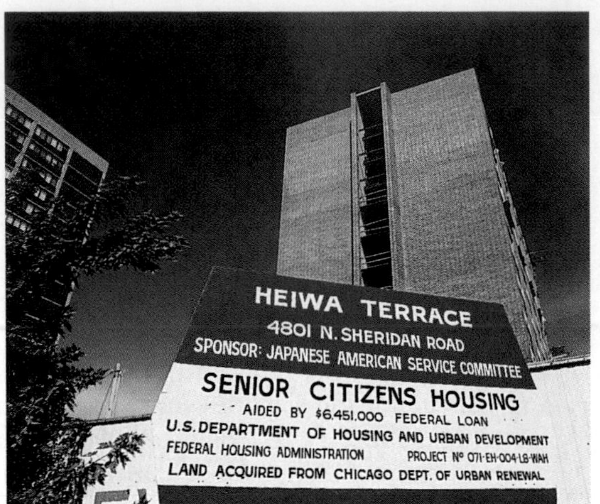

Senior citizens housing built by the Japanese community with funding from the Department of Housing and Urban Development (HUD), upon land received from the City of Chicago's Department of Urban Renewal.

stimulating home environment—the kind of home life that more affluent preschoolers typically enjoy. Head Start represents an important weapon in the government's attempt to break the transfer of poverty from one generation to the next, and many observers agree that it has worked well. The 1990 Head Start budget totaled $1.9 billion.

AFDC

Aid to Families with Dependent Children is monetary assistance. Cash payments are made to supplement food, shelter, and clothing for the dependent children of the poor. In 1990, AFDC payments totaled $19.8 billion, $10.1 billion coming from the federal government. State governments have the authority to specify who is eligibile for AFDC, and their eligibility requirements have been controversial.

Until recently, only families with a nonworking and single parent qualified. The unintended consequence of this eligibility requirement was that some fathers abandoned the household in order to allow the mother to qualify for AFDC assistance.

The Family Support Act of 1988 changed some aspects of the AFDC program. It extended coverage, at least for six months, to two-parent poor families in which the principal wage earner is unemployed. It also obliges AFDC recipients to participate in job training programs.

THE NEGATIVE INCOME TAX ALTERNATIVE

Negative income tax

Government cash payments to the poor—an income tax in reverse—that is linked to the income levels of the poor. The cash payments decrease as income levels increase. The payments are designed to provide a minimum level of income to the poor.

One way to reduce poverty and the costs of administering poverty programs is to devise a system that *automatically* provides those in poverty with enough money to maintain a minimum standard of living and, at the same time, allows the poor to earn as much as possible without penalty.

Many economists regard the **negative income tax** as such a scheme. They see it as the most attractive alternative to an overburdened and underfunded poverty program. Economists are particularly impressed with its political cleanliness and simplicity. It can be administered routinely by the Internal Revenue Service. It actually creates an incentive to work. It avoids the stigma of hand-outs.

TABLE 8 The Negative Income Tax Applied (tax = 50%)

Independent Income	Net Negative [−] or Positive [+] Tax	After-Tax Income
$ 0	$−10,000	$10,000
5,000	−7,500	12,500
10,000	−5,000	15,000
20,000	0	20,000
25,000	+2,500	22,500
30,000	+5,000	25,000

How does it work? Suppose the government sets the minimum income level for a family of four at $10,000 and taxes all income at 50 percent. Corresponding incomes, taxes, and after-tax incomes are shown in Table 8.

If the household earns no income, it *receives* a negative tax of $10,000 from the government—just as you would receive a tax refund from the IRS—which, added to the household's zero independent income represents total after-tax income.

If the household earned $5,000, it pays a 50 percent tax on that income like everyone else. On April 15, the household calculates the $5,000 × 50% = $2,500 tax due. This leaves the household with an after-tax *independently-derived* income of $2,500. But it still receives the $10,000 negative income tax, so that total after-tax income is $12,500. As far as the IRS is concerned, its net payment to the household is $7,500 representing the $10,000 paid out as negative tax and the $2,500 it receives in taxes.

Suppose the household's independent income is $20,000. Its tax obligation [$20,000 × 50%] now equals the $10,000 negative income tax. The household and the IRS break even. The household's after-tax income is its independent income. The IRS pays nothing to the household.

If the household's independent income increases to $30,000, it pays $30,000 × 50% = $15,000 to the IRS, but receives $10,000, so that its after-tax income is $25,000. The IRS clears $5,000.

As you see, there is beauty in simplicity. All households, including the poorest, have a strong incentive to work. The more income earned, the higher is the household's after-tax income. Moreover, the poor are assured a minimum after-tax income of $10,000—it can vary, of course—and the entire operation avoids government meddling in the lives of the people.

A negative income tax sets a threshold poverty level and gives cash payments to those who fall below the threshold. Will such a system eliminate the reasons for poverty?

To some economists, the attractive features of the negative income tax are precisely the source of its weakness! From a macroeconomic perspective, the real problem of the poor is not that they have less income than others, but that they *produce* less income than others. The negative income tax ignores this crucial distinction. Anthropologists Ruth and Oscar Lewis in their life study of poverty recognized that a "culture of poverty" sets the poor apart from others and keeps the poor locked in poverty.

To undo such a cultural stranglehold requires more than adding to household income. It requires a radical change in the poor's perception of themselves, of their future, and of the society they live in. To bring about such change requires large investments in the economic and social environments of the poor. Higher private incomes alone cannot address these needs.

ADDED PERSPECTIVE

Poverty Is About Real People

MARSHALLTOWN, Iowa This city of 25,000 sits amid cornfields and factories in the center of a state that has been riding out the recession with one of the lowest unemployment levels in the country. Yet around 2,000 poor people here are getting help of some kind from the welfare system, from vouchers to heat a house to a regular welfare check.

This is not the South Bronx or Appalachia, where poverty often is attributed to culture or behavior, to racism or reckless childbearing.

But Marshalltown shows with unusual clarity other powerful forces that make welfare and poverty hard to escape anywhere: the nation's proliferation of low-wage jobs and two decades of falling wages, especially for the least skilled, in terms of what they can buy.

Diana Kuchenreuther, 34 years old, single, the mother of three children, has been working for two years and trying to get off the dole, but she is still desperately poor. Her home is an apartment in a big rundown house in a working-class neighborhood. Her entrance is on the side, over a concrete slab cluttered with two wobbly kitchen chairs and the jetsam of children.

Inside, the drain of the sink in the one bathroom hasn't worked for a couple of years, and the toilet leaked until a friend patched a crack in the bowl. The old carpet on the staircase is foul and torn. The upstairs ceiling leaks in the rain. The place has two bedrooms, one for Ms. Kuchenreuther, Phillip, 9, and Aimmee, 7, the other for Lucinda, 13. The rent is $260 a month.

Although dependence on welfare is concentrated in inner cities, a majority of recipients live in suburbs, small towns like this one, and rural areas around the country. And although black and Hispanic people receive welfare out of proportion to their numbers, more white people, including Ms. Kuchenreuther, spend time on it than members of any other group.

Some common patterns of welfare are evident here. Ninety-one percent of the Marshall County households that receive Aid to Families with Dependent Children are headed by women, many of them victims of abusive or runaway men. Forty percent of the women on welfare in Iowa had their first children as teenagers, and 16 percent dropped out of high school.

But no one can blame racism for poverty here. Ninety-eight percent of the 38,000 people of Marshall County, of which Marshalltown is the seat, are white, as are nearly all the families on welfare.

In big cities and the rural South, welfare and poverty might feed on themselves in spreading through neighborhoods. Here, poverty stays indoors. Marshalltown is not rich, but it is barren of slums, and the poor live next to the middle class. The crime and drug problems of the inner cities are, by comparison, insignificant here. . . .

Ms. Kuchenreuther and other people interviewed are at various stages of the struggle with poverty, welfare, and the low-wage economy. She is paid $4.80 an hour as a nurse's aide. She often works up to four hours of overtime a day and earns as much as $350 a week. She no longer receives a cash welfare grant, but she remains eligible for $177 a month in food stamps, and she is in line for a government-subsidized house that should cost her no more than she pays now.

Ms. Kuchenreuther said she loves working and caring for the elderly. But she is trapped by her wages. "People say, 'Why don't you move out of this house?' " she said. "I can't afford to."

She said she wants to become a registered nurse, which would pay $12 an hour. But that means a couple of years of full-time schooling, giving up her work and going back to living almost entirely on welfare. . . .

Christine Anderson: A Temporary Tool to Earn a Degree

For Christine Anderson, 25, the welfare system is not a permanent crutch, but a tool to escape the quicksand of a life of low-wage jobs. She wants to be a social worker.

With the aid of welfare and a federal grant for college students from families with low incomes, Ms. Anderson has spent a year at Marshalltown Community College working toward a two-year associate's degree. With high grades so far, she hopes to keep getting grants and subsidies and eventually earn a master's degree in social work, which could lead to a job paying enough to support herself and her daughter, Burgundy.

Ms. Anderson, who was born in Wisconsin, moved in with her father in Des Moines at 11 after her parents divorced. At 13 she was sent to her father's parents in South Dakota, who sent her to a Seventh-Day Adventist boarding school near Bismarck, SD. She was valedictorian of a class of 17.

Lacking money for college, she became a hostess in a restaurant and took up with a waiter. "I did an irresponsible thing," she said. "I got pregnant." She said the waiter fled to Colorado. She took a job at another restaurant in Lincoln, NB, had her baby, enrolled at the University of Nebraska, and lasted a month. "I didn't know about welfare," she said. "I was trying to work, go to college, pay a baby-sitter and breast-feed my baby."

She went to Topeka, KS, and found a job as a receptionist with an engineering firm. In three years, she was making $7.50 an hour. But fighting bulimia, a severe eating disorder, she moved to Marshalltown to be closer to her mother and in 1989 enrolled in the welfare system.

The system has helped her take control of her life, she said. Her apartment is bright and clean. In her living room, she has 12 potted plants, her 6-year-old daughter's toys tucked in corners, and school drawings on the wall. "I do not present myself as poor white trash," she said.

But there are many things Ms. Anderson does not have, from a corkscrew to a sofa. She does without a telephone. She changes the oil in her car herself. If short of cash for gas, she gets it with food stamps: If the change due on a food-stamp purchase is less than $1, merchants pay in money, so Ms. Anderson goes from store to store buying 5-cent mints, accumulating enough coins to buy gas.

She feels the stigma of being on welfare—she receives $361 in AFDC payments a month, $118 in food stamps, a subsidy of $199 on her monthly rent of $303, and Medicaid. When she prepares to pay in the supermarket, she keeps the food-stamp book in her purse as she tears out the coupons.

"Someone on my softball team was bitching because I was too tan," she said. "'Oh, I forgot, Christine, you don't have a real life,' she said. That was someone who got a free car when she got married and gets free rent from living with her in-laws."

She is irked that she lets it get to her. She worked for more than four years and paid taxes. "I don't feel guilty about taking *your* money," she said. "I'm not taking *your* money. I'm taking my own."

JoAnn Earnest: A Refuge in Bad Times

JoAnn Earnest, 37, and Roger Bunting, 31, together for two-and-a-half years, say they want to be self-sufficient. He has just started a business, and she would like to start one. But they find the economy blowing against them and the welfare system a refuge.

"I'm tired of all this," Mr. Bunting said. As an able-bodied male without children, he is ineligible for welfare, but he benefits from the help Ms. Earnest gets.

"Nobody should get nothing for nothing," he said. "Russia was a welfare state since 1917, and look what it got them." But it is hard to get along without it, too. "In the winter," he said, "we don't make nothing. She's the one that makes everything happen then."

Most mornings, Ms. Earnest gets up at 5 o'clock. A woman who works in a meat-packing plant brings in her mildly retarded 6-year-old son. Ms. Earnest watches the boy for $50 a week, income she reports to the authorities. The boy curls up with his blanket on the living room rug, and Ms. Earnest goes back to bed for an hour or so. Then she gets up and puts on one of her three pairs of pants.

"I could use some more pants," she says. Her shoes are one of two pairs she wears. She has another pair she doesn't use, high heels that she bought on sale for $5.

She awakens Brandy, her 3-year-old daughter by another man, and then gets up Mr. Bunting if he has any work to do. Since quitting a job making pallets that paid the state's minimum wage of $4.65 an hour, Mr. Bunting has invested in three dump trucks for less than $2,000 to start a business.

He runs advertisements in a local paper. One says, "Hauling and Odd Jobs." The other says, "Black Dirt." The black dirt, good for gardens, comes from the 35-acre backyard. "Want to see a rural ghetto?" he said, gesturing out a back window. Mounds of metallic debris and vehicles parts obscure the view of the property, which is owned by Mr. Bunting's father.

Mr. Bunting said that one month recently he earned four times what he could earn from the minimum wage. But in June, he said, he made nothing at all. In times like that, Ms. Earnest is the sole source of income. Besides her pay from watching the boy, she and Brandy are allotted $200 a month in food stamps and $357 a month in AFDC.

The Mid-Iowa Community Action Program, a service for the poor that is financed in part by the federal government, provides about $40 a month in food coupons for Brandy under the federal Women's, Infants, and Children program and vouchers for part of the heating bill. It also insulated the house.

Brandy turned three on June 18, a threshold age for the youngest child of parents on welfare in Iowa. At that point, parents are beckoned to the state's job service for counseling and possible placement. If they do not show up, they can lose all but the food stamps and AFDC that their children need.

Ms. Earnest said she is not afraid to work. Earlier, while rearing three other children—daughters 18 and 19, and a son, 21—she worked in a nursing home as a housekeeper, in a garment factory, and in a woodworking shop. All the jobs paid less than $5 an hour, but living was easier then.

She had a husband who was a machine operator in a factory. But he went to jail in 1983 for burglary, and she went on welfare for three years. They are separated now and he is somewhere in South Dakota. She said she went back on welfare a few months before Brandy was born because her doctor told her the varnish and paint fumes in the wood shop could endanger her pregnancy. . . .

Glenda Schmidt: Shaky Prospects, Uncertain Pay

Glenda Schmidt, 39, did the right things to get off welfare, getting trained for a job and taking one as a nurse's aide. But hers is not only a low-wage job. Like many of the economy's new jobs, it is part-time and irregular. She never really knows when she will be beckoned to work.

Mrs. Schmidt fits one stereotype of women on welfare but not another. She has five children, ages 9 to 23, which has qualified her for AFDC and food stamps on and off, depending on her husband's success with his work. Under a special program in Iowa, parents, married or not, can get AFDC if both are at home, one or both are unemployed, and at least one has been working.

One the other hand, she has had a long and stable marriage, after one that lasted seven months and produced her first child. Every day she carries a lunch to her husband, Robert, who is 43, at the garage where he is trying to start a machinery repair business.

Mrs. Schmidt seems weary and worn sitting in front of a large television console in the living room of her small, rented brick house. She said Mr. Schmidt bought the television in better times. Because she works, her benefits were cut, and now her big concern is how she will pay for the family's medicine when the Medicaid coverage that came with welfare ends this fall.

She now pays only $1 for each prescription. She takes medicine for an inflamed stomach, for anxiety, for hypertension, and migraine headaches. Until a couple of months ago, she was taking an antidepressant. The Schmidts' 9-year-old daughter needs medicine for a urinary problem that alone costs $180 a month. Mr. Schmidt, who has had three heart attacks, takes nitroglycerin. But he is a Vietnam War veteran, so he gets free medical care.

Mrs. Schmidt's anxiety arises in part from trying to wean herself from welfare. Several years ago she went to school to learn to be a nurse's aide. Last October, she landed a job at a local hospital that pays $5.77 an hour and about 50 cents more for night work. The work, however, is unpredictable, and she does not take the hospital's health benefits because they would cost her $53 a week, or half her pay many weeks. . . .

At the end of June the Schmidts had $300 in bills, for rent, light, garbage collection and telephone service, and nothing to pay them with. She still receives food stamps, $209 in June, but her $495 in AFDC was cut off the month after she started work.

She scrimps. "I don't buy lipstick," she said. "I don't buy fingernail polish. Now shampoo, that's a necessity. I get that for 89 cents." She drives a 1979 Plymouth Horizon to work, but it has problems with its gears, and the emergency brake is unreliable. The car is not insured.

Mr. Schmidt has been a truck driver for years, but needs less-stressful work because of his health. But business for his new repair business is slow, and he may have to give it up.

"I guess I worry if I'm doing things right," Mrs. Schmidt said.

Source: "Lives of Unexpected Poverty in Center of Land of Plenty," by Peter T. Kilborn. *The New York Times*, July 7, 1992.

CHAPTER REVIEW

1. People's incomes come in the form of wages, interest, rent, or profit, or some combination of these.

2. The Lorenz curve provides a graphic view of income distribution. The Lorenz curve matches deciles or quintiles of a population with the percentage of total income that each decile or quintile receives.

3. A Gini coefficient gives a numerical measure of income distribution. The coefficient is calculated by taking the ratio of the area lying between the diagonal and the Lorenz curve to the area beneath the diagonal. Thus, a low Gini coefficient indicates high income equality, while Gini coefficients closer to one indicate high income inequality.

4. Income inequality tends to be greater in less developed countries than in the industrially advanced countries. The greater inequality in less developed countries may reflect both the colonial legacy many of these countries share and the narrow range of employment opportunities available to workers.

5. Net wealth is far more unevenly distributed than is income. The richest 5 percent of the U.S. population holds 50 percent of personal savings. The bottom 50 percent holds only 1 percent of net wealth in the United States in 1973.

6. A case for income equality can be built around the randomness of personal misfortune that often translates into a low income. The philosopher John Rawls argues that the fear of ending up at the bottom of the income distribution in a society "in the making" will push people to opt for income equality. Marxists argue for income equality based on the premise that the establishment of private property rights happens through theft. Another argument can be generated based on the notion that an equal distribution of income maximizes utility.

7. A case for income inequality derives from the notion that taking income away from the very productive in society will cause these people to be less productive and make the economy less efficient. Furthermore, since the rich do most of the saving in the economy, they also do most of the investing, which contributes to economic growth. Faster economic growth actually benefits the poor.

8. Many economists think of poverty as a relative concept. Others define poverty in terms of basic needs—the minimal acceptable physical standard of living that people should have.

9. The percentage of people below the poverty threshold fell dramatically between 1959 and 1969 and has risen slightly since then. A disproportionate number of those who are poor belong to minority and single-female-headed households.

10. The war on poverty has been fought on a variety of fronts since the mid-1960s. Medicaid, food stamps, other food assistance, housing assistance, home energy assistance, the Head Start program, and Aid to Families with Dependent Children are examples of programs intended to aid the poor.

11. A negative income tax is another approach to attacking poverty by guaranteeing supplemental payments to people whose income falls below some predetermined minimum. The negative income tax preserves incentives for poor people to work. However, if people are poor because of an inability to produce income, then a negative income tax cannot by itself solve the complex problem poverty presents.

KEY TERMS

Lorenz curve
Gini coefficient
Wealth
Life-cycle wealth

Median income
Poverty threshold
Cash assistance
In-kind assistance
Negative income tax

QUESTIONS

1. What is a Lorenz curve? How does it illustrate income inequality?

2. What is a Gini coefficient? What is its relationship to a Lorenz curve?

3. Suppose an economy of only five people generates a national income of $100,000. Suppose Leslie Langston earns $4,000; Lynn Canfield, $8,000; Kristin Hersh, $18,000; Paul Wood, $25,000; and Carol Spears, $45,000. Draw a Lorenz curve that represents the economy's income distribution.

4. How does income distribution in the United States in the 1990s compare to the income distribution pattern 20 years before?

5. How does income distribution in the United States compare to income distribution in European economies? In Canada? In Japan?

6. How does income distribution in the industrially advanced economies compare to income distribution in the less developed economies? Explain the difference.

7. Discuss at least two different ways of defining poverty. Which, if either, is superior? Which is commonly used?

8. What are some of the characteristics of heads-of-households in families that fall below the poverty threshold?

9. What arguments support the idea of income inequality?

10. What arguments support the idea of income equality?

11. Distinguish between in-kind assistance and cash assistance to the poor. Why would the president prefer to provide in-kind assistance?

12. Do you think cash and in-kind assistance can eliminate poverty?

13. What is a negative income tax? Why do some people prefer it to government assistance as an instrument of income redistribution?

14. Distinguish between income and wealth. Which shows greater inequality?

PART 5
EMPLOYMENT, INFLATION, AND FISCAL POLICY

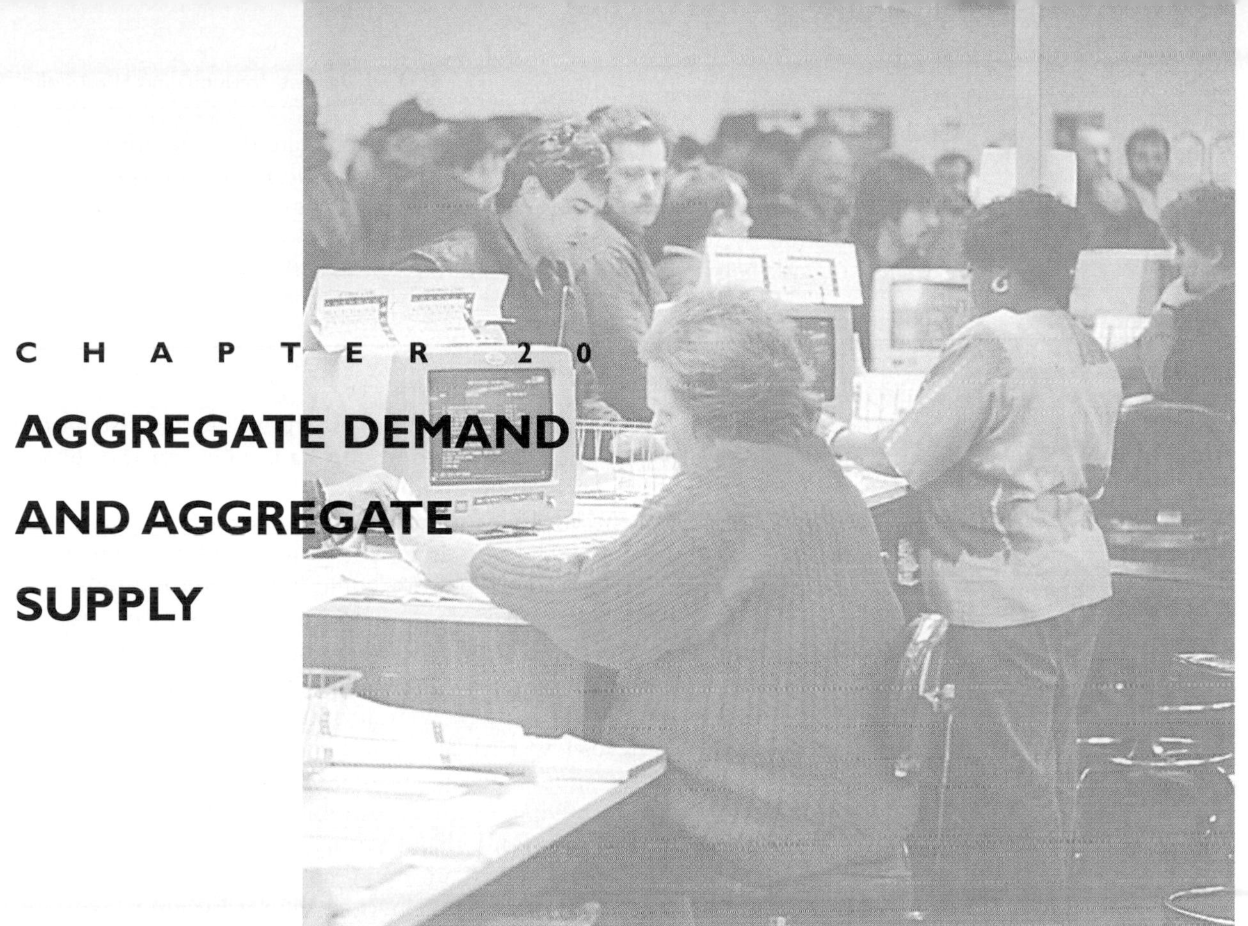

CHAPTER 20
AGGREGATE DEMAND AND AGGREGATE SUPPLY

CHAPTER PREVIEW

We learned in Chapter 1 that economics is divided into two main branches—microeconomics and macroeconomics. Microeconomics focuses on the economic behavior of individual units, such as consumers, households, firms, and industries, while macroeconomics focuses on the economy as a whole. Sometimes, macroeconomics is referred to as aggregate economic analysis because the economy is analyzed as an aggregation of consumers, households, firms, and industries. This chapter introduces you to some of the tools of macroeconomic analysis and to some of the macroeconomic questions to be answered.

After studying this chapter, you should be able to:
- Describe the phases of the business cycle.
- Explain how gross domestic product (GDP) is used to measure a country's economic performance.
- Adjust GDP figures for changes in price levels using the CPI and the GDP deflator.
- Distinguish between nominal and real GDP.
- Draw a graph to describe aggregate supply and aggregate demand.
- Account for the three segments of the aggregate supply curve.

- Give reasons for the downward slope of the aggregate demand curve.
- Show how the economy moves toward macroeconomic equilibrium.
- Explain why an economy can be in equilibrium with either unemployment or inflation present.
- Distinguish between demand-pull and cost-push inflation.

Suppose you've been out of work for four months, and spent the first month trying unsuccessfully to find a job like the one you had. Then, in the second month you lowered your sights and were willing to take a job that at least had some potential. Finally, in the last two months of being out of work, you were willing to take anything at all. The last thing you want to hear is somebody telling you that if you *really* wanted a job, you would hustle and find one.

Most likely, you didn't lose your job through any fault of your own. It wasn't because your wages were too high or because you didn't give the job 100 percent of your talents and energies. It was simply because people cut back on buying the goods you and your coworkers were making. After all, if people buy fewer automobiles, Ford needs fewer M.B.A.'s and engineers.

The trouble with finding another job is not that you aren't hustling. It may be that people are not only buying fewer automobiles, they are also buying fewer of everything. It isn't just Ford that has cut back on its work force. Cutting back employment may be a nationwide phenomenon. With firms everywhere in the economy downsizing production, who is hiring?

Recession

A phase in the business cycle in which the decline in the economy's real GDP persists for at least a half-year. A recession is marked by relatively high unemployment.

Depression

Severe recession.

That's why the job placement agencies you have tried are crowded with people like you. Electricians who worked on residential housing construction are out of work because people are buying fewer houses. Airline pilots lose their jobs because people are flying less. Retail stores are cutting down on their sales staffs because fewer people are shopping. The economy could be producing more, but isn't. People could be consuming more, but aren't. More workers than those employed could be working, but aren't. Economists identify this economic malaise as a **recession** if the decline in GDP persists for six consecutive months.

A relatively long and deep recession is sometimes described as a **depression.** The distinction is meant to convey a difference like that between first and second degree burns: how intense is the inflicted pain.

WHY RECESSION? WHY PROSPERITY?

The business cycle consists of four phases—at the top we have prosperity, then a downturn followed by recession and, finally, recovery.

But why recession? Why do so many people who are willing and able to work lose their jobs? Why do people cut back their consumption? What triggers recession, and how does an economy climb out of the economic doldrums?

Depressed enough? Well, picture a different and much more pleasant scenario. Suppose you are working your regular shift at Ford and the plant manager asks you, almost begs you, to work overtime. Apparently, people are buying more automobiles than Ford and the other automakers had anticipated. You also learn that General Motors needs more workers and is offering wages that are higher than you are earning at Ford. You point this out to your plant manager,

The only people with a job in this Newark office of New Jersey's Department of Unemployment Insurance are those behind the desks. Everyone else is either lining up to register for unemployment insurance or, having registered and searched in vain for jobs, to collect their unemployment compensation checks. Tension sometimes runs high when eligibility for unemployment compensation is questioned.

who immediately matches the General Motors offer. Under these circumstances, morale among management and labor at Ford is understandably high.

But suppose that people are not only buying more automobiles, they are also trying to buy more of everything. They are demanding more residential housing than is available on the market, so more electricians and carpenters are put to work. More people are flying, so more flight crews are operating. More people are crowding into department stores, as if every day were the day before Christmas. Everywhere in the economy, excess demand for goods and services drives prices up. Trying to take advantage of this robust nationwide consumer demand, producers look for more workers, even hiring workers away from each other. They don't mind paying higher wages under these circumstances. Producing more is paramount. And suppose more goods and services are produced until all available resources—land, labor, and capital—are fully employed. What happens if the unrelenting demand for goods and services in the now fully employed economy continues? Prices would rise like a hot-air balloon!

Prosperity

A phase in the business cycle marked by a relatively high level of real GDP, full employment, and inflation.

Inflation

An increase in the price level.

Economists define such a period of economic activity as **prosperity**—an economic boom. And an overall increase in prices is called **inflation.**

But why prosperity and inflation? Why do people try to consume more goods and services than producers have planned to produce? Why can people, without much hustle at all, find almost any kind of job at good wages? Sound attractive? Alas, prosperity, like recession, never lasts.

The Business Cycle

Business cycle

Alternating periods of growth and decline in an economy's GDP.

Trough

Bottom of a business cycle.

Recovery

A phase in the business cycle, following a recession, in which real GDP increases and unemployment declines.

Historical experience shows that our economy roller-coasters from periods of prosperity and inflation to periods of recession, then, recovering from recession, it heads back again to prosperity and inflation. Economists describe this roller coaster pattern of economic activity as the **business cycle.** Figure 1 depicts the course an economy takes through such a cycle.

The vertical axis records the economy's production of goods and services, that is, the economy's output. The horizontal axis records time, measured in years.

The first phase of the cycle depicted in Figure 1 is recession, that time period when the economy's unemployment rate is greatest and output declines to the cycle's minimum level (or **trough**). The **recovery** phase follows reces-

Prosperity is a lot more fun than recession! Malls, such as this one, are typically teeming with people eager to spend their money. It's the day before Christmas every day of the week. Shopkeepers are busy selling and replacing rapidly depleted inventory stocks.

Peak

Top of a business cycle.

Downturn

A phase in the business cycle in which real GDP declines, inflation moderates, and unemployment emerges.

sion. During a recovery, output increases, unemployment decreases, and pressure on the economy's price level begins to build. In time, recovery evolves into the prosperity phase where output reaches its maximum level (or **peak**), the labor force is fully employed, and increasing pressure on prices is likely to generate inflation. Unable to sustain prosperity, the economy enters its **downturn** phase. Output falls, unemployment once again reappears, and inflation tends to moderate as the downturn becomes recession. The business cycle has run its course and the cyclical process repeats, although no two business cycles are quite identical. The number of months in any given phase of the cycle, as well as the output levels of peaks and troughs, vary from cycle to cycle.

FIGURE 1 **The Business Cycle**

The national economy moves through four phases of the business cycle: recession, recovery, prosperity, and the downturn. The cycles repeat. The trend line depicts long-run economic growth.

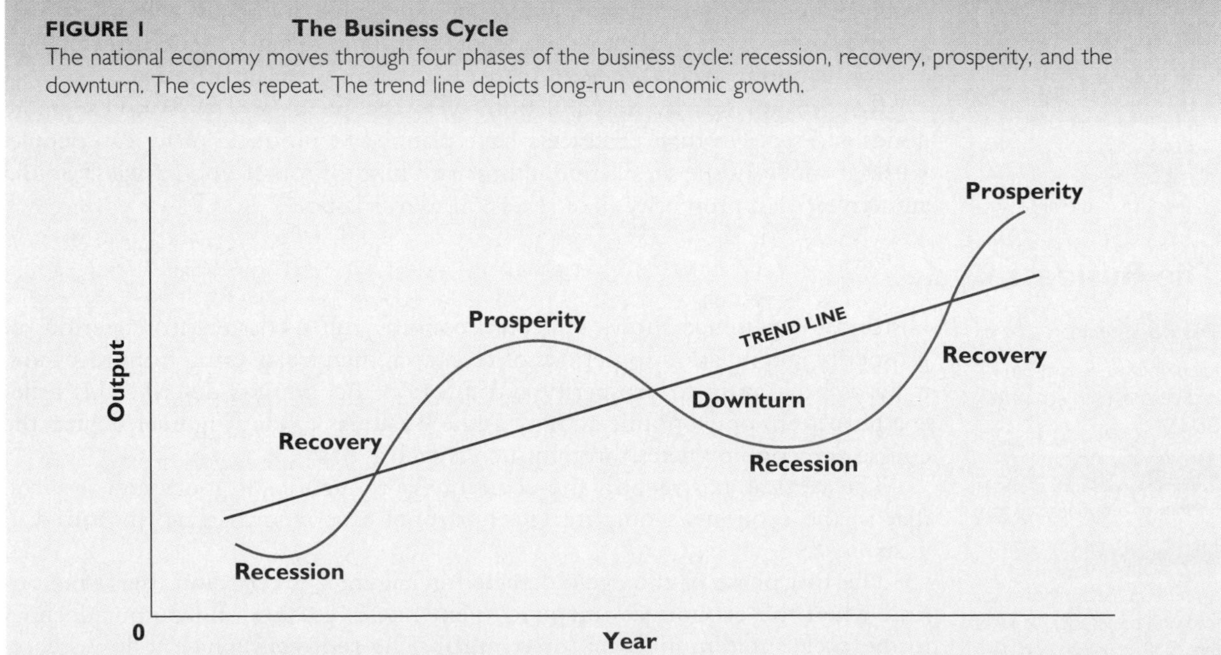

Economic Growth

A trend line drawn through economic cycles over time has a positive slope, indicating that the economy's capacity grows over time.

Note the upward-sloping trend line cutting through the cycle. It traces the economy's output performance over the course of a business cycle, measured either from recession to recession or from prosperity to prosperity. The upward-sloping character of the trend line signifies economic growth. It shows that the economy's output—production of goods and services—increases, cycle after cycle. The steeper the trend line, the higher is the economy's rate of growth. When no growth occurs, the trend line is horizontal.

What causes economic growth? What factors contribute to the increase in the production of goods and services cycle after cycle? Addressing this question (along with questions concerning the economy's cyclical behavior) is what the study of macroeconomics is about.

Understanding why cycles and growth occur is important not just to macroeconomists who study them, but to you and everyone like you who hope to work for and achieve a growing and reasonable standard of living. Can we harness the disturbing swings in our business cycles? That is to say, can we moderate the inflationary pressures on the economy when it is on the upswing of the business cycle, pressing upon full employment? Can we moderate the inevitable unemployment that occurs when the economy, after reaching its peak, begins its slide into recession? Can we also learn how to engineer an attractive rate of economic growth?

MEASURING THE NATIONAL ECONOMY

Gross domestic product (GDP)

Total value of all final goods and services, measured in current market prices, produced in the economy during a year.

Let's look into these questions. Where do we begin? Perhaps the first thing we ought to do is define precisely what we mean by the economy's output and compare the different ways we go about measuring it.

The definition is simple enough: The economy's output, or **gross domestic product (GDP),** is the *total value, measured in current market prices, of all final goods and services produced in the economy during a given year.*

Let's analyze this definition phrase by phrase. Consider first "final goods and services." This refers to everything produced—from acorn squash to Ziploc® bags—that is not itself used to produce other goods. For example, if we produce and eat an acorn squash, it's a final good and counted in GDP. But if we use the acorn squash to make an acorn squash pie, then it's the pie that's counted in GDP, not the acorn squash. After all, we don't want to count the acorn squash twice! The pie is the *final* good, not the acorn squash.

What about "during a given year"? This phrase refers to a specific calendar year. An acorn squash pie baked on December 31, 1995, is counted as part of 1995 GDP. An acorn squash pie produced the next day is counted as part of 1996 GDP. If more pies, along with other goods and services, are produced in 1996 than were produced in 1995, the rate of GDP growth in 1996 is greater than zero.

What about "measured in current market prices"? This phrase refers to the pie's price in the year it was made. If your grandmother tells you that when she was a young lass, acorn squash pies sold for $0.25, it doesn't mean that an acorn squash pie baked in 1995 and priced at $7 adds only $0.25 to 1995 GDP! It's the $7—the current market price—that counts.

What about "produced in the economy"? That's the *domestic* part of gross domestic product. It makes no difference who produces the pie—a U.S.-owned company in Philadelphia or a Canadian-owned company in Davenport, Iowa—it's counted as part of the GDP as long as it is produced domestically, that is, produced in the United States. On the other hand, a pie made by a U.S-owned company in Halifax, Nova Scotia, is not counted as part of U.S. gross domestic product. It's counted in Canada's gross domestic product.

Suppose the 1992 GDP in the United States adds up to $6,000 billion, twice the $3,000 billion GDP that was produced in 1981. Does this doubling of GDP in a little over a decade indicate that we really doubled our production of goods and services?

GDP can increase due either to an increase in prices, an increase in output, or a combination of both.

Not necessarily. Over time, prices have drifted upward. That is, it may have been the *prices* of pies and other goods and services, not necessarily the *number* of pies and other goods and services produced, that have increased. Since GDP for any year measures the value—in *current* market prices—of that year's production of final goods and services, price changes alone might have changed the size of GDP over time.

Consider this simple example. Imagine an economy where the only good produced is corn. If total production in 1985 were 100 bushels, and if the 1985 price of corn were $2 per bushel, then GDP in 1985 would be $200.

Now suppose, for some reason, the price of corn a decade later doubled to $4 per bushel, while production remained at 100 bushels. The 1995 GDP, measuring all final goods and services at 1995 market prices, would increase to $400. Even though *real* production in the economy remains unchanged—100 bushels is still 100 bushels—the economy's GDP doubled. Under these conditions, would it make any sense to describe the 1995 economy as being twice as large as the 1985 economy? Not really. After all, eating $4 corn is no more satisfying than eating $2 corn. And even though a $400 GDP is twice the $200 GDP, people are still eating only 100 bushels of corn.

Adjusting for Prices

If we want to use GDP as a reliable measure of how well an economy performs—in producing goods and services over time—we must devise some way of eliminating the effect of price changes. To compare GDP in different years, we want to remove the effect of inflation. Economists have created a number of price indexes to do just that! The indexes transform **nominal GDP**—GDP unadjusted for price changes—into **real GDP**—GDP adjusted for price changes. The consumer price index and the GDP deflator are the two indexes most used. How do they work?

Nominal GDP

GDP measured in terms of current market prices—that is, the price level at the time of measurement. (It is not adjusted for inflation.)

Real GDP

GDP adjusted for changes in the price level.

Consumer price index

A measure comparing the prices of consumer goods and services that a household typically purchases to the prices of those goods and services purchased in a base year.

THE CONSUMER PRICE INDEX (CPI)

Let's start with the **consumer price index.** Pick a year—any year will do—as a point of reference or **base year.** Let's pick 1987. Suppose in 1987 we shopped for a basket of goods and services that represented what a typical consumer in an urban household buys. The items we put in the basket probably wouldn't include caviar or yachts but would include clothing, food, fuel, and a variety of household goods and services, such as kitchen appliances, transportation, and health care. Suppose that when we took that basket to the cash register, it cost $350. Using 1987 as our base year, the $350 converts to a price level index of 100, $P = 100$.

ADDED PERSPECTIVE

Prices Down the Years

The pound sterling, whose independence some British politicians are hell-bent on preserving, does not have a proud record as a store of value or unit of account. Retail-price indices show that it would take 40 of today's pounds to equal one of 1900s, 30 to equal one of 1930s, and 10 to equal one of 1960s. Such inflation masks the way that the real prices of different, familiar things have changed over time.

For instance, there is currently much moaning in Britain about the price of railway tickets. Yet our table of contemporary and adjusted prices shows how a return trip to Scotland today costs little more than a third, in real terms, of what it did in 1960. By applying the British retail-price index to contemporary prices, the table shows which of an eclectic choice of buys have become more or less expensive since 1900.

Some general points emerge:

- Where technology has greatly improved the supply of something that remains essentially unchanged, such as a telephone call or a flight to Nairobi, the falls in price are eye-opening.
- Where technology changes the product almost as much as the means of making it, real prices tend to remain stable. The Ford car or the sophisticated camera are examples: The increasing cleverness of the product offsets the cleverness of its production.
- Things involving much unautomatable labor—like a theatre ticket, a hotel room, or a three-course dinner—have tended to rise in real terms over the years.
- Prosperity boosts the price of "positional goods" disproportionately. These are goods which derive part of their value from their exclusivity. Note the different shifts in the prices of expensive and cheap opera or theatre tickets, or the rocketing price of a Dunhill pipe. The price of a Monet is an extreme example of the same phenomenon.
- Quite often the prices of government services in 1900 and 1990 are similar, after an intervening dip in the middle years of this century. Examples are postage stamps, university tuition, and underground tickets. A golden age of subsidy showing through here?
- The price of *The Times* shows the same sort of constancy as that of milk or a pound of potatoes. *The Economist* was either a bargain during the 1960s, or has become a positional good of late.
- The price of gold is fickle. The price of coal has gone mad.

Prices in Britain since 1900
Actual and (in bold) revalued to 1990 prices, £

	1900	1930	1960	1990
Railway fare London to Glasgow 2nd class, return	1.66 **66.40**	5.00 **156.25**	8.40 **84.00**	59.00 **59.00**
Atlantic crossing, by ship (to New York) cheapest Cunard ticket available	12.33(a) **674.00**	16.00(b) **516.80**	67.00 **670.00**	970.00 **970.00**
Atlantic crossing, by air London to New York (return) cheapest ticket available	n/a	n/a	154.35 **1,543.50**	323.00 **323.00**
London to Nairobi by air (return) cheapest ticket available	n/a	178.20 **5,562.50**	199.30 **1,993.00**	642.00 **642.00**
Bottle of whisky including tax	.18(c) **6.74**	.71(d) **20.31**	1.95(e) **19.31**	8.80 **8.80**
Car Ford, cheapest model	225(f) **10,238**	170 **5,313**	494 **4,940**	6,180 **6,180**
Monet painting of Waterloo Bridge, "Effet de soleil" (oil on canvas, 1903)	793(g) **34,496**	1,744(h) **67,144**	20,000 **200,000**	4,000,000 **4,000,000**
English dinner at The Savoy Soup, main course, pudding, coffee	.38(i) **15.20**	.78 **24.38**	2.38 **23.80**	28.75 **28.75**
Top of the range camera Sanderson, Leica, Nikon	20.00 **800.00**	18.60 **581.25**	145.00 **1,450**	1,200 **1,200**
Telephone call, 3 minutes London to Glasgow	.25(j) **8.93**	.33 **10.31**	.13 **1.30**	.41 **.41**

Prices in Britain since 1900 **Actual and (in bold) revalued to 1990 prices, £**	**1900**	**1930**	**1960**	**1990**
Telephone call, 3 minutes	n/a	15.00	3.00	2.33
London to New York		**468.75**	**30.00**	**2.33**
Opera ticket	.13	.33	.18	3.00
at Covent Garden, least expensive	**5.20**	**10.31**	**1.80**	**3.00**
Opera ticket	1.50	1.40	2.10	101.00
at Covent Garden, most expensive	**60.00**	**43.75**	**21.00**	**101.00**
Household coal,	1.18	1.24	4.22	120.66
per short ton	**47.20**	**38.75**	**42.20**	**120.66**
The Economist	.03	.05	.08	1.60
	1.20	**1.56**	**.75**	**1.60**
Theatre ticket	.08(k)	.08(l)	.30	7.50
at Theatre Royal, least expensive	**1.86**	**2.58**	**3.00**	**7.50**
Theatre ticket	.60(k)	.75(l)	1.50	25.00
at Theatre Royal, most expensive	**13.98**	**24.23**	**15.00**	**25.00**
Gold,	4.24	4.25	12.56	209.16(m)
per oz	**169.60**	**132.81**	**125.60**	**209.16**
Hotel room, single	n/a	1.50	6.00	189.00
at Hyde Park Hotel		**46.88**	**60.00**	**189.00**
Undergraduate fee for one year	48.88	36.75	70.10	1,675.00
at King's College, London University	**1,955.20**	**1,148.44**	**701.00**	**1,675.00**
Most expensive Jaguar,	n/a	310(h)	2,197	43,200
two-seater		**11,935**	**21,970**	**43,200**
Pair of men's handmade shoes	.84(n)	1.99	4.98(o)	125.00
	30.00	**62.19**	**72.21**	**125.00**
Standard Dunhill pipe	.38(p)	1.25	8.38	108.00
	14.63	**39.13**	**83.80**	**108.00**
Men's suit	n/a	4.20(g)	30.00	269.00
Daks 2-piece		**99.62**	**300.00**	**269.00**
Taxi ride	.03	.11	.11	1.60
one mile	**1.20**	**1.25**	**1.13**	**1.60**
Lighter,	1.75(r)	2.25	7.25	185.00
gold-plated	**41.66**	**70.31**	**72.50**	**185.00**
Potatoes	.02	.02	.08	.91
per 7 lbs.	**.71**	**.77**	**.80**	**.91**
Actual and (in bold) revalued to 1990 prices, pence				
Bread, unsliced loaf	0.5	0.7	2.4	42
per 400g	**18**	**27**	**24**	**42**
Milk	0.7	1.2	3.3	30
per pint	**26**	**38**	**33**	**30**
Postage stamp	.42	.42	1.25	22
London to Scotland	**17**	**13**	**12.5**	**22**
Postage stamp	.01	.63	1.25	37
London to America	**.40**	**19.5**	**12.5**	**37**
The Times	0.83(n)	0.83	3.3	35
	33	**25.9**	**33**	**35**
Underground ticket	0.83	0.63	2.08	.70
Victoria to South Kensington	**33**	**20**	**20.8**	**70**
Mars bar	n/a	.80	2.5	21
		31	**25**	**21**

Source: *The Economist*, December 22, 1990, p. 116.

Base year

The reference year with which prices in other years are compared in a price index.

Price level

A measure of prices in one year expressed in relation to prices of a base year.

Now suppose in the following year, 1988, we purchase the same basket of consumer items and their cost again sums to \$350. Some prices may have risen, but just enough to offset those that declined. The 1988 consumer price index, then, is $P = 100$.

An unchanging **price level** is a rarity. Let's suppose, instead, that the basket purchased in 1988 adds up to \$385. That is, the items in the basket remain unchanged, but the total cost of the items increased by \$35. The 1988 CPI, measured against the 1987 base year of 100, is now 110 ($P = \$385/\$350 \times 100$). What does a 1988 $P = 110$ indicate? It shows that from 1987 to 1988, the cost of the goods and services that consumers typically buy increased by 10 percent.

The CPI for any year is constructed by calculating the ratio between the cost of the basket for that year and its cost in the base year. We can shop for the same basket in 1995, calculate its cost and draw the comparison to the 1987 cost to derive the 1995 CPI. Or we can go back to 1952, calculate the basket's cost in 1952 prices, then compare it to the 1987 cost to derive the 1952 CPI.

The usefulness of such comparisons, however, diminishes the more distant a year is from the base year. Why? First, new goods and services appear on the market every year. Over time, the consumer basket of a base year becomes increasingly less representative of the things consumers buy. For example, if we used a 1952 base year, we could not have included personal computers, CDs, or VCRs that are typical consumer purchases today. Second, the quality of the items in the basket changes as well. The automobile in a 1952 basket is not the same as the automobile we drive today. Power steering, power brakes, seat belts, radial tires, and air bags make price comparisons between the two less meaningful. Third, the importance of specific items in the basket changes over time. Food purchases may have accounted for 40 percent of the consumer basket in 1952 but only 25 percent in 1995. If food prices increase more rapidly than other prices in 1995 and if we still count their importance at 40 percent of the basket, then the influence of food prices in 1995 is exaggerated.

That is why the Bureau of Labor Statistics (BLS) of the U.S. Department of Labor, which is charged with the task of composing the CPI, periodically updates the base year. When it does so, it also revises the specific items and their importance in the consumer basket.

THE GDP DEFLATOR

GDP deflator

A measure comparing the prices of all goods and services produced in the economy during a given year to the prices of those goods and services purchased in a base year.

The CPI measures only prices of consumer items. There are other price indexes that include different sets of items. For example, price indexes are constructed for farm goods, producer goods, crude materials, services, capital equipment, and export goods.

The most inclusive of all price indexes is the **GDP deflator.** It contains not only the prices of consumer goods and services, but prices of producer goods, investment goods, exports and imports, as well as goods and services purchased by government. It is the price index generally used to differentiate nominal GDP and real GDP.

From Nominal to Real GDP

The GDP deflator converts nominal GDP, measured in current prices for any year, to real GDP, which is adjusted for price changes. Economists sometimes refer to real GDP as GDP expressed in constant dollars.

TABLE 1 Converting Nominal GDP into Real GDP, 1983–93 ($ billions, 1987 = 100)

	Nominal GDP	GDP Deflator	Real GDP
1983	$3,405.0	87.2	$3,906.6
1984	3,777.2	91.0	4,148.5
1985	4,038.7	94.4	4,279.8
1986	4,268.6	96.9	4,404.5
1987	4,540.0	100.0	4,540.0
1988	4,900.4	103.9	4,716.5
1989	5,250.8	108.5	4,838.0
1990	5,546.1	113.3	4,897.3
1991	5,722.9	117.6	4,861.4
1992	6,038.5	121.9	4,986.3
1993	6,343.4	123.5	5,134.5

Source: *Economic Report of the President,* 1994 (Washington, D.C.: U.S. Government Printing Office, 1994), pp. 268–272

The conversion formula is

$$\text{Real GDP} = \frac{\text{nominal GDP} \times 100}{\text{GDP deflator}}$$

Let's see how it works. Table 1 traces the conversion of nominal GDP into real GDP for the period 1983–93.

Using 1987 as the base year, 1987 nominal and real GDP are identical. But look at 1988. Nominal GDP increased from $4,540 billion in 1987 to $4,900.4 billion in 1988, or by $360.4 billion. Not all of that $360.4 billion represented an increase in real production of goods and services. Part of it simply reflected the higher prices in 1988. But how much?

In 1988, the GDP deflator was 103.9 (rounding from 103.85). The formula to convert 1988 nominal GDP to real GDP—measuring 1988 GDP in 1987 prices—is

$$\frac{\$4{,}900.4 \times 100}{103.9} = \$4{,}716.5$$

We can now calculate how much of that $360.4 billion increase in 1988 GDP represented more real goods and services and how much simply reflected an increase in prices. The increase in real GDP was $4,900.4 – $4,716.5, or $183.9 billion. The remaining $176.5 billion increase was simply the result of higher prices.

If you were describing the 1987–88 change in GDP to a friend, which number would you use? Would you say that GDP increased from $4,540.0 billion to $4,900.4 billion, or would you choose to compare the $4,540 billion to $4,716.5 billion? Both are honest-to-goodness changes in GDP. They just represent different evaluations. One set includes changes in both production and prices, the other includes just changes in production. If what you mean to convey to your friend is how much better off people were in 1988 than in 1987, wouldn't changes in real GDP be the appropriate one to use?

Look at Table 1. Again, differences between nominal and real GDP growth rates are rather striking. If we calculate the economy's 1983–93 performance in nominal GDP, the economy's annual growth rate was 6.5 percent. But if the calculation is made for real GDP, the growth rate was 2.8 percent. Which GDP we choose to express, then, makes a difference.

DERIVING EQUILIBRIUM GDP IN THE AGGREGATE DEMAND AND SUPPLY MODEL

Understanding the difference between nominal and real GDP for 1993 still doesn't tell us why 1993 GDP ended up being what it was. Why was 1993 nominal GDP $6,343.3 billion? Why not $4,000 billion or $7,000 billion? What determines its size? Why did nominal GDP increase from $6,038.5 billion in 1992 to $6,343.3 billion in 1993? And why did the GDP deflator increase from 120.9 to 123.5?

Several competing theories explain how the equilibrium levels of GDP are derived. We will examine some in detail in later chapters. But for now, we focus on one—the aggregate demand and aggregate supply model—to explain how GDP is determined.

The aggregate demand and aggregate supply model is a good place to start. It bears some similarity to the demand and supply model we used to explain equilibrium price and quantity of goods and services. In the case of fish, we saw how the downward-sloping demand curve for fish intersected the upward-sloping supply curve of fish to determine its price and quantity. In what appears to be an analogy, the downward-sloping aggregate demand curve intersects the upward-sloping aggregate supply curve to determine the economy's price level and GDP.

But there the similarity ends. The factors that cause the demand curves in both models to slope downward are quite different. The factors explaining why the supply curves in both models are upward-sloping are different as well.

The demand curve for fish slopes downward because a decrease in the price of fish is assumed to occur while all other prices remain unchanged. Fish, then, becomes *relatively* cheaper. As a result, people increase the quantity demanded of fish.

This cause-and-effect analysis cannot explain why the aggregate demand curve slopes downward. After all, the price level reflects all prices, so when it falls, *all* prices are assumed to fall. As a result, the relative prices of fish and everything else remain unchanged. If people demand more of everything, it cannot be because everything becomes relatively cheaper.

Aggregate supply

The total quantity of goods and services that firms in the economy are willing to supply at varying price levels.

Aggregate demand

The total quantity of goods and services demanded by households, firms, foreigners, and government at varying price levels.

What are the forces governing the aggregate demand and supply model? **Aggregate supply** is the total supply of goods and services that all firms in the national economy are willing to offer at varying price levels. **Aggregate demand** is the total quantity demanded of these goods and services by households, firms, foreigners, and government at those varying price levels.

Panel *a* in Figure 2 shows the relationship between aggregate supply and the price level. Panel *b* in Figure 2 shows the relationship between aggregate demand and the price level.

FIGURE 2 **Aggregate Supply and Aggregate Demand**

The aggregate supply curve in panel *a* shows the aggregate quantity of goods and services that firms are willing to supply at varying price levels. For levels of real GDP within the range \$0 to \$4 trillion, the price level remains unchanged at 100. Beyond \$4 trillion, increases in real GDP are accompanied by rising price levels. At real GDP = \$5 trillion, *P* = 120. Full employment real GDP is \$5.5 trillion. The aggregate supply curve becomes vertical at that point. An increase in the price level beyond *P* = 130 is not accompanied by increases in real GDP.

The downward-sloping aggregate demand curve in panel *b* shows the aggregate quantity demanded at varying price levels. For example, an increase in the price level from *P* = 100 to *P* = 120 is accompanied by a decrease in the aggregate quantity demanded, from \$6 trillion to \$4.5 trillion.

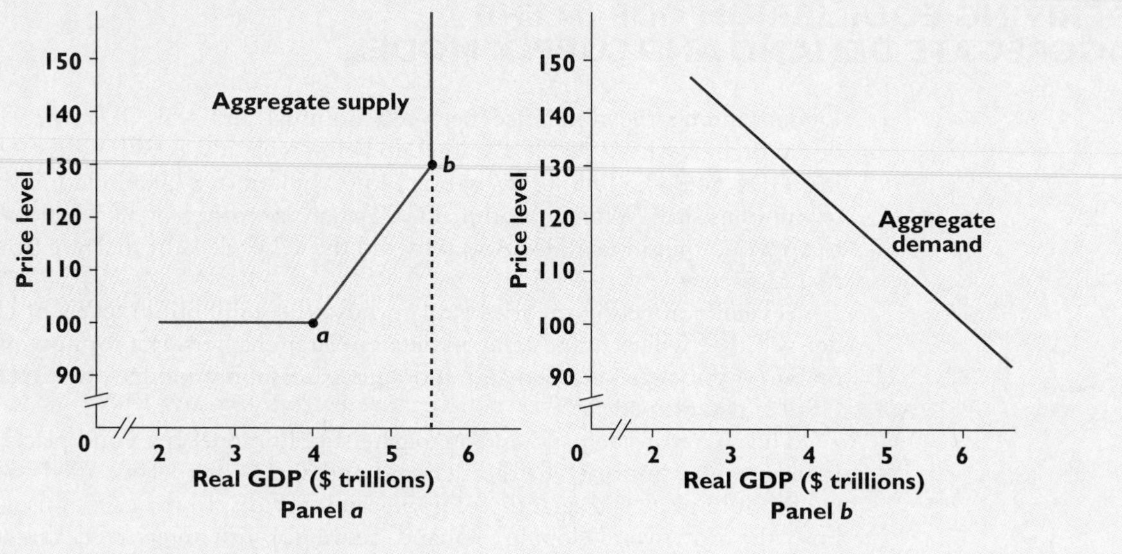

Explaining Aggregate Supply

Look at the economy's aggregate supply curve in panel *a*. Three distinct segments are apparent. The horizontal segment shows that real GDP can increase without affecting the economy's price level. The increase along the curve toward point *a* exerts no pressure on prices because, within that range of real GDP, there are quantities of unemployed resources to draw upon. That is, unemployed labor, unused land, and idle factories and machinery can all be put to work.

The upward-sloping segment of the supply curve depicts a positive relationship between real GDP and the price level. Within this range of real GDP, firms that want to increase production find it more and more difficult to locate unused resources. And the scarcer the resource, the higher its price.

The vertical segment marks the full employment level of real GDP. All resources are fully employed so that real GDP cannot increase. Any apparent increase in GDP beyond point *b* on the aggregate supply curve, then, must be nominal and completely due to price increases. Let's look at aggregate supply in a little more detail.

THE HORIZONTAL SEGMENT

Why the horizontal segment? For any level of GDP in this range—that is, far below full employment—there are ready supplies of unused resources. All these idle resources can be put to work before there is any upward pressure on prices. For example, the economy can increase aggregate supply—the production of goods and services—say, from \$3 trillion to \$4 trillion GDP, without prices going up. Producers can hire more workers without having to raise the wage rate. They can use more capital without having to pay higher interest rates because unused capital in the form of unused plant and machinery is already available. As you see in panel *a*, any increase in real GDP within the range \$0 to \$4 trillion can occur with the price level remaining unchanged at $P = 100$.

THE UPWARD-SLOPING SEGMENT

The aggregrate supply curve's three segments correspond to different levels of GDP—with high levels of unemployment in the flat segment and full employment in the vertical segment. Aggregate demand slopes down as a function of the price level, since spending tends to increase as the price level decreases.

What about aggregate supply beyond \$4 trillion? It becomes upward-sloping. Increases in output are linked to increases in the price level. Why? Because unused resources become less available at higher levels of real GDP. Faced with the difficulty of finding ready resources, firms resort to offering higher prices for them. For example, to get more labor, firms are willing to pay higher wages. These higher wages increase the cost of production, which in turn raises the prices of goods produced. Beyond \$4 trillion GDP, the price level begins to rise above $P = 100$. The higher the level of GDP—say, \$4.5 trillion—the greater is the economy's absorption of the dwindling unused resources and the more intense is the upward pressure on the price level. At GDP = \$5 trillion, $P = 120$.

The upward-sloping relationship between aggregate supply and the price level can be explained in another way. Instead of dwindling unused resources pushing up prices, increasing prices can pull up resource costs. Suppose the price level increases from $P = 120$ to $P = 130$. As the spread between prices and costs widens, producers earn higher profits. Higher profits attract new firms into production and stimulate existing firms to produce more. The higher production levels tap into unused resource availability, driving resource costs upward.

THE VERTICAL SEGMENT

When resources are fully employed, aggregate supply reaches an impassable limit. Full employment is shown in panel *a* of Figure 2 at \$5.5 trillion GDP. At that level of real GDP, producers may try to hire more workers, but how can they? They can bid away *already* employed workers from each other by offering higher wage rates. But what one producer gains in output by hiring a worker away from another, the other loses. In the end, competition among producers for already employed resources can succeed only in raising the economy's price level. Its aggregate supply remains unchanged. In our example, real GDP stays constant at \$5.5 trillion.

Explaining Aggregate Demand

The aggregate demand curve shown in panel *b* is downward-sloping. For example, as the price level increases from $P = 100$ to $P = 120$, aggregate demand of households, firms, foreigners, and government falls from \$6 trillion to \$4.5 trillion. Why? Because increases in the price level affect people's real wealth, their lending and borrowing activity, and the nation's trade with other nations in such a way that the demand for goods and services produced in the economy declines.

REAL WEALTH EFFECT

Consider the effect of a price level increase on the value of people's wealth, and the effect of changes in the value of wealth on aggregate demand. Suppose your own wealth consisted of $100,000 held in the form of cash, bank deposits, and government bonds. You know that, if needed, these holdings can be cashed in, allowing you to buy $100,000 of real goods and services. In fact, that is how you view your wealth.

But suppose while you are holding these financial assets, the economy's price level increases. Videotape recorders that formerly cost $400 now cost $480. Automobiles that formerly cost $16,000 now cost $18,500. With prices rising everywhere, what happens to the real worth of your $100,000? It can no longer buy the same quantity of real goods and services, can it?

That is, the *real* value of your $100,000 wealth decreases. You feel yourself becoming less wealthy. And you're not mistaken! To replenish the value of your real wealth, you would save more and consume less. Everybody reacts the same way. In other words, when the price level increases, the quantity demanded by most people for goods and services in the economy falls.

INTEREST RATE EFFECT

When prices rise, the purchasing power of the dollar falls. People find that they need more money just to buy the same quantity of goods and services. How do they acquire that additional money? Many borrow, leaving unpaid monthly credit card balances. This increased demand for borrowed money raises the cost of borrowing. We refer to the cost of borrowing as the interest rate.

Consider the effect of the higher interest rate on aggregate demand. Very few people buy homes with cash. Typically, high-priced items like homes and automobiles are purchased with borrowed money. The higher the interest rate, the higher is the real price of the home or automobile.

Suppose a rise in the price level causes mortgage rates to increase from 10 percent to 15 percent per year. Monthly payments on a home with a $100,000 mortgage, carrying a 20-year loan at 10 percent, are $965.03. At 15 percent, these monthly payments jump to $1,316.79. Wouldn't you suppose that difference would cut many prospective home buyers out of the market?

Students, too, feel the pinch of higher interest rates. Wouldn't the number of students attending college be affected by higher interest rates on student loans? Even the quantities demanded of restaurant lunches, concert tickets, and designer jeans are linked to the interest rate. Many people pay for these items with Visa, MasterCard, or Discover cards. These plastic cards allow people to build up interest-carrying debt. If interest rates on these cards rise, people tend to cut back on these purchases, depressing the aggregate quantity of goods and services demanded.

Firms' demands for investment goods are sensitive to the interest rate as well. A firm contemplating an investment in new machinery may calculate making 15 percent profit on the investment. If the interest rate is 10 percent, the 5 percent spread between profit and the interest rate may be sufficient inducement to buy the new machinery. If the interest rate rises to 15 percent, the firm's demand for the new machinery disappears along with the spread, contributing to the decrease in quantity demanded.

INTERNATIONAL TRADE EFFECT

Suppose the price level in the United States rises while price levels elsewhere in the world remain unchanged. Wouldn't we tend to buy more foreign goods and services and reduce the demands for our own goods? After all, when prices for domestically produced goods such as wines, lumber, and automobiles increase while other nations' prices remain unchanged, wouldn't French wines, Canadian lumber, and Japanese automobiles become more attractive? Our demand for imports would rise, our demand for domestic goods would fall.

At the same time, the French, Canadians, and Japanese would find our now higher-priced exports less attractive. Many wouldn't buy them. The quantity demanded of our goods and services, then, would fall.

Shifts in the Aggregate Demand and Aggregate Supply Curves

Let's again consider the analogy between the demand and supply model used to explain equilibrium price and quantity of fish that we developed in Chapter 3 and the model of aggregate demand and aggregate supply that we are using to explain equilibrium GDP and price level. In Chapter 3, we distinguished between *changes in quantity demanded* (or *quantity supplied*) of fish—that is, changes along the demand (or supply) curve—and *changes in demand* (or *supply*) of fish—that is, shifts in the demand (or supply) curve.

Let's now draw that same distinction for changes in the aggregate quantity demanded (or supplied) and shifts in the aggregate demand (or aggregate supply) curve.

SHIFTS IN THE AGGREGATE DEMAND CURVE

The aggregate demand curve relates the quantity of goods and services demanded in the economy to varying price levels. A change in the quantity of goods and services demanded at a particular price level, however, is represented by a shift in the curve itself. Figure 3, panel *a*, maps two shifts in aggregate demand. What could cause such shifts to occur?

Aggregate demand shifts to the right when spending increases and shifts to the left when spending decreases. Aggregate supply increases or shifts to the right as resource availability increases. Any factor that reduces resource availability causes the aggregate supply curve to shift to the left, indicating a decrease.

Suppose the government decides to overhaul our economy's infrastructure. It programs major construction on highways, bridges, railroad lines, airports, research hospitals, public housing, and other facilities that are in the public domain. These programs represent new investment demands that shift the aggregate demand curve to the right, from *AD* to *AD*′.

Or consider what would happen to aggregate demand when incomes abroad increase. Canadians, with higher incomes, buy more U.S. imports, shifting our *AD* curve to the right. If we decide to consume more goods and services ourselves—even when prices remain unchanged—aggregate demand increases.

What would cause a change in our consumption behavior? A tax cut could do it or perhaps changes in our expectations of future income. After all, if we expect to have more money in the future, we may feel more comfortable about buying more today by borrowing or saving less.

Just reverse the direction of change in these factors and the aggregate demand curve shifts to the left, from *AD* to *AD*″. For example, a cut in government spending, a decrease in income abroad, an increase in taxes, or an expectation that future income will fall would all tend to lower aggregate quantity demanded at every price level.

FIGURE 3 **Shifts in Aggregate Demand and Aggregate Supply**
The aggregate demand curve in panel *a* shifts with changes in government spending, foreign incomes, and consumer or firms' expectations about the future. The aggregate demand curve increases—shifts to the right—when incomes, expectations, and government spending rise. It decreases—shifts to the left—when they fall.

The aggregate supply curve in panel *b* shifts with changes in the availability of resources. More resources shift the aggregate supply curve to the right.

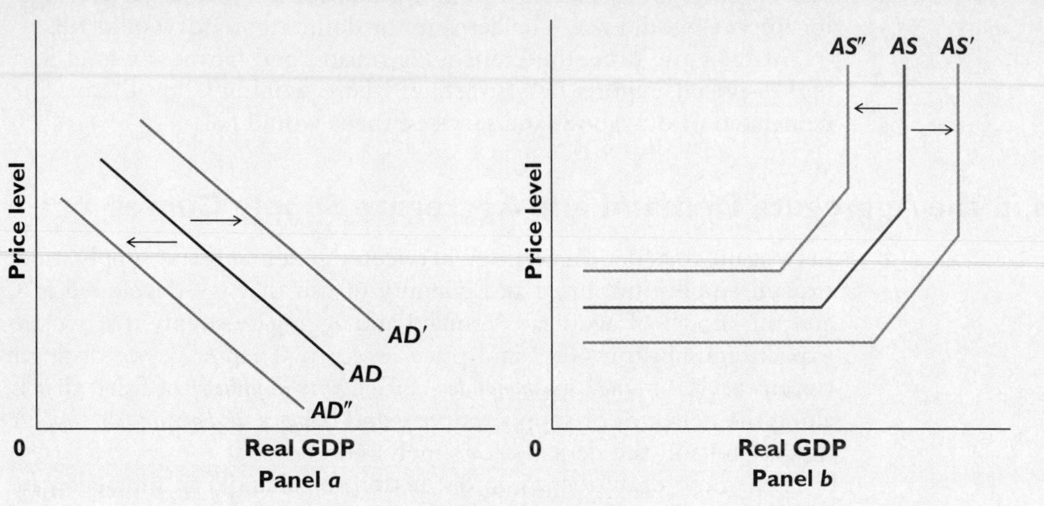

SHIFTS IN THE AGGREGATE SUPPLY CURVE

One of the principal factors accounting for a shift in the aggregate supply curve from *AS* to *AS′* in panel *b* is an increase in resource availability. Simply put: More workers, more land, more capital, and more entrepreneurial energies—no matter what the price level—result in greater aggregate supply. The prices of these resources affect aggregate supply as well. If wage rates or interest rates or rents decrease while the economy's price level remains unchanged, profit margins will expand, making producers more willing to supply greater quantities of goods and services.

Anything that reduces resource availability or increases the prices of resources would, of course, have the opposite effect, that is, would shift the aggregate supply curve from *AS* to *AS″*.

MACROECONOMIC EQUILIBRIUM

Let's bring both aggregate demand and aggregate supply together in a national market for goods and services. This is done in Figure 4.

Does it look familiar? As with all markets, Figure 4 expresses a relationship between price and quantity. The vertical axis measures the economy's price level. The horizontal axis measures real GDP.

We can now explain—at least according to the aggregate demand and aggregate supply model—why 1993 real GDP was $5,134.5 billion. The quantity of aggregate demand equaled the quantity of aggregate supply at $5,134.5 bil-

FIGURE 4
Achieving Macroeconomic Equilibrium
Macroequilibrium is achieved when aggregate supply, *AS*, and aggregate demand *AD*, intersect at real GDP = $5,134.5 billion and *P* = 123.5. At higher price levels, such as *P* = 130, excess aggregate quantity supplied would emerge, depressing the price level. At lower price levels, excess aggregate quantity demanded would emerge, forcing the price level to increase.

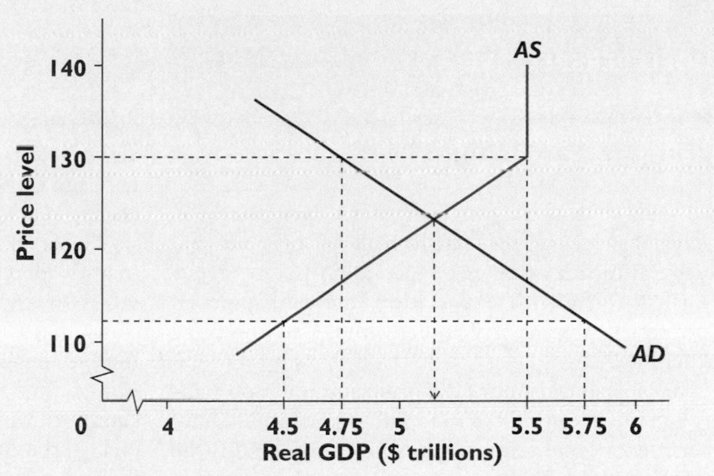

Macroequilibrium

The level of real GDP and the price level that equate the aggregate quantity demanded and the aggregate quantity supplied.

lion real GDP. The equilibrium price level was *P* = 123.5. *This* **macroequilibrium** *position for 1993 persisted only as long as the aggregate demand and aggregate supply curves remained unchanged.*

To illustrate why the economy gravitates towards an equilibrium of $5,134.5 billion real GNP and *P* = 123.5, let's suppose the economy were not in equilibrium. Instead, suppose the price level were *P* = 130. What happens? With that price level, consumers, firms, government, and foreigners demand fewer goods and services. We see in Figure 4 that at *P* = 130, the aggregate quantity demanded falls to $4,750 billion.

What about aggregate supply? How would firms react to the higher price level? At *P* = 130, they are willing to produce more GDP. The aggregate quantity of GDP that firms are willing to supply increases to $5,500 billion.

A problem now emerges. At *P* = 130, the aggregate quantity demanded is insufficient to absorb the aggregate quantity supplied, generating an excess aggregate supply of $5,500 − $4,750 = $750 billion GDP. Competition among suppliers will force overall prices downward. That is, given the aggregate demand and aggregate supply curves in Figure 4, the economy is unable to sustain a price level of 130.

Now suppose the price level is 112. What happens? The aggregate quantity demanded is $5,750 billion and the aggregate quantity of GDP that firms are willing to supply is $4,500 billion. Competition among the demanders—consumers, firms, government, and foreigners—now forces the price level upward.

Where do the price level and GDP come to rest? The aggregate quantity demanded and aggregate quantity supplied equate at $5,134.5 billion GDP and P = 123.5. Macroequilibrium is achieved.

EQUILIBRIUM, INFLATION, AND UNEMPLOYMENT

Macroeconomists use this simple aggregate demand and supply model of GDP and price level to show how an economy can move from stable to rising price levels, and from unemployment to full employment. For example, it gives us

ADDED PERSPECTIVE

"If Winter Comes, Can Spring Be Far Behind?"

The 18th century English poet Percy Bysshe Shelly, finding beauty in the harsh realities of cold and stormy autumns and winters, ends his poem *Ode to the West Wind* with expectation and perhaps even promise: "Oh wind, if Winter comes, Can Spring be far behind?"

How harsh must our economic autumns and winters be? Do economists find anything beautiful about a harsh economic winter? And how far behind is the promising spring?

Recent swings in the business cycle are shown in the accompanying table. Since the Great Depression of the 1930s, the U.S. economy experienced ten recessions, some steeper than others, but all marked by hard times, with high rates of unemployment and declining real GDP.

Those are a lot of months of hard times. In more than 20 percent of our economic life, we find ourselves struggling through the downturns and recession phases of a business cycle. The brighter side of the picture is that for almost 80 percent of our economic life, we bask in the economic springs and summers of recovery and prosperity. If we can't change the flow of these economic seasons, can we at least change their length? Or perhaps, modify the harshness of economic autumns and winters?

Recessions since 1945

Recession of	Duration (months)	Depth Decline in Real GDP (percent)	Peak Rate of Unemployment
1945	8		4.3
1948–49	11		7.9
1953–54	10	–3.0	6.1
1957–58	8	–.3.5	7.5
1960–61	10	–1.0	7.1
1969–70	11	–1.1	6.1
1973–75	16	–4.3	9.0
1980	6	–3.4	7.6
1981–82	16	–2.6	10.8
1990–92	30		7.3

Source: NBER and the Federal Reserve Bank of Boston.

some understanding of the economic forces that were at work during the depression of the 1930s, during the war-related recovery of the 1940s, during the Vietnam-induced inflation of the 1960s, during the OPEC-induced inflation of the 1970s and early 1980s, and during the recession and economic stagnation of the early 1990s.

The Depression of the 1930s

The 1930s produced one of the poorest GDP performance records in our economic history. For most of the decade, real GDP was either falling or recovering slightly, only to fall once again. It fell by 30 percent in the first four years of the decade, recovered to its 1929 level by 1937, but fell again in 1939. Nobody had any reason to feel optimistic about the future. Unemployment was massive.

FIGURE 5 **Aggregate Demand and Aggregate Supply during the Depression and War Period**

The 1930s depression GDP equilibrium occurred at the intersection of the aggregate demand curve, *AD*, and the aggregate supply curve, *AS*, in panel *a*. The demand created by the war in Europe shifted the aggregate demand curve from *AD* to *AD'*, creating a new macroequilibrium at a higher level of GDP. The extension of the war to the Pacific shifted the aggregate demand curve even further to the right, to *AD"*, creating a new macroequilibrium at a much higher price level.

The transfer of men and women out of civilian employment into the armed forces shifted the aggregate supply curve to the left, from *AS* to *AS'*, increasing further the pressure on the price level.

The dramatic increase in the price of crude oil during the 1970s and early 1980s pushed overall costs of production upward, which shifted the aggregate supply curve of panel *b* to the left. A new equilibrium was obtained at a lower level of real GDP and at a higher price level.

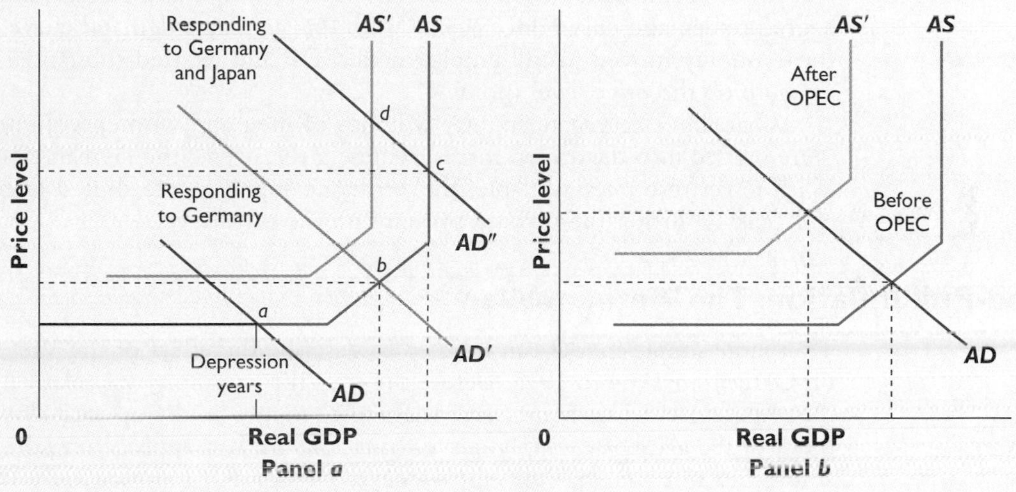

The Great Depression was marked by aggregate demand that was insufficient to achieve a full-employment GDP. The beginning of World War II caused the aggregate demand curve to shift to the right while aggregate supply shifted to the left. Both GDP and the price level increased.

It rose from 3.2 percent in 1929 to a peak of 25.2 percent in 1933. It fell to 14.3 percent by 1937, only to climb back to 19.1 percent in 1938. How would you have felt about our economic future on New Year's Day, 1939?

By December 1939, however, the fate of the world had changed. Germany invaded Poland in September, bringing Europe to war. Moving swiftly westward, German forces took Holland and Belgium, then overtook an ill-prepared France. Paris fell without a single shot fired.

The German war against England, however, was another matter. German warplanes, in unending waves, crossed the English channel during the cold winter of 1940 to strike at England's aircraft factories on its eastern coast. English cities, including London, absorbed almost daily bombings. England's Prime Minister, Winston Churchill, appealed to the United States for material support. We obliged with what he was later to describe as the most generous response any nation afforded another in recorded history. These events of 1939 and 1940 changed the pace and direction of our national economy significantly.

Figure 5, panel *b*, illustrates the impact on GDP of the 1930s depression and of our later wartime commitment.

Consider, first, the effects of a shift in aggregate demand on the economy's prewar position. The prewar depression GDP equilibrium is shown where the aggregate demand curve, *AD*, cuts the aggregate supply curve, *AS*, at point *a* along its horizontal range. With double-digit unemployment and substantial plant capacity remaining idle, real GDP could increase considerably without putting any pressure on the price level.

But the war in Europe changed all that. Our idle factories were put to work producing tanks, fighter planes, cannons, armored cars, aircraft carriers, battleships, munitions, and millions of uniforms. Army bases were built overnight, and entirely new military-related factories mushroomed to meet the demands of war. Government's war-related spending shifted the aggregate demand curve outward to the right, to *AD′*, creating a new GDP equilibrium at point *b* and a higher price level.

The Japanese attack on Pearl Harbor in December 1941 and the subsequent war in the Pacific added even more to the demand for war materials, shifting the aggregate demand curve once again. With the aggregate demand curve at *AD″*, the economy moved to full employment GDP and exerted substantial upward pressure on the price level (point *c*).

What about aggregate supply? Millions of men and women volunteered or were drafted into the armed forces, reducing the size of the civilian labor force. With fewer resources available, the aggregate supply curve shifted from *AS* to *AS′*, raising further the upward pressure on the price level.

Demand-Pull Inflation: The Vietnam War

That same simple model can be used to describe the effect of the Vietnam war on GDP from 1964 to 1975. Before the war, the economy was relatively vigorous. Aggregate demand intersected aggregate supply on the upward-sloping segment of the aggregate supply curve. In fact, GDP was approaching the impassable limits imposed by full employment, but for the moment only moderate pressure was being exerted on the price level.

But in just three years, 1965 to 1968, government spending on defense increased from \$100.1 billion to \$144.1 billion. The aggregate demand curve shifted to the right, pressing GDP to its limit and forcing the price level upward. In fact, the price level during the 1965–75 decade rose from 72.8 to 125.8 (1972 = 100). Economists refer to such price inflation as **demand-pull inflation** because the factor contributing most to the rising price level was the increased demand for military goods and the subsequent rightward shift of the aggregate demand curve. This shift *pulled* GDP to full employment and *pulled* the price level up along the vertical segment of the aggregate supply curve.

Demand-pull inflation

Inflation caused primarily by an increase in aggregate demand.

Cost-Push Inflation: The OPEC Legacy

The aggregate demand and aggregate supply model of panel *b*, Figure 5 may help explain the puzzling phenomenon of concurrent inflation and unemployment—economists call it **stagflation**—during the 1970s and 1980s. The model illustrates the inflation and unemployment effects generated by the oil-producing countries, particularly those associated with the Organization of Petroleum Exporting Countries (OPEC).

Stagflation

A period of stagnating real GDP, inflation, and relatively high levels of unemployment.

In October 1973, the price of Arabian Light Crude oil was \$2.10 per barrel. By November 1974, OPEC had cut oil production substantially and raised the price to \$10.46. By January 1979, the price had drifted upward to \$13.34. While the economy was still trying to adjust to this greater than fivefold price increase, a second major oil price shock hit us broadside. By April 1980, OPEC had raised the price to $28, and by January 1982 to $34.

The impact of these OPEC-designed oil price increases on the costs of producing almost *everything* in our economy—and in the rest of the world—shifted the aggregate supply curve from *AS* to *AS'*. As the model illustrates, GDP declined while the price level increased. The OPEC-induced inflation is described as **cost-push inflation** because the factor contributing most to the rising price level was the increase in cost of a basic good and the subsequent shift to the left of the aggregate supply curve.

Cost-push inflation

Inflation caused primarily by a decrease in aggregate supply.

Recession and Economic Stagnation of the 1990s

For the half-decade preceding the 1990–91 recession, the economy was performing about as well as it ever had in the past quarter century. A number of factors contributed to the relatively high rates of economic growth and low rates of inflation and unemployment. First, the 1986 tax reform fueled consumers' demands for goods and services. In addition, banks and other financial institutions accommodated consumers' tastes for more goods and services by providing ready credit. The financial system also provided the credit for large **leveraged buyouts** and extensive office building. The commercial real estate boom created many construction jobs. Expectations that the good times would continue added even more strength to an already strong aggregate demand.

Leveraged buyout

A primarily debt-financed purchase of all the stock or assets of a company.

But the economic storm clouds were gathering. After all, the tax reform that created tax breaks for many also created the largest government deficits in history. By the end of the 1980s, these deficits became a primary political issue. The government simply couldn't continue with business as usual. In an attempt to harness the deficits, the federal government reduced its revenue-sharing with state and local governments, who in turn were unwilling or unable to raise their own taxes to compensate for the lost revenues. Instead, they downsized their budgets by cutting their demands for goods and services. The end of the Soviet Union and the cold war triggered a cut in our demands for military goods and services. Many defense workers became unemployed in the early 1990s.

Consumers, too, felt the pressures to curb spending. The easy credit that banks made available to them led to exceptionally high levels of consumer debt, so that by the end of the 1980s these consumers had little choice but to change their consumption behavior. And just as expectations can reinforce the good times when times are good, so can they reinforce caution when the economy appears less buoyant.

But consumers weren't the only ones assuming debt in the 1980s. Many firms went into considerable debt by buying new assets and acquiring others through leveraged buyouts. If the economic growth of the 1980s had continued into the 1990s, the revenues these firms needed to service their debts would have been available. But the recession of 1990–91 and the economic sluggishness that followed cut sharply into their revenue flows, making it difficult—and in some cases impossible—for them to pay their debts. Many responded by trimming their work force.

The recession of the early 1990s can best be explained as resulting from a decrease in aggregate demand.

How do these events play out in the aggregate demand and aggregate supply model of Figure 5? The recession and economic stagnation of the early 1990s can be explained by focusing on aggregate demand. Assuming a given aggregate supply curve, the recession could be viewed as the consequence of an inward shift of aggregate demand—that is, from a period of full employment with mod-

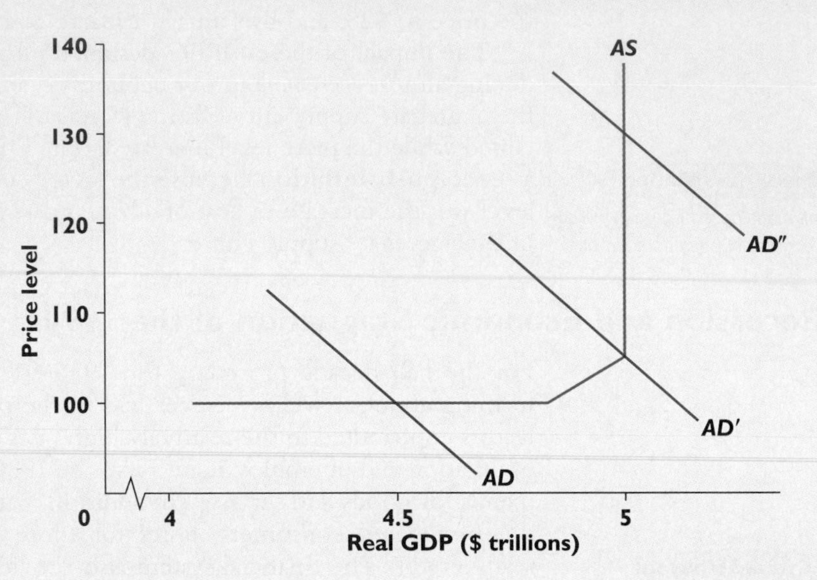

FIGURE 6
Obtaining Full-Employment GDP without Inflation
There is no reason to suppose that the aggregate demand curve will necessarily intersect the aggregate supply curve at a level of real GDP consistent with full employment and no inflation. If the aggregate demand curve is *AD*, unemployment results. On the other hand, if the aggregate demand curve were *AD*″, inflation results. The government can intervene—adding to or cutting its spending and taxes—to shift the aggregate demand to *AD*′, where full employment occurs with moderate inflation—that is, at *P* = 105.

erate inflation to one with lower levels of real GDP, higher levels of unemployment, and even more moderate inflation.

CAN WE AVOID UNEMPLOYMENT AND INFLATION?

Government policies can be developed to work against the problems of unemployment and inflation. Government can increase aggregate demand to combat unemployment and decrease aggregate demand to combat inflation.

If government had a wish list, it would certainly include an economy in equilibrium at full employment with no inflation. In fact, that GDP condition would appear on almost everyone's wish list, wouldn't it? But how realistic are wish lists? Is there anything government can do to make wishes come true? Look at Figure 6.

The aggregate supply curve, *AS*, creates three different GDP levels of equilibrium with the three different aggregate demand curves, *AD*, *AD*′, and *AD*″.

If aggregate demand in the Figure 6 economy were described by *AD*, then real GDP would come to rest at $4,500 billion, $500 billion below the economy's full-employment real GDP. The price level would be 100. If, on the other hand, aggregate demand were *AD*′, the level of equilibrium GDP would be at full employment at $5,000 billion. The price level would be 105. If aggregate demand were *AD*″, the level of equilibrium GDP, already at full employment, would stay at $5,000 billion, but the price level would rise to 130.

Now if government had a choice in the matter, it would no doubt wish for the aggregate demand curve, *AD*′. But wishing, as you know, doesn't always make a wish come true! Why suppose that because the *desired* aggregate demand curve is *AD*′, the independently derived demands for goods and services by households, firms, foreigners, and government will actually generate an aggregate demand of *AD*′? The unsettling fact is that there is no more reason to expect aggregate demand to be *AD*′ than *AD*, *AD*″, or any other aggregate demand curve that can be mapped in Figure 6.

Suppose, for example, that aggregate demand were *AD*. Must the economy, saddled with that level of aggregate demand, accept the consequences? Is there any way to move aggregate demand to *AD'*? That's where some economists believe the government should come into the picture. One way the government can shift aggregate demand to AD' is by increasing its own spending. And it isn't necessary to start a war to do this! *Any* increase in government spending will do the job. How about increased spending on the economy's infrastructure? Or health care? Or education? You can surely think of a few other ways too. The options are almost unlimited.

Other government policies can influence aggregate demand as well. Reducing income taxes, for example, puts more money in the hands of people who will then spend part of it on more goods and services. That spending shifts the aggregate demand curve to the right. If government cuts the corporate income tax, it leaves corporations with higher after-tax income, which may increase demands for investment goods. That, too, shifts the aggregate demand curve.

Can there be *too much* aggregate demand in the economy? If the aggregate demand curve generated by households, firms, foreigners, and government were *AD"* instead of *AD'*, it would push real GNP to full employment at $5,000 billion, but not without pushing the price level up to *P* = 130. In other words, the aggregate demand curve *AD"* creates inflation.

What could the government do under these conditions? The appropriate policy would be to reverse gears, to reduce government spending and increase taxes. Either strategy could shift the aggregate demand curve to the left, from *AD"* to *AD'*.

To many, these government actions seem very simple, almost mechanical. Add spending or reduce taxes to increase aggregate demand. Reduce government spending or increase taxes to cut aggregate demand. But the truth is that our real economy isn't nearly as manageable as the aggregate demand and aggregate supply model suggests. Figure 6 is about as simple an abstraction of the world we live in as economists can design. In the real world it is difficult enough just to identify full-employment real GDP, let alone create a government policy that puts aggregate demand right on the mark.

Why then bother with the model? Because it is still a useful first approximation of the world we live in. Understanding aggregate demand and aggregate supply gives us a useful handle in understanding the basic movements of the primary factors in our national economy. It allows us to see how problems of unemployment and inflation can emerge, and how the government might intervene to orchestrate change. At least it's a start!

CHAPTER REVIEW

1. The business cycle is the way the economy expands during a period of prosperity, which is often accompanied by inflation, and the way it contracts during a period of recession, which is accompanied by high levels of unemployment. The transition from a period of prosperity to a recession is called a downturn, while the transition back to prosperity is called a recovery.

2. Macroeconomic analysis is conducted at the level of the national economy. Macroeconomists attempt to explain and to predict changes in the business

cycle. They also try to explain what causes economic growth over time. Gross domestic product (GDP) is a variable that macroeconomists track closely to measure economic growth.

3. GDP is an accurate measure of the economy's productive potential only if prices stay constant. The CPI and the GDP deflator can be used to adjust GDP figures for changes in the price level.

4. Aggregate demand and aggregate supply can be measured in real terms. The price level can be measured with the GDP deflator. Aggregate demand and aggregate supply can then be plotted with respect to the price level.

5. Aggregate supply is flat at low levels of GDP, reflecting unemployed resources. The upward-sloping segment can be explained by the upward pressure exerted on prices by firms bidding for scarce resources, causing both costs of production and prices to increase. Alternatively, a sudden increase in prices can trigger increased profits, an expansion in output, and another increase in prices due to higher costs. The vertical segment corresponds to full employment. Real GDP cannot exceed the full employment level.

6. The aggregate demand curve is downward-sloping because a decrease in the price level will cause an increase in spending. At a lower price level, real wealth increases, interest rates decrease, and exports increase. Each of these changes causes an increase in aggregate demand.

7. Macroeconomic equilibrium occurs at the intersection of the aggregate demand and aggregate supply curves. At the equilibrium price level, all the goods and services supplied in the economy are purchased.

8. Aggregate demand and aggregate supply can be used to represent macroeconomic equilibrium situations where either unemployment or inflation are present. High levels of unemployment in the economy are represented by the intersection of aggregate demand and aggregate supply on the flat portion of the aggregate supply curve. Demand-pull inflation is shown by a shift in the aggregate demand curve to an intersection with aggregate supply in its vertical segment.

9. Cost-push inflation can be shown by a shift of the aggregate supply curve to the left. Any level of real GDP is more costly to produce after such a shift.

10. Government policies shift the aggregate demand curve in particular ways in order to combat inflation and unemployment.

KEY TERMS

Recession
Depression
Prosperity
Inflation
Business cycle
Trough
Recovery
Peak
Downturn
Gross domestic product (GDP)
Nominal GDP
Real GDP
Consumer price index
Base year
Price level
GDP deflator

Aggregate supply
Aggregate demand
Macroequilibrium
Demand-pull inflation
Stagflation
Cost-push inflation
Leveraged buyouts

QUESTIONS

1. What is macroeconomics?

2. Describe the phases of the business cycle. In what ways is the business cycle illustrated in Figure 1 like a roller coaster ride? In what ways is it different? (*Hint*: What does the trend line look like on a roller coaster ride?)

3. How do economists measure an economy's performance?

4. What is the difference between nominal and real GDP?

5. What is a consumer price index? How is it constructed? Why does the index become increasingly unreliable over time?

6. What is the difference between a consumer price index and a GDP deflator?

7. Which price index is generally used to transform nominal GDP into real GDP? Write the conversion formula.

8. What is aggregate demand? Draw an aggregate demand curve and explain its shape. What factors influence aggregate demand?

9. What is aggregate supply? Draw an aggregate supply curve and explain its shape. What factors influence aggregate supply?

10. What does macroequilibrium mean?

11. Draw a diagram illustrating macroequilibrium at less than full employment. Give an example.

12. What is demand-pull inflation? Draw a diagram illustrating such an inflation. Give an example.

13. What is cost-push inflation? What might cause it? Give an example of a period in the United States when this occurred.

14. What can the government do to change macroeconomic equilibrium?

15. If you were teaching economics, how would you explain the Great Depression (assume your students know the *AD/AS* model).

16. Graph the economy's macroequilibrium position, using the following data.

Price Level	Aggregate Demand	Aggregate Supply
160	$1,000	$7,000
150	2,000	7,000
140	3,000	7,000
130	4,000	6,000
120	5,000	5,000
110	6,000	4,000
100	7,000	3,000

17. Suppose aggregate supply shifts to the left by $2,000 at each price level. What happens to the economy's macroequilibrium position?

18. Suppose aggregate demand shifts to the right by $4,000 at each price level. What happens to the economy's macroequilibrium position?

19. Compute real GDP for 1973 to 1979 from the following data.

	GDP Deflator (1972 = 100)	Nominal GDP ($ billions)
1973	106	$1,349.6
1974	115	1,458.6
1975	126	1,585.9
1976	132	1,768.4
1977	140	1,974.1
1978	150	2,232.7
1979	163	2,488.6

20. Compute the percentage change in nominal GDP, 1973 to 1979, and compare it to the percentage change in real GDP growth over the same period.

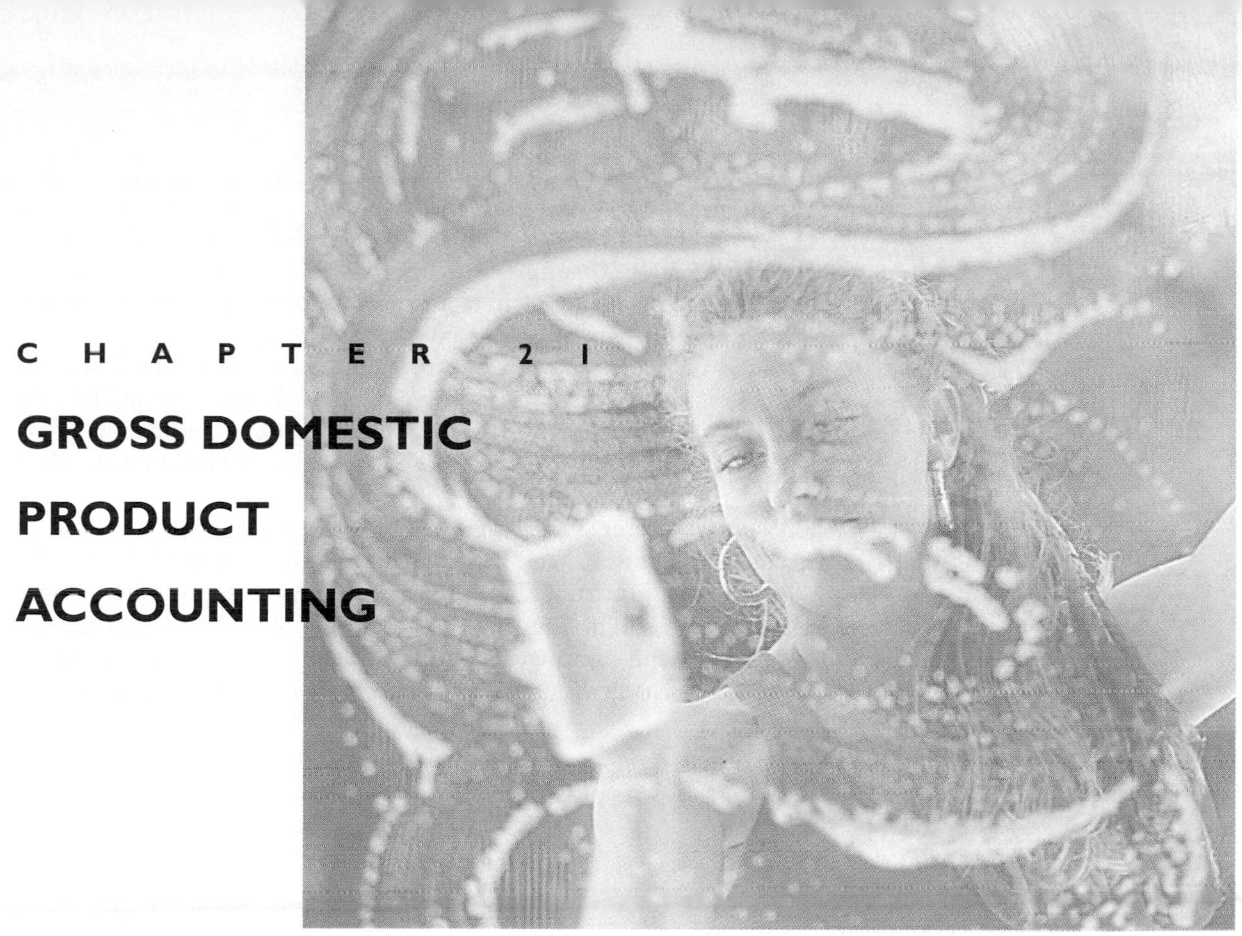

CHAPTER 21

GROSS DOMESTIC PRODUCT ACCOUNTING

CHAPTER PREVIEW

Gross domestic product was introduced in the previous chapter as the principal measure of macroeconomic performance. This chapter identifies the component parts of GDP and describes their significance. We will use the circular flow model to show how gross domestic product can be viewed either as a flow of goods and services or as an equivalent flow of money income. These two approaches to GDP are called the expenditure approach and the income approach.

After studying this chapter, you should be able to:

- Explain the equivalence between flows of money income and flows of goods, services, and resources.
- Categorize goods and services produced by firms as intended for consumption, investment, export, and government.
- Distinguish between durable and nondurable consumer goods.
- Contrast the relative magnitudes of the components of GDP.
- Explain how economists bring GDP and national income into accord.
- Understand the arithmetic relationship of the derivative measures of GDP.
- Explain why GDP might be viewed as an imperfect measure of overall economic activity in a country.

Imagine yourself in a Las Vegas casino playing the quarter slot machines. Suppose that every time you put a quarter into a machine, you win a quarter. No more, no less. It may not be much fun after a while, but it does show how a simple mechanism can generate a circular flow of money. The quarter travels from you, through the machine, back to you, again and again.

Economists see GDP moving through the national economy in much the same way. The slot machines are our firms and households, the quarters are the goods and services as well as the resources and money. The circular flow travels from households to firms back to households again, and repeats. Look at Figure 1.

Households such as your own supply firms with resources in the form of labor, capital, entrepreneurship, and land. That's the quarters fed into the slot machine. What do the firms do? They transform these resources into goods and services which, in the end, flow back to the households. And just as the slot machine took quarters and returned quarters, *the value of the resources that households supply to firms is precisely the value they receive back in the form of goods and services.*

FIGURE 1
The Circular Flow of GDP
The circular flow of GDP shows the interdependence of households and firms. Households supply their resources—labor, capital, land, entrepreneurship—to the firms in the resource market and, in turn, demand in the product market the goods and services produced by the firms. The firms go to the resource market to demand resources that households supply and, in turn, provide households with the goods and services produced for the product market.

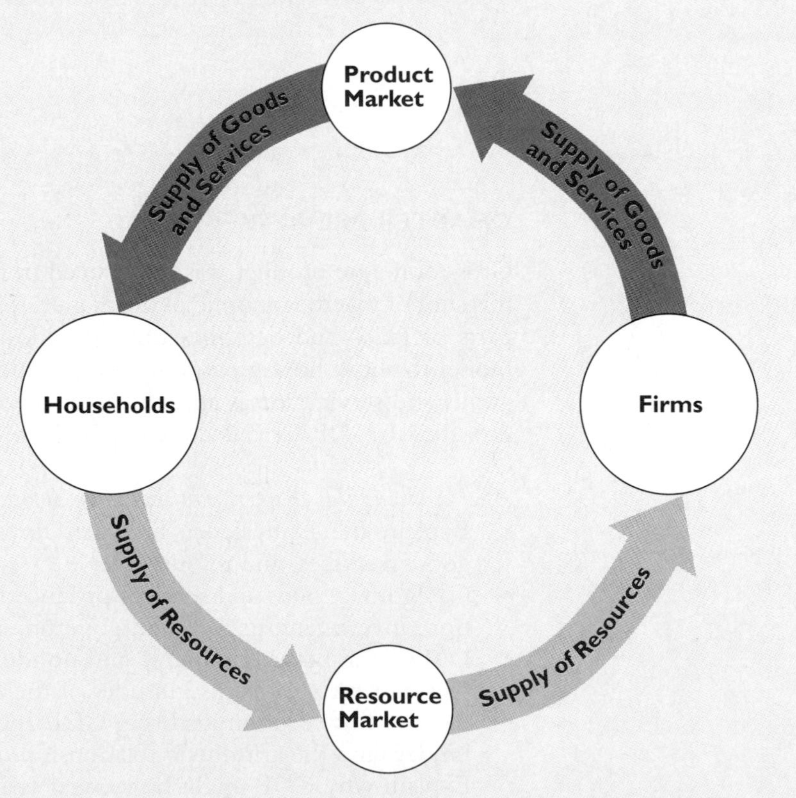

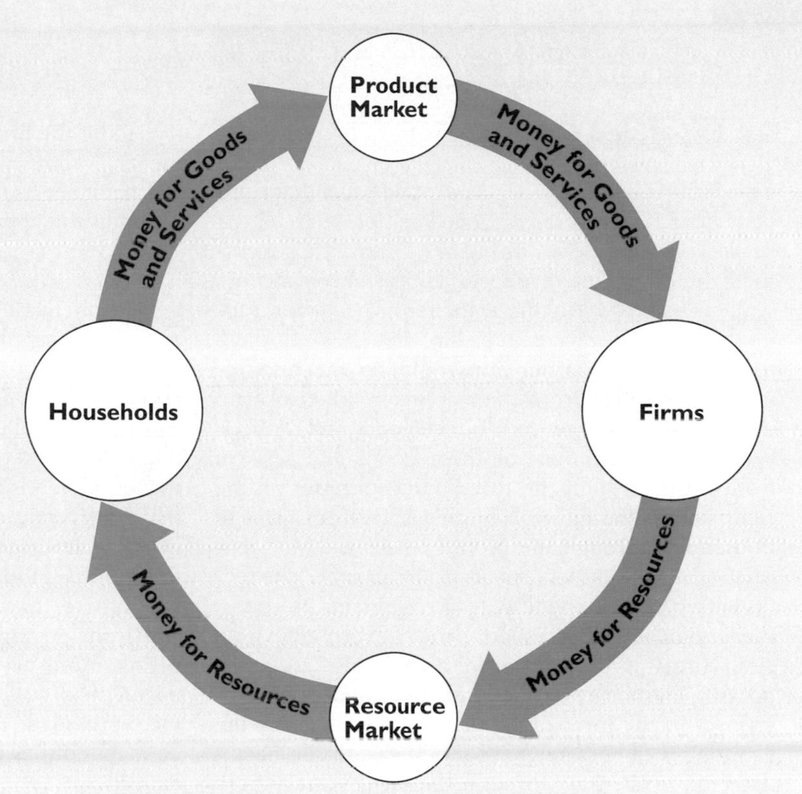

FIGURE 2
The Circular Flow of Money
Start with the flow of money—in the form of wages, interest, rent, and profit—that firms in the resource market pay to households for resources supplied. These resource payments are the incomes that enable households to purchase goods and services from firms. The money circuit is completed when the payments flow from households, through the product market, to the firms for the goods and services they supply.

Circular flow of goods, services, and resources
The movement of goods and services from firms to households, and of resources from households to firms.

Circular flow of money
The movement of income in the form of resource payments from firms to households, and of income in the form of revenue from households to firms.

But here the analogy to the slot machine ends. The **circular flow of goods, services, and resources** is not a game of chance. Households don't bet their resources in the hope of winning goods and services. They supply their resources because firms pay them to do so. Firms pay wages for the labor supplied by households. They pay interest for the capital supplied, rent for the land supplied, and profit for the entrepreneurship provided. These payments make up household incomes. Look at Figure 2, which shows the **circular flow of money.**

As you see, what firms pay out, they get right back. How? Households use the money they receive in the form of income to buy the goods and services that firms produce. After all, firms aren't in business to give goods and services away. They sell them in the product market; households buy them. The money ends up, once again, in the hands of firms. It's a money merry-go-round.

TWO APPROACHES TO CALCULATING GDP

As you already know, gross domestic product (GDP) is a measure of the total value of all final goods and services produced in the economy in a given year. One way of calculating GDP for, say, 1995 is to add up the market value of all

ADDED PERSPECTIVE

An Expanded Circular Flow

The figure, illustrating the income and expenditure approaches to GDP, is an expanded version of the circular flow models shown in Figures 1 and 2. A government sector and international trade have been added.

Let's begin by looking at the resources (labor, capital, land, and entrepreneurship) that flow through the yellow artery from households to the resource market, and then from the resource market to firms that use the resources to produce goods and services. Now follow the flow of these goods and services from firms through the three orange arteries on the right side of the figure. The first leads from firms to households through the product market. These represent the households' private consumption. The second artery carries the flow to government. Note that the goods and services flow that government buys from firms is passed on to households (as public goods). The third artery carries the flow of goods and services in the form of exports from firms to foreign economies. The foreign economies' contribution is depicted in the flow through the orange artery from the foreign economies to households. The difference between the import and export flows represents net exports. Finally, some of the firms' output flow is absorbed by the firms themselves in the form of investment. Combined, these flows of goods and services, all channeled through orange arteries, make up the expenditures approach in the circular flow model:

$$C + I + G + (X - M)$$

The circular flow model also depicts a counterbalancing money flow carried through green arteries that represent payments made by households, government, firms, and the foreign economies for goods and services received. Note the three green arteries that carry money flows from households to firms for the goods and services purchased on the product market, from households to government in the form of taxes, and from households to foreign economies for imports. Households receive money from firms in the form of payments flows for resources provided and from government in the form of transfer payments. Firms pay taxes to government and receive a payments flow from government for goods and services provided. Firms also receive money from foreign economies in the form of a payments flow for exports.

What about saving and investment? The money that households set aside as saving is equal to the value of the goods and services firms set aside for investment.

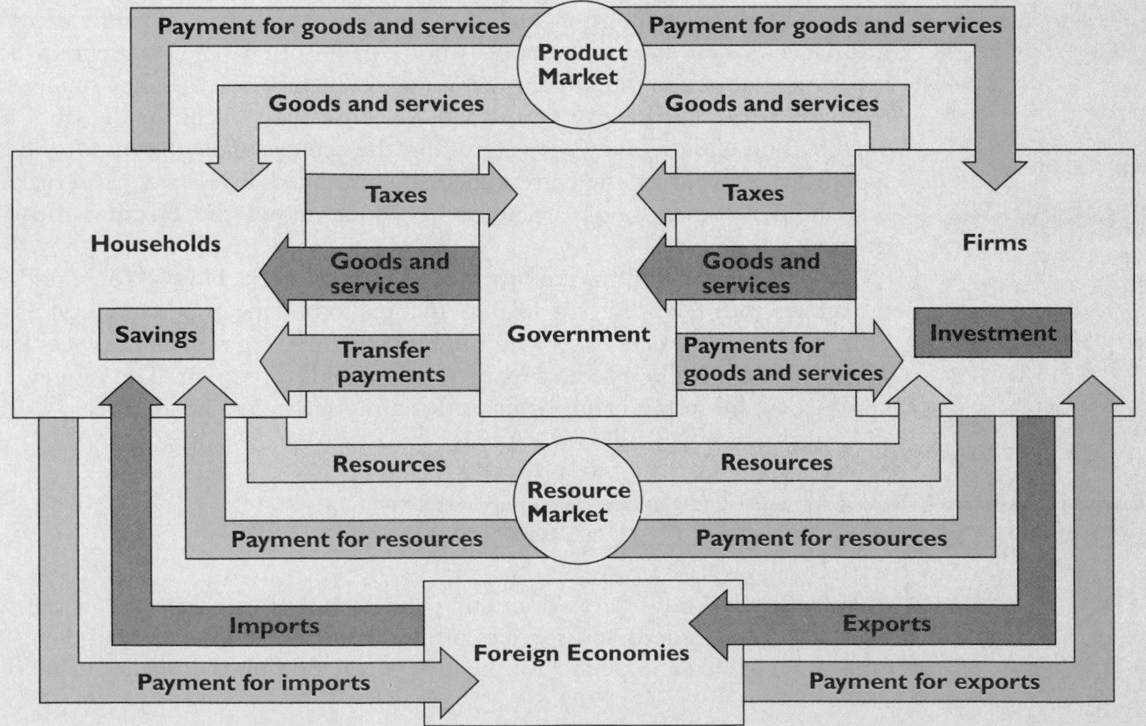

final goods and services produced in 1995. Another way is to add up the total value of the resources used in producing the 1995 final goods and services. The values should be equivalent. After all, goods and services reflect the value of the resources used to make them.

Economists calculate GDP both ways. They add up the total value of all final goods and services produced in the economy in a given year and add up the total value of the resources used in making these goods and services. The former calculation is called the *expenditure approach* to GDP, the latter is called the *income approach* to GDP.

THE EXPENDITURE APPROACH

Counting Final Goods and Services

Expenditure approach

A method that adds all expenditures made for final goods and services by households, firms, and government.

Measuring GDP as the value of all *final* goods and services produced represents the expenditures approach to calculating GDP. Only final goods and services are counted in order to avoid double counting.

Let's start with the **expenditure approach.** One of the first concerns you have adding up the market prices of all final goods and services is to make certain the goods and services whose prices you add are, in fact, *final* goods and services. If you simply add the prices of all goods and services produced in the year, you end up double counting—counting some goods and services more than once. How so? Table 1 illustrates the point.

How much market value is contributed to GDP in Table 1? As you see, five different firms are involved in producing woolen sweaters. In the first, wool is actually being produced on the sheep. Let's suppose the value of the wool, determined by the market price of wool-still-on-the-hoof, is $4. A second firm, producing bulk wool, pays the sheep owner $4—its market price—for the sheep's wool. After shearing, washing, drying, and sizing the wool, the second firm sells it at the $7 bulk wool price.

A knitting mill buys the wool and knits it into a fine wool fabric. At the end of this third stage of economic activity, the market price of the fabric is $13. It is sold to a sweater-making firm that fashions it into a wool sweater, priced at $20.

The firm-to-firm process is finally completed with the sale of the sweater by a clothing store. Here, the sweater is put on display, and a salesperson finally sells it, gift wrapped, for $50.

How do we transfer the information of Table 1 into GDP? We don't simply add up the total values of the goods and services produced by the five firms

TABLE 1 Market Value and Value-Added of Goods Produced

Firm	Good	Market Value	Value Added by Firm
1. Sheep ranch	Wool on sheep	$ 4	$ 4
2. Shearing sheep	Bulk wool	7	3
3. Knitting mill	Wool fabric	13	6
4. Manufacturing	Sweater	20	7
5. Store	Sweater	50	30
TOTAL		$94	$50

to get \$94. That \$94 counts the \$4 raw wool five times over. The \$4 makes up part of the value of the \$7 price of bulk wool, is counted again as part of the value of the \$13 price of the fabric, is counted once more as part of the \$20 price of the manufactured sweater, and counted again as part of the sweater's \$50 retail price at the store.

Final goods

Goods purchased for final use, not for resale.

How do we overcome overcounting? By counting only values of **final goods** produced, that is, *goods that are not resold.* The only good not resold in Table 1 is the \$50 sweater. What about the raw wool, the bulk wool, the fabric, and the sweater in the sweater factory? These are **intermediate goods,** goods sold by firms to other firms. They are goods used to produce other goods. Their values are accounted for in the value of the final good.

Intermediate goods

Goods used to produce other goods.

Another way of arriving at the \$50 value that is counted as part of GDP is by considering only the **value added** by each of the five firms of Table 1. Look at column 4.

Value added

The difference between the value of a good that a firm produces and the value of the goods the firm uses to produce it.

The sheep ranch, where the wool is actually grown, *adds* \$4 to value. The firm producing bulk wool, buys the wool for \$4 and *adds* \$3 to its value. The knitting mill buys the bulk wool for \$7 and *adds* \$6 to its value. The sweater firm buys the \$13 fabric and *adds* \$7 to its value. Finally, the store buys the sweater for \$20 and *adds* \$30 to its value. The firms' *value added* sums to \$50. That is precisely the market value of the *final* good.

Four Expenditure Categories of GDP

What kinds of final goods and services are produced in our economy, and who buys them? Economists classify final goods and services according to whether they are produced to satisfy (1) consumption demands by households, (2) investment demands by firms, (3) demands by government, or (4) exports minus imports (net exports)—that is, the demands by foreigners for our goods and services minus our demands for foreign goods and services.

Personal consumption expenditures

All goods and services bought by households.

All final goods and services that make up GDP, then, can be expressed in the form

$$GDP = C + I + G + (X - M)$$

Gross private domestic investment

The purchase by firms of plant, equipment, and inventory goods.

where C is **personal consumption expenditures,** I is **gross private domestic investment,** G is **government purchases,** and $(X - M)$ is **net exports,** or exports minus imports.

What did 1994 GDP add up to? Look at Table 2.

GDP equals \$6,738.4 billion. Look at the sums and specific character of the goods and services in each of the expenditure categories.

Government purchases

All goods and services bought by government.

PERSONAL CONSUMPTION EXPENDITURES

Net exports

An economy's exports to other economies, minus its imports from other economies.

The \$4,628.4 billion personal consumption expenditures make up 68.7 percent of the \$6,738.4 billion 1994 GDP. These are the goods and services consumed directly by households. They are grouped into categories of durable goods, nondurable goods, and services.

Durable goods

Goods which are expected to last at least a year.

Durable goods account for \$591.5 billion. These include familiar household items such as kitchen appliances, television sets, carpeting, personal computers, washing machines, and lawn mowers. Durables include, as well, automobiles, electric saws, and hearing aids.

TABLE 2 Expenditure Approach to 1994 GDP ($ billions)

C	=	Personal Consumption Expenditures		$4,628.4
		Durable goods	591.5	
		Nondurable goods	1,394.3	
		Services	2,642.7	
I	=	Gross Private Domestic Investment		1,032.9
		Nonresidential	697.6	
		Residential	283.0	
		Change in business inventory	52.2	
G	=	Government Purchases		1,175.3
		Federal	437.3	
		Defense	292.3	
		Nondefense	145.0	
		State and local	738.0	
$X - M$	=	Net Exports of Goods and Services		−98.2
		Exports	718.7	
		Imports	(816.9)	
GDP	=	Gross Domestic Product		6,738.4

Source: *Survey of Current Business* (Washington, D.C.: U.S. Department of Commerce, March 1995). pp. 1–3.

What sets durables apart from other consumption goods and services? Essentially, their durability. Unlike tuna salad sandwiches, they're not consumed soon after being produced. A refrigerator, for example, once produced, outlasts years of tuna salad sandwiches. Of course, all refrigerators eventually wear out. But it takes time. Economists describe a durable good as one that is expected to last at least a year. For example, a new Ford *is expected* to last more than a year. Even if Alice Gorman buys it today and totals it this afternoon on the way home from the dealership, it is still classified as a durable good.

Purchases of durable goods help economists identify the phases of the business cycle. During recessions, consumers tend to hang on to their durables (say, by getting them repaired) so that sales of new durables are relatively weak. As prosperity returns, consumers are more inclined to discard old durables than to repair them. As a result, sales of new durables are relatively strong.

Nondurable goods

Goods which are expected to last less than a year.

What about **nondurable goods?** These include goods that are consumed within a relatively short period of time, usually less than a year, such as food, clothing, gasoline, drugs, tobacco, and toiletries. Some things are easy to classify as nondurables—like bananas—whereas it may take years to consume some spices. Also many of us wear clothes and shoes for more than a year, yet the U.S. Department of Commerce classifies them as nondurables. Households spend more on nondurables than on durables. In fact, the value of nondurables consumed in 1994—$1,394.3 billion—was more than twice the value of durable items.

Services

Productive activities that are instantaneously consumed.

Services are intangible (nonphysical) consumption items that are consumed as they are being produced. Think about health care. You consume your doctor's service precisely when it is being given. An Economics 101 lecture is con-

If it's peach preserves you want, it's peach preserves you'll get. Hours before the supermarket opens, employees are busy restocking shelves with hundreds of nondurable items for your convenience, such as peach preserves, canned tuna, microwave popcorn, and fresh broccoli. In 1994, $1,394.3 billion of nondurable goods was produced and consumed in the United States.

sumed as your professor lectures. The Chicago Symphony is consumed as Daniel Barenboim conducts.

Some industries (often those that produce durable goods) produce services as well. AT&T, for example, sells telephones (durable goods) and telephone calls (services). Sears sells washing machines (durable goods) and washing machine repair (service). As you see in Table 2, we spend more on services—$2,642.7 billion—than we do on durable and nondurable goods combined.

GROSS PRIVATE DOMESTIC INVESTMENT

Not all production of final goods and services in 1994 was consumed by households. Some goods and services—$1,032.9 billion of the $6,738.4 billion—were actually purchased by firms themselves in the form of gross private domestic investment. What kind of goods? The oil rigs produced in 1994 by firms that make oil drilling equipment were bought by Exxon and Texaco, not by you. The rigs are used by the oil companies to produce energy for households. Construction companies built automobile plants for General Motors and Ford, not for households. These plants turn out the automobiles demanded by households.

The goods that firms buy from each other are classified as new structures (or plants) and equipment. Some plant and equipment purchases merely replace plants and equipment that have worn out producing consumption goods. But some purchases are made to increase the quantity of plants and equipment in use. For example, United Airlines bought aircraft to replace those no longer usable. But they also bought aircraft to expand their fleet.

What about residential investment? Houses and apartment buildings produced in 1994 and used as residences are classified as investment goods, even though a case can be made to classify a homeowner's house—as we do a homeowner's automobile—as a durable consumption good.

Inventory investment

Stocks of finished goods and raw materials that firms keep in reserve to facilitate production and sales.

Changes in business inventories are counted as **inventory investment.** Why? Inventories are unsold output. Firms keep stocks of finished final goods, as well as stocks of resources used to produce those goods, in reserve in order to promote efficiency in production and sales. How can a clothing store expect to sell sweaters if it doesn't stock a variety of styles, sizes, and colors? How can Goodyear Tires expect to run a smooth production line if it doesn't stock the raw materials used in manufacturing tires?

Gross private domestic investment includes expenditures on new factories, tools, and machinery, as well as expenditures to replace worn-out plants and equipment, expenditures on residential structures, and the cost of changes in inventories.

What does the $52.2 billion business inventory change in 1994 signify? That some goods produced in 1994 were *added* to 1994 inventory—that is, they were produced in 1994 but not sold in that year.

Business inventory changes, positive or negative, are not always intended. Suppose that Rockport Shoes planned to produce and sell $200 million of shoes in 1994, but by year's end was able to sell only $180 million. The remaining unsold $20 million would be recorded as an addition to business inventory, even though Rockport intended the shoes for sale, not inventory. Rockport would end up with more shoes in inventory than it wanted.

GOVERNMENT PURCHASES

Be sure that you are able to describe the sorts of goods and services that government purchases.

Government, too, is a buyer of goods and services. In 1994 federal, state, and local government purchases amounted to $1,175.3 billion, or 17.4 percent of the economy's $6,738.4 billion production of goods and services. The largest slice of federal government purchases—$292.3 billion—went to national defense. It bought food and clothing for the armed forces, F-15 fighter planes, Bradley tanks, Navy uniforms, and countless other military hardware and software items that make up our military preparedness.

Defense goods were not the federal government's only purchases. It also bought interstate highways, drydocks, post offices, and services such as justice, transportation, and education. It spent money on Amtrak service, for example, and airport construction. Without federal spending on these items, many people could not afford to travel.

Yet, in spite of all the media attention focused on the appetite of the federal government, the biggest government spender doesn't live in Washington, D. C. State and local government expenditures account for approximately 60 percent of all government spending. These expenditures and the means used by governments to finance them are described in later chapters.

NET EXPORTS OF GOODS AND SERVICES

The final item in the expenditure approach to GDP is net exports. We produced for export $718.7 billion of goods and services. How does this item affect our GDP account?

We include exports in calculating GDP because they represent goods and services we produced, even though they do not appear as part of our own expenditures. On the other hand, the imported goods and services we buy from other economies are part of our expenditures even though we didn't produce them. In calculating GDP by the expenditure approach, we include exports and subtract imports. In 1994, net exports—the difference between exports and imports—was negative, a minus $98.2 billion.

THE INCOME APPROACH

Income approach

Method which adds all the incomes earned in the production of final goods and services.

An alternative approach to calculating GDP is the **income approach.** How does this differ from the expenditure approach? Instead of determining GDP by computing the total value of all final goods and services produced in the econ-

ADDED PERSPECTIVE

Is the 1991 Composition of GDP for the United States Unique?

Suppose we hadn't seen the detailed composition of 1994 GDP shown in Table 1. Could we have guessed it? Probably, if we had access to GDP data for any other year. The consumption, investment, government, and net exports shares of GDP change very little from year to year, as Table A indicates.

The annual rate of real GDP growth in the United States for 1960 to 1990 was 3.1 percent. In the 20-year period 1960 to 1980, the consumption share of GDP varied within one percentage point. Investment varied by only 2.4 percent throughout the entire period, and perhaps more surprisingly, government purchases of goods and services varied by no more than 2.3 percent.

Not only do these shares remain fairly stable over time, but they seem to reflect the composition of GDP for most other market economies as well. Look at Table B.

The variations, although greater, are still remarkably narrow. Except for Germany, Ireland, and Mexico, the consumption share of the GDP in these countries varies within a narrow 4.2 percent. And except for Israel, the government's share of GDP is within a 5.3 percent range. The high-level expenditure on defense and on the absorption of immigrants accounts for Israel's abnormally high negative net exports and government expenditures.

TABLE A
U.S. Gross Domestic Product: 1960–1990 ($ billion and percent)

	1960	1970	1980	1990
Nominal GDP	513.4	1,010.7	2,708.0	5,513.8
Real GDP	1,973.2	2,875.8	3,776.3	4,884.9
Consumption	64.7	64.0	64.6	67.8
Investment	15.3	14.9	17.3	14.6
Government	19.4	21.0	18.7	18.9
Net Exports	0.5	0.1	− 0.5	− 1.4
	100.0	100.0	100.0	100.0

Source: *Economic Report of the President, 1992,* Washington, D.C., February, 1992, pp. 298–302.

Discussion

Compare the data in Table A and B. Is there any category of expenditure in which the United States is markedly different from other countries? How would you account for these differences, if any?

TABLE B
Composition of GDP for Selected Economies: 1991 (%)

	Consumption	Investment	Government	Net Exports
Spain	64.0	26.7	15.9	−6.6
Italy	62.5	20.4	17.7	−0.5
France	60.1	21.0	18.6	0.3
Britain	64.1	15.7	21.2	−1.0
Germany	52.7	22.1	17.9	7.2
Canada	59.9	21.9	20.6	−1.9
Mexico	66.0	19.7	10.7	3.6
Turkey	61.8	22.8	16.0	−0.5
Israel	61.0	22.5	30.0	−16.5
Ireland	56.0	17.0	16.0	9.0

Source: *Economist Intelligence Unit,* No. 4, London, England (by country).

TABLE 3
1994 National Income
($ billions)

Compensation of employees		$4,004.6
Wages and salaries	$3,279.0	
Supplements	725.6	
Rental Income		27.7
Corporate profit		542.7
Net interest		409.7
Proprietors' income		473.7
Farm	39.5	
Nonfarm	434.2	
NATIONAL INCOME		$5,458.4

Source: *Survey of Current Business* (Washington, D.C.: U.S. Department of Commerce, March 1995), p. 3.

The income approach measures GDP as the total payments made to households that furnish the resources used to produce the final goods and services.

National income

The sum of all payments made to resource owners for the use of their resources.

omy, the income approach computes the total payments made to households that provide the resources used in producing the final goods and services.

The resources used in production—labor, capital, land, and entrepreneurship—receive income payments in the form of wages and salaries, interest, rent, and profit. These income payments are rearranged in GDP accounting into five categories: (1) the compensation of employees, (2) interest, (3) corporate profit, (4) rental income, and (5) proprietors' income. The sum of these income payments is **national income**.

National income for 1994 is shown in Table 3.

National income equaled $5,458.4 billion. Look at the sums and specific character of each of the income categories shown in Table 3.

Compensation of Employees

In every morning rush hour, an incredible crush of people make their way to work. They spend their working life producing the economy's goods and services. Some work production lines as hourly workers earning wages, others sit behind desks as salaried workers pushing the paper flow that modern production requires. Still others might be journalists, teachers, or fire fighters.

In 1994 firms, organizations, and government entities paid out to their employees $3,279.0 billion in wages and salaries, and another $725.6 billion in fringe benefits, such as bonuses, paid vacations, and contributions to employees' Social Security. All that *compensation of employees* was money paid for labor supplied.

No surprise, then, that our national economy appears to be labor-generated. After all, the $4,004.6 billion income payment to workers accounts for 73.4 percent of our national income. That percentage hasn't changed much over the years.

Interest

How is capital incorporated into the income approach to GDP? People who provide firms with capital—for example, by buying interest-bearing bonds issued by the firms—receive *interest,* just as people who provide labor services receive wages and salaries. Firms also borrow capital from banks, which in turn borrow from individual savers. In each case, interest is earned. In 1994, $409.7 billion was received by people in the form of interest.

Rent

Rent is the payment for use of property. The most common property forms are land, housing, and office space. People using their own property typically don't pay themselves rent, but the rent is nonetheless estimated in GDP accounting and counted along with contractual rental leases. Imputed rents associated with owner-occupied dwellings are also counted. In 1994 these rental forms amounted to $98.9 billion.

But charged against this $98.9 billion rental income is the owners' $71.1 billion depreciation of their rental property. As a result, 1994 net rental income is $27.7 billion.

Corporate Profit

Corporate profit represents the return to owners of incorporated firms. Part of corporate profit is distributed to stockholders as *dividends,* part is retained by the corporation as investment, and a third part ends up with government as corporate taxes. The income approach to GDP includes all of corporate profit, which in 1994, amounted to $542.7 billion.

What about the income of corporate managers? These are the people making key corporate decisions. Are their incomes included as part of corporate profit? No. Their incomes, typically salaries, are counted as employee compensation.

Proprietors' Income

Although our economy is dominated by large corporations, the largest number are unincorporated firms. Many people own their own businesses, earning income for the goods and services they produce. How are these incomes classified? They don't fall into the category of corporate profit because the firms are not corporations. They aren't wages or salaries because owners don't hire themselves as employees. They obviously aren't rent or interest. They are regarded as *proprietors' income.*

Imagine an ethnic restaurant in Brooklyn owned and operated by a husband and wife. They work hard, save their pennies, rent the premises, and set up a 12-table restaurant. They prepare the meals, serve, and clean up after a 14-hour workday. They grossed $172,000 in 1994. But they must also pay rent and utilities, buy ingredients for meals, and repair wear and tear on their plant and equipment. After paying out all 1994 expenses, they ended up with a net income of $44,000. Economists define that net income as proprietors' income. In 1994 unincorporated firms generated $473.7 billion for their owners.

BRINGING GDP AND NATIONAL INCOME INTO ACCORD

How do economists reconcile differences between the $6,738.4 billion 1994 GDP and the $5,458.4 billion 1994 national income? First they derive gross domestic product (GDP), then subtract two items from it, depreciation of capital and indirect business taxes.

From GDP TO GNP

Gross national product (GNP) is equal to GDP plus payments to Americans who are overseas, minus payments to foreigners who work in the United States.

Gross National Product (GNP)

The market value of all final goods and services in an economy produced by resources owned by people of that economy, regardless of where the resources are located.

The difference between GDP and **gross national product (GNP)** is ownership and location. Gross domestic product measures location, that is, what is produced and earned *in the domestic economy*. In 1994 GDP equaled $6,738.4 billion. Gross national product, on the other hand, measures ownership, that is, what the *nation's people and their property* produce and earn. In 1994 GNP was $6,726.9 billion. If the nation's entire resources were employed wholly within the economy, then, GDP would be exactly the same as GNP.

The reality, however, is that some U.S. workers and other resources are employed outside the country. And some of the resources employed in this country are not owned by U.S. citizens. The value of the automobiles produced by a General Motors plant in Spain is not included in our GDP (it is counted in Spain's GDP). On the other hand, it is included in our GNP. Conversely, a Nissan plant's output in Tennessee is part of our GDP, but not our GNP. In 1994 foreign workers and the property owned by foreigners in the United States created $178.6 billion of income that was included in our GDP but excluded from our GNP. On the other hand, the $167.1 billion of 1994 U.S. assets abroad and income earned by U.S. citizens working in foreign economies were excluded from our GDP but included in our GNP.

From GDP TO NDP

To create the 1994 GDP of $6,738.4 billion, people were busy turning out, day after day, automobiles and computers, corn and health care. They worked in factories, hospitals, and on farms. They welded frames, operated tractors, and took x-rays. These factories, hospitals, welding machines, tractors, and x-ray machines—along with other factories and machinery—make up the capital stock in our economy. Wouldn't you think that during 1994 part of this capital stock would be used up producing the economy's 1994 GDP? After all, nothing is forever. Machines in use wear out as do hospitals and factories.

Shouldn't they be replaced? Typically, they are. During 1994 *new* factories and machinery were produced. New hospitals were built, new tractors manufactured, and new automobile assembly lines constructed.

But if the value of all investment goods produced in 1994 only replaces the value of the capital stock used up in 1994, then 1994 GDP may be giving us an inflated view of our economy's 1994 performance.

Capital depreciation

The value of existing capital stock used up in the process of producing goods and services.

Net domestic product (NDP)

GDP minus capital depreciation.

For example, suppose each of two fishermen caught 1,000 pounds of fish, but one used 100 pounds of fish bait to do the catching, the other 500 pounds of fish bait. Wouldn't the difference in their *used-up capital* influence your evaluation of their performance? Or suppose we discover that firms in 1994 used up $1,000 billion, not $715.3 billion, of plant and equipment to produce the $6,738.4 billion GDP. Wouldn't that give us a very different reading of the economy's 1994 performance?

By deducting used-up capital, or **capital depreciation,** *d,* from GDP we derive **net domestic product, NDP.**

TABLE 4 Influence of Capital Depreciation on the Growth Rate of NDP ($ billions)

	GDP	Rate of GDP Growth	Capital Depreciation	NDP	Rate of NDP Growth
1994	$6,738.4		$715.3	$6,023.1	
1995	7,075.3	5.0 %	600.0	6,475.3	7.5 %
1995	7,075.3	5.0 %	700.0	6,375.3	5.8 %
1995	7,075.3	5.0 %	800.0	6,275.3	4.2 %

$$NDP = GDP - d$$

By way of illustration, let's compare the 1994–95 growth rates of NDP, assuming different hypothetical values for capital depreciation and rates of GDP growth.

As you see in Table 4, the 5 percent rate of GDP growth could be coupled with a 7.5 percent, a 5.8 percent, and a 4.2 percent growth rate of NDP, depending upon how much plant and equipment is used up in the process of producing the $7,075.3 billion GDP. Which of the two rates of growth, GDP or NDP, would you consider the more informative measure of the economy's performance?

From NDP to National Income

The reduction of NDP to national income involves removing indirect business taxes—that is, general sales taxes, excise taxes, customs duties, business property taxes, and license fees—from the NDP accounts. They are called "indirect" taxes because they are not levied on the firm directly, but on the good or service. Why must we remove them from NDP to get national income? Because they are embodied in the price of the good or service. And because government is not viewed as a resource, or factor of production, these tax revenues to government are not viewed as compensation for production. That is, the taxes are not paid to any factor of production.

As we saw in Table 3, payments to households for resources provided defines national income. It is the sum of wages and salaries, corporate profit, rent, interest, and proprietors' income. The exclusion of indirect taxes from the NDP accounts, then, generates national income.

Why bother measuring national income? Isn't NDP a good enough measure? National income provides us with more specific information. It offers, in some instances, a much sharper picture of the population's economic well-being. After all, national income is what eventually ends up in people's hands.

GDP, GNP, NDP, and National Income for 1994

Table 5 summarizes the relationships between GDP, GNP, NDP, and national income for 1994.

TABLE 5
The Relationship between Gross Domestic Product, Gross National Product, Net National Product, and National Income: 1994 ($ billions)

	Gross Domestic Product	$6,738.4
minus	Factor payments to the rest of the world	−178.6
plus	Factor payments from the rest of the world	167.1
equals	Gross National Product	$6,726.9
minus	Capital depreciation	715.3
equals	Net National Product*	$6,011.6
minus	Indirect business taxes	−553.2
equals	National Income	$5,458.4

*NNP=NDP+net factor income from the rest of the world.

PERSONAL INCOME AND PERSONAL DISPOSABLE INCOME

Personal income

National income, plus income received but not earned, minus income earned but not received.

National income is what people earn. **Personal income,** on the other hand, is what they receive. What people receive in any year is not always equal to what they earn. Consider, for example, the income earned and received by corporate shareholders in 1994.

Since shareholders own the corporation, what they earn as shareholders is the profit the corporation makes. But shareholders don't end up with that profit. First, the corporation is obliged to pay corporate income tax. What it pays out in taxes, its shareholders don't receive. Second, the corporation typically retains some of its after-tax profit for its own internal investment. What it retains for investment, its shareholders don't receive. And finally, the corporation is obliged to contribute to Social Security. That represents yet another deduction from corporate earnings that its shareholders don't receive.

What about employees? They don't bring home total employee compensation either. Employees are obliged to pay Social Security taxes as well. They end up, then, with less than the full measure of their earnings.

On the other hand, some people in 1994 received more income than they earned. How is that possible? People received income from government in the form of retirement benefits, veteran benefits, unemployment insurance benefits, disability payments, Aid to Families with Dependent Children, and subsidies to farmers. Economists refer to this form of income as **transfer payments** because the government—acting as receiver and dispenser of income—transfers income from taxpayers (who earned the income in the first place by providing resources) to those receiving benefits. These income transfers, prior to the actual transfers, are counted as part of national income because they represent income earned. They are not counted as national income again when they end up in the hands of the benefit recipients.

Transfer payments

Income received but not earned.

Personal income represents what households actually receive as income, while personal disposable income nets out taxes paid to federal, state, and local governments from personal income. Personal disposable income can be either spent or saved.

Another form of income is the interest people receive on the government savings bonds, notes, and bills they own. This interest is part of their personal income, but is not included in national income. Why not? Because the bonds, notes, and bills that government sold to them were primarily incurred to finance *past* recessions and defense, which—however essential they *were*—were not income-yielding in 1994. That is, the interest paid out by government in 1994 had no equivalent 1994 income source.

In 1994 the economy's $5,701.7 billion of personal income exceeded the $5,458.4 billion of national income.

Households, however, were not free to dispose of the entire $5,701.7 billion personal income as they wish. Why not? Because they are still obligated to pay direct taxes to federal, state, and local governments. What remains after subtracting these taxes out of personal income is **disposable personal income.** In 1994, this disposable personal income was $4,959.6 billion. It is what households have at their disposal to spend on final goods and services or to save.

Disposable personal income
Personal income minus direct taxes.

HOW COMPREHENSIVE IS GDP?

Does GDP really measure everything produced in the national economy? Is what we produce an adequate measure of our economic well-being? GDP tries to measure everything that *appears on the market*. But not everything produced in the economy gets onto the market. And there are things that contribute to our economic well-being that aren't even produced.

Value of Housework

One of the most glaring exclusions from GDP accounts is the value of housework done by householders. Nobody with any sense at all would argue that housework is any less a productive activity contributing to our economic well-being than, say, manufacturing automobiles. In fact, housework is included in GDP accounts as long as it isn't done by a member of the household. Hired housekeepers, nannies, and cooks working in households are either employees or else self-employed persons earning incomes for productive services that are counted in GDP. In most cases, however, the housekeepers, nannies, and cooks are the householders themselves, and because their productive labor is not supplied through a market—they are neither employees nor self-employed—their contributions are not recorded in GDP accounts.

Is this woman a homemaker scrubbing away on the shower door in her bathroom or a hired domestic scrubbing away on the same shower door? Although it's the same woman, the same scrubbing, and the same shower door in both scenarios, the second represents activity that contributes to GDP, the first does not.

One explanation for the omission is that GDP was never meant to measure all productive activity in the economy, and anyway, housework is extremely difficult if not impossible to evaluate. On the other hand, economists have found ways to include other forms of nonmarket productive activity in GDP. Is it really more difficult to impute value to housework than to impute value to goods produced and consumed by farm families on family farms? Yet, GDP includes farmers' self-consumed food, but not the value of housework.

The Underground Economy

Some economic activities other than housework also do not get reported—and for good reason. Drug trafficking, money laundering, bribery, prostitution, fraud, illegal gambling, and burglary are activities that aren't negotiated openly in the marketplace. Yet they represent sets of demanders and suppliers, and they generate unreported incomes that can be sizable.

Other activities, legal and mainstream, go unreported by people trying to evade taxes. There is ample opportunity for people who receive payments for service, such as lawyers, physicians, consultants, domestics, tailors, car mechanics, baby-sitters, and taxi drivers, to understate income earned.

Underground economy

The unreported or illegal production of goods and services in the economy that is not counted in GDP.

A driving force of the **underground economy** is tax avoidance. If you and a friend swap services ("I'll fix your car if you paint my house") you both avoid paying taxes. But the car repair and painting are not counted in GDP. Your 9 to 5 economic activity may be counted, but your moonlighting, after-hours informal activities are not.

A growing population of legal and illegal immigrants has swelled the not-so-mainstream workforce. Many earn less than minimum wages in off-the-books entry-level jobs such as sidewalk vendors of electronics, jewelry, and flowers; as casual labor in sweatshops and construction; doing illegal piecework at home; and as domestics. Many immigrants apply their entrepreneurial talents in flea markets, greengrocers, and the garment trade. These activities go unreported. Illegal immigrants are sought-after workers by some employers because, typically, they work for lower-than-prevailing-rate market wages and, because they're working illegally, the employer makes no contribution to the workers' Social Security or unemployment insurance.

How sizable is this unreported underground economy? Some economists estimate it at 10 percent of GDP. Professor Peter Gutmann of Baruch College estimated that $902 billion—$261 billion illegal, $641 billion legal—of U.S. economic activity was underground in 1993, representing 13 percent of GDP. Other economists believe that underground activity in the United States is closer to 25 percent. In some European economies, the underground economy is estimated as high as 40 percent.

Leisure

What about the economic value of leisure? What about reading a book, or taking a walk, or playing baseball, or visiting friends? The fact that people choose to spend time consuming some quantity of leisure over producing and consuming more final goods and services indicates that adding up the market value of goods and services may not give us the whole picture of a person's or a society's economic well-being. Going to a Dodgers-Expos game on Sunday afternoon is

ADDED PERSPECTIVE

Underground Economy Doing Thriving Business

What does skid row in Nashville tell us about the American economy? Or drug smuggling in Belize, the black market in Cuba, or one of those sleazy traveling carnival games? Or even the little-known research department of the Internal Revenue Service that delves primarily into how people cheat on taxes?

A lot, says Bruce Wiegand. Wiegand, a sociologist at the University of Wisconsin at Whitewater, has made his career the study of what is diplomatically called the underground economy. It is also known as the black market, the informal sector, and the parallel economy.

According to Wiegand, that shady, off-the-books economy may be one of America's largest and fastest-growing industries.

It includes drug dealers, teenage baby-sitters, physicians who ask patients to pay in cash, flea market operators, moonlighting carpenters, small businessmen who inflate their deductions, and multinational corporations that fudge on the value of goods transferred between their far-flung subsidiaries.

According to the IRS estimates, the tax gap in America now amounts to $110 billion. That figure, which has grown from less than $30 billion in 1973, is the difference between what the federal government receives in taxes and what the best heads at the IRS think it ought to get.

The IRS traditionally recovers about 15 percent of that gap. But Wiegand, who used to work as a research analyst for the IRS, thinks that agency estimates may be too low. "I'm not sure anyone really knows for sure. My guess is that the underground economy is about 25 percent the size of the national economy, and that does not include the illegal sector, like drugs and prostitution," he said.

The illicit underground economy—activities such as drugs and loan-sharking that are by their nature illegal—is probably only about a third the size of the legal underground economy, which comprises otherwise legal enterprises that simply cheat on taxes.

He also thinks the current recession has resulted in considerable growth of the black market. "With the middle class in trouble today, the underground economy has probably moved out of the ghetto and increased considerably," he said.

The black market really began with Prohibition in 1920, after the 18th Amendment banned booze, and entrepreneurs such as Al Capone began smuggling it to a thirsty public. Prohibition was repealed in 1933, but depression era shortages of goods and money and then World War II restrictions resulted in a thriving underground economy.

After the war, the big-city ghettos became the reservoir of the underground economy, because for many entrepreneurial blacks, that was the only way to survive, scholars say.

Middle-class whites began to rediscover the black market in the 1970s, and according to Wiegand, it was finally noticed by economists late in that decade.

"After all the years IRS denied it had a big tax-avoidance problem, they suddenly decided there was a problem," Wiegand said. The agency appealed to Congress for more enforcement powers.

However, by then the underground economy was too widespread to be stopped, and the net effect of the tax reform was to increase the federal budget deficit, Wiegand said.

IRS estimates on tax avoidance give some clues to the nature of the underground economy. Individuals account for an estimated 75 percent of tax cheating and corporations 25 percent, according to the most recent IRS research reports.

Among individuals who file federal tax returns, almost 57 percent underreport income. The biggest offenders are sole proprietorships (including doctors, lawyers, accountants, sweatshops, and operators of cottage industries), at almost 20 percent of the national total.

Informal suppliers, such as flea market merchants, account for 9 percent, and the underreporting of capital gains by people wealthy enough to claim them accounts for almost 8 percent.

The best compliance, as might be suspected, is by employees who have their income reported to the IRS on their annual W-2 forms. They account for only 1.7 percent of the cheating.

Discussion

What are the principal contributors to the illegal underground economy in the United States? What are the principal contributors to the legal underground economy? Which is larger?

Source: "Underground Economy Doing Thriving Business," by David Young. *Chicago Tribune*, July 10, 1992.

purchased entertainment and included in GDP, but playing tennis with friends on that same afternoon is not.

Quality of Goods and Services

People chronically complain about how our goods and services don't live up to their advertised claims. What's the real value of a new automobile, advertised as high quality, when its transmission fails four days after the warranty runs out? How commonplace is that experience? What value should we place on a toaster that cannot be repaired because there are no shops to service the toaster?

Notwithstanding these and tens of thousands more complaints, quality has nevertheless improved dramatically over time. While transmissions do sometimes go out and toasters become instant junk when one part malfunctions, most of the goods and services we consume have increased in quality and serviceability. Radial tires are considerably more durable than the tires available 25 years ago. Automobiles are more reliable, microwave ovens more convenient, and home furnaces more efficient than they ever were. New technologies make health care more accessible and more successful. Higher quality goods are continuously replacing inferior ones even though they do not always meet our more demanding expectations. These quality improvements may not register in our GDP accounts because the prices of the higher quality goods may actually be less than the prices of the inferior goods they replace.

Costs of Environmental Damage

While firms keep churning out the goods and services that make up our GDP, they churn out pollution that fouls our environment as well. No-deposit bottles and aluminum cans not only contribute to our convenience but to littering our physical space. Automobiles provide us with valued mobility but also with rush-hour traffic, noise, and carbon monoxide. We have polluted air, land, and water, and our poor record in cleaning up our atmosphere threatens to damage the ozone layer that protects us from excessive radiation. We allowed soil erosion to replace forests in parts of our deforested landscape. Destruction of habitat and species follow. How do these negative attributes of our quest for more goods and services fit into our system of GDP accounts? The cleaning-up expenses associated with the pollution we create contribute to GDP, but the actual pollution created is not subtracted.

Although that's precisely how our GDP accounting works, there's something inherently wrong with this system of accounting. After all, if we were to allocate all our resources to producing and cleaning up garbage, we would end up with a GDP and no goods or services!

In the last 25 years, the government has legislated environmental codes and standards that firms are required to observe. Pollution control has been costly. Billions of dollars that could have been invested in new plant and machinery has been spent instead on pollution control devices. On the other hand, ignoring the effects of economic activity on the environment merely postpones payment and increases the damage.

The polluting activities of the recently defunct communist states were nothing short of horrendous. They simply ignored the environmental effects of their polluting factories. Investing almost nothing in pollution control for decades, it is no longer possible for them to postpone the difficult task of cleaning up a

GDP measures only final goods and services produced that reach the market. Productive activities like housework performed by householders and illegal activities relegated to the underground economy are not included in our GDP calculations. The value of leisure time, which has increased in recent decades, improvements in the quality of goods and services, and the costs of environmental damage are also not included in GDP calculations.

costly environmental mess. Perhaps the communist economists should have seen the U.S. television commercial advertising automobile air filters. It showed a mechanic in the foreground holding an air filter to the screen, while in the background we saw an automobile with its hood raised and engine smoking: The mechanic looks straight at the viewer and says: "You can pay me now (the air filter), or pay me later (the engine)."

Do exclusions from GDP measurement of such items as the value of housework, leisure, and the underground economy seriously undermine the usefulness economists ascribe to GDP accounting? Not really. Having a measure of real GDP that can accurately depict recessions and recoveries is worth the exclusion of some economic activities that are incapable of being accurately measured on a consistent basis. Simply put: The few items excluded involve too much guesswork. What we end up with is a measure of GDP sufficiently comprehensive to be a highly reliable indicator of the changes in the overall performance of the economy.

CHAPTER REVIEW

1. The circular flow model shows firms as producers of goods and services that are purchased by households. Households earn money income by supplying resources to firms. The flow of money in the economy is equivalent to the flows of goods, services, and resources.

2. The equivalence of these flows leads to two approaches to measuring gross domestic product. GDP can be computed by either the expenditure approach or the income approach.

3. Approximately 68 percent of the 1994 GDP for the United States consisted of consumption goods and services.

4. Gross private domestic investment includes goods used by firms to produce other goods and services, investment in structures, and changes in inventories.

5. Net exports represent the difference between exports and imports.

6. Government purchases of goods and services account for approximately 20 percent of GDP.

7. Payments to workers accounted for more than 74 percent of national income in 1994. Interest income, rental income, corporate profit, and proprietors' income represent the remaining components of national income.

8. GNP can be derived from GDP by adding payments to U.S. factors of production located overseas and subtracting payments to foreign factors of production located in the United States. If depreciation and indirect business taxes are subtracted from GDP, we are left with national income.

9. Derivative measures calculated from national income include personal income and personal disposable income.

10. The gross domestic product accounts fail to include economic activity such as value of housework performed by householders and the value of production in the underground economy. GDP also fails to account for improvements in the quality of goods and environmental costs.

KEY TERMS

Circular flow of goods, services, and resources
Circular flow of money
Expenditure approach
Final goods
Intermediate goods
Value added
Personal consumption expenditures
Gross private domestic investment
Government purchases
Net exports
Durable goods
Nondurable goods
Services
Inventory investment
Income approach
National income
Gross national product (GNP)
Capital depreciation
Net domestic product (NDP)
Personal income
Transfer payments
Disposable personal income
Underground economy

QUESTIONS

1. Sketch a circular flow model of goods, services, and resources through households and firms. Explain the role resource and product markets play.

2. Sketch the circular flow model of money through households and firms. Explain the role resource and product markets play.

3. What categories of expenditures are included in the expenditure approach to calculating GDP?

4. What categories of income are included in the income approach to calculating GDP?

5. Distinguish between GDP and GNP.

6. How does the problem of double counting arise in calculating GDP and how is it corrected?

7. Distinguish between intermediate and final goods.

8. Distinguish between durable goods, nondurable goods, and services.

9. What is an investment good? Why are some investment goods unintended?

10. How do economists bring GDP and national income into accord?

11. How does GDP differ from NDP? From national income?

12. In what ways do NDP and national income provide more specific information about an economy's performance than does GDP?

13. What are some of the limitations in using GDP as a measuring rod of our economic well-being?

14. Use the following data to calculate GDP, GNP, NDP, national income, personal income, and personal disposable income.

Personal consumption expenditures	$800
Interest	80
Corporate profit	120
Government purchases	300
Depreciation	80
Rent	40
Gross private domestic investment	100
Compensation of employees	920
Exports	100
Imports	60
Indirect business taxes	70
Proprietors' income	110
Income tax	100
Income earned but not received	120
Income received but not earned	140
Receipt of factor incomes from the rest of the world	60
Payment of factor incomes to the rest of the world	50

15. Suppose, in the following year, the changes in economic activity that occur in question 14 are:

Durable goods	+30
Business inventory	+10
Imports	+20
Income tax	+10

What effect would these changes have on GDP?

16. If Madonna married her personal bodyguard, what effect might it have on national income? Under what circumstances would it affect national income? Under what circumstances would it not affect national income?

17. Professor Kangoh Lee asks his students at Towson State University, "Suppose that in an economy, real consumption, real investment, and real government purchases remain the same from one year to another, while the real trade deficit increases. Can we conclude that real GDP must fall during the same period?" Explain.

CHAPTER 22

BUILDING THE KEYNESIAN MODEL: CONSUMPTION AND INVESTMENT

CHAPTER PREVIEW

The gross domestic product for any given year represents an equilibrium between the production decisions firms make and the spending decisions firms, consumers, and governments make. Spending decisions are expressed as either consumption or investment. This chapter considers a variety of hypotheses concerning consumption behavior before exploring the nature of investment decision making.

After studying this chapter, you should be able to:

- Discuss Keynes' absolute income hypothesis.
- Define the marginal propensity to consume.
- Describe Duesenberry's relative income hypothesis.
- Explain Friedman's permanent income hypothesis of consumption.
- Use real-world examples to explain the life-cycle hypothesis of consumption.
- Explain what causes the consumption function to shift.
- Write an equation for the consumption function and the saving function.
- Discuss the determinants of autonomous investment.
- Explain the volatile nature of investment.

If we could put a satellite in space to observe every person's activity in the marketplace, we would be watching millions of people deciding what kinds of goods to consume. At the same time, we would be watching millions of other people deciding what consumption goods to produce. We would also see that these people make these consumption-spending and consumption-production decisions *simultaneously and independently of each other.*

The fact that producers and consumers make their production and consumption decisions simultaneously and independently of each other may explain why an economy slides into recession or rockets to prosperity. Think about it. How can producers know that what they produce for consumption is what consumers want to consume? And if they're off the mark, what happens? For example, suppose Beth Dollins, Nike's CEO, decides to produce 1 million pairs of cross-training shoes, but when these shoes reach the market, consumers decide to buy only 600,000 pairs. Suppose, at the same time, that Paola Flygare, producer of the Flygare fiberglass bass boat, produces 8,000 boats only to discover later that consumers take less than 3,000 off the market. And suppose that their experiences are common among producers. That is, consumers *just aren't buying enough of everything produced.* The most plausible consequence in this scenario is a cutback in overall production (decrease in real GDP) and an increase in the economy's unemployment.

Let's now change the scenario. Suppose that Beth Dollins' decision to produce 1 million pairs of cross-training shoes is still off-base, but this time it's because consumers want to buy more pairs of shoes than Dollins produced. Suppose also that Paola Flygare's decision to produce 8,000 bass boats is substantially less than the number of boats consumers want. And to complete the picture, let's suppose other producers discover that they, too, underproduced for the market. Now the problem is reversed: *Producers are not producing as much as people want to consume.* The most plausible consequence of this scenario is greater overall production (increase in real GDP) and a decrease in the economy's unemployment.

The uncomplicated fact that production and consumption decisions are made simultaneously and independently of each other is critically important in understanding the forces that determine the level of real GDP in the Keynesian model.

WHAT DETERMINES CONSUMPTION SPENDING?

How do people choose their level of consumption spending? What factors are involved in their decisions to increase or decrease the amount of goods and services they consume? Are we just creatures of habit? Or impulse?

If you had to guess the single, most important factor influencing a person's consumption spending, you would probably be right on the first try. It's the level of a person's disposable income. (For now, let's assume no government spending or taxes so that a person's income is the same as his or her disposable income.) You would also be right to suppose that rich people consume more than poor people because rich people have more income. You don't have to be a Nobel Laureate in economics to figure that out! Economists refer to this simple, but powerful, relationship between consumption and income as the **consumption function.** It is written as

Consumption function

The relationship between consumption and income.

You're looking at a woman who this morning received a 10 percent increase in her salary. She's on her lunch break now. She just came from a travel agency where she bought her dream vacation to Costa Rica, but is now busy upgrading her tennis game (she thinks!) by buying a higher quality shoe.

$$C = f(Y)$$

where C represents consumption and Y represents income. It means that consumption is a function of income, or in other words, that the amount of consumption depends on the amount of income.

Let's use real numbers to illustrate this relationship. Suppose Brenda Nielsen, a manager at Record Swap, enjoys a $1,000 raise in salary. What would happen to her consumption? Does it increase by the $1,000? Or by less? And if less, by how much less? A number of hypotheses have been offered to explain how changes in an individual's income and, taken collectively, changes in national income affect individual and national consumption.

Keynes' Absolute Income Hypothesis

Keynes' absolute income hypothesis suggests that consumption increases as income increases, but at a decreasing rate. Be sure that you understand why, if people behave as Keynes suggested, poor people consume a higher percentage of their income than the rich.

John Maynard Keynes, whose 1936 book, *The General Theory of Employment, Interest and Money*, became the bedrock upon which Keynesian economics was built, advanced the hypothesis that although people who earn high incomes spend more on consumption than people who earn less, they are less inclined to spend as much *out of a given increase in income* than those earning less. For example, Madonna's consumption spending is greater than Brenda's. Yet, if both were given $1,000, Madonna would likely spend less of the $1,000 on consumption than Brenda.

Why? Keynes believed that consumption behavior reflects a psychological law that links changes in our consumption spending to the absolute levels of our income. He explains:

The fundamental psychological law, upon which we are entitled to depend with great confidence both a priori *from our knowledge of human nature and from the detailed facts of experience, is that men are disposed, as a rule and on the average, to increase their consumption as their income increases, but not by as much as their increase in their income. A higher absolute level of income will tend, as a rule, to widen the gap between income and consumption. For the satisfaction of the immediate primary needs of a man and his family is usually a stronger motive than the motives towards accumulation, which only acquire effective sway when the margin of comfort has been attained.*

TABLE 1
The Marginal Propensity to Consume

Total Income (Y)	Change in Income	Consumption (C)	Change in Consumption	Marginal Propensity to Consume (MPC)
0		$ 500		
$1,000	$1,000	1,400	$900	0.90
2,000	1,000	2,200	800	0.80
3,000	1,000	2,900	700	0.70
4,000	1,000	3,500	600	0.60
5,000	1,000	4,000	500	0.50

Absolute income hypothesis

As national income increases, consumption spending increases, but by diminishing amounts. That is, as national income increases, the MPC decreases.

Does this **absolute income hypothesis** seem reasonable to you? Imagine a millionaire receiving a gift of $500. It's unlikely that you would find him running off to buy more food, clothing, or shelter. He would probably just add the $500 to his savings. Why? In Keynes' view, the millionaire's "margin of comfort" is already provided, and the "stronger motive" guiding his behavior, then, becomes "accumulation."

But suppose the $500 were given to an inner-city welfare recipient. What do you suppose he would do? Consult his broker? Do you think he would save a penny? Wouldn't the "immediate primary needs of himself and family"—as Keynes aptly put it—lead straight to consumption?

AN INDIVIDUAL'S MARGINAL PROPENSITY TO CONSUME

Let's pursue Keynes' idea further. Keynes believed that if Brenda's income were increased by increments, say, of $1,000—getting richer with every $1,000 added—the amount she would spend on consumption *out of each additional $1,000* would decrease.

Table 1 and Figure 1 illustrate this point.

Look what happens to Brenda's level of consumption as her income increases in increments of $1,000 from $0 to $5,000. Her consumption increases as well, but note the incremental changes. The first $1,000 addition to income—raising income from $0 to $1,000—induces a change in consumption from $500 to $1,400, or by $900. Keynes defines the change in consumption induced by a change in income as the **marginal propensity to consume, MPC.**

Marginal propensity to consume (MPC)

The ratio of the change in consumption spending to a given change in income.

$$MPC = \frac{\text{change in } C}{\text{change in } Y}$$

The marginal propensity to consume, MPC, is a quantifiable and behaviorial relationship. It measures our inclination, Keynes calls it our propensity, to consume *specific* amounts out of *specific* income changes.

At the income level of $1,000, the marginal propensity to consume is ($1,400 – $500)/($1,000 – $0) = 0.90.

What happens to consumption when the second $1,000 of income is added? Consumption increases from $1,400 to $2,200, or $800. Therefore, at Y = $2,000, Brenda's MPC is ($2,200 – $1,400)/($2,000 – $1,000) = 0.80. Brenda increases consumption, but by less than she did before, just as Keynes would have predicted. Her MPC falls from 0.90 to 0.80.

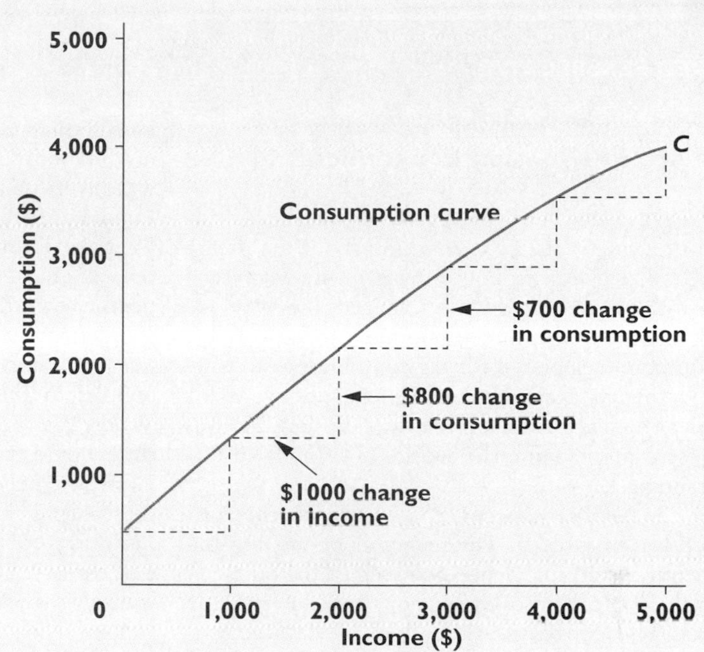

FIGURE 1
The Individual's Marginal Propensity to Consume
The marginal propensity to consume measures the slope of the consumption function. It is the ratio of the change in consumption to the change in income. When income increases by \$1,000—from \$1,000 to \$2,000—the change in consumption is \$2,200 – \$1,400 = \$800. MPC is (\$2,200 – \$1,400)/(\$2,000 – \$1,000) = 0.80. Note how consumption spending increases by diminishing amounts as the income level increases, tracing out the curvature of the consumption curve, C.

Note what's going on. As more units of \$1,000 are added to Brenda's income, her total consumption continues to increase, but each time by lesser amounts. At $Y = \$3{,}000$, $C = \$2{,}900$ and the corresponding MPC = 0.70. At $Y = \$4{,}000$, $C = \$3{,}500$ and MPC = 0.60, and so on. *MPC falls as the absolute level of income increases.*

THE NATION'S MARGINAL PROPENSITY TO CONSUME

To Keynes, national economies behave like individuals. Just as Brenda's MPC depends upon the level of her income, so does a nation's MPC depend upon its level of national income. Table 2 and Figure 2 describe Keynes' view of the nation's consumption behavior.

The nation has its own MPC. When national income increases from \$300 billion to \$400 billion, national consumption increases by \$360 – \$300 = \$60 billion. At $Y = \$400$ billion, MPC = 0.60. Look at the MPC column. As the absolute level of national income increases, the nation's MPC decreases.

Given Keynes' absolute income hypothesis, the consumption function becomes flatter as income increases.

Look at Figure 2. Note the step increases along the consumption curve, *C*. They become increasingly smaller as national income increases; the curve flattens out to almost no increase at all at high levels of national income.

The nation's consumption curve reflects Keynes' *absolute* income hypothesis. It shows that the nation's MPC depends upon the *absolute* level of national income. Does this make sense? Do you find Keynes' view of consumption spending behavior convincing?

If your intuition tells you Keynes was right, you would be dead wrong! Five years after Keynes' *General Theory of Employment, Interest and Money* appeared, Simon Kuznets published his *National Income and Its Composition,* which pioneered analysis of national income data. (He won the Nobel Prize in Economics

ADDED PERSPECTIVE

John Maynard Keynes: Founding Father of Keynesian Economics

In much the same way that Isaac Newton in the 17th century changed the way we think about the physical world, Keynesians believe that in the 20th century John Maynard Keynes changed the way we think about the world of economics.

Although celebrated for his contributions to economic theory, Keynes' creative energies were focused primarily on solving real-world issues. He was interested in changing the world, not simply in understanding it.

In the 1930s the economic world Keynes observed was in turmoil. The reality of a persisting and deepening economic depression seemed to contradict everything economists knew about how an economy works. The conventional wisdom of classical economics argued that depression was only a short-run, temporary departure from full-employment equilibrium and that in the long run the economy would return to it. Keynes' response to this conventional wisdom was that "in the long run, we're all dead."

But Keynes really didn't see the issue—what to do about the depression—as a matter of patience. He was convinced that the economy could not correct itself even in the very long run and explained his reasoning in *The General Theory of Employment, Interest and Money* (1936). *The General Theory* offered an entirely new set of ideas about macroeconomics which, almost instantaneously, became a new school of economic thought. There was ready acceptance of his ideas among the bright, young economists in Britain and in the United States, in part because of the collapse of confidence in classical economics during the depression but also because Keynes was already Britain's preeminent economist. Had he proposed that the world was flat, many of his fellow economists would probably have given him the benefit of the doubt and flattened their globes.

From the very beginning, Keynes was an intellectual phenomenon. Born and raised in Cambridge (his father, Neville, was an economics professor) and schooled at Eton, he returned to Cambridge to do his undergraduate studies at King's College in mathematics and philosophy (which resulted in a highly esteemed book on the theory of probability). His mentor, Alfred Marshall, persuaded him to switch to economics.

Although a rising star at Cambridge, Keynes did not limit himself to academic research. The real world was his natural venue. He divided his time between London and Cambridge, working in London at the Treasury during the week and lecturing at Cambridge on weekends. Quickly establishing a formidable reputation at the Treasury, he became a major participant in international diplomacy, a task he initially relished but later came to dislike. He was the chief economic counsel to the British delegation at Versailles after World War I and there warned against a peace treaty that would impose harsh retribution on defeated Germany, believing that such a policy would ensure the collapse of the European economy. Angered that his ideas were totally disregarded by the framers of the peace treaty, he published them in a much acclaimed, scathing attack on the treaty, *The Economic Consequences of the Peace* (1920), a book that established his worldwide reputation. *A Tract on Monetary Reform* (1923) and *The Economic Consequences of Mr. Churchill* (1925), both policy-oriented works, followed. His two-volume work *A Treatise on Money* (1930) established him as the heir apparent to Marshall. During all this time, Keynes was editor of *The Economic Journal,* the premier scholarly research journal in Britain (and, arguably, the world). In 1944, as the principal architect of the Bretton Woods agreement, he once again tried to prepare Europe and the United States for the difficult task of reconstructing a stable world economy in the aftermath of war.

Keynes' reputation, associations, and activities stretched beyond the circles of academic, financial, diplomatic, and political elites. He was also a celebrated member of Britain's artistic society. He was married to Lydia Lopokovia, a well-known ballerina, and was a member of London's illustrious (and perhaps infamous) Bloomsbury set, which included such eminent personalities as Lytton Strachey, E. M. Forster, and Virginia Woolf.

Keynes also put his financial wizardry to work in stock speculations, which he made in the early morning by phone while still in bed, and which made him a millionaire. While bursar of King's College, he speculated on the college's behalf, increasing its endowment tenfold.

Although new ideas have come to challenge Keynesian economics, many Keynesians still revere him as Shakespeare's Anthony did of Caesar: "Here was a Caesar! When comes such another?"

TABLE 2
The Nation's Marginal Propensity to Consume ($ billions)

National Income (Y)	Change in National Income	Consumption (C)	Change in Consumption	Marginal Propensity to Consume (MPC)
$ 0		$ 60		
100	$100	150	$90	0.90
200	100	230	80	0.80
300	100	300	70	0.70
400	100	360	60	0.60
500	100	410	50	0.50

in 1971 for his work.) Kuznets' findings—as well as the mountains of empirical research that followed—showed that, in spite of intuition, *a nation's MPC tends to remain fairly constant regardless of the absolute level of national income.* Where did Keynes go wrong?

Duesenberry's Relative Income Hypothesis

James Duesenberry offered an alternative income hypothesis. Every economy, whatever its level of national income, includes people earning different incomes. Knowing someone's absolute income tells us little about that person's income

FIGURE 2
The Nation's Marginal Propensity to Consume
Note the similarity between the individual's marginal propensity to consume of Figure 1 and the nation's. When the national income increases, national consumption increases as well, but by diminishing amounts. MPC decreases from 0.90 to 0.50 as national income increases from $0 to $500 billion, tracing out the upward-sloping consumption curve, C.

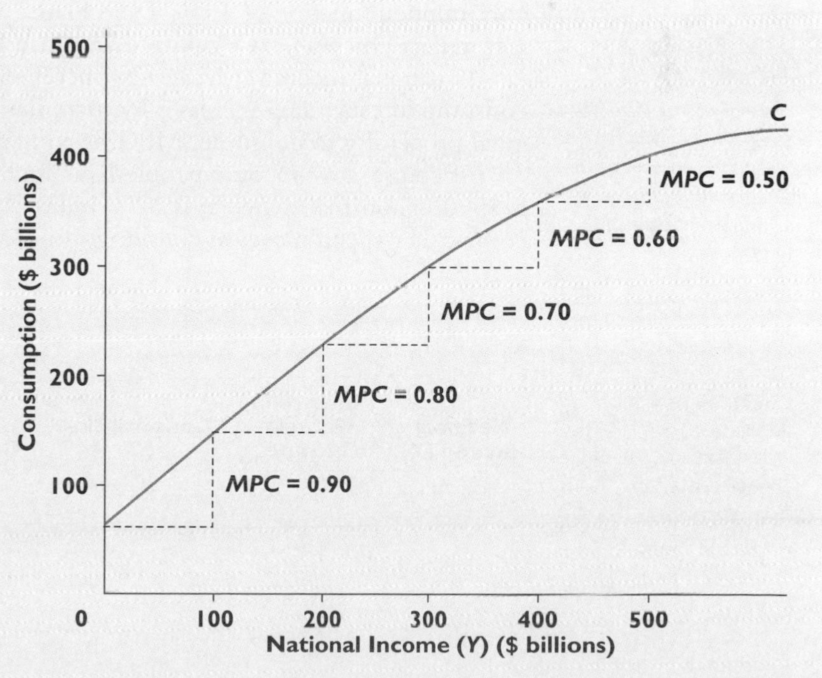

When national income increases, everyone's income increases approximately proportionately. Since relative incomes are unchanged, the MPC for people in different income classes are unchanged as well. Duesenberry's hypothesis suggests a consumption function with a constant slope.

status. For example, Brenda earning $20,000 a year would be considered a low-income person if others in the economy earned more, say $40,000 and $80,000. On the other hand, that same $20,000 makes her a high-income person if others in the economy earn less, say, $5,000 and $10,000.

If Brenda's income doubled to $40,000, but at the same time everybody else's income also doubled—say, from $40,000 to $80,000 and from $80,000 to $160,000—then Brenda, at $40,000 income, would still be regarded as low-income.

The distinction between Brenda's relative income (that is, income relative to other incomes) and her absolute income level provided Duesenberry with an alternative view of the consumption function. It explains why the marginal propensity to consume in the economy does not decline as national income increases—as Keynes believed it does—but instead remains constant.

According to Duesenberry, *consumption spending is rooted in status*. High-income people not only consume more goods and services than others, they set consumption standards for everybody else. They own the most comfortable homes, drive the most expensive cars, enjoy the newest consumer technologies, and read *Architectural Digest* without feeling deprived.

Everybody else takes their cues from the rich. The middle-income people try to stay within reach. Low-income people struggle to keep their consumption within sight of middle-income consumption. For example, if Brenda's MPC were 0.80 at an income of $20,000, it would remain 0.80 even if her income doubled to $40,000 *as long as her relative income position remains unchanged.* If everybody's income doubles so that their relative income positions remain unchanged, then everybody's MPCs remain unchanged. That's how Duesenberry explains why, contrary to what Keynes thought, the nation's MPC is constant while national income increases.

The logic is compelling and is supported by historical data as well. Keynes' consumption function of Table 2 and Figure 2 is modified in Table 3 and Figure 3 to reflect Duesenberry's **relative income hypothesis.**

Relative income hypothesis

As national income increases, consumption spending increases as well, always by the same amount. That is, as national income increases, MPC remains constant.

As national income increases by increments of $100 billion, the economy's consumption spending increases by increments of $80 billion. That is, the marginal propensity to consume, MPC, is constant at 0.80.

Of course, low-income people have higher incomes when national income is $500 billion than when it is $200 billion. And because they have higher incomes, they spend more on consumption. But because their relative income has

TABLE 3 Constant Marginal Propensity to Consume ($ billions)

National Income (Y)	Change in National Income	Consumption (C)	Change in Consumption	Marginal Propensity to Consume (MPC)
$ 0		$ 60		
100	$100	140	$80	0.80
200	100	220	80	0.80
300	100	300	80	0.80
400	100	380	80	0.80
500	100	460	80	0.80

FIGURE 3
The Marginal Propensity to Consume Remains Constant
With every $100 billion increase in national income, the nation's consumption spending increases by $80 billion, tracing out a straight-line consumption curve, *C*. The *MPC* = 0.80 at every level of national income.

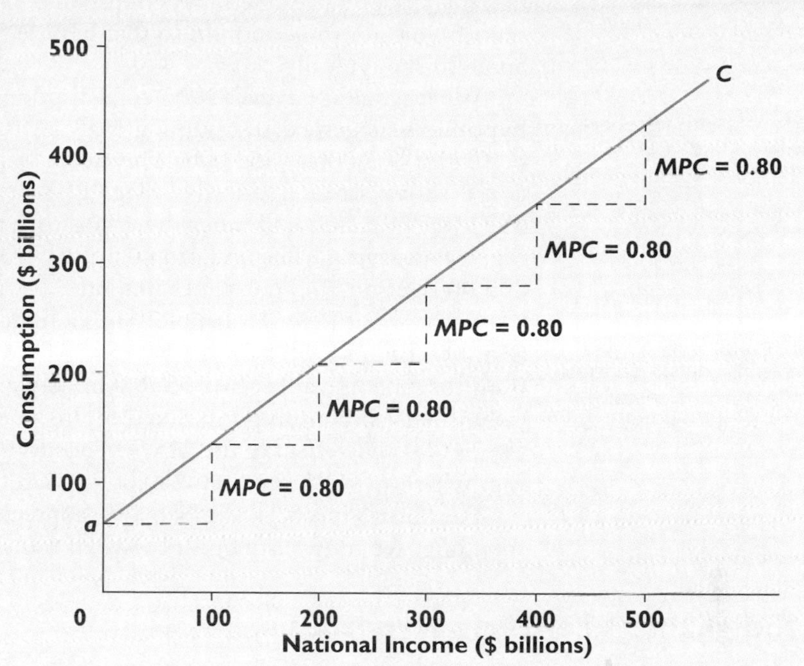

Permanent income hypothesis

A person's consumption spending is related to his or her permanent income.

Life-cycle hypothesis

Typically, a person's MPC is relatively high during young adulthood, decreases during the middle-age years, and increases when the person is near or in retirement.

not changed—everyone, rich and poor, is richer—their MPC, and the economy's, remain unchanged.

Notice the steplike increases in consumption in Figure 3. Because MPC = 0.80, every dollar increase in income generates an $0.80 increase in consumption—the steps are the same height—so that the consumption curve, *C*, is a straight line.

Economists have continued to study the consumption function, providing additional insights into our consumption behavior. The two most influential are Milton Friedman's **permanent income hypothesis** (1957) and Franco Modigliani's **life-cycle hypothesis** (1963).

Friedman's Permanent Income Hypothesis

Permanent income

Permanent income is the regular income a person expects to earn annually. It may differ by some unexpected gain or loss from the actual income earned.

Transitory income

The unexpected gain or loss of income that a person experiences. It is the difference between a person's regular and actual income in any year.

Milton Friedman, who won the Nobel Prize in economics in 1977, believes people distinguish between their regular income and the income they may happen to make (or lose) in any one year. He refers to regular income as **permanent income,** and to the unanticipated income that adds to (or subtracts from) the permanent income as **transitory income.**

Why make these distinctions? Because, according to Friedman, how much we spend on consumption depends strictly on our permanent income.

Why? Why doesn't transitory income contribute to our consumption spending? Because people don't usually go about changing life-styles when they suffer a temporary loss of income or even when they enjoy a temporary gain. Consumption spending is generally tied to long-run earning capacity.

Imagine two people, Natasha Rubel and Peter Holsapple each earning $50,000 in 1995. But suppose Natasha, a self-employed artist who conducts arttherapy classes for teachers and counselors, had a bad year. A broken leg put her out of work for three months so that her 1995 income was $15,000 less than the $65,000 she typically earns.

What would Natasha's 1995 consumption look like? The permanent income hypothesis suggests that, assuming MPC = 0.80, Natasha's consumption would be 0.80 × $65,000 = $52,000. The effect of her negative $15,000 transitory income shows up as reduced saving. Her saving in 1995 becomes $50,000 − $52,000 = −$2,000. Her negative transitory income creates, then, negative saving, or dissaving. The important point is that she still thinks of herself as a $65,000 person, and consumes like one.

Milton Friedman argues that consumption depends on long-run or permanent income, not transitory income.

What about Peter Holsapple? He's a high school teacher who typically earns $35,000. But in 1995 he received a $15,000 teaching award. Would this $15,000 transitory income affect his $35,000 life-style? Not likely. Assuming his MPC = 0.80, his 1995 consumption, fixed by his permanent income, is 0.80 × $35,000 = $28,000. The effect of the $15,000 positive transitory income shows up as saving, which in 1995 becomes $50,000 − $28,000 = $22,000.

Friedman's point is simple. To appreciate what influences consumption spending, we must distinguish between transitory and permanent income.

Modigliani's Life-Cycle Hypothesis

Be certain that you can explain how consumption, as a fraction of income, is likely to change over a person's lifetime.

Franco Modigliani of MIT, who won the Nobel Prize in Economics in 1985, makes his own observation about our consumption behavior. He identifies three consumption phases—young adults, middle age, and near or in retirement—in a person's life-cycle. Each specific phase has its specific MPC.

The MPC for young adults is relatively high. They are busy building families and careers. They buy first homes, first new automobiles, stocks of household durables, sets of clothing for growing children, and streams of services. These items tend to eat quickly into their modest incomes.

When they become middle-aged, enjoying their highest and most rapidly growing incomes, their consumption spending also increases, but modestly at least compared to earlier years. After all, their homes are virtually mortgage-free, their car payments not nearly so demanding, their children finally graduating

That sticker price tells them what they already suspected: It's hard to save with a growing family. But they really do need that station wagon. The kids have to be driven to school, to after-school activities, and the neighborhood kids are typically part of that scene.

from college, and the basics of life already taken care of. They tend to consume more because they earn more, but the ratio of changes in consumption to changes in income tends to fall. That is, their MPC falls.

In the third phase, nearing or in retirement, their MPC tends to rise. Why? Their incomes don't grow very much, and in many cases, actually decline. But what about their consumption? They become more careful about their spending, but habits are hard to break. People don't change their life-styles that much.

Modigliani explains why differing MPCs over a person's life-cycle are still consistent with the observed stability in our national MPC. As long as birth and death rates are relatively stable, the percent of population passing through these three consumption phases at any time remains stable as well.

Autonomous Consumption Spending

The idea that consumption depends primarily on the level of income is so consistent with our experience that very few people have trouble making the connection. But consumption based on income is not the whole story. Look again at Figure 3.

When $Y = 0$, $C = \$60$ billion. Some consumption is autonomous, that is, independent of the level of income. Economists call it **autonomous consumption.**

Autonomous consumption
Consumption spending that is independent of the level of income.

Why autonomous? Because some consumption spending is simply unavoidable. The spending takes place regardless of the level of income. For example, we might spend less on food, clothing, and shelter when our incomes fall, but there are limits to how deeply we can cut into our consumption of these basics. At some point, we simply cannot consume less and still survive. We make some minimum consumption spending even if we have to borrow, use our savings, or sell off part of our assets. Put simply: If we have no other means of putting food on the table, we may sometimes be forced to sell the table! That explains why in the economy of Figure 3, when income is zero, autonomous consumption is positive. The consumption curve, C, in Figure 3 begins at a, above the origin on the vertical axis, at $60 billion.

Shifts in the Consumption Curve

Look at the consumption curve, C, in Figure 4. A change in national income from, say, $200 billion to $300 billion induces a change of $80 billion in consumption—from $220 billion to $300 billion. We see this change in consumption as a movement *along the consumption curve C.*

But consumption spending can change even when the level of national income remains unchanged. These changes in consumption are caused by shifts in the consumption curve itself. What factors shift the consumption curve in Figure 4 upward from C to C'? What could trigger an upward shift in the curve from C to C'?

REAL ASSET AND MONEY HOLDINGS

Suppose Sara Cook wins the $12 million Florida state lottery. That's everyone's fantasy! And suppose she decides to keep her $50,000 job at DisneyWorld. It's hard to believe that her lottery winnings would not *eventually* affect her con-

FIGURE 4
Shifts in the Consumption Curve
Shifts in the consumption curve are distinguished from movements along the curve. The shifts are unrelated to changes in national income. Among the principal factors causing the shifts in the consumption curve are changes in the economy's asset and money holdings, in people's expectations of price changes, in the interest rate, and in taxation. Anything that causes autonomous consumption to change will shift the consumption curve.

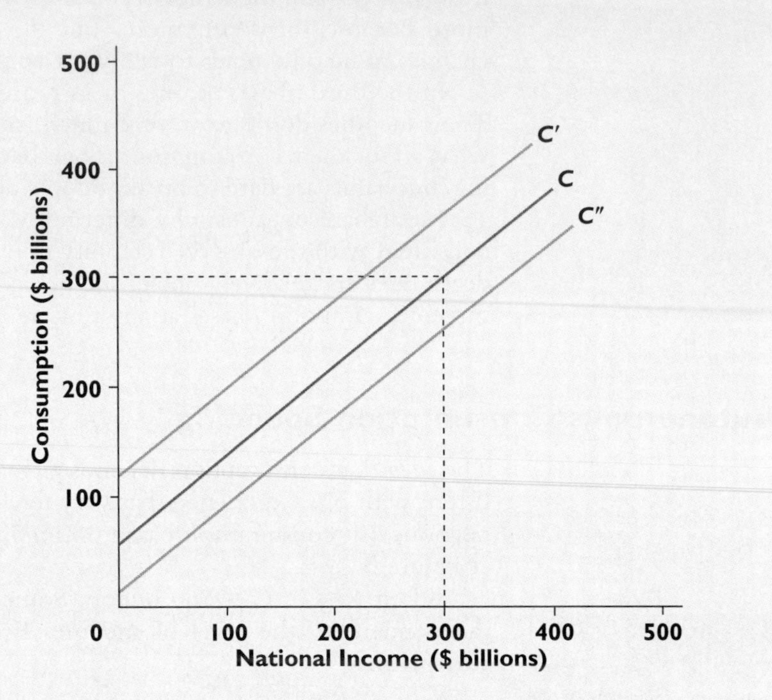

sumption spending. The probability is high that even though she continued to work at her $50,000 job, she would end up consuming more goods and services than before.

The consumption curve will shift upward if real asset and money holdings increase, if people expect prices to increase, if interest rates decrease, and if taxes decrease.

Or suppose George Paaswell, who rents a studio apartment in midtown Manhattan, inherits a mortgage-free house on Park Avenue. That's not exactly $12 million, but to George, it's a real asset of considerable value. Wouldn't you think an inheritance like that would affect his consumption spending?

Suppose people's real assets and money holdings in the economy increase. National consumption spending should increase as well. These increases are shown in Figure 4 as an upward shift in the consumption curve from C to C'. A decrease in the nation's real asset or money holdings would have the opposite effect, shifting the curve from C to C''.

EXPECTATIONS OF PRICE CHANGES

People are always anticipating the future. Suppose, for some reason, they expect inflation to increase from 3 to 12 percent in one year and to continue in double digits for the following six years. Wouldn't it be smart for people, *even though they don't expect their income to change,* to increase the level of their consumption spending now, before the expected inflation hits? Such an increase shifts the consumption curve from C to C′.

CREDIT AND INTEREST RATES

People's consumption of relatively costly durables, such as automobiles, personal computers, and major kitchen appliances is typically financed by interest-carrying credit. For many, interest payments on these items make up a significant part of their monthly expenditures. If, then, credit were made more available or if the credit terms were made more attractive, say, by a cut in the interest rate, wouldn't people increase their consumption spending even if their incomes haven't changed? The consumption curve would shift upward from C to C'.

TAXATION

We are all obligated to pay taxes. But how much? Suppose the government decides to cut the income tax. Then imagine Meg Weinbaum's delight when she discovers more dollars in her pay envelope at the end of the week, even though her salary remains unchanged. What do you suppose she would do with the extra money? Spend some of it, wouldn't she? She and many millions more would shift the consumption curve from C to C'. If their pay envelopes were lighter because of increased taxes, the consumption curve would shift from C to C''.

THE CONSUMPTION EQUATION

Be sure that you understand that this equation is simply the equation for a straight line, with consumption as the dependent variable, national income as the independent variable, and a slope equal to the marginal propensity to consume.

As you see, there are two key factors influencing the character of our consumption spending. Keynes' conception of the marginal propensity to consume, and the insightful modifications to the consumption function that followed—by Duesenberry, Friedman, and Modigliani—show that our level of consumption spending is primarily determined by our level of income. Economists refer to this consumption as *induced* consumption, meaning induced by the level of income. A second factor contributing to consumption spending is autonomous consumption.

Adding autonomous consumption to consumption spending induced by income generates a specific form of the consumption function:

$$C = a + bY$$

where a equals autonomous consumption spending, b equals marginal propensity to consume, and Y equals level of national income.

Let's see how the equation is used to determine how much consumption spending occurs when $Y = \$800$ billion, MPC = 0.80, and $a = \$60$ billion. We simply plug the appropriate values into the equation:

$$\begin{aligned} C &= a + bY \\ &= \$60 \text{ billion} + 0.8(\$800 \text{ billion}) \\ &= \$60 \text{ billion} + \$640 \text{ billion} \\ &= \$700 \text{ billion} \end{aligned}$$

When national income is \$900 billion—assuming MPC and autonomous consumption remain unchanged—consumption spending is \$780 billion.

WHAT DETERMINES THE LEVEL OF SAVING?

People do two things with their income. They either spend it on consumption or they do *not* spend it on consumption. When people make a decision about one, they automatically make a decision about the other. After all, if you decide

ADDED PERSPECTIVE

The Long and Short of It: The Consumption Function in the United States

	National Income ($ billions)	Private Consumption ($ billions)	C/Y
1991	$5,062.8	$3,889.1	76.8%
1990	4,929.8	3,742.6	75.9
1989	4,673.7	3,517.9	75.3
1988	4,374.3	3,296.1	75.4
1985	3,599.1	2,667.4	74.1
1980	2,430.2	1,748.1	71.9
1975	1,439.2	1,024.9	71.5
1970	928.0	646.5	69.7

Panel *a* of the figure plots national income and consumption data for the United States for selected years during the period 1970–91. The data trace out a straight-line consumption curve, *which appears to run through the origin.* The curve shows average propensities to consume—that is, *C/Y,* falling within the range 0.697 and 0.768.

This data-constructed consumption function (see table) seems to contradict the consumption function depicted in the text—such as Figure 3—which shows the consumption curve intercepting the vertical axis above the origin.

Which function is correct? The answer is both! The seeming contradiction between the two is resolved by noting that the straight-line-through-the-origin consumption function is a long-run function, while the intercept-above-the-origin function represents a short-run consumption function.

Panel *b* shows how the two functions relate. Look at the short-run consumption curve, *C*. It depicts the relationship between national income and consumption *for the short-run period of 1970*. For example, the actual levels of national income and consumption for 1970, as shown in the accompanying table, are $928 billion and $646.5 billion. Now suppose that in 1970 national income was not $928 billion but, say, $1,439.2 billion. At that level of national income, the short-run consumption function for 1970 shows that consumption would have been at point *b*—$825 billion. One more example: If national income in 1970 had been $2,000 billion, consumption in 1970 would have been $980 billion (point *b*).

But suppose that after five years of continuing economic growth, people's holdings of wealth and their permanent income increase, shifting the short-

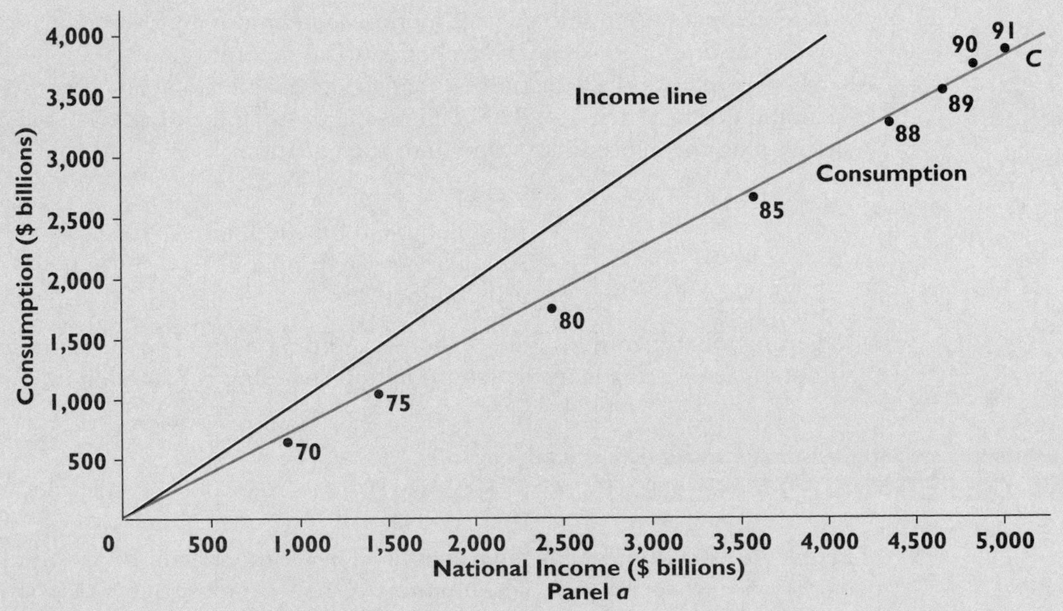

Panel *a*

run consumption function from C to C'. In 1975, then, actual levels of national income and consumption in 1975 are $1,439.2 billion and $1,024.9 billion, respectively. Compare this actual $1,024.9 billion to the $825 billion plotted in the short-run consumption curve, C, for 1970. *The difference is explained in the shifts in short-run consumption curves that take place over the long run,* in this case, the five periods 1970–75. In 1975, people consume $1,024.9 billion, not $825 billion, because they are wealthier than they were in 1970.

Panel *b* shows a series of short-run consumption curves—one for each year of actual data shown in the accompanying table—that identify actual points on the short-run curves. The long-run consumption function of panel *a*, then, is connecting the points of the series of short run consumption functions.

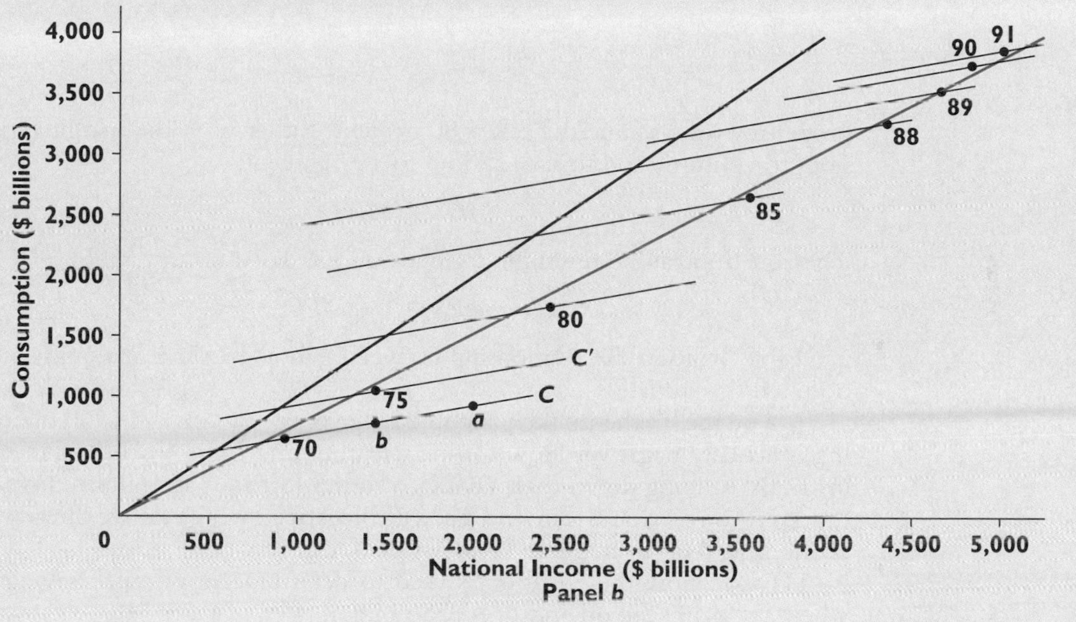

Panel *b*

to spend 80 percent of your income, you have also made a decision *not* to spend 20 percent, haven't you? The income *not* spent on consumption is defined as **saving.**

Saving

That part of national income not spent on consumption.

$$S = Y - C$$

That's the economy's saving equation. Moreover, in the same way that we derive the marginal propensity to consume, we derive as well the **marginal propensity to save, MPS.** The MPS measures the change in saving generated by a change in income.

Marginal propensity to save (MPS)

The change in saving induced by a change in income.

$$MPS = \frac{\text{change in } S}{\text{change in } Y}$$

What we don't spend, we save. If MPC = 0.80, then MPS = 0.20. Why? Because if our marginal propensity to consume is 80 percent of any additional income, then it stands to reason that our marginal propensity is to save the rest. That's the remaining 20 percent.

We could just as well have stated the relationship between MPC and MPS the other way. That is, if we save 20 percent of any additional income, then our

TABLE 4
Marginal Propensity to Save ($ billions)

Y	Change in Y	C	S	MPC	MPS
$ 0		$ 60	$−60		
100	$100	140	−40	0.80	0.20
200	100	220	−20	0.80	0.20
300	100	300	0	0.80	0.20
400	100	380	20	0.80	0.20
500	100	460	40	0.80	0.20

propensity to consume the rest is 80 percent. Either way, the marginal propensities to consume and to save add up to 100 percent.

$$MPC + MPS = 1$$

The equation can be rewritten to focus on the derivation of MPS.

$$MPS = 1 - MPC$$

Table 4 shows the relationship between national saving, national consumption, MPC, and MPS.

As you see, in the unlikely income range of Y = $0 to Y = $200 billion, saving is actually negative. How can people consume more than their income allows? By running down their savings or other forms of accumulated wealth. In this same way, nations can end up with negative saving. As we already noted, economists refer to negative saving as dissaving.

Be sure that you can derive the saving function from the consumption function, realizing that national income is equal to consumption plus savings.

Let's see how the equation is used to determine how much saving occurs when Y = $400 billion and C = $380 billion.

$$\begin{aligned} S &= Y - C \\ &= \$400 \text{ billion} - \$380 \text{ billion} \\ &= \$\ 20 \text{ billion} \end{aligned}$$

When Y = $500 billion and C = $460 billion, then S = $40 billion. Throughout the income range Y = $0 to Y = $500 billion in Table 4, saving increases by $20 billion for every $100 billion increase in national income. MPS is constant at 0.20.

Figure 5, panels *a* and *b,* translates the consumption and saving data of Table 4 into graphic form.

In panel *a,* the 45° diagonal line serves as a point of reference. Since $Y = C + S$, every point on the 45° line equates the level of Y measured on the horizontal axis to the level of $C + S$ measured on the vertical axis. For example, *g* on the diagonal measures $100 on both axes. The **45° line,** measuring $Y = C + S$, is also called the *income curve.*

45° line

A line, drawn at a 45° angle, showing all points at which the distance to the horizontal axis equals the distance to the vertical axis.

How do we derive the level of saving in panel *a*? Look, for example, at Y = $400 billion. By using the equation $S = Y - C$, and substituting $(a + bY)$ for C, we derive

$$\begin{aligned} S &= Y - (a + bY) \\ &= \$400 \text{ billion} - [\$60 \text{ billion} + (0.8 \text{ x } \$400 \text{ billion})] \\ &= \$20 \text{ billion} \end{aligned}$$

FIGURE 5
The Saving Curve
Saving is defined as income not spent on consumption. When Y is less than \$300 billion, C is greater than Y so that saving is negative, that is, the nation is dissaving. Saving is zero at \$300 billion, and then positive and increasing as national income increases beyond \$300 billion. Panel *a* shows saving as the difference between the income and consumption curves. Panel *b* depicts the saving curve.

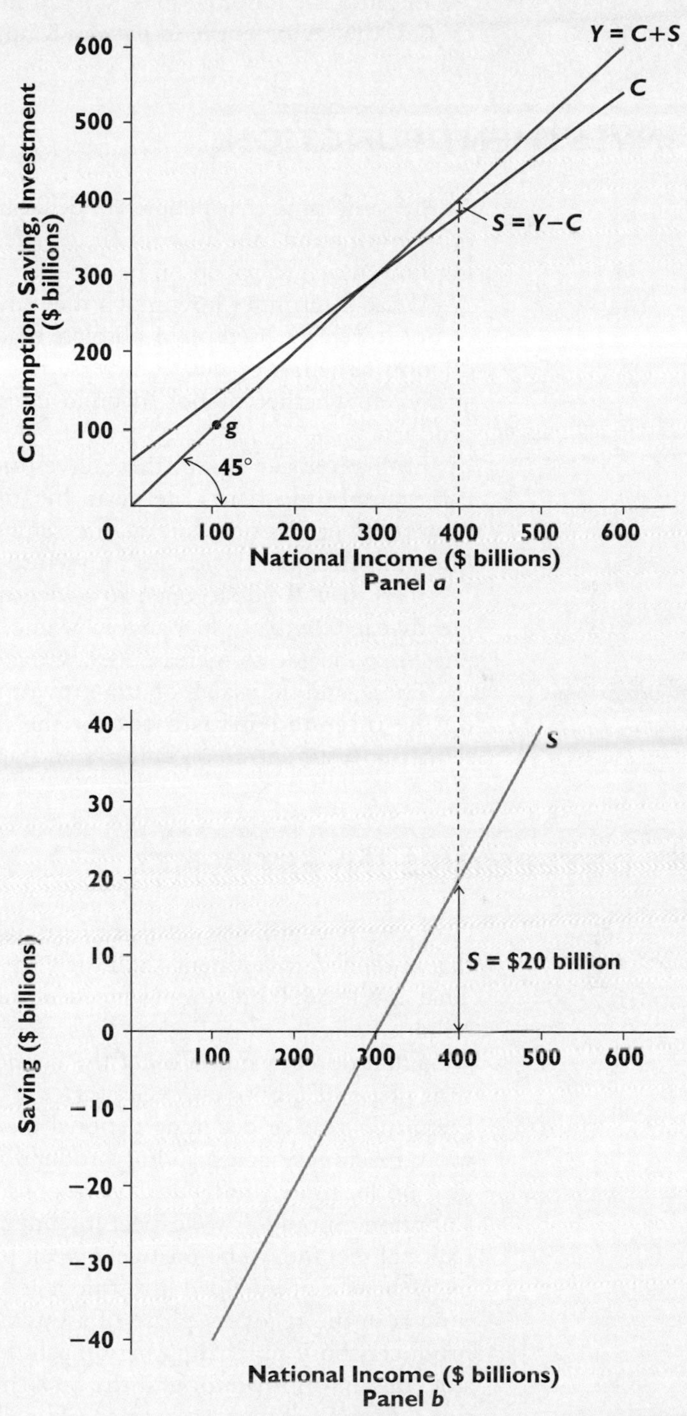

Now look at Y = \$400 billion in panel *b* of Figure 5. Panel *b* is another way of looking at panel *a*, showing only the saving curve which, as we have seen in panel *a*, is derived from subtracting consumption from national income. At Y = \$400 billion, the \$20 billion difference between Y and C, shown in panel *a*, shows up as \$20 billion in the saving curve of panel *b*.

Because the absolute ($Y - C$) gap in panel *a* increases as the level of Y increases, the saving curve in panel *b* is upward-sloping.

THE INVESTMENT FUNCTION

At the same time that people are deciding how much of their income to spend on consumption and how much to save, producers in the economy are deciding how much to spend on new investment.

What determines how much they invest? Producers have to decide whether or not to replace used up or obsolete machinery, whether or not to expand production, whether or not to increase raw material or finished goods inventories, and even whether or not to build completely new facilities for entirely new products.

Each producer makes these investment decisions independently of others. For example, the giant Caterpillar, Inc., in Peoria, Illinois, may decide to expand its forklift production line at the same time that a small retail bookstore in Phoenix, Arizona, decides to move into larger space.

Sears may decide to open an outlet in Raleigh, North Carolina. The Artistic Headwear Company in Bangor, Maine, protecting itself from inadequate supplies, may decide to increase its raw material inventories.

Intended investment

Investment spending that producers intend to undertake.

These, and thousands of other investment decisions made by producers make up the **intended investment** for the national economy. As we shall see, intended investment doesn't always end up realized.

WHAT DETERMINES INVESTMENT?

Consider two different levels of national income: Does your intuition tell you that intended investment should be greater when national income is higher? That at $Y = \$800$ billion, producers would tend to invest more than at $Y = \$500$ billion?

Then think again. What if the economy at $Y = \$800$ billion is in a downturn phase of a business cycle; that the year before, Y was \$900 billion. Why, then, in a year of declining national income should producers consider buying more machinery or expanding production lines or building new factories? Why gear up for more production when consumers are not gearing up for more consumption. Shouldn't we expect intended investment, even at the higher level of national income, to be relatively weak under these bleak conditions?

What about intended investment at $Y = \$500$ billion? Suppose the economy now is in the recovery phase of a business cycle. Wouldn't you expect to find producers busy purchasing new machinery, adding more production lines, and stocking up on inventories if the \$500 billion is \$100 billion more than the national income of the year before? After all, people with growing incomes are also people whose consumption spending is growing. Intended investment under these spirited conditions would tend to be relatively high.

It would seem then that the level of national income doesn't play the decisive role in determining investment that it plays in determining consumption spending. Figure 6 illustrates this point, showing investment as autonomous, that is, independent of the level of national income.

FIGURE 6
The Investment Curve
The investment curve is horizontal, independent of the level of national income. Intended investment is $75 billion at every level of national income.

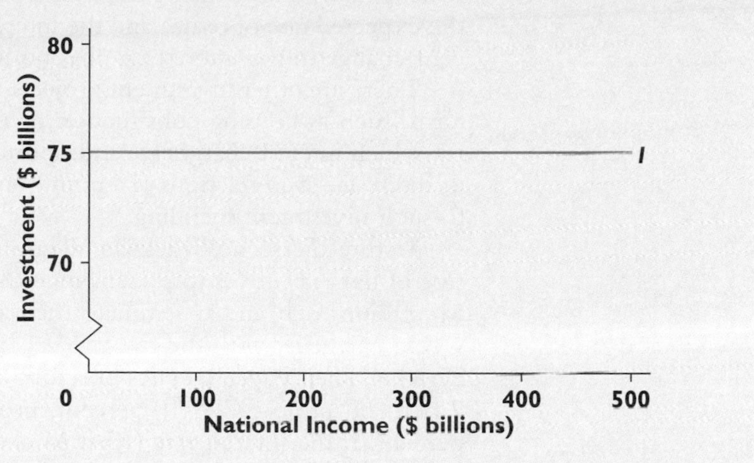

Intended investment is relatively independent of the level of national income.

The investment curve, I, is a horizontal straight line. If $I =$ $75 billion, it is $75 billion regardless of the level of national income. For example, when $Y =$ $100, $I =$ $75 billion. When $Y =$ $200 billion, $I =$ $75 billion. And so on.

Determinants of Investment

Autonomous investment

Investment that is independent of the level of income.

But why $75 billion? What factors determine the size of the economy's **autonomous investment?** There are four principal determinants of autonomous investment: the level of technology, the rate of interest, expectations of future economic growth, and the rate of capacity utilization.

LEVEL OF TECHNOLOGY

The introduction of new technologies is one of the mainsprings of investment. For example, when the railroad displaced water transport as the principal means of long-distance transportation, it sparked massive investment spending not only in the railroad industry, but in the secondary industries that grew up alongside it. Investments in mining, steel, lumber, and construction were needed to feed the expanding railroads. But that was only the surface of railroad-led investment. The railroads opened up the West, generating decades of spectacular investment spending in roads and commercial and residential building, as well as in goods that filled these new structures.

Similar technological leaps, such as the automobile, steam power, electricity, the telephone, petrochemicals, television, nuclear energy, drugs, computers, and genetic engineering have produced, in their own times, extensive networks of investment spending.

Not only is there no connection between these technological breakthroughs and the levels of national income they feed, but it is also impossible to fit them into any defined timetable. Like volcanoes, they seem to erupt in their own time and place.

THE INTEREST RATE

Producers undertake investment when they believe that the rate of return generated by the investment will exceed the interest rate, that is, the cost of borrowing investment funds. For some types of investment, the difference between the expected rate of return and the interest rate is so wide that even a 4 or 5 percent change in the interest rate has no influence on the investment decisions.

There are other investment projects, however, typically large-scale and long-term, such as housing construction or expansion of automobile assembly lines, for which interest charges are an important cost factor. Slight changes in the rate of interest—even fractions of a point—may be a sufficient incentive or deterrent to such investment spending.

Picture the scene. Michelle Vlasminski, CEO of Michelle Enterprises, asks five of her executives to present investment projects which would cost roughly $1 million each and to estimate their expected rate of return. The following week, Michelle, with the five projects in hand, considers which, if any, to undertake. Their expected rates of return are: project A = 12 percent, project B = 7 percent, project C = 10 percent, project D = 9 percent, and project E = 8 percent. If the interest rate (what Michelle pays to borrow investment funds) is 15 percent, which, if any, investment project will she accept? None, of course. She would not borrow at a 15 percent interest rate if she can get, at best, only a 12 percent rate of return.

What if the interest rate is 11 percent? Then, project A is feasible. If the interest rate is 9.5 percent, then both projects A and C are advantageous. At 8.5 percent interest, projects A, C, and D increase the profitability of her firm. As you can see, a lower interest rate makes more investment projects feasible. In other words, there is an inverse relationship between the rate of interest and the quantity of investment spending.

That's what panel *a* of Figure 7 depicts.

The demand curve for investment in the economy as a whole is downward-sloping. That is, as the interest rate falls, the quantity demanded of investment

FIGURE 7 **The Effect of Changes in the Rate of Interest on the Level of Investment**

In panel *a*, the level of investment is determined by the interest rate. The demand curve for investment, *D*, is downward-sloping. As the rate of interest decreases from 8 to 6 percent, the level of investment in the economy increases from $75 billion to $80 billion. This increase in investment is depicted in panel *b* as an upward shift in the investment curve, from $75 billion to $80 billion.

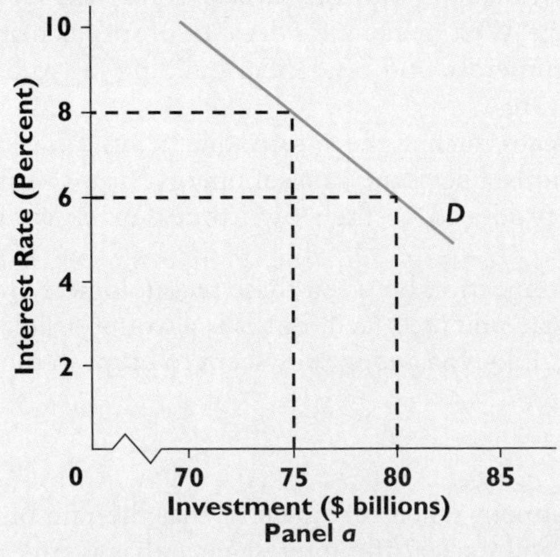

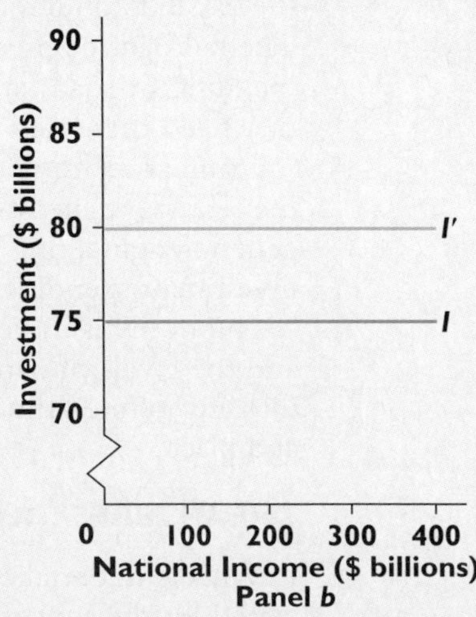

increases. For example, when the rate falls from 8 to 6 percent, investment increases from $75 billion to $80 billion. *Note that this increase in investment has nothing to do with changes in national income.* This new level of investment is represented, in panel *b*, by the upward shift of the investment curve from *I* to *I*′, from $75 billion to $80 billion.

EXPECTATIONS OF FUTURE ECONOMIC GROWTH

Investment spending reflects how producers view the future. They expand production lines or build entirely new factories if they expect sales to grow. What influences expectations?

Many producers base their expectations of the future on past experience. If the economy grew rapidly in the past, many producers—lacking any contrary information—expect it to continue to grow rapidly in the future. If they expect it to grow, they prepare for the growth by increasing investment spending. On the other hand, if the economy was sluggish in the past, these same producers would expect it to continue being sluggish. Investment spending may be the furthest thing from their minds. That is to say, investment spending takes its cue from past performance. It's the changes in national income and the projections of those changes into the future, not the absolute level of national income, that influence producers.

RATE OF CAPACITY UTILIZATION

Be sure that you can explain how changes in technology, changes in the interest rate, changes in the growth of national income, and changes in the rate of capacity utilization influence autonomous investment.

Producers seldom choose to operate at 100 percent capacity. Why not? Because to produce at capacity reduces their ability to expand production on demand. They typically choose a capacity utilization rate that gives them some short-run flexibility. For example, by operating at 85 percent capacity, they can increase production by as much as 15 percent without having to wait for new machinery or raw material inventories. In the highly competitive business world, differences of months, weeks, or even days can make the difference between success and failure.

There is, however, a cost to flexibility. Carrying excess productive capacity can be an expensive way of overcoming short-run production bottlenecks. How much flexibility producers end up choosing, then, influences the economy's level of investment. For producers who choose to operate close to full capacity, a moderate increase in sales may shift them quickly into strong investment spending.

The Volatile Nature of Investment

Any one of the above factors can excite or depress the level of investment. In some years, these factors pull in opposite directions. For example, the interest rate may increase at the same time a new round of technologically induced investments are introduced. One stimulates, the other dampens investment spending.

On the other hand, there are times when, *by chance,* these factors work in unison. A fall in the interest rate combines with an increase in the rate of technological change, with a shift to greater capacity utilization, and with impressive economic growth. In such a situation, dramatic upward shifts in the investment curve occur.

The investment curve in Figure 8 shows the possible volatility of investment spending in the U.S. economy.

In some years, a specific combination of factors influencing investment drives the level of investment to new heights, only to be followed by a sharp

FIGURE 8 **The Volatility of Investment**

Unlike consumption, which is fairly stable over time, investment is subject to erratic fluctuations even through very short periods of time. The economic and technological factors that influence investment can sometimes create the conditions for rapid expansion of investment and, just as quickly, reverse to cause investment to fall just as rapidly, as we see in the annual rate of change in real investment spending over the years 1960 to 1992.

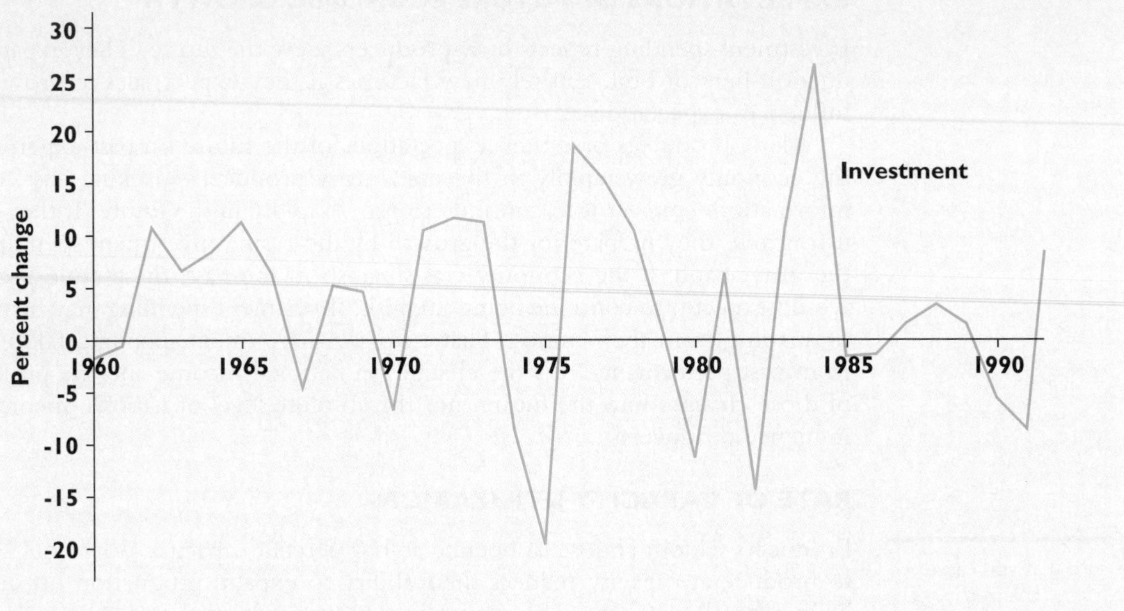

Source: *Economic Report of the President, 1994*, United States Government Printing Office, Washington, D.C., 1994, p. 270.

plunge in investment driven by a reversal in those same factors. Most of the time, the direction—let alone the levels—investment will take is, for everyone, a big unknown.

COMBINING CONSUMPTION SPENDING AND INVESTMENT SPENDING

Let's pause for a moment. The two principal building blocks in the Keynesian model—consumption and investment spending—have been put in position. What follows next is an analysis of the relationship between consumption and investment spending that explains how the Keynesian model derives national income.

That's the task we assign to the following chapter. It should be viewed as a continuation or second half of this chapter since both chapters develop the Keynesian model of national income determination.

CHAPTER REVIEW

1. The consumption function relates the level of consumption to income. It is reasonable to think that as income increases, consumption increases also.

2. Keynes' absolute income hypothesis suggests that as income increases, consumption increases, but at a decreasing rate. Keynes believed that the rich have a lower marginal propensity to consume than do the poor. Extending his theory from individuals to the national economy, Keynes argued that a nation's marginal propensity to consume depends on the absolute level of national income.

3. Empirical work on the national marginal propensity to consume by Simon Kuznets found that contrary to Keynes' hypothesis, the nation's marginal propensity to consume is constant. Duesenberry's relative income hypothesis helps to explain Kuznets' empirical finding. When national income increases and relative incomes remain unchanged, the marginal propensity to consume for the nation is unchanged. Duesenberry's hypothesis suggests a straight-line consumption function.

4. Friedman's permanent income hypothesis distinguishes between permanent income and transitory income. Friedman argues that consumption is dependent on permanent income.

5. Modigliani's life cycle hypothesis of consumption behavior suggests that a person's marginal propensity to consume changes during one's lifetime. Young people tend to have high marginal propensities to consume. People in middle age have lower marginal propensities to consume. When they are in retirement, the MPC increases again.

6. Autonomous consumption is independent of income. Shifts in the consumption function involve changes in autonomous consumption. The consumption function shifts due to changes in real asset and money holdings, expectations of changes in the price level, changes in interest rates, and changes in taxes.

7. The consumption equation expresses consumption as a linear function of national income, with an intercept equal to autonomous consumption and a slope equal to the marginal propensity to consume.

8. The saving equation is $S = Y - C$. The marginal propensity to save is $1 - MPC$.

9. Changes in investment tend to be unrelated to the level of national income. Investment is regarded as autonomous. Variables that influence investment include technological change, interest rate changes, changes in the rate of growth of national income, and the rate of capacity utilization. Autonomous investment can be quite volatile.

KEY TERMS

Consumption function
Absolute income hypothesis
Marginal propensity to consume (MPC)
Relative income hypothesis
Permanent income hypothesis
Life-cycle hypothesis
Permanent income
Transitory income
Autonomous consumption
Saving
Marginal propensity to save (MPS)
45° line
Intended investment
Autonomous investment

QUESTIONS

1. What is the consumption function?

2. How does Keynes' comment: "The satisfaction of the immediate primary needs of a man and his family is usually a stronger motive than the motives toward accumulation" relate to his absolute income hypothesis?

3. Accepting the absolute income hypothesis, would you expect the MPC in the U.S. economy in 1995 to be higher, lower, or about the same as the MPC in the Haitian 1995 economy? Why? How would it compare to the MPC in the U.S. economy in 1925?

4. Accepting the relative income hypothesis, would you expect the MPC in the U.S. economy in 1995 to be higher, lower, or the same as the MPC in the U.S. economy in 1925? Why?

5. Give an example of transitory income. What effect does this income have on the marginal propensity to consume?

6. What is autonomous consumption?

7. Why would a change in asset or money holdings shift the consumption curve?

8. What factor explains movements along the consumption curve?

9. Why is MPC + MPS always equal to one?

10. What is dissaving? Describe a situation that would create dissaving in an economy.

11. What factors determine autonomous investment?

12. Draw a graph depicting consumption for an economy through the range $Y = \$100$ billion to $Y = \$500$ when autonomous consumption is \$100 billion and MPC = 0.6.

13. Using the following table, calculate MPC and saving at each national income level.

National Income ($ billions)	Consumption ($ billions)
$ 0	$ 50
100	100
200	150
300	200
400	250
500	300
600	350

C H A P T E R 2 3

EQUILIBRIUM NATIONAL INCOME IN THE KEYNESIAN MODEL

CHAPTER PREVIEW

We have carefully examined consumption, saving, and investment behavior in the prior chapter. Now with the analytical tools we developed there, it is time to examine the manner in which independent consumption and saving decisions by households interact with the production and investment decisions of business firms to move the economy to a macroeconomic equilibrium. We'll also show how an economy moves from one equilibrium to another, given changes in investment and consumption. The Keynesian model that we continue to develop embodies the multiplier principle, whereby any change in spending in the economy is magnified over and over as new spending becomes new income and the change in income leads to subsequent rounds of spending.

After studying this chapter, you should be able to:

- Explain why consumption spending and investment spending are interdependent.
- Show how changes in inventories cause the level of national income to move toward an equilibrium.
- Tell the difference between intended investment and actual investment.
- Justify that the condition for equilibrium is that saving must equal intended investment.

- Explain the logic of the multiplier.
- Show the paradox of thrift using a numerical example.

Which blade in a pair of scissors cuts the cloth? Silly question? The answer is apparent, isn't it? Both blades do the cutting. It is almost inconceivable to suppose that one blade alone can do the cutting. That's what Alfred Marshall, the celebrated 19th century economist, said when asked if demand or costs of production determines equilibrium price. His reply (*Principles of Economics,* 1891)—using the scissors metaphor—was that both, equally, and in particular, *the interaction of both,* determines equilibrium price.

About a half-century later, a similar question was asked about the determination of the equilibrium level of national income. Which blade does the cutting? Is it **aggregate expenditure**—that is, spending by consumers on consumption goods, spending by businesses on investment goods, spending by government, and spending by foreigners on net exports—or aggregate supply? You might think that by this time the answer was obvious. But Marshall's most renowned student, J. M. Keynes, while acknowledging that the interaction of aggregate expenditures and aggregate supply determines the equilibrium level of national income, still felt that—using Marshall's scissors metaphor again—one blade in particular is responsible for most of the cutting. That blade, he was convinced, is aggregate expenditures.

Aggregate expenditure
Spending by consumers on consumption goods, spending by businesses on investment goods, spending by government, and spending by foreigners on net exports.

Why he was so convinced is the subject of this chapter. What determines the equilibrium level of national income was an important issue for Keynes then—and is perhaps for ourselves today—because he believed that the economy is always heading toward equilibrium (even if it might never get there) and that its equilibrium level might be a rather troublesome one. Keynes was trying to explain why the 1930s economy was mired down in depression and massive unemployment. If he could figure out how an economy's equilibrium level ends up being a depression, he thought, then maybe he could figure out how an economy can be extricated from that situation. That is, is it possible to change an equilibrium level?

Let's see how Keynes (and the Keynesians who followed) built an economic model to represent an economy heading toward or being in equilibrium. Let's first make some simplifying assumptions about the economy in this model so that we can focus on the primary forces that Keynes believed determine the economy's level of national income. Although aggregate expenditures include consumption, investment, government spending, and net exports, let's assume no government spending or foreign trade. Aggregate expenditures then become consumption spending and investment spending alone. Our assumption excluding government, and therefore taxes, also means that disposable income is the same as total income since people pay no taxes.

INTERACTION BETWEEN CONSUMERS AND PRODUCERS IN THE KEYNESIAN MODEL

In the Keynesian model, two very different kinds of people are always at work making decisions concerning consumption spending, saving, and investment that affect each other. As we saw in the previous chapter, people, acting as consumers, spend part of their income on consumption and save the rest. This is represented in

$$Y = C + S$$

At the same time, other people, acting as producers, produce both consumption goods and investment goods, partly in response to and partly in anticipation of the demands that consumers make for consumption goods and producers make for investment goods. This is represented in

$$Y = C + I_i$$

Now suppose, *by chance,* that the autonomous investment producers intend to make equals the same billions of dollars that consumers actually save out of their income. It follows, then, that what producers intend to produce for consumption ($C_i = Y - I_i$) turns out to be precisely what consumers intend to consume, ($C_i = Y - S$). (The subscript i indicates intention as distinct from actual.) This perfect match between intended investment and savings is written as,

$$I_i = S$$

It is purely by chance that what producers intend to produce for consumption will equal what consumers intend to consume.

Perhaps it is worthwhile to note again that the $I_i = S$ equation is a chance event arrived at, in this illustration, by decision making on the part of producers and consumers that unbeknownst to both created the perfect fit. After all, the producers of investment goods do not know *with certainty* what people who do the saving are intending to save. Nor can the people making saving decisions take into consideration what the producers of investment goods, responding to or anticipating investment demand, are intending to produce.

How fortunate, then, if this chance event generates for both producers and consumers the condition in which all consumption, investment, and saving intentions in the economy are realized!

In the Keynesian model, the $I = S$ equation describes the economy in macroequilibrium. After all, no excess demand or supply exists. All the consumption goods supplied by producers are taken off the market by consumers; aggregate expenditures equal aggregate supply.

But what if the intended autonomous investment of producers is not equal to the saving people choose to make?

THE ECONOMY MOVES TOWARD EQUILIBRIUM

Equilibrium level of national income

$C + I_i = C + S$, where saving equals intended investment.

The national economy, if not already in equilibrium, is always moving toward it. *But not by chance.* Let's suppose the economy is at $Y = \$900$ billion, which is *not* the **equilibrium level of national income.** Suppose as well that autonomous consumption is \$60 billion and MPC = 0.80. Consumption spending, then, is

$$C = \$60 + (0.80 \times \$900) = \$780$$

Suppose also that the producers in the economy have decided that of the \$900 billion of goods they produced, \$100 billion is intended for investment. That's their intended investment demand.

$$I_i = \$100$$

It's hard to tell just by looking at this warehouse scene whether business is so good that these drums of inventory are all that's left of a larger inventory stock producers want to keep, or whether they are sitting around the warehouse because, business being so bad, they couldn't be sold. In the one case, national income will increase, in the other, it will decrease.

How Consumers and Producers Behave When Y = $900 Billion

Let's focus on how consumers and producers behave under these circumstances. What do consumers do at Y = $900 billion? What do the producers do at Y = $900 billion? These two sets of people make their consumption and investment decisions simultaneously and independently of each other. We can imagine them thinking through their choices and reacting to realized and unrealized outcomes.

Table 1 summarizes their behavior.

Look at the top row of Table 1. The left-hand side, describing consumers' behavior, simply spells out the fact that consumers divide their income Y = $900 billion into $C + S$. The right-hand side, describing producers' behavior, shows that producers, responding to and anticipating demands for consumption and investment goods, divide their production of Y = $900 billion into $C + I_i$.

At this level of national income, producers produce more consumer goods than consumers are prepared to buy. The consumer goods that remain unpurchased become an unwanted investment in inventories.

But how much of the $Y = C + S$ is in the form of C, and how much of the $Y = C + I_i$ is in the form of C? The consumption equation, $C = a + bY$, provides part of the answer. At Y = $900 billion, consumers spend [$60 + (0.8 × $900)] = $780 billion on consumption. They save, then, $120 billion.

But producers have other ideas. At Y = $900 billion, they intend to invest $100 billion. That means they intend to produce for consumption $800 billion. They immediately run into a vexing problem. How can they sell $800 billion, when consumers are prepared to buy up only $780 billion? They can't.

TABLE 1 Consumers' and Producers' Intentions and Activities, by Stages, when Y = $900 billion

Consumers	Producers
Y = $900 $Y = C + S$	Y = $900 $Y = C + I_i$
$C = a + bY$	I_i = $100
C = $60 + .8($Y$) = $60 +.8($900) = $780	$C = Y - I_i$ = $900 – $100 = $800
$S = Y - C$ = $900 – $780 = $120	I_a = $120

ADDED PERSPECTIVE

Interview with the Author's Brother, Irving Gottheil, CEO of the Artistic Hat Company, Montreal, Canada

FG: Let's talk about business. What's going on this year? Are you doing anything different?

IG: We're coming out with new colors and new styles. And producing a lot more hats.

FG: Who decides how many hats to produce?

IG: I do! Come to think about it, it's also the firms I sell to. After all, they retail the hats. You know, the big ones like the Hudson Bay Company, the T. Eaton Company, Zeller's Incorporated, Sears, and Kmart. Then there are the hundreds of boutique shops across Canada.

FG: How do these firms know how many hats to order?

IG: Well, when you get right down to it, it's a guessing game. They have to anticipate what consumers want. It's hard. We really can't get into the consumer's head. Of course, we hope to get on their heads.

FG: Be more specific.

IG: Well . . . we make decisions on the basis of what we think people will demand. And what they demand depends upon a lot of things. For example, if it's a cold winter (like last year) they buy. Remember three years ago? It hardly snowed. People didn't need hats. Only Santa Claus wore a hat! We ended up with an overload of unsold inventory. You saw the problem when you were in Montreal that February. Who wore hats? We couldn't give them away. It was a bad year. Some years are really bad for other reasons. Remember when I moved the factory from 124 McGill Street to 5445 de Gaspe Street? I doubled my space expecting a great season. It was a heck of a decision. I was wrong! How did I know the economy was going into a recession. What a recession! I took an awful beating.

FG: What about Sears and Hudson Bay?

IG: They took a beating too! Listen, they're no *mavens* [maven is a sage]. They were left holding half the hats they ordered. By the way, this is a good year despite the warm weather. It goes to show you. You think you know, and you don't.

FG: What's in store for next year?

IG: I'm optimistic. Not crazy optimistic, but optimistic. The factory is running now at full capacity. I'm even replacing the stamping presses I bought in Milan, Italy, just two years ago. Technology changes so quickly in this business. There's a new press out of Sweden that is top of the line. I figure it will cut my stamping press labor costs by 25 percent. Oh yes, those handmade aluminum molds from England . . . a company in Toronto does the same quality work and is much less expensive. I'm going to give them a try.

FG: Looks like you're banking on a lot of people buying hats.

IG: That's right! But you know, Freddie, it's always risky. Someone has to make the decision on how much to produce. And that someone is me. Next year? I need cold weather. I can use an ice age. By the way, why these questions?

FG: I will use them in the book as an example of firms making decisions concerning production of consumption and investment goods. You're my consumption goods decision-maker.

IG: Spell my name right!

FG: Any message for my students?

IG: Yeah. Stay out of the hat business!

FG: How about giving the student who scores the highest grade in my economics class a hat as a prize?

IG: Let's wait until the end of the season, OK? If the season's bad, I could give your entire class hats!

What happens to the $800 – $780 = $20 billion of consumption goods that are produced but remain unsold? Retail stores, unable to move these $20 billion across the counter as final goods, discover they have more inventory than they want. Their shelves are crammed with these unsold goods, many boxed in stockrooms and warehouses. That is to say, *although produced as consumption goods, the $20 billion—by default—become investment goods* in the form of **unwanted inventories.**

Unwanted inventories

Goods produced for consumption that remain unsold.

In other words, producers intended to invest $100 billion, but their **actual investment,** I_a, turns out to be $120 billion, that is, $20 billion more than intended investment, I_i.

Actual investment

Investment spending that producers actually make—that is, intended investment (investment spending that producers intend to undertake), plus or minus unintended changes in inventories.

$$I_a > I_i$$

As you can see, whether producers' investment intentions are realized or not depends on what consumers do. After all, how much people choose to consume out of their income dictates how much of what producers produce for consumption gets sold.

You can imagine what happens next. Retail stores, saddled with unwanted inventories, scale down their orders for resupply. After all, why reorder when they can't sell what they already have? Producers, in turn, feeling the pinch of fewer reorders, will be unable to maintain production levels.

What follows next? Both retailers and producers lay off workers. And there's nothing employers or workers can do about it. What room is there for compromise? With consumption and investment functions being what they are, the $900 billion level of national income simply cannot support employment for all the workers. Unemployment results. With fewer people working, production and income falls.

How Consumers and Producers Behave When Y = $700 Billion

Now let's suppose national income is not at Y = $900 billion but at Y = $700 billion. What happens to consumer and producer intentions at Y = $700 billion? Look at Table 2.

As you see, the basic consumption and investment functions, $C = \$60 + 0.8Y$ and $I_i = \$100$, remain unchanged. Consumers still spend $60 billion on autonomous consumption and 0.80 of national income. Producers still intend to invest $100 billion.

TABLE 2 Consumers' and Producers' Intentions and Activities, by Stages, when Y = $700 billion

Consumers	Producers
$Y = \$700$ $Y = C + S$	$Y = \$700$ $Y = C + I_i$
$C = a + bY$	$I_i = \$100$
$C = \$60 + .8(Y)$ $= \$60 + .8(\$700)$ $= \$620$	$C = Y - I_i$ $= \$700 - \$100$ $= \$600$
$S = Y - C$ $= \$700 - \$620$ $= \$80$	$I_a = \$80$

When national income is \$700 billion, consumers want to purchase \$20 billion more of consumer goods than producers are planning to produce. As a result, producers' inventories are depleted.

But note what has changed. The level of national income is \$700 billion and a very different set of circumstances emerges. Consumers now spend [\$60 + (0.8 × \$700)] = \$620 billion on consumption goods. Producers, on the other hand, intending to invest \$100 billion in new factories, new equipment, new vehicles, and so on, produce only \$700 – \$100 = \$600 billion of consumption goods.

What happens now? With consumers spending \$620 billion on consumption, but finding only \$600 billion of consumption goods available, producers and retail stores will find that inventories *they had wanted to hold as investment* end up sold as consumption goods.

Picture, for example, David Tietlebaum's Poster and Frame store. Its wall- and free-standing shelves are filled with stocks of posters. People can walk into the store and choose, as well, from among precut lucite, steel, and wood frames. As you can well imagine, it would be very difficult for David to sell framed posters if he didn't have a ready supply on hand—that is, on inventory—of posters and frames. (Recall, inventories are part of investment.)

How does David fit into the Y = \$700 billion scenario? Because consumers spend \$620 billion on consumption goods while producers only produce \$600 billion of consumption goods, David discovers, along with many other producers and retailers, that the inventories they want *and need* will be reduced. In response, David will reorder greater quantities of posters and frames from the producers of posters and frames, not only to meet consumption needs, but to restock depleted inventories.

Once again, intended investment will be unrealized. But this time, actual investment will be less than intended.

$$I_a < I_i$$

You can bet producers will be more than delighted! Retail stores will be on the phones pleading with them for more goods. Producers, in response, will hire more workers. With more workers producing goods and earning incomes, national income rises above \$700 billion.

How Consumers and Producers Behave When *Y* = \$800 Billion

Let's now suppose national income is at Y = \$800 billion. How would consumers and producers behave? Look at Table 3.

TABLE 3 Consumers' and Producers' Intentions and Activities, by Stages, when Y = \$800 billion

Consumers	Producers
$Y = \$800$	$Y = \$800$
$Y = C + S$	$Y = C + I_i$
$C = a + bY$	$I_i = 100$
$C = \$60 + .8(Y)$	$C = Y - I_i$
$= \$60 + .8(\$800)$	$= \$800 - \$100$
$= \$700$	$= \$700$
$S = Y - C$	$I_a = \$100$
$= \$800 - \$700$	
$= \$100$	

When consumers purchase exactly the amount of consumer goods that producers produce, the macroeconomy is in equilibrium. Be sure that you understand why intended investment, actual investment, and saving are all equal when the economy is in equilibrium.

The consumption and investment functions remain unchanged. Look what consumers do now. Consumption spending is [\$60 + (0.8 × \$800)] = \$700 billion. Producers, still intending to invest \$100 billion, produce \$700 billion of consumption goods.

Although producers really didn't know with certainty what consumers intended to do with their incomes, and consumers really didn't know what producers intended to produce, the match is perfect. People's consumption spending turns out to be exactly what producers have produced for consumption. At Y = \$800 billion, producers responding to or anticipating investment demand, intend to invest \$100 billion and end up actually investing \$100 billion.

$$I_i = I_a$$

Retail stores sell the consumption goods that they had hoped to sell and have left as inventory precisely what they want. What will they do? They will reorder from producers exactly what they had ordered before—no more, no less. Why order more? The market gives no indication that they could sell more than \$700 billion. But why order less when experience tells them the market will absorb \$700 billion?

Producers, then, will maintain their production level at \$800 billion. They will keep in employment precisely that number of workers who produce the \$800 billion. At Y = \$800 billion, there is no incentive for producers or consumers to change what they do. *The economy is in equilibrium.*

EQUILIBRIUM NATIONAL INCOME

Aggregate expenditure curve (AE)

A curve that shows the quantity of aggregate expenditures at different levels of national income or GDP.

Panels *a* and *b* of Figure 1 illustrate the Keynesian model that Tables 1, 2, and 3 describe. They depict the economy moving to national income equilibrium.

Look at panel *a*. The upward-sloping, straight-line consumption curve, C, is a straight line because the marginal propensity to consume is constant—intersects the vertical axis at \$60 billion. The intended investment curve I_i = \$100 billion, which is independent of the level of national income, is added to the consumption curve to generate the $C + I_i$ curve, which is the **aggregate expenditure curve, *AE*.** (At every level of Y, AE differs from C by \$100 billion of investment demand.)

The 45° income line (or $C + S$ curve) in panel *a* represents the economy's total production. Recall in the GDP accounting chapter our analysis of the income and expenditure approaches to national income accounting. There we saw that national income can be derived either by adding up income ($C + S$) or by adding up expenditures, that is, consumers' and producers' spending on consumption and investment goods ($AE = C + I_i$). Note that the 45° income (or $C + S$) line intersects the AE (or $C + I_i$) curve at *e*, where Y = \$800 billion. *The intersection identifies the economy's equilibrium position.*

Suppose the economy is operating at a lower than equilibrium income and production level, say, at Y = \$700 billion. What happens? At Y = \$700 billion, producers still intend to invest \$100 billion, which is the distance marked off by *ac* in panel *a*, while consumers save (Y - C) or *cb*, which is \$700 - [\$60 + (0.80 × \$700)] = \$80 billion. That is, the quantity demanded by consumers of consumption goods at Y = \$700 billion is greater than the quantity of consumption goods supplied by producers.

FIGURE 1
The Equilibrium Level of National Income
In panel *a*, the economy is in equilibrium at *e*, where $Y = \$800$ billion. When national income is below equilibrium, say at $Y = \$700$, aggregate expenditure, that is, people's consumption spending plus producers' intended investment spending, $AE = C + I_i$, is greater than the \$700 billion national income, $C + S$. As a result, part of the producers' intended investment, *ab*, is not realized, driving national income up to \$800 billion. When national income is above equilibrium, say at *g*, where $Y = \$900$, aggregate expenditure, $AE = C + I_i$ at *h*, is less than the \$900 billion national income. The difference, *gh*, drives national income down to \$800 billion.

Panel *b* focuses on the relationship between saving and intended investment. The inequalities, $S > I_i$ and $I_i > S$, drive national income to its \$800 billion equilibrium level.

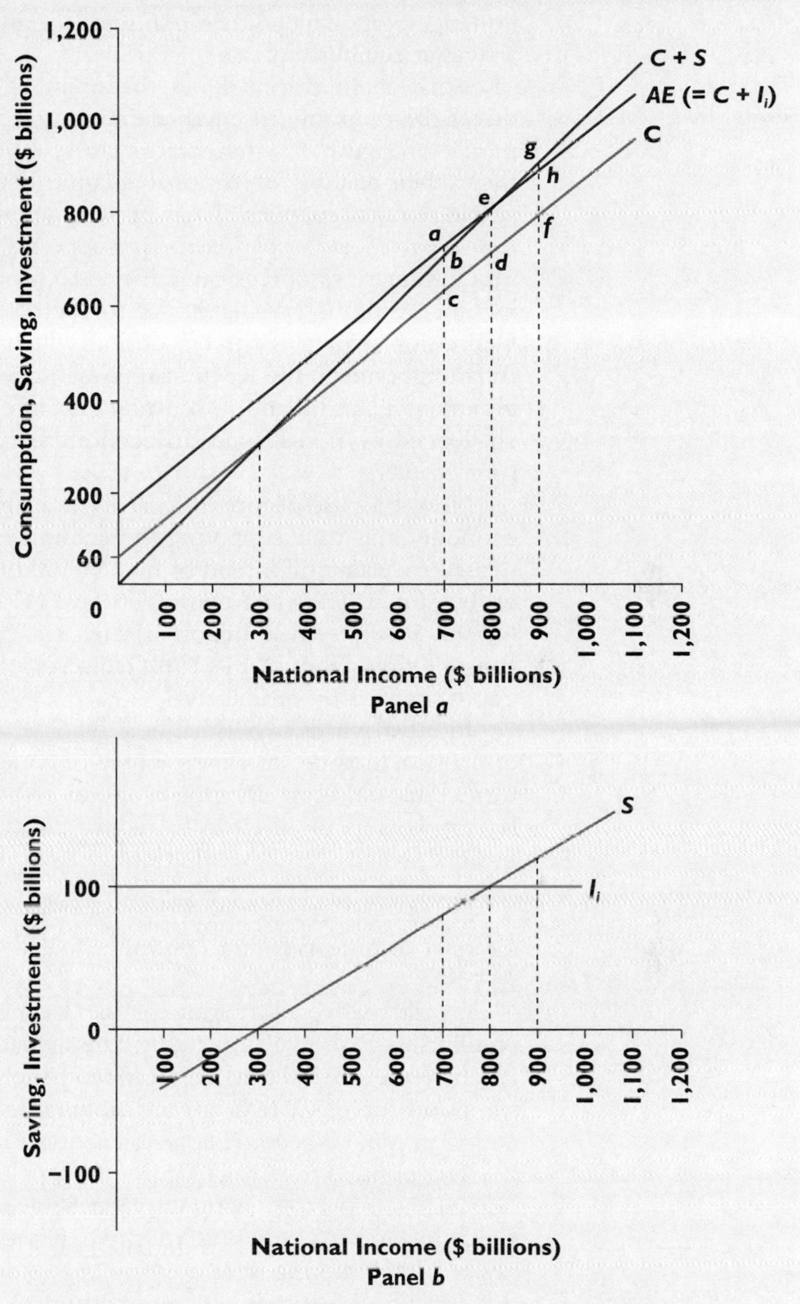

The result? Consumers buy up \$20 billion of inventory (the purchase by consumers of the inventory converts that inventory from investment goods to consumption goods) and producers respond by hiring more workers to replace the \$20 billion depleted inventories. More workers means more income. That is to say, national income increases. In a nutshell, when

$$I_i > S$$

Y increases *and continues to increase until* $I_i = S$. Note where $I_i = S$. At \$800 billion, aggregate expenditures AE equals aggregate output $C + S$. The economy arrives at equilibrium.

What about prices? Does the strain of excess aggregate expenditure that drives the economy to equilibrium also force up prices? Not in the Keynesian model of Figure 1 where prices are assumed constant. Keynesians choose to focus their analysis of national income determination in an environment of ample resource supplies. Their primary interest is in *linking investment and saving to real income and employment*. By supposing the availability of ample resource supplies, more resources can be used to produce more goods (and create more income) without causing prices to increase. This was the case in the Great Depression, which is the era during which Keynes wrote the *General Theory*. Inflation occurs in the Keynesian model only after the economy reaches full employment. (This inflation occurring only after full employment is reached idea is challenged by non-Keynesian economists but we hold that discussion until a later chapter.)

Now let's use Figure 1 to analyze a different nonequilibrium state of the economy, this time supposing the economy is at $Y =$ \$900 billion. What happens? Producers still intend to invest \$100 billion, which is the distance marked off by *hf* in panel *a*, and consumers save $(Y - C)$ or *gf*, which is \$900 – [\$60 + (0.80 × \$900)] = \$120 billion. That is, the quantity demanded by consumers of consumption goods at $Y =$ \$900 billion is less than the quantity of consumption goods supplied by producers.

In other words, when national income is greater than the equilibrium level of national income, an excess supply of consumption goods emerges and inventories build up. How does the economy respond to this excess supply? Producers lay off workers in an effort to reduce unwanted inventories. Incomes fall. In a nutshell, when

$$S > I_i$$

national income falls and continues to fall until it reaches equilibrium where $I_i = S$.

An alternative illustration of the Keynesian approach to national income equilibrium is shown in panel *b*. The upward-sloping saving curve, S, of panel *b* depicts the vertical distance between panel *a*'s income curve, $C + S$, and consumption curve, C. It is upward-sloping because the distances between $C + S$ and C in panel *a* become larger as national income increases.

The planned investment curve in panel *b* is a horizontal curve at \$100 billion. It intersects the saving curve at \$800 billion, the equilibrium level of national income. As panel *b* shows, when national income is below equilibrium, say at \$700 billion, $S < I_i$, creating excess demand for consumption goods that drives national income up to equilibrium. When national income is above equilibrium, say at \$900 billion, $S > I_i$, creating excess supply of consumption goods that drives national income down to equilibrium.

CHANGES IN INVESTMENT CHANGE NATIONAL INCOME EQUILIBRIUM

There is no reason to suppose, *as long as the consumption function and the investment demand function remain unchanged*, that the level of national income would move

TABLE 4 Consumers' and Producers' Intentions and Activities, by stages, when Investment Increases to $130 Billion and Y = $800 Billion

Consumers	Producers
$Y = \$800$	$Y = \$800$
$Y = C + S$	$Y = C + I_i$
$C = a + bY$	$I_i = \$130$
$C = \$60 + .8(Y)$ $= \$60 + .8(\$800)$ $= \$700$	$C = Y - I_i$ $= \$800 - \$130$ $= \$670$
$S = Y - C$ $= \$800 - \$700$ $= 100$	$I_a = \$100$

away from equilibrium at $800 billion. As long as aggregate expenditure, that is, consumers' spending on consumption goods and producers' spending on investment goods exactly matches consumption goods and investment goods production, there is no incentive for producers to increase or decrease their production. Inventories would not be too large or too small. That's what an equilibrium position implies.

But functions do, in fact, change. We noted in the prior chapter how volatile investment can be, and it is not unreasonable to expect that the investment demand function will shift up or down, perhaps even before the economy reaches an equilibrium position.

Suppose producers decide to take advantage of new technologies and add an additional $30 billion to planned investment spending. Intended investment increases, then, from $100 billion to $130 billion.

As we see in Table 4, the $800 billion equilibrium level of national income is no longer tenable.

Intended investment is now $130 billion. How does that affect the equilibrium level of national income? At $Y =$ $800 billion, consumers will still want to spend $700 billion on consumption. But since producers now intend to invest $130 billion of the $800 billion they produce, they supply only $670 billion of consumption goods. That simply isn't enough for consumers.

What will consumers do? What can they do? They will, of course, consume the $670 billion in consumption goods that producers supplied. In addition, they will buy up $30 billion of the inventories that producers had intended to hold as investment. That is to say, consumers convert intended investment into consumption goods. (Imagine the stripped window displays in retail stores after consumers buy up $30 billion of inventories.) The result is that actual investment ends up being $30 billion less than intended investment.

How will the retailers respond? By faxing producers to replenish their depleted inventories. The producers, excited by this surge in orders, hire more workers. National income increases beyond $800 billion.

Y = $950 Billion: The New Equilibrium

We trace the economy's path to a higher equilibrium level in Figure 2.

The consumption and investment spending curve, which is really the aggregate expenditure curve, *AE*, shifts from $C + I_i$ (with $I_i =$ $100 billion) to $C +$

FIGURE 2
Deriving Equilibrium at Y = \$950 Billion
If producers' intended investment spending is \$100 billion then, $S = I_i$ (= *ed*) at *e* where equilibrium Y = \$800 billion. If producers' intended investment spending were to increase to \$130 billion, then at Y = \$800 billion, $I_i > S$ (*jd* – *ed* = *je*). National income would increase to *e'*, the new equilibrium level of \$950 billion where $I_i = S$ = \$130 billion (*e'd'*).

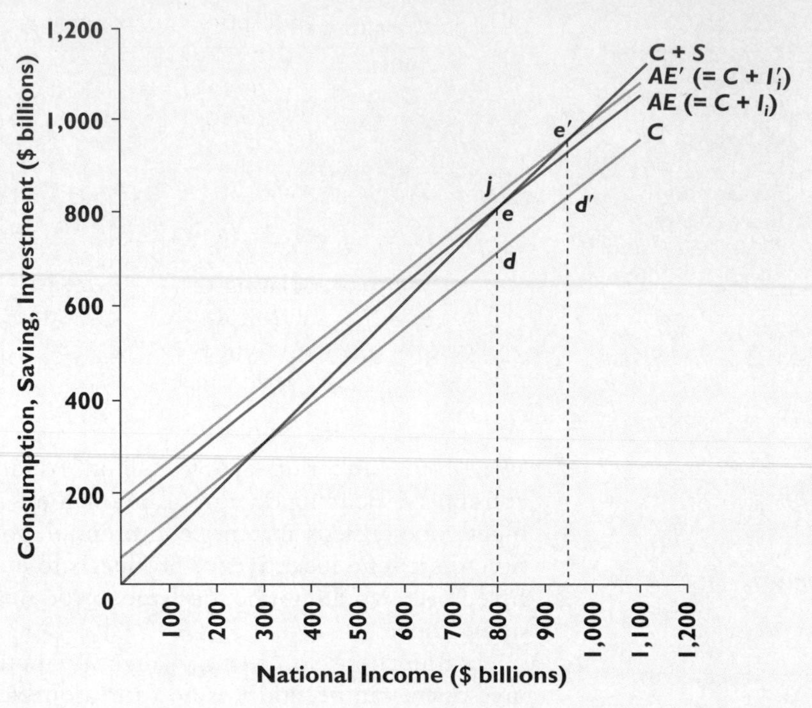

I_i' (with I_i' = \$130 billion). How does the shift affect the equilibrium level of national income?

Look at Y = \$800 billion. Before the shift, $I_i = S$ (the distance *ed*). The economy is in equilibrium. After the shift, saving is still *ed,* but intended investment is *jd*. In other words, $I_i > S$. The result: excess demand for consumption goods at Y = \$800 billion propels national income upward.

An increase in intended investment leads to an even larger increase in the equilibrium level of national income.

But to where? The new equilibrium level of national income is at \$950 billion. Here, both saving and intended investment are \$130 billion (this is the distance *e'd'*, which is the same distance as *jd*). Table 5 lays out the particulars of this new equilibrium position.

TABLE 5
Consumers' and Producers' Intentions and Activities, by stages, with I_i = \$130 Billion and Y = \$950 Billion

Consumers	Producers
Y = \$950 $Y = C + S$	Y = \$950 $Y = C + I_i$
$C = a + bY$	I_i = \$130
C = \$60 + .8(Y) = \$60 + .8(\$950) = \$820	$C = Y - I_i$ = \$950 – \$130 = \$820
$S = Y - C$ = \$950 – \$820 = \$130	I_a = \$130

Look at the left column. At $Y = \$950$ billion, consumers intend to spend \$820 billion on consumption goods and save the remaining \$130 billion. The right column shows that producers, responding to and anticipating the demand for investment goods, intend to invest \$130 billion and produce \$820 billion of consumption. The $I_i = S$ equilibrium condition is met:

$$I_i = S = \$130$$

An Alternative Method of Calculating Equilibrium

A quick way of calculating the equilibrium level of national income, given specific values for (1) autonomous consumption, (2) MPC, and (3) intended investment, is to substitute $(a + bY)$ for C into the aggregate expenditure equation $Y = C + I_i$. For example, since

in equilibrium	$Y = C + I_i$
and	$C = \$60 + .8Y$
and	$I_i = \$130$
then	$Y = (\$60 + .8Y) + \$130$

Subtracting $0.8Y$ from both sides reduces the equation to

$$.2Y = \$60 + \$130 - \$190$$

Finally, dividing both sides by 0.2 reduces the equation to

$$Y - \$950$$

Change any of the values for autonomous consumption, MPC, or intended investment, and a new equilibrium level of national income results.

THE INCOME MULTIPLIER

Investment is the most volatile component of aggregate spending in the economy.

What's likely to change? Consumption spending has tended to be more stable than investment spending in the past. The MPC can be counted on to remain pretty much unchanged. Autonomous consumption, a creature of habit, is hardly likely to change either. Investment spending, on the other hand, is considered rather volatile.

Keynesians identify changes in investment spending as the key to our understanding of why national income changes. Changes in investment have highly magnified effects on national income.

Income multiplier

The multiple by which income changes as a result of a change in investment spending.

For example, we saw in Table 5 that a \$30 billion increase in investment spending generated an increase in national income five times that size, from \$800 billion to \$950 billion, or by \$150 billion.

Economists define the change in national income that is generated by a change in investment as the **income multiplier.** It is written

$$\text{multiplier} = \frac{\text{change in } Y}{\text{change in } I}$$

Deriving the Multiplier

But why precisely five-fold, as in the case of Table 5? *The degree of multiplication depends on the marginal propensity to consume.*

Necessity is the mother of invention. It may not be an earth-shattering technology, but this tennis restringing apparatus makes life so much more pleasant (and productive) for those who, particularly during the summer months, have to work long hours restringing rackets.

Let's consider once more the $30 billion increase in investment spending. It reflects, we supposed, a series of new technologies that were introduced at one time into the economy. Let's follow through the impact on the level of national income of one such technological change, say, a $1,000 investment.

Suppose John Flygare, the owner of a tennis shop in Evanston, Illinois, reads an article in *Sports Illustrated* describing a new machine that restrings tennis rackets in half the time it formerly took. The new technology costs $1,000. Suppose John decides to make the investment.

Let's trace the sequence of events that follow that $1,000 increase in investment. First, a *new* order is placed for the machine. John's decision to invest represents a *new* order for Bradley Hastings, the machinist and inventor of the restringing equipment. He produces the machine, sells it to John, and ends up with a $1,000 increase in income. Of course, John ends up with a new machine.

What do you suppose Bradley does with the additional $1,000 income earned? Since we suppose MPC = 0.80, we know, then, that he increases his consumption spending by $800. Let's suppose he spends $800 on a custom-made waterbed.

The multiplier expansion of national income results from successive rounds of additions to real output, additions to income, and additions to spending and saving.

Think about what follows. The carpenter, Jay Malin, makes the bed and earns $800, which represents for him an addition to income. Once again, real output and real income are created simultaneously. And, of course, Jay will do with his new income what Bradley did with his—spend part, and save the rest. With MPC = 0.80, $640 of the $800 is put to consumption spending.

The sequence of additions to real output, additions to income, and additions to consumption spending and saving is shown in Table 6.

The initial $1,000 change in investment spending sets in motion a chain of events that creates—in successive rounds of income earning, consumption spending, and saving—a $5,000 change in national income. And, as you see, it creates also waterbeds, violins, computers, health care, auto repair, space heaters, and a host of other real outputs whose total value is $5,000.

Note that as economic activity progresses through the successive rounds, the additions to national income become smaller and smaller. For at each round, some of the income is set aside as saving. The lower the MPC (or the higher the MPS), the greater is the sum set aside.

TABLE 6 The Making of the Income Multiplier

Round	Change in I_i	Output	Y	C	S
1	$1,000	Restringer	$1,000.00	$ 800.00	$ 200.00
2		Waterbed	800.00	640.00	160.00
3		Violin	640.00	512.00	128.00
4		Computer	512.00	409.60	102.40
5		Health care	409.60	327.68	81.92
6		Auto repair	327.68	262.14	65.54
7		Space heater	262.14	209.71	52.43
.			.	.	.
.			.	.	.
.			.	.	.
n					
	$1,000	$5,000.00	$5,000.00	$4,000.00	$1,000.00

THE ALGEBRA OF THE INCOME MULTIPLIER

As we see in Table 6, the total income created is the sum of a series of incomes, each one reduced in the succeeding round by the MPS, that is, by 0.20. The series for the $1,000 change in investment, then, is written as

$$\$1{,}000 + (0.8 \times \$1{,}000) + [0.8\ (0.8 \times \$1{,}000)] + \cdots$$

More generally, this is written

$$\$1{,}000 + \$1{,}000\ (MPC) + \$1{,}000\ (MPC^2)$$

The initial $1,000 change in spending is multiplied by

$$1 + MPC + MPC^2 + MPC^3 + \cdots MPC^n$$

where n represents the nth round of spending. (The next round of spending, the nth + 1, is so close to zero that it becomes totally unimportant.)

Finally, the generalized sum reduces to

$$\frac{1}{1 - MPC}$$

Since (1 - MPC) = MPS,

$$\frac{1}{1 - MPC} = \frac{1}{MPS}$$

Why does national income increase five times as much as the increase in investment spending? If MPC = 0.80, then

$$\frac{1}{1 - 0.80} = \frac{1}{0.20} = \frac{1}{2/10} = 5$$

You can see, then, what happens to national income when $30 billion is added to investment. With MPC = 0.80, the economy generates a $30 billion

× 5 = \$150 billion increase in national income. Were investment to increase by \$100 billion, national income would increase by \$500 billion.

What If MPC Were 0.90?

Suppose MPC = 0.90. What would happen to the level of national income if the same \$30 billion of investment were added to the economy? The income multiplier now becomes

$$\frac{1}{1-0.90} = 10$$

With \$30 billion of investment added, national income increases by \$300 billion. In a nutshell, any change in MPC changes the income multiplier and consequently the level of national income that the investment would generate.

The Income Multiplier Works in Either Direction

Just as increases in investment spending stimulate the economy, cuts in investment spending drag it down. Suppose an increase in the rate of interest shifts the demand curve for investment from \$100 billion to \$75 billion.

The income multiplier now works in reverse. In the first round of the cutback, national income falls by \$25 billion. People whose employment had been supported by the \$25 billion investment find themselves with \$25 billion less income. But that \$25 billion had financed 25 × 0.80 = \$20 billion of consumption spending, which was the source of second-round income. That, too, now disappears, creating in turn successive cuts in income and consumption through to the *n*th round. What is the total loss of national income? With a multiplier of 5 (MPC = 0.80), the \$25 billion investment cutback decreases national income by \$25 billion × 5 = \$125 billion. National income falls from \$800 billion to a new equilibrium level of \$675 billion. This is shown in Figure 3.

The shift in *AE* from $C + I_i$ to $C + I_i'$ reflects the \$25 billion decrease in investment. Now, $C + I_i'$ intersects the $C + S$ curve at e', creating a new equilibrium level of national income at \$675 billion.

THE PARADOX OF THRIFT

The paradox of thrift

The more people try to save, the more income falls, leaving them with no more and perhaps with even less saving.

Suppose people, afraid that their economic future is not nearly as promising as they once thought, decide to put a higher percentage of their income into saving. Increased saving, they feel, would provide greater economic security. But does their shift out of consumption spending to higher saving really provide them with greater economic security? Do they *really* end up saving more? Not necessarily. In fact, by *trying* to save more, they may actually end up saving less, or at least saving no more. That's what economists call the **paradox of thrift.** But why should trying to save more lead to no greater saving and perhaps even less? The answer depends on how income (and production) responds to a change in saving.

Suppose people decide to increase their saving by \$30 billion whatever the level of national income. And suppose the economy is in equilibrium at \$800 billion. What happens?

ADDED PERSPECTIVE

GM's Money Machine

As General Motors' decision to sell its Powertrain foundry in Tilton begins to sink in, the question arises, Just how important is GM to the area?

"Let's not try to wrap what could happen in a pretty package with pretty ribbon," said state representative Bill Black, R-Danville. "If that foundry closes and we can't find a buyer, devastating is not, perhaps, a strong enough word as to what it would do to the area's economy."

Though no economic impact study has been done on the importance of the foundry, most officials agree with Black that a closing would devastate Danville and much of Vermilion County. And economists have studied similar situations enough to offer a thumbnail sketch of the foundry's local influence.

GM's annual payroll for its more than 1,300 employees—about $60 million, according to the United Auto Workers union—probably has the most dramatic and direct impact in the area, said Steve Downing, an economics instructor at Danville Area Community College.

Those dollars, in turn, multiply out into the economy, say Downing and other economists, supporting more dollars and more jobs.

For every payroll dollar at the foundry, Downing guesses that about four more are generated throughout the area.

According to federal statistics, the foundry's $60 million payroll would make up roughly 5 percent of Vermilion County's entire personal income in 1990, which was $1.29 billion.

And the state has estimated that those dollars, on top of production costs paid by GM, have helped create three spinoff jobs in the community tied to every foundry job.

So the foundry's 1,300 employees help support the jobs of roughly 3,900 other workers in the area, from the dozens of local industries and businesses that service the foundry to the waitresses and cooks at area restaurants.

"The foundry is integrally linked to the community from its payroll point of view as well as the subcontractors that provide services to it," said Thomas Byrket, president of the Danville Area Chamber of Commerce.

"It is also linked to the entire corridor along Interstate 74, east and west, Champaign and Indianapolis," Byrket said. "There is no question that it is a major player in east central Illinois, central Illinois and western and central Indiana."

Whether the foundry closes or finds a buyer, the change does not bode well for local governments, most of which rely heavily on local property taxes.

The direct effect is deceptively small. For example, the village of Tilton, like other small villages in the area, does not levy a property tax.

But a utility tax it has proposed for the foundry was to have helped fund a major sewer project in the village. The future of that effort seems questionable now.

According to the Vermilion County treasurer's office, the Danville school district, in dire budget straits of its own, is the biggest direct recipient of property tax revenues.

But projections show the district getting less than 1 percent, about $96,000, of its property tax revenues from the foundry next year.

One taxing body, however, seems to be anticipating that the loss of the foundry could erode the overall tax base if workers sell and move away.

Last week, Vermilion County finance committee board members cited exactly that fear in pre-emptively rejecting salary increases for some employees.

Even so, exact property taxes paid by employees and the benefits those revenues bring to county and municipal governments are difficult to gauge.

"This ripples out into our economy in more ways than are imaginable," Downing said.

Discussion

Steve Downing, an economics instructor at Danville Area Community College, estimates that every foundry dollar supports four more dollars in the community. If his estimate is accurate, what is the marginal propensity to consume in Danville?

Source: *The Champaign-Urbana News Gazette*, March 1, 1992.

FIGURE 3
The Multiplier Working in Reverse
When MPC = 0.80, the income multiplier is 5. If the economy is in equilibrium at Y = \$800 billion, then a \$25 billion decrease in investment shifts the aggregate expenditure curve $AE = C + I_i$ to $AE' = C + I'_i$, and the equilibrium level of national income from e to e′, that is, from \$800 billion to \$675 billion. For every \$1 cut from investment spending, the income multiplier creates a \$5 cut in national income.

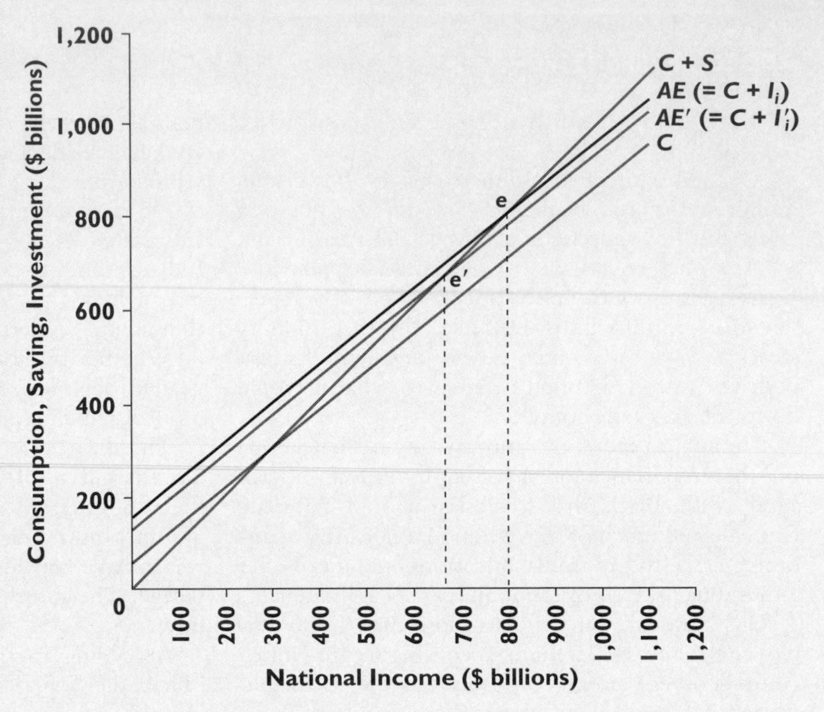

In the Keynesian model, an increase in saving serves to decrease consumption spending, causing a multiplier contraction in national income. At the new equilibrium level of national income, saving is the same as it was originally. By trying to save more, we end up saving the same amount.

Figure 4, panel *a* illustrates the effect of that intention to save on the equilibrium level of national income. The saving curve shifts upward, from S to S', causing the equilibrium level of national income to fall from \$800 billion to \$650 billion. Follow the logic. Before the saving-curve shift, people intended to save \$100 billion, and producers intended to invest \$100 billion.

$$S = I_i = \$100$$

With the shift to S', people *intend* to save \$130 billion at Y = \$800 billion. But can they? If producers still intend to invest only \$100 billion, then

$$S > I_i$$

The economy slips into reverse gear. National income falls. The multiplier, when applied to the \$30 billion increase in saving (\$30 billion cut in consumption), generates a 5 × \$30 billion fall in national income. The new equilibrium level of national income is \$650 billion. At \$650 billion

$$S = I_i = \$100$$

Do you see what has happened? Since people's decision to increase saving to \$130 billion caused a fall in national income, they cannot save \$130 billion! There's the paradox. *The more people try to save, the more they force a fall in national income, which in spite of their intentions, results in the level of saving remaining unchanged.*

If we relax the assumption that the investment curve is horizontal and instead assume that it is upward-sloping, then the consequences of attempting to

FIGURE 4 **The Paradox of Thrift**

The intentions of people in panel *a* to save more out of their income shifts the saving curve to the left, from *S* to *S'*. But their intentions will not be realized because the shift will cause the equilibrium level of national income to fall from $800 billion to $650 billion, leaving saving unchanged and equal to investment spending at $100 billion.

In panel *b*, the investment curve is upward-sloping, so that the shift in the saving curve from *S* to *S'* not only causes the equilibrium level of national income to fall from $800 billion to $550 billion but saving to fall from $100 billion to $75 billion.

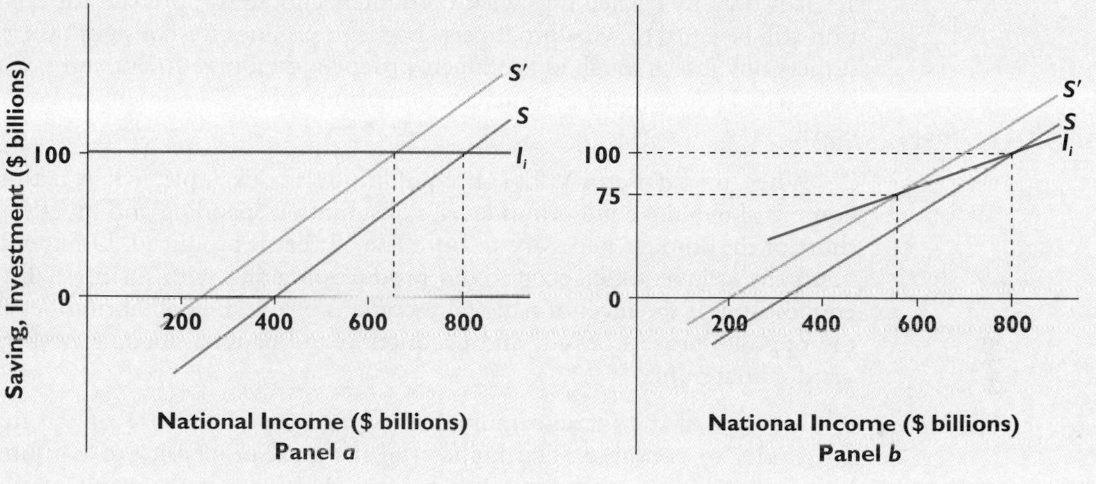

increase saving are even more severe. Look at panel *b*. Because the investment curve is upward-sloping, the shift in the saving curve from *S* to *S'* results not only in a lower equilibrium level of national income but in a fall in the level of investment. And since $S = I_i$ in equilibrium, the paradox now reads: *The more people try to save, the less they end up saving.*

The discovery of this thrift paradox was nothing short of revolutionary. While its economic logic, at least according to the Keynesian model, is perfectly sound, its philosophic implications for policy are rather troublesome, and for some economists downright unacceptable.

For the paradox of Figure 4 challenges the folk wisdom that many of us believe. Benjamin Franklin taught us that a penny saved is a penny earned. The Keynesian model now tells us that a penny saved can cause a depression! Thrift is no longer an unqualified virtue.

Do Keynesians believe that increased saving is *always* detrimental to our economic health? Not by a long shot. If accompanied by increased investment, increased saving is both inevitable and desirable. After all, if intended investment increases to $130 billion along with intended saving, national income increases to $950 billion. The increased saving that people intended to make is actually made. And we're all the better for it. But if saving increases unattended by a complementary increase in intended investment, Keynesians see economic trouble.

We have given up many beliefs since our early childhood with only half a struggle. Most of us abandoned Santa Claus long before we abandoned the

Christmas stocking. The tooth fairy lost out even before our permanent teeth came in. But abandoning the belief that personal thrift is *always* personally rewarding and that it *always* promotes the well-being of society is quite another matter. Our instincts instruct us differently.

CHAPTER REVIEW

1. It is only by chance that what consumers choose to purchase for consumption will be equal to what producers choose to produce for consumption. If consumers buy just as much as producers produce, then investment and saving will be equal. The economy is in macroequilibrium when investment and saving are equal.

2. When the economy is not in equilibrium, for example, when national income is above the equilibrium level, consumption spending and investment fall short of the amount necessary to purchase all that is produced. Unintended investment in inventories occurs, and production along with income fall toward equilibrium. If the level of national income is below the equilibrium level, then the opposite process occurs, and production and national income both rise toward equilibrium.

3. The size of the income multiplier depends upon the size of the marginal propensity to consume. The higher the marginal propensity to consume, the bigger the income multiplier. The income multiplier is the result of an initial change in spending being spent and respent, over and over, each time multiplied by the marginal propensity to consume.

4. Just as an increase in investment causes the equilibrium level of national income to rise, a decrease in investment causes the equilibrium level of national income to fall. Again, the multiplier is at work, but in reverse. Any decrease in investment causes a multiplier decrease in the equilibrium level of national income.

5. The paradox of thrift suggests that by trying to save more, people end up saving the same. An increase in saving represents a decrease in consumption, which sets off a multiplier decrease in the equilibrium level of national income. At the new equilibrium, saving is the same as it was at the original equilibrium level of national income.

KEY TERMS

Aggregate expenditure
Equilibrium level of national income
Unwanted inventories
Actual investment
Aggregate expenditure curve (AE)
Income multiplier
The paradox of thrift

QUESTIONS

1. What conditions describe macroequilibrium in the Keynesian model?

2. Describe what happens to the level of national income when intended investment is greater than actual investment.

3. Describe what happens to the level of national income when intended investment is greater than saving.

4. The creation of unwanted inventories or the depletion of wanted inventories signals coming changes in the level of national income. Explain why.

5. What role, if any, do prices play in the Keynesian model of national income determination? Why?

6. What effect would an upward shift in investment have on the equilibrium level of national income?

7. Describe how the income multiplier works.

8. Suppose a $10 billion increase in investment spending by Goodyear Tire generates a $10 billion increase in national income. What can you say about the income multiplier? What would MPC be?

9. What is paradoxical about the paradox of thrift?

10. What effect would a $50 billion decrease in investment spending have on national income when MPS is 0.40?

11. Suppose investment spending increases by $200. Calculate the effect of that increase on the first five rounds of changes in income, changes in consumption, and changes in saving. Assume an MPC of 0.80. Illustrate these changes by describing the changes in real output (use your imagination).

Round	*Y*	*C*	*S*
1			
2			
3			
4			
5			

12. Draw a graph depicting an economy with the following characteristics: Autonomous consumption = $10 billion, MPC = 0.90, and intended investment = $25 billion. What would be the economy's equilibrium level of national income?

13. Professor Arvind Jaggi asks his students at Franklin and Marshall College the following question: Upon hearing that Boeing Corporation received a massive order for commercial aircraft from the Saudi Arabian government, the governor of Washington optimistically proclaimed the order to be a massive boon not only for Boeing but for the entire state. Using insights from the income multiplier phenomenon, explain the reasons for the governor's enthusiasm.

Appendix Opening the Keynesian Model to Foreign Trade

At the beginning of this chapter, we made it clear that we would deliberately exclude government spending and foreign trade from our analysis of national income determination even though we knew that both government spending and net exports are an integral part of aggregate expenditures. The reason for the exclusion? Simplicity of analysis. What we wanted to do was show, in as uncomplicated a fashion as possible, how aggregate expenditures determine the equilibrium level of national income. To do that, we assumed an economy with no government spending or foreign trade.

But let's relax those assumptions now. Let's consider here the role exports and imports play in determining the equilibrium level of national income.

THE IMPACT OF EXPORTS ON NATIONAL INCOME DETERMINATION

Consider first the impact of exports. Our exports to other countries create production and income in the United States in precisely the same way as production and income are created by Americans buying those goods in the United States. *It makes no difference where the buyers are located.* For example, Canadian teenagers in Montreal buying American-made Nike cross training shoes create production and income in the United States in precisely the same way as a teenager in Philadelphia does buying those shoes.

But aggregate expenditures ($AE = C + I$) in the Keynesian model includes one and not the other. Since the Philadelphia teenager's spending on the Nike shoes is already accounted for in aggregate expenditures as part of consumption (C), the Canadian consumption of the American exports (X) must be added as a new component of American aggregate expenditures.

How do exports affect the equilibrium level of national income? Look at Table A1.

Suppose $60 billion of exports are added to aggregate expenditures. What was once $AE = C + I$ is now $AE' = C + I + X$. This upward shift in national income is shown in panel *a* of Figure A1. What happens to the equilibrium level of national income? It increases from $800 billion to $1,100 billion.

TABLE A1 National Income Determination, Before and After $60 Billion of Exports

Y	$C + I = AE$	$C + I + X = AE'$
$ 600	$ 540 + $100 = $ 640	$ 540 + $100 + $60 = $ 700
700	620 + 100 = 720	620 + 100 + 60 = 780
800	700 + 100 = **800**	700 + 100 + 60 = 860
900	780 + 100 = 880	780 + 100 + 60 = 940
1,000	860 + 100 = 960	860 + 100 + 60 = 1,020
1,100	940 + 100 = 1,040	940 + 100 + 60 = **1,100**
1,200	1,020 + 100 = 1,120	1,020 + 100 + 60 = 1,180

FIGURE A1
The Impact of Foreign Trade on National Income Determination
Panel *a* shows the effect of adding $60 billion of exports—the aggregate expenditure curve shifts upward from *AE* to *AE'*. As a result, the equilibrium level of national income increases from $800 billion to $1,100 billion.

Panel *b* shows the independent impact of $20 billion of imports. They cause the aggregate expenditure curve to shift down from *AE* to *AE"*. The effect is to reduce equilibrium national income from $800 billion to $700 billion.

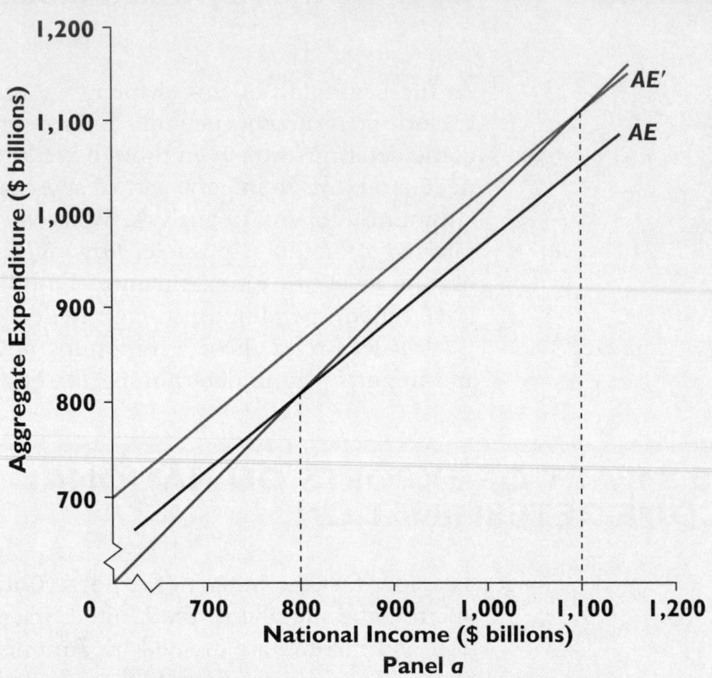

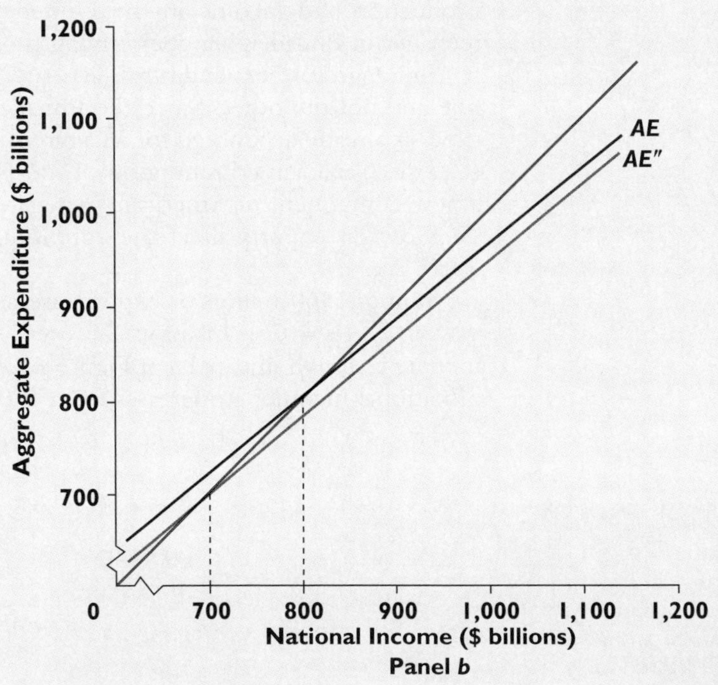

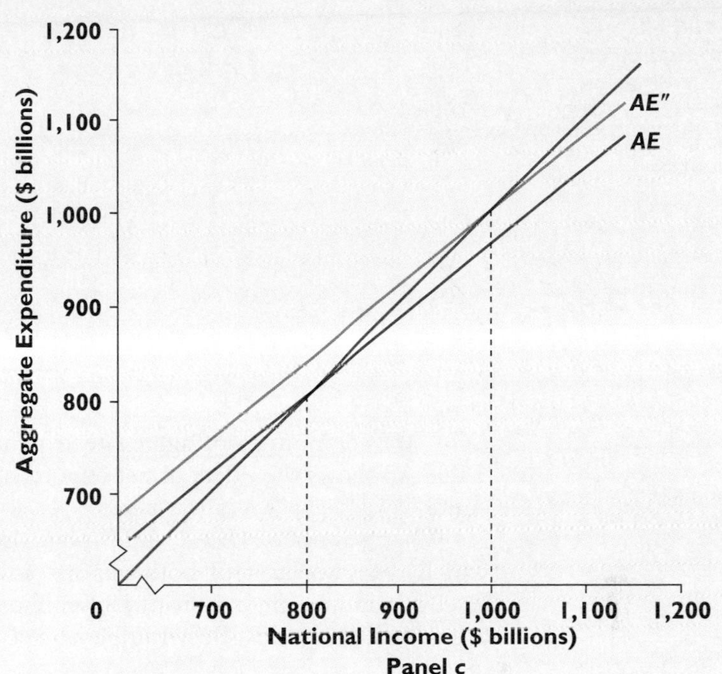

FIGURE A1 (*Continued*)
Panel *c* shows the joint effect of $60 billion of exports and $20 billion of exports. They combine to make $40 billion of net exports, which are a source of aggregate expenditure. As a result of this increased spending, the aggregate expenditure curve shifts up from *AE* to *AE″*. Equilibrium national income increases from $800 billion to $1,000 billion.

THE IMPACT OF IMPORTS ON NATIONAL INCOME DETERMINATION

Let's now look at the impact of imports (M) on aggregate expenditures. Suppose exports are zero but imports into the United States amount to $20 billion. The Philadelphia teenager, for example, buys not only the American-made Nike shoes but a pair of hockey skates made in Canada. While his purchase of the Nike shoes creates production and income in the United States, his purchase of the hockey skates creates production and income in Canada. And because both the shoes and skates are part of his consumption, *they are both included in aggregate expenditures.*

In other words, aggregate expenditures in the United States now overstates the production and income created in the United States. To correct this overstatement, imports are subtracted from aggregate expenditures. This is shown in Table A2.

What was once $AE = C + I$ is now $AE'' = C + I - M$. Look what happens to the equilibrium level of national income when aggregate expenditures are adjusted for imports. It decreases from $800 billion to $700 billion. This downward shift in national income is shown in panel *b* of Figure A1.

THE NET IMPACT OF EXPORTS AND IMPORTS ON NATIONAL INCOME DETERMINATION

Let's now consider an economy with *both* exports and imports. Assuming the same levels of exports and imports used in Tables A1 and A2, the net exports

TABLE A2
National Income Determination, Before and After $20 Billion of Imports

Y	C + I = AE	C + I − M = AE″
$ 600	$ 540 + $100 = $ 640	$ 540 + $100 − $20 = $ 620
700	620 + 100 = 720	620 + 100 − 20 = **700**
800	700 + 100 = **800**	700 + 100 − 20 = 780
900	780 + 100 = 880	780 + 100 − 20 = 860
1,000	860 + 100 = 960	860 + 100 − 20 = 940
1,100	940 + 100 = 1,040	940 + 100 − 20 = 1,020
1,200	1,020 + 100 = 1,120	1,020 + 100 − 20 = 1,100

$(X - M)$ component of aggregate expenditures is ($60 − $20) = $40 billion. Table A3 shows the effect of net exports on the equilibrium level of national income.

What was once $AE = C + I$ is now $AE^* = C + I + (X - M)$. Net exports—which takes account of both exports and imports—increases the equilibrium level of national income from $800 billion to $1,000 billion. This upward shift in national income is shown in panel *c* of Figure A1.

WHAT INFLUENCES FOREIGN TRADE?

Economic Performance

It stands to reason, doesn't it, that if the Mexican economy is growing rapidly, Mexicans will have more income to spend and some of it will be spent buying more goods from the United States. In other words, how much Americans are able to export depends not only on the American ability to produce goods but on the ability of other economies to buy them. Wishing our trading partners well is really wishing ourselves well! After all, if our net exports increase, our aggregate expenditures and national income increase. Of course, when our own economy prospers, American incomes increase, consumption increases, including spending on imports. You can see why our trading partners should wish us well. After all, they prosper when we do. It's a win/win situation for all of us.

TABLE A3
National Income Determination, Before and After $40 Billion of Net Exports

Y	C + I = AE	C + I + (X − M) = AE*
$ 600	$ 540 + $100 = $ 640	$ 540 + $100 + $40 = $ 680
700	620 + 100 = 720	620 + 100 + 40 = 760
800	700 + 100 = **800**	700 + 100 + 40 = 840
900	780 + 100 = 880	780 + 100 + 40 = 920
1,000	860 + 100 = 960	860 + 100 + 40 = **1,000**
1,100	940 + 100 = 1,040	940 + 100 + 40 = 1,080
1,200	1,020 + 100 = 1,120	1,020 + 100 + 40 = 1,160

Barriers to Trade

Because whatever we export is always someone else's imports, there is the possibility (and likelihood) that somebody in the importing economy may be adversely affected by our exports. For example, if American-made Nike shoes are exported to Mexico, Mexican shoe producers may find it more difficult to sell their shoes in Mexico. What can they do? They can try to persuade the Mexican government to place a tariff (which is a tax on imports) on shoes. Why would the government do it? To protect employment in the Mexican economy. Does it work? Are Mexican jobs really protected by tariffs? Not likely.

Look beyond Mexico's own borders. Mexican tariffs reduce the net exports of Mexico's trading partners which reduce their aggregate expenditures, national incomes, and abilities to import. So while employment in the Mexican shoe industry may be protected, other Mexicans, working in export industries, may lose their jobs.

In the long run, it is unclear whether the Mexican government can really protect its overall employment by erecting trade barriers. And since economies may retaliate against tariffs by creating their own—"if you erect barriers against my goods, I'll erect barriers against yours"—in the end, everyone's aggregate expenditures and national incomes fall.

Cooler minds and more constructive economic reasoning seems to have prevailed during the past 50 years. The world's trading partners have successfully negotiated a series of agreements on tariffs and trade that created a relatively higher degree of openness to foreign trade.

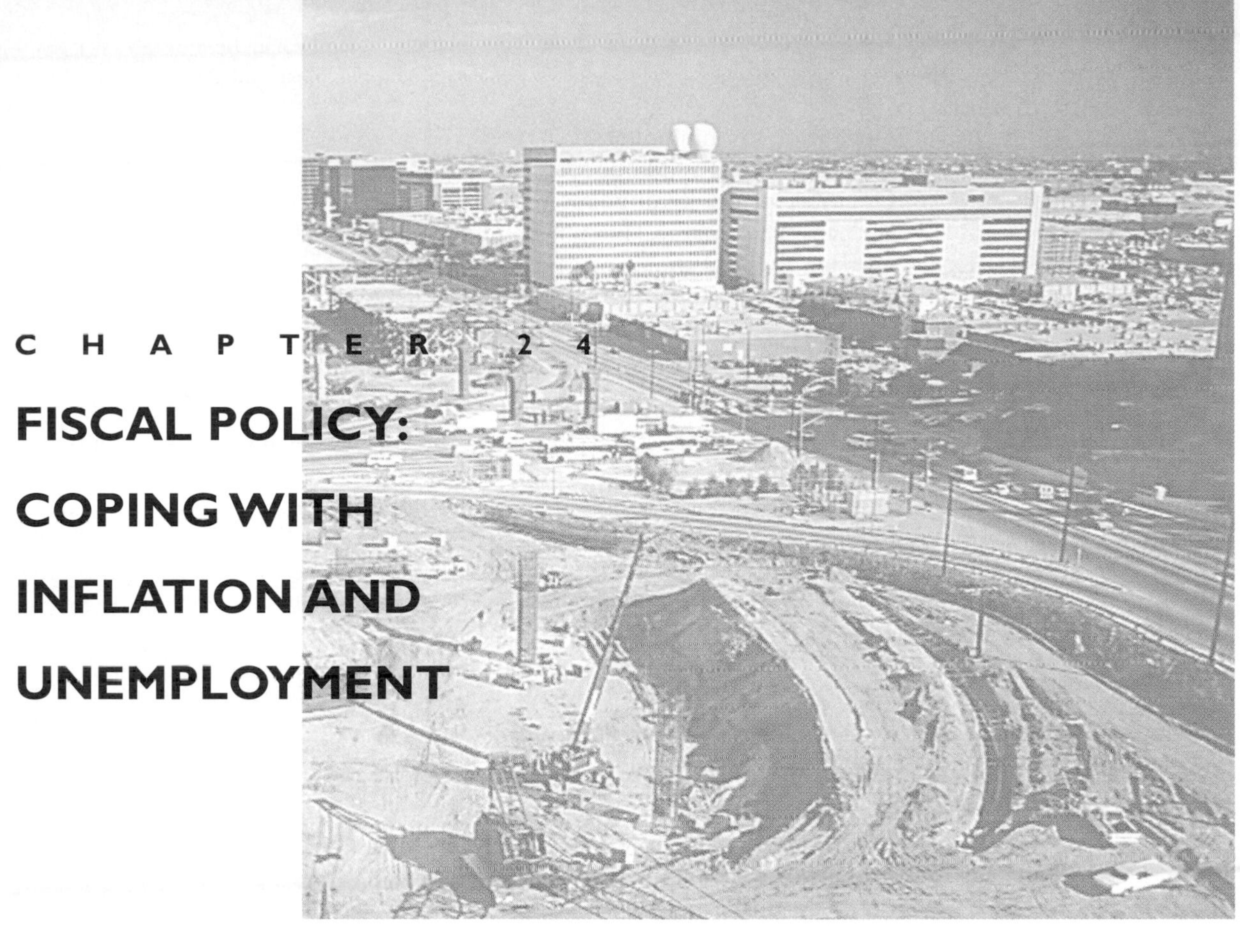

CHAPTER 24

FISCAL POLICY: COPING WITH INFLATION AND UNEMPLOYMENT

CHAPTER PREVIEW

So far we have considered how the economy adjusts from one equilibrium to another. We haven't said anything about the characteristics of the equilibrium. Is there a problem with unemployment? Is inflation troublesome? These are important questions to consider since we know from historical experience that there is the potential for persistent problems of unemployment and inflation. In this chapter we examine the circumstances under which either unemployment or inflation could exist, and the fiscal policy options that are available to the government when it attempts to combat these economic problems.

After studying this chapter, you should be able to:

- Describe the different types of unemployment that can exist.
- Calculate the unemployment rate, given the appropriate data.
- Explain what the term natural rate of unemployment means.
- Distinguish between winners and losers from inflation.
- Point to ways by which people can avoid being harmed by inflation.
- Identify both recessionary gaps and inflationary gaps using the Keynesian model.
- Suggest ways that government spending can be altered to close a recessionary or inflationary gap.

- Derive the tax multiplier.
- Derive the balanced budget multiplier.
- Describe various fiscal policy options for closing recessionary and inflationary gaps that embody different assumptions about the size of the deficit.
- Explain how the choice of a fiscal policy is inherently a choice about the size of the government sector.

As we discussed in the last chapter, only three factors—autonomous consumption, intended investment, and the marginal propensity to consume—dictate precisely where the level of national income will come to rest. That understanding is a good foundation upon which to build added dimensions. As we saw, tens of millions of consumers and producers, each acting independently, make consumption and investment decisions that drive the economy toward equilibrium.

WHAT'S SO GREAT ABOUT BEING IN EQUILIBRIUM?

But what's so great about being in equilibrium? What's really so great about people consuming and investing what they intended to consume and invest? Perhaps their intentions weren't very good in the first place! After all, poor people intend to consume very little and, because they are poor, actually do consume very little. Do you suppose they're happy about the fact that their intentions were realized? When the economy is in equilibrium, it can sometimes be distressful.

In the economy described in the last chapter, we first assumed that at equilibrium $Y =$ \$800 billion. Consumers chose to spend \$700 billion on consumption, precisely the amount that producers, acting independently, chose to produce for consumption. As a result, the actual investment producers made was exactly what they intended to make.

But is $Y =$ \$800 billion, itself, particularly attractive? Were people, in fact, satisfied with their lot? *Equilibrium tells us nothing about satisfaction* or the general state of the economy.

EQUILIBRIUM AND FULL EMPLOYMENT

The Keynesian model holds out the potential for the economy to be in equilibrium with high unemployment.

Let's consider the relationship between the economy's equilibrium position and the level of national income that would support full employment. *For an economy to be in equilibrium and at the same time at full employment is, in the Keynesian model, strictly a matter of historical accident.* After all, the equilibrium position is determined by the consumers' and producers' specific consumption and investment decisions, and these have little to do with how large the labor force is or how many of those in the labor force are actually working.

The economy can be in equilibrium and at the same time still be unable to provide employment to those wanting jobs. In fact, that's precisely what Keynes saw in the 1930s. He and millions of other people who experienced unemployment or who had to live under its threat didn't think that kind of national income equilibrium was anything to celebrate.

Identifying Unemployment

When is an economy at full employment? When *everybody* is working? Although this sounds like a reasonable enough criterion, it's far from being useful. Why? Because there are always some people who, at prevailing wage rates *choose* not to work. Suppose, for example, that Brian Vargo, an auto repair mechanic, refuses to work unless he is paid $1,000 per hour. Who would hire him at that wage? It would be silly, then, to count him among the unemployed. In defining full employment, therefore, we need to look at the reasons why people may not have jobs.

THE FRICTIONALLY UNEMPLOYED

What about people who voluntarily quit a job to spend time looking for a better one? Most people, particularly in the early years of their working life, are relatively mobile. They are always thinking about the possibilities of an upward move. They may have read about the prospects in Alaska, or heard about the new Japanese auto plant being built in Tennessee. Their antennas are always up, searching for new and better employment.

Many times, they do more than think about changing jobs. They actually do it. A real lead or a passed-over promotion could trigger their decision to quit. They gamble on improvement. For a short period—days, weeks, or perhaps even months—they explore their opportunities. It takes energy and patience. Some may decide to return to school to complete a degree or develop new technical skills.

How would you classify these "between jobs" people? Economists use the term **frictional unemployment** to convey the idea that job switching for job improvement is seldom smooth or instantaneous, but is quite natural in a dynamic economy.

Frictional unemployment

Relatively brief periods of unemployment caused by people deciding to voluntarily quit work in order to seek more attractive employment.

THE STRUCTURALLY UNEMPLOYED

It is quite another matter when workers wake up one morning to find their jobs gone because of a technological change in the production process or because of a change in demand for the goods they were producing. And it is hardly a comfort to them to know that both technological change and changes in demand are quite natural phenomena in a dynamic economy. Economists describe such a loss of jobs as **structural unemployment.**

Structural unemployment

Unemployment that results from fundamental technological changes in production, or from the substitution of new goods for customary ones.

When a new technology displaces an old one, it typically displaces the old technology's operators as well. For example, when the steam-driven locomotive was the principal mode of moving passengers and freight across the country, railroad firemen were needed to fuel the engines. But when the railroads switched from steam to diesel, these formerly indispensable firemen became technologically obsolete.

The firemen soon discovered they weren't alone. As rail transportation gave way to trucks and airplanes, many locomotive engineers, porters, stationmasters, switch operators, rail repairmen, and others employed in the manufacture of rails, locomotives, boxcars, refrigerator cars, and railway stations found themselves out of work. What could they do? Not every ex-railway worker can pilot a Boeing 747.

Changes in consumer tastes, too, destroy jobs. Wisconsin farmers lost their farms and employment when consumer preferences shifted from butter to margarine. When people switched from reading newspapers to watching television, a stream of editors, columnists, reporters, printing press workers, and newspaper vendors found themselves out of work. Should we not watch television because editors need jobs?

What do you suppose will happen to fur trappers, traders, tanners, and furcoat makers if activists struggling for animal rights succeed in convincing millions of consumers? What happens to tobacco workers when people stop smoking? When people in France switch from wine to Coke—and they seem to be doing so in increasing numbers—vineyard workers in southern France join the ranks of the structurally unemployed.

Unemployment-creating changes in technology and consumer taste strike workers indiscriminately—no industry or worker is immune—but the impact of such change falls particularly hard on older workers. After all, they acquired years of on-the-job experience to match a specific technology. When the technology changes, their work experience and skills often count for zero. What can they do? It is difficult for them to start over again. They find themselves competing for lower-paying jobs against the preferred, younger workers.

There usually are jobs available when there is structural unemployment. The problem is not a widespread shortage of employment opportunities in the economy, but that typically many structurally unemployed workers do not meet the qualifications required for the available jobs.

Can we avoid structural unemployment? Only by avoiding the modern conveniences of life such as central heating, paved streets, electric lights, personal computers, and vacuum cleaners. That is to say, if people are to enjoy the benefits that advanced technology affords, then the pain of structural unemployment has to be paid. But for those who pay it, the question always is: Why me?

THE CYCLICALLY UNEMPLOYED

Why me? is the same question asked by people who lose their jobs not to technological change but because the economy happens to be languishing in a downturn or recession phase of a business cycle. In these economically depressed phases, many businesses are forced to cut back on production and consequently cut back as well on the number of workers they are able to employ.

Cyclical unemployment
Unemployment associated with the downturn and recession phases of the business cycle.

Economists define this kind of joblessness as **cyclical unemployment** because it is governed by the rhythms of the business cycle; increasing as the cycle moves into its recession phase and decreasing as it moves out.

If you're among the unfortunate workers who are cyclically unemployed during some part of the recession, you would probably find it difficult to get a new job. After all, who is hiring during recessions? You may be eager to work, but eagerness is not the issue.

ADDED PERSPECTIVE

From John Steinbeck's *Cannery Row*

It was a lazy day. Willard was going to have to work hard to get up any excitement. "I think you're a coward, too. You want to make something of that?" Joey didn't answer. Willard changed his tactics. "Where's your old man now?" he asked in a conversational tone.

"He's dead," said Joey.

"Oh yeah? I didn't hear. What'd he die of?"

For a moment Joey was silent. He knew Willard knew but he couldn't let on he knew, not without fighting Willard, and Joey was afraid of Willard.

"He committed—he killed himself."

"Yeah?" Willard put on a long face. "How'd he do it?"

"He took rat poison."

Willard's voice shrieked with laughter. "What'd he think— he was a rat?"

Joey chuckled a little at the joke, just enough, that is.

"He must of thought he was a rat," Willard cried. "Did he go crawling around like this—look, Joey—like this? Did he wrinkle up his nose like this? Did he have a big old long tail?" Willard was helpless with laughter. "Why'n't he just get a rat trap and put his head in it?" They laughed themselves out on that one, Willard really wore it out. Then he probed for another joke. "What'd he look like when he took it—like this?" He crossed his eyes and opened his mouth and stuck out his tongue.

"He was sick all day," said Joey. "He didn't die 'til the middle of the night. It hurt him."

Willard said, "What'd he do it for?"

"He couldn't get a job," said Joey. "Nearly a year he couldn't get a job. And you know a funny thing? The next morning a guy come around to give him a job."

Discussion

Judging from that snippet of conversation, would you describe Joey's father as having been a discouraged worker? Why or why not?

THE DISCOURAGED WORKER

How long can you search for a job without becoming totally discouraged and give up? Many of the unemployed do just that. Perhaps you would too if, day after day, week after week, you confront only rejection? After a while you may no longer even think of yourself as a worker or as part of the labor force. Many **discouraged workers** end up in a nonwork culture and remain permanently separated from the productive society. And once in that culture, it may take more than the availability of jobs to get them back into productive life.

Discouraged workers

Unemployed people who give up looking for work after experiencing persistent rejection in their attempts to find work.

THE UNDEREMPLOYED WORKER

Take the case of Nancy Krasnow, an aeronautical engineer who once earned $60,000 working for Lockheed in Los Angeles. In the midst of a recession, Lockheed laid her off, along with 2,000 of her coworkers. After months of fruitless job searching, and with savings close to zero, Nancy's only viable prospect (other than slipping into the world of the discouraged worker) was flipping hamburgers at McDonald's, which earns her slightly more than minimum wages. Reluctantly, she sets aside her talents and experience and takes the job. But what is she now, an aeronautical engineer or a hamburger flipper?

If she were asked whether she was unemployed and looking for a job, how does she answer? The fact is that she *is* employed. But how would *you* define her status? In periods of recession, the number of people who end up as discouraged workers or among the **underemployed workers** can be rather significant.

Underemployed workers

Workers employed in jobs that do not utilize their productive talents or experience.

TABLE 1 Number of Workers and Types of Unemployment

Number of workers	10,250
Frictional unemployment	150
Structural unemployment	200
Cyclical unemployment	500
Discouraged workers	250
Underemployment	300

Calculating an Economy's Rate of Unemployment

Imagine an economy with the employment/unemployment characteristics shown in Table 1.

How would you go about determining the economy's rate of unemployment? Do you simply sum up the unemployed—that is, the 150 + 200 + 500 = 850 and divide by the total number of workers? That reckoning would generate an unemployment rate of 850/10,250 = 8.3 percent.

But what about the 300 underemployed? A tough call, isn't it? After all, is an aeronautical engineer flipping hamburgers at McDonald's really employed? If you're inclined to answer no and count such workers among the unemployed, the economy's unemployment rate increases to 1,150/10,250 = 11.2 percent.

But look again at Table 1. There are 250 discouraged workers who have no jobs. Are you prepared to write them off the list of unemployed because they have given up looking? If you include them, the rate of unemployment increases to 1,400/10,250 = 13.7 percent. As you see, the unemployment rate for the Table 1 economy depends on your decision about who appropriately belongs in the unemployment pool.

The BLS Definition of Unemployment

How does the rate of unemployment you choose as being appropriate compare to the rate chosen by the Bureau of Labor Statistics (BLS) of the U.S. Department of Labor? Each month, the Bureau conducts a nationwide employment survey of 60,000 households. The critical question asked is: *Are you presently gainfully employed or actively seeking employment?* Only those answering yes are counted in the labor force. That is, according to the BLS, the **labor force** consists of working people plus the unemployed who are looking for work.

Labor force

People who are gainfully employed or actively seeking employment.

Suppose, for example, that Elisa Kilhafer, a housewife in St. Louis, Missouri, is surveyed by the BLS and reports that she is neither gainfully employed nor looking for work. According to the BLS, Elisa is neither unemployed nor a part of the labor force. On the other hand, if she had said that she was looking for work but couldn't find any, she would be counted not only among the unemployed but also as a member of the labor force.

The BLS calculates the unemployment rate as the number of people seeking work divided by the labor force.

How does the BLS treat the underemployed? As long as the underemployed are working somewhere at some job, they are counted as employed and in the labor force. Discouraged workers, on the other hand, are viewed differently. Why? Because it makes no difference to the BLS *why* discouraged workers have no jobs. The fact that they are not actively looking is reason enough to exclude them from the labor force and from the lists of the unemployed.

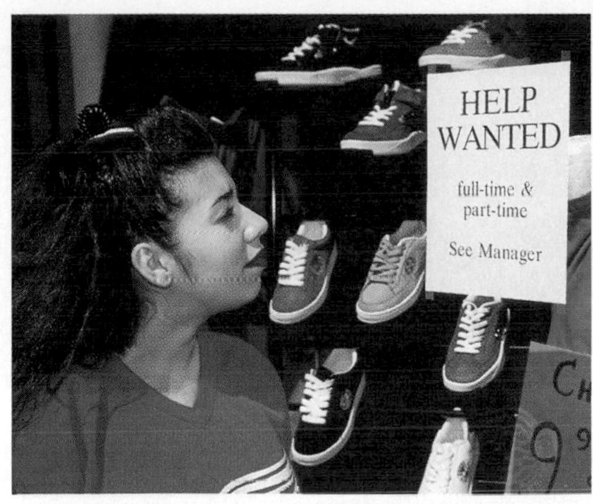

This woman graduated *magna cum laude* from Syracuse University and was hoping to find a job in her field of expertise: computer science. But nobody seems to be hiring. Disappointed, she is seriously considering this job as salesperson. If she takes it, how will the BLS classify her employment status?

According to the BLS, then, the labor force in Table 1 is 10,250 – 250 discouraged workers = 10,000. The number of workers unemployed—now excluding discouraged and underemployed workers—is 150 + 200 + 500 = 850. The BLS-derived rate of unemployment is 8.5 percent.

The Natural Rate of Unemployment

The economy is at full employment when the unemployment rate is equal to the natural rate.

Natural rate of unemployment

The rate of unemployment caused by frictional plus structural unemployment in the economy.

Full employment

An employment level in which the actual rate of unemployment in the economy is equal to the economy's natural rate of unemployment.

Does a 8.5 percent unemployment rate signal that the economy is 850 jobs short of full employment? Not exactly. Economists recognize that some of that 850 unemployment is natural, that is, it does not necessarily reflect an economy unable to absorb its unemployment. After all, they argue, even if the economy of Table 1 were bursting with energy and demand for workers outstripped supply, there would still be workers looking for better positions, and others displaced from their jobs because of technological improvements. If we accept the fact that these forms of unemployment are both natural and inevitable, then—setting that unemployment aside—if all other workers are employed, the economy is at full employment.

The 350 frictionally and structurally unemployed of Table 1 make up what economists describe as the economy's 3.5 percent **natural rate of unemployment.** What remains are the 500 cyclically unemployed, accounting for 5.0 percent of the labor force.

Economists distinguish between the 8.5 percent actual rate of unemployment, the 3.5 percent natural rate, and the 5.0 percent rate of cyclical unemployment. *To economists, the economy is at full employment when the actual rate of unemployment equals the natural rate.* Put differently, the economy is considered to be at **full employment** when the rate of cyclical unemployment is zero.

Full Employment Level

Let's apply the concept of full employment to the Keynesian aggregate supply curve developed in the aggregate demand and aggregate supply chapter and redrawn in Figure 1.

The shape of the aggregate supply curve reflects the Keynesian view (expressed in the last chapter) that the price level is constant at low levels of em-

FIGURE 1 **The Full-Employment Level of the Aggregate Supply Curve**
Within the real GDP range of $0 to $1,000 billion, GDP can increase without triggering an increase in the economy's price level. This is depicted by the horizontal segment of the aggregate supply curve at $P = 100$.

Beyond that point, producers must offer higher wage rates to induce more people into the labor force. Higher wages cause higher price levels, shown in the upward-sloping segment of the aggregate supply curve. At GDP = $1,500 billion, everyone who is capable of working at *any* wage rate is working. No further increase in the price level can generate more real GDP. That is why the aggregate supply curve becomes perfectly vertical at $1,500 billion.

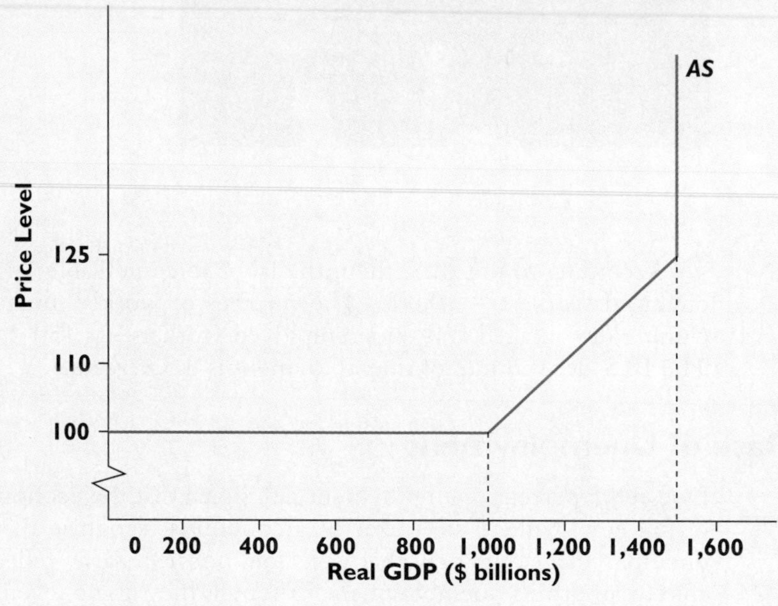

The aggregate supply curve shows a constant price level at low levels of income and employment. The price level rises as full employment is approached.

ployment. Output and income can increase anywhere along the horizontal segment without any upward pressure on the price level because there is a ready pool of unemployed workers to draw upon at current wage rates.

The price level is constant only up to a level of $1,000 billion. From $1,000 billion to $1,500 billion, the price level rises from $P = 100$ to $P = 125$. At *GDP* = $1,000 billion, everyone willing to work at the current wage rate is employed. There are others in the economy who are not working but would be willing to work—but only at wage rates higher than the current rate. If they can't get the higher rates, they prefer not to be members of the labor force.

How, then, can the economy get beyond $1,000 billion; to say, $1,100 billion? By inducing more people into employment with higher wage rates. But higher wage rates raise the cost of producing goods, and with varying degrees of success, producers pass these higher costs on to consumers by raising prices. In the end, higher wage rates are accompanied by higher prices. Note that at $1,100 billion, $P = 105$. *In other words, national income and employment both increase, but only under conditions of price level increases.*

That's why the aggregate supply curve slopes upward within the range $Y =$ $1,000 billion to $Y =$ $1,500 billion. Increases in both GDP and employment occur, but only with increasing doses of inflation.

What happens beyond $1,500 billion? *There is no beyond $1,500 billion.* At $1,500 billion, the aggregate supply curve becomes vertical. The economy's em-

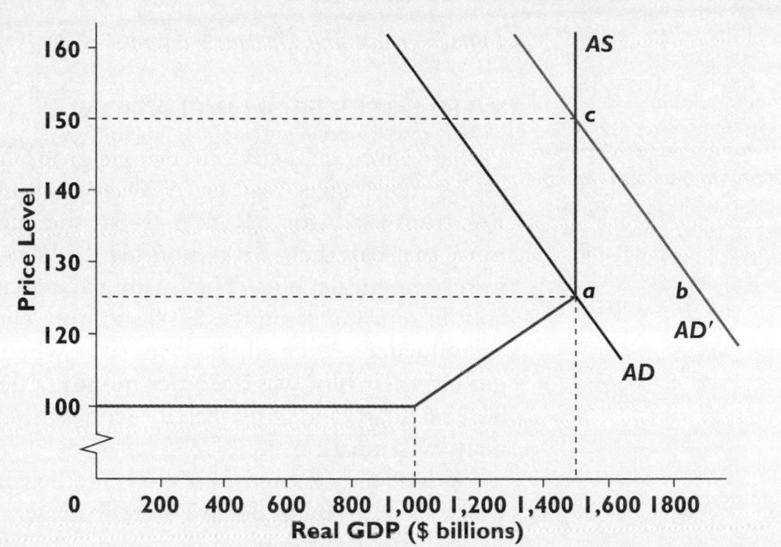

FIGURE 2
Effects of an Increase in Aggregate Demand on Full-Employment National Income
The shift in aggregate demand from *AD* (point *a*) to *AD′* creates excess aggregate demand—aggregate quantity demanded minus aggregate quantity supplied—at $P = 125$ (point *b*). Since output and income at $Y =$ \$1,500 billion are already at full-employment level, the pressures of excess aggregate demand force prices upward to $P = 150$ (point *c*).

ployment potential is *fully* exhausted. There are no more workers available at any wage rate to increase national income. The only increase that occurs at \$1,500 billion is in prices. This is illustrated in Figure 2.

The \$1,500 billion full-employment equilibrium level of national income is shown at point *a*. Let's now suppose aggregate demand increases from *AD* to *AD′*.

Look what happens to income and prices. At the price level $P = 125$, the quantity of output demanded, point *b* on *AD′*, is now greater than the quantity supplied. Although production of goods and services cannot increase beyond \$1,500 (the economy's maximum output is depicted by the vertical segment of the aggregate supply curve), the prices of the goods and services can. Excess aggregate demand at the price level $P = 125$ drives the price level up along the *AD′* curve from point *b* to point *c*, where a new equilibrium occurs at \$1,500 billion and $P = 150$.

UNDERSTANDING INFLATION

Suppose you were living in the economy of Figure 2 and could choose between GDP = \$900 billion and $P = 100$ (moderate unemployment with no inflation) and GDP = \$1,500 billion and $P = 125$ (full employment with inflation), which would you choose? If you are like most people, you would probably choose the second option because you can more easily identify with the pain associated with being out of a job than you can with the pain associated with inflation. Unlike unemployment, whose victims are personal and recognizable, inflation covers the economy like a fog, affecting everything and everybody, making it sometimes difficult to distinguish victims from nonvictims. In fact, there are victims but there are also many in the economy who actually benefit from inflation.

Winners and Losers of Inflation

Inflation redistributes people's incomes. Who wins in this redistribution? Who loses?

WHO LOSES FROM INFLATION?

Losers from inflation include people on fixed incomes, savers, and landlords.

Perhaps more than any other single group, people living on fixed incomes, such as retirees, have reason to worry about inflation. Why? Listen to Tina Eckstrom's sad story. Back in 1954, she and her husband bought a deferred annuity that cost them $100 monthly. In 1994, it started to pay them $700 a month in retirement benefits. They were excited about the prospect of living comfortably in retirement on the $700 monthly check, along with the savings they had accumulated. After all, back in 1954 when they put their retirement plans together, their rent was $125 per month, a new automobile was $1,500, milk was $0.25 a quart, and a first-run movie was $0.35. What they didn't factor into their plans was inflation.

When they retired in 1994, they began to receive their $700 each month. But their retirement dreams were shattered. Why? The $700 doesn't come close to covering their condominium rent, and a new car—now at $16,000—is simply out of the question. They, along with millions of other people *who live on fixed incomes* are big losers of inflation.

For the same reason, some landlords worry about inflation, especially the ones whose incomes are tied to long-term rental leases. If they confront years of inflation, they lose badly. So too do workers who accepted union-negotiated, multiyear, fixed-wage contracts. Imagine how you would feel if you were working for minimum wages during the 1980s. The annual inflation rate was 4.6 percent, and the minimum wage was fixed at $3.25. If your minimum-wage job allowed you to buy $100 worth of groceries in 1980, by 1990 you could buy only $63.70 worth of groceries (assuming the price of groceries went up at the same rate as the price level).

Savers can lose as well. How? Suppose you saved $100 last year, giving up the option of buying a $100 pair of Nike cross-training shoes. This year, you decide to use the savings to buy the shoes. You withdraw $105 from the bank—your savings earned five percent interest—only to discover that the shoes now cost $110. While your money was in the bank, inflation was 10 percent. You're in a relatively worse position. Imagine if you had saved $10,000, not $100.

Remember Benjamin Franklin's comment: A penny saved is a penny earned. Think about it. In inflationary times, it simply isn't true.

WHO GAINS FROM INFLATION?

Winners from inflation include borrowers and the government.

Not everyone loses from inflation. Borrowers, for example, are among those who benefit. Let's consider those shoes again. Suppose that the year before you had spotted them sitting in a store window on sale at $100. Not having the money, you visited your neighborhood bank to borrow $100 at 5 percent interest. This year, you repay the bank with interest and come away a winner. Why? *Inflation!* Had you waited until this year to buy the shoes, with inflation at 10 percent it would have cost you $110. Of course, if inflation works in favor of borrowers, it works against lenders. What you won through inflation, the bank lost.

Let's paint another scenario. Suppose you considered buying a beautiful, brick ranch house sitting on a $\frac{1}{4}$-acre lot. It had three bedrooms, two baths, a sunken living room with fireplace, a large study, wood-floored dining room, and a two-car garage. The owner, anxious to sell, will accept $140,000. The bank offers you a 30-year, fixed-rate mortgage at $6\frac{1}{2}$ percent. Your monthly payments amount to $850. That's $300 more than the two-bedroom apartment you now rent, but the difference in comfort is so striking that you decide to buy the house. Six years later you drive by your old apartment building and notice a For Rent sign sitting on the front lawn. What shocks you is the advertised rent: $885 per month! More than your present monthly mortgage payments. You may have made silly purchases in your lifetime, but the house, thanks to 10 percent per year inflation, was not one of them. You come away a winner.

What ends up as gains from inflation to borrowers like yourself also works for government. After all, government is the largest single borrower. Interest payments every year on its $4 trillion national debt exceed $200 billion. And just as your $850 mortgage payments every month became less and less burdensome through inflation, so too does inflation, with time, reduce the *real* cost to government of carrying the national debt.

Inflation could help the government in yet another way. If prices of goods and services increase at about the same rate as wage rates and other sources of income, then real incomes remain virtually unchanged. That is to say, higher incomes will buy the same quantity of groceries. On the other hand, you may end up paying more income tax. Why? Because a higher money income may put you in a higher tax bracket. Suppose, for example, that 10 years ago, your income was $40,000 and the last $1,000 of it—the fortieth $1,000—was taxed at 20 percent; you paid $200 tax on it. Now, after 10 years of inflation, you earn $75,000, and the last $1,000 of it—the seventy-fifth $1,000—is taxed at 31 percent. You now pay $310 tax on that $1,000. You have been bumped into a higher tax bracket, even though the $75,000 buys the same groceries now as the $40,000 did 10 years ago. In other words, even though your real income remains the same, your disposable income decreases because government collects more.

MODERATING THE WINS AND LOSSES

If inflation is correctly anticipated, then steps can be taken to decrease its adverse impact.

Wouldn't you think that habitual losers of inflation would get tired of losing and try to do something about it? Many do, and succeed. For example, many banks offer home mortgages whose rates vary directly with the rate of inflation. Instead of charging $6\frac{1}{2}$ percent on a 30-year mortgage, they may charge 5 percent *plus the inflation rate.* In this way, they check the loss of future income through inflation. Unions understand as well that they could end up being big losers if they sign multiyear (typically three) fixed-wage contracts. Most union contracts now include a built-in cost-of-living adjustment (COLA) that covers the rate of inflation. Even taxpayers now can get some relief from "bracket creep" because the federal government recently adjusted the income levels associated with tax brackets to the rate of inflation.

LIVING IN A WORLD OF INFLATION AND UNEMPLOYMENT

Look at the economy of Figure 3. It's in equilibrium at $Y = \$800$ billion, where aggregate expenditure, in the form of the consumption and investment curve (*AE*), intersects the 45-degree line. But note: that's $700 billion below the economy's $1,500 billion full-employment level.

FIGURE 3 **Identifying the Recessionary Gap**

The full-employment national income level is Y = $1,500 billion. The equilibrium level of national income—governed by autonomous consumption, intended investment, and the marginal propensity to consume—is Y = $800 billion, where $C + I_i = C + S$. That is, the economy comes to rest at $700 billion short of full employment.

With MPC = 0.80, the income multiplier is 5. An additional aggregate expenditure of $140 billion, shown in *hg*, would be sufficient to drive the equilibrium level up by $700 billion to full employment Y = $1,500 billion. This $140 billion aggregate expenditure requirement defines the recessionary gap.

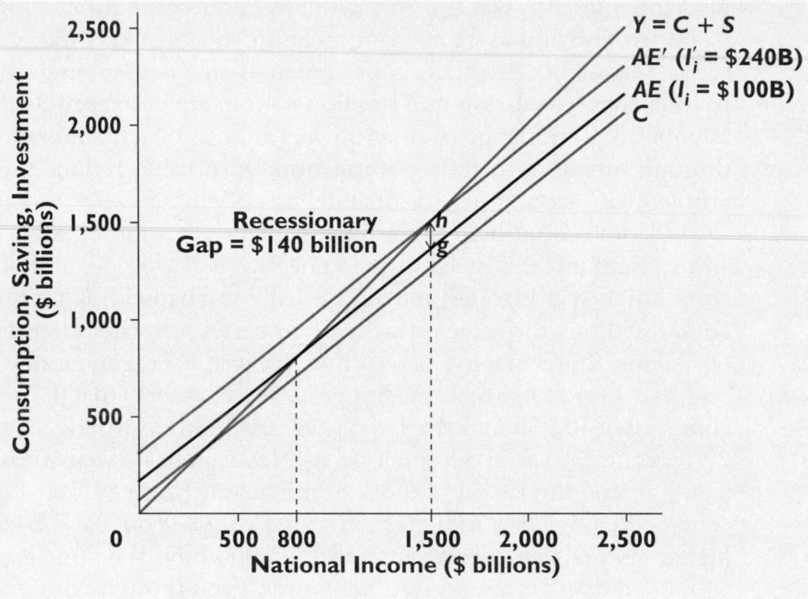

At Y = $800 billion, firms responding to or anticipating demands for consumption and investment goods continue to produce $700 billion of consumption goods and $100 billion of investment goods, and if at the same time, consumers continue to spend $700 billion on consumption and save $100 billion, then the number of people employed in the economy remains stuck at less than full employment. Moreover, there is no reason for those unemployed to expect to find employment no matter how hard they may try.

Wouldn't it be cruel, under these circumstances, to accuse people willing to work but unable to find a job of being lazy or listless? If they can convince an employer to hire them, it likely means that they have displaced other workers in a game of employment musical chairs. After all, at Y = $800 billion, only so many workers will be employed.

Identifying the Recessionary Gap

An economy that is operating below its full-employment capacity is experiencing a recessionary gap.

A $700 billion national income deficiency separates the Y = $800 billion equilibrium level from the Y = $1,500 billion full-employment level. What it takes to drive the equilibrium level of national income up to full employment is more aggregate expenditure; how much more depends principally on the marginal propensity to consume. For example, if MPC = 0.80 and generates an income multiplier of 5, then it would take an additional spending of $140 billion—

ADDED PERSPECTIVE

J. M. Keynes and Say's Law

For the economy as a whole, the total quantity of goods and services supplied equals the total quantity of goods and services demanded, because the very act of producing goods and services for supply necessitates the purchase and use of resources to produce them. The incomes that the resource owners earn producing the goods and services are used by the resource owners to purchase them. In other words, supply always creates its own demand.

This statement of the classical argument—*supply creates its own demand*—is known as Say's law, named after the 19th century French economist Jean Baptiste Say, who was among the first to maintain that *general* overproduction or underconsumption in the economy was impossible. It is possible that the quantity supplied can exceed quantity demanded in specific markets. But since the total value of all goods supplied creates an equivalent total value of all goods demanded, if an excess supply exists in some markets, an excess demand equivalent in value to the excess supply must exist in other markets. Eventually, competitive forces and flexible prices establish equilibrium in all markets.

Say's law applied to the capital market means that, in the long run, the quantity of capital supplied equals the quantity of capital demanded. In other words, saving equals investment. If saving is greater than investment in the short run, the interest rate will fall to equate saving and investment. If investment is greater than saving in the short run, the interest rate will increase to equate saving and investment.

Applied to the labor market, it means that unemployment may exist, but only in the short run. Given enough time, demand and supply forces in the labor market will adjust to bring about full employment.

During the Great Depression of the 1930s, the persistence of extraordinarily high unemployment and chronic deficiency in investment demand seemed to undermine the validity of Say's law. The idea that supply creates its own demand didn't seem to reflect the depressing conditions of oversupply of both goods and resources. Investment demand, it seemed, was insufficient to absorb the availability of saving. What went wrong with Say's law? Why didn't it work?

According to J. M. Keynes, Say's law didn't work because the assumptions underlying Say's law are fallacious. With few exceptions, markets are not competitive nor are prices flexible.

In the labor market, for example, Keynes believed that unions dominate supply— little if any competition exists among workers supplying labor—while large corporate firms dominate demand, providing little competition among themselves for labor. Moreover, the wages that the noncompetitive labor market generate are anything but flexible. Unions and workers typically reject wage cuts even if it means accepting unemployment. And Keynes argued that even if the unions and workers accept wage cuts, unemployment still persists. Why? Because wage cuts decrease workers' incomes and consequently decrease their demand for consumer goods. Firms react to the decrease in consumer demand by cutting employment.

In the capital market the rate of interest is not effective in equating the quantity of capital supplied to the quantity of capital demanded—that is, saving to equal investment. To Keynes, investment demand depends less upon low interest rates or the availability of saving, than on the expectation of a continuing robust economy.

If Keynes' view of labor and capital markets, interest rates, wages, and employment is right, what's left of Say's law? According to Keynesians, not very much!

Recessionary gap

The amount by which aggregate expenditure falls short of the level needed to generate equilibrium national income at full employment without inflation.

which is the amount represented by the distance *hg* in Figure 3—to shift the equilibrium level of national income up from Y = \$800 billion to Y = \$1,500 billion. This \$140 billion deficiency in aggregate expenditures is called the **recessionary gap.**

In Figure 3, the recessionary gap reflects the difference between the \$100 billion that producers invest (investment being part of aggregate expenditures) and the \$240 billion total investment demand required to bring equilibrium to full employment.

FIGURE 4 **Identifying the Inflationary Gap**

The full-employment national income level is $Y = \$1,500$ billion. The equilibrium level of national income—governed by autonomous consumption, intended investment, and marginal propensity to consume—is $Y = \$2,200$ billion, where $C + I_i = C + S$. That is, the economy comes to rest at \$700 billion beyond the full-employment level of national income. This \$2,200 – \$1,500 = \$700 billion gap is strictly price inflation. No more goods and services are produced in the economy beyond $Y = \$1,500$ billion.

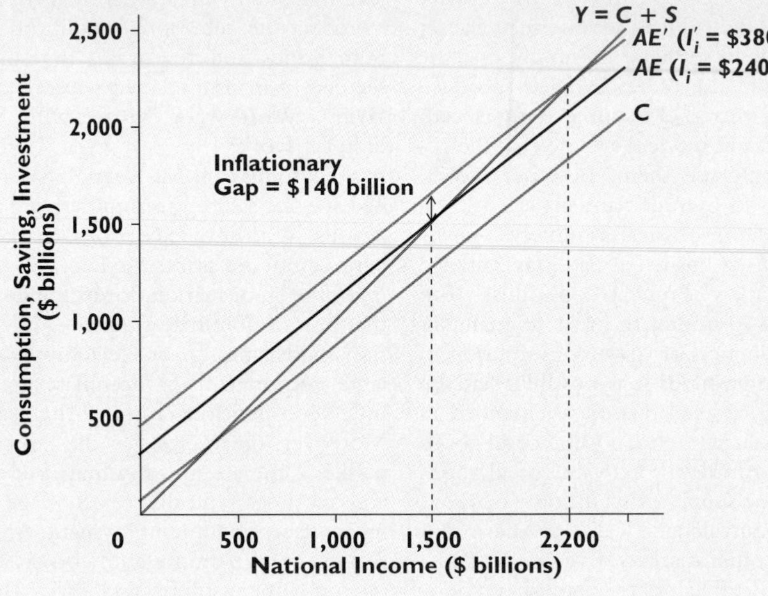

The fact that many people are jobless when producers invest only \$100 billion is unfortunate, not only for the unemployed but for producers as well. After all, they would love to produce more. But they confront the economy's consumption and investment spending, which tells them that producing more would be foolhardy. They can't be expected to increase investment when there's no evidence that demand exists for the investment goods. That is to say, neither the unemployed nor the producers can be faulted for the economy's recessionary gap.

Identifying the Inflationary Gap

An economy that is operating above its full-employment capacity is experiencing an inflationary gap.

Figure 4 presents an altogether different picture of the economy. Here, aggregate expenditures (consumption and investment functions) propel the economy to an equilibrium level of $Y = \$2,200$ billion.

Think about it. How can the economy be in equilibrium at $Y = \$2,200$ billion when the full-employment level is at $Y = \$1,500$ billion? That is to say, how can the economy create more than \$1,500 billion in goods and services? The answer: It can't. What then explains the difference between the \$1,500 billion full-employment level and the \$2,200 billion equilibrium level? Inflation, meaning that national income above the \$1,500 billion level reflects only price increases.

What would it take to bring the economy to equilibrium at full employment without inflation? Assuming again that MPC = 0.80 and the income multiplier

This clover-leaf construction segment of the city's new expressway will not only make driving through and around the city easier and less time consuming, but the multiple jobs it creates will furnish incomes for people who will buy the cars that will use the new expressway.

is 5, a $140 billion cut in aggregate expenditures would draw the equilibrium level of national income down by $700 billion to the Y = $1,500 billion full-employment level. This need for a $140 billion aggregate expenditures cutback defines the economy's **inflationary gap.**

CLOSING RECESSIONARY AND INFLATIONARY GAPS

Inflationary gap

The amount by which aggregate expenditure exceeds the aggregate expenditure level needed to generate equilibrium national income at full employment without inflation.

Suppose the President asks for your advice. The economy he confronts is the recessionary one of Figure 3 and his goal is to bring the economy to equilibrium at full employment. What do you tell him?

How about presidential persuasion? You could advise the President to invite the economy's most influential producers to a White House breakfast and there explain the importance of increasing aggregate expenditures.

It would be marvelous if all it took was a little presidential sweet talk to get producers to add another $140 billion to investment. But even producers who voted twice for the President couldn't justify a penny more investment when the economy is already in equilibrium at Y = $800 billion. Where, then, do you find the $140 billion?

Government Combats Recession

One answer is government. If nobody else will do it, government can. How does government get into a $140 billion investment business? It designs a public investment package that totals $140 billion. In ten minutes the President can probably come up with projects that would completely close the recessionary gap.

There are always more superhighways to build, more public housing to construct, more pollution control facilities to finance, more space shots to make, more health care schemes to fund, and more defense to procure. In fact, the least of his problems would seem to be finding suitable projects to absorb the $140 billion.

What about Congress? Would it go along? Members of Congress have to be sensitive to voters' concerns back home, and among their concerns in times of recession are jobs.

FIGURE 5 **Closing the Recessionary Gap**

Panel *a* depicts national income at its equilibrium level of Y = \$800 billion, where $C + I_i = C + S$. Intended investment is realized at \$100 billion. People's consumption spending and goods produced for consumption are identical at \$700 billion.

Panel *b* depicts the same Y = \$800 billion equilibrium level as shown in panel *a*, except now government intervenes by adding G = \$140 billion to aggregate expenditure. This shifts the equilibrium level of national income up from Y = \$800 billion to the full employment Y = \$1,500 billion. At Y = \$1,500 billion, intended investment is still realized at \$100 billion, but now people's consumption spending, as well as goods produced for consumption, increases to \$1,260 billion.

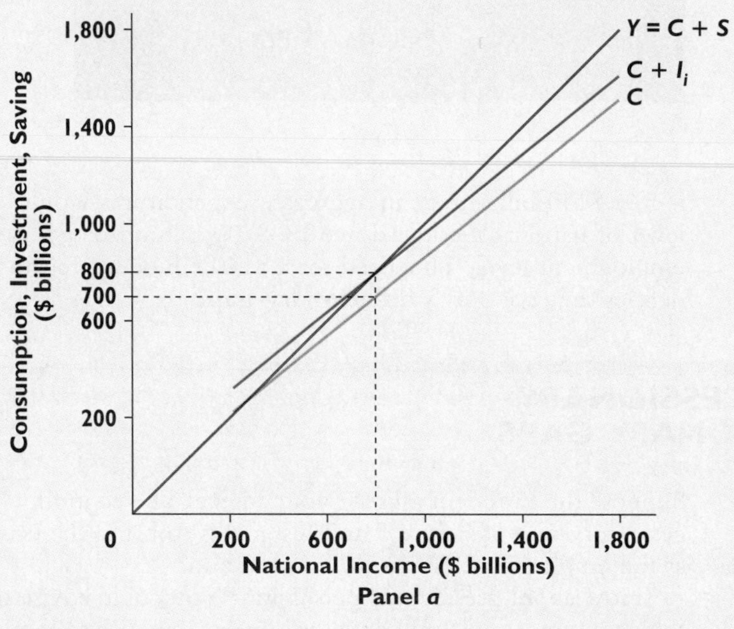

Panel *a*

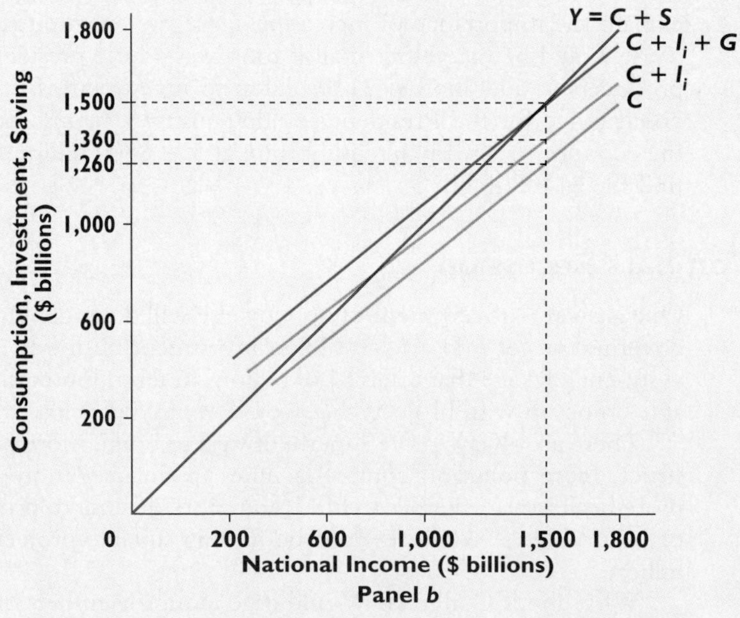

Panel *b*

The government now becomes an integral part of the economy's aggregate expenditures. What was once $AE = C + I_i$, is now $AE = C + I_i + G$, the G representing government purchases of goods and services.

Suppose the President asks you to brief the White House staff on your $140 billion recommendation. You prepare Figure 5 that shows, in panel *a,* the economy struggling along without the $140 billion of government spending on goods and services, and in panel *b,* how the economy fares with the government spending.

They would see the difference immediately. Panel *a*'s economy is in equilibrium at $Y =$ $800 billion. Panel *b*'s economy is in equilibrium at $Y =$ $1,500 billion.

But you can mention other points of interest. Panel *a* is strictly an economy of private aggregate expenditures $(C + I_i)$. There is no government intervention in the economy. By contrast, panel *b* is an economy with *both* private aggregate expenditures and government spending $(C + I_i + G)$.

How does the private sector portion of aggregate expenditure $(C + I_i)$ fare in the economy of panel *b*? With the economy at full employment, more income is earned. In fact, the private sector in panel *b* is actually more robust than the private sector in panel *a.*

You can see this by comparing private aggregate expenditure in the two equilibrium situations. It increases from $(C + I_i) =$ $800 billion in panel *a* to $[(C + I_i + G) - G] =$ $1,500 – $140 = $1,360 billion in panel *b.*

Note also how people's consumption spending increases. It grows from $C =$ [$60 + (.8 × $800)] = $700 billion in panel *a* to $C =$ [$60 + (.8 × $1,500)] = $1,260 billion in panel *b.* What about private investment? Producers end up investing $100 billion, as they intended, in both economies.

Who, then, loses? According to Keynesians, nobody! The $140 billion of government spending is at the expense of no one. The government created jobs *without competing with those already employed in the private sector.* Why, then, should anyone, including the President, object to the government-spending strategy of closing the recessionary gap?

Government Spending Is Not Problem-Free

Once started, government spending is hard to stop.

Critics of the Keynesian view of closing a recessionary gap offer a series of objections. First, they warn that once the $140 billion of government spending is introduced into the economy, it takes on a life-force of its own. *Once in, always in.* Whether it is needed to close recessionary gaps in subsequent years or not, the politics of the spending—such as defense and road-building—guarantees its continuity. In addition, *once in, always grows.* That is, $140 billion of government spending today, because of the vested political interests it creates, might push to $500 billion in a decade.

Second, they insist that Keynesians fail to appreciate the self-correcting nature of the economy. Given sufficient time, market forces will shift the private sector investment function of panel *a* in Figure 5 upward to the right, narrowing the recessionary gap. For example, changes in prices and wage rates may make investment more attractive to producers. Time also takes its toll on the economy's machinery and physical plants. Eventually, they must be replaced, and thus contribute also to the upsurge in demand for investment.

Third, they note the obvious: Government spending is not cost-free. The funding for $140 billion in government spending must come from somewhere

ADDED PERSPECTIVE

The Historical Record on Deficit Budgets Undermines the Idea that They Are Strictly Tools of Countercyclical Fiscal Policy

Back in 1980, economist Irwin Kellner, writing about Keynes and deficits, said: "Those who have written about Keynes in an effort to interpret his writings have drawn the conclusion that budget deficits are quite acceptable during periods of economic slack. I would agree. Some authors believe that Keynes had a cavalier attitude toward budget deficits, pointing to the views of many of his disciples who assert that deficits do not matter. With this I would disagree. If Keynes did not place great emphasis on the implications of a budget deficit beyond that of stimulating the economy, it is simply because he believed that deficits should not be used as a main tool of economic policy, and when they were, they were to be used during periods of slack. It is Keynes' followers and the politicians whom they educated that are to blame for the 'cavalier' attitude toward budget deficits that subsequently developed in the 1950s and 1960s."

Whether Kellner is right or wrong about Keynes, Keynesians, and the budget, the table looks at the record on deficits and surpluses.

	Total ($ billion)		
Year	Receipts	Outlays	Surplus or Deficit
1929	$ 3.9	$ 3.1	$ 0.7
1933	2.0	4.6	−2.6
1939	6.3	9.1	−2.8
1940	6.5	9.5	−2.9
1941	8.7	13.7	−4.9
1942	14.6	35.1	−20.5
1943	24.0	78.6	−54.6
1944	43.7	91.3	−47.6
1945	45.2	92.7	−47.6
1947	38.5	34.5	4.0
1948	41.6	29.8	11.8
1949	39.4	38.8	0.6
1950	39.4	42.6	−3.1
1951	51.6	45.5	6.1
1952	66.2	67.7	−1.5
1953	69.6	76.1	−6.5
1954	69.7	70.9	−1.2
1955	65.5	68.4	−3.0
1956	74.6	70.6	3.9
1957	80.0	76.6	3.4
1958	79.6	82.4	−2.8
1959	79.2	92.1	−12.8
1960	92.5	92.2	0.3
1961	94.4	97.7	−3.3
1962	99.7	106.8	−7.1
1963	106.6	111.3	−4.8
1964	112.6	118.5	−5.9
1965	116.8	118.2	−1.4

	Total ($ billion)		
Year	Receipts	Outlays	Surplus or Deficit
1966	$ 130.8	$ 134.5	$ −3.7
1967	148.8	157.5	−8.6
1968	153.0	178.1	−25.2
1969	186.9	183.6	3.2
1970	192.8	195.6	−2.8
1971	187.1	210.2	−23.0
1972	207.3	230.7	−23.4
1973	230.8	245.7	−14.9
1974	263.2	269.4	−6.1
1975	279.1	332.3	−53.2
1976	298.1	371.8	−73.7
1977	355.6	409.2	−53.7
1978	399.6	458.7	−59.2
1979	463.3	503.5	−40.2
1980	517.1	590.9	−73.8
1981	599.3	678.2	−79.0
1982	617.8	745.8	−128.0
1983	600.6	808.4	−207.8
1984	666.5	851.8	−185.4
1985	734.1	946.4	−212.3
1986	769.1	990.3	−221.2
1987	854.1	1,003.9	−149.8
1988	909.0	1,064.1	−155.2
1989	990.7	1,143.2	−152.5
1990	1,031.3	1,252.7	−221.4
1991	1,054.3	1,323.8	−269.5
1992	1,091.6	1,381.8	−290.2
1993	1,147.6	1,474.9	−327.3

During the 1940s, 1950s, and 1960s, 22 of the 30 years had deficit budgets. Since then, from 1970 through 1993, *every year* was a deficit year. In other words, only eight of the 53 years since 1940 had surplus budgets. Obviously, in the many years of robust economic growth during that period, the budget was still generating deficits. As Kellner noted, the data do not support the idea that deficits necessarily reflect countercyclical fiscal policy.

Adapted from Irwin L. Kellner, *Economic Report* (New York: Manufactures Hanover Trust Company, November 1980); and *Statistical Abstract of the United States, 1994* (Washington, D.C.: U.S. Department of Commerce, 1994).

and, too often, it is debt-financed. Apart from the other objections to spending, this debt financing—the national debt—places a new burden on the economy that can sap the vitality of the economy's future.

Closing the Inflationary Gap

Government spending can be reduced in order to eliminate an inflationary gap.

Let's modify our story a little. Let's consider an aggregate expenditure combination where I_i = \$100 billion, G = \$280 billion, autonomous consumption = \$60 billion, and MPC = 0.80. The equilibrium level of national income is [(\$60 + 0.80Y) + \$100 + \$280] = \$2,200 billion. This is shown in Figure 6.

Unemployment is no longer a worry, but the President has a new headache: inflation. After all, full employment occurs at \$1,500 billion. Any national income level beyond \$1,500 billion must be a result of higher prices.

Suppose the President wants to close the inflationary gap. Is it possible? After all, producers are not about to change their investment plans just because the President wants to curb inflation. How, then, to go about bringing prices down? That is, how can the equilibrium level of national income be brought back to Y = \$1,500 billion?

FIGURE 6 **Closing the Inflationary Gap**

The equilibrium level of national income is at Y = \$2,200 billion, which is \$700 billion beyond full-employment national income. To reduce inflationary pressure, \$140 billion of government spending is cut, shown as a fall in G, which creates a new $C + I_i + G' = C + S$ equilibrium at Y = \$1,500 billion.

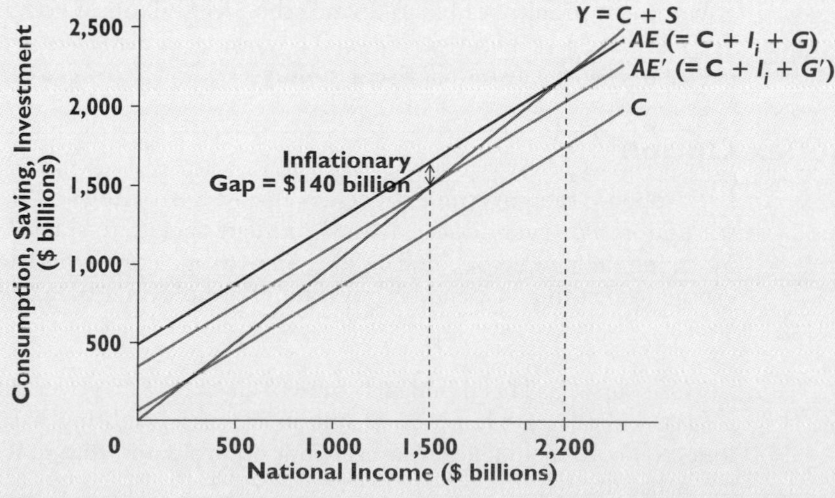

If consumers won't cut their spending on consumption and producers won't cut their spending on investment goods, the President must cut government spending. It means, of course, less highway construction, less public housing, and less defense spending. You can imagine, can't you, some strong resistance back home! If it's *your* highway, *your* public housing, or *your* defense factory that gets cut, then *your* voice will get heard in Congress. For this reason, Congress may be less willing to go along with curbing inflation than it would be in promoting full employment.

How much cutting is necessary? The inflationary gap in the economy of Figure 6 is \$140 billion, measured by the vertical distance between $AE = C + I_i + G$ and $AE' = C + I_i + G'$. With an income multiplier of 5, reducing government spending from \$280 billion to \$140 billion shifts the level of national income back by [(\$280 − \$140) × 5] = \$700 billion, that is, from equilibrium at full employment with inflation to equilibrium at full employment without inflation.

MAKING FISCAL POLICY

Let's again consider the recessionary gap of Figure 5. Knowing that government spending of \$140 billion will drive national income from \$800 billion to the desired \$1,500 billion is an important initial step in the formation of fiscal policy. But that information doesn't tell us where the government *gets* the \$140 billion. It doesn't materialize out of nowhere.

Perhaps the first thing the President considers is taxation. If the government needs \$1, it can raise taxes by \$1. If it needs \$140 billion, then it simply taxes the people \$140 billion. Of course, the people always have the final say. If taxes become too burdensome, it may be the last time the President sees the inside of the White House.

Suppose the President shows a strong reluctance to tax. Is it hopeless? Not yet. The government can borrow the \$140 billion. From whom? From people like you who are willing to lend the government money in exchange for its interest-bearing IOUs. These IOUs take the form of government securities, such as Treasury bills, notes, and bonds. As long as the interest rate the government offers on these securities is competitive with the rate in the private market, the government should be able to finance the \$140 billion of government spending.

Fiscal policy

Government spending and taxation policy to achieve macroeconomic goals of full employment without inflation.

The use of government spending and taxation to make changes in the level of national income is what economists call **fiscal policy.**

Choosing the Tax Option

Let's suppose the government decides against borrowing and instead chooses the tax option. For every dollar the government decides to spend, it gets that dollar by taxing the people one dollar. This one-to-one correspondence between government spending, G, and tax revenue, T, results in a **balanced budget.**

Balanced budget

Government spending equals tax revenues.

$$G = T$$

Of course, balanced budgets come in all sizes. The government can program a \$100 billion, or even a \$500 billion recession-fighting balanced budget. As long as it collects in taxes what it spends on programs, that is, if $G = T$, the budget is balanced.

Full Employment, Zero Inflation, *and* a Balanced Budget

If the President insists on a balanced budget, he cannot simply inject $140 billion of government spending into the economy and allow the income multiplier to shift the equilibrium level of national income from $Y =$ $800 billion to $Y =$ $1,500 billion. He now has to worry about the effects of financing the $140 billion spending with taxes.

If government imposes a tax, most people would be scrambling about trying to come up with the money to pay it. Where would they find it? Obviously, right at home. To pay the tax, people will have to consume less and save less. But consuming less during recession adversely affects the level of national income. And that's a new problem. To increase the level of national income, the government increases its spending. But to finance its spending, it taxes the people, which reduces the level of national income.

Does the negative impact of higher taxes on national income simply cancel out the positive impact of government spending? Not at all. Any increase in the government's balanced budget—that is, government spending and taxes increase by the same amount—actually adds to the level of national income. This may sound like a paradox, so let's take a closer look.

DERIVING THE TAX MULTIPLIER

The answer is linked to the relationship between the income multiplier and the tax multiplier. Like the income multiplier, which magnifies the effect of government spending on the level of national income, the **tax multiplier** magnifies the effect of taxes on the level of national income. *But income magnification from taxes is the weaker of the two.* Why?

Tax multiplier

The multiple by which the equilibrium level of national income changes when a dollar change in taxes occurs. The multiple depends upon the marginal propensity to consume. The equation for the tax multiplier is −MPC/(1 − MPC).

An increase in taxes reduces people's disposable income, causes consumption to fall, and results in a multiple contraction in GDP. The tax multiplier is smaller than the income multiplier. Can you explain why?

Suppose Bob Diener, an attorney working for the FBI in Santa Fe, earns $50,000 annually. And suppose that in the recessionary, before-tax economy of Figure 5, he spent [$500 + (0.8 × $50,000)] = $40,500 of that income on consumption and put the remaining $9,500 into savings.

Now suppose Congress agrees with the President and imposes a 20 percent income tax. Come April 15th, Bob is obligated to transfer $50,000 × .20 = $10,000 of his income to the government. Where would he get it? Would he take it all from savings? Or all from consumption? Neither is likely.

In fact, we know precisely how much he will draw from each source. Since his MPC = 0.80 and MPS = 0.20, he will give up $8,000 of what would have been consumption spending and $2,000 of what would have been saved.

That $8,000 cutback in consumption sends shock waves through the economy. After all, what Bob no longer spends on consumption, others no longer earn as income.

Picture the scene. Unaccustomed to being frugal, Bob must nonetheless cut back. But where? Suppose that among the consumption items he picks to trim are his catered parties. Prior to the tax, he had spent $1,000 annually on catering. He now cuts that out completely.

The first to feel the effect of his consumption cut is, of course, his caterer, Ayala Donchin. Ayala now discovers she has $1,000 less income, and with less income she consumes less herself. How much less? With MPC = 0.80, she cuts her consumption by 0.80 × $1,000 = $800. That, in turn, means $800 less income for some other person. And so this shock wave, initiated by a $1,000 cut in catering, continues.

You should see a *tax-induced multiplier* at work. But note what triggers the rollback in income. It is Bob's $8,000 cutback in consumption, not the entire $10,000 tax. After all, $2,000 of the $10,000 tax came from his would-be savings. Only $8,000 would have gone through the income stream. The multiplying factor associated with such a tax multiplier when MPC = 0.80, is

$$\frac{-MPC}{1-MPC} = \frac{-0.80}{1-0.80} = \frac{\text{change in } Y}{\text{change in } T} = -4$$

The $10,000 tax, then, generates a $10,000 × –4 = $40,000 decline in national income.

GOVERNMENT USES THE $10,000 TAX FOR $10,000 OF SPENDING

The government now has Bob's $10,000 in tax revenue. What does it do with the tax? If it were to save $2,000 and spend the remaining $8,000 on, say, sewage repair, then the income multiplier effect of that spending would exactly offset the $40,000 cut in national income induced by the tax. That is, if the government saved $2,000, the net effect on national income of a $10,000 increase in taxes and spending, $G = T$, would be zero.

But the government doesn't save. It spends the entire $10,000 of Bob's taxes. The income multiplier effect is not on $8,000, but on the entire $10,000. The income multiplier on that $10,000, with MPC = 0.80, is 5.

$$\frac{1}{1-MPC} = \frac{1}{1-0.80} = \frac{\text{change in } Y}{\text{change in } G} = 5$$

The increase in national income that government creates by spending the $10,000 is $10,000 × 5 = $50,000.

The Balanced Budget Multiplier

In brief, things aren't always what they seem. When the government levies a $10,000 tax on people's income and puts the $10,000 back into the economy, national income does not remain the same. It expands. A $10,000 balanced budget has an expansionary effect on the level of national income.

The balanced budget increase that the increase in taxes and in government spending produces is precisely equal to the increase in national income. For example, a $10,000 increase in both G and T generates a $50,000 – $40,000 = $10,000 expansion of national income. We get this result from

$$\frac{1}{1-MPC} - \frac{MPC}{1-MPC} = \frac{1}{0.2} - \frac{0.8}{0.2} = 5 - 4 = 1$$

subtracting the government's tax multiplier of 4, operating on T, from the income multiplier of 5, operating on G. This gives us a **balanced budget multiplier** of 5 – 4 = 1. *No matter what the specific income multiplier and tax multiplier may be, the balanced budget multiplier always equals 1.*

Balanced budget multiplier

The effect on the equilibrium level of national income of an equal change in government spending and taxes. The balanced budget multiplier is 1.

Balancing the Budget at $140 Billion

Suppose the President recommends a $140 billion balanced budget. Its effect on national income, then, is a matter of simple arithmetic. With a balanced budget multiplier equal to 1, national income increases by $140 billion.

The tax multiplier applied to a \$140 billion $G = T$ budget reduces national income by \$140 × 4 = \$560 billion. But at the same time the government gets the \$140 billion tax revenue and converts it into \$140 billion of government spending. The effect of that spending on the economy adds \$140 × 5 = \$700 billion to national income.

What do we end up with? The net effect on the economy of the \$140 billion $G = T$ is a \$700 – \$560 = \$140 billion increase in national income. As we already know, it is precisely the size of the balanced budget. But is it enough to pull the economy out of recession?

How to Get to Full Employment National Income and Balance the Budget

The only way to drive the recessionary economy of Figure 5 out of its equilibrium position at Y = \$800 billion to a Y = \$1,500 billion equilibrium at full employment, *and balance the budget at the same time,* is to generate a government budget of \$700 billion—that is, \$700 billion of taxes and \$700 billion of government spending. This budget produces the desired \$700 billion increase in national income.

But that's strong fiscal policy! You can see why the President, bent on full employment, might think twice about balancing the budget. What would you advise?

Just a Spoonful of Deficit Makes the Medicine Go Down

It's worth exploring other ways to bring the economy out of recession. Why not modify the balanced budget slightly? Or perhaps even more than slightly. The government has several fiscal policy options. Look at Table 2.

Every fiscal policy budget option in Table 2 produces the same results. In each, national income increases by the targeted \$700 billion. That is, each budget option completely closes the \$700 billion recessionary gap.

The first option, $G = T$ at \$700 billion, does the job. Moreover, it creates no budget deficit. But a \$700 billion tax may be more than Congress is willing to impose.

If $G = T$ at \$700 billion is unacceptable, the President can choose the second fiscal policy option, that is, couple a \$100 billion tax revenue with \$220 billion of government spending. That budget combination creates the targeted \$700 billion increase in national income, but it also creates a \$120 billion **budget deficit,** $G > T$.

Budget deficit

Government spending exceeds tax revenues.

TABLE 2
Sample Budget Options to Close a Recessionary Gap (\$ billions)

Option	Government Spending	Tax Revenue	Deficit Budget	Target Change in Income
1	\$700	\$700	\$ 0	\$700
2	220	100	120	700
3	180	50	130	700
4	140	0	140	700

A variety of combinations of government spending increases and tax increases will eliminate a recessionary gap.

The third option couples $50 billion tax revenue with a higher level ($180 billion) of government spending. This lower tax budget (compared to the first and second options) may look attractive, but the drawback is that it creates a larger budget deficit, $130 billion. The fourth fiscal policy option is tax free! The income multiplier (of 5) applied to $140 billion of government spending creates the targeted $700 billion increase in national income. But the economy is saddled with a $140 billion budget deficit as well.

Why even think of such complex combinations of government spending and taxes when the simple balanced budget at $700 billion would do? Because the President and Congress may find it more acceptable politically to have deficit budgets than a balanced budget that depends on $700 billion in taxes. On the other hand, the fourth option would work, but it might be more deficit than the President is willing to tolerate politically.

Is the only issue in choosing a fiscal policy option, then, the political future of Congress and the President? Are their chances for getting reelected and their personal tolerance for taxing and borrowing all that matter? Not really. Another consideration is at issue.

How Mixed Is the Mixed Economy?

The choice of a fiscal policy combination of spending and taxes is part of a choice of the degree to which we want government involved in the economy.

Although all the fiscal policy budget options of Table 2 lead to $Y = \$1{,}500$ billion at full employment, they don't all produce the same mix of government and private sector economic activity.

For example, if the President chooses the first option from Table 1—the balanced budget option at $G = T = \$700$ billion—government becomes a major participant in the national economy. This is an important consideration that the President and Congress must address. As you know, much of the political debate in the United States and other countries focuses on this one issue: How much government is the right amount of government?

Creating Surplus Budgets

A surplus budget is used to combat an inflationary gap and causes national income to decrease because tax revenues are greater than government spending.

Let's look again at the economy of Figure 6. An inflationary gap of $240 billion creates an equilibrium level of national income that is $700 billion *higher* than the full-employment equilibrium level of $1,500 billion. What fiscal policy measures should the President pursue now? The government has several options. Look at Table 3.

The first option reduces both taxes and government spending by $700 billion. Note the negative signs. They indicate cuts. The balanced budget multiplier, with both taxes and government spending cut by $700 billion, reduces national income by the targeted (negative) $700 billion. But that's about as drastic a fiscal policy as the government could possibly design. People would love to see their taxes cut substantially, but cutting $700 billion out of government spending would probably mean the end of interstate repairs, research support for the Centers for Disease Control, all funding of higher education, job-retraining programs, and severe cuts in almost everything else that government does. It would probably be politically unworkable.

Other fiscal policy options are shown in Table 3. For example, in the second option, the government reduces spending by $220 billion and taxes by $100

TABLE 3
Sample Budget Options to Close an Inflationary Gap ($ billions)

Option	Government Spending	Tax Revenue	Surplus Budget	Target ΔY
1	–$700	–$700	$ 0	–$700
2	–220	–100	120	–700
3	–100	50	150	–700
4	–140	0	140	–700

Budget surplus
Tax revenues exceed government spending.

billion—creating a **budget surplus,** $T > G$, of $120 billion. That reduces national income by the targeted $700 billion.

If the government chooses, it can cut government spending and at the same time *raise* taxes. Each reduces national income. For example, in the third option, applying the tax multiplier of –4 to a $50 billion increase in taxes reduces national income by $200 billion. Applying the income multiplier of 5 to a $100 billion cut in government spending reduces national income by an additional $500 billion. The combined effect of the government spending cut and tax increase reduces national income by the targeted $700 billion. Or the government can choose the fourth option, that is, not to increase taxes at all but rely exclusively on decreasing government spending by $140 billion to reduce national income by the targeted $700 billion.

Are Fiscal Policy Options Really That Straightforward?

Are our fiscal policy options really that simple? Does the President really face recessionary gaps and inflationary gaps that emerge—as Figures 5 and 6 show—when equilibrium levels of national income deviate from no inflation, full-employment levels? Can the President and Congress play with taxes and spending to close those gaps with balanced budgets, deficit budgets, and surplus budgets such as those shown in Tables 2 and 3?

Many economists believe that the Keynesian model of national income determination and the fiscal policy prescriptions (to close recessionary and inflationary gaps) that follow from it are accurate enough reflections of our economic reality to make them useful. As a policy adviser, you may find that the President may be not only a good listener and a quick learner, but interested to know what *other* economic models are available.

It will not take the President long to discover that there are many competing approaches to national income determination, that there really is no consensus among economists concerning the "correct" income determination model or the "correct" fiscal policy.

The President has a dilemma, doesn't he? After all, the Keynesian model may have viable alternatives. What advice should he accept? We will return to this obviously important question in later chapters when we consider alternative views on economic stabilization policy. For now, it is important to understand how the Keynesian model works. After all, it has dominated economic thinking on issues of inflation and unemployment ever since the 1930s and still influences a great deal of economic thinking today.

CHAPTER REVIEW

1. For an economy to be in equilibrium tells us very little about the general state of the economy. In fact, for an economy to be in equilibrium at full employment would be purely accidental in the Keynesian model. Keynes' model allows for an economy to be in equilibrium with high levels of unemployment.

2. The types of unemployment that can exist include frictional unemployment, structural unemployment, cyclical unemployment, discouraged workers, and the underemployed. The Bureau of Labor Statistics calculates the rate of unemployment by conducting a survey in which it asks people whether they are working or seeking employment. People who answer yes to this question are part of the labor force. The number of people who are seeking work, divided by the labor force, and expressed as a percentage, is the unemployment rate.

3. The natural rate of unemployment consists of workers who are frictionally and structurally unemployed. Full employment exists when the unemployment rate is equal to the natural rate. Full employment is represented by the vertical portion of the Keynesian aggregate supply curve. As wage rates increase, more workers can be attracted to the labor force, up to a point where the aggregate supply curve becomes vertical.

4. Some groups of people are hurt by inflation while others are helped. Those who are hurt by inflation include people living on fixed incomes, landlords, and savers. Those who gain from inflation include borrowers and the government, which is a major borrower. Bankers have developed ways to moderate their losses from inflation. Unions bargain for cost-of-living allowances in their wage contracts to protect themselves from the erosion of real wages.

5. A recessionary gap exists when the equilibrium level of national income is below the full-employment level. The amount by which spending must increase in order to achieve full employment is the recessionary gap. An inflationary gap exists when the equilibrium level of national income is above the full-employment level. The inflationary gap is the amount by which spending must decrease in order to achieve full employment.

6. A recessionary gap can be closed by government spending. When the government spends, a multiple expansion in national income arises. Government spending is not without its problems. For one, it may raise the deficit. Also, it is possible that the economy will adjust back to full employment automatically, without any government spending.

7. Cuts in government spending are the means by which inflationary gaps can be closed. The problem with cuts in government spending is that those who are hurt by the cuts will oppose them, so that Congress and the President are less likely to follow through.

8. Fiscal policy involves choosing both the level of government spending and the level of taxation. A recessionary gap can be eliminated by a simultaneous increase in government spending and taxes to match the size of the recessionary gap. This result derives from the balanced budget multiplier which equals 1. A variety of fiscal policy options to close recessionary gaps exist. Gaps can be closed in such a way as to leave the deficit unchanged or they can be closed with var-

ious-sized budget deficits. Closing an inflationary gap involves the creation of a surplus budget where tax revenues exceed government spending.

9. Not all economists accept the idea that fiscal policy can be an effective tool for stabilizing the economy at a full-employment level of national income.

KEY TERMS

Frictional unemployment
Structural unemployment
Cyclical unemployment
Discouraged workers
Underemployed workers
Labor force
Natural rate of unemployment
Full employment
Recessionary gap
Inflationary gap
Fiscal policy
Balanced budget
Tax multiplier
Balanced budget multiplier
Budget deficit
Budget surplus

QUESTIONS

1. Why are people not always delighted when national income finally reaches its equilibrium level?

2. What is frictional unemployment? Why is it not regarded as a serious economic problem?

3. What is structural unemployment? Why is such unemployment particularly hard on older workers? Cite examples.

4. What is cyclical unemployment? Why is it difficult for people who are cyclically unemployed to find jobs?

5. Who are discouraged workers? Underemployed workers? Are they counted as part of the labor force? As part of the unemployed?

6. What is the relationship between the full-employment level in an economy and the economy's natural rate of unemployment?

7. Who are the winners and losers of inflation?

8. Professor Scott Fausti asks his students at South Dakota State University to answer the following question: Assume Harry receives a $10,000 bank loan. The loan is due at the end of one year. The interest charge is 10 percent and the inflation rate is 4 percent per year. Who benefits from the inflation, Harry or the bank? Explain.

9. Draw graphs showing recessionary and inflationary gaps and explain how these gaps emerge.

10. What fiscal policy measures can the government employ to close a recessionary gap? An inflationary gap?

11. What is a tax multiplier? How does it differ from the income multiplier?

12. What effect would a $100 billion tax cut have on the level of national income, assuming MPC = 0.50?

13. Why is the balanced budget multiplier always equal to 1?

14. Why shouldn't the government *always* program a balanced budget?

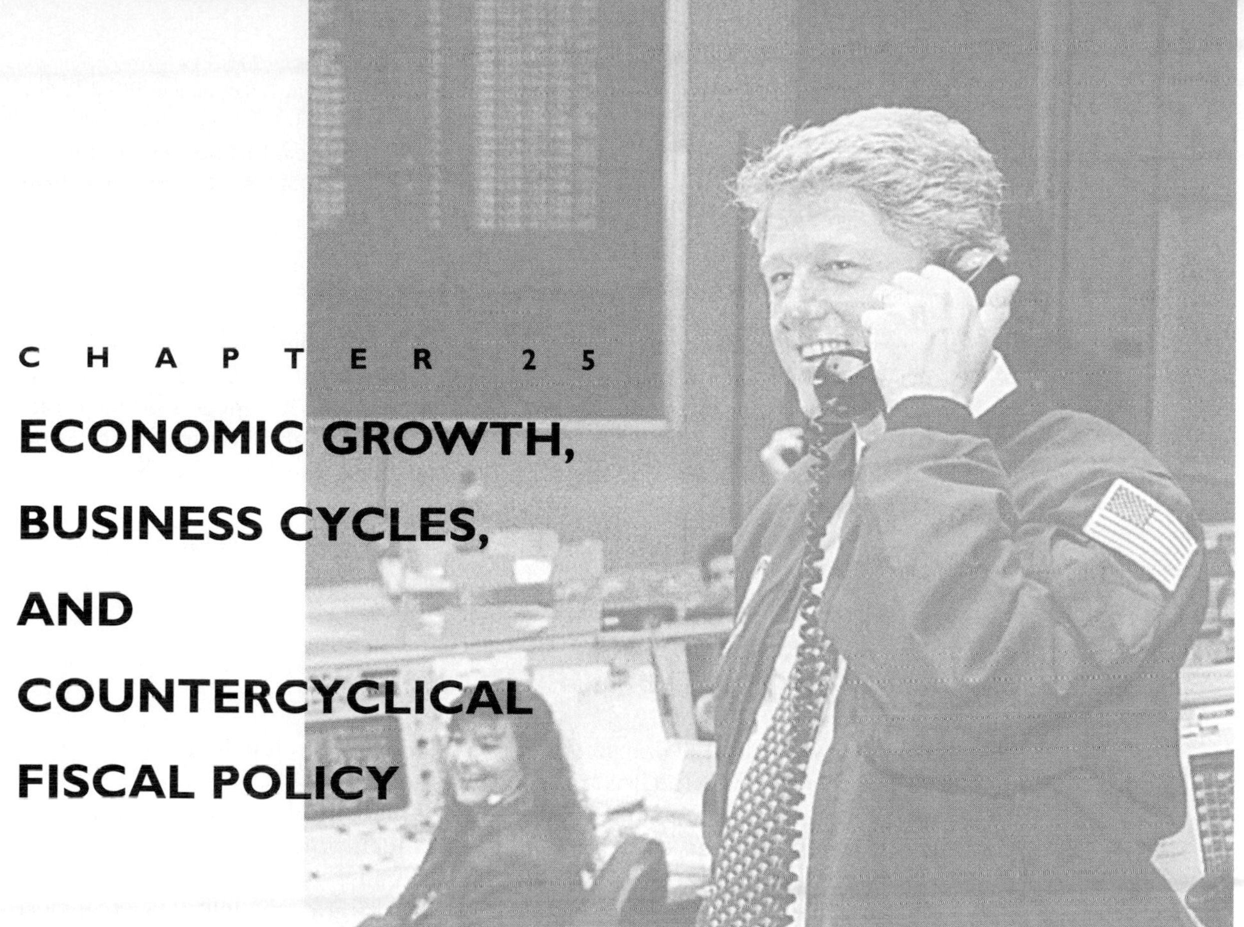

C H A P T E R 25

ECONOMIC GROWTH, BUSINESS CYCLES, AND COUNTERCYCLICAL FISCAL POLICY

CHAPTER PREVIEW

So far our analysis of the macroeconomy has been set entirely in an equilibrium framework. The economy is either in equilibrium or moving toward equilibrium. We have said little about the tendency of economies to grow over time, to sometimes shrink, and to experience periodic episodes of boom and bust—economic cycles. What accounts for economic growth? How do we explain the cycles that are observed in the macroeconomy's performance? These questions and others will be addressed in this chapter.

After studying this chapter, you should be able to:

- Discuss the sources of long-run economic growth.
- Explain the role of the capital-output ratio in the growth process.
- Compare the factors contributing to U.S. economic growth in the period since World War II.
- Draw a graph to depict the business cycle and describe each of its phases.
- List and explain the external theories of economic cycles.
- Account for the possibility of internal cycles in the economy.
- Define the accelerator.
- Describe the interaction of the multiplier and accelerator.

- Contrast traditional theories of business cycles with real business cycle theory.
- Point out problems with the design and implementation of countercyclical fiscal policies.

Have you heard about the fellow who, enjoying the effects of his seventh martini, accidentally slipped off a 35-story penthouse sun deck? While falling to earth, he passed an open window on the second floor. A college student looking out the window asked the unfortunate fellow in flight, "How's life treating you?" Summing up quickly, the falling man replied, "So far, so good!"

Is there a moral to this devilish story? If there is, it may be that it is sometimes difficult to tell just where we are and where we're heading.

HOW DO WE KNOW THE ECONOMY IS REALLY HEADING TOWARD EQUILIBRIUM?

Because economic changes are continuous, it is difficult to know whether an economy is in or moving toward equilibrium.

How do we really know whether an economy in motion is moving toward equilibrium? All we actually observe is its motion.

If national income equilibrium is more a theoretical construct than an observed reality, why do economists spend so much time analyzing it? Isn't that what we did in the previous two chapters? Because understanding a simplified economy, which is assumed to approach equilibrium, can tell us a great deal about how a real economy—even one that never approaches equilibrium—works.

Keynesian analysis of national income equilibrium allows us to see how changes in investment can generate changes in national income and employment. When government is brought into the analysis, we can measure its impact on national income and employment as well. These cause-and-effect relationships are significant findings that apply to *any* economy, whether it is in equilibrium or not.

If an economy is not in or moving toward equilibrium, what, then, is it doing? Perhaps the only thing we can say with some degree of confidence is that it is never at rest; it is in a continuous state of motion.

LONG-RUN ECONOMIC GROWTH

Let's look at the continuous motion path of the U.S. economy through the years 1900–90. What do you see?

What must strike you about Figure 1 is the coupling of year-to-year fluctuations in GDP with a pronounced long-run upward thrust. The long-term average annual growth rate of real GDP is 3.5 percent (a doubling of GDP every generation).

What Causes Economic Growth?

What causes long-run **economic growth?** If you look at the title page of Adam Smith's *Wealth of Nations*—published in 1776 and still very readable—you will

FIGURE 1 **U.S. Economic Performance 1900–90**

From 1900 to 1990, U.S. real GDP, measured in 1972 dollars, increased approximately 15-fold. But year-to-year changes over the period deviated from the approximate 3.5 average rate of growth, and in some years the deviations were considerable. What stands out sharply is the real GDP decline during the 1930s—the years of the Great Depression.

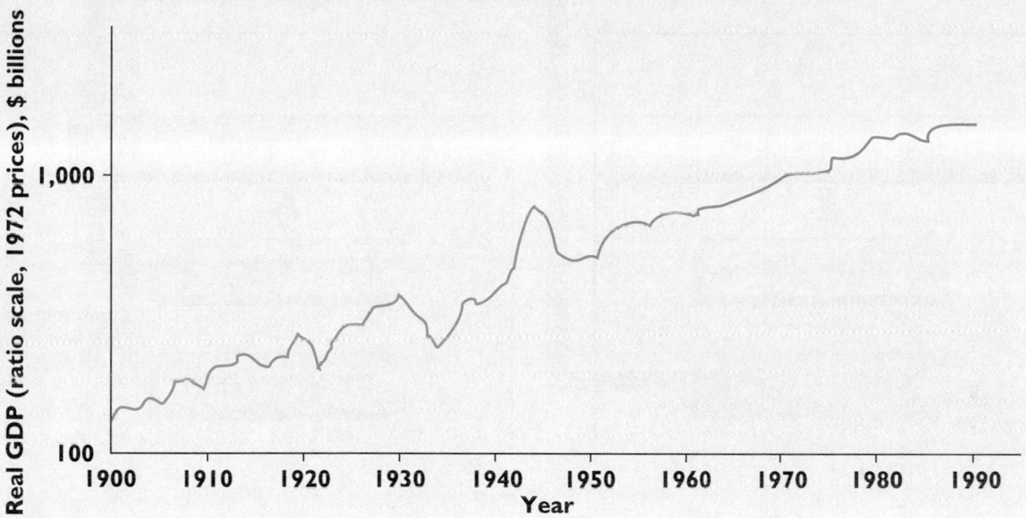

Economic growth

An increase in real GDP, typically expressed as an annual rate of real GDP growth.

discover that its complete title is *An Enquiry into the Nature and Causes of the Wealth of Nations.* Smith struggled with the same question we ask about our economy today, and interestingly, what economists today know about the causes of long-run economic growth is not terribly dissimilar from the insightful observations Smith made over 200 years ago.

Economic growth can result from increases in the size of the labor force, specialization and division of labor, increases in the stock of capital, and improvements in technology.

Adam Smith identified four principal factors that contribute to a nation's economic growth: (1) the size of its labor force, (2) the degree of labor specialization (or division of labor), (3) the size of its capital stock, and (4) the level of its technology.

That is to say, if more people are employed, more goods and services are produced. If people are better educated, they can produce more goods and services. If they use more capital, the goods and services they produce increase even more. And the more advanced the level of technology, the higher is their productivity.

Labor productivity

The quantity of GDP produced per worker, typically measured in quantity of GDP per hour of labor.

But what determines the size of an economy's capital stock, or the quality of its labor, or the level of its technology? *At bedrock, it is the saving and investment decisions that people in the economy make.* Investment in research and development creates the economy's future technology. Investment in education and job-training, as well as job experience determines the quality of its future workers. And investment in plant and machinery enhances **labor productivity.**

A Simple Model of Economic Growth

Figure 2 depicts an economy in long-run economic growth. To highlight the effect of changes in capital stock on GDP, we suppose that the quantity of labor,

FIGURE 2 **The Growth Process**

In year 1, a $400 capital stock generates a $100 GDP. One-fifth, or $20 of the $100 GDP, is put into investment, which appears as an addition to capital stock in year 2. The $420 capital stock in year 2 generates $105 GDP, creating a rate of economic growth of 5 percent.

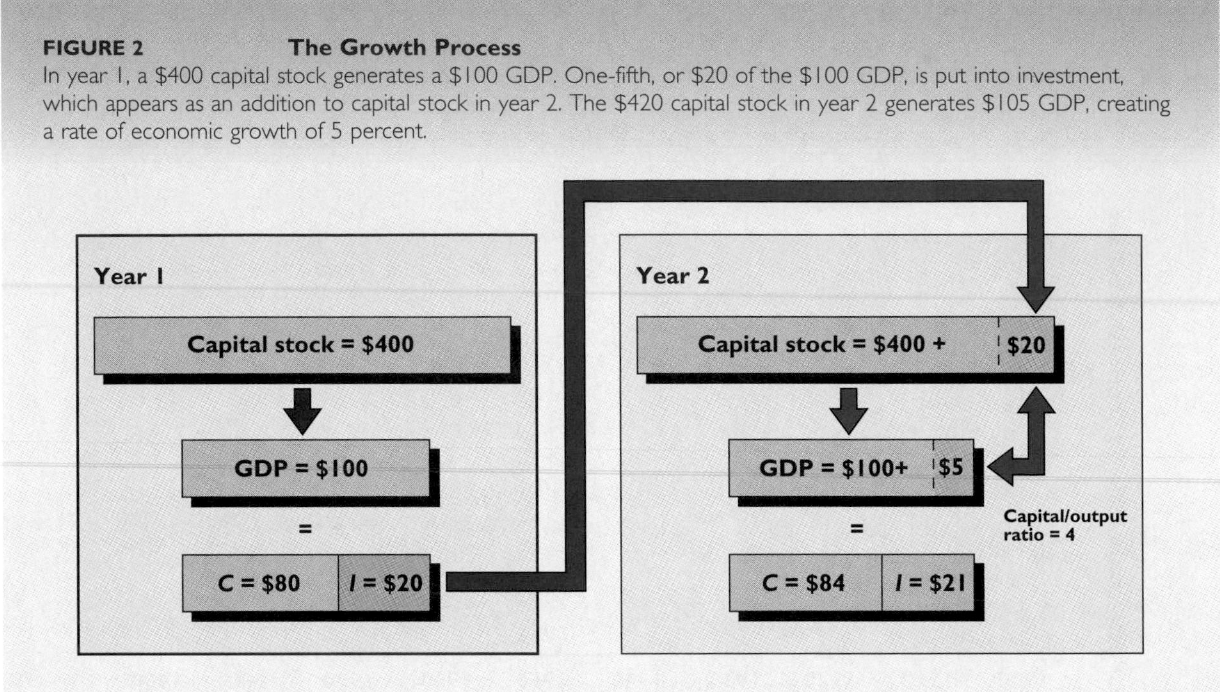

the degree of labor specialization, and the level of technology remain unchanged. Let's also suppose that people in the Figure 2 economy choose to save 20 percent of their income, which is precisely what producers choose to invest ($S = I$).

Let's start with a $400 capital stock that is used to produce an annual GDP of $100. Economists in describing this linkage of capital stock to GDP, typically assume the **capital/output ratio** is constant. In the Figure 2 economy, the ratio is $400/$100 = 4.

Capital/output ratio
The ratio of capital stock to GDP.

Look also at the composition of GDP. We again assume no government or foreign sector. Of the $100 GDP, $80 is in the form of consumption goods, *C*. The remaining $20 is investment goods, *I*. The $20 of investment adds to the economy's capital stock. In other words, because producers decide to invest $20 in year 1, the economy's $400 capital stock, assuming no depreciation, increases to $420 in year 2.

The capital/output ratio tells us how many dollars of capital are required to produce a dollar's worth of output.

How much annual GDP can the economy now produce with a capital stock of $420? With a capital/output ratio of 4, the economy in year 2 is capable of generating an annual GDP of $420/4 = $105. That is, the added $20 to capital stock makes an additional $5 of GDP possible. The potential rate of GDP growth, *g*, then, for this simple economy is 5 percent.

$$\frac{GDP_2}{GDP_1} = \frac{105}{100} = 1.05$$

Let's trace the GDP growth path into the following year. What do people do with a GDP of $105? If they continue to save and invest 20 percent of GDP, then next year's investment will be $105 × .20 = $21, raising the economy's capital stock to $420 + $21 = $441 and GDP to $441/4 = $110.25.

If in each succeeding year, people save and invest 20 percent of GDP, and if the capital/output ratio remains at 4, then the long-run annual rate of GDP growth is 5 percent. As you see, in this simplified model of the growth process, growth depends strictly on the level of investment and on the capital/output ratio.

Is the model *too* simple? Is it unrealistic, for example, to suppose that the size of the labor force and the level of technology never change and that depreciation of capital stock is zero? How would a steady stream of new workers added each year to the economy affect the rate of GDP growth? How would changes in technology affect the economy's growth? Remember that technological change not only raises the level of productivity among workers—the quantity of goods a worker produces in an hour—but it may change the capital/output ratio as well.

If depreciation of capital stock during production of GDP is greater than zero—a more reasonable assumption than zero—then a \$20 investment doesn't raise capital stock by fully \$20. Economists distinguish the *net* additions to capital stock from the total investment people make.

If changes in the economy's capital stock, changes in the quantity of labor, changes in technology, as well as changes in efficiency and scale of production occur at the same time, then the cumulative effect of such changes is bound to affect the long-run rate of GDP growth.

In the real world, these changes occur incessantly. If we want to understand "the nature and causes of the wealth of nations," as Adam Smith phrased the issue, we must consider the role each of these major factors plays in the growth process.

Factors Contributing to U.S. Economic Growth

The Council of Economic Advisers and the Department of Labor estimate the factors contributing to the 1947–92 U.S. GDP growth. Their findings are shown in Table 1.

Technological change seems to have accounted for most of the increase in GDP from 1947 to 1973, while capital accumulation accounted for most of the growth from 1973 to 1992.

The factors identified by the Council of Economic Advisers and the Department of Labor and the estimates they offer are clearly more explanatory than the analysis offered by the simple investment model of GDP growth. Table 1 estimates a 3.94 percent average annual rate of GDP growth for the 1947–73 period and a more moderate 2.3 percent rate for the 1973–92 period.

What explains these rates? The most significant factor in the 1947–73 period was technological change. It alone generated 1.63 percent of economic growth, or explained 1.63/3.94 = 41.3 percent of the recorded 3.94 percent growth rate. *Working smarter seems to be more effective than working harder.*

TABLE 1 Sources of U.S. Growth, 1947–92

Source	1947 to 1973	1973 to 1992
Labor inputs	1.01	0.88
Capital inputs	1.45	1.07
Technological change	1.63	0.40
Adjustments	–0.14	–0.40
Total (GDP growth)	3.94	2.30

Source: Council of Economic Advisers, *Economic Report of the President* (Washington, D.C.: U.S. Government Printing Office, 1994), p. 44.

Another 1.45 percent of the 3.94 percent annual growth, or 36.8 percent of the total contributions to growth, was attributed to increases in the quantity of capital (or size of the capital stock). Labor inputs accounted for 25.6 percent of the 3.94 rate.

But note how the contributions of the sources shifted for the 1973–92 period. Capital inputs dominated, 1.07 percent out of the total 2.3 percent, and technological change's contribution fell dramatically, accounting for only $.40/2.3 = 17.4$ percent of the 2.3 average annual rate.

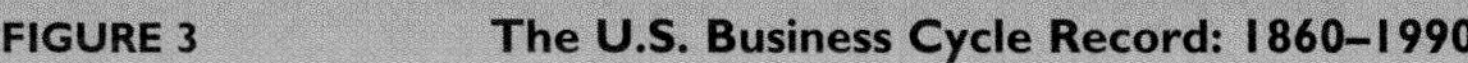

THE BUSINESS CYCLE

Look again at Figure 1, this time focusing not on the dominant, long-run, upward thrust of the GDP growth path, but instead on the path's twists and turns. As you see, in some years the path rose steeply, while in others the incline was more moderate. There were also years in which the path dipped, that is, real GDP was actually declining.

Figure 3 tells the same story but shows the twists and turns as year-to-year deviations from a horizontal trend line that depicts the economy's long-run average annual growth rate (1860–1990).

These deviations *seem* to map out a picture of recurring cycles, that is, periods of rapid GDP growth followed by periods of less rapid GDP growth, or even decline. Some of the cycles appear to be mild while others seem particularly severe. It isn't hard to pick out the depression of the 1930s and the sharp recovery after World War II, is it?

FIGURE 3 **The U.S. Business Cycle Record: 1860–1990**

The year-to-year change in GDP is depicted as percent deviation from the long-term trend growth rate. Sharp upturns are clearly marked by the Civil War, World War II, the Korean War, and the Vietnam War. The Great Depression of the 1930s and the sharp economic recovery following World War II dominate the picture.

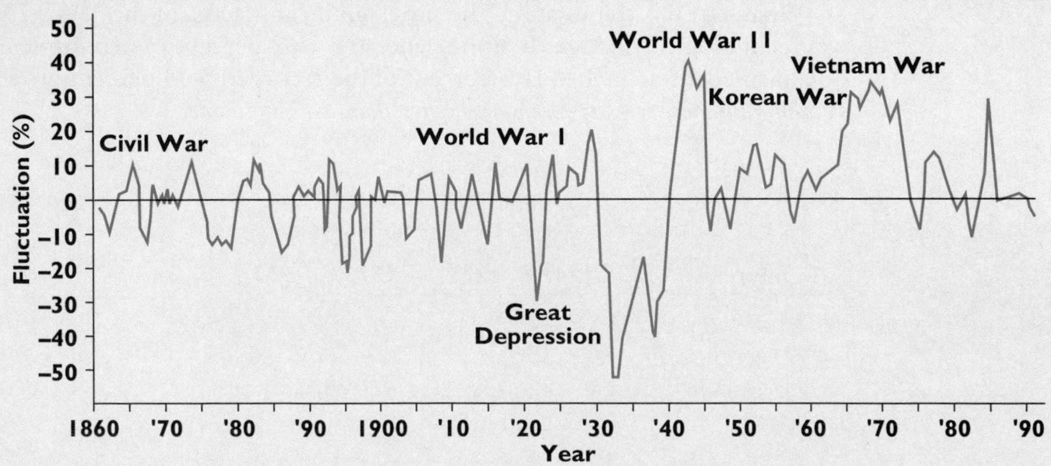

Source: Ameritrust Company, Cleveland, Ohio.

Although economists have no trouble identifying the major business cycles during the 1860–1990 period, they are hard pressed to agree on *why* the cycles occur.

TRADITIONAL THEORIES OF THE BUSINESS CYCLE

What economists do agree on is that there is no one cycle or one explanation for cycles (some economists are even reluctant to acknowledge the existence of cycles, contending that just because the economy has its twists and turns does not mean it cycles through them).

Different economic cycles can either counteract each other or they can reinforce each other.

Some cycles are thought to be triggered by *external,* random events, such as wars, changes in climate, population booms, clustering of innovations, changes in consumer confidence, changes in government spending, or changes in international exchange rates. Other cycles are thought to be *internal* to the economy—like seasons of the year—natural consequences of essentially normal economic activity.

Identifying cycles and their causes is tricky business. For example, a cycle whose upward and downward swings appear to be moderate may in fact be a composite of a set of not-so-moderate cycles whose phases—recessions, recovery, prosperity, downturn—by chance, counteract each other. One cycle's recession phase may overlap another's prosperity phase. Thus, the appearance of a moderate cycle. On the other hand, a cycle that leads to economic depression, such as the Great Depression of the 1930s, may in fact be a composite of moderate cycles whose phases, by chance, are synchronized. One cycle's recession phase overlaps another's recession phase, producing exaggerated twists and turns in the economy's growth path.

Let's examine some of these internal and external cycle theories to see if any fit into the historical record mapped out in Figure 3.

External Theories of Cycles

Some theories linking cycles to random events seem plausible. Others appear far less plausible, and still others seem to be downright silly. Yet, even the silly ones can sometimes make sense. Consider, for example, William Stanley Jevons' sunspot theory of cycles.

THE SUNSPOT THEORY

To explain the English economy's erratic growth path, Jevons linked the economy's movements to the earth's path through the solar system. The causation he found ran from cosmic influences on weather, to weather influences on agricultural yields, and finally to the influences of these yields on the nation's economic performance.

Jevons noted that good harvests occur when the number of sunspots, nuclear storms on the sun, are at a minimum. The resulting abundant food supply lowers food prices and raises real incomes and employment. The national economy prospers.

But when the number of sunspots reaches a maximum, the economic consequences are reversed. Poor climate produces poor crops, higher food prices, lower real incomes, and greater unemployment. Jevons observed:

If, then, the English money market is naturally fitted to swing or roll in periods of ten or eleven years, comparatively slight variations in the goodness of harvest repeated at like intervals would suffice to produce these alternations of depression, activity, excitement, and collapse which undoubtedly occur in marked succession.

Ingenious, wasn't he? But the explanatory value of Jevons' business cycle theory seems pretty much confined to agricultural economies. What relevance could it have to our economy today? After all, the "harvests" of automobiles, VCRs, dishwashers, and financial services seem to have little to do with nuclear explosions on the sun.

WAR-INDUCED CYCLES

Are we destined always to go to war? From time immemorial, wars have been viewed as innate to the human experience. Admittedly, the evidence is frightfully confirming. Whether or not wars can be avoided, economists have long observed a link between wars and business cycles.

Does such a link make sense? Think about it. Wars create instantaneous demands for all kinds of goods and services. Once the decision is made to go to war, supporting the war effort becomes high priority. Armies need to be staffed, fed, clothed, housed, transported, equipped, and mended.

That requires considerable spending. You can see the income multiplier working overtime. In each of our major wars—the 1861–65 Civil War, the 1914–18 World War I, the 1939–45 World War II, the 1950–53 Korean War, the 1964–74 Vietnam War—military production spurred the economy into rapid expansion. And in at least some, if not all of them, the end of war brought an end to the economy's war-induced prosperity.

Many economic historians believe that the Civil War powered the North's conversion to industrialization. It stimulated the expansion of the iron and steel, textile, food packing, shipbuilding, milling, petroleum, and mining industries.

These war-induced demands stopped abruptly when Robert E. Lee surrendered at Appomattox. The economic consequences were equally abrupt. The northern states experienced a sudden, although short-lived, downturn.

Look again at Figure 3. Note the link between wars and economic upturns. For World War I, World War II, and the Korean War, the war-induced expansion came *when the economy was in the downswing or trough phase of an already existing cycle*. We were still in the throes of the Great Depression when Japan attacked Pearl Harbor in 1941.

In fact, the link between war and economic prosperity is so suggestive that some economists—Marxists, in particular—are inclined to believe that some wars were engineered principally to get us out of economic crises!

But most economists are unwilling to suppose that war conspiracies account for the economy's recovery from a cycle's trough. More likely, these war-induced cycles are random shocks to an economy already in continuous cyclical motion.

POPULATION-INDUCED CYCLES

Wars are not the only random events that can affect an economy's growth path. Economists have recognized that a sudden rise in the rate of population growth, perhaps timed by war-delayed marriages, can set off a round of economic activity that generates its own business cycle.

"Give this much to the Luftwaffe. When it knocked down our buildings, it didn't replace them with anything more offensive than rubble. We did that." Prince Charles (talking in 1987 about the German bombing of London in 1940, and the housing construction that took place in the aftermath of the war)

Consider, for example, the aftermath of World War II. Between 1946 and 1952, a record number of marriages was soon followed by a record number of babies. The baby boom forced households out of one-bedroom city apartments into suburban housing. The mushrooming of new suburbs stimulated investments in road networks, sewage systems, shopping centers, public transport, public utilities, libraries, churches, and parks. The family station wagon became the symbol of the population explosion. These investments, nurtured by the income multiplier, sustained the upswing phase of the population cycle.

How long does it take a population cycle to run its course? Does the cycle repeat? Since baby boom children have their own children, the cycle repeats. But not all baby-boomers have babies, and certainly not all at the same time, nor in the same numbers. There is, then, a "spreading out" effect. A second wave of the cycle appears, but in a much weaker form. The third wave is even more so. And so on.

THE HOUSING CYCLE

Another externally induced cycle is the 15- to 20-year housing cycle, also known as the Kuznets cycle, named for Nobel Laureate Simon Kuznets, who pioneered research on the relationship between cycles and housing construction.

How do housing cycles originate? What could touch off an extraordinarily large investment in housing within a relatively short period of time? Imagine what happened to the demand for housing in 1992 after Hurricane Andrew hit south Florida. The calamities of nature, Midwest floods and California earthquakes, may be the most obvious, but certainly they are not the only causes of housing cycles.

For example, if interest rates were unusually high for an unusually long period of time, housing construction would suffer. If people don't buy houses, they tend also not to buy house furnishings. Picture the income multiplier at work. When interest rates finally fall, mortgage payments once again become affordable. Housing investment booms to satisfy the backlog of housing and housing-related demands.

But at some point the investment slows down and the cycle's downturn phase begins. Like the population cycle, the housing cycle reappears with far less

ADDED PERSPECTIVE

Guilt by Association? Do Dips in Housing Starts *Cause* Recessions?

There's a difference between association and causation. If the causal argument—a fall in housing construction causes recession—is not convincing, then at least the association of recessions with housing starts in the figure is. Look at the dips in housing starts from 1945 to 1990. Prior to 1970, the beginning of recessions tends to follow immediately upon dips in housing starts. Suggestive, isn't it?

On the other hand, during the 1970s and 1980s, the lead/lag relationship all but disappears. The two major recessions occur during the downturns in housing starts. While economists tend to agree that changes in housing starts do affect the economy's performance, they do not all view such changes as the principal agent generating recession.

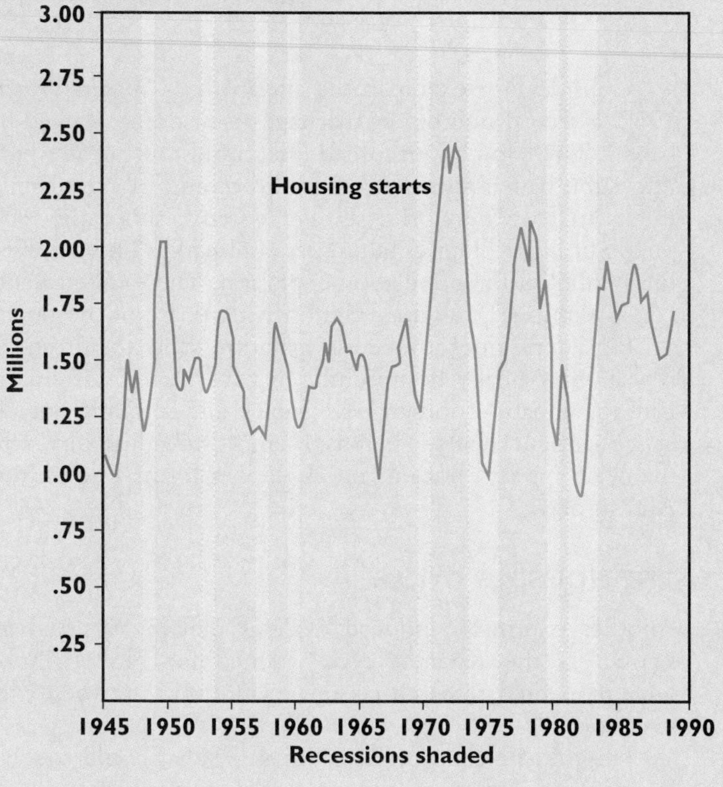

Source: Lehmann, M., *The Wall Street Journal Workbook*, Instructor's Edition (Homewood, IL: Irwin, 1990), p. 57.

intensity. After all, not all housing depreciates at once. Some houses seem to last forever, others, poorly built or maintained, are torn down much sooner. Typically, a first-wave housing cycle lasts 15 to 20 years.

THE INNOVATION CYCLE

Like housing and baby boom investments, innovations are sometimes introduced into an economy in clusters and thus produce their own variety of cycle. What accounts for a clustering of innovations?

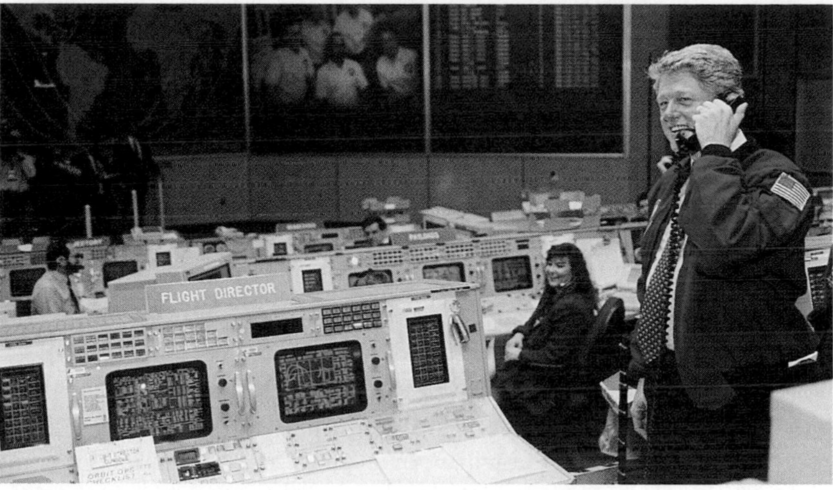

President Bill Clinton talks to the crew of STS-60 aboard the Space Shuttle Discovery at Johnson Space Center on February 7, 1994, in Houston, Texas.

The innovation cycle is caused by spurts of investment associated with new innovation.

Joseph Schumpeter explained innovation clustering by identifying specific innovations that create major breakthroughs in technology. These pioneering innovations require not only massive investment themselves but promote a host of supporting innovations that together create an economic upswing that could last as long as 60 years.

What do these innovations look like? We live in their shadow. The railroad, automobile, petrochemical, television, nuclear energy, computer, genetic engineering, and space technologies are innovations that changed the character of our economy. Each, in its time, stimulated the development of entirely new industries that dictated for generations the specific pace and direction of our economic life.

Consider, for example, the railroad. It revolutionized the size of our markets and, therefore, almost everything marketable. It created industries where none could have existed before, bringing millions of previously remote idle acres into the productive economy.

Yet even the mighty railroad ultimately exhausted its potential. What happens to the economy when the initial investment momentum subsides? The income multiplier effect of reduced demand and employment triggers the downturn phase of this long-wave innovation cycle.

The automobile and the myriad industries it fostered created its own long-wave cycle. Petrochemicals and television followed, creating superstructures of investments that revolutionized the way we live. Are space and genetic engineering innovations now about to revolutionize our economic life? What kinds of earthbound investments will space inspire?

Internal Cycles

Many economists believe that cycles need not wait upon wars or population explosions for momentum. The economy's continuous motion is *inherently* cyclical. But why should this be so?

We know something about the income multiplier. It tells us that any change in the level of investment triggers a series of changes in people's incomes. It explains how we move from one specific equilibrium level of national income to

The multiplier causes national income to increase, which necessitates an increase in investment and further expansion of national income that can lead to the creation of a cycle.

another. That makes sense as far as it goes, *but it doesn't go far enough*. The very change in national income that the original change in investment generated *now feeds back to generate changes in investment*.

Why should a change in national income feed back to induce a new change in investment? Think about it. When national income increases, business people see investment opportunities. Expecting sales to increase, they add to their inventories, buy new machinery, or expand their physical plant.

In other words, changes in investment and changes in national income are mutually reinforcing, and it is the mutual reinforcement that gives the economy its cyclical character. Just how does this mutual reinforcement work?

THE ACCELERATION PRINCIPLE

Let's begin our analysis of mutual reinforcement by explaining the accelerator, that is, the impact of a change in national income on the level of investment.

The investment decision that producers make depends, in part, on their reactions to past economic performance. For example, suppose national income in 1995 was less than national income in 1994. Then producers in 1996, believing that past performance is some indicator of future performance, may be inclined to trim back their investment spending in 1996. On the other hand, if national income in 1995 was higher than it was in 1994, producers in 1996, reacting to the economy's past performance, may be inclined to raise the level of their investment spending in 1996.

Accelerator

A relationship between the level of investment and the change in the level of national income.

Economists refer to such past-performance-sparked investment as *induced investment*. Where does the accelerator come into this discussion? The **accelerator, α**, specifies the relationship between the *level* of induced investment and the *change* in national income. For example, an accelerator of 1.5 indicates that induced investment in any year is 1.5 times the change in national income that occurred in the previous year. In other words, a $20 billion change in national income creates an induced investment of $30 billion.

Let's now see how this accelerator concept is used to explain the business cycle. Imagine an economy characterized by the following six assumptions:

1. The economy is in equilibrium in year 1. National income is $1,500 billion, consumption is $1,200 billion, and autonomous investment is $300 billion.
2. MPC equals 0.80; the income multiplier is 5.
3. $C_t = (MPC)Y_{t-1}$. Consumption in year t is equal to MPC times the income of the previous year.
4. Autonomous investment, I_t, is $300 billion in years 0 and 1, and $310 billion every year thereafter.
5. Induced investment, $I_t' = \alpha(Y_{t-1} - Y_{t-2})$. Aside from autonomous investment that occurs each year, an additional investment induced by changes that occurred in national income during the previous year occurs.
6. The accelerator, α, is 1.1. Applied to the equation for induced investment, it shows that producers, looking to past performance as an investment guide, make investments equivalent to 110 percent of the change in national income that occurred in the previous year.

Table 2 tracks national income over 25 years.

Look at national income, Y_t. *There's the business cycle*. It increases from $1,500 billion in the initial year to $1,621.43 billion in year 8, falls to $1,448.61 billion

TABLE 2
National Income Over 25 Years

Year	I_t	C_t	I'_t	Y_t	Change in Y
0	300	1,200.00	0.00	1,500.00	
1	300	1,200.00	0.00	1,500.00	
2	310	1,200.00	0.00	1,510.00	
3	310	1,208.00	11.00	1,529.00	19.00
4	310	1,223.20	20.90	1,554.10	25.10
5	310	1,243.28	27.61	1,580.89	26.79
6	310	1,264.71	29.47	1,604.18	23.29
7	310	1,283.34	25.62	1,618.96	14.78
8	310	1,295.17	16.26	1,621.43	2.47
9	310	1,297.15	2.72	1,609.86	−11.57
10	310	1,287.89	−12.73	1,585.16	−24.70
11	310	1,268.13	−27.17	1,550.96	−34.20
12	310	1,240.77	−37.62	1,513.14	−37.82
13	310	1,210.52	−41.60	1,478.92	−34.23
14	310	1,183.14	−37.65	1,455.49	−23.43
15	310	1,164.39	−25.78	1,448.61	−6.87
16	310	1,158.89	−7.56	1,461.33	12.72
17	310	1,169.06	13.99	1,493.05	31.72
18	310	1,194.44	34.89	1,539.34	46.28
19	310	1,231.47	50.91	1,592.38	53.05
20	310	1,273.91	58.35	1,642.26	49.87
21	310	1,313.80	54.86	1,678.67	36.41
22	310	1,342.93	40.05	1,692.98	14.32
23	310	1,354.39	15.75	1,680.13	−12.85
24	310	1,344.11	−14.13	1,639.98	−40.16
25	310	1,311.98	−44.18	1,577.80	−62.17

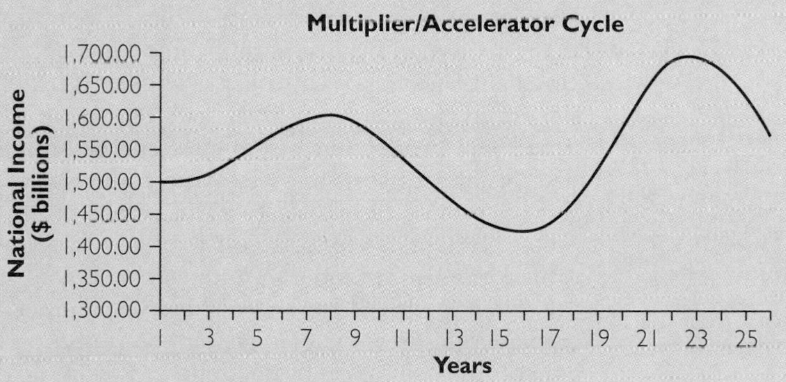

in year 15, and peaks again at $1,692.98 in year 22. What triggers the cycle? A $10 billion increase in autonomous investment in year 2. That's it!

Look at the behavior of producers and consumers during the second year. Consumption is $1,200 billion. What about induced investment? It is equal to 110 percent of the change in national income that occurred in the previous year—that is, in year 1. Since there was no change in national income from year 0 to year 1, induced investment, $\alpha(Y_1 - Y_0) = 0$. As a result, national income in this second year is $1,200 + $310 + 0 = $1,510 billion.

The seeds of the cycle have been planted. That $10 billion increase in national income in year 2 generates a $\alpha(Y_2 - Y_1) =$ $11 billion increase in induced investment in year 3. Note that consumption increases as well. After all, it is 0.8 of last year's income, which increased from $1,500 billion to $1,510 billion. Autonomous investment remains at $310 billion. As a result, national income in year 3 is $1,208 + $310 + $11 = $1,529 billion.

The $19 billion increase in national income during year 3 excites producers to add $\alpha(Y_3 - Y_2) =$ $20.90 billion of induced investment in year 4. The $19 billion increase in income also fuels greater consumption. As a result, national income in year 4 is $1,223.20 + $310 + $20.90 = $1,554.10 billion.

Do the interrelationships between consumption, induced investment, and national income create rising national incomes forever? Not so. The signal of trouble ahead occurs in year 6. Although national income did increase by $23.29 billion, that was less than the $26.79 billion increase of the year before. In other words, the *source that fuels induced investment was beginning to weaken.* That weakening dampens increases in income which further weakens induced investment.

By year 9, induced investment shrinks to $2.72 billion, so that national income in that year actually falls. The slide in national income continues until year 15 which marks the recovery phase.

REAL BUSINESS CYCLE THEORY

Real business cycle theorists reject the notion of a regular business cycle.

Some economists challenge the idea that internal or external cycles exist (even though their own theory is called the real business cycle). They believe that the idea of an economy actually moving through regular and distinct phases of a business cycle is a misreading of our economic reality. They argue that the economy is highly dynamic and competitive, operating close to if not at full employment, and that what other economists, mainly Keynesians, diagnose as cycles are in fact variations in the rate of growth of a full employment economy. (Imagine a production possibilities curve shifting outward year after year but with a different size shift each year.) These variations—tracing out an uneven growth path of twists and turns or, more appropriately, robust spurts, not-so-robust spurts and, very occasionally, short, moderate dips in real GDP—are what is misconceived of as the business cycle.

The principal factor shaping the unevenness (not cycles) in the economy's growth path, they argue, is the random injection by firms of individually minor but still large numbers of unconnected technological changes that cumulatively raise the level of productivity in the economy. They emphasize both the *large numbers of minor, unconnected technological changes* and their *randomness.*

Consider first their idea that technological change in the economy is the result of numerous minor innovations that occur regularly in all industries. This characterization of technological change is consistent with their view that the economy is both dynamic and competitive. The key to success and to ultimate survival for the great numbers of firms that compete is to develop or at least adopt new technology. *New technology raises real productivity,* which allows for lower costs and prices. Firms that don't adopt new technology cannot be price competitive with those that do. In the end, they drop out of the market. The real productivity increases that occur in this competitive environment make up the increase in the economy's real GDP.

Second, the randomness of these technological changes accounts for the variations in year-to-year increases in real productivity. For example, one year may bring in a host of technological changes followed by a year with relatively few changes. These changes are independent of each other. Their frequency and numbers are randomly distributed over time and space.

Compare this characterization of technological change to the one described in Joseph Schumpeter's innovation business cycle theory. Schumpeter assumes that technological change typically is clustered and connected, triggered by a few, very major innovative investments that represent breakthroughs in technology. These clustered innovation investments create the economic activity that causes the dramatic upswing phase in the innovation cycle theory. In time and sequence, the economic impact of these clustered investments peaks then weakens, bringing the cycle into its downturn phase.

In other words, while both views—the Schumpeterian innovation cycle and the real business cycle—focus on technological change, the former projects clear and discernable business cycles while the latter sees no such cyclical pattern, only unevenness in the economy's growth path.

The difference between traditional theories of the business cycle—from the external cycles, such as the housing or war-induced cycles, to the internal cycles, such as the interaction between the multiplier and accelerator—and real business cycle theory is the role assigned to government. While economists associated with traditional business cycle theories, in particular with the internally generated ones, see cycles as a problem and government as an instrument to correct the problem, real business cycle theorists see the unevenness in the economy's growth path not as a problem but as a natural, anticipated, and positive outcome of technological change and increased productivity. That is, in the one case government is viewed as a contributor to the economy's long-run growth and stability while in the other it is viewed as a long-run economic growth obstructionist. (A more complete analysis of the competing theories and ideas concerning the proper role of government awaits us in the chapter, Can Government Really Stabilize the Economy?)

COUNTERCYCLICAL FISCAL POLICY

Uncertainty clouds decisions about whether to undertake countercyclical fiscal policy, what magnitude of policy measure is necessary, and how a fiscal policy should be timed.

The real business cycle theory notwithstanding, let us recall from the last chapter how fiscal policy was used to close inflationary and recessionary gaps and now put that policy to work on business cycles, whatever their origin. The idea is the same, but the problems of fiscal policy management become a little more complicated.

For example, picture a White House cabinet meeting back in 1991, a year of recession. President Bush was concerned about the state of the economy. Economic growth was negative and the rate of unemployment continued to rise. It was abundantly clear to him that the economy was in recession. Congress was

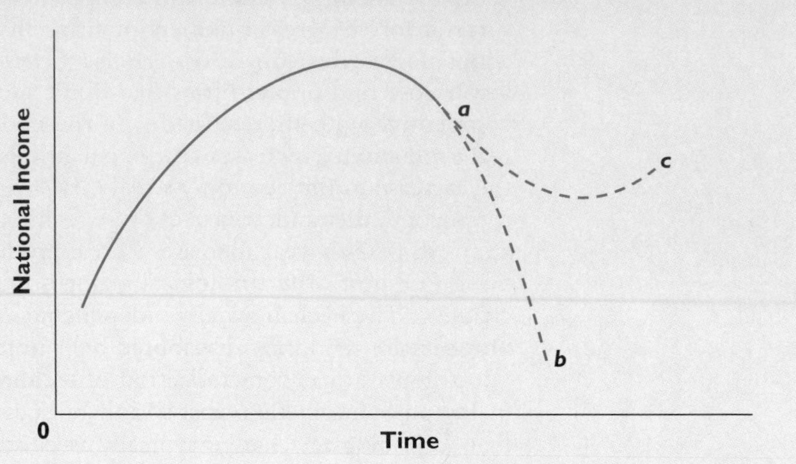

FIGURE 4
Designing Countercyclical Policy
At the time when policy is being discussed, the economy at *a* is in recession. Whether the economy will follow the *ab* or *ac* path through the cycle is unknown to policymakers. Each path has its own (and different) appropriate policy.

anxious to enact fiscal policy to counteract the recessionary forces operating on the economy.

President Bush, along with every member of his cabinet—as well as everyone who has read the chapter on fiscal policy—knew what fiscal policy Keynesians would use to close a recessionary gap. He knew that the government should either increase spending or reduce taxes. If the government is willing to incur large budgetary deficits, it could do both. Yet Michael Boskin, an economist from Stanford who chaired the President's Council of Economic Advisers, was reluctant to push ahead with these **countercyclical fiscal policy** measures and made his views known at the cabinet meeting. He was uncertain whether the intensity of the recession in 1991 deserved a budgetary deficit response.

Countercyclical fiscal policy
Fiscal policy designed to moderate the severity of the business cycle.

Suppose that, to make his point, he went to the chalkboard in the cabinet room and drew Figure 4.

The economy that morning, he says, is positioned at *a*. That is clearly recession. What is less clear is where the economy is heading. If the cyclical path that the economy will take is along the dotted line *ab,* then perhaps countercyclical fiscal policy would be appropriate. But if the actual cyclical path is along dotted line *ac,* then countercyclical fiscal policy may not only be unnecessary but counterproductive.

If it is *ac,* he explains, the economy will work its own way out of the recession. At some point in the cycle, he emphasizes, the economy turns around on its own. *The problem is knowing just where the turning point is.* If the government opts for strong countercyclical policy, he says, it may in fact contribute to inflationary problems that are "just around the corner." The dynamics of the multiplier-accelerator interaction alone will drive the economy to full employment and, most likely, into inflation. With the added measure of countercyclical fiscal policy, the recovery phase may become overcharged, leading quickly to high rates of inflation. In other words, Boskin warns, countercyclical policy at *a* in an *ac* cycle may be overkill.

"But what if the economy is on the *ab* path?" asks the President. "Then," replies Boskin, "countercyclical measures are appropriate. Although how much budgetary deficit is needed," he adds, "is another question."

Everyone stares at Figure 4. Jack Kemp, the Secretary of Housing and Urban Development, thinks aloud: "Figure 4 explains a lot, yet not enough." Everyone agrees. It isn't enough to know where the economy is on the cycle—although that alone is difficult to gauge—but we have to be fairly confident as well that we know the path the economy is taking into the future. Deciding *when* to use *how much* countercyclical policy is crucial in avoiding fiscal overkill or underkill.

"It seems to me," says President Bush, attempting to lift the cabinet's deflating spirits, "that practicing good fiscal policy is much like doing good comedy: *it's all in the timing!*"

Administrative lag

The time interval between deciding on an appropriate policy and the execution of that policy.

"There's still another problem," Boskin warns. "There is **administrative lag** to think about. After all, if we decide this morning to increase government spending by $100 billion because that's the appropriate sum today given our position on the cycle, we can't simply put the $100 billion to work tomorrow. We would have to design realistic spending programs for the $100 billion, such as new interstate highways, new hospitals, new schools, new defense technology, that are acceptable to the Congress, and that takes time. It also takes time for the Senate and the House of Representatives to enact legislation, and even more time for legislated appropriations to get into the hands of people who will use the $100 billion. By the time the $100 billion is actually disbursed, the economy may be in a different position in a different phase of the cycle entirely. In other words, the administrative lag time, however unavoidable, may itself undermine the effectiveness of countercyclical fiscal policy."

But asks Vice President Quayle, "What if the economy's position at *a* is not simply in the downturn phase of a multiplier-accelerator cycle but is instead the result of a recovery phase of the multiplier-accelerator cycle riding on a strong downturn phase of an innovation cycle?" "That's also quite possible," Boskin replies, "and the countercyclical measures we already discussed are, under these conditions, much less appropriate. That is to say, the unemployment could be more structural than cyclical. Major job retraining programs for the unemployed would be more appropriate than the traditional forms of fiscal policy."

"But I've heard there's no such thing as a business cycle!" adds Secretary of State James Baker, "So why the excitement? I'm told the economy's growth path is naturally uneven, reflecting the increase in real productivity that is associated with current levels of technological change. In all probability, those levels will change tomorrow. Is there any truth to this argument, Michael?" The president's chief economic adviser nods his head and replies, "Jim, the truth is that there is a lot of theorizing going on out there about cycles and growth, some making good sense, some less so, but all of them struggling to understand the real world. It's not easy to understand. Whether it's a real cycle phase or merely a dip in an uneven growth path, I think we are still looking at recession."

"And the buck stops here," the President mutters to himself. He knows that the countercyclical policy problems of timing, of administrative lag, of identifying where on the cycle's phase the economy is, and what path it will follow applies as well to closing inflationary gaps. He also knows that however helpful a team of economists may be, they are no substitute for a crystal ball!

CHAPTER REVIEW

1. The Keynesian analysis of macroeconomic equilibrium allows us to pinpoint cause-and-effect relationships among changes in investment, national income,

and employment, as well as the impact of government on the macroeconomy. These cause-and-effect relationships hold up for any economy, whether it is in equilibrium or not.

2. Adam Smith explored the causes of economic growth in his book *The Wealth of Nations*. The four principal factors that Smith identified as responsible for economic growth in the late 18th century are still relevant today. They are the size of the labor force, the degree of labor specialization, the size of the capital stock, and the level of technology.

3. Given a constant capital/output ratio, increases in the capital stock that arise each year through saving and investment will generate continuous growth in output. For example, the U.S. economy grew at an average annual rate of 3.94 percent from 1947 to 1973, and at only 2.3 percent per year from 1973 to 1992. The sources of growth were of different magnitudes between these two periods as well.

4. By looking at the U.S. real GDP performance from 1860–1990 we can discern the business cycle. Periods of growth in real GDP are followed by periods of decline, to be followed again by periods of growth. Many traditional theories for the business cycle exist. Among these are external cycles such as Jevons' sunspot theory, war-induced cycles, population-induced cycles, the housing cycle, and Schumpeter's innovation cycle. An example of an internal cycle is the multiplier-accelerator cycle. The multiplier-accelerator cycle suggests that an economy can be inherently cyclical.

5. Real business cycle theorists believe that there is no such thing as a business cycle composed of regular and distinct phases. Rather, they believe that the economy is highly dynamic and operates close to if not at full employment. What many economists diagnose as business cycles are really just sharp changes in the rate of economic growth. Economic growth rates are highly variable because of random technological changes.

6. Countercyclical fiscal policy is aimed at stemming downturns in economic activity (though it can also be used to combat inflation). The appropriate fiscal policy response to a recessionary downturn is to increase the budget deficit, either with tax cuts or spending increases or both. Whether or not countercyclical policies are necessary is uncertain in many cases. It is also uncertain how large a deficit is needed to make a particular countercyclical policy effective. Moreover, timing a countercyclical policy is difficult given the existence of administrative lag.

KEY TERMS

Economic growth
Labor productivity
Capital/output ratio
Accelerator
Countercyclical fiscal policy
Administrative lag

QUESTIONS

1. What are the principal factors contributing to U.S. economic growth in the latter half of the 20th century?

2. What is a trend growth rate?

3. What is an externally induced cycle? Give some examples.

4. Suppose the government prepares for war during the prosperity phase of a cycle. What effect would the war preparation activity most likely have on real GDP, employment, and inflation?

5. Suppose war preparation occurred during the trough phase of a cycle. What effect would it most likely have on real GDP, employment, and inflation?

6. Explain why a population cycle tends to dampen out over time?

7. What causes an innovation cycle?

8. What is an internally generated cycle?

9. What is the acceleration principle? How does it differ from the income multiplier?

10. Explain how interactions of the multiplier and accelerator generate cycles of national income.

11. Real business cycle theory is not a theory about cycles. Explain.

12. In the end, effective countercyclical fiscal policy relies on guesswork. Explain.

13. How does administrative lag undermine the effectiveness of countercyclical fiscal policy?

14. The long-term trend growth rate for the following set of GDPs is 2.7 percent.

Year	GDP
0	100.0
1	102.5
2	105.6
3	106.6
4	110.9
5	111.2

Graph the deviation of the economic growth rate from the trend line for each year.

PART 6
MONEY, BANKING, AND MONETARY POLICY

C H A P T E R 2 6

MONEY

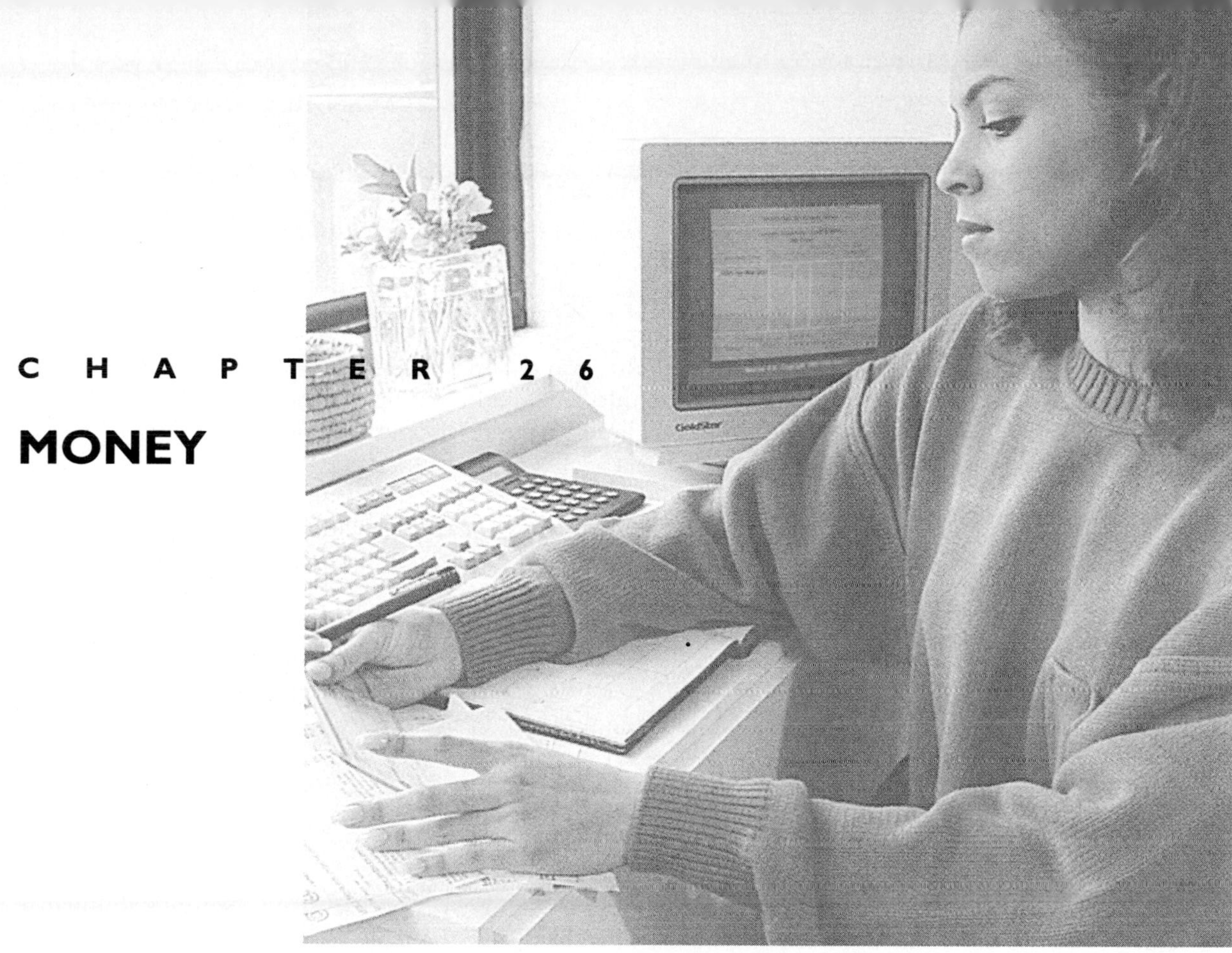

CHAPTER PREVIEW

It probably seems a little strange to have come so far in an economics course with little more than a mention of money. But it isn't strange really. After all, economics studies the way people allocate scarce resources to satisfy their wants, which is far broader than the study of the way people use money. However, money certainly plays a big role in economic affairs and it deserves our careful attention. This chapter and the following two chapters are devoted to gaining an understanding of the functions of money and the institutions that have been created to govern the use and distribution of money.

After studying this chapter, you should be able to:

- Explain why money has replaced barter.
- List the desirable characteristics and functions of money.
- Distinguish between gold-backed money and fiat money.
- Explain the liquidity characteristic of our money supply.
- Give a reason for the rapid growth of the money supply during the 1970s.
- Connect the classical view of money demand with the equation of exchange and the quantity theory of money.
- Explain monetarism.

- Contrast the Keynesian view of money demand with the classical view of money demand.
- Describe how money can affect real GDP, according to the Keynesian view.

Indulge yourself! Imagine that you are on a desert island that is loaded with fruits and berries, rabbits and exotic fowl, and teeming with a wide variety of fish always accessible in the shallows of the island's crystal clear lagoons. All at your disposal.

Sounds marvelous, doesn't it? Now suppose, during the late hours of a summer afternoon, while leisurely digging for truffles with your pet pig, you chance upon a treasure chest filled with 1,000 gold coins. Each bears the imprint of an ancient Spanish realm.

An exciting find? Well, perhaps. What would you do with the coins? You couldn't eat them, wear them, or sleep on or under them, could you? They may be beautiful to look at, but so too are clouds! You may end up deciding that a sensible thing to do with the find would be to bury it again.

THE BEGINNINGS OF EXCHANGE

Suppose, months later, another person arrives on the island. Nature's abundance is now shared. You both agree to divide the daily chores: You pick berries, he does the hunting and fishing. At the end of each day, you exchange the rewards of your specialized labor. For example, one bowl of berries for one fish. Or one egg for two fruit, depending, say, on the time required to produce these goods.

Barter

The exchange of one good for another, without the use of money.

If one of you were an economist, you would know straight away that this kind of direct goods-for-goods exchange is defined as **barter.**

Now suppose a third person appears. This situation creates even more possibilities for specialization, doesn't it? The chores are now divided among three. One specializes in fishing, another in berry and fruit picking, while the third hunts. You set up a flourishing three-way barter exchange.

Let's add a fourth person. And a fifth. Berry and fruit picking are divided, and egg gathering, once handled by the person raising fowls, becomes a specialized activity. Barter exchange now becomes a little more complex, and exchange-matching problems are bound to occur.

For example, suppose the egg gatherer wants to exchange eggs for berries, but the berry picker, worried about cholesterol, is not an egg eater. Or suppose the berry picker wants rabbit for dinner, but the hunter has no taste for berries, preferring eggs instead. You can see the problems.

If they all got together in one place at one time they could probably straighten out this no-match exchange mess. But it would still involve some degree of risk taking. After all, the hunter would have to accept unwanted eggs in exchange for rabbit in the hope of later exchanging those eggs for berries. He would like to have prior knowledge, however, that the berry picker will really want eggs. That's a lot of indirect arranging to do.

Barter requires a double coincidence of wants.

As you see, barter can be an excellent means of exchanging goods as long as the people and goods involved are few and simple. But it breaks down quickly when the numbers increase. To function effectively, barter requires *the double coincidence* of each party to the exchange wanting precisely what the other has to offer. That's difficult to achieve among five people, impossible among five thousand.

THE INVENTION OF MONEY

Money

Any commonly accepted good that acts as a medium of exchange, a measure of value, and a store of value.

Why would eggs be a poor choice as a form of money?

If you find yourself stuck in a barter situation, what can you do? One solution—common to all societies—is to pick one of the available goods as a medium of exchange, that is, **money.** All other goods are measured in units of the one selected. Suppose the choice is eggs. By common consent, eggs are the accepted currency. A rabbit exchanges for 14 eggs, a peahen exchanges for 10, a basket of berries for two, and a banana exchanges one for one.

This wouldn't last very long. People will quickly discover that eggs are a poor money form. They are too fragile. If the hunter sells three rabbits and receives in exchange 42 eggs, most likely many would break before the day is out. There goes the money! How would you feel walking about with 42 eggs in your pocket?

Money must be *durable* and *portable*. Eggs are out on both counts. What about fish? They are too perishable. You wouldn't want to keep that money form in your pocket for very long, would you?

Rabbits? They are more durable than eggs or fish, but how would you buy an egg with a unit of rabbit? How could you measure out one-fourteenth of a rabbit? And what would you do with the remaining thirteen-fourteenths? You see the problem: money must be *divisible* as well.

Another problem with rabbits as a money form is that some rabbits are big and fluffy, others are not. Some are cute, others less so. As long as some are preferred to others, people will tend to hoard preferred rabbits and use only the less preferred ones as money. In such cases, then, not all of the money form actually serves as money. To overcome this problem, the units of any money form selected must be *identical,* or homogeneous.

There's still another problem with rabbits. They breed like rabbits! If rabbits are money, it becomes impossible to control the money supply. The supply of fish and eggs, too, can be expanded without much effort. If money is to serve as a reliable store of value, its supply, at least in the short run, must be fairly *stable.*

As you can see, almost any choice on the island creates a problem. But we all do the best we can. Some Native Americans, before Europeans arrived, used wampum, strings of beads made of shells, as money. During the Colonial period, fish, furs, corn, cattle, whiskey and, at various times, even gunpowder was used as money.

Elsewhere, other goods served as the medium of exchange. In the South Pacific, the tiny island of Yap came to use large stone wheels, one of them 12 feet in diameter, as its money form. In Homer's day, cattle were used as money. The ancient Egyptians used necklaces, hatchets, and daggers. U.S. prisoners of war during World War II used cigarettes. In fact, most common goods, including beans, fishhooks, pearls, cocoa seeds, nails, rum, tea, pepper, sheep, pigs, dates, salt, rice, sugar, skins, silk, reindeer, and whale teeth have served somewhere at some time as money.

Gold as Money

Economies tend to select whatever goods they have that come closest to satisfying the prerequisites for perfect money. What money form would *you* choose if

ADDED PERSPECTIVE

Fluffy Rabbits and Gresham's Law

It seems reasonable, doesn't it, that if rabbits were money and the price of a video rental were two rabbits, you would use the two least attractive rabbits from your rabbit stock to rent the video? Or imagine if you were a lawyer and charged three rabbits per hour, the three you receive from your client would probably be scrawny looking. After all, why would anyone give up the more attractive rabbits from their money supply? In other words, if the economy's money supply consisted of 1,000 rabbits, half adorable and fluffy, the other half cross-eyed and scruffy, only the 500 cross-eyed, scruffy ones would actually circulate as money.

Or suppose the economy's money form was gold, but unscrupulous people minted coins of fool's gold as well as coins of pure gold. Wouldn't you very quickly become expert in detecting which of the coins in your supply were pure and which were debased? And if there were 1,000 coins—500 pure and 500 debased—wouldn't everybody use only the debased coins as money, hoarding the pure coins? That is, the money supply used in everyday transactions would end up being only the 500 debased coins.

Debasing coins was a practice almost as old as coinage itself. Sir Thomas Gresham, a 16th century merchant and advisor to the English crown observed that *bad money drives out good.* He observed that debased coinage drove the good coins not only out of circulation, but out of Britain. He wrote to Queen Elizabeth:

Ytt may please your majesty to understande, thatt the first occasion of the fall of exchange did growe by the Kinges majesty, your latte ffather, in abasinge the quoyne ffrome vi ounces fine too iii ounces fine ... which was the occasion that all your fine gold was convayed ought of this your realme.

Difficult to read old English? This passage explains why gold was conveyed out of Britain. Elizabeth's father, Henry VIII, had debased the coinage. Gresham's observation prompted the 19th century economist H. D. MacLeod to write, "As he was the first to perceive that a bad and debased currency is the cause of the disappearance of good money, we are only doing what is just in claiming this great fundamental law of the currency by his name."

Discussion
What happens to the price level when good money drives out bad money?

Gold has the kinds of characteristics one would want for money.

you were on the desert island? Think about it. If homogeneity, divisibility, portability, durability, and unchanging supply count, what about that gold buried among the truffles? Before exchange, it was useless. Now it appears to satisfy all five prerequisites.

1. Its supply—the 1,000 coins—is fixed. In the real world, supplies of gold are hard to come by. People have searched the globe for gold, but whatever the discovery, even the San Francisco Gold Rush of 1849, year-to-year additions to total stock have been less than dramatic. Gold is just hard to find.
2. It's perfectly homogeneous. Gold is gold. One ounce is identical to any other. No ounce is preferred to another.
3. It's incredibly durable. Just try destroying a nugget of gold. It doesn't rot, rust, fade, overripen, or dry up. Its luster withstands the elements of time.
4. It's perfectly divisible. Gold can be melted down and remolded into any shape or size. Think of gold jewelry. Gold nuggets can be reduced to standard-sized ounces, and ounces cut to minute fractions. Gold dust is still gold.
5. It's portable. It can be held, pocketed, or carried about. There's a limit, of course, to the quantity a person could carry, but for most people, the quantities required are quite manageable.

Because gold has these marvelous physical properties, it satisfies the primary functions of money. That is, it serves as (1) a *medium of exchange* (accepted as payment for any purchase), (2) a *measure of value* (serves as a yardstick for measuring the value of other goods), and (3) a *store of value* (a means of holding wealth from one time period to another).

Its divisibility, portability, and homogeneity make gold a perfect medium of exchange and measure of value. Its durability and relative scarcity make it an excellent store of value. People feel confident that they can store it away knowing that when they choose to spend it, it will buy as much as it would today. In this sense, money transfers goods from our past to the present and from our present into the future.

Gold-Backed Paper as Money

With paper functioning as money, there's no need for gold.

If the island switched its money form to gold, it would not be the first economy to do so. In fact, gold coinage dates back to the eighth century B.C. when coins were issued by the Kingdom of Lydia, by the Greek coastal cities, and by the Persian Empire.

Exchanging rabbits for gold, eggs for gold, and fish for gold works very well. In time, gold becomes the most recognizable good in the economy. Even children know how it works. It is carried about, stored away, traded for real goods, borrowed, and loaned. It represents the *power* to purchase any good at any time.

But somebody comes up with a new idea. Why not print paper money to represent the gold? It's more convenient than carrying the physical gold around. It can be easily tucked away in a pocket or purse, and simply by printing higher numbers on the paper, can be made to represent great quantities of gold. Of course, a unit of paper money would be backed by a specific quantity of gold so that paper money could always be cashed—converted back—for gold.

It's a revolutionary idea, almost as revolutionary as gold money itself. If it works, why not? What, then, should we do with the physical gold? Bury it once more! As long as people have confidence that paper money will serve the functions of money, then "it's as good as gold."

Fiat, or Paper Money

Fiat Money

Paper money which is not backed by or convertible into any good.

One good idea leads to another. Suppose a violent storm washes away the entire supply of gold. Does the island lose its money? Not at all. Why couldn't the paper or **fiat money** still continue to serve as the medium of exchange? Is the gold backing really necessary? As long as everyone continues, as before, to accept the paper as money—why worry?

Still, there is reason for concern. If we no longer link the quantity of paper money to a specific quantity of gold, then what's to limit the supply of paper money? Nothing. It seems reasonable to suppose that people, knowing that money serves as a store of value only if its supply is relatively stable, would be careful about overprinting paper money. But sometimes reason is of no avail. There is a temptation for economies to print more money. If a society chooses fiat money as its money form, then it must be particularly vigilant about controlling the quantity of money.

MONEY IN A MODERN ECONOMY

When was the last time you saw a gold coin, let alone bought anything with it? What, then, do we use as our money form? For a start, look in your pocket.

Banking hours? 24 hours a day, 7 days a week! Thanks to modern technology, liquidity has become as easy to acquire as candy bars and soft drinks.

Currency
Coins and paper money.

Our Federal Reserve Notes are fiat money.

Coins and dollar bills are money in the form of **currency.** Look closely at the dollar bill. Although it says in bold and large print: "The United States of America," it is not government-issued currency. It is, instead, issued by our central bank, the Federal Reserve System (commonly referred to as the Fed). The dollar bill is a Federal Reserve Note. In your pocket, it represents the Fed's IOU. Why do we hold it? Read the fine print. It says: "This note is legal tender for all debts, public and private." That is to say, the Fed assures you that the dollar (its note) can be used by you or by anyone else as a medium of exchange and as payment for debts. Nowhere on the bill does it say anything about gold, because there is no gold backing it. The dollar bill is fiat money.

It works. No one hesitates to accept the dollar bill as payment for pizza, popcorn, or photographic equipment. We can even buy other nations' currencies with it. Canadians gladly accept our dollars in exchange for theirs. Japanese accept our dollar for their yen. Russians would be thrilled to exchange rubles for dollar bills.

Money and Liquidity

Liquidity
The degree to which an asset can easily be exchanged for money.

If you were to play a word-association game with economists and say "money," chances are they would all respond with "**liquidity.**" Liquidity is what distinguishes money from any other asset form. Liquidity is the ease with which an asset can be converted into a medium of exchange. Look around your room. What assets do you have that can be readily converted into a medium of exchange? How about that dollar bill on your desk? That's instant. The dollar is a perfectly liquid form of asset. That is to say, the dollar, *in its present form,* can be used as a medium of exchange. A pizza maker, for example, will accept your dollar *as is* in exchange for pizza. A physician will accept it as payment for services.

What about your other assets? Consider, for example, your ticket to next week's basketball game? Can you use it now, *in its present form,* to buy a pizza? Not likely. Even if the ticket is refundable, you still must go to the refund office to convert it back into dollars. The ticket, *in its present form,* is not a perfectly liquid form of money. What about your stereo? It's worth something isn't it? But *in its present form,* it is highly illiquid. What about the U.S. savings bond in your top drawer? It's more liquid than your stereo, but not nearly as liquid as your dollar bill.

As you see, each one of those assets in your room—the financial as well as the real goods—can be ordered according to liquidity. Some assets are perfectly liquid, that is, can serve immediately as money. Others are less liquid, representing a less-than-perfect money form. Most are highly illiquid, that is, far removed from a money form.

Money supply

Typically, M1 money. The supply of currency, demand deposits, and traveler's checks used in transactions.

How much money we have, then, depends on how much (or how little) liquidity we accept for a money form. Let's consider the various qualities of money that make up our **money supply.**

The Liquidity Character of Our Money Supply

Do we just add up the dollar bills and coins issued by the Fed to compute our money supply? That is to say, is our money supply simply all currency?

Not quite, although currency is part of our money supply. Consider the other money forms we use as a medium of exchange. If you saw a T-shirt you liked, what kind of money would you use to make the purchase? Most likely, currency. But how do you pay your rent? If you're like most people, you write a check on your checking account. The landlord accepts it as payment. As far as the landlord is concerned, your check is money.

THE M1 MONEY SUPPLY

In fact, the check is the most commonly used money form. Most working people receive their wages and salaries in the form of checks. Corporations pay out dividends by check. Most large ticket items are bought by check. How do you pay your telephone bill? How did you pay your college tuition? Next time you're in line at the supermarket, watch the cashier. Three-bag purchases are typically paid for by check.

How many checks you are able to write depends, of course, on the size of your checking account. That is, your checking account balance represents your money supply.

After all, if you were asked to add up your own money supply, wouldn't you count the dollars and cents you have in your pocket, and then add the money you have on deposit in your checking account?

M1 money supply

The supply of the most immediate form of money. It includes currency, demand deposits, and travelers' checks.

Economists describe these money forms as **M1 money.** M1 money is highly liquid (immediately available) money. Currency is about as liquid as money could be. Checking accounts? Banks are legally obligated to give you any fraction or all of your deposit immediately *upon demand.* That's pretty liquid, and that is why economists describe checking account balances as demand deposits.

Traveler's checks, too, are M1 money. Think about it. There are times when traveler's checks are more convenient and even more liquid than checks drawn on local banks. They are particularly useful when we're away from home. If you were in Italy, for example, you would probably find it easier to buy a leather jacket with a traveler's check than with a check drawn on your local bank. The Italian merchant may not know much about your bank balance at home but has confidence that the traveler's check you offer can be readily converted into Italian lire.

M2 money supply

M1 money plus less-immediate forms of money, such as savings accounts, money market mutual accounts, money market deposit accounts, repurchase agreements, and small denomination time deposits.

THE M2 MONEY SUPPLY

A broader definition of money is **M2.** M2 money includes M1 money and more. How much more? What about your savings account? Is it money? Yes.

But savings accounts are not as liquid as checking accounts. You are not at liberty to withdraw your money on demand from your savings account. It may surprise you, but banks are legally entitled to 30 days' notice before being obligated to release your funds to you. That is why economists describe savings accounts as time deposits. Still, as you have probably experienced, banks seldom exercise the 30-day notice privilege.

Savings accounts are not only not as immediate a money form as M1, but are not as serviceable a medium of exchange either. For example, you cannot pay your rent with a check drawn on your savings account.

Why, then, bother with savings accounts? Because traditionally they yield higher rates of interest to depositors than checking accounts.

There is a wide variety of M2 money forms. For example, banks created the certificate of deposit, or CD, which is a less immediate form of money than savings deposits but provides a higher rate of interest.

Investment companies, too, offer a form of M2 money. They got into the banking business in the early 1970s by creating money market mutual funds, or MMMFs, which they invest by purchasing government securities and business debt. When the investment companies first developed these funds, banks were prohibited by state law from paying interest rates on savings accounts above a state-determined maximum (typically 5 or 6 percent). Investment companies, not subject to that constraint, offered a higher rate of interest on their MMMFs. People took advantage of this higher-interest-yielding form of savings even though they were less convenient. Money market mutual funds were less accessible than savings accounts, with restrictions on the number of withdrawals allowed each month, or a minimum size of $500 or $1,000 for each withdrawal. Many funds still have these restrictions, but the trend has been toward greater accessibility. Today, it is possible to write a check against your money market mutual fund just as you would against your checking account. And after the interest rate ceilings were lifted in 1980, banks responded to the competition by creating money market deposit accounts, or MMDAs.

As you see, M1 and the broader M2 are both highly liquid, yet some of the components of M2 are clearly less liquid than M1. The trade-off between them seems clear enough: immediately available money versus higher-interest-earning money. In recent years new financial innovations introduced by banks and other financial institutions have blurred the M1 and M2 money distinction considerably.

For example, prior to the 1970s, commercial banks were the only financial institutions that provided checking account services. Now that's changed. Savings and loan associations (S&Ls) and credit unions now provide interest-earning checking accounts as well. Savings and loan associations created the NOW account, or negotiable order of withdrawal, which allows you to use your savings account with them as an honest-to-goodness checking account. In other words, you can earn interest *and* have checking account services in the same deposit. Not to be outdone, credit unions created the share-draft account, their version of NOW.

Banks didn't sit idly by. They responded by creating the ATS account, or automatic transfer of savings, which allowed depositors to automatically transfer funds from savings to checking when their checking accounts were depleted, thereby providing interest-earning checking accounts that are equivalent to NOW accounts. In these ways, *M2 money is beginning to look more and more like M1 money*. In fact, NOW and ATS accounts are checking account-like deposits that are now considered to be part of the M1 money supply.

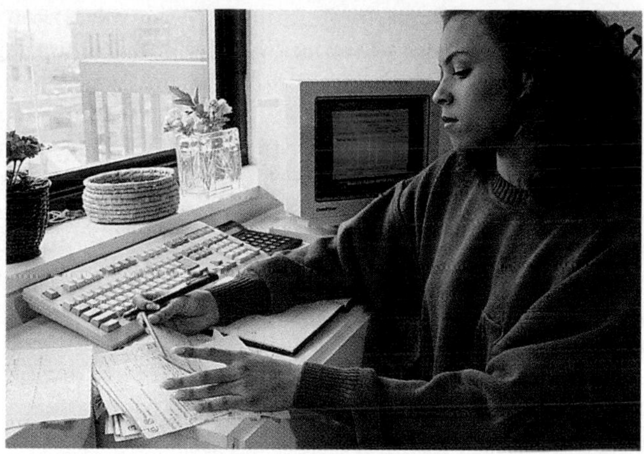

Bills, bills, and more bills! This college graduate, like so many other people her age and older, is trying to figure out a way of "making it through the month" without having to cash in her $500 certificate of deposit, a graduation gift from her parents. Can she live on M1 or must she resort to M2?

THE M3 MONEY SUPPLY

M3 money supply

M2 money plus large denomination time deposits and large denomination repurchase agreements.

An even broader concept of money is M3. The **M3 money supply** includes M2 money, as well as a set of other money forms that have less liquidity than M2. For example, M3 includes large-denomination ($100,000 or more) time deposits, typically in the form of certificates of deposit held in banks and other financial institutions.

M3 includes as well overnight repurchase agreements. These provide still another interest-earning option that is easily convertible to immediate money. The agreement allows banks to create securities and sell them (principally to large corporations), with the agreement that the banks will repurchase the securities the following day at slightly higher prices. Why would banks be interested in getting their hands on corporate money *for just one night?* Because if the sum were hundreds of millions of dollars, they could earn a considerable amount of interest while most people were asleep. The interest banks earn on this overnight access to corporate money more than compensates them for the higher buy-back price they agree to pay.

Money and "Near" Money

If you received a $100 U.S. savings bond as a birthday gift, would you regard it as a money gift? Would you treat it the same way you would a gift of $100? Have you ever sold a U.S. savings bond before its maturity date? If you have, you know why it isn't a perfectly reliable money form or store of value. Although you can sell the bond anytime at *some* price, the price it will fetch on the bond market will be less than the stated maturity value.

What about corporate bonds? Is an AT&T bond any more reliable a money form than a U.S. savings bond? It too is marketable (and therefore convertible into cash), but at what price? There is even greater risk attached to the corporate bond. Economists refer to these financial assets as near money.

What Isn't Money?

When you think about it, what isn't money? After all, can't you really convert any asset you own into money? Couldn't you sell your wristwatch at *some* price?

That's why pawnshops are in business. They allow you to convert your belongings (or someone else's!) into money by purchasing them from you. But do you really think of your watch as a form of money?

Unquestionably, people regard their checking accounts as money. That's what they look at when they worry about making it through the month. They know they can always dip into savings, but savings is something they prefer to protect. It was never really intended as a medium of exchange. Few people think of their homes as money even though second mortgages are not an uncommon way of financing expenditures.

Nevertheless, every asset we own is potential money. At some price, it can be converted into money. Still, we make distinctions between our money, near money, and nonmoney assets, don't we? These distinctions, however problematical, depend not only upon how liquid these assets are, but also upon the intended purpose we ascribe to them.

What about your Visa and MasterCard? Are they money? Not at all. They may be accepted as readily as money, but the reason these cards are honored at shops, restaurants, and hotels is because merchants expect to be paid by the financial institution that issued the card. Eventually, you pay off your bill by writing a check to the financial institution or bank that issued the card. But without an adequate checking account, Visa would soon discover that the credit receipt it received with your signature on it was virtually worthless.

Credit cards are often more convenient than writing checks. Because we travel farther and more frequently than we ever did, these plastic cards have become indispensible. They are readily accepted in other cities and even in other countries by people who would otherwise refuse a check on an unknown bank. And the best part of all is that every time you use a credit card, you receive an interest-free loan for a month or two. You don't need to have money in hand (or in your checking account) until the time comes to pay the bill.

Adding Up Our Money Supply

Table 1 totals the M1, M2, and M3 money supply for the 1993 U.S. economy.

Look at currency, the money form most people would describe as money. It amounts to less than 8 percent of the M3 money supply. It is not even the dominant money form of M1.

Much of the M2 money supply growth since the 1960s, and particularly through the 1970s, can be explained by the introduction of money market mutual funds and deposit accounts into the banking system. They were the right money form for the right people at the right time. People favored an asset that could perform both as investment and as reasonably accessible money. As we see in Figure 1, M2 has grown considerably faster since 1960 than any other money form.

Another factor that contributed to the rapid growth of M2 during the 1970s was the sluggish stock market. High-interest-yielding accounts looked good compared to the stock market performance. People shifted out of the stock market into these M2 money forms.

Although the broadest notion of money supply—M3—amounts to $4,172 billion, unless otherwise specified, *economists mean M1 when they refer to money*. It is what people and businesses use in their day-to-day market transactions.

TABLE 1
1993 U.S. Money Supply ($ billions)

M1		**$1,074**
Currency	$307	
Traveler's checks	8	
Demand deposits	361	
Other checkable deposits	389	
M2		**$3,512**
M1	$1,074	
Savings deposits, MMDAs	1,199	
MMMFs	336	
Small time deposits	830	
Repurchase agreements	73	
M3		**$4,172**
M2	$3,512	
Large time deposits	242	
Term repurchase agreements	229	
MMFs: institutional	189	

Source: *Federal Reserve Bulletin*, Table 1.21., September 1993, p. A14. (Washington, D.C.: Federal Reserve).

FIGURE 1 **Growth of U.S. Money: 1970–93**
M1 money increased from $215 billion in 1970 to $1,074 billion in 1993, or by an annual rate of 7 percent. M2 grew more rapidly, from $628 billion in 1970 to $3,512 billion in 1993, or by an annual rate of 8.4 percent.

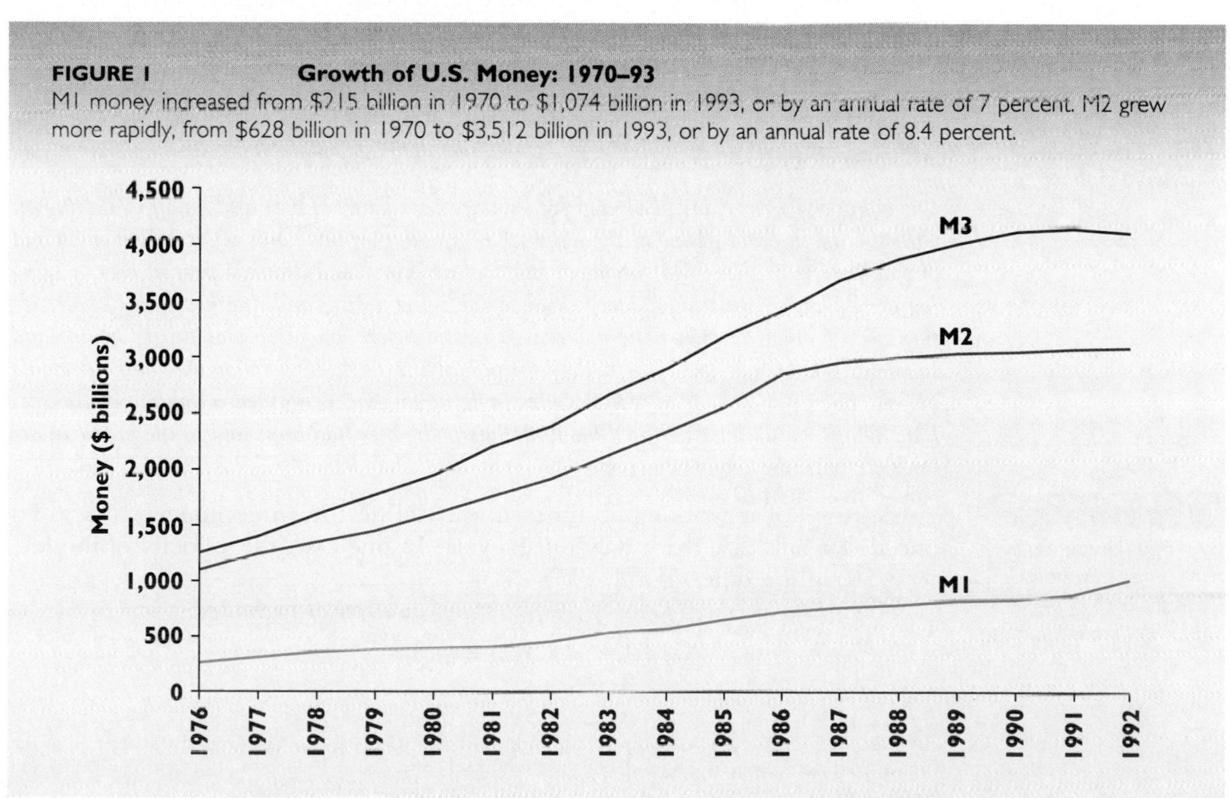

THE QUANTITY THEORY OF MONEY

In the quantity theory of money, the price level is a function of the supply of money.

How does the money supply affect prices? To show the money-price connection, imagine an economy consisting exclusively of 100 apple trees producing a real GDP of 5,000 apples. Suppose also that the economy's money supply is $10,000. Under these conditions, the price of apples is $2. The total value of the apples (or nominal GDP), is 5,000 × $2 = $10,000.

The equation of exchange relating the economy's price level, *P,* the quantity of goods, *Q,* and the money supply, *M,* is written as

$$P = \frac{M}{Q}$$

If the money supply doubles to $20,000, and Q doesn't change, the price level doubles to $20,000/5,000 = $4. If the money supply falls to $5,000, and Q is still unchanged, the price level falls to $5,000/5,000 = $1.

Look at the other correspondences in the equation of exchange. If Q (real GDP) doubles from 5,000 to 10,000 apples and *M* doesn't change, the price level falls to $10,000/10,000 = $1. And if the price level increases to $4 while *Q* is 5,000 apples, we know that the money supply, *M,* must be $20,000. Simple enough?

The Velocity of Money

Velocity of money

The average number of times per year each dollar is used to transact an exchange.

Actually, it's too simple. The equation of exchange shown in our apple illustration above does not take into account the **velocity of money.** The price level depends not only on Q (real GDP) and *M* (the quantity of money), but also on velocity—that is, on the number of times a dollar is used during a year transacting Q.

D. H. Robertson illustrates the importance of money velocity in a rather amusing story.

*On Kentucky Derby day, Bob and Joe invested in a barrel of beer and set off to Lexington with the intention of selling at the racetrack at a dollar a pint. On the way, Bob, who had one dollar left in the world, began to feel a great thirst, and drank a pint of beer, paying Joe the dollar. A little later, Joe yielded to the same desire, and drank a pint of beer, returning the dollar to Bob. The day was hot, and before long Bob was thirsty again, and so, a little later was Joe. When they arrived at the track, the dollar was back in Bob's pocket: but the beer was all gone. One single dollar had performed a volume of transactions which would have required many dollars if the beer had been sold to the public in accordance with the original intention.**

Equation of exchange

MV = PQ. The quantity of money times its velocity equals the quantity of goods and services produced times their prices.

A busy dollar working 50 times a year can do the same money-work as 50 one-dollar bills that work only once a year. In one case, the velocity of money, *V,* is 50, in the other, it is 1.

Adding the velocity of money completes the ***equation of exchange.***

$$MV = PQ$$

*Source: D. H. Robertson, *Money,* (New York: Harcourt, 1922), p. 35. The original text referred to the famous Derby at Epsom, in England, not the Kentucky Derby, and to shillings, not dollars. The Derby and currency were changed here to make the illustration more familiar to the reader.

Consider once more the apple economy. If Q = 5,000 apples, M = \$10,000, and V = 8, the price level P skyrockets to \$16. The velocity of money, as you see, can be important.

The equation of exchange includes the velocity of money, which represents how often the money supply is spent and re-spent in a given period of time.

Although the equation of exchange seems to be a matter of simple arithmetic, economists are nowhere near agreeing on how changes in M, for example, *really* affect P. Some economists, notably Keynesians, believe that if a change in M occurs, it may not only affect P, as we see in the equation of exchange, but also and at the same time affect Q. If that happens, then the one-to-one correspondence between M and P in the equation of exchange is lost. They also see an interdependence between changes in M and changes in V. That is, changes in M cause changes in V. On the other hand, classical economists disagree, arguing that the velocity of money is unchanging, regardless of changes in M, P, or Q.

Classical and Keynesian economists offer two opposing views on the characteristics of V and on the interdependence of the variables in the equation of exchange. Their differing views lead to differing theories concerning the relationship between money and prices.

The Classical View

The classical view of the relationships among money, real GDP, money velocity, and prices fits into the broader picture that classical economists present of an economy in equilibrium at full-employment GDP. Real GDP—Q in the equation of exchange—depends upon the amount of resources available in the economy. If the amounts of resources do not change—a condition supposed by classical economists for short run equilibrium—Q does not change. Prices, on the other hand, are flexible in the classical world, adjusting the value of the goods produced, Q, to the money supply.

What about the velocity of money? According to classical economists, the velocity of money is fairly stable. After all, they argue, people tend not to change the way they use money.

Think about it. How much money we need to purchase the goods and services we buy in a year depends, in part, on how often we get paid during the year. Suppose Kirsten Gentry earns \$52,000 annually and is paid that \$52,000 in one lump sum, say, on December 31. That is, there is only one payday per year. She would use that \$52,000 a dollar at a time throughout the year to buy goods and services. On the other hand, suppose there were 52 paydays per year so that she received \$1,000 weekly. In that case, the same \$1,000, used over and over in each of the 52 weeks, could buy the same \$52,000 worth of goods and services. That is to say, \$1,000 M, with V = 52 can transact for as many goods and services as \$52,000 M with V = 1. As long as the number of paydays is an established practice in the economy, velocity remains fairly stable.

Our spending and saving behavior is habitual as well. As impulsive as we think we are, the truth of the matter is that we use approximately the same quantity of money week after week to buy our goods and services, and even on exceptional occasions such as vacations and holidays, our spending is fairly conventional.

Quantity theory of money

$P = MV/Q$. The equation specifying the direct relationship between the money supply and prices.

Classical economists convert the equation of exchange into a **quantity theory of money.** Since they believe that both V and Q are constants for an economy in short-run equilibrium, the equation of exchange becomes a theory in which the *quantity of money explains prices*.

$$P = \frac{MV}{Q}$$

Causality is clear and mechanical. If M increases, then because V and Q are constants, the price level, P, increases.

For the sake of argument, even if the economy tends to be at full employment, there is nothing that compels us to believe that Q must remain constant *in the long run*. In fact, there's good reason to suppose it doesn't. Why not? Because in the long run, the supply of resources available, such as labor and capital, increases. And since classical economists believe that the economy operates at full employment (always using its available resources and the most advanced technology), then with more resources used, more Q is produced.

To illustrate the classical view of the relationship between money and prices in the long run, let's suppose that the economy's resource supply increases by 5 percent every year.

The simple proportionality between money and prices supposed in short-run equilibrium breaks down. With more resources available every year, full-employment Q increases every year by 5 percent. How does that full-employment Q growth affect prices? If the money supply M grows by 5 percent every year as well, then with velocity constant, the price level remains unchanged year after year. If, on the other hand, M grows at 7 percent while Q grows at 5 percent, then the price level, P, increases by 2 percent (inflation) every year. And if M's growth is lower than Q's, say, 3 percent compared to Q's 5 percent, then P falls (deflation) by 2 percent. Classical economists saw the quantity theory of money as proof that money cannot influence how much we produce, but does influence the prices of the goods we produce.

Monetarism: A Modification of the Classical View

The idea that money velocity is constant was challenged in the 1970s by economists *within the classical tradition*. Their reformulation of the classical view on money became known as monetarism.

In a sense, the monetarist view of money was an attempt to rescue the classical view from the onslaught of empirical evidence that showed that M1 money velocity was anything but constant. Look at Figure 2.

As you see, M1 money velocity is quite erratic. Its long-run trend was downward until the 1950s, then reversed and rose steadily until the mid 1980s. Since then, it has been even more erratic.

Monetarists accept the idea that velocity is not constant, nonetheless they believe that it is still highly predictable, well-behaved, and independent of money supply.

They explain the steady increase in money velocity since the 1950s by pointing to the technological changes associated with the transactions demand for money. For example, the use of computers speeds up the banking process. Also, the widespread use of credit cards allows people to buy and sell goods and services with less cash and lower bank balances relative to nominal GDP. The result: higher money velocity. Since technologies in money and banking are still developing and pay periods are becoming more frequent, monetarists believe it is reasonable to predict increases in velocity over time, and for the short run at least, they believe the increases will be well-behaved.

FIGURE 2 **Historical Record of Money Velocity**

Until World War II, the velocity of money drifted downward, with some short-run upward swings, from approximately 4.0 in the 1920s to 2.0 in 1945. The trend reverses dramatically thereafter, increasing, with some short-run downturns, from 2.0 in 1945 to approximately 6.5 in 1990.

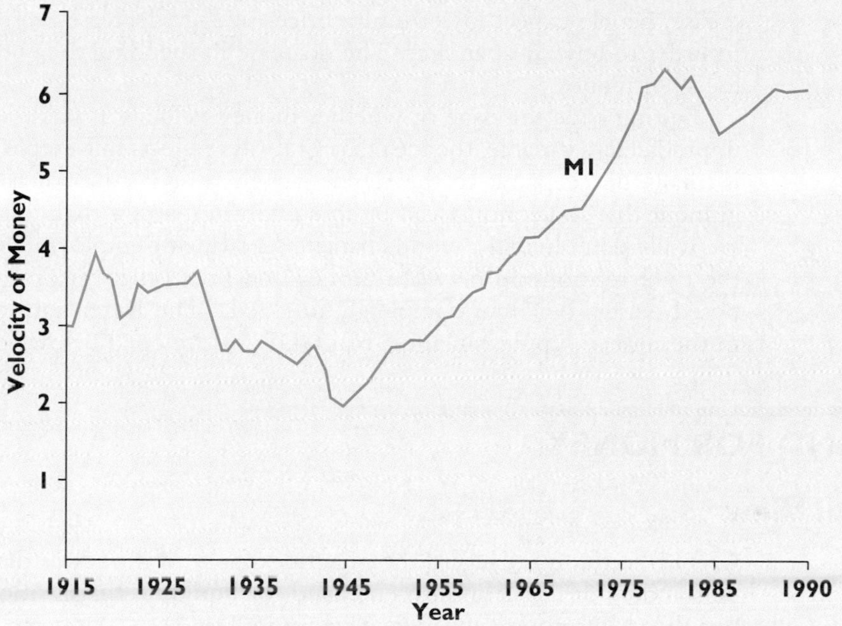

Sources: *Long-Term Economic Growth, 1860–1970* (Washington, D.C.: U.S. Government Printing Office, 1973); and *Economic Report of the President* (Washington, D.C.: U.S. Government Printing Office, January 1993).

Monetarists believe that even though velocity isn't constant, it is predictable.

If money velocity is known—that is, relatively stable and highly predictable—and if Q is at full-employment real GDP, then the quantity theory of money—expressing the relationship between money and prices—remains intact. In the end the monetarist version of the quantity theory of money still leads to the same classical conclusion: Although money cannot influence how much we produce, it does influence the prices of the goods and services we produce.

The Keynesian View

Keynesians believe that an increase in the money supply can lower interest rates, increase investment, and increase real GDP because the economy is not always at full employment.

Keynesians offer a different view of the quantity theory of money. They reject the idea that V is either stable or predictable and that Q always reflects full-employment GDP. If they're right—that is, if V is neither stable nor predictable and if Q is not necessarily at full employment—then changes in the supply of money may end up affecting more than prices. They may affect Q as well.

Consider first how Keynesians view the velocity of money. They do not challenge the classical or monetarist view that payment schedules and patterns of spending and saving are basically stable. What they do challenge, however, is that these are the principal determinants of money velocity.

What is missing? To Keynesians, velocity is also affected by changes in people's *expectations*. A price increase, for example, may lead to an increase in money velocity. Why? Because people typically expect past performance to continue into the future. If prices increase, people will expect them to increase again, that is, they expect future prices will be higher. In that case, people will buy more now to avoid the higher future prices. In other words, price increases today can change spending habits today. To accommodate the increase in spending, the velocity of money increases.

What reduces velocity? The same logic is applied. This time, if prices decrease, people expect lower future prices so they decrease present consumption in order to buy cheaper later. The decrease in spending today decreases the velocity of money.

Setting aside the issue of whether money velocity is stable or predictable or unpredictably variable, the idea that Q always reflects full-employment real GDP is totally unacceptable to the Keynesians because it contradicts their central argument that an economy can be in equilibrium at less than full employment. If we really don't live in a world characterized by full-employment real GDP, then the tight relationship between money and prices that classical economists supposed existed becomes completely unglued. (The Keynesian idea that changes in the money supply can affect real GDP is developed below.)

THE DEMAND FOR MONEY

The Classical View

Classical economists regard the quantity theory of money as the key to our understanding of the economy's demand for liquidity, that is, money. The quantity theory of money equation is transposed to

$$M = \frac{PQ}{V}$$

Since PQ is nominal GDP (the quantity of goods produced multiplied by the price level) and since classical economists assume V is constant, the quantity of money demanded by households and businesses to transact the buying and selling of the goods produced is derived by dividing nominal GDP by the velocity of money. That's it!

Transactions demand for money

The quantity of money demanded by households and businesses to transact its buying and selling of goods and services.

This **transactions demand for money** is the only motive classical economists see for anyone demanding money. If either the price level or real GDP increase, more money would be demanded to meet the needs of increasing nominal GDP.

The Keynesian View

Keynesian economists see a more complex set of motives influencing the demand for money. They identify three principal motives for demanding money. These are the transactions motive (which classical and monetarist economists accept as the only motive), the precautionary motive, and the speculative motive.

THE TRANSACTIONS MOTIVE

Keynesians, like monetarists, believe in a transactions demand for money.

People hold money (liquid assets) to transact purchases they expect to make. That's fairly classical, but Keynesians explain it somewhat differently. To Keynesians, people prefer to avoid the inconvenience of having to convert their nonmoney assets into money every time they decide to buy something. Can you imagine the headache converting nonmoney assets into money every time you buy a tuna sandwich? People learn, then, to hold a specific quantity of money for the groceries, theater tickets, gasoline, clothes, film, and other items they habitually purchase. The quantity of money demanded to satisfy its transactions needs increases with the level of nominal GDP. The more people buy, the more money they need to make the purchases.

But money can also be held as a store of value not used in day-to-day transactions. And there's the difference. The money that people choose to hold in this form, unlike money serving transaction needs, is "couch-potato" money, idle money, or inactive money.

This distinction between active and inactive money is central to how Keynesians view the demand for money. It explains why they do not see, as classical economists do, a one-to-one correspondence between changes in PQ and changes in the transactions demand for money. Keynesians do not assume that the velocity of money is constant, well-behaved, or predictable. Instead, they believe that the *transactions demand for money influences the velocity of money.* Their reasoning? Look at the quantity theory of money equation once again.

$$MV = PQ$$

Let's start with a fixed money supply in the economy. Suppose producers decide to increase investment. Consider the effect of that increase on the right-hand side of the equation, PQ. The increased investment (raising aggregate expenditures) stimulates the economy to higher real GDP (that is, higher Q) so that PQ increases.

Now consider the left-hand side of the equation. That increase in PQ generates an increase in the transactions demand for money. After all, as more economic activity occurs, more money is needed to transact the increased activity. But if the supply of money is fixed, how can people get the additional money they need?

The answer is that with the money supply fixed, the increase in the transactions demand for money can only be satisfied by increases in the velocity of money. The fixed supply of money works harder every day (turns over at a faster rate). Simply put: If MV increases to accommodate the increase in PQ—keeping $MV = PQ$—*and if M is fixed,* then it is V that increases. But how do you get the velocity of money to increase?

Here's where the difference between active and inactive money comes in. The people who demand more money to transact business go to money markets to borrow. Visualize the market. The demand curve for money shifts upward, the money supply curve remains fixed. What happens? The interest rate increases. Now people who have been holding onto the couch-potato part of the money supply are attracted by the higher interest rate and lend the couch-potato money to the demanders. That part of the fixed supply of money has changed hands and is now actively transacting business. Although the total money supply remains unchanged, its velocity has increased.

THE PRECAUTIONARY MOTIVE

People also hold money as insurance against *unexpected* needs. Let's suppose Joel Spencer plans a trip that he estimates will cost \$1,000. Is that the quantity of money he will take along? Most unlikely. Joel will probably add another \$100 *just in case.* More cautious people may add more. The motive? Precautionary.

And what about unexpected problems? A smashed fender needs repair. A broken furnace. A slipped disc that keeps you out of work for three weeks. A pink slip in your pay envelope. All is possible and, at *some* time, most probable. People hold money, giving up interest-bearing accounts, just to cover these eventualities.

THE SPECULATIVE MOTIVE

As the interest rate decreases, the quantity of money people will hold increases.

Another major consideration for demanding money is the speculative motive. As we saw, people have the choice of holding their assets either in the form of active money or nonactive money such as interest-bearing notes, bills, and CDs. How much they choose to hold of each depends on the interest rate. Look at Figure 3.

Why is the speculative demand curve for money downward-sloping? If the rate of interest were high, say, i_1, people would choose to hold only M_1 and use the rest of their money to buy interest-bearing assets. After all, the opportunity cost of holding more than M_1 is the relatively high i_1 interest rate.

But if the interest rate fell to i_2, people would most likely shift out of holding interest-bearing assets into holding money. In Figure 3, the quantity of money demanded increases to M_2. Why? Because the opportunity costs associated with holding money and holding interest-paying assets have changed. Holding money now costs less because the interest-to-be-earned is less. Holding the now lower-interest-yielding assets increases the cost of not having the money immediately available to take advantage of any unforeseen good prospect that may arise suddenly. That is to say, when interest rates fall, people feel more inclined to *speculate*. According to Keynesians, then, the demand for money is not just to satisfy people's transactions and precautionary needs, but to satisfy their speculative proclivities as well.

FIGURE 3
The Speculative Demand For Money
When the interest rate falls, people shift out of interest-yielding asset holdings into holding money. And because the interest rate falls, the opportunity cost of holding money also falls. Why favor money? The primary reason is speculation. The interest rate could either continue to fall, remain unchanged, or rise. In the expectation that it may rise, holding money (instead of nonmoney assets) puts moneyholders in a better position to take advantage of any future rise in the interest rate.

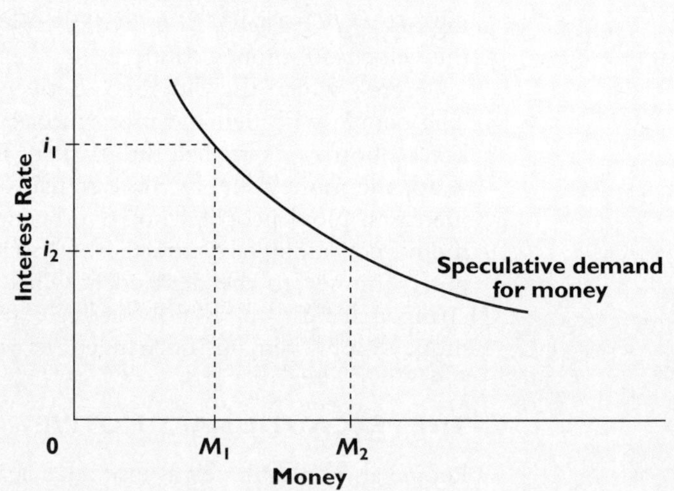

FIGURE 4 **Money Affects Real GDP**

Follow the sequence of events through panels *a*, *b*, and *c*. When the money supply increases from MS_1 to MS_2, the interest rate falls from i_1 to i_2, which increases the quantity demanded of investment goods from I_1 to I_2. This increase in investment shifts aggregate demand from AD_1 to AD_2. The result is an increase in real GDP from GDP_1 to GDP_2.

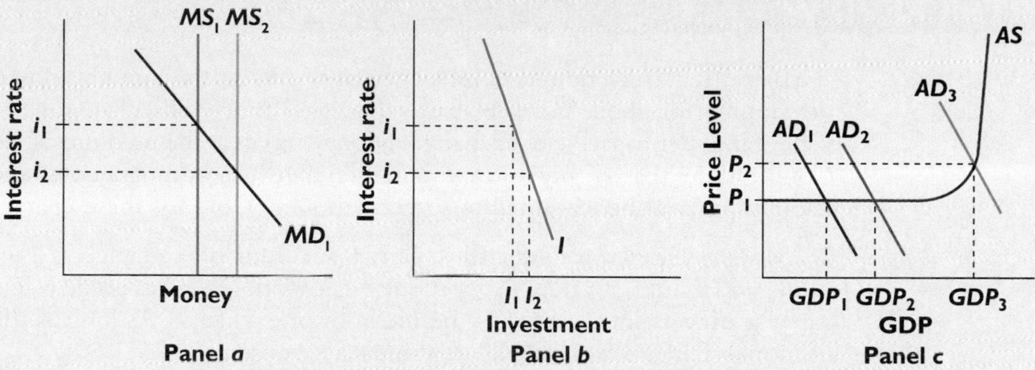

MONEY AFFECTS REAL GDP

We are now prepared to explain why Keynesians believe money affects real GDP. Look at Figure 4.

Suppose the money supply increases from MS_1 to MS_2. (The demand curve is assumed to be MD_1.) The effect of that increase lowers the equilibrium interest rate from i_1 to i_2, as shown in panel *a*. The fall in the interest rate increases the investment spending from I_1 to I_2, which is shown in panel *b*. (Note the steepness of the investment curve. It reflects the Keynesian view that changes in investment are relatively insensitive to changes in the interest rate.) Since investment is an integral part of aggregate demand, the increase in investment shifts the aggregate demand curve to the right, from AD_1 to AD_2, shown in panel *c*. And because Keynesians believe that the economy typically operates below the full-employment level, the shift in aggregate demand raises real GDP from GDP_1 to GDP_2.

What about the price level? If the shift in aggregate demand and the consequent change in real GDP occur along the horizontal segment of the aggregate supply curve—and that's how Keynesians view the world—the price level remains unaffected by changes in money supply. A different outcome would occur, however, if the economy were operating along the upward-sloping segment of the aggregate supply curve. In this situation, an increase in the money supply that raises aggregate demand to AD_3 raises both real GDP and prices.

The cause-and-effect sequence depicted in panels *a*, *b*, and *c* can be made to show what happens when the money supply falls. Interest rates (in panel *b*) increase, which reduces the quantity of investment undertaken in the economy. The fall in investment, in turn, shifts the aggregate demand curve to the left, thus decreasing real GDP.

How do classical and monetarists view the linkages shown in Figure 4? They believe that the investment curve (in panel *b*) is much more sensitive to changes in the interest rate than Keynesians suppose. Since they also believe that the economy operates at full-employment real GDP—that is, along the vertical segment of *AS*—any increase in the money supply (which lowers the interest rate and raises the quantity of investment and consequently aggregate demand), can only end up raising the price level. Nominal GDP increases, but real GDP does not.

CHAPTER REVIEW

1. Barter requires a double coincidence of wants. As the number of people and the number of goods increase, barter becomes more difficult. Money was invented in order to facilitate exchange. Money serves as the medium of exchange. Commodities that are durable and portable, divisible, homogeneous, and have a stable supply are better-suited to serve as money. Gold has these characteristics.

2. Money serves three functions. It is a medium of exchange, a measure of value, and a store of value. Paper money can work as well as gold, as long as the paper is universally accepted as the medium of exchange. As long as the supply of money remains fairly stable, its value stays constant.

3. Money is a liquid asset because it can be exchanged easily for other assets. The money supply is arranged into different component parts depending on liquidity. M1 is the most liquid form of money—cash and checking accounts. M2 includes savings accounts, certificates of deposit, money market mutual funds, money market deposit accounts, NOW accounts, share-draft accounts, and ATS accounts. M3 includes less-liquid forms of money.

4. In a breakdown of the nearly 5 trillion dollars in the money supply, currency forms a very small part. Most of our money supply is in savings accounts.

5. Classical economists believe that the demand for money is tied to transactions demand. If output is constant at full employment and velocity is constant, then the transactions demand for money depends on the price level. Moreover, the price level depends on the quantity of money in circulation when full employment exists and velocity is constant. These relationships are given by the equation of exchange, $MV = PY$.

6. Monetarists use the equation of exchange with the knowledge that velocity can be variable. They believe that $MV = PY$ can be a good tool for analysis because velocity is predictable even though it is variable.

7. Keynesians have a more complex view of money demand. They believe that money demand reflects the transactions demand for money plus the precautionary motive and the speculative motive.

8. Keynesians believe that money can affect the level of real GDP. An increase in the money supply will cause a decrease in interest rates which leads to an increase in investment and a multiplier increase in real GDP. Monetarists believe that increases in the money supply cause prices to increase because the economy is continuously at full employment.

KEY TERMS

Barter
Money
Fiat money
Currency
Liquidity
Money supply

M1 money supply
M2 money supply
M3 money supply
Velocity of money
Equation of exchange
Quantity theory of money
Transactions demand for money

QUESTIONS

1. Why does barter exchange become increasingly less useful as the number of people engaged in exchange increases?

2. What are the essential properties of money?

3. What are the three principal functions of money?

4. What are the principal components of M1, M2, and M3 money?

5. What is the relationship between money and liquidity?

6. What is "near money"?

7. Are Visa and MasterCard balances part of M1? Why or why not?

8. What is money velocity?

9. How do the classical and Keynesian views of money velocity differ?

10. In the classical view, what is the principal reason for people demanding money?

11. In the Keynesian view, what are the principal reasons for people demanding money?

12. Why does the quantity demanded of interest-yielding assets fall and the quantity demanded of money increase when the interest rate falls?

13. Explain graphically how the interest rate affects the Keynesian demand for money.

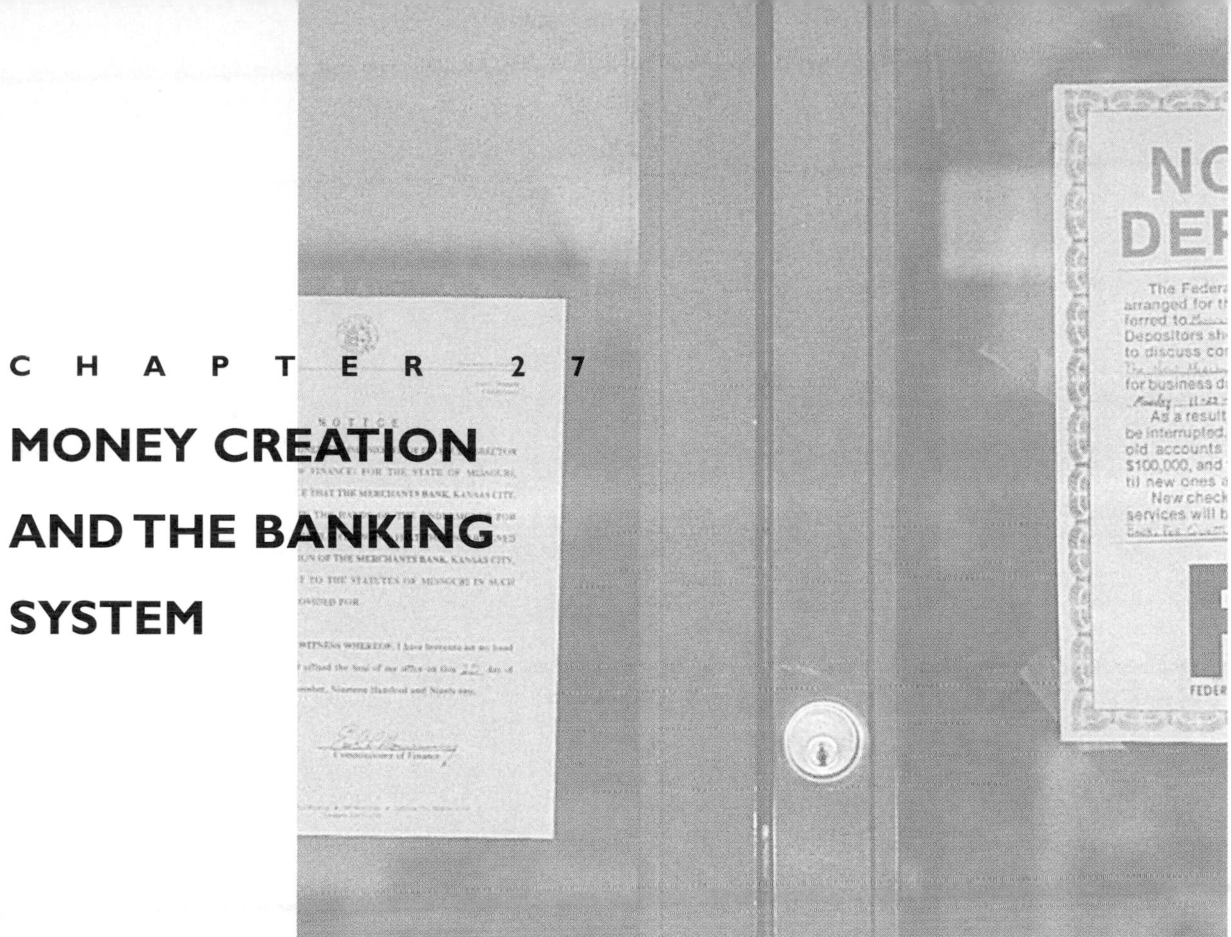

CHAPTER 27

MONEY CREATION AND THE BANKING SYSTEM

CHAPTER PREVIEW

By now we have a good idea of the characteristics and functions of money and some of the theories of the demand for money. This chapter focuses on the supply of money. You will learn how the banking system can take new deposits of money and actually create more money from these deposits. The banking system can destroy money too. Money creation and money destruction shift the money supply function and cause changes in the interest rate. Interest rate changes cause changes in the level of investment. Thus, you will come to appreciate the critical role that the banking system plays in determining the level of investment and the level of national income.

After studying this chapter, you should be able to:

- Explain the concept of a fractional reserve banking system.
- Describe how banks can create money by making loans based on new deposits.
- Calculate the amount of money a banking system can create given a new deposit and the legal reserve requirement.
- Give reasons why banks might keep excess reserves.
- Explain how the money supply shrinks when loans are repaid.

- Discuss the reasons for bank failures.
- Justify the need for deposit insurance and bank audits.
- Recount events associated with a rise in bank and savings and loan association failures during the 1980s.
- Show how a central bank can help to stabilize the banking system and manipulate the money supply to dampen the business cycle.

If you don't believe in magic, this chapter may make you change your mind. The magic performed is the creation of money. Like pulling a rabbit out of a hat, money seemingly appears from nowhere. Not only does the magician make money appear, but the money created ends up in the hands of those who have reason to use it.

THE FRACTIONAL RESERVE SYSTEM

Under normal circumstances a bank need not keep all of its deposits on hand as reserves in order to meet the daily demands of depositors for cash.

Let's start our analysis of money creation with a simple tale. Imagine a premodern economy where gold is used to satisfy the people's transactions and precautionary money needs. But here, life can be quite "nasty, brutish, and short," particularly for those holding large quantities of gold. People in this economy-without-banks have a problem. Where do they put their gold for safekeeping?

Amar Bazazz is the answer. Why him? He owns a deep cave and an enormous, unfriendly dog. He uses the cave as a depository where people can keep their gold. With the dog pacing the cave's entrance, nobody would dare try their luck.

Amar charges depositors 10 percent per year for guarding the gold they deposit in his cave. They regard that percentage as an insurance premium.

Sounds uneventful so far, but the plot thickens. What people don't know is that Amar is addicted to gambling. Every night, he takes some of the deposited gold to the casino in the next town and loses it all in a matter of hours. In fact, he gambles away fully 80 percent of the deposits in the cave.

But what he discovers, to his shock, is that it doesn't really matter. Nobody is the wiser! Everybody thinks their gold is in the cave, and when they come to withdraw some of it—few withdrew all, and certainly not everyone at once—*enough* is always there. Gold is gold. Perfectly homogeneous. That's the way Amar Bazazz makes his living, earning 10 percent per year on gold that isn't there.

Let's now suppose that in the twilight of his life, Amar confesses his gambling to his only son who, although shocked at the disclosure, is quick enough to see the possibilities. Inheriting the cave and the dog's ferocious pups, he goes into his father's gold-keeping business.

Amar's son doesn't gamble in casinos. Instead, he takes the deposited gold to other towns and gambles there on what he thinks are sound investments. In this way he earns money both by safekeeping the gold *and* on the investments. To get his hands on more gold, he lowers the security rate he charges to 5 percent. People are so moved by his generosity, they elect him mayor.

He is a smart businessman. He holds to a sound fractional reserve rule. He always keeps 20 percent of the deposited gold in reserve to handle the transactions demands of the depositors. That, of course, still leaves 80 percent free for investments. He even hires people to locate good investment projects for him.

To encourage growth in his investment business, he not only cuts the security rate to zero but offers to pay his depositors a small percentage to deposit their gold in his cave. For fear they would think him insane, he comes clean! He tells them about his father's gambling, his own investments, and explains how the security of their deposits is guaranteed in a **fractional reserve system.**

Fractional reserve system

A banking system that provides people immediate access to their deposits, but that allows banks to hold only a fraction of those deposits in reserve.

Should the depositors panic? Should they be concerned that only 20 percent of their gold deposits are in reserve? Not at all. They accept his assurance that they can get their entire deposit returned upon demand. Some even refer to their deposits as *demand deposits*. It works. Now they actually draw interest on their entire deposit although only a fraction of their gold is being safely kept in the cave.

Who said life can't be wonderful? The tale may be simple, *but this is essentially the basis of all modern banking.*

HOW BANKS CREATE MONEY

Let's update the story to a modern economy. Suppose we want to go into the banking business. What would it take? What would we do? Why do it?

The last question is easy. The reason people go into banking is to earn profit. Bankers are like barbers, automobile makers, and coal mining entrepreneurs. They cut hair, make automobiles, and dig coal because that's how they make a profit. Bankers hope to make a profit by borrowing your money at low prices and lending it to others at higher prices. That's all there is to it. Nothing really complicated.

Well, let's do it! Let's set up the Paris First National Bank (PFN) in downtown Paris, Texas. We pick out an imposing, gray stone building. We hire cashiers, loan officers, and other staff personnel. We're ready.

Attracting Depositors

We run a series of radio and television commercials inviting depositors to bank at PFN. The commercials also invite people looking for bank loans to come by.

Let's suppose Jeff Kaufman decides to bank with PFN. He opens a checking account by depositing $1,000. He knows, of course, that he can withdraw that sum of M1 money any time he pleases. It is, after all, a demand deposit.

Balance sheet

The bank's statement of liabilities (what it owes) and assets (what it owns).

PFN's **balance sheet**—a summary of the bank's assets (what it has) and liabilities (what it owes)—after this initial $1,000 demand deposit is:

Paris First National Bank

Assets		Liabilities	
Reserves	$1,000	Demand Deposits	$1,000

Look at PFN's assets and liabilities. Its assets, held by the bank as reserves in its vaults, are $1,000. What does that mean? Simply that it has Jeff Kaufman's $1,000 in cash. Is the bank, then, $1,000 richer than it was before Kaufman came in? No. Although it has the $1,000, it also has a $1,000 obligation to give the money back to Kaufman. In fact, Kaufman can demand the money back any time he pleases. The bank may *use* the money, but it's not theirs. It's Jeff

This couple may not know it, but they are in the process of *creating* money. By taking out a $200,000 loan to start up a gourmet ice-cream business, they create new jobs that in turn create new incomes and new demand deposits. These demand deposits are new M1 money.

Kaufman's. In fact, if you ask Kaufman how much money he has, he would tell you. It's $1,000.

Making Loans

Demand deposits are only half of PFN's business. Loans are the other. PFN makes a profit only on the loans it provides, not on its deposits. So PFN is now willing and able to lend money, but it can only do so if borrowers show up. And they do. Some borrow to finance consumption purchases, such as automobiles and houses, others borrow to finance business investments.

Let's suppose Matt Taylor approaches the bank with an idea of setting up a Japanese food carry-out. His presentation to the bank is impressive. He explains that there are many pizza, taco, hot dog and hamburger places in town, as well as Chinese restaurants. But no one offers Japanese food. He has also done his homework. He shows that he could renovate a vacated Pizza Hut for $800 and make a 25 percent profit in the first year. What he needs is an $800 loan.

PFN likes the idea and loans Matt $800 at an interest rate of 10 percent. In fact, $800 is the maximum it can loan because, by law, banks are required to keep 20 percent of their demand deposits on reserve, either in their own vaults or at the Federal Reserve Bank. The Federal Reserve decides what the **legal reserve requirement** will be. The 20 percent legal reserve requirement in this story is only hypothetical. In fact, the legal reserve requirement that the Fed actually picks for our economy is typically less than 10 percent. (We'll say more about the Federal Reserve later.)

Legal reserve requirement

Percent of demand deposits banks and other financial intermediaries are required to keep in cash reserves.

Let's look at PFN's balance sheet after the loan is made.

Paris First National Bank

Assets		Liabilities	
Reserves	$1,000	Demand Deposits	$1,800
Loans	800		

Note what happens to the bank's assets. They change from $1,000 in reserves to $1,800 in reserves and loans. By agreeing to loan Matt $800, PFN has a new asset in the form of Matt's signed $800 IOU to the bank (shown as the $800 loan in the asset column of the balance sheet). What does PFN give Matt Taylor in return? The bank opens an $800 demand deposit for him. Note what's hap-

ADDED PERSPECTIVE

Banker to the Poor

Bernardo Santa Maria is an unlikely banker. He does not own a blue suit, and he refuses to wear a tie. Sporting a threadbare cardigan and neatly pressed corduroy pants, Santa Maria glances at his datebook before setting off for early-morning business meetings. Trudging uphill through the narrow streets of the Mercado Lanza, one of the busiest outdoor markets in Bolivia's capital, La Paz, he pauses for breath before greeting a group of ragged street vendors, his most valued and trusted clients.

Santa Maria works for Banco Solidario SA (BancoSol), Latin America's first private, profit-oriented commercial bank for the poor. His 600 clients include such microentrepreneurs as self-employed artisans and Aymara Indian women who sell candy bars and batteries on just about every street corner. "And they don't like to see their bankers in ties and business suits. It makes them frightened and too deferential," says the 38-year-old banker, who is known as Don Bernardo or *joven* (young man) by his clients in the market.

For five years, Santa Maria was a loan officer for Prodema, a Bolivian program supported by the United States Agency for International Development and other groups. Prodema, whose full name is Micro-Enterprise Promotion and Development Assistance, was the first organization in Bolivia to lend small sums of money to tiny enterprises run by shantytown dwellers.

The heads of Prodema believed that the only way to operate their project on a long-term basis was to turn it into a profit-making institution. In January, a group of Bolivian and foreign investors representing private foundations and aid agencies opened BancoSol, which will take over Prodema's loan program.

Depending on the size of their enterprises, microentrepreneurs can apply for loans of $25 to $300 to buy materials or hire employees. Supporters of the bank say that it represents a revolution in Third World development schemes, which generally work on a nonprofit, charitable basis.

"Conventional aid programs often collapse when the donations dry up, and that's why it's getting harder and harder to convince people to donate money for projects in the developing world," said Canadian businessman Martin Connell, who is on the bank's board of directors and who recently invested in the project.

Critics charge that the 42 percent annual interest rate set by BancoSol is too high and threatens the livelihood of borrowers. Santa Maria says that the rate is as high as it is because small loans mean large overhead costs.

His clients prefer the BancoSol system to other loan programs because BancoSol makes its loans in local currency. Many nonprofit lenders make their loans in U.S. dollars, and if inflation goes up or there is a devaluation in the Bolivian currency, the borrower is forced to repay the loan at the higher dollar rate.

"This bank is all about compromise," said Pancho Otero, BancoSol's managing director. "In this venture, we have the do-gooder social scientists, who don't wear ties, meeting the do-gooder businessmen, who do wear ties. And the chemistry is wonderful, because they are working together to alleviate poverty."

Every Monday morning, Santa Maria's clients line up to make their weekly payments. Prodema has had a 99 percent repayment rate in the past five years. Victor Luna, who operates a small photo lab and hat shop in a makeshift stall, has received seven loans from BancoSol in four years. The first, around $50, enabled him to double his business. Luna, whose loans now average $250 twice a year, says that he would rather pay the BancoSol interest rate than the 10 percent a day charged by loan sharks and co-signers.

Santa Maria, a former schoolteacher and sociologist, says that BancoSol's system works because it resembles the *pasanaka,* a traditional loan system based on group-repayment schemes. Borrowers are divided into "solidarity" groups to help insure that their loans are repaid. Francisca Lujanda Llanes, who sells tomatoes in the Lanza market, belongs to the Cochalitas solidarity group, so called because it is made up of Quechua women from Cochabamba. Women currently make up more than 70 percent of BancoSol's clients. When one of the six women in the group cannot make a weekly payment, the others chip in. "We lend to save the group," says Llanes, "If someone can't make a payment, then we all lose."

Discussion

Why would the poor pay a 42 percent annual rate of interest to BancoSol and think they're getting a good deal?

Source: *Globe and Mail* (Toronto), February 20, 1992. Reprinted with permission.

pened. *The loan creates the demand deposit.* There is now $1,800 in demand deposits, up from $1,000 before the loan. That is, loans create money.

Does the bank give Matt the $800 in currency? Not likely. Instead, it gives Matt a checkbook—like yours—and the right to write checks up to the amount of the $800 demand deposit. It really makes no difference to Matt whether he has checking privileges or currency. It's still M1 money. He can just as easily write checks as use currency to buy labor and materials needed for the carry-out.

The Interaction of Deposits and Loans

Suppose Matt Taylor hires Charlie Dold, a skilled carpenter, who can do the work for $800. Dold completes the project in a week. Taylor, satisfied with the job, writes out a check to Dold for $800. Dold accepts the check as his week's income and deposits it in *his* bank, Paris Second National (PSN).

Let's see what happens to the balance sheet at the Paris First National Bank after the check clears.

Paris First National Bank

Assets		Liabilities	
Reserves	$200	Demand Deposits	$1,000
Loans	800		

The $800 check to Charlie Dold wipes out Matt's $800 demand deposit at PFN. The bank's total demand deposits fall from $1,800 to $1,000. At the same time, PFN's reserves fall from $1,000 to $200. After all, PFN paid out $800 to the Paris Second National Bank.

Let's now look at PSN's balance sheet.

Paris Second National Bank

Assets		Liabilities	
Reserves	$800	Demand Deposits	$800

Dold's $800 demand deposit creates an $800 asset and an $800 liability for PSN. Imagine a conversation between Jeff Kaufman and Charlie Dold. Dold could ask, "How much money do you have?" Jeff would respond, "$1,000 in Paris First National. What about yourself?" Charlie would reply, "$800, in Paris Second National." They are both right. *What was once $1,000 in Kaufman's pocket now becomes, through the banking process, $1,800 of money in the form of demand deposits.*

Of course, PSN doesn't sit on Dold's $800 demand deposit. It is eager to loan. Let's now suppose Laura Spears, a city park district director, wants to refinish her old 1936 Packard. She plans to sell it on the antique car market and needs a loan of $640 to rebuild the engine and transmission. She's sure she can make a 50 percent profit on the car, and after checking out her car and the market, PSN agrees. Laura Spears gets the loan. Let's look at PSN's revised balance sheet, right after the loan has been credited to Laura's checking account.

Paris Second National Bank

Assets		Liabilities	
Reserves	$800	Demand Deposits	$1,440
Loans	640		

The two depositors in PSN are Charlie Dold (with $800) and now Laura Spears (with a new account set up in her name for $640 which is the amount of her loan). *Remember, the loan creates the new demand deposit.* Let's suppose Spears hires Balty Deley, a mechanic with a passion for classic automobiles, to rebuild the engine and transmission for the agreed $640. He is paid with a PSN check, which he promptly deposits in his bank, the Paris Third National (PTN).

Once Laura writes a check to Balty for $640 and the check clears PSN, her demand deposit at PSN is wiped out. The bank's new balance sheet now looks like this.

Paris Second National Bank

Assets		**Liabilities**	
Reserves	$160	Demand Deposits	$800
Loans	640		

Look at its assets. Reserves are reduced from $800 to $160 (it paid out $640, the amount of Laura's check) and has $640 in loans. *Note:* Its $160 in reserves is 20 percent of its $800 demand deposit. In other words, PSN is also completely loaned out. That's precisely what PSN had hoped for. It makes profit on the $640 loan.

What about PTN after Balty deposited Laura's $640 check? Look at its balance sheet.

Paris Third National Bank

Assets		**Liabilities**	
Reserves	$640	Demand Deposits	$640

PTN, too, is now ready and able to loan money. Like other banks, it is obligated to keep at least 20 percent of its demand deposits in reserve, which entitles it to loan out a maximum of $512.

Do you see what's happening throughout the banking system? Kaufman's original $1,000 demand deposit in PFN set in motion a chain reaction of loans and demand deposits that created not only a series of new money but also bank loans that make the creation of real goods, such as carry-out restaurants and rebuilt cars, possible.

What does it take to create money? There are three prerequisites.

Financial intermediaries

Firms that accept deposits from savers and use those deposits to make loans to borrowers.

First, there must be a fractional reserve system operating within **financial intermediaries,** such as banks, savings and loan associations, or credit unions, that are able to loan out some fraction of their deposits.

Second, there must be people willing to make demand deposits.

Third, there must be borrowers prepared to take out consumption loans or loans to finance investment projects.

Without borrowers like Matt Taylor, Jeff Kaufman's original $1,000 demand deposit in the PFN would remain completely sterile.

Banks create money by turning the reserves they acquire with new deposits into loans. These loans become new deposits for other banks that make more loans. Each set of loans is a fraction of the new deposits acquired, in turn, by the banks.

HOW MUCH MONEY CAN THE BANKING SYSTEM ULTIMATELY CREATE?

Let's add up the creation of money that takes place in the first 10 rounds of our example, from the initial deposit made in the Paris First National Bank through to one placed in the Paris Tenth National Bank.

Total Demand Deposits in the Banking System after 10 Rounds of Deposits and Loans

Bank	Demand Deposits
Paris First National	$1,000.00
Paris Second National	800.00
Paris Third National	640.00
Paris Fourth National	512.00
Paris Fifth National	409.60
Paris Sixth National	327.68
Paris Seventh National	262.14
Paris Eighth National	209.72
Paris Ninth National	167.77
Paris Tenth National	134.22
TOTAL M1	$4,463.13

After 10 rounds, the initial $1,000 deposited by Jeff Kaufman had triggered a series of financial transactions that created an additional $3,463.13 of M1 money. But the process continues. With a new demand deposit of $134.22, the Paris Tenth National can loan out $107.38. As long as there is a sufficient number of people willing to borrow, each demand deposit created by a preceding loan creates the reserves for the succeeding one. With the legal reserve requirement, LRR, set at 20 percent, the *total* amount of money—the initial $1,000 plus all the money potentially created by the banking system—is

$$M = \frac{ID}{LRR}$$

where M is the total demand deposits in the banking system, ID is the initial deposit, and LRR is the legal reserve requirement. When $ID = \$1,000$ and $LRR = 20$ percent, M is $5,000.

$$M = \frac{ID}{LRR} = \frac{\$1,000}{.20} = \$5,000$$

It's a pretty neat system, isn't it? That's why economists marvel at its performance. When you think about it, it's almost magical.

Let's sum up. How is money created? Borrowing creates it, automatically, when the borrower's checking account at a bank is credited as a result of a loan. Why do borrowers demand money? To produce goods and services. So there we have it. The banking system is perfectly synchronized with real world production. As more goods and services are produced, the banking system automatically creates the equivalent money.

POTENTIAL MONEY MULTIPLIER

Of course, the amount of money that is created depends on the legal reserve requirement and upon borrowers *actually* utilizing the maximum permissible loans. If $LRR = 10$ percent, a demand deposit of $1,000 will generate—assuming willing borrowers—an increase in the money supply of $10,000. If LRR increases to 50 percent, the money supply grows by only $2,000.

Another way of describing this process of money creation is by developing

Potential money multiplier

The increase in the money supply that is potentially generated by a change in demand deposits.

the concept of the banking system's **potential money multiplier,** m. It is simply

$$m = \frac{1}{LRR}$$

When *LRR* = 20 percent, the potential money multiplier is 1/0.2 = 5. That is, a new demand deposit of $1,000 placed in any bank can potentially support $5,000 of demand deposits.

LIVING WITH EXCESS RESERVES

Why do we call it a "potential" money multiplier? Because we can't always assume that there will always be sufficient borrowers to take advantage of the available loanable reserves. Suppose Jeff Kaufman deposits $1,000 in PFN, but only $400 is demanded by Matt Taylor. Although PFN is willing and able to loan twice that sum, the potential simply isn't realized. What happens?

Look at PFN's revised balance sheet.

Paris First National Bank

Assets		Liabilities	
Required Reserves	$200	Demand Deposits	$1,000
Excess Reserves	400		
Loans	400		

Kaufman's $1,000 shows up, as before, as the PFN bank's liability. But look at its assets' composition. Although the legally required reserve remains $200, PFN's *actual* reserves are $600. It holds, then, **excess reserves**, reserves in excess of those legally required, of $400.

Excess reserves

The quantity of reserves held by a bank in excess of the legally required amount.

The presence of excess reserves changes how much money the banking system *actually* creates. With PFN now loaning out only $400, the second-round demand deposits in PSN fall to $400. Even if every other bank in the series loans out the maximum permissible, the money created by Kaufman's initial $1,000 deposit shrinks from $4,000 to 400/0.20 = $2,000. Adding Kaufman's own $1,000, the total demand deposits in the banking system are $3,000 instead of $5,000.

Cautious banks may choose to hold excess reserves instead of lending them.

But this $3,000 assumes that no other bank aside from PFN holds excess reserves. That's a strong assumption. If other banks, too, do not loan out the maximum permissible, then the actual demand deposits created in the economy by Kaufman's original $1,000 deposit could be most any sum less than $5,000.

The role played by the borrower in money creation cannot be overstated. *Without someone actually coming into the bank to demand a loan, there is no process of money creation.*

REVERSING THE MONEY CREATION PROCESS

In our example, we have focused on Kaufman's initial $1,000 demand deposit, and for good reason. We were interested in understanding the mechanics of creation and the simplicity of the example was useful.

Obviously, Jeff Kaufman cannot be PFN's only depositor. Let's add 2,000 more depositors. Now look at PFN's new, fully expanded balance sheet.

By raising the legal reserve requirement, the Federal Reserve System forces banks to hold repaid loans as required reserves instead of lending the funds again.

Paris First National Bank

Assets		Liabilities	
Required Reserves	$ 4,000,000	Demand Deposits	$20,000,000
Loans	16,000,000		

PFN is a thriving bank. Deposits are $20 million. Look at its asset position. With the legal reserve requirement at 20 percent, PFN is fully loaned out. The bank has $4 million in required reserves and the remaining $16 million of its assets in outstanding loans.

Why 20 percent? Because, in our illustrative scenario, that's what the Federal Reserve instructs. Let's change the instruction. Let's now suppose that the Federal Reserve increases the legal reserve requirement from 20 to 40 percent. All financial intermediaries—commercial banks, savings and loan associations, and credit unions—are obliged to comply. How would PFN react?

It knows what it has to do. It must raise its reserves from $4 million to $8 million. But how? By converting loans back into reserves. Perhaps the least painful way of converting loans into reserves is to wait until some of them are paid off—every day some of them are being paid off—and instead of loaning them out again, keep them in reserves.

Imagine the bank's loan department at work loaning money and then recovering loans that come due. By redirecting some of this flow, the bank can pull in the reins. In the end, its balance sheet is revised.

Paris First National Bank

Assets		Liabilities	
Required Reserves	$ 8,000,000	Demand Deposits	$20,000,000
Loans	12,000,000		

Nothing, of course, changes in the PFN bank's liabilities. Demand deposits remain at $20 million. But look at its asset position. The bank shifted $4 million out of loans into reserves to comply with Federal Reserve instructions. Its loan position contracted from $16 million to $12 million.

With a potential money multiplier of 5, that's an awful lot of money shrinkage. That is, the Fed's effect on PFN alone reduced the economy's money by $4 million × 5 = $20 million. With 15,000 banks operating in the United States, that's an awful lot of play in the money supply. It makes you appreciate the Fed's awesome power.

WHY BANKS SOMETIMES FAIL

Banks fail when they make a large number of bad loans.

Suppose Matt Taylor's Japanese carry-out restaurant is less than a great success. Because people still prefer hamburgers to Matt's sushi, he is in a mess of trouble. But so, too, is the PFN bank. What seemed at first like a great idea to both Taylor and PFN just didn't work out.

What, then, happens to PFN's $800 loan to Taylor? As much as Taylor would like to, he simply can't repay it. He used the bank's money in an honest effort, but ended up with a lot of unsold sushi and little money. When the carry-out finally closes, the bank can claim its used equipment. And that's about it.

Most likely, the bank survives the Taylor folly. After all, PFN has a diversified loan portfolio and can absorb a loss here and there. In fact, it probably expected something, somewhere, to go afoul. If you were the bank, wouldn't you? Not *everything* works out as planned. That's life.

But what if Taylor's failure was the bank's usual experience—the rule, not the exception? What if too many of PFN's loans to promising business ventures turn out to be not so promising? How many loan defaults can PFN absorb without running into problems of survival itself? Upon occasion, banks do fail.

Any failure is an unhappy event. Everyone associated with the enterprise suffers. Some never recover. But when a bank fails, not only do bank owners and bank staff lose the money they invested in the bank and their jobs, but the people who deposited money in the bank discover they no longer have deposits.

Unfair, isn't it? People who deposit money in banks don't regard themselves as being in the banking business. That was not the intent of their deposit. Yet, *unless they are protected in some way,* they become unsuspecting partners in the bank's financial losses.

Moreover, any bank failure can undermine an entire banking system. Imagine a rumor spreading that a bank just failed completely, wiping out its depositors' money. How secure would you feel about your own bank deposit? After all, what happens to one bank could happen to any other. Could yours be next? How could you protect yourself? You would probably do what everyone else was doing. Run quickly to withdraw your money.

Such a run on the bank creates the very problem it tries to avoid. Obviously, no bank, including your own, can expect to satisfy all deposit withdrawal requests at once, even though it is legally obligated to do so. It keeps less than 100 percent in reserve. The entire banking system could collapse if people lose confidence in its ability to function.

The United States has had bank runs brought about by numerous bank failures. It happened in 1907 and triggered an economic downturn. Then, in March 1933, people panicked and set off a run on the banks that forced President Roosevelt to declare an unprecedented week-long "bank holiday." The bank shutdown was meant to calm the troubled financial waters and to signal that government would come to the people's rescue.

SAFEGUARDING THE SYSTEM

When banks fail and people panic, how can the banking system protect itself from its inherently explosive vulnerability? Is there no way to protect depositors from the frightening consequences of bank failure?

The Federal Deposit Insurance Corporation

Federal Deposit Insurance Corporation (FDIC)

A government insurance agency that provides depositors in FDIC-participating banks 100 percent coverage on their first $100,000 of deposits.

Why not an insurance policy? Why can't banks insure demand deposits just as you insure your automobile? If your automobile disappears, you're covered. Well, if a bank fails and your demand deposits disappear, you're covered as well.

That's precisely what the **FDIC—Federal Deposit Insurance Corporation**—does. It insures all demand deposit accounts up to $100,000 in banks choosing FDIC protection. The protection costs the participating bank an insurance premium that represents only a small percentage of their deposits. It makes sense for depositors and banks. Most everyone, including Jeff Kaufman, can now relax. If PFN goes under, no small depositor is hurt.

ADDED PERSPECTIVE

Federal Deposit Insurance and Moral Hazard

Congress created the Federal Deposit Insurance Corporation in 1933 and followed it up a year later with the Federal Savings and Loan Insurance Corporation. Both corporations were designed to protect depositors from incurring losses in the event of a bank failure. Prior to the creation of these federal deposit corporations, banks had been plagued by capricious, rumor-fed, panic runs on deposits.

In many instances, such runs made prophecies about a bank's insolvency self-fulfilling. Since banks don't typically hold reserves sufficient to meet all their depositors' claims, a sudden burst of withdrawals in any bank by a large number of its depositors might leave the bank short of cash. In an attempt to raise immediate cash to cover depositors' withdrawal demands, the bank might be forced to borrow short term at very high interest rates or even to sell some of its assets at relatively low prices. Both measures can result in substantial losses for the bank. If large enough, the losses can lead to the very bank failure that depositors fear.

The idea of federal deposit insurance was to prevent such a sequence of events from happening. Once people understood that their deposits were safe even if the bank failed, fear of bank failure need no longer lead inexorably to panic withdrawals and bank runs. In this way, federal deposit insurance prevents bank failures.

This attribute of federal deposit insurance seems incontestable. But what proponents for deposit insurance didn't factor into their analysis was the moral hazard that deposit insurance creates. Moral hazard refers to the costs to society that arise from people changing their behavior—sometimes in unanticipated and personally irresponsible ways—in response to agreements, contracts, or legislation that affects them directly.

For example, by insuring depositors against loss, federal deposit insurance reduces the cost to banks of taking risks. People have less reason to worry about the safety of their deposits and as a result, banks have less incentive to avoid high-risk, speculative investment. In other words, federal deposit insurance may actually encourage bank behavior that leads to bank failure. In the end, the costs of moral hazard arising from this kind of personally irresponsible behavior are borne by the deposit insurance corporations, which shift the costs, ultimately, to the unsuspecting public.

Appreciating the applicability of moral hazard costs to deposit insurance, Gerald P. O'Driscoll, Jr., the vice president of the Federal Reserve Bank of Dallas, concluded that, "Deposit insurance is a major culprit in the current wave of bank failures."

Federal deposit insurance appears to be, then, a dual-edged sword. It injects a degree of stability in the banking system because it prevents bank runs based on unfounded fears. At the same time, it gives banks a greater incentive to operate in ways that we all need to worry about.

Discussion

The FDIC was created to reduce the risks of banking. Yet, it may end up actually increasing that risk. Explain why.

Source: *The Margin*, September/October 1989.

The FDIC, which is a government-owned corporation, was created in 1933, too late for the tens of thousands of people who had been financially wiped out by bank failures in the Great Depression. Today, bank failures still occur, but their sting has been localized and most of the depositors are compensated.

Bank Audits and Examinations

But why "close the barn door *after* the horse escapes"? While the FDIC is the insuring institution that protects depositors against bank failure, why allow a financially unsound bank to get into trouble in the first place?

Bank audits and examinations are designed to prevent bank failure. The task of auditing and examining falls upon the FDIC, which regularly evaluates bank

FIGURE 1 **Bank Failures**

For years after the Great Depression the number of bank failures was insignificant. All that changed in the 1980s. With the recession of 1982, bank failures increased dramatically. In 1988 alone there were more bank failures than the combined total for the previous 25 years.

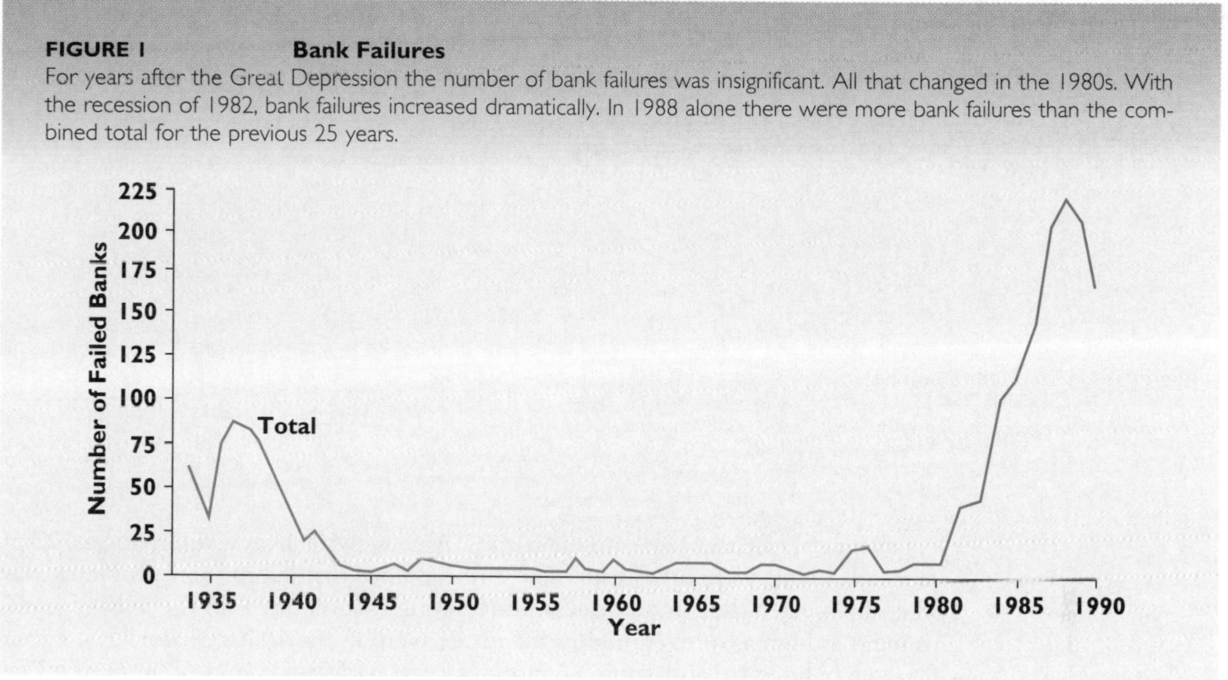

performance to detect weaknesses in operations. Recognized early enough, serious damage can be avoided.

Still, Banks Do Go Under

Falling farm prices and land values, bad loans to Mexico and other developing countries, and risky investments were all factors contributing to the higher rate of bank failures in the 1980s and 1990s.

Bank failures used to be rare events, as we see in Figure 1. Only 43 of approximately 14,000 banks failed in the 1950s. That is less than five failures per year. The number per decade increased during the 1960s to 63, and to 83 during the 1970s. Still, less than ten failures per year.

In the early 1980s, however, bank failures became somewhat more visible. In 1981 alone, 48 banks went under. Many were small, located in rural communities, but a few were large banks involving substantial sums of money and numbers of people. Why the increase?

THE BANK DEBACLE OF THE 1980s AND 1990s

These bank failures reflected the severe shocks that troubled specific sectors of our real economy, such as agriculture. High farm prices in the 1970s misled many farmers. As land values rose to reflect these higher prices, farmers brought more land under cultivation, bought more machinery, and expanded production. They financed these activities with loans extended to them by accommodating banks that acccepted the price-inflated land as collateral for the loans.

The honeymoon ended abruptly when farm prices and land values collapsed in the early 1980s. Many farmers, caught between falling farm prices and rising costs, went bankrupt and defaulted on their bank loans. Some unfortunate banks, whose loan portfolios were heavily involved in these farm ventures, could not survive.

TABLE 1
Bank Failures, Selected States 1987–1989

State	Failures	State	Failures	State	Failures
Texas	296	Nebraska	8	Ohio	2
Oklahoma	66	Arizona	7	Alabama	2
Louisiana	46	Missouri	7	Idaho	1
Colorado	30	Illinois	6	Kentucky	1
Kansas	19	Montana	6	Michigan	1
Minnesota	19	Alaska	5	Mississippi	1
California	12	Arkansas	5	Pennsylvania	1
Iowa	12	New York	5	Oregon	1
Florida	11	Utah	5	Wyoming	1

Source: Federal Deposit Insurance Corporation, *Annual Report*, 1989 (Washington, D.C., 1989) p. 11.

What about the large urban banks? A few, with heavy international loan commitments, were hit as well. The circumstance that led to their problems was the unexpected slide in oil prices. Anticipating that oil prices in the 1980s would remain as high as or even higher than they were in the 1970s, major U.S. banks loaned billions to oil-export economies such as Mexico and Venezuela. The banks anticipated that the oil economies would have no problems meeting their interest and loan obligations.

But they guessed wrong. The dramatic fall in oil prices during the 1980s sent many of the oil exporters, even Saudi Arabia, into deficit. Mexico alone incurred a \$100 billion bank debt, and after the first shock of falling oil prices, it was forced to seek new terms on its loan repayments. To press its need for loan restructuring, Mexico even threatened default.

Mexico was not alone among the less-developed economies seeking relief from excessive loan obligations. Brazil, for example, had to borrow extensively during the 1970s to finance its trade deficit—the difference between its imports and exports. Here, too, oil was at the heart of the problem. OPEC's ability to increase the price of oil tenfold during the 1970s accounted for the dramatic rise in Brazil's oil import bill and, consequently, in its trade deficit.

The connection between the plight of agriculture and the oil industry and bank failures shows up clearly in the numbers of bank failures by state for the latter part of the 1980s. Look at Table 1.

Note the large number of failures in the oil-based economies of Texas, Oklahoma, and Louisiana. Look also at bank failures in the farm states of Iowa, Kansas, Florida, California, and Minnesota. The disproportionality is striking, isn't it?

EVEN THE MIGHTY FALL

Perhaps the most dramatic bank failure of the 1980s was the demise of Chicago's Continental Illinois Bank. The cause of its death: "overdosing" on high-risk loans. In one dramatic but fatal move, Continental enhanced its loan portfolio by buying up more than \$1 billion in loans from the Penn Square Bank of Oklahoma City. Continental believed it was acquiring high-performing assets. In fact, the Penn Square loans were basically unsound. The loss was more than Continental could digest.

The FDIC took Continental over and, to everyone's surprise and the depositors' delight, announced it would cover *every* deposit, not just accounts under $100,000. It then tried to sell Continental to another bank. But even at bargain prices, no bank showed any interest. In the end, the FDIC invested billions of its own money to make the bank solvent once again.

Why didn't the FDIC just allow Continental to fold, as it did the smaller rural banks? Size was the difference. The FDIC's decision to keep Continental alive was taken to protect the confidence people place in our banking system. In the view of the FDIC, Continental was simply too important a bank to be allowed to go under.

THE SAVINGS AND LOAN DEBACLE OF THE 1980s AND 1990s

What about savings and loan associations (S&Ls)? They, too, felt the sting of financial bankruptcy. Look at Figure 2.

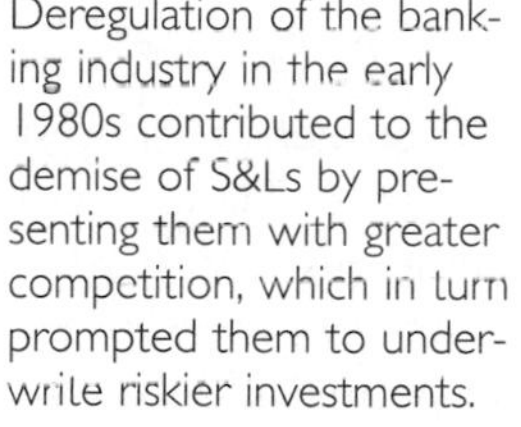
Deregulation of the banking industry in the early 1980s contributed to the demise of S&Ls by presenting them with greater competition, which in turn prompted them to underwrite riskier investments.

Why the dramatic growth in S&L failures in the 1980s? Prior to the 1980s, S&Ls were busy providing long-term (20- to 30 year) mortgages to private homeowners. They had a virtual monopoly in the home mortgage market because government regulations prohibited banks from competing in that market and prohibited S&Ls from competing in any other. And because government also set ceilings on the interest rate that banks and S&Ls were allowed to pay depositors (Regulation Q), S&Ls enjoyed the spin-off effect of competing with banks for depositors at relatively low rates of interest, while making loans to homeowners at much higher mortgage rates. In other words, long-term, private residential mortgage loans were not only fairly safe investments for the S&Ls, but were quite lucrative as well.

But deregulation of economic activity became the new focus of government policy during the 1980s and the undoing of the S&Ls. Among the industries affected by deregulation was banking. The deregulation created an open-season banking environment. Investment houses, such as Merrill Lynch, were allowed to compete with banks and S&Ls for depositors. They offered money market mutual funds at rates higher than those offered by banks and S&Ls. These funds

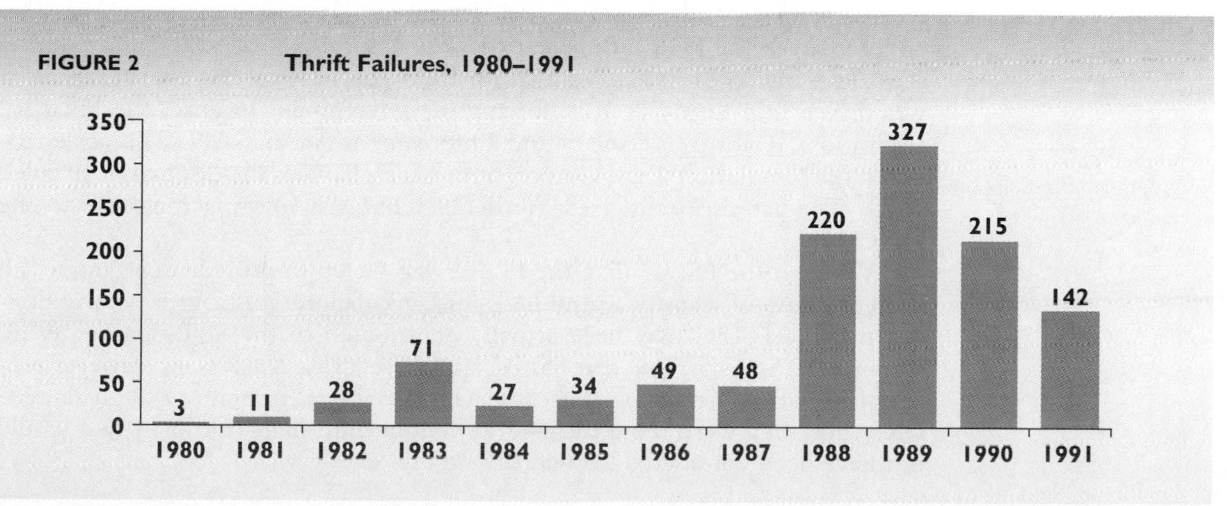

FIGURE 2 **Thrift Failures, 1980–1991**

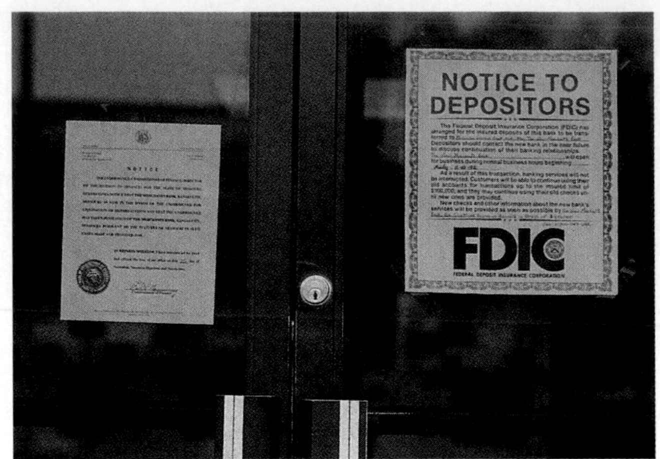

This notice announces the closing of a neighborhood bank. Sad enough, but not nearly as sad as the announcements used to be when banks were not covered by FDIC and the notice simply announced that depositors were "out of luck" (and out of money!)

gave depositors the best of two worlds: sound investments at attractive interest rates and the privilege of using these funds as checking accounts. To create a level playing field for banks and S&Ls, the government also discarded Regulation Q so that banks and S&Ls now had the opportunity to raise interest rates to keep their depositors from switching to the competing investment houses. These events sealed the fate of many S&Ls.

Why? Because the S&Ls were locked into fixed, long-term mortgage loans at rates that were often lower than the rates they now had to pay depositors. To recoup losses, they moved into new loan markets, such as speculative land development, that earned more, *but were much riskier* than the private, residential home mortgage market they had once dominated.

Another factor contributing to the S&Ls' demise was the substantial fraud that crept into their deregulated banking environment. "Loans" were made to S&L management friends and families that, upon later investigation, amounted to outright theft. In the end, as Figure 2 shows, disaster struck. By 1987 a third of them had gone bankrupt.

What about their depositors? They were protected by the government-created FSLIC—Federal Savings and Loan Insurance Corporation—the S&L counterpart to the FDIC. But the extraordinary number of S&L failures during the 1980s and 1990s was too much for the FSLIC to absorb. The FSLIC itself was driven into financial crisis, forcing the government to enact the Financial Institutions Reform, Recovery and Enforcement Act in 1989. The act established the Resolution Trust Corporation, which handles the disposal of all failed S&Ls. The act also transferred the defunct FSLIC's insuring functions to the FDIC.

Although the FSLIC (like the FDIC) was set up to provide depositors with some measure of security against S&L (or bank) failure, it is somewhat paradoxical that the FSLIC may have actually contributed to the S&L demise. Why? Because the S&Ls, having that FSLIC-backed security, had less incentive to prevent failure from occurring. That is, having the FSLIC insurance as a guaranteed safety net, they were more inclined to venture into high-risk loans that would not have been considered loanworthy otherwise.

CONTROLLING THE FINANCIAL INSTITUTIONS THAT CONTROL THE MONEY SUPPLY

Georges Clemenceau, the French statesman who served as War Minister during the First World War once remarked: "War is too important to be left to the generals." Had he looked at the banking system, he might well have added: "And the money supply is too important to be left to the banks."

Few economists would disagree. We have seen how the banking system, almost by magic, creates money.

But the relationship between the money that financial institutions are willing and able to create and the economy's need for the money is *not always* one to one.

Paradoxical as it may seem, it is when the economy most needs injections of money that the financial institutions are most reluctant to supply it. And only when the economy least needs it, do they show a willingness—sometimes an eagerness—to offer money.

And that's a problem. In periods of prosperity when prices, wage rates, interest rates, employment, and consumer spending are relatively high, banks, S&Ls, and credit unions feel confident in the economy's future and, therefore, in borrowers' ability to repay loans. Under these conditions, most bankers are anxious to lend the maximum permissible. Such loan behavior, coupled to the money multiplier, creates maximum permissible supplies of money. But it is precisely in the heady times of prosperity, with the economy already at full employment, that maximum permissible money can push the economy into unintended inflation.

On the other hand, in periods of recession when prices, wage rates, interest rates, employment, and consumer spending are relatively low, the financial institutions' expectations of the economy's future change from confidence to caution. Their loan policies, reflecting this change, become increasingly hesitant. Their concern now is to minimize loan defaults. They are more willing, then, to hold greater excess reserves. In other words, precisely when the economy could use more investment money, banks and other financial institutions are more inclined to forego the opportunities of creating money.

Frustrating, isn't it? The marvelous invention of modern banking allows us to create the money supply to promote maximum real goods production. Sometimes, however, it overindulges, and at other times it denies that supply and exacerbates the economy's bouts with inflation and unemployment.

If the financial institutions cannot be counted upon to create the proper money flows to foster economic activity with minimal inflation and unemployment, then perhaps *some* control over their control of the money supply is needed. That's where the Federal Reserve System comes in.

CHAPTER REVIEW

1. Fractional reserve banking is based on the idea that a bank need not keep all of its deposits on hand as reserves. Loans can be made based on deposits, with only a fraction of the deposits held as reserves. In this way, a bank can earn interest on loans while paying depositors interest for their deposits.

2. A fractional reserve banking system is able to create money. When a bank receives a new deposit, it can loan a portion of this deposit, leaving enough of the deposit on hand to satisfy the reserve requirement. The borrower spends the proceeds from the loan. These expenditures end up as a new deposit in a second bank. The second bank is able to loan a fraction of its new deposit. And in this way, a sequence of events occurs that causes the money supply to expand by a multiple of the original deposit.

3. The banking system can create new deposits equal to the initial demand deposit divided by the legal reserve requirement. The potential money multiplier is given by the reciprocal of the legal reserve requirement. The money supply may not expand to the extent suggested by the potential money multiplier because banks may elect to hold some of their excess reserves, people may not want to borrow, and not all the loans made find their way back into bank deposits.

4. The money creation process can run in reverse. When loans are paid back, checks are written on bank accounts, which decreases deposits and forces banks holding loans up to their legal reserve requirements to reduce their loans. The potential money multiplier can be used to calculate the extent to which the money supply will shrink as deposits decrease.

5. Banks sometimes fail when a large portion of the loans they have made are not repaid. When people learn of bank failures, they tend to become nervous about their own deposits and withdraw them. As deposits are withdrawn, loans must be called in and the money supply shrinks. Serious bank failures can trigger waves of failures and drastic reductions in the money supply.

6. Federal deposit insurance is intended to insure depositors of the safety of their deposits so they won't be easily inclined to withdraw their funds. Bank audits and examination help improve faith in the banking system by making certain that the bank operates according to sound principles and legislated regulations.

7. In spite of FDIC and bank auditing on a regular basis, banks do fail sometimes. During the 1980s and the first years of the 1990s, bank failure rates rose significantly. Savings and loan associations also went through a difficult period during the 1980s as banks began to compete with them for customers in the home mortgage market. S&L failures were so extensive in the 1980s that a special government-sponsored corporation, the Resolution Trust Corporation, had to be established in order to dispose of the failed S&Ls.

8. If left to their own devices, financial intermediaries would tend to make downturns in the business cycle more pronounced and upturns more extreme. During a downturn, a bank or other intermediary is less likely to lend for fear of not being repaid. The money supply shrinks as outstanding loans are repaid, causing the interest rate to rise and investment to fall. Thus, the downturn is more severe. During an economic expansion, banks are more inclined to lend, which causes the money supply to grow more rapidly than otherwise, resulting in lower interest rates and more borrowing. As the economy approaches full employment, there is upward pressure on the price level.

KEY TERMS

- Fractional reserve system
- Balance sheet
- Legal reserve requirement
- Financial intermediaries
- Potential money multiplier
- Excess reserves
- Federal Deposit Insurance Corporation (FDIC)

QUESTIONS

1. Why was Amar Bazazz able to convince people who deposited gold in his cave for safekeeping that it was all there when, in fact, he had gambled most of it away?

2. What relationship is there between the Amar Bazazz story and the fundamentals of modern banking?

3. Why is it important to have a legal reserve requirement imposed on banks? What could happen to the banking system if there were no such requirement?

4. What is the potential money multiplier? Why is it called potential?

5. What are the three principal requirements for the banking system to create money?

6. What is the significance of calling the deposits you make in your checking account *demand deposits?*

7. Explain how a new demand deposit of $100 can potentially create $500 of new money if the legal reserve requirement is 20 percent.

8. If the legal reserve requirement is 50 percent, how much new money could the $100 deposit create?

9. How does a bank end up with excess reserves?

10. Suppose your neighborhood bank has no excess reserves and the legal reserve requirement is raised from 20 percent to 50 percent. What must it do to conform to the new requirement?

11. What can cause a bank to fail?

12. What has been the record of bank failures in the United States over the past four decades?

13. Which states have been hardest hit by bank failures? Why?

14. What safeguards have we created to protect ourselves against the fall-out of bank failure?

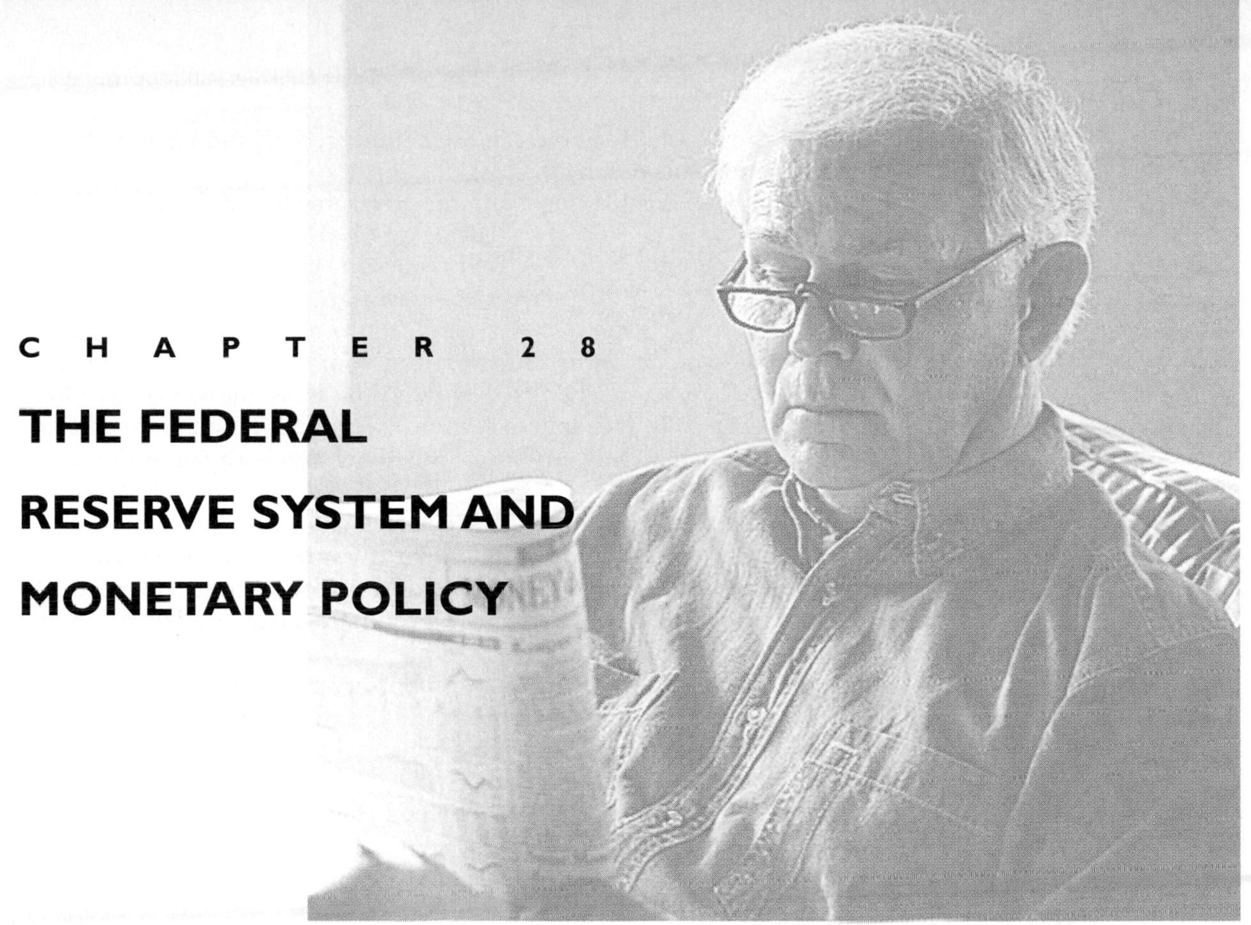

CHAPTER 28

THE FEDERAL RESERVE SYSTEM AND MONETARY POLICY

CHAPTER PREVIEW

Armed with our knowledge of the banking system's ability to create and destroy money, we're ready to consider ways that a central bank can manipulate the money creation and destruction processes in order to moderate the business cycle. The history of central banking in the United States is a colorful one. The United States has not always had a central bank. And the central banking system that we now have is unlike any other in the world. But the tools used by central banks are essentially similar in all nations. This chapter should give you a good understanding of the way monetary policy operates in the United States and in other industrialized countries.

After studying this chapter, you should be able to:

- Provide an account of the history of money and banking in the United States.
- Describe the organizational structure of the Federal Reserve System.
- List the functions of the Federal Reserve System.
- Discuss the different instruments of control over the money supply used by the Federal Reserve System.
- Contrast a money supply target with an interest rate target as policy options.

- Show how the Federal Reserve can use countercyclical monetary policy to influence the macroeconomy.
- Explain why the Federal Reserve and the government may have conflicting policy goals.

If there is anything you've learned in school, in your home, and in your daily life, it is that we are a society that jealously cherishes individual freedom. Freedom to travel around. Freedom to say what we please. Freedom to take any job we like or none at all. Only *very* reluctantly do we agree to compromise our personal freedoms.

We resisted the regulation of our money system. We allowed private banks guided by the profit motive to determine their own reserve requirements, and we allowed interest rates, which govern the quantity of money demanded and supplied in our economy, to be determined in an unregulated market by an unregulated banking system.

American resistance to control over our monetary system finally broke down in the early part of the twentieth century. It had become unmistakably clear that unregulated banking had too often triggered financial panics that endangered the economic well-being of nearly everyone.

The core problem until this century seemed to be the money system itself. *From the very beginning of our Republic, through the 19th century, the overriding and chronic money problem we faced was the banks' inclination to overissue currency.* The early and hesitant attempts by Congress to curb the banks' appetite to overissue repeatedly ended in failure, and finally led to the enactment of the more assertive Federal Reserve Act of 1913. We need to consider the principal historical events that led to the creation of the Federal Reserve.

A GLIMPSE AT HISTORY

Bank note

A promissory note issued by a bank that is a pledge to redeem the note for a specific amount of gold or silver. The terms of redemption are specified on the note.

In colonial times, before banks printed their own **bank notes,** our money was simply a collection of foreign currencies. The French guinea, the Spanish pistole, and the English crown, among many others, circulated as money on the streets of New York, Baltimore, Philadelphia, and Boston. They were exchanged readily for each other. The nation had no currency of its own. But the system worked.

Continental Notes

Continental Notes diminished in value because too many were issued.

Then came the American Revolution. It transformed our money system as well as our political system. It took a great deal of money to recruit, equip, feed, and pay a growing army. The Continental Congress, pressed for funds, turned to the states. But little help was forthcoming. With no real alternative, the Continental Congress took to the printing presses.

Between 1775 and 1780, $242 million of Continental Notes, our first real money, were printed. Since Congress had no taxing authority, it turned to the printing press for money. As the quantity of Continentals multiplied, their value depreciated. In 1777 they traded 2 for 1 against silver. By 1779, as more and more of these notes came on the market, the exchange rate jumped to 20 to 1.

By 1781, with printing presses still churning them out, the notes traded 1,000 to 1 against silver. Continentals were rapidly becoming worthless.

To create some semblance of monetary order, Thomas Jefferson proposed a new money, based on the Spanish dollar, metrically divisible, and *backed by gold and silver.* His recommendations were accepted by the Continental Congress, and in 1786, the government established the dollar as the country's unit of account.

The Chartering of State Banks

The Bank of North America was the first bank chartered in the United States.

But who was to supply the dollars, and how many of them? In those pre-banking years, this simple money system became increasingly incapable of providing adequate supplies to satisfy our monetary needs. Farmers pushing westward needed credit to finance their homesteads. Businesspeople back east sought credit to expand their growing manufacturing operations. Some form of banking system that could offer credit was not only desirable but became imperative.

In 1781 the Bank of North America, chartered by the State of Pennsylvania, was formed. It was the first bank in the United States to accept deposits and issue bank notes. Soon, other **state-chartered banks** sprang up—the Bank of New York and the Massachusetts Bank in 1784—each printing and issuing its own bank notes. Table 1 traces the growth of state-chartered banks.

State-chartered bank

A commercial bank that receives its charter or license to function from a state government and is subject to the laws of that state.

With each new bank issuing its own bank notes, with no established rule on specie backing, and with little discipline on what should be acceptable collateral, was there any way the government could have controlled the banks' control of the money supply? Should it have tried?

There were opposing views on this issue. Some felt that the states had the right to charter banks and that banks should have the right to issue notes unimpeded by the federal government. They were very reluctant to interfere with a bank's freedom to give or not give credit. They did not like the idea of creating a government monitor over the money supply. But others, no less supportive of a banking system, were still worried about the unconstrained behavior of the banks. They were fearful that these profit-making, state-chartered banks would end up overissuing bank notes which would undermine the stability of the monetary system.

TABLE 1
Growth of State Banks: 1784–1860 ($ millions)

	Number of Banks	Capital
1784	3	$ 2.1
1801	31	22.4
1805	75	40.4
1811	88	42.6
1816	246	89.8
1829	329	110.1
1839	840	327.1
1859	1,476	402.9

Source: U.S. Bureau of the Census, *Historical Statistics of the United States, 1789–1945* (Washington, D.C.: U.S. Government Printing Office, 1949) pp. 261-3.

The First Bank of the United States

The worriers prevailed. In 1790, Congress proposed that the Bank of North America take on the functions of a central bank. Its primary function would be to control the economy's money supply. It would have the power to dictate what banks could and could not do. The idea of central banking was anything but novel. Central banks were already functioning in Sweden, England, and Holland.

An alternative proposal was put forward by Alexander Hamilton. Instead of the state-chartered Bank of North America acting as the country's central bank, he proposed the creation of a **nationally chartered bank** which would exercise control over the nation's money supply *and* be authorized to extend credit to the government.

Nationally chartered bank

A commercial bank that receives its charter from the Comptroller of the Currency and is subject to federal law as well as the laws of the state in which it operates.

Thomas Jefferson and James Madison opposed the idea of a central bank altogether because, in their view, establishing a central bank exceeded the powers of the federal government under the strict interpretation of the constitution. Moreover, they were convinced that central bank activity would favor the already powerful northern merchant class.

Congress bought the Hamilton plan. In 1791, it set up the First Bank of the United States. The bank's charter was designed to expire after 20 years but could be renewed by Congress.

The First Bank of the United States was able to control the money supply by presenting state banks with their notes for repayment in gold and silver.

Actually, the First Bank of the United States performed reasonably well. It served as the government's fiscal agent and even succeeded in dampening the inclination of the state-chartered banks to overissue notes. How? Since many of the state bank notes found their way to the First Bank, the Bank could present the notes to the state banks for payment in gold or silver. Aware of this prospect, the state banks became more careful about issuing bank notes in excess of their gold and silver.

The Second Bank of the United States

Andrew Jackson opposed the Second Bank of the United States on constitutional grounds.

And yet in 1811, when the time came to renew its charter, Congress declined to do so. The advocates of states' rights won out. Over the next five years, the number of state-chartered banks almost tripled, from 88 in 1811 to 246 in 1816. Left without a central bank's restraining influence on the issuance of bank notes, bank note depreciation and fraud became rather commonplace. By 1814, most banks had suspended specie payment. That is, they would no longer convert paper bank notes into gold and silver. Would you put your gold into such a bank?

It didn't take Congress long to regret having disposed of the First Bank. It became painfully clear that something had to be done to stabilize the money supply. The answer, just five years after the demise of the First Bank, was to establish the Second Bank of the United States. This time, Congress gave the national bank the right to issue its own notes. These soon became the most widely accepted currency in the nation, preferred to the less-trusted notes of the state-chartered banks.

When the Second Bank took on the task of making specie payment in exchange for its notes, it confronted strong regional resistance. Many state banks in the West and South catered to the unrestrained money demands of farmers, merchants, and land speculators. Many banks ended up holding excessive quantities of overvalued real estate collateral which they, in turn, used to fuel their bank note issues.

Recognizing the weakness of these issues, the Second Bank pressed for sounder specie backing. The southern and western banks balked, viewing this pressure as discriminatory. Animosity toward the Second Bank intensified when it instructed northern banks not to accept bank notes from the southern and western banks which could not back their currency with gold and silver.

Like the First Bank, the Second Bank's performance record was laudable. And like the First, it was abandoned. When Andrew Jackson, an opponent of central banking, was reelected to the Presidency in 1832, the Second Bank's constitutionality was an election issue and its fate was virtually sealed. Jackson shifted Treasury funds from the Second Bank back to state banks, which undermined the Second Bank's ability to control the issuance of notes by state banks. By 1836 it had become just another bank in Pennsylvania.

From the demise of the Second Bank as a central bank until Congress passed the National Banking Act in 1864, the economy's money supply was once again left in the hands of the state banks. And once again, unsound loans and overissuing of notes led to an unhealthy climate of unreliable money. The Civil War pressured Congress to "rediscover" central banking.

The National Banking Act

The National Banking Act encouraged state banks to change to national charters as a way of raising funds for the federal government to finance the Civil War.

The cost of the Civil War pushed Congress far beyond its financial capabilities. The steady outflow of specie from the Treasury made it impossible for it to continue buying back its notes. Congress reluctantly allowed the Treasury to begin to print money. The Treasury printed Greenbacks, so called because of the ink used on the back side of the notes. They became the economy's most common, but rapidly depreciating, currency.

Once again, the government faced two classic problems: How to provide itself with the financial resources it needed to carry on the affairs of government and, at the same time, stabilize the monetary system. This time, it came up with a novel idea that ultimately was legislated in 1864 as the National Banking Act.

The idea was to develop a national banking *system*. The act created a new office, Comptroller of the Currency, housed in the Treasury, which chartered national banks. A national bank had to buy Treasury bonds equal to one-third of its capital, and could issue notes only in proportion to its Treasury bond holdings.

Now how do you reestablish people's confidence in the banking system? Banks were no longer allowed to accept real estate as collateral for loans, nor lend more than 10 percent of the value of their capital stock to any single borrower. Also, each bank was required to provide financial reports to the Comptroller of the Currency and was subject to periodic bank audits.

To encourage state banks to switch over to the national system, the Comptroller levied a 10 percent annual tax on state-chartered bank-note issues. This was a steep tax, but there wasn't a rush to conversion. For one thing, not all state-chartered banks could afford the minimal capital required to obtain a national charter. As a result, state-chartered and nationally chartered banks coexisted within the banking industry.

The National Banking Act did tighten the money supply, but it was by no means the banking industry's panacea. It could not stem the credit expansion that banks generated by holding each other's deposits. This practice of credit expansion heightened the banking system's volatility.

For example, in winter when farmers' demands for funds were relatively weak, country banks would deposit some of their reserves in the larger city banks to earn interest. Counting these deposits as their own reserves, the city banks would create new loans.

Then came spring. Farmers, now ready to get back into the fields, needed money for seed and equipment. The country banks, ready to service farmers, withdrew their over-winter deposits from city banks, leaving them with much depleted reserves. There was nothing city banks could do but call in outstanding loans. At times, these wholesale shifts of deposits touched off financial panics and recessions.

THE KNICKERBOCKER TRUST DISASTER

The 1907 Knickerbocker disaster was the final straw that broke the camel's back. Both state and national banks, along with mushrooming financial trusts, were caught up in a whirlwind of speculative loans. In October, frightened depositors looked in horror at the collapse of the Knickerbocker Trust Company, a highly reputable and seemingly sound financial institution. The thought in everyone's mind—as it would have been in yours—was, Who's next? Panic spread. People ran to their banks to withdraw their deposits, and hard-pressed banks in turn scrambled for liquidity by calling in outstanding loans. Investment projects, in various stages of incompletion, were all-at-once suspended. Sound businesses, drained dry of credit, were forced into bankruptcy. The result was almost instant recession.

Once again, Congress was forced to intervene. This time, with Knickerbocker still fresh in mind, Congress broadened its concerns from simply coping with the chronic problems of overissue of bank notes and inadequate collateral to include a newly perceived menace, the overreach of powerful financial trusts. The response came in the form of the Federal Reserve Act of 1913.

THE FEDERAL RESERVE SYSTEM

Federal Reserve System (the Fed)
The central bank of the United States.

The Federal Reserve Act of 1913 created the **Federal Reserve System,** commonly referred to as the Fed. Why the Federal Reserve *System* and not the Federal Reserve *Bank?* The Fed was designed as a system because Congress

Alan Greenspan, Chairman of the Federal Reserve System, explaining the Fed's monetary policy to the Joint Economic Committee of the U.S. Congress. The Fed is primarily concerned about the rate of inflation.

FIGURE 1 The Geography of the Federal Reserve System

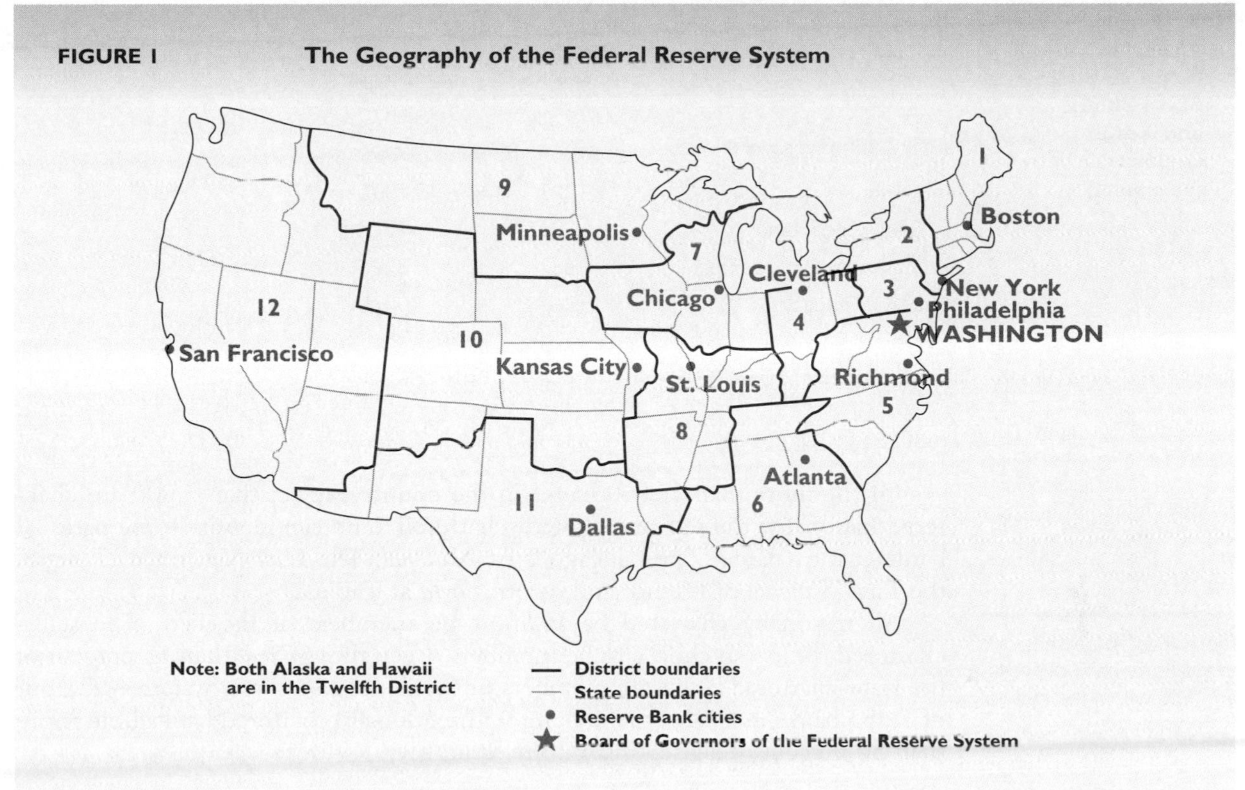

wanted a decentralized central bank. The decentralization was essentially geographic, reflecting people's desire for regional monetary independence.

The Federal Reserve System consists of 12 District Banks that are owned by the member banks in their districts.

The need for such regional autonomy has since dissipated, but the structure remains intact. The Fed's structure is simple. It consists of 12 District Federal Reserve Banks, each serving a region of the country. The larger District Federal Reserve Banks have smaller branches. Under this arrangement, a bank in a specific district would use its own District Federal Reserve as its central bank. In this way, banks in Omaha, Nebraska, or Ocala, Florida would not have to depend upon banking decisions made in New York. Figure 1 maps the geographic domain of the 12 District Federal Reserve Banks and their locations.

Who Owns the Fed?

Unlike the Bank of Canada, the Bank of France, the Bank of England, and other central banks in democratic market economies, the Federal Reserve System is not owned by the government. Although created by and responsible to Congress, the Fed pursues an independent monetary policy which at times can conflict with government's economic policy. For example, the government may be pursuing a stimulative fiscal policy (lower taxes, increase government spending) while the Fed may be more interested in controlling inflation.

Who owns the Fed, then, if not the government? Each District Federal Reserve Bank is owned by its member banks. Each member bank contributes 3 percent of its capital stock to the Federal Reserve Bank in its district and another 3 percent is subject to call by the Fed.

TABLE 2 National Banks, State Banks, and Total Deposits: 1993 ($ billions)

	Number of Banks	Deposits
Total	13,221	$4,707.2
Commercial Banks	10,957	3,705.9
National	3,303	2,100.5
State (Fed member)	971	727.6
State (nonFed member)	6,682	877.9
Savings Institutions	2,264	1,001.0

Source: Federal Deposit Insurance Corporation, *Statistics on Banking, 1993* (Washington, D.C.: FDIC, April 1994), p. B23.

Of the more than 12,000 banks in the country, fewer than 5,000 are chartered nationally; the rest remain state-chartered. You can identify some national banks just by name. The Chicago First *National,* The First *National* of Toledo, the First *National* of Fresno, and so on. Look at Table 2.

More than 50 percent of the nation's bank deposits are held within the Federal Reserve System.

All nationally chartered banks must be members of the Fed. The state-chartered banks can choose to be members. Even though less than 13 percent of the state-chartered banks are members of the Federal Reserve System—971 out of 7,653 banks in 1993—they, along with nationally chartered banks hold more than 50 percent of all deposits in our economy.

The Fed's Purpose and Organization

The Federal Reserve System's main charge is to safeguard the proper functioning of our money system. It is the watchdog of our money supply, our interest rates, and the economy's price level.

Obviously, if it's going to do that job at all, it has to monitor the activities of the nation's financial institutions, anticipate what they will do, prevent them from doing some things, encourage them to do others, and do all this without interfering too much in the conduct of private business. Impossible? Some people think so. But these same people are unable to imagine a modern economy operating without a central bank.

The Fed's organizational structure is not very complicated. Look at Figure 2.

The nucleus of the Federal Reserve System is its Board of Governors, which meets in Washington, D.C. The Board consists of seven members, appointed by the President and confirmed by the Senate. Each serves a 14-year term. Appointments are staggered, one every other year, so that no President or Senate session can manipulate the composition of the board. This also ensures continuity. The Chairman is a board member appointed by the President to a four-year term. Chairmen may be reappointed, but they cannot serve longer than their 14 years on the Board.

Chairmen of the Board of Governors of the Fed typically overlap presidential administrations.

Typically, chairmen are reappointed for lengthy periods that overlap Republican and Democratic presidents. Paul Volcker, who preceded current Chairman Alan Greenspan, was appointed by Jimmy Carter and twice reappointed by Ronald Reagan. Greenspan has continued into the Clinton administration. Much earlier, William McChesney Martin chaired through the Eisenhower, Kennedy, and Johnson administrations and even into the early Nixon years.

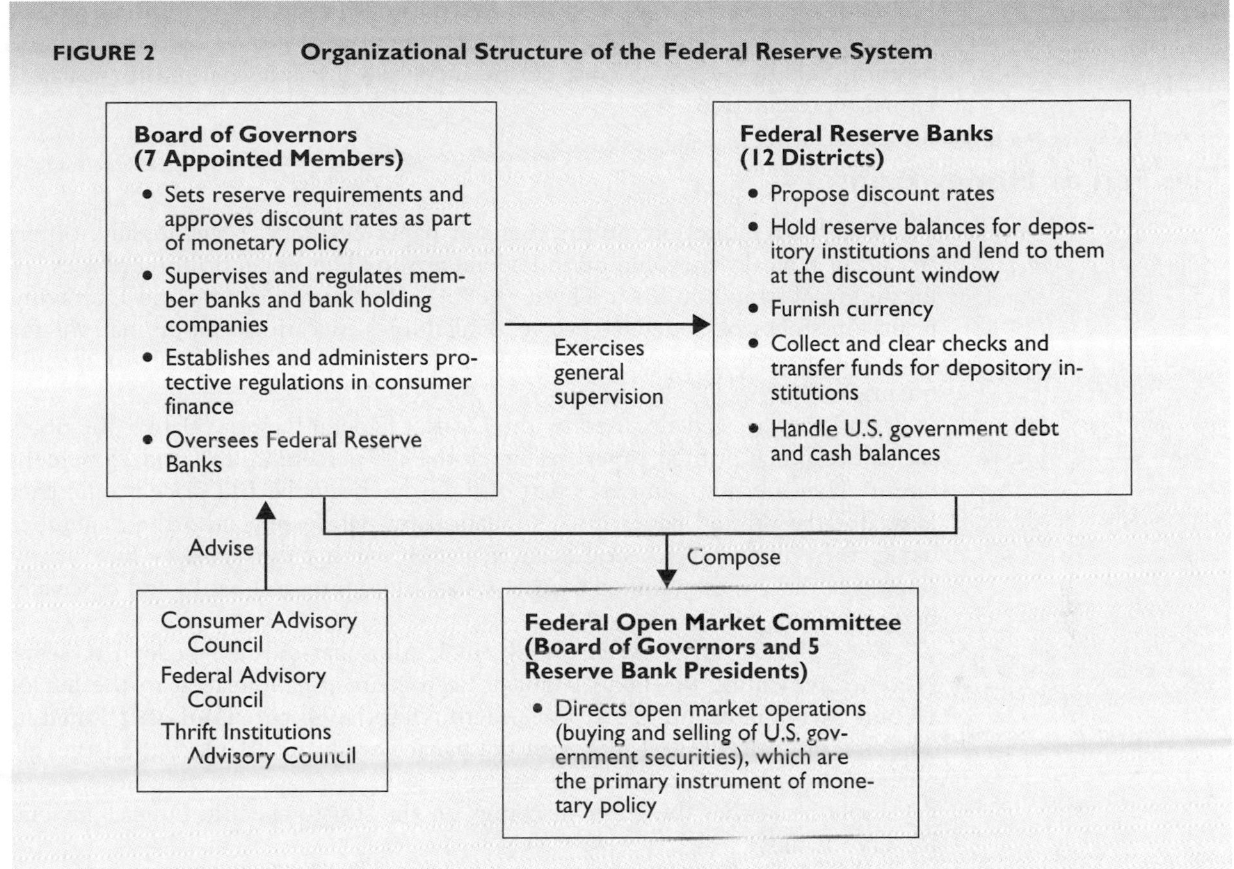

FIGURE 2 Organizational Structure of the Federal Reserve System
Board of Governors (7 Appointed Members)
• Sets reserve requirements and approves discount rates as part of monetary policy
• Supervises and regulates member banks and bank holding companies
• Establishes and administers protective regulations in consumer finance
• Oversees Federal Reserve Banks
Exercises general supervision
Federal Reserve Banks (12 Districts)
• Propose discount rates
• Hold reserve balances for depository institutions and lend to them at the discount window
• Furnish currency
• Collect and clear checks and transfer funds for depository institutions
• Handle U.S. government debt and cash balances
Advise
Compose
Consumer Advisory Council
Federal Advisory Council
Thrift Institutions Advisory Council
Federal Open Market Committee (Board of Governors and 5 Reserve Bank Presidents)
• Directs open market operations (buying and selling of U.S. government securities), which are the primary instrument of monetary policy

Source: Board of Governors of the Federal Reserve System, Division of Support Services, *Purposes & Functions,* 1984.

More often than not, Board members are drawn from within the banking industry, either from commercial banks or from the Fed's District Banks. Volcker, for example, came from the New York Fed. Such ties to banking experience can be both helpful and problematic. While members must understand the complexities of banking, their strong connection to the industry seems to compromise, for some people, their role as guardians of the public trust. But not all come from banking. Arthur Burns, for example, left his professorship at Columbia University to serve as chairman during the late Nixon years.

DISTRICT FEDERAL RESERVE BANKS

The 12 District Banks make up the second tier of the Fed's structure. Each is managed by a board of nine directors, six chosen by the member banks of the district, the other three appointed by the Board of Governors. The President of each district bank is selected by its nine directors.

Federal Open Market Committee

The Fed's principal decision-making body, charged with executing the Fed's open market operations.

FEDERAL OPEN MARKET COMMITTEE

The nerve center of the Fed is its **Federal Open Market Committee.** Here, the Fed exercises monetary control over the economy through its open market operations (discussed below). The 12-person committee is composed of all seven members of the Board of Governors who each have one vote, as do the

President of the New York Fed, and four District Presidents who rotate voting on the Committee. Its composition reflects the power of the Board, the unique position held by the New York District Fed, and the Fed's commitment to regional representation.

The Fed as Money Printer

The Fed has a monopoly on printing our paper currency. Occasionally, others try it, but typically they end up in Federal prison. The actual printing presses are located in Washington D.C. There, the U.S. Bureau of Printing and Engraving prints up stocks of Federal Reserve Bank Notes in various denominations for each District Bank. These are stored until the District Banks call for specific quantities.

Until they are actually used by the District Federal Reserve Banks, the notes are just so much printed paper (really, cloth—75 percent cotton and 25 percent linen). They are not counted as part of the money supply. But once the District Feds put the printed paper into circulation by transferring it to their member banks, the printed paper becomes currency. How much currency we have at any one time, then, is determined by the wishes of commercial banks and especially the public.

We all know what currency looks like. All dollar bills are Federal Reserve Notes, representing the Fed's liability. Each bears a seal—placed to the left of George Washington on the $1 bill—identifying the District Bank that issued it. The fine print on the seal spells out the particular District Bank, but a large, alphabet letter makes identification easier.

Table 3 matches the letter markings on the seal to specific District Federal Reserve Banks.

Check the seals on your own dollar bills. How many different District Federal Bank notes do you have? Chances are that out of five notes in your wallet, two or three will be different bank issues. How do you suppose the San Francisco Fed's note ends up in a Boston wallet? Or a Kansas City Fed's ends up

TABLE 3
Identifying Letters and District Banks

Letter	Federal Reserve Bank of
A	Boston
B	New York
C	Philadelphia
D	Cleveland
E	Richmond
F	Atlanta
G	Chicago
H	St. Louis
I	Minneapolis
J	Kansas City
K	Dallas
L	San Francisco

in Dallas? We are an open, active, and wide-ranging economy. When you can fly from Los Angeles to New York in less than six hours, it doesn't take long for currency to travel across the country.

The Fed as the Bankers' Bank

The Fed is the bankers' bank because it holds their reserves, provides banks with currency and loans, and clears their checks.

The Federal Reserve System is often called the bankers' bank because it provides specific services to its member banks that in some respects are like the services banks provide to us. For example, member banks can create their own accounts at the Fed allowing them to deposit and withdraw their funds on demand. They can even borrow from the Fed, just as we borrow from banks. The Fed provides them with check-clearing services and, of course, with currency.

HOLDING BANK RESERVES

As you know, banks are obligated to keep some fraction of their demand deposits in reserve. But they can hold reserves in excess of the reserve requirement set by the Fed. Suppose the Paris First National Bank (PFN), a member of the Federal Reserve System, with $1,000,000 in demand deposits, holds $300,000 in reserve, $200,000 more than the 10 percent legal reserve requirement.

What does it do with the $300,000? Some of it, say $75,000, stays in Paris in PFN's vaults. The remaining $225,000 is sent to Dallas where it is deposited in PFN's account at the Dallas Fed, just as you deposit money in your account at your own bank. PFN can always add to or subtract from its account at the Dallas Fed.

PROVIDING BANKS WITH CURRENCY AND LOANS

Suppose PFN finds that its depositors are demanding much more currency than it has available in Paris. What does it do? It simply calls the District Federal Reserve Bank in Dallas. The Dallas Fed ships the currency in an armored car (or mails it, insured of course!) to PFN and deducts that amount from PFN's deposits at the Dallas Fed.

If, on the other hand, PFN discovers that the amount of currency it has on hand is abnormally large, it can transfer some of it to the Dallas Fed. The Fed then simply credits PFN's account with that amount. This is the same process you go through with your bank.

Now suppose the PFN wants to make a loan to Shara Gingold but has no excess reserves it can draw upon. It holds only the legally required reserves. Are PFN and Shara out of luck? Not necessarily. PFN can borrow from the Dallas Fed just as we can borrow from banks. If the Dallas Fed decides to make the loan to PFN, it charges PFN an interest rate on the loan—called the **discount rate**—just as we are charged an interest rate on bank loans. Obviously, the discount rate charged to PFN would have to be lower than the rate of interest PFN charges Shara if Shara is to get the loan.

Discount rate

The interest rate which the Fed charges banks that borrow reserves from it.

Why is the Fed so generous? These Fed loans to member banks provide the Fed not only with a means to service member banks, but also with a means to control what banks do.

CLEARING BANKS' CHECKS

Suppose Brian Mosley, watching David Letterman on TV one night, sees a Rock Classics commercial for five Billy Bragg CDs and decides to get them. He writes a check for $49.95 on his bank, the First National of Cincinnati, FNC, and mails the check to Rock Classics in Athens, Georgia. He expects the CDs in six weeks.

Figure 3 traces the sequence of bank transactions that Brian triggers with his $49.95 check. Two days after it is mailed, Brian's check arrives in Athens. Rock Classics deposits the check in its account at the First National of Athens, FNA. Rock Classics's account at FNA is richer by $49.95.

It never occurs to Rock Classics that FNA would refuse Brian's check. But why not? Why should an Athens bank accept a check drawn on a bank in Cincinnati? How does the Athens bank collect the $49.95 from Cincinnati?

Here's where the Federal Reserve System comes in. FNA transfers the check to its District Federal Reserve Bank, the Atlanta Fed, for deposit. FNA now has an additional $49.95 on deposit at the Atlanta Fed and the Atlanta Fed now has Brian's check. What does the Atlanta Fed do? It wants to be reimbursed. After all, its liabilities to FNA just increased by $49.95.

The Atlanta Fed transfers the check to the Cleveland Fed and informs the Interdistrict Settlement Fund in Washington about the transfer. The Fund cred-

FIGURE 3 **Bank Transactions Triggered by Brian's Purchase**

The circular flow of Brian Mosley's $49.95 check through Rock Classics, the First National Bank of Cincinnati, the First National Bank of Athens, the Atlanta Fed, and the Cleveland Fed.

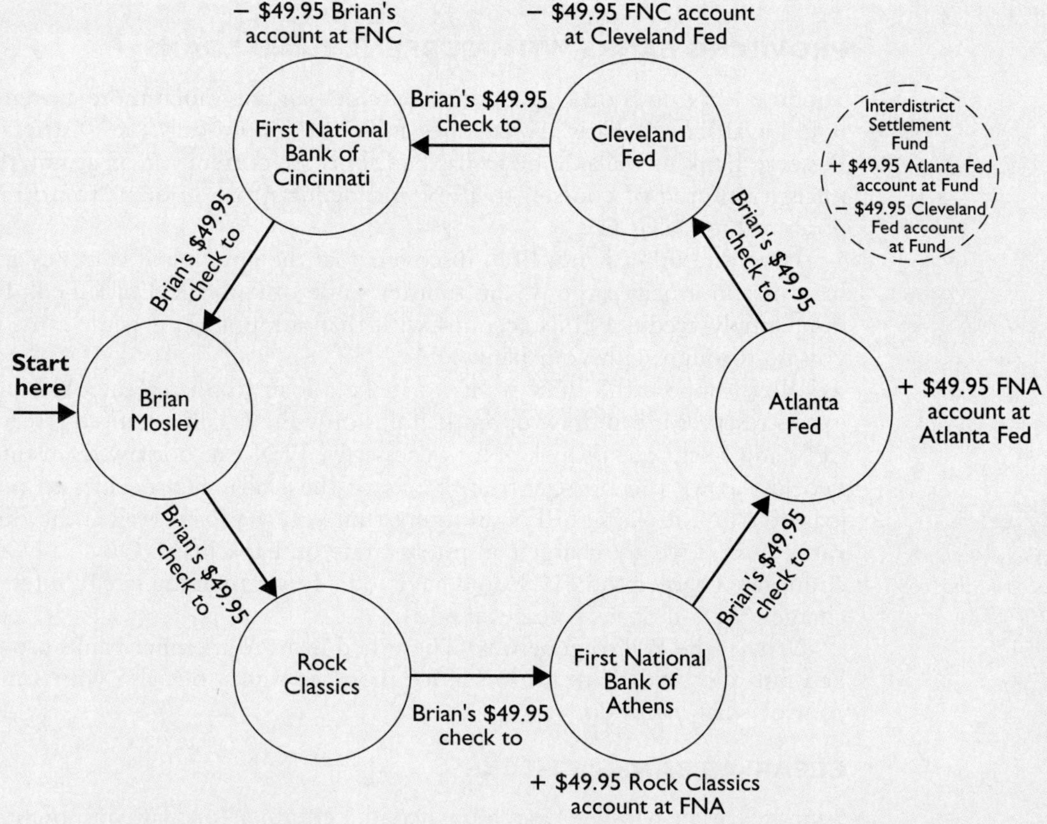

its the Atlanta Fed's account at the Fund by $49.95—the Atlanta Fed is now reimbursed—and debits the Cleveland Fed's account at the Fund by $49.95.

What does the Cleveland Fed do? It deducts $49.95 from the First National Bank of Cincinnati's account with it. The FNC, in turn, gets reimbursed by reducing Brian Mosley's account by $49.95. The trail ends with the cancelled check sent back to Brian.

Imagine how busy the banks, the District Feds, and the Fund must be on any banking day. Millions of accounts in banks, at the District Feds, and at the Fund are in a state of constant change. The Fed processes over 30 billion of these "migrating" checks each year, serving millions of people and businesses. It is hard to imagine how our economy could survive without such an arrangement.

CONTROLLING THE MONEY SUPPLY

An increase in the money supply lowers the interest rate, causing an increase in investment and an increase in GDP. A decrease in the money supply has the opposite effect.

As we noted earlier, a primary function of the Fed is to control the money supply. Focusing on the flow of money in the economy allows the Fed to exercise some control over the economy's price level, interest rates, and level of employment. What the Fed hopes to achieve by all this control activity is the promotion of the economy's stability and growth. Look at Figure 4. It depicts the way the Fed can influence real GDP, that is, engage in countercyclical policy.

Look at the sequence of events that occurs when money supply increases. First, an increase in the money supply from M_1 to M_2 causes the interest rate to fall from i_1 to i_2. That fall in the interest rate causes the quantity demanded of investment to increase from I_1 to I_2. Finally, the increase in investment spending shifts the aggregate demand curve from AD_1 to AD_2, which increases the level of real GDP in this illustration.

Of course, what goes up, can come down. By reversing policy on the money supply, the Fed can engineer a decrease in the price level. How? Imagine aggregate demand at AD_3. By decreasing the money supply, the interest rate rises,

FIGURE 4 **From Changes in the Money Supply to Changes in Real GDP**

An increase in the money supply from M_1 to M_2 lowers the interest rate from i_1 to i_2. This fall in the interest rate raises investment spending from I_1 to I_2, which shifts the aggregate demand curve from AD_1 to AD_2. As a result, real GDP increases from GDP_1 to GDP_2.

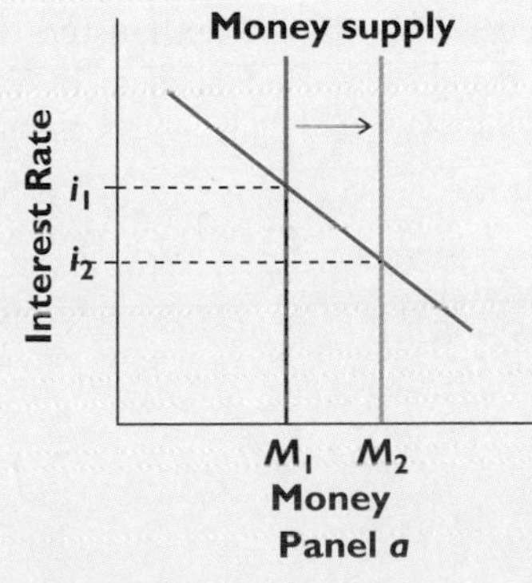

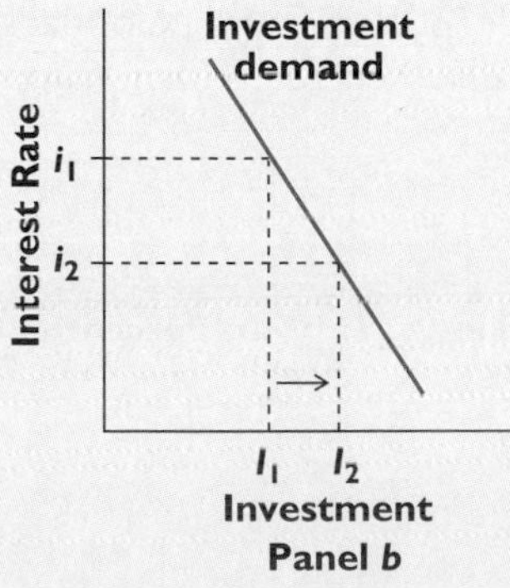

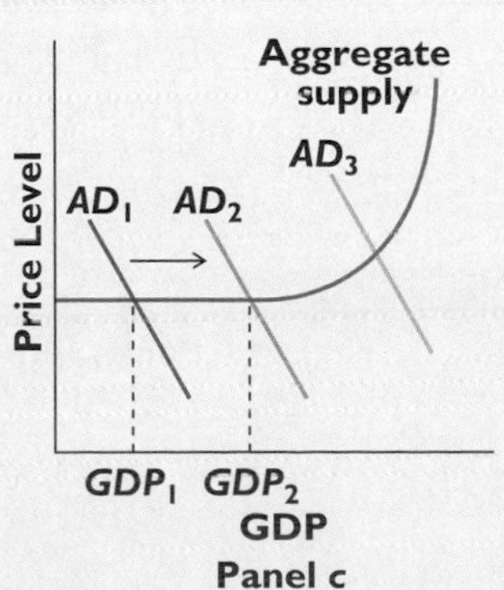

Countercyclical monetary policy
Policy directives used by the Fed to moderate swings in the business cycle.

investment falls, and aggregate demand falls, causing the price level to fall. As you see, the Fed's key to controlling GDP and the price level—the heart and soul of **countercyclical monetary policy**—is controlling the money supply.

How does the Fed control the money supply? It relies upon three instruments: reserve requirements, the discount rate, and open market operations.

Changing the Legal Reserve Requirement

Reserve requirement
The minimum amount of reserves the Fed requires a bank to hold, based on a percentage of the bank's total deposit liabilities.

By lowering the **reserve requirement,** the Fed can trigger a new series of additional loans and deposits throughout the banking system. For example, lowering the reserve requirement allows banks to make more loans. More borrowers mean greater real production in the economy.

If the Fed wants to curb production, it can increase the reserve requirement and restrict loans and thereby decrease the money supply. In this way, the economy's money supply can be expanded or contracted at the Fed's discretion. In times of recession, the Fed can lower the reserve requirement. In times of full employment and inflation, it can raise it. But there's a hitch to its effectiveness. Even if the Fed lowers the reserve requirement to increase the money supply, there is no guarantee that the money supply will increase. Why not? Because it depends upon whether borrowers are willing to take up the new loans that the Fed now makes possible. If borrowers, for their own reasons, choose not to borrow, then the Fed can lower the legal reserve requirement all it wants without changing the money supply by one penny.

By raising the legal reserve requirement, the Fed restricts banks' abilities to make loans.

The legal reserve requirement set by the Fed applies not only to banks but, since the enactment of the Depository Institutions Deregulation and Monetary Control Act of 1980, also to savings and loan associations and credit unions, whether state or nationally chartered or whether or not they are members of the Fed.

Table 4 shows that the reserve requirement imposed on banks by the Fed depends on the size of a bank's total deposits.

Although the Fed's ability to change the reserve requirement would seem to be an effective tool to control money supply, it is rarely used. Why not? Because it creates uncertainty that banks prefer to avoid. For example, every time the Fed raises the requirement, it forces banks to contract outstanding loans. This can be highly disruptive to both banks and borrowers.

Changing the Discount Rate

The Fed can change the discount rate it charges banks who borrow from the Fed. For example, if Paris First National's excess reserves are exhausted, it can approach the Dallas Fed for a loan. Suppose the Dallas Fed agrees. It charges

TABLE 4 Reserve Requirements (July 1994)

Banks with Checking Account Balances	Percent of Checking Account Deposits
$0 to $51.9 million	3
more than $51.9 million	10

Source: Board of Governors of the Federal Reserve System, *Federal Reserve Bulletin* (Washington, D.C., July 1994), p. A9.

TABLE 5 Change in the Dallas Fed's Accounts after Providing a $5,000 Loan to PFN

Assets	Liabilities
Loan to PFN +$5,000	Reserve deposit of PFN +$5,000

PFN a discount rate, determined by the Fed. PFN will borrow from the Fed only if the discount rate it is obliged to pay is less than the interest rate it charges its borrowers. The spread between these two rates determines the banks' eagerness to borrow from the Fed.

A decrease in the discount rate makes it easier for member banks to augment their reserves by borrowing from the Fed. This will cause the money supply to grow.

If there is a recession and the Fed wants to encourage banks to provide loans in the economy, it lowers its discount rate. On the other hand, if the economy is inflationary, the Fed would want to restrict bank lending. It does so by raising the discount rate.

How are the Fed's loans to banks transacted? See, in Table 5, how the accounts of both the Dallas Fed and PFN change after a $5,000 Fed loan is made to PFN.

In making the loan to PFN, the Dallas Fed simply creates a $5,000 deposit in PFN's account. That's potentially *new* money that never existed before. *The Fed brought it into being by simply changing its assets and liabilities.* The PFN, with $5,000 added to its total reserves, can now make additional loans, the amount depending upon the reserve requirement. Table 6 shows how the Dallas Fed's loan affects PFN's account.

If the reserve requirement were 20 percent, then PFN's new $5,000 reserve allows PFN to loan out $4,000. That *may* trigger a series of deposits and loans throughout the banking system that could potentially raise the economy's money supply by

$$\$5{,}000 \times \frac{1}{.20} = \$25{,}000$$

What do discount rates look like in the real world? How frequently do they change? Look at Table 7.

As you see, the Fed is very much disposed to change its discount rate. Changes are sometimes as frequent as weekly. These changes not only affect the

TABLE 6 Change in PFN's Accounts after Receiving a $5,000 Loan from the Dallas Fed

Assets	Liabilities
Reserves at the Fed +$5,000	Borrowing from Fed +$5,000

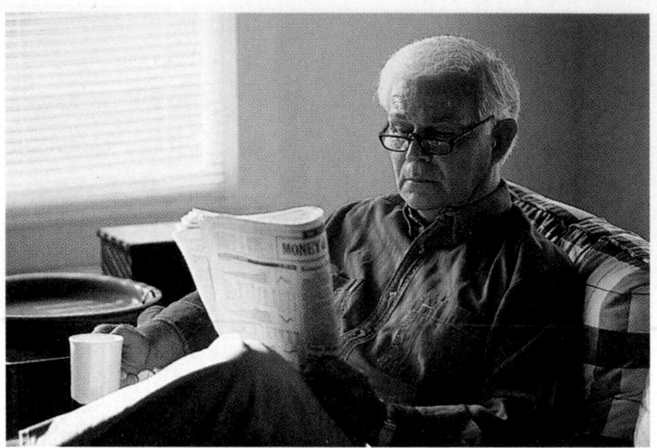

Interested in knowing what the Fed's discount rate is today? Or the federal funds market rate? Just consult *The Wall Street Journal*, or *The New York Times*, or perhaps your own daily newspaper. That's what this man is doing in the comfort of his home.

percent spread that banks earn on a Fed loan but, no less important, reflect the Fed's thinking about the money supply. That's important information to banks, perhaps enough to make them reconsider their own loan behavior.

Federal funds market

The market in which banks lend and borrow reserves from each other for very short periods of time, usually overnight.

Federal funds rate

The interest rate on loans made by banks in the federal funds market.

In practice, however, the Fed has become increasingly reluctant to provide member banks with excess reserves to expand their loans, encouraging them instead to use the **federal funds market.** What is this market?

Suppose Paris First National, at the close of a brisk banking day, discovers that it is $100,000 short of reserves the Fed requires it to hold. And suppose at the close of that same day, Paris Second National discovers that it holds $100,000 in excess reserves at the Dallas Fed.

Consider PFN's line of action. It must borrow to cover its $100,000 reserve deficit. It can call the Dallas Fed and borrow the $100,000 from it—paying the discount rate to the Fed. Or, it can borrow PSN's $100,000 of excess reserves at the Dallas Fed for the day—paying the **federal funds rate** to PSN. Why

TABLE 7 **Federal Reserve Bank of New York Discount Rates: 1978–94**

[Percent per year. Rates for short-term adjustment credit. For rates applicable to other types of discount window credit, see source. See also *Historical Statistics, Colonial Times to 1970*, series X, pp. 454-455]

Effective Date	Rate	Effective Date	Rate	Effective Date	Rate	Effective Date	Rate
1980: Feb. 15	13	Dec. 4	12	Nov. 21	$8\frac{1}{2}$	1989: Feb. 24	7
May 30	12	1982: July 20	$11\frac{1}{2}$	Dec. 24	8	1990: Dec. 19	$6\frac{1}{2}$
June 13	11	Aug. 2	11	1985: May 20	$7\frac{1}{2}$	1991: Feb. 1	6
July 28	10	Aug. 16	$10\frac{1}{2}$	1986: March 7	7	April 30	$5\frac{1}{2}$
Sept. 26	11	Aug. 27	10	April 21	$6\frac{1}{2}$	Sept. 13	5
Nov. 17	12	Oct. 12	$9\frac{1}{2}$	July 11	6	Nov. 6	$4\frac{1}{2}$
Dec. 5	13	Nov. 22	9	Aug. 21	$5\frac{1}{2}$	Dec. 20	$3\frac{1}{2}$
1981: May 5	14	Dec. 15	$8\frac{1}{2}$	1987: Sept. 4	6	1992: July 2	3
Nov. 2	13	1984: April 9	9	1988: Aug. 9	$6\frac{1}{2}$	May 2, 1994	3

Source: *Statistical Abstract of the United States, 1994* (Washington, D.C.: U.S. Department of Commerce, 1994), p. 507.

TABLE 8
Change in the Fed's Accounts after Buying $10 Million of Securities from PFN ($ millions)

Assets	Liabilities
Government securities +$10	PFN's reserve +$10

wouldn't Paris Second National want to make money on its excess reserves for the day?

Imagine thousands of daily transactions involving interbank loans and borrowings of excess reserves. It is a more common practice than borrowing directly from the Fed. Typically, the federal funds rate is slightly higher than the discount rate.

Engaging in Open Market Operations

Open market operations
The buying and selling of government bonds by the Federal Open Market Committee.

The most effective and frequently used tool the Fed has at its disposal to change the economy's money supply is its **open market operations**—that is, *its buying and selling operations in the government securities market.* The Fed's operating rule is simple: It buys government securities on the open market when it wants to increase the money supply and sells some of its government securities when it wants to reduce the economy's money supply.

When the Fed purchases government securities, it increases banks' reserves and makes possible an increase in the money supply. When the Fed sells government securities, it decreases banks' reserves and makes possible a decrease in the money supply.

The nerve center of the Fed's securities buying and selling activity is located in its Federal Open Market Committee (FOMC), which issues directives to the securities trading desk at the Federal Reserve Bank of New York. Suppose the FOMC wants to increase the money supply and decides to buy $10 million of government securities. Where would it find the security sellers? Who are they?

If you owned government securities, wouldn't you be willing to sell them if the Fed met your price? Suppose you owned a $1,000 government bond and discovered that the Fed was willing to pay $1,100 for it. Would you sell? You may not be the only one who would take the deal. Many corporations and most banks own government securities for the same reason you do; they pay interest. And like you, they would sell their interest-bearing securities if the price were right.

The market price of government securities is determined, like the price of most goods, by buyers and sellers operating in the market. The securities market is described as *open* because securities holders and would-be securities holders freely negotiate the prices of securities.

TABLE 9
Change in PFN's Accounts after Selling $10 Million of Securities to the Fed ($ millions)

Assets	Liabilities
Government securities –$10	No change
Reserves at Fed +$10	

TABLE 10
Change in PFN's Accounts after Maria Sells $10 Million of Securities ($ millions)

Assets	Liabilities
Cash reserves +$10	Demand deposits +$10

The FOMC enters the securities market to purchase $10 million of securities. Suppose the Paris First National Bank decides to sell $10 million of the securities it owns. Tables 8 and 9 trace the effect of the sale on the Fed's and PFN's accounts.

PFN transfers $10 million of its securities to the Fed. The Fed now owns them. Look at the Fed's new asset position. It has increased by $10 million. However, the securities are hardly a gift. The Fed pays for the securities by adding $10 million to PFN's reserves at the Fed. This appears as a $10 million increase in the Fed's liabilities to PFN.

What about PFN? Table 9 describes the change in its accounts.

Note the change in PFN's asset position. Before, it held $10 million in interest-bearing government securities. It now holds, instead, $10 million in excess reserves at the Fed. *These new excess reserves can be used by PFN to support $10 million in additional loans.*

That's precisely why the Fed went on the open market to buy the securities. It wanted to increase the economy's money supply. If sufficient numbers of borrowers can be found, the $10 million of increased reserves at PFN will trigger ($10 million × 1/0.20) = $50 million more in deposits throughout the banking system. That's a $50 million increase in the economy's money supply. And that's precisely what the Fed had in mind.

But suppose the Fed bought the $10 million of securities from individuals, not from PFN. Would it change the results? Yes, but only slightly. Let's trace the sale of these securities by supposing, for simplicity's sake, that only one person, Maria Snarski, sold the securities to the Fed.

What happens now? Maria sells her $10 million of securities on the open market. The Fed buys them. She receives a check, made out by the Fed, for $10 million. She deposits the check in her account at PFN.

What does PFN do with it? Look at Table 10.

Maria's $10 million deposit increases PFN's assets and liabilities by $10 million. PFN sends the $10 million check to the Fed for collection. The Fed credits PFN's account at the Fed by $10 million. We see this recorded in Table 11.

TABLE 11
Change in the Fed's Accounts after Buying $10 Million of Securities from Maria ($ millions)

Assets	Liabilities
Government securities +$10	PFN's reserves +$10

ADDED PERSPECTIVE

The Honorable Martha Seger: Ex-Fed Governor Tells it Like it Is

The Margin: You taught about the Fed in the classroom before joining it. Were there any differences between the Fed of economic textbooks and what you found when you actually became a member of the board?

Martha Seger: The biggest difference between the Fed as the textbook writers describe it and how it actually works is that it's just about a hundred times more tough to make the decisions. There isn't some cute little formula to use, even though the Fed has a tremendous computer system and 350 or so researchers with all sorts of Ph.D.'s in finance, economics, math, and econometrics. You can't just run some econometric model and have the policy answer pop out.

In the final analysis, the decisions have to be made by the Governors and not by the staffers. I guess the only way I can describe it is to say that it's much more difficult and involves much more judgment than the average textbook would suggest. Making monetary policy is much more an art than a science—it's not a science at all.

Could you give us a little of the flavor of an FOMC meeting? Are the discussions heated or is there an air of calm deliberation? What goes on?

At the beginning of the meeting, you have a report from Fed staffers on what's been happening to monetary policy since the last FOMC meeting. You get a chance to compare what the FOMC had told the staff to do with the actions it actually carried out.

Then there is a staff presentation on their view of the economic outlook. Then they would go around the table and everyone who is at the meeting—the seven members of the Board of Governors plus all 12 district bank presidents—gets a chance to ask a question of the staff about their forecast. During this period some of the participants may challenge the staff forecast. It's not heated, but I would say it's an open discussion, an open exchange of views, questions, comments. Then after that's done, they go around the table and people can give a little spiel on how they see the economy. The president of the Chicago bank might say, "Well, I met some guy from Ford Motor last week and he said that they just revised downward their sales forecast for next year or they're changing their production schedules and knocking them all down." That sort of thing would be discussed.

In addition to the discussions at the meeting, members are also given two books of materials, called the "Green Books," prior to the meeting with reports and analyses about the economy. They also receive the "Blue Book," which outlines monetary policy options. The "Blue Book" usually spells out three options: option A, option B, option C. Then one of the staffers in the monetary affairs section would make the presentation on those options and what you might get in terms of monetary growth and what would happen to the federal funds rate and other interest rates if you chose A, or you chose B, or C. Again, that's information, not always accurate, but still it was presented. And then there would be a discussion after that presentation by the members about the options and about the assumptions, and people would express their views about which ones they thought were most reasonable. And then we would have a break and go for coffee and doughnuts.

While we were relaxing, the chairman would go off with this staffer who was basically in charge of the "Blue Book," and they would prepare a proposed Directive for the group to consider. The Directive gives instructions to the Fed's staff for how to conduct open market operations until the next FOMC meeting. They would draft the Directive based on what they thought they were hearing from everybody. In other words, they would try to get some sense of where the bulk of the feeling is, the bulk of the sentiment. They would write something up, and then they would come back, and then this draft Directive would be distributed. Alan would talk about the proposed policy for the period ahead, again until the next FOMC meeting, and what he thought would be appropriate. Then everybody else could talk about his or her views and then finally we would have an up or down vote on it. You could either vote in favor of supporting that Directive or you could vote against it—you could be a dissenter. All the votes were recorded. You could also write something up to be put in the minutes, so later on people could go back and see why you disagreed with all those wise folks. So that's basically what goes on.

Source: *The Margin*, Spring 1992.

TABLE 12 Change in PFN's Accounts after Buying $10 Million of Securities ($ millions)

Assets	Liabilities
Reserves at the Fed −$10	No change
Government securities +$10	

The increase of $10 million in reserves allows PFN to loan out $8 million—rather than $10 million as in the previous example—and begin the process of money creation throughout the banking system. As you see, that process occurs whether the Fed buys securities from the bank directly or from individuals like Maria.

Now suppose the economy is in an inflationary phase and the Fed decides to reduce the money supply. How would it do it? It just reverses its open market operations. It *sells* securities instead of buying them. Banks, corporations, and individuals buy them from the Fed if the price is right. Let's suppose again that PFN gets into the act. This time it decides to buy securities from the Fed. What would it do? Look at Table 12.

PFN writes out a $10 million check to the Fed. PFN pays for these additional securities out of its reserves (i.e., the Fed reduces PFN's reserves by $10 million). So far, the only change has been in the composition of assets PFN holds. With $10 million fewer reserves, PFN is not in a position to loan $10 million. This eliminates a series of loans and deposits which ordinarily might take place throughout the banking system. The reduction in credit available to consumers and businesses is likely to reduce spending. Not a bad outcome if the economy were in its inflationary phase.

The results would be the same if Maria Snarski, Merrill Lynch, or Nike Corporation did the buying.

CONTROLLING THE INTEREST RATE: THE FED'S ALTERNATIVE TARGET OPTION

If the Fed chooses a money supply target, then the interest rate may vary if money demand shifts.

The idea of targeting the money supply in order to control interest rates, investment, aggregate demand, and ultimately real GDP makes sense in the simple world of Figure 4. That world *assumes* the Fed knows where the demand curve for money is positioned. After all, if its position weren't known, the Fed couldn't possibly associate specific changes in the money supply to specific changes in the interest rate. Without that specificity, the Fed's ability to execute policy weakens.

What, then, can it do? Look at Figure 5, panels *a* and *b* (a modification of Figure 4, panel *a*). This view of the economy yields new target options for the Fed.

Choosing the Money Supply Option

Look first at panel *a*. Suppose the Fed decides to target the money supply at M_{s1}. It uses its tools—the reserve requirement, the discount rate, and open market

FIGURE 5 **Fed's Target Options**
If the Fed targets the supply of money at M_{s1}, as we see in panel *a*, then it cannot control the interest rate, for that depends on the positioning of the demand curve for money. If, on the other hand, it targets the interest rate at i_1, and if the demand curve for money is M_{d1}, as we see in panel *b*, then the Fed loses control over the supply of money.

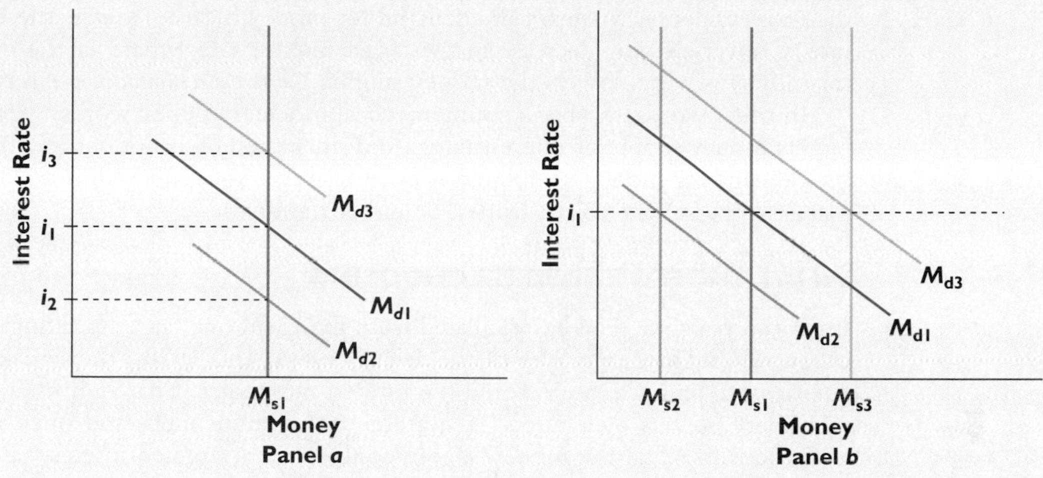

operations—to create M_{s1}. If the Fed believes that the demand curve for money is M_{d1}, then it knows that the interest rate will be i_1. But the truth of the matter is that the Fed lives, as we all do, in a world of uncertainty. It doesn't *really* know the position of the demand curve for money, in which direction it may shift, or how often it shifts, even for the short run. For example, if after fixing the money supply at M_{s1}, the money demand curve turns out to be M_{d2} or M_{d3} and not the M_{d1} curve the Fed anticipated, then the interest rate that results could vary between i_2 and i_3. That variation could create a new set of problems for the Fed. At, say, i_2, producers may want to invest more than the Fed anticipated or considers desirable. Simply put: *If the Fed chooses to target the money supply, it cannot at the same time control the interest rate.*

Choosing the Interest Rate Option

The Fed, instead, can choose to target the interest rate, allowing the money supply to take its course. We see the consequences of this option in Figure 5, panel *b*.

If the Fed chooses an interest rate target, then the money supply may have to vary considerably to maintain the target.

Suppose the Fed, using reserve requirements, discount rates, and open market operations, wishes to fix the interest rate at i_1. If the demand curve for money is M_{d1}, then the money supply must be set at M_{s1} (quantity of money demanded equals quantity of money supplied in equilibrium). But what if the Fed guesses incorrectly and the demand curve for money is not M_{d1}, but, say, M_{d2} or M_{d3}? Now the money supply, in order to keep the interest rate fixed at i_1, must be M_{s2} or M_{s3}. Once again, the Fed may confront problems it didn't anticipate. That is, it may end up with a money supply it really doesn't want. But it has no alternative. *By choosing to target the interest rate, it loses control over the money supply.*

Is There *Really* a Preferred Target Option?

You see the Fed's dilemma, don't you? *It faces an opportunity cost no matter which option it chooses.* But is the opportunity cost really debilitating? After all, even though the Fed loses some control over the interest rate once it targets money supply, *the interest rate still moves in the appropriate direction.* That is, any increase in the money supply, whatever the demand for money may be, lowers the interest rate. Conversely, any decrease in the target interest rate, whatever the demand for money may be, lowers the money supply. *Correct directional movement counts!*

In other words, the Fed's countercyclical monetary policy works, whether it targets money supply or interest rates. And since the Fed is not entirely blind to the demand for money, the actual opportunity cost associated with either target may, except in very volatile times, be rather minimal.

WHAT THE FED ENDED UP CHOOSING

Over the years, the Fed has vacillated from fixing on one target to fixing on another. Through the decades of the 1950s, 1960s, and 1970s, the Fed kept an anxious eye on both, but favored the interest rate target. That is, it used its discretionary powers over reserve requirements, discount rates, and open market operations to make the money supply conform to a targeted interest rate. The linkages were understood and expected. GDP depends upon aggregate demand, which depends upon investment, which depends upon the interest rate.

But by 1980, with Paul Volcker as Chairman of the Fed, the Fed's focus shifted to the money supply. Worried about persisting high inflation, the plan was to target money supply in order to bring inflation under control. It understood that the unavoidable consequence of lowering the money supply was rising interest rates. But in the 1980s, the Fed felt that higher interest rates were not only tolerable but desirable. After all, higher rates would reduce investment and aggregate demand, easing pressure on inflation.

The Fed's monetary target shifted once again in the late 1980s and 1990s. In 1989, the Fed became less concerned about inflation and worried more about recession. This time, Chairman Alan Greenspan sought to bring interest rates down, ignoring the swing it might create in the money supply. The Fed hoped that lower interest rates would stimulate investment, aggregate demand, and real GDP. Inflation? It was now the lesser of the problems.

Ancillary Tools Available to the Fed

Aside from the Big Three—the reserve requirement, the discount rate, and open market operations—the Fed can exercise some additional control over the money market by controlling margin requirements on financing of stock market purchases, and by exercising moral suasion. But these are strictly the Fed's utility players in the major league game of money control.

CONTROLLING STOCK MARKET MARGIN REQUIREMENTS

You've heard stories, haven't you, about the "killings" people make on the stock market? Sometimes, the lure of the market can be downright intoxicating, blurring our vision of reality. In truth, playing the stock market is about as reliable a way of getting rich quickly as playing the tables at Las Vegas or betting on the horses at Churchill Downs.

Here's how it's supposed to work. If you have real inside information as many people suppose they do, or have a strong sense of the market's moods as many more people feel they have, then speculating on the market is a nice, clean way of making money. For example, if you believe that the price of Xerox stock, now at $50 per share on the New York Stock Exchange, will reach $60 by this time next year, it pays to buy Xerox. If you bought $50,000 worth of Xerox, you would end up netting $10,000.

But how do you get your hands on $50,000? Here's the trick. Just go to Paris First National and borrow $40,000. Why would PFN loan you $40,000? Because you can offer the $50,000 Xerox stock as collateral on the $40,000 loan. All you have to put up of your own money, then, is $10,000.

If you have speculated correctly, you end up making $10,000 on a $10,000 personal investment. That's a cool 100 percent. Even adjusting for the interest on the $40,000 loan, that's a mighty fine percentage.

Where's the catch? Everybody in the stock market business knows that what goes up can come down. Suppose Xerox falls from $50 to $30 two months after your purchase. Your stock is now worth $30,000. Not only has your $10,000 expected profit evaporated, but PFN realizes it can only recover $30,000 of its $40,000 loan.

What does it do? PFN may choose to take the $30,000 rather than chance waiting for an upswing in prices. A speculative loss of $10,000, or even more, may not trouble a bank whose loan portfolios are basically sound. But if the bank's assets were dominated by an array of loans to stock market speculators, then even moderate downward movements in stock prices can do the bank in.

And if the banking system, itself, is heavily into loans supported by stock market collateral, then any downward movement in stock prices that frightens banks enough to sell off their stock collateral will drive stock prices down even further. It may not take much to trigger a stock market panic.

That's precisely what happened in the stock market crash of 1929. When the dust clouds of that infamous October cleared, it was obvious that loans made on stock market collateral were as uncontrollable as a runaway locomotive on the downside of a mountain. As J. M. Keynes so aptly noted just a few years after the crash:

Speculators may do no harm as bubbles on a steady stream of enterprise. But the position is serious when enterprise becomes the bubble on a whirlpool of speculation.

If it didn't make sense before, it certainly made sense after the crash that some control over the banking system's holding of stock market collateral was required. The Federal Reserve seemed to be the logical choice.

Margin requirement

The maximum percentage of the cost of a stock that can be borrowed from a bank or any other financial institution, with the stock offered as collateral.

The Fed was called upon to establish stock market **margin requirements,** the fraction of the stock's price that must be put up by the person buying the stock. In the Xerox PFN example, the margin was ($50,000 – $40,000)/$50,000 = 20 percent. How has the Fed used this margin requirement as a selective control device? Look at Table 13.

During the war years 1940–45, inflationary pressures built up in the economy. How did the Fed respond? By raising margins from 50 to 100 percent to discourage speculative bank loans. After all, the more loans, the more the banking system would fuel the inflation.

At other times, for example during the recessions of 1949 and 1953, the Fed cut the margins back to 50 percent to help bolster a lackluster economy. The reduced margins gave banks the green light to grant stock-supported loans. The

TABLE 13 Federal Reserve's Margin Requirements: 1940–94 (percent)

Date	Margin	Date	Margin
1940	50	1960	70
1942	75	1962	50
1945	100	1963	70
1947	75	1970	65
1953	50	1972	65
1955	50	1974	50
1958	90	1994	50

Source: *Banking and Monetary Statistics, 1940–1970* (Washington, D.C.: Board of Governors of the Federal Reserve System, 1975) pp. 799; and *Federal Reserve Bulletin*, July 1994, p. A27.

Fed hoped that by this action such loans would create new deposits, new money, and new jobs.

MORAL SUASION

We have all used some form of moral suasion on friends and foes to promote a particular idea. How many times have you heard your high school teacher say before an exam: "No copying from your neighbor." Sometimes, this admonition would be followed by a threat: "Those found cheating will be suspended from school."

Did it work? Sometimes, on some people. The problem with relying on moral suasion is that in the final analysis it relies entirely on morality and persuasion. But that's what the Fed sometimes uses to encourage or discourage bank loans.

For example, the Chairman of the Board of Governors may explain in a television interview that the Fed hopes banks show more restraint in providing consumer credit because inflation is a problem. Sometimes these expressions of concern take the form of official Fed policy statements or direct appeals by way of letters to thousands of bank presidents.

Whatever its form, these pronouncements rely on voluntary compliance. They may seem weak as instruments of policy, but they are always supported by the unspoken threat that if moral suasion doesn't work, the Fed can always resort to more reliable instruments. Moral suasion, then, can be viewed as an omen of things to come. And banks take note.

THE FED'S COUNTERCYCLICAL MONETARY POLICY

Let's put the analysis of the Fed's operating tools into the context of the Fed's countercyclical monetary policy. When you think about it, the Fed and the government can be described as partners in a "shock-absorbing" business, protecting us against the bumps of unemployment and inflation. The government manages its activity through its budget, adding or cutting taxes and spending as the occasion warrants. The Fed works either through the banking system directly or indirectly through its open market operations.

ADDED PERSPECTIVE

An Interview with the Fed's Alan Blinder

Alan Blinder, the new vice chairman of the Federal Reserve Board, denied that there's any rift between him and Fed Chairman Alan Greenspan. But he didn't back away from his recent declaration, unusually candid for a central banker, that the Fed must in the short run choose between more unemployment and more inflation.

Mr. Blinder caused a stir at a recent Fed conference on unemployment at Jackson Hole, WY, by saying flatly that the Fed should worry about both unemployment and inflation. "I said what I meant. I meant what I said," an unrepentant Mr. Blinder said in a speech yesterday, though he complained that some accounts mischaracterized his remarks.

Although Mr. Blinder voted to raise interest rates by half a percentage point in August, he has been criticized for being insufficiently tough on inflation in his public utterances and continuing to say the things he did when he was a Princeton University economics professor and an economic adviser to President Clinton.

Mr. Blinder yesterday answered questions for *The Wall Street Journal*. Here are some excerpts:

Q: You got a lot of attention for what you said at Jackson Hole, probably more than you wanted.

A: Quite a bit more than I wanted.

Q: What point were you trying to make?

A: What central banks do affects employment and real economic activity in the short run. I thought it was appropriate to keep that in mind, as the Federal Reserve Act directs us to do. There is some controversy around the world now, with the prevailing view being in some quarters that the central bank should ignore the short-run effects on employment and only focus on its long-run inflation objective. I was disputing that.

Q: One economist has said: "The data do indicate a short-term trade-off [between inflation and employment], but that is an ephemeral relationship, and all the evidence we have suggests that to whatever extent there is such a relationship in the very short term, it very quickly dissipates. Monetary policy which fails to focus on the long-term requirement of achieving price stability is inevitably going to find itself in a position where inflation emerges. . . ."

A: I can guess who said that.

Q: Yes, Alan Greenspan. Isn't that different in emphasis from what you've been saying?

A: Yes, it's different in emphasis. I don't think it's different in substance. When this notion that there is a short-run trade-off, but no long-run trade-off is announciated by Alan Greenspan, it usually comes up emphasizing there is no long-run unemployment out at Jackson Hole. I emphasized that there is a short-run trade-off, though no long-run trade-off. It's a difference in emphasis that has to do partly with context and partly with rhetorical style, but it's not a difference in substance. It's two ways of saying the same thing.

Q: So on this point, you and Mr. Greenspan don't have any difference?

A: I don't think so.

Q: Presumably you've talked to him about this.

A: Yes, yesterday.

Q: The Federal Reserve Act directs you to aim for "maximum employment and stable prices." Mr. Greenspan has endorsed a bill to give the Fed a single-minded focus on inflation. You oppose that.

A: That's a theoretical difference that has no operational significance because the law, as it stands today, gives us both objectives.

Q: You chose your words precisely when you said, in answering a question in public Thursday, that there aren't any "currently operational" differences between you and other Fed officials. What does that mean?

A: Whatever philosophical differences or differences in how one thinks the economy operates there may be, they haven't been at the forefront in monetary policy decisions in the short time that I've been at the board, nor do I see them at the forefront any time soon. I don't rule out the possibility that differences . . . could at some future date lead to a clash over policy. It's definitely not imminent.

Q: The harder choices lie ahead. It's easier to agree that a 3 percent interest rate was too low than to decide the point at which the Fed has raised interest rates enough.

A: That's right. I don't rule out the possibility that we've done enough already, and I don't rule out the possibility that we'll have to do more. As events unfold in the coming months, there could be differences of opinion within the Federal Open Market Committee on that.

Q: If we end up with 2.5 percent growth and 3 percent inflation over the next few years, would that satisfy you?

A: Yes, absolutely. Given the hazards in this business, I'll be overjoyed.

FIGURE 6 **The Fed's Countercyclical Operations**
In the recovery and prosperity phases of the cycle, the Fed can contain the money supply by raising the reserve requirement, raising the discount rate, or selling bonds on the open market. In the downturn and recession phases of the cycle, the Fed lowers the reserve requirement, lowers the discount rate, or buys bonds on the open market to increase the supply of money.

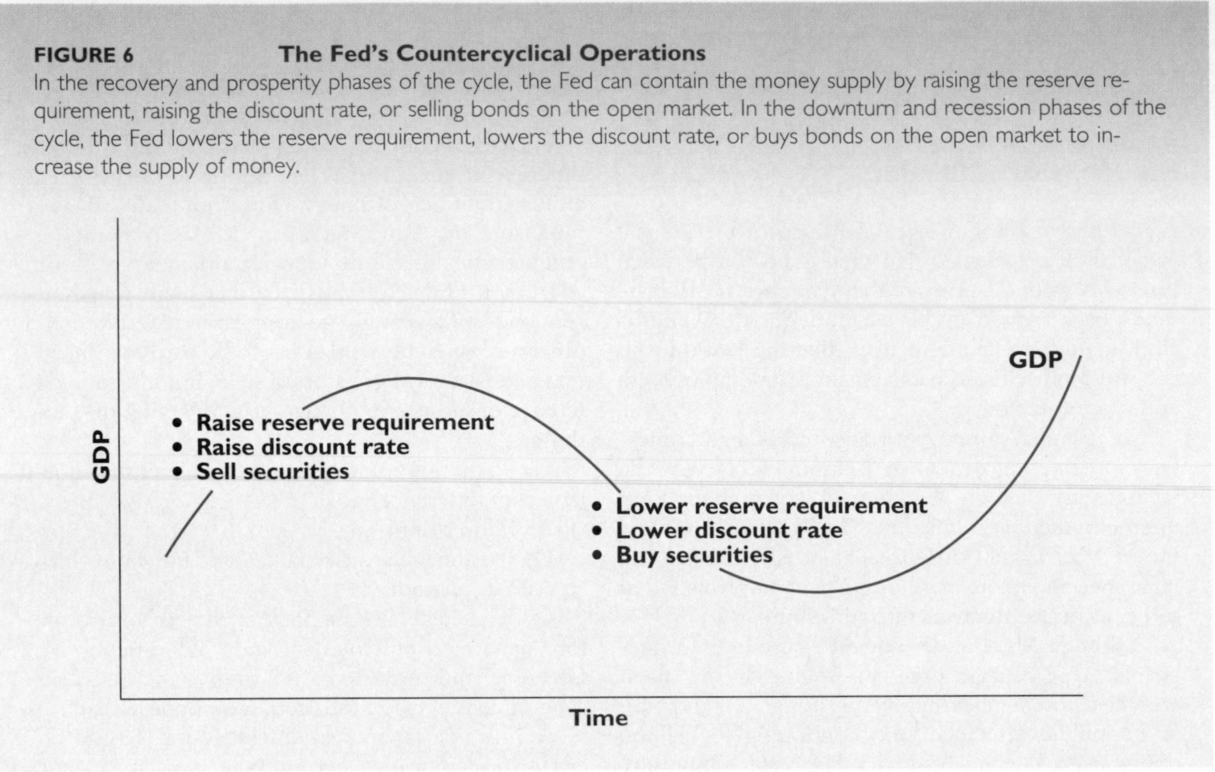

Typically, the Fed and government work in unison, pursuing common goals. For example, when a recession hits, we would expect the government to run a budget deficit by raising the level of its spending or by cutting taxes, or perhaps both. At the same time and for the same reason, we would expect the Fed to reduce the reserve requirements, reduce the discount rate, and buy securities on the open market. All three activities are engineered to promote bank loans. After all, loans create jobs.

What about Fed and government policies during periods of full employment and inflation? Both have the tools to reverse their lines of attack. We would now expect government to create a surplus budget by cutting its own spending and raising taxes. At the same time and for the same reason, we would expect the Fed to raise the reserve requirements, raise the discount rate, and sell securities on the open market. In this way, banks would find it more difficult to loan, easing the inflationary pressures on the economy.

Figure 6 depicts the Fed's countercyclical monetary operations. Although there appears to be symmetry in the Fed's policies during the upswing and downswing phases of the cycle, in fact, there isn't. The Fed is more effective in curbing inflation in periods of prosperity than it is in promoting employment during a recession. Why? Because the Fed can prevent banks from loaning, but it can't force people to borrow.

Does it make sense? Imagine a college without a library. Wouldn't that make it difficult for students to learn? Suppose a library is built. Does access to a library guarantee that students will learn? The facilities may be there, but there is no way to assure that students will use them. In the same way, the Fed can prevent the creation of loans, but can't force loan creation.

Fed and Government Don't Always Agree

Typically, the Fed and the government pursue the same countercyclical policies. However, the Fed is independent and may pursue a different policy than the government, as happened during the early and mid-1980s.

Government budgets are typically financed by taxes. When government decides to spend more, it can simply tax more. It enjoys that as a constitutional right. Yet, interestingly enough, it doesn't always exercise it. Instead, government sometimes finds it more convenient to finance its spending by creating and selling new government securities.

In the past decade, government has financed its $200 billion annual budget deficits principally by creating government securities and selling them, that is, by borrowing. The interest rate it must offer to attract securities buyers is no minor issue. As you would suspect, the government would much rather pay lower than higher interest rates.

But that's not how the Fed views ideal interest rates. It supports high interest rates when it wants to curb inflation and switches to supporting lower interest rates when it promotes employment.

There are times, then, when the Fed's interest rate policy clashes with the government's. During recession, the Fed may be working to lower interest rates so that borrowers will find it more attractive to take up bank loans, while the government, financing a deficit, may find it necessary to offer higher interest rates to sell its securities. Sometimes, their conflicting interests require a series of summit meetings to negotiate an acceptable interest rate strategy. In such cases, it is generally the pressing needs of government that win out.

CHAPTER REVIEW

1. The money supply in colonial America was a mixed bag of different currencies and coins. With the American Revolution came the introduction of a paper money supply that was quickly devalued by overprinting. After independence, state banks began to be chartered. Many feared that these state banks would tend to overissue currency as had occurred during the revolution, thus leading to monetary instability. In part to counter this fear and to serve other monetary functions as well, the First Bank of the United States was established in 1791.

2. Congress refused to renew the charter of the First Bank of the United States in 1811 because of opposition coming mainly from southern and western states, whose representatives perceived the bank to be an unconstitutional money monopoly. Not surprisingly, the number of state banks and bank notes rose dramatically over the next several years. As a result of the ensuing financial instability, the Second Bank of the United States was established in 1816. The Second Bank is widely regarded as having done a good job at promoting a stable economic environment. However, in his second term, Andrew Jackson vowed to destroy the bank, and he succeeded. Apart from the National Banking Act during the Civil War, the history of banking in the United States from the 1830s to the eve of World War I is that of a growing economic power without the direction of a central bank.

3. The Panic of 1907 that followed the Knickerbocker Trust Disaster prompted U.S. political leaders to reconsider the need for a central bank. What evolved out of the political process was the Federal Reserve System, established in 1913. The Federal Reserve System is composed of 12 District Federal Reserve Banks. Each of these district banks is owned by member banks in the district and one required to contribute 3 percent of their capital to the district bank.

4. The main purpose of the Federal Reserve System is to maintain the proper functioning of our money system by regulating the money supply and interest rates, and influencing the price level. The Federal Open Market Committee controls the money supply through open market operations—the purchase and sale of government securities.

5. In order to achieve its purpose, the Fed performs a variety of functions. Among these are printing Federal Reserve Notes, serving as the bankers' bank for member banks, and controlling the money supply. By manipulating the money supply, the Fed can alter interest rates to maintain a countercyclical monetary policy.

6. The Fed has several tools by which it can change the money supply. The reserve requirement can be raised if the Fed wants the money supply to shrink, or be lowered if it wants the money supply to grow. Or, the Fed can increase the discount rate to decrease the money supply and lower it to increase the money supply. The Fed can also sell government securities to decrease the money supply and buy them to expand the money supply.

7. The Fed can choose either an interest rate target or a money supply target. The choice of an interest rate target implies a variable money supply and vice versa. The Fed cannot control both at once because it cannot control money demand. When the Fed is worried about inflation, it sometimes targets the money supply. When the concern is unemployment, the interest rate is usually the target.

8. A number of other tools are available to the Fed to control the money supply. Among these are stock market margin requirements and moral suasion. The Fed tends to be more effective at fighting inflation in high-employment periods than it is at combating unemployment during recessions. It is entirely possible for Fed policy and government policy to work at cross-purposes. For example, the Fed tended to maintain high interest rates through the mid-1980s at a time when the government ran big, expansionary deficits.

KEY TERMS

Bank note
State-chartered bank
Nationally chartered bank
Federal Reserve System (the Fed)
Federal Open Market Committee
Discount rate
Countercyclical monetary policy
Reserve requirement
Federal funds market
Federal funds rate
Open market operations
Margin requirement

QUESTIONS

1. We believe in economic freedom and yet we deny banks the right to make whatever loans they wish to make. Why? What has been our experience with unregulated banking?

2. The *Bank* of England is the central bank of England. The *Bank* of Canada is the central bank of Canada. Why did the Federal Reserve Act of 1913 create the Federal Reserve *System* instead of the Federal Reserve *Bank?*

3. When the Fed sells government bonds, the nation's money supply decreases. Explain how this works. You can construct your own bank transactions, changes in assets and liabilities of the Fed and of banks, to illustrate.

4. What is the discount rate, and how can the Fed use it to control the nation's supply of money?

5. One way the Fed can increase the nation's money supply is by reducing the reserve requirement. Explain how this works. You can construct your own bank transactions, changes in assets and liabilities of banks, to illustrate.

6. Why is the Fed more effective in preventing the money supply from increasing than it is in increasing the money supply?

7. Suppose your bill for a seafood dinner in San Francisco came to $100 and you paid it with a check drawn on your bank, the First National Bank of Boston. Describe the circuit the check would take through banks and District Feds.

8. Who prints currency for whom? How does the currency finally make its way to the thousands of banks operating in the economy?

9. How does a bank's borrowing reserves on the federal funds market differ from borrowing from the Fed? Which interest rates are typically higher?

10. Draw a sequence of figures detailing how an increase in the money supply eventually results in an increase in real GDP.

PART 7
GOVERNMENT AND THE MACROECONOMY

CHAPTER 29

CAN GOVERNMENT REALLY STABILIZE THE ECONOMY?

CHAPTER PREVIEW

By now you probably have the feeling that considerable controversy exists in the field of macroeconomic theory. We have hinted at the controversy a number of times. For example, in the chapter on business cycles many competing theories were advanced. And, in the chapter on money, classical, monetarist, and Keynesian views were contrasted. Keynesians disagree among themselves about the shape of the aggregate supply curve. No one has a monopoly on the truth when it comes to macroeconomic theory. An understanding of the various competing theories helps to build a better understanding of the way the macroeconomy behaves and should contribute to better policies for stabilization. The intent of this chapter is to provide you with a better understanding of the various macroeconomic theories being proposed, debated, tested, and refined by economists.

After studying this chapter, you should be able to:

- State the assumptions that support the classical-school model of the economy.
- Understand the classical school's advocacy for a laissez-faire policy regarding unemployment and inflation.

- Present the Keynesian argument for why unemployment exists.
- Draw a representative Phillips curve and explain its shape.
- Discuss neo-Keynesian policies to cope with unemployment and inflation.
- Present the argument for the vertical long-run Phillips curve.
- Explain what is meant by rational expectations.
- Contrast supply-side policies for economic stabilization with Keynesian policies.
- Describe the automatic stabilizers in the economy.

Most physicians will tell you that in cases they consider life threatening, they will advise the patient as a matter of course to get a second opinion. They do so not because they feel uncomfortable with their own diagnosis, but rather because they know we all live in a world of imperfect information. They realize that their understanding of the human body, however expert, is still subject to error.

A second opinion may confirm the first. But not always. If the first physician consulted advises radical surgery and the second suggests that the medical problem will correct itself, what should the patient do? Consult a third? What if the third physician prescribes a different remedy altogether? Should the patient seek a fourth opinion? How many are enough? Do additional opinions really add to the patient's stock of knowledge? Sometimes, the opinion offered reflects the temperament or set of values of the attending physician. Some physicians are known to be aggressive, immediately recommending a maximalist approach, such as strong drugs or surgery. Other physicians belong to a more conservative school and typically advise a number of approaches, from the least interfering to more interventionist treatments before even thinking about surgery.

THE NATURE OF ECONOMIC ADVICE

Economists' opinions reflect imperfections in the information that they use, as well as differences in ideology among them.

Economists, too, live in a world of very limited information and have a less than perfect understanding of how the economy they study really works. They will readily confess that even after centuries of systematic observation of their subject matter, of data collecting, theory building, empirical testing, and amassing historically relevant material, like physicians, they still arrive at different and sometimes even highly conflicting conclusions and recommendations.

Their opinions reflect a wide array of temperaments and ideologies. Some schools of economic thinking are interventionist by design. These economists are quick to advocate that government and the Fed, sometimes in massive doses, correct what they believe ails the economy. Other economists, looking at the same situation and reflecting a more conservative ideology, will advocate much less interference in the private sector.

It is reasonable to ask if ideology dictates economic policy, or if economic policy is the logical derivative of an ideology-free understanding of how the system works. For example, do conservative economists advocate conservative policy because they are ideologically conservative, or do they become ideologically conservative because they see and accept a particular understanding of how the

The Treasury Department—especially the Secretary of the Treasury—is an important player in economic policy making.

economy behaves? The same question, of course, is asked of interventionist economists. Do their liberal policies simply reflect a preconceived ideology, or is their ideology spun out of a particular understanding of the economy's behavior?

How should we view appointments to the President's Council of Economic Advisers? Economists picked by the more conservative presidents have been known advocates of conservative economic policy. For example, it was not surprising that President Bush would choose Stanford's Michael Boskin to head his Council, or that President Reagan would choose Harvard's Martin Feldstein and, later, Washington University's Murray Weidenbaum, both known and respected conservatives. Nor was it surprising that President Carter picked Brookings Institution's Charles Schultze to head his Council, and President Clinton picked Berkeley's Laura Tyson. Both of the latter economists are known and respected liberals. Isn't that precisely why they were chosen? But how should we read their appointments? Is the expert economic advice that presidents receive from the Council, then, "rigged" from the start?

WHY DOES THE ECONOMY GENERATE INFLATION AND UNEMPLOYMENT?

Some people, listening to expert opinion on economic policy over the years, are convinced there are more views held by economists than there are economists. Admittedly, there's some truth to that conviction, particularly when the focus of discussion is macroeconomic policy. After all, every macroeconomist sees the economic world through a unique lens. Some views are similar to others, but even among these there are important shades of differences.

Yet just as we have come to know schools of painters—French Impressionists, Surrealists, Cubists, Post-Modernists—so too do we find schools of thinking on matters of economic policy. Most economists will agree that the most demanding macroeconomic issue is: *Why do unemployment and inflation exist, and what should be done about them?*

Over the last century, the ideas on issues like inflation and unemployment could be classified according to economic schools of thought. Some of these ideas might be considered a radical departure from the mainstream, such as Marxian economics, while others share many things in common.

Classical economics was the dominant school of thought until midway through the depression of the 1930s when Keynesian economics became conventional wisdom. Monetarism has been around for quite some time, and although its ideas have had some impact on many economists, it has never succeeded in becoming a leading school of thought. In addition to monetarism, some of the schools which might loosely be viewed as contemporary are neo-Keynesian, supply-side, and rational expectations.

In each school of thought there are ideas which have shortcomings, especially in some of the older theories. Sometimes a particular economic theory does not offer an adequate explanation for a situation. In other cases, there are more fundamental difficulties. As we explore these different schools, it is important to follow the thought process involved and also understand where it tends to break down. You may find some appealing ideas in each school. In fact, many economists find considerable value in at least some ideas from each school of thought.

THE CLASSICAL SCHOOL

Classical economics

The school of thought that emphasizes the natural tendency for an economy to move toward equilibrium at full employment without inflation. It argues against government intervention.

The **classical economics** view of how our economy behaves is this: *If the economy were left on its own—without the interference of government or the Fed—it would move toward an equilibrium rate of growth that would produce, with only minor interruptions, full employment without inflation.*

There's something refreshing, isn't there, about this approach to handling inflation and unemployment. After all, what it really argues is that the problems of inflation and unemployment disappear by just doing nothing! That's as simple a policy as you could find.

Moreover, it doesn't make too many demands on our limited skills. Doing nothing is what most of us do well! Or do we? For if it's that simple a matter, why then do we find ourselves continually plagued by inflation and unemploy-

Laura D'Andrea Tyson, Chair of the White House Council of Economic Advisers in the White House briefing room, Friday, August 6, 1993, telling reporters the good news on unemployment. She announced that the nation's unemployment rate fell to 6.8 percent, its best showing in 22 months.

ment? Because, the classical economists argue, in spite of all the advice to the contrary, we still insist upon tampering with the machinery.

This hands-off view rests upon two simple propositions about markets: (1) all markets are basically competitive, and (2) as a result, all prices are flexible upward and downward, approaching equilibrium, if they are not already there.

Why Unemployment?

Classical school economists believe that the economy adjusts quickly back to full employment so no government intervention is necessary.

How do classical economists, then, explain unemployment? In their view, unemployment is only a temporary condition, caused by wage rates climbing above the equilibrium rate. In the long run, however, these above-equilibrium wage rates cannot last. The excess labor supply, the unemployed, competes with those who have jobs, driving the wage rates down to equilibrium and employment levels to full employment. The graphics of the classical view are shown in Figure 1.

Suppose the wage rate lies above the $6 equilibrium, say at $10. The supply curve shows that at $10, 16,000 people are willing to work but only 12,000 people actually find employment. The 4,000 who would be willing to work are out of luck. What happens? The 4,000 compete with those already working, driving the wage rate down. As the wage rate falls toward $6, more people get hired.

How many more? At the $6 equilibrium wage rate, 14,000 people are willing to work and 14,000 are hired. That is, *everyone who is willing to work at the equilibrium wage rate will eventually find employment.* Unemployment disappears.

If classical economists insist that unemployment is only temporary, why do we find unemployment stubbornly persisting in the real world? Because, they argue, people interfere with the competitive process, preventing wage rates from reaching equilibrium. The interference creates the unemployment.

Who interferes? Labor unions, for example, might use their market power to push wage rates above equilibrium levels, but they can only do so at the ex-

FIGURE 1
Classical Determination of Unemployment
The demand curve for labor and the supply curve of labor create employment for 14,000 workers at a wage rate of $6. If the wage rate is above $6, say at $10, the quantity of labor supplied is 16,000 while the quantity of labor demanded is 12,000, creating an excess labor supply (or unemployment) of 4,000. Competition among the employed and unemployed will force the wage rate to $6, erasing the unemployment.

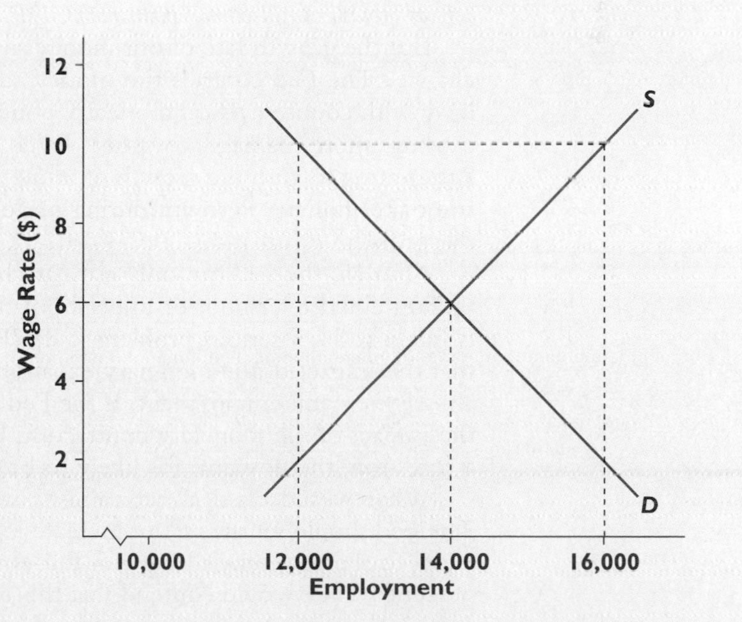

pense of employment. In other words, unions might end up being their own worst enemy.

Congress, too, gets into the act. They create unemployment by imposing minimum wage laws that necessarily cut people out of jobs they otherwise would have taken at less than the minimum wage. The unintended result is painfully clear. The unskilled, teenagers, minorities, and women are big losers.

Stabilization policy

The use of countercyclical monetary and fiscal policy by the government and the Fed to stabilize the economy.

What, then, should government do? The most appropriate countercyclical policy, or **stabilization policy,** in times of unemployment, according to classical economists, is for the *government to do nothing*. The competitive market should be allowed to work its way to equilibrium.

Why Inflation?

How do classical economists explain inflation? Just as unfettered competition in the labor market will always generate full employment, unfettered competition in the market for capital generates the full employment of capital.

If the money supply grows faster than real output, inflation results.

With labor and capital busy at work, the economy produces full-employment real GDP, or Q, as shown in the quantity theory of money equation

$$P = \frac{MV}{Q}$$

Recall that P is the price level, M is money supply, V is money velocity, and Q the quantity of goods and services produced. If resources are fully employed and if money velocity is constant, then the price level, P, depends on the quantity of money, M.

According to classical economists—in a view shared by monetarists— if the growth rate of M equals the Q growth rate, the price level remains unchanged. *Inflation occurs when the annual rate of growth in the money supply exceeds the annual rate of growth of full-employment real GDP.*

But the growth rate of our money supply, they remind us, is not a matter of chance. The Fed controls the money supply, they argue. The Fed is typically busy with countercyclical monetary policy, which more often than not, ends up causing more damage to price level stability than ensuring that stability. Attempting to curb the growth of money in periods of economic expansion and stimulate monetary growth during periods of recession, the Fed often worsens the problem of inflation.

After all, the Fed can only estimate how much money is needed. These estimates could overshoot or undershoot the appropriate money supply. Inflation is likely to be a serious problem if the Fed has increased the money supply so that the impact of the monetary expansion coincides with an economic climate already near full employment. If the Fed has restricted the money supply so that the impact of the monetary contraction happens when the economy is entering a recession, the downturn is likely to be more intense.

What would classical economists or the modern day monetarists suggest? The Fed should set the rate of increase in the money supply to be approximately equal to the economy's long-run full-employment rate of growth (i.e., about 3 percent). They would contend that this noninterventionist policy would tend to reduce the intensity of recessions and promote greater price stability. In other words, *the best countercyclical policy is no countercyclical policy.*

FIGURE 2
Keynesian View of Demand and Prices in the Swimsuit Market
The $30 price curve for swimsuits remains unchanged over the firm's production range. If the demand curve the firm faces is D, it produces 100,000 swimsuits. If the demand curve falls to D′, price remains at $30, but production falls to 80,000.

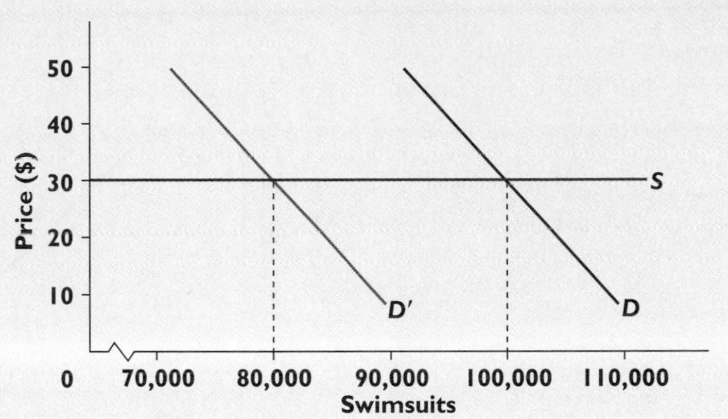

THE KEYNESIAN SCHOOL

Keynesian economics
The school of thought that emphasizes the possibility that an economy can be in equilibrium at less than full employment (or with inflation). It argues that with government intervention, equilibrium at full employment without inflation can be achieved by managing aggregate demand.

Keynesian economics rejects the classical economists' basic premise concerning competitive markets and flexible prices and, therefore, rejects the stream of classical policy implications that follow from it. To Keynesians, monopolies and unions tend to be permanent fixtures in our economy and the prices they create tend to be inflexible, at least downwardly. The classical idea of flexible prices, they argue, is a figment of the imagination.

Figure 2 depicts the Keynesian view of how changes in demand for goods affect production.

Note that prices are inflexible at $30. What *is* flexible is the firm's production level. If the demand curve for swimsuits is *D* in Figure 2, the quantity produced is 100,000. If demand falls to *D*′, production falls to 80,000. Price remains fixed at $30, whether production is 100,000 or 80,000. What happens to employment in the swimsuit industry? It depends on production levels. The firms employ more workers at 100,000 than at 80,000.

Why Unemployment?

Keynesians believe that unemployment results when aggregate demand is insufficient to reach a full-employment level of real GDP.

This downward inflexibility of price in individual markets is built into Keynesian macroeconomic analysis. Aggregate demand determines the level of GDP and therefore the level of employment in the economy.

KEYNESIAN MODEL OF AGGREGATE DEMAND AND AGGREGATE SUPPLY

Panels *a* and *b*, in Figure 3 summarize the Keynesian view.

Aggregate demand in panel *a* is *AD*. The "right-angled" aggregate supply depicted by *AS* reflects the early Keynesian view that the price level does not rise as long as there is any unemployment. Equilibrium real GDP is $900 billion and the price level is $P = 100$.

The same equilibrium condition results in the more familiar Keynesian model of panel *b*. Aggregate demand, *AD*, in panel *a* is depicted as aggregate ex-

FIGURE 3
Aggregate Demand, GDP, and Employment
Given the "right-angled" aggregate supply, *AS*, if aggregate demand is *AD*, the economy in panel *a* is in equilibrium at $900 billion real GDP and price level *P* = 100. This equilibrium condition is depicted also in panel *b*. Aggregate expenditure *AE* = *C* + *I*, intersects aggregate supply, *C* + *S*, at $900 billion *nominal* GDP.

If full employment real GDP is $1,000 billion, then in both panel *a* and panel *b*, the economy is in equilibrium at less than full employment. To achieve full employment without inflation, aggregate demand in panel *a* must shift to the right to *AD′*, and aggregate expenditure in panel *b* must shift to *AE′* = (*C* + *I*)′.

If aggregate demand instead shifts to *AD″*, real GDP stays at $1,000 billion full-employment level but the price level rises to *P* = 110. In panel *b*, if *C* + *I* shifts to (*C* + *I*)″, an inflationary gap of *ab* emerges at nominal GDP equilibrium of $1,100 billion, which is equivalent to panel *a*'s $1,000 real GDP at a price level of 110.

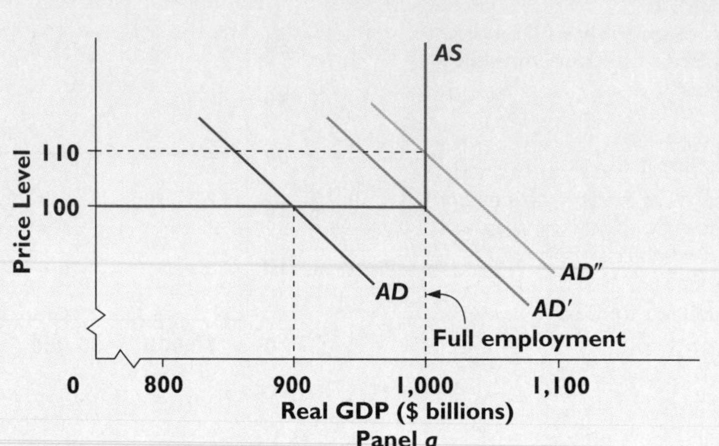

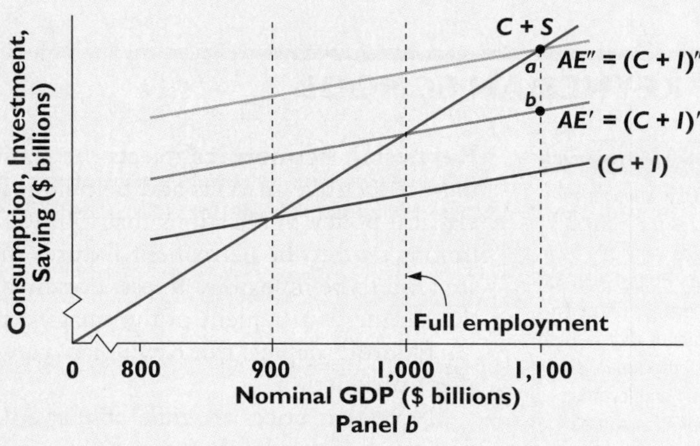

penditures *AE* = *C* + *I,* and aggregate supply, *AS,* is depicted as *C* + *S*. The economy is at equilibrium where the *C* + *I* curve intersects the *C* + *S* curve, that is, at $900 billion. In panel *b*, the price level, which is not explicitly shown, is assumed to be fixed.

Note that in both versions of the Keynesian model, with aggregate demand drawn as *AD* in panel *a* and aggregate expenditures as *AE* = *C* + *I* in panel *b*, equilibrium occurs at less than full-employment GDP. If aggregate demand doesn't change, unemployment is chronic.

That's why Keynesians reject the classical view that competitive markets ultimately drive the economy to full-employment equilibrium and dismiss the countercyclical policy of do nothing, that is, allowing market forces to work, as totally inappropriate.

An economy bogged down at equilibrium with less than full employment is what Keynesians saw in the 1930s, and they believed that depressing condition could recur through the 20th century. Why? To Keynesians, the level of aggregate demand in the 1930s was insufficient to generate full employment. It could happen again.

What, then, should the government do? As we have already shown in earlier chapters dealing with Keynesian countercyclical fiscal policy, the Keynesians focus on aggregate demand. In the model of Figure 3, aggregate demand should be made to shift from AD to AD' (which is the equivalent shift of aggregate expenditures from AE to AE').

THE FULL EMPLOYMENT ACT OF 1946

By the 1940s, government intervention in the economy to generate full employment was widely accepted.

In the midst of the 1930s depression, Keynes was invited to the White House to explain his theory of employment to President Franklin D. Roosevelt. After the meeting, Keynes was asked by fellow economists whether Roosevelt understood the theory. Keynes replied that although the President didn't understand it, the President would "do the right thing" because he seemed ideologically prepared to accept its policy prescriptions.

Keynes was right about Roosevelt's willingness to use the government as a vehicle to shift aggregate demand. The President seemed undisturbed about the new and expanded role that government would play in our economic lives. Although it is unclear whether Roosevelt believed that government spending to create jobs should be a permanent feature in stabilizing the economy, it was clear that he was prepared to create deficit budgets for that purpose. The President called this commitment to full employment a New Deal for the nation.

The economic pain caused by the depression made the New Deal ideology more digestible for many people. In 1946, Congress officially recognized its role as the economy's stabilizer by enacting the epoch-making Full Employment Act.

The Congress hereby declares that it is the continuing policy and responsibility of the Federal Government to use all practical means . . . to foster . . . conditions under which there will be afforded useful employment for those able, willing, and seeking to work, and to promote maximum employment, production, and purchasing power.

This act, a somewhat milder version of an earlier bill that had referred to the people's "right" to employment, indicates the extent to which government had become legitimized as an agency of economic stabilization.

Why Inflation?

Keynesians never expected inflation to be much of a problem, since the economy they knew tended to operate below full employment.

What about inflation? When a house is burning, do you suppose firefighters are bothered by a little rainfall? In the 1930s, when unemployment rates climbed as high as 25 percent of the labor force, Keynesians were little troubled by the prospects of inflation.

Look at Figure 3, panel *a* again. Inflation doesn't occur until aggregate demand shifts to the right, beyond AD', say to AD''. The economy's real GDP cannot increase beyond \$1,000 billion, but the price level rises from $P = 100$ to $P = 110$. That is, a shift in aggregate demand to the right of AD' causes inflation. The same phenomenon is shown in panel *b*. If aggregate expenditures shift to $AE'' = (C + I)''$, an inflationary gap, *ab*, results.

In other words, as long as aggregate demand is less than AD', or $AE' = (C + I)'$, equilibrium GDP falls short of full employment and inflation is of no concern. In fact, fiscal policy can push the economy to full-employment real GDP—where the actual unemployment rate equals the natural rate—without worrying at all about inflation. That is to say, *it never occurred to Keynesians that they would ever have to choose between policies to control unemployment and policies to control inflation.*

THE ECONOMICS OF FINE-TUNING

Countercyclical policy was rather uncomplicated for Keynesian economists. In periods of recession, government creates deficit budgets and the Fed expands the money supply to increase economic activity and decrease the rate of unemployment. In periods of prosperity, government works with surplus budgets and the Fed contracts the money supply to slow the economy and decrease the rate of inflation.

During the Kennedy and Johnson administrations in the 1960s, there was broad consensus among members of the Council of Economic Advisers with respect to which stabilization policy to pursue. It was mostly a matter of how well the policy could be pursued. Keynesian economists such as Arthur Okun, and Nobel laureates Robert Solow, Paul Samuelson, James Tobin, and Lawrence Klein worked at perfecting techniques of economic stabilization. It was, they insisted, a matter of *fine-tuning* the economy.

But these fine-tuners, and the entire school of Keynesian fine-tuning economists, were ill-prepared for the events that beset our economy in the 1970s and 1980s: high rates of unemployment concurrent with high rates of inflation.

NEO-KEYNESIAN SCHOOL

The presence of stagflation during the late 1960s and 1970s sparked the search for new theories to explain the coexistence of unemployment and inflation.

That had to be a puzzlement for Keynesian economists. After all, they see unemployment and inflation as either/or problems, not as concurrent ones. Keynesian countercyclical policy is a one-problem-at-a-time policy. How do you manage two at a time when each problem requires diametrically opposite prescriptions? Wouldn't you think the presence of high rates of unemployment *and* high rates of inflation would have undermined the confidence Keynesians placed in their understanding of how the economy works?

A new term, stagflation, came into vogue in the early 1970s to describe this rather unusual combination of inflation and unemployment. It was an uncomfortable mix of low rates of economic growth, high rates of unemployment, and high inflation.

What had Keynesians gotten wrong in their view of the economy? Why had inflation become a problem long before the economy approached full employment? Was stagflation an exception to the rule, or was the Keynesian view of the economy simply dead wrong?

In retrospect, it appears that the coexistence of inflation and unemployment never was a secret, not even to Keynesians. It was perhaps a situation which caused the Keynesians, still traumatized by the extraordinary unemployment of the Great Depression, to push the issue into the background.

But in 1958, New Zealand economist A. W. Phillips, after studying employment and inflation data for 1861–1957 in Britain, published his findings, which showed the inverse relationship between inflation and unemployment. Historically, inflation rose when unemployment fell. The graphic expression of this inverse relationship became quickly accepted and is known as the **Phillips curve.**

Phillips curve

A graph showing the inverse relationship between the economy's rate of unemployment and rate of inflation.

Phillips' findings, illustrated in Figure 4, forced Keynesians to modify their Figure 3 view of the economy.

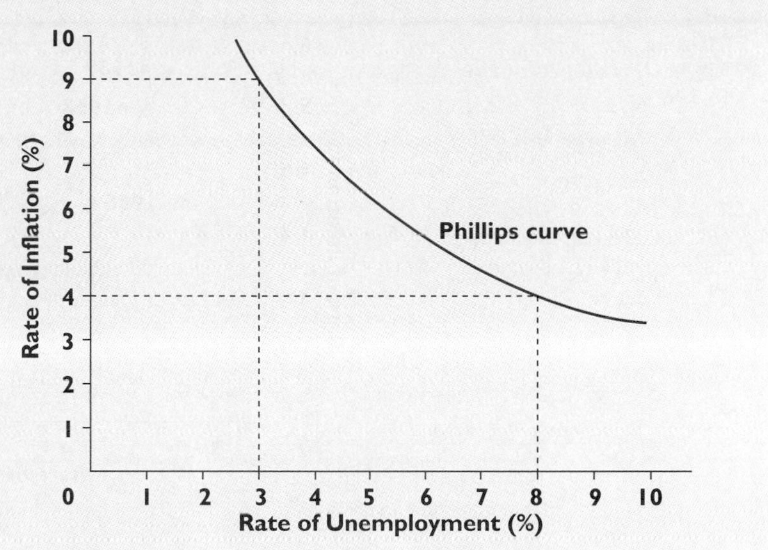

FIGURE 4
The Phillips Curve
The Phillips curve traces a set of combinations of rates of unemployment and inflation. Because these rates are inversely related, the government cannot use fiscal policy to reduce both at the same time. If government chooses to cut the rate of unemployment, it must accept higher inflation. If it chooses to cut inflation, it must accept higher rates of unemployment.

Phillips Curve Trade-offs

Unemployment and inflation rates are inversely related along a Phillips curve.

Keynesians began to see the world in terms of Figure 4 and faced a dilemma they had not before considered. If government and the Fed succeed in reducing unemployment, they exacerbate the problem of inflation. One cure creates the other disease. In Figure 4, you either accept 8 percent unemployment with 4 percent inflation, or 3 percent unemployment with 9 percent inflation. There is no zero unemployment (that is, zero cyclical unemployment) and zero inflation option as the Keynesians had believed.

Incorporating the Phillips curve into the Keynesian aggregate supply curve of Figure 3 produces the neo-Keynesian aggregate supply curve of Figure 5. This is the aggregate supply curve we have been using throughout most of our study of macroeconomics.

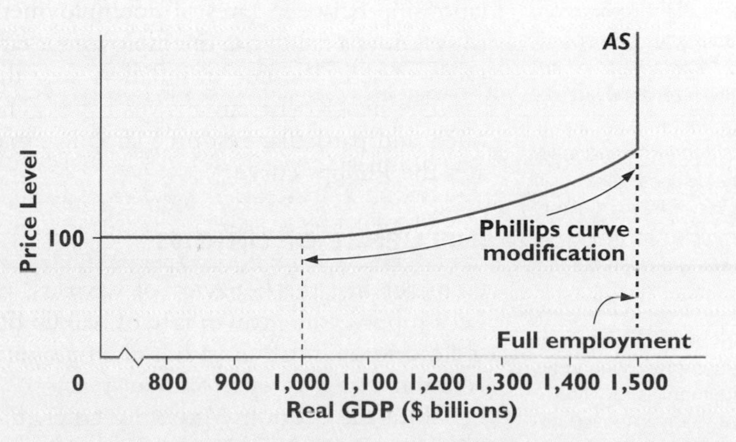

FIGURE 5
The Neo-Keynesian Aggregate Supply Curve
The Phillips curve reflects the intermediate, upward-sloping segment of the Keynesian aggregate supply curve of Figure 3. It shows that increases in real GDP create pressures on the price level *before* reaching full-employment real GDP.

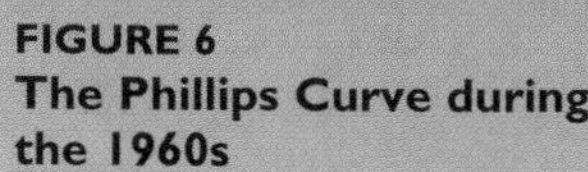

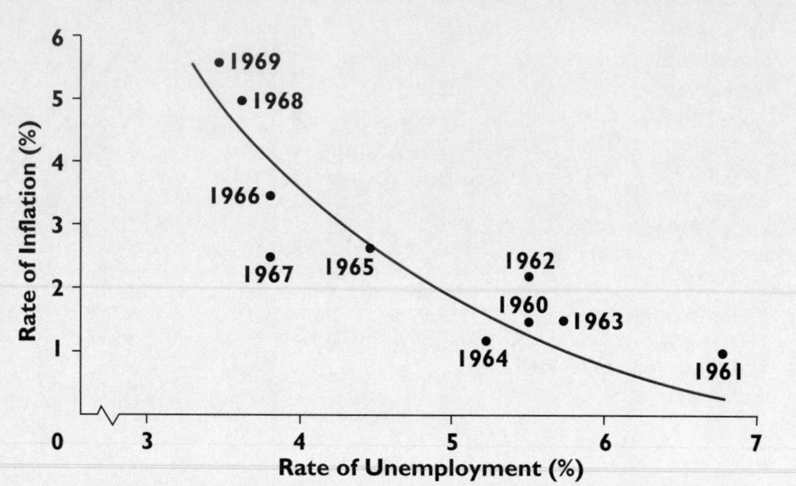

FIGURE 6
The Phillips Curve during the 1960s
The rates of unemployment and inflation in the 1960s map out a well-behaved Phillips curve. Stabilization policy during the 1960s centered on the trade-offs reflected in the Phillips curve.

The horizontal and vertical segments of the aggregate supply curve, shown also in Figure 3, are separated by an intermediate segment that represents the Phillips curve trade-offs. For example, the actual rate of unemployment at \$1,000 billion real GDP is higher than the natural rate. At \$1,500 billion, the actual rate equals the natural rate. If fiscal policy is designed to lower the actual rate of unemployment, real GDP increases, but only at higher price levels. If fiscal policy is designed to lower the price level, then if GDP is within the \$1,000 billion to \$1,500 billion range, it comes at the expense of GDP and employment.

As the Phillips curve of Figure 6 shows, the inflation and unemployment rates experienced during the decade of the 1960s seemed to indicate that the economy was operating on the intermediate segment of the aggregate supply curve.

Note the year-to-year changes in rates of unemployment and inflation. The fall in inflation from 1960 to 1961 was matched with a rise in unemployment. The fall in unemployment from 1965 to 1966 was matched with a rise in inflation. As you see, the 1960s made up a well-defined Phillips curve.

Neo-Keynesian economics
The school of thought that emphasizes the possibility that an economy can be in equilibrium at less than full employment with inflation. It argues that by managing aggregate demand, government can achieve the most acceptable combination of unemployment and inflation.

But putting the statistical evidence aside, how do **neo-Keynesians** explain the Phillips curve? Why should the economy behave this way? Is the inverse relationship between rates of unemployment and rates of inflation *causal?* That is to say, does a fall in the unemployment rate *cause* the rate of inflation to increase? Does a rise in the rate of inflation *cause* the rate of unemployment to decrease?

The neo-Keynesian answer is yes. The market power that unions, monopolies, and particular resource suppliers exercise in their respective markets creates the Phillips curve.

INFLUENCE OF UNIONS

Unions actively bargain for wage increases when unemployment is low and back away from wage demands when unemployment is high.

Consider first the behavior of workers, particularly those organized in unions. Let's suppose the growth rate of real GDP increases from 1.5 to 3.7 percent, but the economy is still short of full employment. How do firms and workers in that economic growth environment react?

With the economy growing faster, firms attempt to increase production by hiring more workers. Unemployment rates fall. How do workers react to falling unemployment rates? Feeling somewhat more secure about their jobs, they shift their focus away from job protection, which made sense when unemployment was high, to wage demands. The firms respond positively to their higher wage demands. Why not? With the economy growing more rapidly, their main concern is retaining their workers. After all, other firms are expanding production as well, and are competing aggressively for more workers by raising wage rates.

Firms' resistance to strong wage pressure weakens for still another reason. During periods of rapid economic growth, they find it easier to pass along higher wage rates in the form of higher prices without having to worry about losing markets. In other words, a decline in the rate of unemployment *causes* higher rates of inflation.

What happens during a recession? When growth rates of GDP fall, say, from 3.7 percent to -1.5 percent, the rate of unemployment rises. Many workers are now more concerned about protecting their jobs than protecting their wage rates, so they accept smaller wage increases.

They're no dummies. They know that when the economy is sluggish, many firms have difficulty keeping production going at the same levels. If workers insist on high wage increases, then the high-wage-paying firms become disadvantaged in competition. Everybody loses. Workers must choose, then, between jobs and wage rates.

When workers accept smaller wage rate increases, they may make it possible for firms to moderate price increases. That is, higher rates of unemployment which accompany declining GDP may slow the economy's rate of inflation.

INFLUENCE OF SUPPLY SHOCKS

As unemployment decreases, bottlenecks can appear in production, driving prices up further.

OPEC's price increases during the 1970s caused the inflation rate to accelerate.

Unusual events may sometimes trigger a resource supply shock that jolts the economy from one position on the Phillips curve to another. For example, in October 1973 OPEC—the petroleum exporting countries—drastically cut the supply of oil to the rest of the world. The result was a tripling of oil prices by January 1974. (The tight control on supply by OPEC continued throughout the decade of the 1970s, tripling the price from $6 a barrel to $18 a barrel by 1979—and almost doubling it again to $34 a barrel in 1982.) The effect on the economic performance of the rest of the world from this oil price increase was immediate and devastating. Many economists attribute the prolonged worldwide stagflation of the 1970s to the supply shock caused by OPEC. The cost of producing and delivering almost all goods and services in the oil-importing economies soared, shifting their aggregate supply curves to the left. The outcome: Price levels increased and real GDP decreased.

The Phillips Curve and Countercyclical Policy

What do Keynesians do now? Is it back to the drawing board? The countercyclical monetary and fiscal policies that were supposed to produce full employment without inflation don't work in economies characterized by the Phillips curve. How do you avoid raising the rate of inflation when pursuing a countercyclical policy aimed at reducing the rate of unemployment during recession?

WAGE AND PRICE CONTROL

One solution is to combine wage and price controls with a Keynesian-style, job-creating policy. Something like muzzling a barking dog—the dog *wants* to bark, but can't.

Wage and price controls worked for Nixon until they were lifted. How do you think asking people not to raise prices or demand higher wages worked for Jimmy Carter?

That's what President Nixon tried in 1971. Facing high rates of inflation caused by the Vietnam war, he imposed wage and price controls. By prohibiting any increase in either prices or wages for 90 days, he hoped that workers and industry would come to accept more stable prices. At the same time, along with the Congress and the Fed, he used monetary and fiscal policies to reduce the economy's unemployment rate.

Many economists were surprised by President Nixon's wage and price controls. Why was a conservative Republican adopting this market-interventionist stabilization policy? After all, controls distort free market signals and create market inefficiencies. Perhaps the President saw the issue as a trade-off between efficiency and stabilization, and chose stabilization.

Did Nixon's wage and price controls work? Not really. They seemed to work during the control period. But when the controls were finally lifted, inflation reappeared. That is to say, the hiatus had no impact on changing the behavior of workers or businesses. President Carter's flirtation with wage and price controls in the late 1970s was far less serious. He asked only for voluntary compliance with wage and price guidelines. His strategy was to slow inflation by recommending that firms cap their price increases to 0.5 percent below the inflation rate of the previous year. Workers were asked to limit wage demands to 7 percent. Such a stabilization policy relies heavily on worker and industry goodwill and common sense. Neither are very powerful weapons. In fact, both inflation and unemployment rates remained relatively high during most of President Carter's years in the White House.

HUMPHREY-HAWKINS ACT OF 1978

Many neo-Keynesian economists saw the futility of trying to hammer both inflation and unemployment to zero. If we can't engineer full employment without inflation, then we must learn to live with *some* inflation and *some* unemployment (unemployment above the natural rate). That is, reality forced economists to accept the new stabilization policy of choosing the *most livable point on the Phillips curve.*

To Congress, the most livable point on the Phillips curve was spelled out in its 1978 enactment of the Full Employment and Balanced Growth Act, commonly referred to as the Humphrey-Hawkins Act. This act, a modified version of Congress' 1946 Full Employment Act, initially identified a 4 percent rate of unemployment and 3 percent inflation as acceptable and reasonable targets. But few economists took it seriously. Why? Because, for the decades of the 1970s and 1980s, these target rates proved to be hopelessly unrealistic.

Almost as soon as neo-Keynesians accepted the Phillips curve as the starting point of stabilization policy, they confronted a new problem. They discovered that the rates of inflation and unemployment in the 1970s and early 1980s seemed to have run completely amuck. By no stretch of the imagination could the 1970s and early 1980s data be fitted into the Phillips curve of Figure 6, or into any downward-sloping Phillips curve for that matter. Look at Figure 7.

How do you draw a Phillips curve in Figure 7? It seems at first glance that the scatter of annual inflation and unemployment rates for the 1970s and 1980s have little in common with the well-behaved Phillips curve of the 1960s. What's left, then, of neo-Keynesian Phillips curve analysis if the data contradict the Phillips curve? Was the 1960s fit simply an accident?

FIGURE 7
Rates of Inflation and Unemployment: 1970–90
During the 1970s and 1980s, the scatter of points depicting combinations of inflation and unemployment rates *seem* to bear no resemblance to the well-defined Phillips curve of the 1960s shown in Figure 6.

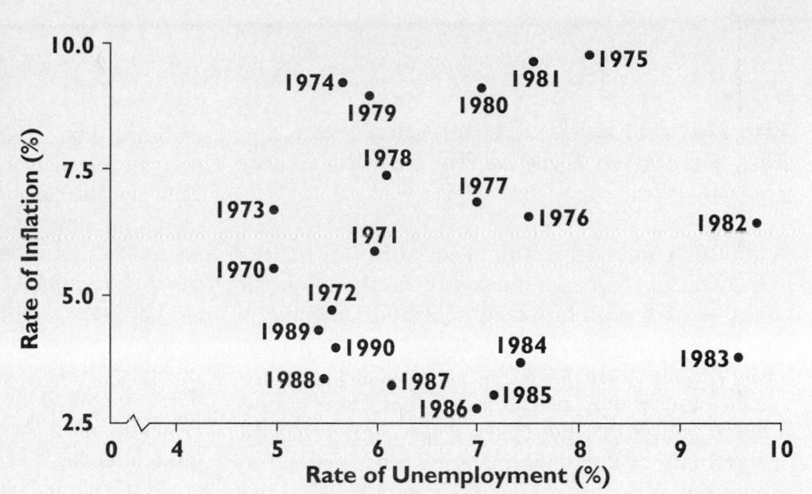

Long-Run Phillips Curves

The Phillips curve of the 1950s and early 1960s seemed to be shifting upward during the late 1960s and 1970s.

Neo-Keynesians took a hard look at the 1970s and 1980s scatter of inflation and unemployment rates and found a Phillips curve hidden among them. Only what they discovered was not a single Phillips curve, but a *set of Phillips curves.* The neo-Keynesian idea that an economy can choose only between a limited set of inflation and unemployment options still holds, except that the set of options shifts over time. Figure 8 illustrates the point.

What had been a set of scatter points in Figure 7 now are points in a set of Phillips curves. What explains the shift from one Phillips curve to another? The principal cause of the shift is the follow-up reaction of workers and firms to the price increases they initially triggered.

FIGURE 8
Shifting Phillips Curve
Neo-Keynesians revised their understanding of how people react to government policy to explain why the data of the 1970s and 1980s can be fitted into a set of Phillips curves.

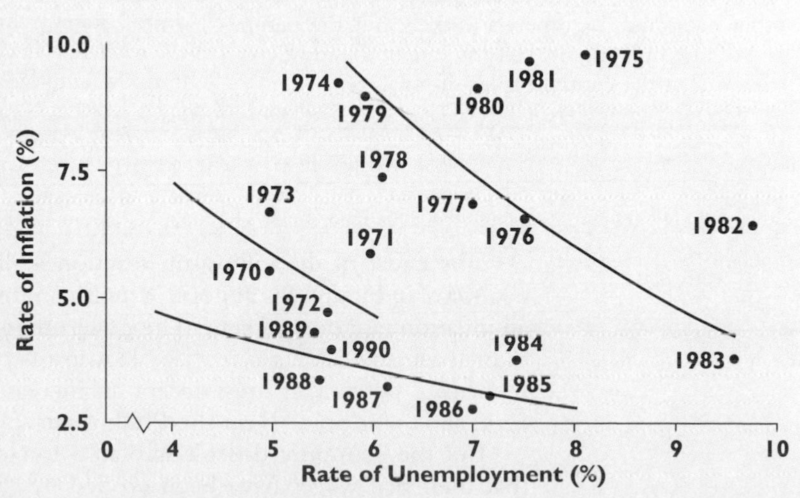

ADDED PERSPECTIVE

The Natural Rate of Unemployment Sets a Bottom Line to the Phillips Curve

James Risen

With little public debate, the Federal Reserve Board is increasingly basing interest rate decisions on the controversial assumption that the nation's unemployment rate cannot be reduced much below 6 percent without igniting inflation.

Fed officials tend to gauge whether the economy is overheating partly by referring to what they call the "natural rate of unemployment." That is defined by economists as the lowest level of unemployment that can be sustained without putting inflationary pressures on the economy.

In the 1970s, economists used a benchmark called "full employment," and it was generally agreed to mean an unemployment rate of about 4 percent. But today, Fed officials and many economists believe that the economy cannot long sustain an unemployment rate below about 6 percent without causing wages and prices to spiral upward.

Fed officials here acknowledged there is still considerable debate about the precise level of "natural" unemployment. Some conservatives believe that it could be as high as 6.5 percent, while others believe it could be slightly under 6 percent. But there is general agreement inside the central bank that U.S. unemployment, which drifted down from 6.9 percent in mid 1993 to 6 percent last June, is very close to the natural rate. That, in turn, helps explain why the Fed has moved repeatedly in recent months to boost interest rates. Fed officials stress that they use many other economic barometers as well, but the natural rate of unemployment is clearly one of the most controversial at the central bank's disposal.

Some Fed officials conceded privately that their increasing reliance on the 6 percent target is politically sensitive because there has been almost no debate in Congress or elsewhere about the new assumption that reducing unemployment to 4 percent or so is no longer a realistic goal.

The new approach is particularly risky since Congress mandated in the 1970s that one of the Fed's priorities had to be achieving "full employment." That mandate is contained in the Humphrey-Hawkins Act, which still provides the technical guidelines the Fed is supposed to follow.

"The natural-rate hypothesis has received near-universal acceptance among academic economists since the 1970s," said Stanford University economist Paul Krugman.

Krugman argued that the natural rate of unemployment has risen during the last generation, in large part because of costly government social programs in the United States and Europe that reduce incentives for the poor to get off welfare and other assistance and return to the work force.

That trend, coupled with the increased importance of education in getting a good job, has led to a sharp rise in long-term unemployment, especially in Europe, Krugman said.

In fact, the natural unemployment rate in Europe is now thought to be about twice the U.S. level. The increase in the United States has been less extreme, in part because American social programs are less generous, Krugman observed.

But it is also because there are fewer governmental restrictions on firing or laying off workers in the United States, which means American employers are less reluctant than their European counterparts to hire new employees.

Source: "Feds's Decision Tied to 'Natural' 6% Jobless Rate," by James Risen. *The Los Angeles Times,* August 29, 1994.

The effect of the follow-up reaction is illustrated in Figure 9. Suppose the economy in Figure 9 is at point *A,* with an unemployment rate of 9 percent and an inflation rate of 4 percent. The government regards 9 percent unemployment as unacceptable. What can it do? If it insists on reducing the rate of unemployment to 7 percent, it must accept an increase in the rate of inflation to 6 percent, shown at point *B* on the Phillips curve *PC*.

But the economy doesn't stay at *B* for long. Why? Because workers learn that their real wages have been eroded by the higher prices they now pay for goods and services. Should they be upset? Wouldn't you be? How do they re-

FIGURE 9
Shifting Phillips Curves
Beginning at point *A* on the Phillips curve *PC*, government policy cuts the rate of unemployment from 9 percent to 7 percent, which causes the rate of inflation to rise from 4 percent to 6 percent. This result is shown as a movement from point *A* to point *B* along the Phillips curve *PC*.

The inflation raises costs and lowers profit, causing firms to cut production and employment, shown as a new combination point *C* (the rate of unemployment is again 9 percent while inflation remains at 6 percent). Point *C* lies on the new Phillips curve *PC'*.

Frustrated, the government tries to restore the 7 percent rate of unemployment, causing the economy to move first to point *D* on *PC'*, then to *E* on *PC''* where the rate of unemployment is back to 9 percent but the rate of inflation has increased to 8 percent. As long as government tries to cut the rate of unemployment below 9 percent, the rate of unemployment will eventually return to 9 percent but the rate of inflation will increase.

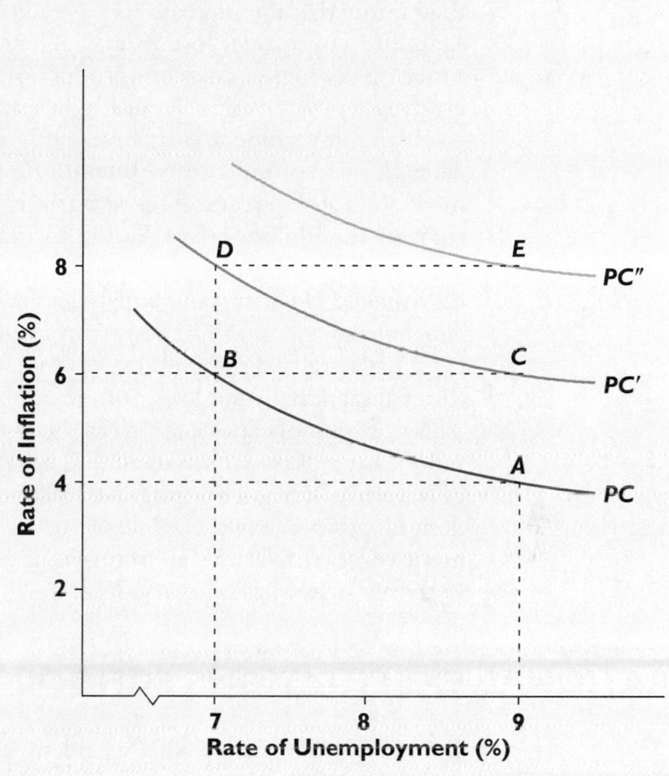

cover lost ground? By bargaining for wages high enough to make up what they lost through increased inflation.

Typically, they succeed. Why? Because firms enjoying higher prices and higher profit worry about losing workers to other firms that are also expanding production. Under these conditions, they are inclined to concede to wage demands.

As workers succeed in bargaining for wage increases during periods of low unemployment, producers cut back production because profit margins are squeezed and unemployment goes up.

But the workers' success is only short-lived. The higher wages raise production costs and lower profits. Production is cut back and workers are laid off. In other words, in the long run the higher rate of inflation causes the unemployment rate to climb again to, say, 9 percent, point *C* in Figure 9.

Good intentions notwithstanding, what has government accomplished by trying to lower the unemployment rate from 9 to 7 percent? The economy shifts from *A* on Phillips curve *PC* to *C* on Phillips curve *PC'*. The unemployment rate is back to 9 percent, but the rate of inflation stays at 6 percent.

Frustrated, the government may try again to cut the rate of unemployment to 7 percent by even stronger fiscal policy. Will it work? As we saw, only in the short run. Movement along Phillips curve PC' from 9 percent to 7 percent unemployment raises the rate of inflation from 6 to 8 percent, that is from C to D.

But workers will not sit idly by. Having learned their painful lesson earlier, they know that the increase to 8 percent inflation reduces their real wages. They again press to recover lost ground. They succeed in raising their wages, but firms suffering the higher costs cut production. The rate of unemployment rises again, creating a new position E on Phillips curve PC''.

If the government insists on reducing the rate of unemployment to 7 percent, the rate of inflation will continue to increase while the rate of unemployment stays at 9 percent. This scenario is illustrated in the repeated shifting to the right of the Phillips curve shown in Figure 9. That is to say, *in the long run the rate of unemployment remains unchanged in spite of government stabilization policy, but the dynamics of the economic activity that the government sets in motion generates accelerating rates of inflation.* The long-run Phillips curve is effectively vertical.

That's pretty disheartening, isn't it? These short-run employment policy victories disappear in the long run, producing in their wake accelerating inflation. The policy implications are clear. Neo-Keynesians show the futility of trying to reduce rates of unemployment and inflation simultaneously. All that's left of stabilization policy is choosing a set of monetary and fiscal policies that achieve a desired position on the Phillips curve. Unless workers, industry, and government resist temptations to improve upon it, any attempt to manipulate a better outcome invites inflationary disaster.

THE RATIONAL EXPECTATIONS SCHOOL

According to rational expectationists, the government should not attempt to lower the unemployment rate.

The 1970s and early 1980s world of stagflation basically broke the Keynesian consensus of the macroeconomic world. Shortly after President Nixon quipped: "We are all Keynesians," many young macroeconomists saw the hollowness of this claim when they looked at the decade of exceptionally high inflation and high unemployment.

Prior to the Nixon era, the only notable conservative voices in macroeconomics were those of the classical economists from an earlier era, and monetarists. As we noted earlier, conservatives believe that the government should abstain from activist fiscal and monetary policies. Their policy prescription is clear and simple: Set money supply growth equal to the economy's real growth rate. That's it! But classical economics and monetarism had a decidedly small presence back in the 1970s.

Rational expectations

The school of thought that emphasizes the impossibility that government can reduce the economy's rate of unemployment by managing aggregate demand. It argues that because people anticipate the consequences of announced government policy and incorporate these anticipated consequences into their present decision making, they end up undermining the policy.

However, when the economy seemed to be stuck in the rut of stagflation and Keynesians no longer seemed to have all the answers, new and challenging conservative ideas quickly emerged. By far the most important set of conservative ideas to blossom and to draw many young adherents was **rational expectations.**

Rational expectations economists challenge the neo-Keynesian view that stabilization policy can have some short-run success, even if it disappears in the long run. They offer a different interpretation of how workers and industry respond to government's fiscal policy. The implications of their view are striking: *There is absolutely nothing government can do, even in the short run, to reduce the economy's unemployment rate.* Compare this view of government's role in the economy to the view held by classical economists. Ends up being pretty much the same, doesn't it? Both advocate a hands-off policy. That's not quite the view

ADDED PERSPECTIVE

An Exchange between a Keynesian and a Rational Expectations (New Classical) Economist

Professor Paul Samuelson, Nobel laureate in Economics, remains, in his words, an "eclectic Keynesian"; he thinks the government can play an important role in guiding the economy. He attacks the new breed of economic conservatives led by Robert Lucas, Thomas Sargent, and Robert Barro. Their New Classical school argues that governments can do no economic good.

Mr. Barro made his name arguing the case that bigger government deficits reduce private sector spending by an exactly offsetting amount. Why? Because people will save money in order to meet the expected increase in their descendants' tax liabilities.

"I burst out laughing when one of the ablest young macroeconomists put this to me," says Mr. Samuelson. He asked whether the young conservative really believed such nonsense. "Indeed I do," was the answer, "and so do all the good economists under 40." "I felt old," says Mr. Samuelson; "The doubt kept asserting itself that maybe in this generation the loss of practical knowledge might be permanent and irreversible." Yet Mr. Samuelson does not dismiss all such theories. Take the distinction between anticipated and unanticipated changes in policy—stressed in work by Messrs. Lucas and Sargent. Modern Keynesians, including Mr. Samuelson, have embraced the idea, adapting it to their own purposes. By such means, the conservatives have pulled all of economics to the right.

Source: Excerpted from "A New Authorised Version for Tomorrow's Policy-Makers," *The Economist*, March 14, 1987.

held by Keynesians or even neo-Keynesians, is it? But why do rational expectations economists believe there is nothing government can do to alleviate unemployment in the short or long run?

Anticipation of Fiscal Policy Undermines the Policy

From past experience, workers know to bargain for a wage increase as soon as an expansionary fiscal policy is announced.

They start with a view, quite different from the neo-Keynesian one, of how people react to the inflationary effects of government job-creating fiscal policy. Rational expectations economists believe that workers are not only rational but are also smart enough to learn from experience how best to overcome the effects of the government's fiscal policy. Workers understand that a Phillips curve exists even if they don't know what a Phillips curve is. Their experience tells them that the government's attempt to lower rates of unemployment is linked to higher rates of inflation. They therefore respond not only to the past inflation that has eroded real wages but, expecting rates of inflation to increase again because of government policy, they incorporate that expectation into their future wage demands. That is, their wage demands include anticipated inflation.

This anticipating factor transforms Figure 9 into Figure 10.

Suppose the economy is at *A*, where the unemployment rate is 9 percent and the rate of inflation is 4 percent. Workers demand a 4 percent wage increase to keep their real wages from eroding.

Suppose government tries to cut unemployment to 7 percent. The economy moves along the Phillips curve to *B*. Inflation is now 6 percent. Now trouble begins. Workers catch on quickly. They don't just try to make up for past inflation losses, but try to *prevent a repeat* of the short-run erosion of real wages.

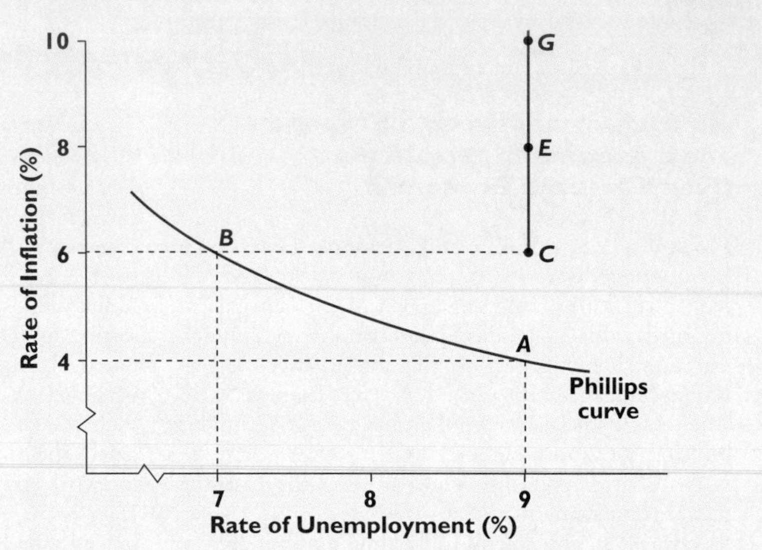

FIGURE 10
Rational Expectations Model
Correctly anticipating the increase in the rate of inflation that is generated by the government's policy to cut the rate of unemployment, workers press for wage demands that cover the anticipated inflation, thereby erasing any short-run gains in profit that firms would have made. As a result the unemployment rate remains unchanged, but the rate of inflation increases. If the government keeps trying to cut the rate of unemployment, the rate of inflation keeps increasing along the vertical path of the Phillips curve.

How do they do that? Because they have seen inflation increase from 4 to 6 percent, they *expect it will continue to increase at that rate*. After all, government's announced policy is to drive unemployment to 7 percent and workers, being rational, know from experience that such a policy causes inflation. So, anticipating that their real wage will fall because of the government's policy, they ask not for 6, but for 8 percent. That is, they try to stay one step ahead of losing out, to preempt any short-run loss.

But firms, too, are rational and incorporate expectations into their decision making. They, too, learn to read the effects of government's fiscal policy on inflation. They also know that workers' demands will *instantaneously* eliminate the short-run price-cost gap, cutting out that source of short-run profit. Losing the incentive to expand production, they don't hire more workers. The unemployment rate, therefore, remains unchanged—frustrating the government's efforts—while the rate of inflation keeps increasing at the expected rate.

This scenario is played out in Figure 10. The economy moves from *B* to *C*. Then from *C* directly to *E*. From *E* directly to *G*. And so on. Look at the shape of the Phillips curve these points map out. It becomes a vertical line at 9 percent unemployment.

Anticipation of Monetary Policy Undermines the Policy

Suppose the Fed, worried about a prolonged recession, decides to increase GDP and employment by increasing the money supply. To do this, it announces a cut in its discount rate. How do people react? Past experience tells them that the Fed's expansionary policy typically is linked to higher rates of inflation. Incorporating that expectation into their plans, workers demand wages that will cover the anticipated inflation. Firms, expecting the rise in inflation, raise their own prices. Banks react to the expected inflation by raising interest rates. The result? Aggregate demand falls because consumer spending declines, especially for big-ticket items which normally involve some borrowing, and because business investment spending declines due to higher interest rates charged by banks.

Firms, facing decreasing aggregate demand, cut back production; anticipating inflation, they raise prices, which feeds inflation and further depresses the demand for goods and services. As a result, the rate of unemployment rises. In other words, anticipation of the effects of the Fed's policy on the economy ends up undermining the policy.

SUPPLY-SIDE ECONOMICS

Supply-side policies are focused on shifting the aggregate supply curve.

Keynesian countercyclical policy focused on what the government can or cannot do to change aggregate demand. Changes in aggregate demand were the principal vehicle for changing real GDP and employment. Phillips curve analysis—by neo-Keynesians and rational expectations economists—took issue with the simplicity of the Keynesian prescriptions, but they too focused on what government spending can or cannot do.

Supply-side economics

The school of thought that emphasizes the possibility of achieving full employment without inflation. It argues that through tax reductions, spending cuts, and deregulation, government creates the proper incentives for the private sector to increase aggregate supply.

An altogether different view on stabilization policy emerged in the early 1980s. The analytic focus of **supply-side economics** shifted from aggregate demand to aggregate supply. The idea was that changes in real GDP can best be achieved by changing the environment that suppliers live in. To supply-siders, whatever makes the suppliers happy tends to make the economy better.

What makes suppliers happy? The supply-side economists' checklist includes lower taxes, less government regulation, less government spending, and less union power in wage determination. In short, everything that promotes profit. It was this view that attracted President Reagan to supply-side economics. He believed, as supply-siders do, that not only do suppliers benefit when these checklist items are addressed, but so does everyone else whose job depends upon successful businesses. During the 1980s, supply-side policy became popularized as "Reaganomics." The idea was that it was possible to lower rates of inflation along with rates of unemployment—an old Keynesian idea—but by working on the supply-side of the economy.

Lower Tax Rates

Supply-side economists emphasize the importance of reducing tax rates. They accept the Keynesian idea that lower tax rates will increase consumer demand, but believe a more important consequence is the added incentive it provides suppliers. For example, lower corporate tax rates increase after-tax profit, which induces suppliers to increase aggregate supply. Lower income tax rates encourage more people to work longer, adding as well to aggregate supply.

Their argument was carried a step further by economist Arthur Laffer, who insisted that high tax rates not only check the expansion of real GDP and employment, but end up producing less tax revenues. His explanation for this unusual outcome is illustrated in Figure 11.

Tax revenues are measured along the horizontal axis, the tax rates along the vertical axis. Consider the most extreme position first. If tax rates were 100 percent, no one would work. GDP is $0, and of course, income tax revenue is $0 as well. If the tax rate is lowered to 75 percent, some people would work, GDP grows, and the tax revenue that GDP generates is $800 billion. If the rate is reduced further, say to 50 percent, GDP increases and tax revenue is $1,300 bil-

FIGURE 11
The Laffer Curve
The Laffer curve reflects the view that when tax rates are too high, lowering them not only creates greater incentive for suppliers to increase production, but ends up generating higher tax revenues as well.

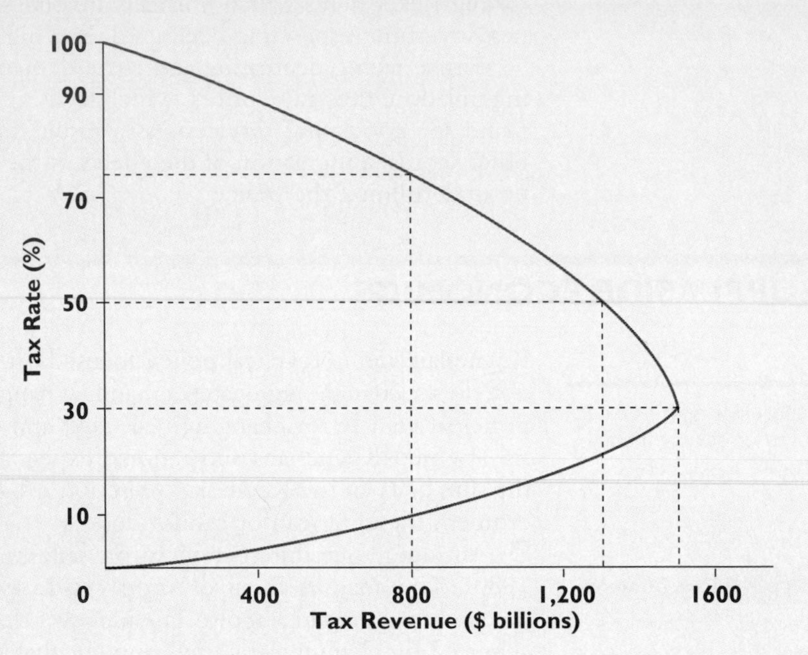

lion. The Laffer curve shows that a tax rate of 30 percent provides suppliers with incentive to produce a GDP large enough to generate a maximum $1,500 billion tax revenue. A lower tax rate, say, at 20 percent, will increase GDP, but end up lowering tax revenue.

Laffer's message was clear. Our tax rate is so high that it stifles incentive and produces less than the maximum tax revenue. By lowering the tax rate, he argued—the key factor in supply-side economics—GDP and tax revenue could grow.

Laffer's argument had considerable weight in President Reagan's decision to change the tax structure. In 1981, Congress passed the Kemp-Roth tax cut which lowered tax rates. The highest marginal tax rate was cut from 70 to 50 percent. In 1986, the Tax Reform Act followed Kemp-Roth's lead, reducing the number of tax brackets to three and cutting the top marginal rate to 31 percent. The two other marginal tax rates were set at 28 and 15 percent.

The result? Not very positive. Tax revenues did not increase, contributing to the exceptionally large budget deficits of the 1980s.

The supply-siders' political clout ended with President Reagan. President Bush's campaign promise, "Read my lips, no new taxes," was compromised early in his administration; although willing to reduce the capital gains tax, he was unable to persuade Congress to go along. President Clinton's tax policy, on the other hand, moves considerably away from supply-side economics.

Less Government Regulation

To supply-siders, the myriad of government regulations affects almost every industry in the economy, reducing productivity and undermining industrial efficiency. Although most regulations are designed to protect consumers, workers, and the environment, they also represent a substantial added cost to suppliers. They stifle creativity and trigger higher prices.

Although supply-siders acknowledge the need for some regulation, they insist that the cure has become worse than the disease. They argue for substantial deregulation of the economy. They have had some success during the Reagan years, especially in banking, energy, and transportation.

Less Government Spending

Supply-siders believe that the government's reliance on its own spending to create employment is not only not a quick fix but is a major contributor to the unemployment problem. Because government typically ends up spending more than it receives in tax revenues, budget deficits grow. These deficits are financed by the sale of government securities—that is, government borrowing—which undermines private sector investment in two ways: First, government competes in the securities market with firms trying to sell their own securities, **crowding out** these firms from the source of funds, and second, the increase in government borrowing drives up the interest rate, crowding out private investment once again. This crowding-out phenomenon checks the rate of economic growth.

Crowding out

A fall in private investment spending caused by an increase in government spending.

Supply-siders argue that if government reduces its spending, more investment capital would be made available at lower rates of interest to private sector suppliers. Combined with lower tax rates and less government regulation, lower government spending produces lower rates of inflation and unemployment. Figure 12 illustrates their view.

The shift in the aggregate supply curve from *AS* to AS_1 that results from supply-side stabilization policy causes a decrease in the price level, from $P = 110$ to $P = 100$, and an increase in GDP from $900 billion to $1,000 billion, cutting the rate of unemployment.

FIGURE 12
Supply-Side Effects on Unemployment and Inflation
If aggregate supply shifts to the right from *AS* to AS_1, real GDP increases from $900 billion to $1,000 billion while the price level falls from $P = 110$ to $P = 100$.

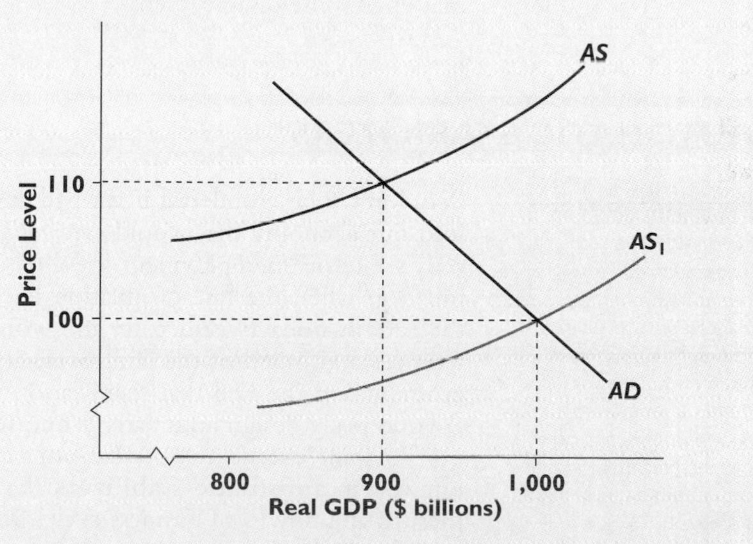

IS THERE A MACRO CONSENSUS?

Though some views among macroeconomists overlap considerably, there is hardly a consensus.

Who is right on stabilization policy has as many answers as there are economists with views on stabilization. Macroeconomic models—classical economics, the Keynesian $C + I = C + S$, the aggregate demand and aggregate supply, the short-run and long-run Phillips curves, rational expectations, and supply-side—all generate outcomes that differ and, depending on one's economic ideology, can be compelling. In other words, not everyone agrees with any one "correct" stabilization policy.

Yet real world events of the 1970s, 1980s, and 1990s have brought macroeconomists together, notwithstanding the specific policy disagreements that make interesting bedfellows. For example, rational expectations economists and neo-Keynesians share the same view concerning government's ability to change the economy's long-run employment position. They both demonstrate its futility. They see stabilization policy—what we can do with rates of inflation and unemployment—as constrained. Their observations are not entirely revolutionary. Classical economists came to the same conclusions, insisting that even well-intentioned government interference in the economy was not only futile but counterproductive.

Note what supply-siders and Keynesians agree and disagree on. They agree that with the correct approach to stabilization policy, it is possible to reduce both the rate of unemployment and the rate of inflation. But supply-siders and Keynesians disagree on the correct approach to stabilization. The Keynesians focus on changing aggregate demand, supply-siders focus on changing aggregate supply.

Even among Keynesians, there is disagreement about what government can and cannot do to promote employment, although they all share the belief that government has a positive role. Some Keynesians are convinced that government can create policy to increase employment without causing inflation. Others take a different view. They accept the validity of the Phillips curve, which requires us to make choices between employment and inflation. And among those economists, what policies the government should pursue is still a matter of some disagreement.

AUTOMATIC STABILIZERS

Automatic stabilizers

Structures in the economy that tend to add to aggregate demand when the economy is in recession, and subtract from aggregate demand when the economy is inflationary. Unemployment insurance payments and benefits, and the progressive income tax are two such automatic stabilizers.

Wouldn't it be wonderful if we had an economic stabilization thermostat built into our economy that would *automatically* create employment when the economy's rate of unemployment grew to unacceptable levels and *automatically* cut inflation when the rate of inflation became too high? It would mute much of the activist-nonactivist debate, and would set aside much of the ideological differences and much of the controversial, discretionary decision making by government and the Fed that stabilization policy demands. But is it possible? Can anyone really design automatic economic stabilizers?

To some extent, that's what our economy already has. We have built into our system **automatic stabilizers** that kick in at the right times to moderate the ups and downs of business cycles. One of the principal stabilizers is the unemployment insurance system. The other is our income and corporate tax structure. How do they work?

Unemployment Insurance

When people work, they contribute part of their earnings *indirectly* to an unemployment insurance program. Although employers, not workers, actually pay the insurance, employers are reimbursed, at least in part, by paying workers lower wages. That is, workers would probably earn higher wage rates if employers were not obligated to pay the insurance. The point is that while workers are working at jobs, part of their income is siphoned off by employer-employee contributions to the unemployment insurance program.

On the other hand, when workers are unemployed, they receive income payments in the form of unemployment insurance benefits from that program. This simple and practical spreading of workers' incomes more evenly over the business cycle not only makes life more tolerable for affected workers but acts as an automatic stabilizer in the economy.

Consider the prosperity phase of a business cycle. With unemployment approaching the natural rate and wage rates rising along with the price level, the one thing you don't want to encourage is more consumer spending. But that's just what happens when wages increase. Unemployment insurance payments (leaving less take-home dollars in the paychecks than would otherwise be the case) come to the rescue. With less income, people spend less, which modifies somewhat the upward pressure on prices.

On the other hand, in the recession phase of the cycle, the unemployment insurance program automatically pumps more spending into the economy. People out of work find their earning power considerably diminished, but those who are eligible for unemployment benefits now have some spending power. In this respect, spending does not decrease as much as it would without the unemployment insurance benefits. This ultimately means fewer workers lose their jobs, which translates into less unemployment than would otherwise have occurred.

Personal and Corporate Income Taxes

Our personal income tax structure has a built-in stabilizing feature as well. The tax structure is progressive, meaning that as income increases, the percentage of income paid to taxes increases. How does it work? When incomes and real GDP increase during a prosperity phase, taxes increase at an even higher rate, leaving less disposable income in the hands of people. With less income, people spend less. That's good news because less spending dampens the inflationary pressure on the economy.

During a recession when income and real GDP are falling, less is collected in taxes. Disposable income and spending do not fall as fast. That's good news as well, because the less spending falls, the less real GDP will fall, and consequently, fewer workers will lose their jobs. This means unemployment will not increase as much as it would have in the absence of these automatic stabilizers.

Unemployment insurance and the tax system automatically exert a countercyclical influence over the economy.

Our corporate income tax structure operates the same way. In fact, economists consider the corporate profit tax to be the most countercyclical of all automatic stabilizers. In the prosperity phases of the cycle, corporate profits tend to increase faster than any other income form. In recessions, they tend to decrease faster. As a result, corporations pay considerably more taxes in inflationary periods than in recessions.

CHAPTER REVIEW

1. Since economists work with imperfect information and have different temperaments and ideologies, they don't always agree. Liberal economists tend to advocate greater intervention in the economy, while conservative economists advocate little or no intervention. Presidents typically choose economic advisers who reflect their own ideologies.

2. Macroeconomic theorists have focused most of their attention on why unemployment and inflation exist and what can be done about them. Different schools of thought have developed around this issue. The classical school believes that unemployment is, at worst, a temporary phenomenon. They believe that markets are competitive and that prices are flexible up and down, always moving toward an equilibrium. The appropriate policy for dealing with unemployment is to not intervene. To classical economists, inflation is purely the result of too much money being circulated. In order for prices to remain stable, the rate of growth of the money supply should match the rate of growth of real GDP.

3. Keynesian economists argue that prices are downwardly rigid and markets are not competitive. A decrease in demand leads to a decrease in output rather than a decrease in price. Under these circumstances, unemployment can persist indefinitely if nothing is done. Increases in government spending, decreases in taxes, and increases in the money supply are all appropriate policies for combating unemployment according to Keynesians. As long as the economy is at or below full employment, inflation is not a worry for Keynesians.

4. However, during the 1970s and 1980s, high rates of unemployment and inflation coexisted. The term stagflation was coined to describe this unhappy coincidence. The Phillips curve was used to explain how higher rates of inflation could be traded for lower rates of unemployment. That is to say, as unemployment decreases, inflation increases. Neo-Keynesians developed an aggregate supply curve with an upward-sloping segment that displays how the price level increases as full employment is reached.

5. The Phillips curve relationship is explained by neo-Keynesians as the result of market power held by unions, monopolies, and particular resource suppliers. For example, as GDP grows more rapidly, unemployment falls and unions are in an excellent position to bargain for wage increases that, in turn, contribute to price increases. When unemployment increases, unions back away from demands for higher wages and inflationary pressures dampen. A supply shock can cause upward pressure on price levels as well.

6. Wage and price controls have been tried without much success, as neo-Keynesian policies to cope with the simultaneous existence of high levels of unemployment and inflation. Over time, enthusiasm for the Phillips curve model, as it was originally proposed, has waned. The data for the late 1960s through the 1980s show that the Phillips curve seemed to be shifting upward over time, sug-

gesting trade-offs between ever-higher rates of unemployment and inflation. Moreover, government policies aimed at lowering unemployment rates below a certain level did not seem to work in the long run. The long-run Phillips curve seemed to be vertical at a particular level of unemployment; any decrease in the unemployment rate was met by worker demands for higher wages in anticipation of higher inflation which, in turn, would cause unemployment to rise again.

7. Rational expectations theorists argue that there is no trade-off between unemployment and inflation as suggested by the Phillips curve model. The Phillips curve is, for all intents and purposes, vertical at whatever rate of unemployment prevails. As soon as the government announces expansionary policies to cut unemployment, workers demand and get wage increases. Thus, the policy doesn't work even temporarily.

8. Supply-side economists argue that the best way to attack the problem of unemployment and inflation is by implementing policies that will move the aggregate supply curve to the right more rapidly over time. Such policies include lower tax rates, less government regulation, and less government spending.

9. To the question, "Is there a macro consensus?" we must answer no. While there are areas of agreement between economists from different schools of thought, there is nothing like general agreement. Even within schools of thought there are significant divergences of opinion about the nature of economic problems like unemployment and inflation, and the policies to solve these problems.

10. To some extent, the economy can stabilize itself automatically. Unemployment insurance is one automatic stabilizer. During a recession, when unemployment increases, greater amounts of unemployment insurance are paid, thus propping up aggregate demand somewhat. At full employment these payments are lower, thus relieving inflationary pressure. The personal and corporate income taxes work similarly. During periods of high unemployment, total tax receipts are lower, because the progressive nature of the tax structure allows people to keep a larger percentage of their earnings. When the economy is at full employment, tax revenues rise, and as people move into higher tax brackets, they have smaller percentages of their total earnings to spend, which relieves some of the inflationary pressure.

KEY TERMS

Classical economics
Stabilization policy
Keynesian economics
Phillips curve
Neo-Keynesian economics
Rational expectations
Supply-side economics
Crowding out
Automatic stabilizers

QUESTIONS

1. Imagine yourself at dinner with a Keynesian and a classical economist. The conversation turns to why the economy is experiencing high unemployment and what the government ought to do about it. How would the Keynesian ex-

plain the unemployment and what policies would she advocate? The classical economist would no doubt disagree with both the explanation and the policy prescription. What would he argue and why?

2. Professor Martin Feldstein chaired President Reagan's first Council of Economic Advisers. He was never a serious consideration when President Clinton picked his Council. Why?

3. Keynesian economists were fine-tuning the economy during the 1960s, but found their policies ineffectual in the 1970s. Why?

4. "The key to any economic stabilization is managing aggregate demand." Keynesians and neo-Keynesians would agree with that statement, even though they see quite different outcomes stemming from such management. Discuss.

5. To supply-siders, the key to any economic stabilization is managing aggregate supply. What kinds of policy do they advocate and what outcomes do they expect to achieve?

6. In 1958, A. W. Phillips published his celebrated article introducing the Phillips curve. It changed the way economists think about stabilization policy. Why?

7. "Unions make it difficult for government to reduce the rate of unemployment." Discuss the logic underscoring this view and show how it relates to the Phillips curve.

8. "In periods of inflation, any attempt by the Fed to increase real GDP through increases in the money supply ends up only in increasing the rate of inflation." What school of economists makes this point? How do they make their argument?

9. "To rational expectations economists, it makes no difference whether we think in terms of the short run or the long run: Government cannot reduce the rate of unemployment, period." Explain.

10. "Government may *try* to increase employment and output by increasing its spending, but it just crowds out private investment and ends up reducing employment and output." Discuss.

11. "To *some* extent, automatic stabilizers work." What are they supposed to do, and why do they work?

12. What is the Laffer curve? What impact did it have on government policy?

13. Explain why unemployment insurance is a good example of an automatic stabilizer.

14. "The Fed should just increase the money supply at the same rate that the full-employment economy grows, and the government should desist from any stabilizing urges." What school of thought would make such a suggestion and how do economists of that school justify that prescription?

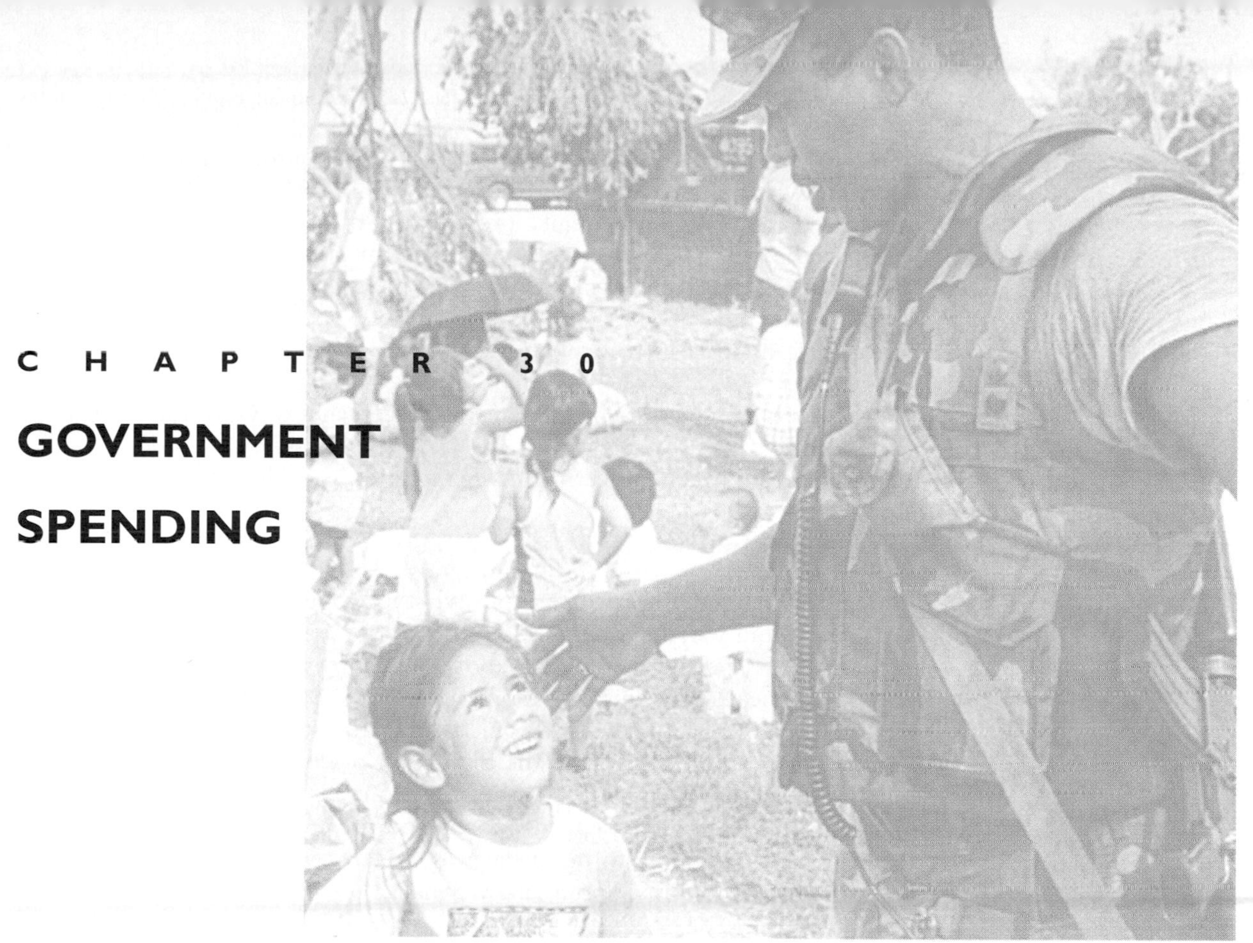

C H A P T E R 3 0

GOVERNMENT SPENDING

CHAPTER PREVIEW

Thus far in our examination of macroeconomics, we have considered government spending used as a tool for countercyclical policy. If unemployment is too high, then government spending can be increased to lower it and vice versa. But the level of government spending is a controversial issue in and of itself. In the absence of the usefulness of government spending as a tool for countercyclical policy, would we want any government spending at all? For nearly all of us, the answer is yes. Some level of government spending is necessary. But what level exists now? What does government spending buy for us? Should the level and allocation of government spending be altered? All these questions are considered in the pages that follow.

After studying this chapter, you should be able to:

- Present a public goods argument to justify government spending.
- Give examples of transfer payments.
- Describe the relative size of different components of government spending.
- Explain why it is difficult to determine how much to spend on security.
- Outline the history of government involvement in education in the United States.

- Discuss government's role in the provision of transportation services.
- Explain why farmers get help from the government.
- List the areas of public assistance provided by the government.
- Discuss the way Social Security operates in this country.
- Contrast the level of Social Security payments in the United States with other countries.
- Propose a hypothesis to explain the growth of government spending over time.
- Rank levels of government spending as percentages of GDP for the OECD countries.
- Explain the impact of government spending on the allocation of resources.

There will *always* be public debate about whether government spends too much or too little, about whether it taxes too much or too little, and whether the kinds of things it does and the way it goes about collecting revenues to pay for what it does represents the best that government can or should do.

These debates are a vital part of our democratic process. We not only have the right to raise these issues, but the obligation of deciding upon them. *These are not strictly economic decisions.* Whether government's role in our economy is too large or too small often depends more upon the cultural, political, religious, and social values we bring to the debate, as well as our property interests, than it does upon the economic arguments we make.

GOVERNMENT SPENDING AND COUNTERCYCLICAL FISCAL POLICY

There are more fundamental reasons for government spending than just countercyclical fiscal policy.

Perhaps the first question we should ask is: *Why government spending at all?* Why, for example, is government in the business of providing interstate roads, street lights, education, national defense, and public parks? We have already seen in our analysis of countercyclical fiscal policy the usefulness of government spending to achieve target employment and GDP levels. Government spending is a vital part of aggregate demand. But is government spending strictly a matter of countercyclical fiscal policy?

Do we really need that bridge? If you don't live and work in that area, you may be inclined to vote against this government project. If you had to cross that highway every day to work, you may vote differently. That's the difficulty in deciding how much government spending is appropriate for the nation.

It would seem unreasonable to argue that the only reason government builds city streets is because the dollars spent on street construction generate—through the income multiplier—desired levels of GDP and employment. Think about it. Wouldn't we need city streets even if the economy were at full employment GDP? But why rely on government to provide the streets? Why don't we rely on the market to produce the city streets just as we rely on it to produce automobiles?

GOVERNMENT SPENDING AND PUBLIC GOODS

Market failure can occur when the market provides inadequate quantities of a good.

Auto makers produce automobiles because people demand them. People demand them because the personal benefits they derive from an automobile are greater than the personal costs they incur buying it. That's also why raincoats, strawberries, and CDs are produced. In each case, people compare the benefits they derive against the costs they incur. Look at your own collection of household items. Didn't you calculate, perhaps subconsciously, benefits and costs before making each purchase? Why, then, can't you make the same kind of personal cost-benefit calculation for a city street?

Hard to even imagine such a calculation, isn't it? After all, no matter how much you may personally benefit from a city street, the cost of buying one is far beyond your personal means. If each of us relied exclusively on the market to determine what to buy, we would all end up with lots of strawberries and no city streets.

How, then, do we overcome the market's failure to provide us with goods and services, such as city streets, sewage systems, and police protection? By replacing the market with government. How does it work?

Public Goods

Consider the small community of Logan Square with a population of 20,000. Suppose that a network of city streets would cost the community $40 million. And suppose that the personal benefit each of the 20,000 people derives from the network is $5,000. The community's total benefit, then, is $100 million or $2\frac{1}{2}$ times its cost of production. In other words, the street project is economically sound. But how do you get it built?

Suppose Doug Dubson, the mayor of Logan Square, calls a town meeting to discuss the economic costs and benefits of the project. He asks each resident to contribute $2,000. The community accepts the mayor's estimate of a $5,000 personal benefit. But Denise Miller, a Logan Square psychiatrist, has another idea. She figures that if everyone *except her* contributes $2,000, the streets will be built anyway and she will still be able to use them. She doesn't feel too guilty about not contributing because she reasons that even if she uses the streets, it's not at her neighbors' expense. They each still end up deriving a $5,000 benefit. What Denise doesn't count on, however, is that everyone has the same idea. The result is that nobody makes a $2,000 contribution and, consequently, no streets are built.

Frustrated, the mayor calls another town meeting. This time, he brings along Paul Budin, an economic consultant, to discuss the unhappy outcome. Paul spells out the differences between a public good, such as a city street, and a private good, such as an automobile. When you buy an automobile, he explains, you exercise exclusive control over its use. *You* have the keys. If others use it, they do so at your expense. That is, their use rivals your own. After all, if they drive the automobile, you walk. The same with your raincoat. You have exclusive control over its use. If someone else uses it, it's at your expense. They're dry, you're wet.

The exclusivity and rival-use properties of private goods are absent in public goods. A city street is a *nonexclusive* good. That is, street owners (or taxpayers) cannot exclude nonowners (or nontaxpayers) from using the streets. There are no keys to city streets. Once built, everybody has open access to them. A street is also a *nonrival* good. If you use the street, it's not at the expense of others.

Public goods are nonexclusive and nonrival goods.

The nonexclusivity and nonrival properties of public goods, Paul Budin explains, means that Logan Square will never get city streets if people rely on markets, because there is no way to exclude anyone who has not paid for the streets from deriving equal benefits. Each individual therefore waits for everybody else to pay for them. If Logan Square wants city streets, it must bypass the market. That bypass is government spending. We rely on government to provide the streets and to tax the community accordingly.

How many private goods individuals buy on the market and how many public goods they buy through the system of government spending and taxation, he tells them, is a matter of individual choice. That's what the ballot box allows each person in Logan Square to do: elect a mayor to represent the levels and character of government spending they want.

GOVERNMENT SPENDING AND TRANSFER PAYMENTS

Not all government spending is designed to satisfy our need for public goods or as a tool of countercyclical fiscal policy. Some government spending simply transfers income from some people—government taxes them—to other people—government pays them. These transfer payments are typically in the form of government services, price subsidies, and cash payments. They are intended to moderate the harshness of poverty among low-income people and, in some cases, to moderate the economic distress suffered by groups such as farmers, whose income source has been undermined by adverse changes in market conditions.

Transfer payments shift income from one group in society to another.

Government is also in the business of administering Social Security, an obligatory social insurance program (also known as OASDI, or Old-Age, Survivors, and Disability Insurance). The program provides benefits to retired people, spouses of people in the program who have died, and disabled people. Every working person who contributes to Social Security—contributions are matched by employers—receives Social Security benefits.

The contributions are held in a specifically earmarked trust fund. Social Security contributions and benefits are transfer payments. Income is transferred from the young (who typically pay into the trust fund more than they receive from it) to the elderly (who typically receive more from the trust fund than they pay into it), even though the payers themselves regard their own contributions to the trust fund more as personal savings than as part of a transfer payment system.

GOVERNMENT SPENDING AND THE PUBLIC DEBT

Each year, government makes interest payments to people who own the public debt. The debt is in the form of Treasury bills, notes, and bonds and is held not only by individuals, but by banks, corporations, the Federal Reserve, other government agencies, and foreigners. A more detailed analysis of the government's debt is offered in the next chapter.

HOW MUCH DOES GOVERNMENT SPEND?

Most of the federal government's spending is focused on transfers, while state and local spending is mostly for purchases of goods and services.

Table 1 shows the total government spending for 1992.

Slightly more than half of total government spending is in the form of purchases of goods and services. At the federal level, purchases made up only 30.8 percent of spending, while transfer payments and interest accounted for 55.4 percent. The federal government also provided state and local governments with $173 billion of grants. Over 80 percent of state and local spending is for purchases of goods and services. What do federal, state, and local governments buy? Table 2 details government spending by function.

Before deciding whether government is too big or too small, we should know what government really does. We should know how government has grown. We should know how much of total government spending is federal and how much is state and local, and how these shares have changed over time. It may be interesting as well to compare our government's spending to spending by governments of other democratic market economies.

Let's start our descriptive analysis of government spending by examining the major items that absorb most of our tax dollars.

SECURITY

There are some public goods that government provides that seem to be almost beyond public controversy. One of these is national security. How many peo-

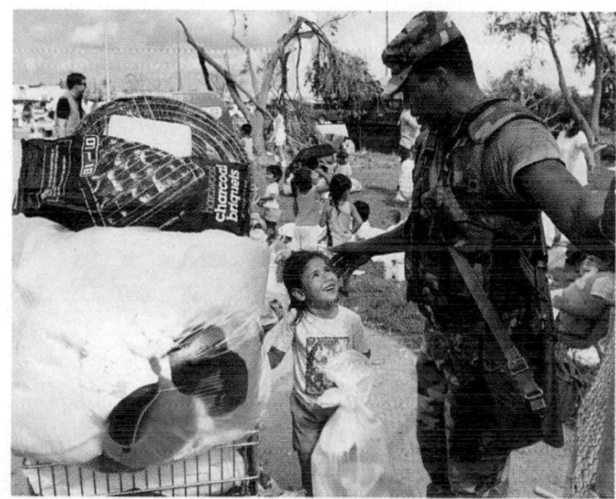

In August, 1992, five-year-old Anabel Pacheco of Homestead, Florida, thanks a U.S. soldier from Fort Bragg, N.C., who provided security and civil order for her, her family, and their community in the aftermath of Hurricane Andrew.

TABLE 1 Federal, State, and Local Government Spending: 1992 ($ billions)

	Federal	State and Local	Total
Purchases	$ 449.2	$ 666.0	$1,115.2
Transfer payments	621.8	233.6	855.4
Grants-in-aid to state and local governments	173.0	—	173.0
Interest	186.5	−43.8	142.7
Other	26.2	−33.3	−7.1
Total	$1,456.7	822.5	$2,279.2

Source: *Survey of Current Business*, February, 1993 (Washington, D.C.: U.S. Department of Commerce), p. 13.

As a percentage of GDP, federal spending for defense has actually fallen since 1960.

ple do you know who contest our need for a reliable national defense? How many people would advocate leaving defense preparedness to individual purchases in the marketplace? There appears to be a wide consensus that national security properly belongs in the federal government's domain.

Some of our security is managed by other levels of government. Local governments, for example, provide police protection to safeguard our communities.

TABLE 2 Government Spending in 1990, by Function ($ billions)

	Federal	State and Local
Security, national defense	$ 315.5	$ —
Security, civilian protection	5.6	70.5
Veterans' benefits and services	34.0	—
International affairs	16.8	—
Education	21.1	280.7
Transportation	30.5	63.7
Natural resources	7.6	6.6
Energy	3.3	−3.4*
Space	13.0	—
Agriculture	16.8	3.8
Income support, Social Security, and welfare	555.6	126.7
Health and hospitals	17.4	30.3
Housing and community services	19.8	16.5
Net interest	177.5	−5.0**
Central executive, legislative, and judicial activities	19.2	45.8
Others	16.4	62.6
Total	$1,270.1	$689.8

Note: The minus figures represent subsidies less current surplus of government enterprises (*), or transfer payments and net interest paid less dividends (**).

Source: *Survey of Current Business*, January 1992 (Washington, D.C.: U.S. Department of Commerce), pp. 50, 52.

ADDED PERSPECTIVE

The Cost of Property

In the euphoria generated by the collapse of communism in Europe the advice-givers from the West have tended to overlook a simple truth: It is costly to define and enforce a system of private property rights. Capitalism is expensive.

Definition and enforcement of private property rights for individuals is accomplished through a mixture of private and public expenditures. We make these expenditures every day, so we tend not to notice them. That is not to trivialize the resource investment. Individual property rights are defined by both an ethical code and a formal legal order. The relative importance of each varies by state, by tribe, by ethnicity. At most, the ethical code and legal order merely define the *de jure* allocation of property rights. However, the *de facto* distribution of property rights may differ greatly from the *de jure* distribution if individuals disregard the law and the social code of conduct. "Thou shalt not steal from thy neighbor" defines a system of property rights, but it does not guarantee those rights.

Enforcement of individuals' property rights claims is ultimately the responsibility of the state. However, much enforcement of private property rights is efficiently conducted by individuals. As the accompanying table reveals, Americans spent billions of dollars in 1985 to protect against theft in its various guises. The vast preponderance of the resource expenditure is made privately.

Individuals spend billions per year on locks. Consider car locks for a moment. A simple switch or button is all it would take to turn over an engine or open a hood or trunk lid. Interior hood releases, locking trunks, and key-activated ignitions are all theft-prevention measures that add considerably to the cost of a vehicle. We purchase titles to real property and title searches for previously owned real estate. Residential insurance against burglary and theft is a $100 million industry. Commercial investments in theft prevention consume well over $150 billion each year. Business insurance against stealing by employees is a multi-billion dollar expense.

There is good news. The dollar magnitude of the resource expenditure in theft prevention appears large, but as a fraction of gross national product it is relatively small. For example, GNP in 1985 was a shade over $4 trillion. Indeed, perhaps much of the reason why our GNP is so large is our willingness to spend resources to define and enforce property rights.

GOVERNMENT EXPENDITURE	
Organized Crime	
Organized crime investigations (FBI)	$124,120,000
Labor racketeering & organized crime	6,101,000
White Collar Crime	
Government fraud	45,240,000
Labor matters	1,160,000
Public corruption	37,120,000
Financial crimes	126,440,000
Other	5,800,000
Personal Crimes Investigations	
Extortion/Hobbs Act (commercial)	15,080,000
Bank robbery and related crimes	55,680,000
Theft of controlled substances	1,160,000
General Government Crimes Investigations	6,960,000
General Property Crimes Investigations	
Thefts from interstate shipments	12,760,000
Interstate transport of stolen vehicles and aircraft	18,560,000
Interstate transport of stolen property	33,640,000
Racketeer influenced and corrupt organizations	3,480,000
Police	
Police protection	4,867,991,900
Corrections	2,882,229,800
Judicial/Legal	2,226,795,600
Protection Against Restraint of Trade/Fraud	
Federal Trade Commission	18,355,000
Department of Justice (Antitrust Division)	41,357,000
Securities and Exchange Commission	26,334,250
EDUCATIONAL	
Locks	
Offices (Instructional and Staff)	
Elementary and secondary	15,239,000
Higher education	13,278,675
Desks (Instructional and Staff)	
Elementary and secondary	397,837
Higher education	313,377
Dorm Rooms and mailboxes	5,442,483

Library Book Theft Detection Devices	
Equipment (not including installation)	9,000,000
Installation (including wiring)	937,953
Power (5/mo. × 16,162 libraries)	969,720
PRIVATE EXPENDITURE	
Residential Investments	
Locks	
Vehicles	
Passenger cars	$1,035,077,080
Trucks	441,816,720
Motor homes	21,888,290
Travel trailers	1,228,578
Folding camping trailers	532,038
Truck camper shells	102,258
Houses/Apartments	
Privately owned, 1-family houses	94,550,400
Privately owned, 2-4 unit housing	7,877,100
Privately owned, 5+ unit housing	6,546,540
Miscellaneous	
Suitcase locks	91,726,518
Safe deposit boxes	2,859,405,100
Burglar Alarms	882,000,000
Titles	
Vehicles	90,342,500
New residential & non-resid. bldgs.	1,116,680,400
Transferred property	1,160,374,600
Residential Insurance	
Premiums paid for insurance against burglary/theft	122,000,000
COMMERCIAL INVESTMENTS	
Locks	
Buildings/Office/Desks	
Buildings	61,362,896
Churches	3,459,610
Hotel rooms	12,500,000
Business entrance doors	46,624,820
Offices	5,180,879
Desks	3,830,474
Commercial Insurance	
Premiums paid for surety and fidelity insurance	2,853,000,000
Business Access	
Burglar alarm systems (10 yr. est. life)	2,621,749,700
Guards	148,400,930,000
Passes/ID (1 yr. est. life)	3,132,908,500
Gates (10 yr. est. life)	1,319,119,400
Surveillance cameras (10 yr. est. life)	989,339,250
Guard dogs (5 yr. est. life)	32,977,984

Source: Excerpted from *The Wall Street Journal*, September 18, 1991.

State police cast a wider security net. Our National Guard is administered by state governments and is sometimes called upon to assist local police. The 1992 Los Angeles riots came to an end only after the National Guard was called in by the governor after consultation with the President.

Although federal, state, and local governments provide for national defense and local and statewide police protection, not all our security is provided by government. Banks, for example, have their own private security system. So do universities. Even shopping malls have theirs. Many corporations hire security guards to protect their property and some even provide personnel protection. Superdomes, Silverdomes, Wrigley Field, and Fenway Park all have their own privately run security forces.

How Much Security Is Enough?

But how much security, private or government, is enough? Can we ever be *too* well protected? How many times have you heard someone say about our police, "They're always around except when you need them!" If there's any substance to the charge, it may signal a need for more police. But how many more? Do you want them around everywhere, all the time?

TABLE 3 Government Spending on Security: 1990 ($ billions)

	Federal	State and Local	Total
National defense	$315.5	$ —	$315.5
Police	4.2	31.4	35.6
Corrections	1.3	25.6	26.9
Total	321.0	57.0	378.0

Source: *Survey of Current Business,* January 1992 (Washington, D.C.: U.S. Department of Commerce), pp. 48–52.

Doesn't our personal security also depend upon what we do with security offenders? What kinds of correction facilities—local jails, state prisons, federal penitentiaries—should we build? What should we do with offenders once they are incarcerated? Should we try to rehabilitate them? That could be expensive. Perhaps the least expensive policy is to hang them immediately after sentencing! Ridiculous? Society has done it for centuries. Many countries still do it. Remember: *Whatever form and level of security we choose, determined by whatever sets of values we hold, carries a price tag that can be compared with those for alternative security systems.*

How would *you* go about deciding how much to spend on what? That's what Congress and the White House must do. That's also what state and local governments must do.

How Much Security Do We Buy?

Table 3 records the security package purchased by federal, state, and local governments for 1990.

In 1990, federal, state, and local governments spent $378 billion on national defense, police, and corrections. Police protection is administered principally by our local governments. National defense, on the other hand, is the monopoly of the federal government.

Look at Table 4, which tracks the growth of national defense spending.

National defense spending, measured in current dollars, grew at an annual rate of 6.4 percent during the period 1960–90. Those are the dollar amounts and rates of growth typically reported and discussed in our national debates on de-

TABLE 4 Growth of National Defense Spending: 1960–90 ($ billions)

	Defense Outlay			
Year	Current $	1982 $	Defense as Percent of Federal Budget	Defense as Percent of GDP
1960	$ 18.1	$192.1	52.2	9.5
1970	81.7	225.6	41.8	8.3
1980	134.0	164.0	22.7	5.0
1990	315.5	234.2	24.8	5.7

Source: *Statistical Abstract of the United States, 1990,* p. 330; and *Survey of Current Business,* January, 1992 (Washington, D.C.: U.S. Department of Commerce), p. 50.

fense spending. But measured in terms of constant dollars, the annual rate of growth in defense spending is only 0.7 percent. That's a mighty different picture of the 1960–90 defense spending growth, isn't it?

Looking at the ratio of defense spending to total federal government spending, or at the ratio of defense spending to GDP offers another perspective. The defense share of both total federal spending and GDP actually *declined* from 1960 to 1980 and rose only slightly during the 1980s. The 1960 and 1990 comparisons are striking. The ratio of defense spending to total federal spending fell from 52.2 to 24.8 percent, the ratio of defense spending to GDP fell from 9.5 to 5.7 percent.

VETERANS' BENEFITS AND SERVICES

Veterans are men and women who have served in our armed forces. When they retire from active duty, they take with them entitlements—benefits and services—that Congress has granted. These entitlements represent "payment now for past security provided."

What do the entitlements include? The major item is disability and survivor compensation. But it also provides for education and medical care. In 1990, veterans' benefits and services amounted to $34 billion.

INTERNATIONAL AID

What about international aid to the less-developed countries? Many people in government believe that providing our allies with economic and military aid is as much a security item as the purchase of a Bradley tank. Others view and support the aid as part of a jobs-creation program. After all, most of the economic aid is used to purchase our own agricultural and manufacturing output. Still others are inclined to view the aid as a transfer payment, that is, as an expression of our humanitarian concern.

How much does aid amount to? In 1990, $16.8 billion was spent, $3.6 billion on the conduct of foreign affairs and informational activities and $13.2 billion on economic aid.

EDUCATION

It's about as American as apple pie to regard primary education as belonging in the public domain. Such a belief has deep roots in our society. To most people, access to education is a right.

Spending on Education

How much government spends each year on education is partly determined by school enrollments. But spending is also dependent upon the quality of the education we demand. What determines quality? The skills and training of our teachers, of course. The number of school days per year. Class size is also a factor, as well as the physical facilities available, such as space and classroom equip-

TABLE 5 Government Spending on Education: 1960–90 ($ 1990 billions)

	Elementary and Secondary	Colleges and Universities	Total Spending on Education
1960	$ 67.5	$16.9	$ 84.4
1970	136.8	54.6	191.4
1980	157.0	68.8	225.8
1990	198.6	92.2	290.8

Source: *Statistical Abstract of the United States, 1991* (Washington, D.C.: U.S. Department of Commerce, 1991), p. 134.

ment. What's our track record on spending? Table 5 traces the growth of government spending on education from 1960 to 1990.

Measured in constant dollars, government spending on education over the period 1960–90 grew at an annual rate of 4.2 percent. Spending on colleges and universities grew more rapidly than spending on elementary and secondary education, 5.8 percent compared to 3.7 percent per year.

How much each of the government levels spends on education is shown for 1990 in Table 6.

As you see, most of the spending on education is handled by state and local governments, not only for elementary and secondary schools but for colleges and universities as well.

TRANSPORTATION, NATURAL RESOURCES, ENERGY, AND SPACE

Interstate highways, county roads, city streets, canals, bridges, sewage systems, street lighting, city playgrounds, national parks, and zoos are just a few in a long list of public goods that government has assumed responsibility for over the years. Some are traditional public goods, with long histories, others are of more recent vintage, such as space exploration and securing strategic reserves of crude oil.

Transportation

It's probably just as hard to imagine a highway that is privately owned as it is to imagine living in an economy without the highway. But like government

TABLE 6 Federal and State and Local Government Spending on Education ($ billions)

	Federal	State and Local	Total
Elementary and Secondary	$ 8.5	$210.4	$218.9
Colleges and Universities	8.3	53.9	61.9
Libraries and Research	4.4	16.3	20.7
Total	$21.2	$280.6	$301.8

Source: *Survey of Current Business*, January 1992 (Washington, D.C.: U.S. Department of Commerce), pp. 48–52.

spending on security and education, the question with highways and streets always is: How much spending is appropriate?

The answer is never without controversy. As small communities grow into large metropolitan suburbs, and as our incomes permit us to become increasingly mobile, we need to build and maintain more city streets, more bridges, more expressways, more bypasses, more county, state, and interstate highways.

Our international airports are seemingly always expanding their capacities as they must if we insist on making greater use of air transportation. Do you know of any major airport that is not thought of as overcrowded and outmoded?

Natural Resources

And what about government spending on conservation and natural resources? The government's right to spend in these areas is almost never disputed. Although spending is minor compared to security, education, and transportation, the same question confronts us concerning natural resources: How much is appropriate?

How much should we spend caring for our national, state, and county parks, our wildlife preserves, government forests, minerals, and agriculture lands? How much for promoting such projects as land reclamation, irrigation, drainage, and flood control?

There are competing interests that press for different levels of spending on our environment. Environmental groups such as the Sierra Club are actively engaged in promoting greater public concern and raising money to preseve our natural resources. They are opposed by people who are more interested in committing our resources to economic development. The issue, in the short run, is whether we can afford not to develop these resources. The long-run issue, according to conservation groups, is whether we might not all lose out if we allow them to be developed.

Energy

In 1973, OPEC engineered a dramatic increase in the price of international oil by sharply curtailing the flow of oil supplies to world markets. The impact on our economy was devastating. Many economists attribute the recessions and inflations of the 1970s and 1980s to escalating oil prices and shortages. After all, we are a high oil-consuming society and have come to rely on imports for over 50 percent of our oil needs.

Our vulnerability to the OPEC oil producers and the belief that they had manipulated supplies to pursue political as well as economic advantage—to our disadvantage—made us increasingly receptive to the idea that government has a legitimate role to play in stabilizing the supply of energy in our economy. Our national energy program includes promoting energy conservation, providing information and regulation, aiding in the exploration of new sources, and securing an emergency supply which can be used in periods of critical shortages. But how much government spending on these programs is appropriate?

Space

If 500 years ago government spending had not included "space exploration," Christopher Columbus might never have ventured beyond the coastal waters of

TABLE 7 Government Spending on Transportation, Natural Resources, Energy, and Space: 1990 ($ billions)

	Federal	State and Local	Total
Transportation	$30.5	$ 71.2	$101.7
Highways	14.5	58.3	72.8
Water	5.0	0.4	5.4
Air	6.6	0.8	7.4
Railroad and transit	4.5	11.6	16.1
Natural resources	5.7	6.6	12.3
Energy	3.3	−3.2	0.1
Space	13.1	—	13.1

Source: *Survey of Current Business*, January 1992 (Washington, D.C.: U.S. Department of Commerce), pp. 48–52.

Southern Europe. But King Ferdinand and Queen Isabella did finance Columbus' expedition and the rest, as they say, is history.

Perhaps some tax-paying Spaniards then complained that such spending was a poor investment, and that there were countless competitive demands being made on the Crown that were more productive. It would be hard to discredit their claim even today.

Twentieth-century space exploration faces the same kinds of charges, and those supporting our space shots and moon landings rely on the same spirit of adventure that put Columbus on our shores. But whether the opportunity costs associated with space exploration makes it a worthwhile investment or not, it is clear both to advocates and opponents of space exploration that if we are to have a space program, government is the appropriate provider. Once again, the question is how much spending.

Spending on Transportation, Natural Resources, Energy, and Space

Federal, state, and local government spending on transportation, natural resources, and energy for 1990 is shown in Table 7.

Over $100 billion was spent on transportation, with the lion's share being handled by state and local governments. The highway system alone accounted for over 70 percent of all government spending on transportation. No surprise, is it? Is there a road you travel on that isn't under repair or doesn't need repair?

Imagine yourself president of the United States, or senator from North Dakota, or governor of Tennessee, or mayor of New Orleans. You would probably have a tough time cutting a penny from any of Table 7's spending. Where, for example, would you use your red pencil? Every item has a history, a *raison d'etre*. You would probably have a difficult time turning aside advocates who press for even higher funding.

AGRICULTURE AND PUBLIC ASSISTANCE

What common denominator is there for government spending on security, education, transportation, natural resources, energy, and space? For each, the target population is everyone. Government does not intentionally target its spending on these items to satisfy any one segment of the population. National defense is intended to defend everyone. Interstate highways are built and maintained for everyone. Elementary and high school education is free and open, and even our community colleges and land-grant universities are open to those who meet the requirements.

Of course, not everyone takes advantage of these public goods to the same degree. Families without children, for example, do not benefit from elementary education in the same way that families with children do. And some people benefit more from an interstate highway than others. There are people who feel more secure with more people in jail. But no one is intentionally short-changed.

But not all government spending is so universal. Some spending is exclusive and targeted to specific segments of the population, and takes the form of goods and services or direct cash payments.

What's the rationale underlying such exclusion? Why is government in the transfer payment business, providing some people with goods, services, and cash, and not others? Perhaps the two most important principles governing such targeted spending are equity and stability.

What should we do about people who simply can't afford the bare necessities of life? Economic equity has always been a concern. Private philanthropy, which at one time was the only institution to address the problems of the destitute, now shares that responsibility with government.

What should we do about people who are not destitute, but are adversely affected by technological change? In some cases, the economic stability of a community or of an entire region is significantly affected. In many of these cases, government has chosen to supplement the incomes of the people who are adversely affected.

Agriculture

Consider, for example, the government's spending on agriculture. It is essentially a transfer payment. The government transfers money received from the general population in the form of taxes to the farm population in the form of subsidies and grants. The primary purpose is to create some measure of stability in the farm economy. But why should government worry about agriculture? Why doesn't government simply allow the market to solve the chronic problem of farm surpluses the way excess supply in other markets is allowed to create new market equilibriums? Because it is thought that farm prices and farm incomes would fall to levels that would not only be acutely painful to many farm families, but would even jeopardize the health of many regional economies.

How does government spending protect the farmer? It establishes minimum prices on particular farm goods, which creates even greater excess supply. The farmers end up much better off because government uses tax revenues to buy up the farmers' excess supply. In a nutshell, that buy-up accounts for much of government spending on agriculture. But government does more. It also grants low-interest loans to farmers who have difficulty obtaining credit elsewhere, and provides financing for farm ownership and utilities.

Public Assistance

Public assistance—the government's welfare program—is a transfer payment intended to moderate the economic hardships facing the poor, the elderly, and the disabled. Government does so by supplementing the incomes of needy people with government-provided goods and services and with direct cash payments.

Government provides goods and services in housing and health care, food stamps and cash payments to families with dependent children, and Supplemental Security Income (SSI) to the elderly and disabled.

HOUSING

Just as government spending in agriculture provides benefits to a target population, so does government spending on housing benefit a target population. The Department of Housing and Urban Development (HUD), for example, finances mortgage insurance programs that help families become homeowners, and facilitates the construction and rehabilitation of rental units. HUD also provides rent-assistance programs for low-income families who otherwise could not afford decent housing. Other government-supported programs that are intended to encourage home ownership, such as those run by the Federal Housing Administration (FHA), provide lower-than-market mortgage rates to first-time buyers who purchase homes that meet FHA requirements.

Why does government target low-income families? And why does it subsidize their rental housing and not, say, their purchase of automobiles? Government spending generally reflects community values. Most people regard housing as an essential good and many are inclined to accept housing assistance as a worthy government undertaking.

MEDICAID

As private health care costs have skyrocketed during the past several decades, many people—particularly the poor and disabled—have been shut out of the health care market. In response, government has intervened, redressing the most serious problems concerning the delivery of health care. Like spending on housing, the issue is equity.

Medicaid

A health care program administered through Social Security that is applicable to low-income and disabled people.

Medicaid is government's health care program targeted primarily toward low-income families, although it also covers people who are elderly, blind, and disabled. It is administered by the states, and is funded jointly by the states and the federal government.

Who qualifies for Medicaid? People who are eligible to receive federally assisted cash welfare payments, such as Aid to Families with Dependent Children. In some states, the coverage is broadened to include specific groups who do not qualify for cash assistance.

The primary emphasis of Medicaid is on institutional care, such as hospitalization and long-term care in nursing homes or provision of skilled nursing home care. Medicaid also covers fee-for-service payments to private physicians, and in some states covers optional services such as dental care and eyeglasses.

AID TO FAMILIES WITH DEPENDENT CHILDREN

Aid to Families with Dependent Children (AFDC)

A cash assistance program designed to aid single-parent families, usually headed by a woman.

Housing and Medicaid are the two most important items in the government's welfare program given in the form of goods and services. The single, most important cash payment assistance is **Aid to Families with Dependent Children (AFDC).** These cash payments are provided jointly by the federal and state governments. Because state government participation in the AFDC program varies widely, the benefits that the poor receive vary from state to state.

Who qualifies for AFDC? Established in 1935, it was designed to provide funds for widows with small children. But as our social environment changed, the program grew to include single-parent families. Typically, these families are headed by women who are unable to work because they must look after their young children. Since 1990, eligibility for AFDC has broadened to include two-parent families, provided the principal breadwinner is unemployed or earns less than the maximum level set by government.

SUPPLEMENTAL SECURITY INCOME

Supplemental Security Income (SSI)
A cash assistance program that aids the elderly, blind, and disabled.

Cash payments are also made to the elderly, blind, and disabled who are unable to work. The **Supplemental Security Income** program is jointly funded by the federal and state governments, who establish the eligibility and payment standards, although most state governments supplement the basic SSI payments.

FOOD STAMPS

Food stamp program
An aid program that provides low-income people with stamps that can be redeemed for food and related items.

How can you guarantee that cash payments will be used by the recipients to buy worthwhile goods and services? Actually, you can't. Once cash payments are made, you rely on the recipient's good judgment. To overcome the problem of possible "improper household management," in 1964 the government initiated a **food stamp program** that controls what people are able to buy. Those eligible for food stamps (the poor, elderly, and disabled) receive a quantity of stamps monthly that are redeemable for goods at most retail stores and supermarkets. In this way, government is better able to get recipients to acquire nutritionally adequate foods.

Spending on Agriculture and Public Assistance

Public assistance spending has been a significant area of growth for total federal spending since 1960.

How much does government spend on agriculture and public assistance? Table 8 shows federal, state, and local government transfer payments to agriculture and public assistance in 1990.

The $241.0 billion of government transfer payments in the form of welfare programs represented 13.1 percent of the government's $1,836.7 billion of total spending. Excluding Medicaid, welfare for the poor and disabled amounted to 6.5 percent of total spending.

The 1960–90 growth of spending on public assistance is shown in Table 9.

TABLE 8 Government Transfer Payments to Agriculture and Public Assistance: 1990 ($ billions)

	Federal	State and Local	Total
Agriculture	$ 16.8	$ 3.8	$ 20.6
Public Assistance	113.5	106.9	220.4
food stamps	14.7	—	
medical care	43.3	75.7	
SSI	12.5	3.8	
AFDC	—	19.8	
other	43.0	7.6	
Total	130.3	110.7	241.0

Source: *Survey of Current Business*, January, 1992 (Washington, D.C.: U.S. Department of Commerce, Table 3.12, pp. 48, 50, 52.

ADDED PERSPECTIVE

Affluent Gain Sizable Benefits from Federal Entitlement Programs

Scott Burns

Entitlements, the largest component of federal spending, now account for about half of federal government spending. These programs include Social Security, Medicare, veterans' benefits, and others.

Few entitlement programs are means-tested; you get the money regardless of your income or assets because, as the word suggests, you are "entitled" to it. Indeed, 75 percent of these funds are passed out without concern for need.

"The scary part of the history of entitlements is the inadvertence of it. It's not a matter of ideology; it's almost entirely accidental," economic historian Neal Howe said.

"No one has ever talked about this. People just assumed that the benefits go to the poor. It takes a long time for public opinion to catch up with common knowledge among the people who measure things," he said.

In a study for the National Taxpayers Union Foundation and based on government data, Howe has examined who gets money from the federal government. He has come to some surprising conclusions.

"A lot of stereotypes we have are based on the idea that government spending is connected to needs. But that isn't so. If you're going to tax people so heavily for this enormous transfer, you'd think it would be well-understood and supported. But when you actually look, there is very little to support how the money is spent."

He has found, for instance, that:

- Nearly $30 billion in federal benefits went to families with incomes of more than $100,000 in 1991.
- $115 billion, almost 22 percent of the total paid out, goes to families with incomes of $50,000 or more.
- $230 billion, more than 43 percent of the total paid out, is received by families with incomes of $30,000 or more.
- Of the $534 billion in benefit spending in fiscal 1991, only 17.8 percent went to families with incomes of $10,000 or less.

While 90 percent of the money from means-tested programs such as AFDC, SSI, and food stamps goes to families with incomes below $20,000, Howe found that money from non-means-tested programs, which accounted for far more federal spending, were "tilted" the other way—toward the affluent.

Households with $100,000 income, for instance, received $2 from Social Security for every $1 received by households with incomes under $10,000. As a result, the overall direction of federal spending is to increase the incomes of those who already have larger-than-average incomes.

Much of that "tilt" occurred in the 1980s. From 1980 to 1991, households with incomes of less than $10,000 experienced a *decline* in real benefit dollars of 7 percent. Households with incomes of $10,000 to $20,000 experienced no increase. Meanwhile, real benefits to more affluent households *increased*. While the typical range of increase was 10 percent to 58 percent, households with incomes over $200,000 saw their real federal benefits double during the period.

If entitlements, particularly the 75 percent that are not means-tested, are the largest single category of government spending now, they are also the fastest growing. Howe points out that an aging population, the bulge of the boomers as they grow older, and advances in longevity all make it inevitable that entitlement programs will be even more of a problem in the future.

His solution? Comprehensive means testing. Instead of capping benefit hikes, as some suggest, or taking other steps that might work to cut benefits to the poor, Howe suggests the establishment of a federal withholding tax on entitlement benefits. A withholding of 7.5 percent of benefits for households with incomes over $30,000, rising 5 percent for each additional $10,000 of income, would have produced annual savings of $33.5 billion in 1991. Phased in over five years, Howe estimates it would reduce spending $71 billion a year by 1996.

But whether all entitlements are means-tested is not the important point. If the distribution of federal spending is, as Howe says, "almost entirely accidental," it is made even more random when you consider another vast but subtle area: Who gets the benefit of income not taxed? What alarms Howe, as with entitlement spending, is "the inadvertence of it."

"Look at the ideas and look at the actual results," he said. "Look at the nontaxability of Social Security. Or the nontaxability of health insurance."

"In the 1940s health insurance was tiny. No one anticipated that it would become what is has become."

Now, billions in annual tax revenue are lost to income tax exclusions that have ballooned over the last 40 years. According to a recent study by the Joint Center for Housing Studies at Harvard University, for instance, tax benefits from home ownership peaked at $1,233 for an average new owner in 1981 and have since declined to $72 in 1992. Deductibility of home mortgage interest and real estate taxes, however, cost the federal government $11.6 billion in 1981 and an estimated $42 billion in 1992 in foregone tax revenue.

The immediate inference: Homeownership exclusions primarily benefit the very affluent. Other income that can escape taxation, such as pension contributions and pension earnings, medical insurance premiums, and other items that were minuscule 40 years ago, now account for mega-billions. (See chart "Major consumer 'tax expenditures'".)

Significantly, the benefits of tax expenditures, like non-means-tested entitlements, also tend to be "tilted" toward the affluent.

Most of what passes for rational political discussion about public needs has no foundation in actual dollars and benefits delivered. What we have created over the last 40 years is an enormous collecting, borrowing, and redistributing machine that is now out of control.

Entitlement Skewed to Well-Off
Amount of federal entitlement funds that went to households of various income levels in 1991. Entitlement allocations are in billions of dollars.

Income Level	Percent Benefits	Dollar Amount
$0–$10,000	17.8%	$ 95.33
$10,000–$20,000	21.7	115.86
$20,000–$30,000	17.2	91.99
$30,000–$50,000	21.8	116.35
$50,000–$100,000	15.9	85.2
$100,000 plus	5.6	29.66

Source: *National Taxpayers Union Foundation.*

Major Consumer 'Tax Expenditures'
All figures in billions of dollars

Item	Amount 1993	Amount 1980
Mortgage interest	$ 42.9	$15.6
Home real estate taxes	12.6	7.3
Step up capital gains at death	46.1	4.7
Exclusion, employer medical insurance	54.1	12.1
Exclusion, Social Security benefits	24.5	8.6
Exclusion of pension		
Contributions, earnings	68.3	19.8
IRA accounts, Keoghs	10.9	1.9
Totals	$259.4	$70.0

Source: *Office of Management of Budget.*

Public assistance increased not only in terms of real dollar expenditures from $15.8 billion in 1960 to $177.8 billion in 1990, but also in terms of the percent of total government spending, from 2.9 percent in 1960 to 11.0 percent in 1990. As you see, Medicaid becomes the major item in the government's public assistance program, increasing from 38.1 percent in 1980 to 53.7 percent in 1990.

TABLE 9
Growth of Public Assistance Programs: 1960–90 ($ 1987 billions)

	Public Assistance	of which Medicaid is	Public Assistance/ Total Spending (%)
1960	$ 15.8	$—	2.9
1970	41.0	14.9	4.3
1980	100.2	38.2	7.5
1990	177.8	95.5	11.0

Source: *Statistical Abstract of the United States, 1982-83*, p. 316, and *ibid., 1985*, p. 356; and *Survey of Current Business*, January 1992 (Washington, D.C.: U.S. Department of Commerce), pp. 50, 52.

SOCIAL INSURANCE

Tables 1 through 9 detail the billions of dollars spent by federal, state, and local governments on public goods and transfer payments. But government handles considerably more money than the discretionary spending indicated in these tables.

Since the 1930s, the government has taken on the functions of an insurance agent, collecting premiums from those who participate in its insurance program and paying out benefits to claimants. These premiums and benefits appear as government taxes and spending—in fact, that's what they are commonly called—but the truth of the matter is that government is principally the agency handling the insurance dollars.

Collecting premiums from the insured and paying out benefits to claimants is precisely what private insurance companies do. Typically, they insure our lives and property. Most homeowners, as you know, insure their homes against losses caused by fire, flood, theft, and in some locations, even earthquakes. The insured pay annual premiums and hope not to be in the position of having to make claims.

Why is government in the insurance business and what does it insure? Government is in the business because it responds to an insurance need that, it feels, had not being adequately served by private insurance. What does it insure? In a nutshell, government insures families against incurring sizable income losses when they retire or when they are disabled or unemployed during their working life. As you can imagine, most people who pay into the government-managed insurance program hope that they do not have to make claims for disability or unemployment.

Social Security

Social Security (OASDI)

A social insurance program that provides benefits, subject to eligibility, to the elderly, disabled, and their dependents.

Be sure that you understand how Social Security is funded and how benefits are paid out.

The core of the government-managed insurance program was established in 1935 when Congress passed the Social Security Act. **Social Security** provides old age and survivor insurance. Payments to the insured or to their surviving dependents were originally intended to supplement incomes, not to be the major source of income. Disability insurance was added to Social Security in 1956, and health insurance—Medicare—was added in 1965.

Social Security—also referred to as **OASDI,** which is an acronym for Old-Age, Survivors, and Disability Insurance—is first and foremost a pension system. There are a host of private pension systems in the marketplace, but none compares with the size and inclusiveness of Social Security. It was designed to provide income security upon retirement to people who would not otherwise have that form of security. Social Security differs from private pension systems in a number of respects.

First, OASDI is compulsory. Wage earners must belong whether they like it or not. Second, Social Security transfers income across income and age groups. How so? Premiums, paid in the form of Social Security taxes, are based on ability to pay. That is, high-wage earners pay more into the system than low-wage earners. But benefits received depend not only on how much a person has paid into the system but also on the number of surviving dependents. As a result, low-wage earners tend to receive more retirement benefits, relative to their contributions, than do high-wage workers. Age is also a factor. Most people today retire with more benefits than Social Security offered, say, a generation ago. But what they paid into the system years ago was determined by what benefits were provided then. In other words, in each year younger workers paying Social Security taxes subsidize those in retirement.

Third, Social Security is a pay-as-you-go system that is financed through a payroll tax, half of which is paid by the worker and the other half by the employer. The revenues from this Social Security tax go into a trust fund from which benefits are paid out. In some years government receives less in Social Security taxes than it pays out in Social Security benefits, in which case it makes up the difference by drawing from its trust fund. In other years, more money comes in than goes out, allowing government to build up the fund.

Unemployment Insurance

Unemployment insurance

A program of income support to eligible workers who are temporarily unemployed.

Unemployment insurance was introduced as a provision of the Social Security Act in 1935. Its main purpose is to provide temporary income support for unemployed workers. How much the unemployed worker receives each week and the number of weeks the unemployed worker is allowed to receive benefits varies from state to state. Unemployment insurance is funded by a 3.5 percent unemployment tax on the first $7,000 of the worker's earnings. This tax is paid by the employer.

Medicare

Medicare

A health care program administered through Social Security that is applicable to everyone over 65 years old.

In 1965, the government added a health care insurance program, **Medicare,** to the Social Security system. Its purpose is to reduce the financial burden of illness on the elderly. The criterion for eligibility is uncomplicated: Medicare covers everyone 65 years of age or older.

Like Social Security's pension program, Medicare's funding is anchored in a trust fund. In any year, workers pay into the Medical Insurance Trust Fund through a payroll tax system which provides the money needed to cover payments to Medicare recipients in that year.

What does Medicare provide? Subject to deductibles and caps, Medicare covers hospitalization, skilled nursing care at home, outpatient care, and physician fees.

Because Medicare is focused primarily on the elderly, who continue to be a growing percentage of our population, and because new, expensive, state-of-the-art technologies are increasingly becoming part of health care, Medicare's trust fund may soon be added to the list of endangered species. How long Medicare can continue to function as a health insurance program without radically changing its structure of revenues and benefits is a problem that ranks among the most critical government faces today.

Social Insurance Payments

The growth of government-managed social insurance over the period 1960–90 is shown in Table 10.

Social insurance payments have increased about fivefold since 1960.

Consider the decade of the 1980s. Adjusting for inflation, social insurance payments increased from $320.6 billion to $384.0 billion, or at an annual rate of 1.8 percent, significantly below the 2.6 percent annual rate of growth of real GDP for the period.

TABLE 10
Social Insurance Payments: 1960–90 ($1987 billions)

	1960	1970	1980	1990
Social Security	$42.3	$110.8	$212.2	$219.5
Medicare	—	20.5	48.8	97.8
Unemployment	10.8	10.0	25.5	18.6
Other	21.1	14.5	34.1	48.1
Total	$74.2	$155.8	$320.6	$384.0

Source: *Statistical Abstract of the United States, 1982-83*, p. 316; and *Statistical Abstract of the United States, 1985*, p. 356; and *Survey of Current Business*, January 1992 (Washington, D.C.: U.S. Department of Commerce), p. 50.

How Do Our Social Security Payments Compare to Those Elsewhere?

Are our Social Security payments out of line? That is to say, is our commitment to Social Security in 1990 frightfully expensive or pitifully low? Or is it just about right? How can we assess the role of Social Security in our economy? Perhaps one way is to compare what we do to what other democratic market economies do. Table 11 does just that.

What do you make of this table? Whatever else can be said about our commitment to social security, it does not appear to be too large. The 10.8 percent of GDP for 1990 is slightly below the average for similar democratic market economies. Perhaps it should give us some comfort to know we're not off the deep end.

INTEREST

The government borrows, accumulates debt, and each year pays interest on that debt. In 1990 the public debt reached $3.2 trillion—$2.8 trillion measured in 1987 dollars—and $177.5 billion—$157.2 billion measured in 1987 dollars—was spent by government on interest payments. Both the size of the debt and the annual interest payments it creates grew considerably in the 1980s. As we see in Table 12, interest represents a growing share of government's total spending.

TABLE 11
Social Security Transfers as a Percent of GDP, U.S. and Selected OECD Economies: 1990

Country	Percent
United States	10.8
Germany	15.3
France	21.4
United Kingdom	12.2
Italy	18.0
Canada	12.6
Japan	11.5
Average	14.7

Source: OECD Economic Outlook, *Historical Statistics 1960-1990*, (Paris, 1992), p. 67.

TABLE 12 Interest Payments, 1960–90 ($1987 billions)

	Debt	Interest	Interest/Federal Spending (%)
1960	$1,117.3	27.2	7.6
1970	1,085.2	42.2	7.2
1980	1,267.4	74.1	8.8
1990	2,839.4	157.2	14.0

Source: *Survey of Current Business*, July 1962, p. 20; July 1972, p. 33; July 1982, pp. 59, 61; January 1992, pp. 50, 52. *Economic Report of the President, 1992* (Washington, D.C.: U.S. Department of Commerce), pp. 385, 391.

IS THE LEVEL OF GOVERNMENT SPENDING TOO HIGH?

Looking back over each of these government spending items, it becomes difficult to advocate wholesale cuts in government spending. Just where would you start? What parts of what programs are expendable?

Every government dollar spent has a purpose. Moreover, every government program has a strong support system buttressed by a determined constituency. It is always possible for government to spend money foolishly, and sometimes that seems to be what it does, but what indicators should we use to gauge whether government spending—federal and state and local—is too big or too small?

Growth of Government Spending

Government spending in 1990 was $1,959.9 billion ($1,743.7 billion in 1987 dollars), 64.8 percent of which was handled in Washington, D.C. How has it grown? Table 13 traces the historical record of total government spending from 1960 to 1990, adjusted for inflation.

Clearly, government spending grew significantly over the course of these 30 years, more than tripling in terms of 1987 dollars. Note that federal spending grew at approximately the same rate as state and local spending. But look at the ratio of total government spending to GDP. While the ratio steadily rose, the increase was rather moderate; in particular, the 1970–90 increase from 33.3 to 35.7 percent. That is to say, government spending has been rising, but by approximately the same rate as our GDP. Is that by chance?

TABLE 13 Government Spending: 1960–90 ($ 1987 billions)

	Total	Federal	State and Local	Total/GDP (%)
1960	$ 550.4	$ 358.1	$192.3	27.9
1970	959.0	582.5	376.5	33.3
1980	1,339.0	839.9	499.1	35.5
1990	1,743.7	1,124.8	618.9	35.7

Source: *Survey of Current Business*, July 1962, p. 20; July 1972, p. 33; July 1982, pp. 59, 61; January, 1992, pp. 50, 52; and *Economic Report of the President, 1992*, p. 300, (Washington, D.C.: U.S. Department of Commerce).

The Peacock-Wiseman Hypothesis

Government spending tends to rise in times of emergency more easily than it falls when the emergency is over.

Not so, claim economists Alan Peacock and Jack Wiseman. They argue that in times of peace and economic tranquility, levels of government spending tend to be constrained by people's view that prevailing levels of spending and taxing, whatever they are, are acceptable upper limits. With GDP growing, tax revenues automatically increase to finance acceptable marginal increases in government spending. Most people are reluctant to move away from these practiced taxing and spending habits.

But in troubled times—periods of economic depression or war—a considerable divergence takes place between what people have long believed are the upper limits to government spending and taxing and what the crisis circumstances dictate. They abandon previously held limits, accepting the divergence as a temporary necessity. However, over time they become accustomed to these new and higher levels. And what was once thought to be temporary, now becomes permanent. In this way government spending and taxes tend to be marked by a pattern of sudden growth followed by plateaus. If the Peacock-Wiseman hypothesis has any validity, then in the long run we should expect a moderate, upward drift in the ratio of government spending to GDP.

SPENDING BY GOVERNMENT IN OTHER ECONOMIES

If Peacock and Wiseman are right, we should expect to see government spending in other democratic market economies look like our own. In fact, that's exactly what we find. Look at Table 14.

If nothing else, Table 14 should dispel the hard-held notion that our government is particularly over indulgent. It isn't more so than other democratic market economies, is it? Look at Japan. Are you surprised to find that its government is as involved in the national economy as ours? Compare Germany's 46.0 percent, France's 49.9 percent, or Italy's 53.0 percent to our own 36.1 percent for 1990.

TABLE 14 Government Spending as a Percent of GDP: U.S. and Selected OECD Economies, 1960–90

	1960	1970	1980	1990
United States	27.6	32.3	33.7	36.1
Japan	18.3	19.4	32.6	32.3
Germany	32.5	38.7	48.5	46.0
France	34.6	38.9	46.1	49.9
United Kingdom	32.6	39.3	44.8	42.1
Italy	30.1	34.2	41.7	53.0
Canada	28.9	35.7	40.5	46.9
Average	28.6	32.8	38.0	42.6

Source: OECD Economic Outlook, *Historical Statistics 1960-1990*, (Paris, 1992), p. 68.

GOVERNMENT SPENDING AND RESOURCE ALLOCATION

Government spending tends to reallocate resources away from private uses when the economy is at full employment.

Look again at Table 13. Do the increases in the ratio of government spending to GDP, 27.9 percent in 1960 to 35.7 percent in 1990, necessarily signal a proportional shift of resources out of the private sector to government? Are we really giving up 35.7 – 27.9 = 7.6 percent more of the resources that produce private goods and services, such as automobiles and television sets, in order to produce more government goods, such as highways and schools?

Not necessarily so. As we showed in Table 1, some of government spending takes the form of public goods—government purchases of goods and services—and some takes the form of transfer payments.

The distinction is important. When government provides a highway, it takes steel, concrete, heavy equipment, man-years of labor, and other resources away from the production of private goods. That is, a reallocation of the economy's resources occurs. Assuming full employment, the highway we enjoy comes at the expense of private goods.

What about the government's transfer payments? Do they involve the same kind of opportunity cost? Not exactly. Consider the government's welfare programs. Government spending on food stamps, or on Aid to Families with Dependent Children does not represent government purchases of goods and services. Government simply engineers a transfer of private goods and services from one group in the economy, the taxpayers, to another, the welfare recipients.

What do welfare recipients do with the transfer payments? They don't buy highways. Their purchases of private goods and services substitute for the taxpayers' purchase of private goods and services. Although these two different groups of people may buy different private goods, the allocation of GDP between private and public goods and services is unaffected.

That is, the character of government's intervention in the allocation process depends on the character of government spending. How significant a share of GDP is in the form of government purchases? In 1990 federal government purchase of goods and services—putting transfer payments and interest aside—amounted to $424.9 billion. If we add $618 billion of state and local government purchases to the federal, total government purchases are $1,042.9 billion. Big? Bigness lies in the eyes of the beholder. The $1,042.9 billion is 18.9 percent of $5,513 billion GDP.

CHAPTER REVIEW

1. The level and composition of government spending will always be topics for debate. Decisions about government spending are value judgments as much as they are economic decisions. Government spending is more than spending in order to counter the business cycle. It also represents spending for public goods—goods that the market would not provide in sufficient quantities because they are nonexclusive and nonrival goods.

2. The government also spends on transfer payments. These include payments for government services, price subsidies, and cash payments to different groups

in our society. One important category of transfer payments is Social Security. Another area of government spending is interest payments on the public debt.

3. When we compare federal with state and local government spending, we find that the federal government spends some 55 percent of its total outlays on transfer payments and interest, and only 31 percent on purchases of goods and services. In contrast, purchases of goods and services comprise 80 percent of state and local government spending.

4. Most federal spending on security is for national defense. State and local spending is split between police and corrections. Tracking federal spending on security shows that it has been falling as a percentage of GDP since World War II.

5. Transportation, natural resources, energy, and space all receive government support. Though the debate over spending in these areas is fierce, each area has its own history and reasons for existence. Spending in these areas is hard to cut.

6. Spending on agriculture and public assistance is more exclusive than spending on defense, education, or transportation. Agriculture receives public money because farm incomes might suffer significantly otherwise, jeopardizing the health of regional economies. Public assistance shows up as spending on housing, Medicaid, Aid to Families with Dependent Children, Supplemental Security Income, and food stamps. Public assistance as a percentage of total spending by government has grown from 2.9 percent in 1960 to 11 percent in 1990.

7. Social Security is a compulsory program that transfers income across income and age groups. Low-wage earners tend to receive more benefits relative to their contributions than do high-wage earners. Younger workers paying Social Security taxes subsidize people in retirement who receive benefits. Unemployment insurance is another type of government social insurance program. Medicare provides health insurance for the elderly, and like Social Security, is funded via a trust fund.

8. Interest payments on the government debt are a growing percentage of federal spending, rising from about 7 percent in the 1960s and 1970s to 14 percent by 1990.

9. Government spending has increased from about 28 percent of GDP in 1960 to some 36 percent of GDP in 1990. According to the Peacock-Wiseman hypothesis, government spending tends to rise most rapidly in periods of emergency, like wars and depressions, and then stay at these new, higher levels.

10. As a share of GDP, federal, state, and local purchases amounted to about 19 percent in 1990. To the extent that government spending moves resources away from the provision of private goods to public goods, resource allocation is affected.

KEY TERMS

Medicaid
Aid to Families with Dependent Children (AFDC)
Supplemental Security Income (SSI)
Food stamp program
Social Security (OASDI)
Unemployment insurance
Medicare

QUESTIONS

1. What are the principal purposes of government spending?

2. What are the most important spending items of the federal government? Of state and local governments?

3. Explain why each of the following is either a private good or a public good: traffic lights, roller blades, a city park, a chicken salad sandwich, a tennis racket, national defense, a coastal lighthouse.

4. The federal government provides the funding for national defense. Why doesn't it also provide the funding for public schools?

5. What is a transfer payment? Why does the government engage in such transfers?

6. The significance of government spending in our economy depends on whether we record the spending in constant or current dollars, in absolute levels of spending or ratios of spending to GDP. Discuss.

7. Why is some of the federal government's spending on agriculture considered a transfer payment?

8. What is the principal difference between Medicare and Medicaid?

9. What does the Peacock-Wiseman hypothesis attempt to explain?

10. "Government that governs least governs best." Do you agree?

11. Is the level of government spending too high? How has it grown? How does it compare to government spending in other industrial economies?

12. Explain how government spending on transfer payments and on the purchase of public goods and services generates different patterns of resource allocations between public and private goods and services.

C H A P T E R 3 1

FINANCING GOVERNMENT: TAXES AND DEBT

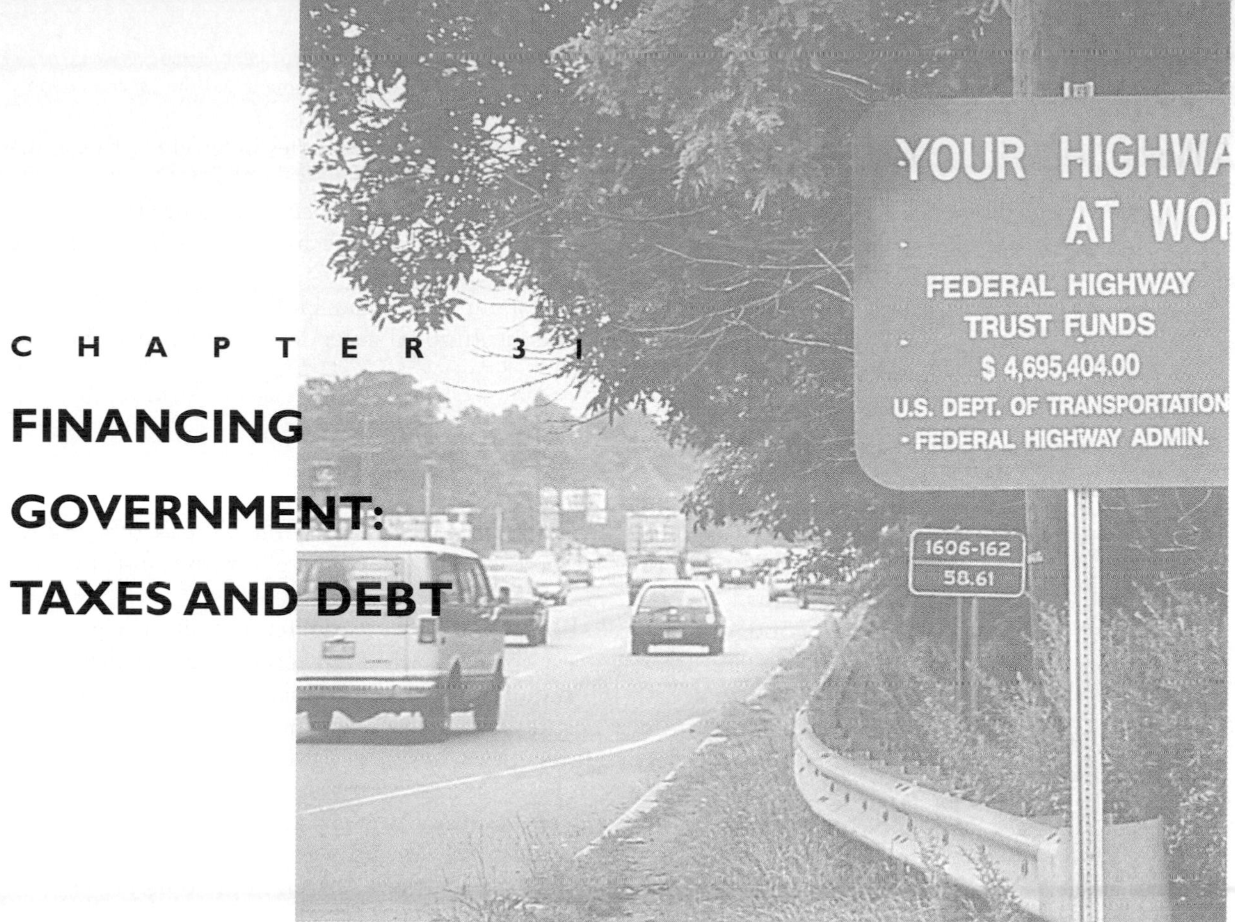

CHAPTER PREVIEW

The last chapter presented a fairly detailed listing of the kinds of goods and services the government purchases and the sort of transfer payments it makes. Now we turn our attention to the way government spending is financed. The government has a choice—it can either tax and pay now for its spending, or it can borrow and pay later. Let's consider the implications of these different approaches to financing government.

After studying this chapter, you should be able to:

- Describe the variety of ways that government has financed its activities over time.
- Discuss different systems of income tax.
- Show that an excise tax is a tax on consumption.
- Distinguish between regressive and progressive taxes.
- Explain what is meant by the marginal tax rate.
- Compare the magnitudes of federal tax revenues with state and local tax revenues.
- Show how government revenues have increased since 1960.
- Describe how government spending can be financed through the sale of government securities.

- Explain why the price of government securities varies inversely with the interest rate.
- Evaluate the danger of a large public debt to our economic health.
- Recount events that led to the massive increase in public debt during the 1980s.
- Account for the failure of the Gramm-Rudman-Hollings Act of 1985.
- Discuss the implications of a constitutional amendment to balance the federal budget.

Few people seriously question our need for national defense, or for universal education, or for most of the items that have become an integral part of our government services. The issue is not our need for public goods, but instead, how to pay for them.

Public goods are not free. If we need an F-16 fighter aircraft or if we need to pave a new city street, we are obliged to give up something else that could have been produced with the resources used to produce the F-16 or pave the city street. The opportunity cost of providing government services can be illustrated in a production possibilities curve. Look at Figure 1.

Producing the F-16 means giving up, say, 500 houses. But how do you get people to give up 500 houses? That is, how is it physically done? Even if people are willing to sacrifice houses for the F-16, how does government go about designing a transfer mechanism that shifts resources from home building to F-16 making?

COMMANDEERING RESOURCES

Governments used to simply take the resources they needed to provide public goods.

The most direct method a government can use to acquire resources is simply to commandeer them. In fact, that's precisely the way governments for centuries have acquired resources. That's how Pharaoh built his pyramids. That's how temple virgins were obtained for sacrifice to the gods.

FIGURE 1
Production Possibilities Curve
The 500 houses, which are the opportunity cost of producing one F-16 aircraft, are depicted in the movement along the production possibilities curve from *a* (3,000 houses and no F-16s) to *b* (2,500 houses and one F-16).

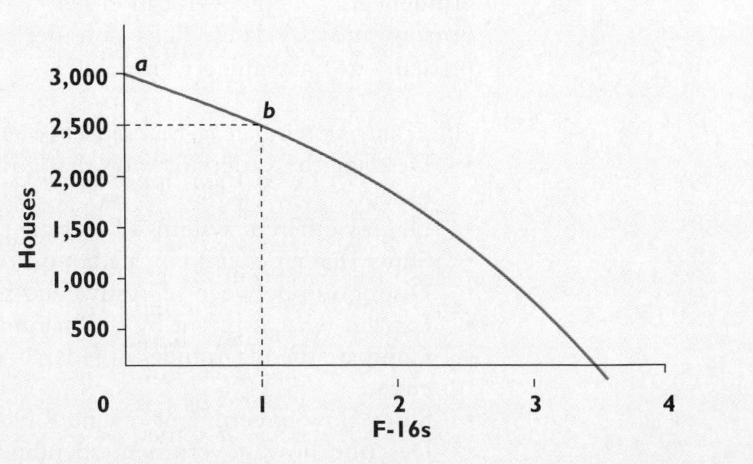

In the economy of Figure 1, the government can just go out to the construction sites, round up a number of construction workers, transport them to the F-16 factories, and set them to work. The result is fewer houses and more F-16s.

Exaggeration? It was customary throughout the Middle Ages for governments to construct road systems by just that kind of commandeering. They institutionalized a system of *corvée* labor, a specific number of days of unpaid labor per year, which people were obliged to provide.

This practice of commandeering resources was particularly widespread in recruiting for the military, and is still used in modern societies for that same purpose. It was common practice throughout the Ottoman Empire for the Turkish government to comb through provincial villages and snatch young men right out of their homes. Those they caught, they took. Few ever returned.

During our Civil War, draft animals, wagons, and food were sometimes commandeered by both southern and northern armies from unlucky farmsteads that happened to be located close by a war zone. In many less-developed countries today, military supplies are supplemented this same way.

Even modern democratic governments haven't completely abandoned this practice of commandeering resources. After all, isn't the military draft simply another form of corvée labor? Army wage rates are not at all related to the draftees' opportunity costs. Although we recently switched from the draft system to an all-volunteer army, some European armies are still recruited through a draft.

Provision for military service aside, there are good reasons why the practice of commandeering has been virtually forsaken by democratic governments as a method of procuring resources. It can be capricious and unpopular, but above all else, it is terribly inefficient. Suppose government decides to produce that F-16 aircraft. Should it really draft construction workers to make it? Do they have the skills? Would *you* fly it?

THE TAX SYSTEM

Money, rather than physical resources, is commandeered through a tax system.

The tax system is an alternative way of shifting resources from the private sector to government. In this system, *government commandeers money, not resources.* Government uses the money in the marketplace to buy what it needs.

There's no need now for the government to run after construction workers or aeronautical engineers. It taxes money away from the general population and *buys* the F-16. Who produces it? An aircraft company, of course. Why shouldn't it? It gets paid by government. The aeronautical engineers, along with everyone else associated with building the F-16, are hired by the company at wage rates that match or better their opportunity cost.

Since people end up—after taxes are imposed—with smaller after-tax incomes, their demand curves for private goods such as houses decrease. This is how resources used in the production of private goods are transferred through the government to the aircraft company.

How much money should government tax away from the people? You might suppose that it depends upon how many F-16s or city streets or other public goods and services it intends to buy. It makes sense, doesn't it, and it is generally the case. But sometimes, cause and effect get reversed. Government can buy only what its tax revenues allow.

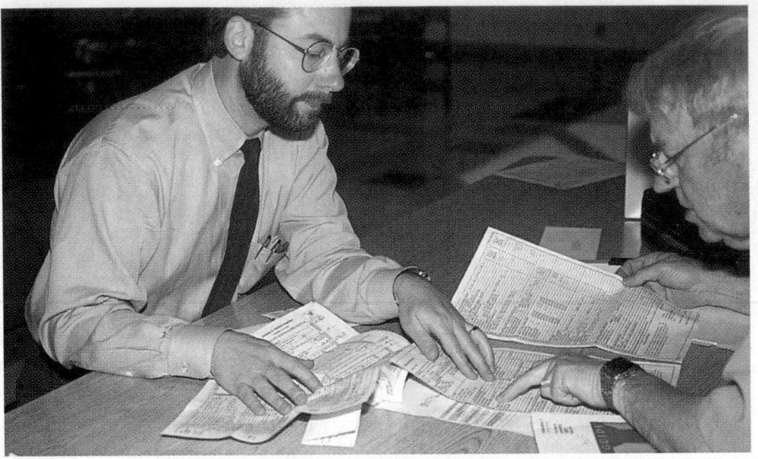

Guess the time of year! You got it! It's tax deadline time: April 15th. This tax consultant is helping a distraught taxpayer figure out just how much he owes the Internal Revenue Service. By the look on his face, you know he's not getting a refund. He has until midnight to post his return.

THERE'S MORE THAN ONE WAY TO LEVY TAXES

Suppose the government decides to spend $100 billion and plans to finance the $100 billion expenditure by taxation. How does it go about taxing? Taxes are not voluntary contributions. The government has to be particularly careful about the method it uses to raise the $100 billion. It has several options.

The Poll (or Head) Tax

Poll tax

A tax of a specific absolute sum levied on every person or every household.

The government can levy a fixed tax, sometimes called a **poll tax,** on every adult in the population. But this tax assumes that all adults can pay. Can they? Some who are unemployed or working at minimum wage may not have the funds. The government will either fall short of needed revenue or be forced to raise the poll tax on the richer adults. The outcome can become more complicated than the government first imagined.

If tax equity—the fairness of the tax—were an issue, the poll tax presents a serious problem. If everyone were taxed the same absolute amount, say, $500, then poorer people end up paying a higher percentage of their income. Economists describe such a tax as **regressive.** The poor pay proportionally more.

Regressive income tax

A tax whose impact varies inversely with the income of the person taxed. Poor people have a higher percent of their income taxed than rich people.

But who are the poor? If the government had little or no information about people's personal incomes, then the poll tax might be the most equitable way of distributing the tax burden. You can see why a poll tax would be an attractive option in some less-developed economies where income data are virtually unknown.

The Income Tax

In most modern economies, however, governments have access to income data. They can tax these incomes in as many ways as their imagination allows, but two options stand out as the most used.

THE PROPORTIONAL INCOME TAX SYSTEM

Proportional income tax

A tax whose rate varies proportionally with the income of the person taxed. Everyone with the same income is taxed at the same rate.

The government can levy a flat-rate tax on personal income, that is, tax a fixed percentage of all incomes. Unlike a poll tax, the rich and poor don't end up paying the same amount. Now the rich obviously pay more. In the **proportional income tax** system, equity is described as paying the *same proportion* of income to taxes.

Consider, for example, two people who work but earn very different incomes. Sandy Roos, an oncology nurse, earns $25,000. Her next-door neighbor, Gary Behrman, is a psychologist earning $50,000. If the flat-tax rate is 20 percent, then the government collects a total of $15,000. Gary, who ends up paying twice the tax Sandy pays, would probably prefer the poll tax. If you were in his shoes, wouldn't you? What about Sandy?

	Income	Tax Rate	Tax Bill
Gary	$50,000	20%	$10,000
Sandy	$25,000	20%	$5,000

THE PROGRESSIVE INCOME TAX SYSTEM

Sandy would probably complain about the flat-tax rate. She would argue that a flat-tax rate, although better than a poll tax, is unfair because the tax burden still falls more heavily upon the poor than upon the rich.

She believes that she suffers a greater loss in giving up 20 percent of her income than Gary does in giving up 20 percent of his. After all, he makes twice her income. She thinks that the enjoyment she derives from the $5,000 she gives up is greater than the enjoyment Gary gives up paying $10,000 tax.

Of course, it is impossible to make interpersonal comparisons of enjoyment. How can she possibly know how he feels about giving up $10,000? But her reasoning is not entirely implausible, is it?

Progressive income tax

A tax whose rate varies directly with the income of the person taxed. Rich people pay a higher tax rate a larger percentage of their income is taxed—than poor people.

At least some governments think not. Instead of taxing a flat rate across incomes, they design a **progressive income tax** structure in which the tax rate on higher incomes increases progressively. For example, the government could tax everyone's first $25,000 at 20 percent, everyone's second $25,000 at 40 percent, everyone's third $25,000 at 50 percent, and all income beyond $75,000 at 60 percent. As you see, the marginal tax rate is steeper in the higher income brackets.

What does Gary Berhman pay under such a progressive tax system? He pays 20 percent on his first $25,000, or $5,000, plus 40 percent, or $10,000, on his second $25,000. His total tax is now $15,000, $5,000 more than he paid before. Sandy's tax remains unchanged at $5,000.

	Income	Tax Rate	Tax Bill
Gary	1st $25,000	20%	$ 5,000
	2nd $25,000	40%	$10,000
			$15,000
Sandy	1st $25,000	20%	$ 5,000

Gary now ends up paying three times the tax Sandy pays. Through this progressive tax system, based on ability to pay, the government hopes to achieve a more equitable sharing of the tax burden. It calculates that Gary's loss of enjoyment in giving up $15,000 now approximates the enjoyment loss incurred by Sandy.

ADDED PERSPECTIVE

Americans' Hostility to Taxes

In an effort to understand the aversion to taxation in the United States, we have compiled data concerning taxation for 14 countries at levels of development comparable to that of the United States. We compare the relative tax burden in each of these countries, the sources of tax revenue, and the degree to which each country's tax structure is progressive—that is, taxes high-income individuals proportionately more than low-income persons. We examine this information in order to gain insight into the reasons why Americans are as hostile as they are to the raising of revenue by the public sector.

The per capita tax level in the United States by no means can be considered high, as Table 1 shows. Of the 14 countries included in our sample, only three countries, Australia, Italy, and the United Kingdom, experienced a lower level of tax per person than did the United States. At the other end of the spectrum, the per capita payment of taxes in Sweden was double the level in the United States, and Denmark had almost the same level as Sweden. The per capita tax level in the United States was about 20 percent *lower* than the average for all 14 of our countries.

The data in the second column of Table 1 reinforce the evidence that by no means are the people in the United States overtaxed. Taxes at all levels of government are expressed in that column as a percentage of each country's level of output, or gross domestic product (GDP). This, in fact, is the best measure of relative taxation since it includes not simply the tax burden but some indication of the ability to pay taxes as well.

The United States is ranked at rock bottom in column 2. Taxation as a percentage of national income is lower in the United States than in any other country. The discrepancy is striking. Whereas taxes represent 30 percent of national income in the United States, taxation in Sweden comes to 56.7 percent, and in Denmark it is 52.0 percent. Though this high percentage might be attributable to the social democratic policies in those countries, even conservatively ruled countries such as Germany and the United Kingdom experience rates of taxation in excess of those in the United States. Thus the data are unambiguous. Compared with other countries, the people in the United States do not pay disproportionately high levels of taxes.

TABLE 1
Tax Revenues, 1987 (per capita and as a percentage of gross domestic product)

	Per Capita in $US	As a % of GDP
United States	5,396	30.0
Japan	5,959	30.2
Australia	3,975	31.3
Canada	5,710	34.5
Italy	4,778	36.2
United Kingdom	4,451	37.5
Germany	6,880	37.6
Austria	6,550	42.3
France	7,099	44.8
Belgium	6,665	46.1
Netherlands	7,012	48.0
Norway	9,546	48.3
Denmark	10,257	52.0
Sweden	10,707	56.7

Source: *Statistical Abstract of the United States, 1991,* Table 1456 (Washington, D.C.: U.S. Department of Commerce).

Table 2 examines the relationship between economic growth and taxes for the same 14 countries discussed above. In this table we have ranked countries by the growth they experienced between 1980 and 1987. We have once again listed the tax to GDP ratio used in Table 1. If the low-tax hypothesis is correct, we would expect to find that the high growth countries should, in general, have low-tax ratios while the low-growth countries should have high tax burdens. Examination of this table, however, suggests that no pattern at all in this relationship is evident. It is true that rapidly growing Japan experienced a low tax to GDP ratio, but the next two most rapidly growing countries, Norway and Denmark, were countries with high tax ratios.

We mobilize the data in Table 3 to test the hypothesis that the form of taxation which is used might be an important determinant of the tax/GDP ratio.

As reported in Table 3 there is not, for the nine countries listed, a statistically significant relationship

TABLE 2
Countries Ranked by Growth in GDP and Tax to GDP Ratio

	Growth in GDP 1980–87	Taxes as a % of GDP 1987
Japan	67.7	30.2
Norway	64.1	48.3
Denmark	57.6	52.0
United Kingdom	57.2	37.5
Canada	57.0	34.5
United States	55.4	30.0
Italy	53.8	36.2
Sweden	51.7	56.7
Australia	50.8	31.3
Germany	50.7	37.6
Belgium	50.5	46.1
Austria	48.9	42.3
France	47.3	44.8
Netherlands	42.1	48.0

$r = -.02823$: not statistically significant.

Source: For data on growth in GDP, *Statistical Abstract of the United States, 1991*, Table 1448; for tax/GDP ratio, see Table 1 (Washington, D.C.: U.S. Department of Commerce).

TABLE 3
Taxes as Percent of GDP, and Individual Income and Taxes on Goods and Services as a Percent of Taxation, 1987

	Tax/GDP	Income	Goods and Services
U.S.	30.0	36.2	16.7
Japan	30.2	24.0	12.9
Canada	34.5	38.7	28.9
Italy	36.2	26.3	26.4
U.K.	37.5	26.6	31.4
Germany	37.6	29.0	25.4
France	44.8	12.7	29.3
Netherlands	48.0	19.7	26.0
Sweden	52.0	37.2	24.1

$r = -0.2364$ $r = 0.4612$

$r^2 = 0.0559$ $r^2 = 0.2127$

Source: For tax/GDP data, see Table 1. For income and taxes on goods and services, *Statistical Abstract of the United States*, Table 1457 (Washington, D.C.: U.S. Department of Commerce).

between the form of taxation and the tax/GDP ratio. Neither use of the income tax nor the sales tax is strongly associated with the level of tax collection. However, this result is heavily influenced by the fact that Sweden, a heavily taxed nation, used the income tax more than any other country. If Sweden were removed from consideration, then the relationship between both of these forms of tax and the tax/GDP ratio would be strongly significant. The income tax becomes associated with low tax/GDP ratios and the sales tax is associated with high levels of that statistic. The United States conforms to that general pattern: a low taxed country, heavily uses the income tax and relies less than most countries listed on sales taxes. Generally, therefore, this table supplies some, but not overwhelmingly strong support, for the view that the form of taxation is related to the extent that taxes are raised.

But is there a relationship between the tax ratio and the degree to which a country employs a progressive tax system? To test this, we provide the data necessary to consider the hypothesis that taxes are politically more acceptable when they are levied according to the ability to pay—that is, the rich (high-income households) pay proportionately more than others. We examine this relationship by employing data compiled by the late Joseph A. Pechman of the Brookings Institution, which indicated effective tax rates at numerous income levels. Our index of progressivity is constructed by subtracting the tax incidence for people earning income equal to that of an average production worker from the tax incidence of an individual earning ten times that level. The larger the number—the greater the difference in tax incidence between the two groups—the greater the degree of progressivity.

There is no ambiguity in Table 4. The statistical association between the index of tax progressivity and the tax/GDP ratio is unambiguously significant. The greater the degree to which tax collection is progressive, the higher is the level of tax collection relative to the GDP. Once again the experience in the United States is completely consistent with the more general pattern. Not only does the United States collect, relatively, the lowest level of taxation, it is also the case that it has the least-progressive tax structure of all those countries listed in the table.

Generally our statistical results are as follows. The United States, compared with other comparably de-

TABLE 4
Index of Tax Progressivity by Country, and Taxes as Share of GDP

	Index of Progressivity	Taxes/GDP
United States	25.5	30.0
Japan	31.6	30.2
Australia	31.3	29.4
Canada	34.5	32.0
Italy	36.2	29.7
United Kingdom	37.5	29.1
Germany	37.6	38.4
France	44.8	47.9
Netherlands	48.0	49.3
Denmark	52.0	32.9
Sweden	56.7	42.1
$r = 0.6685$ $r^2 = 0.4470$		

Source: For data on tax/GDP ratio, see Table 1. Index of tax progressivity computed from Joseph A. Pechman, "Modern Industrial Countries: The Role of the NIT," *Focus*, 12, 3 (Spring 1990), Table 2, p. 34.

veloped countries, is undertaxed, and the taxes which it does collect are less progressive in their source than is the case for any other nation. Internationally, there is no relationship between the extent of taxation and growth rates. But there is at least suggestive evidence that the use of the income tax is negatively associated with the extent of taxation, while sales taxes are positively associated with that variable. Finally, the evidence is strong that tax progressivity is positively associated with tax receipts.

Louis Ferleger
Associate Dean, College of Arts and Sciences and Professor of Economics
University of Massachusetts at Boston

Jay R. Mandle
W. Bradford Wiley Professor of Economics
Colgate University

Discussion

Using Tables 1 to 4, make the case that relative to taxpayers in other democratic market economies, Americans are seemingly hostile to taxes.

Source: *Challenge*, July/August 1991, Vol. 34, No. 4, pp. 53–55. Reprinted by permission of M. E. Sharpe, Inc., Armonk, NY 10504.

Of course, the government can introduce exemptions and allow deductions from all sorts of taxable income. But as you would guess, there will always be some grumbling among some people no matter what exemptions and deductions are allowed and no matter what the tax rates are at various income brackets.

The Corporate Income Tax

Corporate income tax

A tax levied on the corporation's income before dividends are distributed to stockholders.

In most modern democratic economies, governments also tax the income of corporations. They could levy a progressive **corporate income tax,** using the same rationale that justifies imposing a progressive income tax, but there's a complicating factor here. Shareholders of corporations receive income in the form of dividends and since their personal incomes are certainly not identical, the burden of the corporate income tax—whatever its progressivity—would fall unevenly among corporate shareholders.

The Property Tax

Why limit taxes to income and profit? Why not tax wealth? Why shouldn't the government also impose a tax on part or all of a person's wealth?

Taxing wealth could involve the government in the rather messy business of taxing personal belongings, such as furniture, carpets, and household appliances. Or the government could tax financial assets, such as savings deposits, bonds, stocks, and certificates of deposit which would be much easier to evaluate. The government could also tax real estate.

The most commonly taxed wealth holdings are residential, commercial, and industrial properties. Typically, the **property tax** is a flat-rate tax applied to the property's assessed value. In this sense it becomes a proportional wealth tax. That is, people who live in mansions on hilltops pay more than people who live in mobile homes. But how much more? The proportionality of the tax depends on accurate assessments of property values.

Property tax

A tax levied on the value of physical assets such as land, or financial assets such as stock and bonds.

What about financial wealth? Don't we pay taxes on our savings accounts? No! The government typically taxes the *income earned* on savings, which is taxed as personal income, but not the accounts themselves.

Excise Taxes

Aside from taxing personal income, corporate profits, and physical and financial property, the government can levy taxes on specific goods and services that people consume. It has several options.

It can levy (1) a **unit tax**—so many cents per item, (2) a **sales tax**—a percentage of the sales price on every item sold, or (3) **customs duty**—which is simply the sales tax applied to foreign goods imported into the economy. All of these are different kinds of **excise tax.**

Unit tax

A fixed tax in the form of cents or dollars per unit levied on a good or service.

Sales tax

A tax levied in the form of a specific percentage of the value of the good or service.

Customs duty

A sales tax applied to a foreign good or service.

Excise tax

Any tax levied on a good or service, such as a unit tax, a sales tax, or a customs duty.

In any form, the excise tax is regressive. For example, if you fill up your gas tank in New Hampshire, the 24 cents per gallon unit tax on the 20 gallons purchased yields the government $4.80. Dorothy Shelly-Vickers' Porsche at the next pump takes 20 gallons as well and Dorothy pays the same $4.80 tax. But the $4.80 tax Dorothy pays probably represents a smaller percentage of income than it does of yours.

If you are impressed with the $60,000 Porsche and decide to buy one yourself, the 20 percent customs duty paid by the Porsche dealer and passed on to you plus the 10 percent sales tax you pay on the $60,000 purchase nets the government $18,000. The tax is regressive, unrelated to income, but the government probably figures that a new Porsche owner can afford that level of taxation.

The equity issue may not be very disturbing in the matter of Porsches—after all, few of the poor own one—but sales taxes on bread, milk, medicine, and other basics of life do add up and their burden tends to fall more heavily upon the poor. Governments typically exercise moral judgment in levying excise taxes. Some exclude from taxation such items as milk, medicine, and books, and place a relatively high rate on items such as cigarettes and alcohol. Discriminatory? Of course.

Like a poll tax, the excise tax is relatively easy to impose. It doesn't require the government to know much about your income, your corporation's profit, or your property assets. When you buy milk, you pay a tax. When you smoke, you pay a tax. It's as simple as that. For some governments in some economies, its about the only tax they can administer.

THE SOCIAL SECURITY TAX

How your $1,000 of income tax or your $10 sales tax on shoes is used by the government is left to government discretion. It can use these taxes to purchase an F-16 aircraft or an interstate highway. It can use them to retire the national debt. There is no connection between the source of the tax and the purpose it's applied to.

However, unlike corporate and personal income tax, property, estate, gift, and excise taxes, Social Security contributions, commonly referred to as Social Security taxes, are earmarked funds. That is, they are used specifically to finance the benefits that the Social Security system is obligated to pay. The system provides retirement income, survivors income, income to the disabled, and hospital insurance.

The government is simply the Social Security system's collection and disbursement agency. Funds are collected by the government from workers and businesses, and government pays out the benefits.

In any one year, the Social Security taxes collected by the government do not necessarily equal the Social Security payments that the government makes. What happens when there is a surplus? The funds are invested in government bonds which pay interest to the Social Security system.

Although the government acts as the system's agency, it is not simply a conduit of funds. It decides not only on the amount and quality of benefits paid out, but on the form of revenues collected.

ACTUALLY, EVERYTHING IS TAXABLE!

When you think about it, there is probably nothing that can't be taxed. Even love and marriage. Don't we pay marriage license fees? Of course, not everything is. In fact, what gets taxed is surprisingly limited and varies among the forms of government doing the taxing. The federal government, for example, relies almost exclusively on personal income, corporate income, and excise taxes. It collects revenue from its estate and gift taxes, but these are rather minor sums.

Even among the sources it taxes, the federal government is still selective. Not all personal income or corporate income is subject to taxation. The government allows deductions, exemptions, credits, and write-offs that reduce the tax base. Matters of fairness, incentives to work, incentives to save, and incentives to invest influence what government decides.

Some state governments, too, tax personal and corporate income. Among those that do, the variations in rates, progressivity, and what actually gets taxed are great. States also levy their own excise taxes. Local governments rely heavily on property taxes.

Because the federal government taxes two of the most productive revenue sources—personal and corporate income—it shares some of its tax revenues with both state and local governments. Local governments also receive some funding from their state governments.

THE U.S. TAX STRUCTURE

The marginal tax rate applies only to income earned above the cutoff for each bracket.

What does the U.S. tax structure look like? Table 1 describes the federal income tax structure.

Note how the marginal tax rate increases from bracket to bracket, from 15 percent at the lower end to 39.6 percent at the upper end. Progressive? This five-bracket structure, legislated in the 1986 tax reform, replaced a tax structure

TABLE 1
1992 Tax Rate Schedule for Married Persons Filing Jointly

Income Bracket	Percent of Income Taxed	Of the Amount Over
$0 to $38,000	15	
$38,000 to $91,850	28	$38,000
$91,850 to $140,000	31	$91,850
$140,000 to $250,000	36	$140,000
$250,000 and over	39.6	$250,000

Source: Internal Revenue Service, *Instructions for Form 1040* (Washington, D.C.: U.S. Department of the Treasury, 1992), p. 47.

that had more brackets and higher rates. This 1992 structure represents a remarkable change, particularly when compared to the 1959 structure for joint incomes, which had seven income brackets and marginal tax rates that ranged from 0 percent to 91 percent.

FEDERAL, AND STATE AND LOCAL TAX REVENUES

The revenues generated by taxes for the federal, state, and local governments are shown in Table 2.

Income taxes are the biggest source of revenue for the federal government. Sales taxes are the biggest source of revenue for state and local governments.

As you see and perhaps could have guessed, the single, most important tax is the income tax. The lion's share of the income tax goes to the federal government and accounts for almost half of the federal tax revenues. The income tax is also an important source of revenue for state governments, ranking slightly behind the states' sales taxes. Local governments rely almost exclusively upon the property tax for their self-generating revenues. The state and local governments also receive revenues in the form of grants-in-aid from the federal government.

TABLE 2
Federal, State, and Local Government Revenues: 1993 ($ billions)

	Federal	State and Local
Tax revenues	$1,265.7	$891.0
Income tax	505.9	123.3
Estate and gift	12.9	—
Corporate income	143.0	30.3
Sales, excise	48.5	212.4
Custom duties	19.9	—
Property		184.0
Federal revenue sharing	—	186.1
Social Security contributions	517.8	67.8
Other	17.7	87.1

Source: *Survey of Current Business*, August 1994 (Washington, D.C.: U.S. Department of Commerce), p. 16.

Sometimes it's a good idea to remind people that paying taxes—a not too pleasant activity—provides very visible and essential goods and services to the taxpaying public. In this scene, drivers learn that the road they are driving on is made possible through their tax dollars.

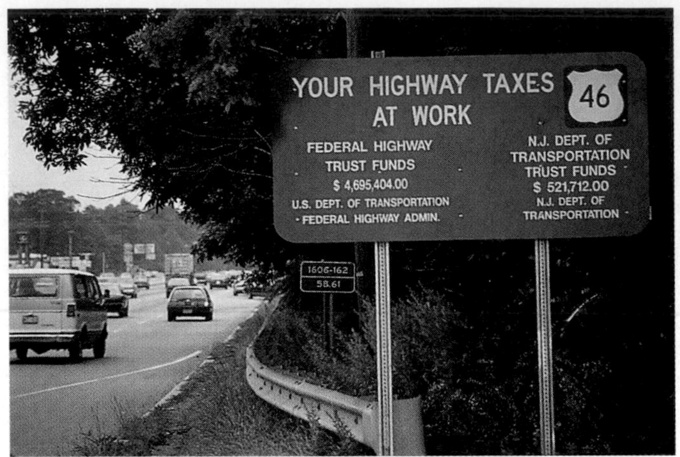

TRACKING GOVERNMENT REVENUES SINCE 1960

Table 3 details federal, and state and local government revenues over the years 1960–93.

Over the 33 years of Table 3, total government receipts measured in 1987 dollars increased at an annual rate of 3.6 percent. The 3.0 percent growth rate for federal receipts was slightly lower than the 4.1 percent growth rate for state and local receipts.

Revenues have increased steadily, for the most part, from 1960 through 1991.

These tax revenue growth rates are less than the growth rates of government spending. For that same period, 1960 to 1993, total government spending measured in 1987 dollars increased at an annual rate of 3.7 percent; the federal spending rate was 3.6 percent, and the state and local rate was 4.2 percent.

The disparities between the growth rates of federal tax revenues and the growth rates of federal spending show up in growing federal budget deficits. By 1993 the total federal revenues of $1,265.7 billion ($1,020.6 billion in 1987 dollars) were $241.3 billion short of the $1,507.0 billion of total federal spending. The federal government incurred deficits in 29 of the 33 years covered in Table

TABLE 3 Federal, State and Local Government Receipts: 1960–93 ($1987 billions)

	Total	Federal	State and Local
1960	$ 533.9	$ 373.1	$185.8
1965	658.4	442.9	254.6
1970	851.7	554.6	366.5
1975	947.0	599.3	458.7
1980	1,151.6	770.9	503.8
1985	1,288.8	835.1	559.9
1990	1,505.5	978.2	644.2
1993	1,735.0	1,020.6	714.4

Source: *Economic Report of the President, 1993* (Washington, D.C.: U.S. Government Printing Office, 1994), pp. 272, 365–66.

3. Over time, the government's annual budgetary deficits grew. In 1993, the federal deficit (measured in 1987 dollars) was more than twice the 1980 deficit.

With federal revenues incapable of providing all the funds the federal government has been spending, how then has the government managed to stay solvent? The answer is deceptively simple. *By borrowing.*

FINANCING GOVERNMENT SPENDING THROUGH DEBT

Treasury securities are simply IOUs issued by the federal government.

When the federal government discovers that its revenues fall short of its planned spending, it instructs the Treasury Department to do precisely what private companies do when they need funds beyond their own resources to finance investment projects—print up interest-bearing IOUs and peddle them on the market.

Every $100 IOU that the Treasury sells transfers $100 to the government from the person who buys it. Why would anyone want to hold the Treasury's IOU? Because it yields interest. Besides, buying a Treasury IOU is not risky business. The U.S. government has never welshed on its IOUs.

Who buys them? Individuals like yourself, commercial banks—actually anyone interested in a secure, interest-bearing investment—and even the Federal Reserve. Look at Table 4.

Wouldn't you think that foreigners, looking for a good way to earn interest, would also consider buying the Treasury IOUs? If enough IOUs are sold, the Treasury covers the deficit created by the difference between government's spending and taxes.

Public debt

The total value of government securities—Treasury bills, notes, and bonds—held by individuals, businesses, other government agencies, and the Federal Reserve.

But solving one problem creates another. Now the government is involved in **public debt.** After all, Treasury IOUs in the hands of others are financial claims against the government. How can the government pay these claims? One way is to raise taxes and use the revenues to redeem the IOUs. But it was insufficient taxes to cover spending that caused the deficit in the first place. The other way is to sell new IOUs to pay off the old ones.

TABLE 4 Ownership of the U.S. Public Debt: 1993 (percent of total)

Federal agencies and trust funds	25.4%
Federal Reserve	7.2
Commercial banks	6.9
Money market funds	1.7
Insurance companies	4.8
Other companies	4.8
State and local governments	12.3
Individual U.S. citizens	6.7
Foreigners	13.1
Others*	15.6

Source: *Federal Reserve Bulletin*, October 1994 (Washington, D.C.), p. A29.

Note: *Others** refers to savings and loan associations, nonprofit institutions, credit unions, mutual savings banks, corporate pension trust funds, certain U.S. Treasury deposit accounts, and federally sponsored agencies.

Treasury Bonds, Bills, and Notes

Government sells a variety of debt forms, principally to satisfy the tastes of debt holders. People who prefer not to tie up their money in long-term debt holdings can buy Treasury bills that mature in three months, six months, or 12 months. These bills are offered in minimum amounts of $10,000 and in multiples of $5,000 above the minimum, which makes them inaccessible to some people.

Longer-term debt is available in the form of Treasury notes and bonds. Because they are sold in denominations as low as $1,000, they are more accessible than Treasury bills. Notes carry maturities of two to ten years. Treasury bonds have a maturity of 30 years.

All Treasury securities (bonds, notes, and bills) are marketable debt. That is, anyone holding a Treasury security who decides to sell it before maturity can offer it for sale on the market.

TRACKING GOVERNMENT DEBT SINCE 1929

The federal government has been in the business of supplementing tax revenues with sales of Treasury bills, notes, and bonds for many, many years. Figure 2 records the federal government's indebtedness.

Look at panel *a*. It's a long hard climb from $16.9 billion to $3,683.4 billion of federal government debt. The debt more than doubled during the 1930s, reflecting government deficits incurred in the Great Depression. The fivefold increase during the 1940s is attributable primarily to the financing of World War II.

Government spending increased faster than tax revenues (when income growth declines, tax revenue growth declines) during the OPEC-induced recession years of the 1970s, resulting in increasing deficits that more than doubled federal government debt. The combination of the tax reforms of 1981 and 1986 (which reduced tax rates) and the recessions of the early 1980s and 1990s doubled the debt once again.

Looking at Ratios, not Dollars

The ratio of debt to GDP for the United States is not out of line with that observed for other countries.

But how horrendous is the debt? Frightening when looked at in terms of absolute dollars, but perhaps less frightening when the debt is viewed as a percentage of GDP. Look at Figure 2, panel *b*.

The ratio of debt to GDP climbed during the early years of the Great Depression, reaching a plateau at approximately 33 percent just before World War II. During the first half of the 1940s, the ratio rocketed above 100 percent and then drifted steadily downward to approximately 40 percent in the 1980s, before climbing again during the 1980s to reach 64 percent in 1991.

Is $3,683.4 billion too large? Is 64 percent of GDP worrisome? Figure 3 records the debt ratios for other democratic market economies.

Because other economies' debt ratios are similar to our own does not necessarily mean our debt ratio or theirs isn't a problem. But it is perhaps noteworthy that our ratios are not out of line. In Italy, the ratio of public sector debt to GDP increased from 88.4 percent in 1986 to 101.8 percent in 1991. Canada's ratio of net public debt to GDP in 1991 was 61.5 percent. As you see in Figure 3, the ratios for Japan and the OECD economies mirror fairly closely the ratios in the United States.

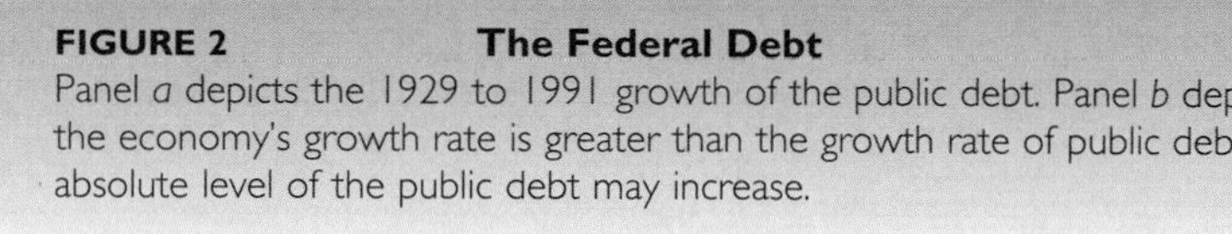

FIGURE 2 **The Federal Debt**

Panel *a* depicts the 1929 to 1991 growth of the public debt. Panel *b* depicts the ratio of the public debt to GDP. If the economy's growth rate is greater than the growth rate of public debt, the debt to GDP ratio falls, even though the absolute level of the public debt may increase.

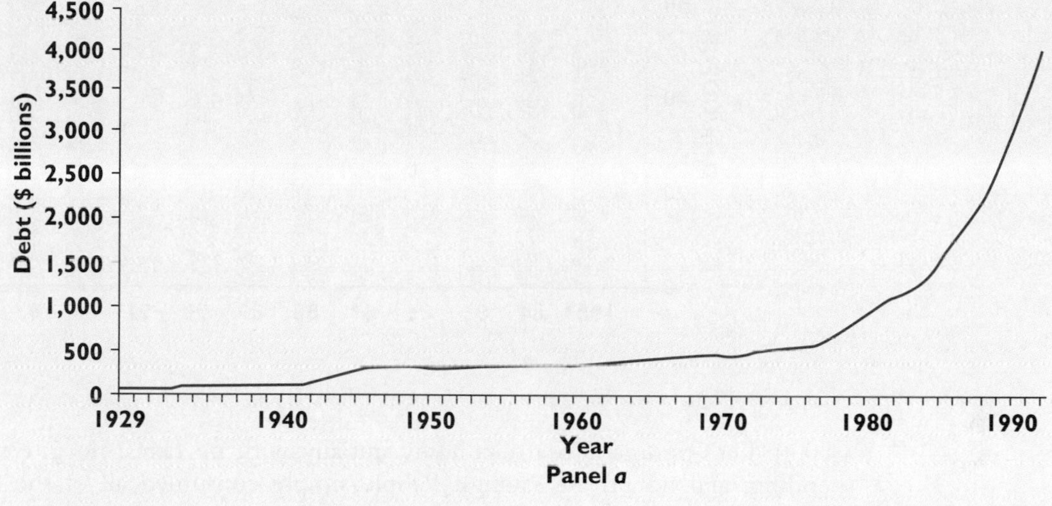

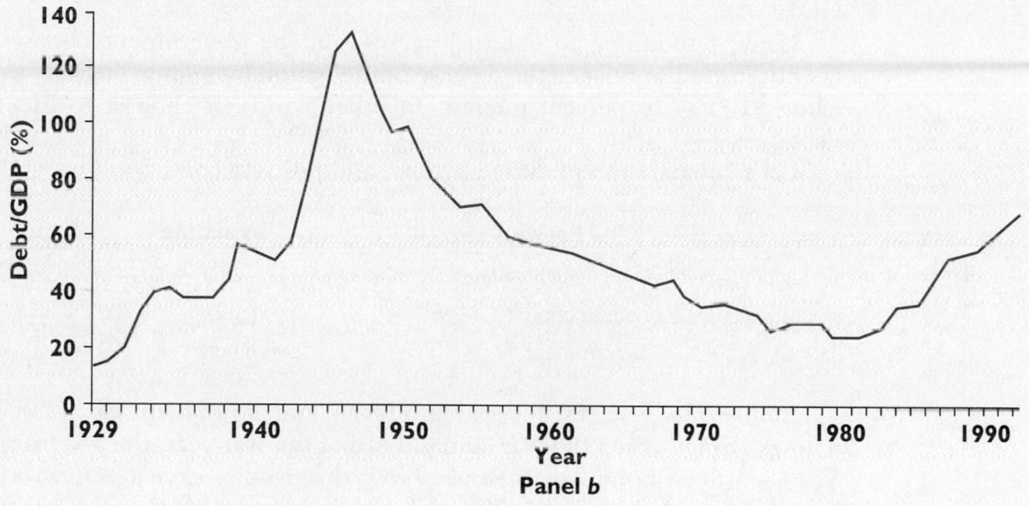

DOES DEBT ENDANGER FUTURE GENERATIONS?

One of the most commonly held views about government debt is that "we can live in debt today, but only at tomorrow's expense." That is, by incurring debt now, we bequeath a debt problem to our children. That's a tough charge to make. And it seems to make a certain amount of sense. After all, *someone* has to pay! If the debtors don't, won't their children have to?

Let's pursue the debt burden argument by examining what happens to debt and the debt burden when a government finances a one-year war by selling bonds. We'll simplify the argument by supposing that prior to the war, GDP was

FIGURE 3
General Government Debt as a Percent of GDP for Japan and OECD Economies
The 60 percent (plus or minus 5 percent) debt/GDP ratio in Japan and other OECD economies is similar to the debt/GDP ratio in the United States.

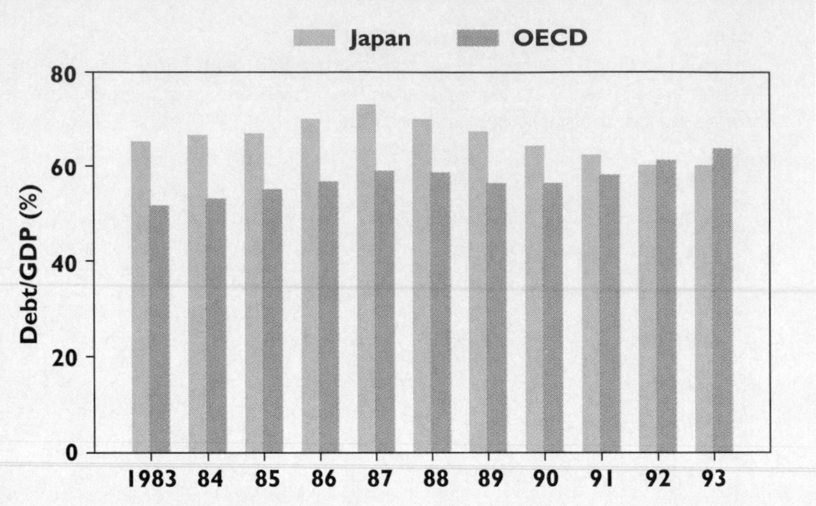

$1,000. Let's assume also an economy initially with no taxes, no government spending, and no private savings. People simply consumed all of the $1,000 GDP.

Now, responding to external aggression, the government chooses not to tax but instead to finance the defense of the nation by selling Treasury bonds totaling $100 at 10 percent interest. In other words, it chooses to incur public debt.

Let's compare the prewar, wartime, and postwar conditions.

Prewar		Wartime	
GDP =	$1,000	GDP =	$1,000
Consumption =	1,000	Consumption =	900
Government =	0	Government =	100

Before the war, the people produced and consumed the $1,000 GDP. Things change when the war comes. During the war year, the government sells $100 worth of bonds to *its people.* Now the people, exchanging $100 for the bonds, can only consume $900. What did government do with the $100? It spent it on the purchase of ships, tanks, aircraft, and armed forces.

Now let's compare the postwar condition to the blissful prewar status.

Prewar		Postwar	
GDP =	$1,000	GDP =	$1,000
Consumption =	1,000	Tax =	−10
Government =	0	GDP − Tax =	$ 990
		Interest =	+10
		Consumption =	$1,000
		Government =	0

It's really not terribly complicated. After the war, GDP remains at $1,000—the quantity of resources remains the same—and the government no longer sells Treasury bonds. But there are $100 worth of bonds *already sold* and the government is obligated to pay the promised 10 percent interest on its $100 debt. That is, government's postwar annual interest payments are $10.

Where does it get the revenue to pay the interest? Suppose it chooses to tax. Now the people, producing and earning $1,000 GDP, can't keep it all. Every year, they pay a $10 tax to government, leaving them with $990. Government now has the money to pay its $10 interest obligation. People who hold the bonds receive the $10 as interest payments; and that $10, coupled with the $990, ends up as $1,000 available to the people for consumption.

What about production? Government spending returns to zero, no need for ships, tanks, or aircraft, so that the economy is producing precisely what it did before the war.

Let's suppose 25 years pass. The government still taxes and pays $10 annually. Suppose also that the people who bought the $100 worth of Treasury bonds 25 years ago have died and bequeathed the bonds to their children. Should the children be thankful? *For what?*

Although their parents left them bonds that yield $10 each year, they left them also the obligation to pay taxes. After all, dead people cannot pay taxes. Are the children any poorer because they must assume the tax obligation? No. What they pay in taxes, they receive in interest payments. Perhaps they are richer on one account. Their parents were wise enough to secure their future by choosing to produce less consumption and more defense back in the war years.

Are There No Problems with Incurring Debt?

Do you feel as if you've been had? That somehow a sleight of hand has taken place? First you see it, then you don't. Not at all. There's no magic, no tricks, no illusions. The debt, held by the people themselves, neither adds to nor subtracts from national production or consumption. But that neutrality doesn't rule out complications.

NOT EVERYONE HOLDS THE DEBT

As long as the debt is held domestically, some individuals in future generations will hold the debt and earn interest, while others will pay the interest.

Although the nation neither gains nor loses, individuals may. For example, not everyone holds the debt. If the bondholders are only the rich, then they alone receive the interest payments. Depending on how many bonds they hold, they may end up receiving more in interest than they pay in taxes. On the other hand, because they hold fewer bonds, poorer people may end up paying more in taxes than they receive in interest. Under these conditions, the debt can indeed be a burden to some. The progressiveness of the income tax and the presence of the corporate income tax might mitigate somewhat the inequity of the burden.

Savings bond

A nonmarketable Treasury bond that is the most commonly held form of public debt.

Government is particularly conscious of this burden effect and has kept a watchful eye on who holds what bonds. For example, it has at times instructed commercial banks to reduce their total debt by divesting some of their bond holdings. That's also why the Treasury created the relatively low-priced **savings bond.** It allows more people to buy and hold government debt.

DEBT PROMOTES "OVERCONSUMPTION"

The debt can also distort our choices of consumption and saving. How? Many people who hold bonds tend to consume more out of their income than they should because they *think* they are wealthier than they really are. They mistakenly view the bonds as their personal assets and as the government's liabilities, without realizing that in the end the government's liabilities are actually their own. They don't realize that the source of the interest they receive is the taxes they must pay. By regarding their bond holdings as part of their savings, they feel they can afford to spend more on consumption. That is, by holding bonds, they end up undersaving and overconsuming.

DEBT CAN CREATE INFLATION

Debt complications can develop if government chooses to finance its debt interest obligations not by taxing people or by issuing and selling more bonds directly to people, but by issuing bonds that are purchased by the Federal Reserve. Since the Fed pays for the bonds by creating an equivalent deposit in the Treasury's account at the Fed, the economy's money supply increases, which may cause prices to rise.

CROWDING OUT PRIVATE INVESTMENT

Debt complications could become even more difficult. If, in order to sell its bonds, the government raises the interest rate on the bonds it offers, it forces private businesses, who must stay competitive as suppliers of bonds in the bond market, to raise the rates they offer on their corporate bonds. That is, financing government spending by government debt makes it more costly for private industry to finance its own investment. As a result, government debt may end up crowding out private investment and slowing economic growth in the private sector.

Some economists who acknowledge this crowding out phenomenon do not necessarily subscribe to the idea that crowding out undermines overall economic growth. After all—to exaggerate their point—is it really detrimental to economic growth if private investments in gambling casinos are crowded out by debt-financed government spending on public schools? The effects of crowding out, then, aren't so much a matter of who crowds out whom, as they are in measuring the relative contributions to economic growth made by the specific private and public investments.

External Debt Is a Different Matter

Domestic consumption may be reduced if significant amounts of the debt are held by foreigners.

Suppose that foreigners, not the people living and working in the economy, buy the government bonds. For example, suppose that Saudi Arabians, attracted by the Treasury's high interest rates, buy a large share of the bonds issued by the U.S. government to finance its 1993 budget deficit.

To simplify, we assume GDP = $1,000 for both the U.S. and the Saudi economies, and that the $100 U.S. government bond issue is bought entirely by the Saudis.

Year of Bond Purchase		Thereafter	
U.S.	Saudi Arabia	U.S.	Saudi Arabia
GDP = $1,000	GDP = $1,000	GDP = $1,000	GDP = $1,000
Government = +100	Bond = −100	Tax = −10	Interest = +10
Consumption = $1,100	Consumption = $ 900	Consumption = $ 990	Consumption = $1,010

What happens to national consumption in each country during the year of the bond purchase? Suppose that a U.S. war effort, which accounts for the 1993 deficit, involves the purchase of $100 of Saudi oil, which is financed by selling $100 worth of bonds to Saudi Arabia. During the war period, U.S. civilian and war consumption increases to $1,100. Americans consume their own $1,000 GDP and the additional $100 Saudi oil which is recorded as government spending, G = $100. The Saudis, now holding the U.S. debt, consume $100 less. Their consumption falls to $900 in the year that they buy the U.S. bond.

Thereafter, the burdens shift. In subsequent years GDP remains $1,000 in each country, but the U.S. government taxes its people $10 to make its annual debt payments to the Saudis. That reduces American consumption to $990. On the other hand, the $10 interest paid to the Saudis allows them to claim $10 of U.S. production, increasing their consumption to $1,010.

External debt
Public debt held by foreigners.

What happens after 25 years? The new generation is still debt-obligated. American children grow up and are taxed to pay the grown-up Saudi children who inherited the $100 worth of bonds. In other words, if government debt is an **external debt,** that is, held outside the country, the debt burden can be passed on to future generations. Of course, the U.S. government can always buy back its own bonds.

ARE DEFICITS AND DEBT INEVITABLE?

Aside from whether or not budget deficits and the public debt burden are really troublesome, what can the government do to reduce deficit and debt levels? Basically, there are only two ways for the government to tackle the problem. It can increase taxes or reduce spending. Everyone in government is aware of these options. But knowing isn't doing. Putting either of these alternatives into action is the difficult part.

Tax Reforms of 1981 and 1986

The intent of the 1981 tax cuts was to spur production, investment, and employment so much that tax revenues would rise significantly to offset the deficit created by the cuts.

Let's look at the tax-design efforts associated with deficit and debt reduction. In 1981 President Ronald Reagan came to the White House with a tax-cutting agenda in mind. He was intent on revising the basic income tax structure by reducing tax brackets and marginal tax rates, and eliminating tax loopholes. This, he hoped, would be coupled with a cut in government spending. He expected the combination to reduce the government's deficit and debt.

Congress responded positively, at least with respect to taxes, by legislating the Economic Recovery Tax Act of 1981 (Kemp-Roth) which cut marginal tax rates. It was less forthcoming on government spending. At the time, the economy was in recession and the idea of leaving more money in the hands of people by cutting tax rates was not only politically popular but made good sense as countercyclical fiscal policy.

President Reagan was convinced that the tax reform would not only stimulate the economy through the demand side—raise aggregate demand—but would stimulate the economy through the supply side—encourage investments and production. He believed the tax rates in the United States were too high and acted as a disincentive to production. Supply-side advocates, delighted with the 1981 tax reform, pushed the argument for tax reduction further, asserting that such a tax move would end up creating more tax revenues. Their arithmetic was elementary. Lower tax rates mean expanded production, employment, and income. More income adds up to more tax revenues.

The Tax Reform Act of 1986 completed the Reagan tax agenda. It lowered the marginal tax rates further, reduced the number of tax brackets, eliminated many tax loopholes, and instituted changes in deductions, exemptions, and capital gains.

Both the 1981 and 1986 tax reforms were integral parts of the President's political agenda, which was to disengage the government from the economic life of the nation. In a sense, the reduction in tax rates was compensation for the elimination of the myriad of specific tax-incentive schemes—deductions, exemptions, allowances, and loopholes—that government discretion allowed. The tax reform not only simplified the tax structure but reduced the government's ability to discriminate with respect to who pays what taxes.

Supply-side expectations notwithstanding, the tax reforms did not do much to increase tax revenues during the 1980s. At the same time, government spending continued to grow. That combination of tax cuts and government spending growth produced in the 1980s the largest annual deficits in the history of the republic. As a result, the public debt increased dramatically.

Gramm-Rudman-Hollings on Government Spending

Most members of Congress understand the need to cut government spending to reduce deficits and debt. The question that paralyzed congressional action on spending was: What gets cut? Everyone was willing to cut spending in areas other than their own. Most major spending items, such as defense, entitlements, and even environment, had some political support. It was politically unwise for members of Congress to jeopardize their own economic interests by assailing others. The result was soaring deficits.

How can Congress break the impasse? Senators Phil Gramm, Warren Rudman, and Ernest Hollings hit on a scheme. If Congress is unable to make the necessary cuts through the normal process of discretionary budget making, then the Gramm-Rudman-Hollings (GRH) Act of 1985 goes into action. Every federal budget item gets cut by the same percentage, indiscriminately and automatically, according to a timetable that eventually will reduce budget deficits to zero.

Why apply across-the-board cuts to government spending? Because it solves the political problem that for years has made spending cuts unimplementable. It allows Congress to make cuts *without having to vote on them.* In this way, no members of Congress can be blamed for losing projects for their districts.

BUT, ALAS, SOME BUDGET ITEMS ARE MORE EQUAL THAN OTHERS

No sooner had Congress voted for the GRH idea, than it tried to change the ground rules. President Reagan and many in Congress, for example, tried to ex-

TABLE 5 GRH Initial (1985) Deficit Targets and Actual Deficits: 1986–91 ($ billions)

	GRH Target Deficit	Actual Deficit
1986	$171.9	$237.9
1987	144.0	169.3
1988	108.0	193.9
1989	72.0	206.1
1990	36.0	220.5
1991	0.0	268.7

Source: *Statistical Abstract of the United States, 1992,* (Washington, D.C.: U.S. Department of Commerce, 1992), p. 315; and *Balanced Budget and Emergency Deficit Control Act of 1985.*

Cutting spending and raising taxes are politically unpalatable to our Congress and to its constituents.

clude defense from the GRH chopping block because, they argued, that item was already critically underbudgeted. Other members of Congress had their own favorites. Many, for example, sought preferential treatment for social welfare items. In the end, GRH didn't work. Table 5 compares the GRH target deficits set at the time GRH was enacted (1985) to actual deficits for 1986 to 1991.

The deficit targets were revised upward in 1987 and again in 1990. But the gap between target and reality was still glaring. For example, the 1987 GRH revision estimated the 1991 deficit at $64 billion, still considerably less than the actual deficit.

A Constitutional Amendment to Balance the Budget?

Some members of Congress, frustrated by the failed attempts to reduce the deficit, sought the answer in a constitutional amendment that would prohibit government, year-to-year, from spending more than it collects in tax revenues. If we are unwilling to raise tax revenues to reduce the deficit, then such an amendment would require the government to cut its spending, regardless of the nation's needs for public goods. This unlinking of government spending to public needs made many in Congress uneasy about supporting the amendment. There may be many ways to skin a cat, but to the dismay of Congress, there are only two ways to reduce the deficit: raise taxes or cut government spending

The Clinton Agenda

President Clinton's economic agenda for the 1990s represents a radical departure from the agenda of the Reagan-Bush years. Abandoning any attempts at innovative schemes, President Clinton has gone back to the simple meat-and-potatoes options. His agenda on the deficit and debt includes tax increases and government spending cuts, reversing the budgetary direction and the political overtones of the Reagan-Bush presidencies.

In the Clinton presidency, government plays a more interventionist role in the economy. For example, the Clinton tax program not only raises tax rates but gives government discretionary powers in deciding which economic activities receive tax breaks and which do not. In legislating government spending cuts, the GRH idea was abandoned and allowance made for discretionary cutting.

The collapse of the Soviet Union, for example, has allowed the government to cut disproportionately into spending on defense. President Clinton also accepted cuts in entitlement programs, while at the same time increasing government spending on infrastructure investments and job retraining. That is, government is playing an activist role, influencing through selective tax and spending programs not only the size of the deficit and debt, but the direction of the economy.

CHAPTER REVIEW

1. The public goods that government provides are not free goods. In the past when a government required resources, it simply commandeered them. More recently, governments have shifted to commandeering money through a tax system rather than commandeering resources directly.

2. Poll taxes are taxes levied on every adult in a population. Income taxes may be proportional or progressive. Corporate income can also be taxed proportionately or progressively. Taxes on wealth include the property tax. Consumption is taxed through excise taxes. Social Security is paid for with earmarked funds collected from workers and their employers.

3. The federal tax structure in the United States has five distinct tax brackets, with rates ranging from 15 to 39.6 percent. As incomes increase, people may move into the next higher tax bracket. Only the amount of income earned over the cutoff is taxed at the higher rate.

4. The income tax is the biggest source of tax revenues for the federal government, representing almost half of federal revenues. Sales taxes account for somewhat more revenue than do income taxes for state and local governments. Between 1960 and 1993, federal, state, and local revenues nearly tripled. However, this was insufficient to cover expenses at the federal level.

5. When the revenue generated by taxes is insufficient to cover the expenses of government, a deficit exists. Government can finance the deficit by selling securities. Securities are like IOUs issued by the government. Essentially, people loan money to the government in return for an interest payment. Government securities are regarded as safe assets since the United States has never failed to pay securities holders either interest or principal.

6. The federal debt has risen enormously since 1929 but so has GDP. The debt/GDP ratio was lower in 1991 than at the end of World War II. Big increases in the debt/GDP ratios are noticeable for the decades of the 1930s, the 1940s, and the 1980s. The debt/GDP ratios for the United States are similar for those observed in other OECD countries.

7. The problems associated with debt include potentially greater inequality in income distribution, the potential for overconsumption, inflation resulting from Fed purchases of bonds, crowding out of private investment, and payments to foreigners who hold the debt.

8. The recent rise in the deficit over the 1980s and the ensuing rise in the debt was the result of decreased taxes and tax rates in 1981 and 1986.

9. The Gramm-Rudman-Hollings Act of 1985 was intended to introduce discipline to the budgetary process by setting targets for the deficit. If Congress

failed to make the spending cuts necessary to achieve the targets, then across-the-board cuts would occur automatically. This act failed to keep the budget deficit in line. A constitutional amendment to balance the budget continues to be discussed, although it would unlink government spending from the nation's needs for public goods.

10. The Clinton administration has pursued a path emphasizing tax increases and spending cuts to balance the budget. Under Clinton's direction the government plays a more interventionist role in the economy, by raising different tax rates by different amounts. The collapse of the Soviet Union has been used to justify cuts in defense spending.

KEY TERMS

Poll tax
Regressive income tax
Proportional income tax
Progressive income tax
Corporate income tax
Property tax
Unit tax
Sales tax
Customs duty
Excise tax
Public debt
Savings bond
External debt

QUESTIONS

1. If the government wants to build a highway, why doesn't it just commandeer the necessary land, labor, and capital to build the highway?

2. What is a poll tax? Why would governments sometimes favor such a tax? Does the tax affect rich people and poor people alike?

3. What is the fundamental difference among regressive, proportional, and progressive tax structures?

4. How does an excise tax differ from an income tax?

5. What is the federal government's most important source of tax revenue? What are the state and local governments' most important sources of tax revenue?

6. What are Treasury securities? Who owns them?

7. What is the relationship between Treasury securities and the public debt?

8. What is the relationship between the public debt and the debt/GDP ratio? How does the U.S. debt ratio compare to the ratios in other democratic market economies?

9. Explain why some economists believe the burden of a public debt cannot be shifted onto future generations.

10. Some economists believe that the public debt may be detrimental to the economy's growth. Explain.

11. How does an externally held public debt differ from an internally held public debt?

12. What were President Reagan and the Congress trying to accomplish by enacting the tax reforms of 1981 and 1986?

13. Why did the Congress pass the Gramm-Rudman-Hollings Act of 1985, and why did it fail to do the job?

14. Suppose you earned $100,000 in income in 1995. Your next-door neighbor earned $25,000. Using the tax structure shown in Table 1—assuming no exemptions, deductions, or credits—how much income tax would you pay? How much would your neighbor pay? Is the income tax structure progressive, regressive, or proportional?

PART 8
THE WORLD ECONOMY

CHAPTER 32

INTERNATIONAL TRADE

CHAPTER PREVIEW

So far we have focused primarily on domestic consumption and production activities. To be sure, some attention has been given to the international character of economic activity. But we haven't developed an economic argument to support international trade, nor have we considered the economic problems that arise from such trade. However, previous chapters have provided the analytic tools necessary for a sophisticated comprehension of international trade and its associated problems. So, let's explore this increasingly critical component of economic behavior.

After studying this chapter, you should be able to:

- Explain how trade can alter the relative prices of goods between two states or two nations.
- Discuss how trade creates only winners in the participating countries.
- Describe how political power can influence the way international prices are set.
- Provide an explanation, in the terms of trade, for the weaker position of less-developed countries vis-à-vis industrialized countries.
- Distinguish between absolute and comparative advantage in international trade.

- Describe the main patterns of international trade.
- Evaluate arguments in favor of restricting international trade.
- Compare and contrast quotas and tariffs as protectionist measures.
- Outline recent efforts to liberalize international trade.
- Explain how economic sanctions are intended to work as an economic weapon.

If you were to drive west during the late summer months, along Trans-Canada Highway 401 through southern Ontario, then cross into Michigan at Port Huron, turn south along Interstate 69, then west again along Interstate 74, through Indiana into central Illinois, you would have to be impressed by the changing heights of the corn stalks you see along the route. They stand under five feet in Ontario, but reach well over eight feet in Illinois. They just don't grow corn in Ontario—or in Michigan or Indiana—the way they do in Illinois.

That's why so many farmers grow corn in Illinois. If you haven't yet tired of driving, you could connect at Champaign onto Interstate 57 south to St. Louis, and just off the highway, see a landscape dotted with pumping oil wells. They are scattered among the corn fields. The pumping machinery keeps churning away, but it doesn't yield much oil. At least, not nearly the barrels generated by the wells in Oklahoma and Texas.

INTRASTATE TRADE

Illinois Corn for Illinois Oil

The straight-line production possibilities curve shows a constant opportunity cost—one bushel of corn for one barrel of oil.

If we were to suppose that the Illinois economy were sealed off from the rest of the world, then Illinois oil producers and corn farmers, if they wanted to trade at all, would be forced to trade among themselves.

How would they arrange a trade? How many bushels of corn, for example, would an oil producer get by trading oil for corn? Assuming perfectly competitive markets, the relative prices of corn and oil are determined by the relative costs of producing corn and oil.

For simplicity's sake, let's suppose that the only production cost is labor and that it takes one hour of Illinois labor to produce either a bushel of corn or a barrel of oil. That is, *the opportunity cost of producing a bushel of corn in Illinois is a barrel of oil, and the opportunity cost of producing a barrel of oil in Illinois is a bushel of corn.* To simplify our model even further, let's also suppose that these opportunity costs apply regardless of the quantities of oil and corn produced. That is, the law of increasing costs is set aside. Suppose, as well, that the total labor supply in Illinois is 200 hours of labor.

Figure 1 represents the two-good production possibilities curve for the Illinois economy. By devoting all its labor to corn production, Illinois can produce 200 bushels of corn. On the other hand, it can produce 200 barrels of oil, or any combination of corn and oil along the production possibilities curve shown in Figure 1. Let's suppose Illinois chooses *A,* 100 bushels and 100 barrels.

Now imagine yourself as one of those Illinois corn farmers. It takes you one hour to produce a bushel of corn. Your next-door neighbor, who owns one of those oil wells along Interstate 57, puts in the same hour to fill a barrel.

FIGURE 1
Illinois Production Possibilities Curve
If all the resources in Illinois, 200 hours of labor, were devoted to the production of oil, its economy could produce 200 barrels. If it chooses to produce one bushel of corn, it must redirect some resources away from oil. It sacrifices one barrel of oil. The opportunity cost of producing a bushel of corn is a barrel of oil.

The production possibilities curve is drawn as a straight line, reflecting the fact that the opportunity cost is one barrel per bushel regardless of the number of bushels or barrels produced. The economy can use its 200 hours of labor to produce any combination of oil and corn, such as 100 bushels of corn and 100 barrels of oil, shown at point *A*.

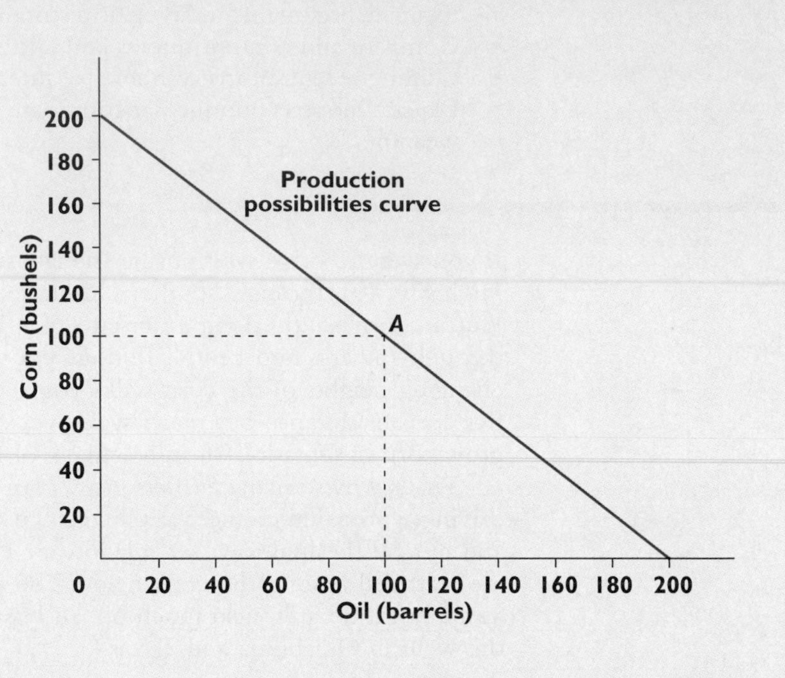

Neither of you, of course, lives on corn or oil alone. It seems only reasonable that you want to exchange corn for oil and she wants to trade oil for corn. The question is, what quantities would exchange for what quantities? Since, in the highly competitive economy of Illinois one hour's labor buys another, you would need to give up a bushel of corn to buy a barrel of oil.

Of course, your neighbor faces the same opportunity costs. In her case, however, she reads the price of corn in terms of barrels of oil she must give up in exchange to buy the corn.

Oklahoma Corn for Oklahoma Oil

The straight-line production possibilities curve here shows the constant opportunity cost of producing oil or corn in Oklahoma—one bushel of corn for 12 barrels of oil.

Let's now suppose, as we did for Illinois, that the Oklahoma economy has 200 hours of labor and is sealed off from the rest of the world. Let's also suppose that Oklahomans, like the folks in Illinois, produce corn and oil. In Oklahoma, however, the labor costs involved in producing corn and oil are substantially different. The corn stalks there look more like Ontario's. It takes not one, but four hours of Oklahoma labor to produce a bushel of corn. Their oil fields, however, are another matter. They are gushers. It takes only 20 minutes of labor to fill up a barrel.

Figure 2 represents Oklahoma's production possibilities. If Oklahoma's 200 hours were devoted to corn production, they would yield 50 bushels. If the 200 hours were devoted to oil production, they would produce 600 barrels. If Oklahomans choose to produce at *A*, they could produce 25 bushels and 300 barrels. Since the quantities of corn and oil exchange according to their relative labor costs—that is, their opportunity costs—one bushel of corn is the labor equivalent of 12 barrels of oil.

FIGURE 2 **Oklahoma Production Possibilities Curve**

If all the resources in Oklahoma, 200 hours of labor, were devoted to the production of oil, the economy could produce 600 barrels. If the 200 hours were devoted to the production of corn, it could produce 50 bushels. The opportunity cost of producing a bushel of corn is 12 barrels of oil. The economy can use its 200 hours of labor to produce any combination of the two, such as 300 barrels of oil and and 25 bushels of corn, shown at point A.

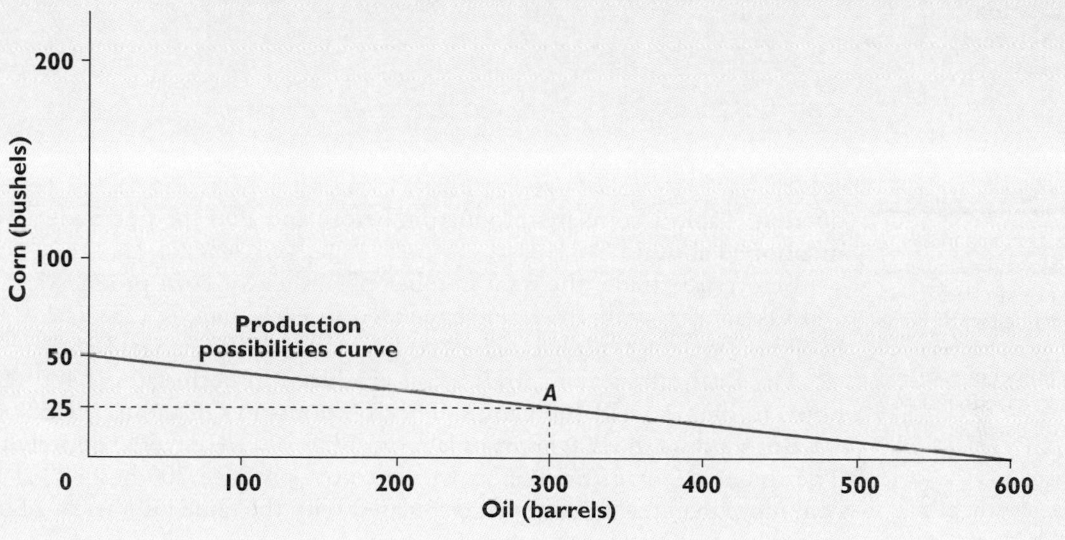

INTERSTATE TRADE

Illinois is the low-opportunity-cost producer of corn. Oklahoma is the low-opportunity-cost producer of oil.

Free trade

International trade that is not encumbered by protectionist government policies such as tariffs and quotas.

Suppose you were an Illinois corn farmer. Given the opportunity, wouldn't you prefer to buy oil in Oklahoma? After all, at Oklahoma prices your bushel would buy 12 times more oil than it could in Illinois. For the same reason, an Oklahoma oil producer would be more than delighted to buy corn in Illinois. At Illinois prices, he takes home three full bushels for his one barrel of oil.

Suppose Illinois and Oklahoma agree on **free trade.** It's no secret what would happen. Oklahoma oil producers would quickly drive Illinois oilers out of business. Think about it. How can any Illinois oiler who has to pay one hour of labor for each barrel compete against a producer who can fill a barrel in 20 minutes?

What about corn producers? Here, the tables are turned. Oklahoma farmers wouldn't stand a chance. By the time they could put a bushel of corn together, the Illinois farmer would have four in the bin.

The Case for Geographic Specialization

The case for geographic specialization, producing corn in Illinois, and oil in Oklahoma, is simple enough: Everybody benefits. We all end up with more corn *and* more oil.

How can we show the benefits? Suppose people in Illinois and Oklahoma collectively spend 400 hours producing corn and oil. Suppose also that these hours are allocated equally between the states and between corn and oil pro-

TABLE 1 Production of Corn and Oil in Illinois and Oklahoma, Before and After Free Trade (bushels and barrels)

	No Trade		Free Trade	
	Corn	Oil	Corn	Oil
Illinois	100	100	200	0
Oklahoma	25	300	0	600
Total	125	400	200	600

Specialization and free trade make the average individual in both Illinois and Oklahoma better off. At a price of three barrels of oil for one bushel of corn, Illinois can have the same amount of corn and three times as much oil. At this price, Oklahoma can have the same amount of oil and four times as much corn.

duction. Table 1 compares production before and after the free trade agreement mentioned above.

Before free trade, the total number of bushels of corn produced in Illinois and Oklahoma, with 100 hours expended in each state, is 125. The 100 hours in Illinois yield 100 bushels. The 100 hours in Oklahoma yield 25.

The total number of barrels of oil produced in both states is 400. The 100 hours in Illinois yield 100 barrels. The 100 hours in Oklahoma yield 300.

But suppose the 200 hours of labor in Illinois were devoted entirely to corn. The results are dramatic. Illinois workers now produce 200 bushels, or 60 percent more than the amount that two states, with the same number of labor hours expended, had produced before free trade.

The oil yields are also impressive. The 200 hours of labor expended in Oklahoma produce 600 barrels, or 50 percent more than the amount the two states, with the same number of labor hours expended, had produced before free trade.

What set of relative prices—barrels in terms of bushels—would they end up with in this interstate trade? If trade were to be profitable for both Illinoisans and Oklahomans, the price should fall somewhere between the 200/200 = 1 barrel per bushel prevailing in Illinois and the 300/25 = 12 barrels per bushel prevailing in Oklahoma.

Let's suppose the price settles at 3 barrels per bushel. Table 2 shows the gains that trade offers to both Illinois and Oklahoma.

Look at Oklahoma's consumption. They produce 600 barrels of oil, keep 300 barrels for themselves, and sell the remaining 300 barrels to Illinois for 300/3 = 100 bushels of corn. They now have four times their pre-trade corn consumption.

TABLE 2 Corn and Oil Consumption in Illinois and Oklahoma, Before and After Free Trade (bushels and barrels)

	No Trade (Production = Consumption)		Free Trade (Production)		Free Trade (Consumption)	
	Corn	Oil	Corn	Oil	Corn	Oil
Illinois	100	100	200	0	100	300
Oklahoma	25	300	0	600	100	300

What about Illinois? Having bought 300 barrels of oil from Oklahoma with 100 of their 200 bushels of corn, they have 100 bushels of corn left. Look at their improved condition. They have 200 more barrels than their pre-trade consumption. In other words, everybody gains!

Impressive? That's why we consume Oklahoma oil, Illinois corn, Washington apples, Michigan automobiles, Georgia peaches, Idaho potatoes, Florida grapefruit, Hawaii pineapples, Ohio steel, Pennsylvania coal, Oregon lumber, New York banking, North Carolina furniture, Iowa hogs, Louisiana sugar, Wyoming cattle, Vermont maple syrup, and California wine.

Nobody Loses?

Specialization entails losses for people who previously earned a living in pursuits other than the specialty.

Are we all always winners? Does nobody lose? Why, then, do we find some people objecting vigorously to free trade? Well, imagine how you would feel if, as an Illinois oil producer, you suddenly discovered an Oklahoma oil producer selling oil in your back yard.

You wouldn't be overjoyed, would you? In fact, you probably couldn't survive the competition. Of course, there's always a place for you farming corn. Still, it isn't entirely painless to give up doing what you know best, oil rigs, and turn to corn farming.

You can count on some oilers trying to prevent Oklahoma oil from coming into Illinois. How could they do that? By exercising political muscle on their Illinois legislators. Nothing really new, is it? That's the primary reason we have protective tariffs.

Of course, if everything else fails, you could always get on a Greyhound bus bound for Tulsa. That's assuming Oklahoma places no restrictions on interstate immigration.

INTERNATIONAL TRADE

The same economic argument that promotes interstate free trade should promote international free trade. After all, why should national boundaries have any bearing on the economic benefits that people derive from free trade?

U.S. merchant seamen are a major contributor to the nation's economic well-being. They navigate our fleets of cargo ships across the seven seas, bringing our manufactured and farm goods to other countries and foreign goods back to our shores.

Suppose, for example, that Mexican workers take only 10 minutes to produce a barrel of oil. That's half the labor cost of producing an Oklahoma barrel. Suppose also that it takes Mexican farmers one hour of labor to produce a bushel of corn.

International specialization

The use of a country's resources to produce specific goods and services, allowing other countries to focus on the production of other goods and services.

The conditons are ripe, now, for exploiting the full benefits of **international specialization** and trade. United States corn for Mexican oil. Why not? *Everybody ends up with more corn and more oil.*

Let's pursue the argument. Table 3 details the before and after conditions of international free trade. The before condition assumes 800 hours of labor spent in production, allocated equally between the two trading partners and between corn and oil production.

Oklahoma oilers now face the same problem Illinois oilers did before interstate trade. How can Oklahoma oilers survive against a more efficient competitor?

Look at the relative prices of corn and oil in the United States and Mexico. Illinois farmers could get three barrels of Oklahoma oil for their bushel of corn. However, if they sold their bushel of corn on the Mexican market at Mexican prices, they could take home six barrels of oil!

Mexican oilers will immediately discover the advantages of international free trade as well. Why should they sell their oil for Mexican corn? The relative prices in Mexico—1,200/200, or six barrels to one bushel—will give the Mexican oiler only 1/6 bushel of corn for his barrel. By selling the Mexican barrel north of the border at U.S. prices, however—that is, at 600/200, or three barrels to one bushel—the Mexican takes home 1/3 bushel of corn. That's twice the quantity of corn that could be obtained in Mexico.

International economic competition will drive both the United States and Mexico to specialize. The United States becomes the corn producer, Mexico becomes the oil producer.

With specialization, total production for both Mexico and the United States increases from 400 bushels of corn and 1,800 barrels of oil to 400 bushels of corn and 2,400 barrels of oil. That's a net gain of 600 barrels of oil.

What set of prices—barrels in terms of bushels—would prevail on the international market? Clearly, it has to be at least three barrels per bushel, otherwise U.S. farmers would do better buying Oklahoma oil. It also has to be no more than six barrels per bushel, because Mexican oilers can purchase a bushel of corn in Mexico for six barrels.

In other words, the international price will fall somewhere between the 600/200 = 3 barrels per bushel prevailing in the United States, and 1,200/200

TABLE 3 Production of Corn and Oil in the United States and Mexico, Before and After Free Trade (bushels and barrels)

	No Trade		Free Trade	
	Corn	Oil	Corn	Oil
United States	200	600	400	0
Mexico	200	1,200	0	2,400
Total	400	1,800	400	2,400

TABLE 4 Corn and Oil Consumption in the United States and Mexico, Before and After Free Trade (bushels and barrels)

	No Trade (Production = Consumption)		Free Trade (Production)		Free Trade (Consumption)	
	Corn	Oil	Corn	Oil	Corn	Oil
United States	200	600	400	0	200	800
Mexico	200	1,200	0	2,400	200	1,600

= 6 barrels per bushel prevailing in Mexico. Any price within that range makes it profitable for both Mexico and the United States to trade. Let's suppose the price is four barrels per bushel.

Table 4 shows what happens to the consumption of corn and oil in the United States and Mexico before and after free international trade.

Look at U.S. consumption. It produces 400 bushels of corn, keeps half and exports the remaining 200 bushels to Mexico in exchange for 800 barrels of oil. Free trade has increased U.S. oil consumption by 800 – 600 = 200 barrels.

What about Mexico? Having bought 200 bushels of corn from the United States with 800 barrels of oil, it is left with 2,400 – 800 = 1,600 barrels, which is 400 barrels more than they had before. Both the United States and Mexico have gained.

ABSOLUTE AND COMPARATIVE ADVANTAGE

Illinois had an absolute advantage in corn production and Oklahoma had an absolute advantage in oil production.

Absolute advantage

A country's ability to produce a good using fewer resources than those the country it trades with uses.

Some trading economies are considered perfect trading partners because each can produce one of the goods with fewer resources than the other, that is, with less labor. Consider, for example, the trading condition we supposed in Table 2. Illinois produces corn with less labor than Oklahoma, while Oklahoma produces oil with less labor than Illinois.

Economists describe each economy engaged in such trade as having an **absolute advantage.** Illinois has an absolute advantage in growing corn, and Oklahoma has an absolute advantage in producing oil. It's easy to think of real-world absolute advantage cases. What about trade of Japan's automobiles for Egypt's cotton? Do you suppose each country has an absolute advantage over the other? Or Colombian coffee for U.S. steel? Or Taiwanese radios for Canadian nickel? Or Czech glass for Russian caviar? Or Israeli oranges for Icelandic fish? Or Dutch tulips for Danish furniture?

Comparative Advantage

Absolute advantage, however, is not always the condition under which nations trade. In fact, absolute advantage is not present when the United States trades corn for Mexican oil (see Table 3 again).

There, Mexico devotes fewer resources than the United States to produce oil—10 minutes per barrel versus one hour per barrel—but the same quantity of resources as the United States to produce corn—both one hour per bushel. The

To determine which country has a comparative advantage in an activity, compare the opportunity costs. The lower opportunity cost producer has a comparative advantage.

United States had no absolute advantage in trading with Mexico. Yet Mexico still gains by specializing in oil.

Why? Why should Mexico bother importing corn from the United States when it can grow its own corn at home using the same quantity of labor that Americans use? The reason is that even though the absolute cost of producing corn in Mexico is the same as it is in the United States, the *opportunity cost of producing corn in Mexico is higher.* The one hour of labor used to produce corn in Mexico could be used to produce 12 barrels of oil. That is, Mexico gives up 12 barrels of oil to get that one bushel of corn. In the United States, Americans give up only one barrel of oil to produce a bushel of corn. In other words, the opportunity cost of producing corn in the United States is considerably lower. This lower opportunity cost is defined by economists as a **comparative advantage** for the United States.

Comparative advantage

A country's ability to produce a good at a lower opportunity cost than the country with which it trades.

The United States has a comparative advantange—lower opportunity cost—in producing corn, and Mexico has a comparative advantage—lower opportunity cost—in producing oil. Both countries gain if each specializes in producing the good that affords it a comparative advantage. Even if Mexico had an absolute advantage over the United States in both corn and oil production, it would still benefit Mexico to abandon producing the good that has the greater opportunity cost—that is, to take advantage of comparative advantage!

How Much Is Gained from Free Trade Depends on Price

The gains from trade depend on the price, or terms of trade. Political power can sometimes manipulate the terms of trade in favor of the more-powerful trading partner.

Look at Table 5. Suppose the international trading price is four barrels per bushel. Look at Mexico's consumption of oil and corn before and after trade. Suppose Mexico, specializing in oil, keeps 1,600 of the 2,400 barrels it produces and trades the remaining 800 barrels to the United States for corn, at 4 barrels per bushel. It ends up, then, with 800/4 = 200 bushels of corn. This 1,600 barrels and 200 bushels compares favorably to the 1,200 barrels and 200 bushels Mexico would have consumed if it did not trade with the United States. In other words, it pays Mexico to give up producing corn even though its corn farmers are as efficient as corn farmers in the United States!

Suppose, however, that the international price is set at five barrels per bushel instead of four. The gains from trade are distributed somewhat differently. At five barrels per bushel, the United States, still producing 400 bushels of corn, keeps half and exports the remaining 200 bushels to Mexico for 1,000 barrels of oil. That's 1,000 - 800 = 200 barrels more than it got from Mexico when the price was four barrels per bushel.

TABLE 5 Corn and Oil Consumption in the U.S. and Mexico, Under Conditions of No Trade and Free Trade

	No Trade		Free Trade			
			4 brls/bu		5 brls/bu	
	Corn	Oil	Corn	Oil	Corn	Oil
United States	200	600	200	800	200	1,000
Mexico	200	1,200	200	1,600	200	1,400

What about Mexico? Having bought 200 bushels of corn from the United States with 1,000 barrels of oil, it is left with 2,400 − 1,000 = 1,400 barrels, which is still more oil than it consumed before free trade. That is, the shift in price from four to five barrels per bushel shifts the gains from free trade to the United States. If the price increases to six barrels per bushel, the gains from trade would shift *completely* to the United States.

Political power sometimes influences international prices and therefore the distribution of gains among the trading nations. During the era of European colonialism in the 17th through 19th centuries, lopsided gains were commonplace. Trade between the colonies and the European colonial powers was often politically engineered, giving the European mother country exclusive rights to markets and at prices designed to shift most of the gains to the colonial power.

Today, it's not so much political power as the market power of supply and demand that determine international prices. An increase in world demand for corn, for example, will have more influence in shifting prices from $2 to $3 per bushel than all the speeches in the Mexican Assembly or the U.S. Congress.

Low price and rapid technological progress work against LDCs that specialize in the export of agricultural commodities.

How many bushels of U.S. corn could Mexico get for a barrel of its oil if world demand for U.S. corn increased, causing corn prices to rise? With higher corn prices, Mexico would have to offer more barrels of oil to purchase a bushel of corn. The distribution of gains from free trade would shift in favor of the United States.

CALCULATING TERMS OF TRADE

Imports

Goods and services bought by people in one country that are produced in other countries.

Exports

Goods and services produced by people in one country that are sold in other countries.

Many of the less-developed countries (LDCs) of Asia, Africa, and Latin America are behind the proverbial eight ball when it comes to international prices and gains from trade. Why? LDC exports, which are typically agricultural, trade on highly competitive markets. Their principal **imports** from the industrially advanced economies, on the other hand, are manufactured goods traded in markets that tend to be far less competitive. As a result, new technologies in agriculture and shifts in demand for agricultural exports over the years have depressed the LDCs' **export** prices more than new technologies in manufacturing and changing demands for manufacturing imports have raised the LDCs' import prices.

The Dilemma of the Less-Developed Countries

Figure 3 illustrates the problem facing the less-developed countries. It shows what happens to cotton and automobile prices when demands and supplies for Egyptian cotton and Japanese automobiles change over time.

Panel *a* shows the increase in world demand for Japanese automobiles, from D to D', and the change in Japanese automobile supply, from S to S'.

What does this mean? It appears that Japan's automobile exports have doubled from two to four million caused by a rather robust shift in demand. During the same decade, new assembly lines and more automation shifted its supply curve of automobiles slightly to the right. The result of these two shifts? The price of Japanese automobiles increased from $10,000 to $12,000.

Panel *b* shows what happens to the price of cotton during the same time period. The slight increase in world demand for Egyptian cotton, from D to D', combined with a large change in its supply, from S to S', results in increased

FIGURE 3 **Japanese Automobile and Egyptian Cotton Exports**

Panel *a* depicts shifts in the demand for and supply of Japanese automobiles. The robust demand shift to the right, from D to D′, combines with a moderate supply shift to the right, from S to S′, to drive the equilibrium price from $10,000 to $12,000.

Panel *b* depicts shifts in the demand for and supply of Egyptian cotton. The moderate demand shift to the right, from D to D′, combines with a robust supply shift to the right, from S to S′, to drive the equilibrium price downward, from $10,000 to $5,000.

Prior to the shifts, an Egyptian cotton producer could buy a Japanese automobile with 1,000 bales of cotton. After the shifts, the Egyptian producer needs 2,400 bales of cotton to buy the same automobile.

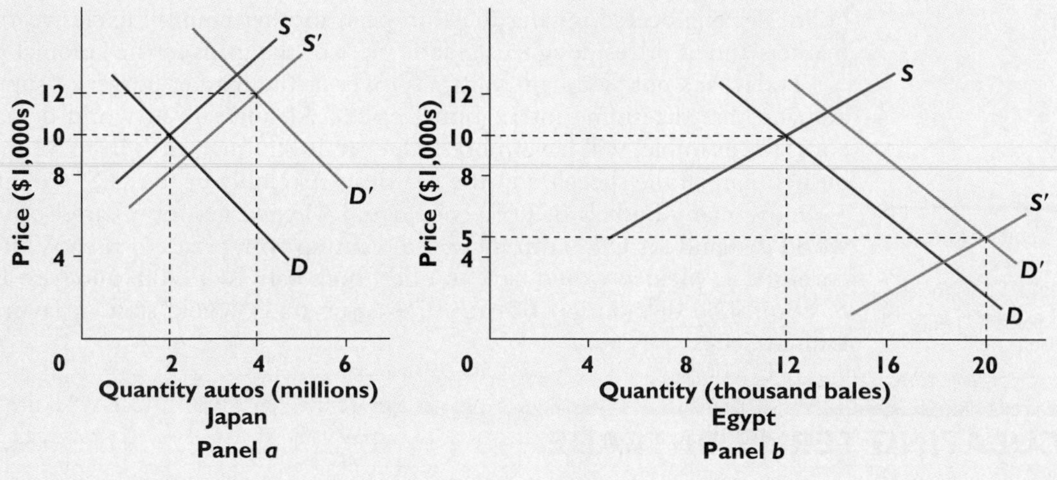

production, from 12 to 20 million bales, and a decrease in the price of Egyptian cotton from $10,000 per 1,000 bales to $5,000 per 1,000 bales. The development of synthetic fibers used as substitutes for cotton certainly didn't help promote the demand for raw cotton.

How many automobiles can Egypt buy with cotton? Originally, Egyptians could buy a Japanese automobile with only 1,000 bales of cotton. Later, after shifts in supply and demand, that same automobile cost Egyptians $12,000/$5,000 = 2.4 × 1,000 bales, or 2,400 bales of cotton.

Economists express Egypt's deteriorating international trade position with Japan, and the rest of the world, in the **terms of trade** equation

Terms of trade

The amount of a good or service (export) that must be given up to buy a unit of another good or service (import). A country's terms of trade is measured by the ratio of the country's export prices to its import prices.

$$\frac{\text{Index of export prices}}{\text{Index of import prices}} \times 100$$

Since, for simplicity's sake, we use Egypt's cotton exports as its representative export, then the index of Egypt's export prices is simply the export price of cotton. In the same way, we use the price of Japanese automobiles as the index of Egypt's import prices. Then, Egypt's original terms of trade equation is

$$\frac{\$10{,}000}{\$10{,}000} \times 100 = 100$$

Later, Egypt's terms of trade equation deteriorates to

TABLE 6
LDCs Terms of Trade For 1992 (1980 = 100)

Significant Deterioration		Moderate Deterioration	
Bolivia	27.3	Mexico	88.4
Burundi	28.3	Zambia	87.2
Ghana	38.6	Egypt	67.4
Kenya	55.2	Indonesia	66.6
Colombia	54.7	Mauritania	73.8

Source: The World Bank, *World Development Report 1994* (New York: Oxford University Press, 1994).

$$\frac{\$5,000}{\$12,000} \times 100 = 41.7$$

Egypt's cotton ends up with only 41.7 percent of its former purchasing power. Of course, the Japanese are delighted. The gains from international trade move in their favor. And there isn't much Egypt can do about it. It simply obeys the dictates of the market. Should Egypt abandon its trade with Japan? Certainly not! Egypt is still better off trading than not trading. After all, the opportunity cost of producing an automobile in Egypt is, more likely than not, greater than the 2,400 bales of cotton it must now pay for the Japanese automobile.

Looking at Real-World Numbers

Striking declines in the terms of trade during the 1980s for developing countries stand in stark contrast to improvements in terms of trade for most industrialized countries.

In point of fact, the terms of trade for Egypt, the index of Egypt's export prices divided by the index of its import prices, fell from 100 in the base year 1980 to 67.4 in 1992. Egypt's problem was typical of the less-developed countries' experiences. World Bank data for 93 LDCs recorded 83 with worsening terms of trade.

Table 6 provides a sample of 12 such LDCs from Asia, Africa, and Latin America.

On the other hand, only five of the 19 industrial market economies reviewed in the World Bank's report suffered declines in their terms of trade. Table 7 records the data for the United States, Japan, Canada, and five major European economies.

TABLE 7
Eight Industrial Market Economies, Terms of Trade for 1988 (1980 = 100)

United States	119	Japan	174
France	108	United Kingdom	101
Germany	118	Netherlands	102
Italy	125	Sweden	114

Source: The World Bank, *World Development Report 1994* (New York: Oxford University Press, 1994).

WHO TRADES WITH WHOM? TRACKING INTERNATIONAL TRADE

The percentage of world GDP accounted for by international trade has increased by nearly five times from 1970 to 1989.

Small wonder that the world's economies are engaged in massive exchanges of almost every kind of familiar and exotic good. We find coffee makers from Germany, food processors from France, television sets from Japan, wool sweaters from Scotland, processed meat from Australia, hockey sticks from Canada, fish from Iceland, medical imaging equipment from Israel, cheese from Switzerland, coffee from Brazil, tin from Bolivia, tea from Sri Lanka, raw rubber from Indonesia, anchovies from Portugal, pistachios from Iran, and shoes from Italy in almost every one of our metropolitan and small-town markets.

They are found as well in markets all over the world. No surprise also that the United States is a major world trading partner. Our imports provide vital markets to many exporting countries. Our own exports of soybeans, steel, automobiles, computers, lumber, aircraft, electrical appliances, coal, chemicals, wheat, movies, machinery, scientific instruments, telecommunications equipment, corn, and banking, shipping, legal, and high-tech services rank among the highly competitive goods and services sold on international markets.

More and more, the world's economies are becoming linked into one unified market network. In 1993, more than 15 percent of the world's GDP made its way onto the international market in the form of exports. That compares to less than 3 percent of the world's GDP in 1970. As communications and transportation technologies become even more advanced and accessible to more economies, we should expect that exports and imports in the 21st century will account for even higher percentages of the world's production.

The more developed countries tend to trade mostly with each other.

The one striking observation we can draw from international trade statistics is that the big guys play with the big guys and even the little ones want to play with the big guys. Look at Table 8.

Approximately two-thirds of world exports in 1993 were exported to the industrially developed countries. The less-developed countries accounted for the remaining one-third. The major markets for the exports of the developed economies were themselves. They absorbed 70.3 percent of their own exports. They also absorbed 57.3 percent of LDC exports.

The Major Leagues

There's no doubt which of the developed economies play in the major leagues. Table 9 lists them in order of their 1993 trade volumes.

TABLE 8 Percent Distribution of Exports to Developed, LDCs, and Other Economies (1993)

	Exports to	
Exporter	**Developed**	**LDCs**
Developed	70.3	28.8
LDCs	57.3	39.8
World	66.2	32.3

Source: *Direction of Trade Statistics, Yearbook, 1994* (Washington, D.C.: International Monetary Fund, 1994).

TABLE 9
1993 Exports and Imports of the Major Developed Economies ($ billions)

	Exports	Imports		Exports	Imports
United States	$464.8	$603.4	Britain	$180.2	$205.4
Germany	362.1	327.0	Italy	168.5	147.5
Japan	362.2	241.6	Netherlands	131.1	115.6
France	209.4	201.8	Canada	144.7	135.3
Belgium	123.1	125.1	Hong Kong	135.3	138.7

Source: *Direction of Trade Statistics, Yearbook 1994* (Washington, D.C.: International Monetary Fund, 1994).

The United States dominates the list. Its $1,068.2 billion trade volume is followed by Germany's $689.1 billion. But, as you see, all 10 countries have annual trade volumes in excess of $240 billion. That puts them in a league by themselves.

The Triple-A Minor Leagues

The 10 leading international traders are followed by 10 others who make up a strong second division but fall well below the majors' trade volumes. Table 10 lists them in order of trade volume.

WHO DOES THE UNITED STATES TRADE WITH?

The United States, Canada, and Mexico are extraordinarily important to each other as trading partners.

There is so much heated discussion over our trade relations with Japan that sometimes we tend to forget that Japan comes in second to our primary trading partner, Canada. Are you surprised? Look at Table 11.

Proximity is important. Trade between Canada and the United States represents the largest trade flow between any two countries in the world. Mexico ranks as our third largest trading partner. The $141.8 billion of U.S. exports to Canada and Mexico in 1993 amounted to only $6 billion less than the combined U.S. exports to Japan, Britain, Germany, the Netherlands, and France.

No wonder many Canadians are upset about our benign neglect of them. Important as they are to us, however, we are much more important to them. The United States alone bought 79.1 percent of Canada's 1993 exports to the world. Our markets also bought as much as 78.3 percent of Mexico's exports.

TABLE 10
1993 Exports and Imports of Trading Countries with Substantial Trade Volumes ($ billions)

	Exports	Imports		Exports	Imports
Denmark	$30.7	$30.5	Switzerland	$58.7	$56.7
Norway	31.9	24.0	Singapore	74.0	85.2
Korea	82.2	83.8	Sweden	49.9	42.7
Spain	63.1	82.3	Russia	29.4	28.4
China	90.9	103.1	Australia	42.7	42.4

Source: *Direction of Trade Statistics, Yearbook 1994* (Washington, D.C.: International Monetary Fund, 1994).

TABLE 11
1993 U.S. Trade with Its Major Trading Partners ($ billions)

	U.S. Exports to	U.S. Imports from		U.S. Exports to	U.S. Imports from
Canada	$100.2	$113.6	Netherlands	$12.8	$ 5.7
Japan	48.0	110.4	France	13.3	15.7
Mexico	41.6	40.8	Korea	14.8	17.8
Britain	26.4	22.4	Italy	6.5	13.8
Germany	19.0	29.5	China	8.7	33.7

Source: *Direction of Trade Statistics, Yearbook 1994* (Washington, D.C.: International Monetary Fund, 1994).

Their import packages, too, carry a clear U.S. stamp. Our exports to Canada added up to 64.9 percent of their total 1993 imports and our exports to Mexico accounted for 68.2 percent of its 1993 total imports. For both neighboring economies, that's an enormous one-country dependence.

The singular importance of the United States to Canada and Mexico is strikingly shown in comparisons to their next-best markets. For example, Canada's $85.3 billion in exports to the United States was followed by its $7.4 billion exports to Japan. Mexico's $37.3 billion exports to the United States towered over its $2.7 billion exports to Canada and $980 million exports to Japan.

DO WE NEED PROTECTION AGAINST FREE TRADE?

Very special circumstances must exist before an argument against free trade can be justified.

No one, not even those who lobby Congress for protection against free trade, would deny the economic benefits that go to international trading partners. The evidence is overwhelming. The arguments made against free trade, then, are made strictly as *exceptions to the rule*. They address particular circumstances.

Ask Oklahoma oil producers how much they benefit when we allow Mexican oil into U.S. markets. The economic pain they suffer is, unquestionably, severe. Although in general the nation gains from free trade—tens of millions of U.S. oil consumers now pay less for oil—some individuals do get hurt.

How do we weigh the widespread, general gains against the particular losses? Should we simply ignore the downside of free trade or is that pushing a good thing too far? How far is far? For example, should we sacrifice gains to protect injured parties? *All* injured parties?

A number of classic arguments have been made against *indiscriminate* free trade. These have had considerable effect not only in persuading Congress to limit trade in specific industries of our economy, but also in persuading other governments to do precisely the same in their economies, and for the same reasons.

The National Security Argument

Suppose France's Mirage is a less costly, more effective fighter aircraft than our own F-16. Should we close down our F-16 factories and import Mirages? Hardly! Although this move might create gains from trade for both the United States and France, we do not want to rely on France for our national survival. Most of the major industrial economies of the world produce their own security systems, even though most understand that their domestic production rules out the gains that would result from international specialization. Production of weapons, munitions, missiles, tanks, submarines, aircraft carriers, cannons, and radar equipment are obvious candidates for protection against free trade on national security grounds.

Some goods, however, are less-obvious candidates, and that's where the national security exception to the free trade rule runs into trouble. It's not terribly difficult, particularly for industry lobbyists, to draw some connection, however indirect, between any producing industry and national security.

As early as 1815 the British Parliament enacted a series of corn laws that established tariffs on grain imports from Europe. Its main objective was to protect the landlord class of England against cheaper European grain. But the national security argument was invoked. Corn law advocates insisted that England must not be beholden to the Europeans for its food supply.

What worked then, works today. Our agricultural industries, too, have invoked the national security argument to protect markets from cheaper imports.

In fact, almost everything can be brought under the umbrella of the national security argument. In times of national crisis, can we really rely on foreign supplies of sheet metal? What about photographic equipment, surveying instruments, lumber, pharmaceuticals, steel fabrication, optical equipment, orthopedic equipment, radio communication systems, and petrochemicals? Shouldn't they, too, qualify for protection on national security grounds?

The Infant-Industries Argument

The trouble with infant industries is that they often refuse to grow up.

Learning curves—time required to gain expertise—apply to new industries just as they do to people. Because of that, it's sometimes unfair to expect a fledgling industry at home to survive free trade competition from its older, more-experienced foreign competitors. It cannot do it. It needs more time. In such circumstances the relative prices of foreign and domestic production shouldn't count.

Protecting infant industries from foreign competition, then, has some validity, because without such protection, many promising industries just wouldn't get started. It's perhaps worthwhile for a country to suffer the higher prices of its own less-efficient new industries in the short run because it expects to gain from greater efficiency and lower prices in the long run.

But how long is the long run? When is an industry's infancy period over? There's the problem. The comforts of protection, once experienced by the infant industry, are difficult to forego. Many, having run the learning curve many times over, are still as inefficient as they were the day protection was granted. Others remain protected under new guises. Our steel industry, for example, was protected as an infant industry over a century ago, and is still protected today. It's an argument that can too easily be abused.

The Cheap Foreign Labor Argument

Cheap labor usually means unproductive labor.

Perhaps the most frequently invoked battle cry against indiscriminate free trade is the injustice of having to compete in markets against foreign firms that employ cheap labor. How can the U.S. textile industry, for example, employing highly paid, unionized labor, compete against textiles imported from Hong Kong, Korea, Jamaica, China, Thailand, Brazil, Mexico, the Philippines, and

Malaysia? Those countries, even if unions exist at all, still pay wage rates considerably below U.S. levels. Some argue that the U.S. textile industry can't compete, and the consequences are declining wages rates, real incomes, employment, and standards of living at home.

You may wonder if that is really so. The cheap foreign labor argument ignores the fact that higher levels of productivity (output per hour), typically accompany the higher wage rates in the United States, so that the wage cost per unit of U.S. manufactured goods is not necessarily higher than the wage cost associated with the foreign good.

If raincoats produced in Hong Kong are less costly because of cheap labor than the raincoats produced in New York, shouldn't we take advantage of the lower price? After all, isn't that precisely why we engage in specialization? Rather than lowering our standard of living, trade with low-wage economies increases the real goods we are able to purchase, so that our living standards should actually improve.

Of course, the widespread, general gains consumers enjoy from such trade are not universally shared. Some people end up losing. Some firms, for example, cannot survive the competition, and their demise is bound to cause disruptive reallocations of labor and capital. That is, people lose jobs and don't always find new ones. Entrepreneurs fail and many never recover. Stockholders lose their investment and many never invest again.

The Diversity of Industry Argument

Some economies have become so highly specialized in one or two production activities that these alone account for a major share of national product and, typically, an even greater share of exports. Think, for example, of Saudi Arabia and oil, or Honduras and bananas. When the prices of their few specialized exports are relatively high, their economies perform well. When prices fall, however, their entire economies suffer.

Since these prices reflect the swings of demand and supply in the international market, in many cases the fate of highly specialized economies is out of their hands. Moreover, if the swings are erratic, these economies also tend to become unpredictable and unstable.

No one wants to live in an unstable world. Good enough reason to diversify industrial production, isn't it? That's where protection comes in.

Many less-developed countries argue for such protection. They understand the costs involved in abandoning specialization, but still prefer the greater economic stability that the protection affords. In their case, it may make sense. However, it is hardly the argument that industries in the United States can make for protection. The United States and Western European economies are already sufficiently diversified.

The Antidumping Argument

Dump some goods in my economy, please!

Some industries seeking protection insist that it is not lack of absolute or comparative advantage on the international market that does them in, but rather the sinister strategies of their foreign competition. Why sinister? Because their foreign competitors dump goods on the market, *priced below cost,* in order to knock them out of the game. Once the competition is eliminated, these sinister producers—now monopolists—will use their monopoly power to raise prices to levels even higher than they were before. That's pretty cheeky, isn't it?

Dumping

Exporting a good or service at a price below its cost of production.

Our Congress thought so, and made **dumping** on our markets illegal. The problem is, how do we go about proving that low-cost foreign goods are priced below cost? One way is to compare the export prices of the foreign producer to the prices it charges in its own domestic market. That's not always easy to do, and sometimes the comparisons are rigged to support inefficient producers here in the United States.

Anyway, what's wrong with trading with producers who export at prices below cost? Wouldn't consumers benefit? If the export-dumping producer later tries to raise prices, wouldn't it only invite competitors back into the market?

The Retaliation Argument

Should we allow other countries free access to our markets if they restrict our exports in theirs? That's rather unfair, isn't it? Yet that's precisely the trading conditions we confront with many of our trading partners. Perhaps the most glaring case of such lopsided access is our trading experience with Japan. Our complaints to them about their restrictive practices seem to fall on deaf ears.

Many U.S. producers, frustrated by Japanese protection of their own domestic markets, call for retaliation. If the Japanese won't allow us free entry into their markets, they argue, we should simply deny them free entry into ours. Since we are a major market for their exports, the retaliation may "encourage" them to rethink their protection strategies.

It may in fact work. With greater access to their markets, our own export and even import volumes would most likely increase, benefiting both ourselves and the Japanese. It may make sense, then, to threaten retaliation—and even in some cases to carry out the threat.

But suppose retaliation doesn't work. If it leaves us with less, not greater trade, it makes no sense at all. After all, even with restricted access to their markets, we still benefit by importing Japanese goods. Otherwise, we wouldn't import them.

THE ECONOMICS OF TRADE PROTECTION

How do we restrict imports? Basically, with tariffs and quotas. What are they, and how do they work?

Tariffs

Tariff

A tax on an imported good.

A tariff raises the price to consumers at the same time that it grants domestic producers a larger share of the market and generates tax revenues.

The **tariff** is a government-imposed tax on imports. It can be levied as a percentage of the import's value or as a specific tax per unit of import. Like any other tax, it becomes government revenue. Although importers pay the tariff to U.S. customs when importing the foreign goods, they typically shift at least part of it onto the consumer by raising the market price that consumers pay. To the consumer, the tariff is invisible. After all, do you really know what percentage of the price you pay for an Italian bike is the tariff on the bike and what percentage represents the price the Italian bike producer actually receives?

How can a tariff on bikes protect our own producers? Let's suppose that bike manufacturers in the United States cannot produce a bike of as high a quality or as inexpensively as manufacturers in Italy. Suppose the Italians can price their bikes in U.S. markets at \$200 (ignoring transport costs), which is \$250 less than the \$450 equilibrium price for U.S. bikes on the U.S. market.

Without the tariff, the U.S. manufacturers are in serious trouble, aren't they? How can they face Italian competition? Why would anyone buy the U.S. product? Now suppose that Congress is persuaded by any one of the protection arguments and slaps a 100 percent tariff, \$200, on all foreign bikes. The U.S. manufacturers would now have a fighting chance of survival. Look at Figure 4.

The supply curve, S_{US}, represents the quantities of bikes that U.S. producers are willing to supply at various prices. The demand curve represents U.S. consumer demand for bikes. If the market were completely insulated from foreign competition, U.S. manufacturers would be busy producing 3 million bikes and selling them at a price of \$450.

Let's now introduce free trade. We assume that Italian producers would be willing to supply any quantity of bikes at a \$200 price. The Italian supply curve on the U.S. market is shown as S_I. Look what happens to U.S. manufacturers.

At a \$200 price, U.S. consumers increase their quantity demanded from 3 to 5 million bikes. Only 1 million of the 5 million, however, would be supplied by U.S. manufacturers. That is, the U.S. firms lose 2 million of their former sales to Italian competitors and now have only 20 percent of this new, flourishing

FIGURE 4 **Tariff-Restricted Trade**

The supply curve, S_{US}, records the quantity of bikes U.S. producers are willing to supply at varying prices. The demand curve records the quantity of bikes Americans are willing to buy at varying prices. With no foreign suppliers, 3 million would be bought and sold at an equilibrium price of \$450.

S_I records the willingness of Italian bike producers to supply any quantity at \$200. When Italian suppliers are allowed to enter the U.S. market, equilibrium price and the quantities of bikes demanded and supplied in the United States change dramatically. Price falls from \$450 to \$200 and the quantity demanded increases to 5 million; 1 million supplied by U.S. producers and 4 million imported from Italy.

If the U.S. government imposes a 100 percent tariff on bikes, the Italian supply curve in the United States becomes $S_I + t$. At a price of \$400, 3.5 million bikes are demanded; 2.5 million supplied by U.S. producers and 1 million imported from Italy. The shaded area shows the U.S. government's tariff revenue.

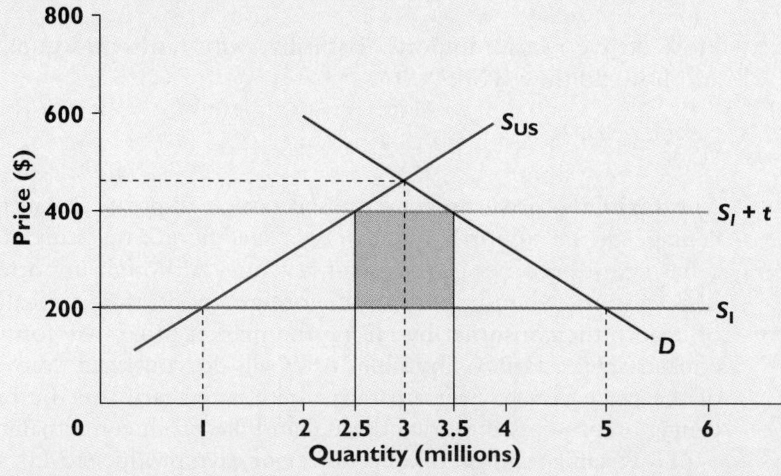

market. We now import 4 million Italian bikes. You can imagine how the U.S. bike manufacturers would react.

When a 100 percent tariff, t, is applied to bikes, the Italian supply curve shifts up to $S_I + t$, the price of Italian bikes in the U.S. market increases to $400, ($200 + t). At this higher price, the quantity demanded by U.S. consumers falls from 5 to 3.5 million. U.S. firms produce 2.5 million, and importers of Italian bikes provide the other million.

In other words, the tariff gives the U.S. bike industry a new lease on life, but only at the expense of the U.S. consumer. What about government? It ends up with a revenue of $200 × 1 million = $200 million, the shaded rectangle in Figure 4.

Quotas

Quota

A limit on the quantity of a specific good that can be imported.

Quotas don't generate revenue for the government, but they do raise the price to consumers and they give domestic producers a larger share of the market.

Sometimes governments prefer to restrict imports by imposing a **quota** instead of a tariff. What's the difference? Tariffs are import taxes added to prices, quotas limit the amount of a good that is allowed into the country at any price.

The outcomes are different. Certainly for the government. With quotas, the government loses its revenue source. Let's suppose that instead of placing a 100 percent tariff on Italian bike imports, the government limits the number of imports to 500,000 units. That's all we're allowed to bring in. Picture the scene. U.S. importers would be busy making long-distance calls to Rome to buy up the 500,000 Italian bikes. These are brought into the U.S. market at the free trade price of $200 each. What happens now? Look at Figure 5.

The supply curve is horizontal until we reach 1.5 million bikes, reflecting 500,000 supplied by Italian producers and 1 million that U.S. producers are willing to supply at $200. At higher prices, the supply curve becomes S', the horizontal sum of the U.S. supply curve, S, and the 500,000 quota.

There we have it. The U.S. producers suffer a slight fall from the quantities they would sell if there were no Italian competitors in the market, from 3 milion to 2.75 million. Quota protection raises the price from $200 to $420, although it is still less than the $450 that would prevail without competition from Italy.

What about the Italian bike producers? They sell their 500,000 quota to importers at $200 per bike. The importers, then, end up with a $420 − $200 = $220 windfall on each bike.

The protection options with the quota are almost countless. With zero quota, price is $450. With an unlimited quota, price falls to the free trade level of $200. Between these extremes, each specific quota yields a unique U.S. production and market price. As with the tariff, there's no magic number that defines every quota. It could be anywhere in that range, depending on the objectives of the government and U.S. producers.

Other Nontariff Barriers

Tariffs and quotas are not the only mechanisms that can be used by domestic producers and by government to reduce imports. The government can also pass a law that specifies highly restrictive health and safety standards that imports must meet. For example, the government can insist that all Italian bikes be dismantled and reassembled by U.S. bike inspectors—at a cost, say, of $75 per bike—to guarantee safety.

FIGURE 5
Quota-Restricted Trade
With no free trade, 3 million bikes are bought and sold in the United States at an equilibrium price of $450. If the U.S. government sets an import quota of 500,000 bikes, the relevant supply curve becomes S′ (which is S + 500,000). The equilibrium price falls to $420, and 3.25 million bikes are bought and sold, of which 2.75 million are produced by U.S. suppliers.

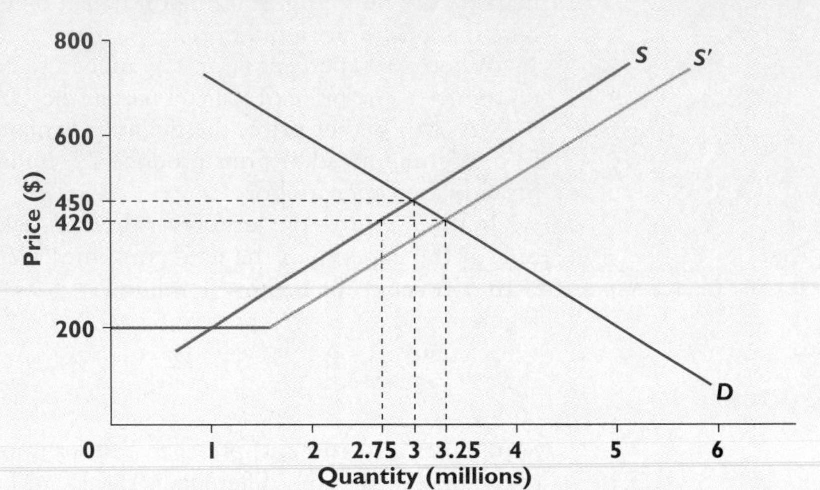

That's not a particularly creative idea. The Japanese once prohibited ski imports because, they maintained, only Japanese skis were suitable for Japanese snow. The Germans disallowed foreign-brewed beer on grounds of health and safety. U.S. beef imports were shut out of European markets because U.S. cattle were fed with government-approved hormones.

Reciprocity
The idea that tariff reductions negotiated between two countries should automatically be extended to all of those countries' trading partners.

In some cases, import barriers are self-imposed by foreign exporters who agree to "voluntarily" limit the quantity of their exports. For example, Japanese automakers voluntarily agreed to limit auto exports to the United States. They understood the alternatives: "Volunteer" or face higher tariffs or lower quotas.

NEGOTIATING TARIFF STRUCTURES

GATT (General Agreement on Tariffs and Trade)
A trade agreement to negotiate reductions in tariffs and other trade barriers and to provide equal and nondiscriminating treatment among members of the agreement. Over 100 countries are members of GATT.

Whatever tariff structure a nation chooses, it would seem only fair that the structure, once established between two trading partners, should apply to all other countries as well. For example, if the United States and France agree to a mutual reduction, from 40 to 25 percent, in their tariffs on imported wine, then a third country, say Portugal, should be allowed to sell its wine in the United States and France at the same 25 percent tariff rate. Otherwise, international trade would be marked by country-to-country discrimination.

This idea of tariff **reciprocity** became the guiding principle industrial nations adopted after World War II in establishing rules of international trade. The aim was both to increase the free movement of goods across national boundaries, and to do so nondiscriminately.

GATT

The General Agreement on Tariffs and Trade (GATT) served as the framework for this multilateral trade objective. Nations came together under GATT rules to negotiate trade policies. Organized in the aftermath of World War II, with 22 nations participating, GATT has grown to 97 member nations

ADDED PERSPECTIVE

How Much Do Barriers to Imports Cost Japanese Consumers?

Mention Japan's trade barriers to its trading partners, and they will leave you in no doubt about their effects. They will point to firms in their countries that cannot price their way into Japanese markets, and lament the profits and jobs that are lost to protectionism.

Such moans are understandable. And yet a hefty chunk of the cost of Japanese protection is paid not by foreigners, but by the Japanese themselves. Trade barriers, which raise the price of foreign goods or keep them out altogether, force consumers to buy more costly domestic alternatives. They also distort firms' inputs, pushing them towards expensive local sources and raising the prices of goods made at home. Indeed, the most persuasive argument for scrapping trade barriers, in Japan or anywhere else, ought to be that they damage protected economies.

So much for the theory. But how much does Japan really pay for its own protection? In a new book (*Measuring the Costs of Protection in Japan*, Institute for International Economics, 1995), three Japanese economists, Yoko Sazanami, Shujiro Urata, and Hiroki Kawai, provide an answer. They compare the price of imports on the dockside (i.e., before tariffs and wholesalers' markups have been added) with the price of Japanese goods at the factory gate. They use the difference to estimate the cost of trade barriers to Japanese consumers.

They conclude that Japanese protection is limited to agricultural products and a few manufacturing industries. Where protection exists, though, it is heavy (see table). They estimate that in 1989 the prices of some foods were several hundred percent higher than import prices. Japanese-made radios and televisions were over 600 percent more expensive than imports. Clothing was marked up by nearly 300 percent; petrol by more than 200 percent.

Difference between Price of Domestic Goods and Imports: 1989 (as % of import price)

	Price Difference	Tariff Rate	Implied Nontariff Barrier Rate
Milled rice	737.1	0.0	737.1
Tea and coffee	718.4	11.9	706.5
Cosmetics	661.6	2.0	659.6
Radios and TVs	607.0	0.0	607.0
Wheat	477.8	0.0	477.8
Soyabeans	423.6	0.0	423.6
Clothing	292.6	10.4	282.2
Petrol	229.0	5.5	223.5

Sources: Y. Sazanami, S. Urata, and H. Kawai; Datastream.

The cost to Japanese consumers totals around 15 trillion yen a year ($110 billion at 1989 exchange rates), or 3.8 percent of GDP. The cost to the Japanese economy as a whole is a good deal smaller, because protection earns profits for domestic producers and tariff revenues for the government. But the estimated damage is still hefty, at about 0.6 percent of Japanese national income. Moreover, say the three economists, these numbers may understate the costs of protection. More foreign competition would force Japanese industry to become more efficient: costs and prices would fall.

In addition, the prices of imports are affected by trade restraints. By making imports scarcer, they create monopoly power for foreign suppliers (as long as imports and domestic goods are not perfect substitutes). This enables them to charge higher prices for their wares in countries that protect local producers.

The conclusion for Japanese consumers (and policy makers) is a sobering one: Trade barriers not only push up the price of Japanese goods, they probably make imports dearer as well.

Source: "Japan's Protection Racket," *The Economist*, January 7, 1995.

plus nine observer nations. It includes all industrial market economies, several from Eastern Europe, and over 50 economies from the less-developed countries. Together, these GATT members represent over 80 percent of all international trade.

GATT's principal objective is to reduce the level of all tariffs. The nondiscriminating provision of GATT is called the *most-favored nation clause*. The clause applies to all member nations. What is offered to one member as a tariff concession, is offered to all.

As you might expect, the United States role in GATT, which is critical to GATT's functioning, reflects Congress' own interest in promoting free trade. In 1962, Congress legislated the Trade Expansion Act, which led to the Kennedy rounds of tariff cuts. Later, the Tokyo round, which cut tariffs further, was negotiated under the authority of the 1974 Trade Reform Act. The most recent GATT round of negotiations, the Uruguay round—tackled the issue of reducing nontariff protective barriers to trade.

GATT Concessions to Less-Developed Countries

GATT is an agreement among member nations that makes tariff concessions that are offered to one member available to all members. LDCs are exempted from reciprocity and are granted even lower tariffs on their exports than the industrialized nations grant to each other.

The less-developed countries were never really happy about GATT. In fact, they were downright annoyed. With good reason. They saw it as strictly a rich nation's club. How could they be excited about lowering their own tariffs when their principal concern was economic development? After all, if the infant-industry argument against free trade had meaning anywhere, didn't it make most sense for them?

GATT got the message. The less-developed countries are exceptions to the GATT rules. Although enjoying most-favored nation status, their exports typically face lower tariffs than industrial nations grant to each other. Moreover, reciprocity rights do not apply to the less-developed countries. They can enjoy the industrial economies' tariff concessions without having to reciprocate.

Customs Unions

Customs union

A set of countries that agree to free trade among themselves and a common trade policy with all other countries.

European Economic Community (EC)

A customs union consisting of France, Italy, Belgium, Holland, Luxembourg, Germany, Britain, Ireland, Denmark, Greece, Spain, Portugal, Iceland, Finland, Sweden, and Austria.

In 1958, the six West European economies of France, Germany, Italy, Holland, Belgium, and Luxembourg established a **customs union**—the **European Economic Community (EC)**—whose special trade arrangements allowed for *complete free trade within the union and a common tariff schedule against the rest of the world.* That's precisely the economic arrangement that exists between Vermont and California, isn't it? In the 1970s, Denmark, England, and Ireland joined the Community. In the 1980s the EC expanded again to include Greece, Spain, and Portugal. In the 1990s, Iceland, Finland, Sweden, and Austria joined.

The objectives of the EC raise fundamental questions that concern the reciprocity principle underlying the GATT agreements. For example, if the United States lowers its tariff against French wine, according to GATT instruction it must also lower its tariff against wine imported from other countries.

The United States is disadvantaged, however, when it comes to competing with French wine in Britain. While French wine comes into Britain tariff free, California wine faces a common EC tariff. That's not fair, say California wineries. The French respond that California wine comes in tariff free to Vermont, French wine doesn't. It's the same, *n'est-ce-pas?* Not exactly. California trade with Vermont is strictly domestic, trade between France and England is still international. *GATT's rules apply only to international trade.*

Free Trade Areas

A variant of the customs union is the **free trade area.** The single difference between it and the customs union, such as the EC, is that the free trade area permits free trade among members, but each is allowed to establish its own tariff

Free trade area

A set of countries that agree to free trade among themselves but are free to pursue independent trade policies with other countries.

policy with respect to nonmembers. In other words, the free trade area permits each member greater independence in trade policy making.

NORTH AMERICAN FREE TRADE AGREEMENT

North American Free Trade Agreement (NAFTA)

A free trade area consisting of Canada, the United States, and Mexico.

By far the most significant trade agreement concluded by the United States is with Canada and Mexico. In 1989 both the U.S. Congress and the Canadian House of Commons enacted the **North American Free Trade Agreement (NAFTA).** Mexico joined NAFTA in 1993, making it the largest free trade area in the world, matching the total production of goods and services of the EC.

NAFTA calls for the elimination of all tariffs, quotas, and other trade barriers within 10 years. Although over 75 percent of Canadian-U.S. trade was tariff-free even before NAFTA, the expansions in both U.S. and Canadian markets that NAFTA is expected to create makes the agreement a very significant economic event for both countries. Canadians gain a considerable advantage *vis-à-vis* other exporting countries in a market ten times the size of its own. On the other hand, the United States, having faced tariff rates in Canada higher than those Canadians faced in the United States prior to NAFTA, gains more when both cut their rates to zero.

Still, NAFTA was not engineered without some political controversy. Although some debate concerning its merits took place in the United States, NAFTA was a major political issue in Canada. The U.S. economy has always been regarded by Canadians as a potentially threatening colossus. Some Canadians feared that free access to each other's markets would result in U.S. production overwhelming their own. But their voices were muted by the logic of comparative advantage. It proved too much for Canadians to ignore.

Mexico's entry into NAFTA generated a somewhat more unsettling promise for the future. Although the expansion of all three markets—Canada, Mexico, and the United States—is seen by all three as an outcome of Mexico's membership in NAFTA, a disquieting note is voiced in the United States and Canada. The issue is low-wage Mexican labor. With tariffs completely eliminated, many worry that low-wage Mexican labor will lure firms, particularly labor-intensive ones, out of Canada and the United States to Mexico. Polluting firms that are forced to adhere to tough Canadian and U.S. environmental regulations will also be attracted to Mexico, where pollution regulations are fewer and poorly enforced.

Advocates of NAFTA respond with compelling arguments of their own. The economic development of Mexico, which NAFTA will assist, not only provides markets for Canadians and Americans, but employment opportunities for Mexicans. In other words, NAFTA can help reduce the illegal immigration flow across the Rio Grande. And the low-wage jobs that Americans and Canadians will lose are precisely the jobs that should be lost in the United States and Canada. The greater production in Canada and the United States that Mexico-included NAFTA generates should be able to reemploy those Canadian and American job-losers in higher paying jobs.

TRACKING TARIFFS SINCE 1860

Some people see a half glass of water as being half empty while others view the same glass as half filled. It's just a matter of how you look at things. The same idea applies when we assess tariffs and trade performance. Look at Figure 6.

FIGURE 6 **Average U.S. Tariff Rates on Imports**
The dramatic increase in the rates during the 1920s and early 1930s evaporated by 1950. Thereafter, the rates steadily declined, and by 1970 were less than 10 percent.

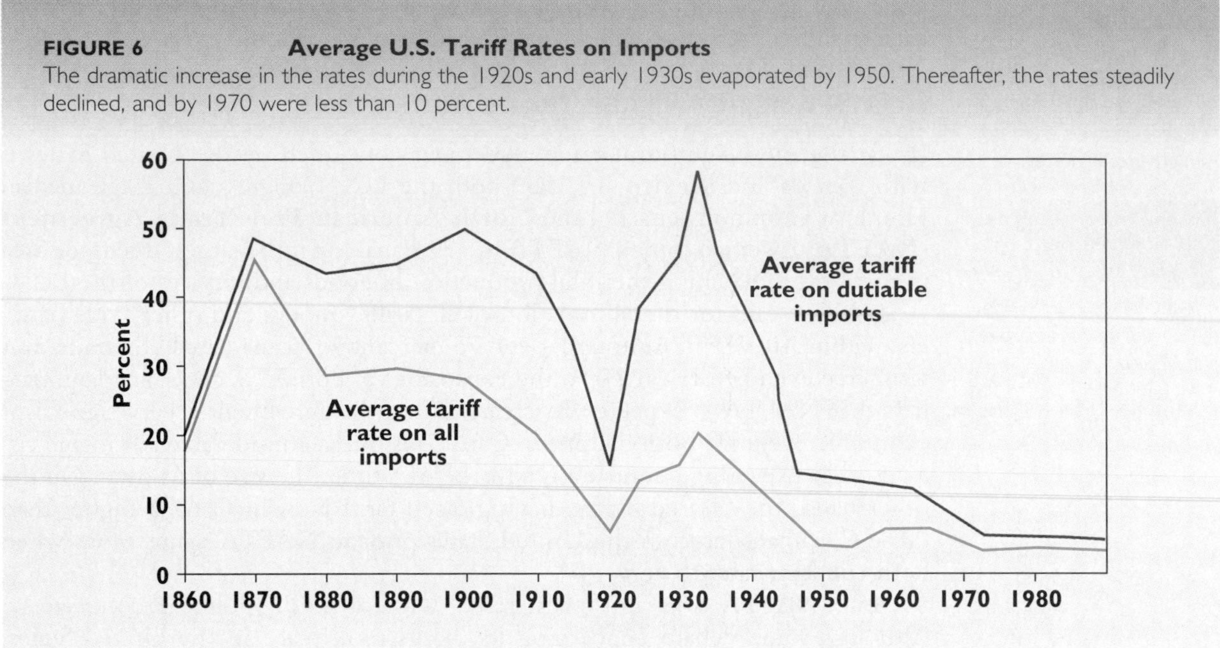

Source: *Economic Report of the President*, January 1989 (Washington, D.C.: U.S. Government Printing Office, 1989), p. 152.

Just a cursory glance shows that whatever our view about whether tariffs are too high or too low, they have clearly dropped dramatically during the past 50 years.

As you see, our tariff history shows some erratic behavior. In earlier years, our international trade policy was clearly protectionist. During the period 1870 to 1890, the average tariff rate on dutiable imports fluctuated only slightly within the 45 percent to 50 percent range. But note how the average tariff rate on all imports steadily declined during the same period, indicating a movement toward freer trade for many imported goods.

The skyrocketing of rates during the 1920s and early 1930s appears as an exception, the direct result of the highly protectionist Fordney-McCumber Tariff Act of 1922 and the Smoot-Hawley Tariff Act of 1930. The Reciprocal Trade Agreement Act of 1934 reversed the upward movement in rates, and by 1950, rates were back to pre-1920 levels. Since 1970, the rates have fallen below 10 percent and continue to decline.

Are our current average tariff rates still too high? For the industrially developed economies of the world, in 1987 the weighted average tariff for industrial goods was 7 percent. The U.S. and Canadian averages were 6 percent. The Japanese average was 8 percent. Are we, then, really out of line? It seems clear that the U.S. economy is not extraordinarily protectionist, at least when compared to other industrial economies.

CHAPTER REVIEW

1. The relative prices of goods in a country (or a state) are determined by the relative costs of producing them. Differences in the relative prices of goods present opportunities for trade between countries (or states). Each trading partner

specializes in the production of the good that it produces most efficiently. Trade provides more of all goods to the trading partners than were formerly available.

2. While free trade makes more of the goods traded available to all trading parties, exporting countries that produce goods that are not specialties may be hurt by the competition from more efficient producers in other countries..

3. National power can sometimes influence the prices set through international trade in such a way that most of the gains from trade are assigned to the more powerful trading partner. However, for most market economies supply and demand forces rather than political power set international prices.

4. Many less-developed economies have difficulty trading in international markets because they specialize in agricultural products that are produced under competitive conditions. Prices of these agricultural exports tend to fall over time relative to industrial products which these countries must buy.

5. Absolute advantage is a term that applies to a country that is more efficient at producing a good than another country. However, gains from trade are potentially available even if one country has an absolute advantage in both types of production over the other country.

6. Patterns in international trade are readily discernible. The large industrialized economies do most of the trading and mostly with each other.

7. The United States' major trading partners are Canada, Japan, and Mexico. The United States is even more important to Canada and Mexico as a trading partner than they are to us.

8. Arguments that favor limits on free trade include the national security argument, the infant-industries argument, the cheap foreign labor argument, the diversity of labor argument, the antidumping argument, and the retaliation argument.

9. Restricting imports is possible through tariffs or quotas. A tariff is a tax on an imported good, which raises its price so as to give domestic producers a larger share of the market. Domestic producers gain at the expense of domestic consumers. Quotas can generate the same results as tariffs with the exception that no tax revenues are collected.

10. The General Agreement on Tariffs and Trade (GATT) seeks to lower tariff barriers. For GATT members, a tariff concession offered to one member must be offered to all. The European Economic Community allows for completely free trade within the union and a common tariff schedule with the rest of the world.

11. GATT members offer LDCs lower tariffs than industrial nations are granted without demanding reciprocity.

12. Tariffs have by no means been constant over time. Tariff levels are determined by the political process.

KEY TERMS

Free trade
International specialization
Absolute advantage
Comparative advantage
Imports
Exports
Terms of trade
Dumping

Tariff
Quota
Reciprocity
General Agreement on Tariffs and Trade (GATT)
Customs union
European Economic Community (EC)
Free trade area
North American Free Trade Agreement (NAFTA)

QUESTIONS

1. Why do nations trade?

2. Georgia exports its peaches to Maine, and Maine exports its lobsters to Georgia. Considering this trade alone, do you suppose Georgia and Maine are trading under conditions of absolute or comparative advantage? Make an educated guess about resource use and opportunity cost in producing those goods in Georgia and Maine.

3. Suppose Canadians can produce a bushel of wheat for half the cost it takes to produce a bushel in Belgium. And they can produce a ton of fish for only one-quarter the Belgium cost. Should Canadians bother trading with Belgium? If not, why not? If they do trade, what should each end up producing?

4. Suppose the cost of producing a bushel of wheat in Canada is $2 and the cost of producing a ton of fish is $20. If Canada and Belgium do decide to trade, what range of international prices—bushels of wheat per ton of fish—would be acceptable to both?

5. Lower tariffs create greater international specialization. Explain.

6. Many Detroit autoworkers do not buy the argument that everybody gains in international trade. What's their point?

7. Suppose Iraq can produce surface-to-surface missiles more efficiently than we can, while we are able to produce artichokes more efficiently than they. Should we specialize in artichokes, trading them for Iraqi missiles? Make the pro and con arguments.

8. The Irish complain that they never got a chance to make automobiles because the English, their major trading partner, are more experienced and therefore more efficient at it. Would-be Irish automakers ask their government to impose a tariff on foreign automobiles to help them get started. Can you make the case supporting their complaint and request?

9. American sport-fishing equipment producers argue that Japanese manufacturers are selling rods, reels, and tackle below Japanese cost in American markets to drive out American competitors. The American producers ask for quotas on such imports. They argue that, without government-imposed quotas on the Japanese sport-fishing equipment, American sportfishermen will ultimately pay more. Can you make the case supporting the American producers' complaint and request?

10. What is reciprocity?

11. What economic arguments can be made to support the idea of the European Economic Community?

12. Canada, Mexico, and the United States have negotiated a free trade agreement. Many Canadians, Mexicans, and Americans opposed the agreement, but even more supported it. Why would anyone oppose it? Or support it?

13. The U.S. demand for, U.S. supply of, and Japanese supply of VCRs are shown in the following schedule.

	United States		Japan
Price	**Quantity Demanded**	**Quantity Supplied**	**Quantity Supplied**
$100	500	100	100
200	400	200	200
300	300	300	300
400	200	400	400
500	100	500	500

If Japanese VCRs were prohibited from entering the United States, what would be the equilibrium price and quantity bought and sold by Americans in the VCR market in the United States?

14. Suppose the United States allowed Japan free trade privileges in the U.S. market. What would happen to the equilibrium price and total quantity of VCRs bought and sold in the U.S. market?

15. Suppose the U.S. imposed a $100 tariff on each Japanese VCR imported. What would happen to the equilibrium price and total quantity bought and sold in the U.S.?

16. Graph the situations described in questions 13 to 15.

CHAPTER 33

EXCHANGE RATES, BALANCE OF PAYMENTS, AND INTERNATIONAL DEBT

CHAPTER PREVIEW

Now that we understand the logic underlying international trade relations, it's time to turn our attention to international trade issues of a financial nature. How do countries pay for imports from other countries that use different currencies? What happens if a country imports more than it exports or vice versa? Aren't many countries in debt to other countries? How did this happen? What are the implications of international debt? You'll have answers for these questions by the end of this chapter.

After studying this chapter you should be able to:

- Explain the buying and selling of currencies on foreign exchange markets.
- Show that an exchange rate is simply the price for a currency in terms of another currency.
- List the factors that influence exchange rates from the demand side and the supply side.
- Give definitions for the terms *appreciation* and *depreciation* of currencies.
- Describe how arbitrage creates mutually consistent exchange rates.
- Discuss the problems with free-floating exchange rates.

- Explain how fixed exchange rates are intended to work and the possible problems that can arise.
- Relate the current account and the capital account in the balance of payments.
- Examine the problems associated with a persistent current account deficit.
- Describe how the United States' current account deficit arose during the 1980s.
- Explain Japan's balance of trade success.
- Contrast the balance of current accounts for oil-rich countries and other less-developed countries.
- Discuss the problems of international debt and debt service from short-run and long-run perspectives.

Suppose you were on vacation on an exotic South Pacific island and there chanced upon a native craftsman finishing off a beautiful teakwood carving of a swordfish. Just the thing you were hoping to find. Suppose you offered to buy it for $10, but the craftsman insisted on 4 yaps. After all, it's the only money he knows. He can buy anything he wants with it. The U.S. dollar? It's as unfamiliar to him as the yap is to you. It's not accepted on the island. You raise the offer to $20, but he won't budge. It's yaps or nothing.

Frustrating, isn't it? But, really, if the craftsman can't use the dollar in his everyday business of life, what good is it to him?

Let's change the scene. Suppose the craftsman was on vacation in Boston and noticed streams of cars heading toward Fenway Park. Upon inquiring, he discovers that they are all going to a Red Sox baseball game. Suppose he joins the crowd just to see how U.S. natives play.

He offers 4 yaps, but the ticket vendor insists on $10. He raises the offer to 6 yaps, but nobody at Fenway Park will take the yaps. They politely explain to him that Bostonians haven't heard of the yap and that it simply won't pass as currency in Boston. He goes away disappointed, never to see Andre Dawson belt one out of the park.

THE MONEY TOWER OF BABEL

It would be convenient if everyone in the world used one currency, but, alas, we don't. The French use French francs. The Swiss use their own francs, the British use the pound, Italians use the lira, Jordanians use the dinar, Israelis use the shekel, Mexicans use the peso, Brazilians use the cruzado, Japanese use the yen, Chinese use the yuan, Spaniards use the peseta, Canadians use the Canadian dollar, and we, of course, use the U.S. dollar. And there are many more economies, each with its own specific currency.

How then do we trade? How do we buy each other's goods? We know why some French fishermen may want to buy Greek boats, but how do they actually go about paying for them? With French francs? Why would Greeks take the francs? Nobody uses francs in Athens. How do the Japanese buy Brazilian coffee? What would a Brazilian want with yen? What would the South Pacific island craftsman do with U.S. dollars?

Every day, every nation's currency is traded on the foreign exchange market for every other nation's currency. The exchange rates those trades generate depend ultimately on the world's demand for each nation's goods and services.

THE FOREIGN EXCHANGE MARKET: THE BUYING AND SELLING OF CURRENCIES

Perhaps the only way we could persuade the South Pacific craftsman to accept U.S. dollars is to find someone on his island who wants U.S. goods and needs U.S. dollars to buy them. Then we could just swap dollars for yaps. It would work. But finding each other, that is, people with dollars looking for yaps meeting people with yaps looking for dollars is too accidental. Yet, *if there were enough such people looking for each other's currencies, we could establish a currency, or* **foreign exchange market,** where people could easily buy dollars with yaps and yaps with dollars.

Foreign exchange market

A market in which currencies of different nations are bought and sold.

That's what the foreign exchange market is all about. Suppose we still want to buy that teakwood swordfish. The islander wants 4 yaps for it. We can now exchange our dollars for yaps on the foreign exchange market. With the purchased yaps, we buy the teakwood carving. But is 4 yaps a reasonable price for the carving? How can we measure its worth in dollars? It would depend on how many dollars it takes to buy a yap.

The price of the yap in terms of dollars depends, like other prices, on market demand and supply. Look at Figure 1.

The foreign exchange market determines how many dollars it takes to buy a yap just as the umbrella market determines how many dollars it takes to buy an umbrella. The equilibrium price of a yap, shown in Figure 1, is $3. If the islander asks 4 yaps for the teakwood swordfish, its price in dollars is $12. Economists define the price of one country's currency, such as the dollar, in terms of another country's currency, such as the yap, as the **exchange rate.**

Exchange rate

The number of units of foreign currency that can be purchased with one unit of domestic currency.

The Demand Curve for Yaps

As the price of yaps in dollars falls, the quantity demanded increases.

If the exchange rate were not $3, but say only $1 per yap, then the 4 yap teakwood carving would be considerably less expensive *in terms of dollars*. And because it's cheaper, we would buy more carvings. That's simply the law of demand, isn't it? But to buy more carvings, we would need more yaps. In Figure 1, the quantity demanded of yaps increases from 30,000 to 50,000 when the exchange rate drops from $3 to $1 per yap. That's why the demand curve for yaps is downward-sloping.

FIGURE 1 Foreign Exchange Market

Keep this in mind when you think about exchange rates: *Americans demand yaps* to buy South Pacific goods and *South Pacific islanders supply yaps* to buy U.S. goods.

The demand curve for yaps, *D*, depicts the demand for yaps at varying rates of exchange, that is, number of dollars required to buy a yap. At $2 per yap, the quantity of yaps demanded is 40,000. At $3 per yap—the yap is now more expensive, that is, people have to give more dollars to buy a yap—the quantity of yaps demanded falls to 30,000.

The supply curve of yaps, *S*, depicts the supply of yaps at varying rates of exchange, dollars for yaps. At $6 per yap—one yap buys a $6 U.S. good—the quantity of yaps supplied by people holding yaps and wanting to buy dollars is 60,000. At $1 per yap—one yap now buys only a $1 U.S. good—the quantity of yaps supplied by people holding yaps and wanting to buy dollars is 10,000.

At $1 per yap, a 50,000 - 10,000 = 40,000 excess demand for yaps emerges, driving up the exchange rate. The market reaches equilibrium at $3 per yap, where the quantity of yaps demanded and supplied is 30,000.

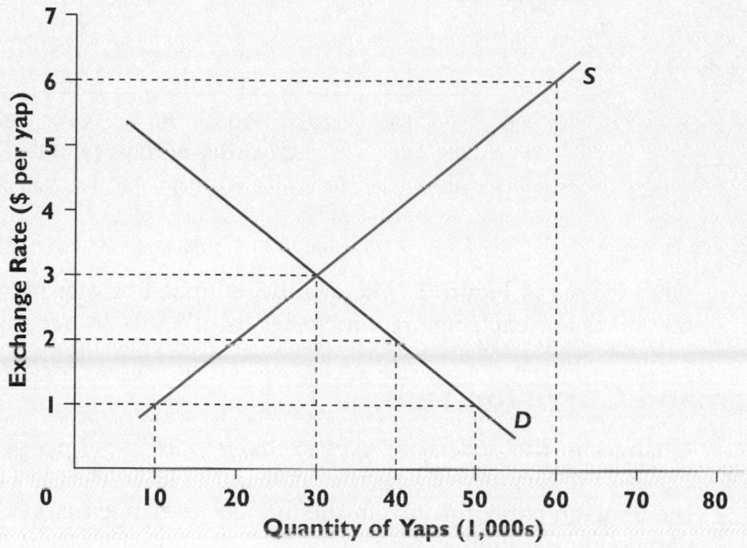

What about the craftsman? Whether the exchange rate is $3 or $1 per yap, that is, whether we end up paying $12 or $4 for the carving, he still ends up with 4 yaps. How does he feel about the exchange rate? If he had any say in the matter, he would probably prefer the $1 per yap. Why? Because at $1 per yap, we buy more of his carvings.

The Supply Curve of Yaps

As the price of yaps in dollars rises, the quantity supplied increases.

What about the supply curve of yaps in Figure 1? The South Pacific islanders supply yaps, exchange them for dollars, to buy our goods. Suppose a South Pacific islander on vacation in New York spots a graphite fishing rod in a window at Macy's. It sells for $60. He immediately translates the price into yaps. After all, that's the currency he's familiar with. At $3 per yap, that rod costs him 20 yaps. Not a bad buy. But at $1 per yap, the rod's price jumps to 60 yaps. It makes a difference.

That's why the supply curve of yaps is upward-sloping. At $3 per yap, South Pacific island people find U.S. goods relatively inexpensive *in terms of yaps* and end up buying more goods. To buy more, they supply yaps for dollars. That's

FIGURE 2
Effect of an Increase in the Demand for Yaps on the Dollars-for-Yaps Rate of Exchange
The demand curve for yaps shifts from D_1 to D_2, reflecting an increase in demand for yap-priced imports. At the old equilibrium exchange rate of $3 per yap, a new 70,000 - 30,000 = 40,000 excess demand for yaps emerges, driving the equilibrium exchange rate from $3 to $5 per yap, where the quantity of yaps demanded and supplied is 50,000.

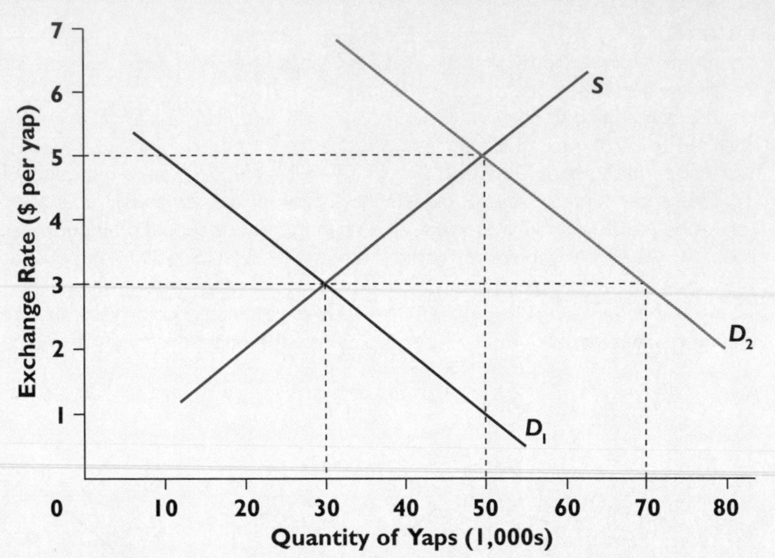

what we see in Figure 1. The quantity supplied of yaps increases from 30,000 to 60,000 as the exchange rate increases from $3 to $6 per yap.

Shifts in the Demand Curve for Yaps

Changes in income, tastes, and interest earnings on the yap influence the foreign demand for yaps.

Changes in the dollars-for-yaps exchange rate cause people demanding yaps to change the quantity of yaps they demand, which is shown as a movement along the demand curve for yaps in the foreign exchange market. But what causes the demand curve itself to shift?

CHANGES IN INCOME

Imagine what would happen to our demand for yaps if our incomes increased by, say, 20 percent. With more dollars in our pockets, we end up buying more goods. Suppose among the more goods we buy are teakwood carvings from the South Pacific islands. To buy more teakwood imports, we need more yaps. Look at Figure 2.

Our demand curve for yaps shifts to the right. As a result, the equilibrium exchange rate increases from $3 to $5 per yap, and the quantity of yaps demanded and supplied on the foreign exchange market increases from 30,000 to 50,000.

CHANGES IN TASTE

What about changes in taste? If teakwood carvings catch on, the increased demand for the carvings creates an increase in the demand for yaps as well. And that puts us right back to Figure 2.

On the other hand, suppose our tastes change from wood carvings to Irish cut glass. What happens to our demand for yaps? The fall in demand for teakwood carvings shifts our demand for yaps to the left, depressing the exchange rate below $3 per yap.

CHANGES IN INTEREST RATES

A fall in the interest rate in the United States or a rise in the interest rate in the South Pacific island will affect the demand for yaps as well. For example, suppose you were looking through the pages of *The Wall Street Journal* and came upon an announcement that the Teakwood Carvings Company, a South Pacific island firm, wants to expand its plant capacity and expects to finance the expansion by offering bonds, in denominations of 10,000 and 20,000 yaps, at a 10 percent rate of interest. If the rate of interest offered by U.S. companies on their corporate bonds is 6 percent, the 4 percent rate spread makes the South Pacific bond rather attractive. Wouldn't you be tempted to buy a 10,000-yap bond?

But how do you go about buying the bond? You first must exchange your dollars for 10,000 yaps and with the purchased yaps, buy the 10,000-yap bond. That shifts the demand curve for yaps to the right. Once again, we are back to Figure 2.

Shifts in the Supply Curve of Yaps

Changes in income, tastes, and relative interest rates influence the supply of yaps in foreign exchange markets.

Just as changes in U.S. incomes, tastes, and interest rates shift the demand curve for yaps, changes in South Pacific incomes, tastes, and interest rates shift the supply curve of yaps. After all, South Pacific islanders are very much like us.

If their incomes increase, wouldn't you expect that they, too, would buy more goods, which might include imports from the United States? Their increase in demand for U.S. goods results in an increase in their demand for U.S. dollars. They buy dollars by supplying yaps. That is, the supply curve for yaps shifts to the right. The effect of this supply shift on the dollars-for-yaps rate of exchange is depicted in Figure 3.

The equilibrium exchange rate decreases from $3 to $2 per yap, and the quantity of yaps demanded and supplied on the foreign exchange market increases from 30,000 to 40,000. And if the interest rate on the island fell,

FIGURE 3
Effect of an Increase in the Supply of Yaps on the Dollars-for-Yaps Rate of Exchange
The supply curve of yaps shifts from S_1 to S_2, reflecting an in crease in demand for dollar-priced imports. At the old equilibrium exchange rate of $3 per yap, a new 50,000 – 30,000 = 20,000 excess supply of yaps emerges, driving the equilibrium exchange rate from $3 to $2 per yap, where the quantity of yaps demanded and supplied is 40,000.

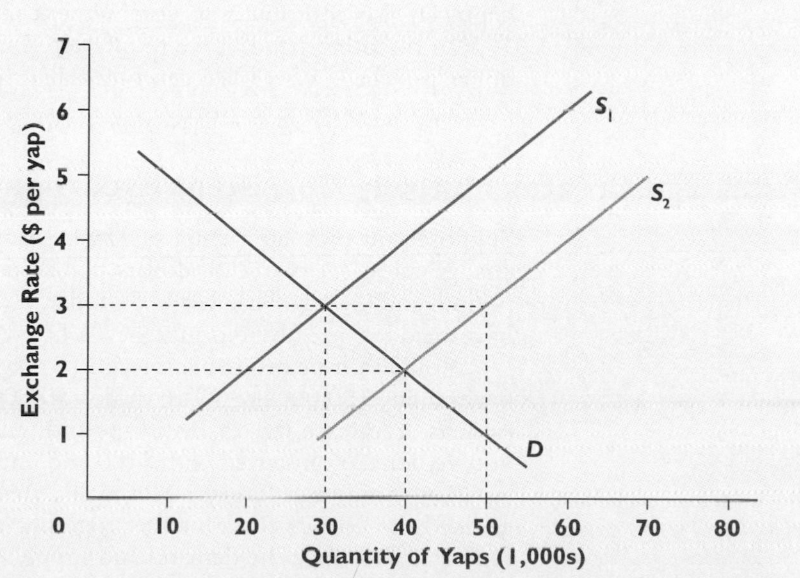

wouldn't that fall encourage islanders to look elsewhere for possible investments? They may end up buying U.S. bonds, which creates a demand for U.S. dollars and a supply of yaps.

FLOATING EXCHANGE RATES

Floating exchange rate

An exchange rate determined strictly by the demands and supplies for a nation's currency.

Imagine a world of economies, all importing and exporting goods from each other, investing in each other's capital markets, and demanding and supplying each other's currencies to carry out these many international transactions. That would create a multiplicity of exchange rates, each one reflecting the specific demand and supply condition for its own national currency.

Such an array of exchange rates would be **floating,** that is, in a continuous state of flux, adjusting always to the changing demand and supply conditions in the international market for goods and capital.

Depreciation and Appreciation

Appreciation

A rise in the price of a nation's currency relative to foreign currencies.

Depreciation

A fall in the price of a nation's currency relative to foreign currencies.

The market forces that determine floating exchange rates are really no different from the market forces that determine the prices of goods such as umbrellas, microwave popcorn, and houses. Yet, curiously, many people seem to be more than just a little confused about the significance of a change in exchange rates.

CBS Evening News' Dan Rather, along with his media friends, report regularly on how the U.S. dollar has fared against other currencies during the week. For example, in reporting the dollar's **appreciation,** meaning we pay fewer dollars for a yap, or the dollar's **depreciation,** meaning we pay more dollars for a yap, they typically go one step further by referring to the appreciation as a *strengthening* of the dollar and to the depreciation as a *weakening* of the dollar.

In other contexts, the words *strength* and *weakness* convey moral attributes. Do they convey the same in foreign exchange markets? Is a weak dollar bad? Not if we're interested in exporting U.S. goods. After all, Italians, who are getting more dollars for their lira buy more U.S. goods. That makes our exporters happy. It also contributes to employment in the United States.

On the other hand, if we're interested in consuming imports, then a strong dollar isn't bad. Why? We can buy Italian imports more cheaply. Our dollar's purchasing power increases.

Arbitrage Creates Mutually Consistent Exchange Rates

Suppose you pick up a copy of *USA Today* and read the following set of exchange rates: (1) two U.S. dollars per British pound, (2) 2,000 lire per British pound, and (3) 1,500 lire per U.S. dollar. You go over it again to make sure you have read it correctly. No mistake. What would you do?

Arbitrage

The practice of buying a foreign currency in one market at a low price and selling it in another at a higher price.

Wouldn't it be profitable for you to take $100 to the foreign exchange market and buy 150,000 lire. With those 150,000 lire, you could then buy 75 British pounds. You take the 75 British pounds and buy 150 U.S. dollars. Look what you've done. You started with $100 and ended up with $150. That's **arbitrage.**

Can you do this forever? Not really. Because others, too, will probably have noticed the chance for arbitrage; together the total buying and selling of currencies will change the demand and supply curves in the foreign exchange market, making all exchange rates mutually consistent with each other.

Problems with Floating Exchange Rates

Changes in exchange rates can mean big headaches for an importer of wood carvings from the South Pacific. Why would a depreciation of the dollar cause particularly bad migraines?

Sometimes free-floating exchange rates are not always desirable. Suppose we are importers of wood carvings and strike a deal with a South Pacific island producer to buy 1,000 pieces at 4 yaps each, the exchange rate at \$3 per yap. We expect, then, to pay \$12,000. Six months later when the 1,000 wood carvings are delivered, we send a check for \$12,000 only to be told that it is now insufficient. Why? Because in the six months between the contract agreement and delivery, the exchange rate changed from \$3 to \$5 per yap. The 4,000 yaps we promised to pay, expecting that they would cost \$12,000, now cost \$20,000. There goes our profit and more.

Of course, the exchange rate could have gone the other way. For example, it could have fallen to \$2 per yap. We would then end up with a windfall. Instead of paying \$12,000 for the 1,000 carvings, we would have to pay only \$8,000.

But our business is importing, not gambling. Floating exchange rates add an element of uncertainty to international trade, making it a less-reliable venture than simple domestic trade. As a result, we probably end up importing and exporting fewer goods than the expected gains from international trade would warrant.

Fixing Exchange Rates

Can we avoid that kind of uncertainty if we plan to engage in international trade? After all, shifts in demand and supply curves that change equilibrium levels of exchange rates simply reflect our changing preferences. Do we really want to interfere with these preferences?

Perhaps the way out of the dilemma is to *fix* exchange rates—to no longer allow them to float—in such a way that uncertainty is reduced to zero, but at the same time allow demand and supply conditions on the market to dictate the quantities of imports and exports.

How can this be done? Look at Figure 4. Panel *a* depicts what happens to the exchange rate over three years of changing demands for island goods when the rate is allowed to float. Look at the first year. Demand, *D,* and supply, *S,* generate an exchange rate of \$3 per yap. The quantity demanded and supplied is 30,000 yaps.

Suppose in the second year, an increase in demand for South Pacific island goods shifts the demand for yaps to the right to D_1. The exchange rate increases to \$4 per yap, and the quantity demanded and supplied increases to 40,000 yaps.

Now suppose in the third year the demand for island goods decreases. This time, the demand curve for yaps shifts to the left to D_2. The exchange rate falls to \$2 per yap and the quantity demanded and supplied decreases to 20,000 yaps.

These roller-coaster exchange rates are precisely what we want to avoid. If the rate can drop from \$4 to \$2 per yap in one year, what's in store for us next year? Will it drop again? Or recover? Who knows? That's the problem, nobody does. Not a very comfortable world if you're an importer or exporter calculating profits and losses on constantly fluctuating exchange rates. But what can we do?

Fixed exchange rate

A rate determined by government and then maintained through the process of buying and selling quantities of its own currency on the foreign exchange market.

Let's bring government into the market. The government announces that it is replacing the floating exchange rate system with an unchanging rate, that is, a **fixed exchange rate.** All international transactions will take place at the gov-

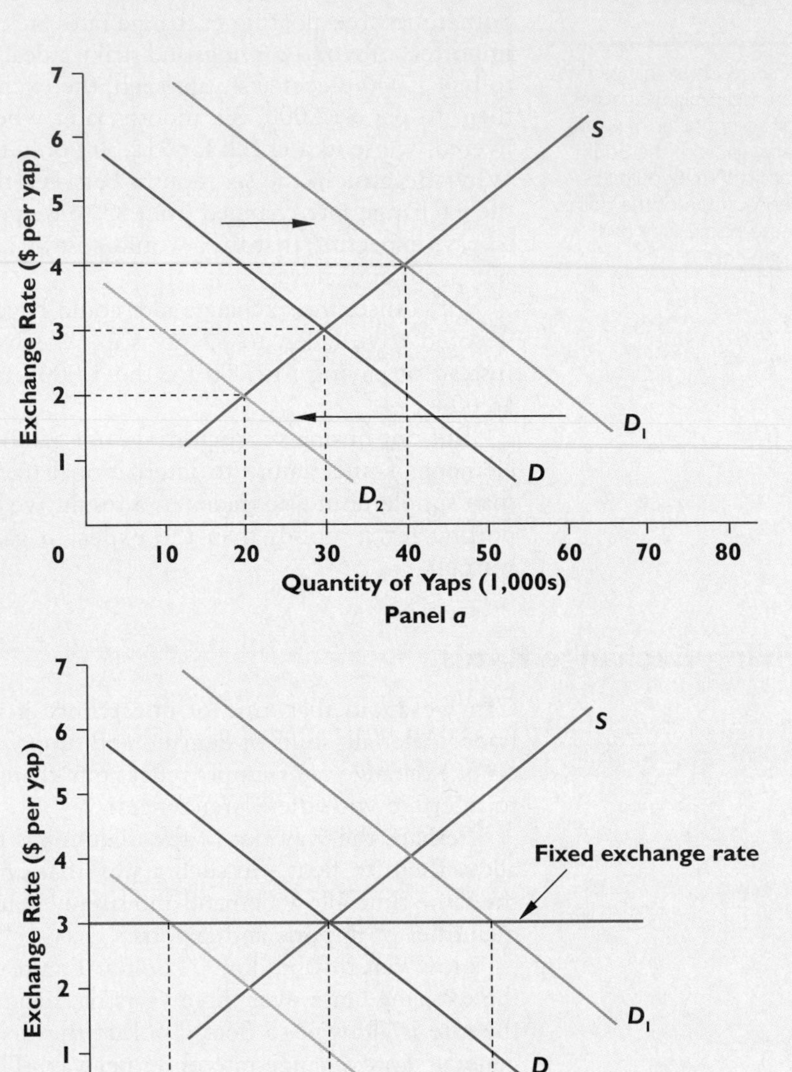

FIGURE 4
Trade under Free and Fixed Exchange Rates
Panel *a* depicts changes in the equilibrium exchange rate—dollars per yap—caused by shifts in the demand curve. In the first year, the demand curve for yaps, *D*, intersects the supply curve of yaps, *S*, to produce an exchange rate of $3 per yap. In the second year, the demand curve shifts to the right, to D_1, driving the exchange rate up to $4 per yap. In the following year, the demand curve falls to D_2, driving the exchange rate down to $2 per yap.

In panel *b*, the U.S. government fixes the exchange rate at $3 per yap and supports that rate regardless of changes in the U.S. demand for yaps.

In the second year, the demand curve D_1 creates an excess demand of 20,000 yaps at the $3 per yap exchange rate. Rather than allowing that excess demand to drive the exchange rate up, the government goes onto the foreign exchange market and supplies 20,000 yaps from its own yap reserve, trading those yaps for dollars at the fixed rate of $3 per yap. The market clears.

In the third year, the demand curve moves left to D_2, creating an excess supply of 20,000 yaps at the $3 per yap exchange rate. Rather than allowing that excess supply to drive the exchange rate down, the government now goes onto the foreign exchange market with $60,000 and demands 20,000 yaps. The market clears.

ernment's fixed rate of exchange. Follow the effects of government intervention in Figure 4, panel *b*. Suppose the government fixes the exchange rate at $3 per yap. How can it keep it fixed at $3 when our demand for imports from the South Pacific island changes?

The first year is no problem. The government doesn't have to intervene. The economy's exports and imports themselves create a set of demand and supply conditions on the exchange rate market that, by chance, drives the rate precisely to the government's fixed rate. The quantity demanded and supplied is 30,000 yaps, and the market clears.

In the second year, demand for South Pacific island goods increases, raising our demand for yaps to D_1. In panel *a,* where the market determined exchange rates, the rate floated up to $4 per yap, but in the panel *b* economy, the rate stays fixed at $3 per yap. Look what happens. At that rate, the quantity demanded becomes 50,000 yaps. However, only 30,000 are supplied. The market now generates an excess demand of 20,000.

How can the government handle the 20,000 yap excess demand pressure on the foreign exchange market? It does so *by coming up with its own supply of yaps.* It goes into the foreign exchange market to exchange its own 20,000 yaps for $60,000. That is, it sells yaps to people with dollars who are looking for yaps. It absorbs the entire excess demand for yaps, relieving pressure on the exchange rate. Of course, to play such a role, the government must have sufficient **foreign exchange reserves.**

Foreign exchange reserves

The stock of foreign currencies a government holds.

Look at panel *b*'s third year. A fall in demand for South Pacific island goods shifts the demand curve for yaps to the left to D_2. At $3 per yap, only 10,000 yaps are demanded but 30,000 are supplied, creating now an excess supply of 20,000 yaps. This time, the government intervenes by supplying $60,000 of its own dollar reserves to buy up the 20,000 excess supply of yaps. We're back where we started. The government has replenished its foreign exchange reserves.

What if the Government Runs Out of Foreign Exchange Reserves?

Figure 4, panel *b* is carefully drawn to allow the third year's excess supply of yaps to replenish the shortage that was created by excess demand for yaps in the second year. Unfortunately, life isn't always that convenient. The economy's foreign exchange reserves can build up far beyond sufficient levels, or can be drawn down to dangerously low levels.

Alternatives to drawing down foreign exchange reserves are adjusting the exchange rate, imposing import controls, imposing exchange controls, and borrowing foreign currencies.

Suppose the excess demand for yaps, shown for only panel *b*'s second year, persists year after year? How long can the government keep digging into its foreign exchange reserves before it comes up empty? And what can it do if it confronts that predicament?

ADJUSTING THE EXCHANGE RATE

Perhaps the simplest remedy is **devaluation** to adjust the fixed exchange rate at a higher level. For example, if the government were to fix the exchange rate at $5 instead of $3 per yap, our exports would rise, our imports would fall, and excess demand for yaps would disappear. The drain on the government's foreign exchange reserves would cease.

Devaluation

Government policy that lowers the nation's exchange rate; its currency instantly is worth less in the foreign exchange market.

IMPOSING IMPORT CONTROLS

A second option is to impose **import controls** by tariff and quota adjustments. By either raising tariffs or lowering quotas, the government can limit imports. Either way, it can shift the economy's demand curve for yaps as far to the left as it needs to bring the quantity of yaps demanded and supplied into line at $3 per yap.

Import controls

Tariffs and quotas used by government to limit a nation's imports.

IMPOSING EXCHANGE CONTROLS

Another way of accomplishing the same goal is for the government to introduce **exchange controls.** It can require exporters earning yaps to turn them over to the government in exchange for dollars at the $3 per yap rate. In this way, gov-

Exchange controls

A system in which government, as the sole depository of foreign currencies, exercises complete control over how these currencies can be used.

ADDED PERSPECTIVE

Tourists at the Mall

Imagine having a cousin George from Calgary, Alberta, Canada who came to visit you in the summer of 1992, bringing with him 254 Canadian dollars that his mother gave him to buy gifts for the Calgary family. Suppose he shopped in your neighborhood mall and the gift shops there were willing to exchange his Canadian dollars for U.S. dollars at the 1992 exchange rate. He would end up buying gifts worth 200 U.S. dollars. Not knowing much about free-floating exchange rates, he would be a little disappointed. Why? Because his mother told him that when she visited your folks back in 1960, she was able to use her 254 Canadian dollars to buy as much as 254 U.S. dollars worth of gifts. What could possibly explain the difference?

Suppose also that at the mall, George and you met a Japanese tourist from Tokyo who also was gift shopping for family back home. You notice that she exchanges 2,480 Japanese yen for $200 U.S. dollars and makes the same purchases your cousin does. While you are all waiting for gift wrapping, she tells you a surprising story. Her mother was here back in 1960 and she, too, bought $200 U.S. of gifts. But her mother had to exchange 7,160 Japanese yen for those gifts! What could possibly explain the difference?

If tourists from Italy, Britain, and Germany were at the mall, what stories would they tell about buying U.S. gifts with lira, pounds, and marks in 1960 and 1992?

Exchange Rates of Selected Countries (currency units per U.S. dollar)

Year	Canadian Dollar	Japanese Yen	French Franc	German Mark	Italian Lira	British Pound
1950	1.06	361	3.50	4.20	625	.36
1955	1.00	361	3.50	4.22	625	.36
1960	1.00	358	4.90	4.17	621	.36
1965	1.08	361	4.90	4.01	625	.36
1970	1.01	358	5.52	3.65	623	.42
1975	1.02	305	4.49	2.62	684	.50
1980	1.19	203	4.52	1.96	931	.42
1985	1.40	201	7.56	2.46	1,679	.69
1990	1.16	134	5.13	1.49	1,130	.52
1992	1.27	124	5.51	1.61	1,471	.66

Source: End-of-year exchange rates from International Monetary Fund, *International Financial Statistics*, Washington, D.C.

ernment ends up with all the yaps in the economy. It then rations them out among importers, keeping the quantity of yaps demanded and supplied in balance.

BORROWING FOREIGN CURRENCIES

Finally, the government can always go into the foreign exchange market and borrow yaps to cover the economy's excess demand for yaps. Sometimes borrowing is the most reasonable option. In periods of crisis, such as wars or famines, the government cannot afford to cut back on basic imports, nor can it easily increase exports. To keep the economy functioning, its best and perhaps only option is to borrow foreign currencies.

But if not held in check, borrowing can lead to problems. Just as doctors who prescribe narcotics to overcome postoperative pain always worry about addiction, so must governments who borrow foreign exchange to overcome economic crises worry about becoming addicted to the habit. Borrowing, and the interest payments that accompany it, can too quickly lock an economy into unmanageable international debt.

BALANCE OF PAYMENTS

Balance of payments

An itemized account of a nation's foreign economic transactions.

An economy's **balance of payments** account provides a statement of the economy's financial transactions with the rest of the world. For example, the U.S. balance of payments account for 1993, shown in Table 1, records the dollars that flowed into the U.S. economy in 1993 from the rest of the world and the dollars that flowed out of the United States to the rest of the world. These flows influence the demand and supply for foreign exchange.

Balance on Current Account

Balance on current account

A category that itemizes a nation's imports and exports of merchandise and services, income receipts and payments on investment, and unilateral transfers.

The **balance on current account** summarizes U.S. trade in goods and services, net investment income, and unilateral transfers that occur during the current year. Exports of goods and services and income receipts on investments abroad represent dollar inflows (+) from the rest of the world. Imports of goods and services and income payments to the rest of the world represent dollar outflows (−).

MERCHANDISE EXPORTS

Look at line 1. The single, most important source of dollar inflow was the $456.9 billion that foreigners paid for our merchandise exports. How do exports contribute to the dollar inflow?

Suppose Dennis Wiziecki, a British engineer from Liverpool, wants to buy a $30,000 Buick LeSabre manufactured in Detroit. He first needs to get his hands on $30,000. After all, that's the currency General Motors wants. How does he get them? By trading his own British pounds for U.S. dollars in the foreign exchange market. That is, the Buick export from the United States creates the demand for U.S. dollars. Dennis buys the $30,000 with his British pounds, then transfers the $30,000 to General Motors in Detroit. That's a $30,000 inflow into the U.S. balance of current account. General Motors in turn exports the Buick to him.

MERCHANDISE IMPORTS

Line 2 records the $589.4 billion outflow from the United States to the rest of the world. That's a lot of dollars going out. Of course, it represents a lot of imports coming in.

How do imports translate into dollar outflow? Well, suppose Carolyn Hatch, a New York tea importer, decides to buy 500 pounds of Darjeeling tea from India. She learns that the Indian tea exporter wants 50 rupees per pound. That adds up to 25,000 rupees. Carolyn obtains 25,000 rupees by going into the foreign exchange market. There, she supplies U.S. dollars in exchange for Indian rupees. This simple transaction represents a U.S. dollar outflow.

TABLE 1 The U.S. Balance of Payments Account, 1993 ($ billions)

Current Account	
1. Merchandise exports	+456.9
2. Merchandise imports	−589.4
3. Balance of trade	−132.5
4. Export of services	+184.8
5. Import of services	−128.0
6. Income receipts on investments	+113.9
7. Income payments on investments	−109.9
8. Unilateral transfers	− 32.1
9. Balance on current account	−103.9
Capital Account	
10. Change in U.S. assets abroad	−147.9
11. Change in foreign assets in U.S.	+230.7
12. Statistical discrepancy	+ 21.1
13. Balance on capital account	+103.9

Source: *Survey of Current Business, June 1994* (Washington, D.C.: U.S. Department of Commerce), p. 66.

BALANCE OF TRADE

Balance of trade

The difference between the value of a nation's merchandise exports and its merchandise imports.

The focus of much discussion and debate on the balance of payments is fixed on the **balance of trade** account, that is, the value of exports minus the value of imports, shown in line 3. The terms we use to describe the balance signal how we view it. For example, when exports are greater than imports, we describe the balance as *favorable*. When imports are greater than exports, the balance is described as *unfavorable*.

In 1993, the value of the goods we exported was $132.5 billion less than the value of the imports of foreign goods we bought. As Figure 5 shows, the United States has been running negative balances of trade since 1975.

Negative balances are seen by American industrial workers as a factor that undermines their economic well-being. If the Japanese must wait patiently in their Buicks and Fords during the Tokyo rush-hour traffic, workers in Detroit do well. On the other hand, if the bumper-to-bumper traffic in Cleveland is a stream of imported Toyotas and Hondas, Detroit becomes a wasteland.

How do you switch from an unfavorable to a favorable balance of trade? Produce better automobiles? Depreciate the exchange rate, U.S. dollars for Japanese yen? Impose import quotas? Increase tariffs? These options are always under discussion, and considerable pressure from American exporters and labor unions is continually being brought to bear on the Congress and the administration.

EXPORT OF SERVICES

Another source of U.S. dollar inflow into the current account was the $184.8 billion export of services, shown in line 4 of Table 1. When Mary Constantine, an account executive in one of Italy's leading advertising agencies, flew from Rome to New York on TWA, she had to purchase the $900 ticket with U.S.

FIGURE 5 **U.S. Balance of Trade, 1950–1993**
The year 1975 marks a watershed in the U.S. balance of trade accounts. It turned from moderate surpluses for most years prior to 1975 to deficits. Note the sharp plunge in the U.S. balance of trade (increases in the annual deficit) from 1983 to 1987, with a slight improvement (more moderate deficits, but deficits nonetheless) thereafter.

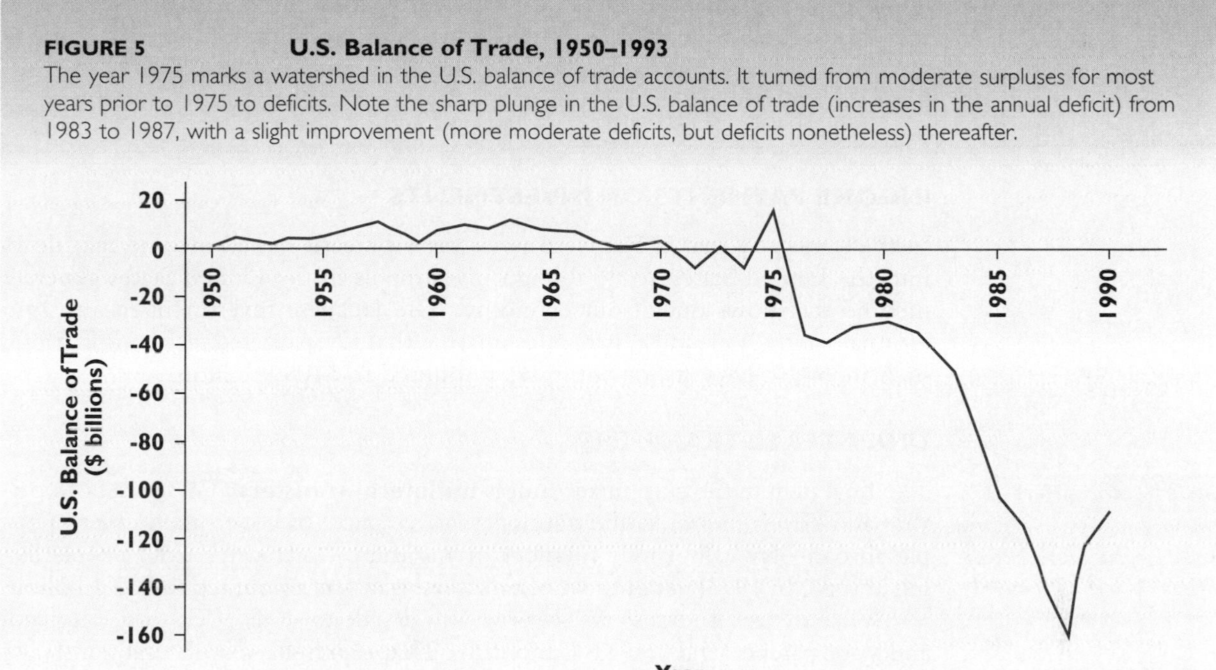

Services can be exported just like merchandise.

dollars. After all, that's the currency TWA demands. To make life somewhat more convenient for its passengers, TWA may accept her Italian lire and itself go into the foreign exchange market, exchanging lire for $900 dollars.

What about exports carried out of the United States by foreigners? For example, when Ryan Walter, a Dubliner, spends his vacation in Cincinnati, that vacation is equivalent to our exporting goods and services to Ireland. If he stays at the Cincinnati Hyatt Hotel, isn't that equivalent to an export of our services? He supplies Irish pounds and demands U.S. dollars for the hotel service. If he takes home a Cincinnati Bengal jacket bought at Riverfront Stadium, isn't that the same as if we exported the jacket to Dublin and he bought it at a shop off St. Stephen's Green?

IMPORT OF SERVICES

What about the $128.0 billion of imported services, shown in line 5? Remember Mary Constantine's flight to New York on TWA? Now suppose, at the same time, Jonathan Richman, a welder from Kenosha, Wisconsin, decides to visit Canada. He buys a deluxe package tour that includes round-trip fares, hotels, and sightseeing trips to Montreal. Just as TWA demanded U.S. currency, Air Canada and Canadian hotels demand Canadian dollars. The travel agent handling the tour takes Jonathan's U.S. dollars to the foreign exchange market and there trades them for the needed Canadian dollars. Jonathan's trip, then, just like the import of Indian tea, represents an outflow of U.S. dollars.

INCOME RECEIPTS ON INVESTMENTS

Many U.S. companies have profitable investments abroad that earn income. For example, United Fruit, a U.S. food conglomerate with investments in Honduran banana plantations earns income each year selling bananas to the rest of the world. Part of the income earned remains in Honduras as additional investment, and part ends up in the United States as income receipts. The $113.9 billion, shown in line 6, is the sum of the income receipts of U.S. investments in the rest of the world.

INCOME PAYMENTS ON INVESTMENTS

In the same way that U.S. investments abroad create annual income that flows into the United States, so do foreign investments in the United States generate income that flows out of our economy. The Japanese investment in an Ohio Honda plant, for example, generates income that is repatriated to Japan. In 1993, such income payments, or outflows, amounted to $109.9 billion.

UNILATERAL TRANSFERS

Unilateral transfers

Transfers of currency made by individuals, businesses, or government of one nation to individuals, businesses, or governments in other nations, with no designated return.

If you choose to study abroad, you will make a unilateral transfer of dollars overseas.

The final item in the current account is **unilateral transfers.** These are both private and government income transfers that we make to governments or to people abroad—typically family members living there—or receive from people living abroad. In 1993, net outflow of unilateral transfers amounted to $32.1 billion.

What are private transfers? Suppose you decide to study at Oxford, England, and your parents send you $100 monthly. That represents a unilateral transfer of dollars. It's described as unilateral because it flows in only one direction—in this case, out of the United States. What do you do with $100? March right down to an Oxford bank to exchange it for British pounds. After all, the local restaurant takes British pounds, not U.S. dollars.

Foreign students studying in the United States create private unilateral dollar transfers that flow in the opposite direction, that is, into the United States. There are thousands of students from the rest of the world on U.S. campuses who exchange their own currencies for U.S. dollars.

Many people living in the United States send money to their families in Europe, Latin America, and the Middle East. Every such transaction represents a unilateral income transfer and enters our balance of payments as an outflow—that is, a supply of dollars that corresponds to a demand for other currencies. After all, relatives in other countries exchange the dollars for their domestic currencies to buy goods and services where they are.

The economic and military aid that the U.S. government provides other governments is an example of a government unilateral transfer. Although such aid represents a dollar outflow, the recipient countries typically use the aid to purchase U.S. goods (adding to our exports). In most cases, all of the dollar outflows associated with the aid come back to the United States as dollar inflows.

BALANCE ON CURRENT ACCOUNT

Line 9 sums up the inflows (+) and outflows (−) on the U.S. current account which, in 1993, amounted to $103.9 billion.

Balance on Capital Account

What about capital account entries? These entries refer to the flow of capital into and out of the United States that takes place when people buy and sell real and financial assets across borders. Consider these kinds of transactions.

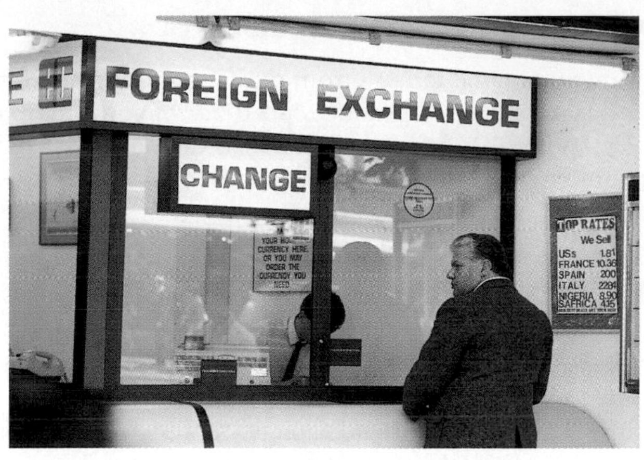

Where do Englishmen travel? Note the sign on the wall. It probably indicates the most commonly traded currencies, at least at that foreign exchange office. If he trades his British pound sterling for Italian lire, he's most likely off to Rome.

CHANGES IN U.S. ASSETS ABROAD

When a U.S. firm sets up shop overseas, dollars flow out of the country.

When a U.S. natural-fiber broom company decides to take advantage of the low labor costs in Mexico to build a factory on the outskirts of Mexico City, it needs pesos to construct the plant, buy and install the machinery, and hire workers. How does the company get the pesos? By supplying dollars on the foreign exchange market (an outflow of dollars) for the needed pesos. In the end, U.S. assets abroad, in the form of a new broom factory in Mexico, increase. Similarly, U.S. assets abroad increase when Exxon builds an oil refinery in Jamaica. The refinery construction creates an outflow of U.S. dollars to purchase the Jamaican dollars.

You don't have to be Exxon or a broom company to own assets abroad. Individuals can buy assets abroad as well. For example, suppose Gary Adelman, a university professor, chanced upon a prospectus at his broker's office describing a new stock issue by an Israeli medical equipment company and bought 50,000 shekels worth of the stock. His assets now include a piece of the Israeli company. But to get that asset, he created an outflow of dollars.

In 1993 the outflow of dollars from the United States that ended up as changes in U.S. assets abroad amounted to $147.9 billion, shown in line 10 of Table 1.

CHANGES IN FOREIGN ASSETS IN THE U.S.

Just as Gary Adelman can buy assets abroad, so can foreigners buy U.S. assets. Imagine a Saudi sheik, sitting in his sumptuous living room in Mecca reading *The Wall Street Journal.* He reads that the U.S. government has put a new issue of its bonds on the market at a 6 percent rate of interest. He decides to buy $10 million of them. But how? He needs U.S. dollars to make the purchase. His broker goes into the foreign exchange market, supplying the sheik's Saudi riyals and demanding 10 million U.S. dollars. The bond is a U.S. asset.

Foreigners buying any U.S. asset—such as Japanese automakers building an Ohio automobile factory—provide an inflow of dollars. In 1993 changes in foreign assets in the United States amounted to $230.7 billion (line 11). As you see, changes in foreign assets in the United States in 1993 were higher than changes in U.S. assets abroad.

Balance on capital account

A category that itemizes changes in foreign asset holdings of the nation and that nation's asset holdings abroad.

BALANCE ON CAPITAL ACCOUNT

Subtracting capital inflows from capital outflows, and introducing a $21.1 billion statistical discrepancy produces a $103.9 billion **balance on capital account,** shown in line 12. As you see, it equals the negative $103.9 billion in the current account.

WHAT IS A BALANCE OF PAYMENTS PROBLEM?

An excess of imports over exports can be covered by foreign currency reserves, the sale of assets, government securities, or by borrowing.

Do U.S. dollar inflows and outflows always cancel each other out? Is it by chance or is there some kind of magic at work bringing these dollar flows into balance? And if current and capital accounts always balance, how can we possibly end up with a balance of payments problem?

The problem associated with the balance of payments is how the balance is obtained. Consider, for example what happens when the outflow of dollars to pay for our imports exceeds the inflow of dollars earned by our exports. Some source of financing has to be found to cover the difference. Foreigners don't export for the love of it. And currencies don't just materialize out of thin air.

How, then, do we cover? There are three alternatives. First, we can dip into our foreign currency reserves. For example, if we import more from Japan than we export to Japan, we can use our yen reserves to cover the difference. Second, the Japanese may decide to buy some of our assets, such as the Sears Building in Chicago. Their supply of yen to buy the dollars needed for the Sears purchase may be just the yen we need to cover the difference between our imports from and exports to them. Third, we can go into the foreign exchange market to borrow the needed yen. Each alternative serves to bring dollar inflows and outflows into balance.

But that's also how we get into trouble! How deep are our currency reserves? How many assets do we really want to sell off? How many foreign currency loans can we take out before foreigners close the door?

Do Trade Imbalances Always Create Problems?

One reason a country might consciously import more than it exports is to accumulate capital.

Governments are not always concerned about trade imbalances even when their economies import considerably more than they export. Why not? Because if an economy's principal imports are in the form of industrial and agricultural machinery, the government may expect that by building up the economy with these imports, the economy will *eventually* expand its export markets. That is, the government believes that imports, properly selected, can contribute to future exports and, therefore, *future* dollar inflows.

Foolhardy? Not really. No one would call a farmer foolhardy for scattering seed during spring sowing. The late summer harvest is expected to more than make up for the cost of seed. If imports modernize the economy's productive capacity and improve its competitiveness in world markets, then greater export sales would make the earlier balance of payments problem a gamble well worth taking.

The problem with such a strategy is that it doesn't always work. There is simply no way of guaranteeing that imports intended to develop the productive base of the economy today translate into exports tomorrow. Too often, governments are too optimistic about their export prospects. They view the future through rose-colored glasses. In the end, what was thought to be a calculated risk becomes a real problem.

In many cases, an economy's deficit on current account may not reflect any government strategy at all, not even a failed one. It may simply record the economy's lackluster export performance, at least compared to its import appetites. But why lackluster and why the appetite?

HOW DEFICITS ON CURRENT ACCOUNT DEVELOP

The Trouble with Being Popular

As foreign companies invest in the United States, their purchases of dollars cause the dollar to appreciate.

It's sometimes hard to stay out of trouble when you're too popular. That may be precisely why the United States sometimes gets into balance of payment difficulties. Paradoxically, it is the strength and stability of the U.S. economy compared to other economies that creates the problem. That's how many economists explain the sharp reversal from favorable balances on current account to deficit ones during the mid-1980s.

Foreigners shopping around the world for attractive investment opportunities found them right here in the United States. In very few other economies did they find such inviting combinations of investment security and reasonable rates of return. Not surprisingly, then, foreigners invested in the U.S. economy, supplying their own currencies on the foreign exchange market and demanding U.S. dollars.

But consider what this popular demand for U.S. dollars does to the U.S. exchange rate. It drives it up. We need fewer U.S. dollars to buy foreign currencies. At the same time, it becomes more expensive for foreigners to buy U.S. dollars. *We now find foreign goods relatively inexpensive in terms of dollars, while foreigners find our goods increasingly expensive in terms of their currencies.* As a result, we import more and export less. If foreigners persist in viewing our economy as a popular domicile for their investments, we may end up with deficits on current account.

The High Cost of High Interest Rates

High interest rates in the United States make dollars attractive for foreigners to hold, which in turn causes the dollar to appreciate.

We can arrive at the same deficit on current account when our interest rates climb above those prevailing in other economies. Canadians, for example, compare interest rates offered at home and abroad and choose those yielding the highest rates. Many individuals, regardless of nationality, invest in securities offering the highest rates. The rising U.S. interest rates in the 1980s shifted the demand curve for the U.S. dollar to the right, driving up the exchange rate on the U.S. dollar. As a result, it made imports more attractive, our exports less attractive.

In this same way, domestically driven monetary policy can inadvertently affect the balance on current account. If the Fed, fighting an inflationary drift in the economy, raises its discount rate, it may trigger an increase in interest rates throughout the U.S. banking system. The effects do not stop at the U.S. borders. If the interest rates in the United States climb above foreign rates, the demand for U.S. dollars will increase. The effects of an appreciated U.S. dollar on our imports and exports create the deficit on current account.

The High Cost of Budgetary Deficits

Keeping in mind this link between exchange rates and interest rates, imagine what happens to the deficit on current account when the government, pursuing

ADDED PERSPECTIVE

The December 1994 Plunge of the Mexican Peso

The roughly 35 percent slide in the value of the Mexican peso against the U.S. dollar in just one month—from just under $.29 per peso on December 19, 1994 to just over $.18 per peso on January 19, 1995—left millions of American investors, as well as Mexican banks, exporters, and working people financially bruised and uncertain about their stake in Mexico's immediate future. Other developing economies in the southern hemisphere, such as Argentina and Brazil, were also affected. For years the Mexican peso was both strong and stable. Why then the December 1994 debacle? What precipitated the peso's decline?

In the 1980s President Carlos Salinas thought he could turn Mexico into another Singapore. Hoping to accelerate economic growth and raise standards of living, he tried to change the focus of Mexico's economy from a system of government-engineered growth to one of open-ended, free-market activity. But for that to happen Mexico needed massive foreign investment, and to attract it President Salinas knew that the peso had to be both strong and stable. For much of the 1980s and 1990s, that's precisely what it was.

Responding to President Salinas' initiatives, American businesses migrated south to Mexico to take advantage of low-wage production. And to a larger extent, American dollars, anticipating great things for the Mexican economy, crossed the border as portfolio investment in Mexican businesses. The Mexican stock market boomed, confirming what foreign investors had anticipated. Mexico's economic successes during the 1980s and 1990s produced a continuing demand for pesos (and supply of dollars) on the foreign exchange market. The peso, fixed by government at $.29, was clearly undervalued. The strength of the peso, the buoyancy of the stock market, and the steady migration of dollars to Mexico were mutually reinforcing. The booming Mexican economy became a lucrative market for American exports, and even though Mexico ran a deficit on its current account—the value of Mexican imports exceeded the value of Mexican exports—the strong dollar inflows kept the peso strong. There seemed to be no reason at all why newly elected President Ernesto Zedillo, who succeeded Salinas in 1994, should not expect to look forward to years of sustained economic growth.

Then, almost overnight, it all unraveled. First, the peasant uprising in early 1994 in Chiapas along with the Mexican government's inept handling of the uprising, and later, two major political murders, made foreign investors nervous. Until then, Mexican politics were an inconsequential matter to foreign investors. Now they became an issue of paramount importance. Uncertainty replaced optimism. The financial markets in both Mexico and the United States responded in predictable ways. The dollar migration to Mexico virtually ceased. Capital began to flow out of Mexico's booming stock market. Stock prices fell. Suddenly, the bloom was off the Mexican economic rose.

To add to Mexico's woes, the Fed raised interest rates in the United States to prevent a resurgence of inflation; to stay competitive (for investment dollars), Mexico was forced to follow suit. The higher interest rates in Mexico put an additional damper on its economic activity. Unemployment rose. With imports still vastly exceeding exports, devaluation of the peso seemed inevitable. But unwilling to renege on a pledge not to devalue, the government supported its deficit on current account by draining Mexico's foreign reserves, allowing them to fall from $29 billion in February to $7 billion in December.

This strategy had no chance of succeeding in an environment of continuing capital outflow and massive imports. To the surprise and dismay of U.S. investors, President Zedillo, on December 20, 1994, finally yielded. The peso was devalued 13 percent. This devaluation, however, did not come close to reflecting investors' altered perceptions of Mexico's new reality. Allowed now to float freely on the foreign exchange market, the value of the peso kept sliding, hitting a low of just under $.18. Among the devaluation victims were:

- *Foreign investors.* Americans held more than $75 billion of Mexican securities. When the peso was devalued, whoever was still holding peso investments, would stand to lose. As well, hundreds of U.S. stock or money market mutual funds that kept a fraction of their assets in Mexico took a direct hit.
- *U.S. exporters.* Mexico's days as a magnet for anything Made in the U.S.A. came to an abrupt end. Living with a much-devalued peso, Mexicans could no longer afford the Lincoln Town Cars,

Dallas Cowboy T-shirts, and Atlantic Records CDs that had become commonplace in Mexican household consumption.

- *Mexican companies.* Higher interest rates put many small Mexican companies on the brink of bankruptcy. Some big ones as well fell upon troubled times, especially those earning pesos and paying debts in dollars.
- *Latin America.* Because some Latin American currencies, including Argentina's peso, were widely considered to be overvalued, the Mexican peso plunge spooked stock markets and drove up interest rates as far away as Buenos Aires and São Paulo. Their own currencies were in danger of crashing.

Was there no stopping the Mexican peso free-fall? Help came from Mexico's NAFTA allies. The United States and Canada provided effective damage control. Believing that the precipitous fall in the peso reflected more an unwarranted investor panic than the real performance of the Mexican economy, Mexico's NAFTA partners came to the peso's rescue by loaning Mexico sufficient U.S. and Canadian dollars to stabilize the price of the peso on the foreign exchange market.

Does the story end happily ever after? In a way, it does. After all, *devaluation is precisely what the Mexican economy needed.* Most economists believe that Mexico's long-run prospects are still as good as President Salinas predicted a decade ago. When the dust clouds of investor anxiety finally settle, economists believe the devalued peso will work its wonders. It should increase Mexico's potential for exports by cutting their prices (in terms of dollars). The weaker peso will also help keep Mexico's imports down, correcting the deficit on its current account. And with more pesos per dollar, Mexican securities will once again attract foreign investors who will see investments in Mexico as cheap buys.

a purely domestic fiscal policy, finances its deficit budget by selling government securities. If it offers a relatively high interest rate to attract buyers, wouldn't foreigners be just as receptive to the securities offer as Americans?

In order to finance budget deficits, interest rates must be maintained at high levels, which causes the dollar to appreciate.

Budgetary deficits can affect exchange rates and, consequently, balances on current account. Moreover, government securities in the hands of foreigners represent IOUs that must be honored. Eventually we will have to either sell off some of our real assets or export goods of equivalent value to pay foreigners holding U.S. securities.

The High Cost of Low Productivity

There's little that the government can do—even correcting for troublemaking monetary and fiscal policies—if the economy's level of productivity, compared to the levels of productivity in other economies, is low and falling. Maintaining export markets becomes increasingly difficult for industries that cannot keep pace with foreign prices and quality. In fact, when confronted by stiff foreign competition, even domestic producers have only an uncertain hold on their own domestic markets.

An economy that has low productivity cannot compete effectively in export markets.

In an economy characterized by low productivity, there are no quick-fix solutions. Unless its industries make the effort to match foreign competition by adopting successful technologies or by creating a more productive culture within its management and labor force, the economy's balance on current account position will steadily worsen.

How serious can a trade imbalance become? How much can an economy borrow or how much of its assets can it sell to finance chronic deficits on current account before pressure builds up to force changes in its exchange rate? Ultimately, depreciation of its rate must occur, making its exports cheaper and its imports more expensive.

But unless a low-productivity economy confronts the problem of its low-level productivity, even exchange rate adjustments won't work in the long run.

TRADE BALANCES: JAPAN, SAUDI ARABIA, MEXICO, AND EGYPT

The Japanese are sometimes described as workaholics. Their work ethic, coupled with their unrelenting export drive, harvested a string of positive annual trade balances over the past 20 years, as Figure 6 shows, that generated an impressive accumulation of dollar reserves. Japan's trade balance in 1993 alone added $141.5 billion to its reserves.

When will the Japanese start to consume more and invest less?

Nor did the Japanese just sit on their sizable reserves. They were used to purchase income-generating properties overseas. (Among its more publicized acquisitions were New York's landmark Rockefeller Plaza and the mega-entertainment properties of MCA.) In 1989 alone, Japan acquired over $50 billion of physical assets in the United States and over $30 billion in Western Europe.

Saudi Arabia's annual trade balances over the 1973–1993 period have little to do with work ethic or export-drive strategy. They result primarily from sky-rocketing oil prices during the 1970s and 1980s. By 1981, the Saudi trade balance reached $82 billion. Although Saudi Arabia opened the floodgates on imports during these decades, investing heavily in infrastructure, building new industries, experimenting with new agricultural technologies, acquiring massive quantities of consumer goods, the value of imports simply couldn't keep pace with Saudi exports. The sudden collapse of oil prices (although never falling to pre-1973 levels) during the mid-1980s accounts for the dramatic dip in the Saudi trade balance depicted in Figure 6.

Mexico, also a major oil exporter, enjoyed enormous export revenues. Yet, its annual trade balances, also shown in Figure 6, were actually negative for most of the 1973 to 1993 years.

What were the Mexicans doing wrong? If anything, they were guessing incorrectly—like almost everyone else—on future oil prices. Expecting oil prices to continue to escalate, Mexicans plunged headlong into massive imports of both capital goods and consumption goods to promote ambitious, government-sponsored development programs. Was such a policy really a mistake? In retrospect, it drove Mexico into severe balance of payments problems, although it also promoted Mexico's impressive 1980s industrialization.

A very different set of trade-balance problems confront most of the non-oil-producing, less-developed countries of the world such as Bangladesh, Kenya, India, Pakistan, Chad, Sri Lanka, Thailand, Sudan, Philippines, Tunisia, Jordan, Tanzania, Guatemala, and Egypt. In most of these countries, annual trade balances through the 1973 to 1993 period were negative for every year.

Egypt's annual trade-balance performance, shown in Figure 6, is typical for the less-developed countries. To varying degrees, many of them face the same export and import problems. First among their trade-balance concerns is their worsening terms of trade. For most, their imports satisfy basic and immediate human needs such as food and energy which are difficult to cut and economic development needs which if cut have dire negative consequences on long-term economic performance. Their exports, typically concentrated in agricultural and mining goods such as cotton, copper, tea, bauxite, bananas, and sugar, are sub-

FIGURE 6 **Trade Balance: Japan, Saudi Arabia, Mexico, and Egypt**

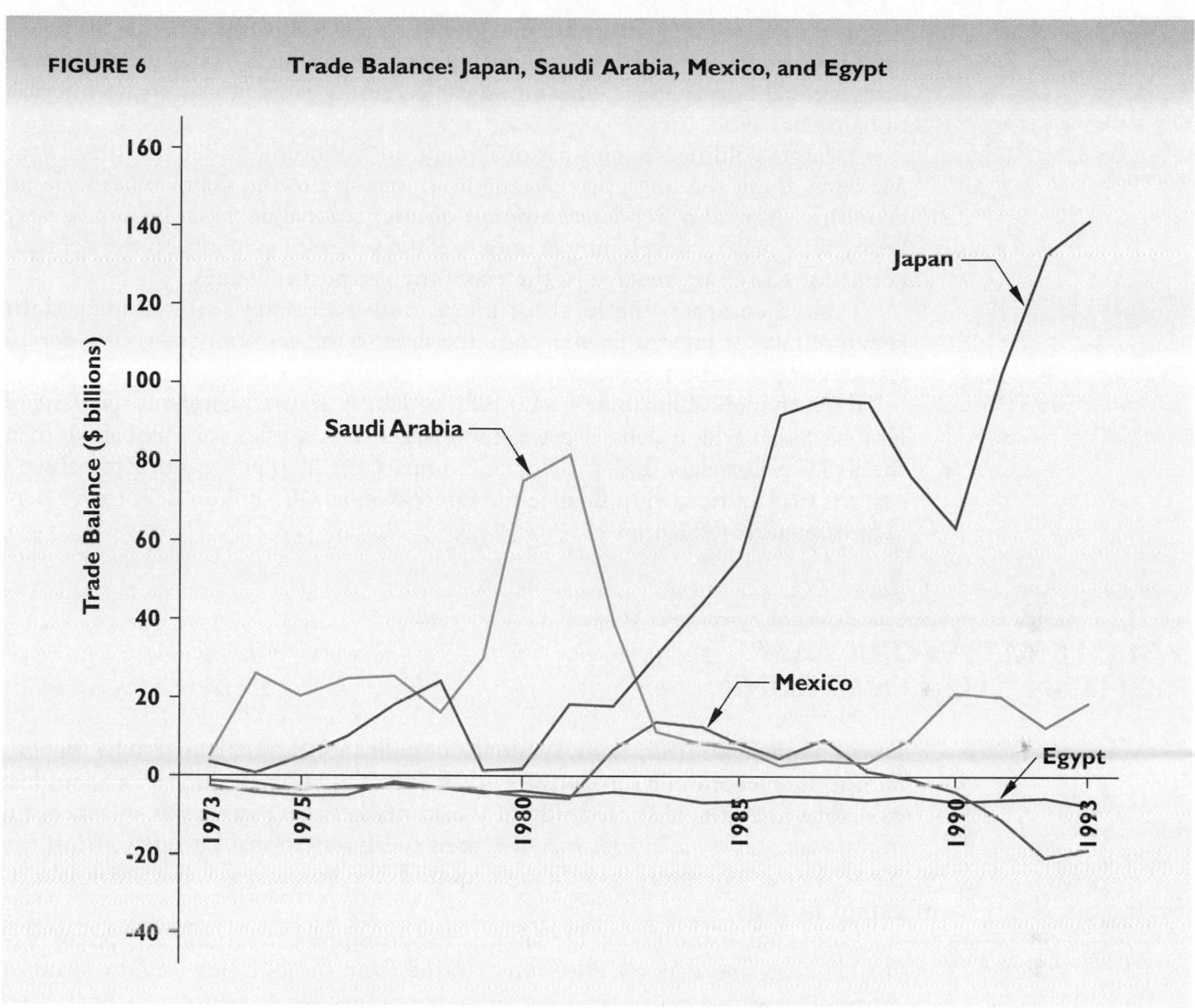

ject to prices that are unreliable and markets that are relatively weak and in some cases disappearing.

As a result, even with stringent exchange and import controls, and with a willingness to devalue currencies, many of these less-developed countries still must end up borrowing abroad to cover their negative trade balances. Who lends to them? Who accepts their IOUs? Many find a market for their government bonds (IOUs) in a variety of lending institutions, including private banks, sympathetic governments, and international agencies such as the World Bank. Together, these outstanding bonds represent sizable international debt that in recent years has come to dominate financial relations between the industrial advanced and less-developed countries.

INTERNATIONAL DEBT

It isn't only the very low-income, low-productivity, less-developed economies that make their way to lending institutions. In many cases, it is economies with higher incomes, among them relatively high performers that still find themselves

International debt

The total amount of outstanding IOUs a nation is obligated to repay other nations and international organizations.

strapped to substantial **international debt.** It doesn't matter whether an economy is borrowing to survive or borrowing to sustain high-gear development—both are still borrowing. If the high-gear economy jams, it can create international debt havoc.

A large volume of international debt in economies such as Brazil's or Mexico's is not the only, or even the best, measure of the debt's burden on an economy. A small or moderate amount of international debt can become a very heavy burden on a developing economy if the interest payments on the debt account for a large percentage of the economy's export revenues.

Debt service

Interest payments on international debt as a percentage of a nation's merchandise exports.

Table 2 compares the levels of international debt and corresponding **debt service** (ratio of interest payments on the debt to the economy's exports) for 10 less-developed debtor economies.

Even though Zimbabwe's $4.0 billion debt is approximately 10 percent of Korea's $43.0 billion debt, it generates a larger debt service for Zimbabwe than the $43.0 billion debt does for Korea. Compare the 32.0 percent of Zimbabwe's exports that are needed to finance the interest on its $4.0 billion debt to 7.4 percent of exports for Korea.

WILL IT ALL WORK OUT RIGHT IN THE *LONG* RUN?

A persistent negative current account balance will lead to a currency depreciation that will eventually lead to a zero current account balance, perhaps at the expense of living standards.

David Hume, an 18th century political philosopher, explained why Spain's demise as an economic superpower was inevitable. Hume argued that Spain lost its ability to compete successfully in world markets because it was so successful in amassing great quantities of gold, then the international currency, from the New World. The more gold Spain acquired, the less able it was to maintain its export markets.

Hume understood why. He saw the relationship between money, prices, exchange rates, and exports. As money, in the form of gold, flowed into Spain, it drove up Spanish prices, making foreign imports less expensive in Spain and Spanish exports more expensive abroad. As a result, Spain's balance on current account became negative, with gold now flowing out of the country. It was as unavoidable as the common cold.

We can apply that same logic to our 20th century economies. In spite of what they try to do, economies with negative balances on current account will find their exchange rates falling. And unless these rates are propped up by government intervention, they will fall to stem the currency outflows. As long as a negative balance exists, the exchange rate will keep on falling. Eventually, the rate will reach the level appropriate to a zero balance on current account. It only takes time.

This automatic correction mechanism, however, may also push the economy into lower living standards. Some people may be pleased when the economy's exchange rate generates a zero trade balance, but it is somewhat less pleasing if the economy cannot afford to provide the majority of its population with the necessities of life.

In many cases, that is indeed what results. If the Egyptian pound, for example, is driven so low relative to the U.S. dollar that its people lose the ability to import needed food, then whatever the equilibrium level of its exchange rate, Egypt's standard of life falls. Equilibrium levels of exchange rates, perhaps inevitable, do not guarantee a desirable outcome.

TABLE 2
Debt Service as a Percentage of Exports: 1992

Low-Level Debt Economies			High-Level Debt Economies		
	Debt	Debt Service		Debt	Debt Service
Ghana	$4.3	26.7	Brazil	$121.8	23.1
Zimbabwe	4.0	32.0	Mexico	113.4	44.4
Ethiopia	4.4	14.2	India	77.0	25.3
Kenya	6.4	27.1	Egypt	40.0	27.1
Sri Lanka	6.4	13.5	Korea	43.0	7.4

Source: *The World Development Report, 1994* (New York: Oxford University Press, 1994) pp. 200–207.

But what's to be done? Is there anything the less-developed economies like Egypt and Zimbabwe can do to correct their international trade and debt problems? Perhaps the starting point is first to understand why their economies look the way they do. That's the task we set for ourselves in the next chapter.

CHAPTER REVIEW

1. Foreign exchange markets allow people to convert their currencies so that they may purchase goods from other countries. The exchange rate is the price set in foreign exchange markets that determines how much of one currency must be exchanged for one unit of another currency. As the exchange rate falls, the quantity demanded of a currency will increase, so the demand curve for a currency is downward-sloping. As the exchange rate for a currency rises, the quantity supplied of the currency will increase, so the supply curve for a currency is upward-sloping.

2. The demand for dollars will increase when incomes abroad increase, when tastes change in favor of U.S. goods and services, and when the interest rate in the U.S. increases. The supply of dollars increases when incomes in the U.S. in crease, when American tastes favor foreign goods, and when interest rates in the U.S. fall relative to interest rates in other countries. Shifts in the demand and supply curves for a currency create changes in the equilibrium exchange rate.

3. The array of exchange rates that is established floats freely as changes occur in the international market for goods and capital. A particular currency appreciates relative to another when it takes less of the currency to purchase the other. Similarly, a currency depreciates relative to another when it takes more of the currency to purchase the other.

4. Fixing exchange rates eliminates the uncertainty that accompanies floating exchange rates, but other problems may arise. The government may have to intervene in currency markets to maintain the stated exchange rate. Suppose the demand for a currency increases, causing an excess demand for it. The government will enter the market and supply needed currency to keep the rate fixed. However, the government's reserves of foreign currencies can run dry stretched in this way.

5. An economy's balance of payments account describes its financial transactions with the rest of the world. The current account adds up exports and im-

ports of merchandise and services, income payments and receipts on investments, and unilateral transfers. The capital account shows the sum of changes in the value of our overseas assets and the value of foreign assets in the United States. The difference between merchandise exports and merchandise imports is the balance of trade. When imports exceed exports there is a balance-of-trade deficit.

6. Exports of services occur when foreigners purchase U.S. services. When Americans travel overseas they create service imports. When we earn income on our investments overseas, an inflow of dollars from the rest of the world is created. Similarly, when foreign companies operating in the United States earn profits, dollars flow abroad. Unilateral transfers are payments by individuals that are sent abroad and exchanged for a foreign currency.

7. The capital account line for changes in U.S. assets abroad shows the extent to which firms in the United States have invested overseas. These investments create an outflow of dollars. Foreign firms' investments in the United States show up as changes in foreign assets in the United States. Such investments create an inflow of dollars.

8. If the outflow of dollars to pay for imports exceeds the inflow of dollars to pay for exports, then the difference must be financed. Four financing options exist. Reserves of foreign currency can be drawn down. Domestic assets can be sold. Government securities can be sold. Or, a country can go into foreign exchange markets and borrow the difference.

9. It may make sense for a country to import more than it exports if the kinds of goods being imported contribute to future gains in productivity.

10. Japan has maintained positive trade balances and invested the inflows of foreign currencies back into overseas assets. The oil-exporting economies were able either to enjoy massive trade surpluses, as did Saudi Arabia, or to import large quantities of capital and consumer goods, as Mexico did. As oil prices fell in the mid 1980s, Mexico experienced balance of payments problems.

11. Developing countries often struggle to maintain their balance of payments due to limited export capacities. Some developing countries, like Egypt, rely on remittances from Egyptian workers in foreign countries to prop up the balance of payments. Sometimes, developing countries must borrow in order to cover their deficits on current account.

12. International debt can become a problem for a developing country if interest payments on the debt take a large percentage of export revenues. The debt service is the percentage of a country's exports that interest payments on the debt represent.

KEY TERMS

Foreign exchange market
Exchange rate
Floating exchange rate
Appreciation
Depreciation
Arbitrage
Fixed exchange rate
Foreign exchange reserves
Import controls
Exchange controls
Balance of payments
Balance on current account

Balance of trade
Unilateral transfers
Balance on capital account
International debt
Devaluation
Debt service

QUESTIONS

1. Why would anyone in Butte, Montana, or Lyons, France, want yaps?

2. How could people get the yaps they want?

3. Suppose the equilibrium exchange rate is $3 per yap. Explain what that rate signifies in terms of quantities of goods imported and exported.

4. What does arbitrage mean, and how does it work?

5. How can the government fix an exchange rate? Can the government fix it at any level, for any length of time? Discuss the limitations that a government faces in maintaining a fixed rate.

6. What control mechanisms can a government introduce to support its exchange rate policy?

7. What are the major categories and items in a balance of payments account?

8. How would each of the following affect the U.S. balance of payments account:
   (a) A Bangladeshi professor at the University of Utah sends $200 to his family living in Bangladesh every month.
   (b) A Japanese businessperson in Nagasaki buys 100 shares of General Motors stock.
   (c) The U.S. government sells 20 Patriot missiles to the Israeli government.
   (d) The U.S. government gives the Russian government 50 million tons of wheat, priced at $3 per ton, in the form of a unilateral transfer.

9. In some cases, a balance of payments problem really isn't a problem at all. Yet, in other cases, it could signal a fundamental problem in the economy. Explain.

10. Some economists argue that our budgetary deficits contribute to our balance of payments problems. How do they make their case?

11. Balance of payments problems and long-term international debt plague the less-developed economies. The two issues are related. Explain.

12. Can Japan go on forever exporting more than it imports? Explain.

13. Suppose the following data represent the international transactions of a South Pacific island economy.

Merchandise exports	$10
Change in foreign assets in the South Pacific island	2
Export of services	5
Income receipts on investment	3
Income payments on investment	−2
Unilateral transfers	−1
Merchandise imports	−8
Change in assets abroad	−5
Imports of services	−1

What is the South Pacific island's balance of trade? What is its balance on current account? What is its balance on capital account? Does the island seem to have a balance of payments problem?

14. Draw demand and supply curves for U.S. dollars and show how each of the following events affects either the demand curve or the supply curve and the rate of exchange. Assume Mexican pesos for U.S. dollars.
   (a) A U.S. manufacturer of slippers moves its factory from New Jersey to Mexico.
   (b) Hilton builds a new 150 room hotel in Acapulco.
   (c) The United States removes its tariff on Mexican carpets.
   (d) Mexican citizens who work in the United States increase the amount of money they send back to their families in Mexico.
   (e) A U.S. economist is hired by a Mexican firm to represent its case on an environmental issue in a Mexican court.

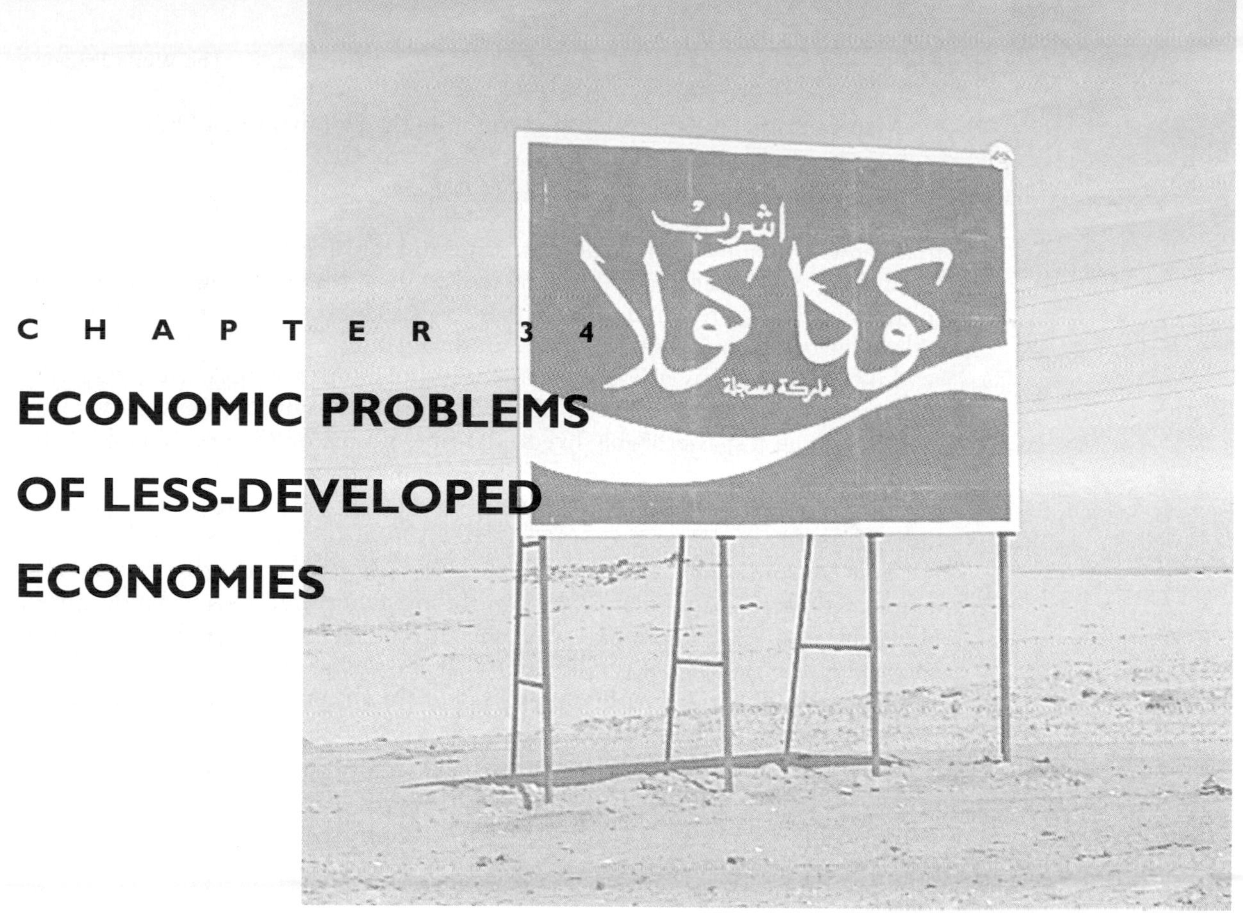

CHAPTER 34

ECONOMIC PROBLEMS OF LESS-DEVELOPED ECONOMIES

CHAPTER PREVIEW

The advent of satellite communications and 24-hour news networks have made it painfully evident that much of the world exists at a standard of living that is vastly lower than ours. The countries comprising the lower end of the world's income distribution are called the less-developed countries. Why are they poor? What can be done to improve the plight of their people? Are some of these countries experiencing success in raising living standards by embarking on development paths? We'll explore these questions in the following pages.

After studying this chapter, you should be able to:

- Explain how the term less-developed countries came into use by economists.
- Describe the variations in economic circumstances that exist among LDCs.
- Show how rapid population growth makes achieving growth in per capita incomes more difficult for LDCs.
- Compare growth in agricultural output with growth in industrial output as a source of GDP growth in the LDCs.
- Discuss the role that investments in human capital play in the development process.
- Give examples of economic dualism.
- List and explain factors that slow down or prevent economic development.

- Map out different strategies for economic development in LDCs.

Imagine two infants born at the very same instant, one in the delivery room of the maternity ward at Barnes Hospital in St. Louis, Missouri, the other in a one-room, earthen floored, mud brick home in El Fashn, a small village along the Nile river in Egypt, about 150 miles south of Cairo.

Like all newborns, these are two beautiful human beings. But, tragically, they face very different futures. The Missouri baby will probably survive the early years and just as probably live to the ripe old age of 85. The El Fashn baby, on the other hand, will have a much less certain chance of surviving to the first birthday, and according to life tables for Egypt, has a life expectancy at birth of only 62 years.

The Missouri baby, like most in the United States, can expect to attend a day-care center, and then at age 5 join the neighborhood kids in kindergarten. Her education is compulsory; she will attend elementary and high school. Moreover, the probability is quite high that she will graduate from some college or university with a degree that prepares her for an intellectually and financially rewarding productive life.

What about her counterpart in Egypt? The El Fashn infant may learn how to read and write, but the chances of her acquiring an advanced degree are rather remote. She will probably marry at an early age, have more than seven children, and work long, hard hours on a few nonirrigated cultivated acres surrounding the village.

Perhaps the most disheartening part of this tale of two cities, at least for the Egyptian baby, is that the story repeats. Her children will probably face similar prospects. The unfairness—isn't it unfair?—continues.

CONFRONTING NATIONAL POVERTY

Being poor is certainly no crime. But *accepting* poverty and allowing it to continue unchecked seems to be, perhaps, not only a crime against the population's impoverished victims, but against those generations of impoverished yet to come. Who's to blame? Obviously, people whose standards of life are not much above physical subsistence don't *choose* to remain poor. The world they inhabit affords them little choice. Is their national poverty, then, inevitable? Is there nothing anyone can do?

Economists, at least since the early 1950s, focused some attention on the issue of persisting national poverty in the economies of Asia, Africa, and Latin America. It was clear in 1950, and even clearer now, that the kinds of problems confronting these economies in their attempt to achieve higher standards of living differ fundamentally from those faced by the industrial economies of the West.

The Language of National Poverty

The language used by economists to describe these economies has changed over time. In the 1950s, economists began to take a hard, closer look at the

Economic backwardness and underdevelopment, terms formerly used to describe the plight of poorer nations, have been replaced by the term less-developed countries.

economies of Asia, Africa, and Latin America. For the first time they were seen as something more than trading posts for our raw materials. During that period, economists were quick to identify their national poverty as endemic, the consequence of economic *backwardness* or *underdevelopment*.

The terms seemed appropriate. The differences between Canada and Egypt, for example, cannot be measured in terms of higher or lower GDP. The real differences are not quantitative, but qualitative. Egypt's inability to raise its standards of living has more to do with its social, political, and economic institutions and with its perceptions of past, present, and future than with lack of effort or personal talents.

Economies that have yet to invest in basic energy, housing, education, or transportation systems, or that have yet to develop legal, financial, and communication systems to support modern ways of producing goods and services simply cannot compete in the same economic world as the industrial economics of the West. In this sense, the terms backwardness and underdevelopment conveyed that idea.

Less-developed countries (LDCs)

Economies of Asia, Africa, and Latin America.

But in the 1960s, economists dropped the terms backwardness and underdevelopment in favor of **less-developed countries (LDCs).** The change reflected the view that backwardness and underdevelopment were terms that were much too prejudicial. After all, many Asian, African, and Latin American societies, although poor and lacking the prerequisites of development, were in other respects the equals of their counterparts in the West. The United Nations, with expanding memberships from the newly independent, former colonics had much to do with promoting this language change.

There Are Important Differences Among the Less-Developed Economies

Sometimes, labels can be misleading. Many of the less-developed economies have, indeed, made considerable progress. For example, in the past 25 years, Brazil, Korea, Singapore, Hong Kong, Israel, Taiwan, and Iran have made rather spectacular leaps in modernizing and developing their economies, achieving for their people substantially higher levels of per capita income. And many other developing economies made moderate progress.

But many others haven't. Some LDCs still seem to be stalled in a mode that keeps yielding, decade after decade, the same kinds of subsistence-level incomes and the same employment opportunities and investment patterns that inhibit them from making even very modest transitions to modernization.

LDC PER CAPITA INCOMES

LDC per capita incomes and growth rates vary widely between countries.

While there is no consensus among economists concerning just what specific level of per capita income or what specific rate of output growth would allow us to identify LDCs, *some* levels and *some* rates are so obviously troublesome that economists have little difficulty making the identification.

Table 1 compares the income performance records of some of the 94 LDCs of the world.

The data in Table 1 are about as striking and painfully clear as any set of income numbers can possibly be. Even though you have to be on guard against translating these incomes into the purchasing power they would represent in our own economy, still would you question the economic impoverishment they suggest?

Look at Ethiopia's $120 and Bangladesh's $170 per capita income for 1988. Consider the per capita income growth rates for these economies over the 1965–88 period. How can an average annual 1.5 percent growth rate for low-income LDCs suggest anything but economic sluggishness?

TABLE 1
1988 per Capita Income and per Capita Average Annual Growth Rate 1965–88 for Selected LDC Economies ($ 1988 U.S.)

	Per Capita Income	Growth Rate of per Capita Income
Low-Income Economies	**$320**	**1.5**
Ethiopia	$120	−0.1
Bangladesh	170	0.4
Zaire	170	−2.1
Zambia	290	−2.1
Pakistan	350	2.5
Kenya	370	1.9
Ghana	400	−2.1
Lower Middle-Income Economies	**$1,380**	**2.6**
Bolivia	570	−0.6
Zimbabwe	650	1.0
Egypt	660	3.6
Morocco	830	2.3
Honduras	860	0.6
Jamaica	1,070	−1.5
Peru	1,300	0.1
Upper Middle-Income Economies	**$3,240**	**2.3**
Algeria	2,360	2.7
Argentina	2,767	0.0
Gabon	2,970	0.9
Venezuela	3,250	−0.9
Trinidad	3,350	0.9
South Korea	3,600	6.8

Source: The World Bank, *World Development Report, 1990* (New York: Oxford University Press, 1990), pp. 178–9.

Note: China and India are not included in Low-Income Economies.

LDC POPULATION GROWTH

With birth rates far surpassing death rates, LDC populations are growing very rapidly.

How successful an economy is in achieving higher per capita incomes depends as much on containing population growth as it does upon promoting higher levels of income. If population grows faster than income, then per capita income falls. It's simple but devastating arithmetic.

Therein lies the LDCs' double-whammy problem. While their economies' income growth has been unimpressive, their population growth has been *too* impressive.

Table 2 records the percentage change in crude birth rates, crude death rates, and average annual population growth for the economies of Table 1.

How should we read Table 2? Crude birth rates measure the number of people born per 1,000 population. Crude death rates measure the number that died per 1,000 population. The difference tells us how many were added to, or subtracted from the 1,000 population over the course of the year.

TABLE 2 Percentage Change in Crude Birth Rates and Crude Death Rates, and Average Annual Population Growth: 1965–88

	Birth Rates		Death Rates		Population Growth Rates	
	1965	1988	1965	1988	1965/88	1980/88
Low Income	**46**	**41**	**21**	**13**	**2.6**	**2.8**
Ethiopia	49	45	27	17	2.7	2.9
Bangladesh	47	40	21	15	2.7	2.8
Zaire	47	45	21	14	2.8	3.1
Ghana	47	45	18	13	2.2	3.4
Pakistan	48	46	21	13	3.1	3.2
Zambia	49	50	20	13	3.0	3.7
Lower Middle	**41**	**30**	**13**	**8**	**2.5**	**2.3**
Bolivia	46	42	21	14	2.5	2.7
Egypt	43	34	19	9	2.1	2.6
Zimbabwe	55	38	17	8	3.1	3.7
Honduras	51	39	17	8	3.2	3.6
Jamaica	38	23	9	6	1.3	1.5
Peru	45	31	16	9	2.8	2.2
Morocco	49	35	18	9	2.5	2.7
Upper Middle	**31**	**26**	**12**	**8**	**2.0**	**1.8**
Algeria	50	37	18	8	3.1	3.1
Gabon	31	42	22	16	3.6	3.9
Argentina	23	21	9	9	1.6	1.4
Korea	35	16	11	6	2.0	1.2
Trinidad	33	26	8	6	1.1	1.7
Venezuela	42	30	8	5	3.5	2.8

Source: The World Bank, *World Development Report, 1990* (New York: Oxford University Press, 1990), pp. 254–7.

As you see, the single, most important factor contributing to Ethiopia's population increase was the decline in its death rate. Although its birth rate fell from 49 to 45 per 1,000 population, these diminishing additions to Ethiopia's population were more than offset by the concurrent fall in its death rate, from 27 to 17 per 1,000 population. That is to say, many more were not dying than were not being born. As a result, population growth rates increased.

Look at the demographic data for the LDCs of Table 2. Declining death rates seem to explain their population increases. Not very surprising. After all, changes in birth rates reflect changes in society's habits and customs, and these tend to be associated with cultural and religious values that are sometimes quite resistant to change. Death rates, on the other hand, can be cut dramatically by simple hygiene and by use of modern technology, such as DDT and penicillin.

What does Zambia's 3.7 percent population increase signal for its per capita income future? It means that Zambia's annual rate of output must grow at 3.7 percent per year just to maintain its $290 per capita 1988 income level.

LDC OUTPUT GROWTH

What's happened to the LDCs' output? Table 3 records LDC production performance for the 23 years, 1965 through 1988.

Industry growth is a greater source of GDP growth for most LDC countries than is agricultural growth.

As you see, output growth in the LDCs for the period 1965–88 was hardly uniform or successful. If we're searching for a way out of the LDC poverty trap, there's not much to cheer about.

For 1965–88, Ghana's and Zaire's 1.4 percent and Zambia's 1.9 percent annual output performances are downright discouraging. Although less than exciting, Ethiopia's 2.7 percent, Bangladesh's 2.4 percent, Argentina's 3.5 percent, and Peru's 3.9 percent show some improvement.

EMPHASIS ON INDUSTRY GROWTH

Table 3 also signals where the LDC emphasis on output growth has been placed. For all—high and low performers alike—industry outperformed agriculture.

For the low-income LDCs, industrial output grew by 4.4 percent per year and agricultural output by 2.0 percent. Kenya's 9.8 percent and Pakistan's 6.4 percent industrial growth were atypical.

OTHER INDICATORS OF THE LDCS' LACK OF ECONOMIC WELL-BEING

Human capital

The investment in workers' knowledge acquired through education, training, and/or experience that enhances their productivity.

The most important contributor to the economic well-being of people in industrial economies has been investments in **human capital.** This refers to investments in people—in education, housing, and promotion of vocational skills to meet the challenges of new and modernizing technology.

But for most economies in Table 3, these human capital investments, however important, are extremely difficult to finance. Because LDCs are barely capable of providing minimal subsistence for their populations, they simply don't have the luxury of devoting the resources necessary to invest in human capital.

TABLE 3 Average Annual Growth Rates in GDP, Agriculture, and Industry, 1965–88 and 1980–88

	GDP		Agriculture		Industry	
	1965-88	**1980-88**	**1965-88**	**1980-88**	**1965-88**	**1980-88**
Low Income	**5.5**	**2.0**	**2.3**	**1.9**	**10.0**	**1.7**
Ethiopia	2.7	1.4	1.2	−1.1	3.5	3.5
Bangladesh	2.4	3.7	1.5	2.1	3.8	4.9
Zaire	1.4	1.9	3.2	2.5		
Kenya	6.4	4.2	4.9	2.8	9.8	2.0
Ghana	1.4	−2.1	1.6	−0.5	1.4	−1.9
Pakistan	5.1	6.5	3.3	4.3	6.4	7.2
Zambia	1.9	0.7	2.2	4.1	2.1	−0.3
Lower Middle	**6.5**	**2.6**	**3.3**	**2.8**	**7.8**	**2.5**
Bolivia	4.5	−1.6	3.8	2.1	3.7	−5.7
Egypt	6.8	5.7	2.7	2.6	6.9	5.1
Zimbabwe	5.0	2.7	2.5	1.7		
Honduras	5.0	1.7	2.0	1.1	6.8	0.8
Jamaica	1.3	0.6	0.5	0.9	−0.1	10.0
Peru	3.9	1.1	1.0	3.6	4.4	0.4
Morocco	5.6	4.2	2.4	6.6	6.1	2.8
Upper Middle	**5.6**	**3.3**	**3.2**	**2.5**	**4.7**	**3.7**
Algeria	6.0	3.5	5.7	5.6	7.1	3.8
Gabon	9.5	−0.2				
Argentina	3.5	−0.2	1.4	1.4	3.3	−0.8
Korea	9.3	9.9	3.0	3.7	16.6	12.6
Trinidad	5.1	−6.1	0.0	4.5	5.0	−8.6
Venezuela	3.7	0.9	3.9	3.8	1.5	−0.1

Source: The World Bank, *World Development Report, 1990* (New York: Oxford University Press, 1990), pp. 204–5.

Although rates of return on education and other investments in human capital are high, many LDCs lack the resources for these most basic types of investments.

Human capital investments, although productive, require considerable time to generate visible results. Better health improves a person's working efficiency. So does more education and better housing. But it takes time.

Table 4 provides some impressive evidence of the high rate of returns on human capital investments, particularly in LDC economies.

As you see, the 28 percent rate of return at the primary level is impressive. Abolishing illiteracy, then, should have the highest priority on any LDC list of productive investment. But that's not easily accomplished. Despite the solid evidence of Table 4, many LDCs still choose to channel investment into the lesser-performing agriculture and industrial sectors because their payoffs are more visible, more direct, and more immediate.

But opting for the visible, direct, and immediate creates for these economies an environment that reproduces much of their national poverty. Table 5 records the problem.

Life expectancy increases as income increases. Witness the changes among economies from the lower income, to the lower middle, and finally to the upper

TABLE 4 Economic Rates of Return in Education (percent)

	Level of Education		
	Primary	Secondary	Higher
Industrial economies	15	11	11
LDC manufacturing exporters	15	13	9
26 other LDCs	28	17	14

Source: The World Bank, *World Development Report 1987* (Washington, D.C.), p. 64.

Note: The economic rates of return on which these averages are based are from studies which, for the most part, refer to the 1970s and early 1980s.

middle. Not unexpected, is it? Look at the infant mortality rates. Do you see the relationship between these rates and the numbers of people per physician? They tell the same story. They are also related to the percent of people having access to safe water.

TABLE 5 Life Expectancy, Infant Mortality per 1,000 People, People per Physician, Percent School-Aged Population in School, and Percent of People with Safe Water

	Life Expectancy	Infant Mortality	People per Physician	Percent of School-Age Population	Percent of People with Safe Water
United States	76	9	416	99	100
Low Income					
Ethiopia	46	99	63,975	26	19
Bangladesh	52	114	6,304	65	81
Zaire	53	75	14,810	59	33
Kenya	60	68	7,388	91	30
Ghana	55	140	8,038	70	57
Pakistan	58	104	1,879	65	56
Zambia	54	72	8,913	80	60
Lower Middle					
Bolivia	55	102	1,630	83	53
Egypt	60	61	834	85	73
Zimbabwe	60	55	7,844	76	66
Peru	63	82	1,078	95	61
Morocco	62	75	5,110	55	61
Upper Middle					
Algeria	65	68	2,433	88	71
Argentina	71	31	336	83	65
Venezuela	70	35	605	61	90

Source: For 1989 data on life expectancy and infant mortality see *Statistical Abstract of the United States, 1990* (Washington, D.C.: U.S. Department of Commerce, 1990), pp. 835-6. For persons per physician, percent population in school, and percent of people having access to safe water, see Ruth L. Sivard, *World Military and Social Expenditures, 1986* (Washington, D.C.: World Priorities, 1992), pp. 32-41.

This Egyptian marketplace, or *suk*, is a commonplace institution in the villages and towns of traditional economies where almost every household item can be purchased: furniture, goat-skin handbags, cheeses, lambs' heads, saffron, lightbulbs, gold jewelry, herbs, eyeglasses, fruits and vegetables, and lately, Chicago Bulls T-shirts.

ECONOMIC DUALISM

Of course, not everybody in the LDCs suffers these basic deprivations. Some live as well as your neighbors. Many LDC doctors, lawyers, merchants, accountants, exporters and importers, manufacturers, hotel owners, bank managers, cosmetics salespeople, customs officials, and government clerks have access to safe water, to hospitals, to education, to decent housing, to telephones, to automobiles, and to a variety of imported durables that make their lives relatively comfortable.

The problem is that such a life style is reserved for the few. Most people in LDCs live in remote villages, in overpopulated cities or on their outskirts, in crowded, squalid shelters. Their employment, if they are employed, is typically in low-productivity agriculture, or marginal service-related jobs.

These two very different worlds exist side by side without affecting each other. Figure 1 illustrates this **economic dualism.**

Economic dualism

The coexistence of two separate and distinct economies within an LDC; one modern, primarily urban, and export-driven, the other traditional, agricultural, and self-sustaining.

The demand curve for workers, *D,* in the traditional sector of panel *a* is relatively low, reflecting low-level capital intensity, traditional technology, and weak prices. The supply curve of labor, *S,* reflects the availability of large numbers of unskilled workers with low opportunity costs willing and even anxious to work at minimum wage rates.

In comparison, the modern sector of panel *b* yields substantially higher wage rates. The demand curve, *D,′* reflects industrial technology applied to the export market, where productivity is higher and prices firmer. Its labor supply curve, *S,′* is relatively steep, reflecting the scarcity of technical skills in the LDCs.

This economic dualism tends to persist because the skills of those in the traditional sector are completely inadequate for the modern sector. They lack the education, the technological culture, and the specific talents, as well as the knowledge needed to obtain them. Although sharing the same geography, they are as far removed from that modern world as they are from the moon. The vast majority of these people are trapped in poverty conditions.

Tables 1 through 5 reveal the unhappy circumstances of LDC economic life.

FIGURE 1 Economic Dualism

In the traditional sector of the LDC, depicted in panel *a*, the demand curve for labor, *D*, is relatively low and flat. The relatively low opportunity costs associated with traditional labor produces the relatively flat supply curve of labor at relatively low wage rates, *S*. The traditional market, then, generates the relatively low equilibrium wage rate, *W*.

The modern sector of the LDC, depicted in panel *b*, contrasts sharply with the traditional sector of panel *a*. The demand curve for labor, *D′*, is higher. The higher opportunity costs associated with the skilled workers in this sector generates a steeper supply curve of labor, *S′*. The equilibrium wage rate is *W′*, considerably higher than *W*.

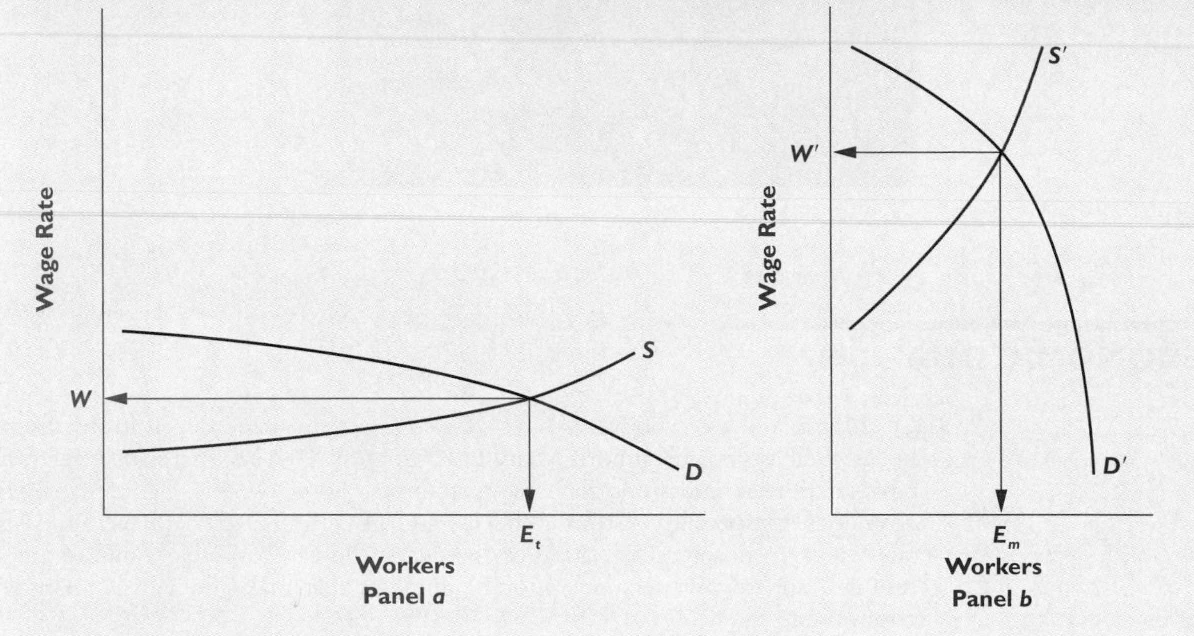

THE ABSENCE OF BASIC PREREQUISITES

Some things are so basic to the proper functioning of an economy and to economic progress in general, and so commonplace in our own economy, that we are sometimes inclined to overlook their importance.

Political Instability

Economic decision making is made vastly more complicated by the uncertainty associated with political instability.

For example, can you imagine how difficult it would be to plan our economic future if we thought that our government could not only be overthrown overnight, but that the character of our political system would change radically with the overthrow?

Laws become meaningless when governments, which displace each other too frequently and by force, are inclined to set aside past government commitments and, at times, even basic property rights. Such political discontinuities must interfere with routine economic decision making, increasing people's uncertainty everywhere in the economy.

For example, how can anyone rely on a military junta or on a revolutionary party government whose political support among the people is always questionable and whose legitimacy can be contested only in disruptive ways? How can such a regime provide confidence in anyone's economic future when its own time horizon is, by past experience, short?

In many LDC economies, juntas, single-party regimes, and puppet-like monarchies are precisely the kinds of governments that hold power. Generals in government are soon deposed by their colonels, and one revolutionary party is undone by another, with each new regime always claiming power on behalf of the people. For many, secret police and political prisoners are a matter of fact.

While some changes in regime may represent new faces in old uniforms or new revolutionary parties replacing old ones, many incoming regimes actually do go about undoing much in the economy.

Nonscientific Perceptions

A no-less fundamental factor inhibiting economic development is the perceptions LDC citizens have concerning their economic status, the societal goals they consider most desirable, and the accepted ways they go about pursuing them. These perceptions reflect both the psychological, religious, and cultural character of LDC economies.

THE POWER OF TRADITIONALISM

LDCs are marked by attitudes among many of their people that leave them disinclined to adopt modern methods of production and distribution that could create surpluses for the market.

Consider Table 2 once more. The high population growth rates are no accident. Large numbers of children are highly desired, particularly sons. The opportunity cost, measured in terms of sacrificed material goods and services, of having large families is clearly understood. *These are choices people make*. They just reflect a different set of accepted values.

Just as people in LDCs are reluctant to exchange large families for more goods, so also are they reluctant to part with known and accepted ways of producing goods for new and more productive ways. Their reliance on custom and tradition is a powerful inhibitor of development. In this respect, too, they differ substantially from the way people in industrial economies view technology. We are quick to discard the familiar when new goods or ways of producing them are offered.

That same healthy respect for custom and tradition works against their willingness to apply scientific methodology to the everyday business of life. Peasants are slow to adopt modern chemistry or even mechanization, and are disinclined to change the kind of crops they cultivate. Even if LDC governments were anxious to help the peasants increase productivity, the governments often confront resistance.

Infrastructure

The basic institutions and public facilities upon which an economy's development depends.

How do you overcome traditionalist perceptions of life or how do you modify the behavior of the ruling regimes? Without applying value judgments to either, they simply are dead weights to economic development. But unless some modification takes place, it is highly unlikely that tradition-bound LDC economies can make the transition to economic modernization.

The Absence of Infrastructure

While overcoming noneconomic barriers is critical to any effort at development, there are several economic barriers that pose equally as insurmountable obstacles. Among them is the conspicuous absence of economic **infrastructure.**

What is infrastructure? When we think about how our own economy works, we tend to take for granted the money and banking system that provides the major investment loans to our nation's businesses; the educational system that turns out the incredible varieties of skills and basic research that actually run our nation's production lines; the extensive transportation and communications system—interstate roads, railroads, airports, canals, telephones, computer lines, postal systems, television—that links almost every piece of our geography into one market; the energy system that powers our factories; and, of course, the market system itself, which brings our nation's goods and services into our households.

Transportation, communication, and energy facilities are necessary prerequisites for successful development programs.

Although the basic systems that make up our economic infrastructure were either completely absent or underdeveloped when the United States became a republic, they are now so second nature to us that we tend to overlook the fact that without them our national productive capacity would suddenly and dramatically collapse.

Imagine transplanting a modern Detroit automobile plant to Chad. Even if U.S. technicians were sent along to put it in place, this major piece of private direct investment would probably do the Chadians little good.

Why? Because physical plants themselves cannot create output. The manufacture of automobiles requires, at the least, a variety of skilled workers, engineers, accountants, salespeople, plant managers, and maintenance crews. Just who in Chad would be qualified? But that's just the beginning.

Who would do the financing? Chadians have always financed purchase of seed for their few acres or bought a milk cow with funds drawn from their own savings or from a moneylender, but neither the moneylender nor the saver is capable of financing an automobile plant. The Chadian banking system is still embryonic.

The plant, of course, requires some energy source. What good is the plant and its state-of-the-art machinery if there is no electricity to power it? Chad simply doesn't have the megawatts. But suppose it did, what's the point of the plant if there are no decent roads in the country?

Obviously, we've only scratched the surface of the problem. Even with a road system, it would still require an accessible service station industry, with ready stocks of fuel, spare parts, repair equipment, and most important, people with completely different sets of skills, to make it work. It gets rather complicated, doesn't it?

Where do all these skilled people come from? Without a modern educational system, the answer is nowhere. Too few colleges in Chad graduate engineers, accountants, and doctors. Its 22 percent literacy rate is critically low. Peasants farming in traditional ways rely upon experience, not education.

To educate people involves not only the monumental task of acquiring compliance—a population willing to send its children to school—but the funds needed to build the schools and to staff them. Where do these funds come from?

As you see, the automobile plant would quickly wither into disuse unless it was accompanied by an expansive set of direct and indirect investments. That's all but impossible. Chadians have neither the material nor human resources to undertake such a tremendous development departure. Chad's poverty trap seems to be rather formidable, doesn't it?

PURSUING STRATEGIES OF DEVELOPMENT

If you were asked to map out a grand strategy for economic development in Chad, just where would you begin? Economists have struggled with this vexing challenge and came up with essentially two competing strategies. Both focus on the task of breaking the vicious circle of underdevelopment that traps the LDCs into national poverty.

The vicious circle of underdevelopment refers to LDCs that are poor because of the underdeveloped state of their economies and that state of underdevelopment persists because they are poor. It's both logical and frustrating. The only way to cut into that self-sustaining trap is by massive doses of infrastructure and accompanying investments. But how? Is there a particular order or sequence of investing that works? Who does what investing? What role does government play? Can the private sector do it alone?

The Big Push

Big push

The development strategy that relies on an integrated network of government-sponsored and financed investments that are introduced into the economy all at once.

One idea that has found a receptive audience among development economists is the **big-push** strategy. It argues that because each potential investment's success depends upon there being a market for its output, none of the potential ever gets realized because none has ready markets.

How do you create ready markets for, say, 1,000 potential investment projects when none exist? By investing in the 1,000 projects *all at once*. That's the idea behind the big push.

For example, a new rubber tire plant would have no chance of succeeding unless it had an automobile plant to serve. Investing in both tire and automobile plants provides the ready market for the tire plant. Investing in road construction provides the beginnings of a market for automobiles and trucks. After all, the tire plant needs trucks to move its raw materials in and its tires out to market. Impossible without a road system, now possible with one. The road construction project itself needs trucks to move its equipment and materials. That, too, becomes a market for the auto plant.

Investments in steel and concrete production now become feasible because each can see a new, ready market. Steel is the primary raw material in automobile production. It is also needed in the construction of the physical plants. Concrete's major market emerges with road construction. Both steel and concrete works, of course, need trucks and automobiles. The automobile market expands.

You can see the connections to investments in the mining industries, can't you? Iron ore, if available, is used in the production of steel. If ore is produced,

This Coca-Cola sign cannot obscure the vast expanse of undeveloped desert that typifies Saudi Arabia. Yet note the electric lines that stretch across the landscape. The Saudis have committed much of their oil revenues to building infrastructure.

it finds a ready market in steel, which in turn becomes a market for automobiles and trucks. Of course, none of this could happen without the infrastructure investment in roads.

HOW BIG MUST A BIG PUSH BE?

The bigger the push, the more investment is involved and the greater is the potential for markets to develop. However, the big push must be carefully orchestrated so that bottlenecks in key economic sectors don't develop.

The bigger the total all-at-once investment commitment, the easier it is to generate ready, attractive markets for each project . And that's the trick. But it's just the first phase. Once the big push is introduced, creating ready markets for the interlocking projects, the growing markets in the economy make many other investment projects attractive.

In other words, the big-push strategy triggers a dynamic swelling of investments in the economy that serves to break through the vicious circle of underdevelopment. There is a critical minimum level required for a big push to set the strategy in motion. The initial projects must be carefully chosen to take advantage of the economy's human and material resources and synchronized to form interlocking markets. And each of the selected projects must be large enough to absorb the other outputs.

Is there an upper bound to a big push? Is bigger always better? The problem with grandiose big-push schemes is not only their cost, but the inevitability of confronting bottlenecks that can stall an otherwise well-planned strategy. Among the first of the serious bottlenecks confronted is the shortage of technical expertise and skilled production-line workers. There are always many in the economy eager to work, but almost as many lacking the simplest of skills required to operate modern technology.

Breakdowns in production lines are common to all economies, but if the skills and materials needed to maintain the lines are too few and spread too thinly across too many big-push projects, the big push becomes distorting and itself distorted. Like a picture puzzle, the pieces must be formed to fit and put together to make the fit, otherwise the picture is lost.

It sometimes pays to think in more modest and reasonable terms rather than pursue a big-push strategy, and to curb an ambitious development appetite in order to guarantee proper digestion.

WHO DOES THE PUSHING?

Big-push economists argue that such an interlocking, balanced set of infrastructure and development investments can only be initiated, financed, and managed by government. Why government? Because such a scheme not only requires long-term planning but its rewards are forthcoming only in the long run. Who else but government has a time horizon big enough to make such investments and wait upon their results?

Entrepreneurs in the private sector cannot be expected to invest long term in an economy with limited investment promise. After all, it is unreasonable to expect them to think that by the time their output is ready for market, there will be a market. What assurances do they have? How are they supposed to know others are thinking the same thoughts? And if they wait upon others to start, nothing starts.

But once the government-sponsored big push gets underway, the private sector is indeed expected to participate. They do so not because they want to develop the economy, but because they now discover a stream of new, profitable opportunities that the big-push strategy created.

WHO FINANCES THE BIG PUSH?

Big-push strategies, depending on their aggressiveness, require enormous national commitments that can sometimes tax an economy beyond its capabilities. Government funds the push because no one else can.

How? Primarily through taxes. But levying even more taxes on an already impoverished people is not only painful but can be destabilizing. Because government's ability to tax incomes is restricted by its lack of effective tax collecting at the source, LDC governments typically rely on sales taxes on consumer goods and on customs duties. The results tend to be regressive. Egypt's attempt in the 1970s to cut government subsidies on food led to riots in Cairo that almost brought the government down.

Less painful to LDCs in the short run, but perhaps more costly in the long run, is government's attempt to finance the big push by external borrowing from foreign private and government lending agencies. Ultimately, LDCs pay for the development they undertake.

The Unbalanced Development Strategy

The competing strategy to the big push relies essentially upon entrepreneurs themselves doing the major part of investing and funding development once projects become potentially profitable.

Forward linkages

Investments in one industry create opportunities for profitable investments in other industries, which use the goods produced in the first as inputs.

Backward linkages

Investments in one industry create demands for inputs that induce investment in other industries to produce those inputs.

How do investments, unprofitable before the strategy, suddenly become profitable? Like the big-push strategy, the profitability of private investment projects depends upon the initial undertaking of infrastructure projects. In this respect, the unbalanced development strategy still counts on government initiative. But unlike the big push, these initial government undertakings are tailored in size and scope. How does it work?

The strategy is based on the idea that every investment, however small, has its own set of **forward and backward linkages** into the economy. Once undertaken, the investment creates new demands and new supplies in the economy. That's the trick. Production projects emerge to satisfy these new demands and their outputs make other previously unfeasible projects feasible. These new projects, now undertaken, create a succeeding round of entirely new demands and new outputs. And so on.

LINKAGES IN SRI LANKA

Unbalanced growth relies on tension between new supply capacity creating new demands that, in turn, prompt new and different supplies.

Imagine the Sri Lankan government thinking about a strategy to get its development process started. Although a world supplier of raw tea, Sri Lanka does not have its own tea processing plants. Its tea is shipped in bulk to the industrial economies and there gets treated.

But no longer. The Sri Lankan government decides that tea is the trigger industry in its development process. It invests in a large, modern processing plant that prepares the raw tea for the consumer market. While the plant goes into construction, a number of Sri Lankans take note.

It becomes quite clear that when the government-owned tea processing plant gets underway, it will need packaging material. A sharp Sri Lankan entrepreneur seizes the opportunity. He can now get into the container business with a ready market. Government doesn't have to worry about packaging. It created the backward linkage.

ADDED PERSPECTIVE

The Road to Better Farming

On present trends, Africa's population will double in the next 20 years, pushing its people on to ever more marginal land. Over-grazed pastures will turn to desert. Topsoil on newly cultivated hillsides will be washed away. Exhausted soil will support fewer crops. And ever more Africans will go hungry.

Or so environmental doomsters claim. Not so, argues a new study by researchers from Britain's Overseas Development Institute and the University of Nairobi. Using colonial records, satellite images, and field research, they have looked at farming in the Machakos district of Kenya, a region of low rainfall and occasional drought, over the period 1930–90. Sixty years ago most farmers kept cattle—for milk, meat, and as a bride price—and grew some grain and pulses. The region faced periodic food shortages: during the 1940s and 1950s it needed regular famine relief. Soil erosion had deeply scarred the landscape.

By 1990 the population had swelled fivefold, to 1.4 million. Result: disaster? No. Total output had risen fifteenfold: more land was under cultivation (by 1979 there was no unclaimed land left) and yields per square kilometer were up tenfold. The "badlands" of the past had been transformed into a landscape of neatly terraced hills and fenced fields.

How did it happen? Most important, Machakos became integrated fairly early—during the 1960s—into the market economy. Farmers diversified from subsistence crops into ones they could trade: coffee, bananas, peas, pawpaws. Under British rule the region's Kamba people had not been allowed to grow coffee in competition with white farmers, or to sell grains outside the area without a permit. After independence in 1963, land reform and the lifting of some state controls encouraged smallholders to invest in higher-value crops—and to conserve soil and water so the land could support them.

Capital for investment came from new opportunities to earn money outside farming. By 1990 most farm families in Machakos had at least one son or daughter earning money from nonfarm work, such as weaving baskets or making carvings for tourists. This helped families buy better tools, fertilizer, drought-resistant strains of maize, and seed for second crops to plant among first ones to take advantage of Kenya's second seasonal rains.

Decent road links to Nairobi, dating from the 1950s, made a huge difference. It became profitable to grow fruit and vegetables as Asian traders began to travel to Machakos to buy crops—and later other goods—for city markets.

Better communications also helped government advisers spread news about new farming methods. Yet expert advice was not the key. Productivity grew fastest between 1960 and 1980, when the government, busy with more promising farming areas, was making no special effort for Machakos. Yet farmers there invested hard in better land and crops: advised or not, they had the incentives, and the means, to gain from doing it.

Source: *The Economist*, December 11, 1993.

But the new container factory can produce more packaging than the government-owned processing plant can absorb. Once in operation, it can diversify its packaging product to satisfy almost every packaging demand. In other words, the development process, triggered by the processing plant, created an imbalance between packaging supply capacity and the government's demand for packaging.

Such an imbalanced development process is preferred by some economists to the balanced development strategy of the big push. Why? Because not only is there a new supply source where one hadn't existed before, but the imbalance will spark new forward and backward linkages through the economy. How does it work?

Since it is no longer necessary for Sri Lankan businesses to import expensive packaging into the economy—domestic supply, employing Sri Lankan labor, is typically less expensive and more accessible—the availability of this domestic supply can make the difference between a profit and a loss to businesses for which packaging is a major input.

Other businesses, now confident about getting access to this new supply, expand their operations. But their expansions create new imbalances between their new supplies and the demands for their goods.

The mutually reinforcing imbalances caused by new supplies creating new demands—forward linkages—and these new demands creating new and different supplies—backward linkages—play off against each other, forming a dynamic chain reaction of economic development.

The attraction of such a development strategy is that it places minimal stress on government. It requires neither a grandiose design nor a grandiose taxing scheme. Like a picture puzzle, the individual linkage pieces make up the development picture, but unlike the puzzle, the actual picture isn't known beforehand.

WHO DOES THE INVESTING?

The key to success in the unbalanced strategy is the role played by entrepreneurs. The idea is that in all societies, in whatever stage of economic development, there are always creative, energetic people who, presented with a chance at enterprise, will take it. Personal commitment is stronger and more reliable than government commitment or reliability.

WHO DOES THE FUNDING?

While government triggers the process by funding and putting into place some of the economy's key infrastructure investments, the primary source of development finance is the private sector. Entrepreneurs themselves are expected either to invest their own savings in their own businesses, or to find the funding in the banking system.

Although, for most LDCs, the banking system is limited or nonexistent, it is precisely the demands for private business loans that create the *rationale* for commerical banking. If domestic banks aren't available, foreign banks, lured by the new prospects, will come in. It's just a matter of time before Sri Lankan entrepreneurs get into the banking business.

FOREIGN DIRECT INVESTMENT

You might think that LDC governments would jump at the chance of having foreign direct investment join in their development programs. After all, foreign direct investment is about the only way an LDC economy can get into development at zero opportunity cost. Figure 2 illustrates its appeal.

Without foreign direct investment, the LDC economy must sacrifice 120 − 90 = 30 consumption goods in order to expand investment goods from 10 to 15. There is no other way. But suppose it now decides to invite foreign investment. If it attracts five units of foreign investment goods, it can stay at 120 consumption and still get 15 investment goods into its development process. Point *C* in Figure 2 is impossible without foreign investment. On the other hand, with the foreign investment the LDC's production possibility curve shifts outward to include *C*.

FIGURE 2
Production Possibilities Curve with Foreign Investment
Without foreign investment, the production possibilities for the LDC economy are restricted to combinations of capital goods and consumption goods along the *AB* curve. Position *C* is an impossible choice. With the added capital resources provided by foreign investments, *C* is attainable.

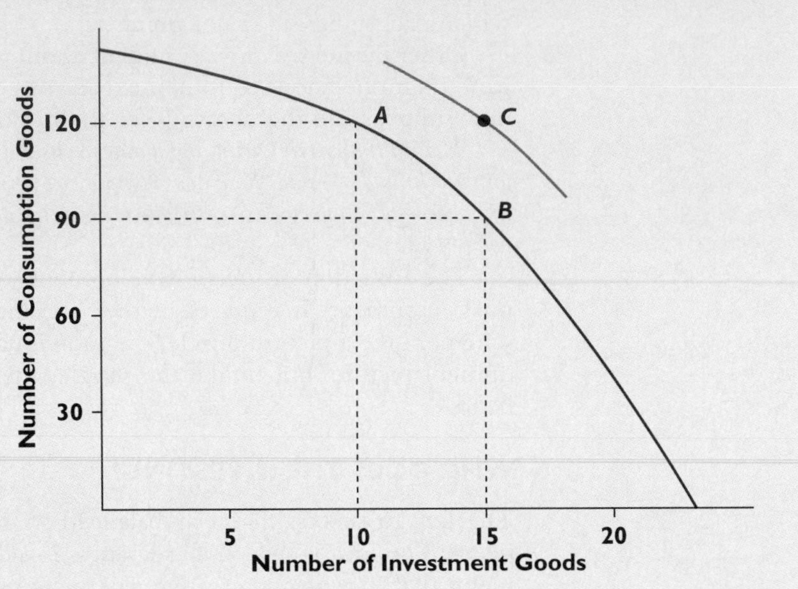

Foreign direct investment typically brings in not only new capital but new expertise. In many cases, it provides the LDCs with markets in the industrial economies that otherwise would be unavailable.

Moreover, foreign direct investment is not an either/or development strategy. It complements both the big push and the unbalanced development strategies. In fact, as a contributor to LDC development, it just seems too good to be true. Yet almost universally, LDC governments have had serious reservations about designing their development programs with a foreign direct investment imprint. Why their reluctance?

Images from the Colonial Past

Foreign direct investment by multinationals conjures up images of colonial power dominance for many LDCs.

The arguments for and against foreign investments are based as much upon emotion as upon economic logic. Many development economists argue that it was the uninvited foreign direct investment of the colonial 19th century that left LDC economies underdeveloped in the first place. The LDCs' inability to pursue domestic industry, they insist, was not a result of failing to provide the human and material resources required, but rather the result of coercive interference by colonial regimes in the LDCs.

By colonial design, LDC economies became economic caricatures, restructured into raw material supply bases for the West. Their entrepreneurs had no freedom to operate, except perhaps in small-scale retail trade or in traditional artisan production. The promising industries were reserved for the colonial power. Managerial skills remained underdeveloped because those employment opportunities, too, were available only to the colonial power.

To some economists, then, it would seem to be the height of irony that after finally gaining independence—in some cases at great human sacrifice—the LDCs were to turn right around and invite back into their economies the colonial powers, even if the economic gains from foreign investments were undeniable.

Yet the contribution that foreign direct investment can make to an LDC development process is just too important to overlook, even for the most reluctant LDCs. Although worried about the consequences of inviting in foreign investment, the LDC governments worry as well about the consequences of not inviting foreign investment in!

What do they do? Most end up with a "yes, but" policy. Yes, foreign investment is wanted, but not without serving LDC designs. Typically, foreign investment in the LDCs is well harnessed. It is subject to more-stringent regulation than is domestic investment. Foreign investors are sometimes excluded from particular fields of activity. In some economies, they are obliged to hire nationals in managerial positions or are required to meet employment quotas. In most cases foreign investors must also accept profit-repatriation ceilings. That is to say, foreign investment is carefully monitored to suit the development objectives of the host economy.

Different developing countries have different attitudes toward foreign direct investment, with some LDCs closely controlling multinationals and others welcoming them, to the extent of offering tax breaks and other inducements.

On the other hand, foreign direct investment in some LDCs, typically the more successful ones, is as welcomed as Santa Claus at Christmas. Some LDCs provide tax holidays—as long as five years free of all domestic taxes—and some have investment subsidies to encourage foreign investment. Many offer duty-free imports of capital goods as added inducements.

FOREIGN ECONOMIC AID

While foreign direct investment is essentially a private sector activity, foreign economic aid—loans and grants—is government to government. Our own aid program is housed in the Department of State and is administered by the Agency for International Development (AID).

Table 6 records the growth of our aid program.

As you see, over 60 percent of our 1946–88 economic aid to LDCs took the form of outright grants. In 1988 these grants accounted for 90.3 percent of our total economic aid package. Typically, aid sponsors basic infrastructure development, but often takes the form of supplementing LDCs' food stocks. Whether aid flows into investment or consumption, it is designed to nudge the LDC off its production possibility curve, just as foreign direct investment took the LDC economy to position *C* in Figure 2.

How generous are we? Although we account for as much as 30 percent of all the economic aid given to the LDCs by western industrial economies, many European countries have given a much higher percent of their GDPs. For ex-

TABLE 6
U.S. Foreign Economic Aid Programs: 1946–88 ($ millions)

	Total	Loans	Grants
Total 1946–88	$212,480	$55,188	$157,292
1970	3,676	1,389	2,288
1975	4,908	1,679	3,229
1980	7,573	1,993	5,580
1988	8,749	852	7,897

Source: *Statistical Abstract of the United States, 1990* (Washington, D.C.: U.S. Department of Commerce, 1990), p. 802.

TABLE 7 LDC Arms Imports and GDP per Capita: 1960–90

	1960	1970	1980	1989	1990
Arms imports ($ billions)	4.1	11.1	37.6	33.2	16.5
GDP per capita ($)	356	499	673	742	762

Source: Ruth L. Sivard, *World Military and Social Expenditures 1993* (Washington, D.C.: World Priorities, 1993), p. 42.

ample, in 1988, Norway's 1.1 percent of GDP, Holland's 0.98 percent, Canada's 0.50 percent, and France's 0.73 percent were higher than our own 0.25 percent.

Still Guns and Butter Issues

Even though economic aid (measured in 1987 dollars) to LDC economies from the West has grown from $19 billion in 1960 to $50 billion in 1990, its net impact on boosting LDC resources has been all but cancelled out by the LDCs' growing propensity to import arms from the West. Look at Table 7.

Arms purchases by LDCs can divert resources from more-productive investment in infrastructure, human capital, and physical capital.

LDC economies, of course, do not have a monopoly on arms purchases. But they can least afford them. During the 1960 to 1989 period, their arms imports increased eightfold, compared to a modest doubling of their per capita GDP. Figure 3 traces the LDC spending on arms imports during the decade 1981–91.

Not too surprisingly, the lion's share of arms imports goes to the Middle East. But note the sharp cutback since 1987 for every region. Among the factors accounting for the downturn are the increasing burden of LDC international debt and the substantial growth in the LDCs' ability to produce their own

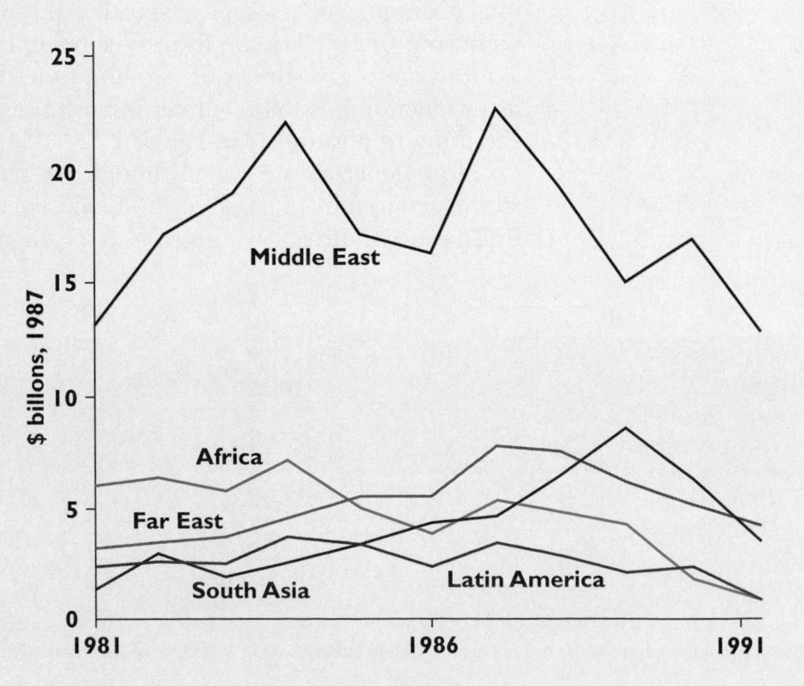

FIGURE 3
Arms Imports of LDCs
Arms imports from the West to the LDCs increases in the early 1980s then falls sharply from 1987. Among the reasons for the fall are the increasing international debt burden of the LDCs and the substitution of domestic arms production for the arms imports.

TABLE 8 The LDCs' Public Expenditures for the Military, Education, and Health: 1970–91 ($ billions 1987, U.S.)

	1970	1980	1991
Military	$59	$102	$121
Health	15	30	50
Education	40	111	124

Source: Ruth L. Sivard, *World Military and Social Expenditures 1993* (Washington, D.C.: World Priorities 1993), p. 42.

arms. This scaling down of arms imports, however, does not signal a scaling down of the LDCs' public expenditures on the military. Look at Table 8.

Military expenditures actually grew in real terms during the 1980–91 period, at an annual rate of 1.7 percent, and represents a use of LDC resources in 1991 that is equal to the resources expended on education and is substantially higher than those allocated to health.

Why this waste of resources? Because for most LDCs, the government's first priority is to stay in power. What good is the development of the economy to the regime in power if the regime isn't around to claim the benefits? Political stability is a costly operation. So too are the many intraregional conflicts. LDC military spending has as much to do with internal control as it does with external military threats. Look at Figure 4.

FIGURE 4 Militarization and Repression in the LDCs: 1982 and 1992

Comparing 1982 to 1992, the number of LDCs under military rule increased, as have the official acts of violence committed against their citizens.

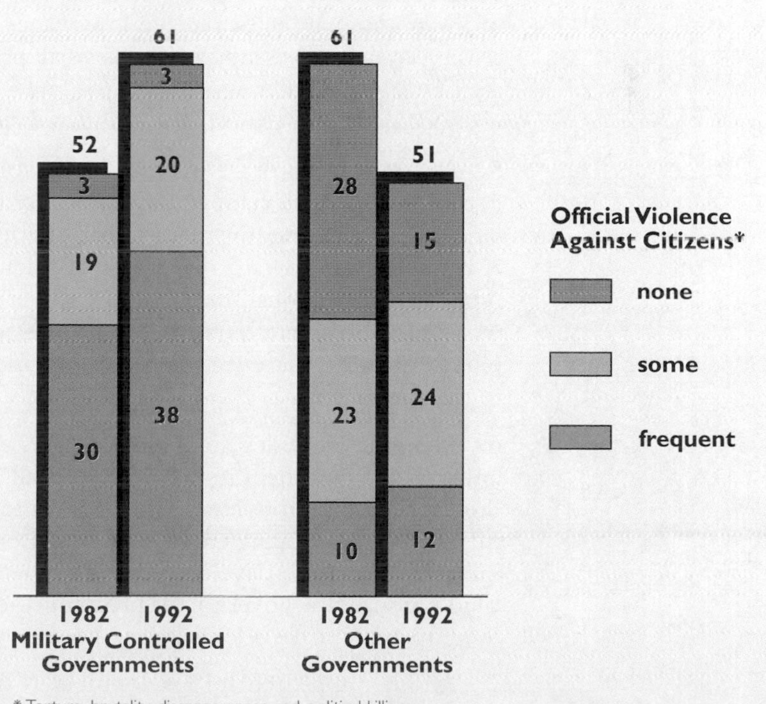

During the decade of 1982–92, the number of LDCs under military control increased from 52 to 61, and official violence against citizens increased as well. It makes the task of breaking through the barriers of national poverty even more difficult.

CHAPTER REVIEW

1. The life prospects of a child born in the United States compared to those of a child born in a developing country like Egypt are very different indeed. Egypt's poverty makes the possibilities for the child born there quite limited compared to those for the American baby. Economists have been concerned with the problem of persistent poverty in the economies of Asia, Africa, and Latin America since the early 1950s.

2. LDC per capita incomes vary substantially from a low of $120 in Ethiopia to a high of $3,600 in South Korea. With few exceptions, these per capita incomes are growing slowly or not at all. Rapid rates of population growth make it very hard for LDCs to raise their per capita incomes. Industry appears to be a more significant source of GDP growth than agriculture.

3. Investments in human capital contribute greatly to the economic well-being of people in industrial economies. However, it is very difficult for LDCs to accomplish these investments. With large segments of their populations close to subsistence, LDCs cannot afford to devote resources to human capital investment.

4. Economic dualism is the term applied to situations in LDCs where a small minority of the population lives on a par with their counterparts in the industrialized countries while the rest of the population is mired in poverty. Workers in the traditional sector receive low wages because of a low level of capital intensity, traditional technology, and weak prices, whereas workers in the modern sector receive higher wages because they work with modern technology and produce goods for export that command higher prices.

5. A combination of factors may be at work in contributing to the poverty experienced in less-developed countries. Political instability often plays an important role by creating uncertainty that interferes with economic decision making. A disinclination toward materialist or scientific perceptions of the world stemming from traditionalism can also hamper development efforts, as can the absence of an adequate infrastructure. For example, peasants will not produce surplus food unless there are transportation and marketing facilities that allow them to sell the surplus.

6. Many different development strategies exist for LDCs. The big-push strategy emphasizes investment in many projects all at once to simultaneously create both the capacity for production and markets for the output. Typically, the government of the developing country orchestrates a big push by coordinating and planning infrastructure, development investment, and financing over the long term. One rationale for government planning and coordination of the big push is that the government has a longer time horizon than do private entrepreneurs.

7. Another approach to development is the unbalanced strategy. Rather than relying on government to direct development efforts, the unbalanced develop-

ment strategy focuses on entrepreneurs themselves doing most of the investment and financing of profitable projects. Government still plays a role by investing in infrastructure. With an infrastructure in place, private entrepreneurs pursue investments that create backward and forward linkages in the economy. New demands and supplies are created through new investment, existing markets expand and new markets are created in the process. This strategy is called unbalanced, because with each new investment an imbalance is created between new supplies prompting new demands. The new demands are called forward linkages, and these new demands result in new supplies called backward linkages.

8. Foreign direct investment can also support economic development. Foreign direct investment allows a developing country to accumulate capital without having to sacrifice consumer goods. The drawback of foreign direct investment is that it bears some resemblance to the colonial activity that dominated many LDCs in years past.

9. Foreign economic aid is another source of funds for development. Governments in the developed world provide aid to governments in LDCs in the form of loans and grants. In the United States, our foreign economic aid programs are administered by the Agency for International Development (AID) in the Department of State.

10. Many LDCs are inclined to import large quantities of arms from the West. These purchases of arms are made in spite of the fact that they are virtually unaffordable. LDC governments invest heavily in arms to maintain political stability and stay in power.

KEY TERMS

Less-developed countries (LDCs)
Human capital
Economic dualism
Infrastructure
Big push
Forward linkage
Backward linkage

QUESTIONS

1. The historical data of falling birth rates and falling death rates in LDCs helps explain the difficulty they face in raising per capita incomes. Explain.

2. What is meant by the LDC poverty trap?

3. What is economic dualism and why does it create a formidable obstacle to national economic development for LDCs?

4. Why is political stability vital to the economic development process?

5. What is economic traditionalism? Compare its characteristics to the modern sector of an economy.

6. Describe the components of an economy's infrastructure. What aspects are lacking in LDCs?

7. Describe the economic logic associated with the big-push development strategy. What are its pitfalls?

8. Describe the economic logic associated with the unbalanced development strategy. What are its pitfalls?

9. Why are some LDC governments reluctant to invite in foreign direct investment? What are the pros and cons of such investment?

10. Show the relationship between foreign direct investment and the economy's production possibilities curve.

11. Professor Miguel Ramirez asks his students at Trinity College to respond to the following problem: Economists, notably those in the World Bank and the IMF, argue that free trade and open markets are important factors contributing to LDC economic growth. On the other hand, American policymakers in the early 19th century—when the United States was beginning to industrialize—pursued a highly protective strategy *vis-à-vis* England, the premier industrial power of the world. Should LDCs follow the advice of World Bank and IMF economists or take their cue from U.S. economic history?

Make your case using economic analyses offered in the chapters on international trade; exchange rates, balance of payments, and international debt; and economic problems of less-developed economies.

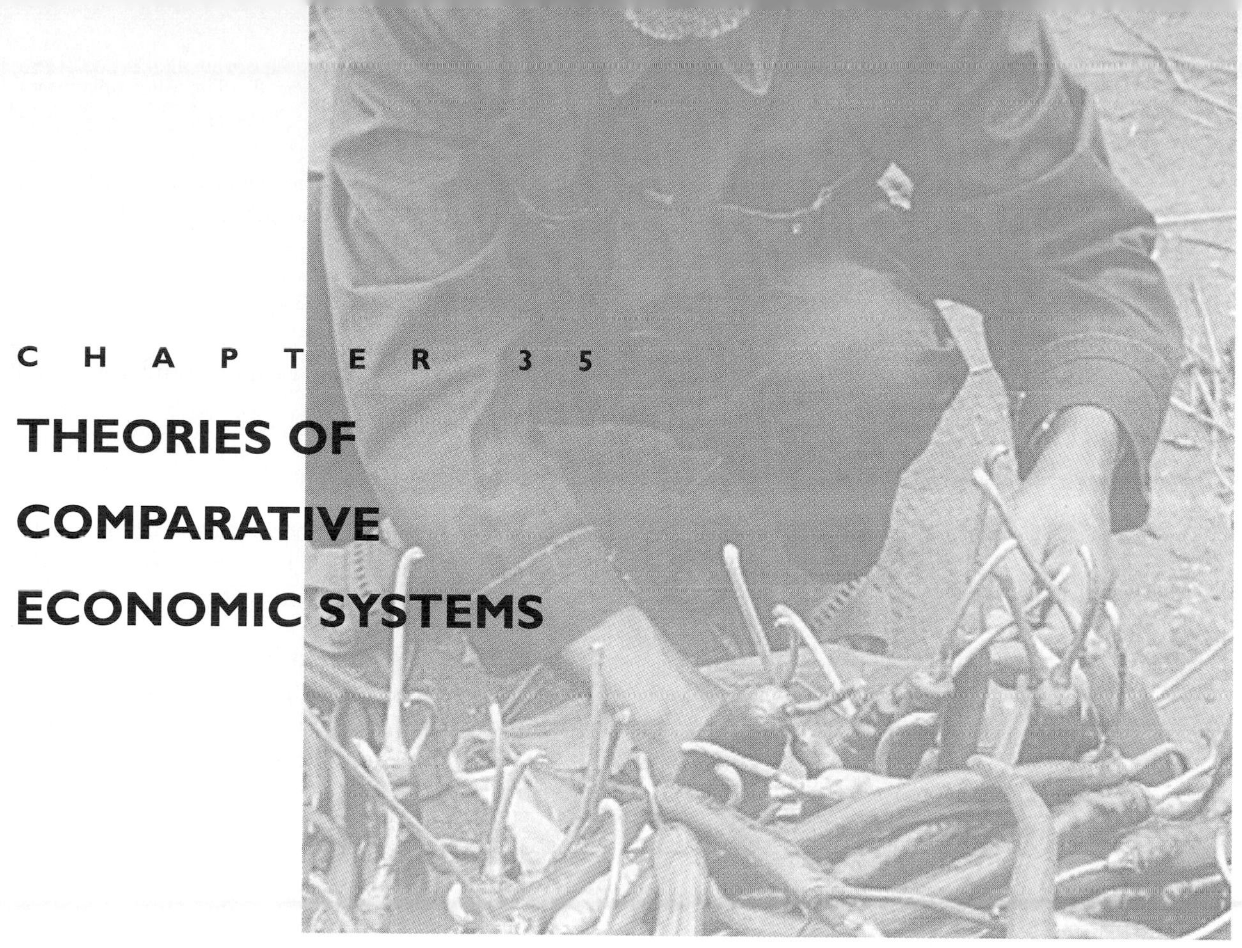

CHAPTER 35
THEORIES OF COMPARATIVE ECONOMIC SYSTEMS

CHAPTER PREVIEW

Until now we've said little about the precise nature of an economic system's organization, except that goods and services are produced and distributed through markets, and that some types of public goods are provided by the government. However, there is substantial variation between countries as to the exact proportions of goods and services that are provided by the private sector and by the public sector. Until recently, the Soviet Union was a country that planned for virtually all goods and services to be provided by the public sector. European countries typically have larger government sectors than does the United States. What accounts for these differences? What are the implications of allocating a greater share of the production and distribution decision making to the state? These questions and others will be explored in the following discussion.

After studying this chapter, you should be able to:

- Explain why Karl Marx believed it was impossible for a country to choose its economic system.
- Outline Marx's stages theory of economic systems.
- Describe the manner in which Marx thought capitalism would be transformed to socialism.

- Define historical materialism.
- Explain why most mainstream economists reject historical materialism as a basis for distinguishing one economic system from another.
- Contrast capitalism with market socialism, and state socialism with fascism.
- Discuss the process of creating an economic plan in a state socialist economy.
- Describe the economic advantages that allegedly arise from fascism compared to capitalism and market socialism.
- Identify the economic systems that correspond to various countries of the world.

There's a story told about a New York garment district entrepreneur who, having worked hard and honestly for many years, bought himself a spanking new 40-foot yacht that carried a crew of four. Excited, he brought his aging mother down to the dock to show her his new possession.

She looked at her proud, happy son sporting a gold-braided naval captain's hat. "What's that?" she asked, pointing to his head. "It's a captain's hat," he beamed, "I'm a captain!" His aging mother replied with much tenderness: "My dear son, by me you're a captain, by you you're a captain, *but by captains,* are you a captain?"

Why this story? Because in 1974 a group of army officers overthrew King Haile Selassie of Ethiopia and, upon taking power, announced the establishment in Ethiopia of a socialist economic system. Imagine Ethiopia's new head of state bringing his aging mother to Addis Ababa to see the great palace, now his residence, and explaining to her that she now lives in a socialist economy. Can't you hear her replying: "My dear son, by me it's a socialist economy, by you it's a socialist economy, *but by socialist economies,* is it a socialist economy?"

Good question! Think about it. Can a tribal people, whose villages are widely scattered throughout a high, central plateau and unyielding desert, whose level of technology has changed little in a thousand years, suddenly transform itself from a primitive agricultural and nomadic economic system into a socialist one?

The same question could have been asked about the Russian Revolution in 1917 which overthrew the Czarist regime. It is not difficult to understand how a small band of Bolsheviks might seize political power, but just how could that small band of revolutionaries transform a premechanized agricultural economy into a workers' socialist state when—aside from all the other problems it had—there were precious few workers in Russia at the time?

TO WHAT EXTENT CAN NATIONS CHOOSE THEIR ECONOMIC SYSTEMS?

Do nations really have the option of choosing among economic systems? Did the 1974 pre-feudal Ethiopia *really* have the option of becoming socialist? What about Russia in 1917? Consider our own options. Suppose the majority of Americans chose to return to an economic system based on the buffalo, can we really switch out of market capitalism to a nomadic system based on herding?

Or is the character of a nation's economic system not a matter of choice at all, but instead an inescapable consequence of its state of technology? That is, are we capitalist *because* our technology imposes that form of system on us? Is Ethiopia's nomadic economic system, then, what it is because of its state of technology?

Feudalism
An economic system in which primary productive property, land, is organized into large, essentially self-supporting estates (or manors).

A few economists believe so. In fact, some hold a completely technology-deterministic view of comparative economic systems. Other economists, while sympathetic to the deterministic view, are willing to grant that nations, at *some* levels of their economic development, can still exercise *some* freedom in choosing the character of their systems. Others economists debunk determinism altogether.

DETERMINISTIC THEORY OF ECONOMIC SYSTEMS

Let's begin our analysis of economic systems by looking first at a determinist theory. Perhaps the most-celebrated theory of economic systems expressing an unqualified deterministic view is Karl Marx's. Marx argues that all societies, in the process of development, *evolve* through a sequential series of stages, each stage reflecting a specific state of technology.

Marx's Stages of Economic Systems

Capitalism
An economic system in which the primary productive property, capital, is owned and managed by individuals.

Socialism
An economic system in which productive property is owned and managed by the state.

This technology-directed evolution transforms societies from primitive communism to **feudalism,** from feudalism to **capitalism,** from capitalism to **socialism,** and finally, from socialism to **communism.** The maturation of each prepares the foundation for its successor. For example, economic activity in feudal society brings into being the rudimentary economic structures that will eventually create capitalism. In the same way, capitalism's economic maturation leads inexorably to socialism. Finally, the stage is set for communism.

The key idea is that one system prepares for the next. *The sequence is completely deterministic.* The idea that socialism can be chosen by a people without the economy first having experienced capitalism was, to Marx, sheer nonsense. That is, it is no more possible for economies to skip systems than it is for an infant to skip childhood on its way to becoming an adult.

Marx's Dialectics

Communism
A stateless economic system in which productive property is owned and managed by the community.

Dialectics
A process describing the simultaneous growth and destruction of economic systems.

Marx explains the transition from one economic system to another in the framework of the **dialectics,** *which is a dynamic process of continuing opposition, of interacting growth, conflict, and destruction.* The process is cast in terms of the thesis, antithesis, and synthesis. How does the process work?

The thesis in Marx's dialectics is a collection of all elements that make up a functional society. The elements include its state of technology, its property relations, its production, distribution, and exchange structures, as well as its politics, philosophy, religion, literature, and culture. These economic and noneconomic elements come together to define the thesis' specific character.

Each thesis contains the seeds of its own destruction. The antithesis represents the basic opposition to the thesis, the essential element of internal conflict. In Marx's dialectics, *the conflict is over property. It is between those who have property and those who don't.* Look at Figure 1.

In the early stage of a thesis, the conflict over property exists but is inconsequential. As the thesis matures, the conflict grows and eventually comes to dom-

FIGURE 1 **Marx's Dialectics**

The thesis is a collection of predominantly complementary elements, although some are conflicting, that identify the thesis' specific vitality and character. As the thesis matures, the conflicting elements within it interact to create antagonisms that eventually undermine the thesis. The conflict, called antithesis, grows to dominate the thesis. Unable to contain the conflict, the thesis explodes. Emerging out of the explosion is a new thesis, called synthesis, with its own specific vitality and character. But it, too, contains conflicting elements that eventually destroy it.

In Marx's dialectics, the conflicting elements are people who own productive property and those who don't. The conflict comes to dominate the economic system, leading eventually to revolution.

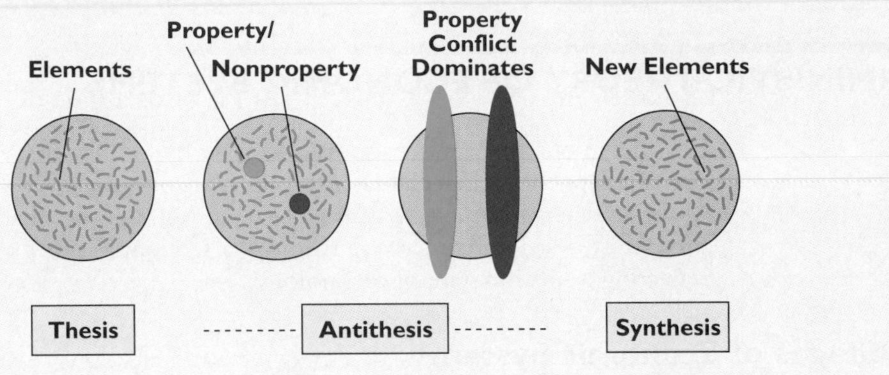

inate it. In the final stages of a thesis, the conflict becomes so intense that the thesis is unable to contain it and, in the end, is destroyed by it. Out of its destruction emerges a new, succeeding thesis—the synthesis—with its own set of elements.

But like the thesis, the synthesis too contains the seeds of its own destruction. Conflict between its property owners (the haves) and nonowners (the have-nots) undermines and eventually destroys the synthesis, replacing it with another. The dialectical process of creation and destruction is the way Marx explains how societies and their economic systems emerge and decay *in a structured sequence.*

How do people, in any economic system, come to acquire property? Marx's answer is simple: *All property is theft.* The haves become haves by taking and holding property by force. They create through their control over society's literature, religion, education, philosophy, and politics a myth of legitimacy that strengthens their claim to property. But in the end, technological change *which they can't control* subverts the importance of their property. New property forms (also acquired by theft and held by force), resulting from new technologies, push aside, sometimes violently, the established property and its owners.

The Transformation from Feudalism to Capitalism

Let's see how Marx's dialectics can be used to explain the transformation from feudalism to capitalism. Land, the basic property of the feudal economic system, belongs to the landlords. The peasant who farms the land is given mere subsistence, while the landowners end up with the surplus. Most of what is produced on the land is consumed directly by the landowners and peasants. Markets and market prices are inconsequential.

The landowners' wealth creates a demand for new types of manufactured goods and the rise of a capitalist class with interests that are opposed to those of the feudal landowners.

As you can imagine, this arrangement is not always struck by mutual consent. Peasants are forced to accept it. After all, they have no real alternatives. They own no land and must work to survive.

But it isn't the peasant that brings about the demise of feudalism. The landowners' riches create demands for new goods that are supplied by a responsive *newly emerging class of merchants and manufacturers*. This newly emerging class represents the antithesis (the ultimate opposition) to feudalism.

These merchants and manufacturers (mostly drawn from the peasant class) are lured by the prospect of profit. They compete with each other, creating new technology and greater quantities of goods that now appear on markets. As they try to expand production further, they confront the myriad of feudal restrictions on commerce. They agitate for unrestricted trade. They invest in roads to expand their markets and their success in market expansion opens up new possibilities for adopting new and even more productive, capital-using technology. Their demand for labor to produce these new manufactured goods provides new opportunities for peasants, challenging the established feudal arrangements.

The economic power of these merchants and manufacturers grows as more profits are converted into new and more productive capitalist technology. Markets and the price system develop to become the new allocative mechanism for production and distribution.

Eventually, the feudal way of production is no match for the vitality of new capitalism. The final death blow to feudalism is revolution, but its downfall really has little to do with cannon fire. It is the outcome of a continuous undermining of existing technology (land-related) by new technology (capital).

The Transformation from Capitalism to Socialism

Technologically advanced capitalists drive out less-advanced firms, eventually shrinking the number of capitalists.

What takes feudalism's place? Capitalism. The new property is capital in the form of factories and machinery. Everything in capitalism—goods, services, people—is bought and sold in markets. The fate of workers? Incessant labor-saving technology creates chronic unemployment that keeps market-determined wages at subsistence levels.

But the same harsh rules of the market apply as well to capitalists. Always competing against each other in the market, capitalists with new technology (and lower prices) drive out those using old technology (at higher prices). Wave after wave of new technology keeps driving capitalists out of business. In the end, the surviving capitalists are few in number, but own empires of capitalist property.

What about the working class? Failed capitalists join the swelling ranks of workers, along with artisans and other skilled craftspeople who are ruined as well by the inescapable competition with low-priced, machine-made goods. Peasants, displaced by mechanized agriculture, leave the farm for the factory, adding their numbers to the working class. Working side-by-side in factories, workers become aware of each other's misery and common fate. *Technology brings them together and imposes class solidarity upon them.*

Ultimately, large numbers of workers end up facing very few capitalists. It becomes self-evident to workers, who compare their high productivity to their common misery, that the capitalist system is their problem. The spark that ignites the workers' revolution is incidental. The inevitable collapse of capitalism, like that of feudalism before it, is the inexorable consequence of a continuous undermining by new technologies of existing ones.

What follows? Capitalism polarized population into workers and capitalists. With capitalists deposed, the enormous productive property that was created under capitalism becomes the property of workers *who constitute the entire society.* Society is no longer divided between haves and have-nots. The source of conflict, property, no longer exists. Marx's dialectical process comes to an end.

The socialist system that follows is a temporary stage before the advent of communism. Workers use property only to reconstruct society, abolishing the market and adapting new production and distribution arrangements. In this period of transition, workers use the state to promote the people's will.

The Transformation from Socialism to Communism

It takes time, but eventually socialism gives way to communism, in which production is organized according to an economic plan. Everyone contributes according to ability and distribution is made according to need. There is no need for a state or for those social institutions that previously supported the propertied class. The state withers away.

NONDETERMINIST THEORY OF ECONOMIC SYSTEMS

As you see, Marx's theory of economic systems leaves absolutely no room for choice. All societies eventually end up communist, but only after evolving through a series of transitional systems. Marxists call Marx's theory of systems historical materialism. That's not what most mainstream economists believe or experience.

To them, economic systems such as capitalism, market socialism, state socialism, and fascism represent alternative ways for modern societies to organize their economic lives. That is, without denying the importance of technology in defining the limits of choice, most economists believe that *the fundamental questions of property, of consumer and state sovereignty, of income distribution, and of the mechanisms used to allocate resources to produce goods and services are still matters of societal choice.*

Most mainstream economists believe that a degree of choice in economic systems exists for most societies.

First of all, societies choose their political systems. Some are democratic, others are authoritarian. Politically democratic societies are inclined to allow the market to determine what goods and services society produces, what technologies are used, and who gets what quantity of goods and services. Property is privately owned.

The choice of market systems and private property by politically democratic societies is not accidental. The underlying principle is individual freedom of expression. Representative government and consumer sovereignty in the marketplace are reflections of that expression. The right of individuals to private property tends to diffuse the economic power associated with owning productive property. This diffusion safeguards political liberty.

By contrast, a society that consents to, or is subjugated by, authoritarian political rule is more inclined to authoritarian economic decision making where state preferences substitute for consumer sovereignty. The state, whether it allows or takes over private property, organizes resource allocation, chooses the goods and services produced, and distributes income. In this environment, state planning mechanisms replace markets.

The underlying principle that authoritarian systems claim as their *modus operandi* is that the state works on behalf of the people. Of course, the state assigns itself the role of being the final arbiter of what people want.

CAPITALISM AND MARKET SOCIALISM COMPARED

Let's look first at capitalism and market socialism, the two economic systems that provide individuals with the right to express economic choice.

Individuals, Markets, and Property

Capitalism is an economic system rooted in private property. Individuals are entitled to use, sell, or lease their property. There are established rules concerning property acquisition (for example, theft is illegal) but, allowing for these rules, capitalist society is typically reluctant to interfere with how individuals use their property or with the income their property generates.

Markets bring property owners and property seekers together. Individual demanders come to markets expressing their willingness to buy property (in the form of goods, services, or resources) at various prices, while individual suppliers come to markets expressing their willingness to supply property (in the form of goods, services, or resources) at various prices. In this way, individuals exchange property at freely negotiated market prices.

Capitalism emphasizes private ownership of re sources and individual liberty whereas market socialism emphasizes state ownership of resources and equality.

Why individuals choose to buy and sell property is their own business. The results to society, however, are monumental. It explains how we end up with certain kinds of goods, services, and resources.

Markets not only direct capitalist production, but income distribution as well. *Individuals who own property also own the rights to the income that the property generates.* These rights are critical to capitalism because *effort and reward are thought to be inexorably linked.* Capitalism allows for income inequities that reflect the inequities of property holdings. Capitalist society can also choose to modify these rights to income by legislating taxes and income transfers.

Market socialism

A socialist system in which the state determines the economy's basic investments, leaving all other production and consumption decisions to individuals who express their preferences for goods and services on the market.

By contrast, **market socialism** *is an economic system rooted in state ownership of all resources, or property, except labor. As in capitalism, individuals in market socialism choose how much labor they are willing to supply at various prices.*

How does market socialism work? Economic sovereignty in market socialism, as in capitalism, rests with the individual and is expressed on the market. Although the state owns the productive property, the socialist market acts like a ballot box, registering decisions that individuals make concerning what they want the state to produce.

Figure 2 shows how markets in capitalism and market socialism work, comparing the role of price signals in capitalism to the role of trial-and-error signals in market socialism.

In panel *a*'s capitalist market, the demand curve for bread, *D*, intersects the supply curve of bread, *S*. The equilibrium price is $2 per loaf, and 1,000 loaves are bought and sold.

FIGURE 2 **Market Socialist Directives**

In the panel *a* capitalist market, demand curve, *D*, and supply curve, *S*, intersect to create an equilibrium price of $2 and quantity of 1,000 breads bought and sold. When the demand for bread falls to *D′*, the price signal works to shift resources out of bread to other goods and services. With demand at *D′*, an excess supply occurs at $2, driving price down to a new equilibrium of $1.50. The quantity of bread bought and sold falls to 700.

In the panel *b* socialist market, the demand curve, *D*, intersects the supply curve at a quantity of 1,000 breads. When the demand for bread falls to *D′*, the excess supply works to shift resources out of bread to other goods and services. With the demand curve at *D′*, the socialist firm, by trial and error, reduces price until the excess supply is eliminated. This occurs at 700 loaves.

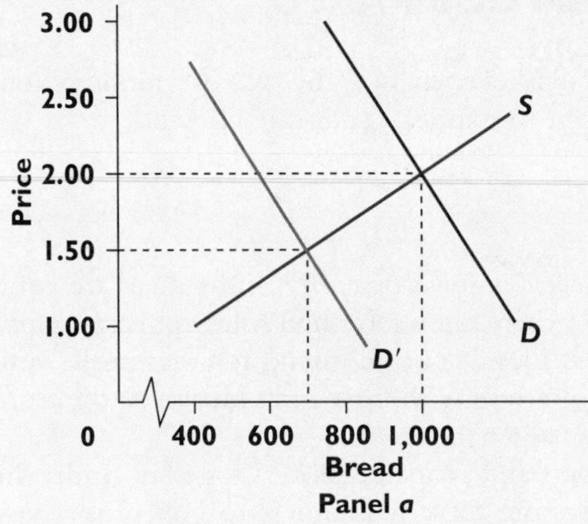

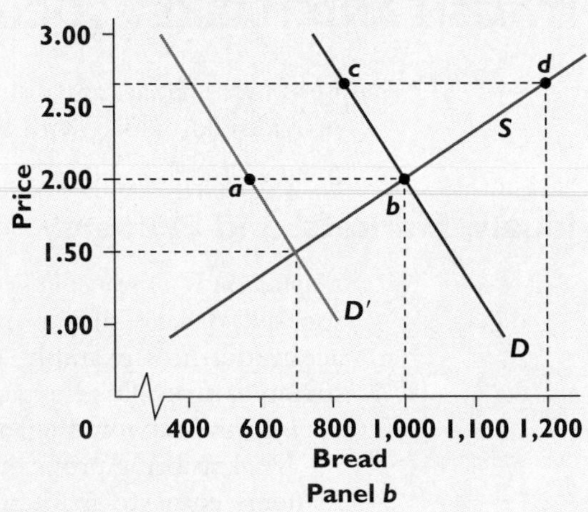

Suppose consumers now want less bread (demand curve falls to *D′*). How is their less-bread-wanted preference satisfied? The simple mechanics of the market—price always signalling whether to produce more or less—is the way a fall in demand for a good eventually becomes translated into a shift of resources away from the production of that good. The equilibrium price falls to $1.50 and the quantity falls to 700.

What about market socialism? Panel *b*'s market socialism illustrates how the same fall in demand for bread results in less bread being produced. The state, owning the bakery, sets price at first by *trial and error.* If shortages develop, it simply raises price. If surpluses develop, it lowers price. Suppose, after several rounds of trial and error, the state bakery arrives at a price of $2 and a quantity of 1,000 loaves.

Note that the demand curve it faces is *D,* reflecting consumer choice. If the bakery had picked a quantity of 400 loaves at its $1 supply price, it would have quickly discovered that it wasn't enough; 700 people wanting a $1 bread would be turned away breadless. The bakery would respond to the excess demand signal by raising price. Suppose it errs in the other direction by setting price at $2.75 and increasing production to 1,200 breads. Now it finds itself with unsold bread (cd). It is a signal to reduce price. Eventually, by *trial and error,* it produces 1,000 loaves.

Now suppose the demand for bread falls to *D′.* What would state bakers do? An excess supply (ab) of $2 bread appears on the market. This excess supply is the signal the state uses to cut price. By trial and error, it discovers that the only

This woman is thinking: "What luck to chance by this outdoor vendor. The State underestimated the demand for sausage and every shop is completely sold out. It will be another week before the State produces enough to meet demand, and if the past is any guide, the price will increase."

price that would bring quantities demanded and supplied into accord is $1.50, precisely the equilibrium price that the capitalist market produces. That is, by trial and error, the state bakery will trim bread production to 700, where the socialist market clears.

As you see, the trial-and-error signal is market socialism's equivalent of capitalism's price signal. In both cases, the too-much-bread message originates with the consumer and works through the market to direct producers' activity. In both cases, the consumer is sovereign.

If market socialist resource allocation merely mimics capitalism's, why bother with market socialism? Why not simply allow capitalism to work its magic producing the proper quantities of goods and services that consumers demand?

Advocates of market socialism would respond by pointing out that state ownership of property rules out individual acquisition of unearned income such as rents and monopoly profit, which, they argue, is commonplace in capitalist society. In this way, market socialism not only creates the goods that capitalism creates, but provides a more equitable income distribution as well.

They cite yet another argument in favor of market socialism. There are some goods whose production ought not be left to consumer discretion. For example, how much investment society undertakes should be made by the state instead of allowing individuals, as capitalism does, to decide through their saving and investment preferences.

But why not let individuals make those investment decisions? Because investment, they believe, is a critical factor influencing the economy's rate of growth. In this one area, they argue, the state is better equipped to serve the long-run economic interests of society than the private investment market would.

Equality versus Liberty

Their different approaches to investment and market signals aside, capitalism and market socialism can be distinguished by the goals they pursue. If any one goal distinguishes market socialism, it is economic equality. The goal that distin-

ADDED PERSPECTIVE

Would Marx Have Subscribed to the State Socialisms That Bear His Name?

V. I. Lenin, the Marxist revolutionary who brought state socialism to Russia in 1917, had a serious problem of socialist legitimacy. After all, if Marx was right about historical materialism, economic determinism, and the dialectical process that charts the evolution of economic systems from feudalism through capitalism to socialism and communism, then how could Lenin claim that workers in 1917 Russia had created the historic socialist revolution?

Marx on Lenin's View of Socialism

Think about it. Russia in 1917 was basically a peasant economy emerging from feudalism where the predominant manufacturers were still the artisan and craft trades. At best, Russian capitalism was embryonic. The technologies associated with the capitalist class, the working class, and the factory system—about which Marx wrote at great length—were virtually nonexistent almost everywhere in Russia. The Russian economy was among the least developed in Europe and aside from the Trans-Siberian railway (a non-Russian enterprise) there was little infrastructure to link the vast Russian continent into a national market. As well, there was no significant Russian working class. Marx would have dismissed as preposterous the idea that a worker's revolution could take place in 1917 Russia. How could it become socialist without first struggling through capitalism?

Good question. How, then, did Lenin manage to convince himself and many others that the revolution he successfully engineered in Russia was both socialist and Marxist? By simply ignoring Marx! Instead of socialism following upon the demise of capitalism, as Marx predicted, Lenin assigned the role of capitalist development to the socialist state he himself created. In other words, Lenin's socialism creates the capitalism that was supposed to have preceded socialism. What role do workers play in the decision-making process? Very little. Their principal task is to concur with the decisions taken by the socialist state.

Would Marx have regarded Lenin's view of socialism as his own? Not by a long shot! Lenin's socialism in Russia had nothing to do with historical materialism, economic determinism, or the dialectical process that explains the evolution of economic systems. According to Marx's own ideas about socialism, Lenin's Russia, although revolutionary, could be neither Marxist nor socialist.

Marx on Mao's China

Mao-Tse-Tung's 1949 socialist revolution in China occurred in an economy even less capitalistic than Lenin's 1917 Russia. Mao, like Lenin before him, paraded Marx as the father figure of the Chinese revolution, but the economic focus of Mao's socialism had nothing to do with Marx's blueprint for socialism. Mao's socialism was built on the Chinese peasantry. That's about as far from Marx as one can get. Mao fantasized that peasants were anxious to convert their precapitalist villages into state-socialist communes (collectives). But Mao had to use the People's Liberation Army to convince the peasants that they were indeed anxious.

China was supposed to leap-frog capitalism, skipping from an agricultural economy based on primitive technologies to a modern agro-industrial economy based on advanced technologies. This leap-frogging was to be initiated and guided by the socialist state. Such leap-frogging was an anathema to Marx's view of how the evolution of economic systems was supposed to take place.

Marx on LDC Socialism

There's not much theoretical distance between Lenin's and Mao's socialism and the schools of state socialism that emerged in the LDCs during the 1950s and 1960s. Castro's socialism in Cuba, Nasser's socialism in Egypt, Boumedienne's socialism in Algeria, Sukarno's socialism in Indonesia, Nkrumah's socialism in Ghana, and Ho Chi Min's socialism in Vietnam are a few of the state socialisms that came to power on the continents of Asia, Africa, and Latin America.

Their socialism, too, had little to do with either the stage of their economic development or the existence of a working class. Whatever ideology these socialist states tried to inculcate, it was generally national in character, rather than the Marxist focus on the working class. Like Lenin's and Mao's state socialism, LDC socialism argued that it acted "on behalf of the people." Too often, the military overthrew one socialist regime to install another, always "on behalf of the people."

"On Behalf of the People?"
How can anyone assess whether a state works "on behalf of the people" when voting privileges are denied outright, or restricted to choosing the only party standing for election? But that's precisely the circumstances facing people in socialist China, socialist Cuba, socialist North Korea, and most other state socialist LDCs.

Where revolutionary governments come to power by displacing others and hold state power "on behalf of the people," the question always is: If the state owns the property, who owns the state?

In Russia, following Lenin's death in 1922, the struggle for socialist leadership between Joseph Stalin and Leon Trotsky ended in 1941 with a pick-axe lodged in Trotsky's head. The reign of Stalin's socialism "on behalf of the people" thereafter went unchallenged. In 1964, 11 years after Stalin's death, Nikita Krushchev, head of the Soviet state, acknowledged that Stalin's rule had been both dictatorial and detrimental to Russia. Yet Stalin ruled for 30 years, supposedly "on behalf of the people." In 1991, both Mikhail Gorbachev, head of the Soviet state, and Boris Yeltsin, President of Russia, denounced all Soviet rulers since the 1917 revolution, including Lenin, as having been undemocratic, and only a year later, amidst the complete disintegration of the Soviet empire, they disavowed not only Soviet socialist history, but each other.

In Cuba, disagreement during the 1960s between socialist revolutionaries Fidel Castro and Che Guevara, Castro's comrade and architect of Cuba's industrialization, led to Guevara's unceremonious departure. Whatever the merits of their positions, the Cuban people had no say in the matter. The control of the Cuban state today remains personal and rests ultimately on Castro's ability to command allegiance from the Cuban military and secret police. Is this what Marx had in mind?

It is unreasonable to suppose that any state socialist regime would not insist that it holds power "on behalf of the people." But just because slave drivers call themselves Marxists doesn't mean their slave systems are socialist.

guishes capitalism is economic liberty. *These are not necessarily incompatible, but when they are, it is the market socialist who comes down on the side of equality and the capitalist who comes down on the side of liberty.*

Economic equality typically refers to the equality of income people receive. There are many reasons why market socialists advocate income equality, but the principal reason is that they feel everybody should have approximately the same. It's an undisguised value judgment. You can either agree or disagree.

Advocates of capitalism object in principle to this goal because it clearly violates the principle of economic liberty. Moreover, the belief that our economic liberty is inseparable from our political liberties is enough reason for them to accept, if not excuse, the economic inequities that the capitalist system may generate. But advocates of capitalism also refer to the connection between economic liberty and economic progress.

However productive people can be, it takes incentives to energize their productivity. Interfere with people's rights to the fruits of their property and the incentives that promote productivity weaken. Everyone is a loser. Why should people expend their energies in productive pursuits when the rewards can be taken from them? Why develop new technology? Why save and invest?

But just as advocates for market socialism don't generally press for absolute income equality, advocates of capitalism acknowledge the need to moderate income inequality. At issue, then, is discovering the ranges of tolerable income shifting and tolerable restrictions on rights to property.

STATE SOCIALISM

Under state socialism, the market is replaced by a plan.

The more commonplace form of socialism in our world experience is not the market socialist model, but the socialisms associated with the former USSR, with China, Cuba, North Korea, and other societies that were designed and executed by politically authoritarian regimes. In each, the state owns the property, makes the decisions on what goods and services are produced, how these goods and services are produced, and who ends up with them. In other words, *the state's decision makers completely replace the market.*

State socialism

A socialist system in which the state decides which goods and services are to be produced and designs and directs an economic plan to produce them.

What is particularly interesting about **state socialism** is that it has been tried. The former USSR (Union of Soviet Socialist Republics)—commonly referred to as Russia—developed a form of state socialism that lasted 75 years. The mystery is not that Russian state socialism lasted 75 years, but that it lasted one day. After all, it is mind-boggling to suppose that a state can allocate millions of workers to jobs that are commensurate with their abilities and interests, produce millions of goods and services that consumers want, and do all that *without the aid of markets!*

It takes a great deal of conceit for a state to believe that it can set aside a market system and be itself the substitute. The beauty of the market system is that no individual has to worry about whether the shoes people want will be produced, or how to produce them, or whether the turkeys people want for Thanksgiving will be in supermarkets, or how to run a turkey farm. Shoes and turkeys will be produced because someone will be smart enough to pick up those demand signals on the market and, lured by the prospect of profit, will get busy producing them. They don't need permission, they don't need to consult with others, they simply do it. That's exactly how millions of goods, in appropriate quantities, get on the market.

Who is daring enough or crazy enough to think that they are capable of playing the role of the market, making simultaneous demand and supply decisions for the millions of goods produced and consumed in the economy, and get it right? Think about it. If there's no market, how would anyone know how many turkeys to produce? If there's no market, how would turkey-feed producers know what quantities to produce? How would truckers know how many trucks will be needed to transport the turkeys and turkey feed? What about fuel supply and motor repair? If trucks break down, there's no turkey for Thanksgiving! The linkages, as you can imagine, are endless.

Is chaos, then, inevitable when the market system no longer functions? Not according to state economic planners. They believe they can personally supervise the production and distribution of millions of goods, in exact quantities, and distribute them to the right people.

Designing the Plan

Economic plan

A set of production targets for all goods and services determined in advance by the state which is consistent with the economy's supply of the resources.

How do they do it? By creating an **economic plan.** Imagine yourself as the chief economic planner for a state socialist system that is given the assignment of constructing an economic plan for the next five years.

Suppose that by revolutionary decree, the economic system has been changed from capitalism to state socialism. Workers are given a revolutionary holiday, all industry is shut down, waiting upon your instruction.

You might begin by collecting all data concerning the economic activity that took place prior to the holiday. The economy is composed of numbers of in-

TABLE 1
Input-Output Table for the Socialist State (Assuming Each Unit Costs $1)

Input/Output	Agriculture	Steel	Textiles	Transport	Households	Total
Agriculture	12	2	8	10	21	53
Steel	4	9	5	14	2	34
Textiles	3	1	6	4	24	38
Transport	7	14	3	10	15	49
Households	27	8	16	11	40	102
Total	53	34	38	49	102	276

dustries. You would want to know where each gets its inputs and where it sells its ouput.

An economic plan requires information about the location and quantities required of inputs and the distribution of output between industries and consumers.

For example, the auto industry bought specific quantities of steel from the steel industry, tires from the tire industry, glass from the glass industry, fabric from the textile industry, and so on. It sold autos to the steel, tire, glass, and textile industries as well. That is to say, industries buy from and sell to each other.

CREATING AN INPUT-OUTPUT TABLE

Assuming the data are complete, each industry provides an account of its total output, including information concerning which industries bought what quantities from other industries, as well as which industries provided what quantities of inputs to which industries. The data also include a household sector that records the people's consumption of goods and their supply of labor.

Input-output table
A table whose rows (read across) record the specific quantities each producing sector sells to itself and to every other producing sector, and whose columns (read down) record the specific quantities each producing sector buys from itself and from every other producing sector.

These industry and household accounts make up an economy's **input-output table.** Although real-world input-output tables would show a matrix of hundreds of industries, Table 1, depicting our newly created state socialism, is simplified to four producing industries and a household sector.

Look at agriculture. It produces a total of 53 units. Reading across the first row of the table, we see that 12 of those 53 units are bought by agriculture itself. Two units are bought by steel. The biggest buyers of agricultural output (principally food), 21 units, are households.

Table 1 also shows exactly what goes into producing 53 units of agriculture. The first column tells us that agriculture uses 12 units of its own output, four units of steel, three units of transport, and employs 27 units of labor from the household sector. As you see, agriculture is a relatively labor-intensive industry.

The column that records agriculture's inputs is not unlike a chef's recipe. To make a unit of agriculture, you mix together 12/53 units of agriculture, 4/53 units of steel, and so on. In the same way, you can read the recipes for making steel or textiles.

SELECTING CONSISTENT PRODUCTION TARGETS

If the state plans to produce 34 units of steel, it needs to plan on producing a unit of textiles (read down the steel column) at the same time, otherwise the steel target will be unachievable. It would be like baking bread without flour. The state also must assign eight workers from the household sector to steel. If a flu epidemic hits the factory, steel production could be jeopardized.

But if steel falls short of its target, how can agriculture achieve its target? Agriculture uses 12 units of steel inputs. What happens to transportation's 49 unit target if it cannot get 14 units of steel? You see how terribly vulnerable every target is to every other?

MAKING UP A PRICE SYSTEM

Suppose Katy Stack were put in charge of steel. It's one thing for her to know that the state, in setting up the Table 1 plan, planned the simultaneous production of those inputs she uses to meet her 34-unit target, but quite another to actually get the inputs to her, on schedule, and in the quantities called for in the steel-producing recipe. She also has to think about getting her steel to steel-using producers.

How do those inputs get to her and how does her steel get to steel users without the guidance of a market? That is to say, who directs the traffic? It just doesn't happen because you will it, or plan it out on paper. An impossible task it seems, particularly if there are thousands of planned goods.

How is it done? The hands-on execution of the plan requires the creation of *make-believe markets and make-believe prices.* Plan prices are make-believe because they bear no relationship whatever to demand or to supply. They are determined arbitrarily. For example, the plan may set the price of steel at \$3 per unit, the price of agricultural output at \$2 per unit, the price of labor at \$4 per person, and so on. It may be wise to price goods according to their costs, but costs, being prices too, are also make-believe. What pricing scheme would work for the economy of Table 1?

For simplicity's sake, let's suppose that all prices are \$1 per unit. A unit of steel is \$1. The price of labor is \$1. If Katy meets her steel target, her total revenue would be \$34. Her total cost also would be \$34. Note that she makes no profit because prices were rigged to create no profit. Is Katy concerned about profit? Of course not. Her concern is meeting her production target.

CREATING THE STATE BANK

How is the plan put into operation? The process starts with the state bank. It functions like any bank in a market economy. It makes loans and accepts deposits. Of course, who gets loans and who makes deposits is all predetermined in the plan. For example, because Katy is targeted with producing \$34 of steel and must have \$34 of steel inputs, the state bank gives Katy a credit of \$34.

Why go through this process? Because that's how the steel industry gets money to buy the inputs needed to produce steel. Prices, money, banks, and loans in state socialist systems may look like our own prices, money, banks, and loans, but in fact, they are very different. They allow Katy to buy and sell just as play money in the game of Monopoly allows you to buy railroads, utilities, and if you're lucky, Boardwalk.

The Plan Goes into Action

Katy now goes to work. She hires eight steel workers and pays them, by check, a total of \$8. She writes more checks to pay for agriculture, for transport, and textiles. When these checks are cashed at the state bank, her account there is drawn down by those amounts. In the end, her checks to pay for steel-making inputs should draw down her entire $34 bank line of credit.

But she also sells steel. Transport uses steel. Gordon Kay, who heads Transport, pays for steel with a $14 check drawn on his own account at the state bank. Katy delivers the steel and deposits the $14 check at the bank. Her account is credited for that amount. If Steel produces its 34-unit target, its deposits should total $34. At the end of the plan's production period, then, Steel's account at the state bank should be right back to where it was at the beginning, with $34.

Each industry does what Steel does. Each has its own account at the state bank, each goes through the motions of buying and selling, knowing of course, that there will be demanders to buy its output and sellers to provide it with the inputs needed. Its only concern is hitting the target.

SETTING UP FALLBACK POSITIONS

The state usually establishes priority industries that must achieve their targets, sometimes at the expense of other industries.

Now that's pretty impressive, don't you think? After all, the combination of the state planning agency and the state bank not only created a workable plan, but made it work. Of course, if some industries can't meet their targets, the neatness and simplicity of the plan disappears. If any critical industry falls considerably short of its target, the results can be downright disastrous.

It doesn't take much to mess up a good plan. When one or two key industries fall short, other industries cannot get sufficient inputs to meet their own targets. And the shortage problem spreads rapidly throughout the plan. The only way the state can safeguard against such a potential disaster is for it to establish priority industries. These industries get their designated supplies even if it means cutting deeply into other industries' supplies.

Typically, that's what happens during the plan's production period. The state's priority industries achieve or come close to achieving their targets. The lower-priority industries lag considerably behind. It takes a lot of emergency shifting, denials of supplies, and redesigning of the original plan. As you would expect, the state's investment goods industries are favored. It's the consumer goods industries that always end up short.

What About Consumers?

The habitual victim of state socialist planning is the consumer. The plan can give priority to the households, but that would defeat the purpose of state socialism. After all, *the idea of economic sovereignty belonging to the state is to allow the state to dictate the levels of investment and consumption.* What its households prefer is not unimportant to the state, but household preferences cannot be allowed to undermine state preferences.

This matter of consumer or household preferences is more complicated than allowing or disallowing expression. As you see in Table 1, what households consume is determined by the state. If the state plan is designed to produce only steel, transport, agriculture, and textiles, then, regardless of household preferences, other goods such as washing machines, CD players, cross-training shoes, and luxury homes are not produced. *Unlike market socialism and capitalism where consumers dictate what producers produce, in state socialism the consumers consume what the state plan dictates.* In one case, it's the dog wagging its tail, in the other, it's the tail wagging its dog.

The employment data of the plan also dictate where people work. As you see, the plan assigns 27 people to agriculture, 8 to steel, 16 to textiles, and so on. With enough people of varying skills and interest, perhaps most could end up working at jobs they prefer. Why shouldn't the state try to satisfy workers' employment preferences? But there are limits. Agriculture will get 27 workers, *whether workers like it or not.*

FASCISM

Fascism

An economic system in which productive property, although owned by individuals, is used to produce goods and service that reflect state preferences.

Fascism was an economic system practiced during the depression years of the 1930s, when Germany and Italy voted their fascist political parties into government and when a civil war in Spain brought a fascist dictator to power.

What distinguishes a fascist system from a capitalist one is that economic sovereignty is vested in the state, not in the people. Although property is privately owned, all decisions concerning what to produce and who gets what are vested in the state. The state decides whether private firms produce breads or bombs. *It organizes business, labor, and government into a cooperative unit to execute its preferences.*

Under fascism, the state organizes business, labor, and government so as to increase rates of economic growth.

Why is such state power accepted by its population? Perhaps the most plausible explanation is that the authoritarian character it reflects is not an anathema to the society's culture. Typically, the fascist economy is the complement system to an authoritarian political society. But it is also justified by its proponents on the grounds that it promotes high rates of economic growth which, they argue, are in society's long-run economic interest.

The fascist economic system, they insist, is more capable of generating economic growth than market socialism or capitalism because these systems are structured to satisfy consumer preferences. The state's preferences, on the other hand, are more future-directed than consumer preferences, and inclined toward investment.

In this sense, fascism is state socialism's next-of-kin. The one difference between it and state socialism is that fascism, based on private property, has functioning markets. The fascist state does not engage in hands-on economic activity, as state socialism does in economic planning, but instead allows private producers and labor, working through markets, to do what the state wants done. Historically, what fascist states want is a high-growth economy.

TABLE 2 **Comparing Economic Systems, According to Ownership of Property, Resource Allocator, and Professed Goal**

	Capitalism	Market Socialism	Fascism	State Socialism
Property Ownership	Private	Private and state	Private	State
Resource Allocator	Market	Market and state	State	State
Professed goal	Economic liberty	Economic equality	Economic growth	Economic growth

SUMMARY CLASSIFICATIONS OF ECONOMIC SYSTEMS

Table 2 summarizes and compares the basic attributes of capitalism, market socialism, fascism, and state socialist systems.

WHERE DO THE WORLD'S ECONOMIES FIT IN?

The state socialist economies of the former USSR and Eastern Europe are in the process of radical transformations, although the eventual outcomes of these changes are anything but certain.

Although no economy represents a *pure* form of any model economic system, some come close, or at least closer, to the pure forms outlined in Table 2 than others. Figure 3 provides a crude measure of where some of the world's economies—the United States, Canada, France, Britain, China, North and South Korea, the former USSR, China, and the former Nazi Germany—are positioned.

Look at our own economy in relation to others. Productive property in the United States is overwhelmingly private, positioning our economy in the upper-right corner of Figure 3. The millions of private proprietorships and corporations get their signals from the market, produce for profit, and make indepen-

FIGURE 3
Comparative Economic Systems
A *pure* capitalist system—100 percent private property with 100 percent of goods and services allocated according to individual preferences—would be located at the upper-right corner. A *pure* socialist state system—zero percent private property (meaning 100 percent state property) with zero percent of goods and services allocated according to individual perferences (meaning 100 percent allocated according to state preferences) would be located at the lower-left corner. A *pure* fascist economic system would be located at the upper-left corner. Note the approximate positions of the United States and Canada. Privatization in the 1980s shifted France and Britain closer to the United States. Nazi Germany represents a fascist economic system.

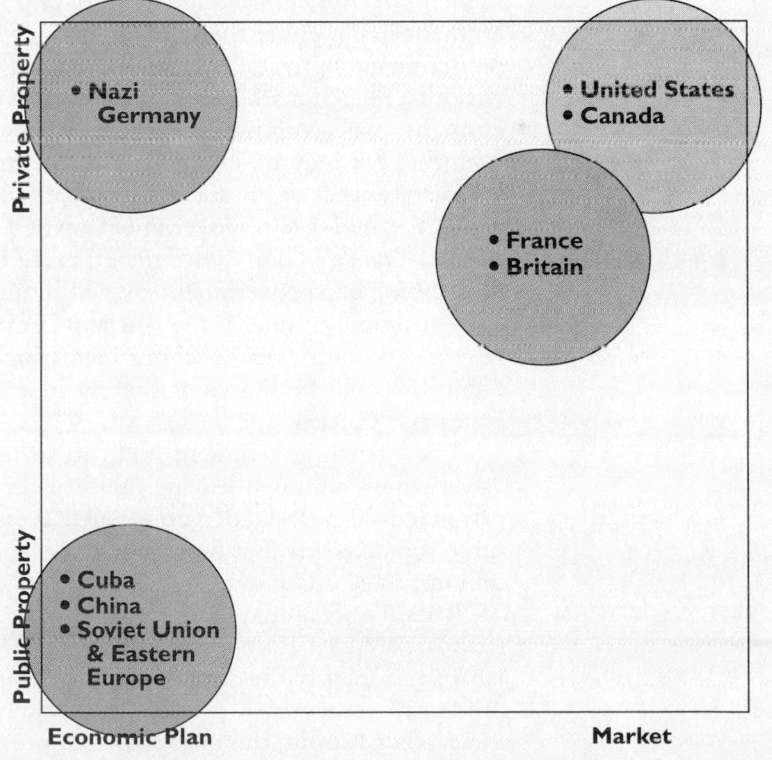

dent investment decisions that, in sum, dictate the character of the economy's growth.

Government-owned and run enterprise still has an important place in our economy. Amtrak, the nation's primary rail system, is owned and run by government. Although some public utilities are private, most are government-owned and run, some by municipalities, others by the state. PBS radio and television is a government network operating in a predominantly private communications industry. Even the government-owned post office competes in a predominantly private industry. Higher education is primarily in the public domain. Many universities and colleges are owned and managed by state and municipal governments.

What about Canada? The Canadian system, reflecting its own history and values, is very similar to our own. Its productive property, too, is overwhelmingly private. Its goods and services, too, are market-determined. Still, Canada's ownership mix bears a uniquely Canadian stamp. Its health care, for example, once similar to ours, is now a government industry, run by its ten provincial governments. Its transcontinental rail system allows government to compete with private enterprise. Government-owned CBC is Canada's principal radio and television network. It competes with CTV and other, smaller private networks. Public utilities are primarily provincial and municipal. Agricultural cooperatives play an important role in the rural economies of the prairie provinces.

Western Europe's economic systems, each specific to its own history and values, are still much more similar than dissimilar. They are clearly capitalist. The French government has a much more important role in economic life than government has in either the United States or Canada. Still, productive property is predominantly private. And French *indicative planning,* once considered the precursor to French market socialism, is little more than a set of guidelines that government expects private industry to achieve. Government targets are announced, but industry compliance is a matter of choice. Market forces in France still dictate what to produce, how to produce, and who gets what.

Privatization

Government divestiture of some of its assets through their sale to private firms and individuals.

In the mid-1980s, government-owned firms produced approximately one-third of France's GDP. Since then, France has embarked upon **privatization,** a dismantling of its government-owned economic operations. By government design—ironically, under the socialist government of François Mitterand—France's economy has become increasingly privatized. Its position, then, in Figure 3 could be shown as shifting in a direction toward that of the United States and Canada.

The French government sold part of its stockholdings in state firms to private owners, although leaving itself still with majority control. For example, it privatized 20 percent of state-owned Renault, France's major auto manufacturer. France's privatization policy affected as well its once state-owned aluminum, steel, computer, insurance, and chemical firms.

Britain's economic system is unmistakably capitalist. Like the economic systems of Western Europe, the United States, Canada, Australia, New Zealand, Japan, and most of the developing economies of Asia, Africa, and Latin America, productive property is principally privately owned and run. In Britain, as in these other nations, the market system prevails.

Government ownership and privatization of industry has been an on-again, off-again activity in Britain since the end of World War II. The Labour Party (socialist) came to power after the war promising to smooth out capitalism's rough edges. It sought no revolution, merely to nationalize the transport, energy, steel, coal, and health care industries. From its inception, Labour's nationalization was challenged. The Conservative government that replaced Labour in 1951 came to power promising privatization. It immediately privatized steel, but left the coal, transport, and health industries still in the government's domain. When Labour became the government in 1967, it renationalized the steel industry. In the 1980s, Margaret Thatcher's conservative government privatized in earnest. Steel was once again denationalized in 1988. The government also sold its British Telecom, British Gas, and British Petroleum. In 1989 it sold its water authorities, and in 1990–91 it sold the electric supply industry.

Look at the positions of the economic systems of Eastern Europe and the Soviet Union *prior to the 1990s*. Their entrenched position in the lower left is a matter of record, even though their economic systems have since been completely dismantled.

The Soviet Union was *the* representative state socialist system. Almost 100 percent of Soviet productive property was state-owned and run. Goods and services were produced according to Gosplan, its planning agency, and its price systems, which were completely divorced from market forces, were instruments used to realize the plan. Gosbank, the state's banking agency, administered the plan's financial accounts. Ownership and management of state farms were identical to ownership and management of industrial factories. Although not at a corner position, the Soviet Union is positioned close to the lower left corner in Figure 3.

Many Soviet peasants had the option of working on state farms or on agricultural collectives. Land used by the collective was government-owned, but farm machinery, houses, barns, livestock, and production belonged to the collective. The collectives exercised more decision-making power than the state farms allowed, but most of their production, prices, and investments were determined by Gosplan.

The economic systems of Eastern Europe were modeled on the Soviet system. Cuba, North Korea, and Vietnam were close copies of Soviet state socialism.

China's state socialism, more peasant-oriented than its Soviet counterpart, survives. The Chinese industrial system is based on state ownership and economic planning. Its rural economy is organized in communes, a variation of the Soviet collective.

The professed goal of these state socialist systems was economic growth. In the 1960s and 1970s, the Soviets seemed almost pathological about catching up to the United States. Were they successful? Although estimates of Soviet economic performance were always controversial, it appeared that the Soviet system was, on this criterion anyway, highly successful.

That judgment all but disappeared in the 1980s. New information, much of it coming from Soviet self-criticism, painted not only an unflattering picture of Soviet economic performance in the 1980s, but a very different picture of its past performance.

The process of state socialist disintegration occurred, as well, throughout the Soviet empire. The East German political state, which dissolved even before Soviet dismemberment, voted to unify itself with capitalist West Germany. State socialist political and economic control in Poland, Hungary, Czechoslovakia, Romania, Albania, and Bulgaria unraveled, creating in each unique directions of economic and political change.

Proudly displaying the peppers produced by his commune, this Chinese peasant will "sell" these vegetables to the State at prices fixed by the State.

Where would the less-developed economies be positioned in Figure 3? Where, for example, would Afghanistan fit? What about Libya, or Saudi Arabia, or Ethiopia, or Chad? These are economies in transition, from nomadic economic activity to basic agricultural production. Some, like Saudi Arabia and Libya, may have modern, foreign-developed, export-directed industry, but these are associated more with the specific export markets they supply than with their own economies. LDCs like those in the Pacific Rim—South Korea, Singapore, Hong Kong, Malaysia—are as capitalist as the U.S. economy.

Where do fascist systems fit in? The most prominent fascist systems were Hitler's Germany, Mussolini's Italy, Franco's Spain, Peron's Argentina, and Salazar's Portugal. There were other less-prominent ones, such as Somoza's Nicaragua, Duvalier's Haiti, and Trujillo's Dominican Republic. They all eventually collapsed. Nazi Germany, structured in 1936, did create employment to push Germany out of depression. But it also pushed them into aggression against Europe in the most barbaric adventure any modern nation has undertaken. In the end, Nazi Germany and its fascist ally Italy were destroyed.

Other fascist states collapsed with the deaths of their fascist leaders. Franco's military victory over Spain's loyalist government brought fascism to Spain in 1936. It ended with his death. Peron's death ended a long reign of Argentinian fascism, although subsequent regimes seem to have been well-schooled in Peronian fascism. Still other fascist regimes, such as Trujillo's Dominican Republic, Duvalier's Haiti, and Somoza's Nicaragua have collapsed under the weight of internal revolt. The only surviving fascist economic system is Paraguay.

CHAPTER REVIEW

1. The extent to which a country can choose its economic system is an intriguing question. Karl Marx believed that no choice existed in this regard. Marx developed a stages theory of economic systems whereby a country's economy

evolved over time through definite and determinate stages, each one reflecting a specific state of technology.

2. Marx's stages ran from primitive communism, through feudalism, capitalism, socialism, and finally, to communism. An economy makes the transition from one stage to the next in the framework of the dialectics. The thesis, or existing set of relations, is marked by the presence of an antithesis that grows to the point at which the thesis can no longer contain it. As a result, the thesis is destroyed and out of its destruction a new thesis, or synthesis, emerges.

3. The transformation from feudalism to capitalism can be explained in the context of Marx's dialectics. The basic form of property under feudalism is land used for agricultural production. This represents the thesis. Opposing the thesis is a growing class of merchants and manufacturers who compete with one another and extend production to new markets. In the process feudal restrictions on their activities are confronted and broken down. Eventually, the merchants and manufacturers grow to the extent that new employment opportunities are offered to peasants, markets become well-developed, and the price system begins to allocate resources. In this way, feudalism is continuously undermined and replaced by capitalism.

4. Capitalism contains its own contradictions in the form of technological change that wipes out small capitalists and causes the ranks of the unemployed to swell over time. Eventually, many workers face a small number of capitalists and the workers rise in revolt, taking over the highly developed productive property created under capitalism. The socialist system that follows the revolution is a brief interlude prior to the advent of communism.

5. Marx's theory of systems is called historical materialism. However, most mainstream economists believe that economies can be organized along alternative lines to be capitalist, market socialist, state socialist, or fascist in character. According to mainstream economists, the choice of an economic system is a societal choice rather than deterministic.

6. Capitalism is an economic system rooted in private property. A rather limited set of rules governs the manner in which people can use their property under capitalism. Property owners also have the right to the income that their property generates, although taxes and transfers can be enacted to modify the market-determined income distribution.

7. Individuals make choices in the market under market socialism just as they do under capitalism. However, the state controls property resources under market socialism. Prices are set by a trial-and-error process so that eventually a market-clearing price is established.

8. Market socialism tends to give greater emphasis to economic equality, while capitalism emphasizes economic liberty. While capitalist economies may moderate income inequality and market socialists don't usually press for perfect income equality, there are ranges of income equality and restrictions on the rights to property that allow us to classify economies as capitalist or market socialist.

9. Under state socialism, the state's decision makers completely replace the market. The former USSR, China, North Korea, and Cuba are examples of state socialist countries marked by the presence of authoritarian regimes. State socialism operates according to an economic plan that is constructed by the use

of data on economic activity in the country. The data can be organized into an input-output table where the various inputs necessary to produce different outputs are shown. Consistent production targets are set, a price system is created, a state bank is established to monitor transactions, and the plan goes into action.

10. Planning in state socialist countries typically gives emphasis to certain key economic sectors. Typically, consumers' preferences take a back seat to the preferences of planners. The intention is to achieve rapid rates of economic growth.

11. Fascism bears some similarity to state socialism, even though property is privately owned. Business, labor, and government are organized into a cooperative unit to execute the preferences of the state. Frequently, the goal is to achieve high rates of economic growth.

12. No pure form of any economic system exists in the world today. The world's systems are hybrids to varying degrees. For example, the United States is predominantly a capitalist economy, even though some enterprises like Amtrak are socialist. The European economies are mostly capitalist, although there is a greater degree of government intervention in their economies than in ours. The USSR used to be the representative state socialist economy. China remains as a state socialist economy. Today, Paraguay is the only example of a truly fascist economy.

KEY TERMS

Feudalism
Capitalism
Socialism
Communism
Dialectics
Market socialism
State socialism
Input-output table
Economic plan
Fascism
Privatization

QUESTIONS

1. How does the deterministic theory of comparative economic systems differ from the nondeterministic theory?

2. Describe Marx's structured sequence of economic systems.

3. The dialectics describes a process of change. How does Marx use the dialectics to explain how economic systems evolve?

4. What distinguishes capitalism from socialism?

5. Compare the priorities that capitalism and socialism assign to economic liberty and economic equality.

6. What distinguishes market socialism from state socialism?

7. What distinguishes fascism from state socialism and from capitalism?

8. What is an input-output table and how is it used in shaping an economic plan?

9. Describe the role played by the state bank in executing a state socialist economic plan.

10. Why do state socialist systems tend to downplay household preferences in economic planning?

11. What is privatization?

GLOSSARY

45° line A line, drawn at a 45° angle, showing all points at which the distance to the horizontal axis equals the distance to the vertical axis.

A

Absolute advantage A country's ability to produce a good using fewer resources than the country it trades with.

Absolute income hypothesis As national income increases, consumption spending increases, but by diminishing amounts—that is, as national income increases, the marginal propensity to consume (MPC) decreases.

Accelerator A relationship between the level of investment and the change in the level of national income.

Accounting profit A firm's total revenue minus its total explicit costs.

Actual investment Investment spending that producers actually make—that is, intended investment (investment spending that producers intend to undertake) plus or minus unintended changes in inventories.

Administrative lag The time interval between deciding on an appropriate policy and the execution of that policy.

Aggregate demand The total quantity of goods and services demanded by households, firms, foreigners, and government at varying price levels.

Aggregate expenditure curve (AE) A curve that shows the quantity of aggregate expenditures at different levels of national income or gross domestic product (GDP).

Aggregate expenditures Spending by consumers on consumption goods, spending by businesses on investment goods, spending by government, and spending by foreigners on net exports.

Aggregate supply The total quantity of goods and services that firms in the economy are willing to supply at varying price levels.

Aid to Families with Dependent Children

(AFDC) A cash assistance program designed to aid single-parent families, usually headed by a woman.

Antitrust policy Laws that foster market competition by prohibiting monopolies and oligopolies from exercising excessive market power.

Appreciation A rise in the price of a nation's currency relative to foreign currencies.

Arbitrage The practice of buying a foreign currency in one market at a low price and selling it in another at a higher price.

Automatic stabilizers Structures in the economy that tend to add to aggregate demand when the economy is in recession and subtract from aggregate demand when the economy is inflationary. Unemployment insurance payments and benefits and the progressive income tax are two such automatic stabilizers.

Autonomous consumption Consumption spending that is independent of the level of income.

Autonomous investment Investment that is independent of the level of income.

Average fixed cost (AFC) Total fixed cost divided by the quantity of goods produced. AFC steadily declines as more of a good is produced.

Average revenue Total revenue divided by the quantity of goods or services sold.

Average total cost (ATC) Total cost divided by the quantity of goods produced. ATC declines, reaches a minimum, and then increases as more of a good is produced.

Average variable cost (AVC) Total variable cost divided by the quantity of goods produced. AVC declines, reaches a minimum, and then increases as more of a good is produced.

B

Backward linkages Investments in one industry create demands for inputs that induce investment in other industries to produce those inputs.

Balance of payments An itemized account of a nation's foreign economic transactions.

Balance of trade The difference between the value of a nation's merchandise exports and its merchandise imports.

Balance on capital account A category that itemizes changes in foreign asset holdings of a nation and that nation's asset holdings abroad.

Balance on current account A category that itemizes a nation's imports and exports of merchandise and services, income receipts and payments on investment, and unilateral transfers.

Balance sheet The bank's statement of liabilities (what it owes) and assets (what it owns).

Balanced budget Government spending equals tax revenues.

Balanced budget multiplier The effect on the equilibrium level of national income of an equal change in government spending and taxes. The balanced budget multiplier is 1.

Balanced oligopoly An oligopoly in which the sales of the leading firms are distributed fairly evenly among them.

Bank note A promissory note issued by a bank that is a pledge to redeem the note for a specific amount of gold or silver. The terms of redemption are specified on the note.

Barter The exchange of one good for another, without the use of money.

Base year The reference year with which prices in other years are compared in a price index.

Big push The development strategy that relies on an integrated network of government-sponsored and financed investments that are introduced into the economy all at once.

Brand loyalty The willingness of consumers to continue buying a good at a price higher than the price of its close substitutes.

Brand multiplication Variations on essentially one good that a firm produces in order to increase its market share.

Budget deficit Government spending exceeds tax revenues.

Budget surplus Tax revenues exceed government spending.

Business cycle Alternating periods of growth and decline in an economy's GDP.

C

Capital Manufactured goods used to make and market other goods and services.

Capital depreciation The value of existing capital stock used up in the process of producing goods and services.

Capital/output ratio The ratio of capital stock to GDP.

Capitalism An economic system in which primary productive property, capital, is owned and managed by individuals. Production of goods and services and distribution of goods and services are determined by market forces. Economic liberty is a highly valued goal.

Cartel A group of firms that collude to limit competition in a market by negotiating and accepting agreed-upon prices and market shares.

Cash assistance Government assistance in the form of cash.

Ceteris paribus The latin phrase meaning "everything else being equal."

Change in demand A change in quantity demanded

of a good that is caused by factors other than a change in the price of that good.

Change in quantity demanded A change in the quantity demanded of a good that is caused solely by a change in the price of that good.

Change in supply A change in quantity supplied of a good that is caused by factors other than a change in the price of that good.

Circular flow model A model of how the economy's resources, money, goods, and services flow between households and firms through resource and product markets.

Circular flow of goods, services, and resources The movement of goods and services from firms to households, and of resources from households to firms.

Circular flow of money The movement of income in the form of resource payments from firms to households, and of income in the form of revenue from households to firms.

Classical economics The school of thought that emphasizes the natural tendency for an economy to move toward equilibrium at full employment without inflation. It argues against government intervention.

Closed shop An arrangement in which a firm may hire only union labor.

Collective bargaining Negotiation between a labor union and a firm employing unionized labor to create a contract concerning wage rates, hours worked, and working conditions.

Collusion The practice of firms to negotiate price and market-share decisions that limit competition in a market.

Communism A stateless economic system in which productive property is owned and managed by the community. People contribute to the production of goods and services according to their abilities, and distribution of the goods and services is made according to their needs.

Comparative advantage A country's ability to produce a good at a lower opportunity cost than the country with which it trades.

Complementary goods Goods that are generally used together; when the price of one increases, the demand for the other decreases.

Concentration ratio A measure of market power. The ratio of total sales of the leading firms in an industry (usually four) to the industry's total sales.

Conglomerate merger A merger between two or more firms in unrelated industries.

Constant returns to scale Costs per unit of production are the same for any level of production. Changes in plant size do not affect the firm's average total cost.

Constant slope of a curve A curve that takes the form of a straight line.

Consumer price index A measure comparing the prices of consumer goods and services that a household typically purchases to the prices of those goods and services purchased in a base year.

Consumer sovereignty The ability of consumers to exercise complete control over what goods and services the economy produces (or doesn't produce) by choosing what goods and services to buy (or not buy).

Consumer surplus The difference between the maximum amount a person would be willing to pay for a good or service and the amount the person actually pays.

Consumption function The relationship between consumption and income.

Contestable market A market in which prices in highly concentrated industries are moderated by the potential threat of firms entering the market.

Corporate bond A corporate IOU. The corporation borrows capital for a specified period of time in exchange for this promise to repay the loan along with an agreed-upon rate of interest.

Corporate income tax A tax levied on the corporation's income before dividends are distributed to stockholders.

Corporation A firm whose legal identity is separate from the people who own shares of its stock. The firm alone, not the people who own it, is responsible for all debts incurred by the firm. The liability of each stockowner is limited only to what he or she has invested in the firm.

Cost-push inflation Inflation caused primarily by a decrease in aggregate supply.

Countercyclical fiscal policy Fiscal policy designed to moderate the severity of the business cycle.

Countercyclical monetary policy Policy directives used by the Fed to moderate swings in the business cycle. The Fed's options are changing the reserve requirements, changing the discount rate, and buying or selling bonds in the open market.

Countervailing power The exercise of market power by an economic bloc is ultimately counteracted by the market power of a competing bloc so that no bloc exercises undue market power.

Craft union A union representing workers of a single occupation, regardless of the industry in which the workers are employed.

Creative destruction Effective competition that exists not among firms within highly concentrated industries but between the highly concentrated industries themselves. Such competition assures competitive prices.

Cross elasticity of demand The ratio of a percentage

change in quantity demanded of one good to a percentage change in the price of another good. Its value expresses the percentage change in quantity demanded of one good generated by a 1 percent change in the price of the other.

Crowding out A fall in private investment spending caused by an increase in government spending.

Currency Coins and paper money.

Customs duty A sales tax applied to a foreign good or service.

Customs union A set of countries that agree to free trade among themselves and a common trade policy with all other countries.

Cyclical unemployment Unemployment associated with the downturn and recession phases of the business cycle.

D

Debt service Interest payments on international debt as a percent of a nation's merchandise exports.

Demand curve A curve that depicts the relationship between price and quantity demanded.

Demand schedule A schedule showing the specific quantity of a good or service that people are willing and able to buy at different prices.

Demand-pull inflation Inflation caused primarily by an increase in aggregate demand.

Dependent variable A variable whose value depends upon the value of another variable.

Depreciation A fall in the price of a nation's currency relative to foreign currencies.

Depression Severe recession.

Deregulation The process of converting a regulated firm into an unregulated firm.

Devaluation Government policy that lowers the nation's exchange rate; its currency instantly is worth less in the foreign exchange market.

Dialectics A process describing the simultaneous growth and destruction of economic systems.

Differential land rent Rent arising from differences in the productivity of land.

Discount rate The interest rate which the Fed charges banks that borrow reserves from it.

Discouraged workers Unemployed people who give up looking for work after experiencing persistent rejection in their attempts to find work.

Discrimination in labor markets The practice by firms that denies qualified workers their marginal revenue product (MRP) either by excluding them from competing in a labor market or by paying them less than other workers with identical skills.

Diseconomies of scale Increases in the firm's average total cost brought about by the disadvantages associated with bureaucracy and the inefficiencies that eventually emerge with increases in the firm's operations.

Disposable personal income Personal income minus direct taxes.

Dividend That part of a corporation's net income that is paid out to its stockholders.

Downturn A phase in the business cycle in which real GDP declines, inflation moderates, and unemployment emerges.

Dumping Exporting a good or service at a price below its cost of production.

Durable goods Goods which are expected to last at least a year.

E

Econometrics The use of statistics to quantify and test economic models.

Economic dualism The coexistence of two separate and distinct economies within a less-developed country (LDC); one modern, primarily urban, and export-driven, the other traditional, agricultural, and self-sustaining.

Economic efficiency The maximum possible production of goods and services generated by the fullest employment of the economy's resources.

Economic growth An increase in real GDP, typically expressed as an annual rate of real GDP growth.

Economic model An abstraction of an economic reality. It can be expressed pictorially, graphically, algebraically, or in words.

Economic plan A set of production targets for all goods and services determined in advance by the state which are consistent with the economy's supply of the resources. The resources are allocated in such a manner (using input-output analysis) as to implement the predetermined production targets.

Economic profit A firm's total revenue minus its total explicit and implicit costs.

Economics The study of how people work together to transform resources into goods and services to satisfy their most pressing wants, and how they distribute these goods and services among themselves.

Economies of scale Decreases in the firm's average total cost brought about by increased specialization and efficiencies in production realized through increases in the scale of the firm's operations.

Elasticity A term economists use to describe sensitivity.

Engel's Law The observation that income elasticities of demand for food are less than one.

Entrepreneur A person who alone assumes the risks and uncertainties of a business. The entrepreneur conceives the idea of the business, decides what factors of production to use, and determines how to market the goods and services produced.

Equation of exchange *MV* = *PQ*. The quantity of money times its velocity equals the quantity of goods and services produced times their prices.

Equilibrium level of national income $C + I_i = C + S$, where saving equals intended investment.

Equilibrium price The price that equates quantity demanded to quantity supplied. If any disturbance from that price occurs, excess demand or excess supply emerges to drive the price back to equilibrium.

Equipment capital The physical plant, machinery, and raw materials that a firm uses in production.

European Economic Community (EC) A customs union consisting of France, Italy, Belgium, Holland, Luxembourg, Germany, Britain, Ireland, Denmark, Greece, Spain, and Portugal.

Excess demand The difference, at a particular price, between quantity demanded and quantity supplied, quantity demanded being the greater.

Excess reserves The quantity of reserves held by a bank in excess of the legally required amount.

Excess supply The difference, at a particular price, between quantity supplied and quantity demanded, quantity supplied being the greater.

Exchange controls A system in which government, as the sole depository of foreign currencies, exercises complete control over how these currencies can be used.

Exchange rate The number of units of foreign currency that can be purchased with one unit of domestic currency.

Excise tax Any tax levied on a good or service, such as a unit tax, a sales tax, or a custom duty.

Expenditure approach A method that adds all expenditures made for final goods and services by households, firms, and government.

Explicit costs The firm's opportunity costs that take the form of cash payments.

Exports Goods and services produced by people in one country that are sold in other countries.

External debt Public debt held by foreigners.

Externalities Unintended costs or benefits that are imposed on unsuspecting people and that result from economic activity initiated by others. Unintended costs are called negative externalities; unintended benefits are called positive externalities.

F

Factor of production Any resource used in a production process. Resources are grouped into labor, land, capital, and entrepreneurship.

Fascism An economic system in which productive property, although owned by individuals, is used to produce goods and services that reflect state preferences. Economic growth is a highly valued goal.

Federal Deposit Insurance Corporation (FDIC) A U.S. government insurance agency that provides depositors in FDIC-participating banks 100 percent coverage on their first $100,000 of deposits.

Federal funds market The market in which banks lend and borrow reserves from each other for very short periods of time, usually overnight.

Federal funds rate The interest rate on loans made by banks in the federal funds market.

Federal Open Market Committee The Fed's principal decision-making body, charged with executing the Fed's open market operations. It also advises the Fed's Board of Governors on policy concerning the reserve requirement and discount rate.

Federal Reserve System (the Fed) The central bank of the United States.

Feudalism An economic system in which primary productive property, land, is organized into large, essentially self-supporting estates (or manors), each owned by a landlord and worked by dependent tenants who, owning no property of their own, are attached to the estates. Hereditary rights to ownership and tenancy perpetuate the arrangement between landlord and tenant.

Fiat money Paper money which is not backed by or convertible into any good.

Final goods Goods purchased for final use, not for resale.

Financial intermediaries Firms that accept deposits from savers and use those deposits to make loans to borrowers.

Firm An economic unit that produces goods and services in the expectation of selling them to households, other firms, or government.

Fiscal policy Government spending and taxation policy to achieve macroeconomic goals of full employment without inflation.

Fixed cost Cost to the firm that does not vary with the quantity of goods produced. The cost is incurred even when the firm does not produce.

Fixed exchange rate A rate determined by government and then maintained through the process of buying and selling quantities of its own currency on the foreign exchange market.

Floating exchange rate An exchange rate determined strictly by the demands and supplies for a nation's currency.

Food stamp program An aid program that provides low-income people with stamps that can be redeemed for food and related items.

Foreign exchange market A market in which currencies of different nations are bought and sold.

Foreign exchange reserves The stock of foreign currencies a government holds.

Forward linkages Investments in one industry create opportunities for profitable investments in other industries, which use the goods produced in the first as inputs.

Fractional reserve system A banking system that provides people immediate access to their deposits, but that allows banks to hold only a fraction of those deposits in reserve.

Free trade International trade that is not encumbered by protectionist government policies such as tariffs and quotas.

Free trade area A set of countries that agree to free trade among themselves but are free to pursue independent trade policies with other countries.

Free-rider Someone who consumes a good or service without paying for it. Typically, the good or service consumed is in the form of a positive externality.

Frictional unemployment Relatively brief periods of unemployment caused by people deciding to voluntarily quit work in order to seek more attractive employment.

Fringe benefits Nonwage compensation that workers receive from employers.

Full employment An employment level in which the actual rate of employment in the economy is equal to the economy's natural rate of unemployment.

G

Game theory A theory of strategy ascribed to firms' behavior in oligopoly. The firms' behavior is mutually interdependent.

GATT (General Agreements on Tariffs and Trade) An agreement to negotiate reductions in tariffs and other trade barriers and to provide equal and nondiscriminating treatment among members of the agreement. Over 100 countries are members of GATT.

GDP deflator A measure comparing the prices of all goods and services produced in the economy during a given year to the prices of those goods and services purchased in a base year.

Gini coefficient A numerical measure of the degree of income inequality in an economy. It ranges from zero, depicting perfect equality, to one, depicting perfect inequality.

Government failure The failure of the government to buy the socially optimal quantity of public goods.

Government purchases All goods and services bought by government.

Gross domestic product (GDP) Total value of all final goods and services, measured in current market prices, produced in the economy during a year.

Gross national product (GNP) The market value of all final goods and services in an economy produced by resources owned by people of that economy, regardless of where the resources are located.

Gross private domestic investment The purchase by firms of plant, equipment, and inventory goods.

H

Horizontal merger A merger between firms producing the same good in the same industry.

Household An economic unit of one or more persons living under one roof that has a source of income and uses it in whatever way it deems fit.

Human capital The investment in workers' knowledge acquired through education, training, and/or experience that enhances their productivity.

I

Implicit costs The firm's opportunity costs of using resources owned or provided by the entrepreneur.

Import controls Tariffs and quotas used by government to limit a nation's imports.

Imports Goods and services bought by people in one country that are produced in other countries.

In-kind assistance Government assistance in the form of direct goods and services, such as Medicaid or food stamps.

Income approach Method which adds all the incomes earned in the production of final goods and services.

Income elastic A 1 percent change in income generates a greater than 1 percent change in quantity demanded.

Income elasticity The ratio of the percentage change in quantity demanded to the percentage change in income. Its value is the percentage change in quantity demanded generated by a 1 percent change in income.

Income inelastic A 1 percent change in income generates a less than 1 percent change in quantity demanded.

Income multiplier The multiple by which income changes as a result of a change in investment spending.

Increasing returns to scale A situation in which a firm's minimum long-run average total cost decreases as the level of production increases.

Independent variable A variable whose value influences the value of another variable.

Industrial union A union representing all workers in a single industry, regardless of each worker's skill or craft.

Industry A collection of firms producing the same good.

Inferior goods Goods for which demand decreases when people's incomes increase.

Inflation An increase in the price level.

Inflationary gap The amount by which aggregate expenditure exceeds the aggregate expenditure level needed to generate equilibrium national income at full employment without inflation.

Infrastructure The basic institutions and public facilities upon which an economy's development depends.

Innovation An idea that eventually takes the form of new, applied technology.

Input-output table A table whose rows (read across) record the specific quantities each producing sector sells to itself and to every other producing sector, and whose columns (read down) record the specific quantities each producing sector buys from itself and from every other producing sector.

Intended investment Investment spending that producers intend to undertake.

Interest rate The price of loanable funds, expressed as an annual percentage return on a dollar of loanable funds.

Intermediate goods Goods used to produce other goods.

International debt The total amount of outstanding IOUs a nation is obligated to repay other nations and international organizations.

International specialization The use of a country's resources to produce specific goods and services, allowing other countries to focus on the production of other goods and services.

Interpersonal comparisons of utility A comparison of the marginal utilities that different people derive from a good or a dollar.

Inventory investment Stocks of finished goods and raw materials that firms keep in reserve to facilitate production and sales.

K

Keynesian economics The school of thought that emphasizes the possibility that an economy can be in equilibrium at less than full employment (or with inflation). It argues that with government intervention, equilibrium at full employment without inflation can be achieved by managing aggregate demand.

Kinked demand curve The demand curve facing a firm in oligopoly; the curve is more elastic when the firm raises price than when it lowers price.

L

Labor The physical and intellectual effort of people engaged in producing goods and services.

Labor efficiency The amount of labor time required to produce a unit of output.

Labor force People over age 16 who are gainfully employed or actively seeking employment.

Labor productivity The quantity of GDP produced per worker, typically measured in quantity of GDP per hour of labor.

Labor specialization The division of labor into specialized activities that allow individuals to be more productive.

Labor union An association of workers, each of whom transfers the right to negotiate wage rates, work hours, and working conditions to the association. In this way, the union presents itself as a single seller of labor on the labor market.

Laissez-faire Government policy of nonintervention in market outcomes. Translated, it means "leave it be."

Land A natural-state resource such as real estate, grasses and forests, and metals and minerals.

Land rent A payment to landowners for the use of land.

Law of demand The inverse relationship between price and quantity demanded of a good or service, *ceteris paribus*.

Law of diminishing marginal utility The idea that as more of a good is consumed, the utility a person derives from each additional unit diminishes.

Law of increasing costs The opportunity cost of producing a good increases as more of the good is produced. The law is based on the fact that not all resources are suited to the production of all goods and that the order of use of a resource in producing a good goes from the most productive resource unit to the least.

Legal reserve requirement Percent of demand deposits banks and other financial intermediaries are required to keep in cash reserves.

Less-developed countries (LDCs) Economies of Asia, Africa, and Latin America.

Leveraged buyouts A primarily debt-financed purchase of all the stock or assets of a company.

Life-cycle hypothesis Typically, a person's MPC is relatively high during young adulthood, decreases during the middle-age years, and increases when the person is near or in retirement.

Life-cycle wealth Wealth in the form of nonmonetary assets, such as a house, automobiles, and personal clothing.

Liquidity The degree to which an asset can easily be exchanged for money.

Liquidity preference The demand for money.

Loanable funds Money that a firm employs to purchase the physical plant, equipment, and raw materials used in production.

Loanable funds market The market in which the demand for and supply of loanable funds determines the rate of interest.

Location rent Rent arising from differences in land distances from the marketplace.

Long run The time interval during which suppliers are able to change the quantity of all the resources they use to produce goods and services.

Lorenz curve A curve depicting an economy's income distribution. It records the percentage of total income that a specific part of the population—typically represented by quintiles ranging from the poorest to richest—receives.

Loss minimization Faced with the certainty of incurring losses, the firm's goal is to incur the lowest loss possible from its production and sale of goods and services.

M

M1 money supply The supply of the most immediate form of money. It includes currency, demand deposits, and traveler's checks.

M2 money supply M1 money plus less immediate forms of money, such as savings accounts, money market mutual accounts, money market deposit accounts, repurchase agreements, and small denomination time deposits.

M3 money supply M2 money plus large denomination time deposits and large denomination repurchase agreements.

Macroeconomics A subarea of economics that analyzes the behavior of the economy as a whole.

Macroequilibrium The level of real GDP and the price level that equate the aggregate quantity demanded and the aggregate quantity supplied.

Margin requirement The maximum percentage of the cost of a stock that can be borrowed from a bank or any other financial institution, with the stock offered as collateral.

Marginal cost (MC) The change in total cost generated by a change in the quantity of a good produced. Typically, MC is used to measure the additional cost incurred by adding one more unit of output to production.

Marginal cost pricing A regulatory agency's policy of pricing a good or service produced by a regulated firm at the firm's marginal cost, $P = MC$.

Marginal externality cost (MEC) The change in an external cost generated by a change in the quantity of a good produced.

Marginal labor cost The change in a firm's total cost that results from adding one more worker to production.

Marginal physical product (MPP) The change in output that results from adding one more unit of a resource, such as labor, to production. MPP is expressed in physical units, such as tons of coal, bushels of wheat, or number of automobiles.

Marginal propensity to consume (MPC) The ratio of the change in consumption spending to a given change in income.

Marginal propensity to save (MPS) The change in saving induced by a change in income.

Marginal revenue The change in total revenue generated by the sale of one additional unit of goods or services.

Marginal revenue product (MRP) The change in total revenue that results from adding one more unit of a resource, such as labor, to production. MRP, which is expressed in dollars, is equal to MPP multiplied by the price of the good.

Marginal revenue product of capital The change in total revenue that results from adding one more dollar of loanable funds to production.

Marginal social cost (MSC) The change in the total cost to society generated by a change in the quantity of a good produced. MSC is equal to the sum of the good's marginal external cost and the marginal cost incurred by the firm producing the good.

Marginal utility The increase in total utility a person derives from consuming an additional unit of a good.

Mark-up profit The profit added to cost to determine price.

Market demand The sum of all individual demands in a market.

Market failure The failure of the market to achieve an optimal allocation of the economy's resources. The failure results from the market's inability to take externalities into account.

Market power A firm's ability to select and control market price and output.

Market share The percent of total market sales produced by a particular firm in a market.

Market socialism A socialist system in which the state determines the economy's basic investments, leaving all other production and consumption decisions to individuals who express their preferences for goods and services on the market. Individual choice and income equality are highly valued goals.

Market structure A set of market characteristics such as number of firms, ease or difficulty of firm entry, and complementarity, or substitutability of goods.

Market-day supply A market situation in which the quantity of a good supplied is fixed, regardless of price.

***MC = MR* rule** The guideline used by a firm to achieve profit maximization.

Median income The midpoint of a society's income distribution, above and below which an equal number of individuals (or families) belong.

Medicaid A health care program administered through Social Security that is applicable to low-income and disabled people.

Medicare A health care program administered through Social Security that is applicable to everyone over 65 years old.

Microeconomics A subarea of economics that analyzes individuals as consumers and producers, and specific firms and industries. It focuses especially on the market behavior of firms and households.

Minimum wage A government-legislated wage rate that becomes the lowest wage rate a firm is legally permitted to offer a worker.

Money Any commonly accepted good that acts as a medium of exchange, a measure of value, and a store of value.

Money supply Typically, M1 money. The supply of currency, demand deposits, and traveler's checks used in transactions.

Monopolistic competition A market structure consisting of many firms producing goods that are close substitutes. Firm entry is possible, but is less open and easy than in perfect competition.

Monopoly A market structure consisting of one firm producing a good that has no close substitutes. Firm entry is impossible.

Monopsony A labor market with only one buyer.

***MU/P* equalization principle** The idea that a person's utility is maximized when the ratios of marginal utility to price for each of the goods consumed are equal.

Multinational corporation A corporation whose production facilities are located in two or more countries. Typically, multinational corporate sales are also international.

Mutual interdependence Any price change made by one firm in the oligopoly affects the pricing behavior of all other firms in the oligopoly.

N

National income The sum of all payments made to resource owners for the use of their resources.

Nationalization Government ownership of a firm or industry. Price and production decisions are made by an administrative agency of the government.

Nationally-chartered bank A commercial bank that receives its charter from the Comptroller of the Currency and is subject to federal law as well as the laws of the state in which it operates.

Natural monopoly The result of a combination of market demand and firm's costs such that only one firm is able to produce profitably in a market.

Natural rate of unemployment The rate of unemployment caused by frictional plus structural unemployment in the economy.

Natural resources The lands, water, metals, minerals, animals, and other gifts of nature that are available for producing goods and services.

Negative income tax Government cash payments to the poor—an income tax in reverse—that is linked to the income levels of the poor. The cash payments decrease as income levels increase. The payments are designed to provide a minimum level of income to the poor.

Neo-Keynesian economics The school of thought that emphasizes the possibility that an economy can be in equilibrium at less than full employment with inflation. It argues that by managing aggregate demand, government can achieve the most acceptable combination of unemployment and inflation.

Net domestic product (NDP) GDP minus capital depreciation.

Net exports An economy's exports to other economies minus its imports from other economies.

Nominal GDP GDP measured in terms of current market prices—that is, the price level at the time of measurement. (It is not adjusted for inflation.)

Noncompeting labor markets Markets whose requirement for specific skills necessarily exclude workers who do not have the required skills.

Nondurable goods Goods which are expected to last less than a year.

Normal good A good whose demand increases or decreases when people's incomes increase or decrease.

Normal profit The entrepreneur's opportunity cost. It is equal to or greater than the income an entrepreneur could receive employing his or her resources elsewhere. Normal profit is included in the firm's costs.

Normative economics A subset of economics founded on value judgments and leading to assertions of what ought to be.

North American Free Trade Agreement (NAFTA) A free trade area consisting of Canada, the United States, and Mexico.

O

Oligopoly A market structure consisting of only a few firms producing goods that are close substitutes.

Open market operations The buying and selling of government bonds by the Federal Open Market Committee.

Opportunity cost The quantity of other goods that must be given up to obtain a good.

Origin A graph's point of reference.

P

Parity price ratio The relationship between prices received by farmers and prices paid by farmers.

Partnership A firm owned by two or more persons who each bear the responsibilities and unlimited liabilities of the firm.

Patent A monopoly right on the use of a specific new technology or on the production of a new good. The monopoly right is awarded to and safeguarded by the government for 17 years to the firm who introduces the new technology or good.

Peak Top of a business cycle.

Per se A judicial standard or criterion by which a firm's size within an industry is considered sufficient evidence for the court to rule against it in an antitrust suit.

Perfect competition A market structure consisting of a large number of firms producing goods that are perfect substitutes. Firm entry is open and easy.

Perfectly contained market A set of goods in which cross elasticities among any two goods in the set are infinite and whose cross elasticities with any other good outside the set are zero.

Permanent income Permanent income is the regular income a person expects to earn annually. It may differ by some unexpected gain or loss from the actual income earned.

Permanent income hypothesis A person's consumption spending is related to his or her permanent income.

Personal consumption expenditures All goods and services bought by households.

Personal income National income plus income received but not earned minus income earned but not received.

Phillips curve A graph showing the inverse relationship between the economy's rate of unemployment and rate of inflation.

Poll tax A tax of a specific absolute sum levied on every person or every household.

Positive economics A subset of economics that analyzes the way the economy actually operates.

Potential money multiplier The increase in the money supply that is potentially generated by a change in demand deposits.

Poverty threshold The level of income below which families are considered to be poor.

Present value The value today of the stream of expected future annual income a property generates. The method of computing present value is to divide the annual income generated, R, by the rate of interest r. That is, $PV = R/r$.

Price ceiling A maximum price set by government below the market-generated equilibrium price.

Price discrimination The practice of offering a specific good or service at different prices to different segments of the market.

Price elastic Quality of the range of a demand curve where elasticities of demand are greater than 1.0. In the elastic range, price cuts increase total revenue and price increases decrease total revenue.

Price elasticity of demand The ratio of the percentage change in quantity demanded to the percentage change in price. Its numerical value expresses the percentage change in quantity demanded generated by a 1 percent change in price.

Price elasticity of supply The ratio of the percentage change in quantity supplied to the percentage change in price. Its numerical value expresses the percentage change in quantity supplied generated by a 1 percent change in price.

Price floor A minimum price set by government above the market-generated equilibrium price.

Price inelastic Quality of the range of a demand curve where elasticities of demand are less than 1.0. In the inelastic range, price cuts decrease total revenue and price increases decrease total revenue.

Price leader A firm whose price decisions are tacitly accepted and followed by other firms in the industry.

Price level A measure of prices in one year expressed in relation to prices of a base year.

Price-maker A firm conscious of the fact that its own activity in the market affects price. The firm has the ability to choose among combinations of price and output.

Price-taker A firm that views market price as a given and considers any activity on its own part as having no influence on that price.

Privatization Government divestiture of some of its assets through their sale to private firms and individuals.

Product differentiation The physical or perceived differences among goods in a market that make them close, but not perfect substitutes for each other.

Production possibilities The various combinations of goods that can be produced in an economy when it uses its available resources and technology efficiently.

Profit Income earned by entrepreneurs.

Profit maximization The primary goal of a firm. The firm strives to achieve the most profit possible from its production and sale of goods or services.

Progressive income tax A tax whose rate varies directly with the income of the person taxed. Rich people pay a higher tax rate—a larger percentage of their income is taxed—than poor people.

Property rights The right to own a good or service and the right to receive the benefits that the use of the good or service provides.

Property tax A tax levied on the value of physical assets, such as land, or financial assets, such as stock and bonds.

Proportional income tax A tax whose rate varies proportionally with the income of the person taxed. Everyone with the same income is taxed at the same rate.

Prosperity A phase in the business cycle marked by a relatively high level of real GDP, full employment, and inflation.

Public choice The view that the behavior of government concerning the production and allocation of public goods is dictated, mainly by the needs of members of government to keep their jobs.

Public debt The total value of government securities—Treasury bills, notes, and bonds—held by individuals, businesses, other government agencies, and the Federal Reserve.

Public good A good whose benefits are not diminished even when additional people consume it and whose benefits cannot be withheld from anyone.

Q

Quantity theory of money $P = MV/Q$. The equation specifying the direct relationship between the money supply and prices.

Quota A limit on the quantity of a specific good that can be imported.

R

Ration coupon A coupon issued by the government entitling the holder to purchase a specific quantity of a good at or below the price ceiling.

Rational expectations The school of thought that emphasizes the impossibility that government can reduce the economy's rate of unemployment by managing aggregate demand. It argues that because people anticipate the consequences of announced government policy and incorporate these anticipated consequences into their present decision making they end up undermining the policy.

Real GDP GDP adjusted for changes in the price level.

Recession A phase in the business cycle in which the decline in the economy's real GDP persists for at least a half-year. A recession is marked by relatively high unemployment.

Recessionary gap The amount by which aggregate expenditure falls short of the level needed to generate equilibrium national income at full employment without inflation.

Reciprocity The idea that tariff reductions negotiated between two countries should automatically be extended to all of those countries' trading partners.

Recovery A phase in the business cycle, following a recession, in which real GDP increases and unemployment declines.

Regressive income tax A tax whose impact varies inversely with the income of the person taxed. Poor people have a higher percent of their income taxed than rich people.

Regulation Although ownership of the regulated firm remains in private hands, pricing and production decisions of the firm are monitored by a regulatory agency directly responsible to the government.

Relative income hypothesis As national income increases, consumption spending increases as well, always by the same amount. That is, as national income increases, MPC remains constant.

Relevant market The set of goods whose cross elasticities with others in the set are relatively high and whose cross elasticities with goods outside the set are relatively low.

Rent The difference between what a productive resource receives as payment for its use in production and the cost of bringing that resource into production.

Rent control Government-set price ceilings on rent.

Reserve requirement The minimum amount of reserves the Fed requires a bank to hold, based on a percentage of the bank's total deposit liabilities.

Return to Monopsony power The difference between the *MRP* and the wage rate of the last worker hired, multiplied by the number of workers hired.

Rule of reason A judicial standard or criterion by which a firm's size within an industry is insufficient evidence for the court to rule against it in an antitrust suit. Evidence must show that the firm actually used its size to violate antitrust laws.

S

Sales tax A tax levied in the form of a specific percentage of the value of the good or service.

Saving That part of national income not spent on consumption.

Scarcity The perpetual state of insufficiency of resources to satisfy people's unlimited wants.

Services Productive activities that are instantaneously consumed.

Short run The time interval during which suppliers are able to change the quantity of some but not all the resources they use to produce goods and services.

Shut down The cessation of the firm's activity. The firm's loss minimization occurs at zero output.

Slope of a curve The ratio of the change in the variable measured on the vertical axis to the corresponding change in the variable measured on the horizontal axis, between two points.

Slope of a tangent The slope of a curve at its point of tangency.

Social Security (OASDI) A social insurance program that provides benefits, subject to eligibility, to the elderly, disabled, and their dependents.

Socialism An economic system in which productive property is owned and managed by the state. Production of goods and services and distribution of goods and services reflect state preferences. Income equality is a highly valued goal.

Sole proprietorship A firm owned by one person who alone bears the responsibilities and unlimited liabilities of the firm.

Special-interest lobby A group organized to influence people in government concerning the costs and benefits of particular public goods.

Stabilization policy The use of countercyclical monetary and fiscal policy by the government and the Fed to stabilize the economy.

Stagflation A period of stagnating real GDP, inflation, and relatively high levels of unemployment.

State socialism A socialist system in which the state decides which goods and services are to be produced and designs and directs an economic plan to produce them. Economic growth is a highly valued goal.

State-chartered bank A commercial bank that receives its charter or licence to function from a state government and is subject to the laws of that state.

Stock Ownership in a corporation, represented by shares that are claims on the firm's assets and earnings.

Stockholder A person who owns stock or shares in a corporation.

Strike The withholding of labor by a union when the collective bargaining process fails to produce a contract that is acceptable to the union.

Structural unemployment Unemployment that results from fundamental technological changes in production, or from the substitution of new goods for customary ones.

Substitute goods Goods that can replace each other. When the price of one increases, the demand for the other increases.

Supplemental Security Income (SSI) A cash assistance program that aids the elderly, blind, and disabled.

Supply curve A curve that depicts the relationship between price and quantity supplied.

Supply schedule A schedule showing the specific quantity of a good or what service suppliers are willing and able to provide at different prices.

Supply-side economics The school of thought that emphasizes the possibility of achieving full employment without inflation. It argues that through tax reductions, spending cuts, and deregulation, government creates the proper incentives for the private sector to increase aggregate supply.

T

Tangent A straight line that touches a curve at only one point.

Target price A minimum price level for specific farm goods that the government sets and guarantees. If the market price falls below this target price, the government pays the farmer the difference between the market and target price for each unit sold.

Tariff A tax on an imported good.

Tax multiplier The multiple by which the equilibrium level of national income changes when a dollar change in taxes occurs. The multiple depends upon the marginal propensity to consume. The equation for the tax multiplier is $-MPC/(1-MPC)$.

Terms of trade The amount of a good or service (export) that must be given up to buy a unit of another good or service (import). A country's terms of trade is measured by the ratio of the country's export prices to its import prices.

The paradox of thrift The more people try to save, the more income falls, leaving them with no more and perhaps with even less saving.

Third parties People upon whom the unintended externalities are imposed.

Total cost Cost to the firm that includes both fixed and variable costs.

Total labor cost Quantity of labor employed multiplied by the wage rate.

Total revenue The price of a good multiplied by the number of units sold.

Total utility The total number of utils a person derives from consuming a specific quantity of a good.

Transactions demand for money The quantity of money demanded by a household or business to transact its buying and selling of goods and services.

Transfer payments Income received but not earned.

Transitory income The unexpected gain or loss of income that a person experiences. It is the difference between a person's regular and actual income in any year.

Trough Bottom of a business cycle.

U

Unbalanced oligopoly An oligopoly in which the sales of the leading firms are distributed unevenly among them.

Underemployed resources The less than full utilization of a resource's productive capabilities.

Underemployed workers Workers employed in jobs that do not utilize their productive talents or experience.

Underground economy The unreported or illegal production of goods and services in the economy that is not counted in GDP.

Unemployment insurance A program of income support to eligible workers who are temporarily unemployed.

Unemployment rate The ratio of unemployment to the labor force.

Unilateral transfers Transfers of currency made by individuals, businesses, or government of one nation to individuals, businesses, or governments in other nations, with no designated return.

Union shop An arrangement in which a firm may hire nonunion labor, but every nonunion worker hired must join the union within a specified period of time.

Unit elastic Elasticity is equal to 1.0. In this range, price cuts or increases do not change total revenue.

Unit tax A fixed tax in the form of cents or dollars per unit levied on a good or service.

Unlimited liability Personal responsibility of the owners for all debts incurred by sole proprietorships or partnerships. The owners' personal wealth is subject to appropriation to pay off the firm's debt.

Unwanted inventories Goods produced for consumption that remain unsold.

Util A fictitious unit of measurement representing how much utility a person obtains from consuming a good.

Utility The satisfaction or enjoyment a person obtains from consuming a good.

Value added The difference between the value of a good that a firm produces and the value of the goods the firm uses to produce it.

Variable costs Costs that vary with the quantity of goods produced. Variable costs include such items as wages and raw materials.

Velocity of money The average number of times per year each dollar is used to transact an exchange.

Vertical merger A merger between firms that have a supplier-purchaser relationship.

Wage rate The price of labor. Typically, the wage rate is calculated in dollars per hour.

Wage-related rent The difference between what a resource receives and what it takes to bring the supply of that resource to market.

Wealth The accumulated assets owned by individuals.

INDEX

A

B

C

F

G

J

K

L

M

N

O

P

Q

R

S

T

TABLE C U.S. MONEY SUPPLY AND INTEREST RATES

Year	M1	M2	M3	Three-Month T-Bill Rate	Prime Rate	Federal Funds Rate
	Billions of Dollars			*Percent*		
1959	140.0	297.8	299.8	3.4	4.5	3.3
1960	140.7	312.3	315.3	2.9	4.8	3.2
1961	145.2	335.5	341.0	2.4	4.5	2.0
1962	147.8	362.7	371.4	2.8	4.5	2.7
1963	153.3	393.2	406.0	3.2	4.5	3.2
1964	160.3	424.8	442.5	3.5	4.5	3.5
1965	167.9	459.3	482.2	4.0	4.5	4.1
1966	172.0	480.0	505.1	4.9	5.6	5.1
1967	183.3	524.3	557.1	4.3	5.6	4.2
1968	197.4	566.3	606.2	5.3	6.3	5.7
1969	203.9	589.5	615.0	6.7	8.0	8.2
1970	214.4	628.1	677.4	6.5	7.9	7.2
1971	228.3	712.7	776.1	4.3	5.7	4.7
1972	249.2	805.2	886.0	4.1	5.3	4.4
1973	262.8	861.0	984.9	7.0	8.0	8.7
1974	274.3	908.5	1070.3	7.9	10.8	10.5
1975	287.5	1023.2	1172.1	5.8	7.9	5.8
1976	306.3	1163.6	1311.7	5.0	6.8	5.0
1977	331.1	1286.5	1472.5	5.3	6.8	5.5
1978	358.2	1388.6	1646.4	7.2	9.1	7.9
1979	382.5	1497.0	1803.9	10.0	12.7	11.2
1980	408.5	1629.3	1988.8	11.5	15.3	13.4
1981	436.3	1793.3	2235.9	14.0	18.9	16.4
1982	474.3	1953.2	2443.2	10.7	14.9	12.3
1983	521.0	2187.6	2696.2	8.6	10.8	9.1
1984	552.1	2377.9	2994.6	9.6	12.0	10.2
1985	619.9	2575.0	3211.6	7.5	9.9	8.1
1986	724.5	2818.2	3497.3	6.0	8.3	6.8
1987	750.1	2920.1	3681.3	5.8	8.2	6.7
1988	787.4	3081.4	3920.4	6.7	9.3	7.6
1989	794.7	3239.8	4067.3	8.1	10.9	9.2
1990	826.4	3353.0	4125.7	7.5	10.0	8.1
1991	897.7	3455.2	4180.4	5.4	8.5	5.7
1992	1024.8	3509.0	4183.0	3.5	6.3	3.5
1993	1128.4	3567.9	4232.0	3.0	6.0	3.0
1994	1147.6	3600.0	4282.4	4.3	7.2	4.2

TABLE D LABOR MARKET DATA

Year	Civilian Labor Force	Civilian Employment	Unemployment	Civilian Unemployment Rate	Civilian Labor Force Participation Rate	Output per Hour (1982=100)
	Millions of Persons			*Percent*		*Index Number*
1959	68.4	64.6	3.7	5.5	59.3	64.6
1960	69.6	65.8	3.9	5.5	59.4	65.6
1961	70.5	65.7	4.7	6.7	59.3	68.1
1962	70.6	66.7	3.9	5.5	58.8	70.5
1963	71.8	67.8	4.1	5.7	58.7	73.3
1964	73.1	69.3	3.8	5.2	58.7	76.5
1965	74.5	71.1	3.4	4.5	58.9	78.6
1966	75.8	72.9	2.9	3.8	59.2	80.7
1967	77.3	74.4	3.0	3.8	59.6	82.8
1968	78.7	75.9	2.8	3.6	59.6	85.3
1969	80.7	77.9	2.8	3.5	60.1	85.8
1970	82.8	78.7	4.1	4.9	60.4	87.0
1971	84.4	79.4	5.0	5.9	60.2	89.8
1972	87.0	82.2	4.9	5.6	60.4	92.7
1973	89.4	85.1	4.4	4.9	60.8	95.0
1974	91.9	86.8	5.2	5.6	61.3	93.2
1975	93.8	85.8	7.9	8.5	61.2	95.5
1976	96.2	88.8	7.4	7.7	61.6	98.3
1977	99.0	92.0	7.0	7.1	62.3	99.9
1978	102.3	96.0	6.2	6.1	63.2	100.5
1979	105.0	98.8	6.1	5.8	63.7	99.4
1980	106.9	99.3	7.6	7.1	63.8	98.6
1981	108.7	100.4	8.3	7.6	63.9	99.9
1982	110.2	99.5	10.7	9.7	64.0	100.0
1983	111.6	100.8	10.7	9.6	64.0	102.3
1984	113.5	105.0	8.5	7.5	64.4	104.8
1985	115.5	107.2	8.3	7.2	64.8	106.3
1986	117.8	109.6	8.2	7.0	65.3	108.5
1987	119.9	112.4	7.4	6.2	65.6	109.6
1988	121.7	115.0	6.7	5.5	65.9	110.7
1989	123.9	117.3	6.5	5.3	66.5	109.9
1990	124.8	117.9	6.9	5.5	66.4	110.7
1991	125.3	116.9	8.4	6.7	66.0	111.8
1992	127.0	117.6	9.4	7.4	66.3	115.5
1993	128.0	119.3	8.7	6.8	66.2	117.2
1994	131.1	123.1	8.0	6.1	66.6	119.9

SOURCE: *Economic Report of the President, February, 1995.*